Oh My Goddess!

OMNIBUS ④

ああっ女神さまっ

STORY AND ART BY
Kosuke Fujishima

TRANSLATION BY
Dana Lewis AND Toren Smith

LETTERING AND TOUCHUP BY
Susie Lee AND Betty Dong
WITH Tom2K

DARK HORSE MANGA

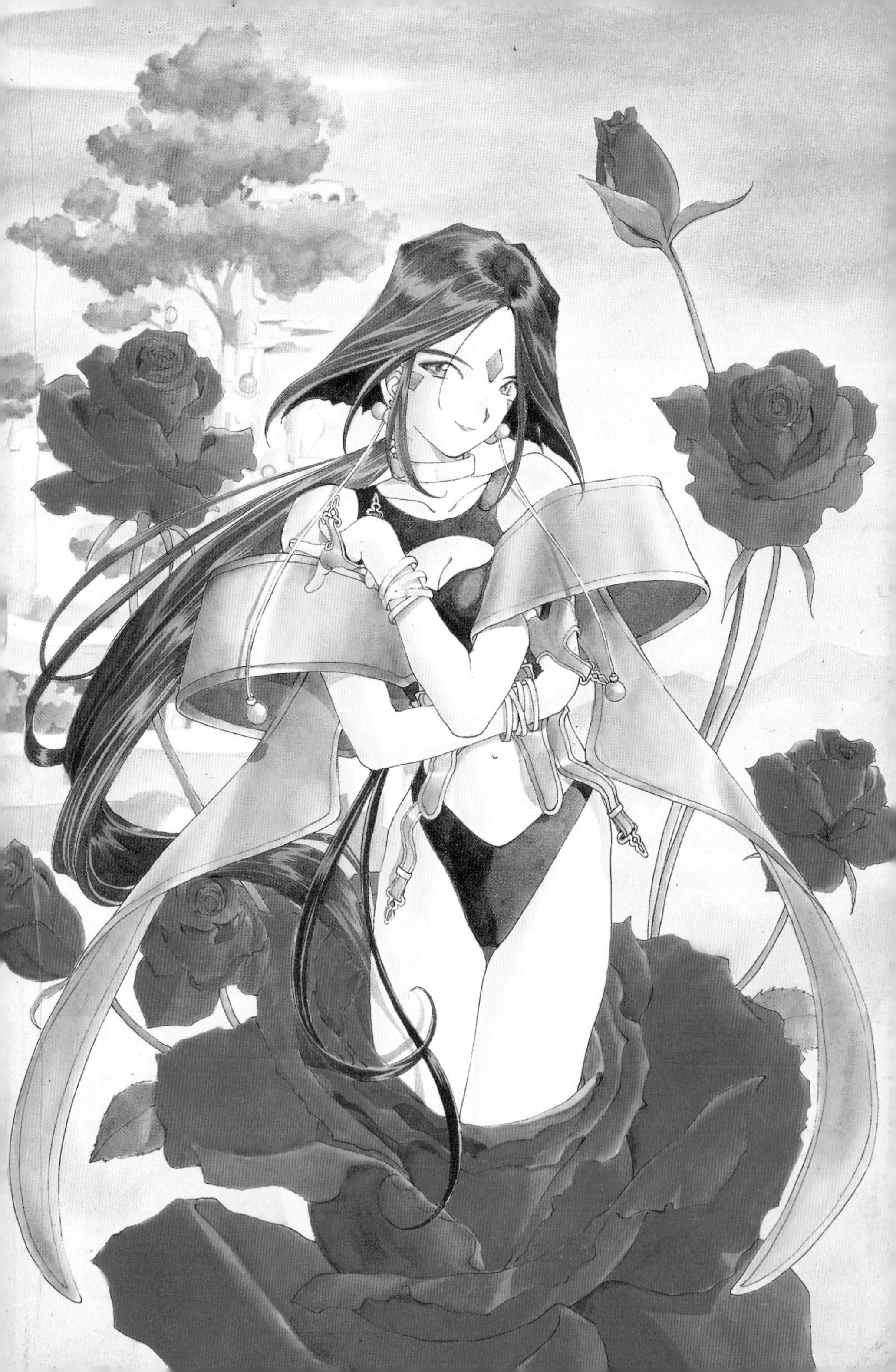

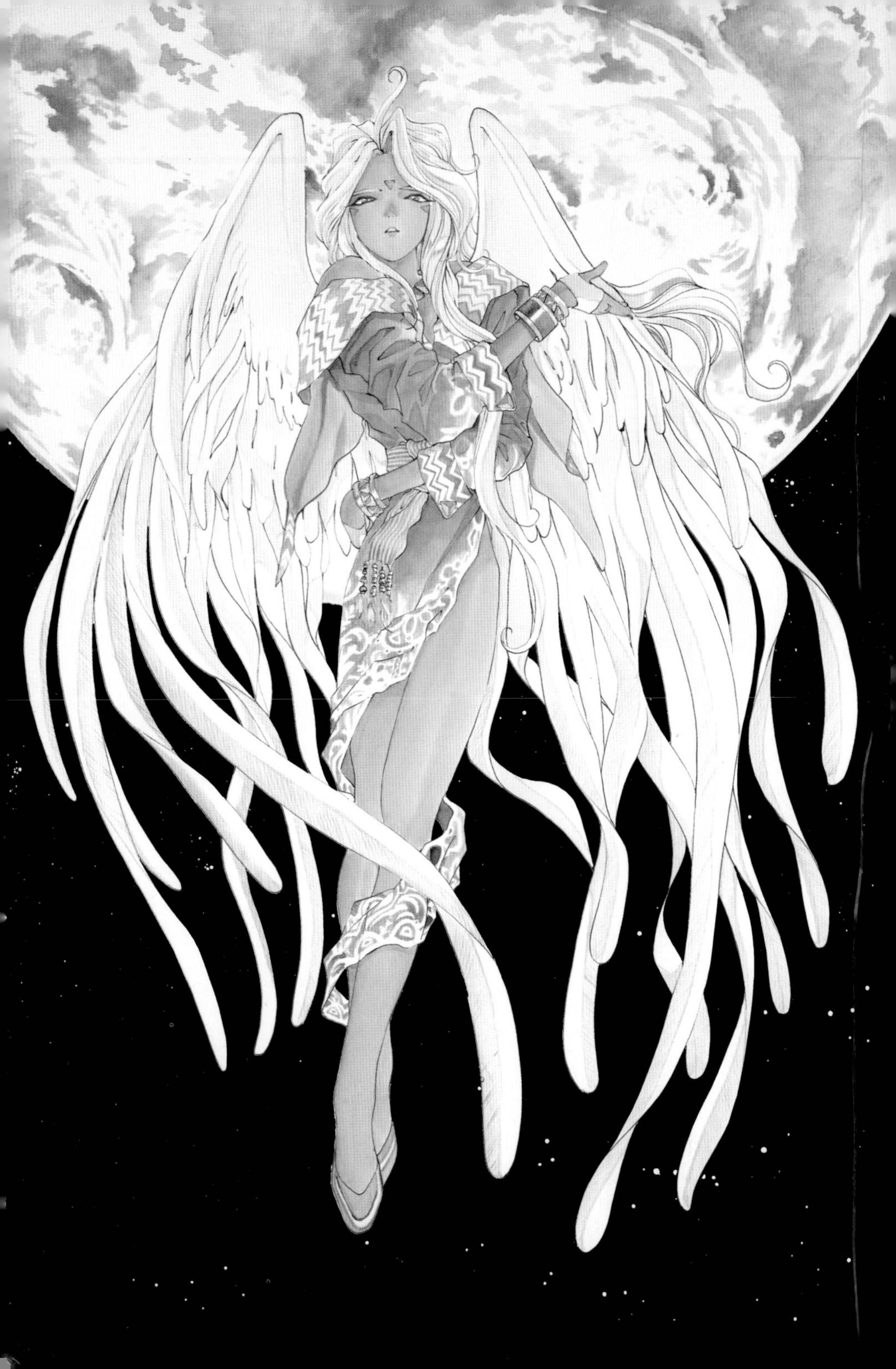

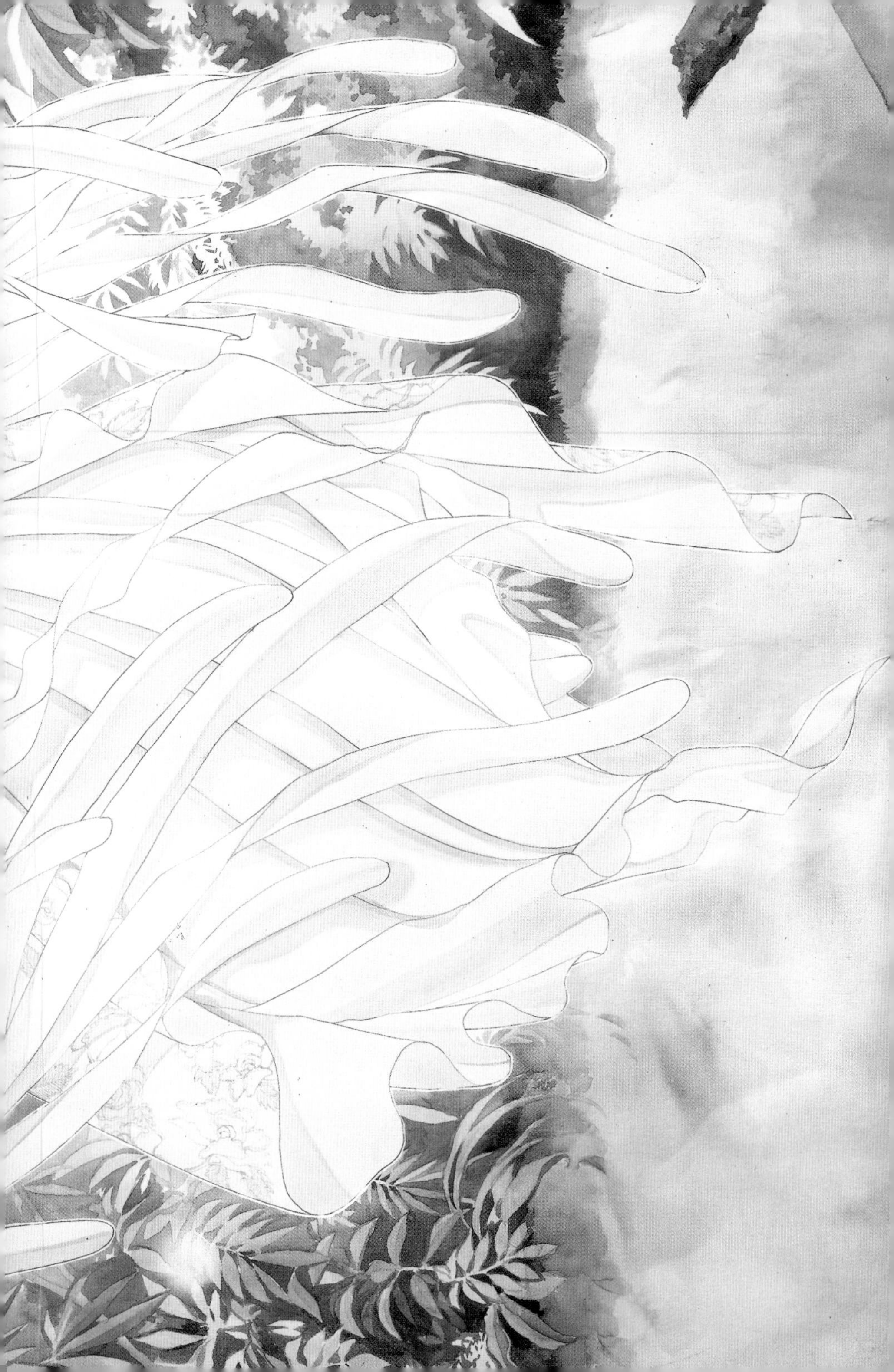

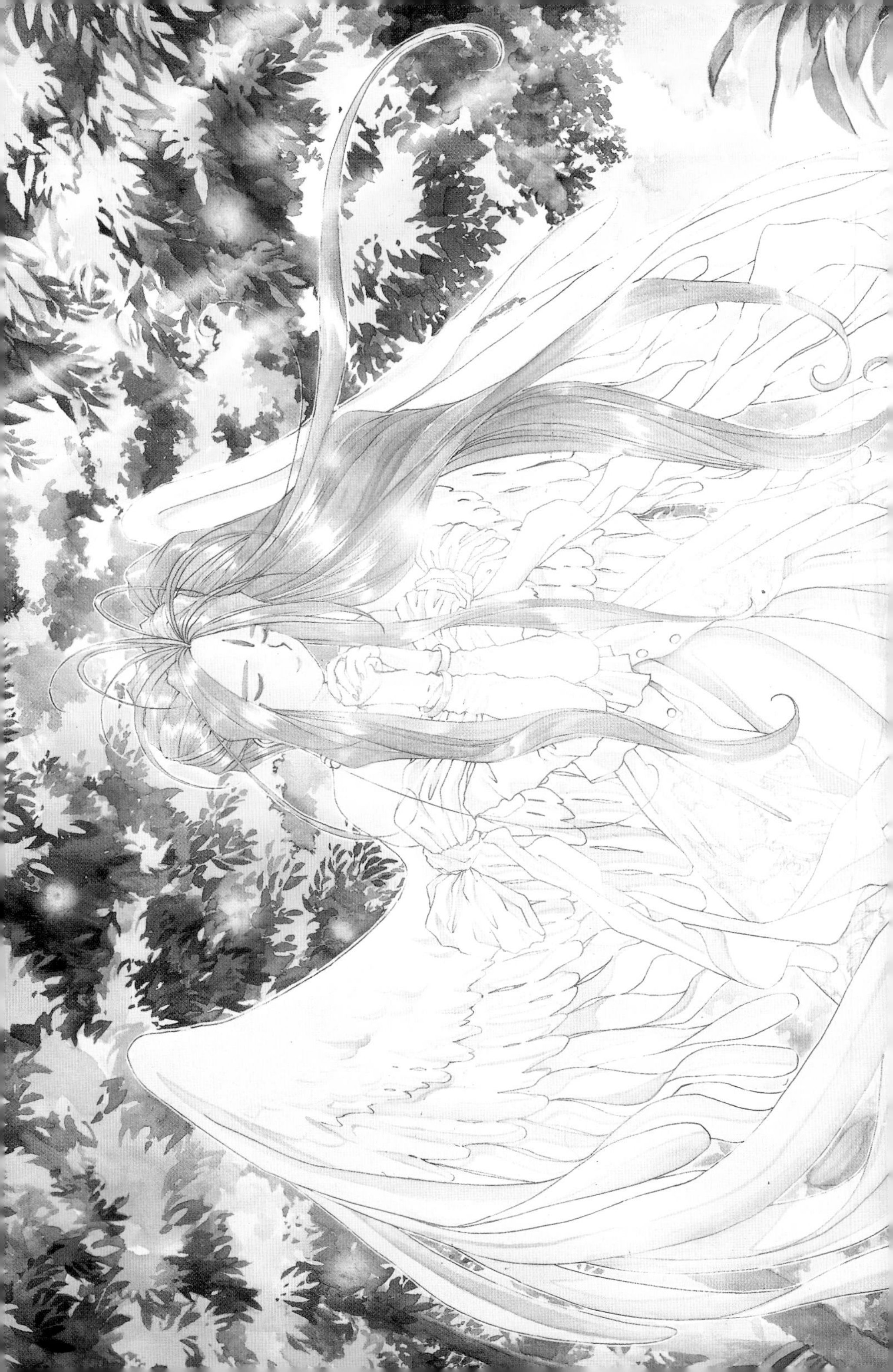

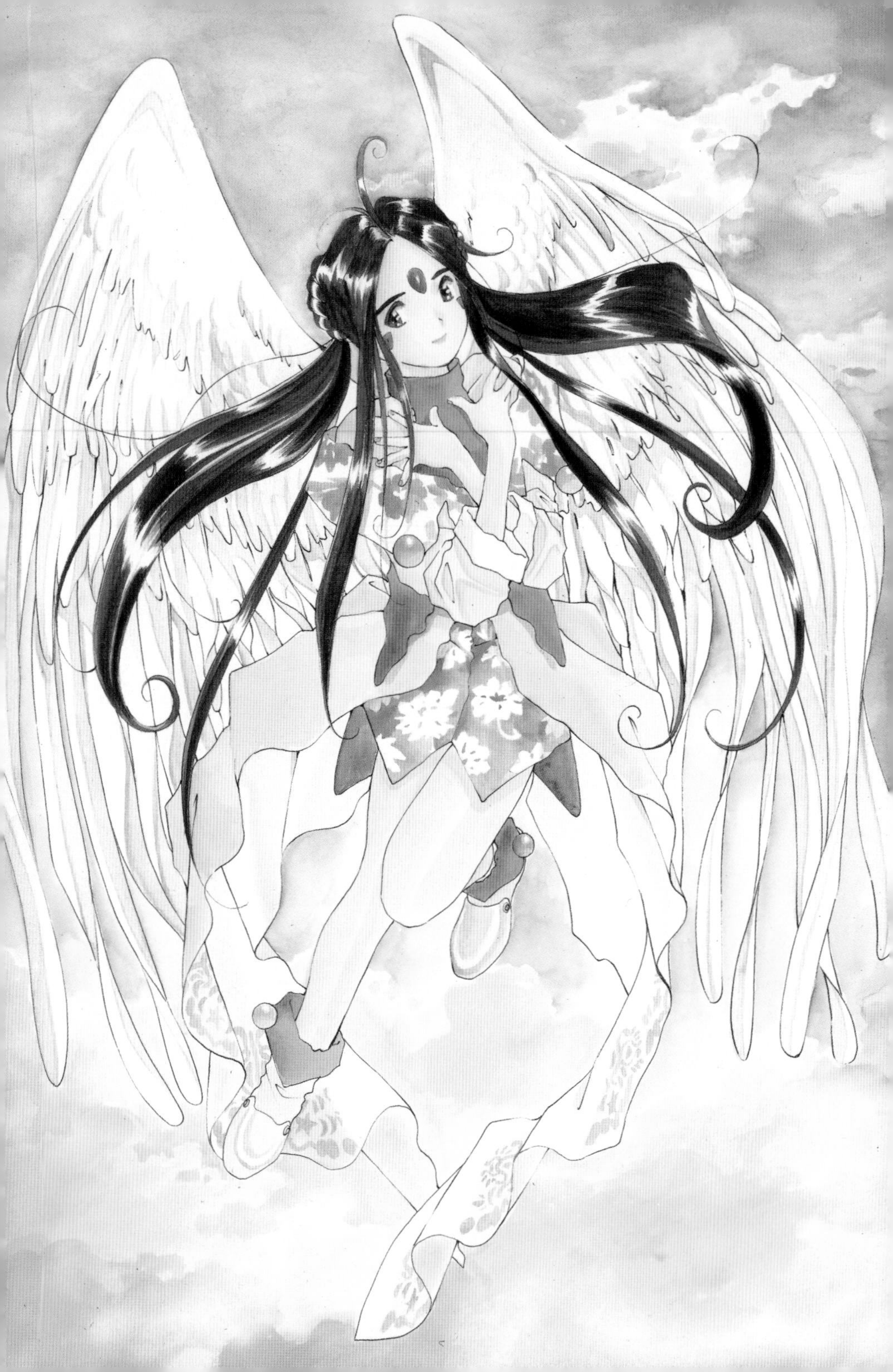

CHAPTER 58

Let's Have Fun

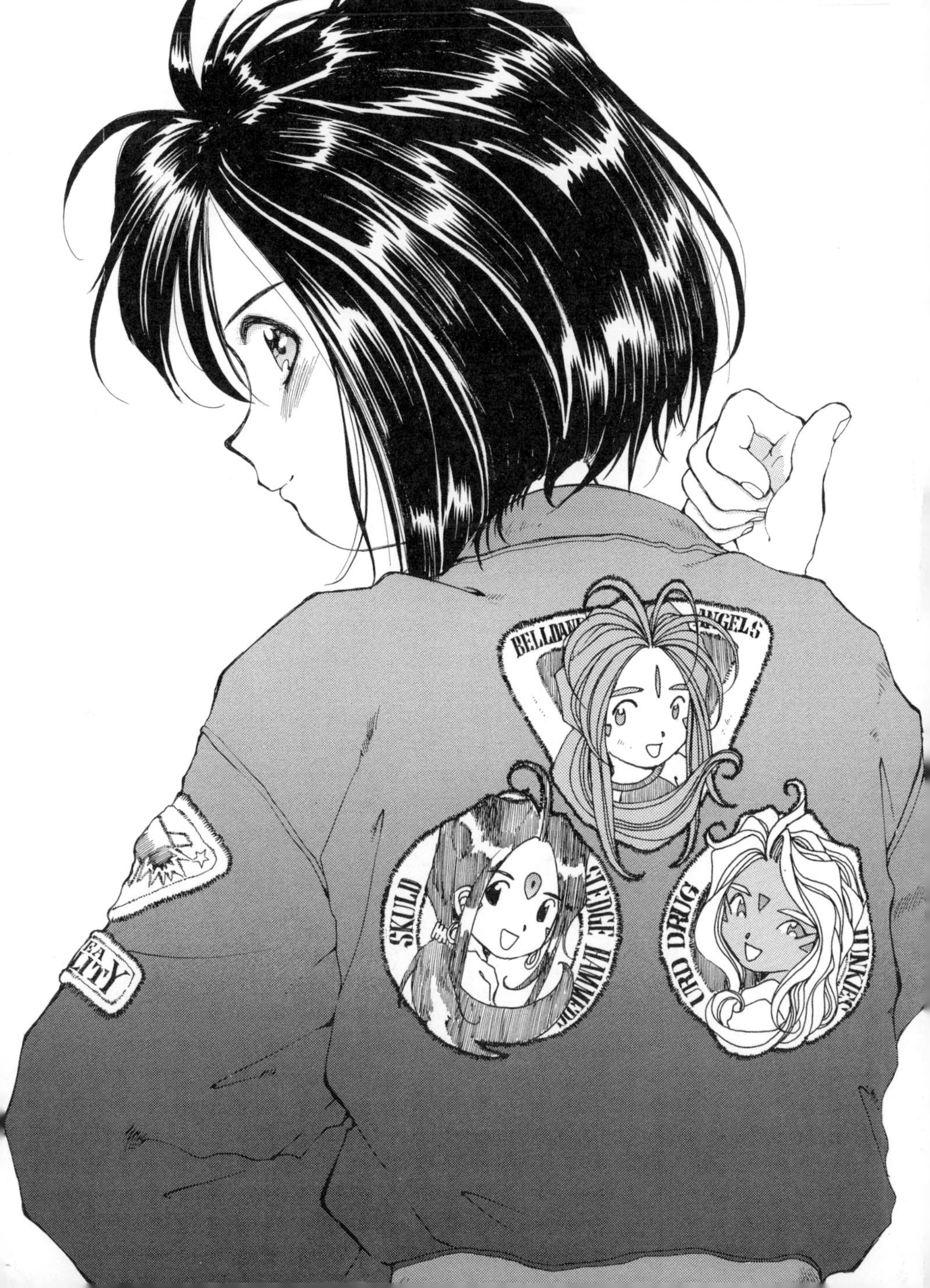
ANGELS
SKULD
URD DRUG

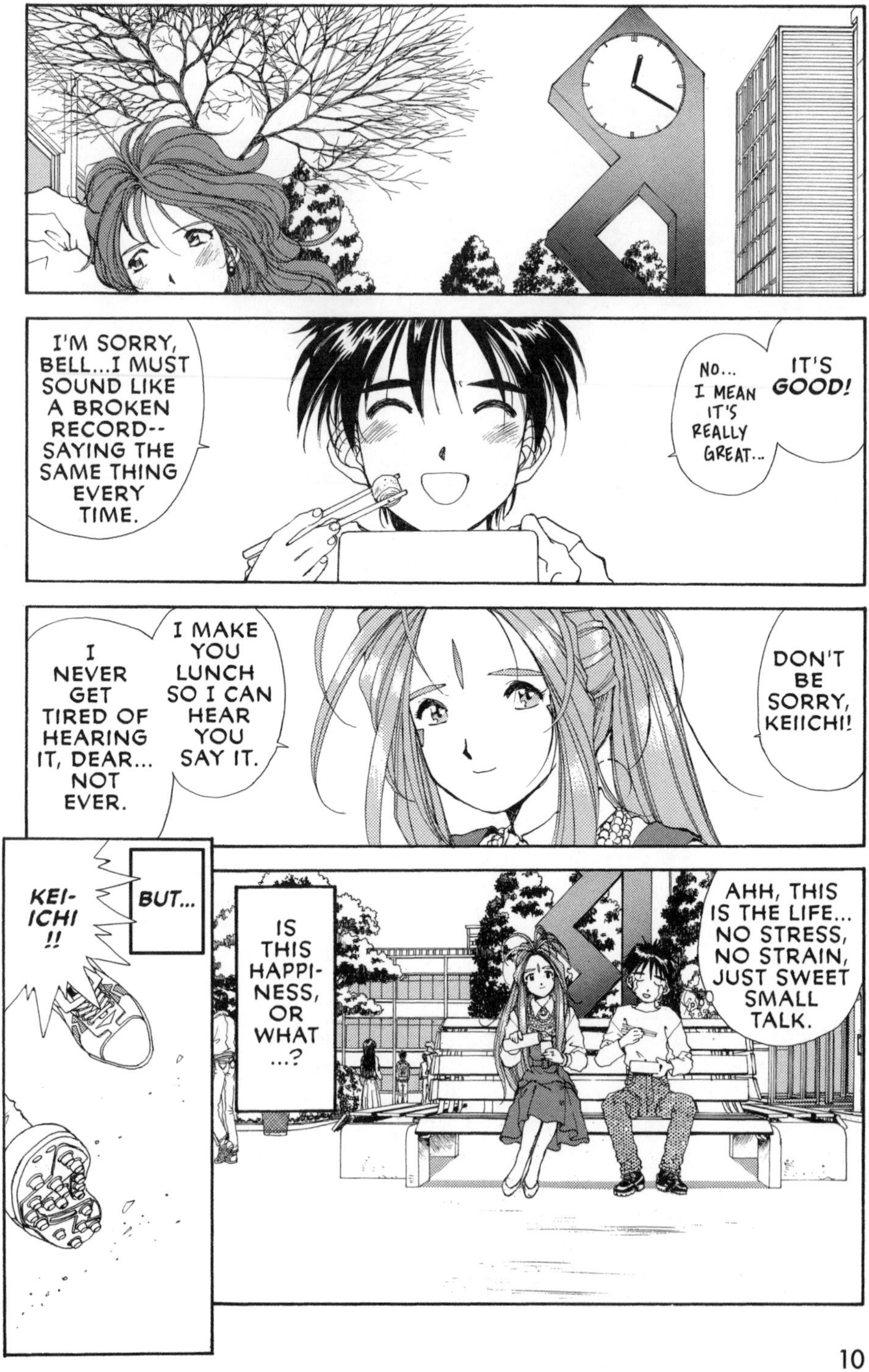
IT'S GOOD!
NO... I MEAN IT'S REALLY GREAT...
I'M SORRY, BELL...I MUST SOUND LIKE A BROKEN RECORD-- SAYING THE SAME THING EVERY TIME.
DON'T BE SORRY, KEIICHI!
I MAKE YOU LUNCH SO I CAN HEAR YOU SAY IT.
I NEVER GET TIRED OF HEARING IT, DEAR... NOT EVER.
AHH, THIS IS THE LIFE... NO STRESS, NO STRAIN, JUST SWEET SMALL TALK.
IS THIS HAPPINESS, OR WHAT ...?
BUT...
KEI-ICHI !!

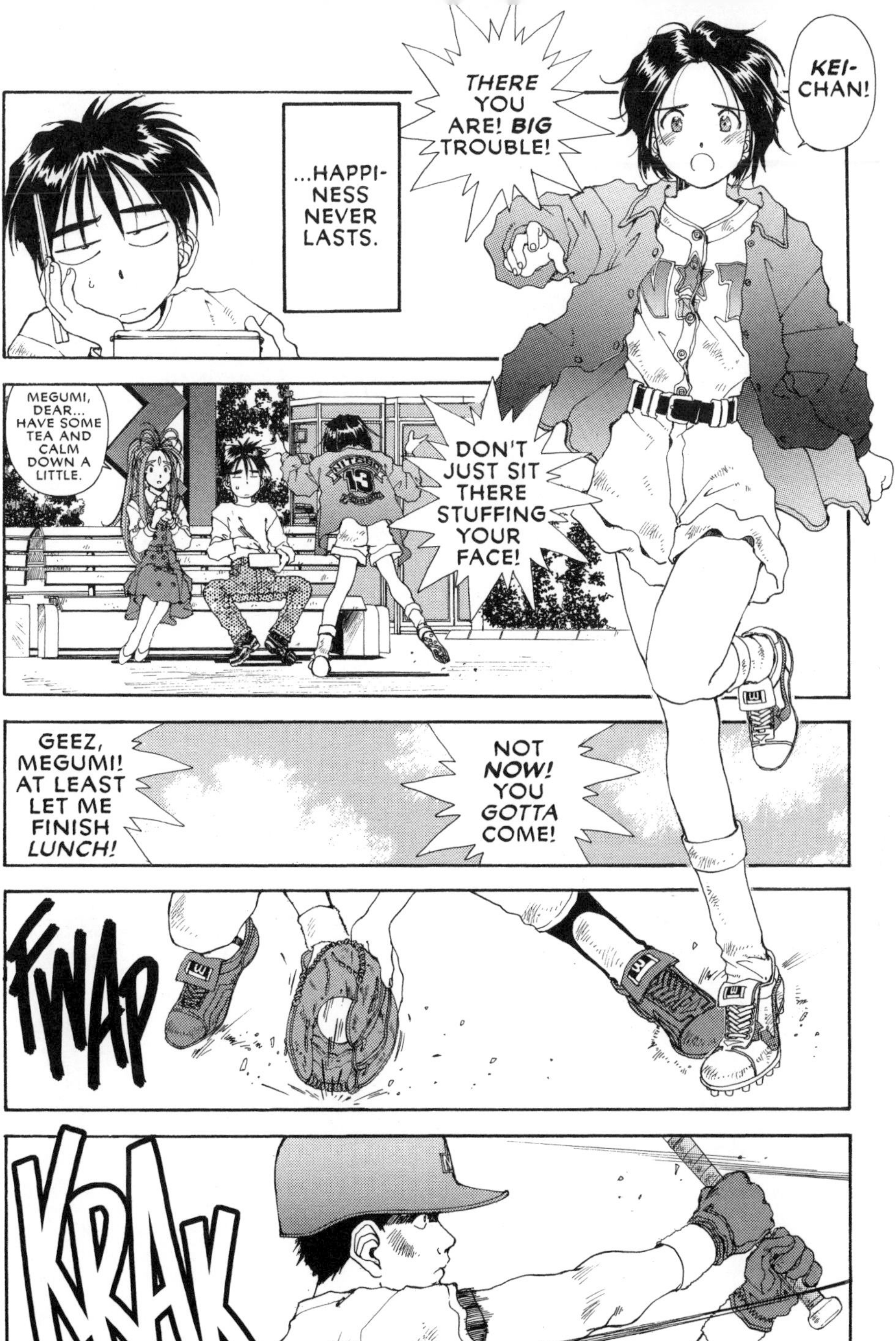
...HAPPINESS NEVER LASTS.
KEI-CHAN!
THERE YOU ARE! BIG TROUBLE!
DON'T JUST SIT THERE STUFFING YOUR FACE!
MEGUMI, DEAR... HAVE SOME TEA AND CALM DOWN A LITTLE.
GEEZ, MEGUMI! AT LEAST LET ME FINISH LUNCH!
NOT NOW! YOU GOTTA COME!
FWAP
KRAK

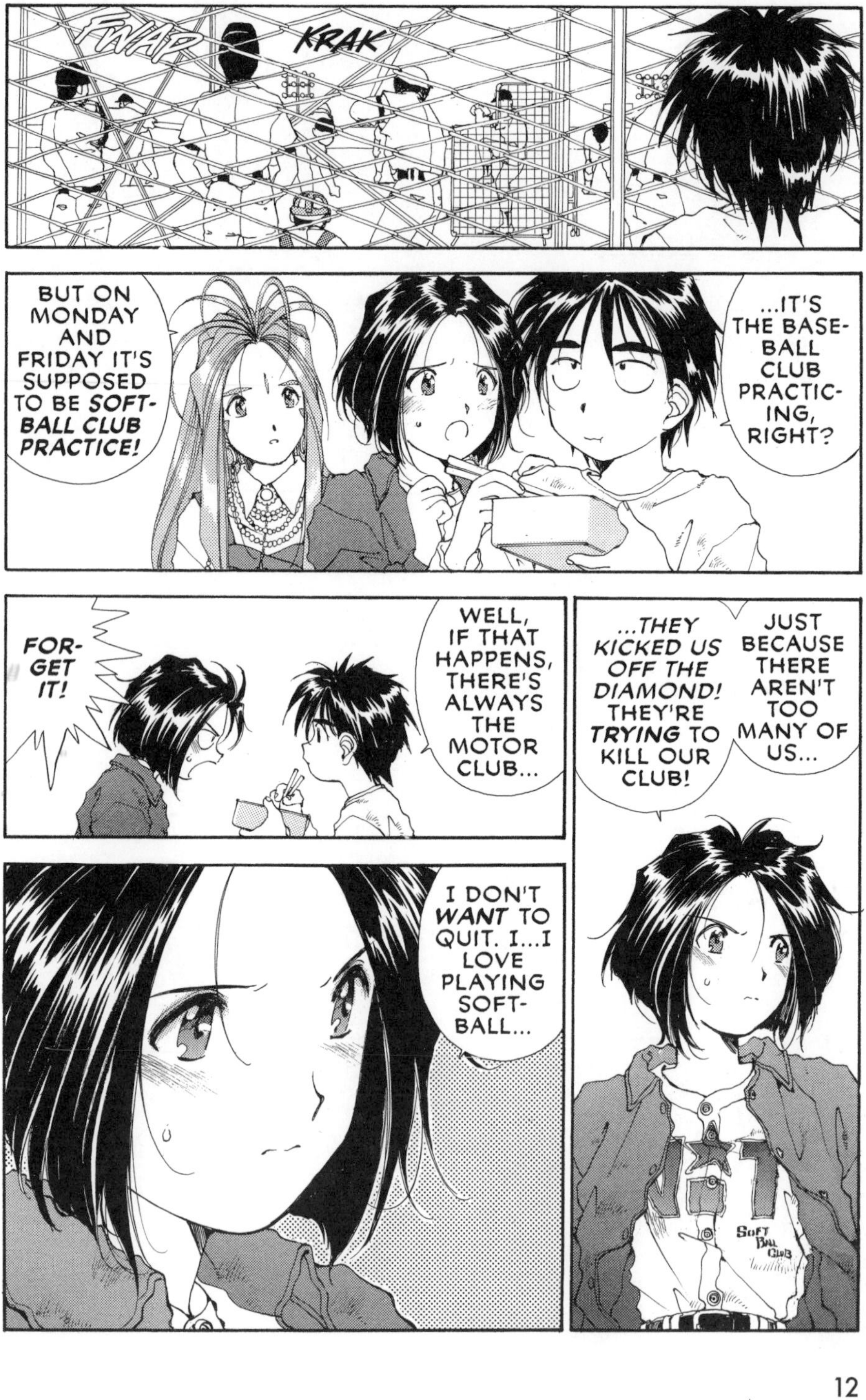
FWAP
KRAK
...IT'S THE BASEBALL CLUB PRACTICING, RIGHT?
BUT ON MONDAY AND FRIDAY IT'S SUPPOSED TO BE *SOFTBALL CLUB PRACTICE!*
JUST BECAUSE THERE AREN'T TOO MANY OF US...
...THEY KICKED US OFF THE DIAMOND! THEY'RE *TRYING* TO KILL OUR CLUB!
SOFT BALL CLUB
WELL, IF THAT HAPPENS, THERE'S ALWAYS THE MOTOR CLUB...
FORGET IT!
I DON'T *WANT* TO QUIT. I...I LOVE PLAYING SOFTBALL...

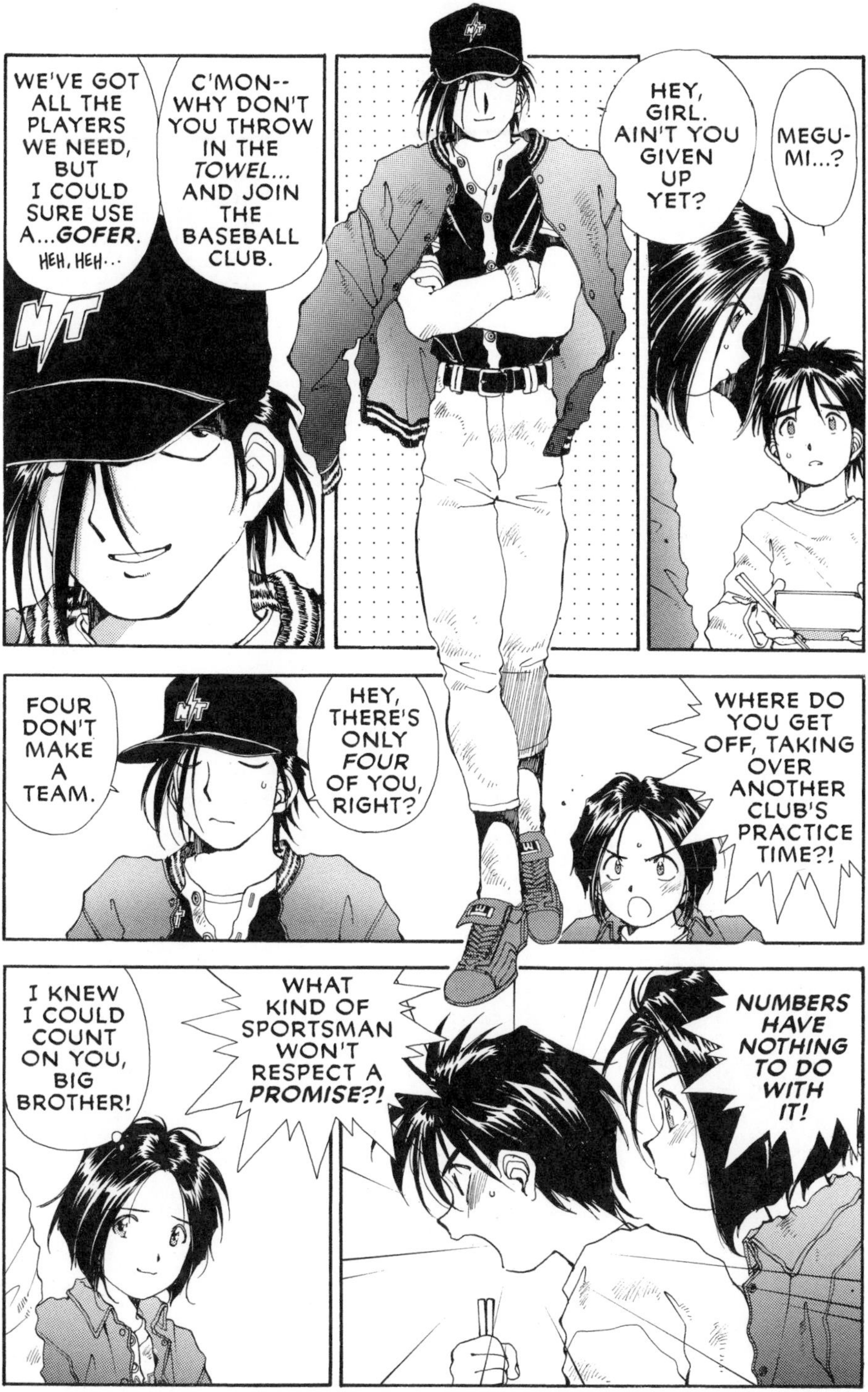
MEGU-MI...?
HEY, GIRL. AIN'T YOU GIVEN UP YET?
C'MON-- WHY DON'T YOU THROW IN THE *TOWEL*... AND JOIN THE BASEBALL CLUB.
WE'VE GOT ALL THE PLAYERS WE NEED, BUT I COULD SURE USE A...**GOFER**. HEH, HEH...
WHERE DO YOU GET OFF, TAKING OVER ANOTHER CLUB'S PRACTICE TIME?!
HEY, THERE'S ONLY *FOUR* OF YOU, RIGHT?
FOUR DON'T MAKE A TEAM.
NUMBERS HAVE NOTHING TO DO WITH IT!
WHAT KIND OF SPORTSMAN WON'T RESPECT A *PROMISE?!*
I KNEW I COULD COUNT ON YOU, BIG BROTHER!

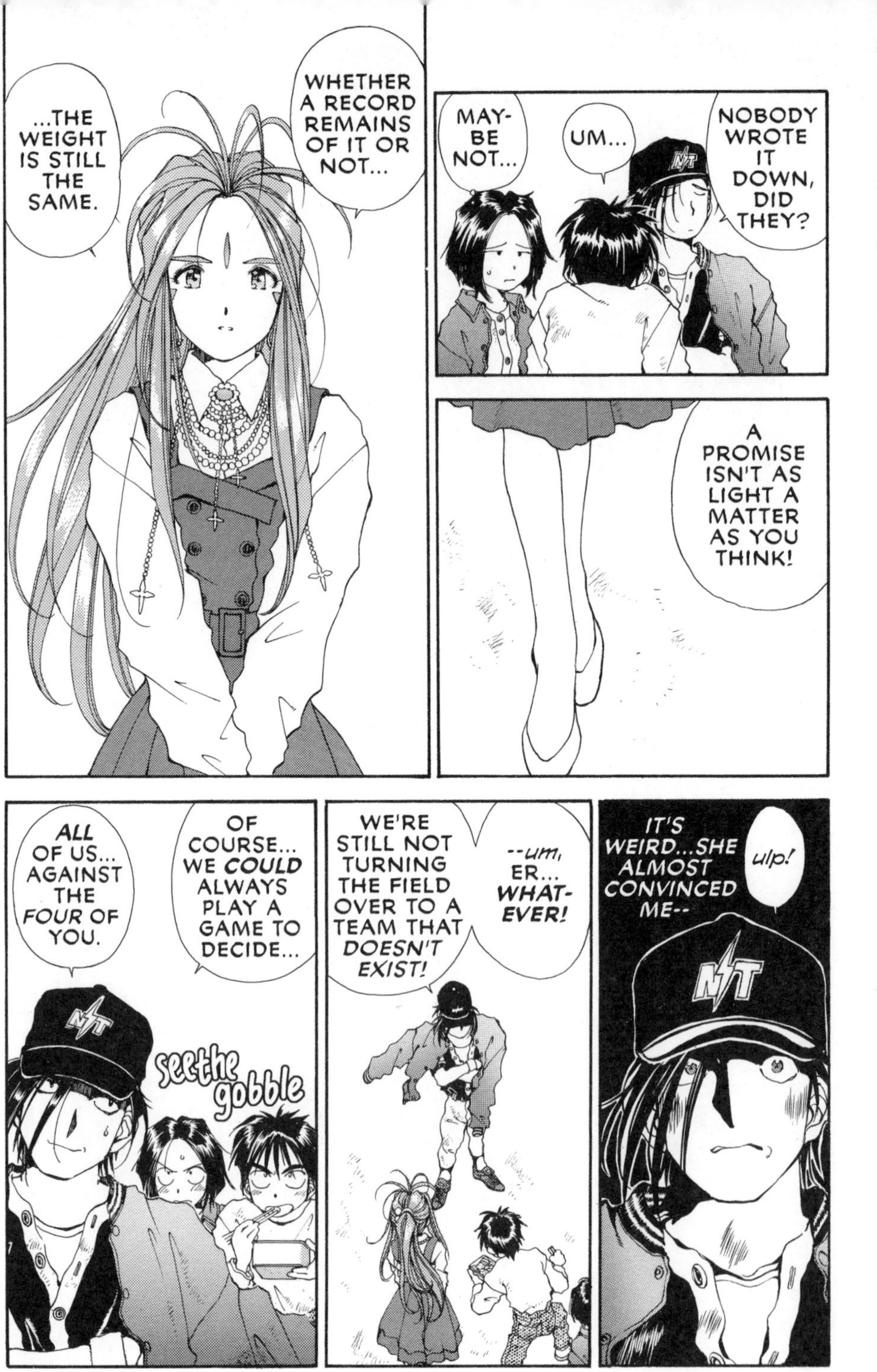
WHETHER A RECORD REMAINS OF IT OR NOT...
...THE WEIGHT IS STILL THE SAME.
NOBODY WROTE IT DOWN, DID THEY?
UM...
MAY-BE NOT...
A PROMISE ISN'T AS LIGHT A MATTER AS YOU THINK!
ALL OF US... AGAINST THE FOUR OF YOU.
OF COURSE... WE COULD ALWAYS PLAY A GAME TO DECIDE...
seethe
gobble
WE'RE STILL NOT TURNING THE FIELD OVER TO A TEAM THAT DOESN'T EXIST!
--um, ER... WHAT-EVER!
IT'S WEIRD...SHE ALMOST CONVINCED ME--
ulp!

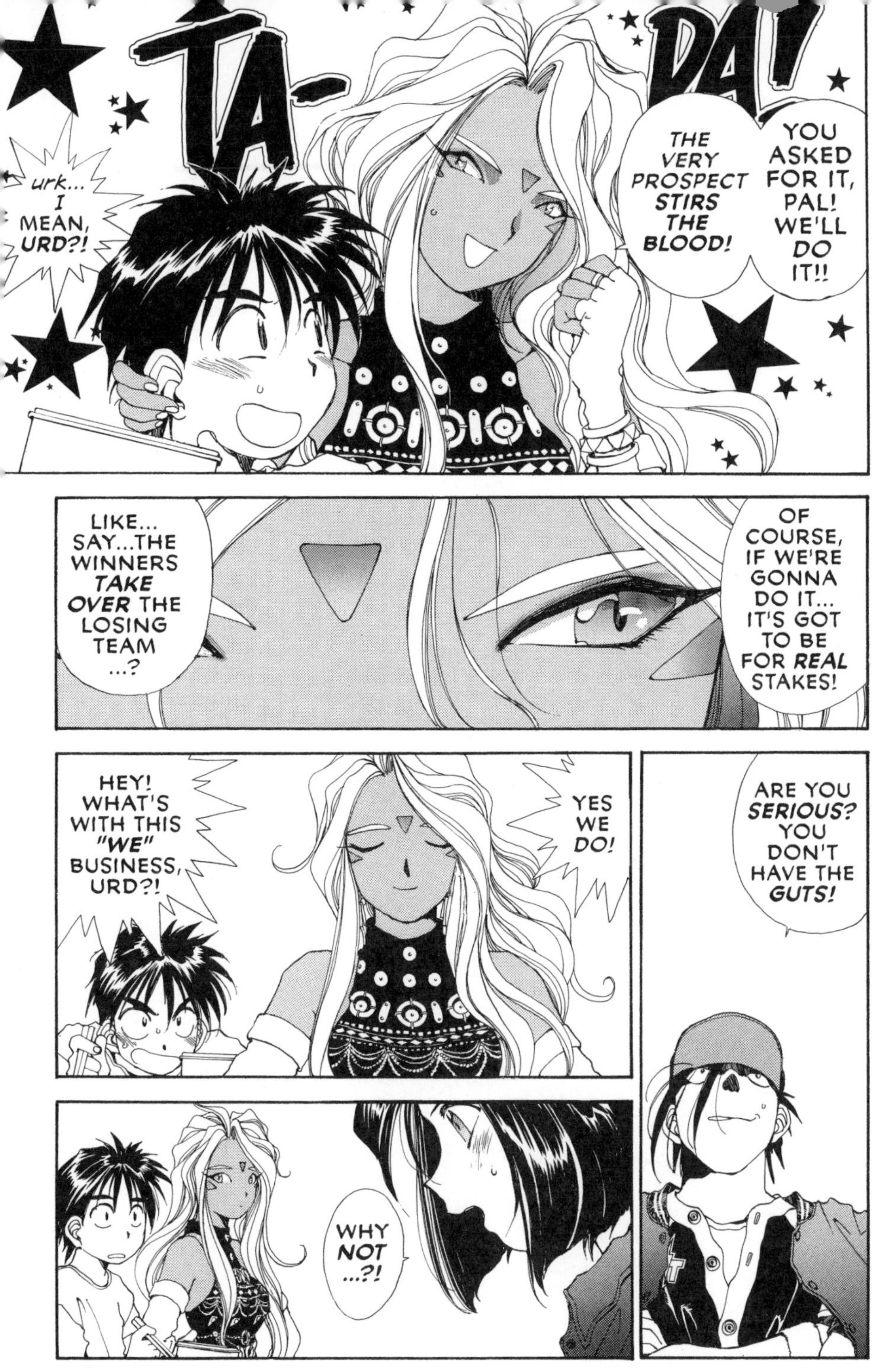
TA-DA!
YOU ASKED FOR IT, PAL! WE'LL DO IT!!
THE VERY PROSPECT STIRS THE BLOOD!
urk... I MEAN, URD?!
OF COURSE, IF WE'RE GONNA DO IT... IT'S GOT TO BE FOR REAL STAKES!
LIKE... SAY...THE WINNERS TAKE OVER THE LOSING TEAM ...?
ARE YOU SERIOUS? YOU DON'T HAVE THE GUTS!
YES WE DO!
HEY! WHAT'S WITH THIS "WE" BUSINESS, URD?!
WHY NOT ...?!

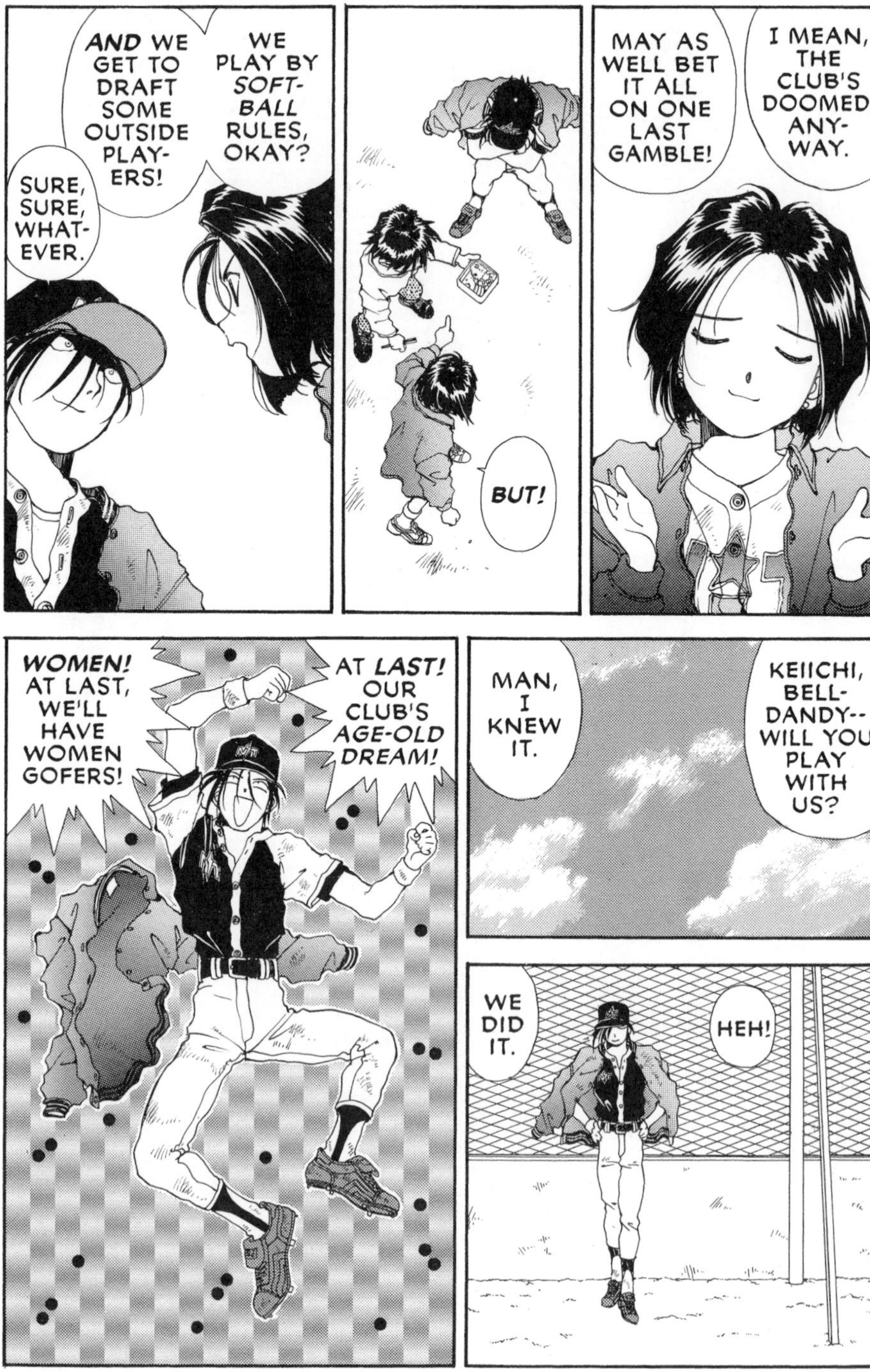
I MEAN, THE CLUB'S DOOMED, ANY-WAY.
MAY AS WELL BET IT ALL ON ONE LAST GAMBLE!
BUT!
WE PLAY BY SOFT-BALL RULES, OKAY?
AND WE GET TO DRAFT SOME OUTSIDE PLAY-ERS!
SURE, SURE, WHAT-EVER.
KEIICHI, BELL-DANDY-- WILL YOU PLAY WITH US?
MAN, I KNEW IT.
HEH!
WE DID IT.
AT LAST! OUR CLUB'S AGE-OLD DREAM!
WOMEN! AT LAST, WE'LL HAVE WOMEN GOFERS!

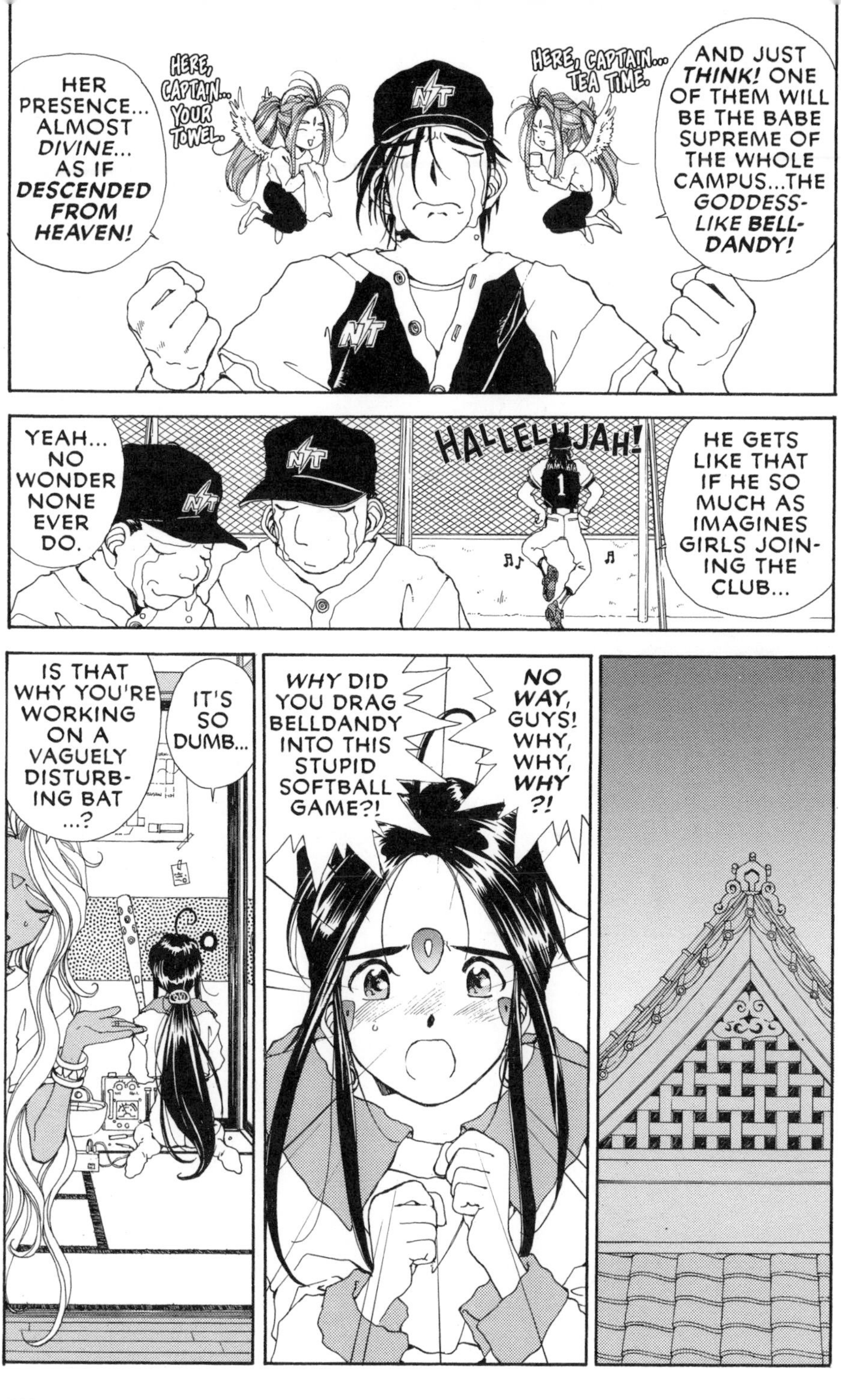
AND JUST THINK! ONE OF THEM WILL BE THE BABE SUPREME OF THE WHOLE CAMPUS...THE GODDESS-LIKE BELLDANDY!
HERE, CAPTAIN... TEA TIME.
HERE, CAPTAIN... YOUR TOWEL.
HER PRESENCE... ALMOST DIVINE... AS IF DESCENDED FROM HEAVEN!
HE GETS LIKE THAT IF HE SO MUCH AS IMAGINES GIRLS JOINING THE CLUB...
HALLELUJAH!
YEAH... NO WONDER NONE EVER DO.
NO WAY, GUYS! WHY, WHY, WHY?!
WHY DID YOU DRAG BELLDANDY INTO THIS STUPID SOFTBALL GAME?!
IT'S SO DUMB...
IS THAT WHY YOU'RE WORKING ON A VAGUELY DISTURBING BAT ...?

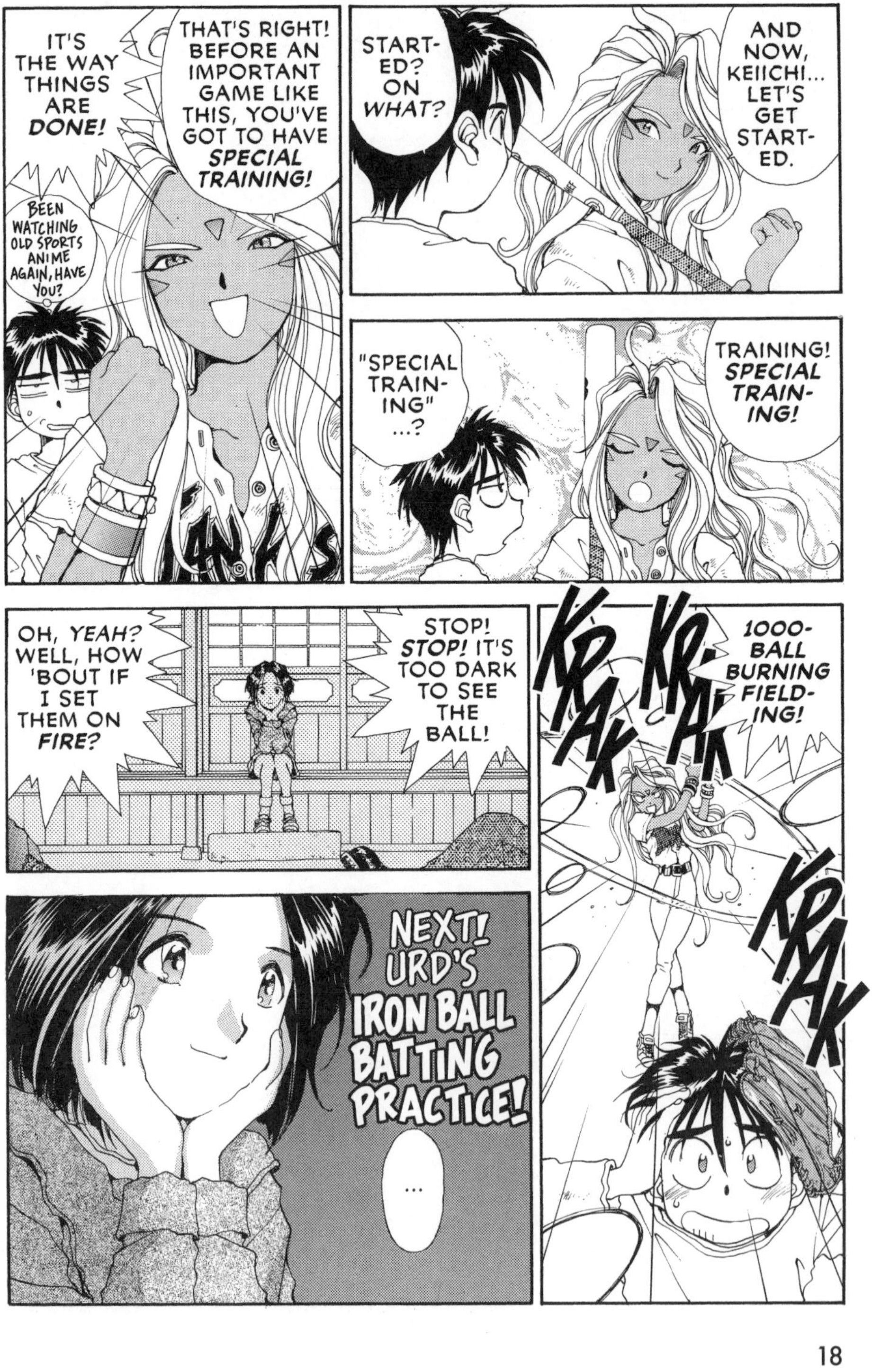
AND NOW, KEIICHI... LET'S GET START-ED.
START-ED? ON WHAT?
TRAINING! SPECIAL TRAIN-ING!
"SPECIAL TRAIN-ING" ...?
THAT'S RIGHT! BEFORE AN IMPORTANT GAME LIKE THIS, YOU'VE GOT TO HAVE SPECIAL TRAINING!
IT'S THE WAY THINGS ARE DONE!
BEEN WATCHING OLD SPORTS ANIME AGAIN, HAVE YOU?
1000-BALL BURNING FIELD-ING!
KRAK
KRAK
KRAK
STOP! STOP! IT'S TOO DARK TO SEE THE BALL!
OH, YEAH? WELL, HOW 'BOUT IF I SET THEM ON FIRE?
NEXT! URD'S IRON BALL BATTING PRACTICE!
...

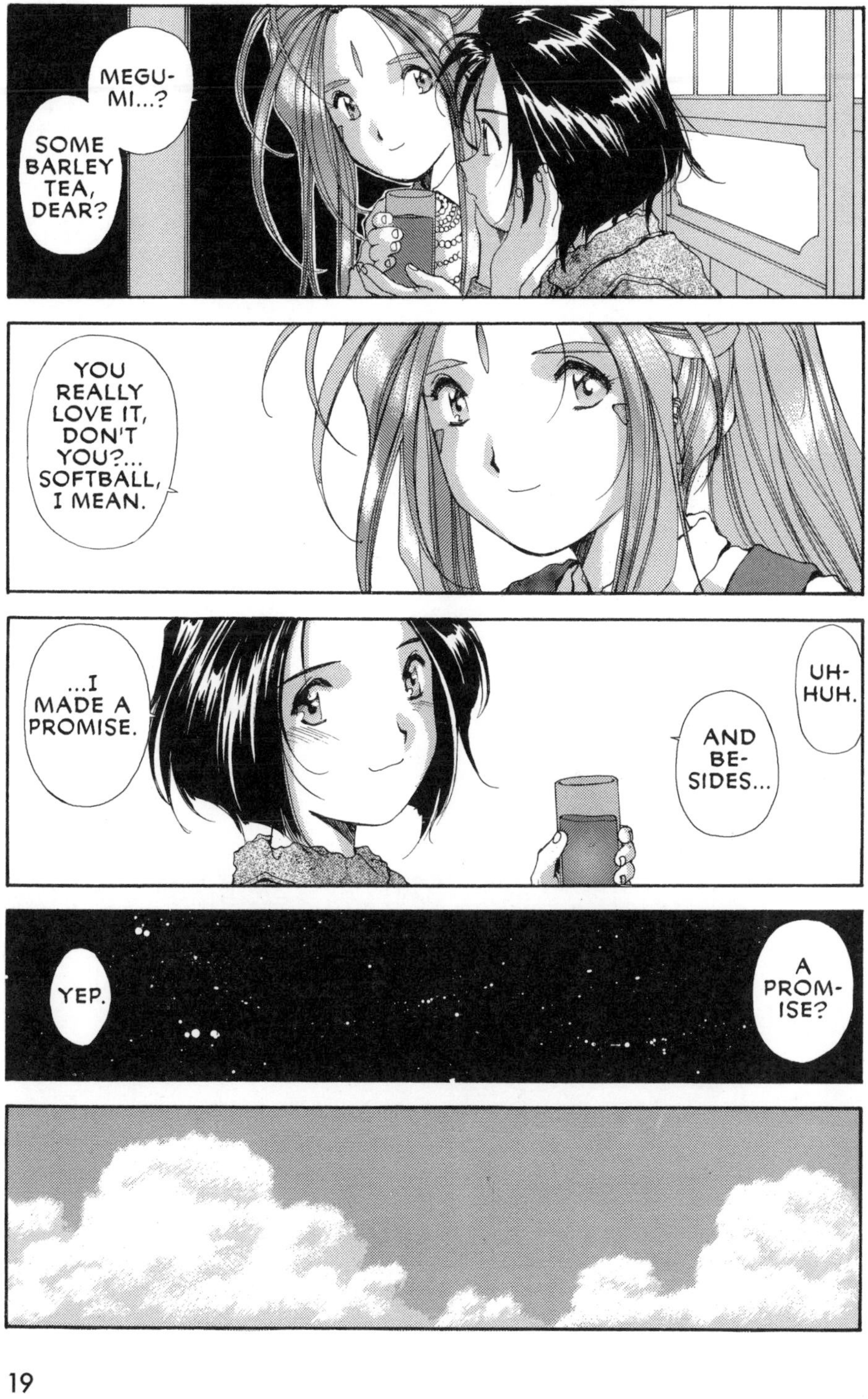
MEGU-MI...?
SOME BARLEY TEA, DEAR?
YOU REALLY LOVE IT, DON'T YOU?... SOFTBALL, I MEAN.
UH-HUH.
AND BE-SIDES...
...I MADE A PROMISE.
A PROM-ISE?
YEP.

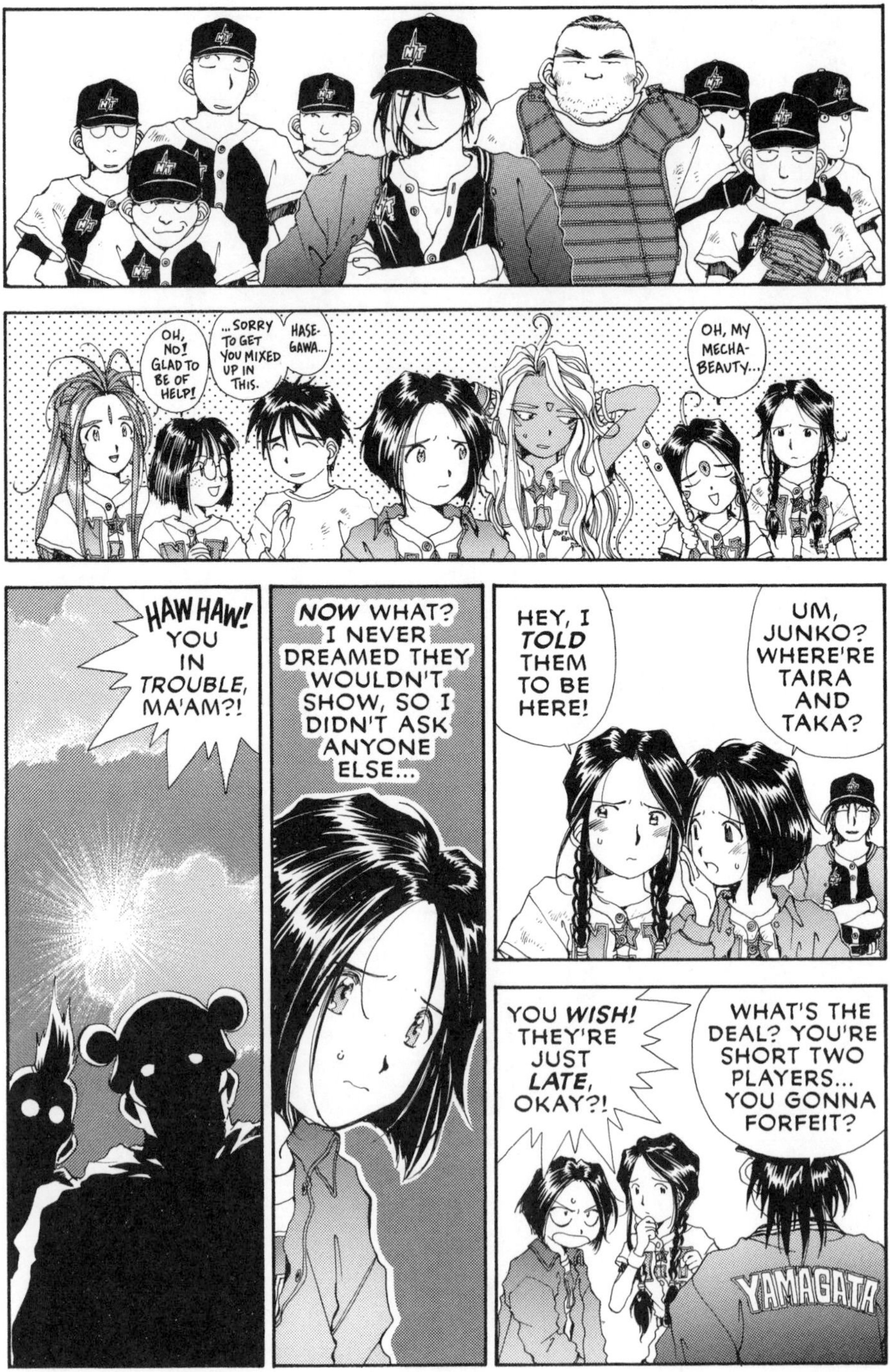
OH, MY MECHA-BEAUTY...
HASE-GAWA...
...SORRY TO GET YOU MIXED UP IN THIS.
OH, NO! GLAD TO BE OF HELP!
UM, JUNKO? WHERE'RE TAIRA AND TAKA?
HEY, I TOLD THEM TO BE HERE!
WHAT'S THE DEAL? YOU'RE SHORT TWO PLAYERS... YOU GONNA FORFEIT?
YOU WISH! THEY'RE JUST LATE, OKAY?!
YAMAGATA
NOW WHAT? I NEVER DREAMED THEY WOULDN'T SHOW, SO I DIDN'T ASK ANYONE ELSE...
HAW HAW! YOU IN TROUBLE, MA'AM?!

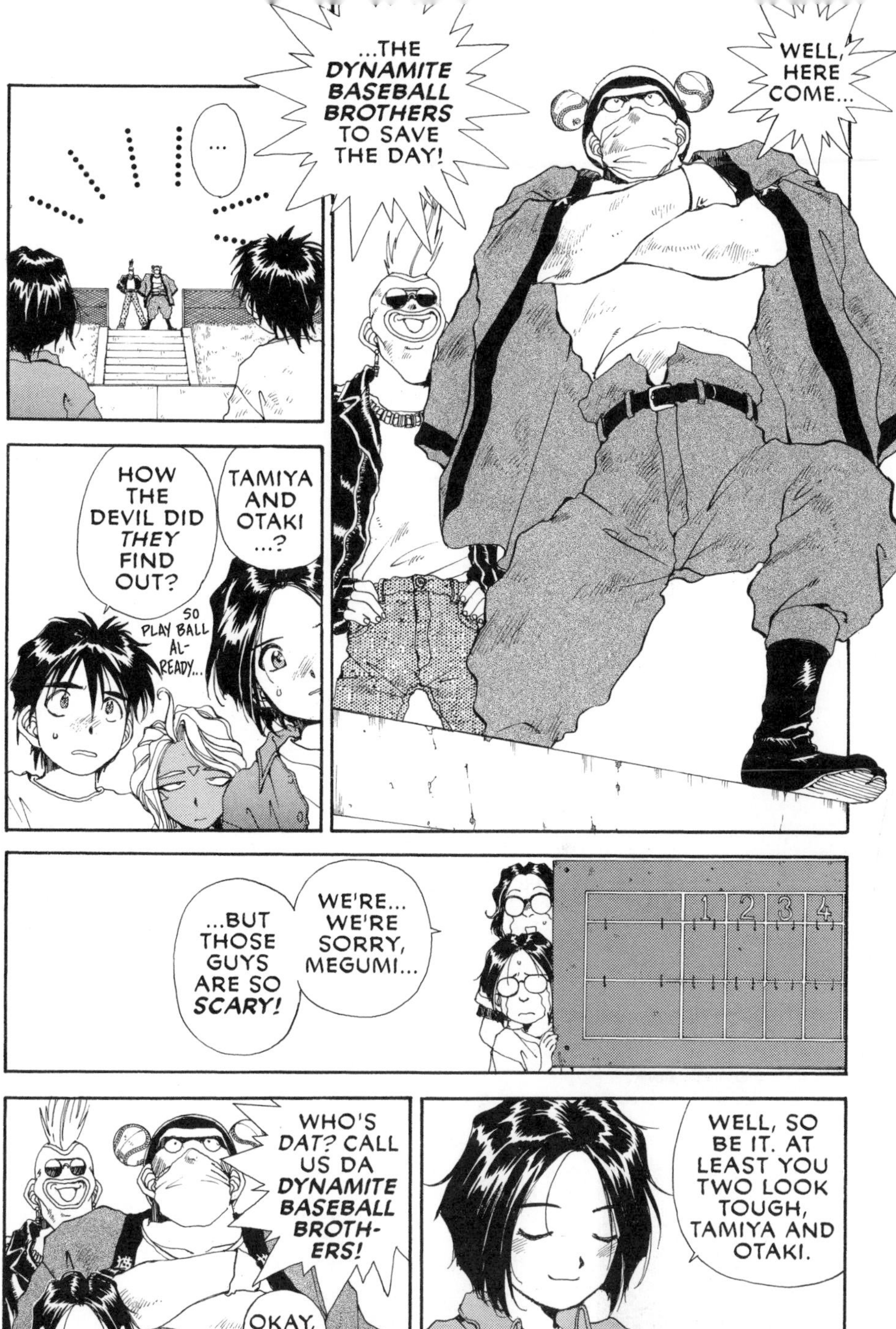
WELL, HERE COME...
...THE DYNAMITE BASEBALL BROTHERS TO SAVE THE DAY!
...
TAMIYA AND OTAKI ...?
HOW THE DEVIL DID THEY FIND OUT?
SO PLAY BALL AL-READY...
WE'RE... WE'RE SORRY, MEGUMI...
...BUT THOSE GUYS ARE SO SCARY!
WELL, SO BE IT. AT LEAST YOU TWO LOOK TOUGH, TAMIYA AND OTAKI.
WHO'S DAT? CALL US DA DYNAMITE BASEBALL BROTH-ERS!
OKAY, OKAY.

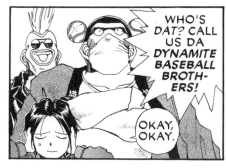

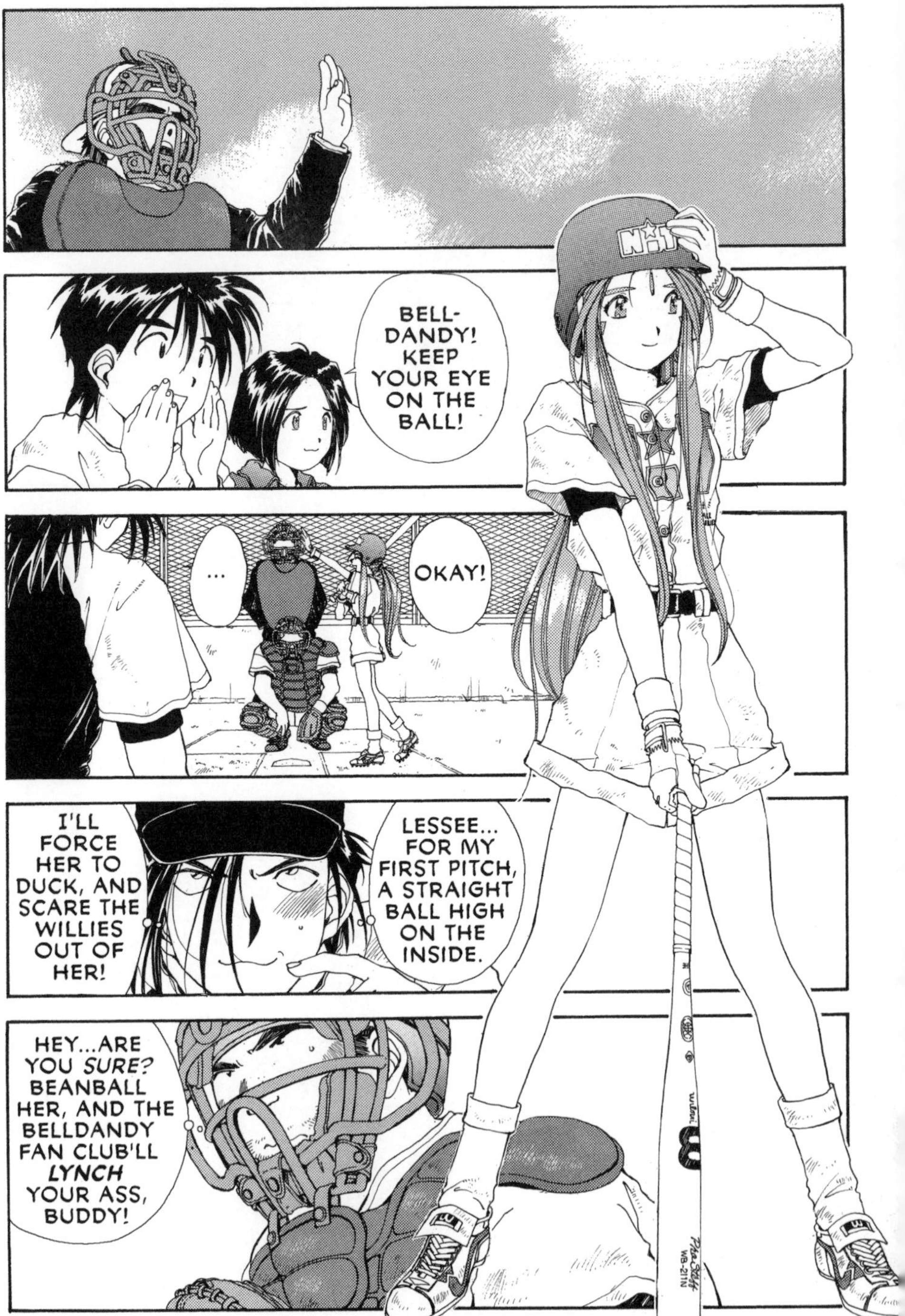
BELL-DANDY! KEEP YOUR EYE ON THE BALL!
OKAY!
...
LESSEE... FOR MY FIRST PITCH, A STRAIGHT BALL HIGH ON THE INSIDE.
I'LL FORCE HER TO DUCK, AND SCARE THE WILLIES OUT OF HER!
HEY...ARE YOU *SURE?* BEANBALL HER, AND THE BELLDANDY FAN CLUB'LL *LYNCH* YOUR ASS, BUDDY!

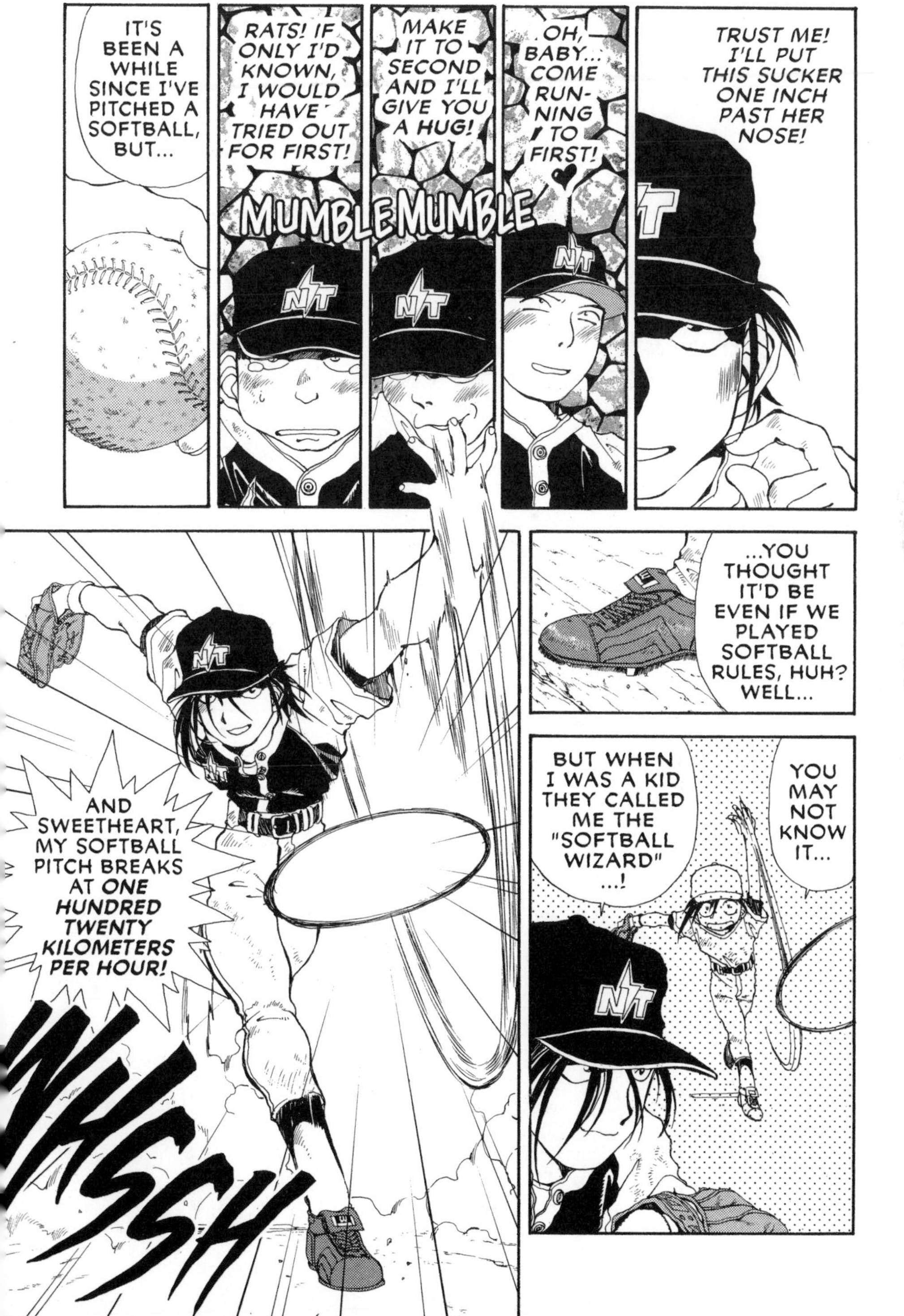

TRUST ME! I'LL PUT THIS SUCKER ONE INCH PAST HER NOSE!
OH, BABY... COME RUN-NING TO FIRST!
MAKE IT TO SECOND AND I'LL GIVE YOU A HUG!
RATS! IF ONLY I'D KNOWN, I WOULD HAVE TRIED OUT FOR FIRST!
MUMBLE MUMBLE
IT'S BEEN A WHILE SINCE I'VE PITCHED A SOFTBALL, BUT...
...YOU THOUGHT IT'D BE EVEN IF WE PLAYED SOFTBALL RULES, HUH? WELL...
YOU MAY NOT KNOW IT...
BUT WHEN I WAS A KID THEY CALLED ME THE "SOFTBALL WIZARD" ...!
AND SWEETHEART, MY SOFTBALL PITCH BREAKS AT ONE HUNDRED TWENTY KILOMETERS PER HOUR!
WHSSH

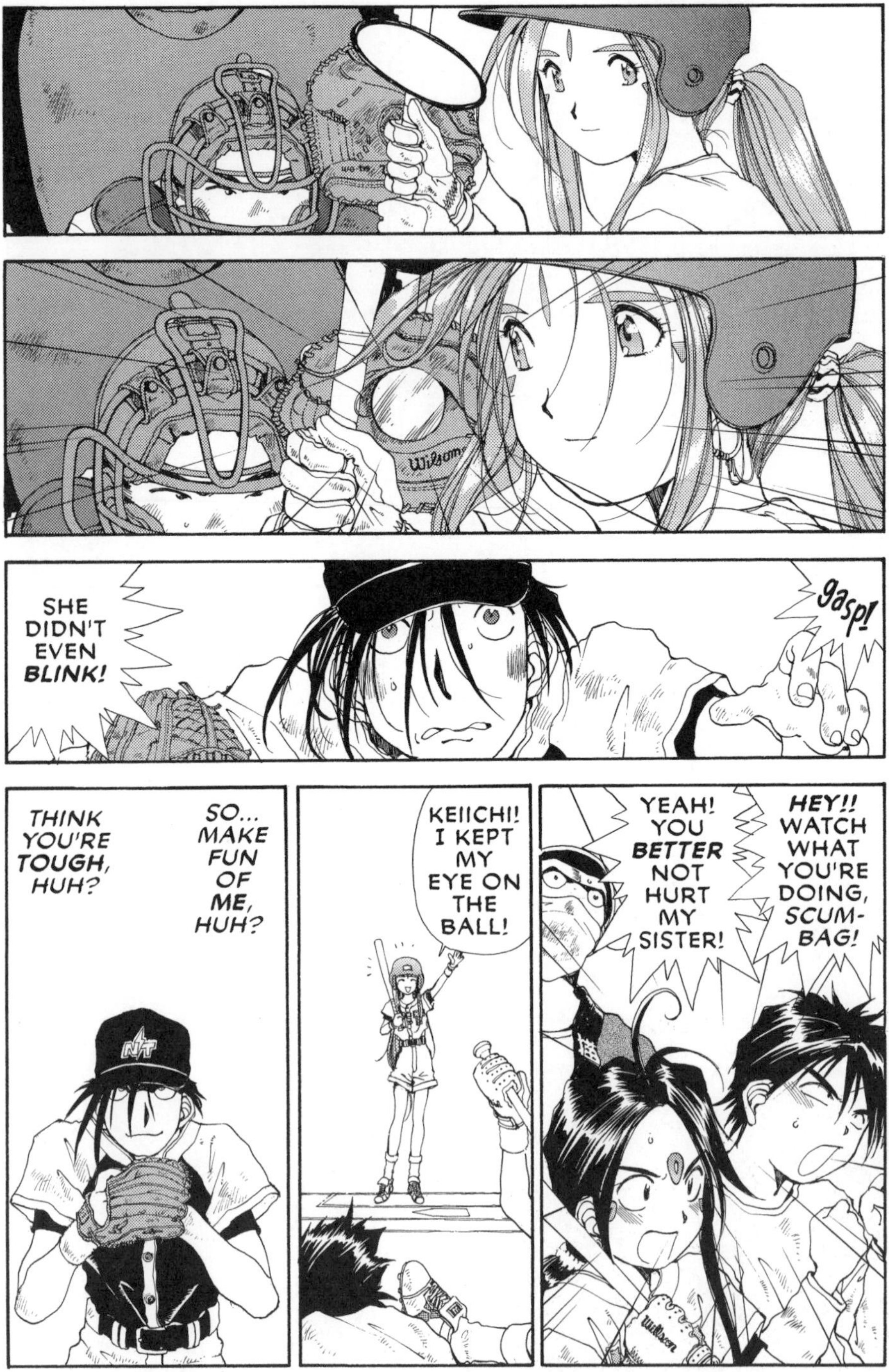
gasp!
SHE DIDN'T EVEN BLINK!
HEY!! WATCH WHAT YOU'RE DOING, SCUM-BAG!
YEAH! YOU BETTER NOT HURT MY SISTER!
KEIICHI! I KEPT MY EYE ON THE BALL!
SO... MAKE FUN OF ME, HUH?
THINK YOU'RE TOUGH, HUH?

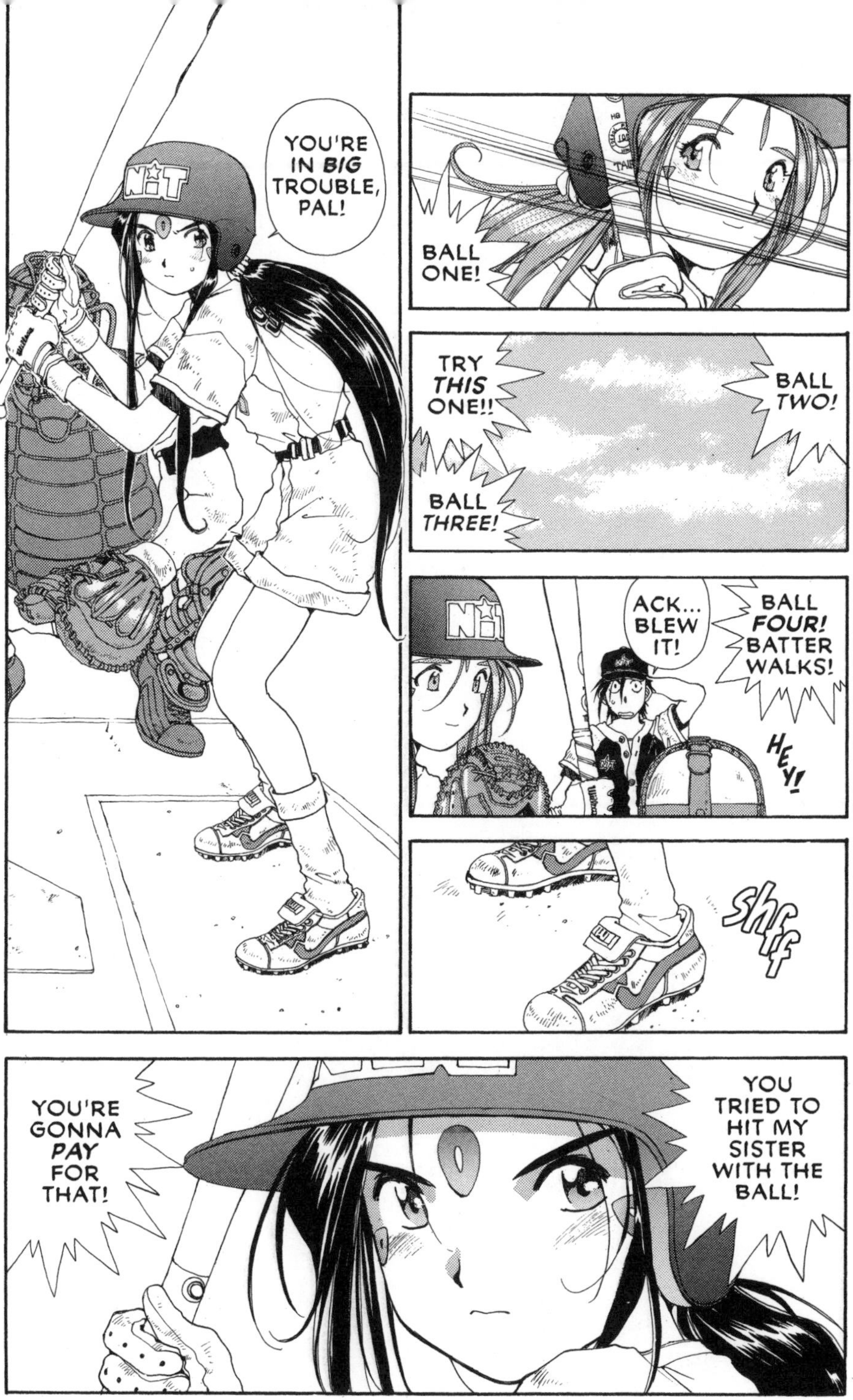
BALL ONE!
TRY THIS ONE!!
BALL TWO!
BALL THREE!
BALL FOUR! BATTER WALKS!
ACK... BLEW IT!
HEY!
SHFF
YOU'RE IN BIG TROUBLE, PAL!
YOU TRIED TO HIT MY SISTER WITH THE BALL!
YOU'RE GONNA PAY FOR THAT!

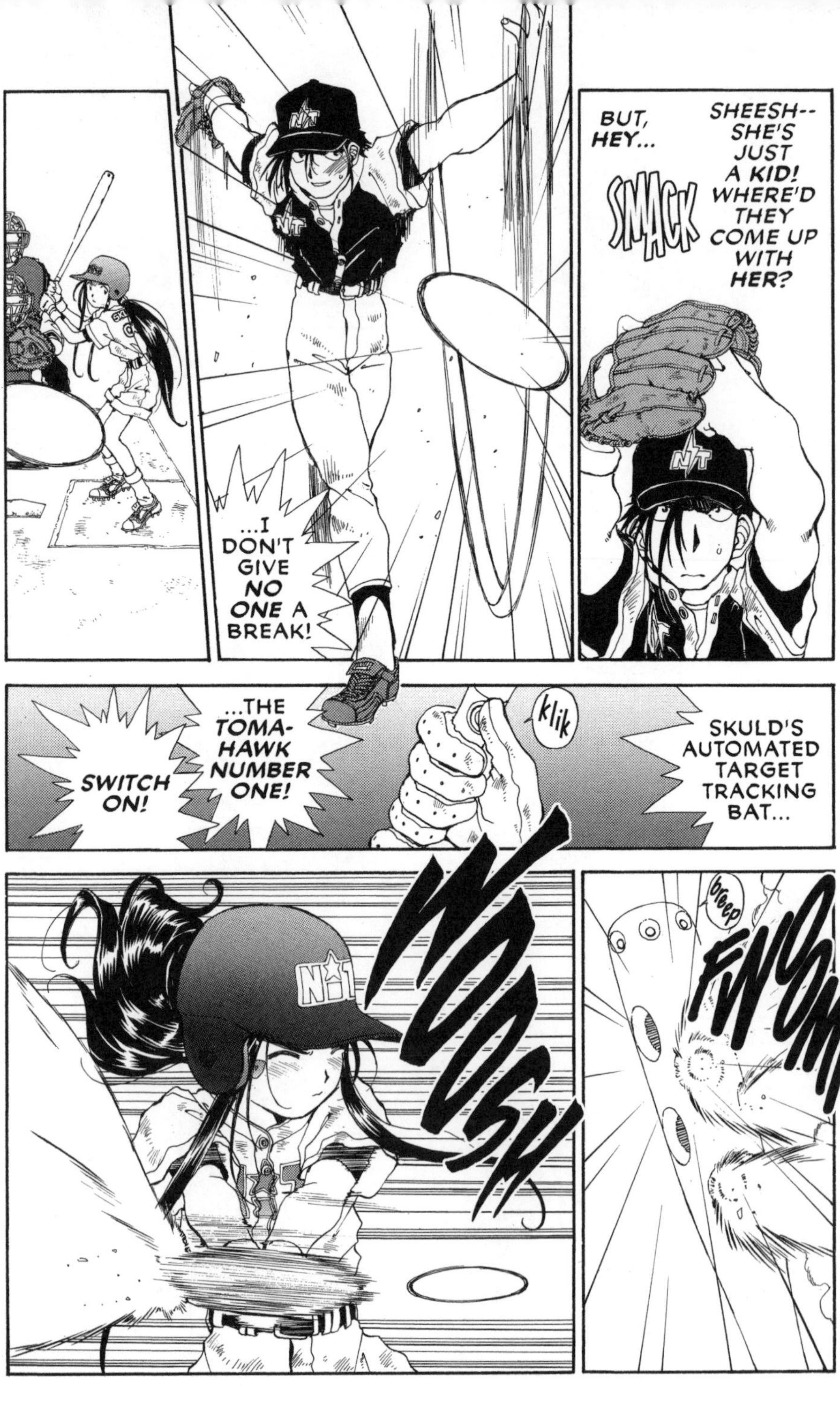
SHEESH-- SHE'S JUST A KID! WHERE'D THEY COME UP WITH HER?
BUT, HEY...
SMACK
...I DON'T GIVE NO ONE A BREAK!
SKULD'S AUTOMATED TARGET TRACKING BAT...
klik
...THE TOMA-HAWK NUMBER ONE!
SWITCH ON!
breep
FWOMP
WHOOSH

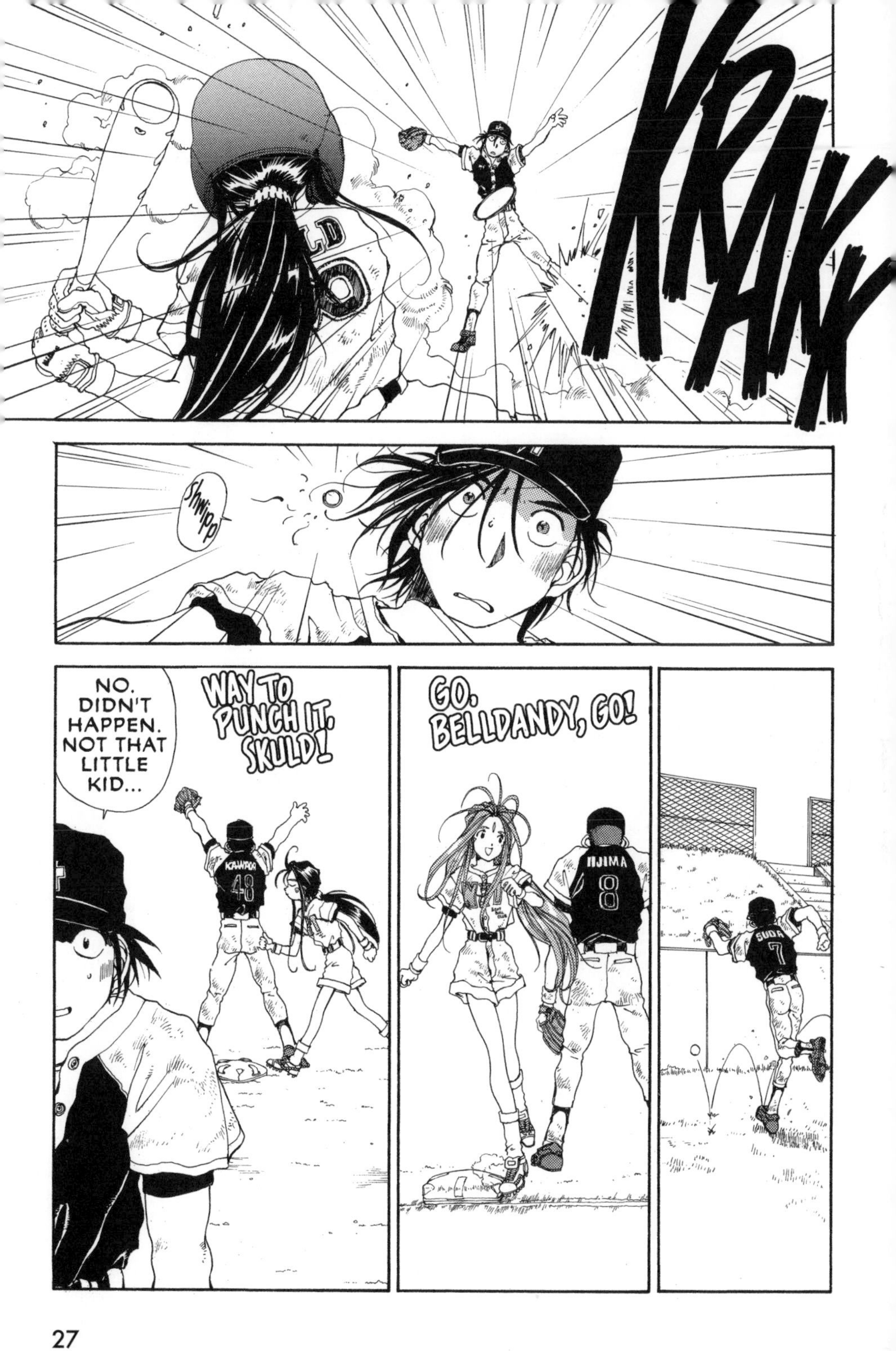
KRAKK
Shwipp
NO. DIDN'T HAPPEN. NOT THAT LITTLE KID...
WAY TO PUNCH IT, SKULD!
GO, BELLDANDY, GO!

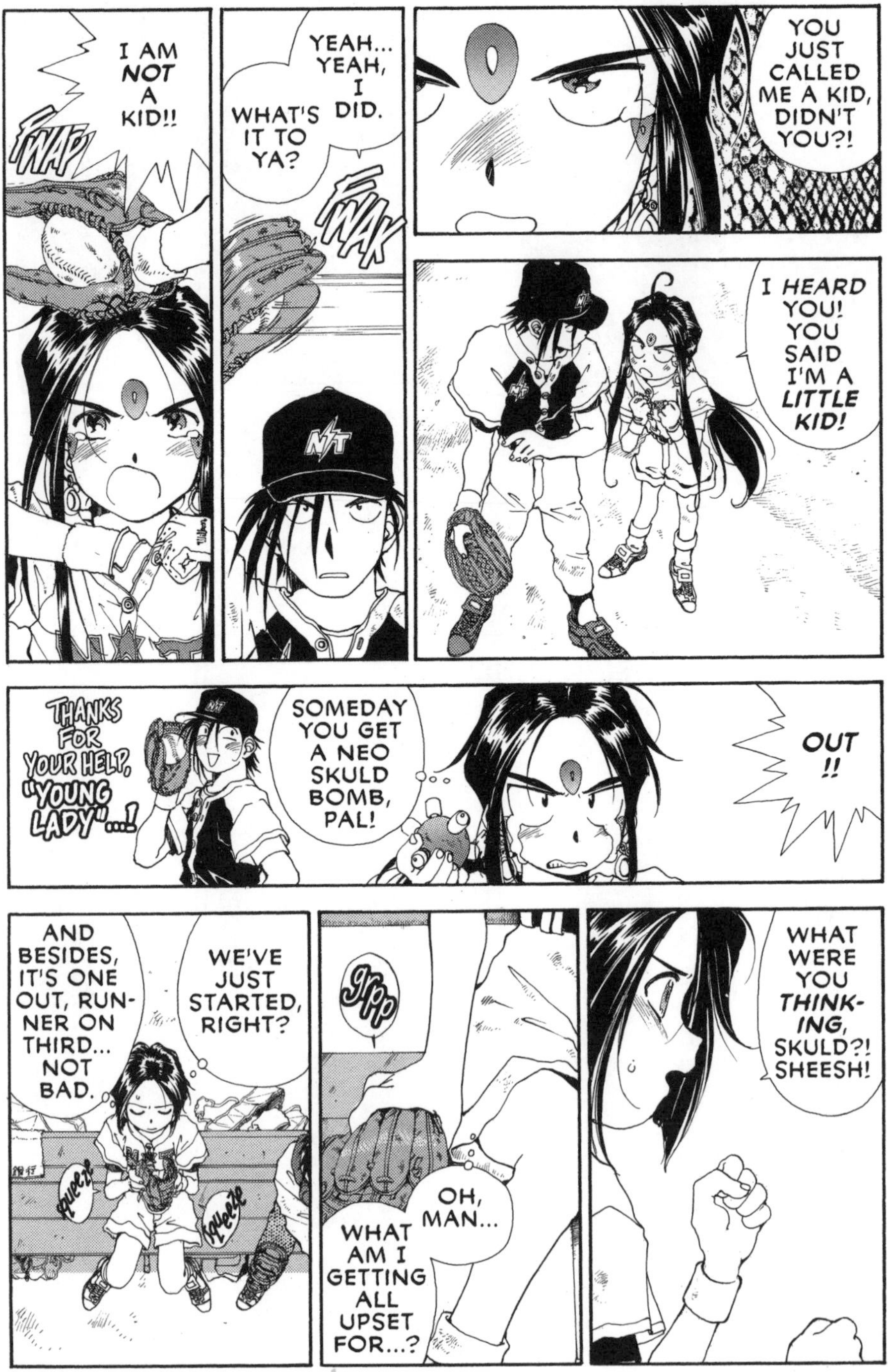
YOU JUST CALLED ME A KID, DIDN'T YOU?!
I *HEARD* YOU! YOU SAID I'M A *LITTLE KID!*
YEAH... YEAH, I DID.
WHAT'S IT TO YA?
FWAK
I AM *NOT* A KID!!
FWAP
OUT !!
SOMEDAY YOU GET A NEO SKULD BOMB, PAL!
THANKS FOR YOUR HELP, "YOUNG LADY"...!
WHAT WERE YOU *THINKING*, SKULD?! SHEESH!
grpp
OH, MAN...
WHAT AM I GETTING ALL UPSET FOR...?
WE'VE JUST STARTED, RIGHT?
AND BESIDES, IT'S ONE OUT, RUNNER ON THIRD... NOT BAD.
squeeze
squeeze

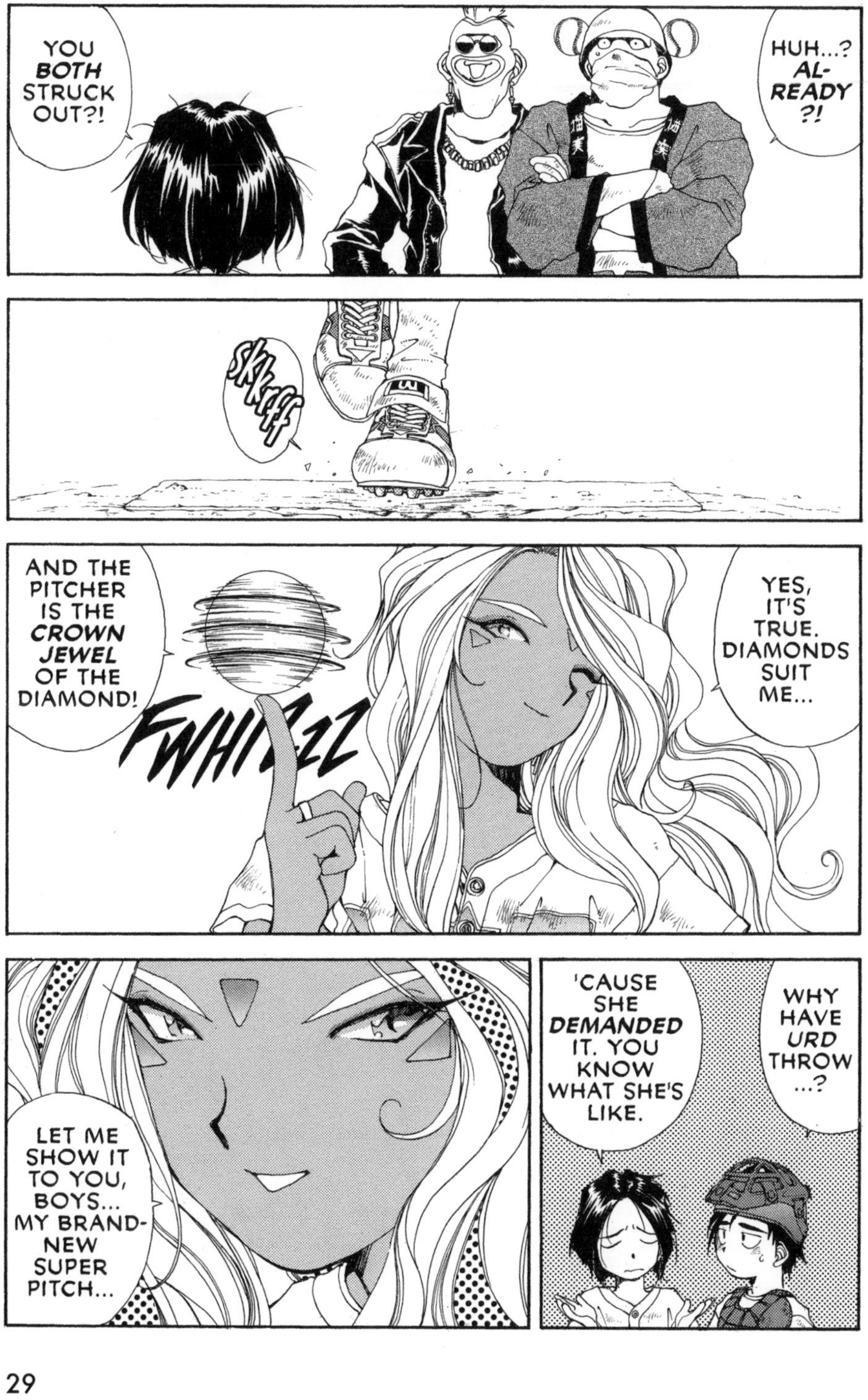
YOU *BOTH* STRUCK OUT?!
HUH...? *AL-READY* ?!
SKKRFF
AND THE PITCHER IS THE *CROWN JEWEL* OF THE DIAMOND!
FWHIZZZ
YES, IT'S TRUE. DIAMONDS SUIT ME...
LET ME SHOW IT TO YOU, BOYS... MY BRAND-NEW SUPER PITCH...
WHY HAVE *URD* THROW ...?
'CAUSE SHE *DEMANDED* IT. YOU KNOW WHAT SHE'S LIKE.

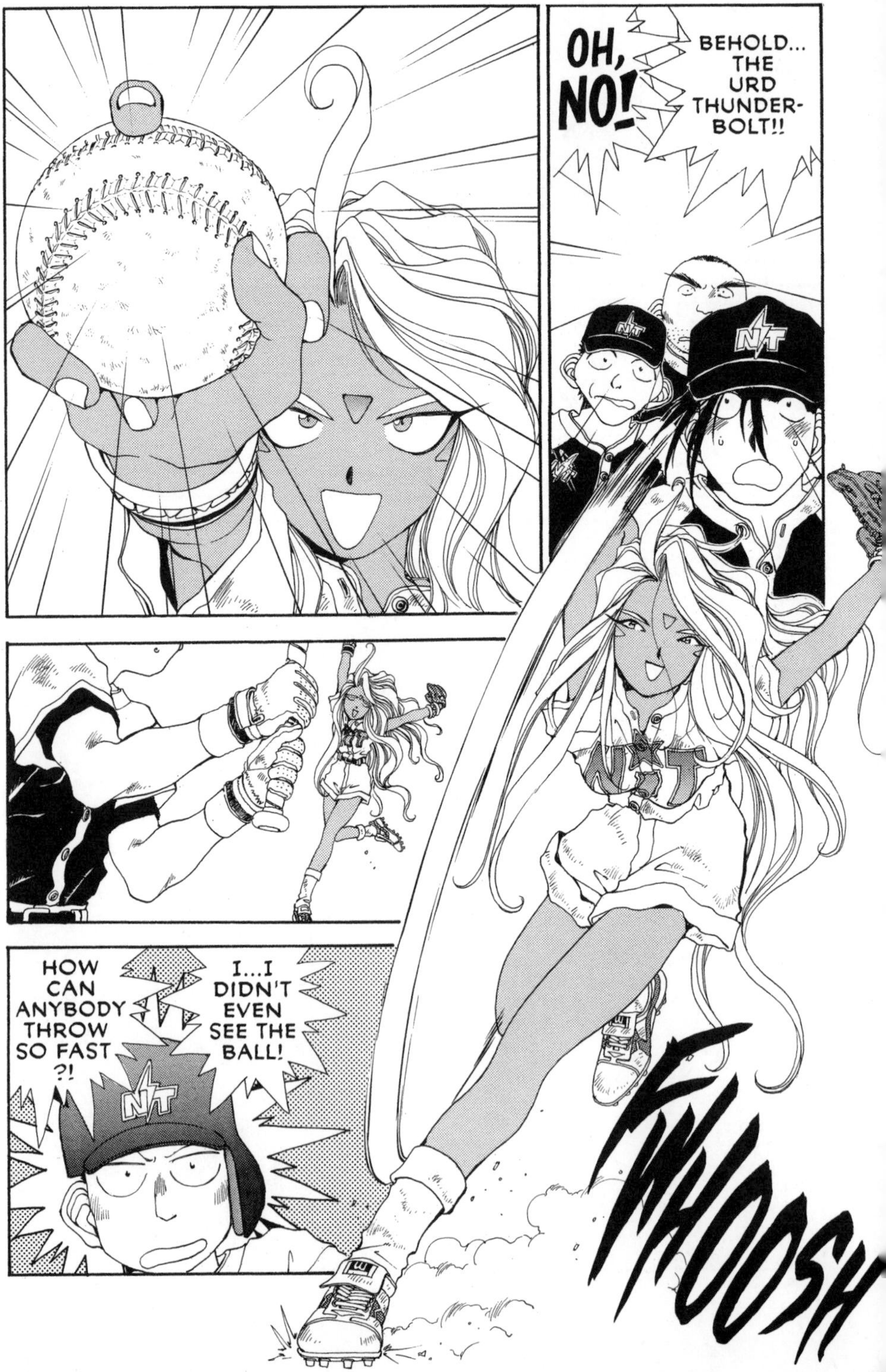
BEHOLD... THE URD THUNDER-BOLT!!
OH, NO!
I...I DIDN'T EVEN SEE THE BALL!
HOW CAN ANYBODY THROW SO FAST?!
WHOOSH

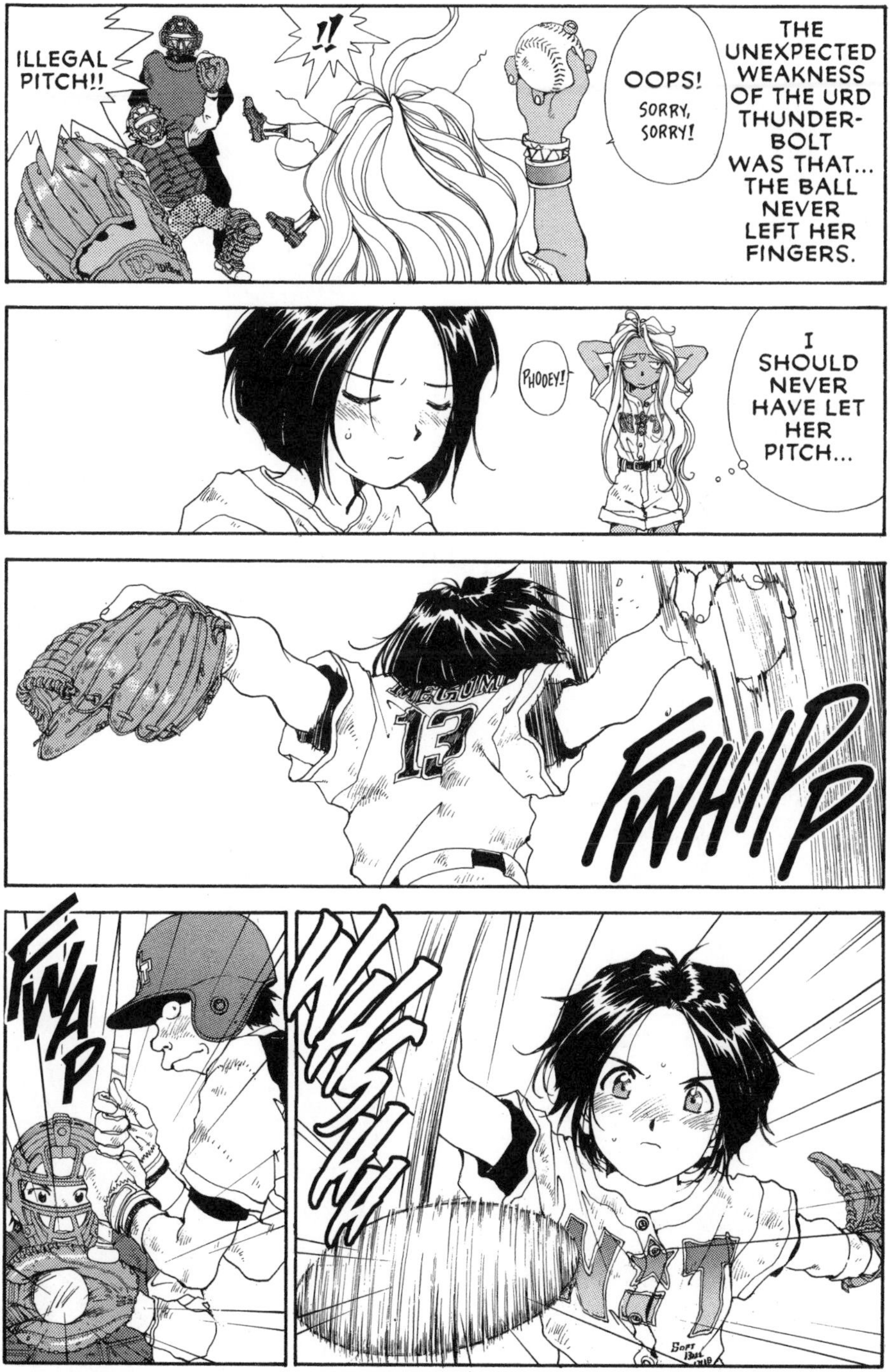
THE UNEXPECTED WEAKNESS OF THE URD THUNDER-BOLT WAS THAT... THE BALL NEVER LEFT HER FINGERS.
OOPS! SORRY, SORRY!
!!
ILLEGAL PITCH!!
I SHOULD NEVER HAVE LET HER PITCH...
PHOOEY!
FWHIP
FWAP

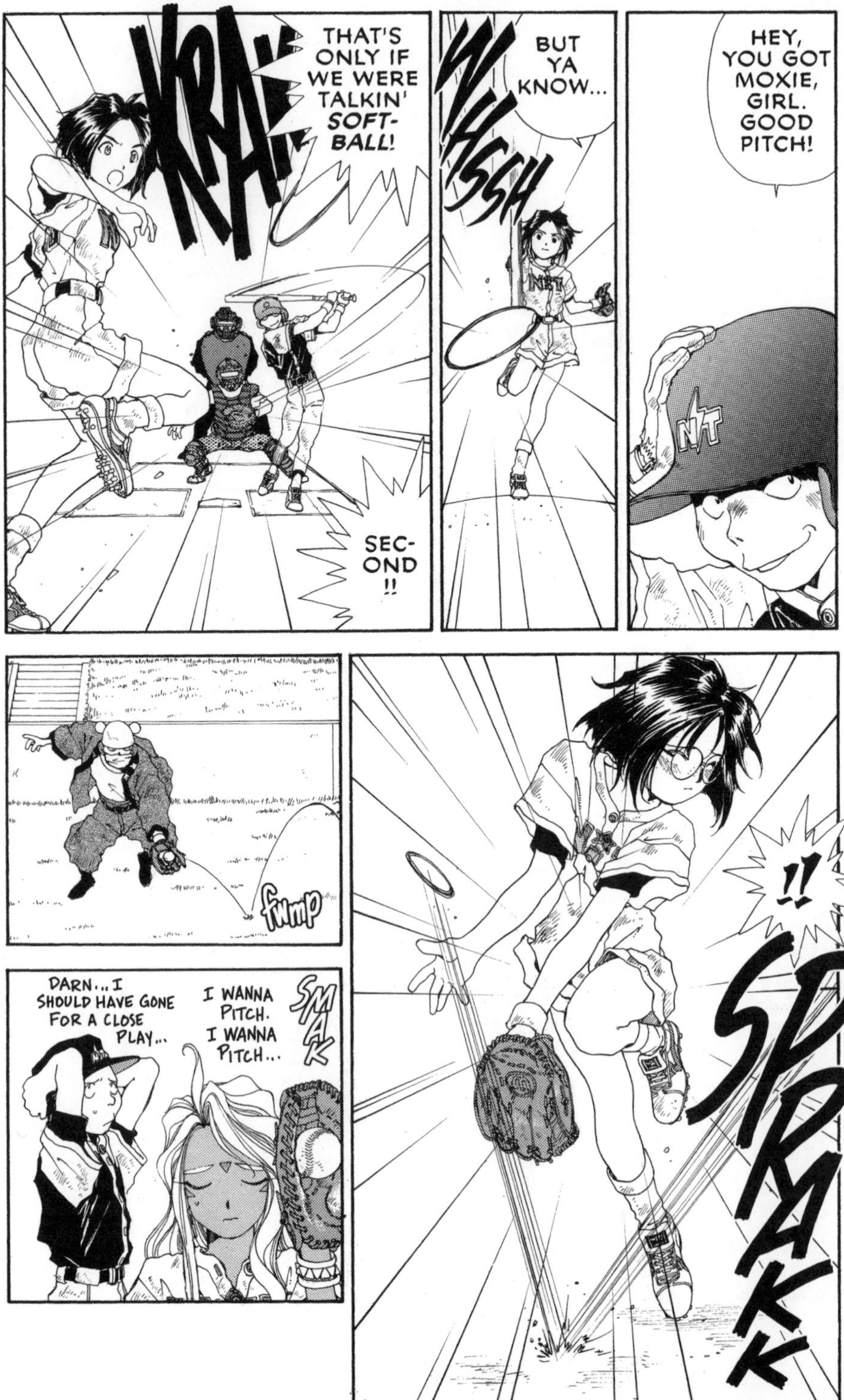
HEY, YOU GOT MOXIE, GIRL. GOOD PITCH!
BUT YA KNOW...
WHHSSH
THAT'S ONLY IF WE WERE TALKIN' *SOFT-BALL*!
KRAK
SEC-OND !!
!!
SPRAKK
fwmp
SMAK
I WANNA PITCH. I WANNA PITCH...
DARN... I SHOULD HAVE GONE FOR A CLOSE PLAY...

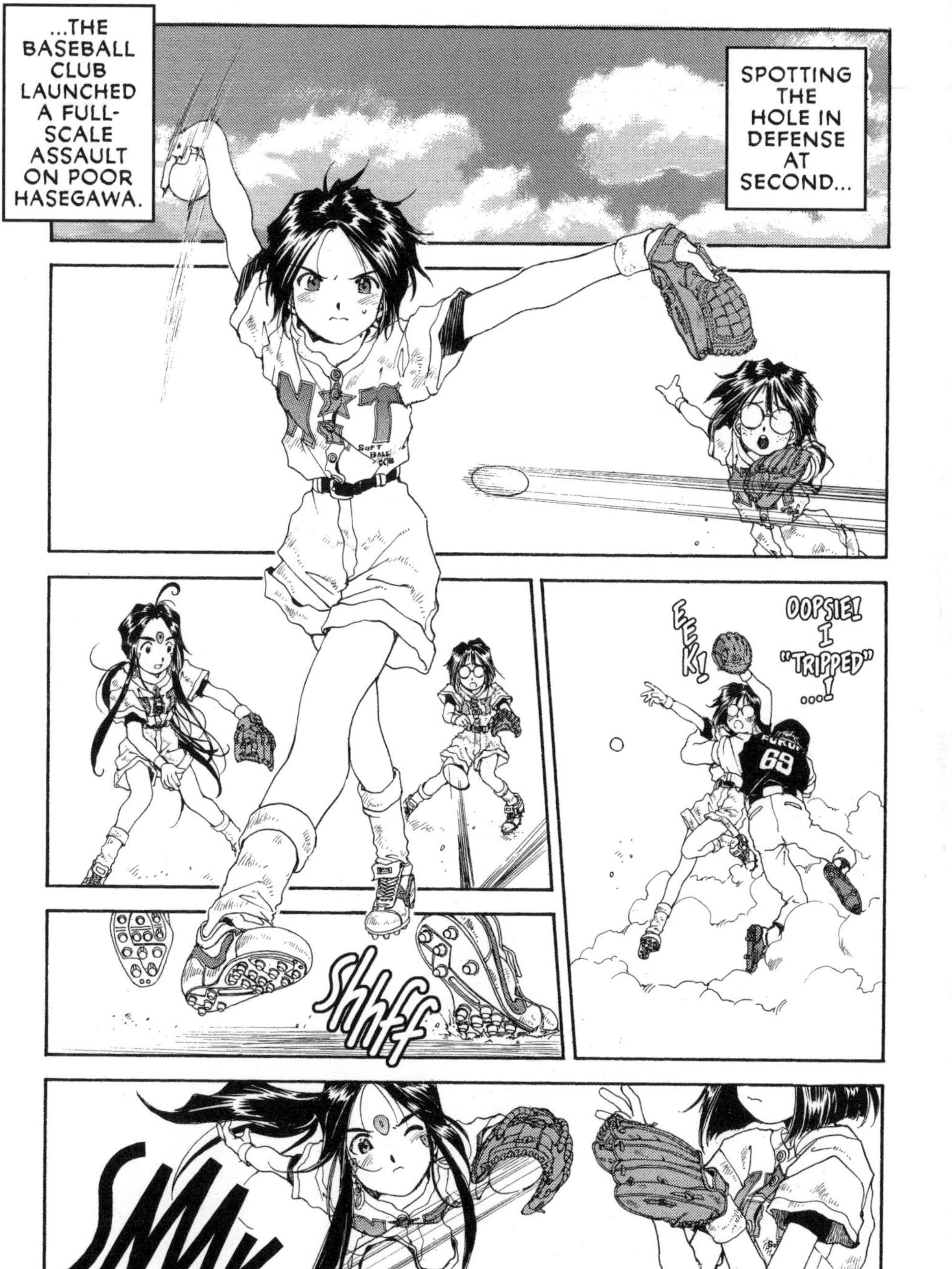
...THE BASEBALL CLUB LAUNCHED A FULL-SCALE ASSAULT ON POOR HASEGAWA.
SPOTTING THE HOLE IN DEFENSE AT SECOND...
SHHFF
EEK!
OOPSIE! I "TRIPPED"...!
SMAK

IT PICKS THEM RIGHT OFF!

HEH HEH... PRETTY COOL, HUH?! AN AUTO-TRACKING GLOVE!

GET YOUR PAWS OFF ME!

FWAKK

YA!EE!

...SKULD-CHAN.

THANKS FOR... COVER-ING ME...

HOW LONG DO YOU PLAN TO STAY THERE ...?

FOR-EVER AN' EVER!! ♥

Smak

TRIPLE PLAY! CHANGE!

HANG IN THERE, SORA!

HEH, HEH... ...THANKS.

	1	2	3	4	5	6	7	8
SOFT	0	1	0					
BASE	4	8	5					

WOW! YOU'RE SO COOL, SKULD!

...um ...

I...

I GUESS IT WAS HOPE-LESS, AFTER ALL.

sigh

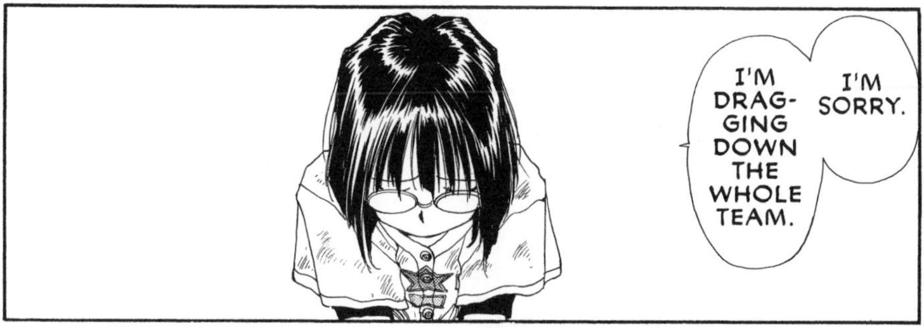
I'M SORRY.
I'M DRAG-GING DOWN THE WHOLE TEAM.

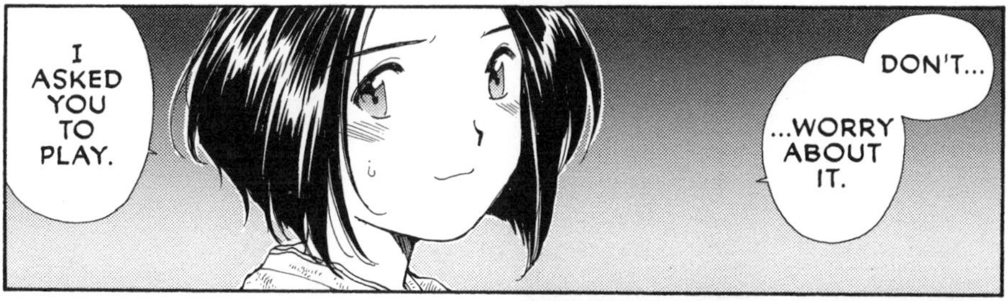
DON'T...
...WORRY ABOUT IT.
I ASKED YOU TO PLAY.

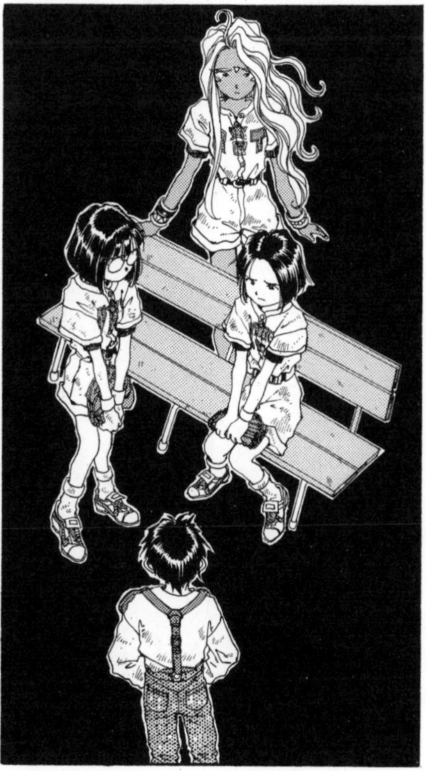

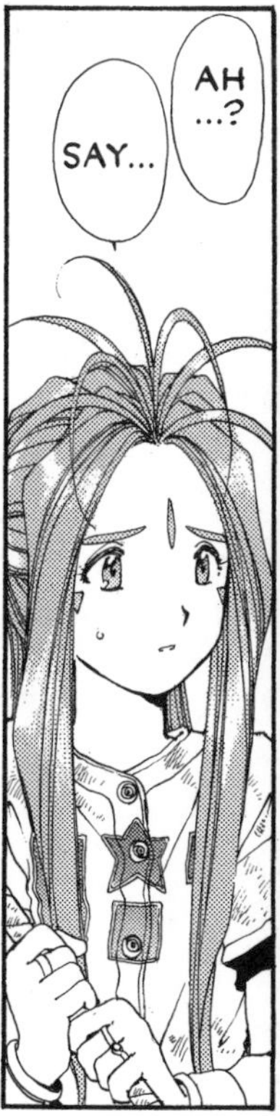
AH ...?
SAY...

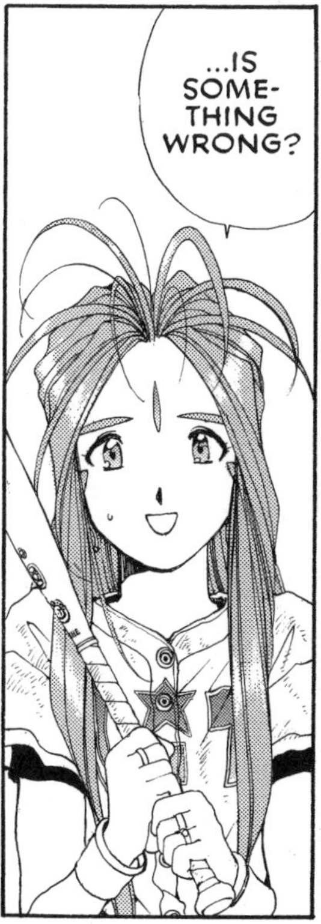
...IS SOME-THING WRONG?

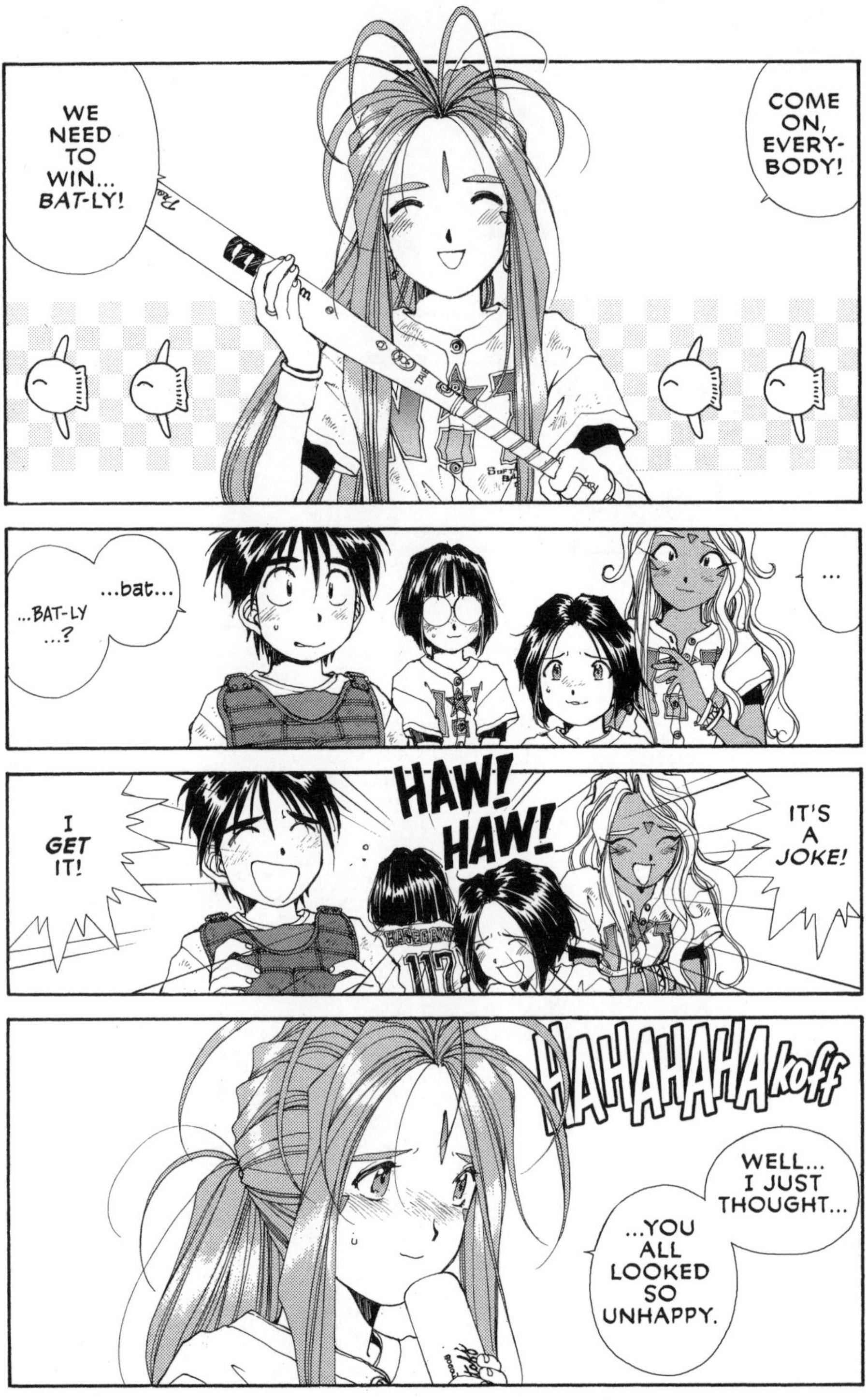
COME ON, EVERY-BODY!
WE NEED TO WIN... BAT-LY!
...
...bat...
...BAT-LY ...?
IT'S A JOKE!
HAW! HAW!
I GET IT!
HAHAHAHAHA koff
WELL... I JUST THOUGHT...
...YOU ALL LOOKED SO UNHAPPY.

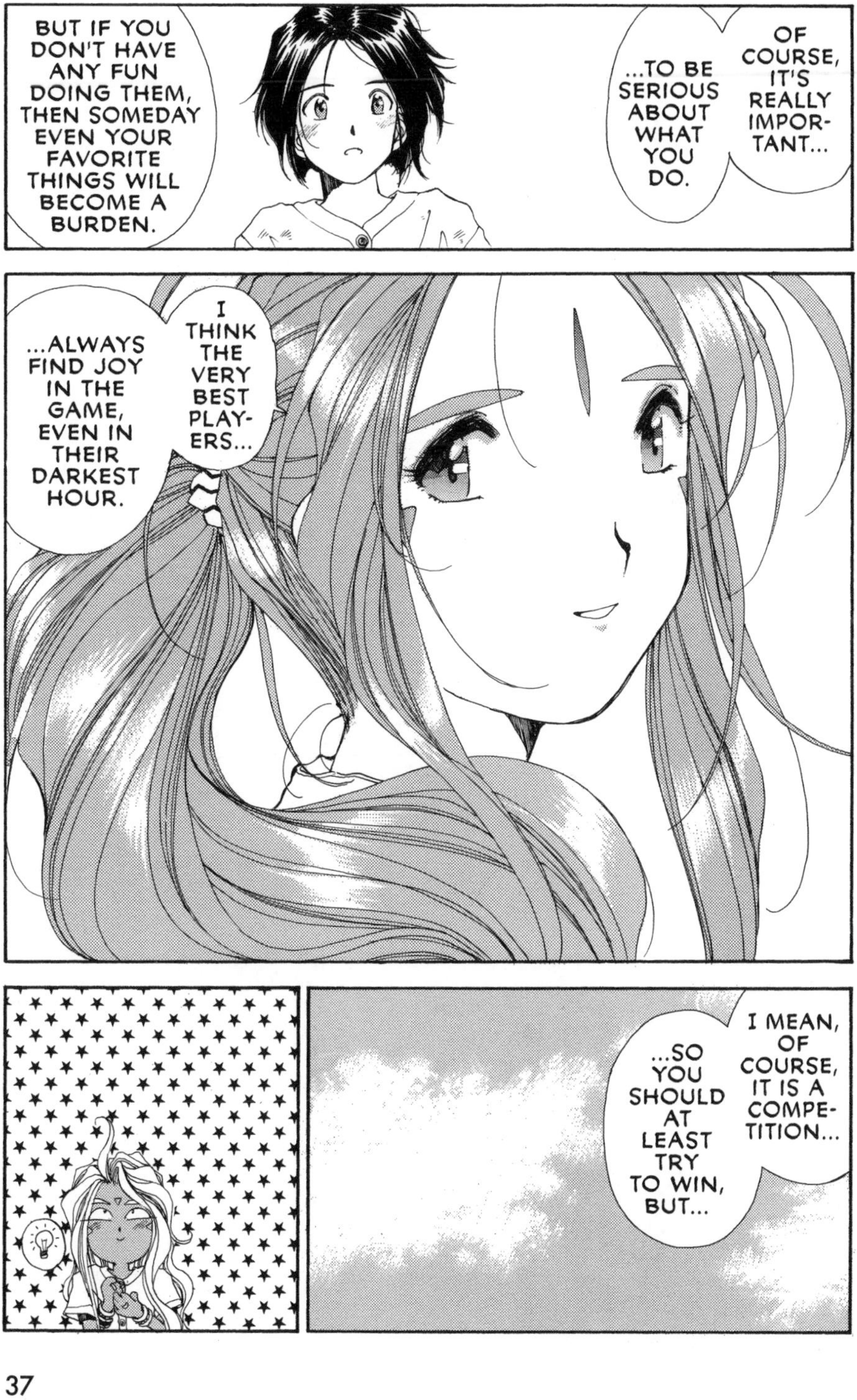
OF COURSE, IT'S REALLY IMPORTANT...
...TO BE SERIOUS ABOUT WHAT YOU DO.
BUT IF YOU DON'T HAVE ANY FUN DOING THEM, THEN SOMEDAY EVEN YOUR FAVORITE THINGS WILL BECOME A BURDEN.
I THINK THE VERY BEST PLAYERS...
...ALWAYS FIND JOY IN THE GAME, EVEN IN THEIR DARKEST HOUR.
I MEAN, OF COURSE, IT IS A COMPETITION...
...SO YOU SHOULD AT LEAST TRY TO WIN, BUT...

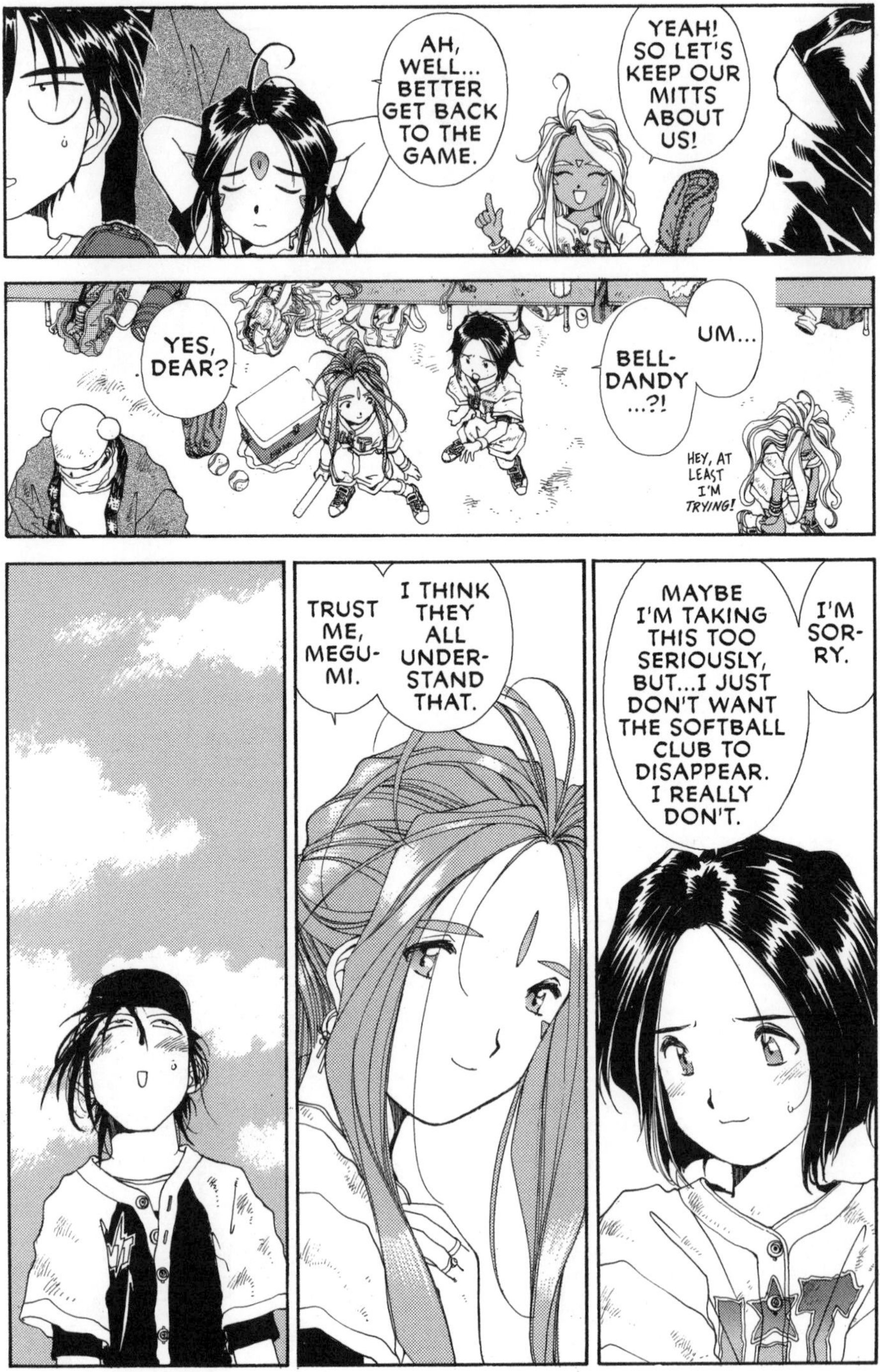
YEAH! SO LET'S KEEP OUR MITTS ABOUT US!
AH, WELL... BETTER GET BACK TO THE GAME.
UM...
BELL-DANDY ...?!
HEY, AT LEAST I'M *TRYING!*
YES, DEAR?
I'M SOR-RY.
MAYBE I'M TAKING THIS TOO SERIOUSLY, BUT...I JUST DON'T WANT THE SOFTBALL CLUB TO DISAPPEAR. I REALLY DON'T.
I THINK THEY ALL UNDER-STAND THAT.
TRUST ME, MEGU-MI.

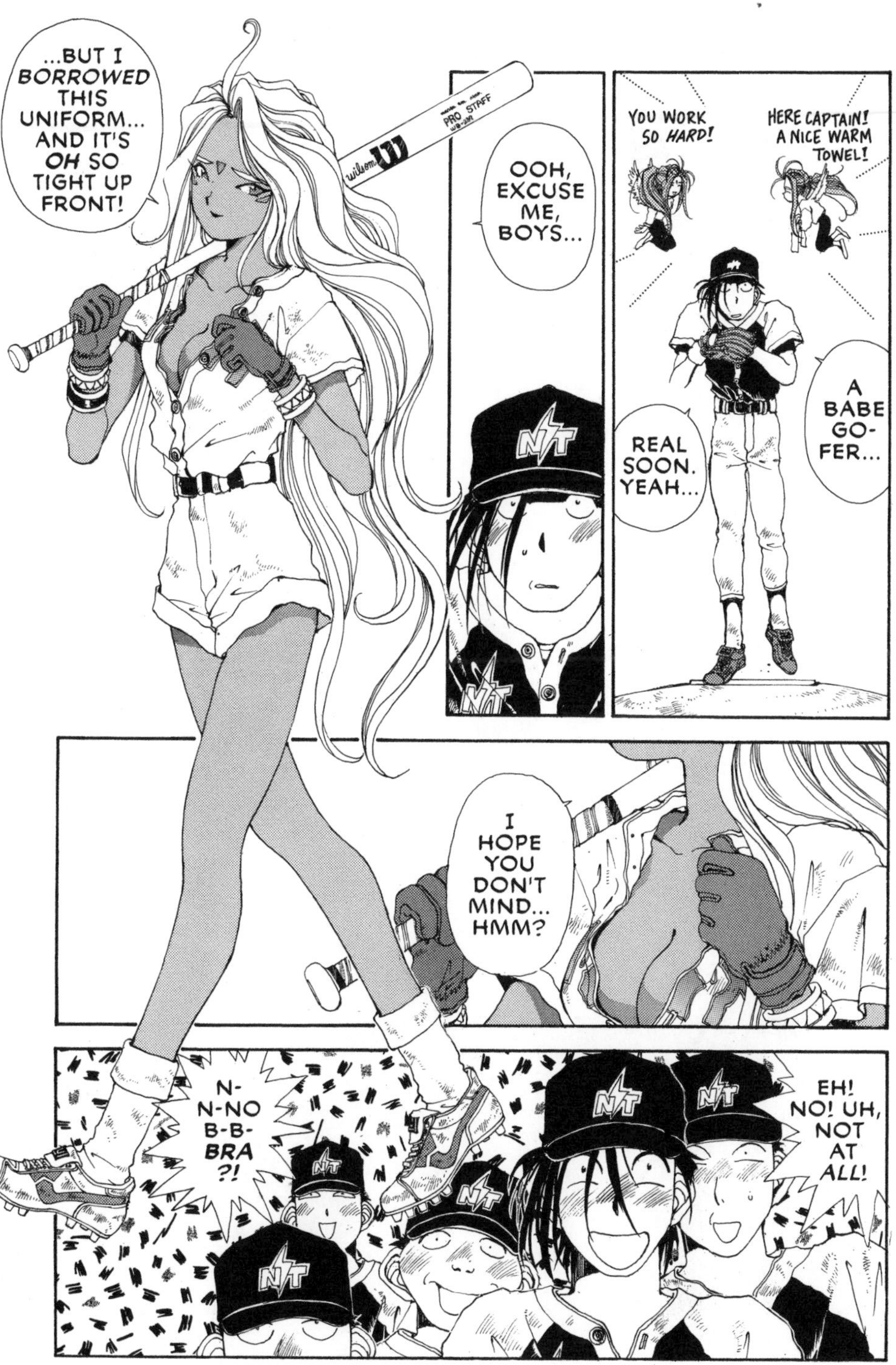
HERE CAPTAIN! A NICE WARM TOWEL!
YOU WORK SO HARD!
A BABE GO-FER...
REAL SOON. YEAH...
OOH, EXCUSE ME, BOYS...
...BUT I BORROWED THIS UNIFORM... AND IT'S OH SO TIGHT UP FRONT!
I HOPE YOU DON'T MIND... HMM?
EH! NO! UH, NOT AT ALL!
N-N-NO B-B-BRA?!

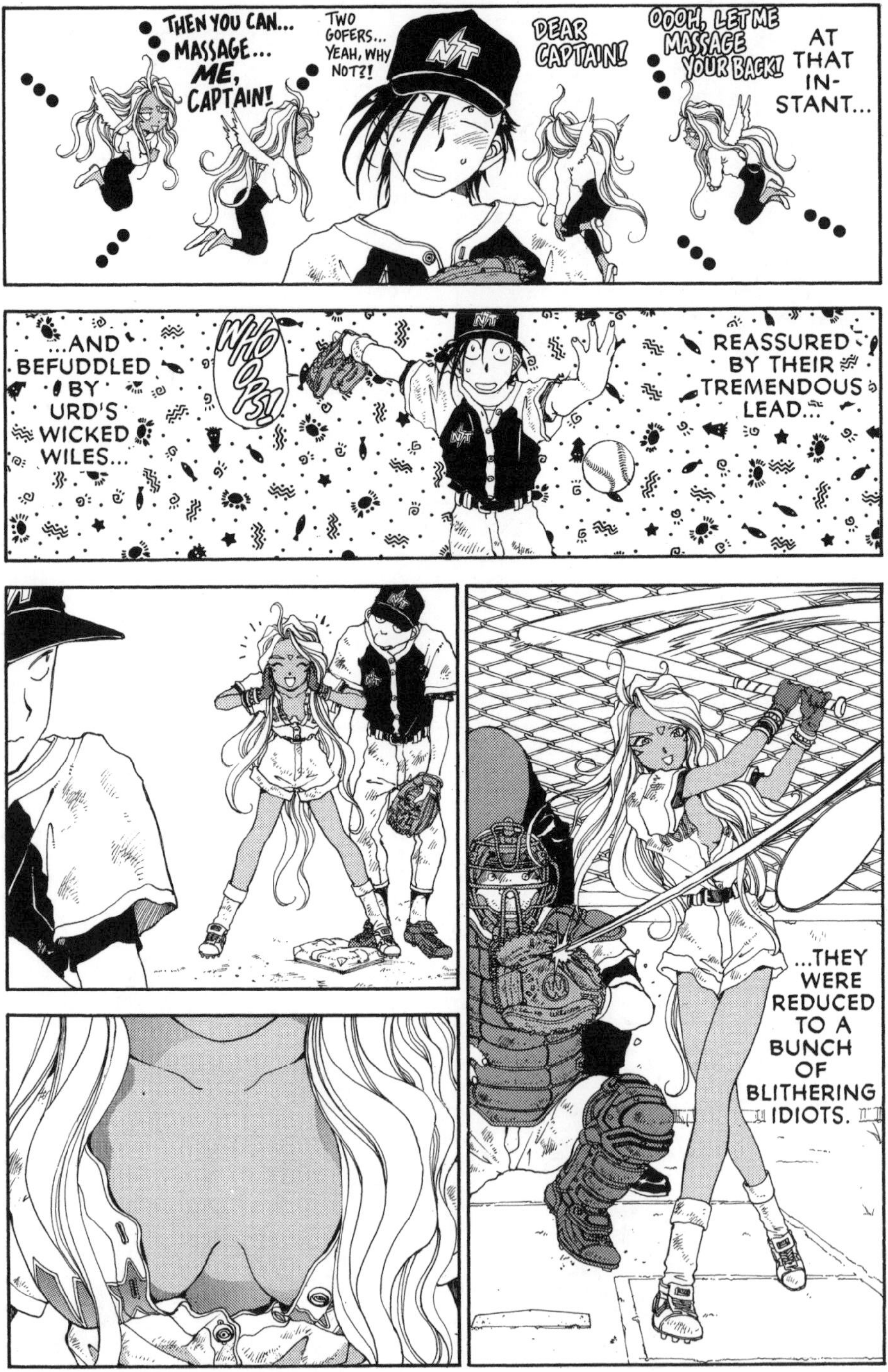
AT THAT IN-STANT...
OOOH, LET ME MASSAGE YOUR BACK!
DEAR CAPTAIN!
TWO GOFERS... YEAH, WHY NOT?!
THEN YOU CAN... MASSAGE... ME, CAPTAIN!
REASSURED BY THEIR TREMENDOUS LEAD...
WHOOPS!
...AND BEFUDDLED BY URD'S WICKED WILES...
...THEY WERE REDUCED TO A BUNCH OF BLITHERING IDIOTS.

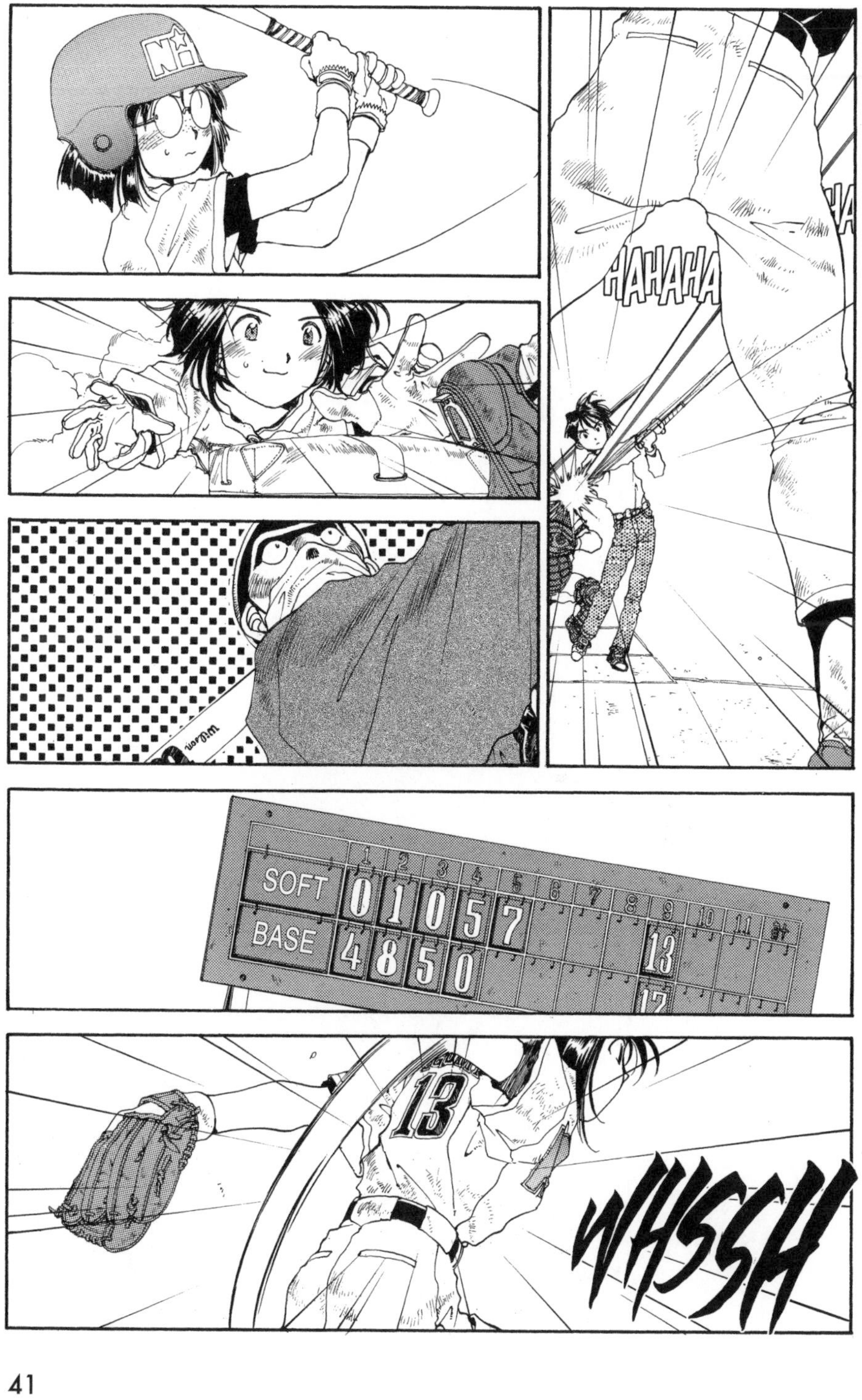
HAHAHA
NH
SOFT 0 1 0 5 7
BASE 4 8 5 0
13
13
WHSSH

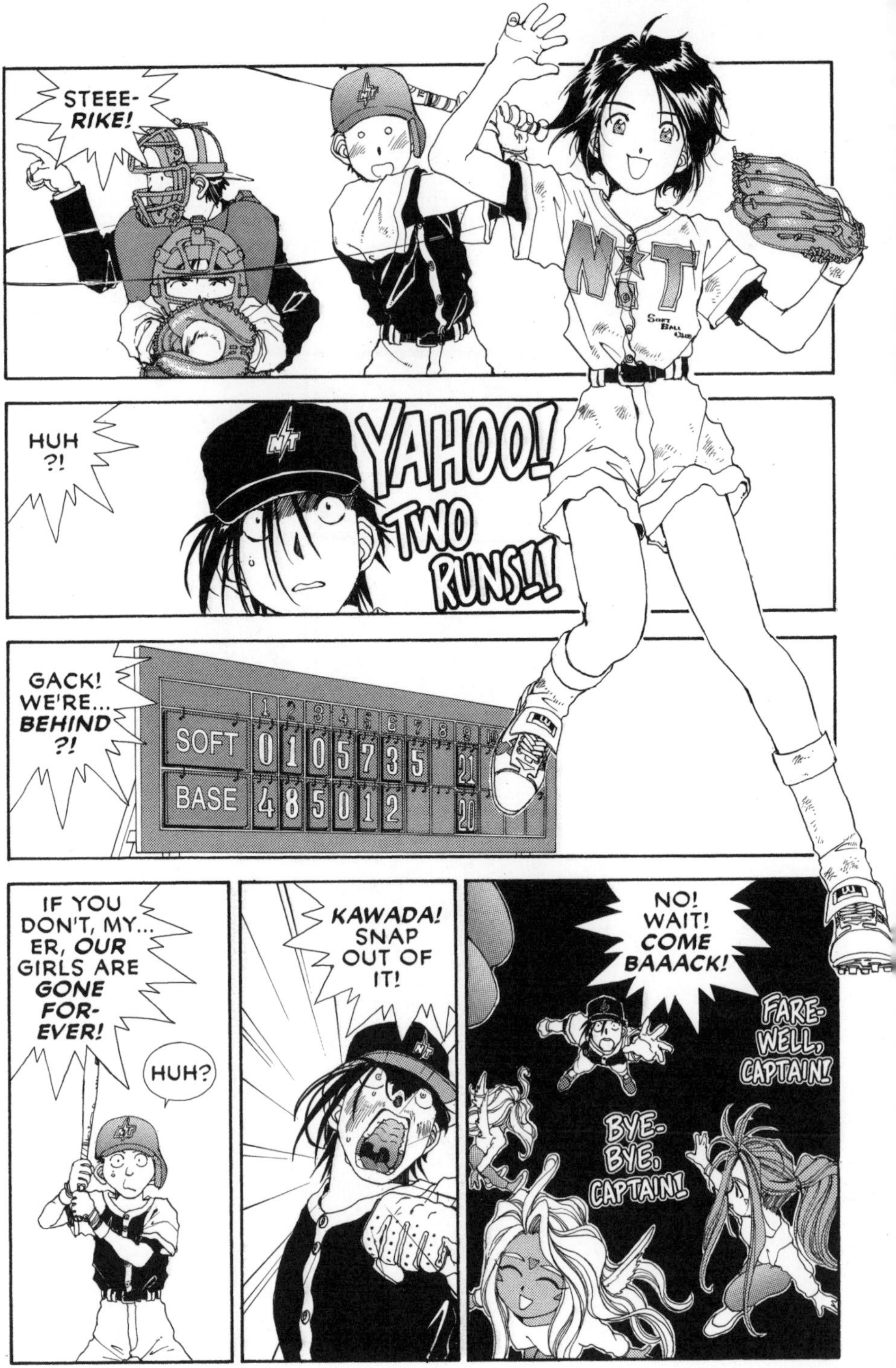
STEEE-RIKE!
HUH ?!
YAHOO! TWO RUNS!!
GACK! WE'RE... BEHIND ?!
SOFT 0 1 0 5 7 3 5 21
BASE 4 8 5 0 1 2 20
IF YOU DON'T, MY... ER, OUR GIRLS ARE GONE FOR-EVER!
HUH?
KAWADA! SNAP OUT OF IT!
NO! WAIT! COME BAAACK!
FARE-WELL, CAPTAIN!
BYE-BYE, CAPTAIN!

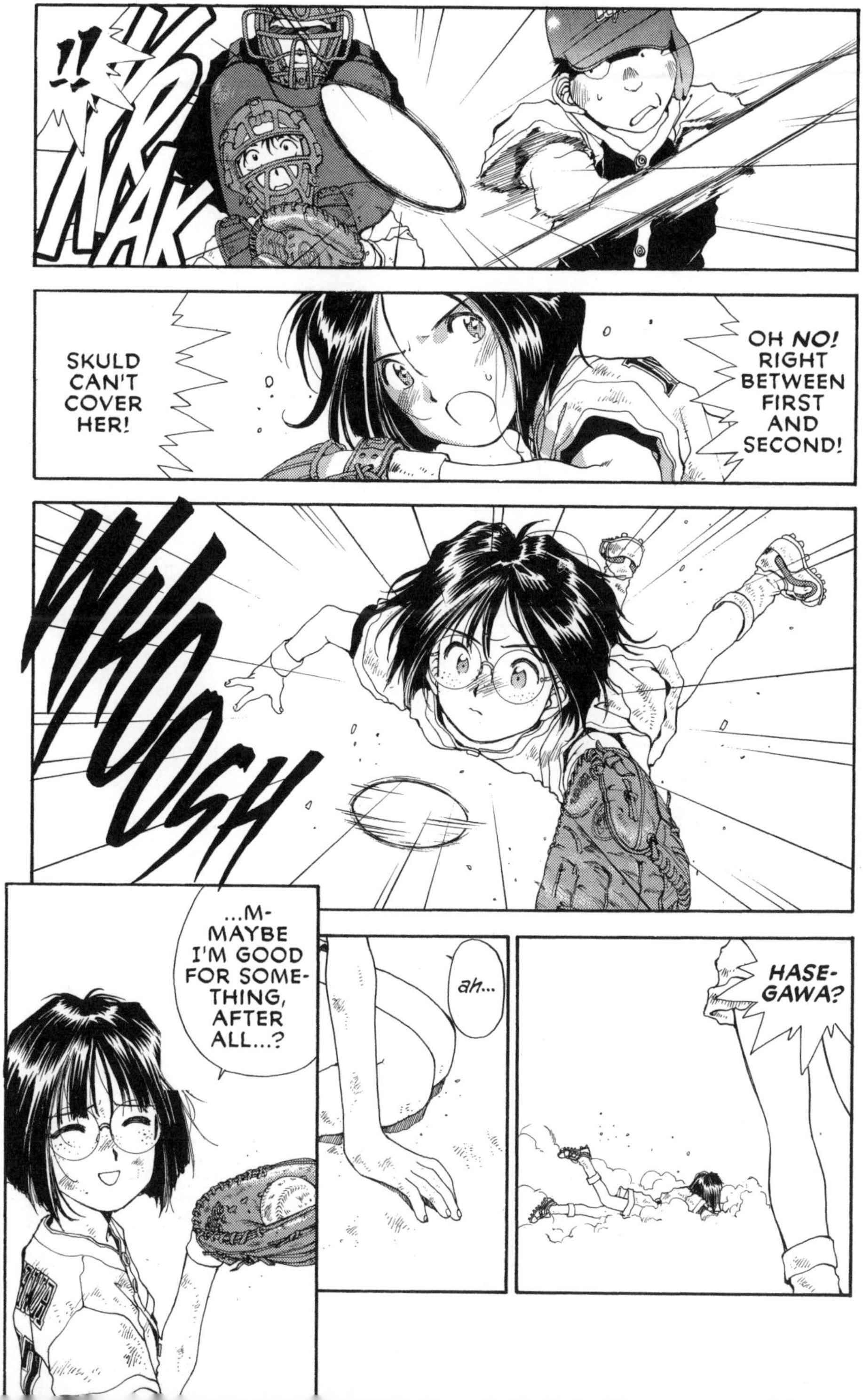
OH NO! RIGHT BETWEEN FIRST AND SECOND!
SKULD CAN'T COVER HER!
WHOOSH
HASE-GAWA?
ah...
...M-MAYBE I'M GOOD FOR SOME-THING, AFTER ALL...?

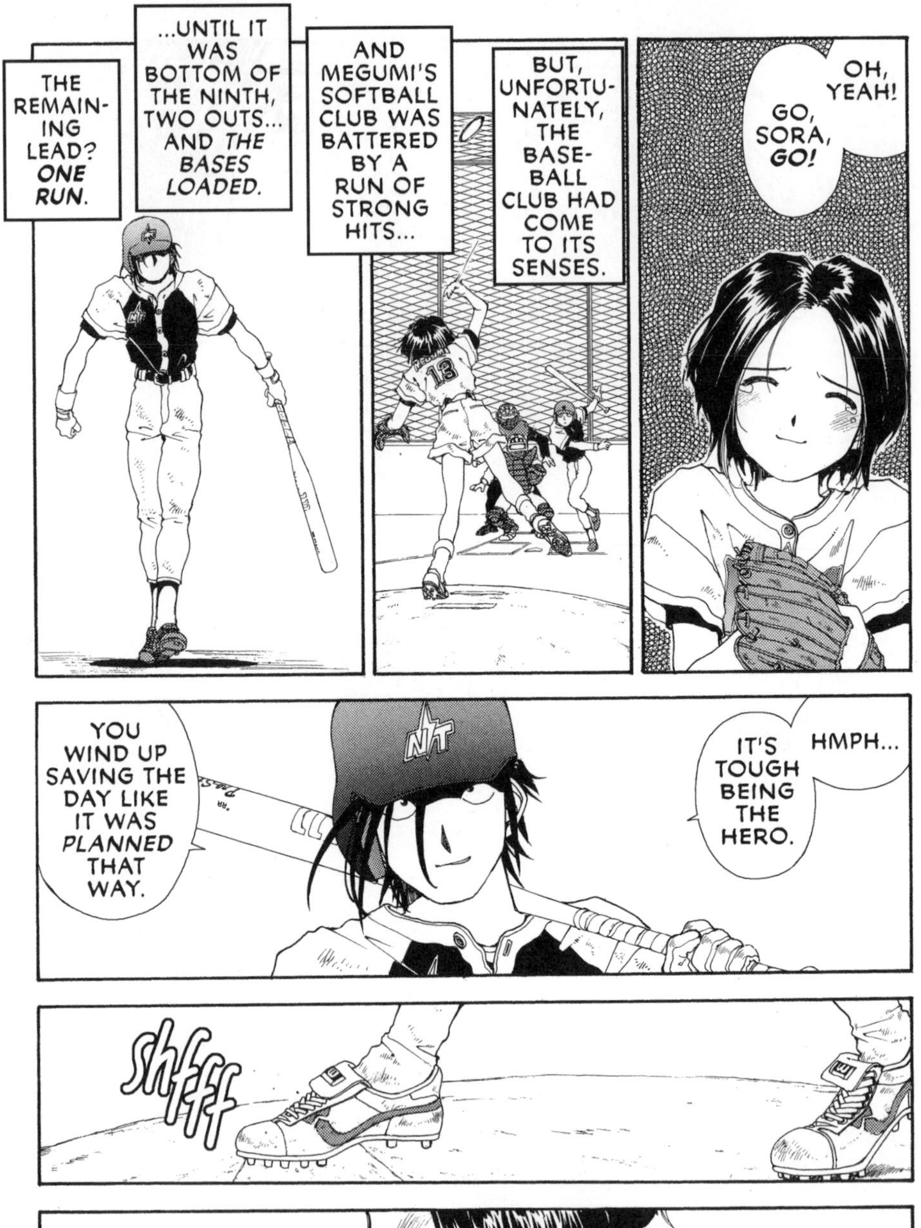

THE REMAINING LEAD? *ONE RUN*.
...UNTIL IT WAS BOTTOM OF THE NINTH, TWO OUTS... AND *THE BASES LOADED*.
AND MEGUMI'S SOFTBALL CLUB WAS BATTERED BY A RUN OF STRONG HITS...
BUT, UNFORTUNATELY, THE BASEBALL CLUB HAD COME TO ITS SENSES.
OH, YEAH!
GO, SORA, *GO!*
YOU WIND UP SAVING THE DAY LIKE IT WAS *PLANNED* THAT WAY.
HMPH...
IT'S TOUGH BEING THE HERO.
shfff
hahh

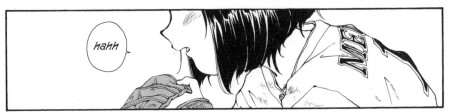

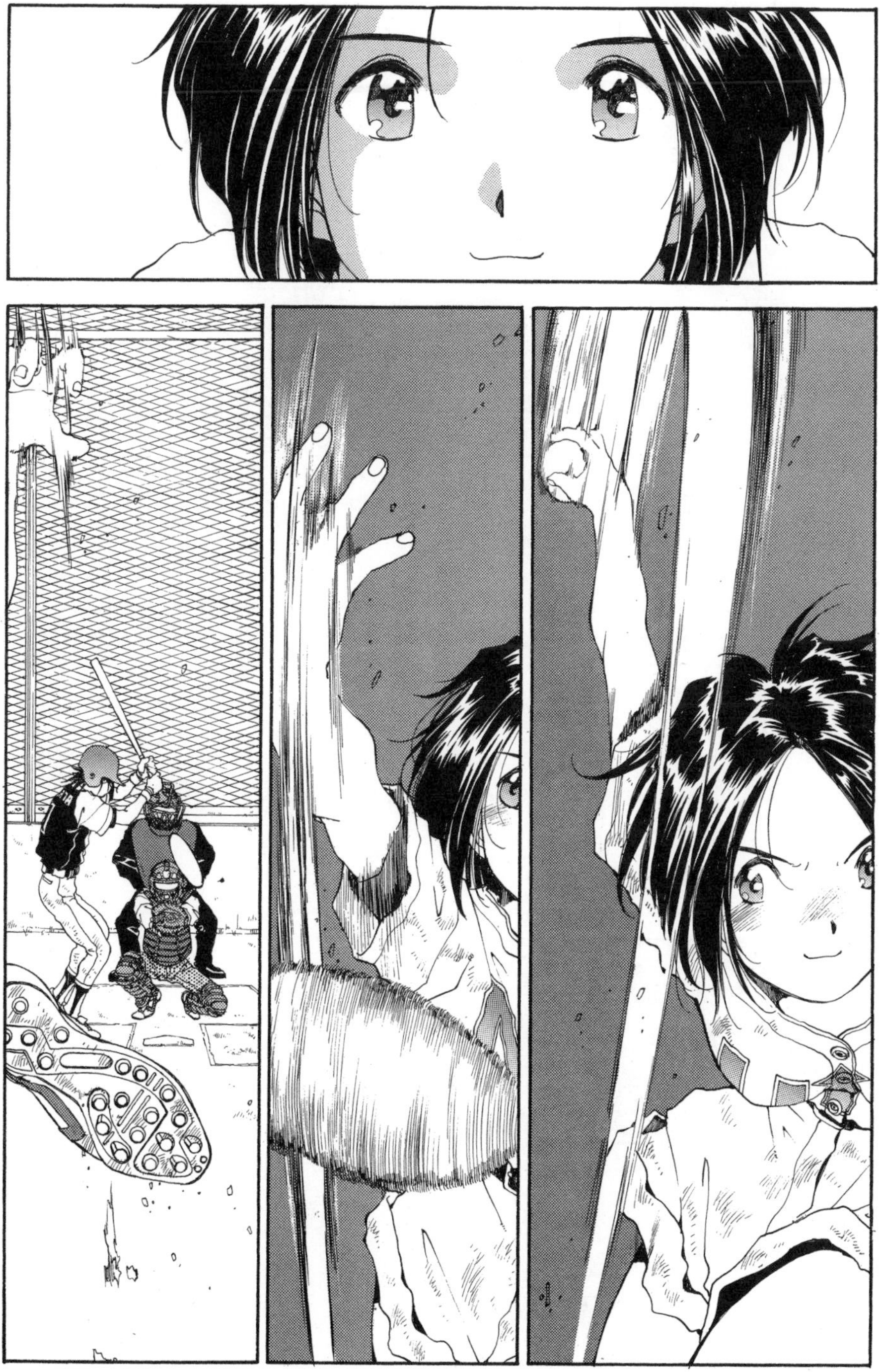

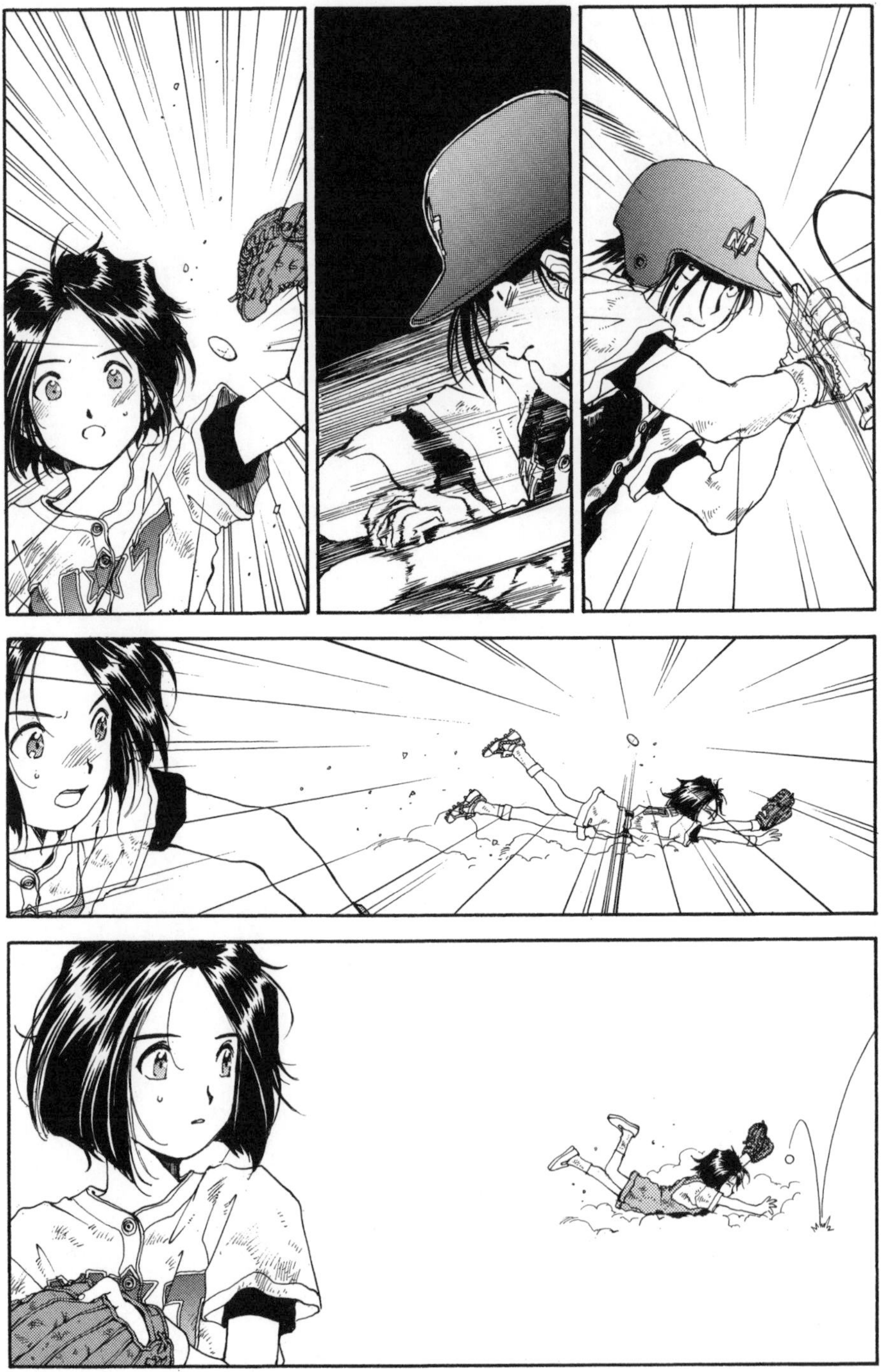

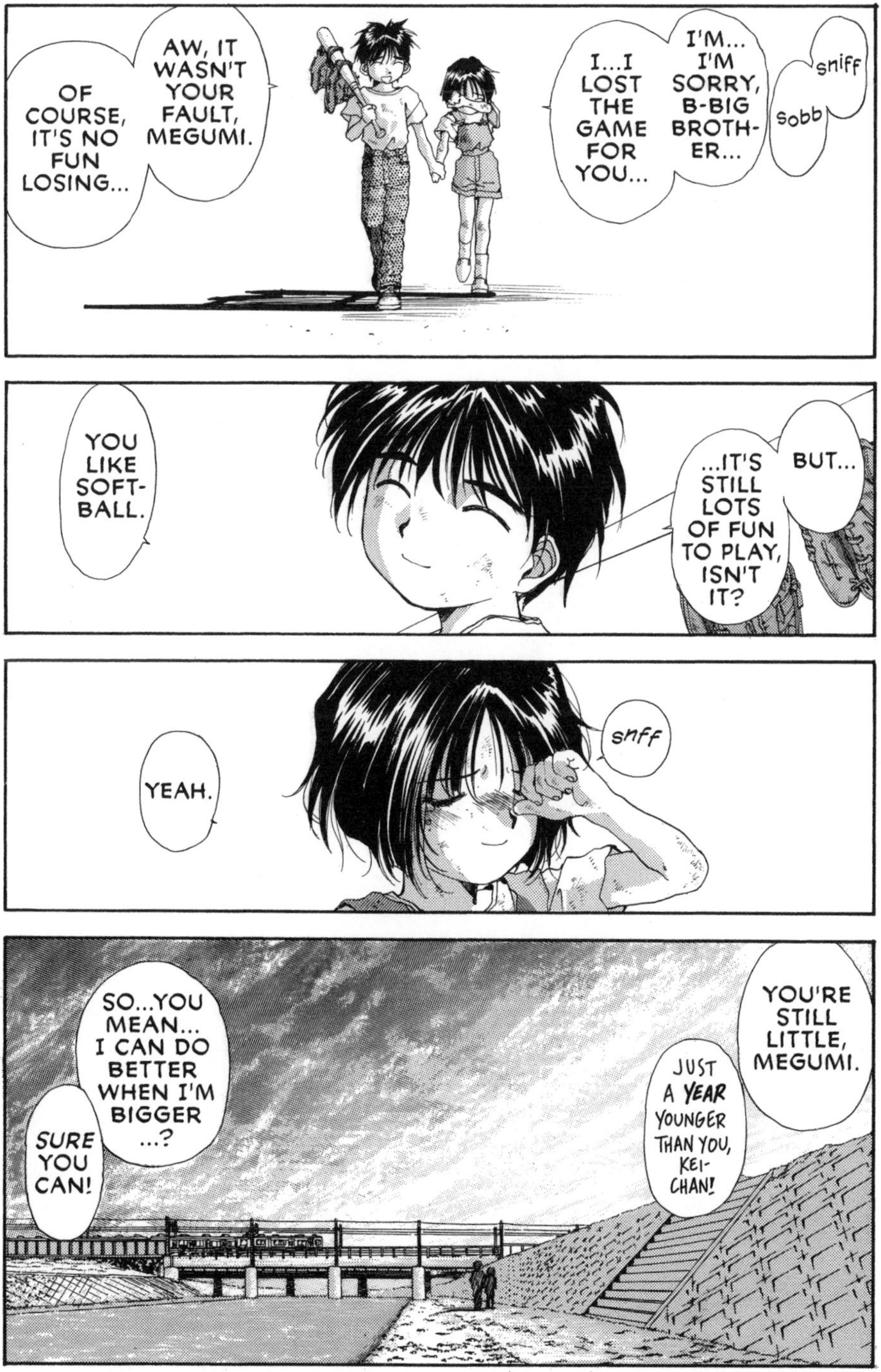
sniff
Sobb
I'M... I'M SORRY, B-BIG BROTHER...
I...I LOST THE GAME FOR YOU...
AW, IT WASN'T YOUR FAULT, MEGUMI.
OF COURSE, IT'S NO FUN LOSING...
BUT...
...IT'S STILL LOTS OF FUN TO PLAY, ISN'T IT?
YOU LIKE SOFT-BALL.
snff
YEAH.
YOU'RE STILL LITTLE, MEGUMI.
JUST A YEAR YOUNGER THAN YOU, KEI-CHAN!
SO...YOU MEAN... I CAN DO BETTER WHEN I'M BIGGER ...?
SURE YOU CAN!

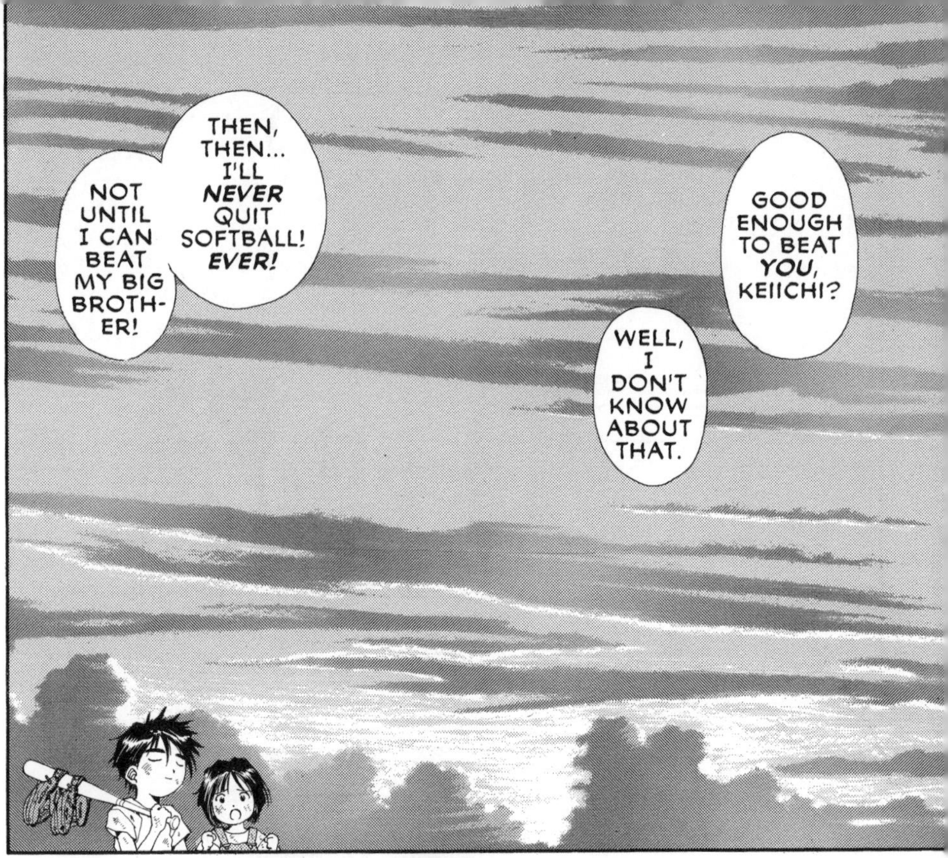
GOOD ENOUGH TO BEAT *YOU*, KEIICHI?
WELL, I DON'T KNOW ABOUT THAT.
THEN, THEN... I'LL *NEVER* QUIT SOFTBALL! *EVER!*
NOT UNTIL I CAN BEAT MY BIG BROTHER!

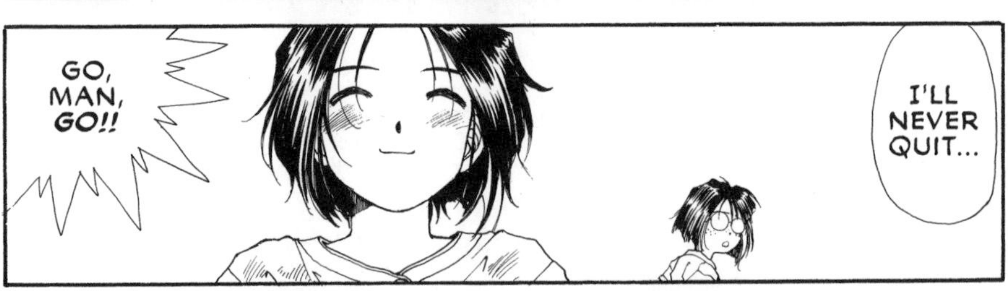
I'LL NEVER QUIT...
GO, MAN, *GO!!*

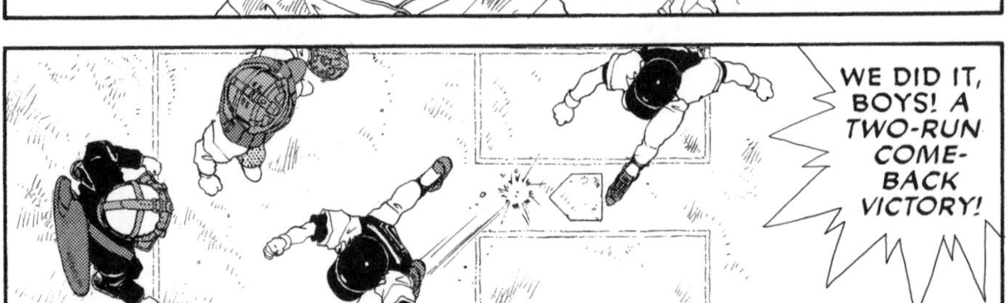
WE DID IT, BOYS! *A TWO-RUN COMEBACK VICTORY!*

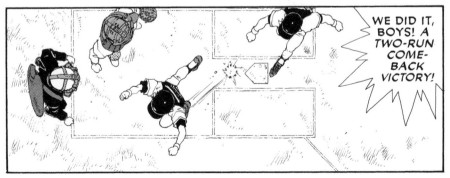

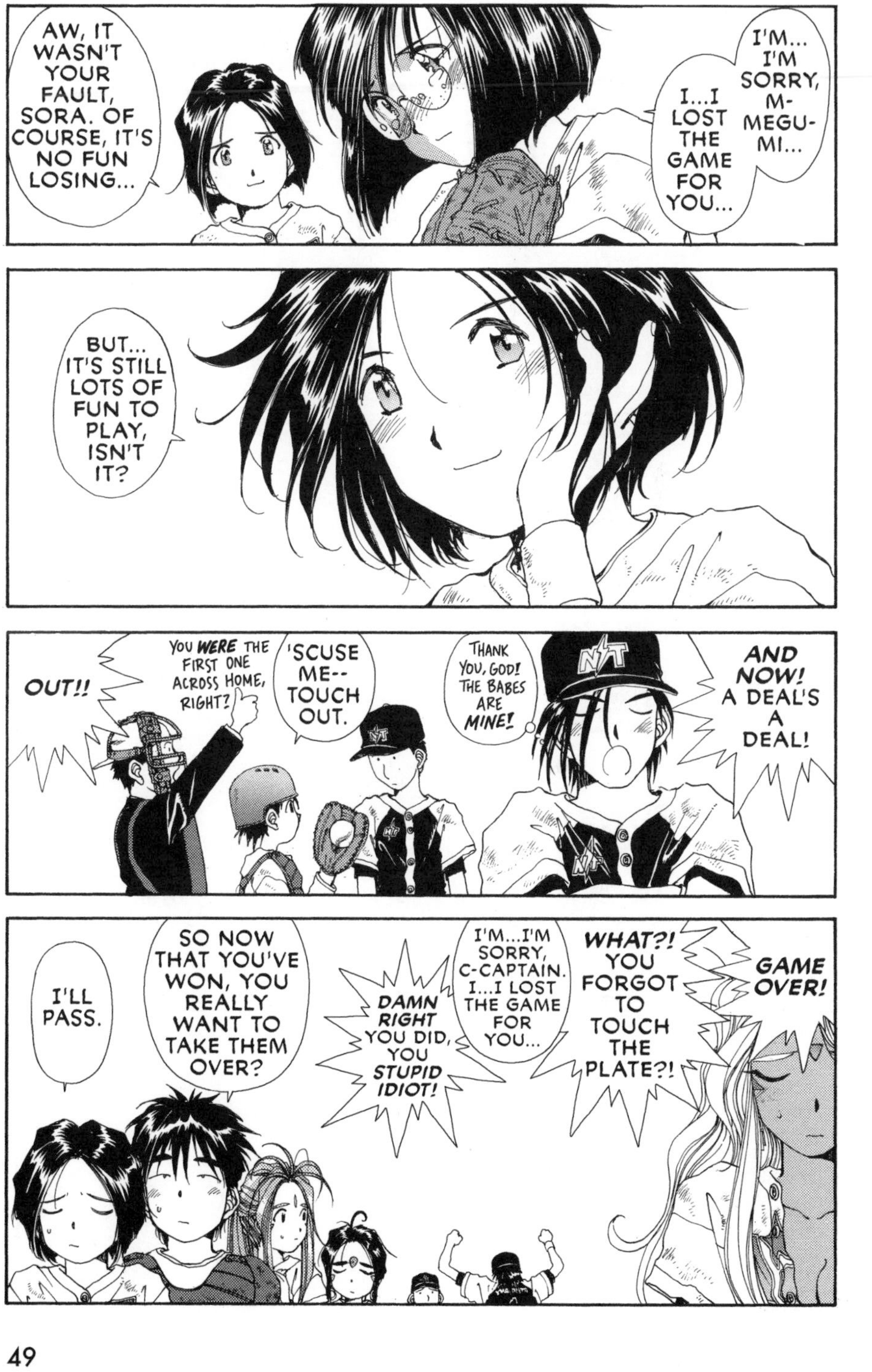
I'M... I'M SORRY, M-MEGU-MI...
I...I LOST THE GAME FOR YOU...
AW, IT WASN'T YOUR FAULT, SORA. OF COURSE, IT'S NO FUN LOSING...
BUT... IT'S STILL LOTS OF FUN TO PLAY, ISN'T IT?
AND NOW! A DEAL'S A DEAL!
THANK YOU, GOD! THE BABES ARE MINE!
'SCUSE ME-- TOUCH OUT.
YOU WERE THE FIRST ONE ACROSS HOME, RIGHT?
OUT!!
GAME OVER!
WHAT?! YOU FORGOT TO TOUCH THE PLATE?!
I'M...I'M SORRY, C-CAPTAIN. I...I LOST THE GAME FOR YOU...
DAMN RIGHT YOU DID, YOU STUPID IDIOT!
SO NOW THAT YOU'VE WON, YOU REALLY WANT TO TAKE THEM OVER?
I'LL PASS.

THE ADVENTURES OF THE MINI-GODDESSES

◆ REVIVAL! A BAND REBORN! ◆

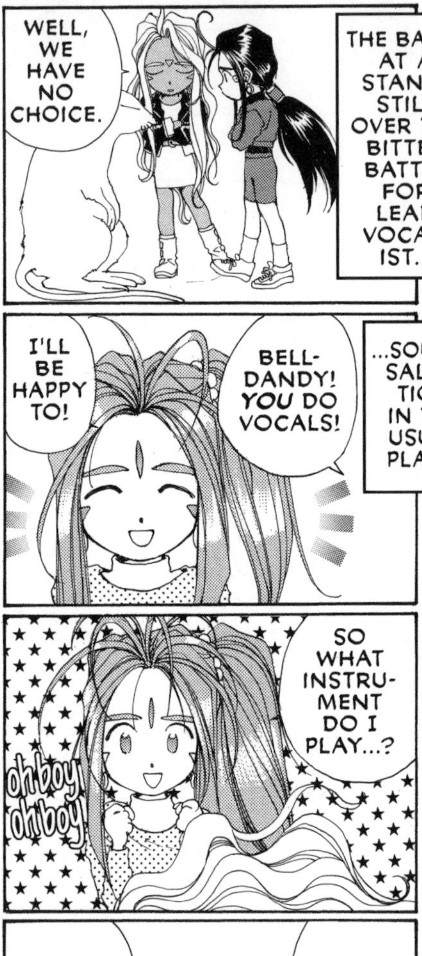
THE BAND, AT A STAND-STILL OVER THE BITTER BATTLE FOR LEAD VOCAL-IST...
WELL, WE HAVE NO CHOICE.
...SOUGHT SALVA-TION IN THE USUAL PLACE.
BELL-DANDY! *YOU* DO VOCALS!
I'LL BE HAPPY TO!
SO WHAT INSTRU-MENT DO I PLAY...?
oh boy oh boy
A VOCALIST *SINGS.*
REALLY? ARE YOU SURE?

◆ THE INVINCIBLE VOCALIST ◆

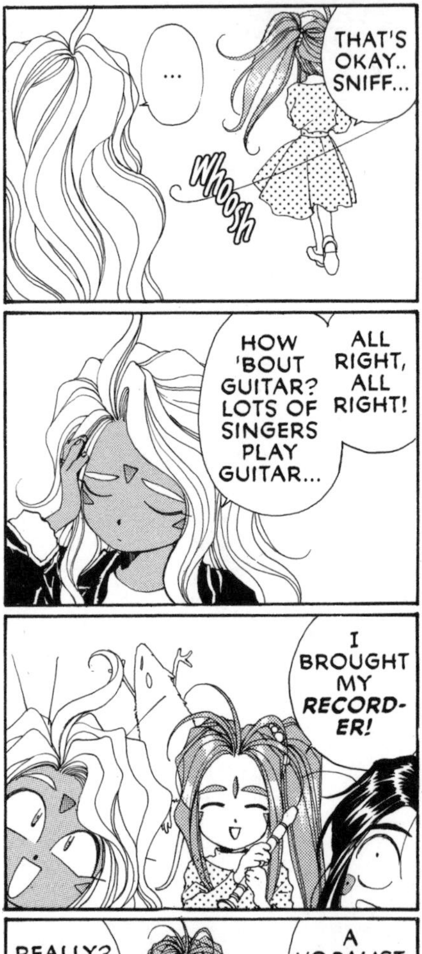
THAT'S OKAY.. SNIFF...
...
whoosh
ALL RIGHT, ALL RIGHT!
HOW 'BOUT GUITAR? LOTS OF SINGERS PLAY GUITAR...
I BROUGHT MY *RECORD-ER!*
A VOCALIST *CAN'T PLAY* THE RECORD-ER.
REALLY? ARE YOU SURE?

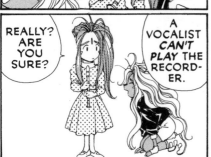

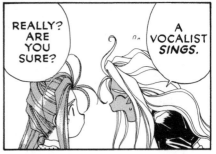

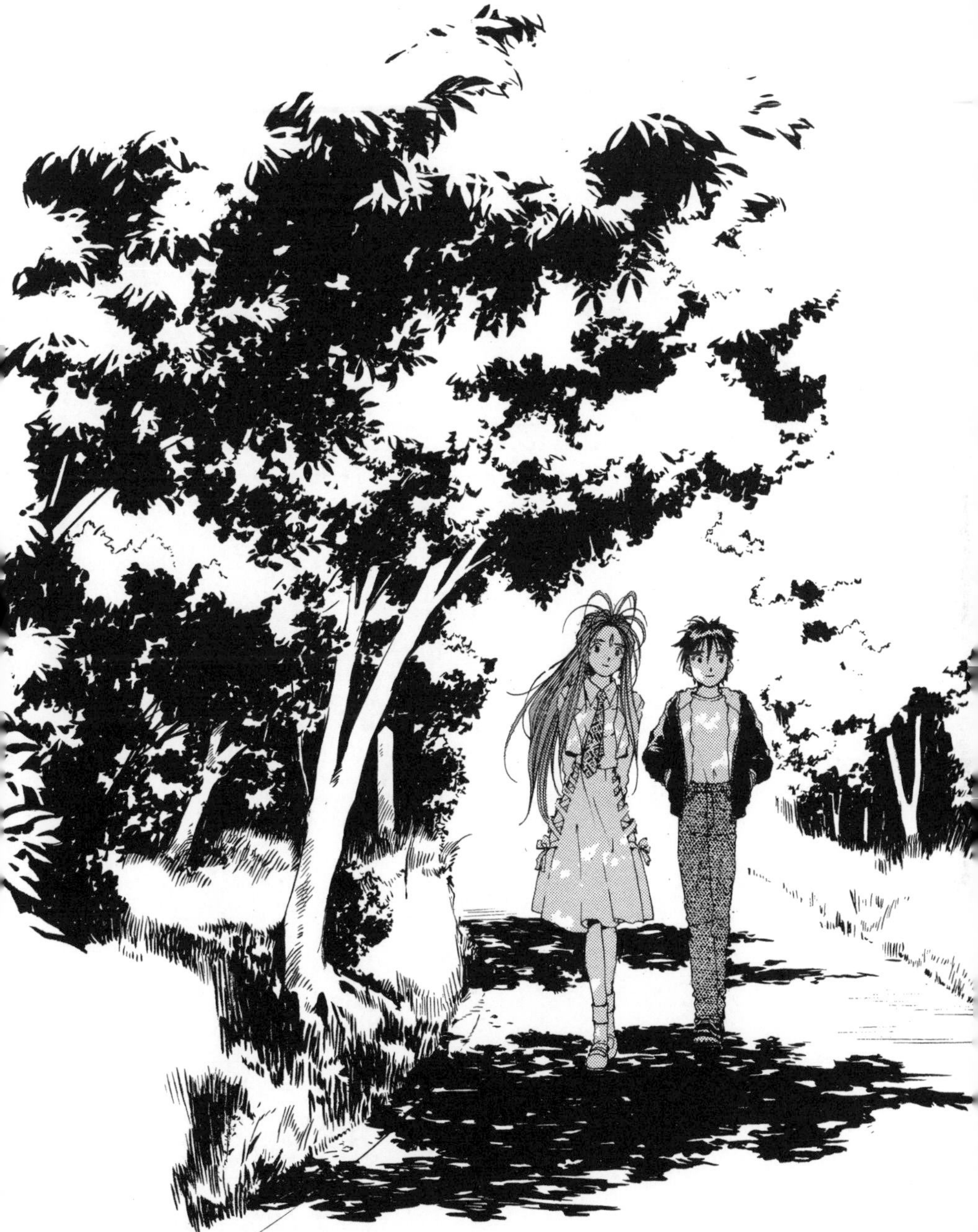

CHAPTER 59

Remember the Sad Times

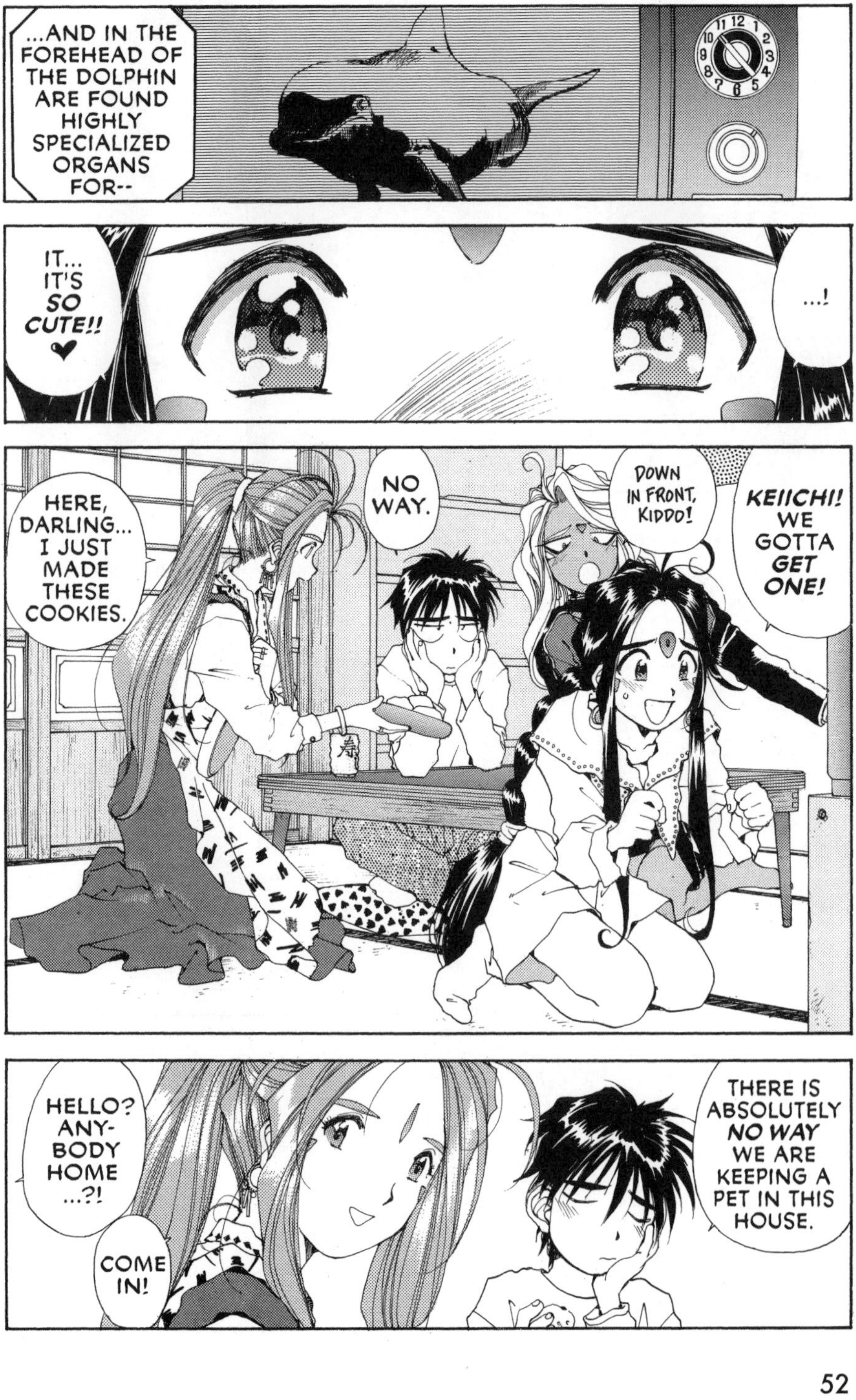
...AND IN THE FOREHEAD OF THE DOLPHIN ARE FOUND HIGHLY SPECIALIZED ORGANS FOR--
...!
IT... IT'S *SO CUTE!!* ❤
KEIICHI! WE GOTTA *GET ONE!*
DOWN IN FRONT, KIDDO!
NO WAY.
HERE, DARLING... I JUST MADE THESE COOKIES.
THERE IS ABSOLUTELY *NO WAY* WE ARE KEEPING A PET IN THIS HOUSE.
HELLO? ANY-BODY HOME ...?!
COME IN!

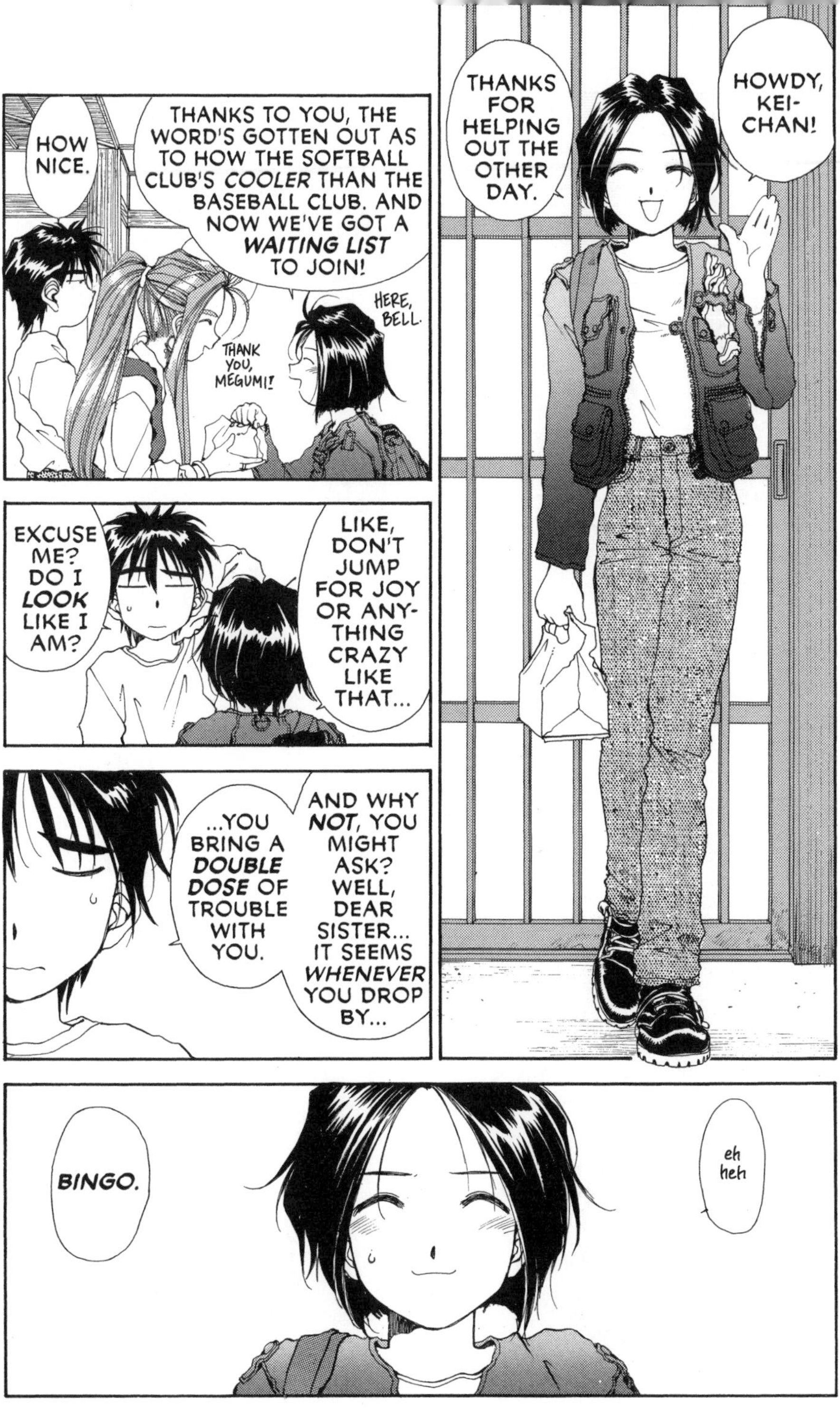
HOWDY, KEI-CHAN!
THANKS FOR HELPING OUT THE OTHER DAY.
THANKS TO YOU, THE WORD'S GOTTEN OUT AS TO HOW THE SOFTBALL CLUB'S *COOLER* THAN THE BASEBALL CLUB. AND NOW WE'VE GOT A ***WAITING LIST*** TO JOIN!
HOW NICE.
HERE, BELL.
THANK YOU, MEGUMI!
LIKE, DON'T JUMP FOR JOY OR ANYTHING CRAZY LIKE THAT...
EXCUSE ME? DO I ***LOOK*** LIKE I AM?
AND WHY ***NOT***, YOU MIGHT ASK? WELL, DEAR SISTER... IT SEEMS ***WHENEVER*** YOU DROP BY...
...YOU BRING A ***DOUBLE DOSE*** OF TROUBLE WITH YOU.
eh heh
BINGO.

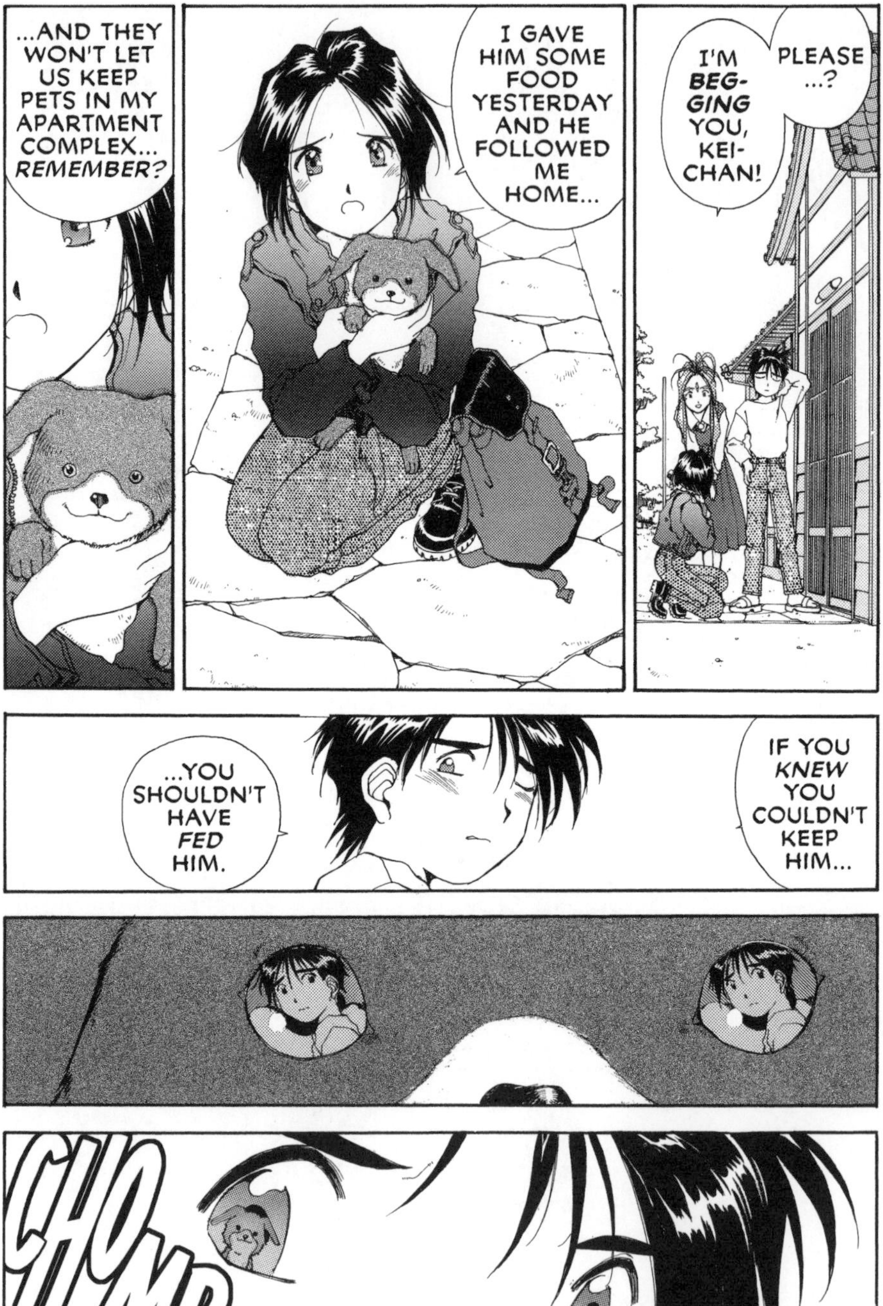
PLEASE ...?
I'M *BEGGING* YOU, KEI-CHAN!
I GAVE HIM SOME FOOD YESTERDAY AND HE FOLLOWED ME HOME...
...AND THEY WON'T LET US KEEP PETS IN MY APARTMENT COMPLEX... *REMEMBER?*
IF YOU *KNEW* YOU COULDN'T KEEP HIM...
...YOU SHOULDN'T HAVE *FED* HIM.
CHOMP

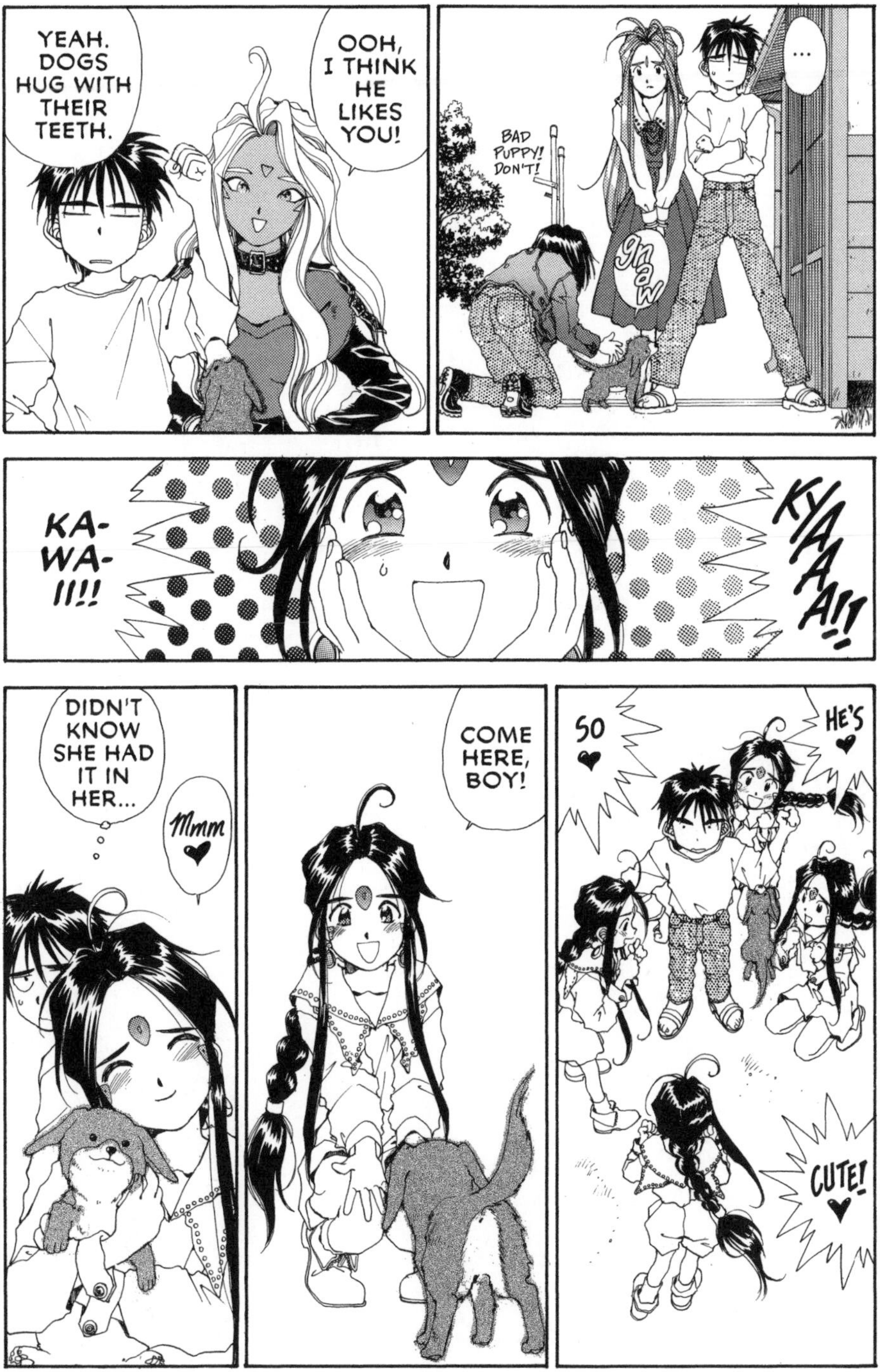
...
BAD PUPPY! DON'T!
gnaw
OOH, I THINK HE LIKES YOU!
YEAH. DOGS HUG WITH THEIR TEETH.
KYAAAA!!!
KA-WA-II!!!
HE'S ♥
SO ♥
CUTE! ♥
COME HERE, BOY!
Mmm ♥
DIDN'T KNOW SHE HAD IT IN HER...

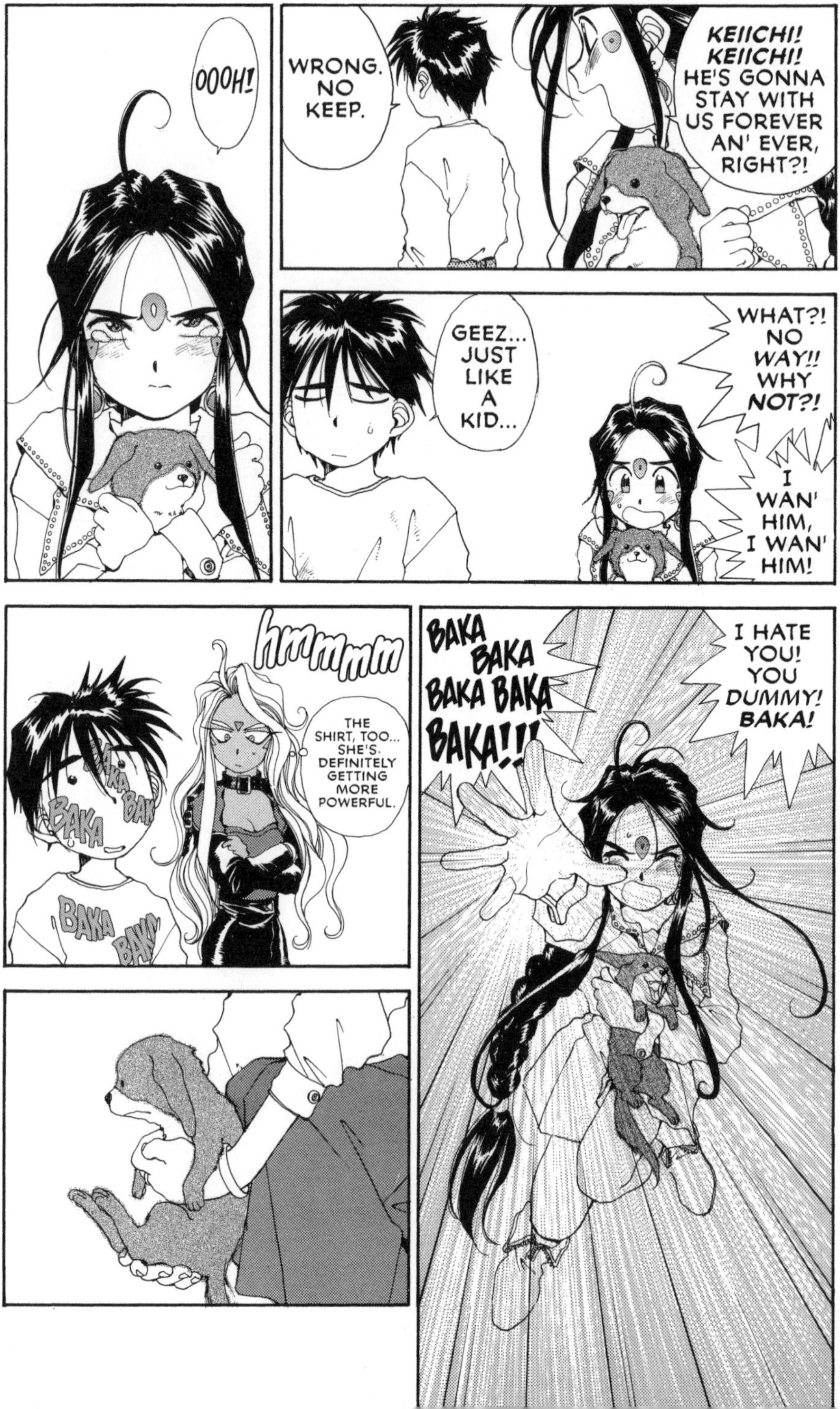
KEIICHI! KEIICHI! HE'S GONNA STAY WITH US FOREVER AN' EVER, RIGHT?!
WRONG. NO KEEP.
WHAT?! NO *WAY!!* WHY *NOT?!*
I WAN' HIM, I WAN' HIM!
GEEZ... JUST LIKE A KID...
OOOH!
I HATE YOU! YOU *DUMMY!* **BAKA!**
BAKA BAKA BAKA BAKA BAKA!!!
hmmmm
THE SHIRT, TOO... SHE'S DEFINITELY GETTING MORE POWERFUL.

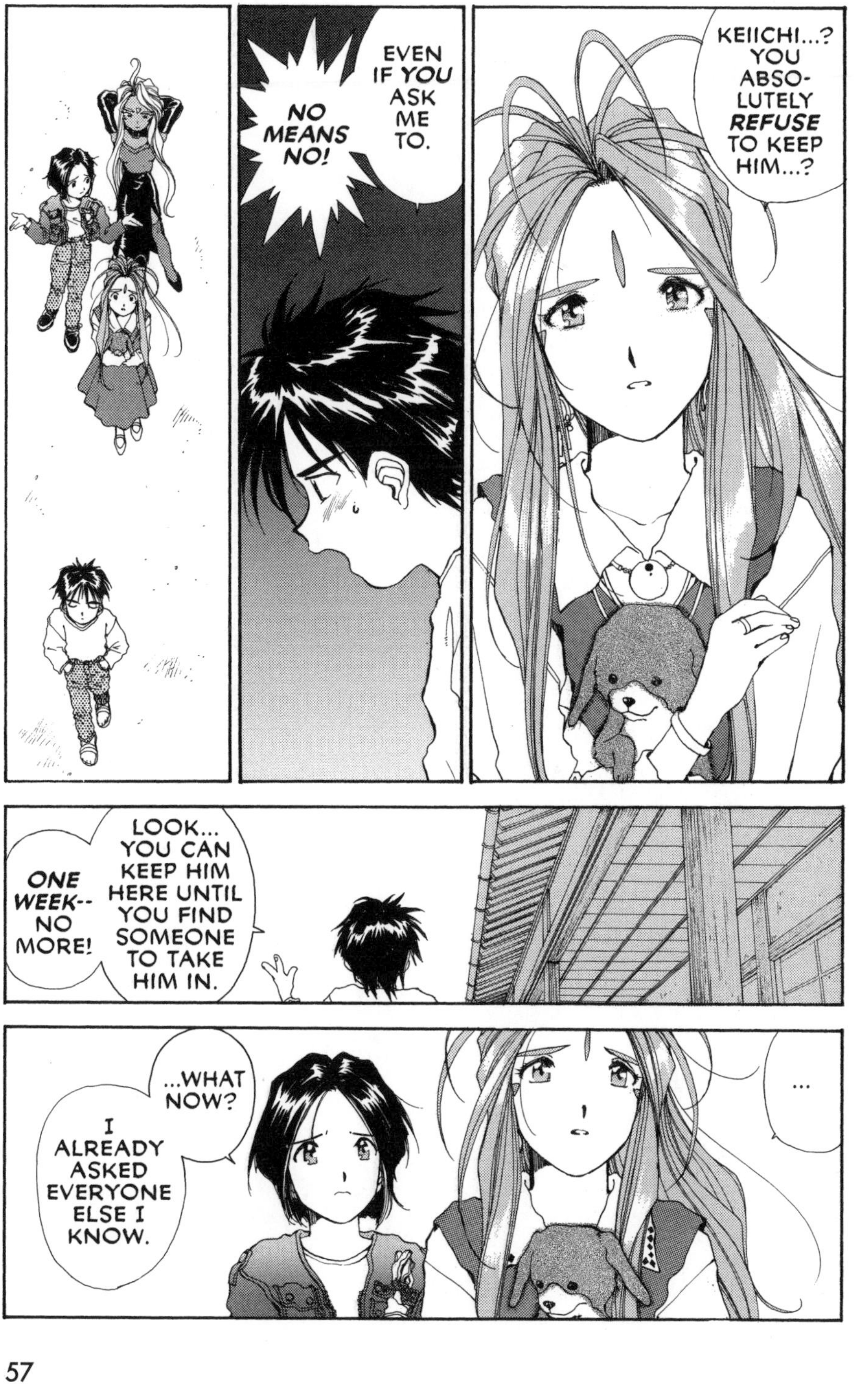
KEIICHI...? YOU ABSO- LUTELY ***REFUSE*** TO KEEP HIM...?
EVEN IF ***YOU*** ASK ME TO.
NO MEANS NO!
LOOK... YOU CAN KEEP HIM HERE UNTIL YOU FIND SOMEONE TO TAKE HIM IN.
ONE WEEK-- NO MORE!
...
...WHAT NOW?
I ALREADY ASKED EVERYONE ELSE I KNOW.

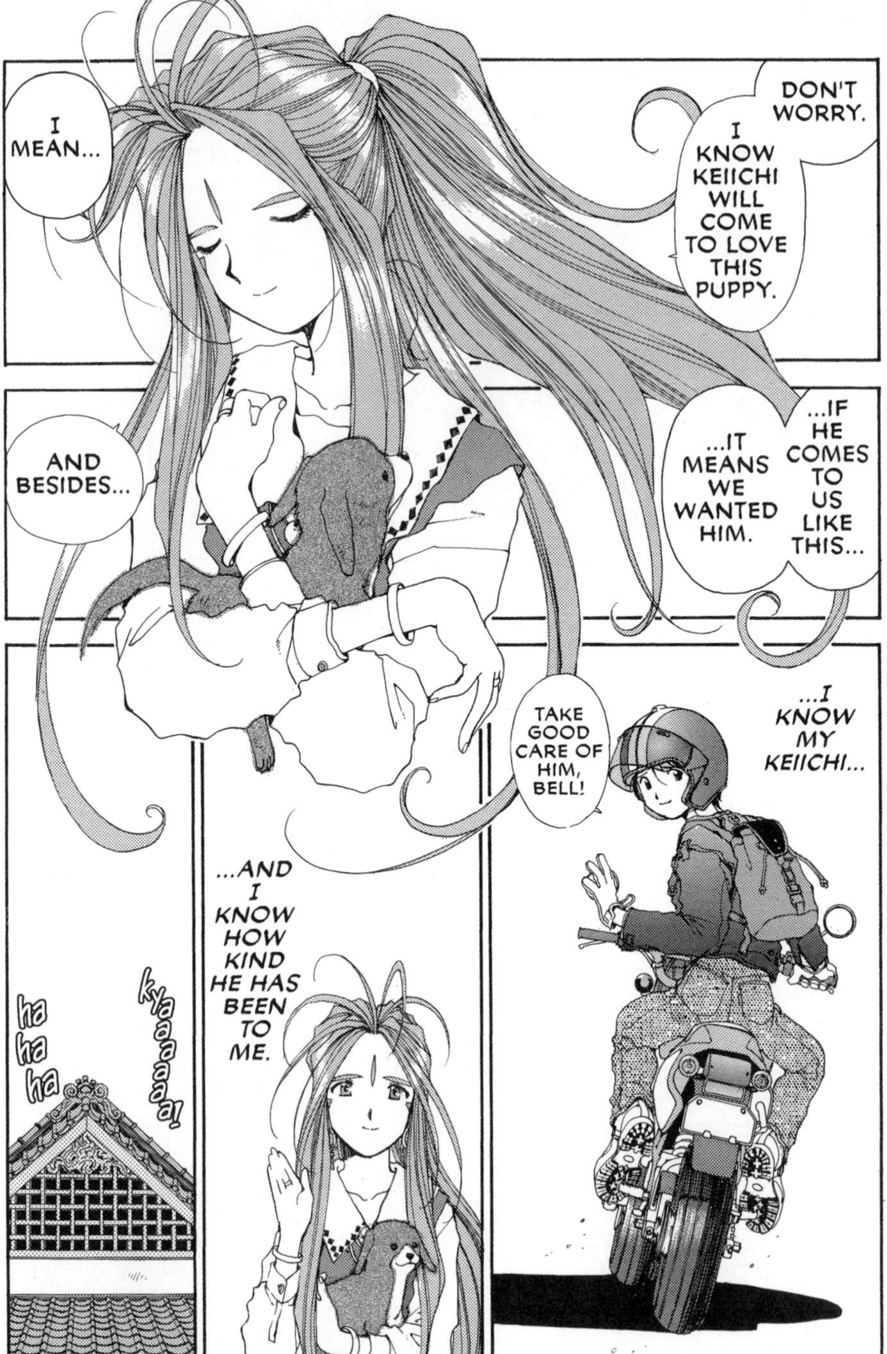
DON'T WORRY. I KNOW KEIICHI WILL COME TO LOVE THIS PUPPY.
I MEAN...
...IF HE COMES TO US LIKE THIS...
...IT MEANS WE WANTED HIM.
AND BESIDES...
...I KNOW MY KEIICHI...
TAKE GOOD CARE OF HIM, BELL!
...AND I KNOW HOW KIND HE HAS BEEN TO ME.
kyaaaaaa!
ha ha ha

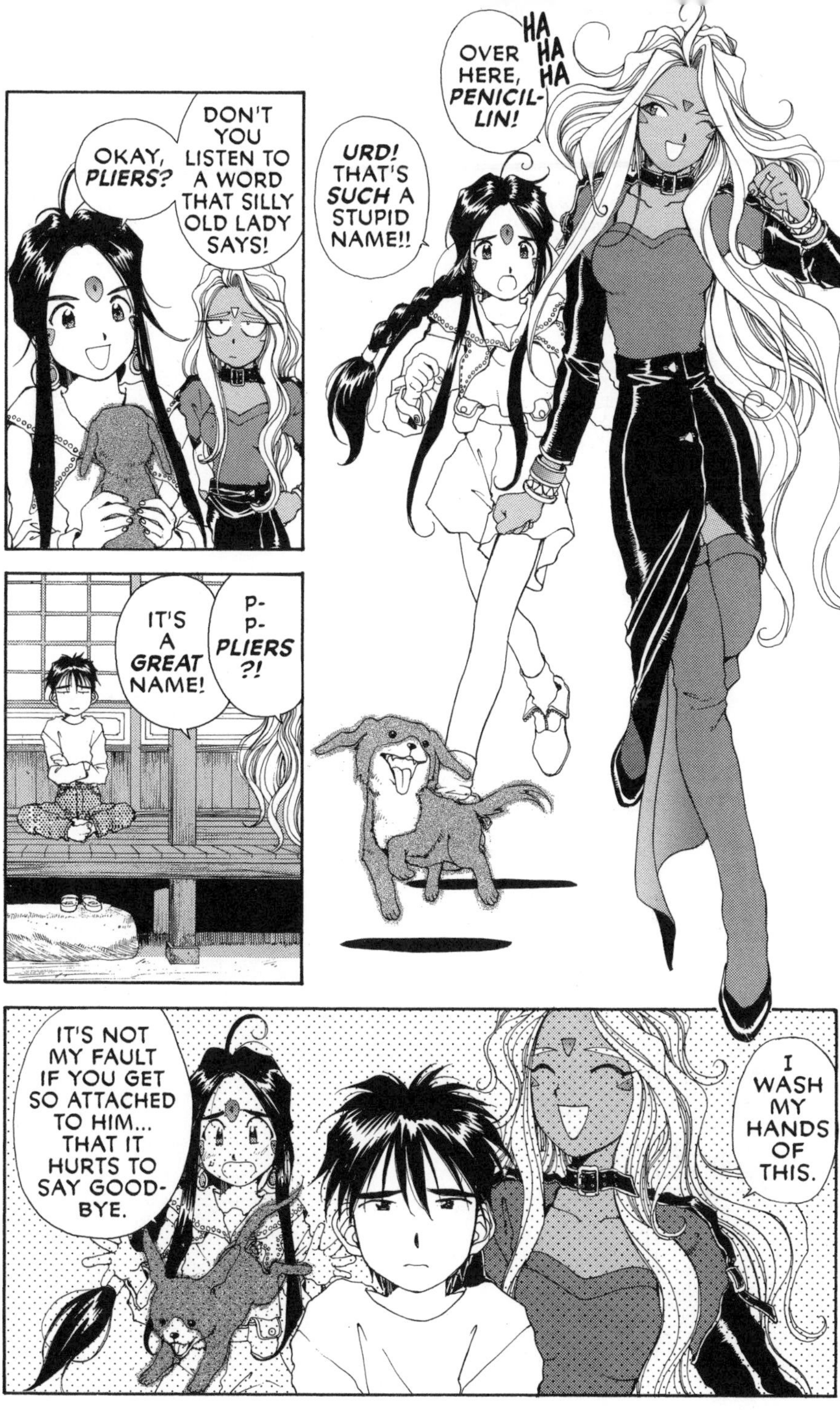
HA HA HA
OVER HERE, PENICIL-LIN!
URD! THAT'S SUCH A STUPID NAME!!
DON'T YOU LISTEN TO A WORD THAT SILLY OLD LADY SAYS!
OKAY, PLIERS?
P-P-PLIERS?!
IT'S A GREAT NAME!
I WASH MY HANDS OF THIS.
IT'S NOT MY FAULT IF YOU GET SO ATTACHED TO HIM... THAT IT HURTS TO SAY GOOD-BYE.

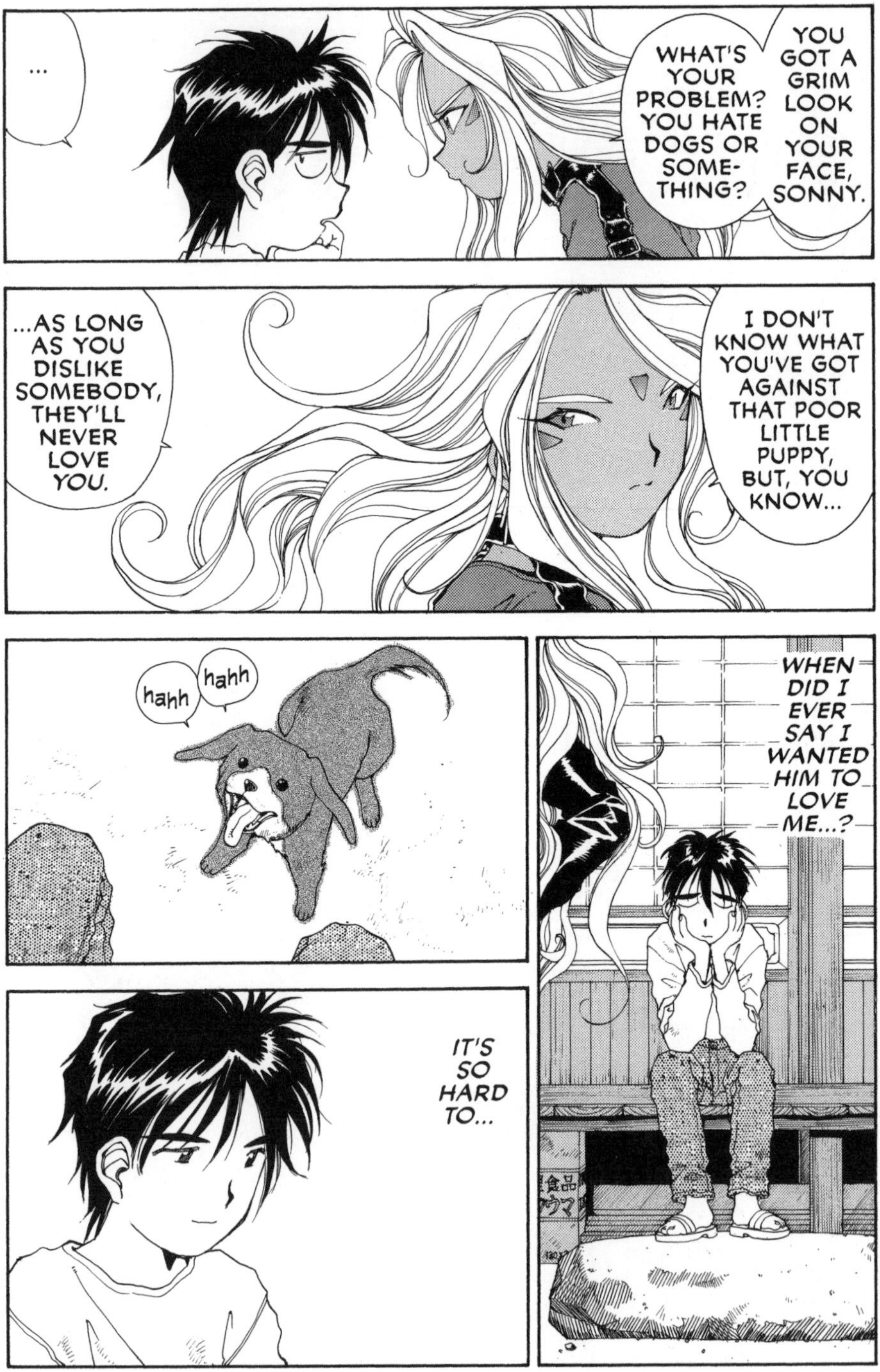
YOU GOT A GRIM LOOK ON YOUR FACE, SONNY.
WHAT'S YOUR PROBLEM? YOU HATE DOGS OR SOME-THING?
...
I DON'T KNOW WHAT YOU'VE GOT AGAINST THAT POOR LITTLE PUPPY, BUT, YOU KNOW...
...AS LONG AS YOU DISLIKE SOMEBODY, THEY'LL NEVER LOVE *YOU*.
WHEN DID I EVER SAY I WANTED HIM TO LOVE ME...?
hahh
hahh
IT'S SO HARD TO...

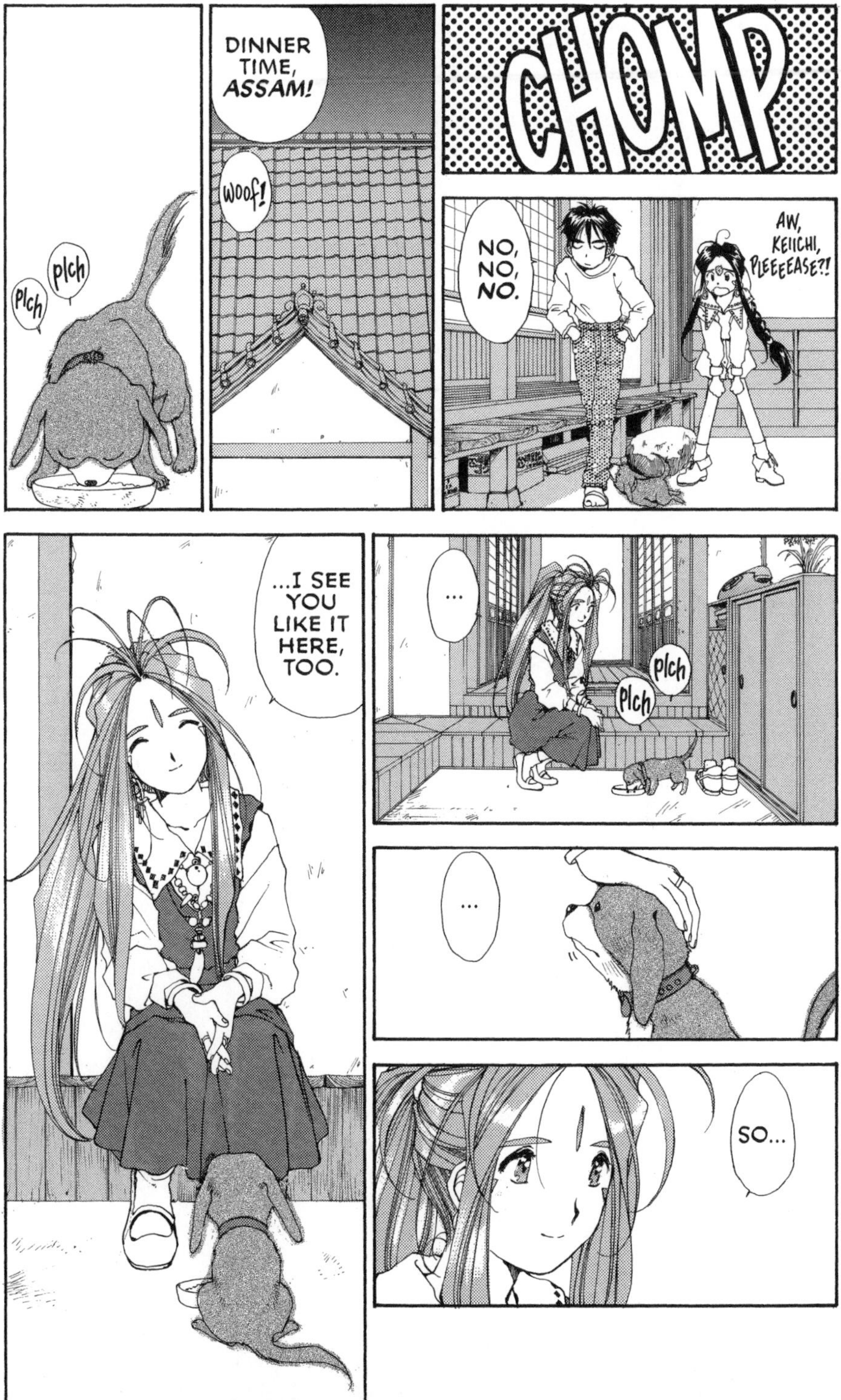
CHOMP
AW, KEIICHI, PLEEEEASE?!
NO, NO, NO.
DINNER TIME, ASSAM!
woof!
plch
plch
...
plch
plch
...
SO...
...I SEE YOU LIKE IT HERE, TOO.

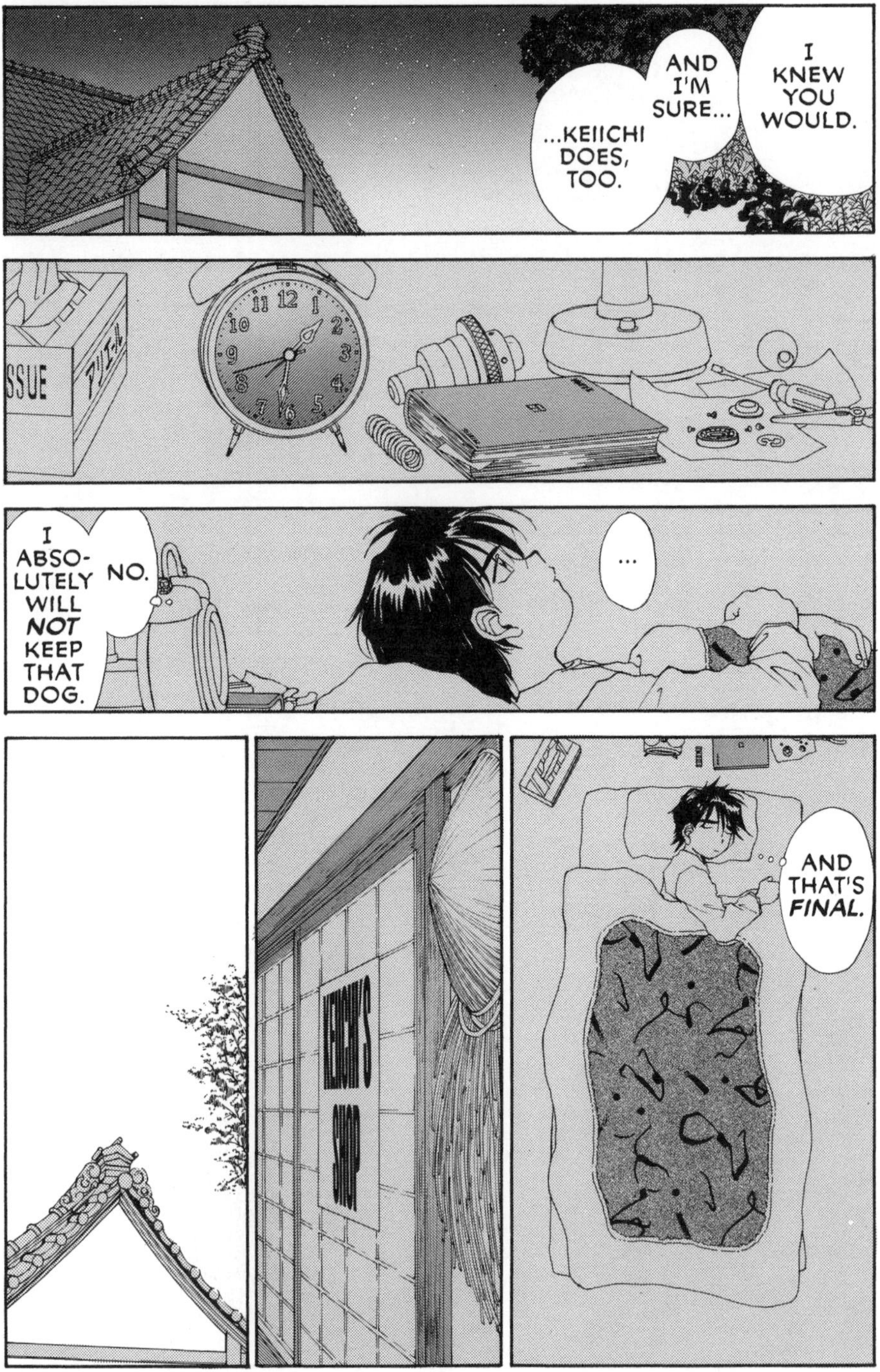

I KNEW YOU WOULD.
AND I'M SURE...
...KEIICHI DOES, TOO.
...
NO.
I ABSO-LUTELY WILL *NOT* KEEP THAT DOG.
AND THAT'S *FINAL.*
KEIICHI'S SHOP

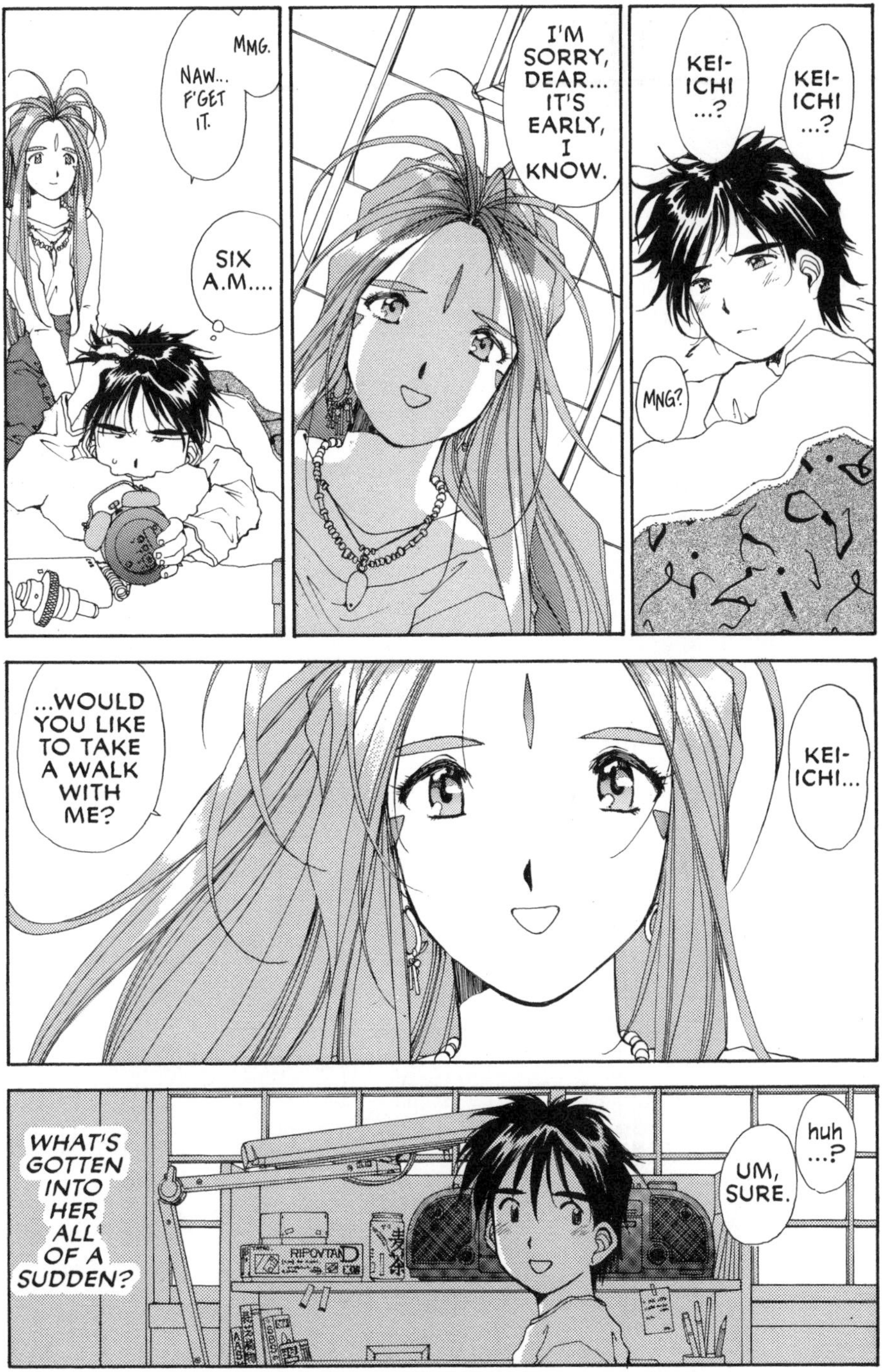
KEI-ICHI ...?
KEI-ICHI ...?
MNG?
I'M SORRY, DEAR... IT'S EARLY, I KNOW.
MMG.
NAW... F'GET IT.
SIX A.M....
KEI-ICHI...
...WOULD YOU LIKE TO TAKE A WALK WITH ME?
huh ...?
UM, SURE.
RIPOVTAN
WHAT'S GOTTEN INTO HER ALL OF A SUDDEN?

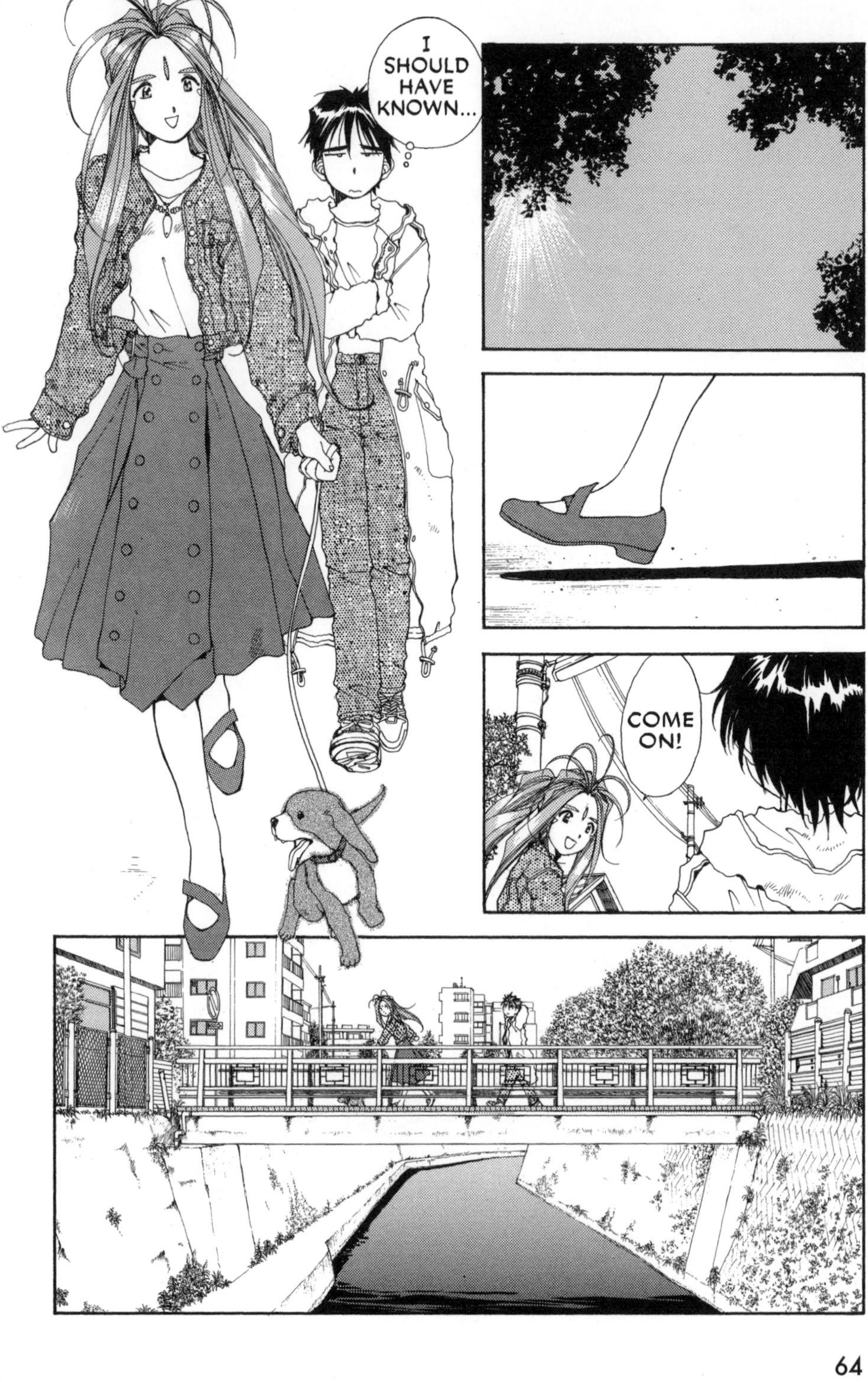
COME ON!
I SHOULD HAVE KNOWN...

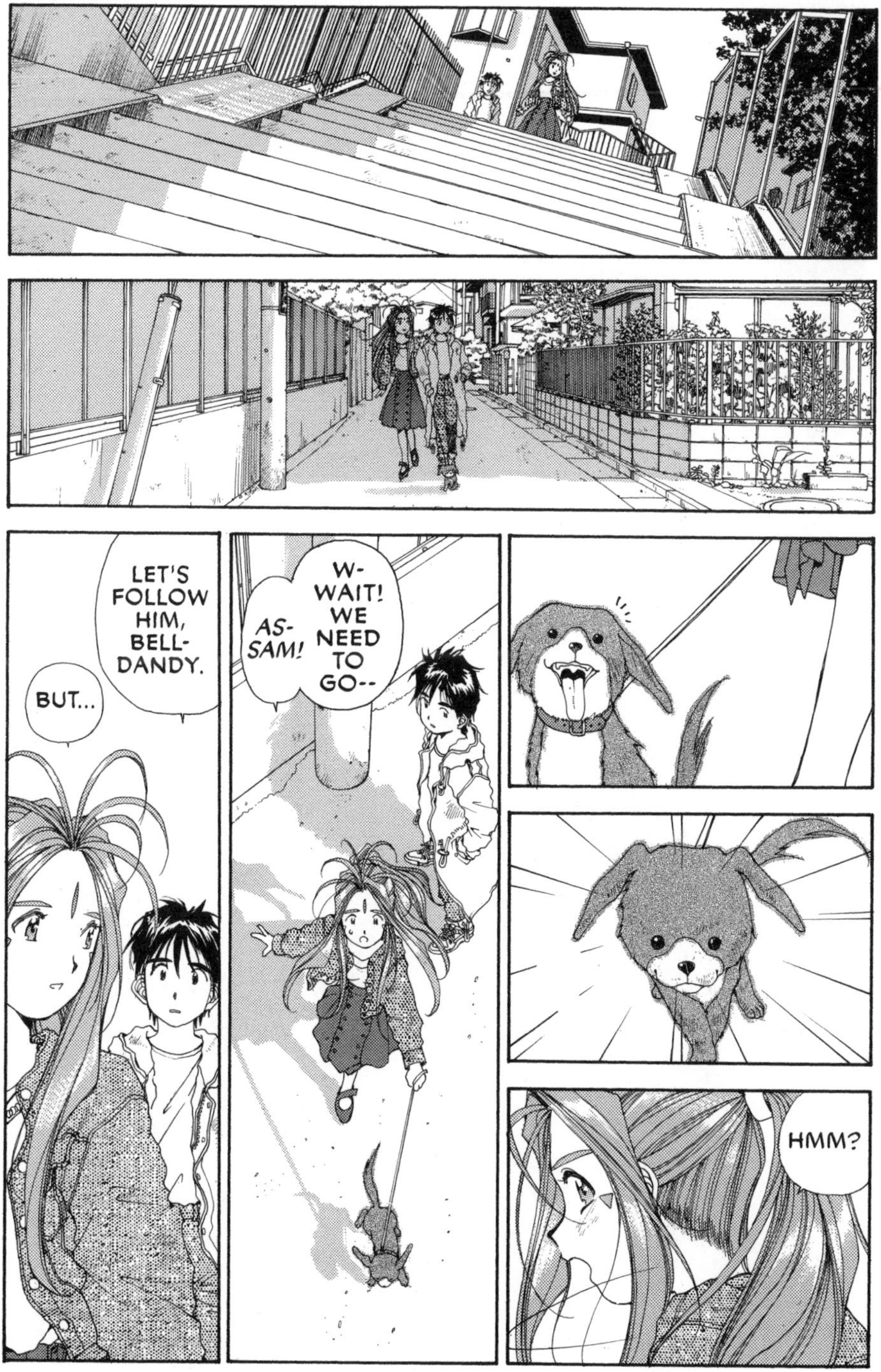
HMM?
W-WAIT! WE NEED TO GO--
AS-SAM!
LET'S FOLLOW HIM, BELL-DANDY.
BUT...

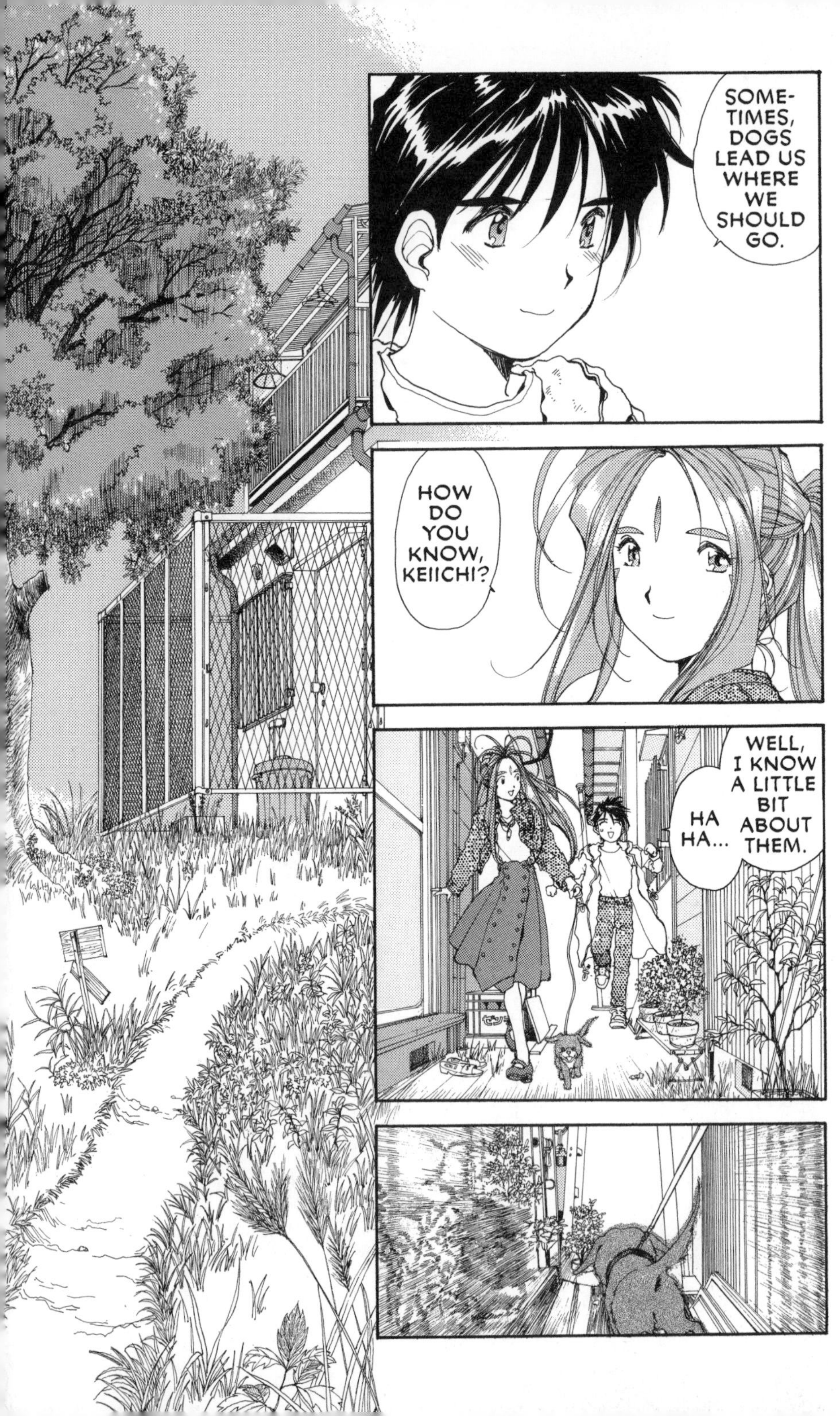
SOME-TIMES, DOGS LEAD US WHERE WE SHOULD GO.
HOW DO YOU KNOW, KEIICHI?
WELL, I KNOW A LITTLE BIT ABOUT THEM.
HA HA...

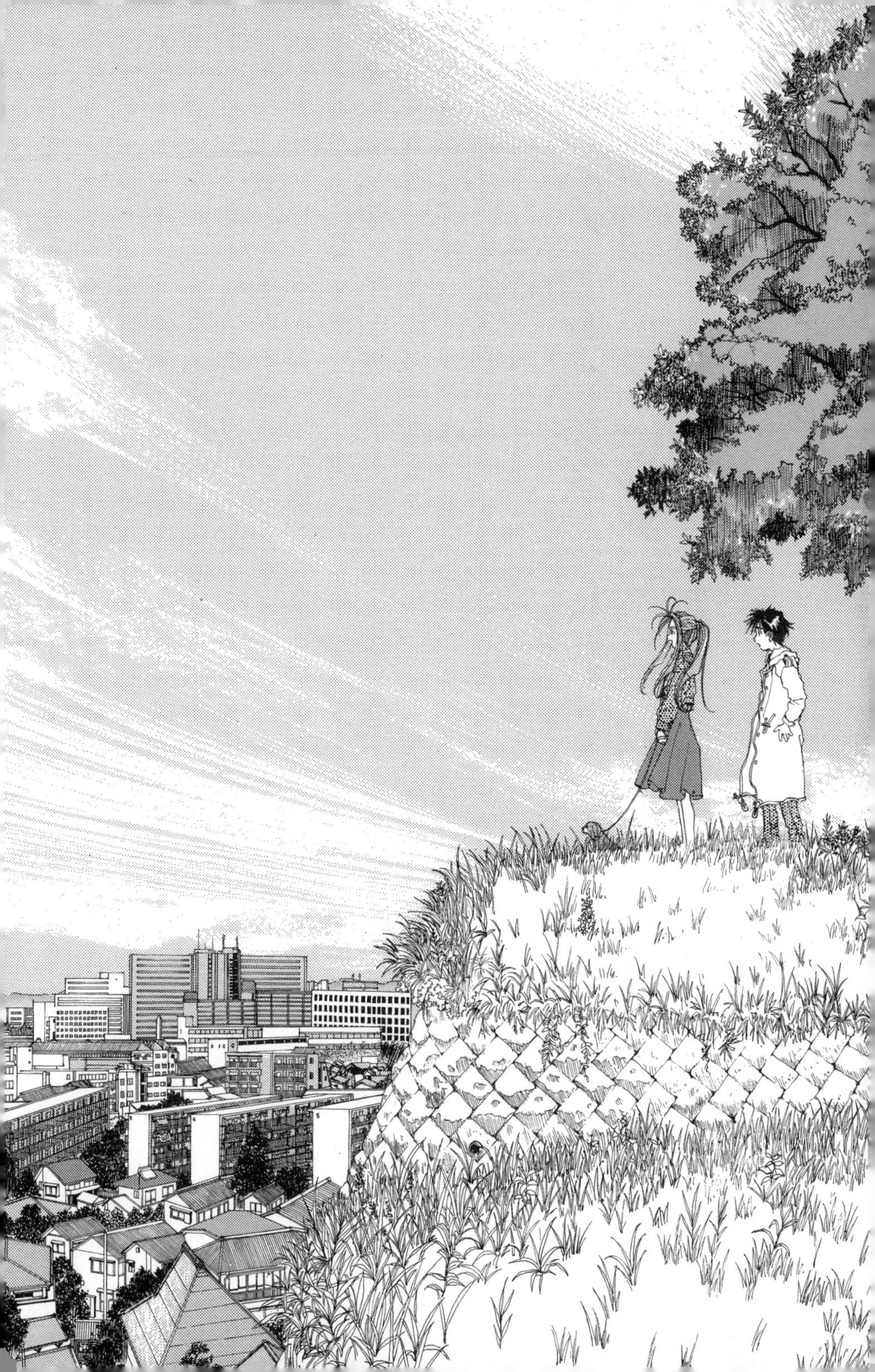

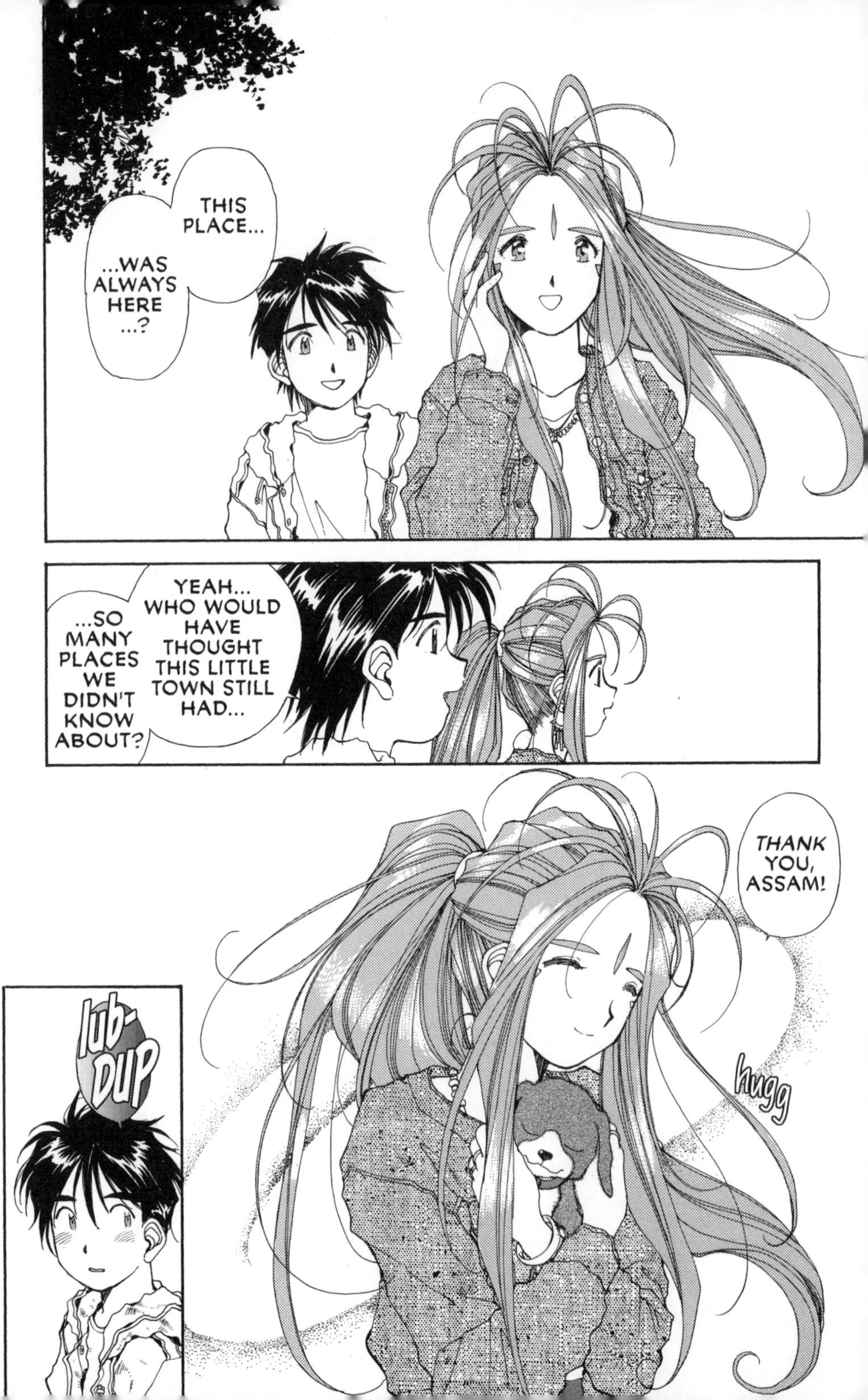
THIS PLACE... ...WAS ALWAYS HERE ...?
YEAH... WHO WOULD HAVE THOUGHT THIS LITTLE TOWN STILL HAD...
...SO MANY PLACES WE DIDN'T KNOW ABOUT?
THANK YOU, ASSAM!
hugg
lub-DUP

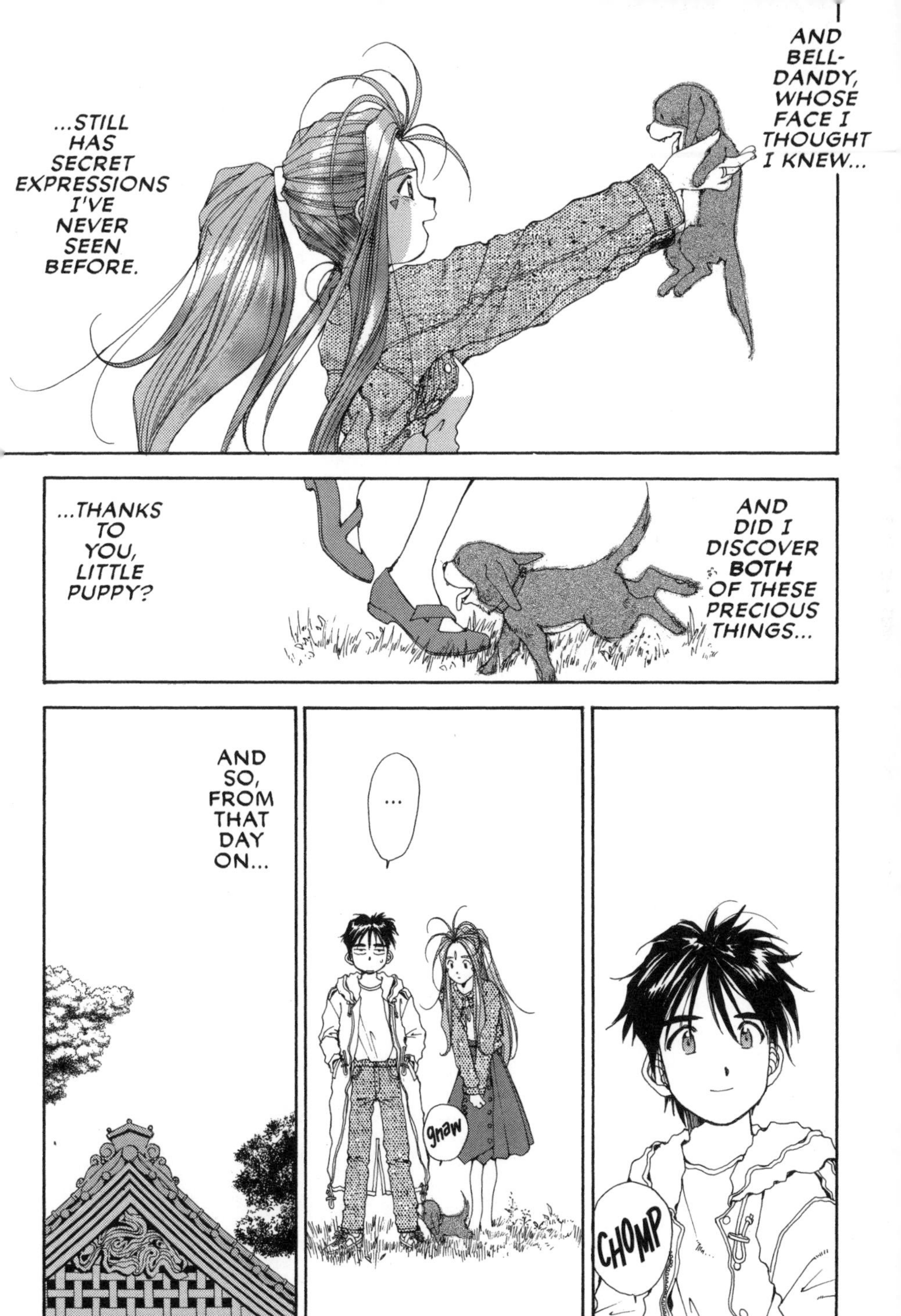
AND BELL-DANDY, WHOSE FACE I THOUGHT I KNEW...
...STILL HAS SECRET EXPRESSIONS I'VE NEVER SEEN BEFORE.
AND DID I DISCOVER **BOTH** OF THESE PRECIOUS THINGS...
...THANKS TO YOU, LITTLE PUPPY?
CHOMP
...
gnaw
AND SO, FROM THAT DAY ON...

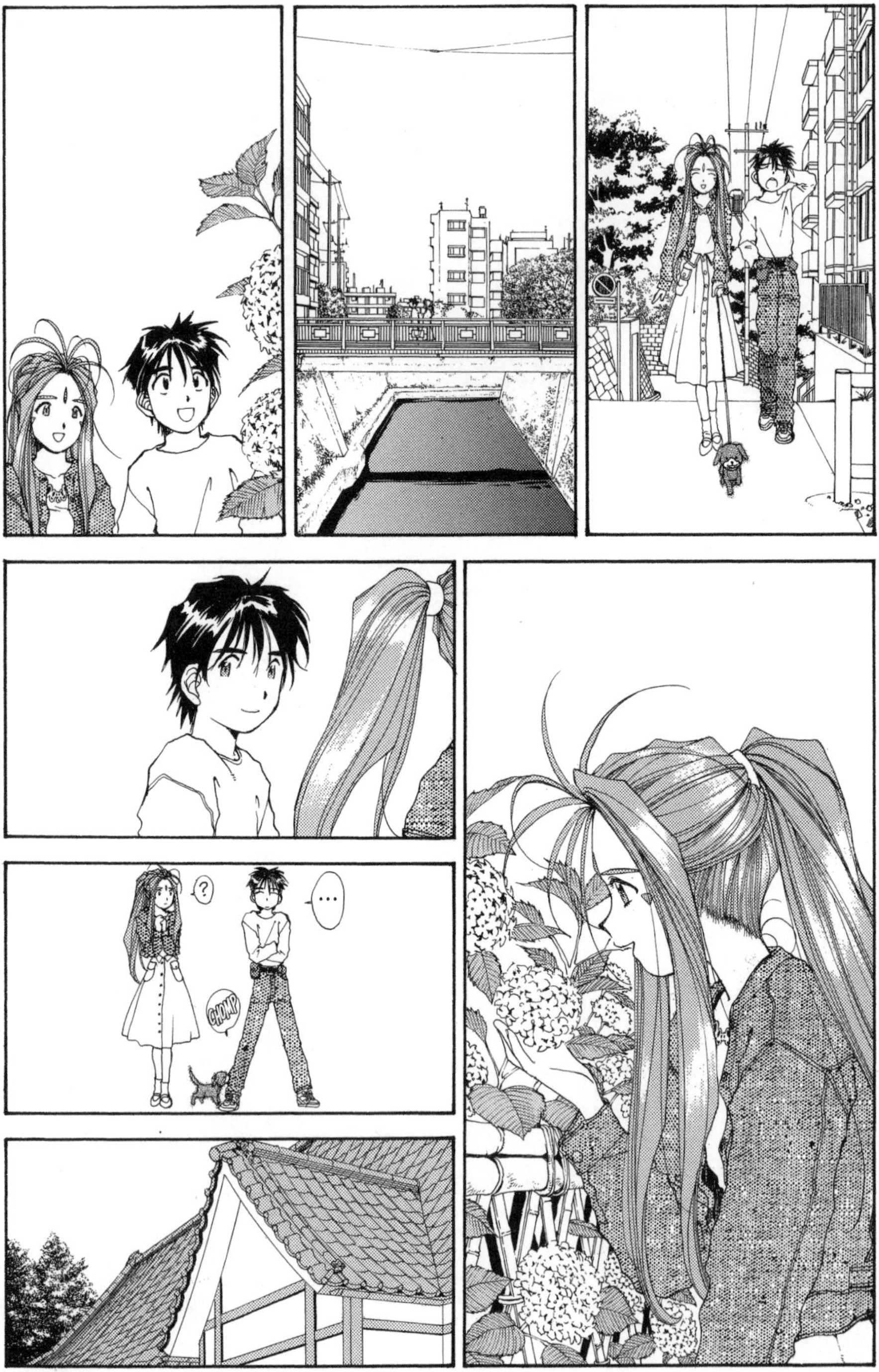
...
?
CHOMP

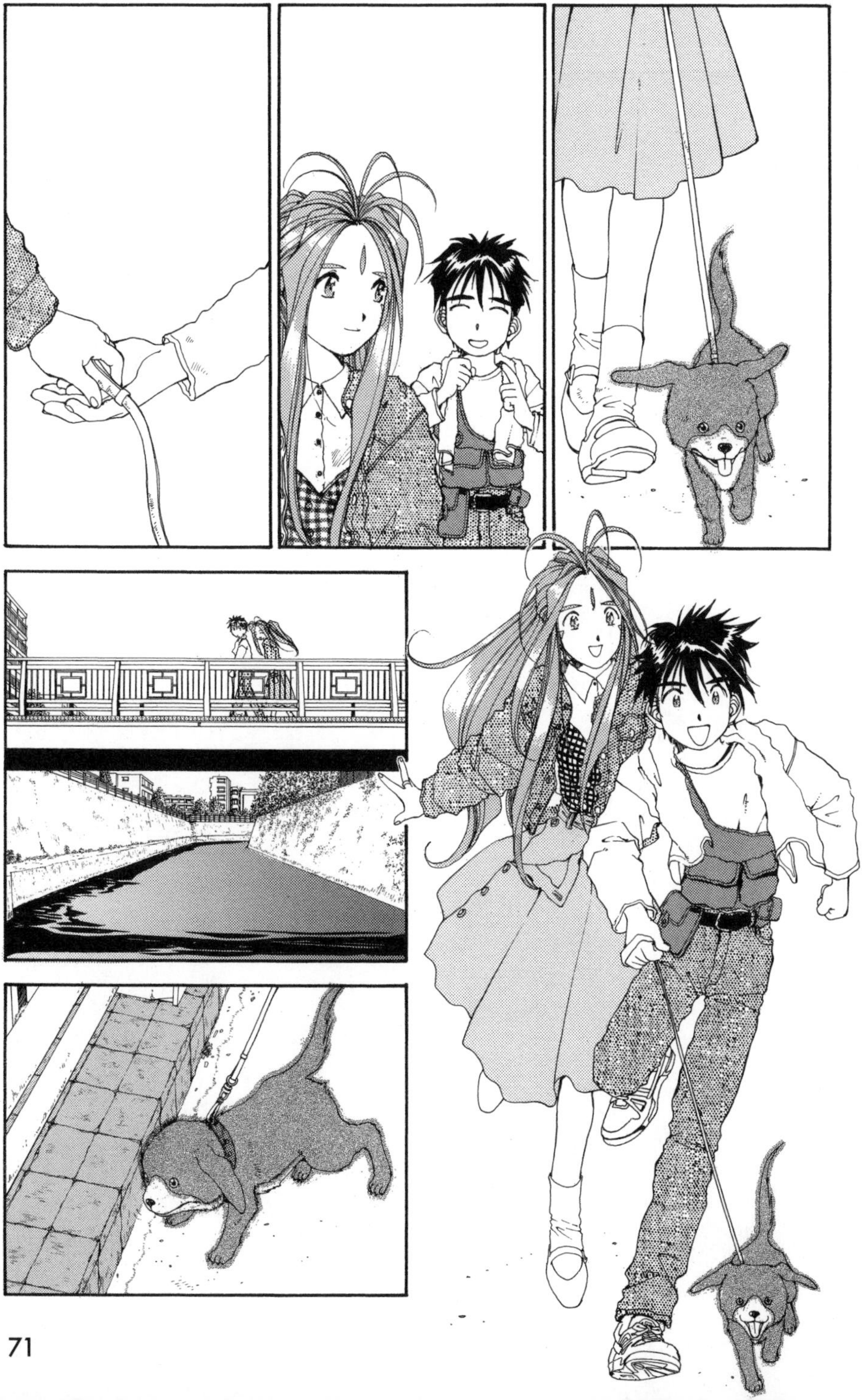

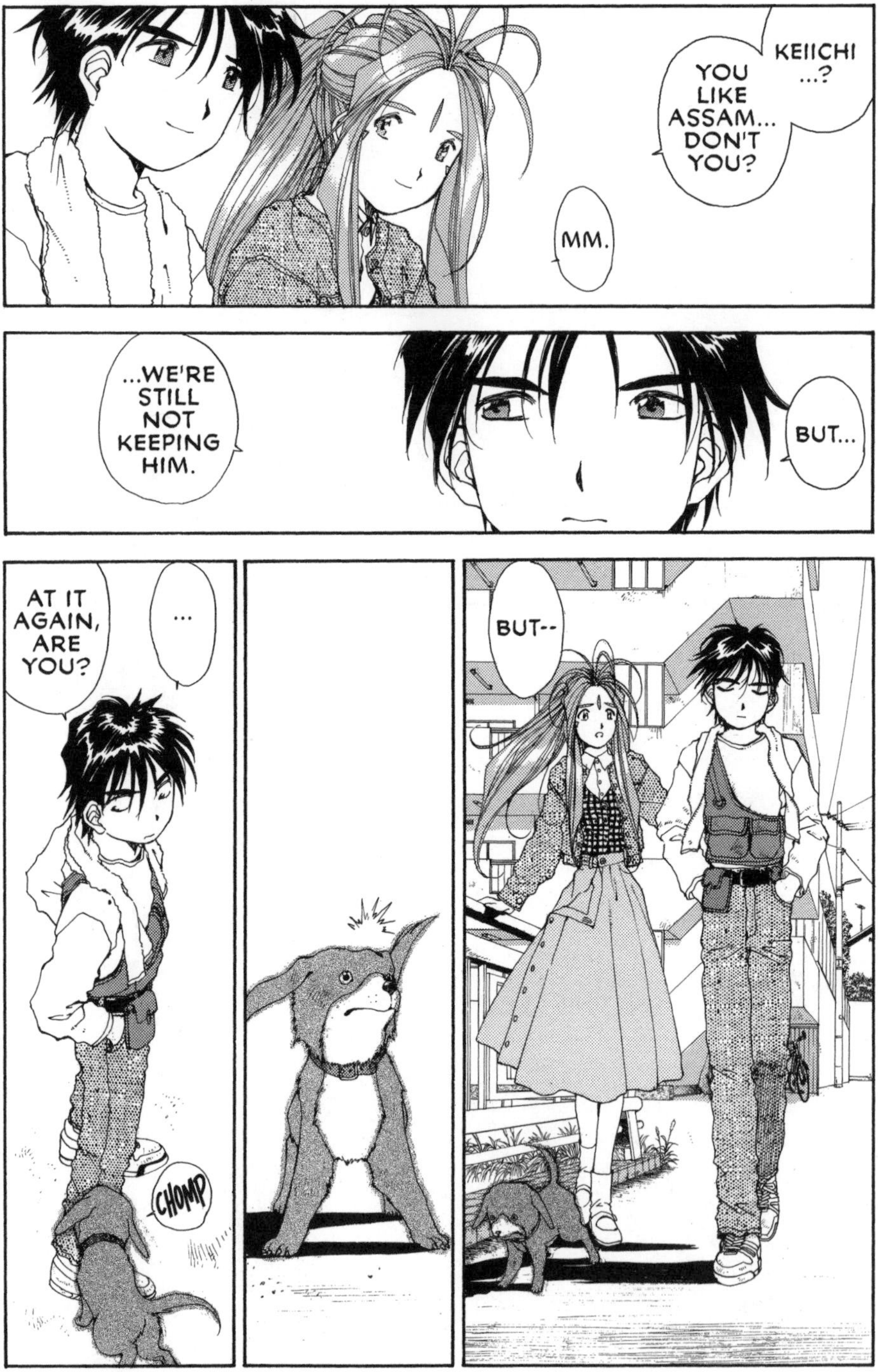
KEIICHI ...?
YOU LIKE ASSAM... DON'T YOU?
MM.
BUT...
...WE'RE STILL NOT KEEPING HIM.
BUT--
...
AT IT AGAIN, ARE YOU?
CHOMP

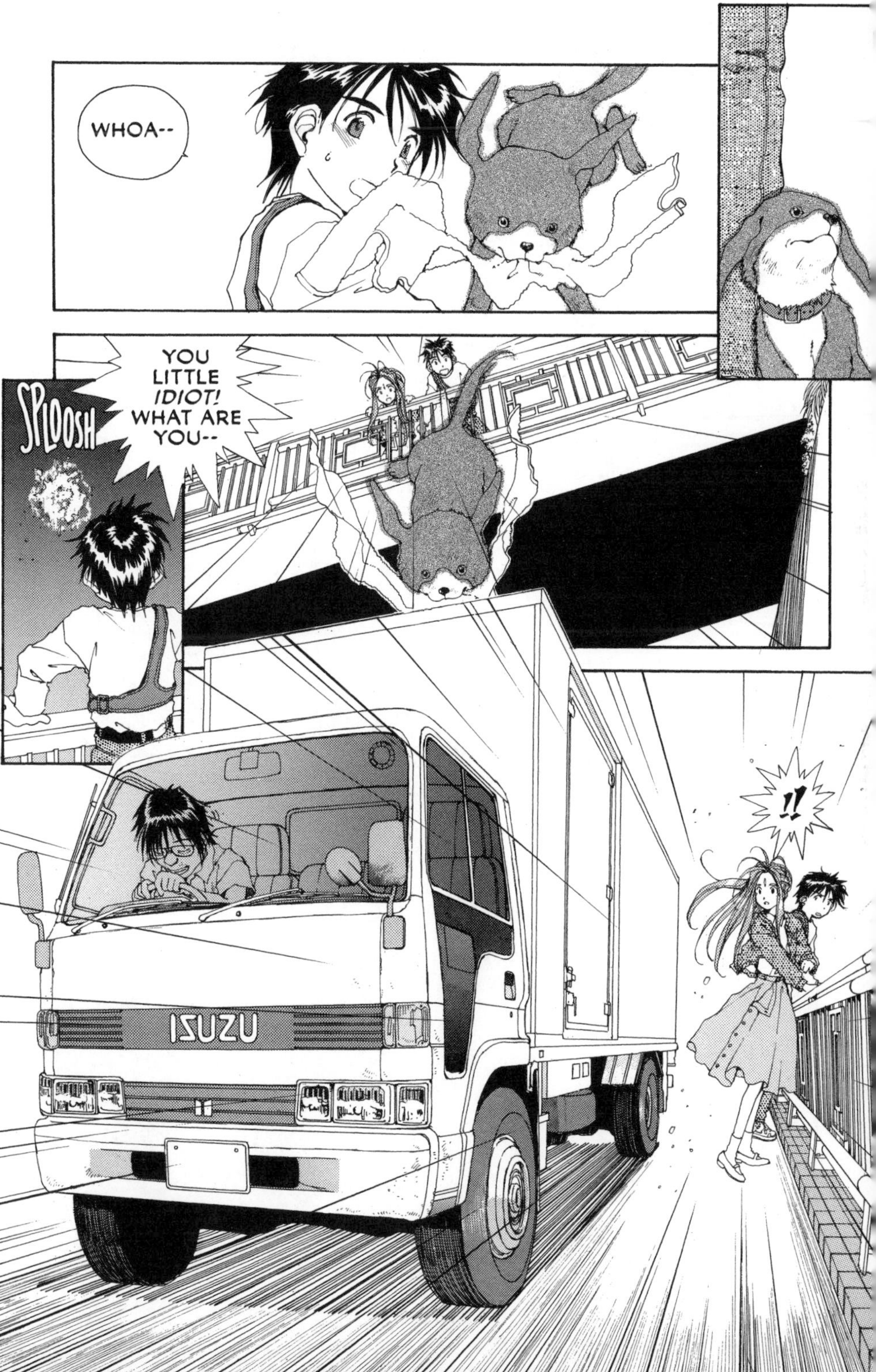
WHOA--
YOU LITTLE IDIOT! WHAT ARE YOU--
SPLOOSH
!!
ISUZU

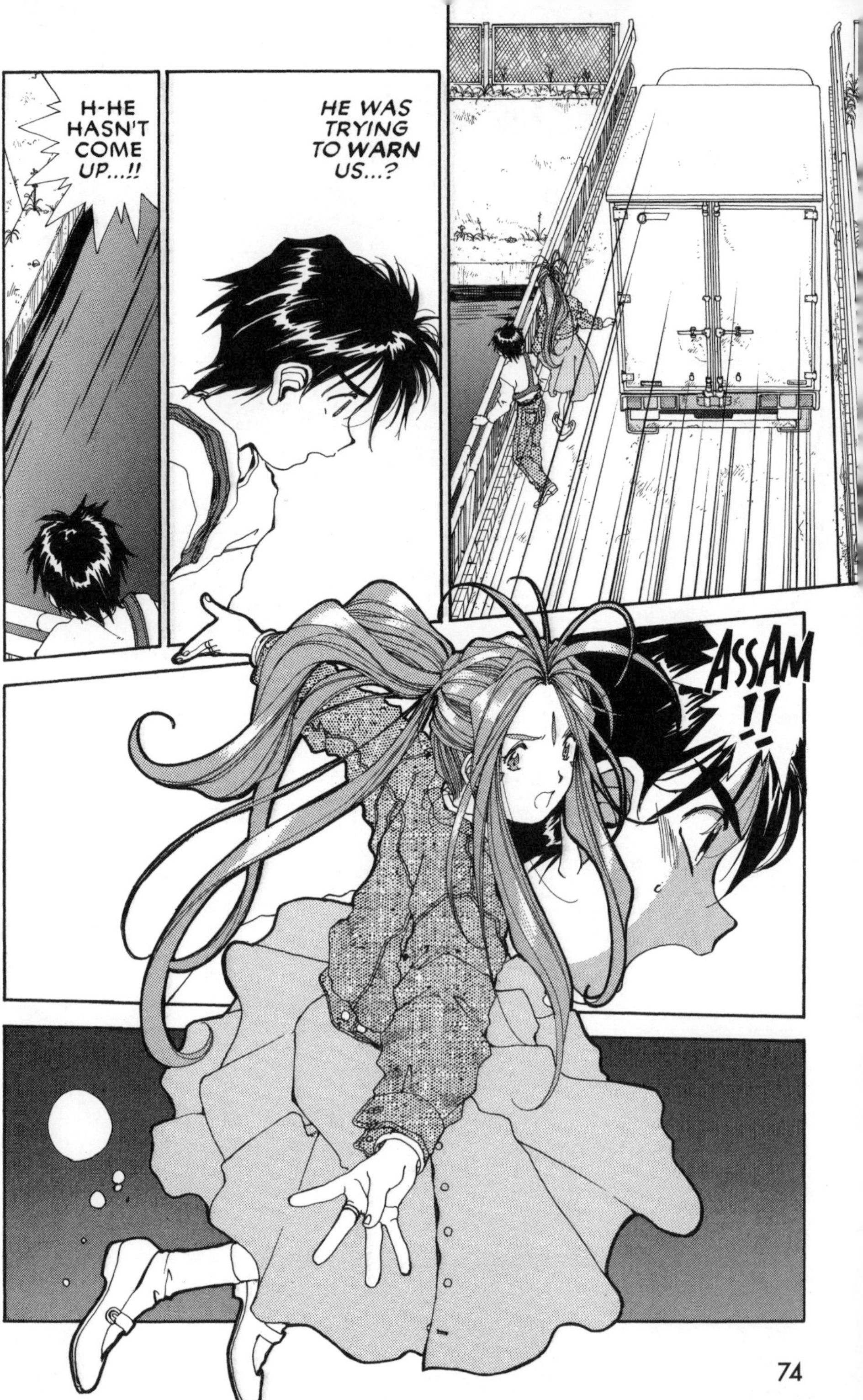
HE WAS TRYING TO WARN US...?
H-HE HASN'T COME UP...!!
ASSAM !!

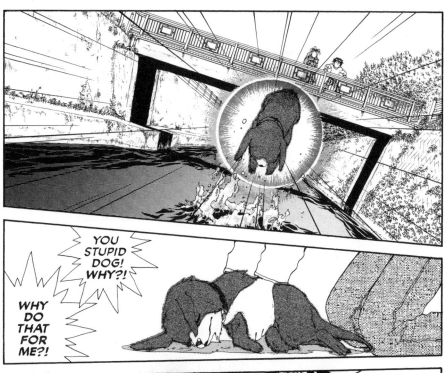

YOU STUPID DOG! WHY?!

WHY DO THAT FOR ME?!

NIHON-MARU!

OH, NO!!

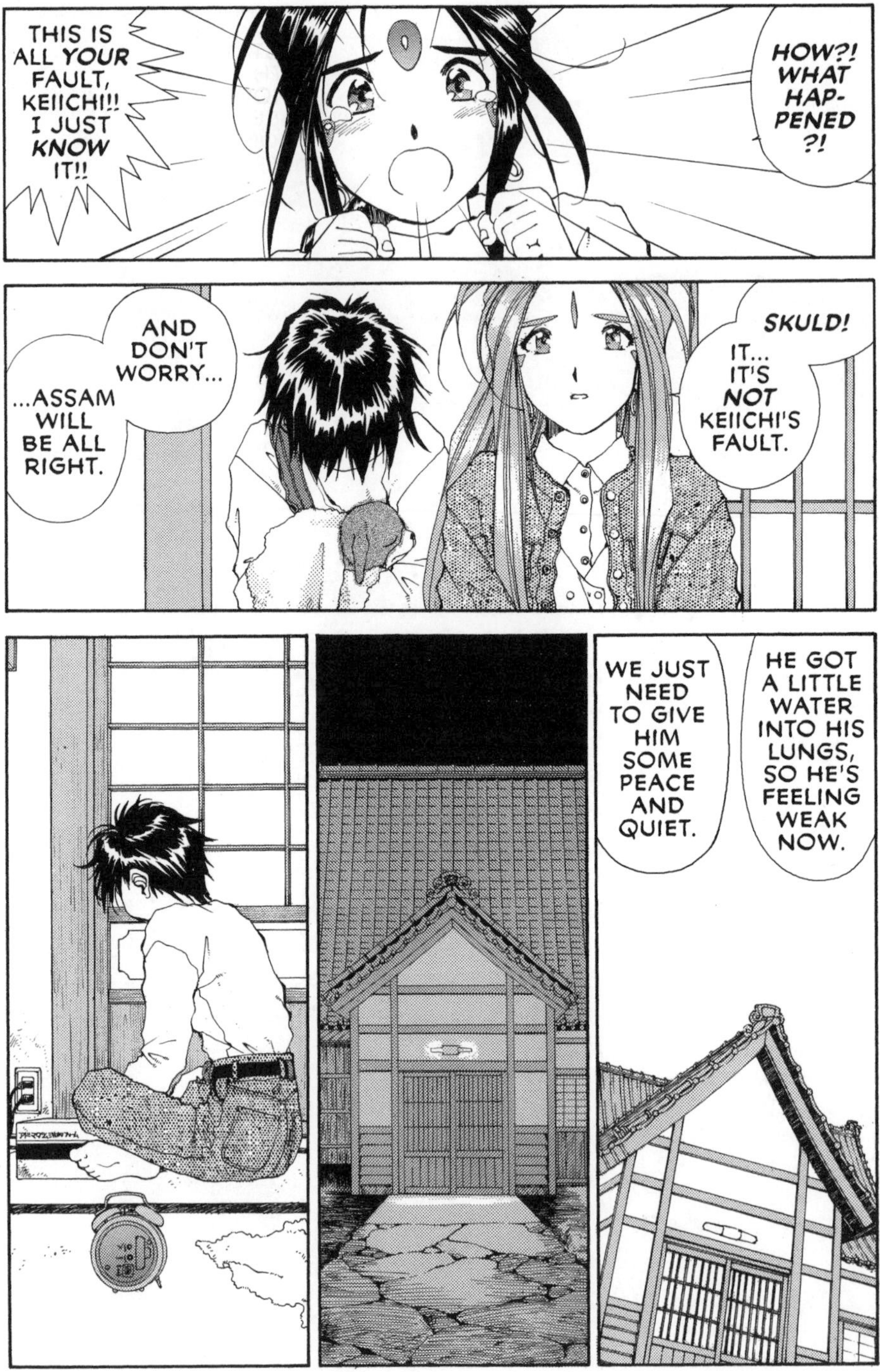
HOW?! WHAT HAP-PENED?!
THIS IS ALL YOUR FAULT, KEIICHI!! I JUST KNOW IT!!
SKULD!
IT... IT'S NOT KEIICHI'S FAULT.
AND DON'T WORRY...
...ASSAM WILL BE ALL RIGHT.
HE GOT A LITTLE WATER INTO HIS LUNGS, SO HE'S FEELING WEAK NOW.
WE JUST NEED TO GIVE HIM SOME PEACE AND QUIET.

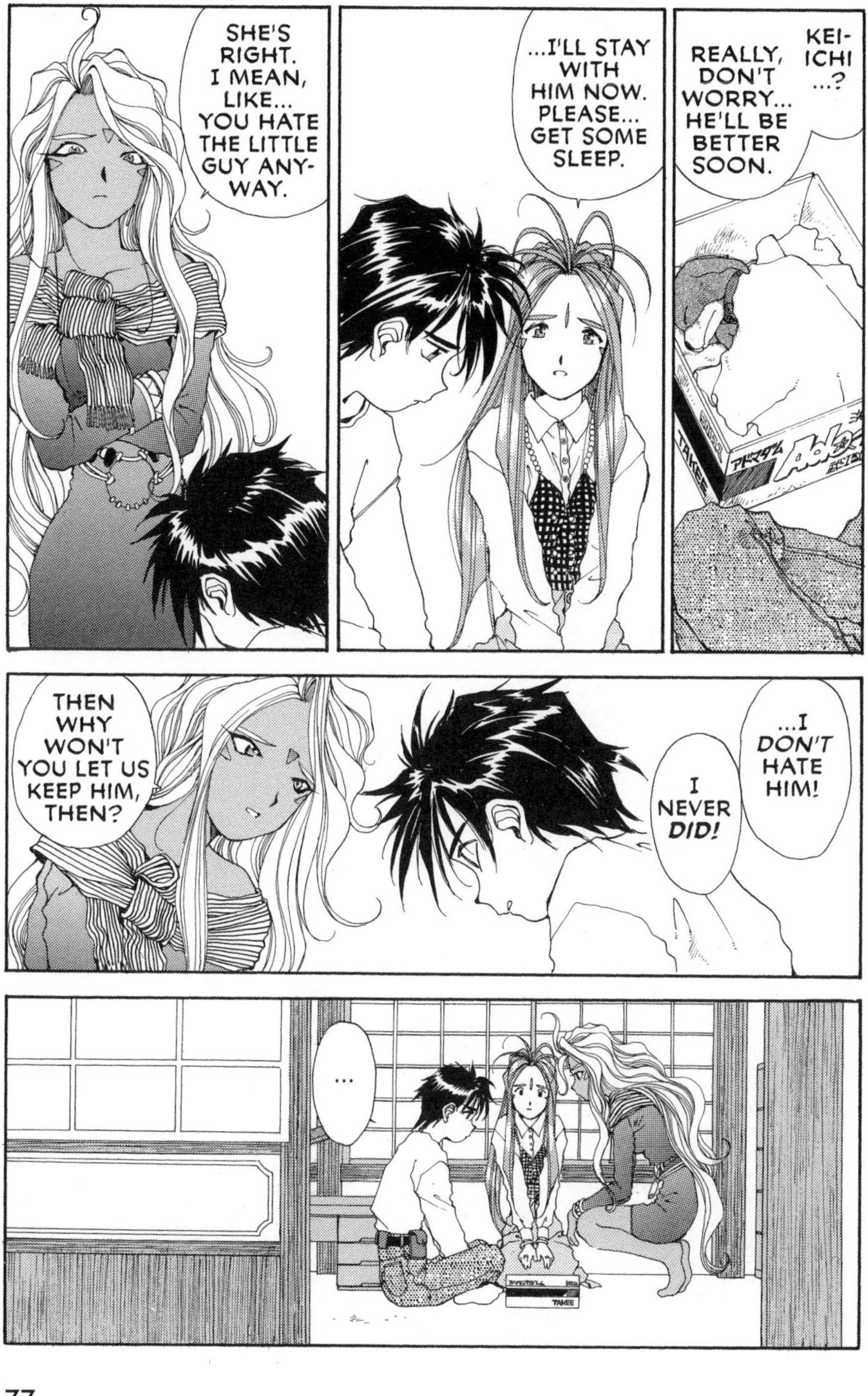
KEI-ICHI ...?
REALLY, DON'T WORRY... HE'LL BE BETTER SOON.
TAKEE
...I'LL STAY WITH HIM NOW. PLEASE... GET SOME SLEEP.
SHE'S RIGHT. I MEAN, LIKE... YOU HATE THE LITTLE GUY ANY-WAY.
...I *DON'T* HATE HIM!
I NEVER *DID!*
THEN WHY WON'T YOU LET US KEEP HIM, THEN?
...
TAKEE

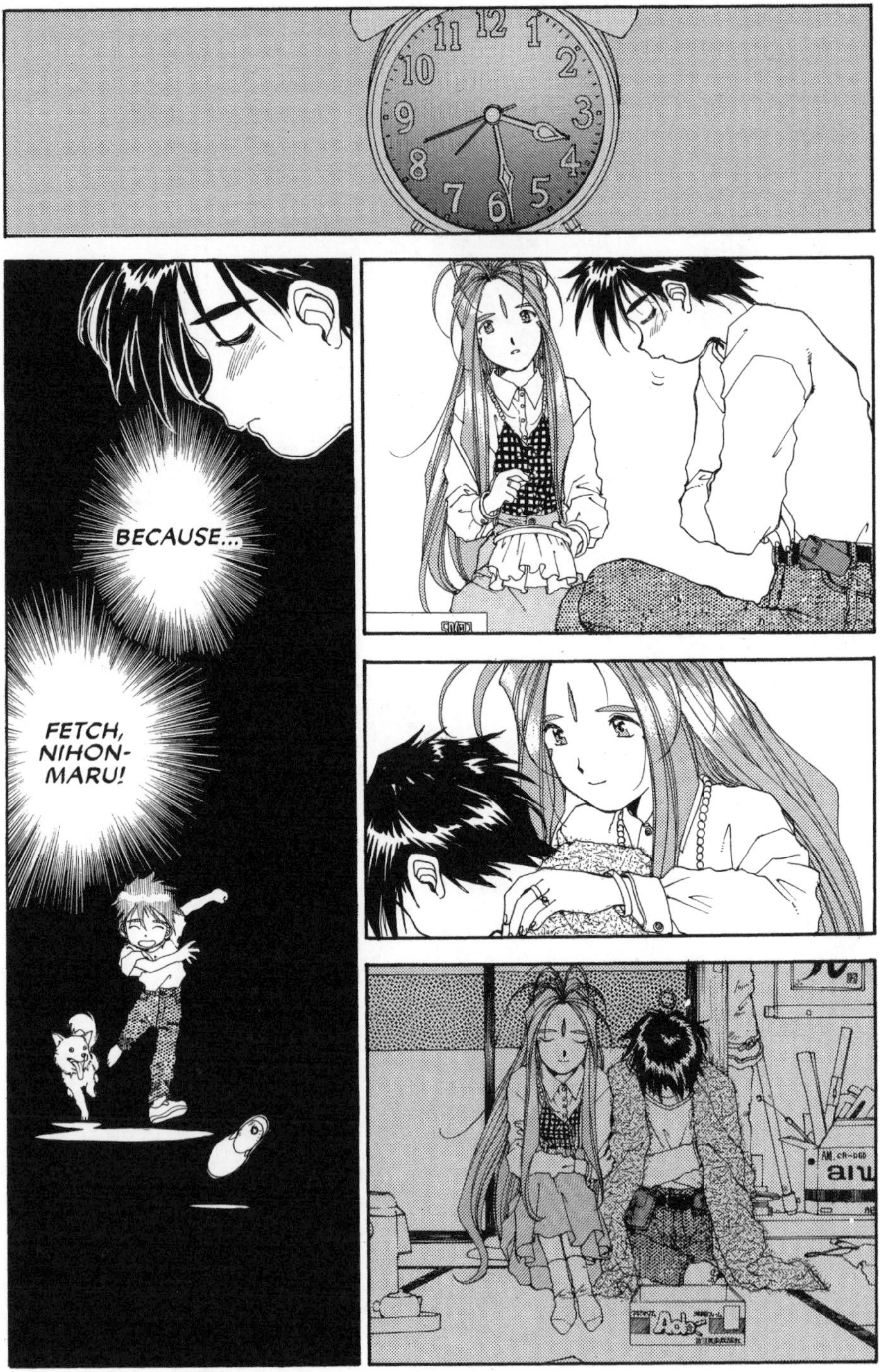
BECAUSE...
FETCH, NIHON-MARU!

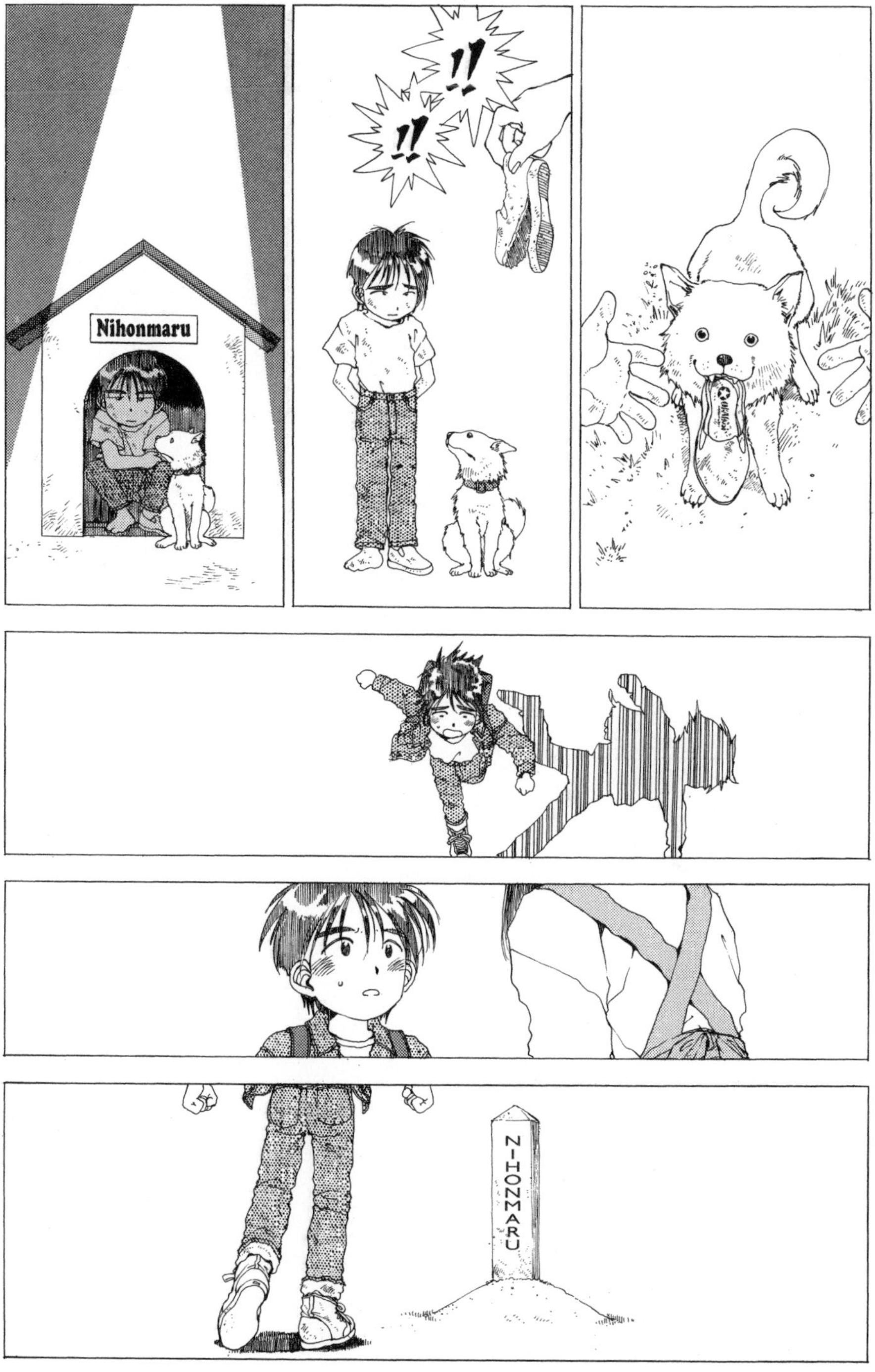
!!
!!
Nihonmaru
NIHONMARU

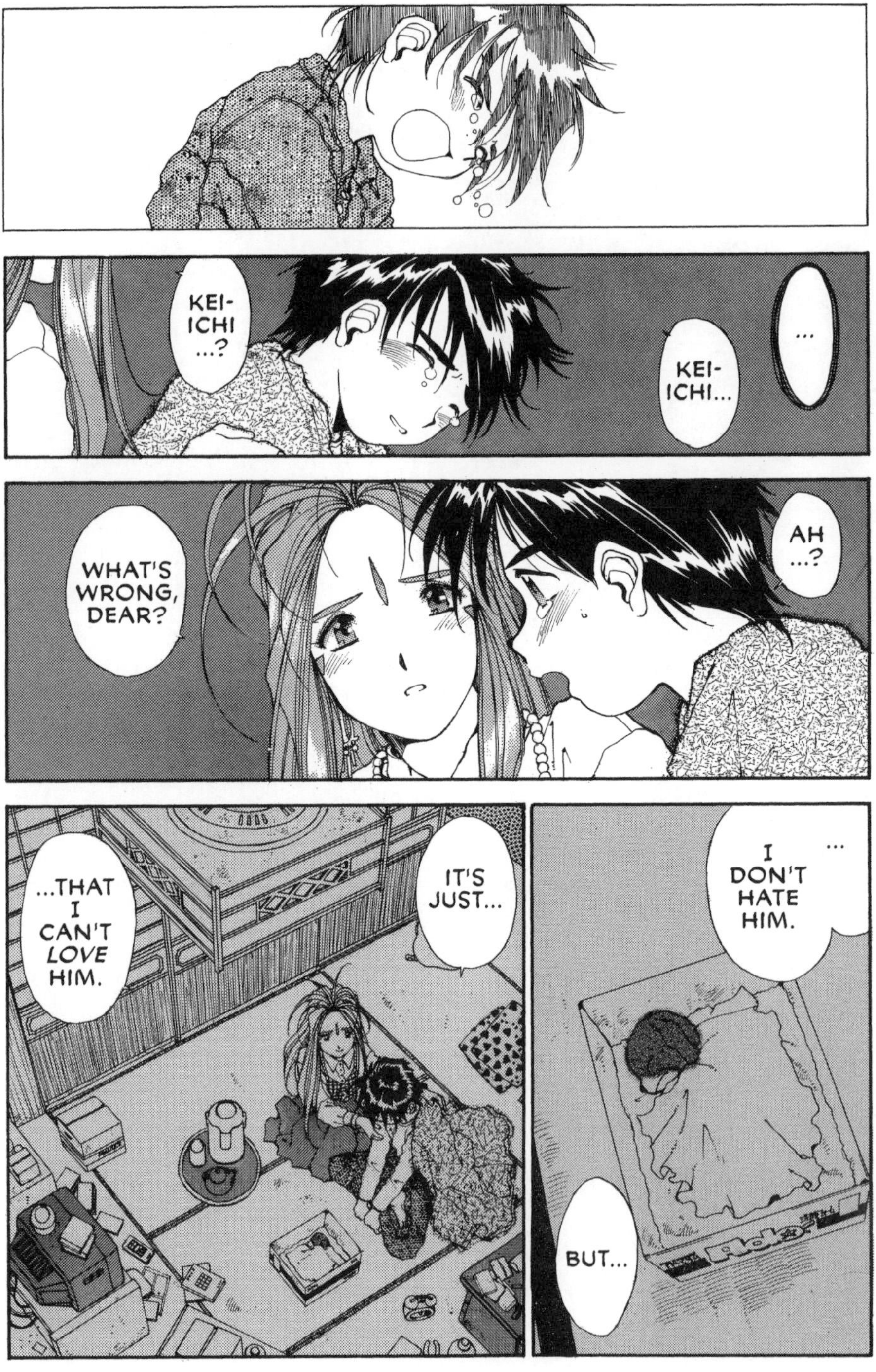
...
KEI-ICHI...
KEI-ICHI ...?
AH ...?
WHAT'S WRONG, DEAR?
... I DON'T HATE HIM.
BUT...
IT'S JUST...
...THAT I CAN'T *LOVE* HIM.

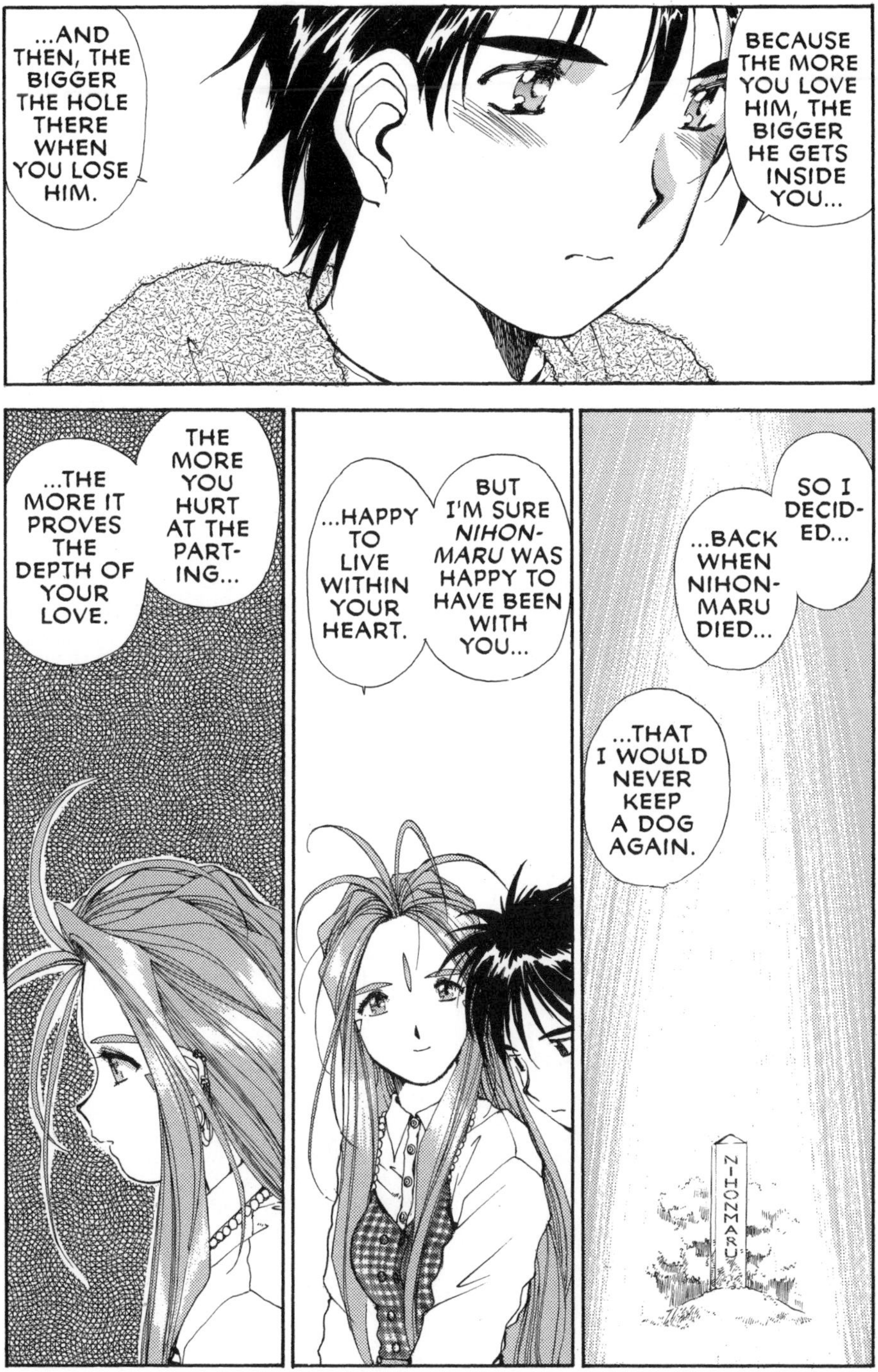
BECAUSE THE MORE YOU LOVE HIM, THE BIGGER HE GETS INSIDE YOU...
...AND THEN, THE BIGGER THE HOLE THERE WHEN YOU LOSE HIM.
SO I DECID-ED...
...BACK WHEN NIHON-MARU DIED...
...THAT I WOULD NEVER KEEP A DOG AGAIN.
NIHONMARU
BUT I'M SURE *NIHON-MARU* WAS HAPPY TO HAVE BEEN WITH YOU...
...HAPPY TO LIVE WITHIN YOUR HEART.
THE MORE YOU HURT AT THE PART-ING...
...THE MORE IT PROVES THE DEPTH OF YOUR LOVE.

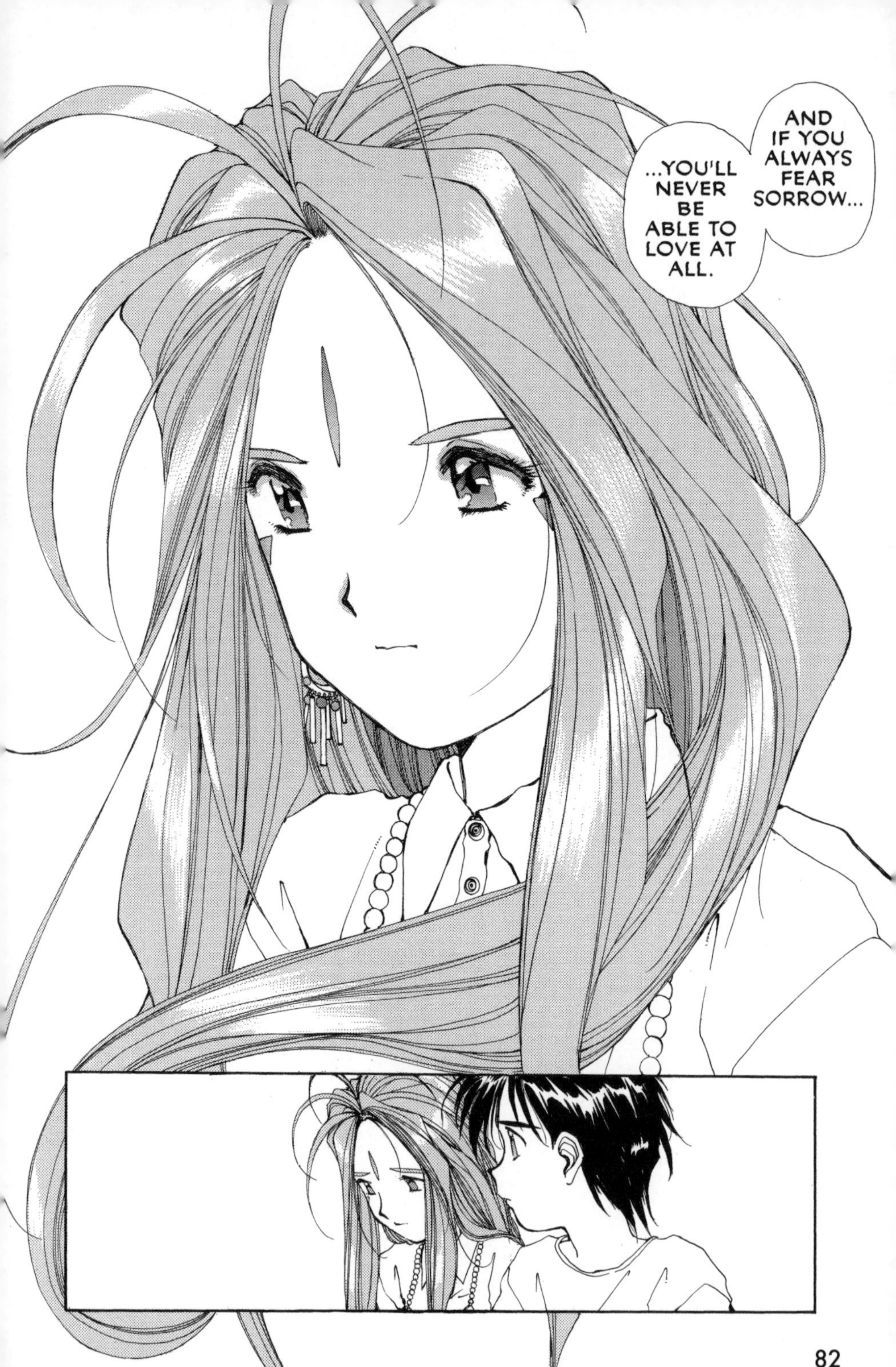
AND IF YOU ALWAYS FEAR SORROW...
...YOU'LL NEVER BE ABLE TO LOVE AT ALL.

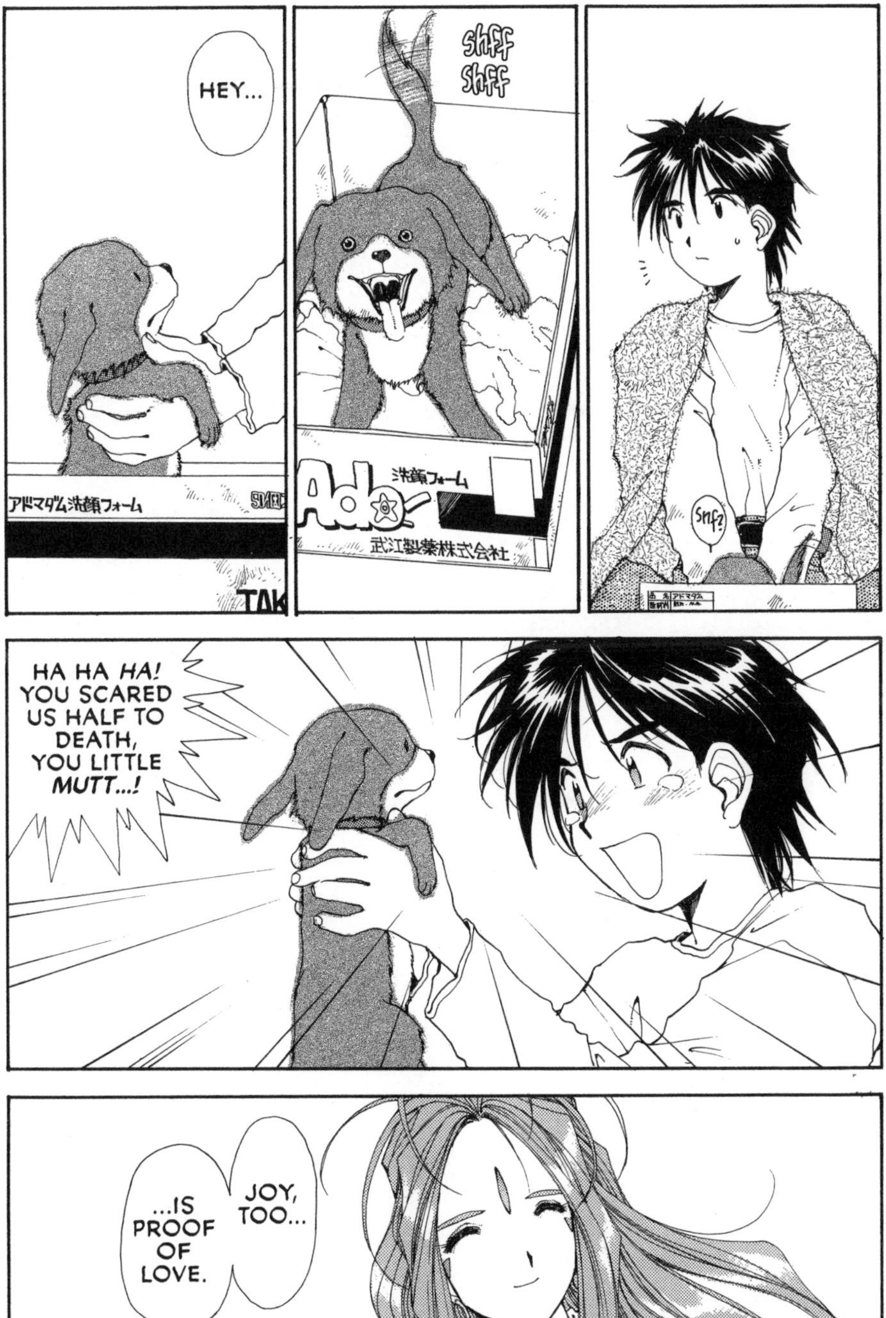
SNF?
SHFF SHFF
Ado
洗顔フォーム
武江製薬株式会社
HEY...
アドマダム洗顔フォーム
TAK
HA HA HA! YOU SCARED US HALF TO DEATH, YOU LITTLE MUTT...!
JOY, TOO...
...IS PROOF OF LOVE.

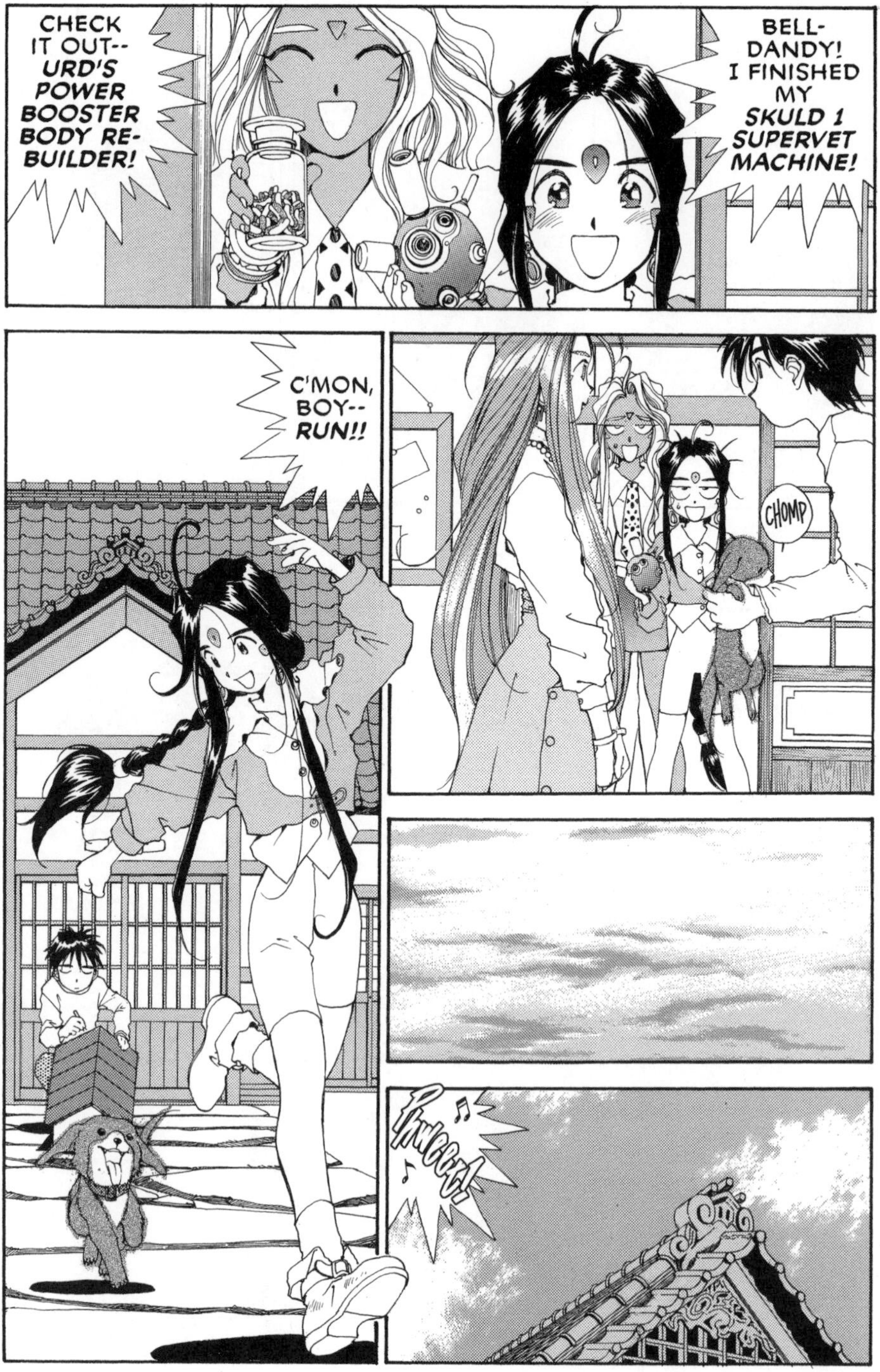
BELL-DANDY! I FINISHED MY *SKULD 1 SUPERVET MACHINE!*
CHECK IT OUT-- *URD'S POWER BOOSTER BODY RE-BUILDER!*
CHOMP
Phweeet!
C'MON, BOY-- *RUN!!*

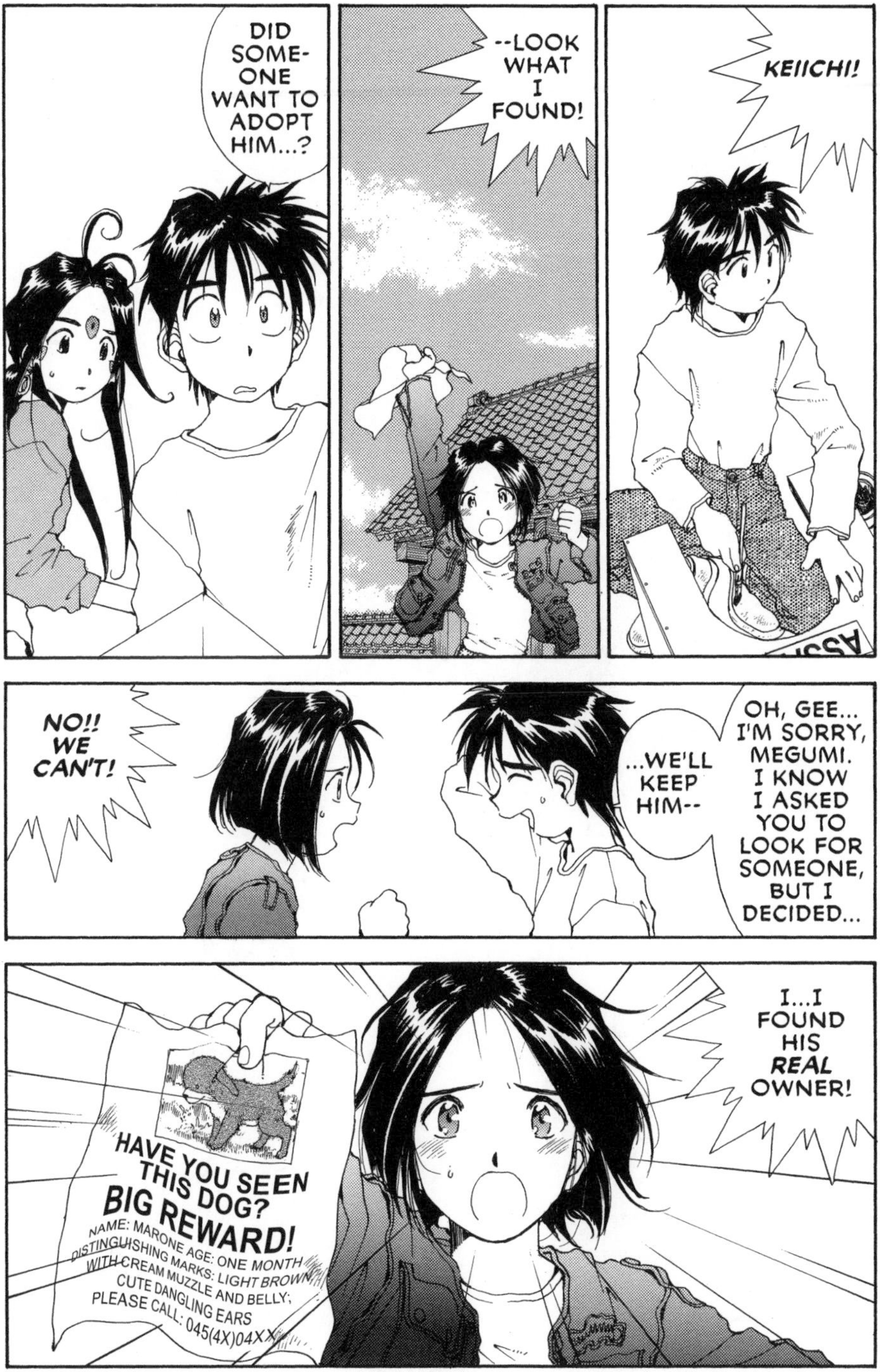
KEIICHI!
--LOOK WHAT I FOUND!
DID SOME-ONE WANT TO ADOPT HIM...?
OH, GEE... I'M SORRY, MEGUMI. I KNOW I ASKED YOU TO LOOK FOR SOMEONE, BUT I DECIDED...
...WE'LL KEEP HIM--
NO!! WE CAN'T!
I...I FOUND HIS REAL OWNER!
HAVE YOU SEEN THIS DOG?
BIG REWARD!
NAME: MARONE AGE: ONE MONTH
DISTINGUISHING MARKS: LIGHT BROWN WITH CREAM MUZZLE AND BELLY; CUTE DANGLING EARS
PLEASE CALL: 045(4X)04XX

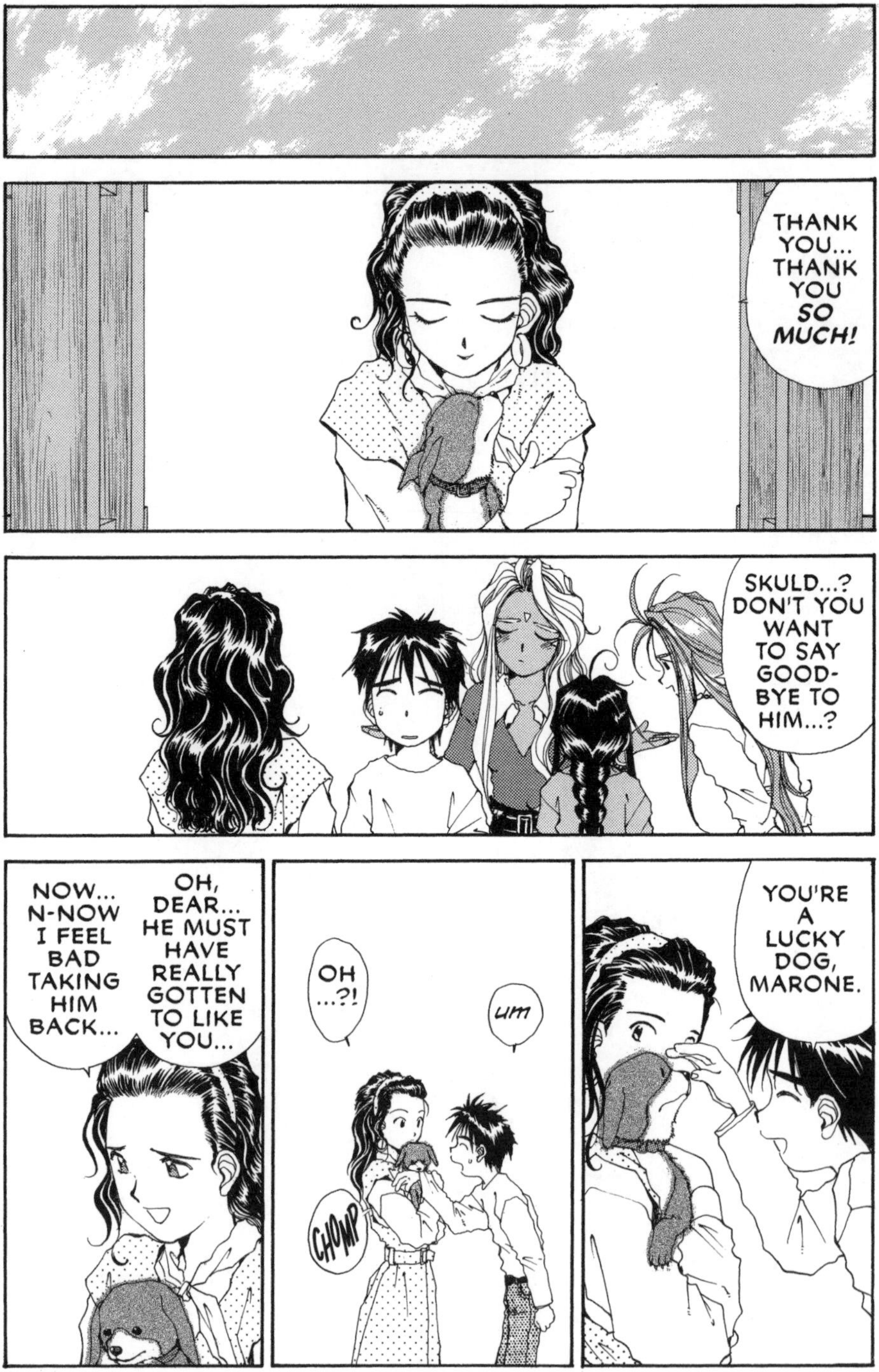
THANK YOU... THANK YOU *SO MUCH!*
SKULD...? DON'T YOU WANT TO SAY GOOD-BYE TO HIM...?
YOU'RE A LUCKY DOG, MARONE.
um
OH ...?!
CHOMP
OH, DEAR... HE MUST HAVE REALLY GOTTEN TO LIKE YOU...
NOW... N-NOW I FEEL BAD TAKING HIM BACK...

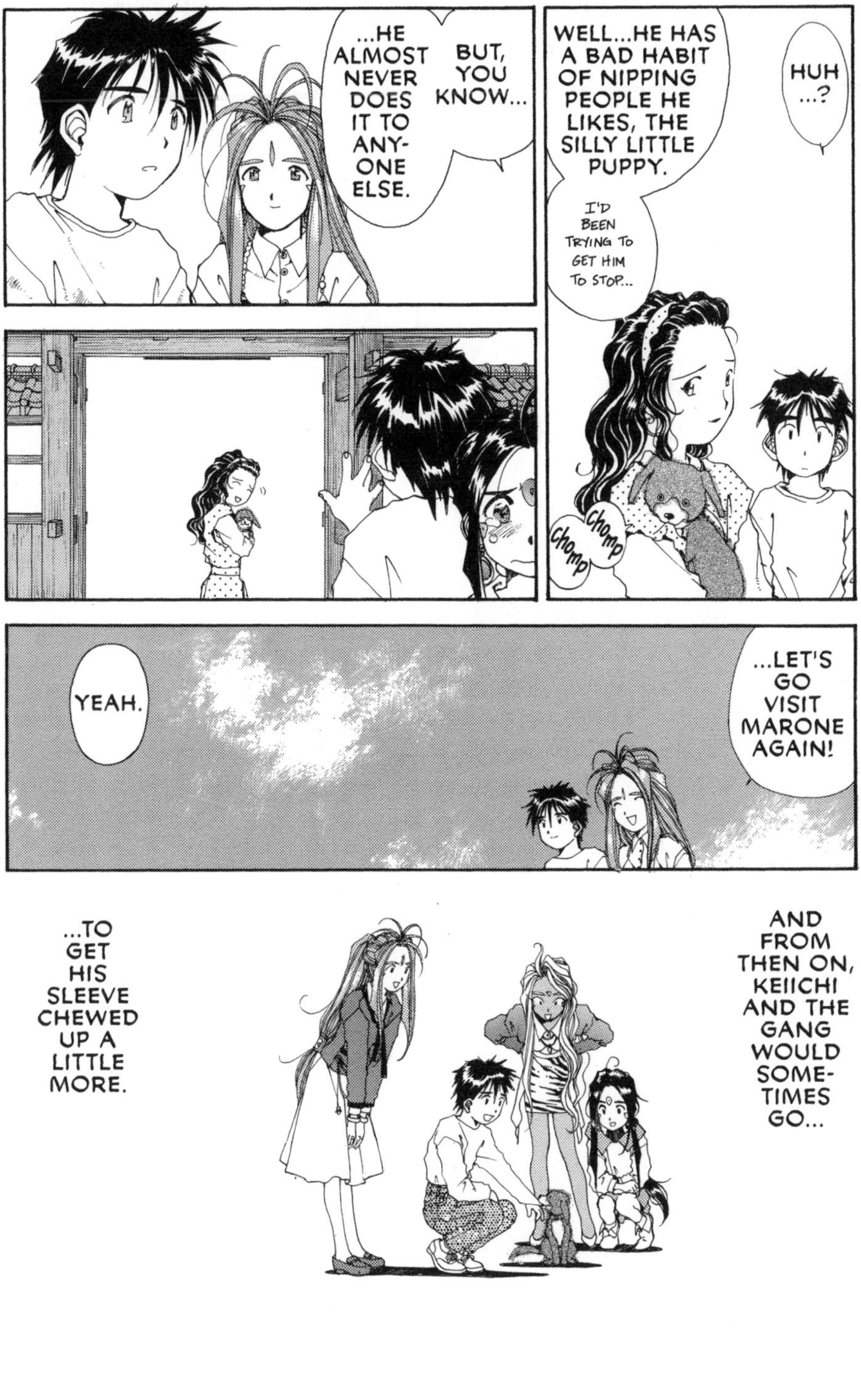
HUH ...?
WELL...HE HAS A BAD HABIT OF NIPPING PEOPLE HE LIKES, THE SILLY LITTLE PUPPY.
I'D BEEN TRYING TO GET HIM TO STOP...
chomp
chomp
BUT, YOU KNOW...
...HE ALMOST NEVER DOES IT TO ANY-ONE ELSE.
...LET'S GO VISIT MARONE AGAIN!
YEAH.
AND FROM THEN ON, KEIICHI AND THE GANG WOULD SOME-TIMES GO...
...TO GET HIS SLEEVE CHEWED UP A LITTLE MORE.

THE ADVENTURES OF THE MINI-GODDESSES

◆BACK AGAIN! THE "OH MY ROCK GODDESS" GRAND PRIX!◆

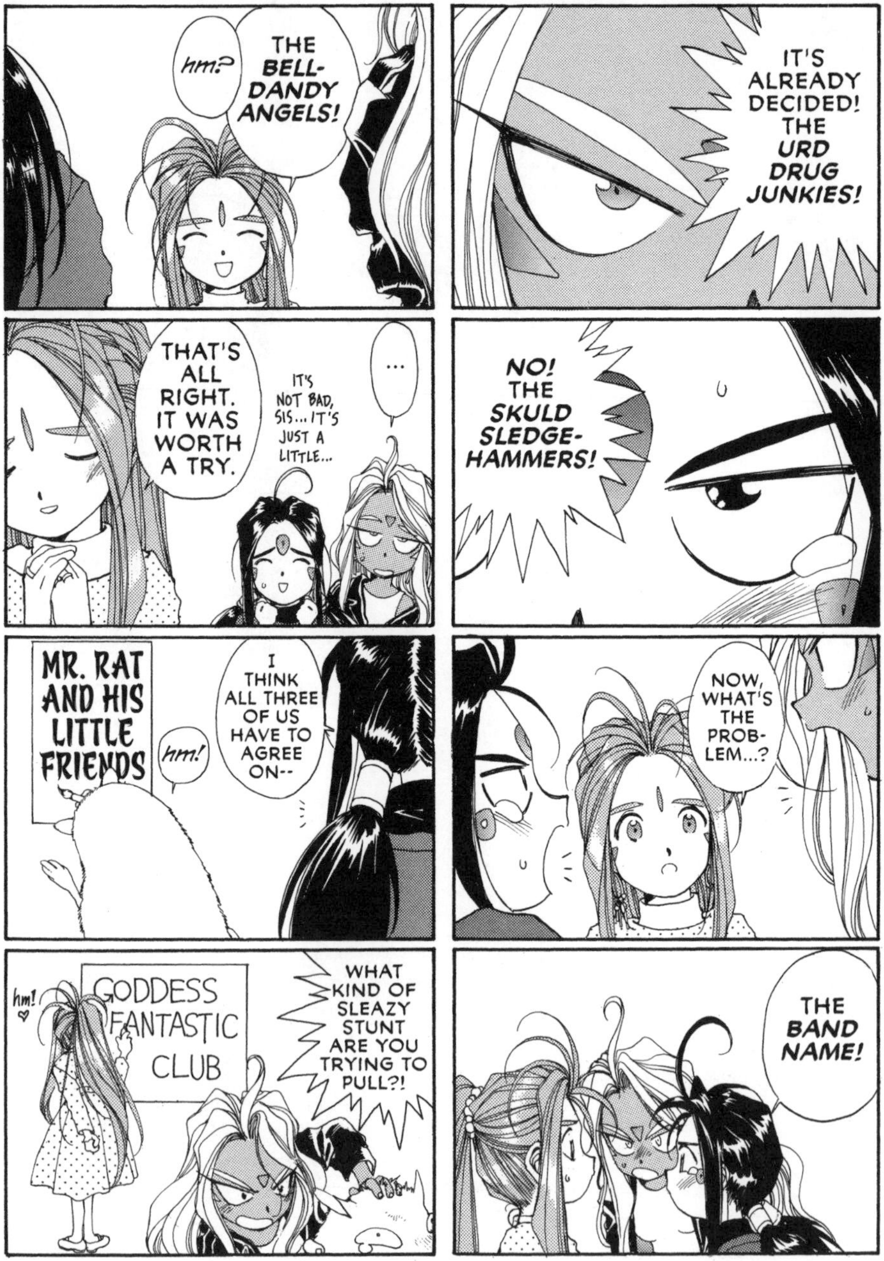

IT'S ALREADY DECIDED! THE URD DRUG JUNKIES!
NO! THE SKULD SLEDGE-HAMMERS!
NOW, WHAT'S THE PROB-LEM...?
THE BAND NAME!
THE BELL-DANDY ANGELS!
hm?
...
IT'S NOT BAD, SIS... IT'S JUST A LITTLE...
THAT'S ALL RIGHT. IT WAS WORTH A TRY.
I THINK ALL THREE OF US HAVE TO AGREE ON--
hm!
MR. RAT AND HIS LITTLE FRIENDS
WHAT KIND OF SLEAZY STUNT ARE YOU TRYING TO PULL?!
GODDESS FANTASTIC CLUB
hm!

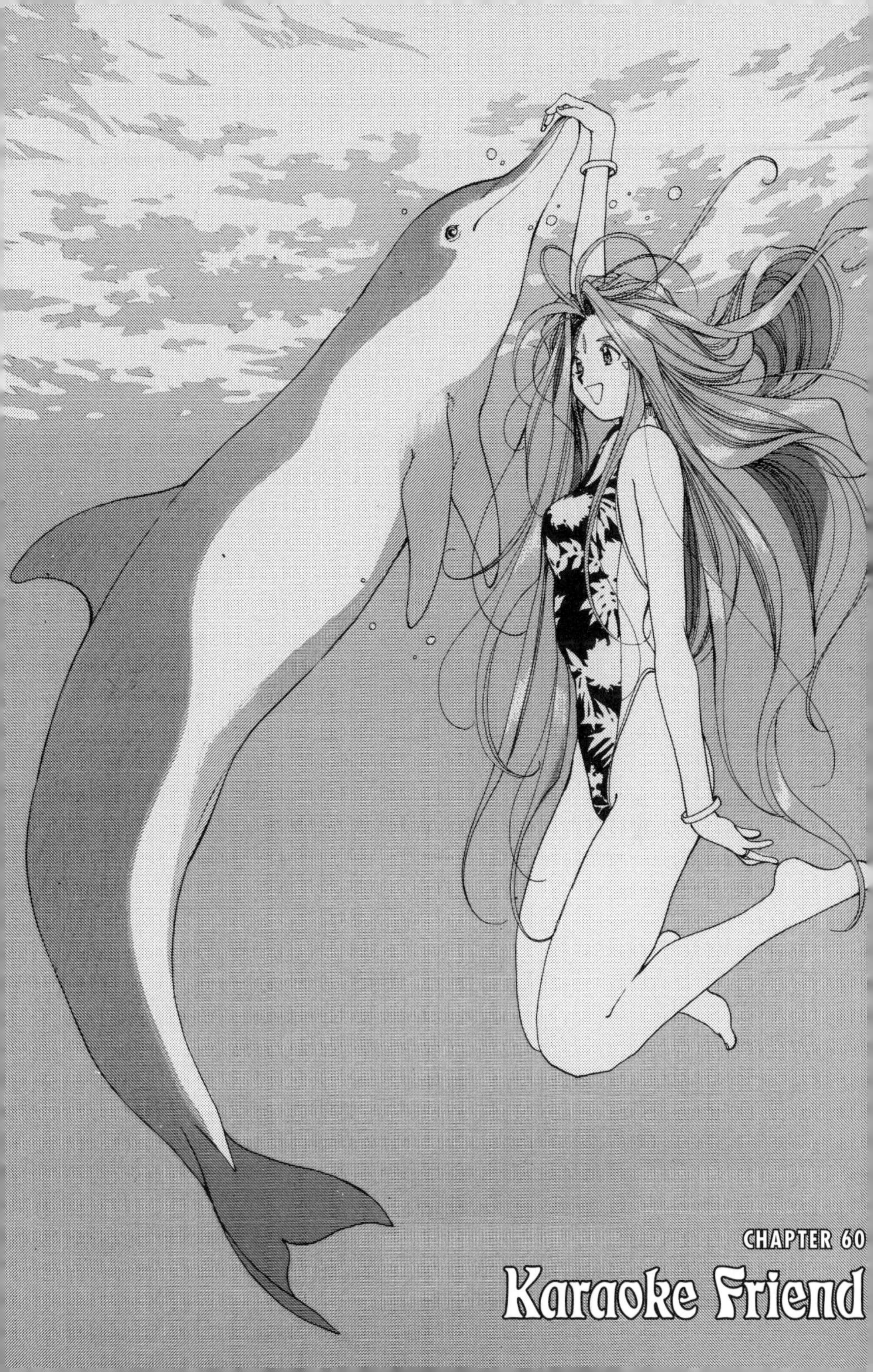

CHAPTER 60

Karaoke Friend

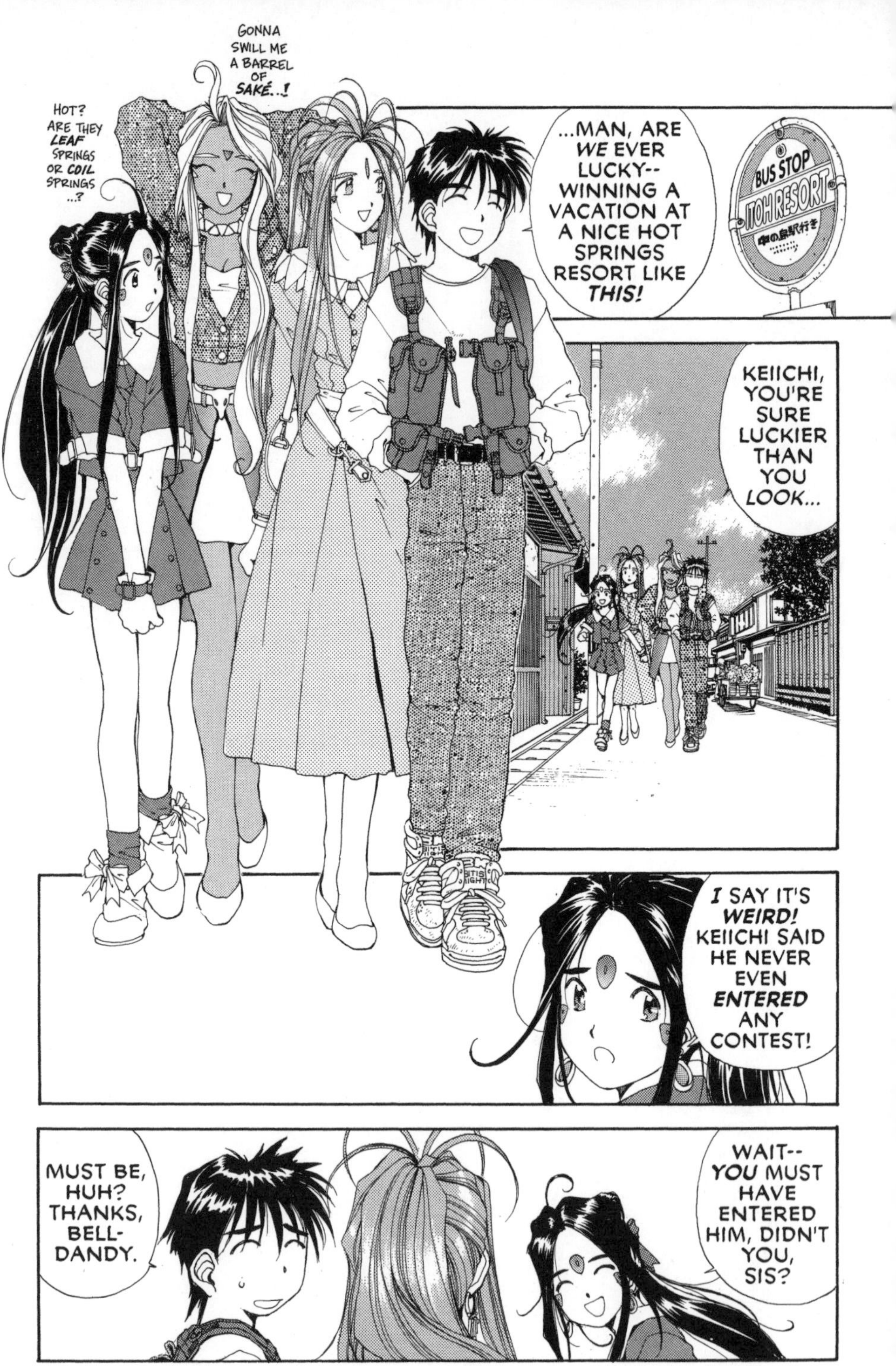
BUS STOP
ITOH RESORT
...MAN, ARE WE EVER LUCKY-- WINNING A VACATION AT A NICE HOT SPRINGS RESORT LIKE THIS!
GONNA SWILL ME A BARREL OF SAKÉ..!
HOT? ARE THEY LEAF SPRINGS OR COIL SPRINGS ...?
KEIICHI, YOU'RE SURE LUCKIER THAN YOU LOOK...
I SAY IT'S WEIRD! KEIICHI SAID HE NEVER EVEN ENTERED ANY CONTEST!
WAIT-- YOU MUST HAVE ENTERED HIM, DIDN'T YOU, SIS?
MUST BE, HUH? THANKS, BELL-DANDY.

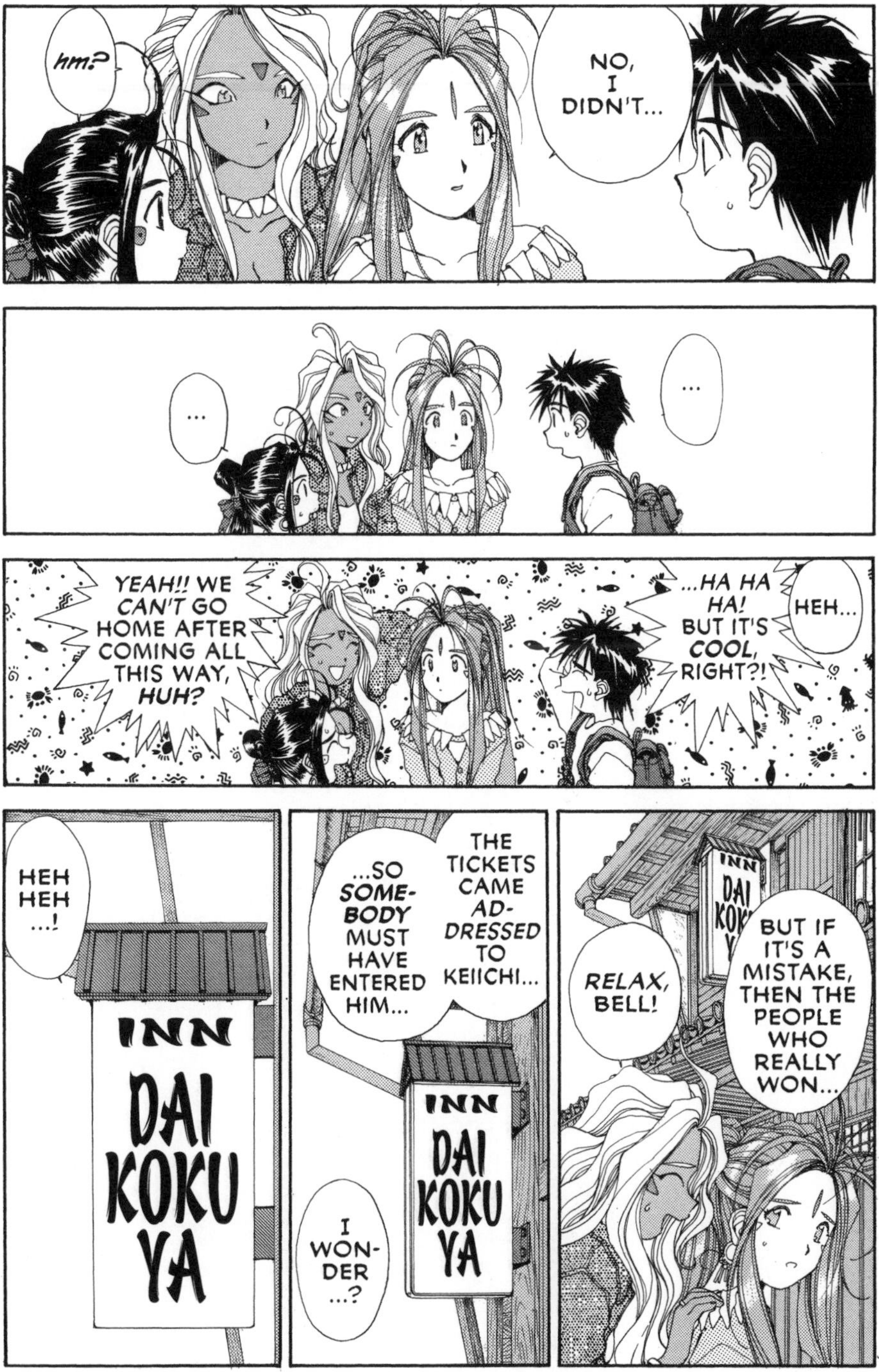

NO, I DIDN'T...
hm?
...
...
HEH...
...HA HA HA! BUT IT'S *COOL*, RIGHT?!
YEAH!! WE *CAN'T* GO HOME AFTER COMING ALL THIS WAY, *HUH?*
BUT IF IT'S A MISTAKE, THEN THE PEOPLE WHO REALLY WON...
RELAX, BELL!
THE TICKETS CAME *AD-DRESSED* TO KEIICHI...
...SO *SOME-BODY* MUST HAVE ENTERED HIM...
INN
DAI KOKU YA
I WON-DER ...?
HEH HEH ...!
INN
DAI KOKU YA

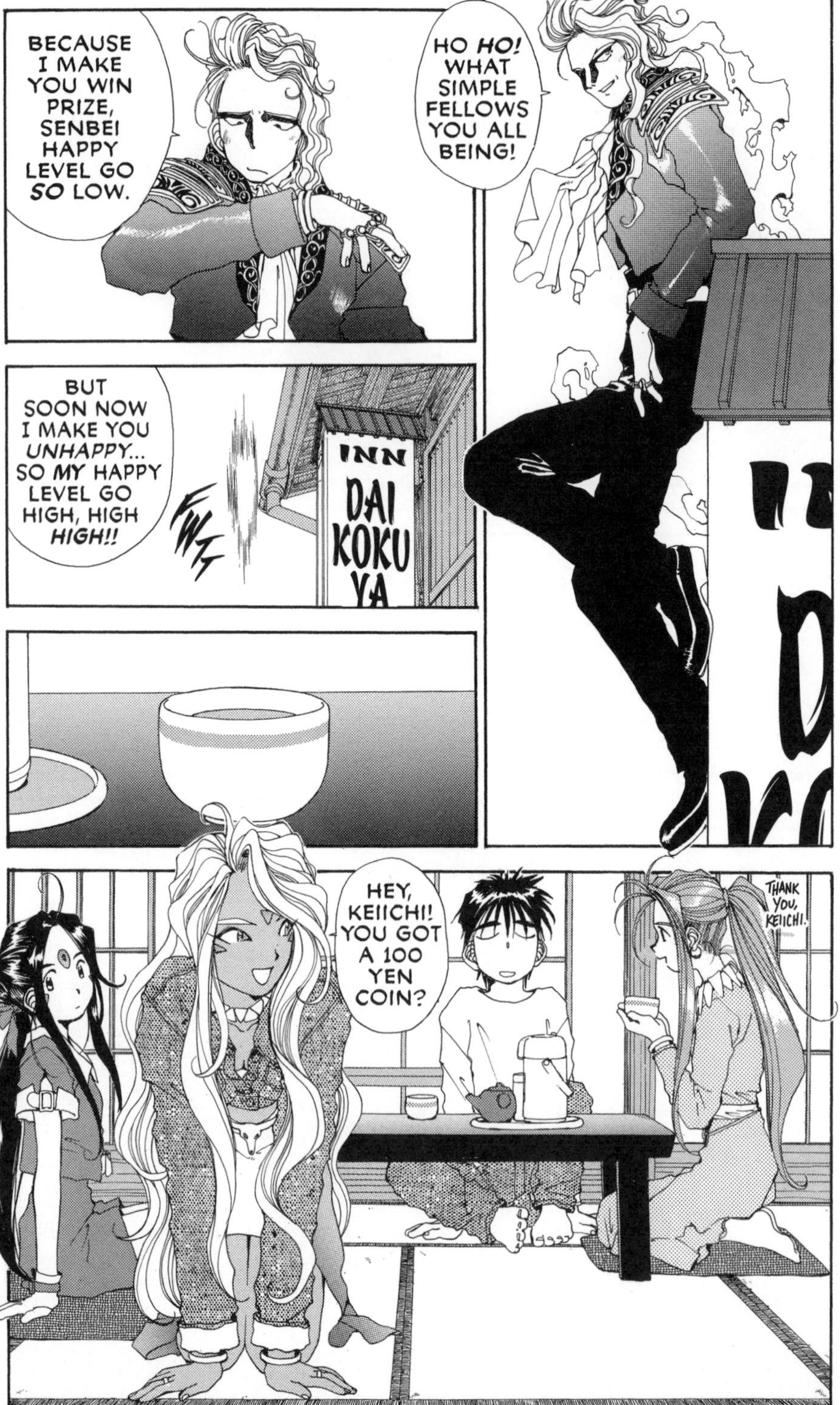
HO HO! WHAT SIMPLE FELLOWS YOU ALL BEING!
BECAUSE I MAKE YOU WIN PRIZE, SENBEI HAPPY LEVEL GO SO LOW.
BUT SOON NOW I MAKE YOU UNHAPPY... SO MY HAPPY LEVEL GO HIGH, HIGH HIGH!!
INN
DAI KOKU YA
THANK YOU, KEIICHI!
HEY, KEIICHI! YOU GOT A 100 YEN COIN?

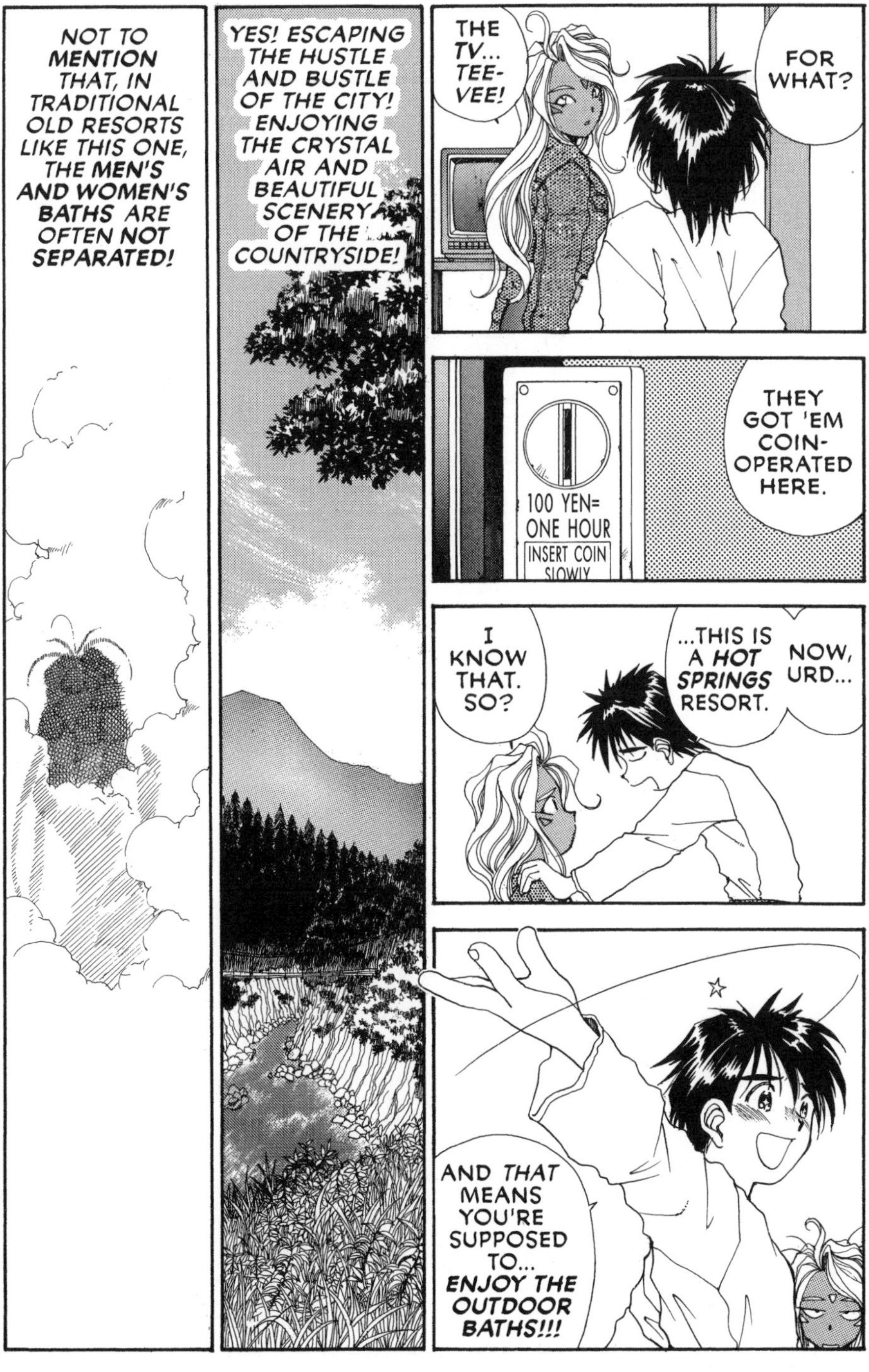
FOR WHAT?
THE TV... TEE-VEE!
THEY GOT 'EM COIN-OPERATED HERE.
100 YEN= ONE HOUR
INSERT COIN SLOWLY
NOW, URD...
...THIS IS A HOT SPRINGS RESORT.
I KNOW THAT. SO?
AND THAT MEANS YOU'RE SUPPOSED TO... ENJOY THE OUTDOOR BATHS!!!
YES! ESCAPING THE HUSTLE AND BUSTLE OF THE CITY! ENJOYING THE CRYSTAL AIR AND BEAUTIFUL SCENERY OF THE COUNTRYSIDE!
NOT TO MENTION THAT, IN TRADITIONAL OLD RESORTS LIKE THIS ONE, THE MEN'S AND WOMEN'S BATHS ARE OFTEN NOT SEPARATED!

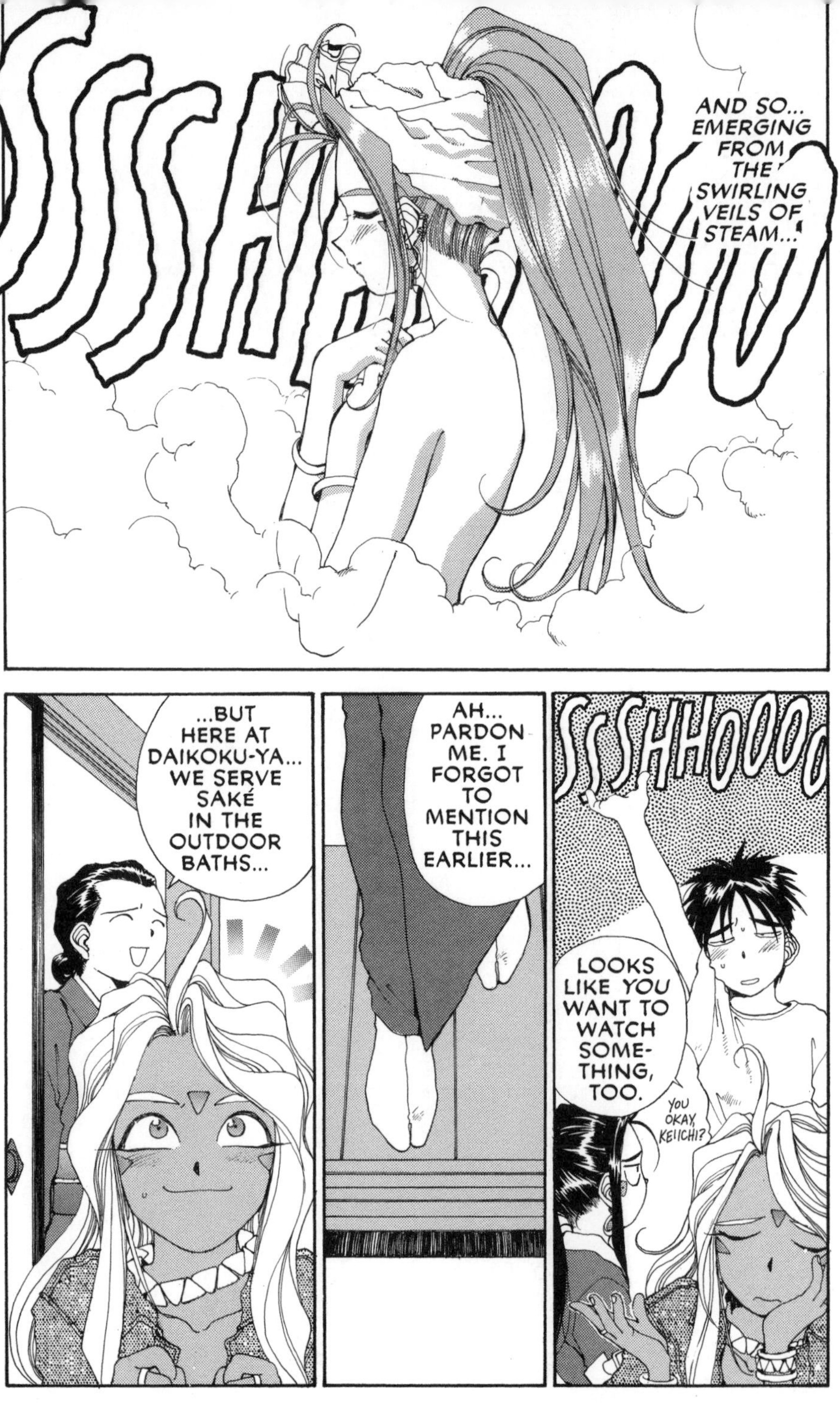
AND SO... EMERGING FROM THE SWIRLING VEILS OF STEAM...
SSSHHOOOO
SSSHHOOOO
LOOKS LIKE YOU WANT TO WATCH SOME-THING, TOO.
YOU OKAY, KEIICHI?
AH... PARDON ME. I FORGOT TO MENTION THIS EARLIER...
...BUT HERE AT DAIKOKU-YA... WE SERVE SAKÉ IN THE OUTDOOR BATHS...

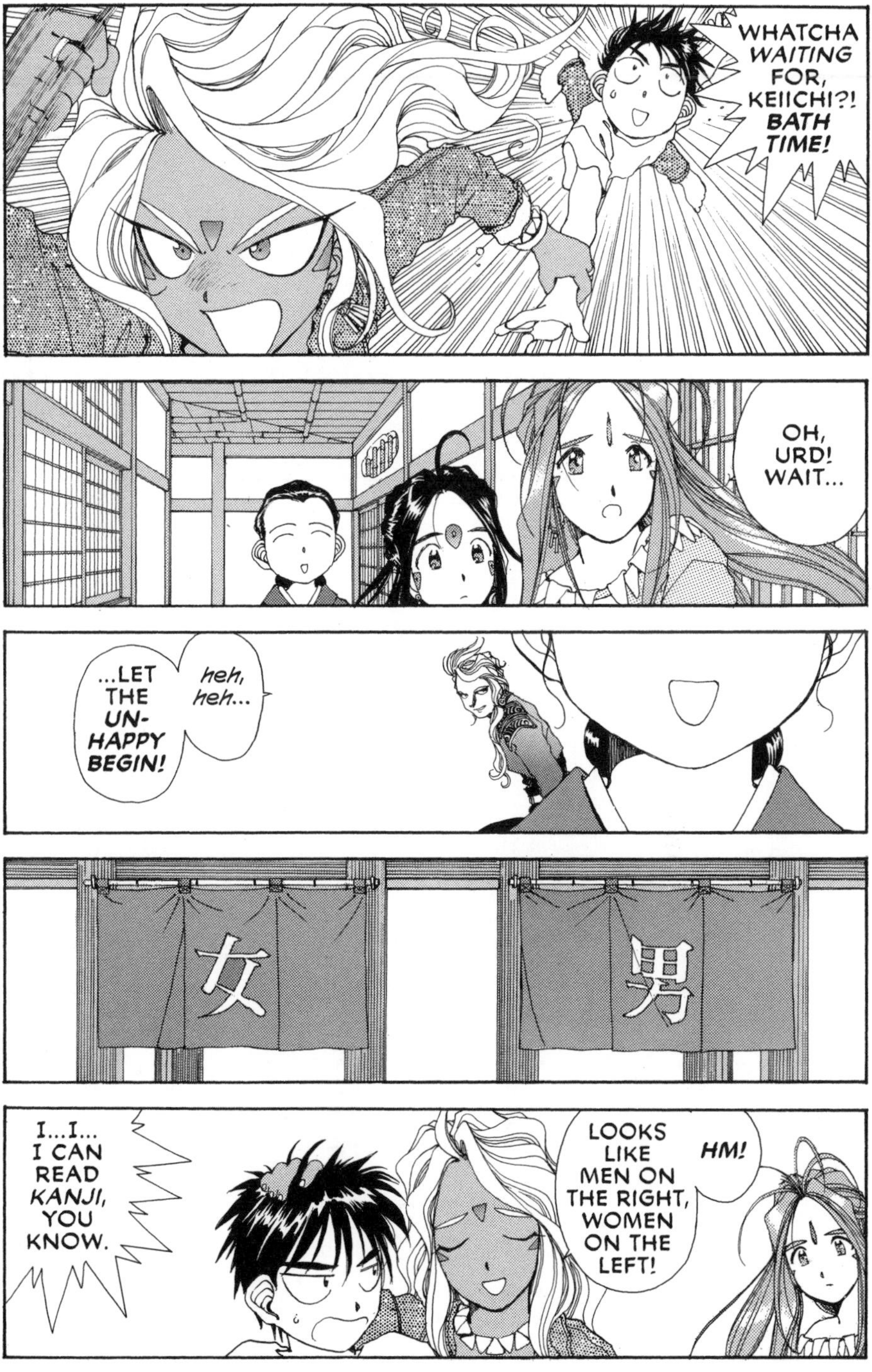
WHATCHA WAITING FOR, KEIICHI?! BATH TIME!
OH, URD! WAIT...
heh, heh...
...LET THE UN-HAPPY BEGIN!
女
男
HM!
LOOKS LIKE MEN ON THE RIGHT, WOMEN ON THE LEFT!
I...I... I CAN READ KANJI, YOU KNOW.

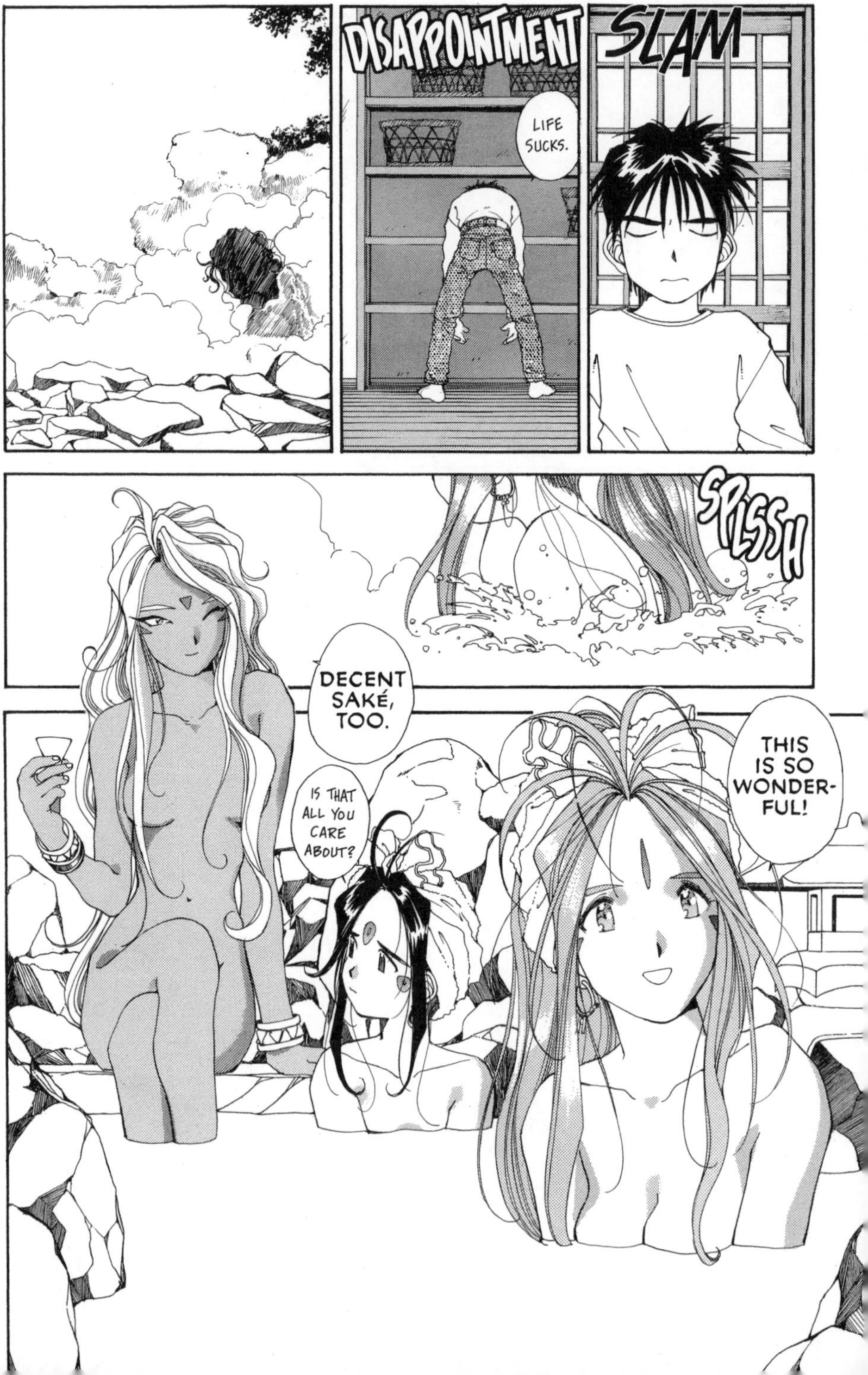
SLAM
DISAPPOINTMENT
LIFE SUCKS.
SPLSSH
THIS IS SO WONDERFUL!
DECENT SAKÉ, TOO.
IS THAT ALL YOU CARE ABOUT?

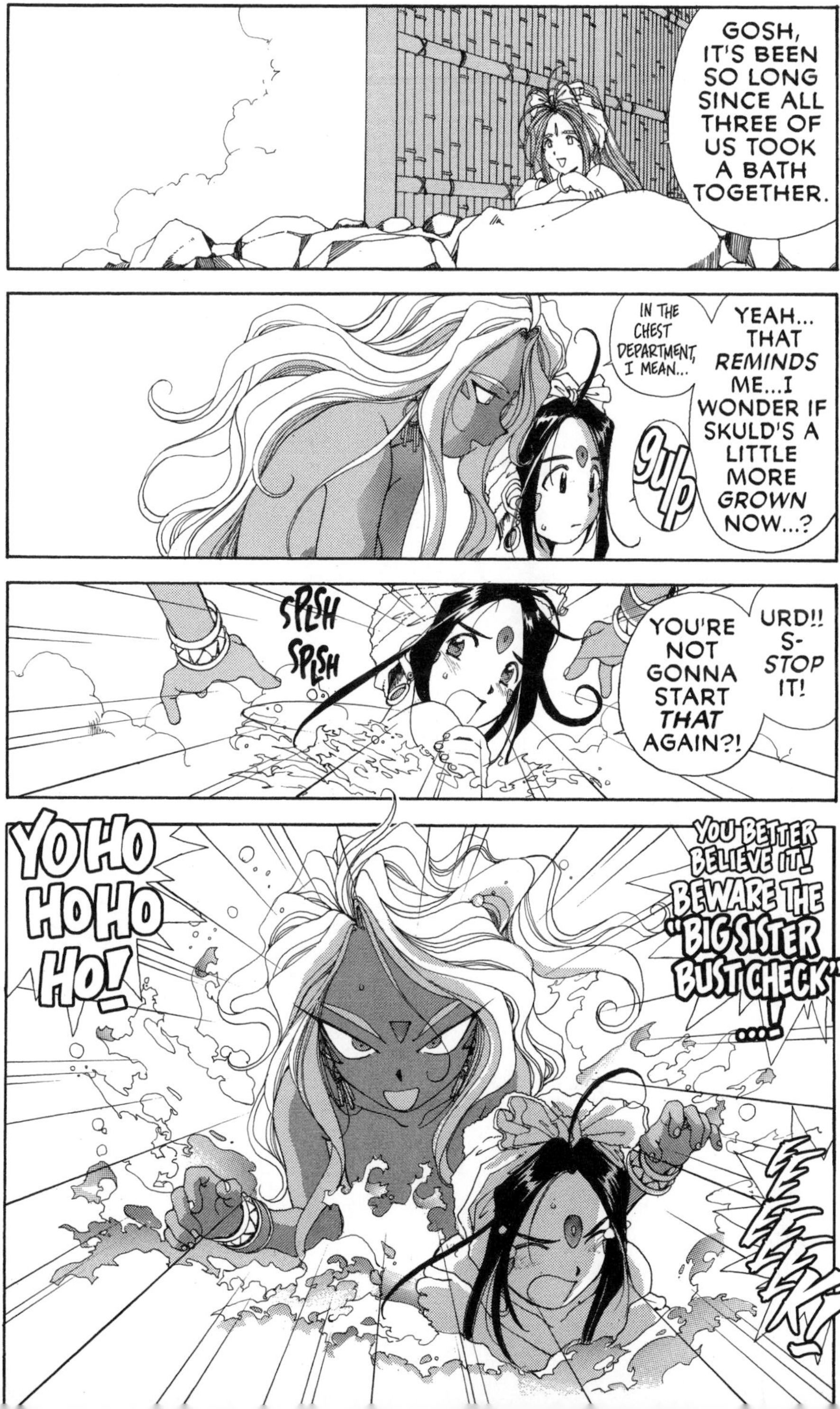
GOSH, IT'S BEEN SO LONG SINCE ALL THREE OF US TOOK A BATH TOGETHER.
YEAH... THAT *REMINDS* ME...I WONDER IF SKULD'S A LITTLE MORE *GROWN* NOW...?
IN THE CHEST DEPARTMENT, I MEAN...
gulp
URD!! S-*STOP* IT!
YOU'RE NOT GONNA START ***THAT*** AGAIN?!
SPLSH
SPLSH
YOU BETTER BELIEVE IT! BEWARE THE "BIG SISTER BUST CHECK"...!
EEEEEK!
YO HO HO HO HO!

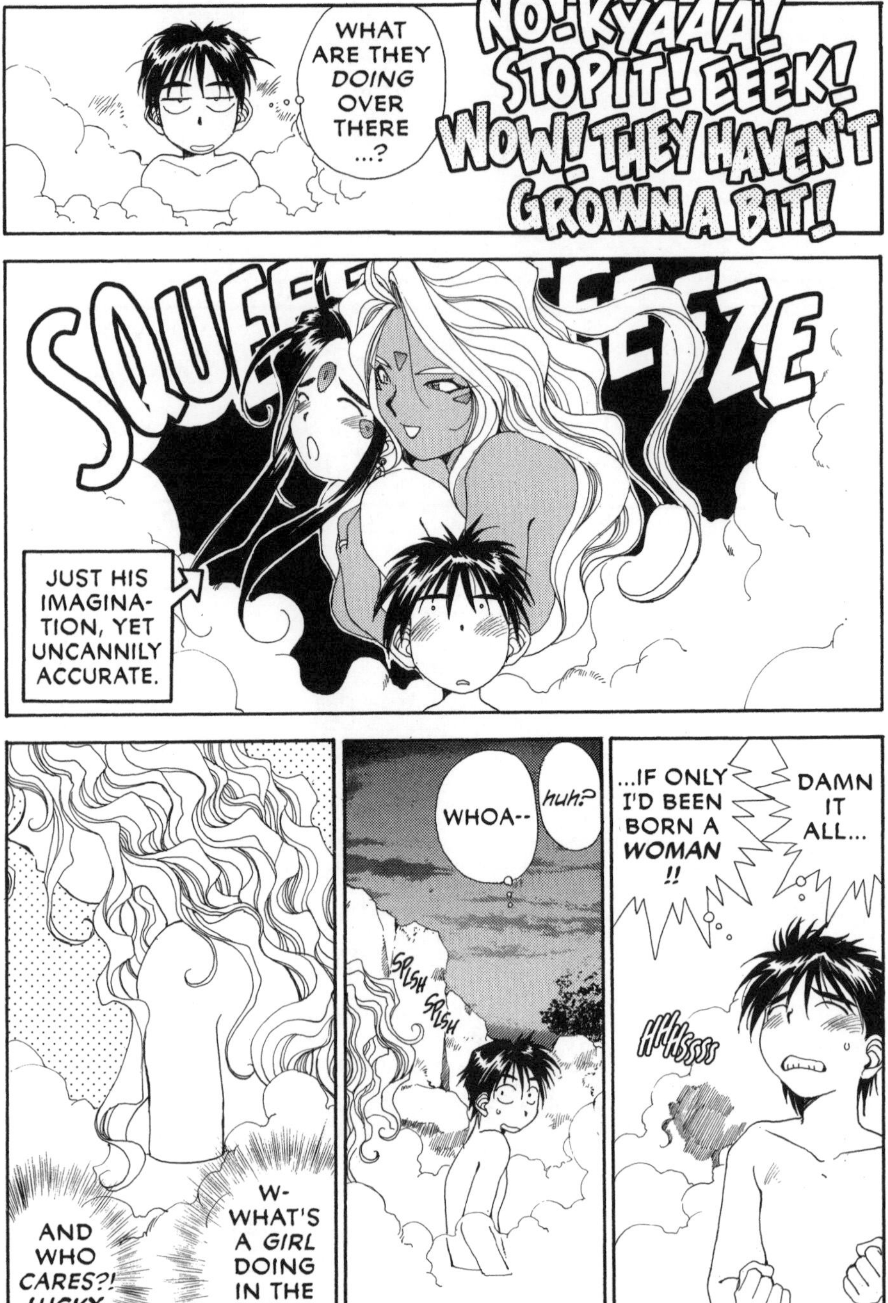
WHAT ARE THEY DOING OVER THERE ...?
NO! KYAAA! STOP IT! EEEK! WOW! THEY HAVEN'T GROWN A BIT!
SQUEEZE
JUST HIS IMAGINATION, YET UNCANNILY ACCURATE.
W-WHAT'S A GIRL DOING IN THE MEN'S BATH?!
AND WHO CARES?! LUCKY !!
WHOA--
huh?
SPLSH SPLSH
DAMN IT ALL...
...IF ONLY I'D BEEN BORN A WOMAN !!
HHHSSSS

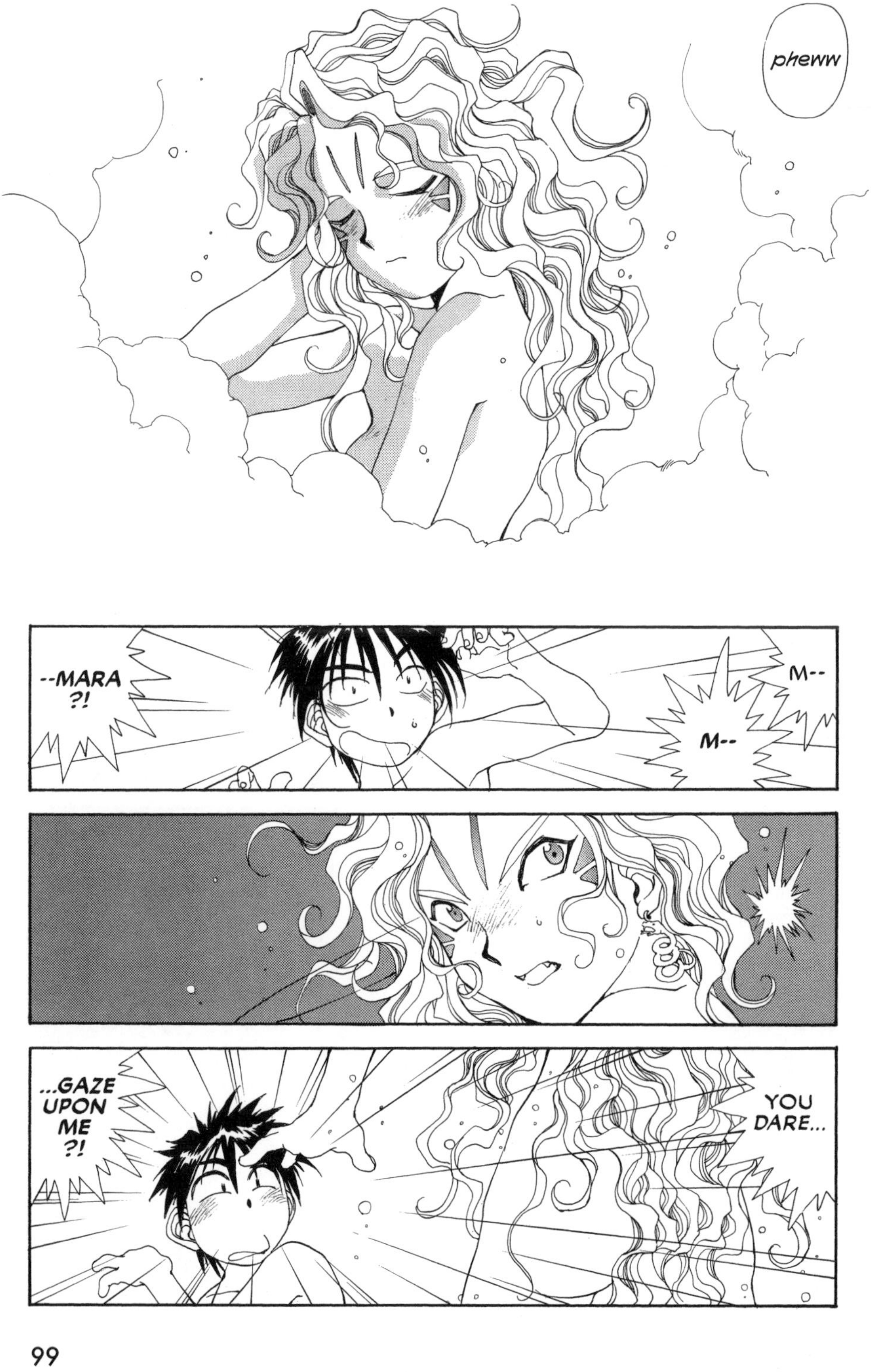
pheww
M-- M--
--MARA ?!
YOU DARE...
...GAZE UPON ME ?!

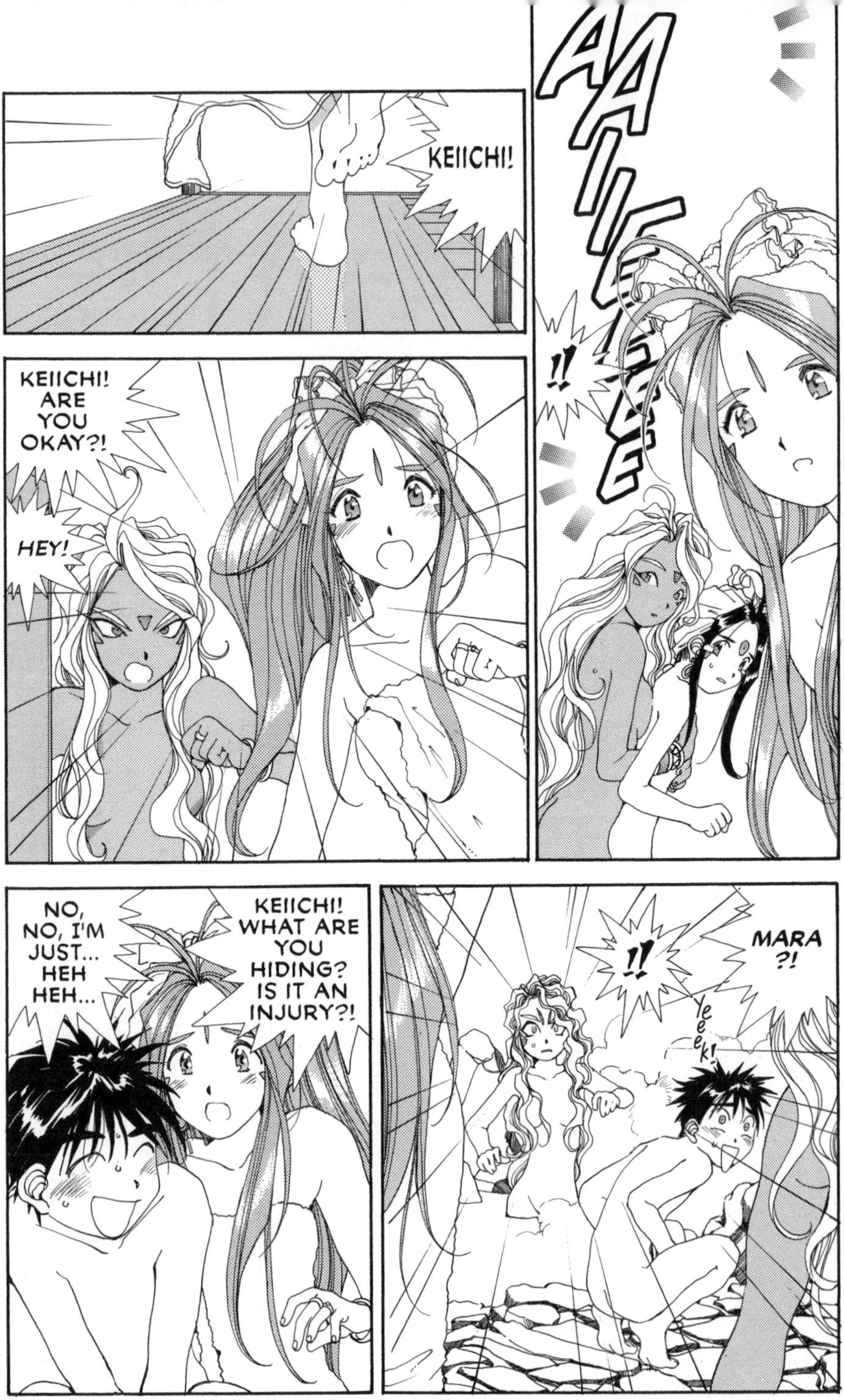
AAIIEEEEE
!!
KEIICHI!
KEIICHI! ARE YOU OKAY?!
HEY!
MARA?!
!!
Yeeeek!
KEIICHI! WHAT ARE YOU HIDING? IS IT AN INJURY?!
NO, NO, I'M JUST... HEH HEH...

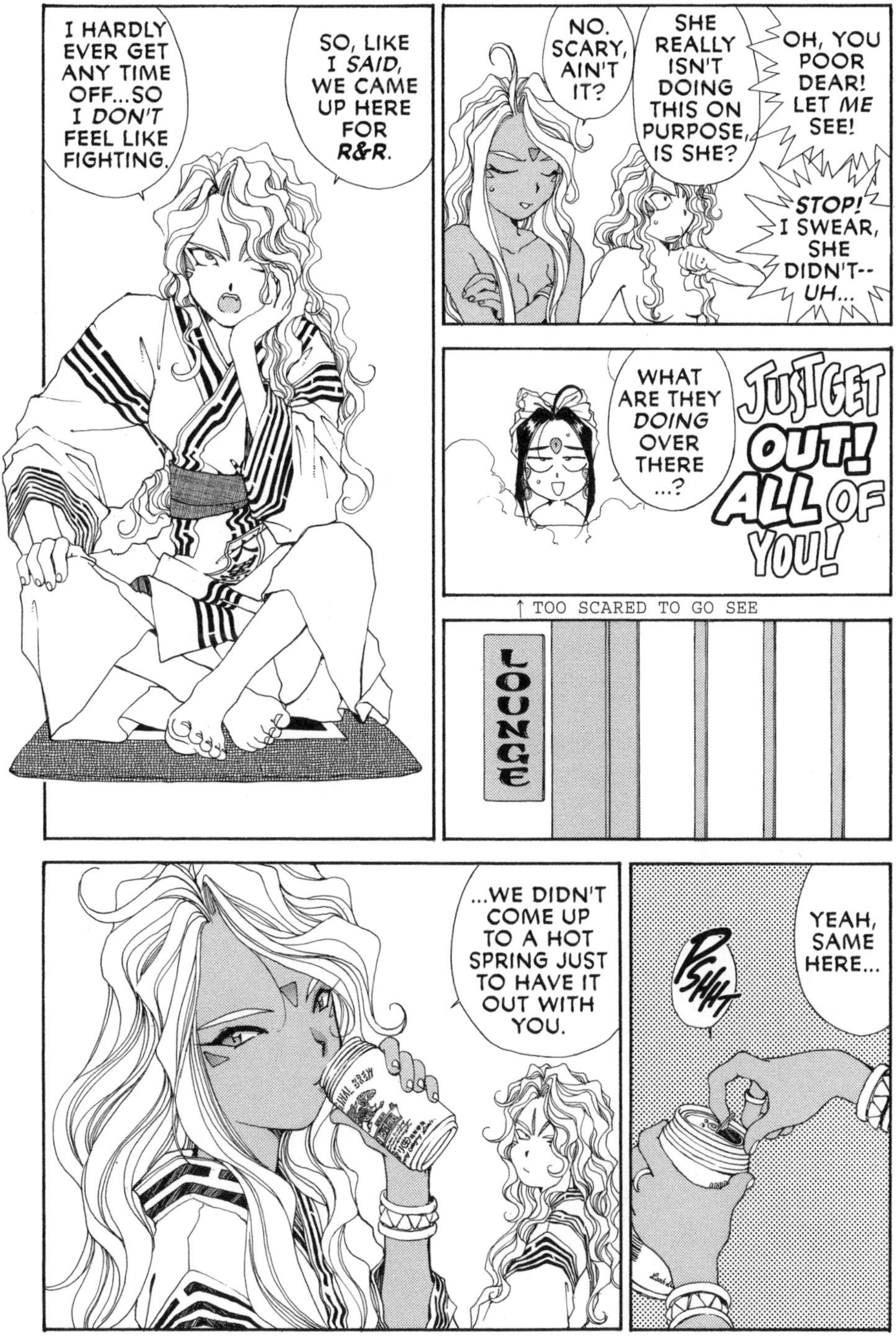
I HARDLY EVER GET ANY TIME OFF...SO I *DON'T* FEEL LIKE FIGHTING.
SO, LIKE I *SAID*, WE CAME UP HERE FOR ***R&R***.
OH, YOU POOR DEAR! LET *ME* SEE!
STOP! I SWEAR, SHE DIDN'T-- *UH*...
SHE REALLY ISN'T DOING THIS ON PURPOSE, IS SHE?
NO. SCARY, AIN'T IT?
WHAT ARE THEY *DOING* OVER THERE ...?
JUST GET OUT! ALL OF YOU!
↑ TOO SCARED TO GO SEE
LOUNGE
...WE DIDN'T COME UP TO A HOT SPRING JUST TO HAVE IT OUT WITH YOU.
PSHHT
YEAH, SAME HERE...

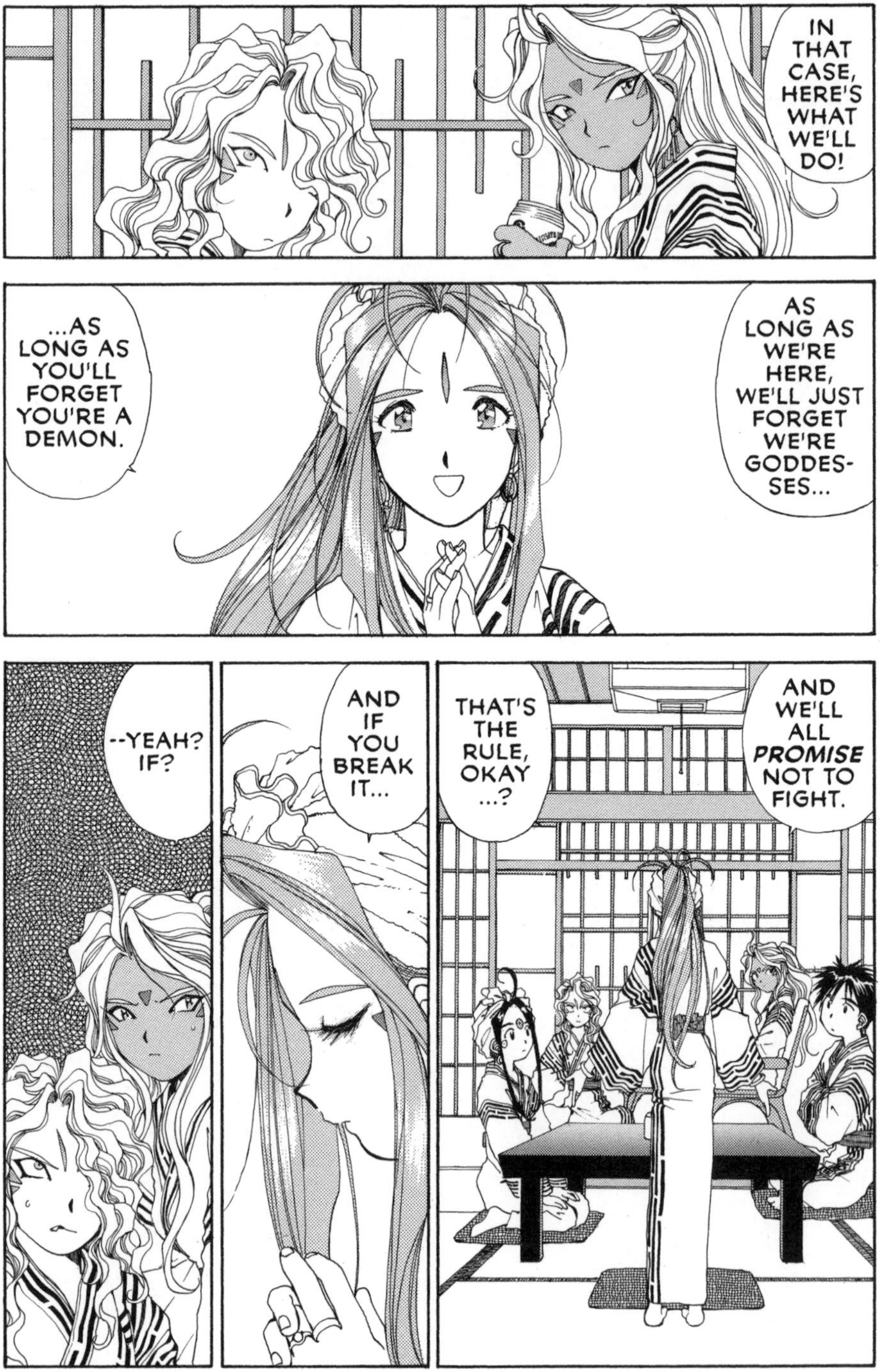
IN THAT CASE, HERE'S WHAT WE'LL DO!
AS LONG AS WE'RE HERE, WE'LL JUST FORGET WE'RE GODDES-SES...
...AS LONG AS YOU'LL FORGET YOU'RE A DEMON.
AND WE'LL ALL *PROMISE* NOT TO FIGHT.
THAT'S THE RULE, OKAY ...?
AND IF YOU BREAK IT...
--YEAH? IF?

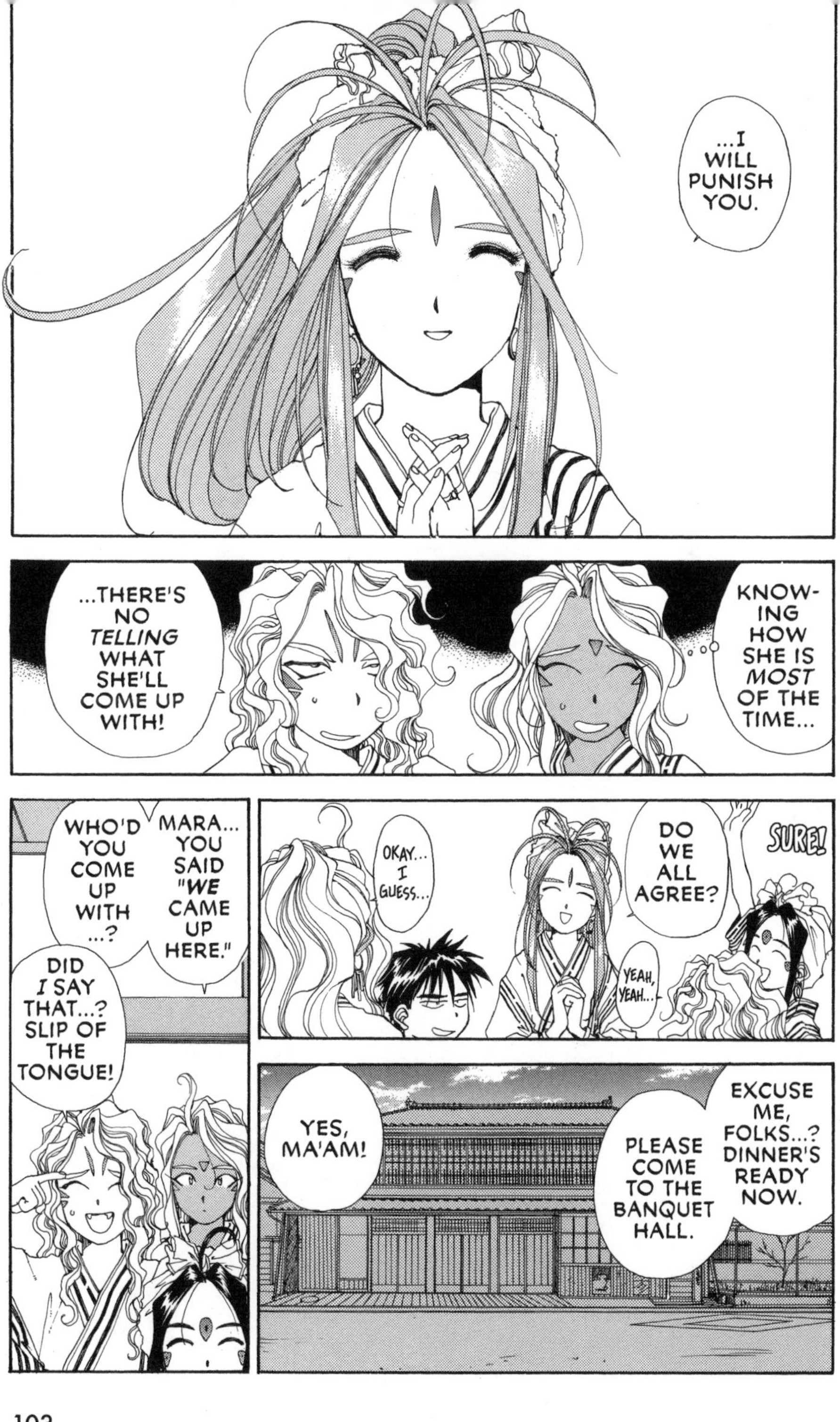
...I WILL PUNISH YOU.
KNOW-ING HOW SHE IS *MOST* OF THE TIME...
...THERE'S NO *TELLING* WHAT SHE'LL COME UP WITH!
DO WE ALL AGREE?
SURE!
OKAY... I GUESS...
YEAH, YEAH...
EXCUSE ME, FOLKS...? DINNER'S READY NOW.
PLEASE COME TO THE BANQUET HALL.
YES, MA'AM!
MARA... YOU SAID "*WE* CAME UP HERE."
WHO'D YOU COME UP WITH ...?
DID *I* SAY THAT...? SLIP OF THE TONGUE!

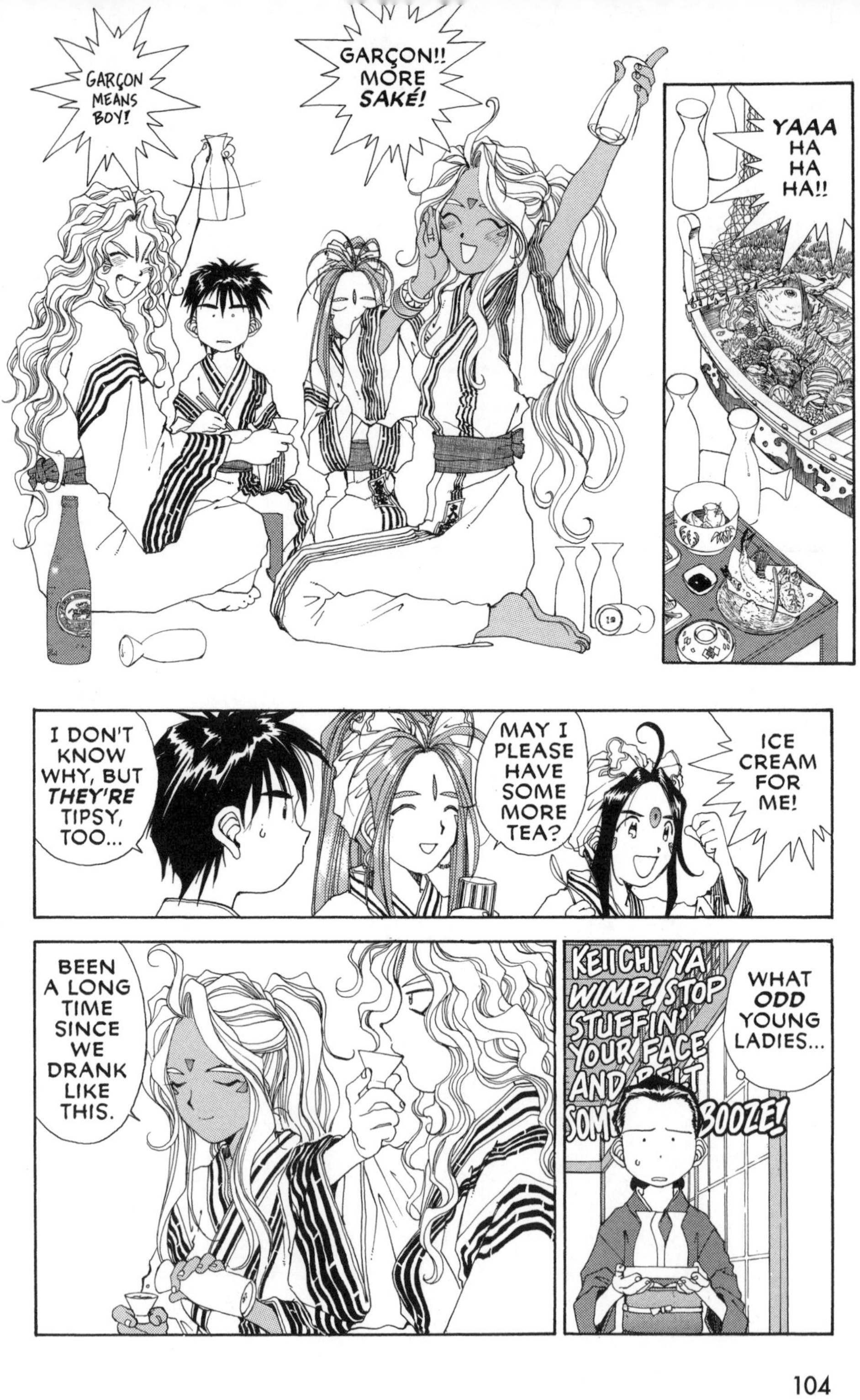
YAAA HA HA HA!!
GARÇON!! MORE SAKÉ!
GARÇON MEANS BOY!
ICE CREAM FOR ME!
MAY I PLEASE HAVE SOME MORE TEA?
I DON'T KNOW WHY, BUT THEY'RE TIPSY, TOO...
WHAT ODD YOUNG LADIES...
KEIICHI YA WIMP! STOP STUFFIN' YOUR FACE AND
BOOZE!
BEEN A LONG TIME SINCE WE DRANK LIKE THIS.

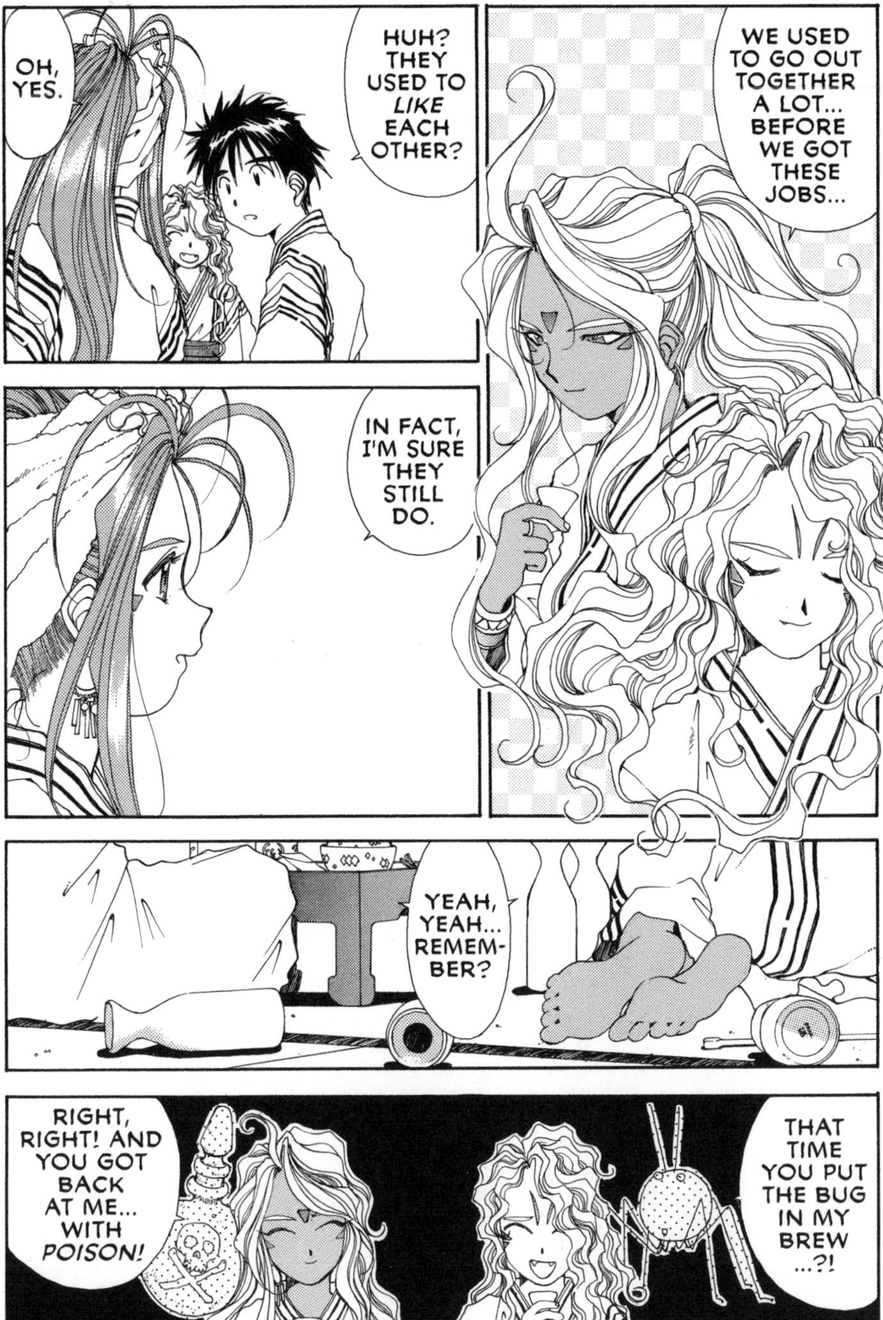
WE USED TO GO OUT TOGETHER A LOT... BEFORE WE GOT THESE JOBS...
HUH? THEY USED TO *LIKE* EACH OTHER?
OH, YES.
IN FACT, I'M SURE THEY STILL DO.
YEAH, YEAH... REMEM-BER?
THAT TIME YOU PUT THE BUG IN MY BREW ...?!
RIGHT, RIGHT! AND YOU GOT BACK AT ME... WITH *POISON!*

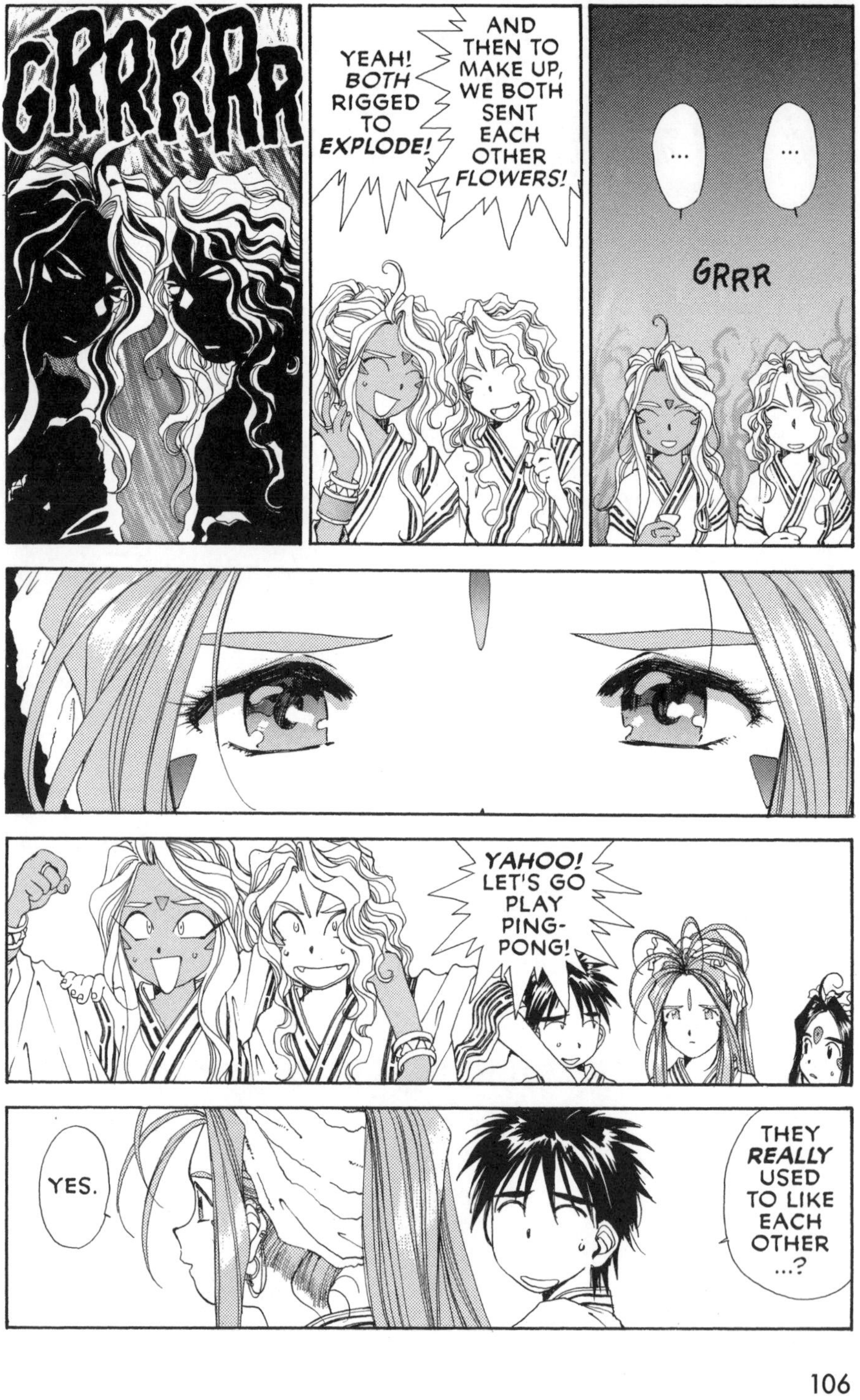
...
...
GRRR
AND THEN TO MAKE UP, WE BOTH SENT EACH OTHER *FLOWERS!*
YEAH! *BOTH* RIGGED TO *EXPLODE!*
GRRRRR
YAHOO! LET'S GO PLAY PING-PONG!
THEY *REALLY* USED TO LIKE EACH OTHER ...?
YES.

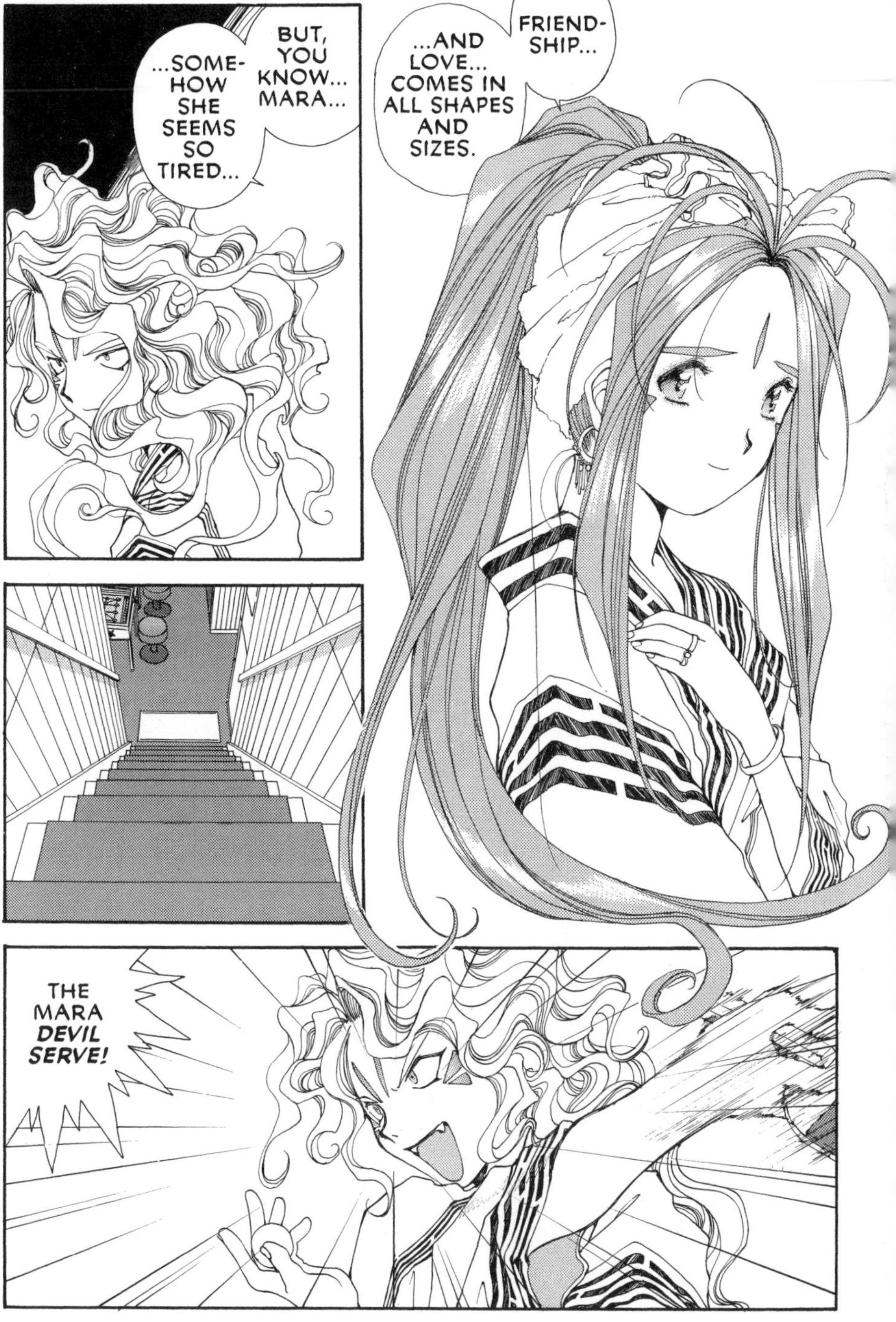
FRIEND-SHIP...
...AND LOVE... COMES IN ALL SHAPES AND SIZES.
BUT, YOU KNOW... MARA...
...SOME-HOW SHE SEEMS SO TIRED...
THE MARA *DEVIL SERVE!*

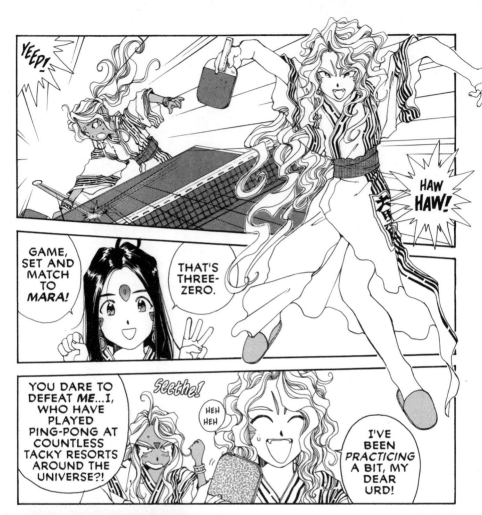

YEEP!

HAW HAW!

GAME, SET AND MATCH TO *MARA!*

THAT'S THREE-ZERO.

YOU DARE TO DEFEAT *ME*...I, WHO HAVE PLAYED PING-PONG AT COUNTLESS TACKY RESORTS AROUND THE UNIVERSE?!

Seethe!

HEH HEH

I'VE BEEN *PRACTICING* A BIT, MY DEAR URD!

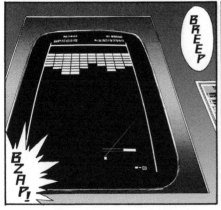

BREEP

BZAP!

THEN I CHALLENGE THEE AT... *VIDEO GAMES!*

MARA'S SO FUNNY, ISN'T SHE!

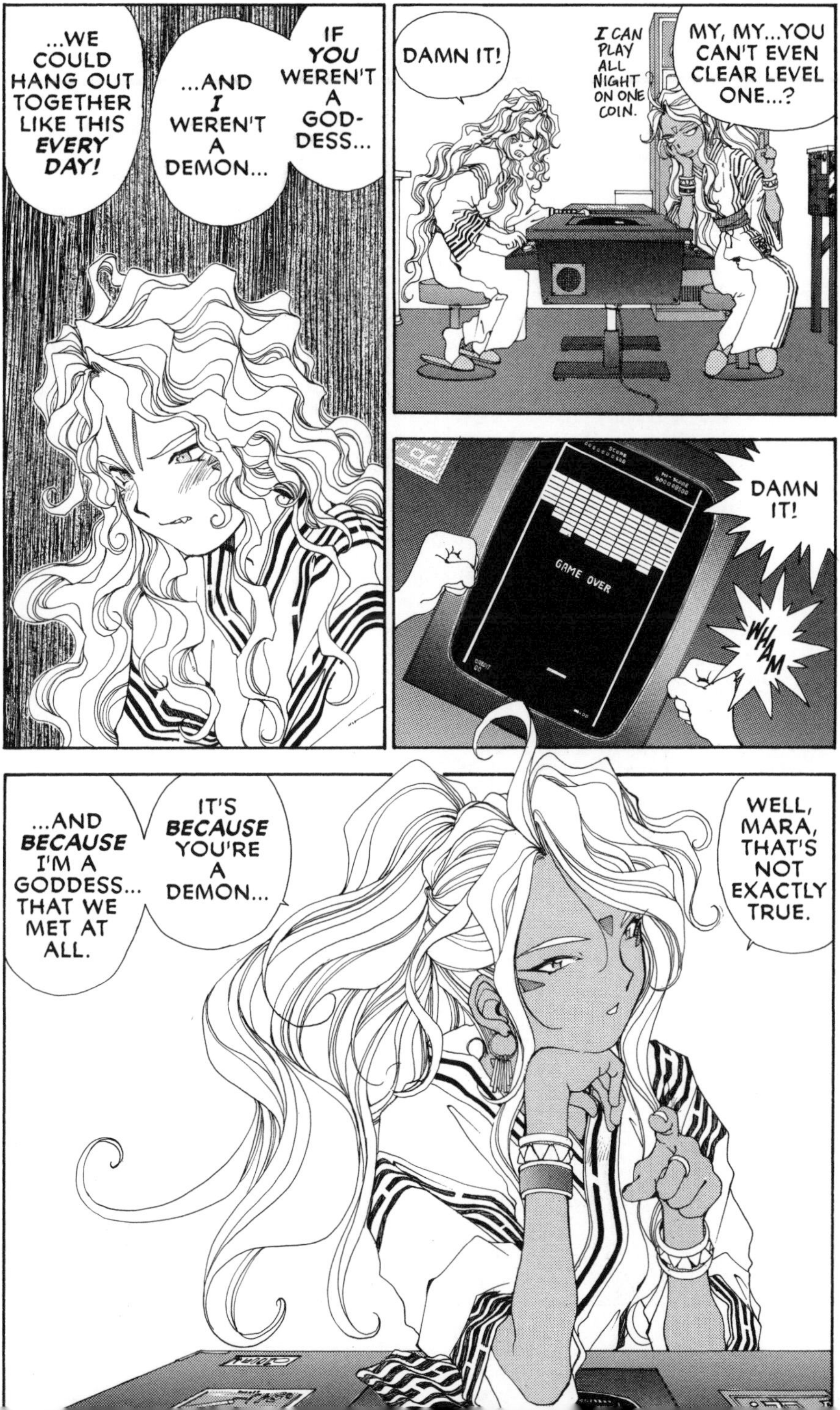

MY, MY...YOU CAN'T EVEN CLEAR LEVEL ONE...?
I CAN PLAY ALL NIGHT ON ONE COIN.
DAMN IT!
GAME OVER
DAMN IT!
WHAM
IF YOU WEREN'T A GODDESS...
...AND I WEREN'T A DEMON...
...WE COULD HANG OUT TOGETHER LIKE THIS EVERY DAY!
WELL, MARA, THAT'S NOT EXACTLY TRUE.
IT'S BECAUSE YOU'RE A DEMON...
...AND BECAUSE I'M A GODDESS... THAT WE MET AT ALL.

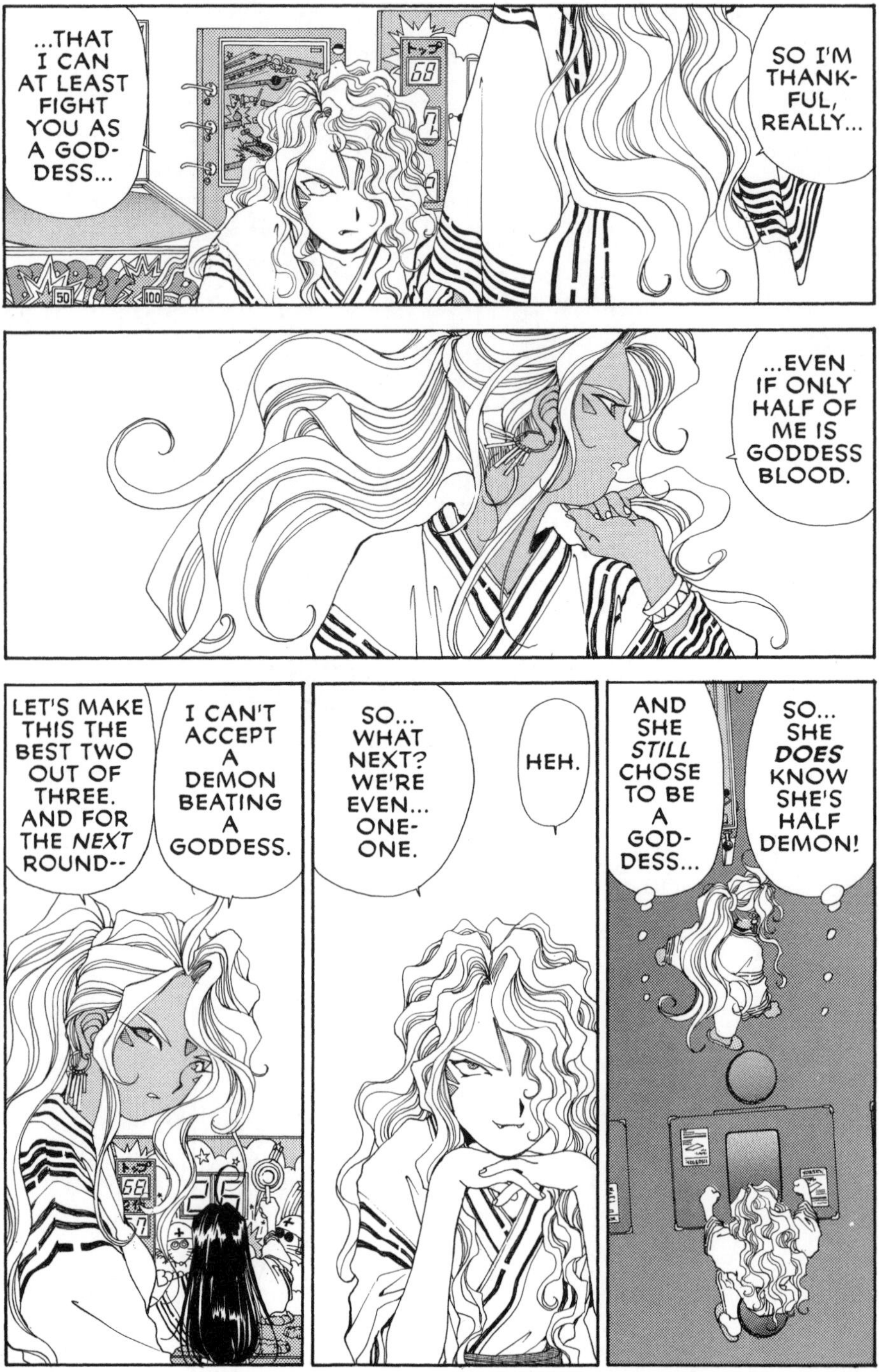
SO I'M THANKFUL, REALLY...
...THAT I CAN AT LEAST FIGHT YOU AS A GODDESS...
...EVEN IF ONLY HALF OF ME IS GODDESS BLOOD.
SO... SHE *DOES* KNOW SHE'S HALF DEMON!
AND SHE *STILL* CHOSE TO BE A GODDESS...
HEH.
SO... WHAT NEXT? WE'RE EVEN... ONE-ONE.
I CAN'T ACCEPT A DEMON BEATING A GODDESS.
LET'S MAKE THIS THE BEST TWO OUT OF THREE. AND FOR THE *NEXT* ROUND--

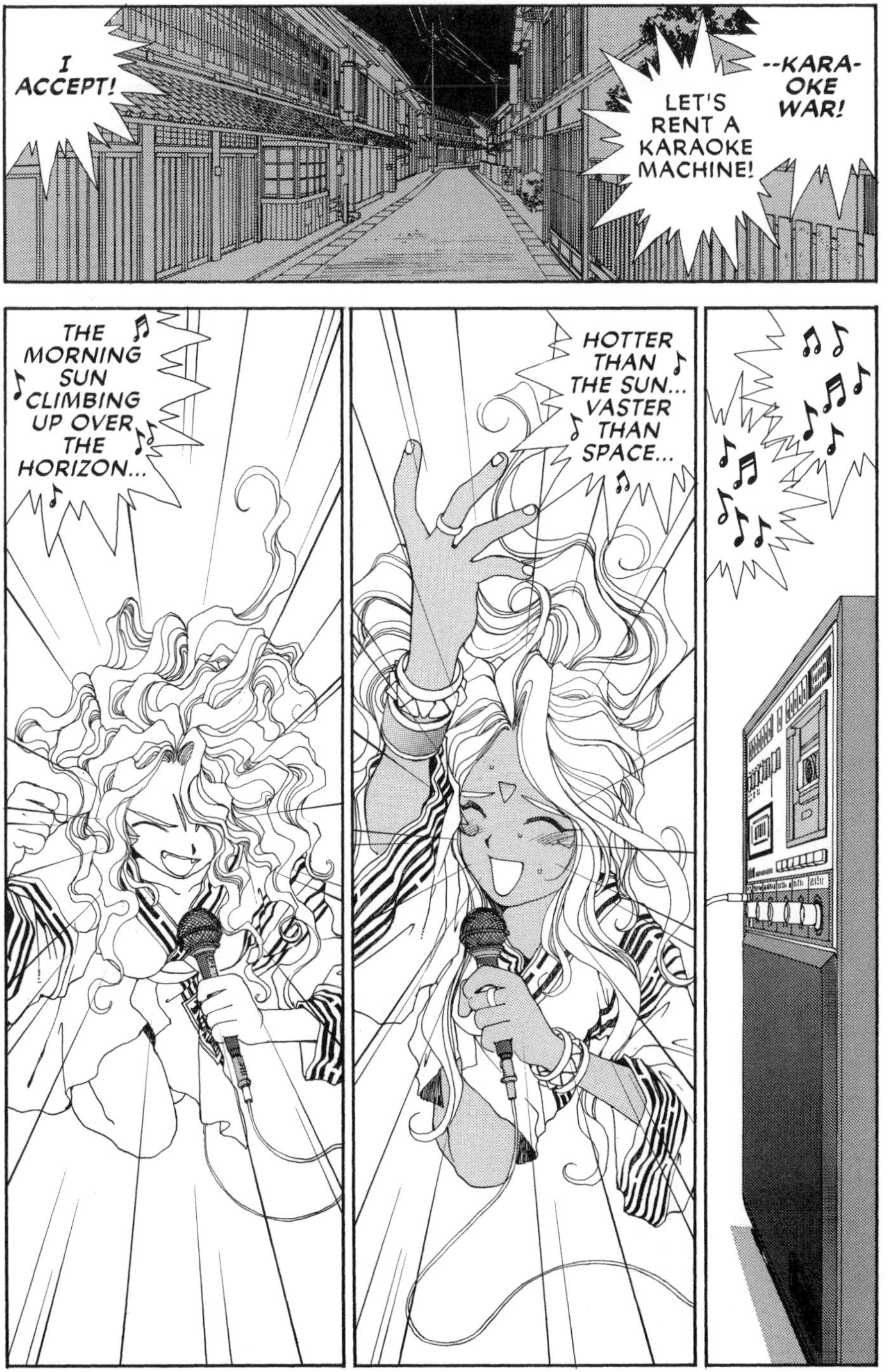
LET'S RENT A KARAOKE MACHINE!
--KARA-OKE WAR!
I ACCEPT!
HOTTER THAN THE SUN... VASTER THAN SPACE...
THE MORNING SUN CLIMBING UP OVER THE HORIZON...

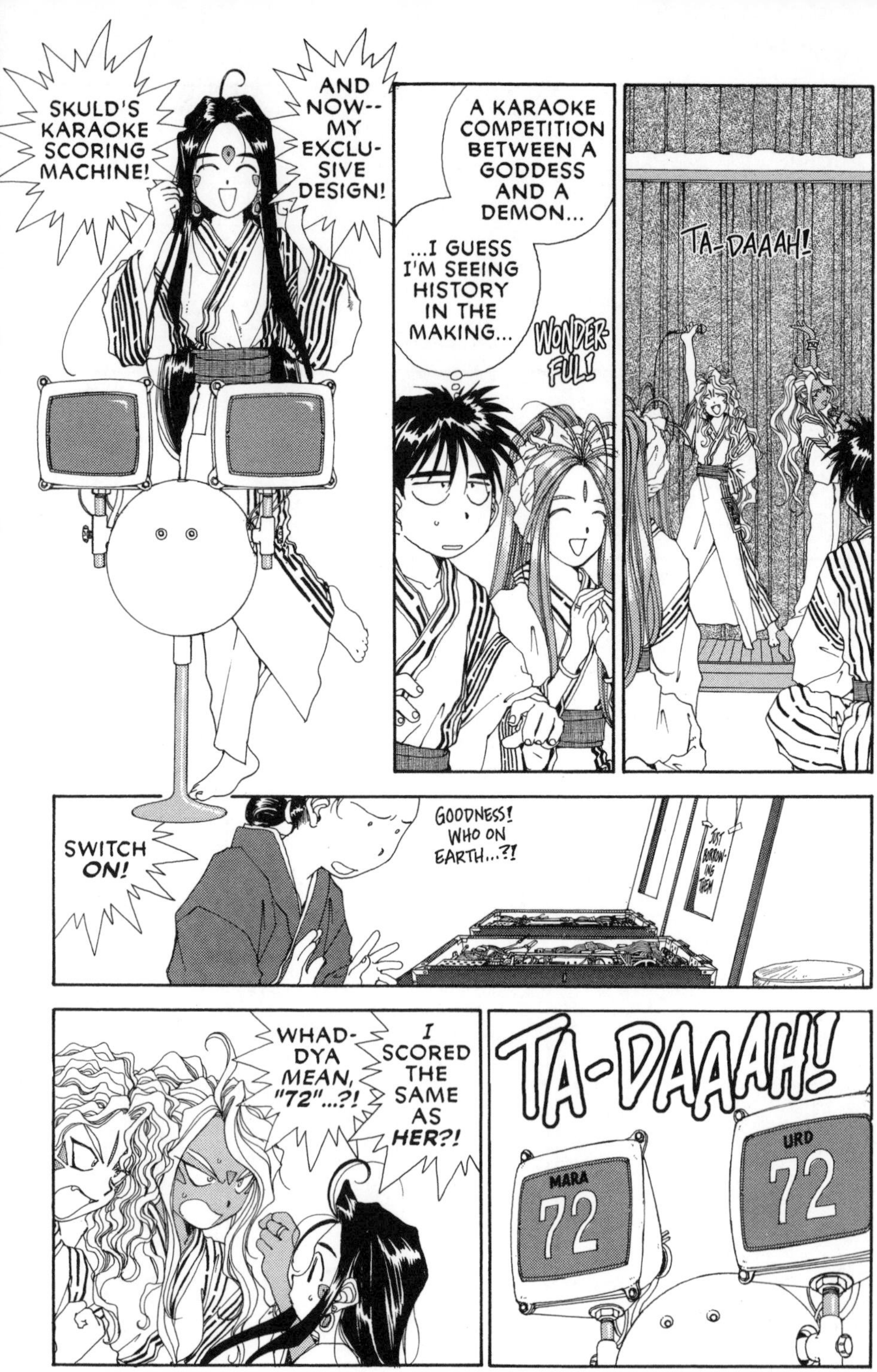
TA-DAAAH!
A KARAOKE COMPETITION BETWEEN A GODDESS AND A DEMON...
...I GUESS I'M SEEING HISTORY IN THE MAKING...
WONDER-FUL!
AND NOW-- MY EXCLU-SIVE DESIGN!
SKULD'S KARAOKE SCORING MACHINE!
SWITCH ON!
GOODNESS! WHO ON EARTH...?!
JUST BORROW-ING THEM
TA-DAAAH!
URD
72
MARA
72
I SCORED THE SAME AS HER?!
WHAD-DYA MEAN, "72"...?!

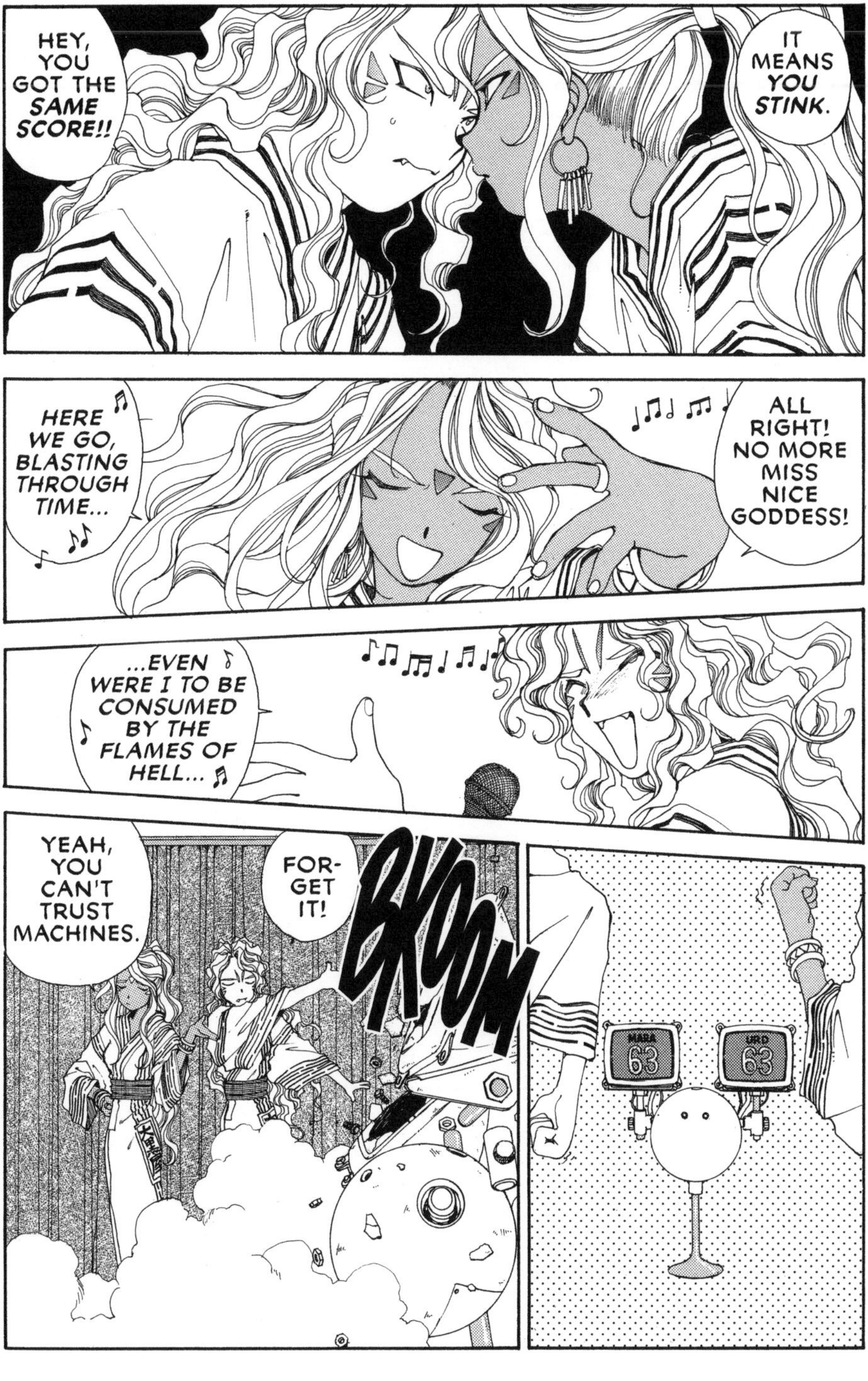
IT MEANS YOU STINK.
HEY, YOU GOT THE SAME SCORE!!
ALL RIGHT! NO MORE MISS NICE GODDESS!
HERE WE GO, BLASTING THROUGH TIME...
...EVEN WERE I TO BE CONSUMED BY THE FLAMES OF HELL...
MARA
63
URD
63
BKOOM
FOR-GET IT!
YEAH, YOU CAN'T TRUST MACHINES.

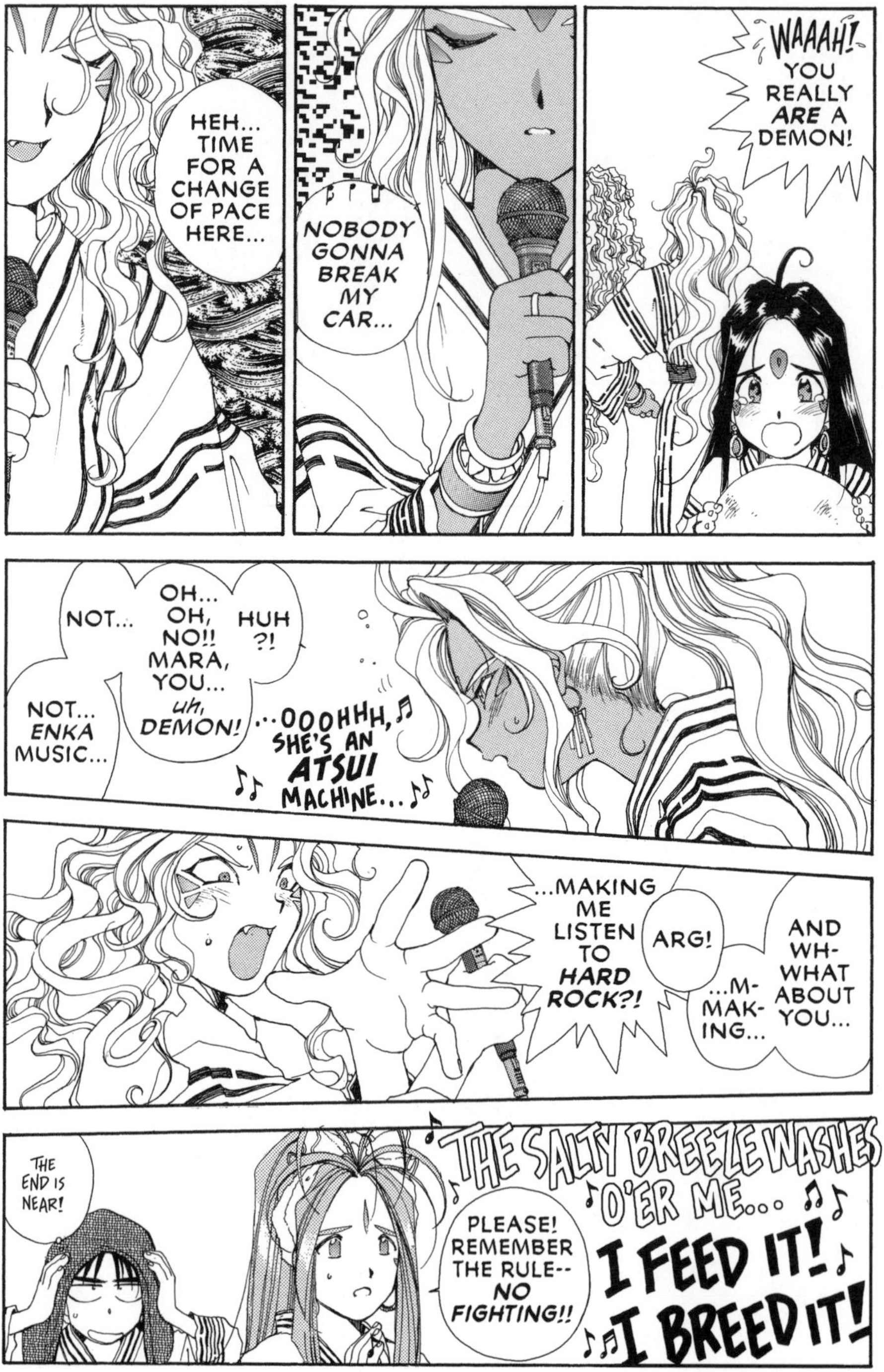
HEH... TIME FOR A CHANGE OF PACE HERE...
NOBODY GONNA BREAK MY CAR...
WAAAH! YOU REALLY ARE A DEMON!
NOT... NOT... ENKA MUSIC...
OH... OH, NO!! MARA, YOU... uh, DEMON!
HUH ?!
...OOOHHH, SHE'S AN ATSUI MACHINE...
...MAKING ME LISTEN TO HARD ROCK?!
ARG!
...M-MAK-ING...
AND WH-WHAT ABOUT YOU...
THE END IS NEAR!
PLEASE! REMEMBER THE RULE-- NO FIGHTING!!
THE SALTY BREEZE WASHES O'ER ME...
I FEED IT! I BREED IT!

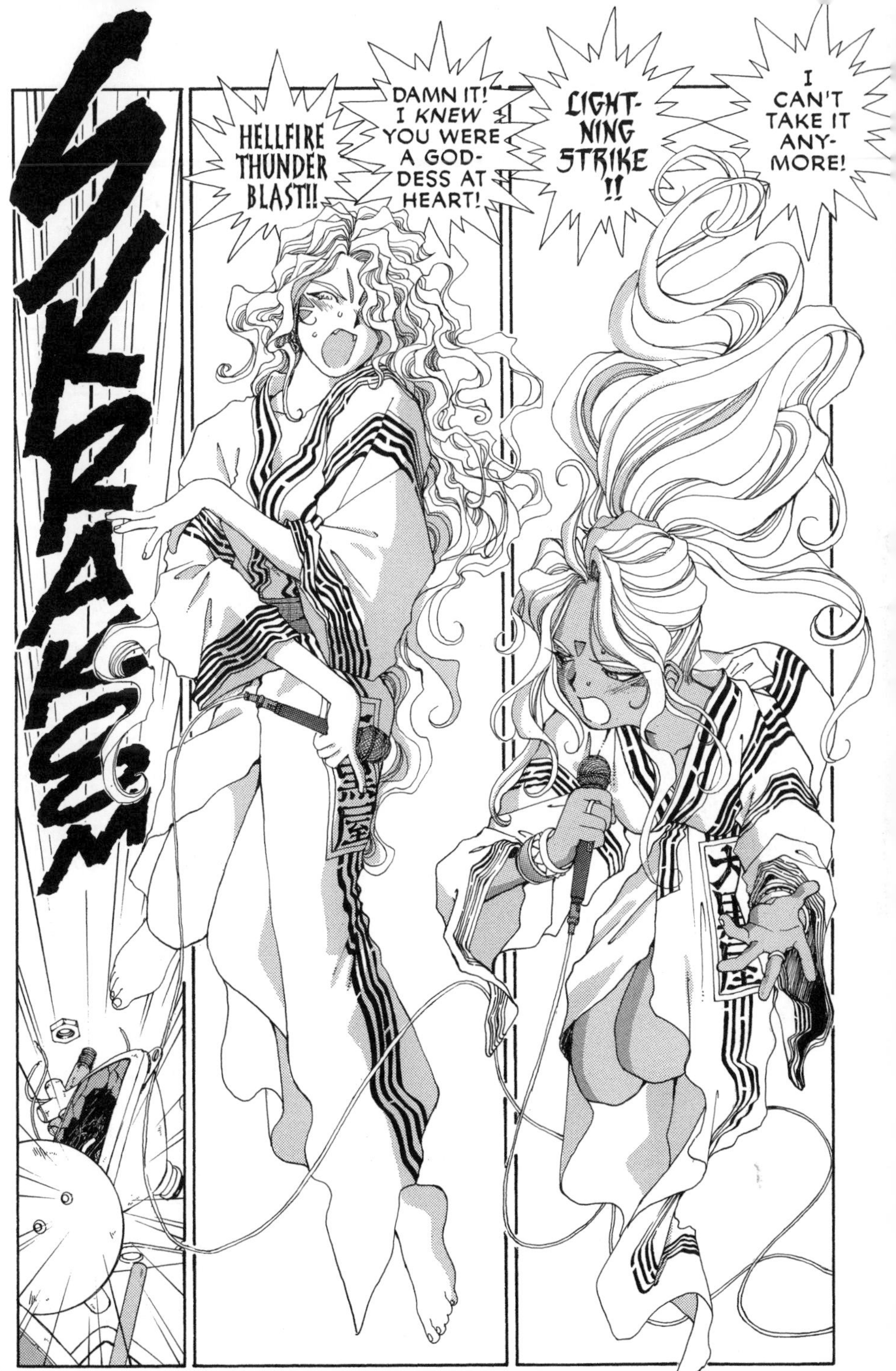
I CAN'T TAKE IT ANY-MORE!
LIGHT-NING STRIKE!!
DAMN IT! I *KNEW* YOU WERE A GOD-DESS AT HEART!
HELLFIRE THUNDER BLAST!!

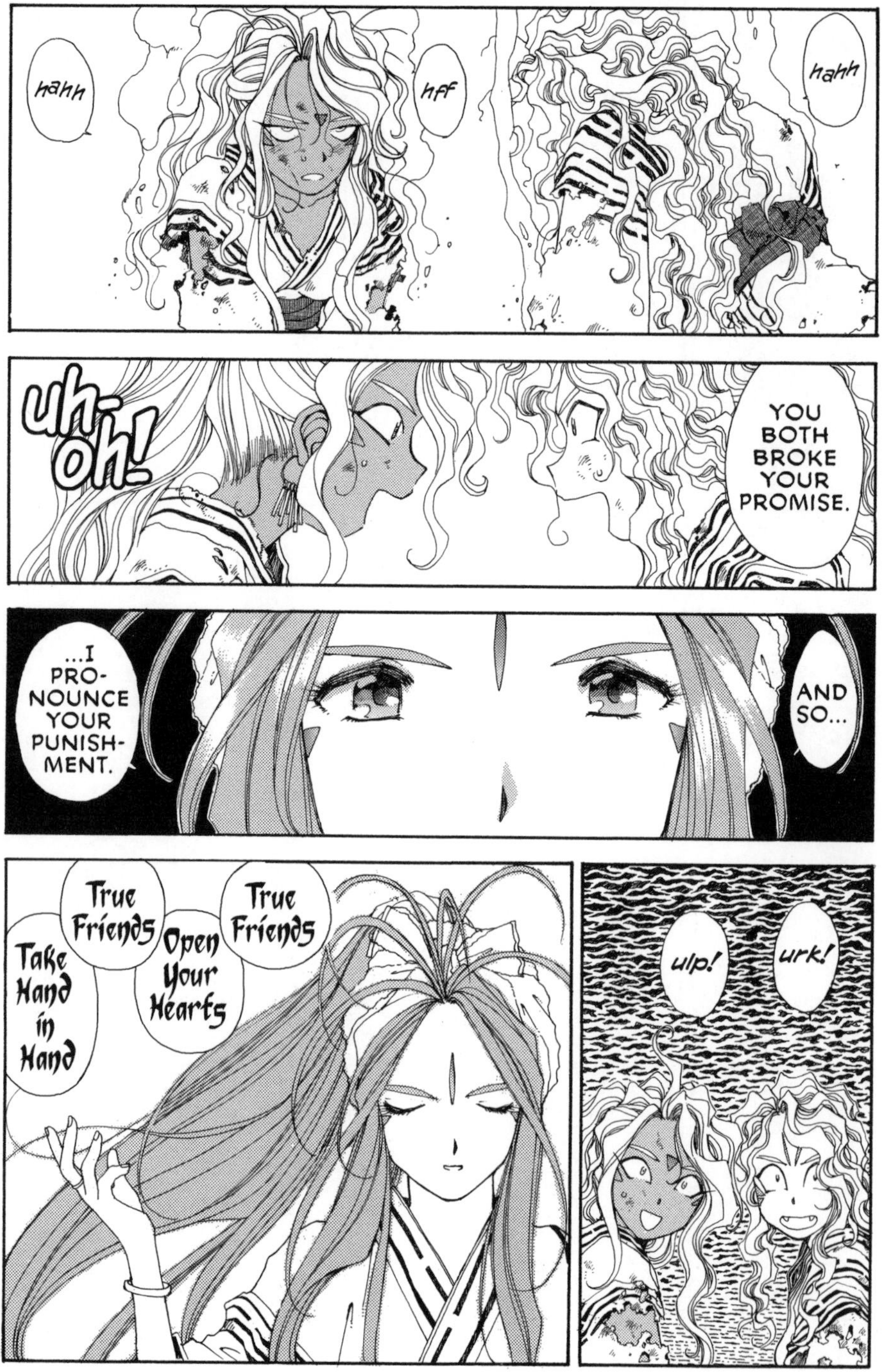
hahh
hff
hahn
YOU BOTH BROKE YOUR PROMISE.
uh-oh!
AND SO...
...I PRONOUNCE YOUR PUNISHMENT.
urk!
ulp!
True Friends
Open Your Hearts
True Friends
Take Hand in Hand

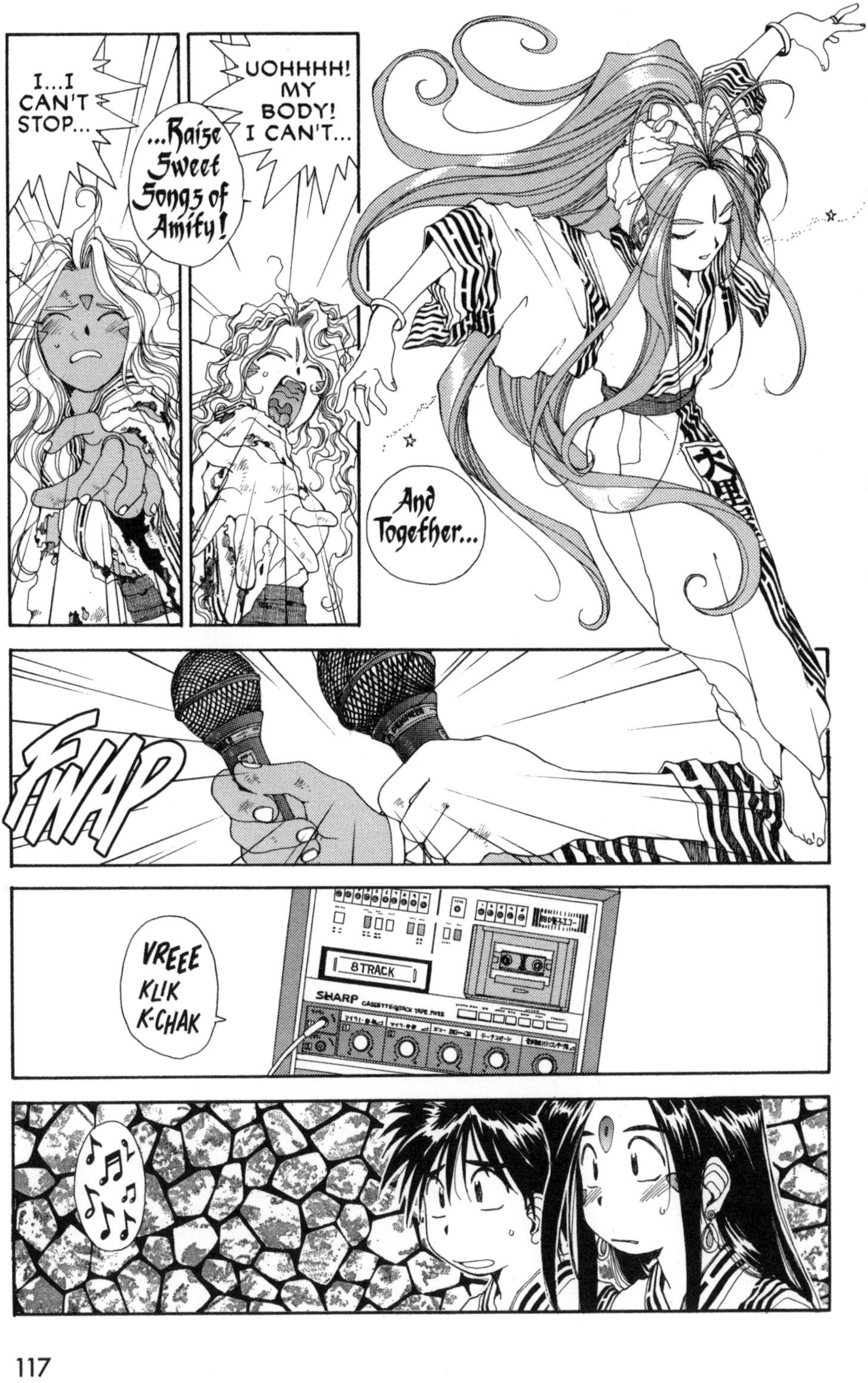
I...I CAN'T STOP...
...Raise Sweet Songs of Amity!
UOHHHH! MY BODY! I CAN'T...
And Together...
FWAP
8TRACK
SHARP
VREEE KLIK K-CHAK

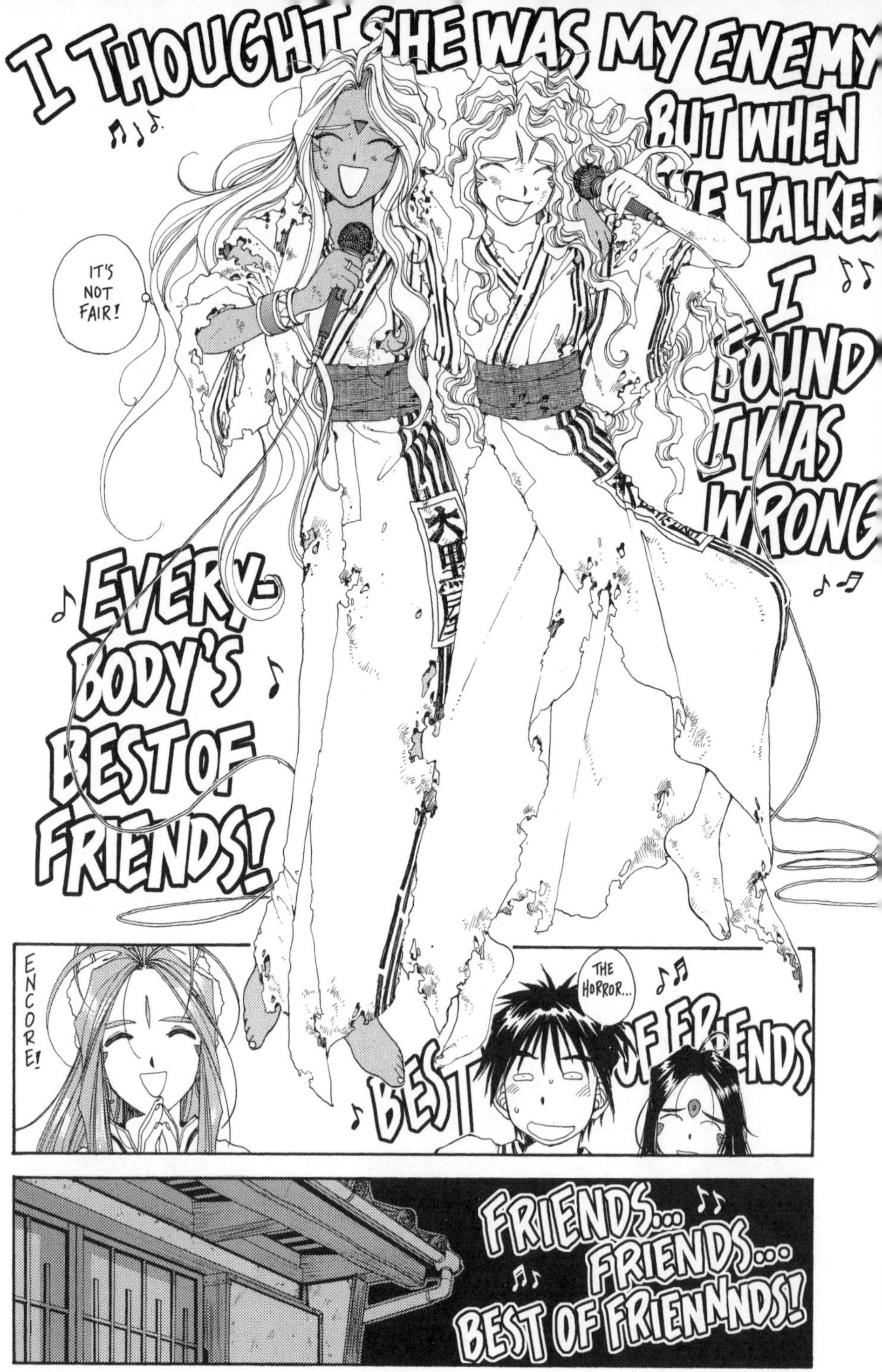
I THOUGHT SHE WAS MY ENEMY
BUT WHEN
TALKED
I FOUND I WAS WRONG
IT'S NOT FAIR!
EVERY-BODY'S BEST OF FRIENDS!
THE HORROR...
BEST OF FRIENDS
ENCORE!
FRIENDS... FRIENDS... BEST OF FRIENNNDS!

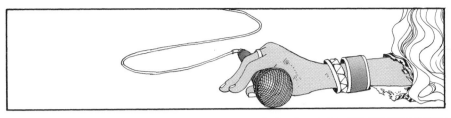

SHEESH...IF SHE HADN'T RESISTED SO MUCH, SHE WOULDN'T HAVE COLLAPSED LIKE THIS...

MARA... I...

...WELL, MY JOB DOESN'T LET ME WISH YOU *LUCK.*

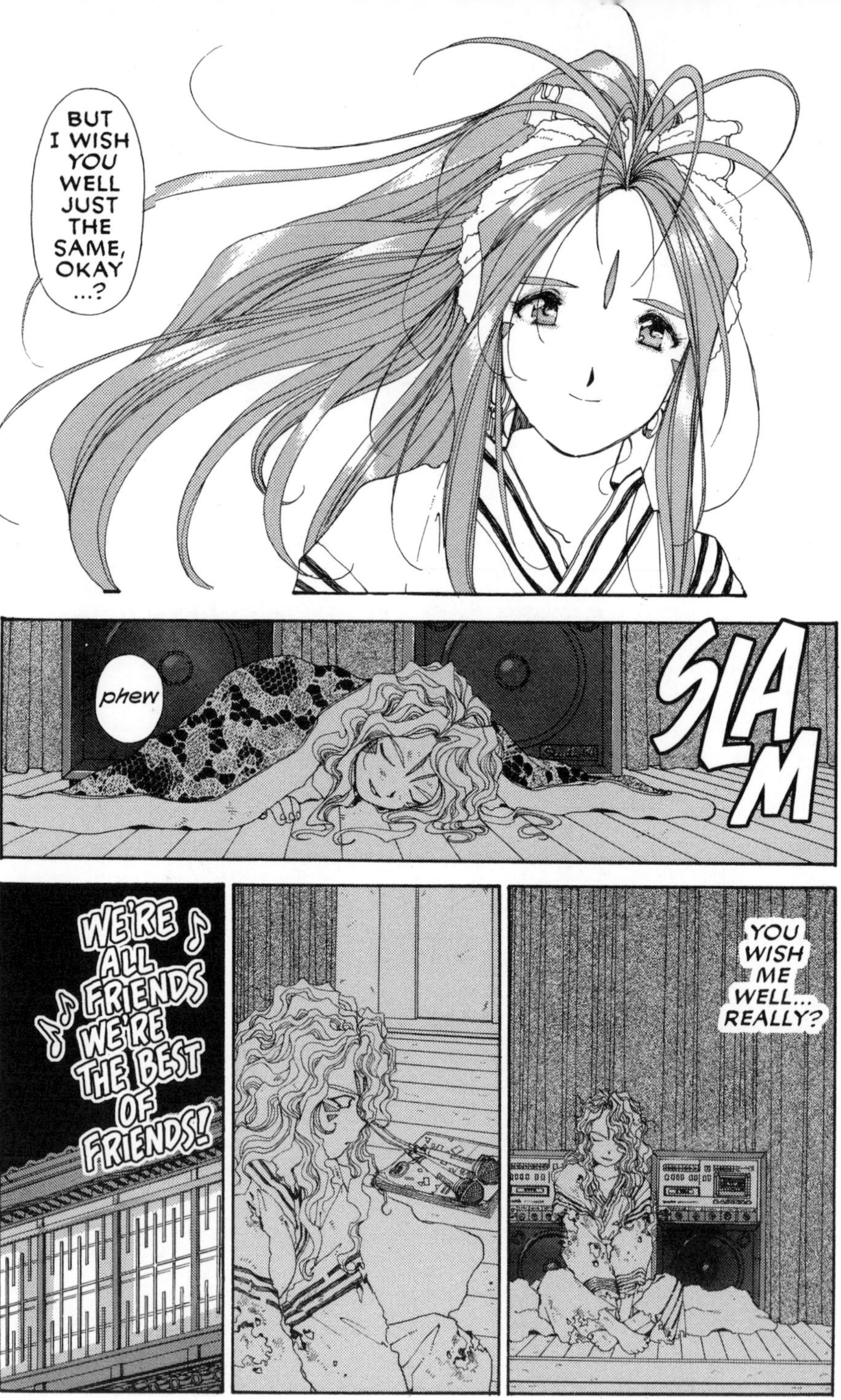
BUT I WISH *YOU* WELL JUST THE SAME, OKAY ...?
SLAM
phew
YOU WISH ME WELL... REALLY?
WE'RE ♪ ALL FRIENDS ♪ WE'RE THE BEST OF FRIENDS!

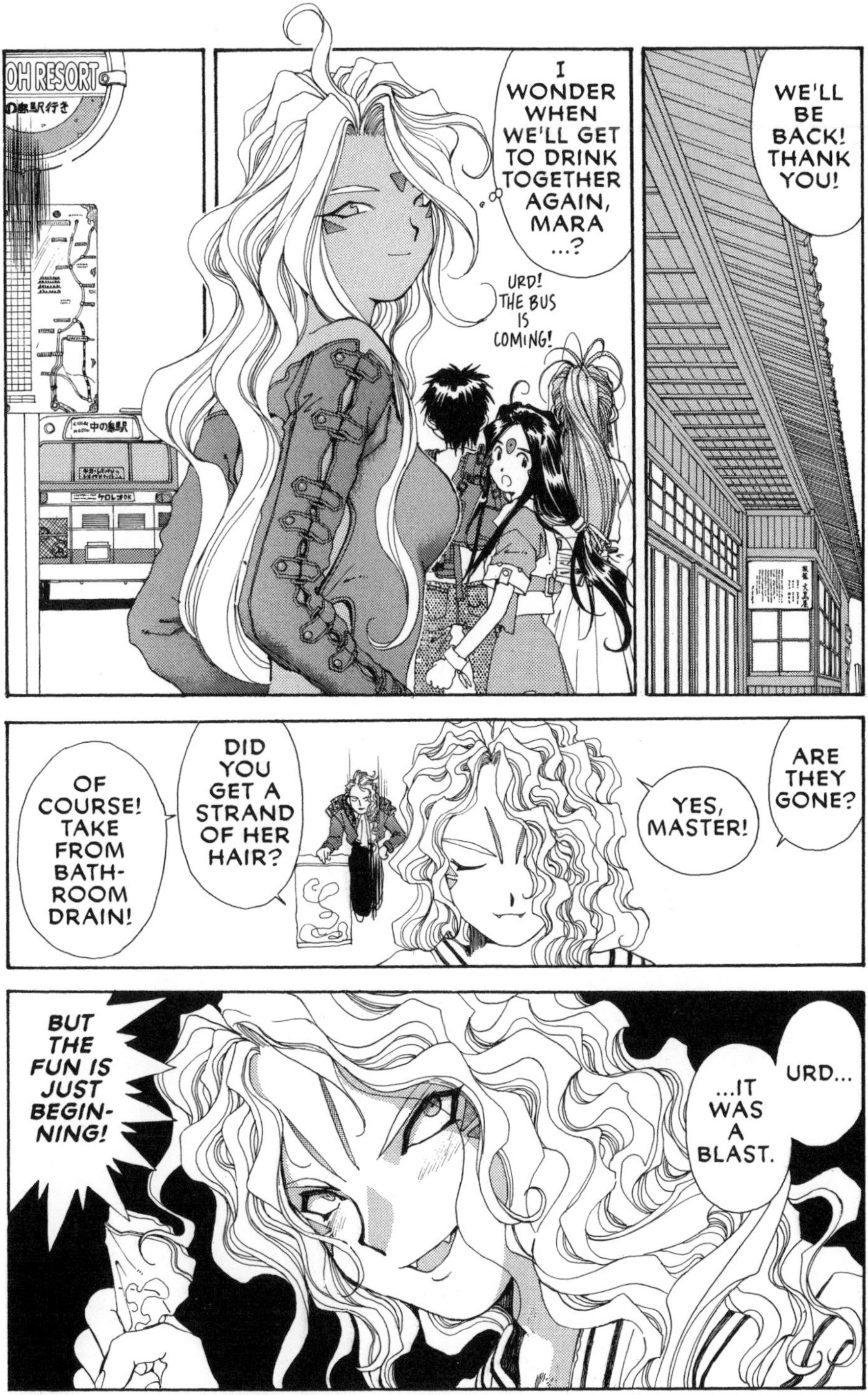
WE'LL BE BACK! THANK YOU!
I WONDER WHEN WE'LL GET TO DRINK TOGETHER AGAIN, MARA ...?
URD! THE BUS IS COMING!
OH RESORT
ARE THEY GONE?
YES, MASTER!
DID YOU GET A STRAND OF HER HAIR?
OF COURSE! TAKE FROM BATH-ROOM DRAIN!
URD...
...IT WAS A BLAST.
BUT THE FUN IS JUST BEGIN-NING!

THE ADVENTURES OF THE MINI-GODDESSES

◆ THE TRAGIC FLYING "V"! AND BELLDANDY! AND MR. RAT! ◆

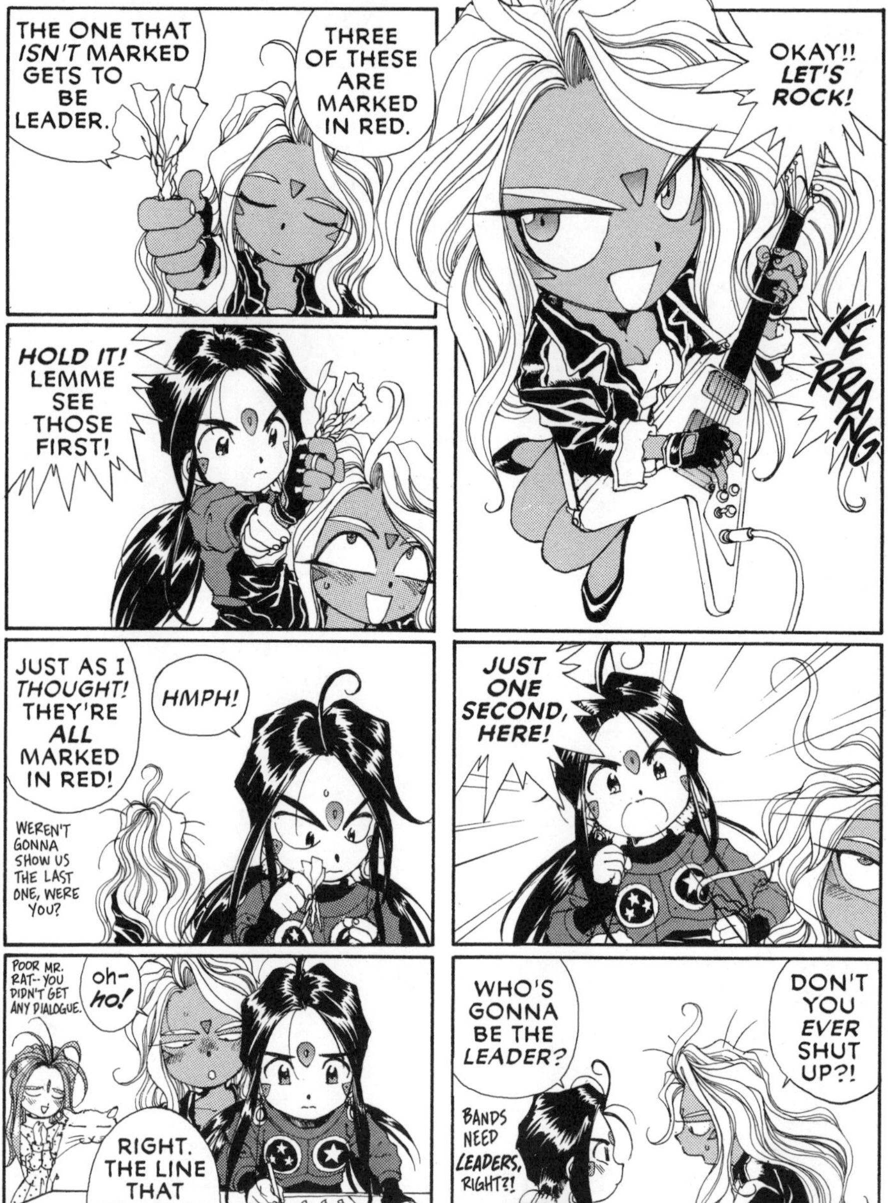

THE ONE THAT ISN'T MARKED GETS TO BE LEADER.
THREE OF THESE ARE MARKED IN RED.
HOLD IT! LEMME SEE THOSE FIRST!
JUST AS I THOUGHT! THEY'RE ALL MARKED IN RED!
HMPH!
WEREN'T GONNA SHOW US THE LAST ONE, WERE YOU?
POOR MR. RAT-- YOU DIDN'T GET ANY DIALOGUE.
oh-ho!
RIGHT. THE LINE THAT TOUCHES A NAME--
OKAY!! LET'S ROCK!
KERRANG
JUST ONE SECOND, HERE!
WHO'S GONNA BE THE LEADER?
BANDS NEED LEADERS, RIGHT?!
DON'T YOU EVER SHUT UP?!

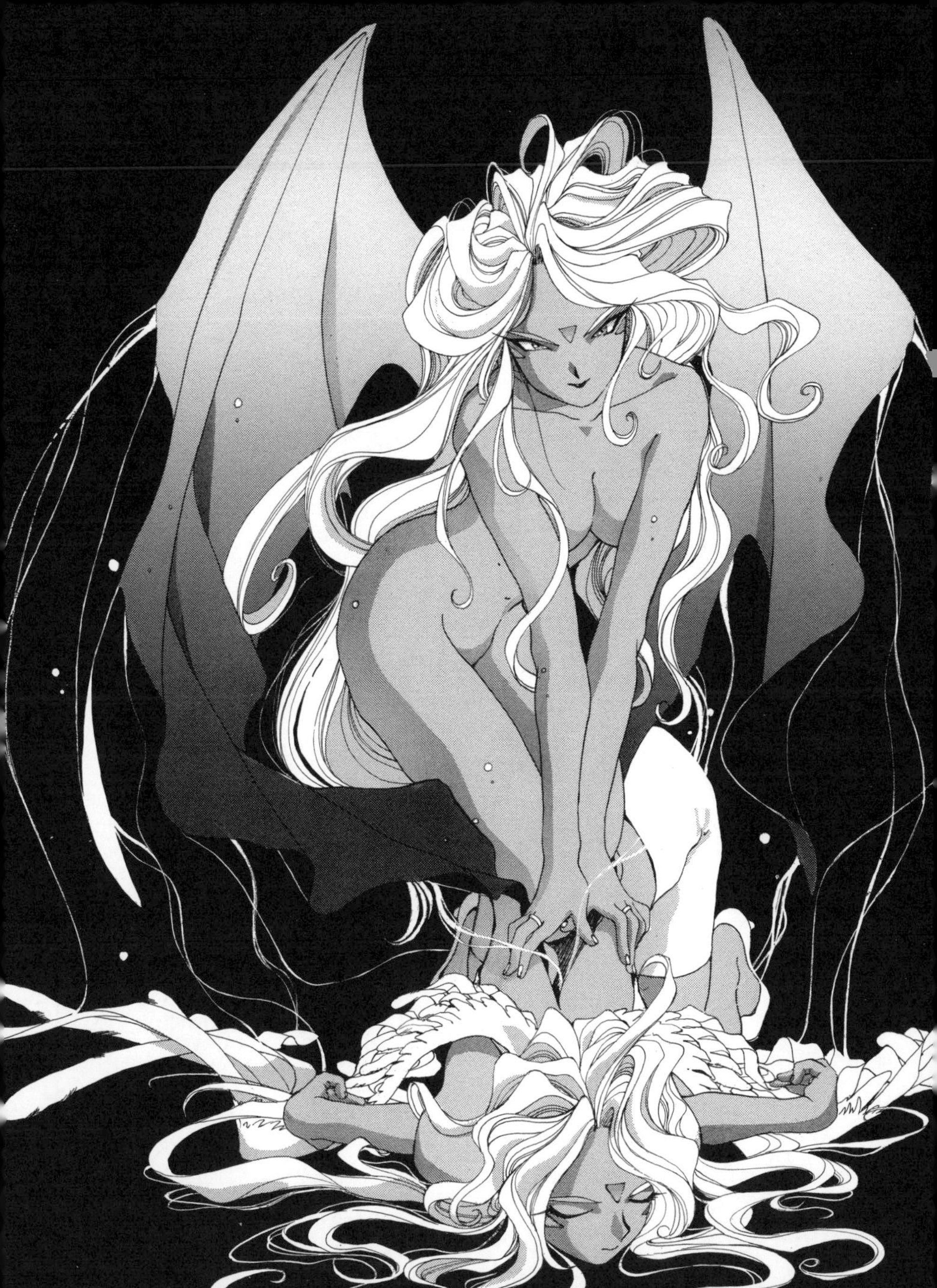

CHAPTER 61

Urd Turns 100% Evil!

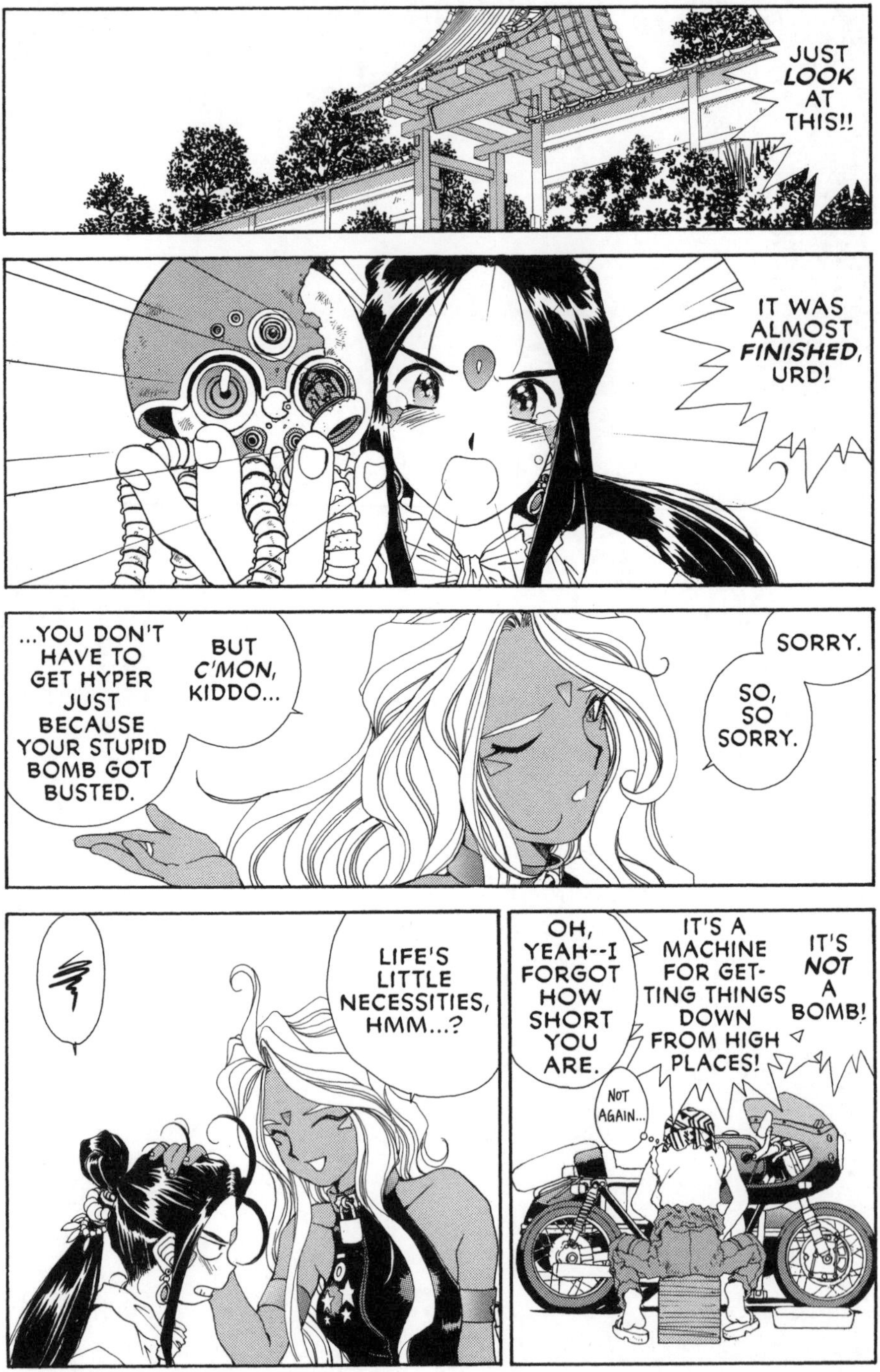
JUST LOOK AT THIS!!
IT WAS ALMOST FINISHED, URD!
SORRY.
SO, SO SORRY.
BUT C'MON, KIDDO...
...YOU DON'T HAVE TO GET HYPER JUST BECAUSE YOUR STUPID BOMB GOT BUSTED.
IT'S NOT A BOMB!
IT'S A MACHINE FOR GETTING THINGS DOWN FROM HIGH PLACES!
OH, YEAH--I FORGOT HOW SHORT YOU ARE.
NOT AGAIN...
LIFE'S LITTLE NECESSITIES, HMM...?

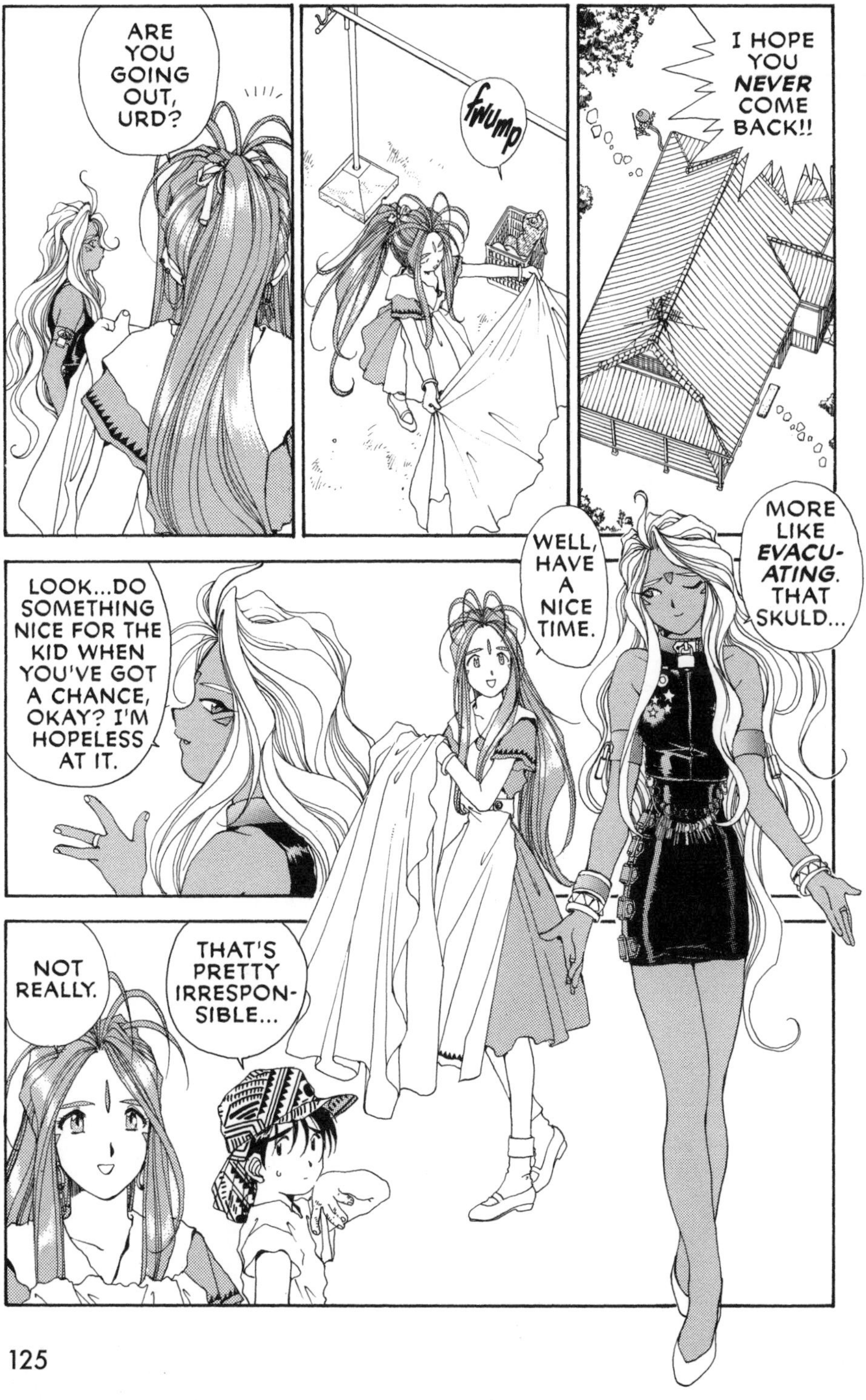
I HOPE YOU *NEVER* COME BACK!!
fwump
ARE YOU GOING OUT, URD?
MORE LIKE *EVACUATING*. THAT SKULD...
WELL, HAVE A NICE TIME.
LOOK...DO SOMETHING NICE FOR THE KID WHEN YOU'VE GOT A CHANCE, OKAY? I'M HOPELESS AT IT.
THAT'S PRETTY IRRESPONSIBLE...
NOT REALLY.

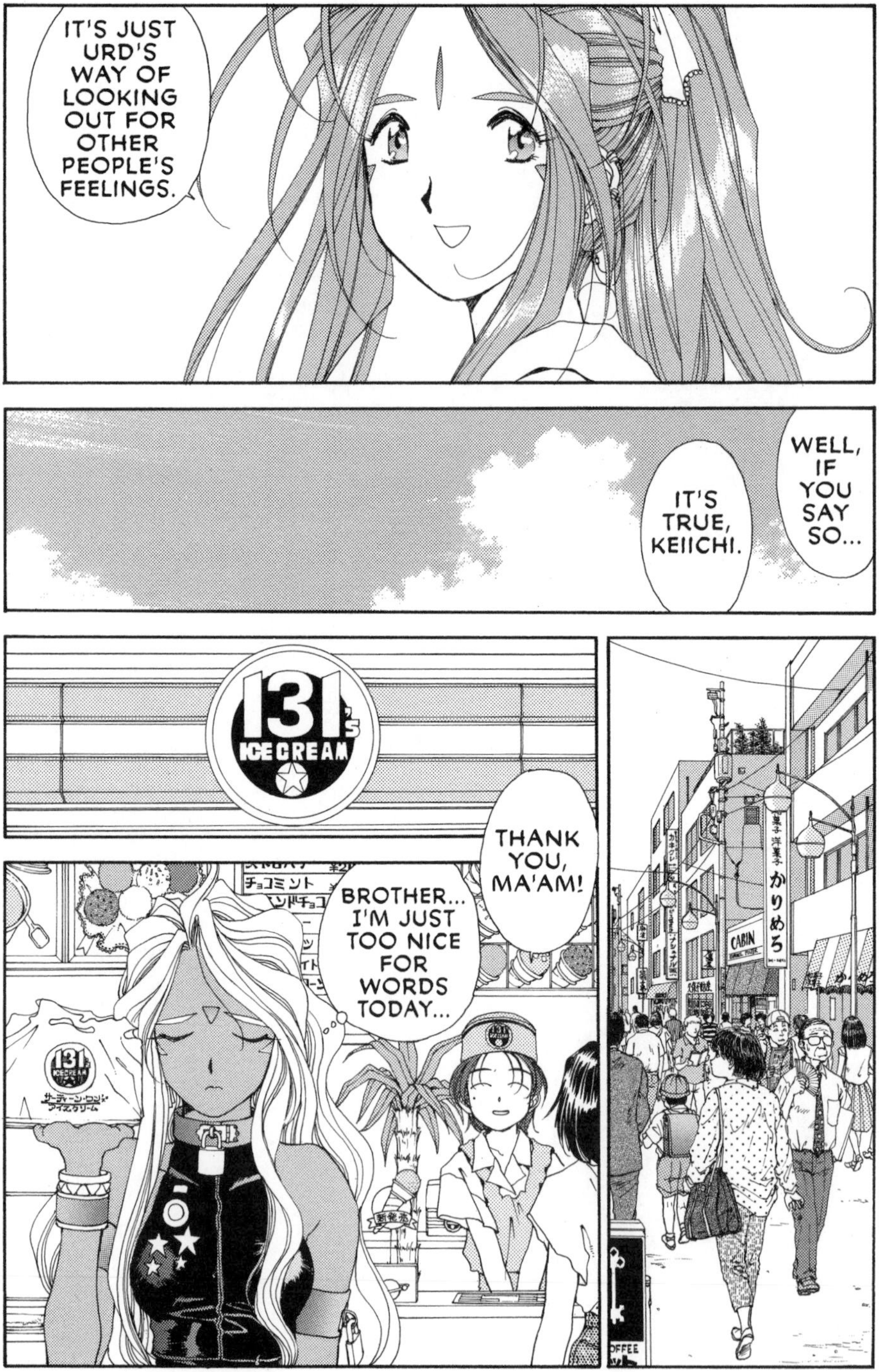
IT'S JUST URD'S WAY OF LOOKING OUT FOR OTHER PEOPLE'S FEELINGS.
WELL, IF YOU SAY SO...
IT'S TRUE, KEIICHI.
菓子洋菓子
かりめろ
CABIN
131's
ICE CREAM
THANK YOU, MA'AM!
BROTHER... I'M JUST TOO NICE FOR WORDS TODAY...
チョコミント

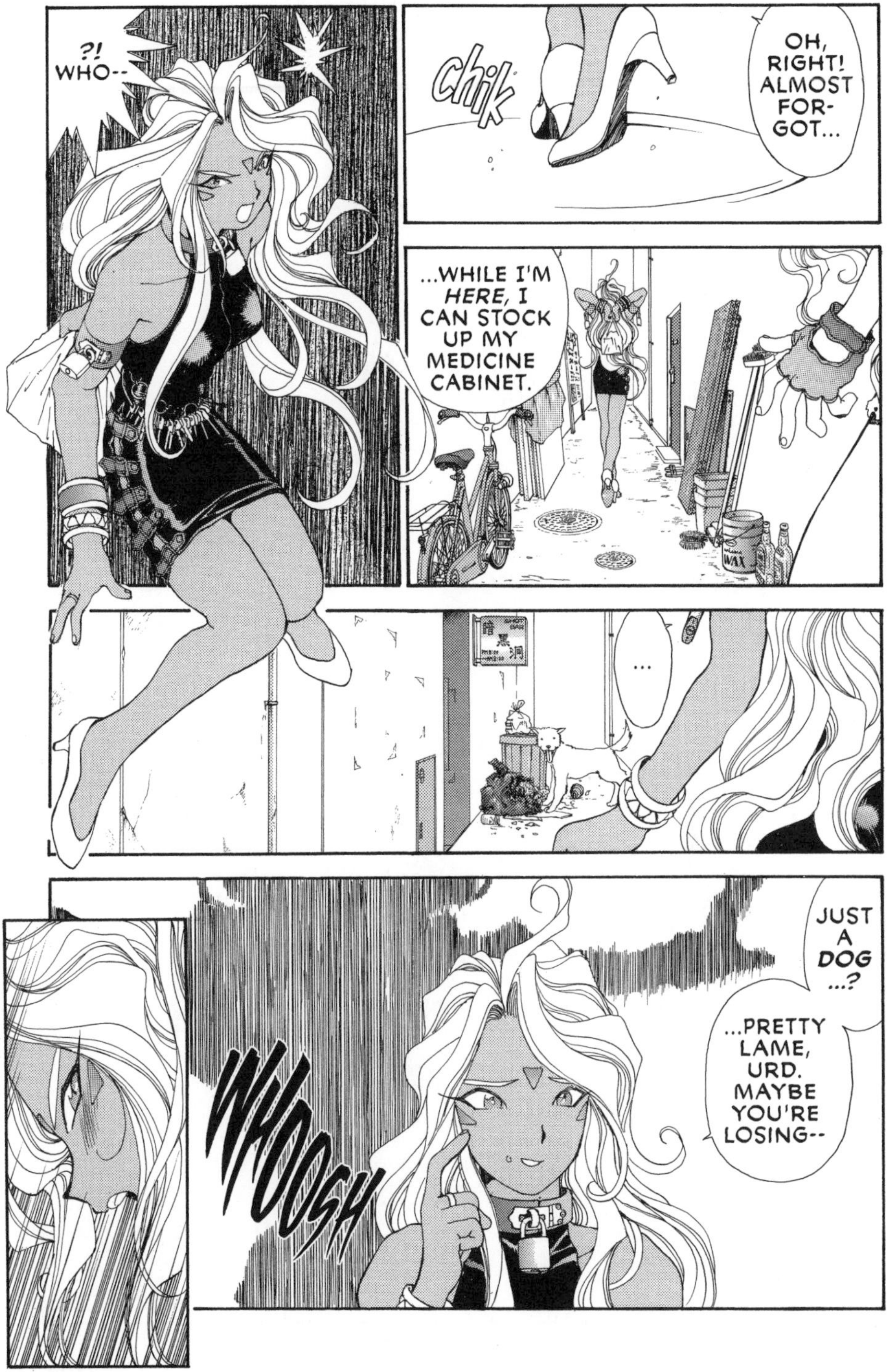
OH, RIGHT! ALMOST FOR- GOT...
chik
...WHILE I'M *HERE,* I CAN STOCK UP MY MEDICINE CABINET.
?! WHO--
...
JUST A *DOG* ...?
...PRETTY LAME, URD. MAYBE YOU'RE LOSING--
WHOOSH

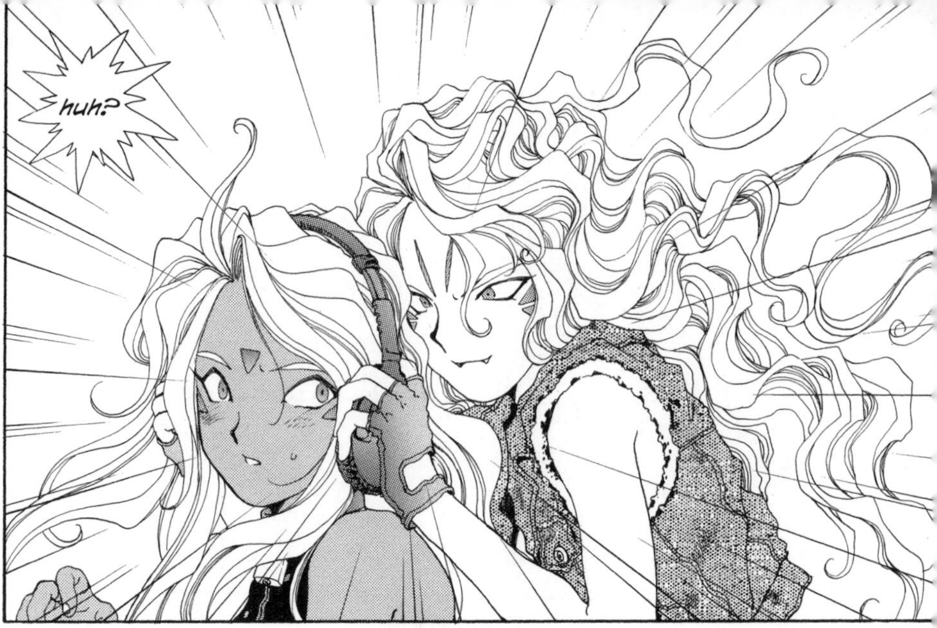
huh?

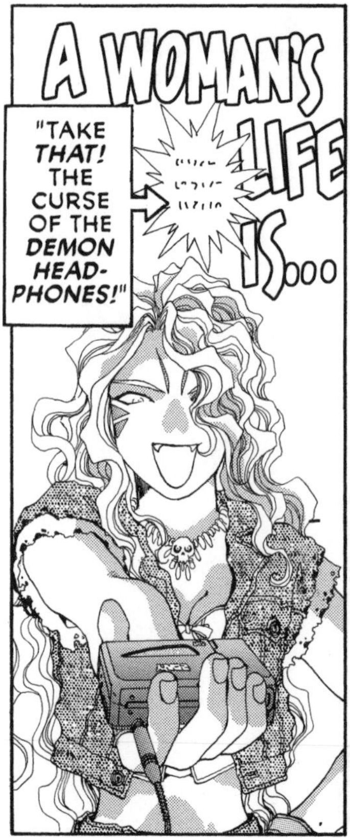
A WOMAN'S
LIFE
IS...
"TAKE THAT! THE CURSE OF THE DEMON HEADPHONES!"

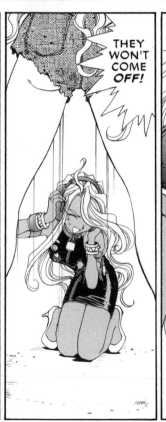

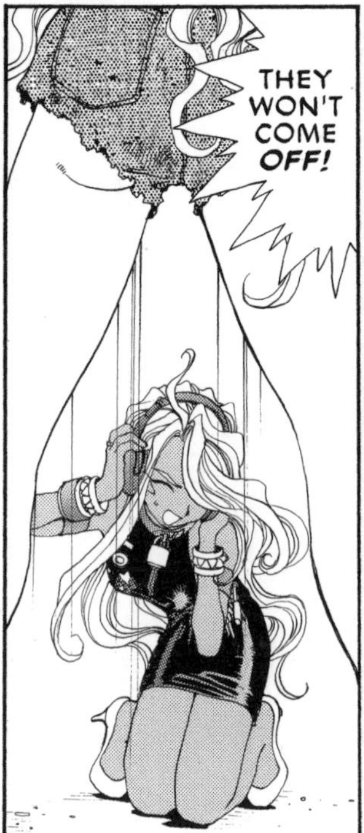
THEY WON'T COME OFF!

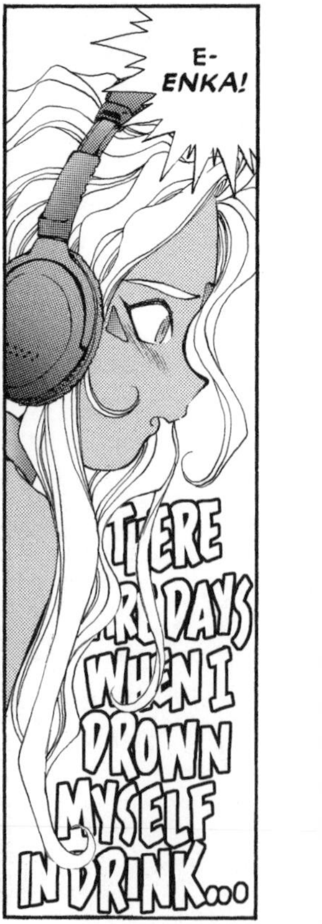
E- ENKA!
THERE
RE DAYS
WHEN I
DROWN
MYSELF
IN DRINK...

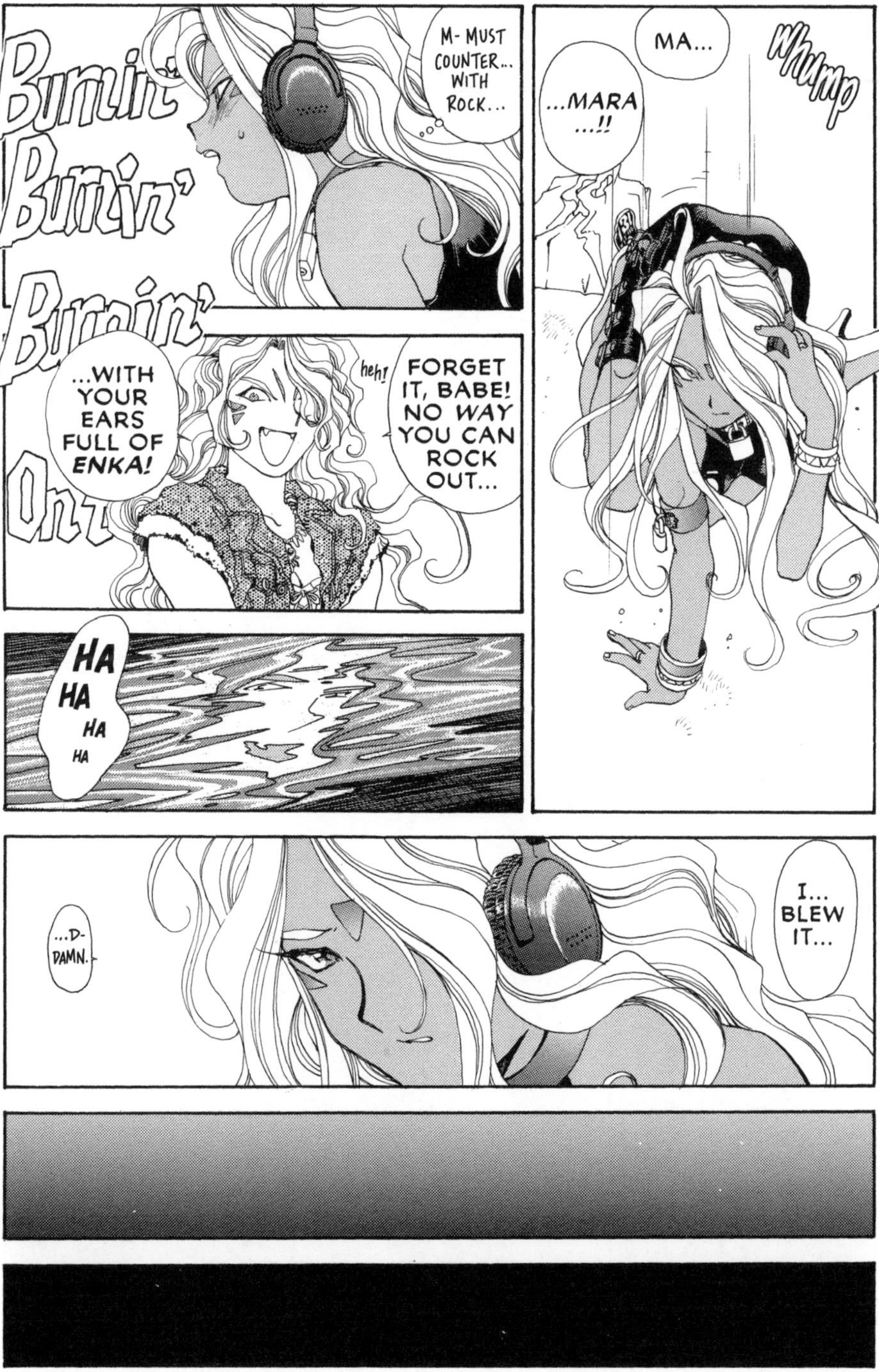
Burnin'
Burnin'
Burnin'
On
M-MUST COUNTER... WITH ROCK...
heh!
FORGET IT, BABE! NO WAY YOU CAN ROCK OUT...
...WITH YOUR EARS FULL OF ENKA!
HA HA HA HA
MA...
...MARA ...!!
Whump
I... BLEW IT...
...D-DAMN.

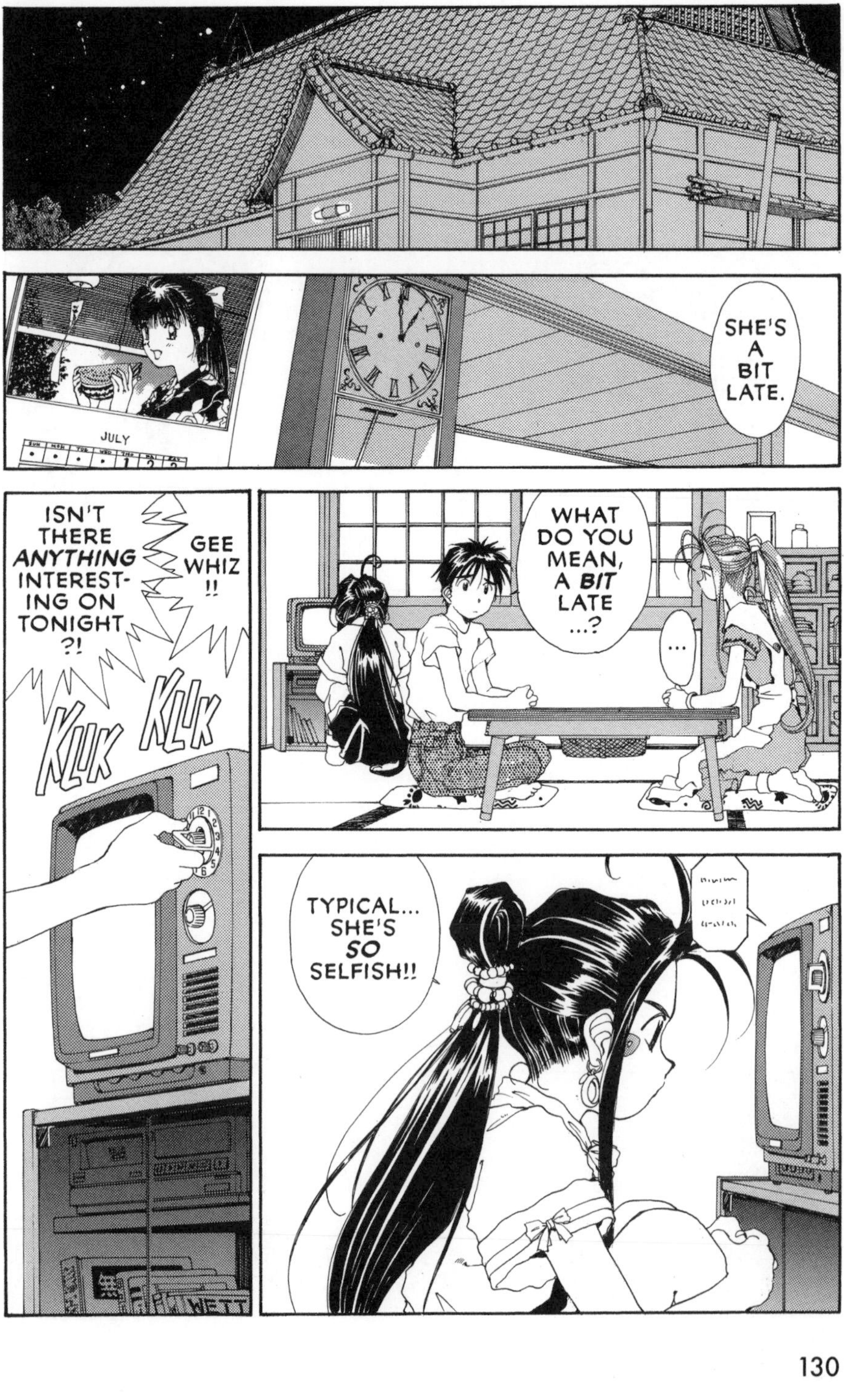
JULY
SHE'S A BIT LATE.
WHAT DO YOU MEAN, A *BIT* LATE ...?
...
TYPICAL... SHE'S *SO* SELFISH!!
GEE WHIZ !!
ISN'T THERE *ANYTHING* INTEREST-ING ON TONIGHT ?!
KLIK KLIK

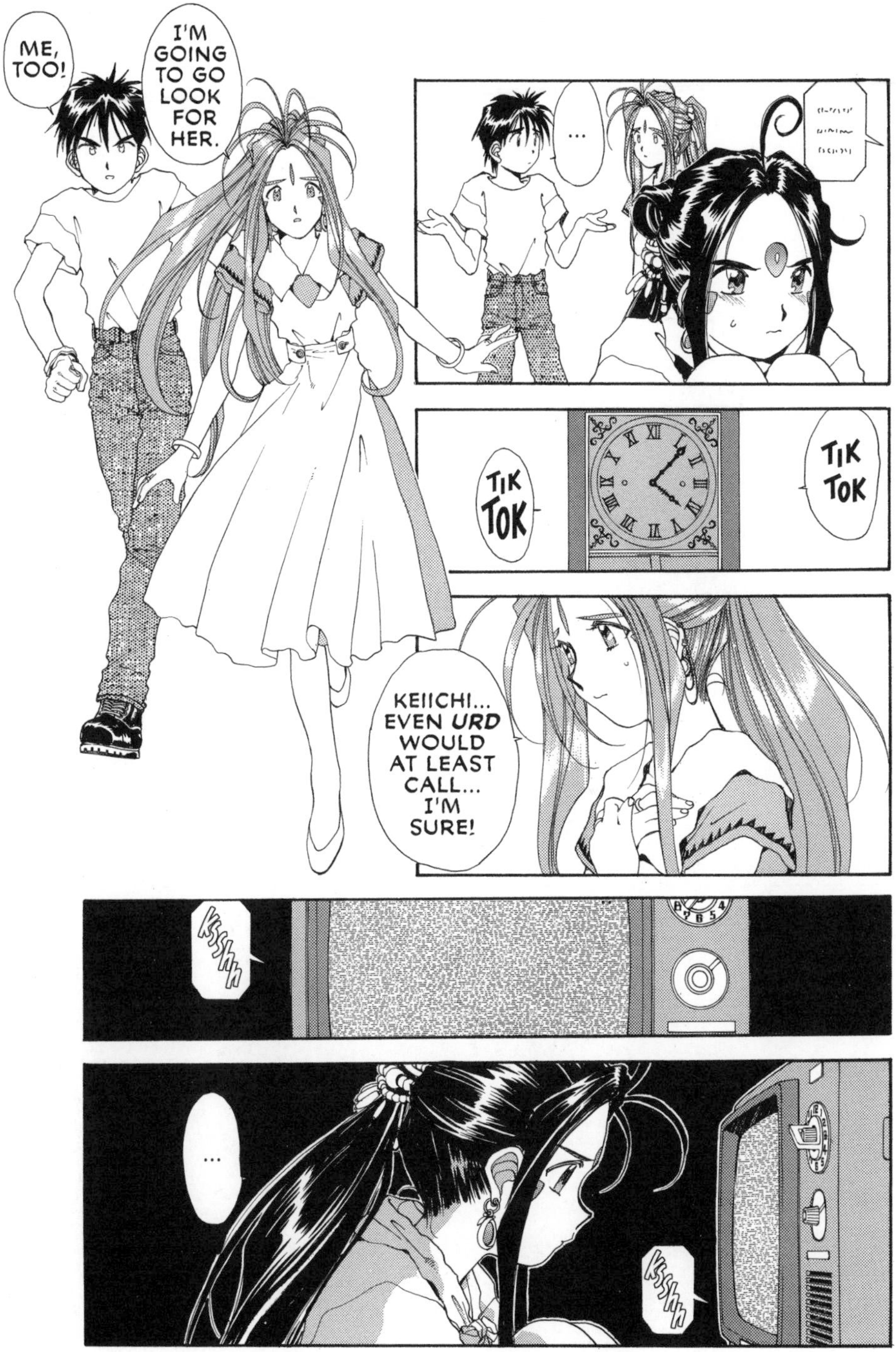
...
TIK TOK
TIK TOK
KEIICHI... EVEN URD WOULD AT LEAST CALL... I'M SURE!
I'M GOING TO GO LOOK FOR HER.
ME, TOO!
KSSHH
...
KSSHH

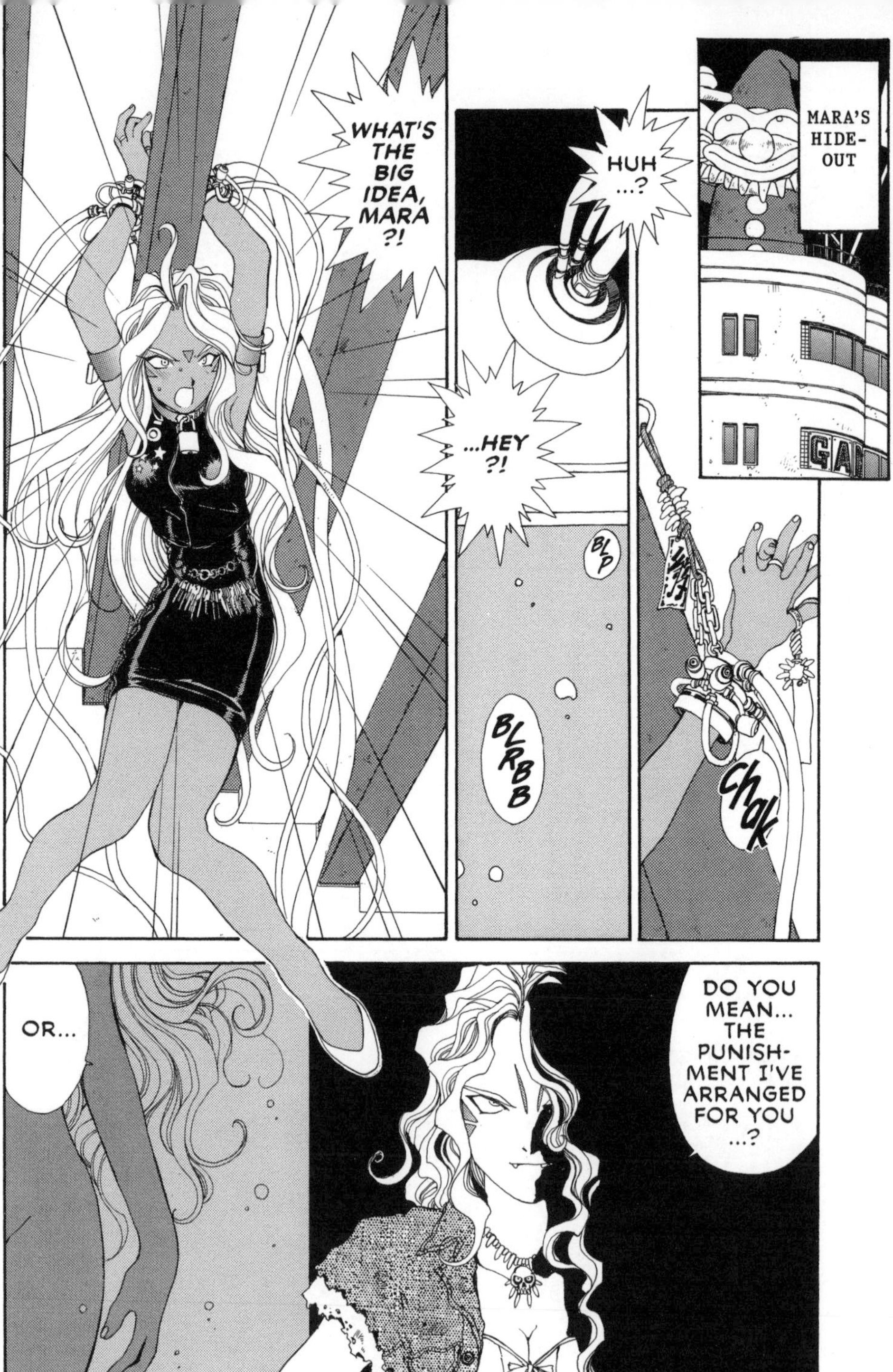

MARA'S HIDE-OUT
CHAK
HUH ...?
...HEY ?!
BLP
BLRBB
WHAT'S THE BIG IDEA, MARA ?!
DO YOU MEAN... THE PUNISHMENT I'VE ARRANGED FOR YOU ...?
OR...

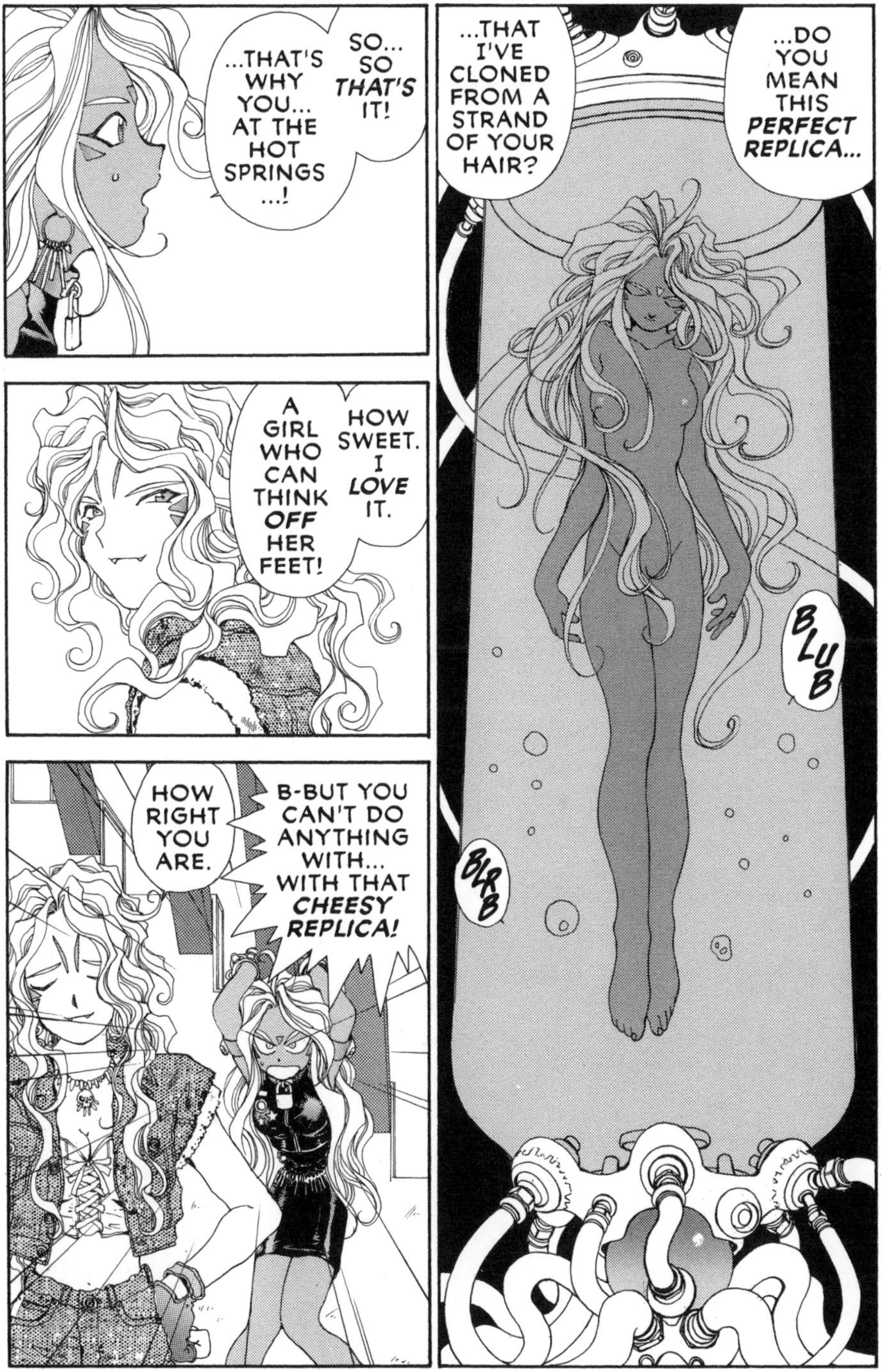
...DO YOU MEAN THIS *PERFECT REPLICA*...
...THAT I'VE CLONED FROM A STRAND OF YOUR HAIR?
BLUB
BLRB
SO... SO *THAT'S* IT!
...THAT'S WHY YOU... AT THE HOT SPRINGS ...!
HOW SWEET. I *LOVE* IT.
A GIRL WHO CAN THINK *OFF* HER FEET!
B-BUT YOU CAN'T DO ANYTHING WITH... WITH THAT *CHEESY REPLICA!*
HOW RIGHT YOU ARE.

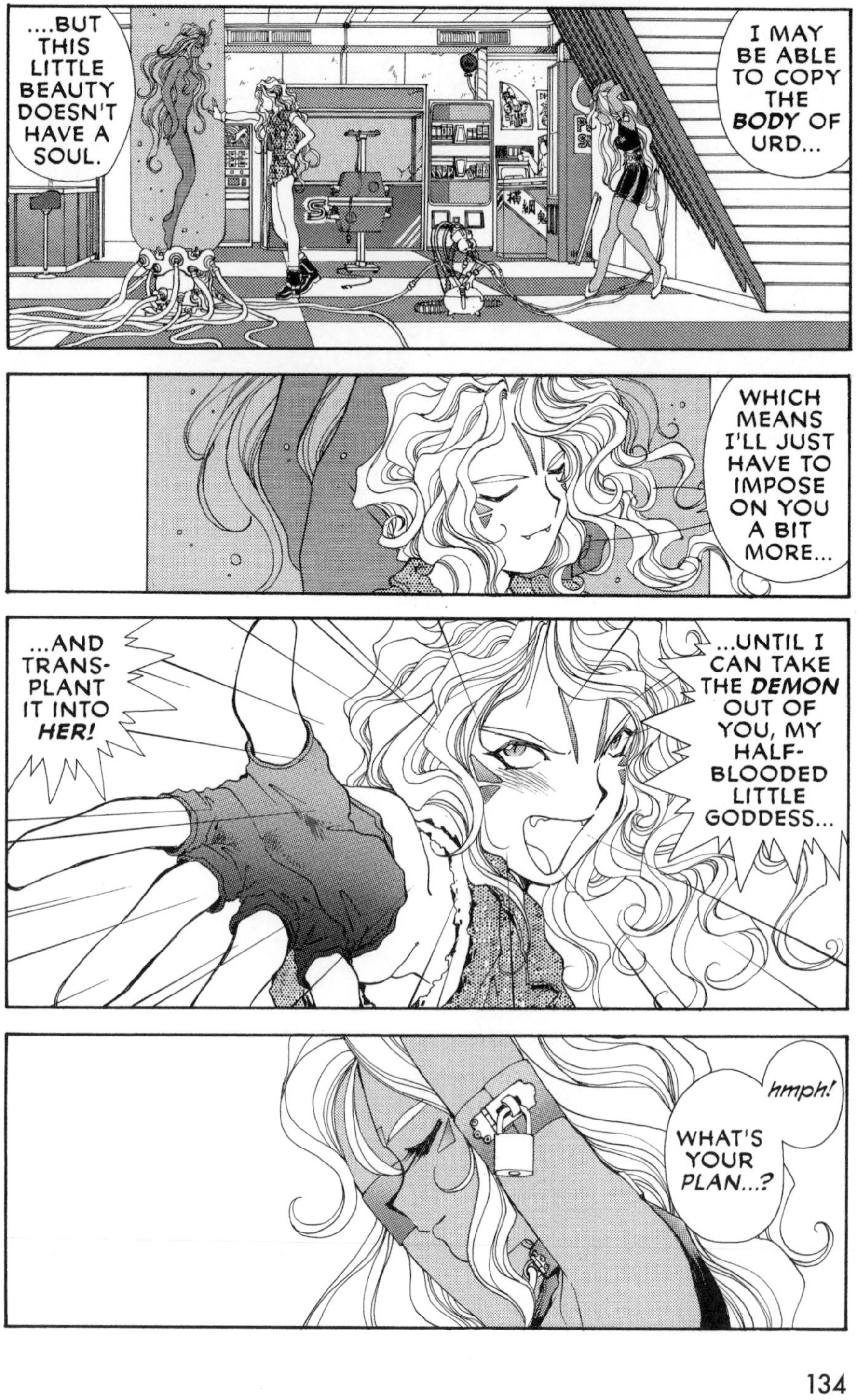
I MAY BE ABLE TO COPY THE *BODY* OF URD...
...BUT THIS LITTLE BEAUTY DOESN'T HAVE A SOUL.
WHICH MEANS I'LL JUST HAVE TO IMPOSE ON YOU A BIT MORE...
...UNTIL I CAN TAKE THE *DEMON* OUT OF YOU, MY HALF-BLOODED LITTLE GODDESS...
...AND TRANS-PLANT IT INTO *HER!*
hmph!
WHAT'S YOUR *PLAN...?*

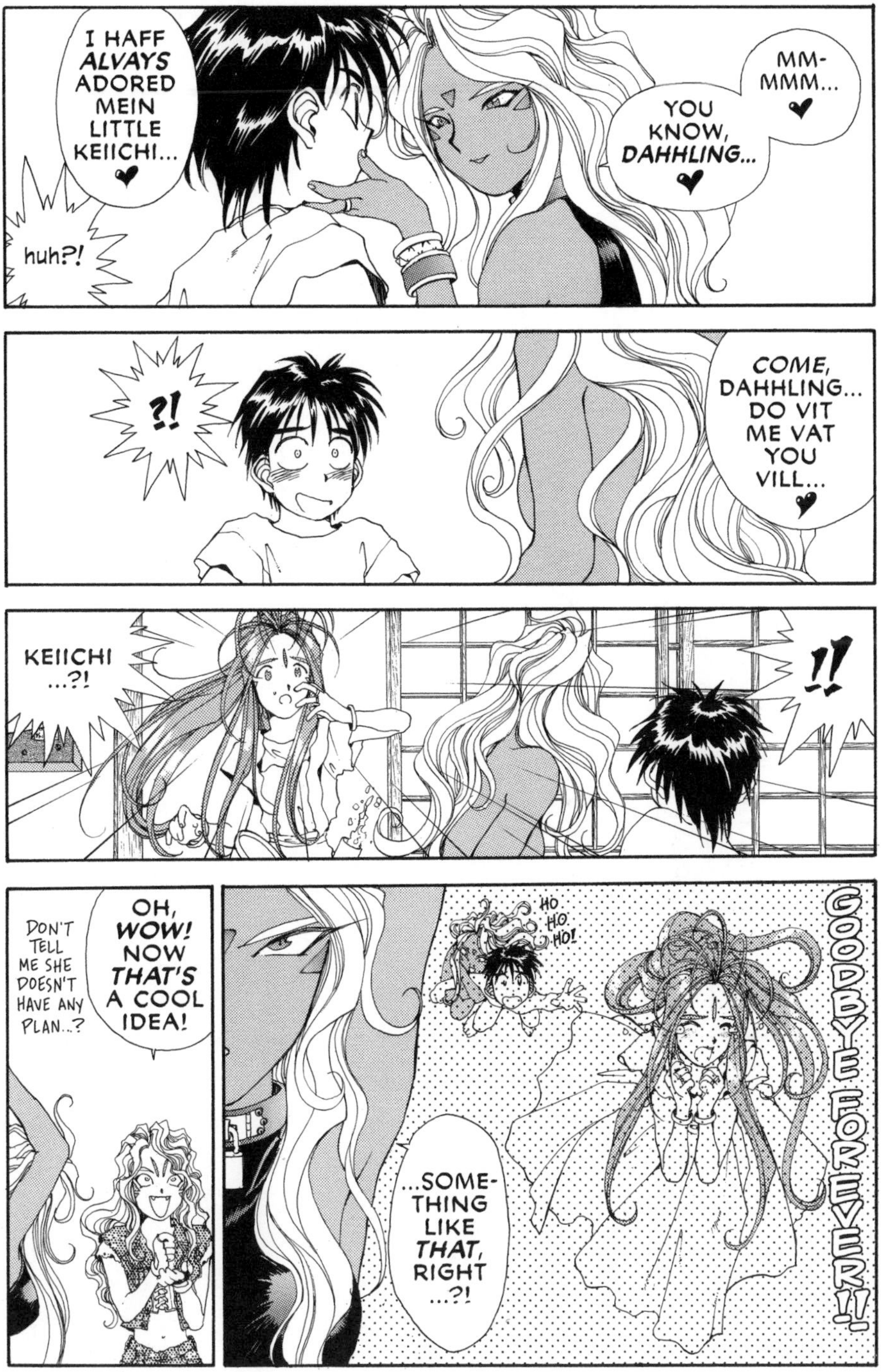
MM-MMM...
YOU KNOW, DAHHLING...
I HAFF ALVAYS ADORED MEIN LITTLE KEIICHI...
huh?!
COME, DAHHLING... DO VIT ME VAT YOU VILL...
?!
!!
KEIICHI ...?!
GOODBYE FOREVER!!
HO HO HO!
...SOMETHING LIKE THAT, RIGHT ...?!
OH, WOW! NOW THAT'S A COOL IDEA!
DON'T TELL ME SHE DOESN'T HAVE ANY PLAN..?

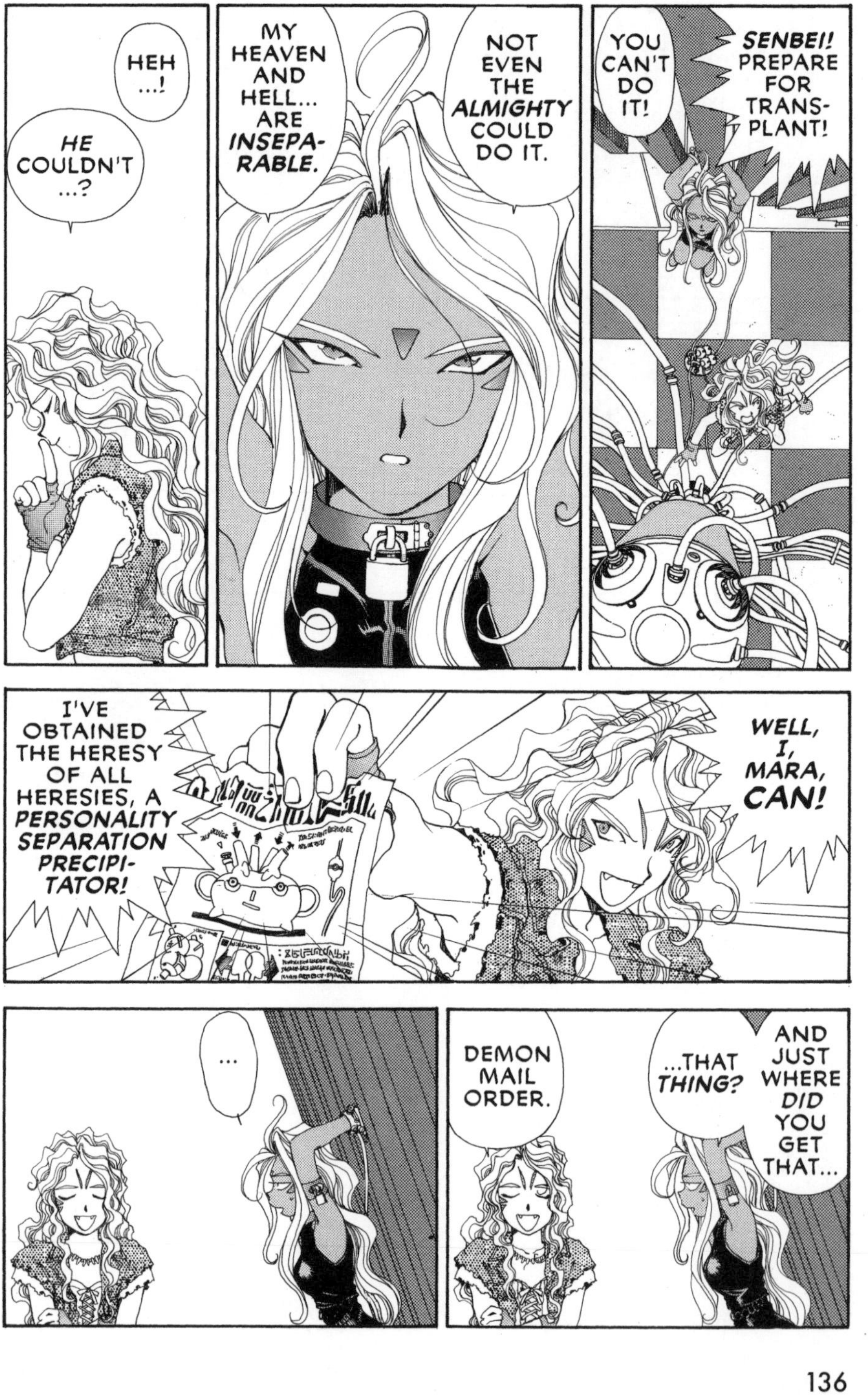
SENBEI! PREPARE FOR TRANS-PLANT!
YOU CAN'T DO IT!
NOT EVEN THE ALMIGHTY COULD DO IT.
MY HEAVEN AND HELL... ARE INSEPA-RABLE.
HEH ...!
HE COULDN'T ...?
WELL, I, MARA, CAN!
I'VE OBTAINED THE HERESY OF ALL HERESIES, A PERSONALITY SEPARATION PRECIPI-TATOR!
AND JUST WHERE DID YOU GET THAT...
...THAT THING?
DEMON MAIL ORDER.
...

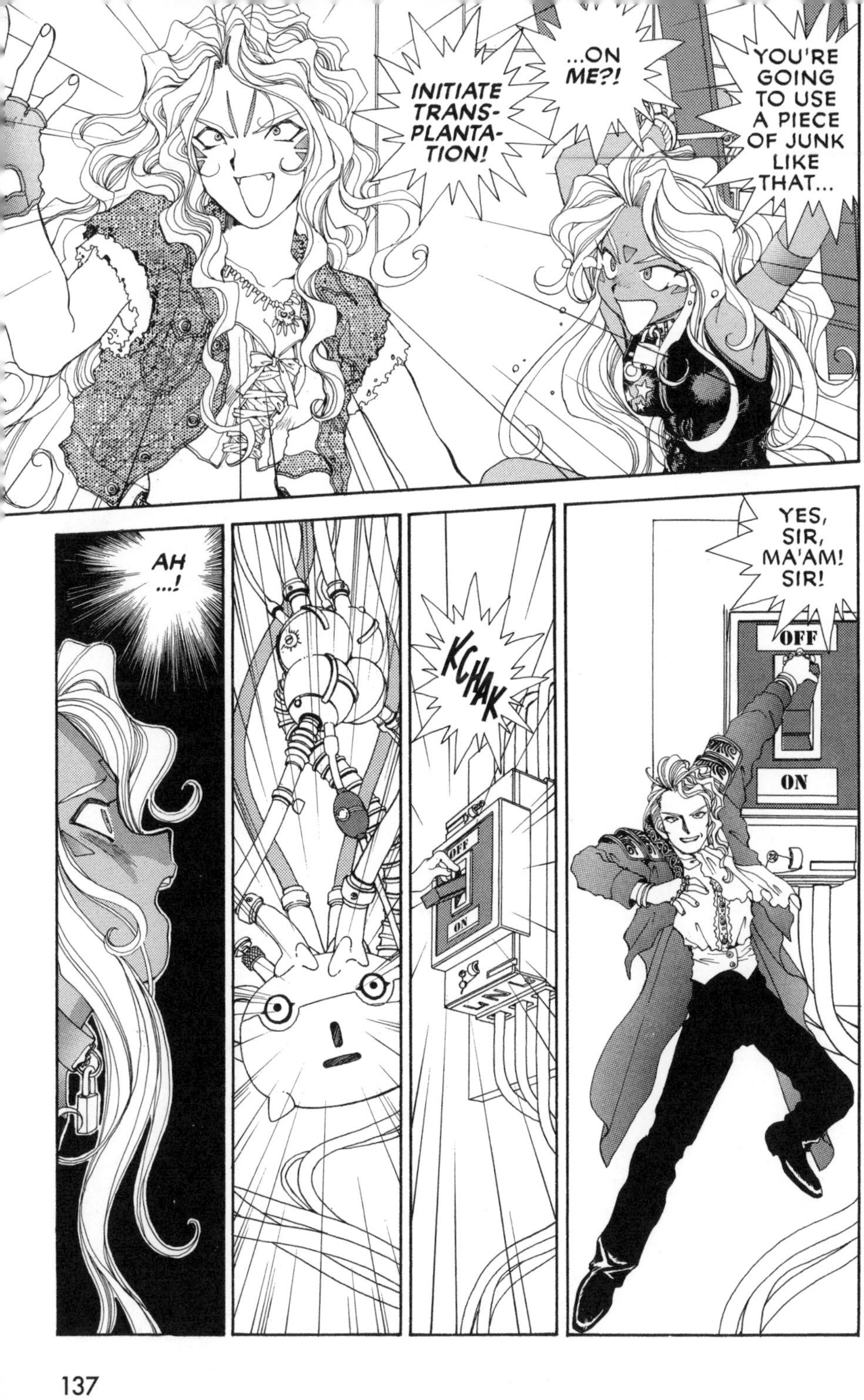
YOU'RE GOING TO USE A PIECE OF JUNK LIKE THAT...
...ON ME?!
INITIATE TRANS-PLANTA-TION!
YES, SIR, MA'AM! SIR!
OFF
ON
KCHAK
OFF
ON
AH ...!

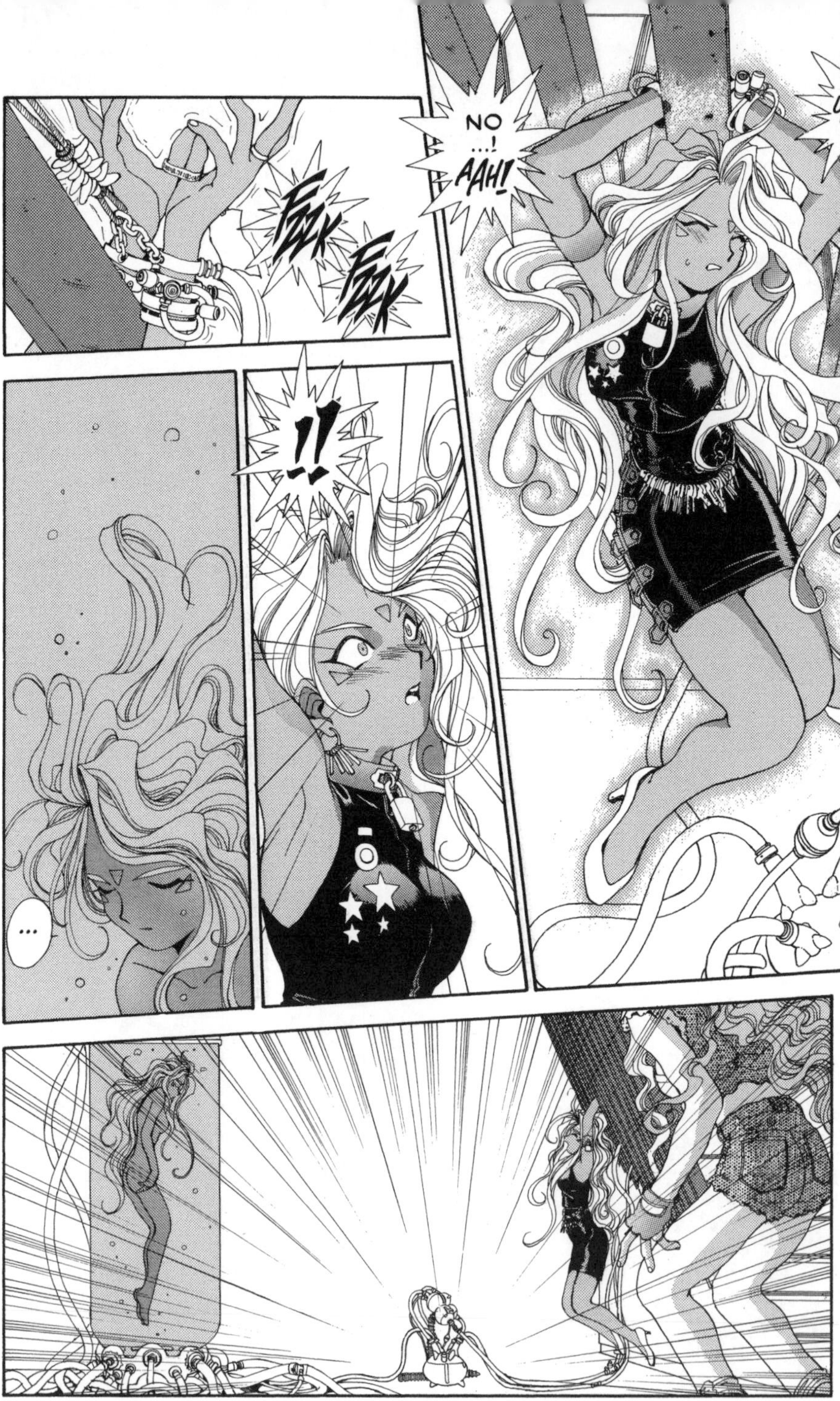
UHN!
NO ...! AAH!
FZZK
FZZK
!!
...

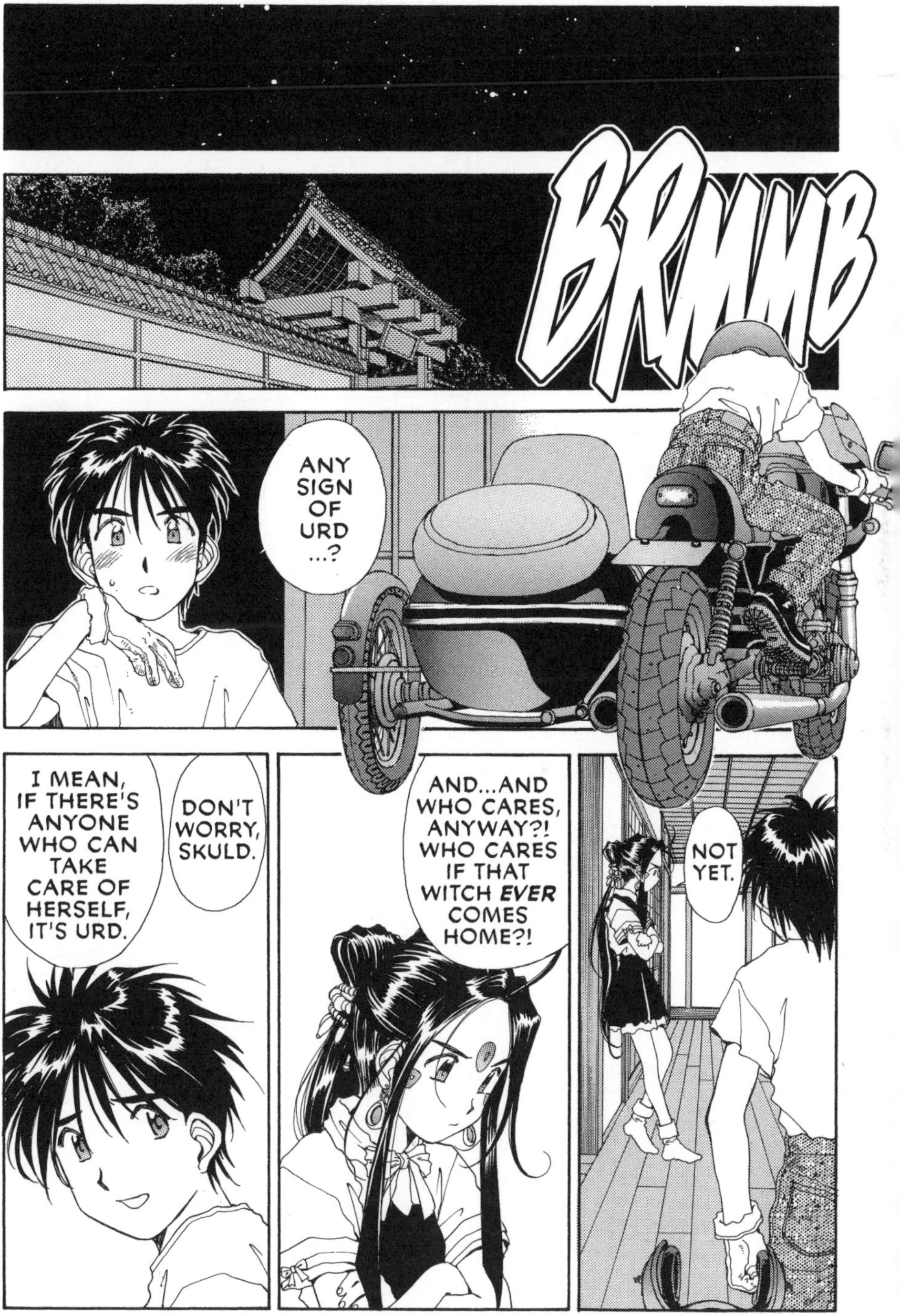
BRMMB
ANY SIGN OF URD ...?
NOT YET.
AND...AND WHO CARES, ANYWAY?! WHO CARES IF THAT WITCH *EVER* COMES HOME?!
DON'T WORRY, SKULD.
I MEAN, IF THERE'S ANYONE WHO CAN TAKE CARE OF HERSELF, IT'S URD.

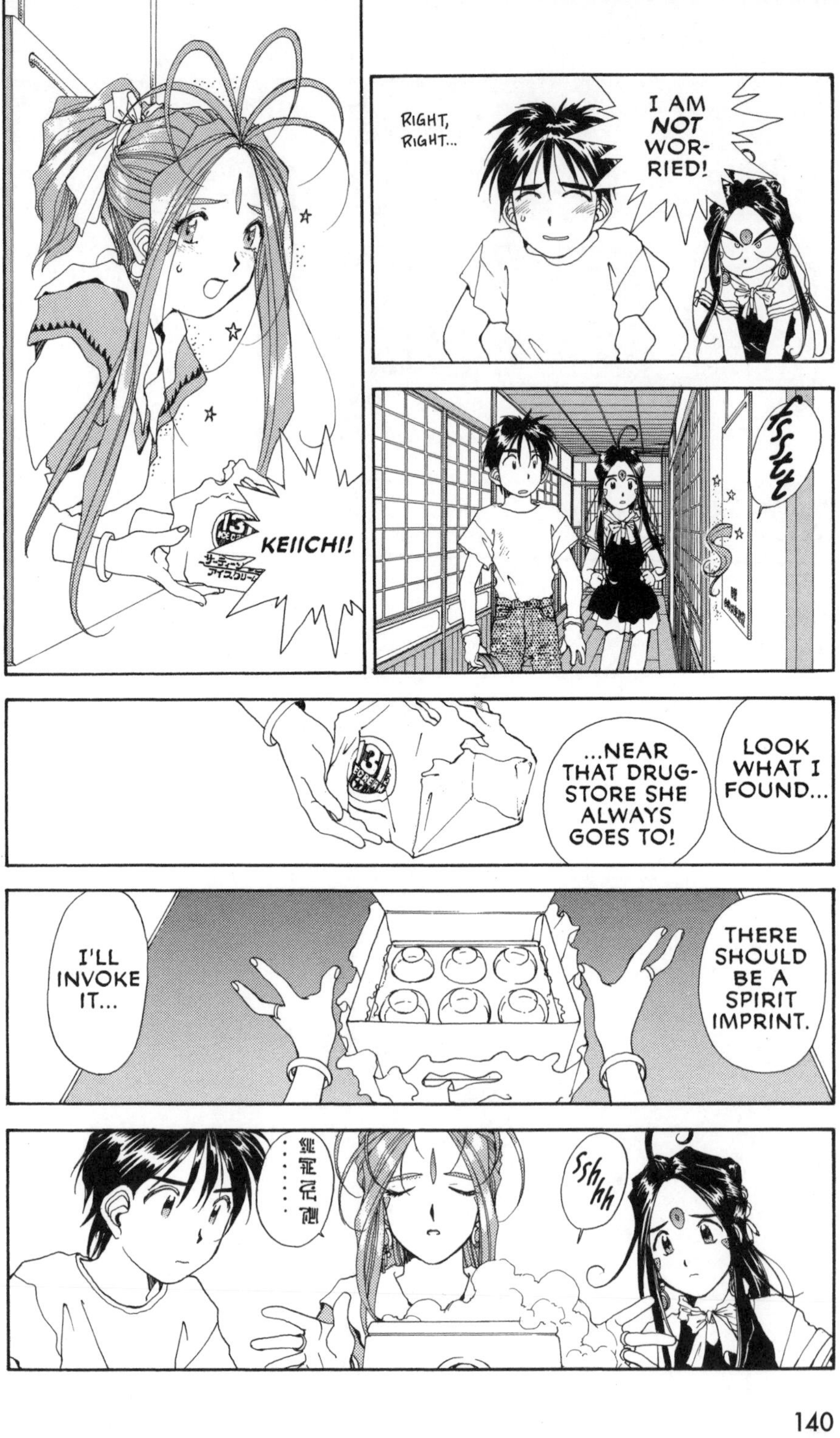
I AM NOT WORRIED!
RIGHT, RIGHT...
KEIICHI!
LOOK WHAT I FOUND...
...NEAR THAT DRUG-STORE SHE ALWAYS GOES TO!
THERE SHOULD BE A SPIRIT IMPRINT.
I'LL INVOKE IT...
Sshhh

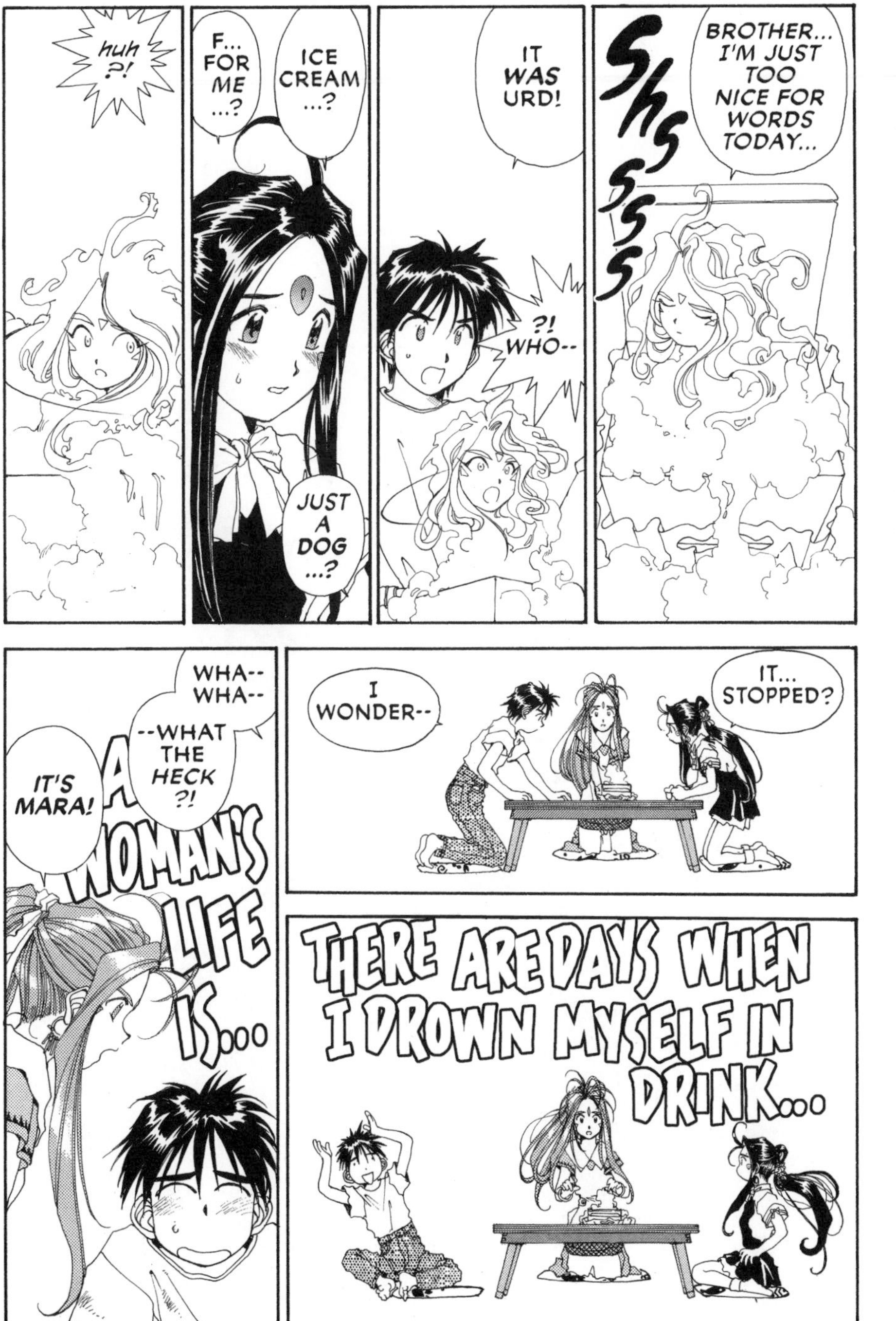
SHSSSSS
BROTHER... I'M JUST TOO NICE FOR WORDS TODAY...
IT WAS URD!
?! WHO--
ICE CREAM ...?
F... FOR ME ...?
JUST A DOG ...?
huh ?!
IT... STOPPED?
I WONDER--
THERE ARE DAYS WHEN I DROWN MYSELF IN DRINK...
WHA-- WHA--
--WHAT THE HECK ?!
IT'S MARA!
A WOMAN'S LIFE IS...

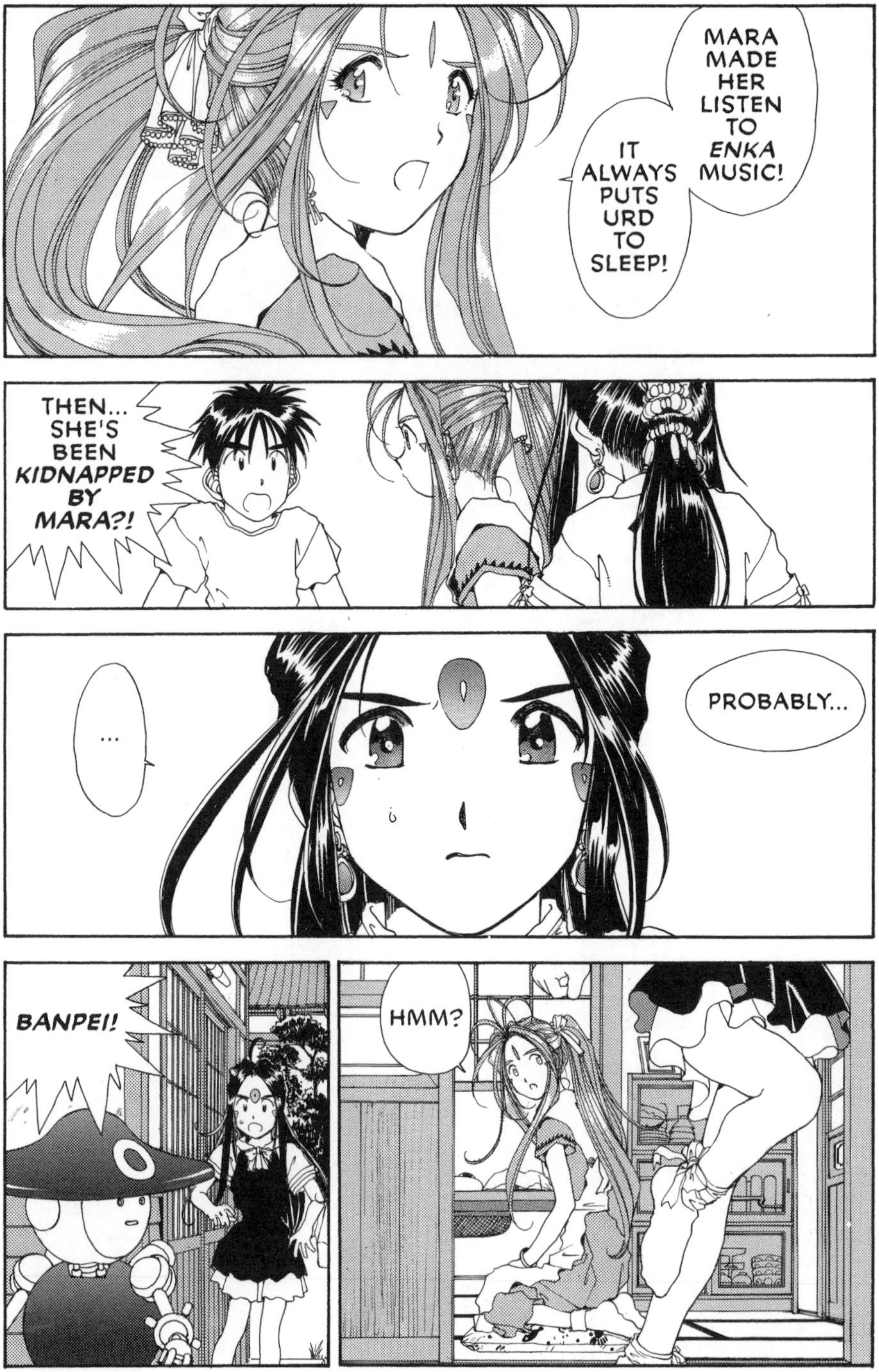
MARA MADE HER LISTEN TO *ENKA* MUSIC!
IT ALWAYS PUTS URD TO SLEEP!
THEN... SHE'S BEEN *KIDNAPPED BY MARA?!*
PROBABLY...
...
HMM?
BANPEI!

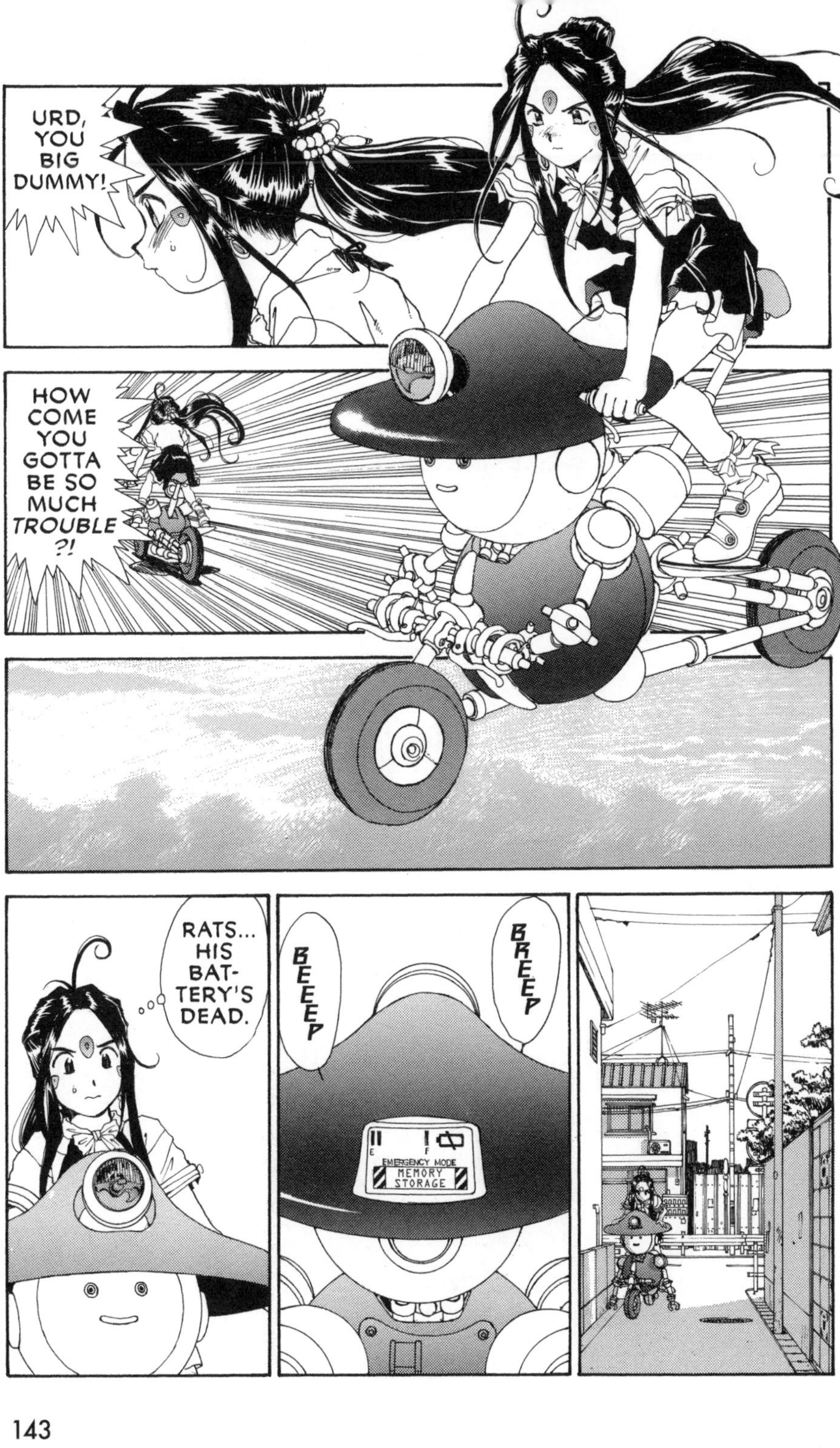
URD, YOU BIG DUMMY!
HOW COME YOU GOTTA BE SO MUCH TROUBLE?!
BREEP
BEEEP
EMERGENCY MODE
MEMORY STORAGE
RATS... HIS BATTERY'S DEAD.

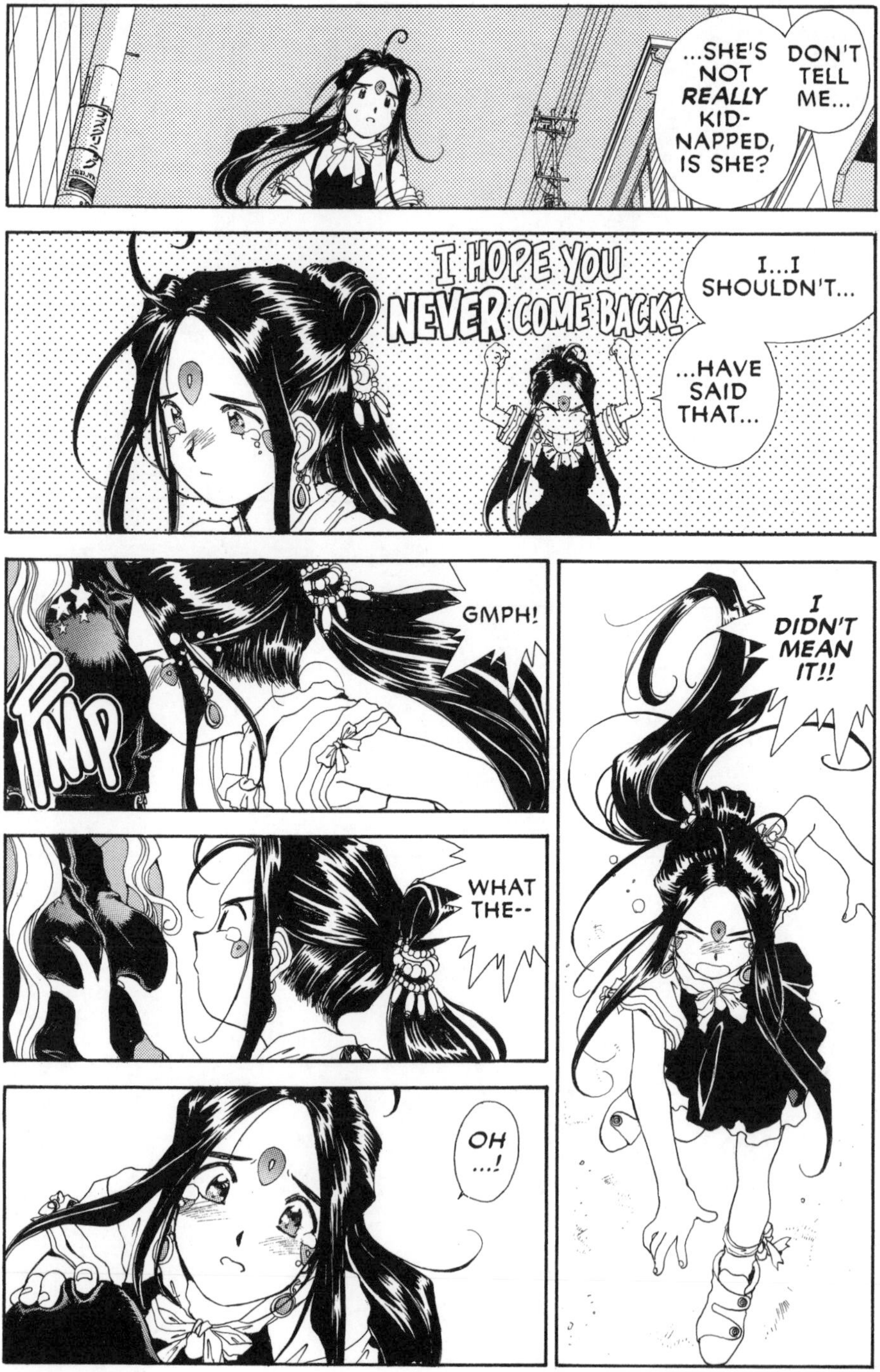
DON'T TELL ME...
...SHE'S NOT REALLY KID-NAPPED, IS SHE?
I...I SHOULDN'T...
...HAVE SAID THAT...
I HOPE YOU NEVER COME BACK!
I DIDN'T MEAN IT!!
GMPH!
FMP
WHAT THE--
OH ...!

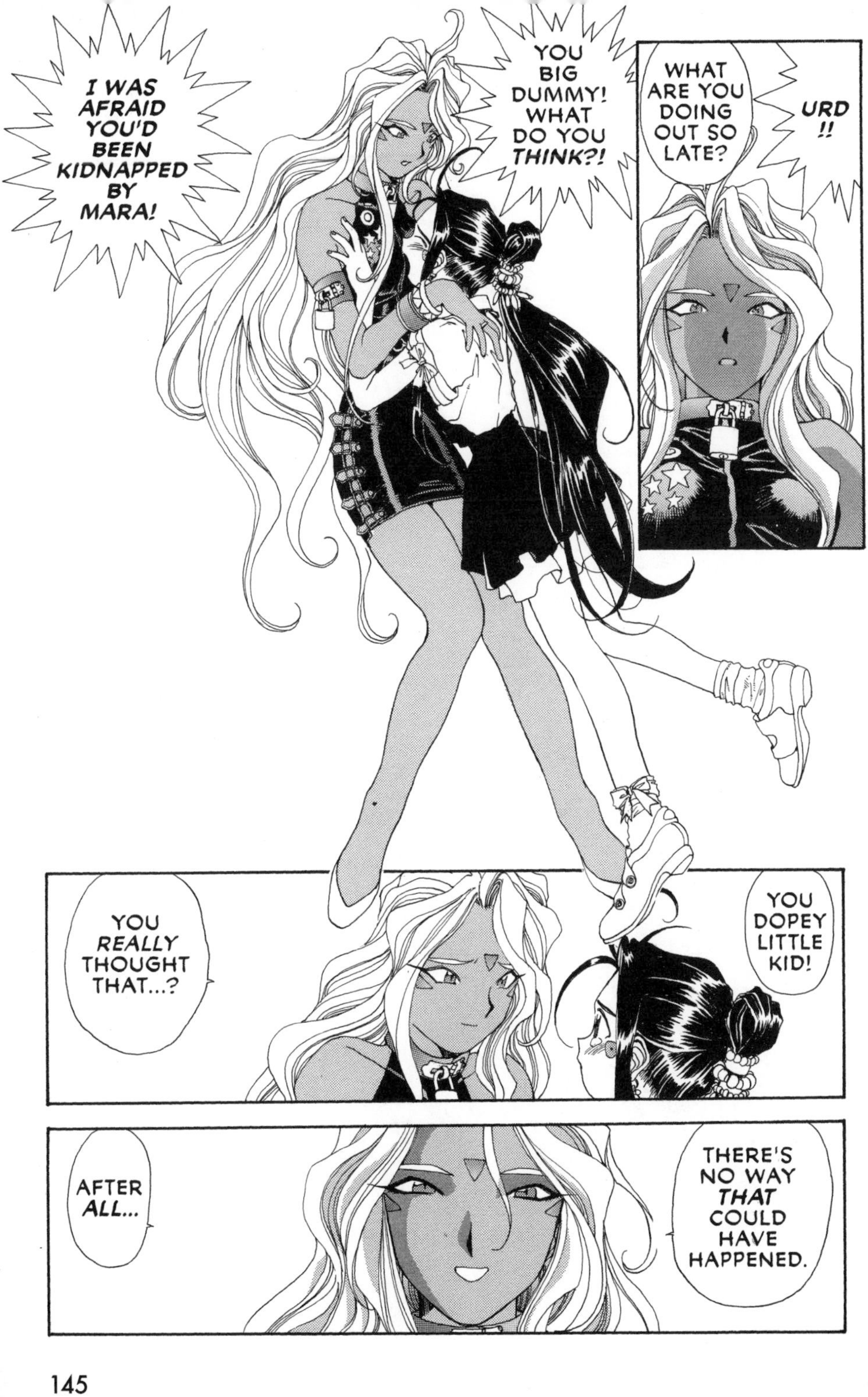

URD !!
WHAT ARE YOU DOING OUT SO LATE?
YOU BIG DUMMY! WHAT DO YOU *THINK?!*
I WAS AFRAID YOU'D BEEN KIDNAPPED BY MARA!
YOU *REALLY* THOUGHT THAT...?
YOU DOPEY LITTLE KID!
AFTER *ALL...*
THERE'S NO WAY *THAT* COULD HAVE HAPPENED.

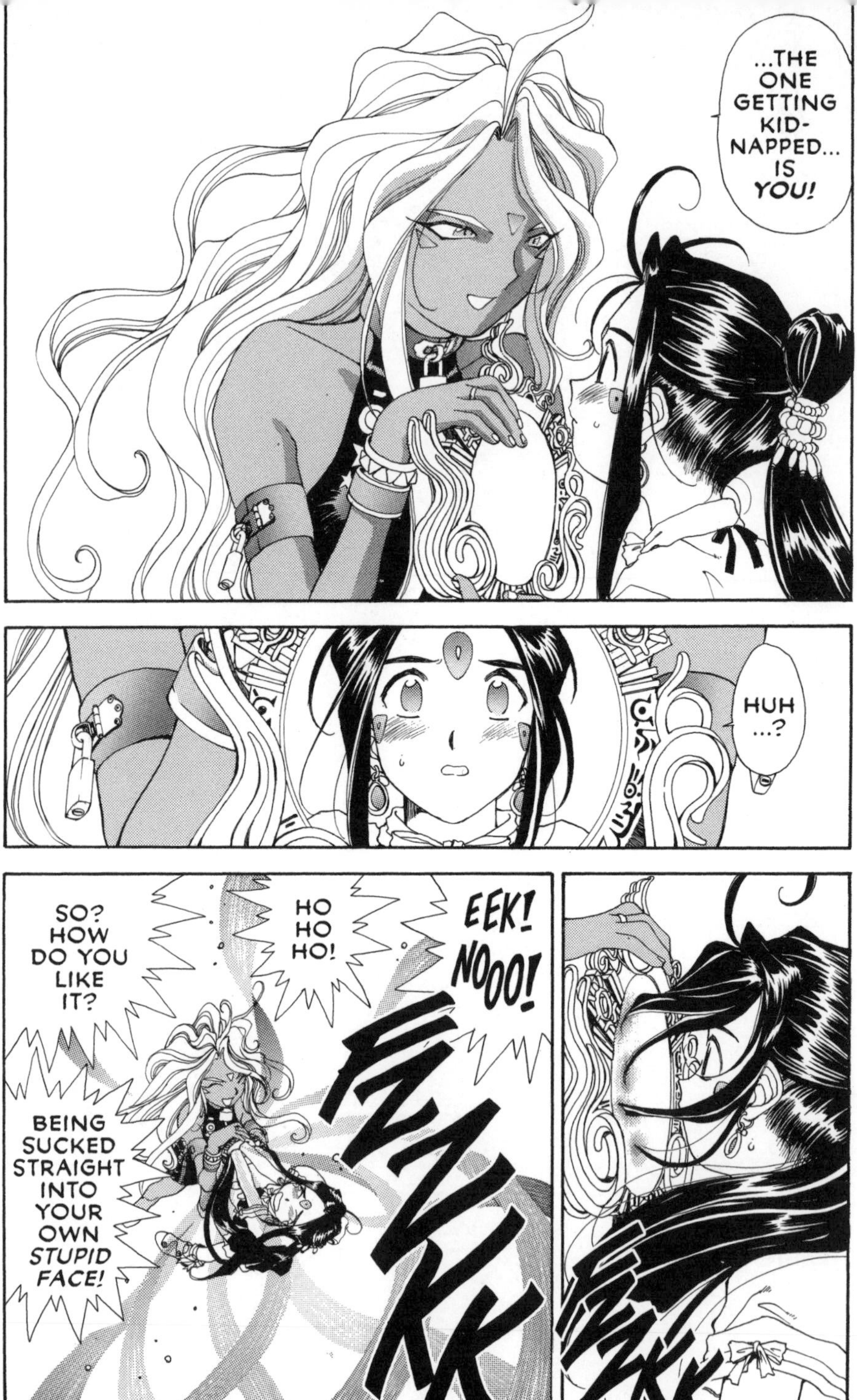
...THE ONE GETTING KID-NAPPED... IS *YOU!*
HUH ...?
EEK! NOOO!
HO HO HO!
SO? HOW DO YOU LIKE IT?
BEING SUCKED STRAIGHT INTO YOUR OWN *STUPID FACE!*

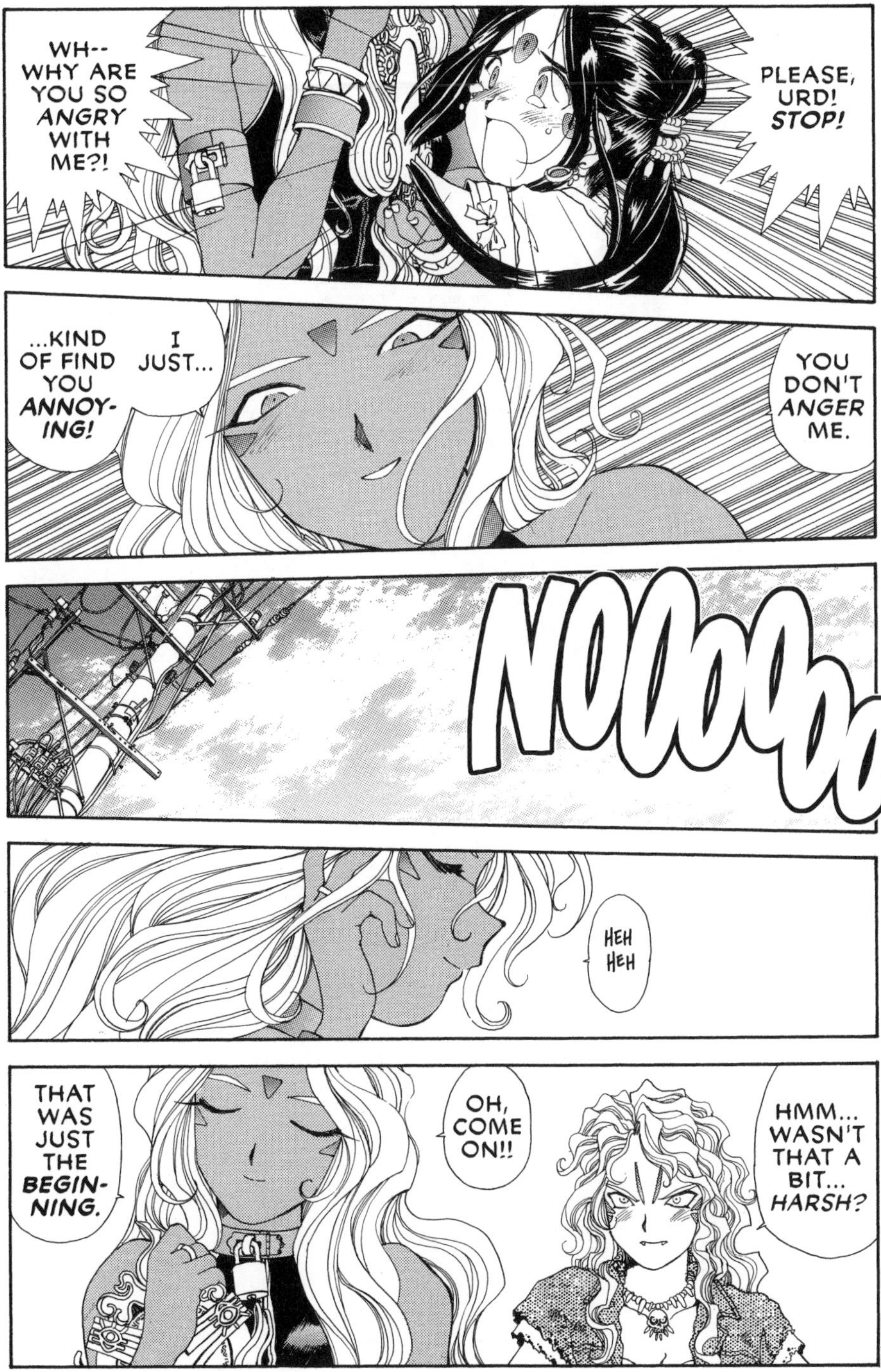
PLEASE, URD! *STOP!*
WH-- WHY ARE YOU SO *ANGRY* WITH ME?!
YOU DON'T *ANGER* ME.
I JUST...
...KIND OF FIND YOU *ANNOYING!*
NOOOOOO
HEH HEH
HMM... WASN'T THAT A BIT... *HARSH?*
OH, COME ON!!
THAT WAS JUST THE *BEGINNING.*

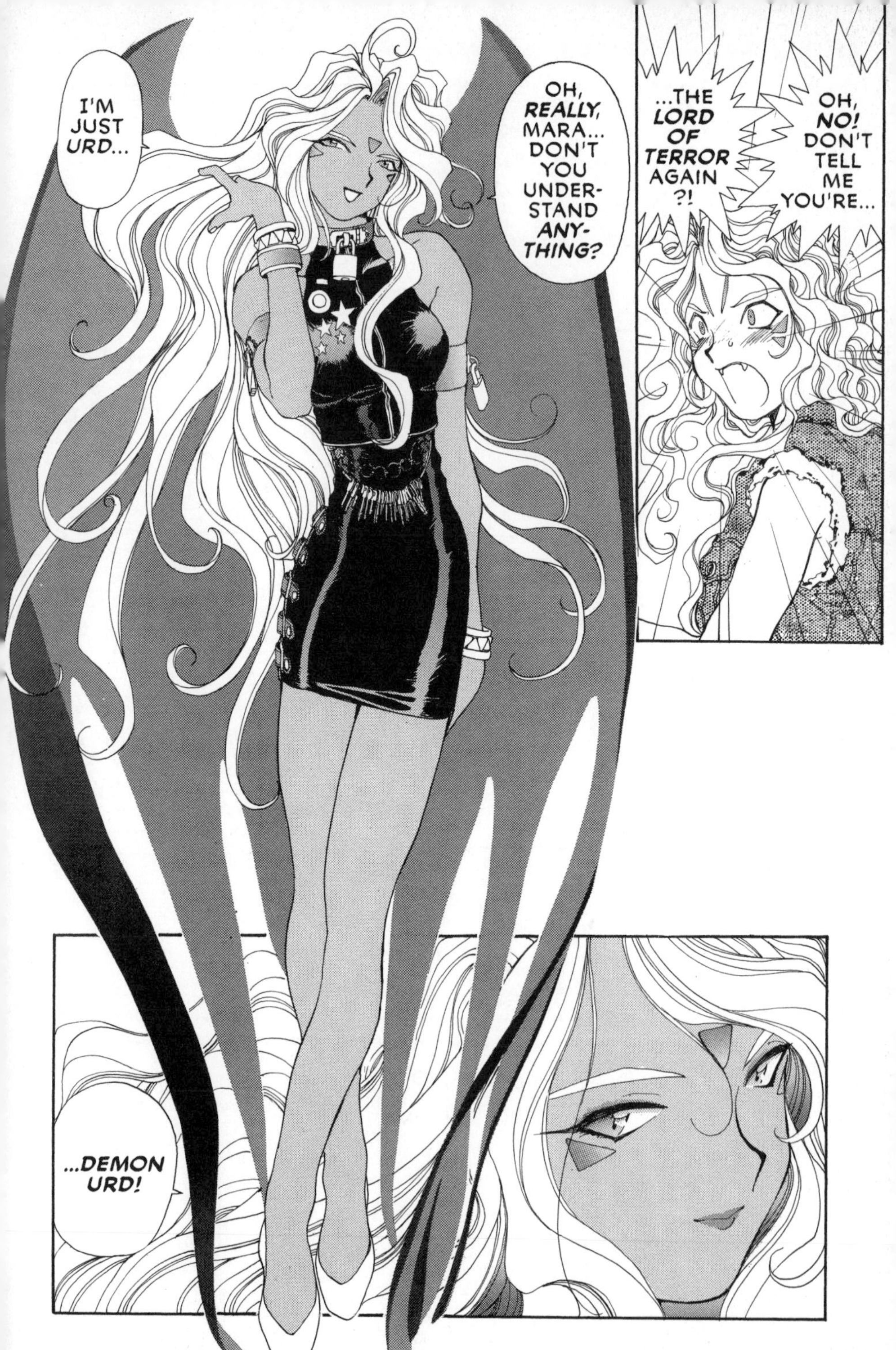
OH, NO! DON'T TELL ME YOU'RE...
...THE LORD OF TERROR AGAIN?!
OH, REALLY, MARA... DON'T YOU UNDERSTAND ANYTHING?
I'M JUST URD...
...DEMON URD!

CHAPTER 62

Skuld Strikes Back!

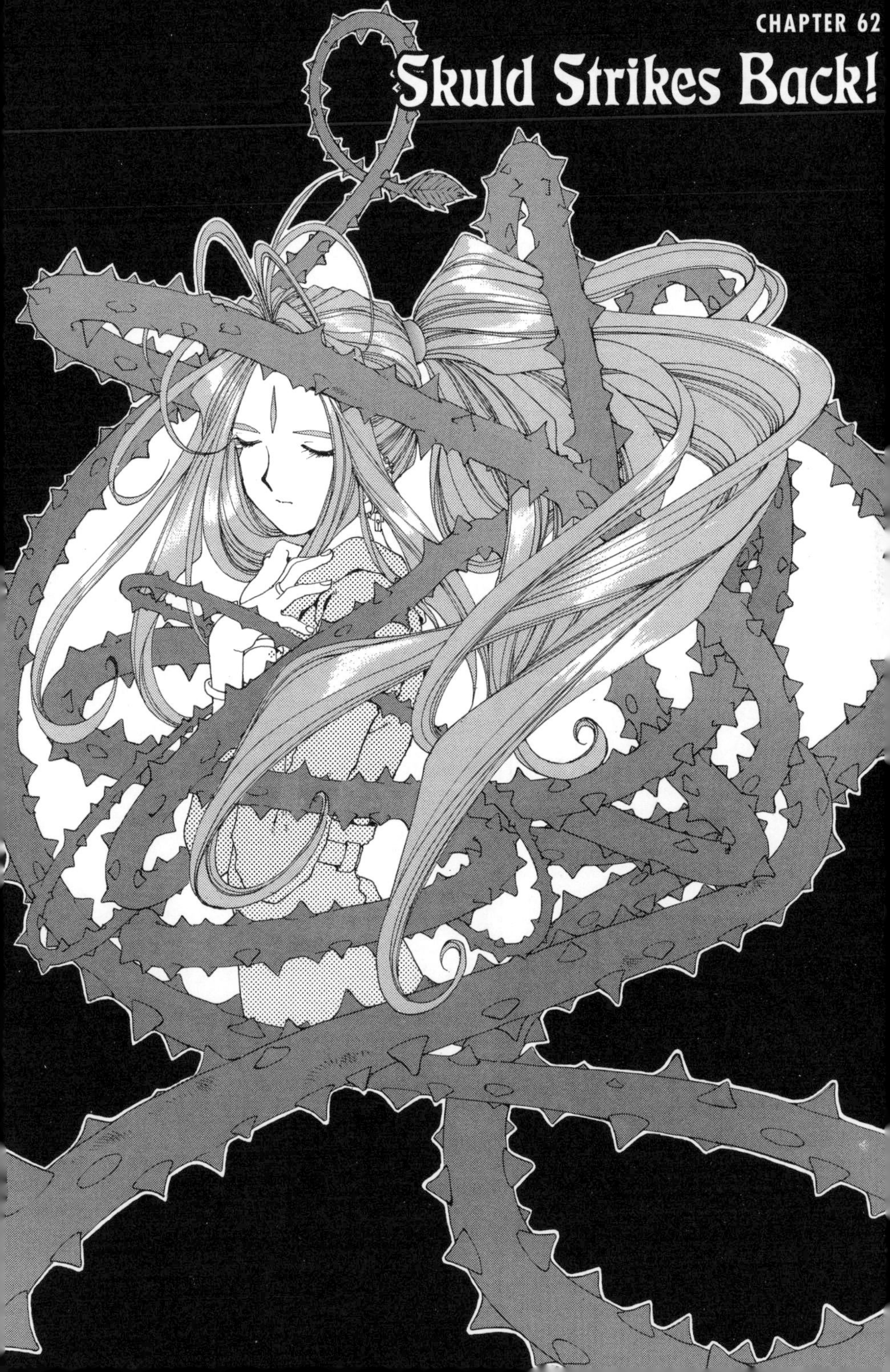

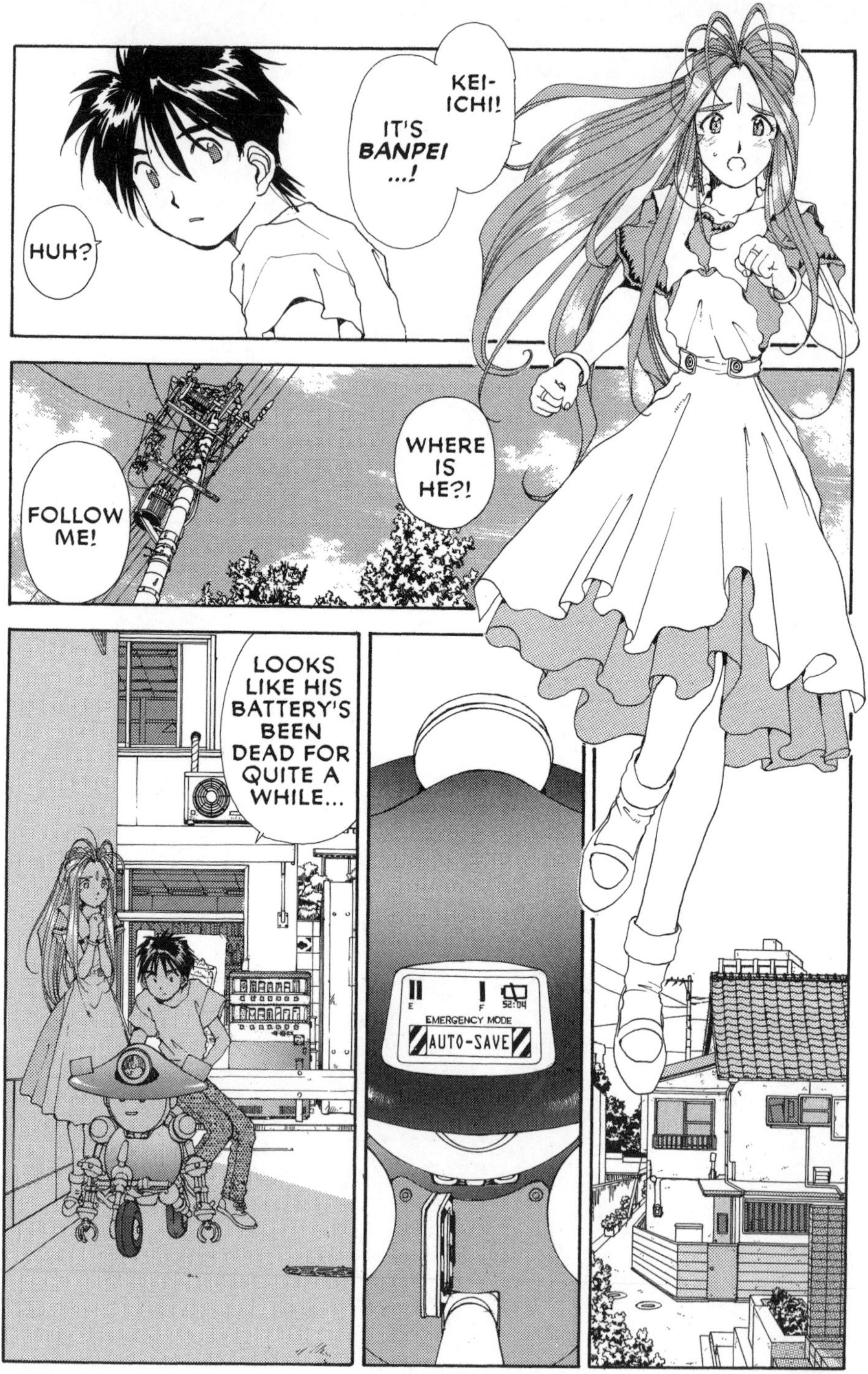
KEI-ICHI! IT'S BANPEI ...!
HUH?
WHERE IS HE?!
FOLLOW ME!
E F 52:04
EMERGENCY MODE
AUTO-SAVE
LOOKS LIKE HIS BATTERY'S BEEN DEAD FOR QUITE A WHILE...

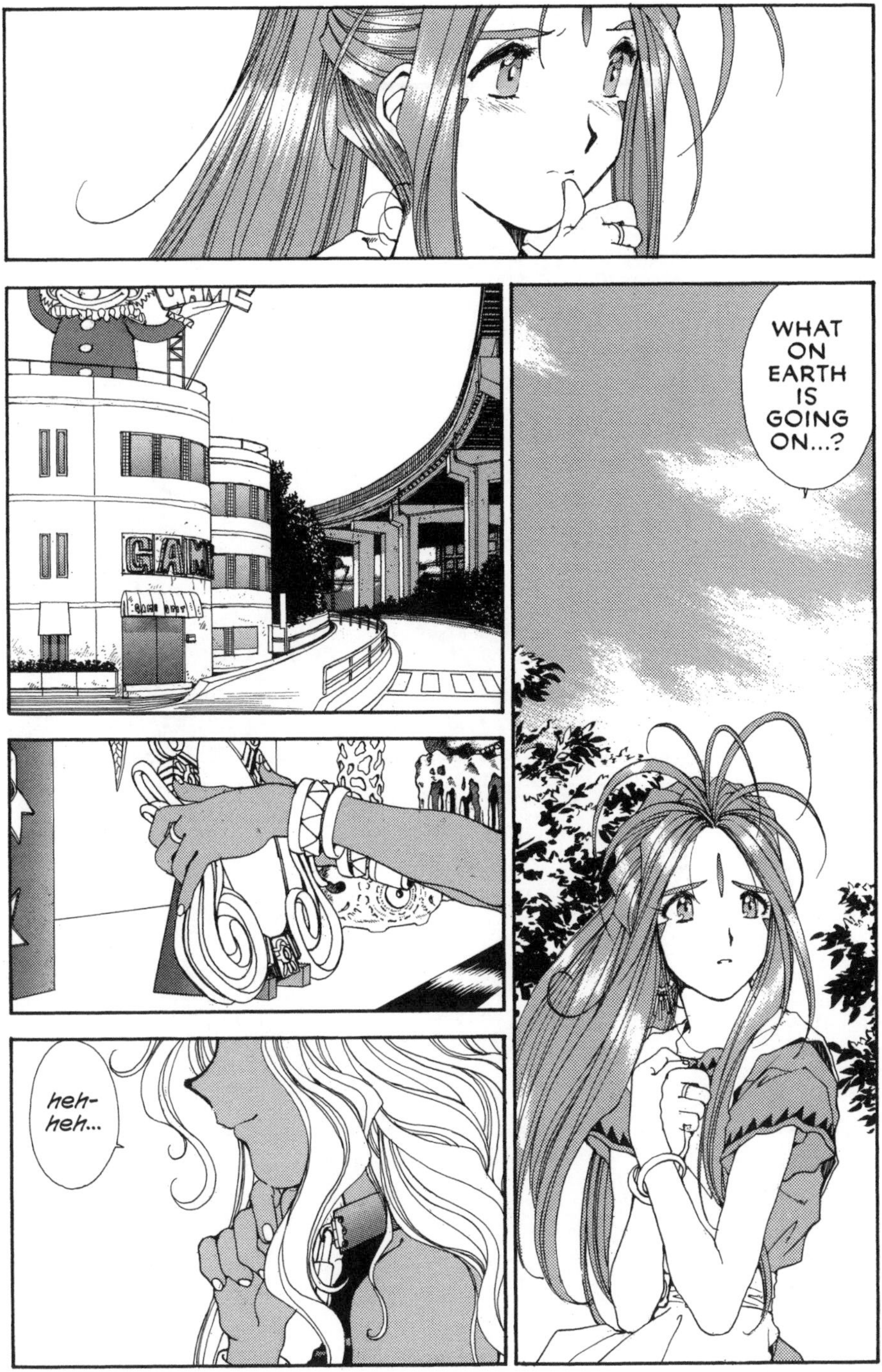
WHAT ON EARTH IS GOING ON...?
heh-heh...

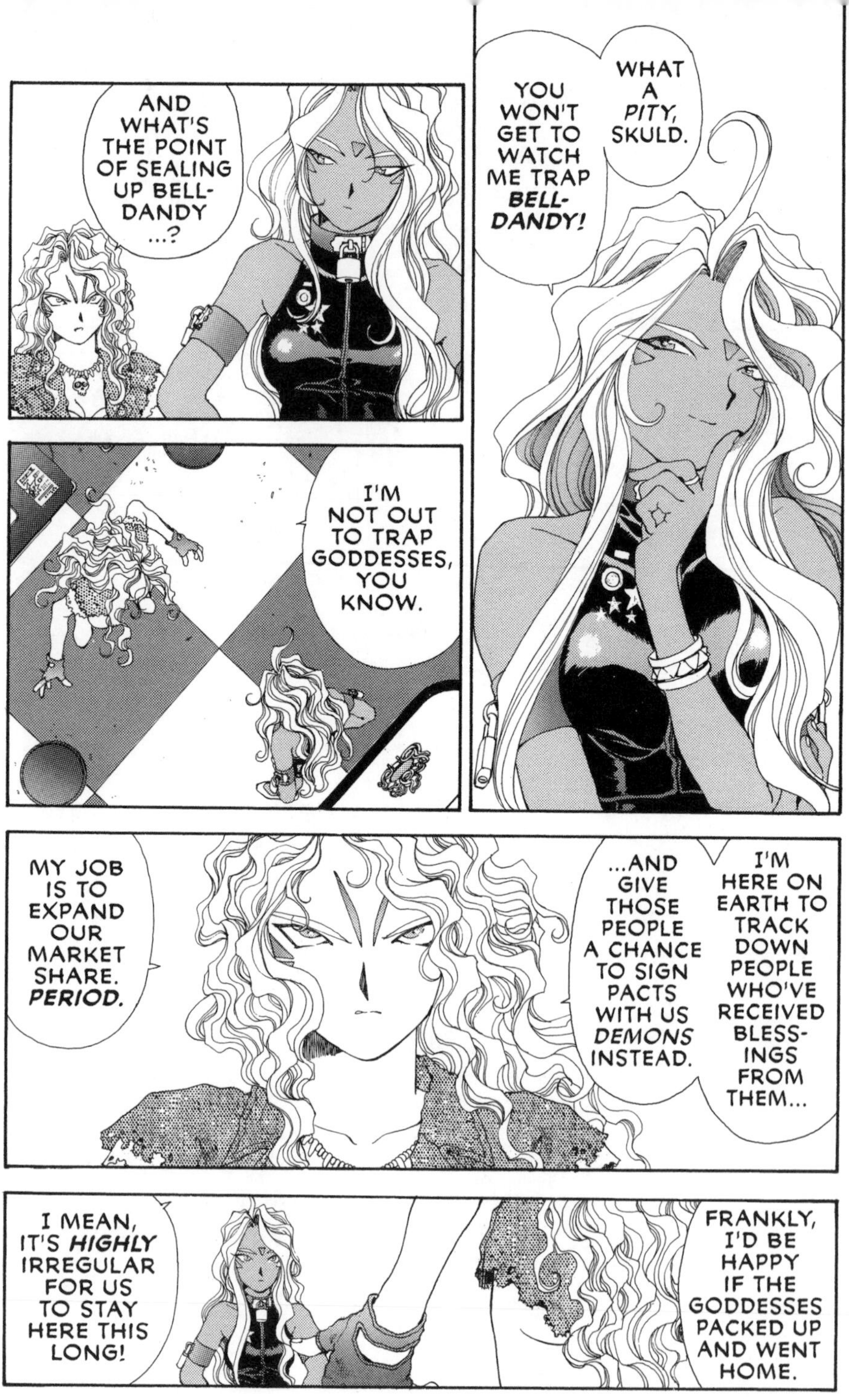
WHAT A *PITY,* SKULD.
YOU WON'T GET TO WATCH ME TRAP ***BELL-DANDY!***
AND WHAT'S THE POINT OF SEALING UP BELL-DANDY ...?
I'M NOT OUT TO TRAP GODDESSES, YOU KNOW.
I'M HERE ON EARTH TO TRACK DOWN PEOPLE WHO'VE RECEIVED BLESS-INGS FROM THEM...
...AND GIVE THOSE PEOPLE A CHANCE TO SIGN PACTS WITH US *DEMONS* INSTEAD.
MY JOB IS TO EXPAND OUR MARKET SHARE. ***PERIOD.***
FRANKLY, I'D BE HAPPY IF THE GODDESSES PACKED UP AND WENT HOME.
I MEAN, IT'S ***HIGHLY*** IRREGULAR FOR US TO STAY HERE THIS LONG!

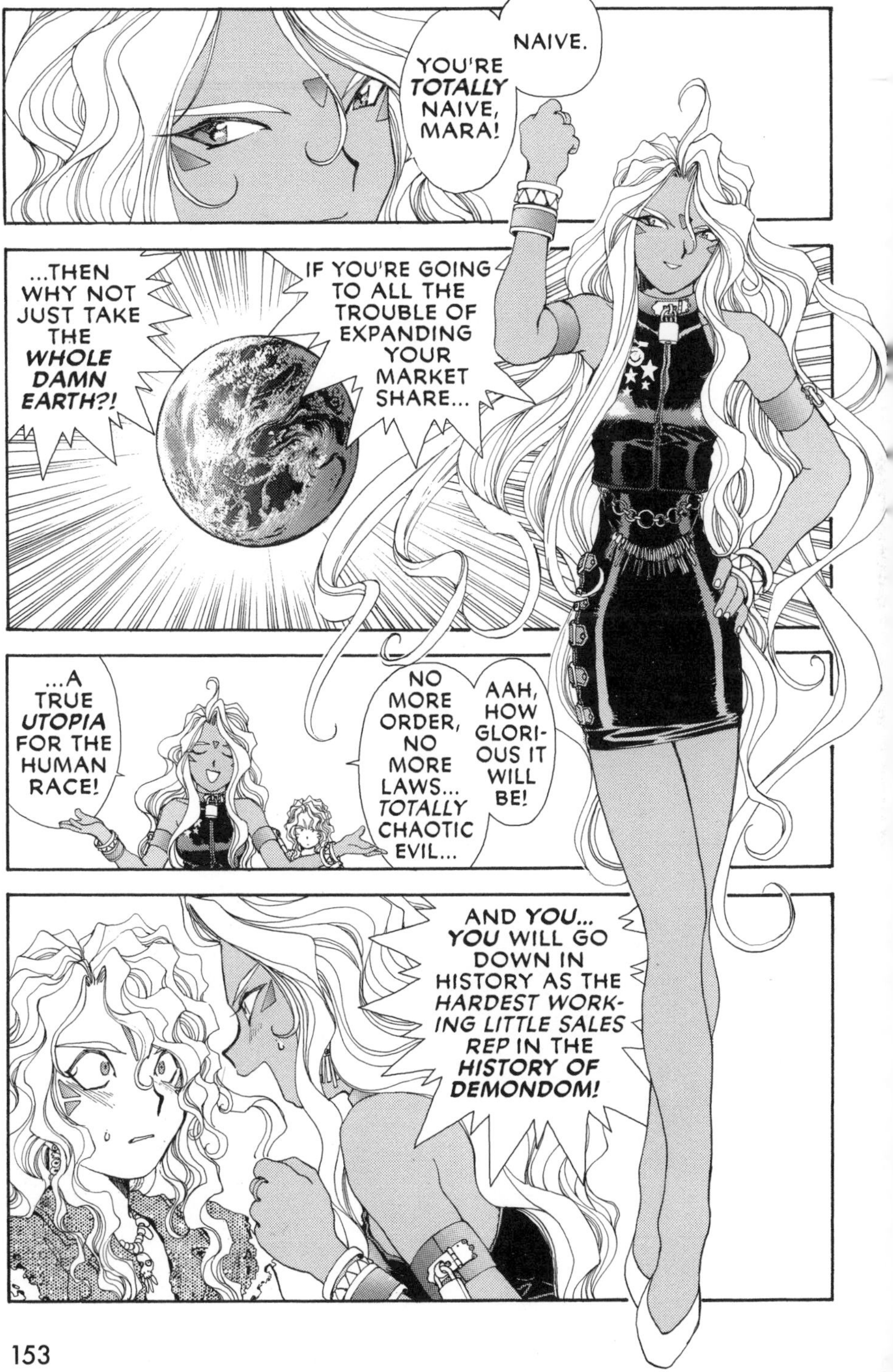
NAIVE.
YOU'RE *TOTALLY* NAIVE, MARA!
IF YOU'RE GOING TO ALL THE TROUBLE OF EXPANDING YOUR MARKET SHARE...
...THEN WHY NOT JUST TAKE THE *WHOLE DAMN EARTH?!*
AAH, HOW GLORIOUS IT WILL BE!
NO MORE ORDER, NO MORE LAWS... *TOTALLY* CHAOTIC EVIL...
...A TRUE *UTOPIA* FOR THE HUMAN RACE!
AND *YOU... YOU* WILL GO DOWN IN HISTORY AS THE *HARDEST WORKING LITTLE SALES REP* IN THE *HISTORY OF DEMONDOM!*

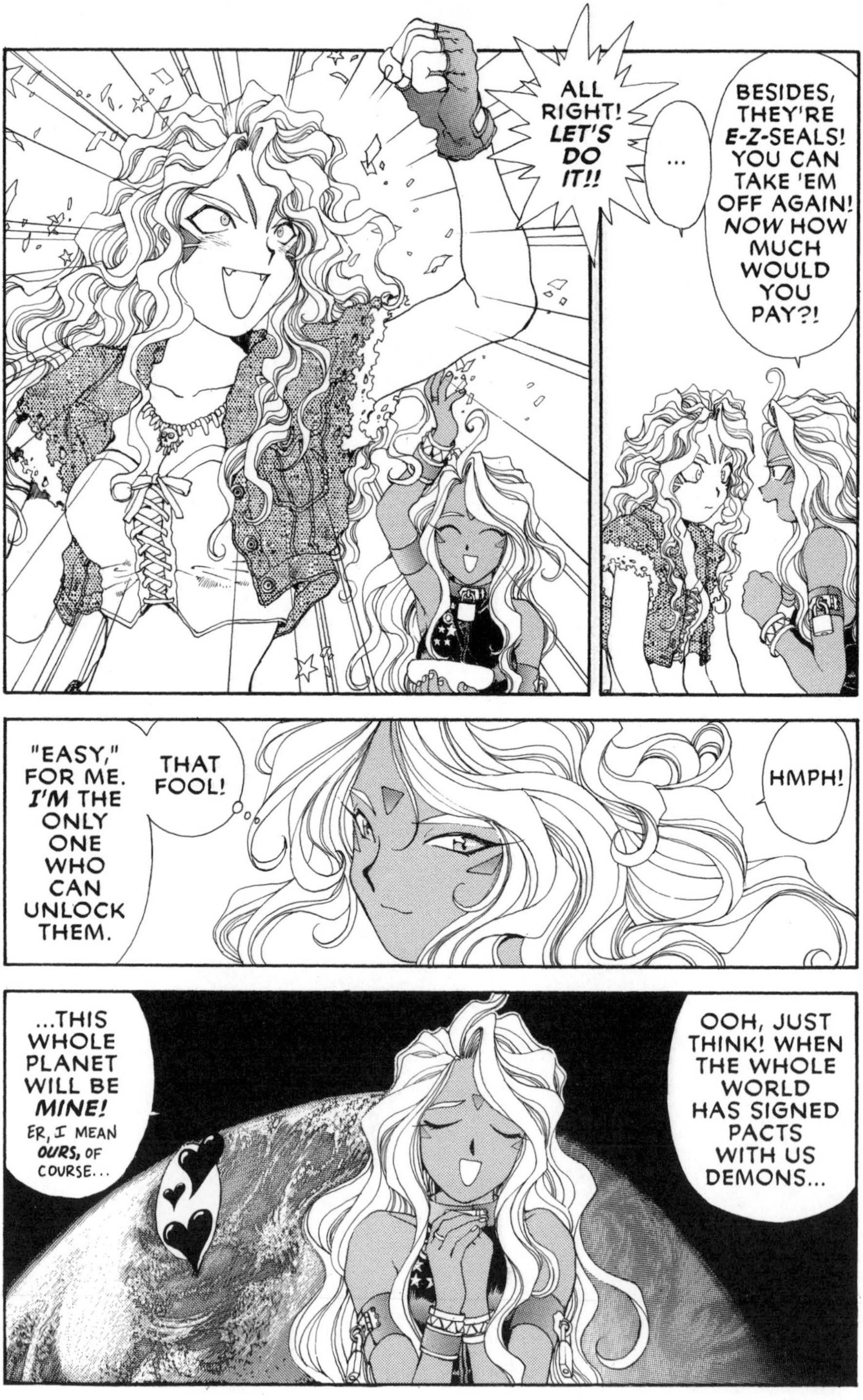
BESIDES, THEY'RE E-Z-SEALS! YOU CAN TAKE 'EM OFF AGAIN! NOW HOW MUCH WOULD YOU PAY?!
...
ALL RIGHT! LET'S DO IT!!
HMPH!
THAT FOOL!
"EASY," FOR ME. I'M THE ONLY ONE WHO CAN UNLOCK THEM.
OOH, JUST THINK! WHEN THE WHOLE WORLD HAS SIGNED PACTS WITH US DEMONS...
...THIS WHOLE PLANET WILL BE MINE!
ER, I MEAN OURS, OF COURSE...

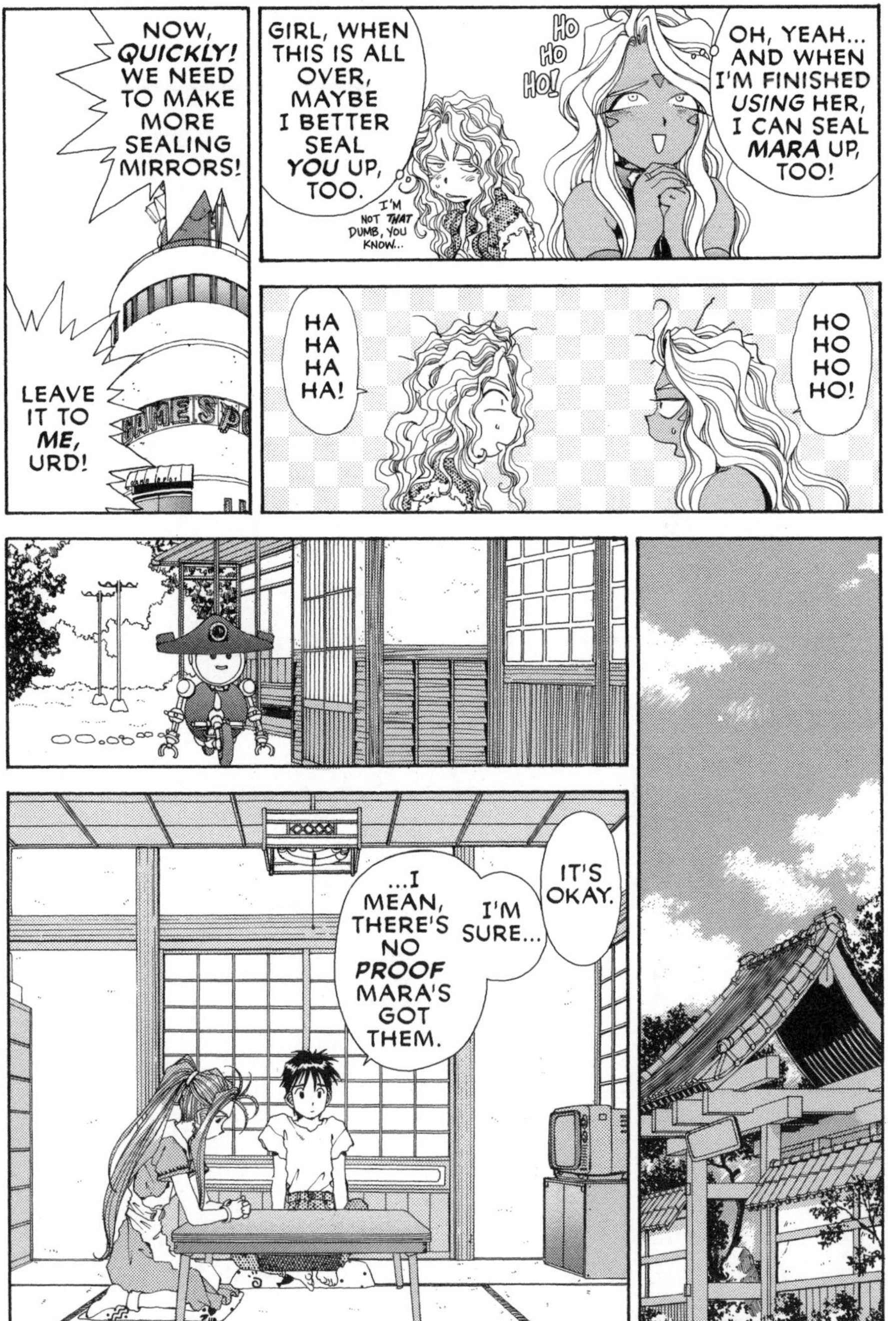
HO HO HO!
OH, YEAH... AND WHEN I'M FINISHED USING HER, I CAN SEAL MARA UP, TOO!
GIRL, WHEN THIS IS ALL OVER, MAYBE I BETTER SEAL YOU UP, TOO.
I'M NOT THAT DUMB, YOU KNOW...
HO HO HO HO!
HA HA HA HA!
NOW, QUICKLY! WE NEED TO MAKE MORE SEALING MIRRORS!
LEAVE IT TO ME, URD!
IT'S OKAY.
I'M SURE...
...I MEAN, THERE'S NO PROOF MARA'S GOT THEM.

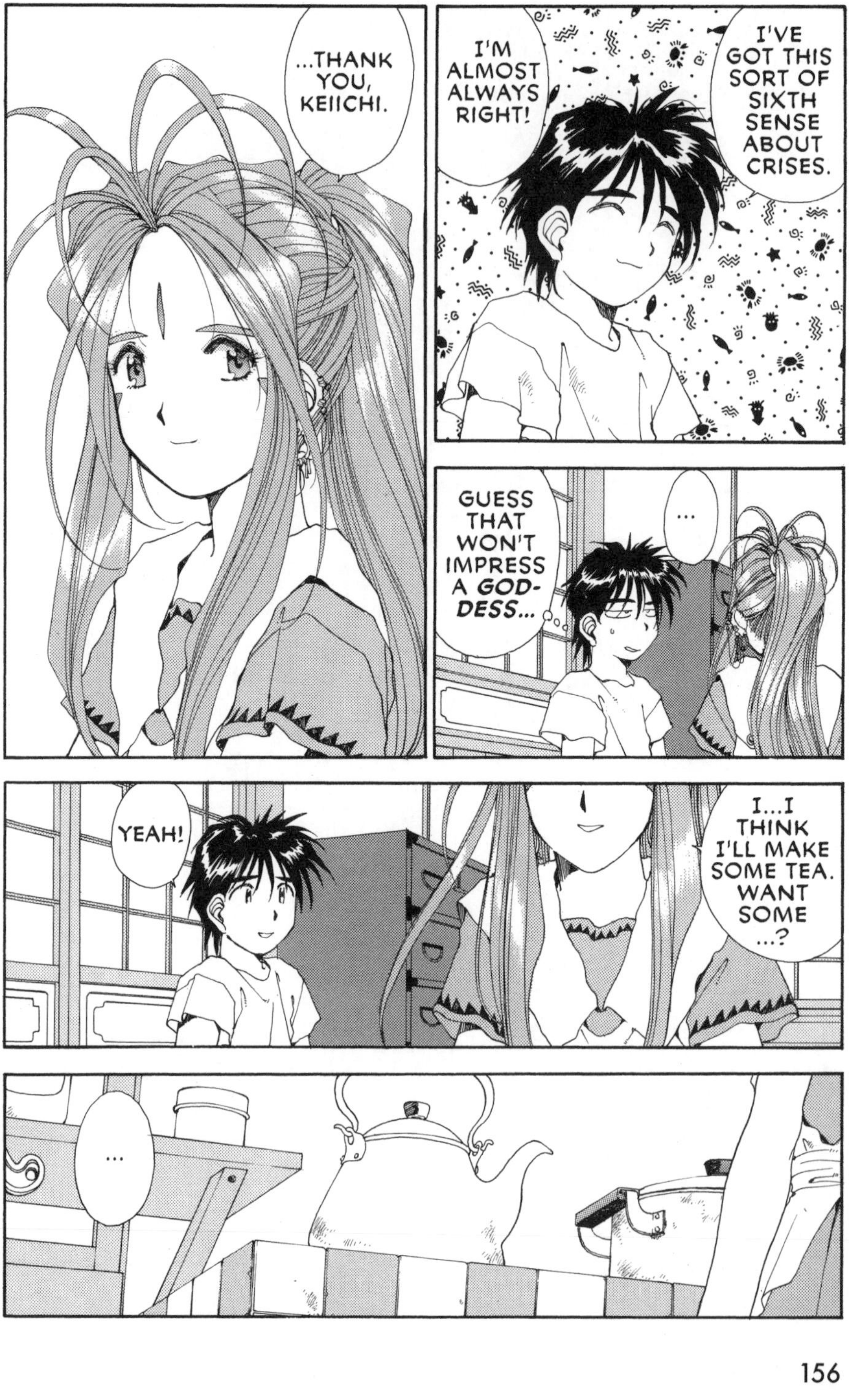

I'VE GOT THIS SORT OF SIXTH SENSE ABOUT CRISES.
I'M ALMOST ALWAYS RIGHT!
...
GUESS THAT WON'T IMPRESS A *GODDESS*...
...THANK YOU, KEIICHI.
I...I THINK I'LL MAKE SOME TEA. WANT SOME ...?
YEAH!
...

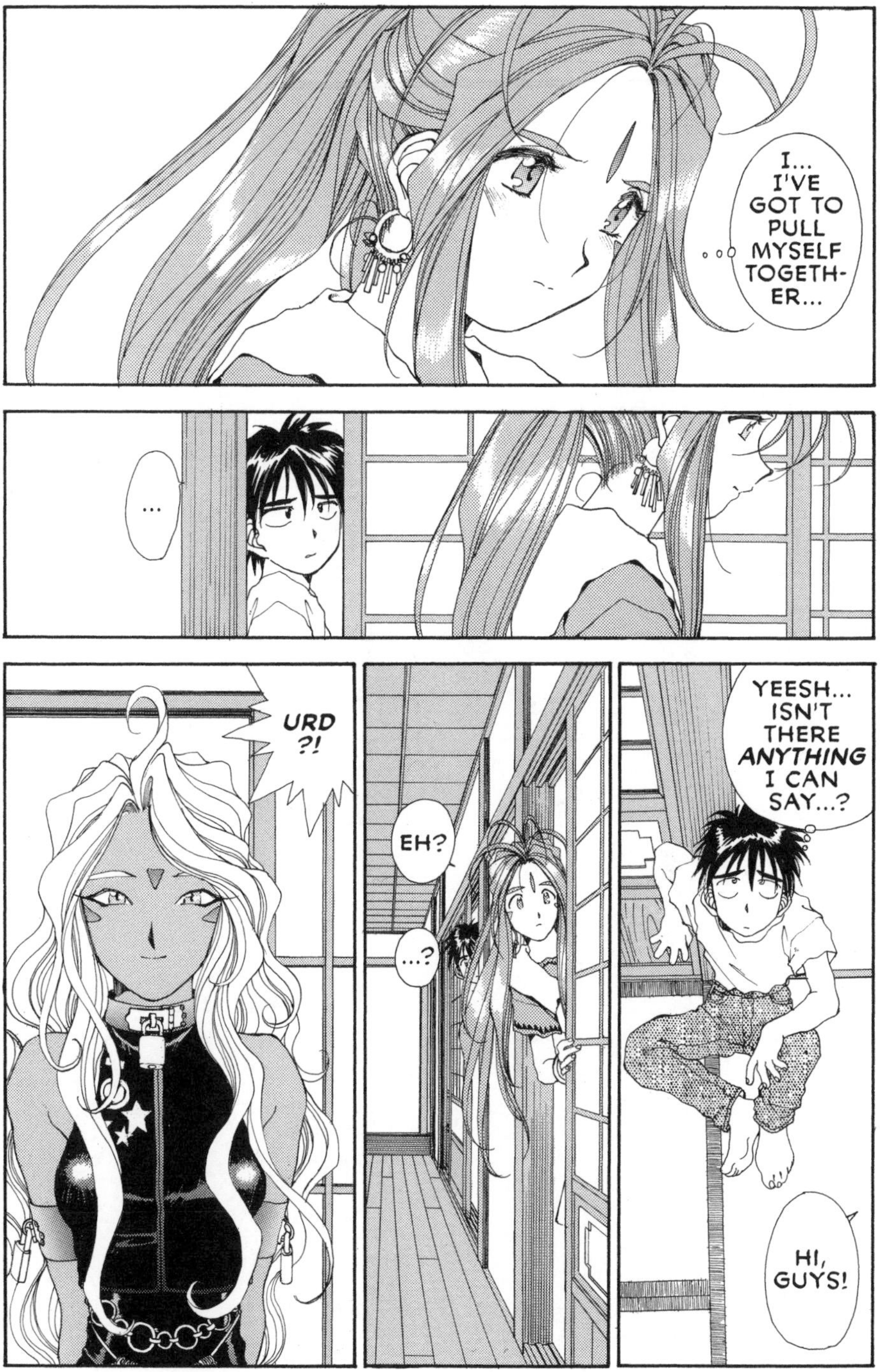
I... I'VE GOT TO PULL MYSELF TOGETHER...
...
YEESH... ISN'T THERE *ANYTHING* I CAN SAY...?
HI, GUYS!
EH?
...?
URD ?!

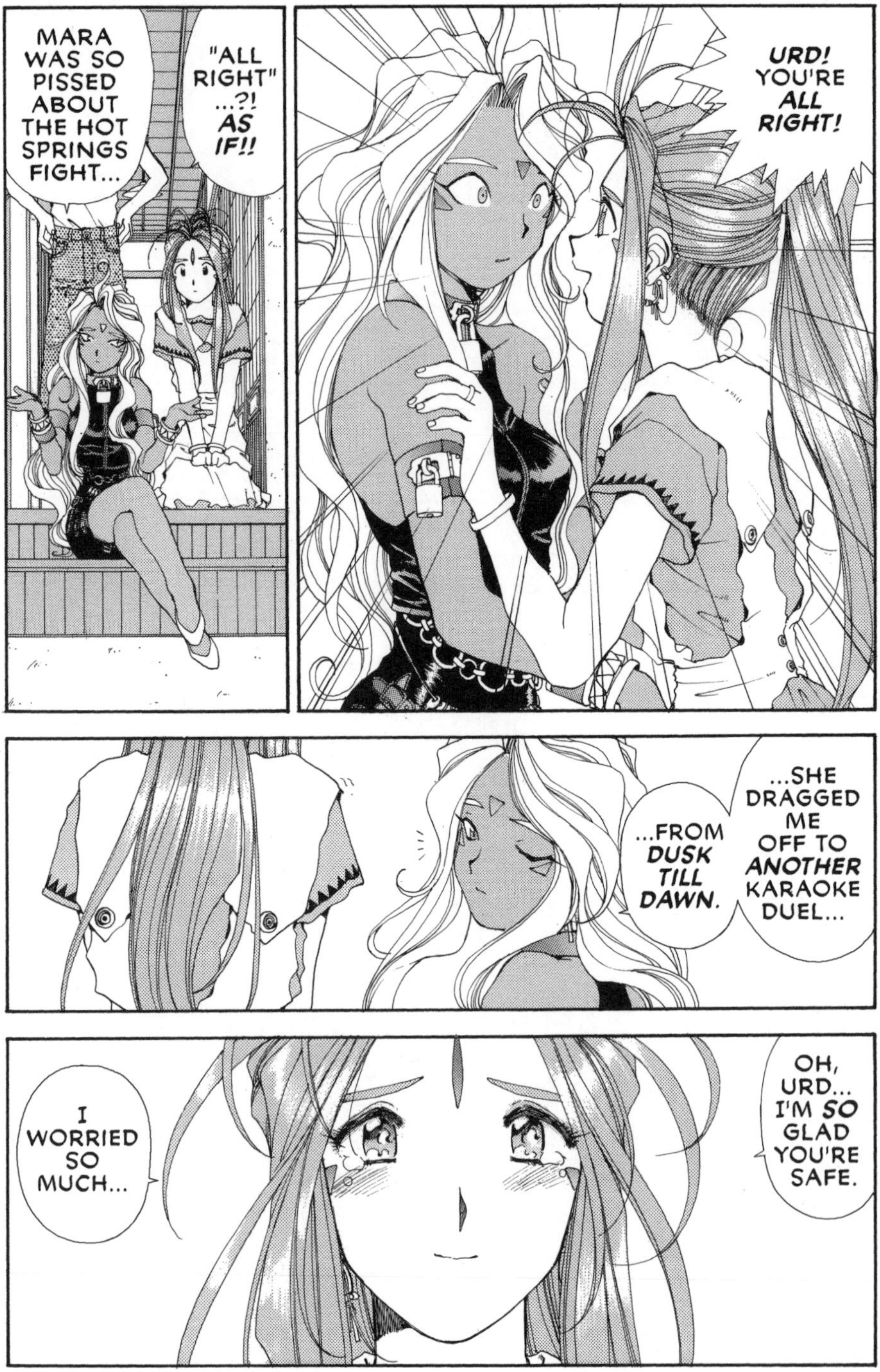
URD! YOU'RE ALL RIGHT!
"ALL RIGHT" ...?! AS IF!!
MARA WAS SO PISSED ABOUT THE HOT SPRINGS FIGHT...
...SHE DRAGGED ME OFF TO ANOTHER KARAOKE DUEL...
...FROM DUSK TILL DAWN.
OH, URD... I'M SO GLAD YOU'RE SAFE.
I WORRIED SO MUCH...

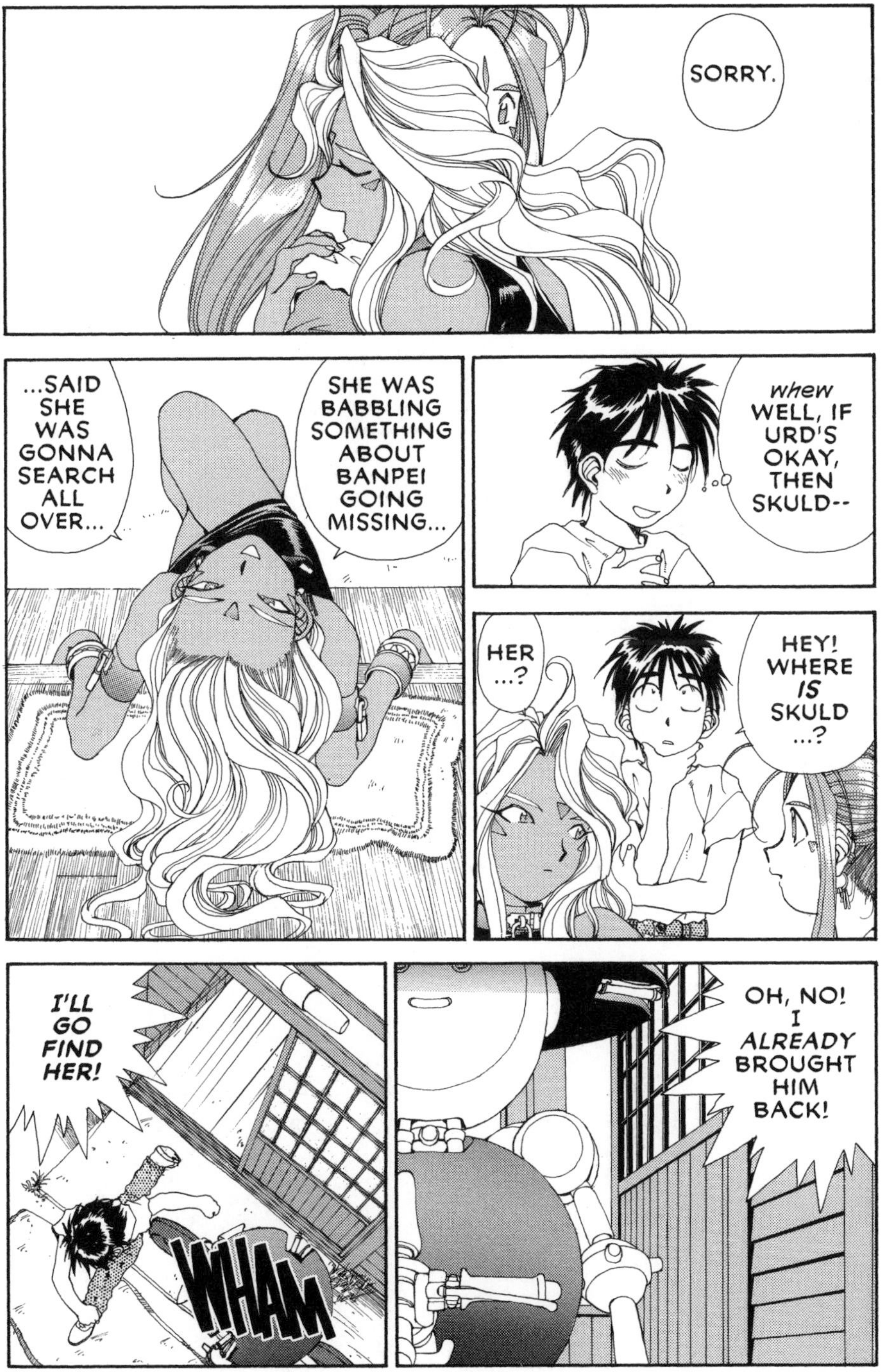
SORRY.
whew WELL, IF URD'S OKAY, THEN SKULD--
HEY! WHERE *IS* SKULD ...?
HER ...?
SHE WAS BABBLING SOMETHING ABOUT BANPEI GOING MISSING...
...SAID SHE WAS GONNA SEARCH ALL OVER...
OH, NO! I *ALREADY* BROUGHT HIM BACK!
I'LL GO FIND HER!
WHAM

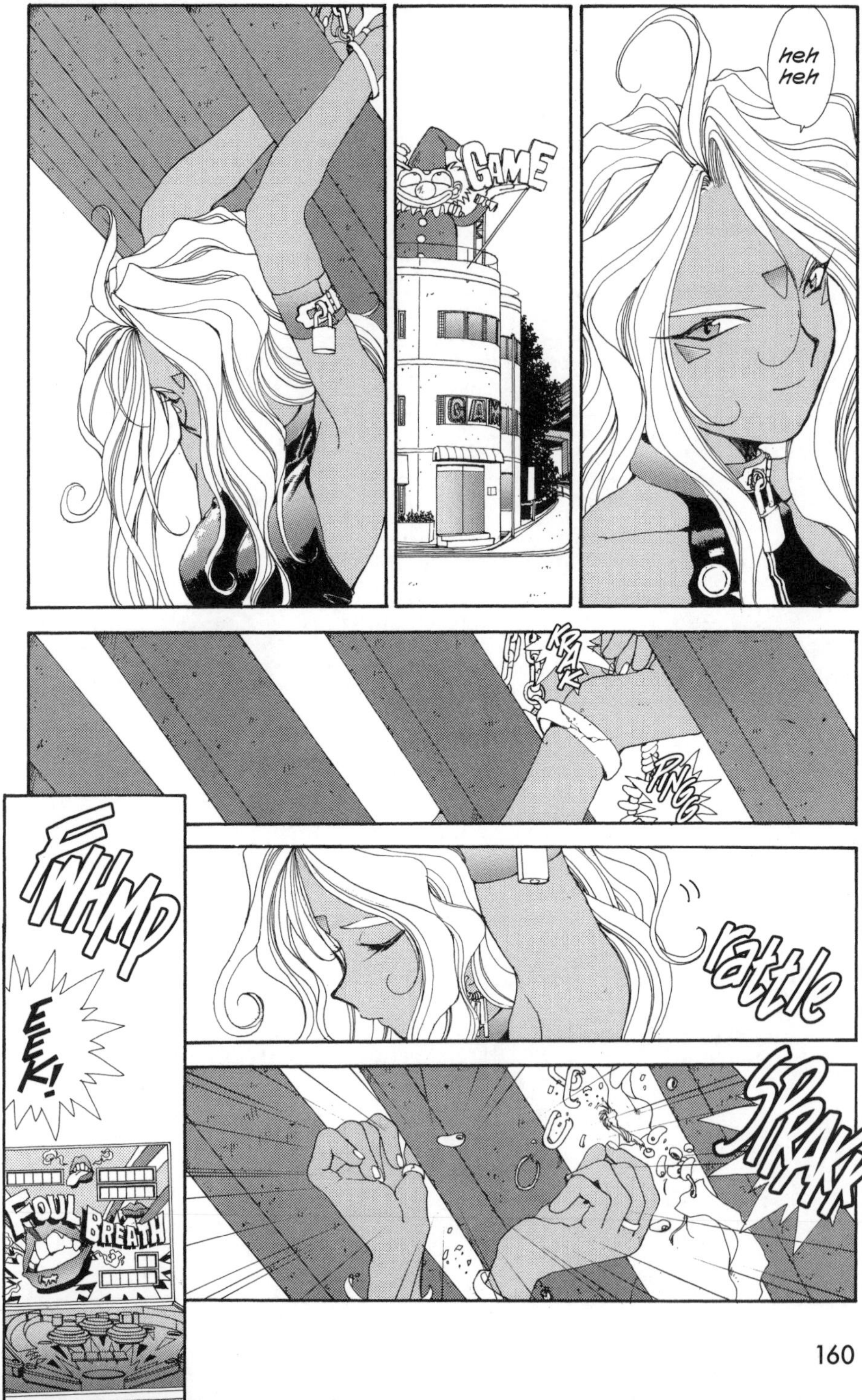
heh heh
GAME
KRAK
PINGG
rattle
SPRAKK
FWHMP
EEEK!
FOUL BREATH

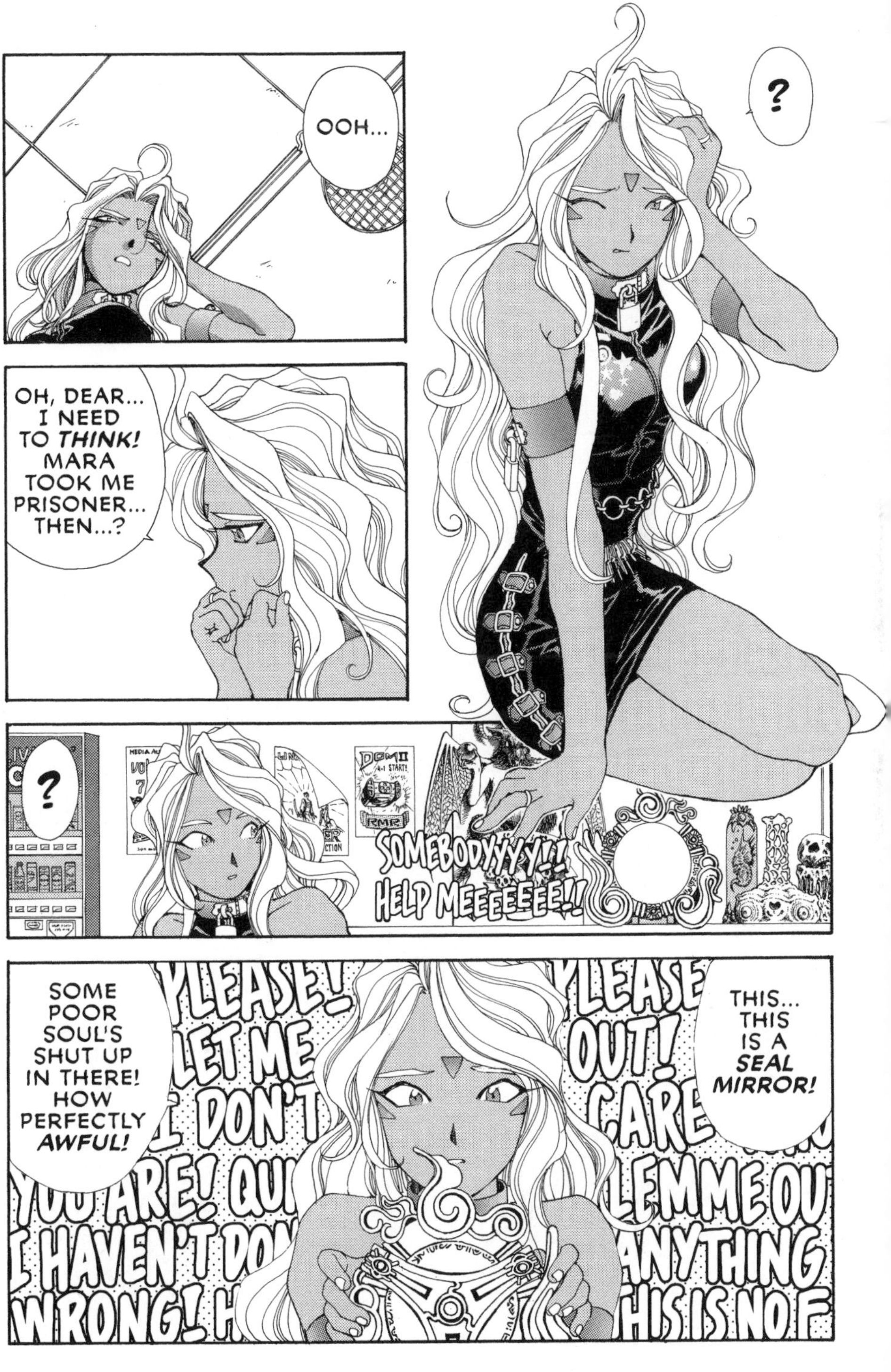
?
OOH...
OH, DEAR... I NEED TO *THINK!* MARA TOOK ME PRISONER... THEN...?
SOMEBODYYYY!! HELP MEEEEEEE!!
?
THIS... THIS IS A *SEAL MIRROR!*
PLEASE! LET ME OUT! I DON'T CARE YOU ARE! LEMME OU I HAVEN'T DON ANYTHING WRONG! THIS IS NOF
SOME POOR SOUL'S SHUT UP IN THERE! HOW PERFECTLY *AWFUL!*

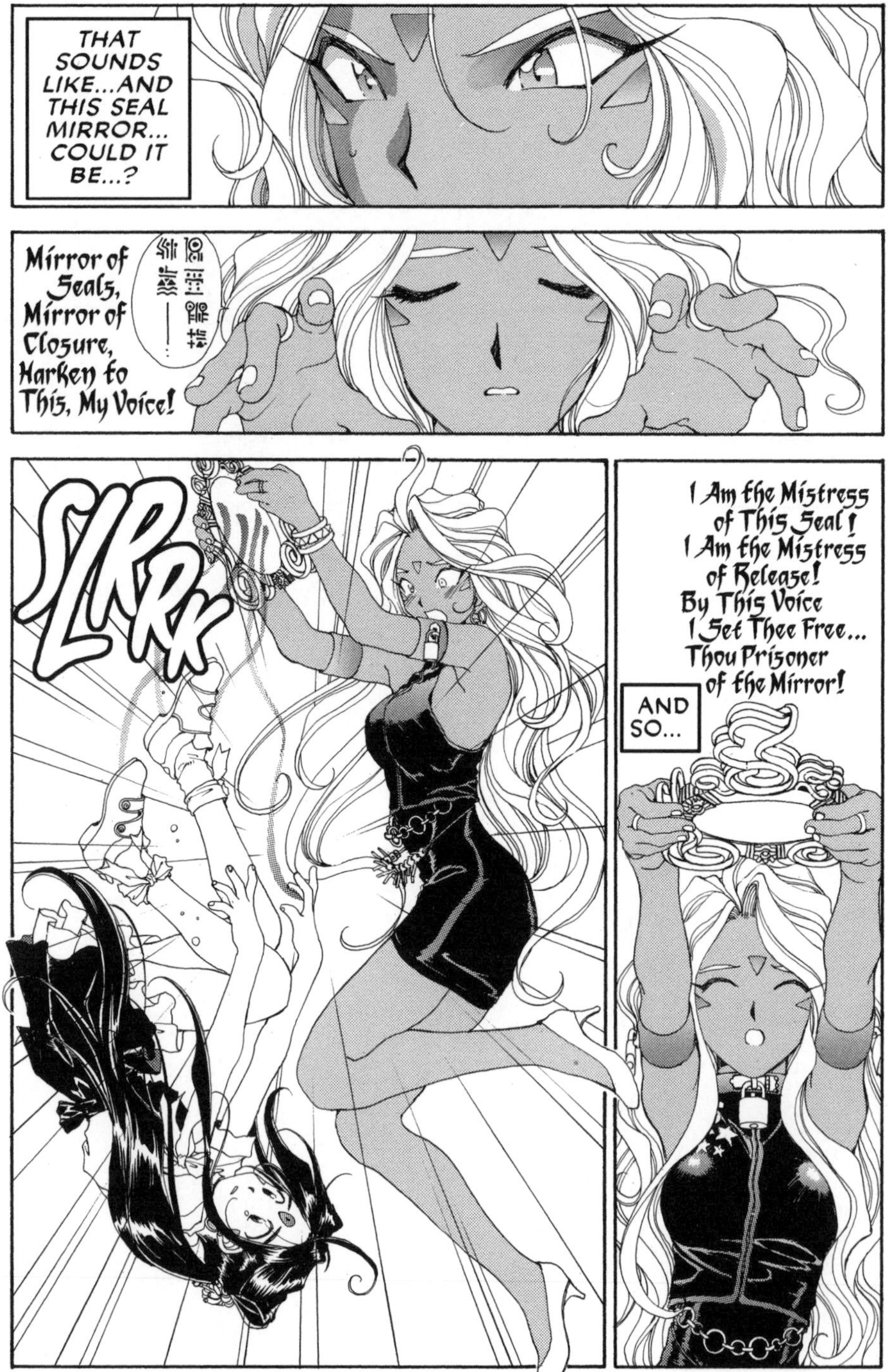
THAT SOUNDS LIKE...AND THIS SEAL MIRROR... COULD IT BE...?
Mirror of Seals, Mirror of Closure, Harken to This, My Voice!
I Am the Mistress of This Seal! I Am the Mistress of Release! By This Voice I Set Thee Free... Thou Prisoner of the Mirror!
AND SO...
SLRRK

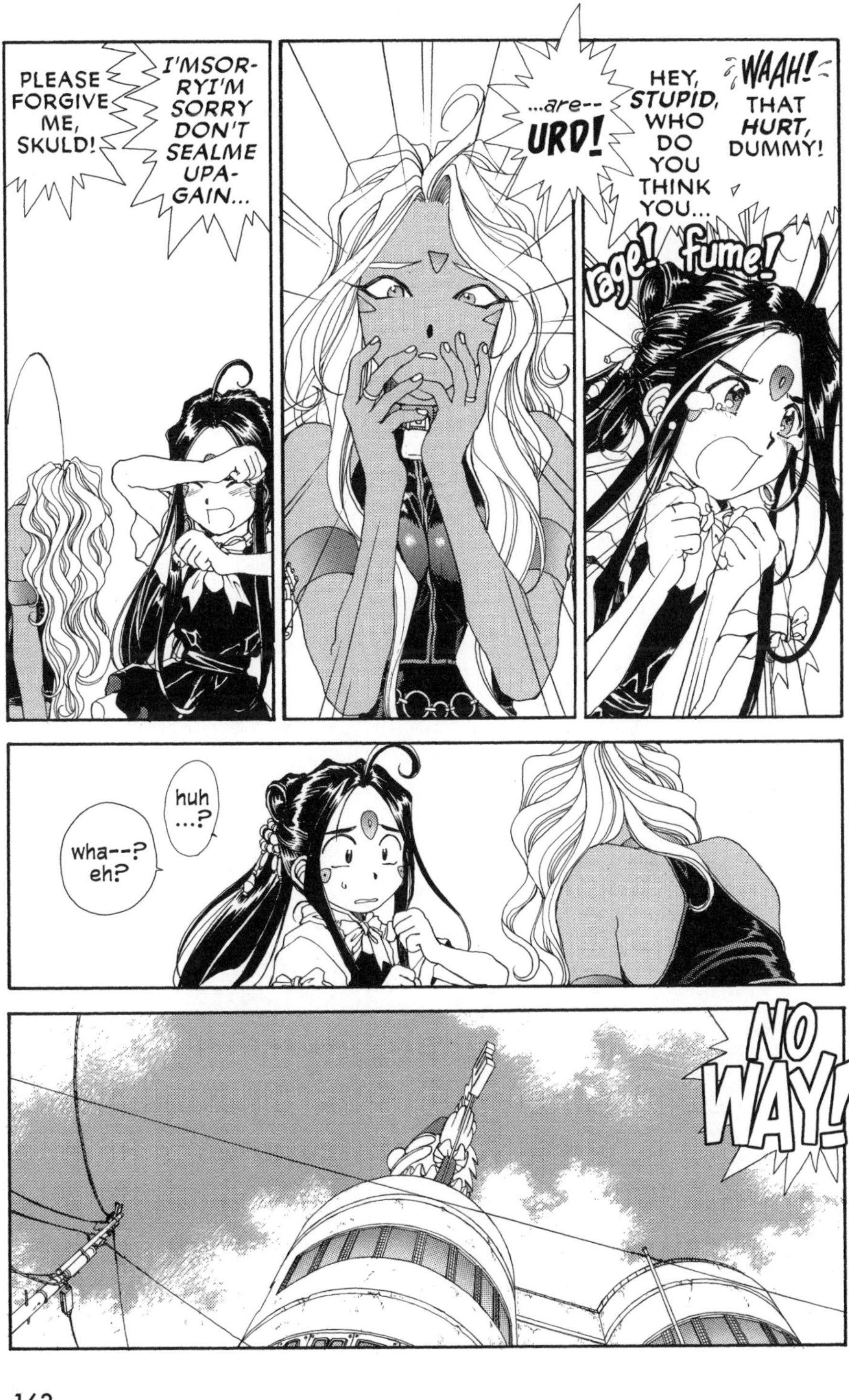
WAAH! THAT HURT, DUMMY!
HEY, STUPID, WHO DO YOU THINK YOU...
...are-- URD!
fume!
rage!
I'MSORRYI'M SORRY DON'T SEALME UPAGAIN...
PLEASE FORGIVE ME, SKULD!
huh ...?
wha--? eh?
NO WAY!

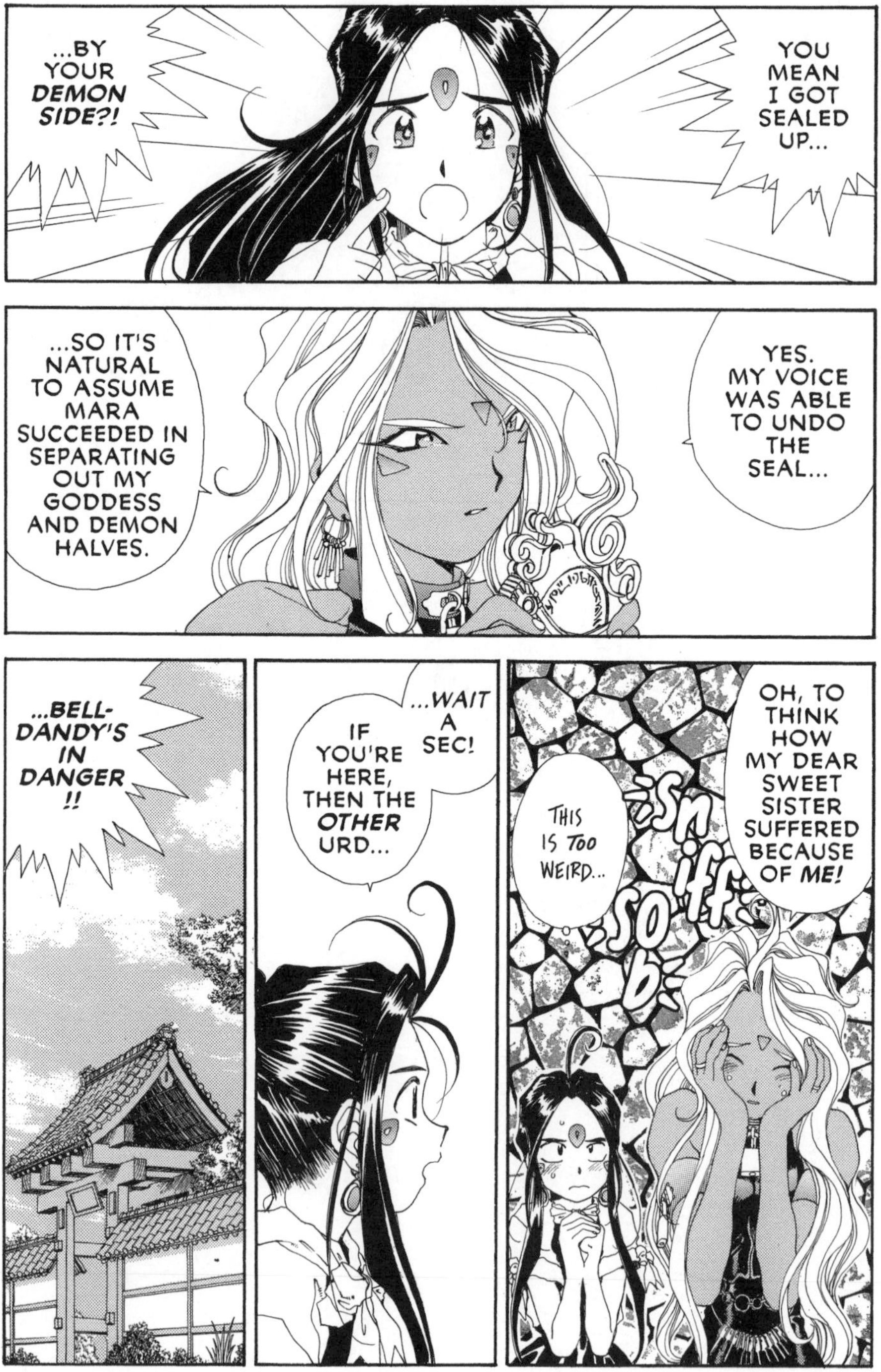
YOU MEAN I GOT SEALED UP...
...BY YOUR DEMON SIDE?!
YES. MY VOICE WAS ABLE TO UNDO THE SEAL...
...SO IT'S NATURAL TO ASSUME MARA SUCCEEDED IN SEPARATING OUT MY GODDESS AND DEMON HALVES.
OH, TO THINK HOW MY DEAR SWEET SISTER SUFFERED BECAUSE OF ME!
SNIFF
SOB
THIS IS TOO WEIRD...
...WAIT A SEC!
IF YOU'RE HERE, THEN THE OTHER URD...
...BELL-DANDY'S IN DANGER!!

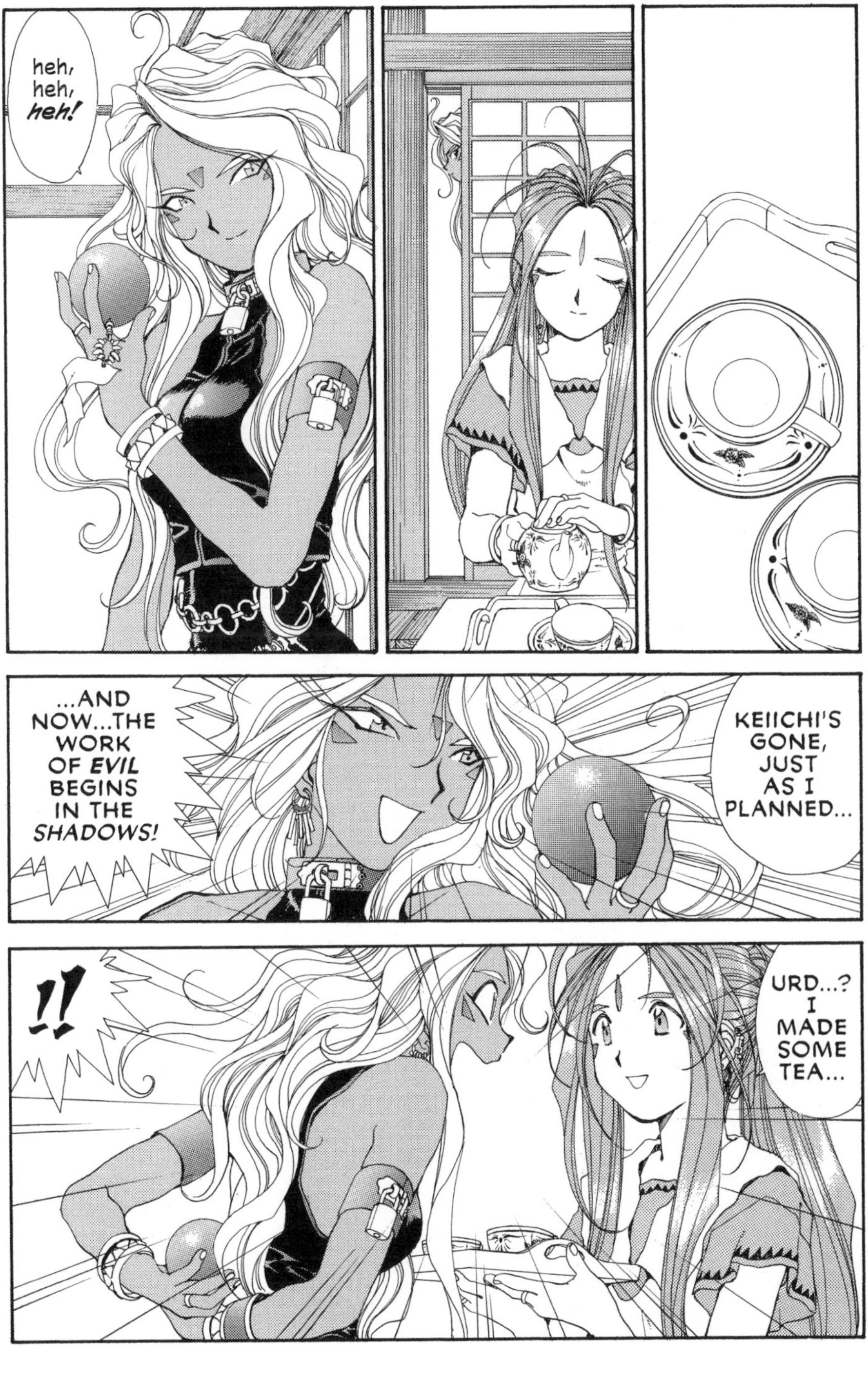
heh, heh, *heh!*
KEIICHI'S GONE, JUST AS I PLANNED...
...AND NOW...THE WORK OF *EVIL* BEGINS IN THE *SHADOWS!*
URD...? I MADE SOME TEA...
!!

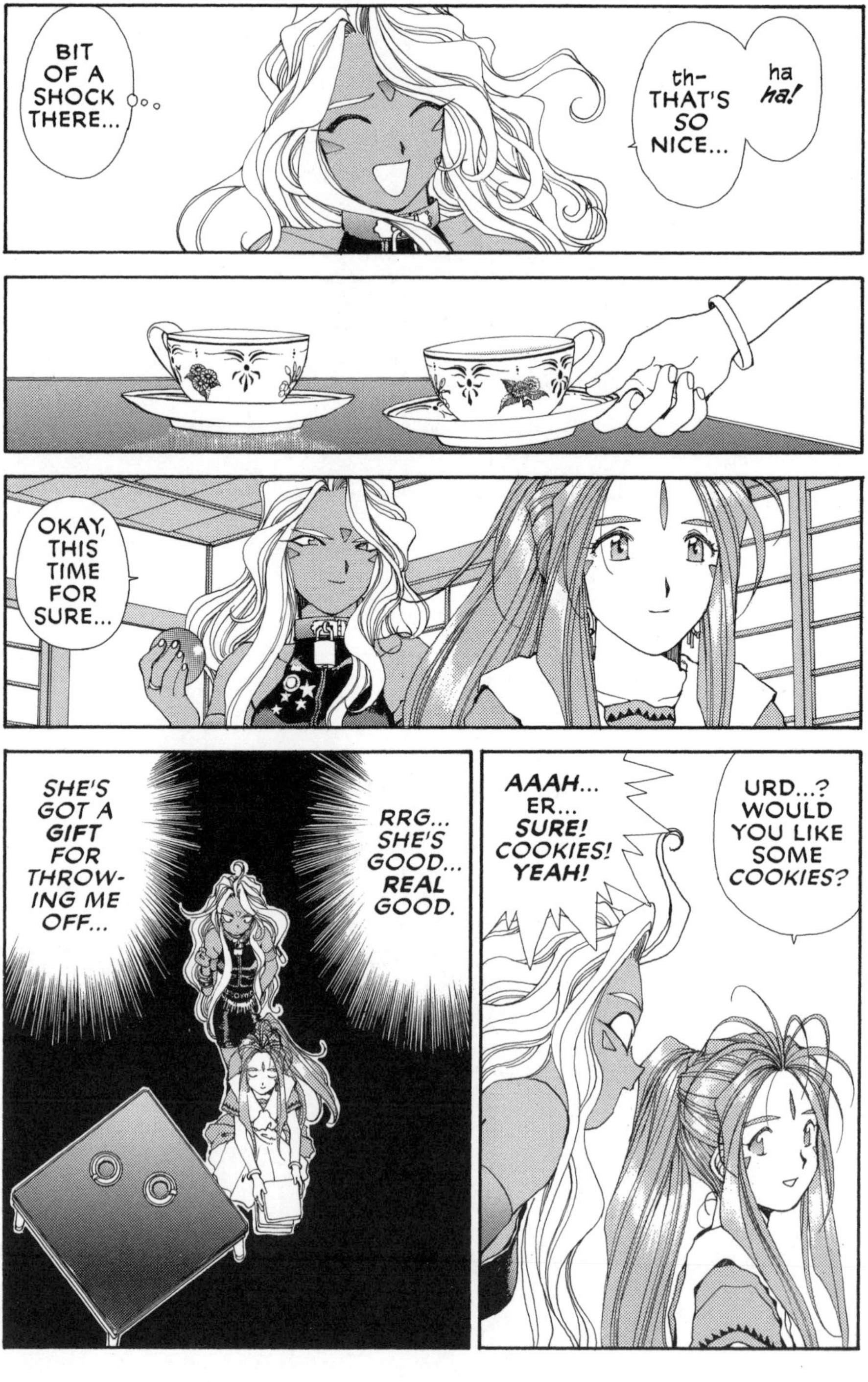
ha ha!
th- THAT'S SO NICE...
BIT OF A SHOCK THERE...
OKAY, THIS TIME FOR SURE...
URD...? WOULD YOU LIKE SOME COOKIES?
AAAH... ER... SURE! COOKIES! YEAH!
RRG... SHE'S GOOD... REAL GOOD.
SHE'S GOT A GIFT FOR THROWING ME OFF...

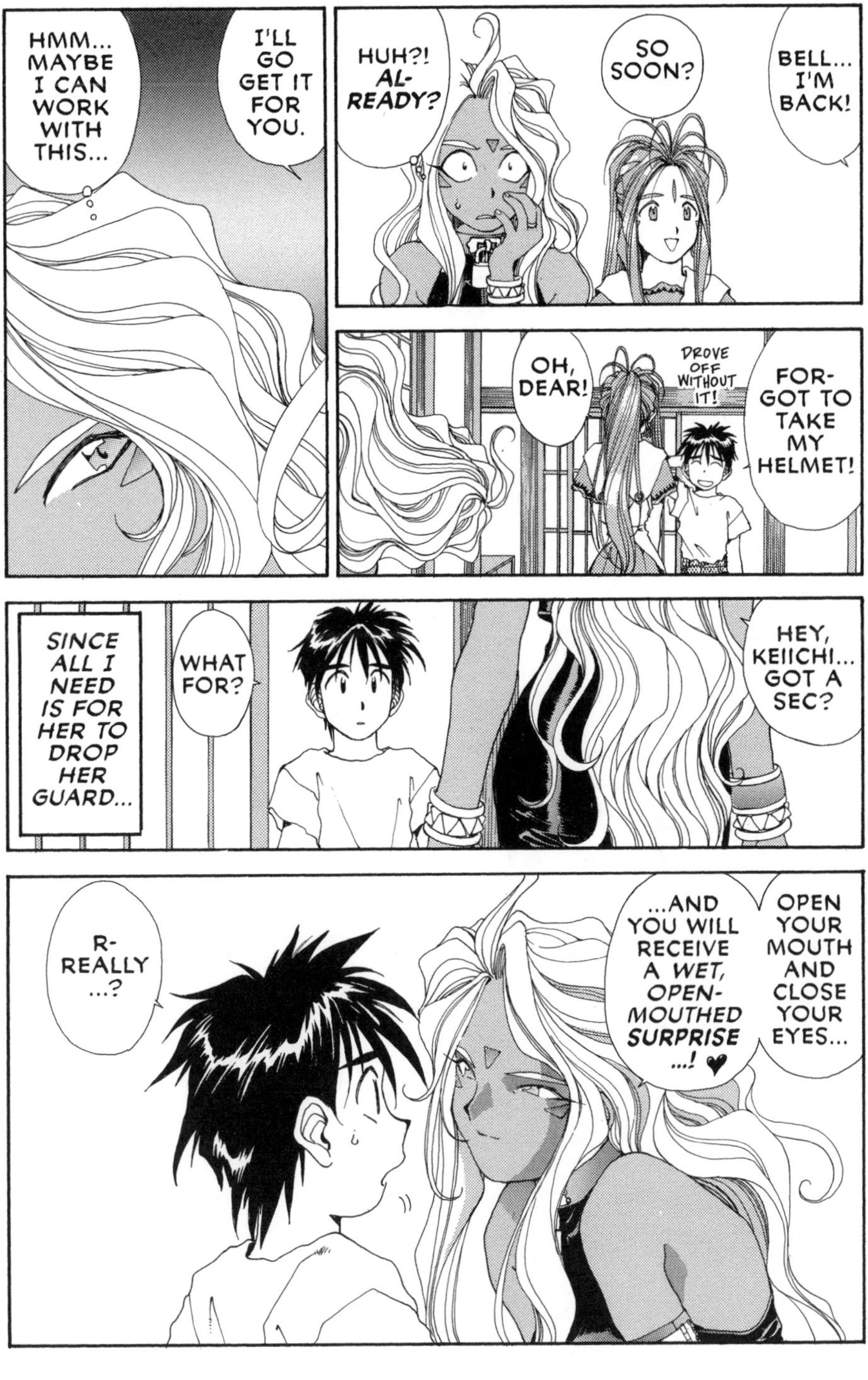
BELL... I'M BACK!
SO SOON?
HUH?! AL-READY?
FOR-GOT TO TAKE MY HELMET!
DROVE OFF WITHOUT IT!
OH, DEAR!
I'LL GO GET IT FOR YOU.
HMM... MAYBE I CAN WORK WITH THIS...
HEY, KEIICHI... GOT A SEC?
WHAT FOR?
SINCE ALL I NEED IS FOR HER TO DROP HER GUARD...
OPEN YOUR MOUTH AND CLOSE YOUR EYES...
...AND YOU WILL RECEIVE A WET, OPEN-MOUTHED SURPRISE ...! ♥
R-REALLY ...?

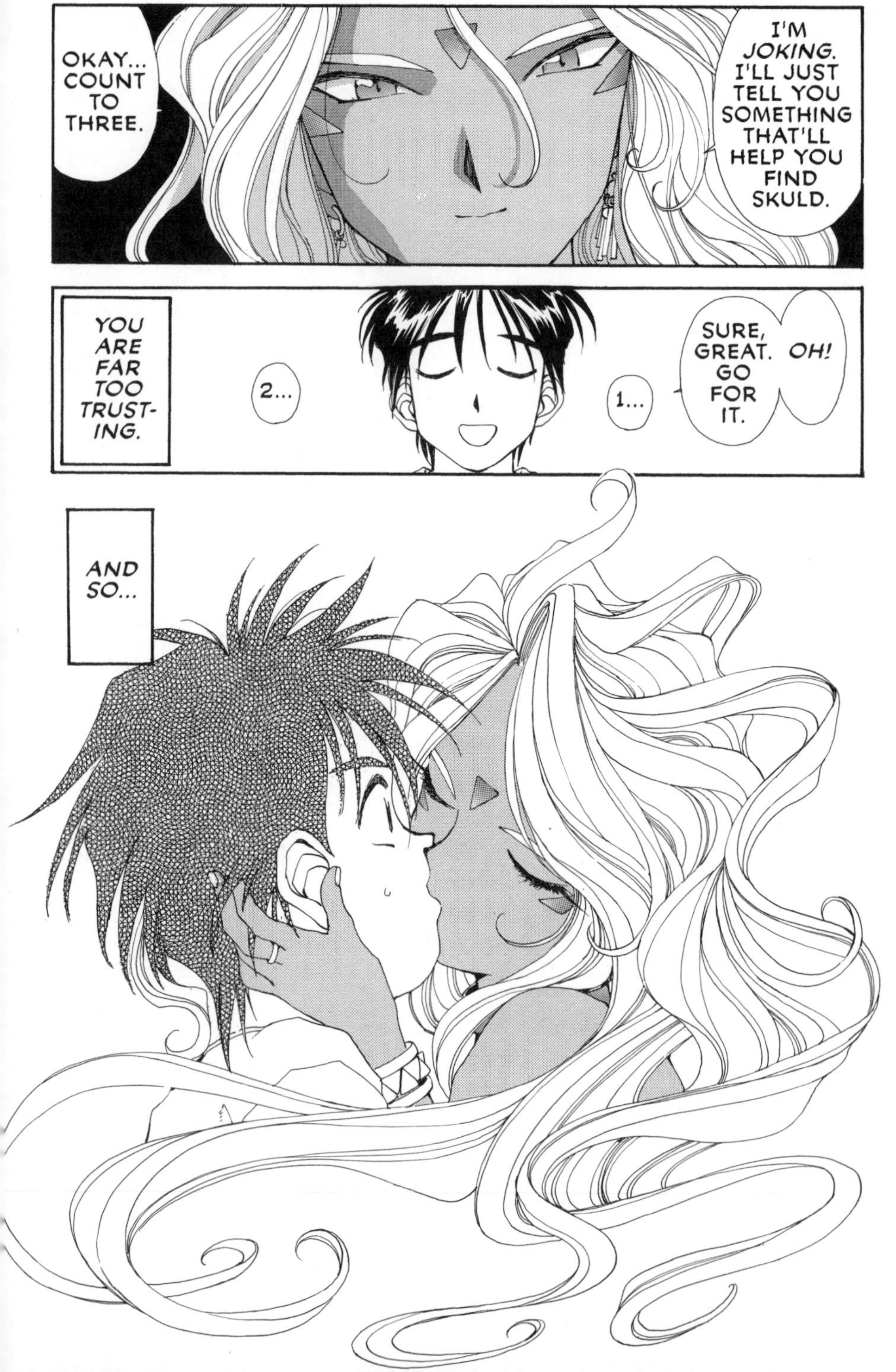

I'M JOKING. I'LL JUST TELL YOU SOMETHING THAT'LL HELP YOU FIND SKULD.
OKAY... COUNT TO THREE.
OH!
SURE, GREAT. GO FOR IT.
1...
2...
YOU ARE FAR TOO TRUSTING.
AND SO...

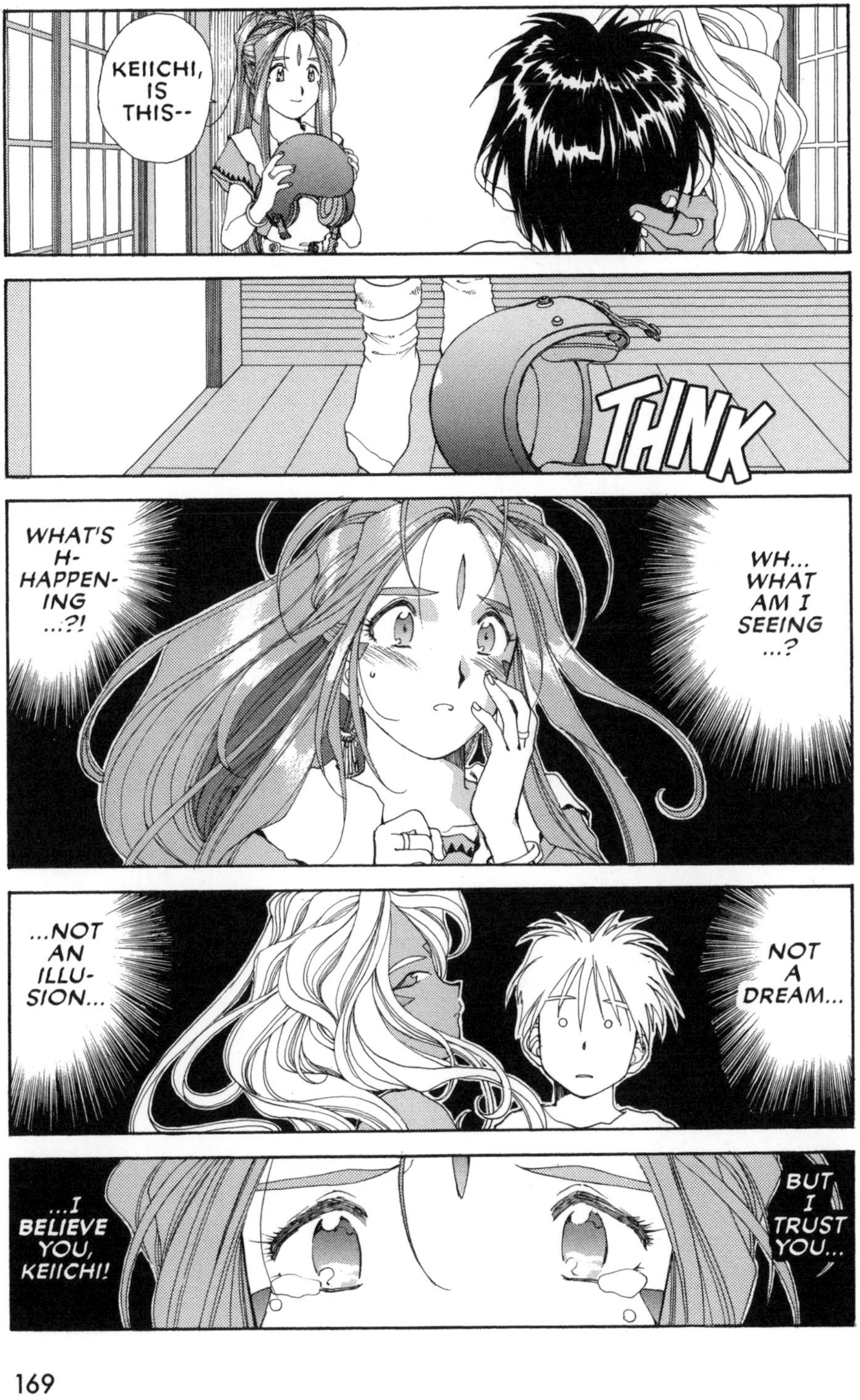
KEIICHI, IS THIS--
THINK
WH... WHAT AM I SEEING ...?
WHAT'S H-HAPPEN-ING ...?!
NOT A DREAM...
...NOT AN ILLU-SION...
BUT I TRUST YOU...
...I BELIEVE YOU, KEIICHI!

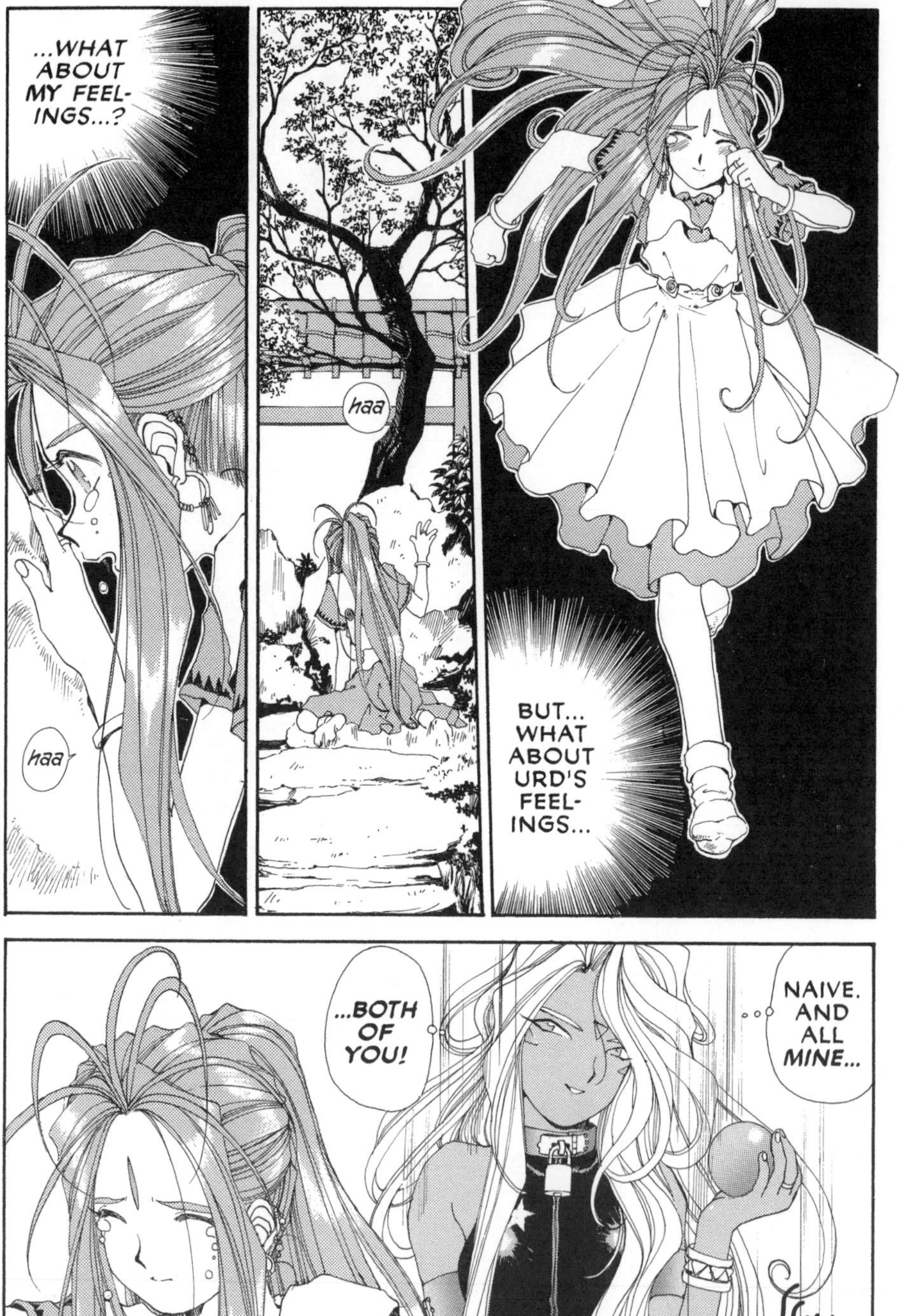

BUT... WHAT ABOUT URD'S FEEL-INGS...
haa
...WHAT ABOUT MY FEEL-INGS...?
haa
NAIVE. AND ALL MINE...
...BOTH OF YOU!
SSHH

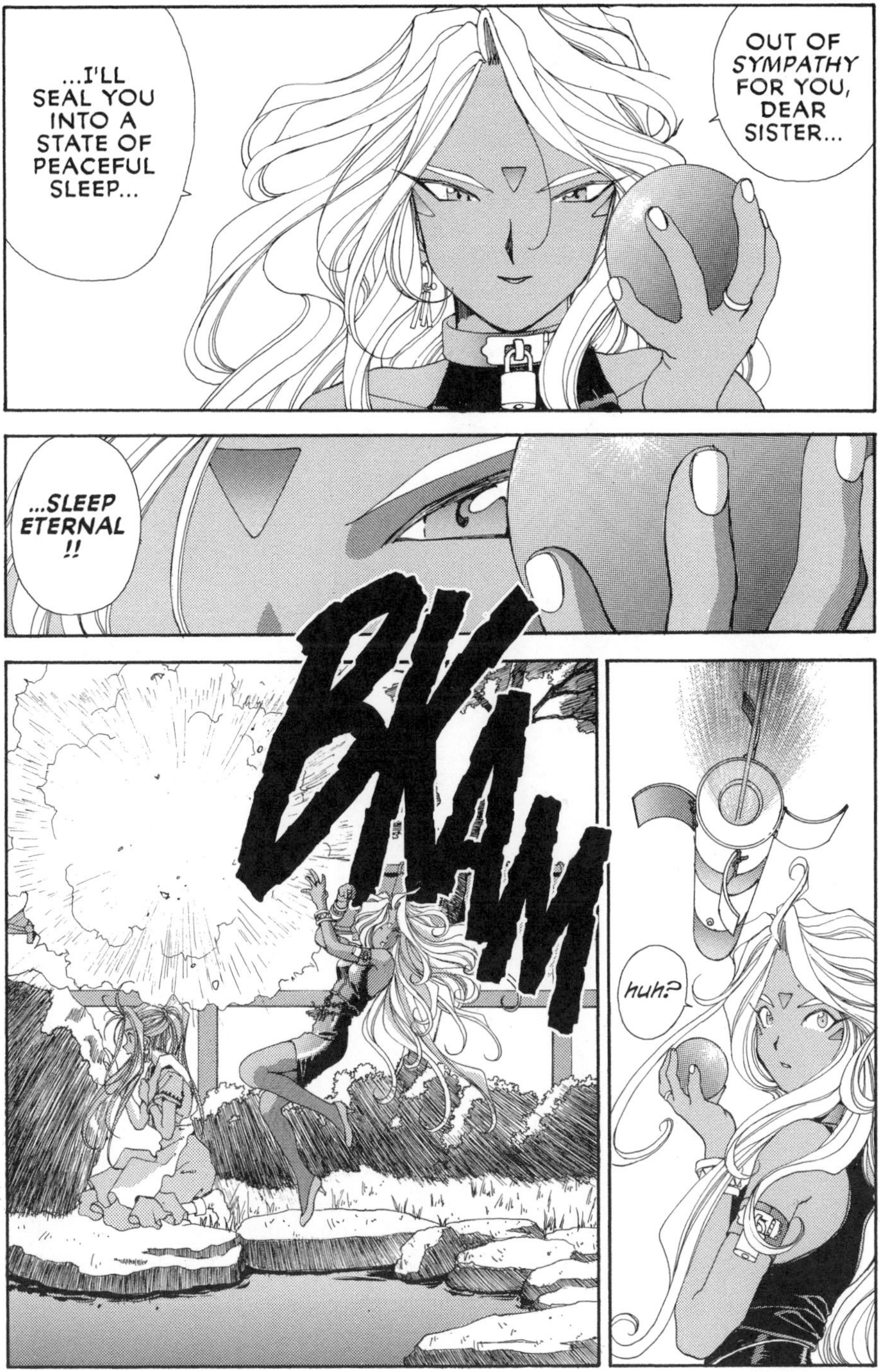
OUT OF SYMPATHY FOR YOU, DEAR SISTER...
...I'LL SEAL YOU INTO A STATE OF PEACEFUL SLEEP...
...SLEEP ETERNAL !!
BKAM
huh?

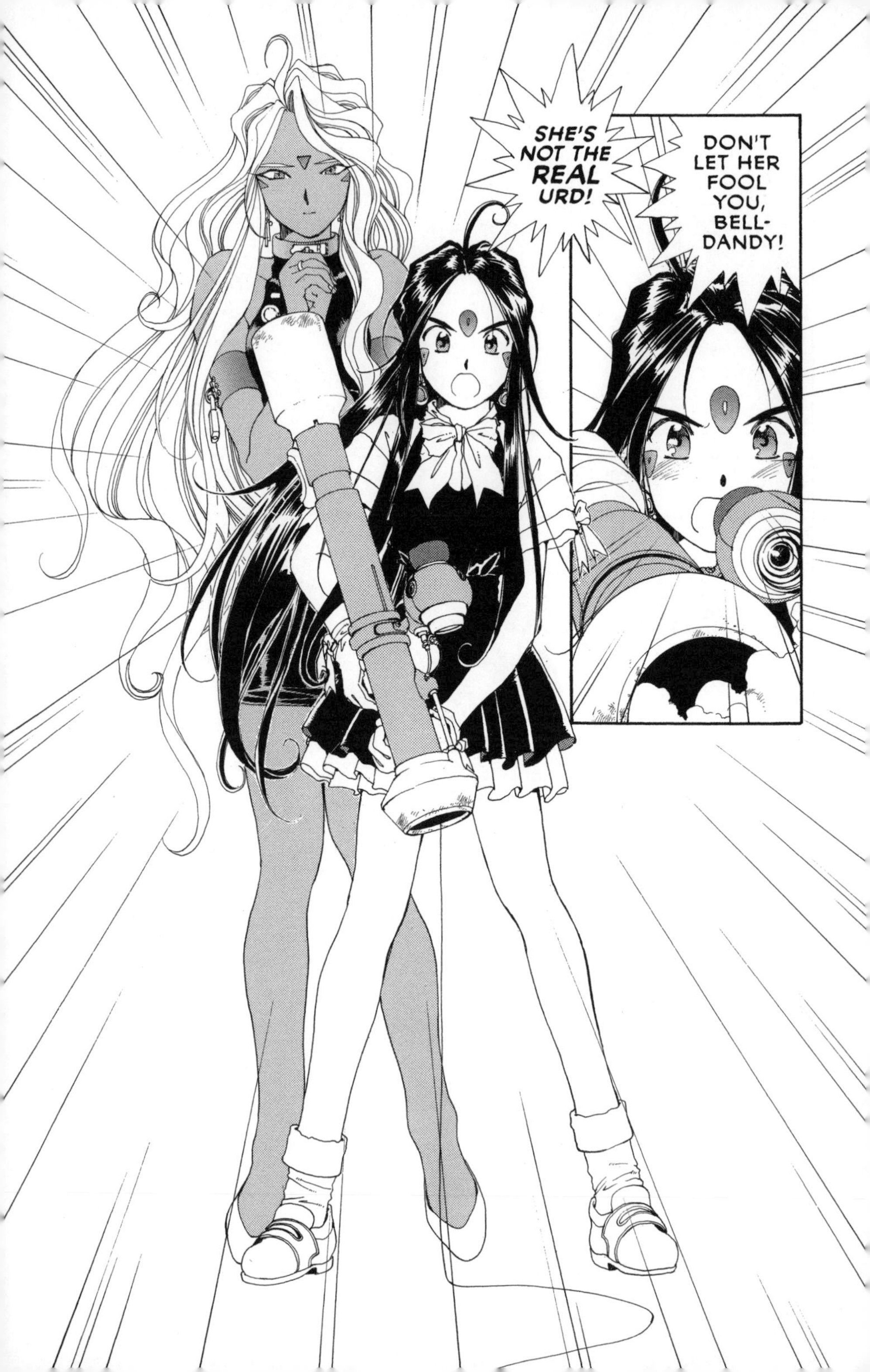
DON'T LET HER FOOL YOU, BELL-DANDY!
SHE'S NOT THE REAL URD!

ADVENTURES OF THE MINI-GODDESSES

FLY FORTH, YOUNG SPIRIT!

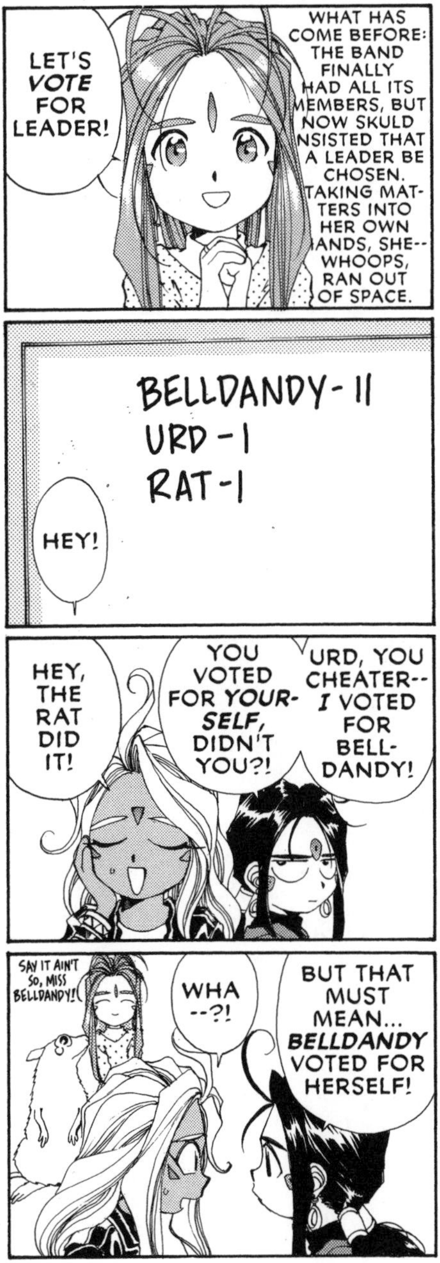
WHAT HAS COME BEFORE: THE BAND FINALLY HAD ALL ITS MEMBERS, BUT NOW SKULD INSISTED THAT A LEADER BE CHOSEN. TAKING MATTERS INTO HER OWN HANDS, SHE-- WHOOPS, RAN OUT OF SPACE.
LET'S *VOTE* FOR LEADER!
BELLDANDY-11
URD-1
RAT-1
HEY!
URD, YOU CHEATER-- *I* VOTED FOR BELLDANDY!
YOU VOTED FOR *YOURSELF*, DIDN'T YOU?!
HEY, THE RAT DID IT!
BUT THAT MUST MEAN... *BELLDANDY* VOTED FOR HERSELF!
WHA--?!
SAY IT AIN'T SO, MISS BELLDANDY!

FLY FORTH, YOUNG SPIRIT! (REVISITED)

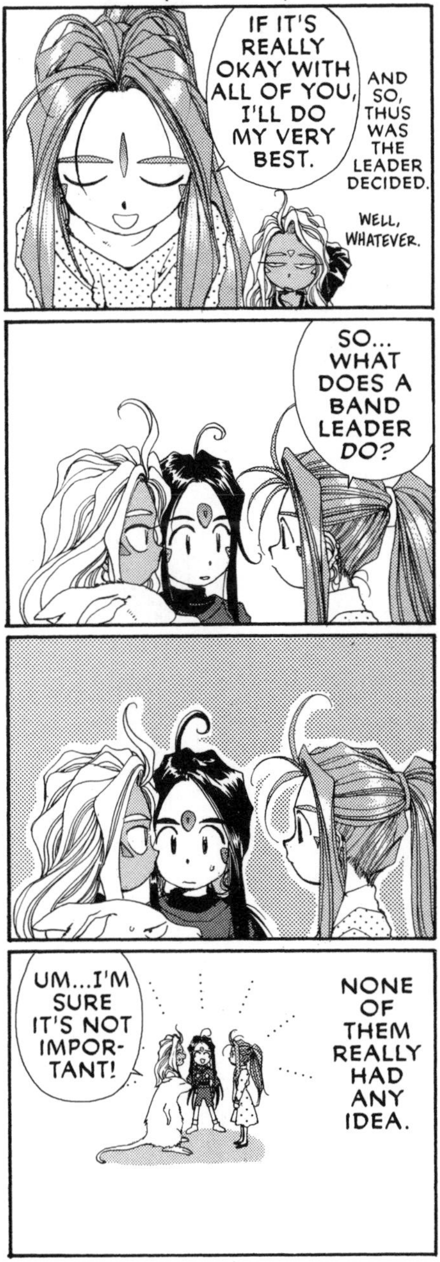
AND SO, THUS WAS THE LEADER DECIDED.
IF IT'S REALLY OKAY WITH ALL OF YOU, I'LL DO MY VERY BEST.
WELL, WHATEVER.
SO... WHAT DOES A BAND LEADER *DO?*
NONE OF THEM REALLY HAD ANY IDEA.
UM...I'M SURE IT'S NOT IMPORTANT!

ADVENTURES OF THE MINI-GODDESSES

◆SO YOU WANT TO KNOW MY NAME?! THEN I'LL TELL YOU!◆

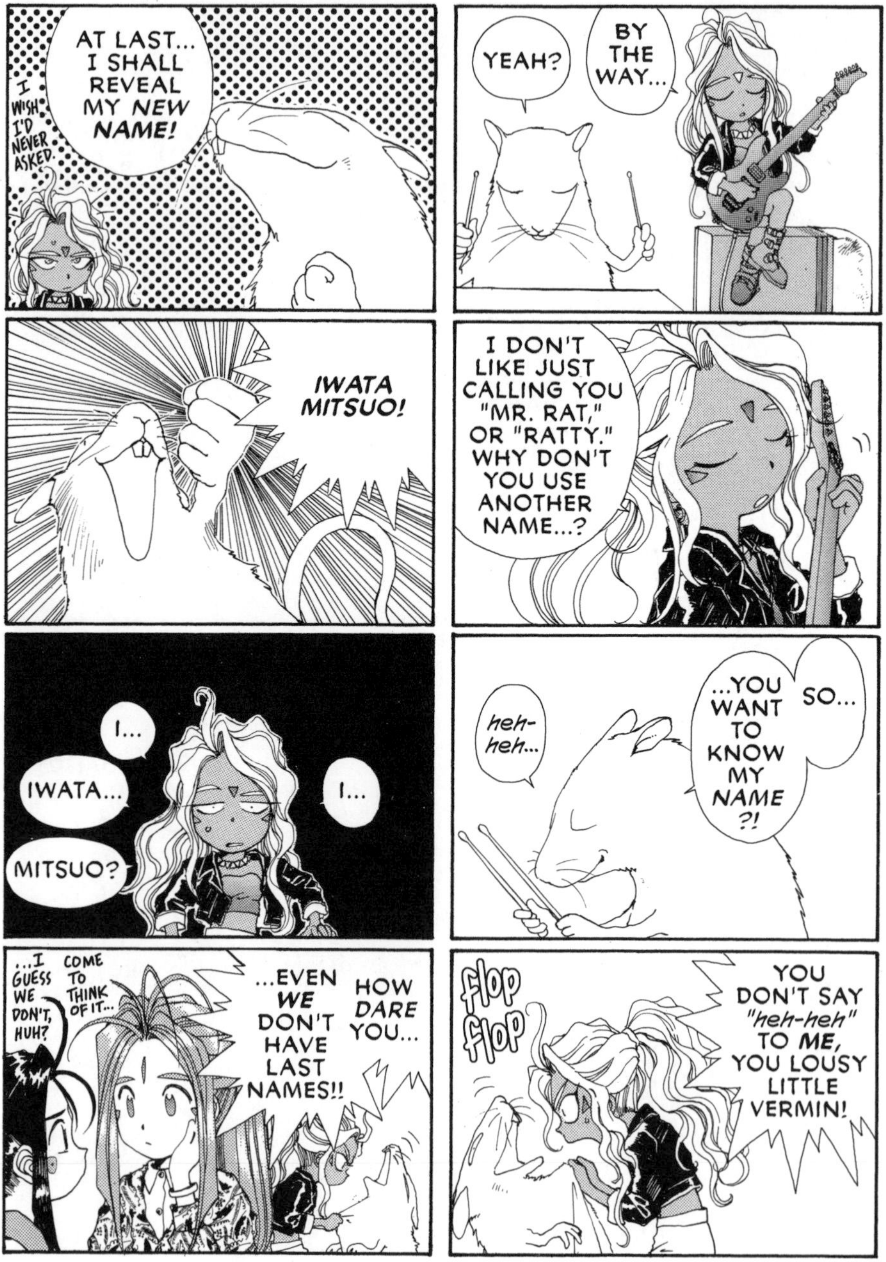
BY THE WAY...
YEAH?
I DON'T LIKE JUST CALLING YOU "MR. RAT," OR "RATTY." WHY DON'T YOU USE ANOTHER NAME...?
SO...
...YOU WANT TO KNOW MY *NAME* ?!
heh-heh...
YOU DON'T SAY *"heh-heh"* TO *ME,* YOU LOUSY LITTLE VERMIN!
flop flop
AT LAST... I SHALL REVEAL MY *NEW NAME!*
I WISH I'D NEVER ASKED.
IWATA MITSUO!
I...
I...
IWATA...
MITSUO?
HOW *DARE* YOU...
...EVEN *WE* DON'T HAVE LAST NAMES!!
COME TO THINK OF IT...
...I GUESS WE DON'T, HUH?

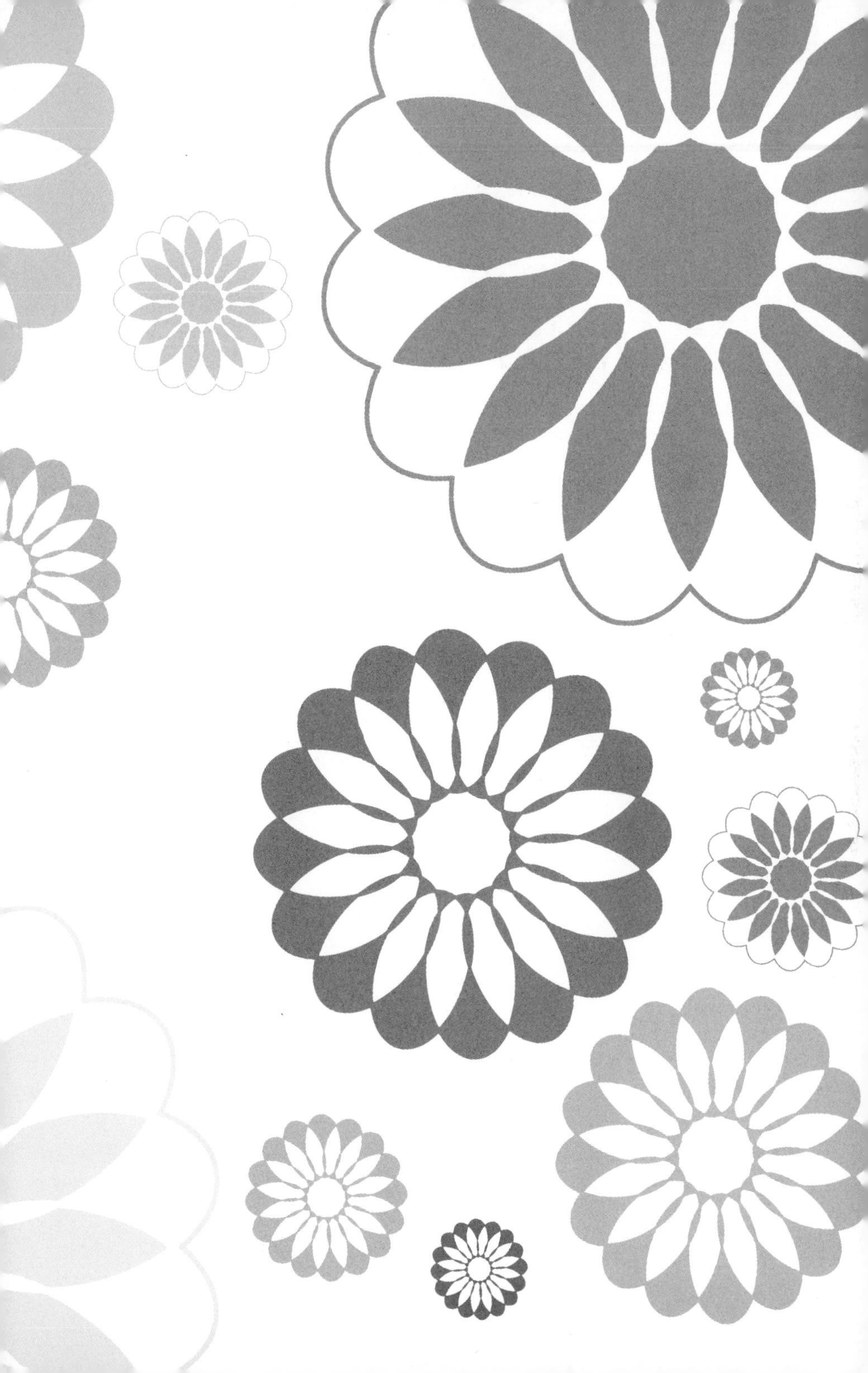

OH MY GODDESS!

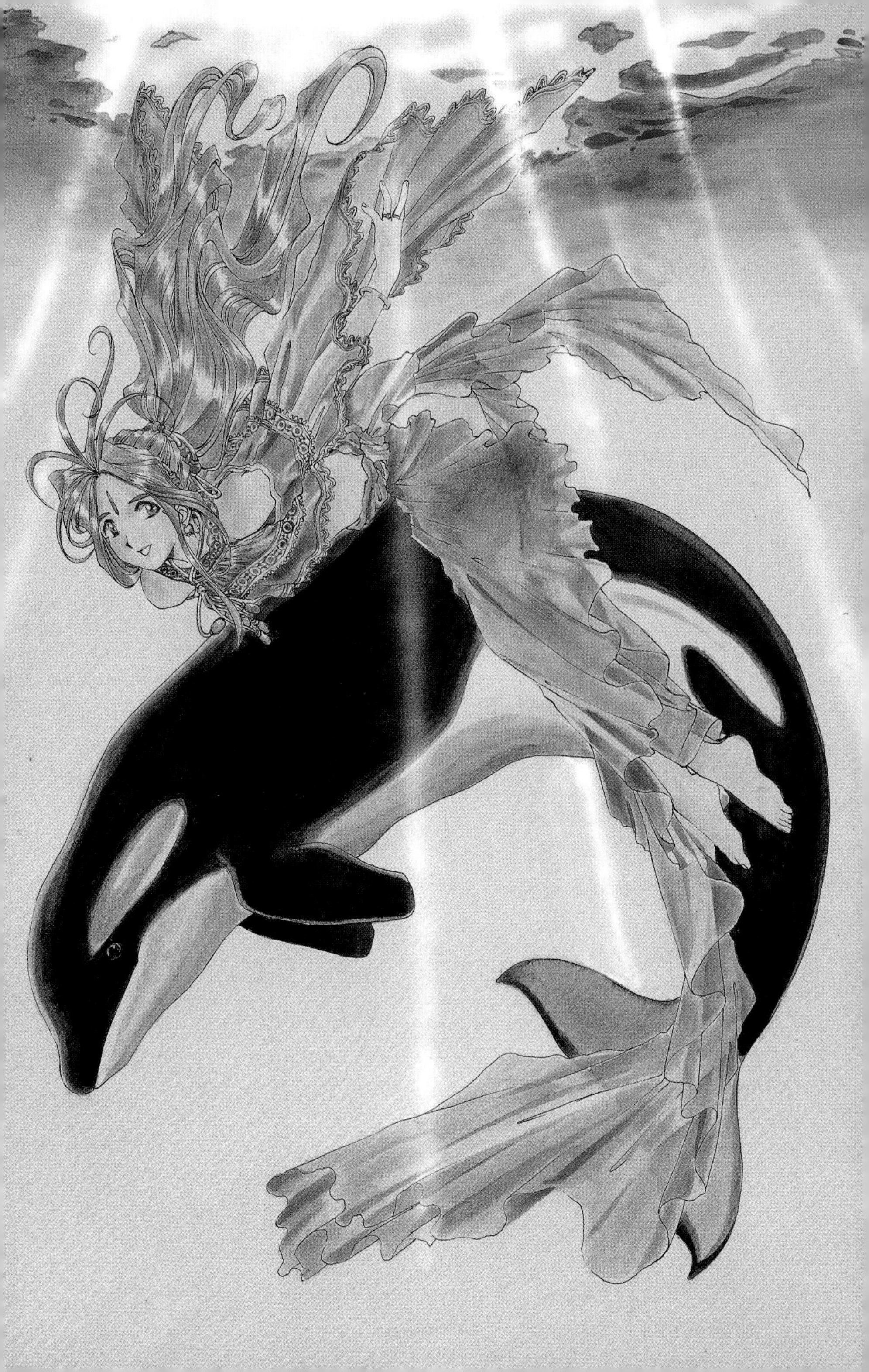

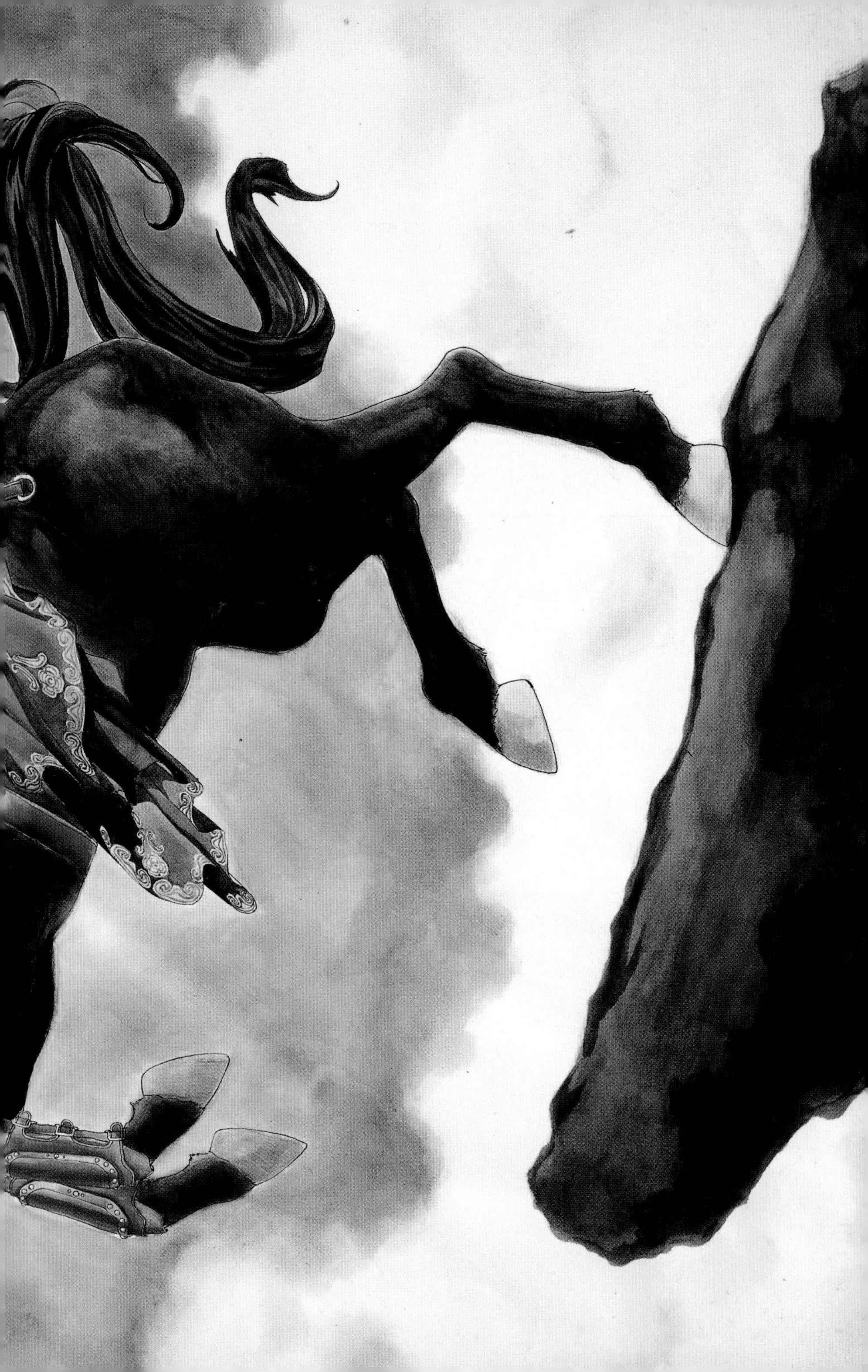

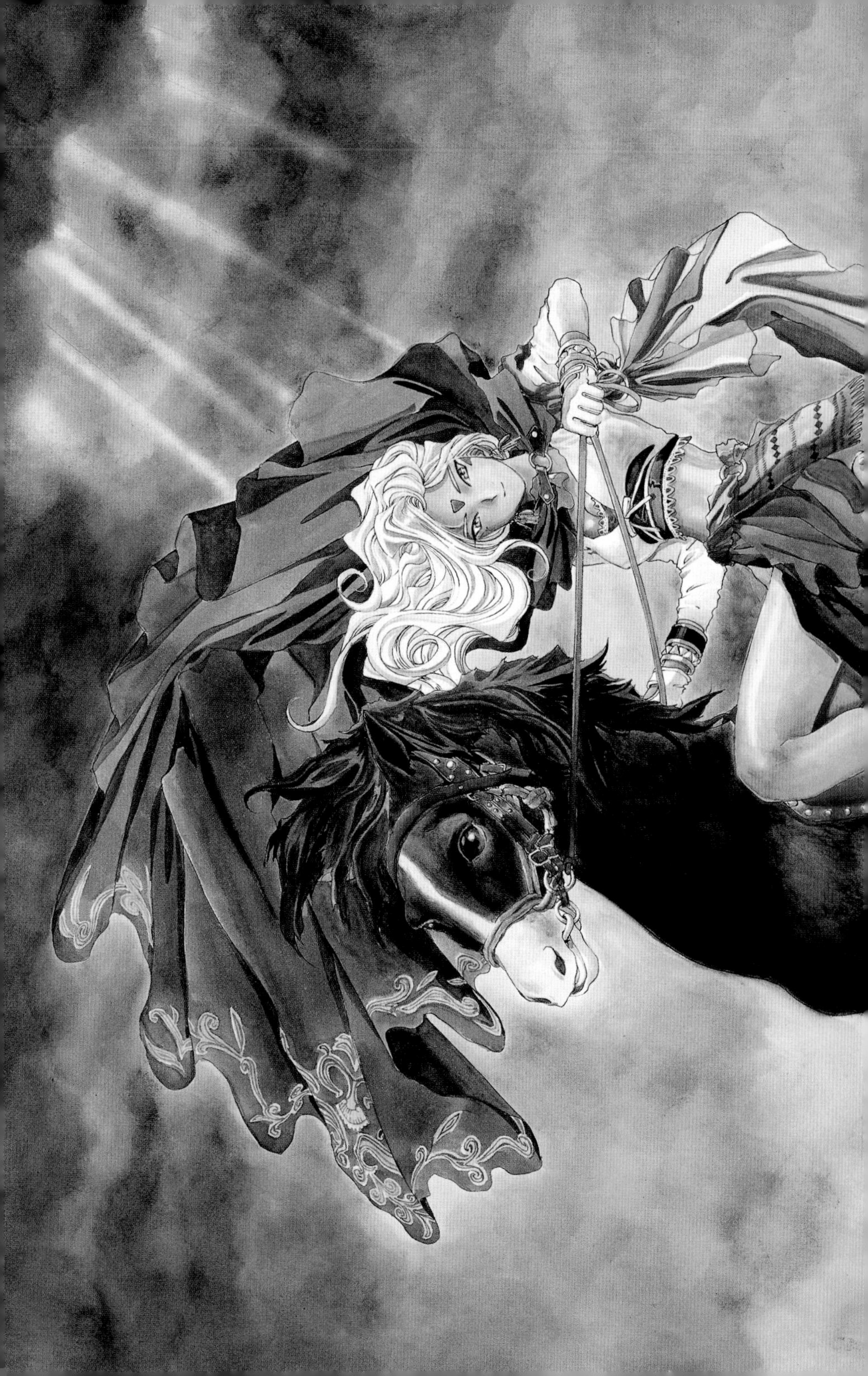

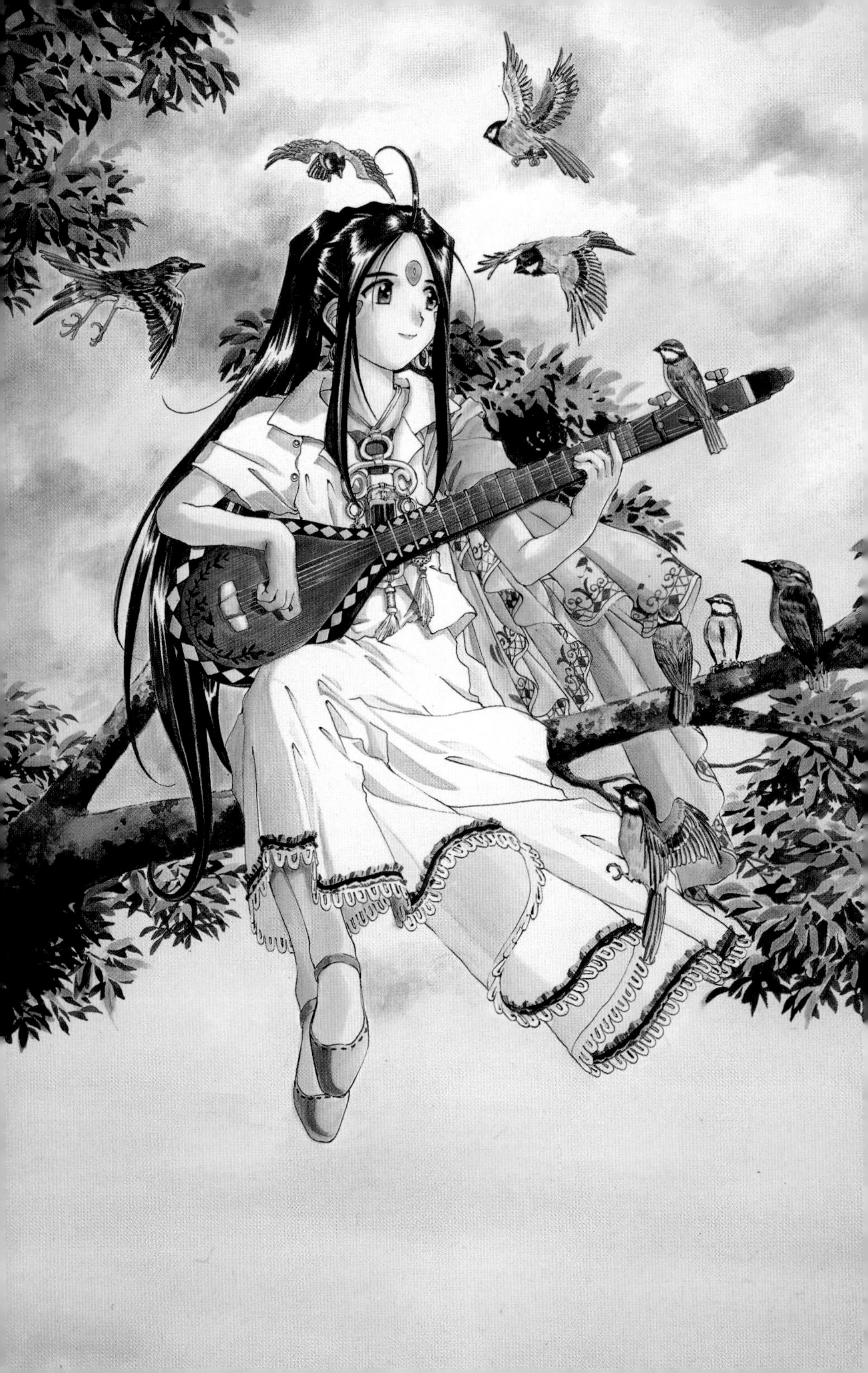

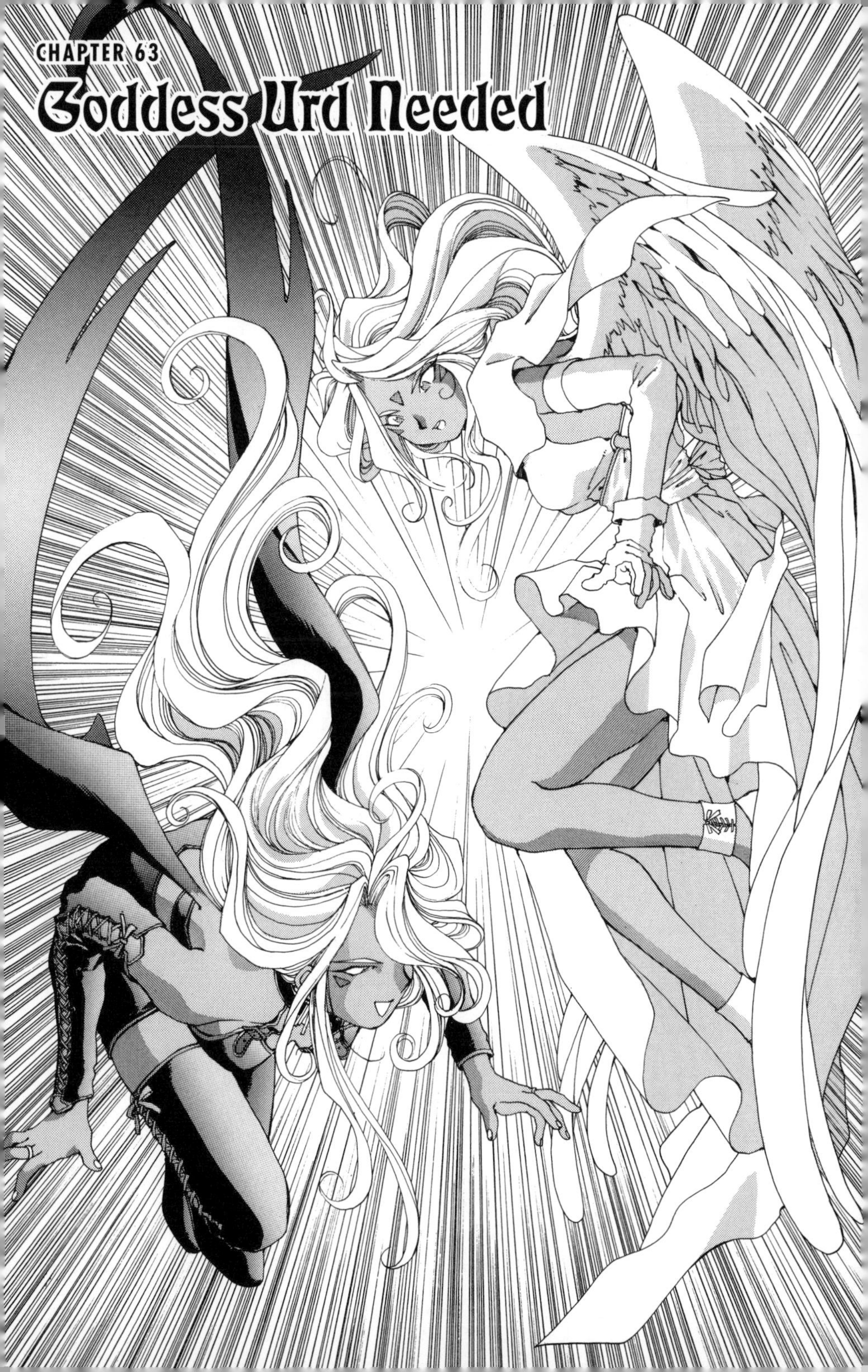
CHAPTER 63
Goddess Urd Needed

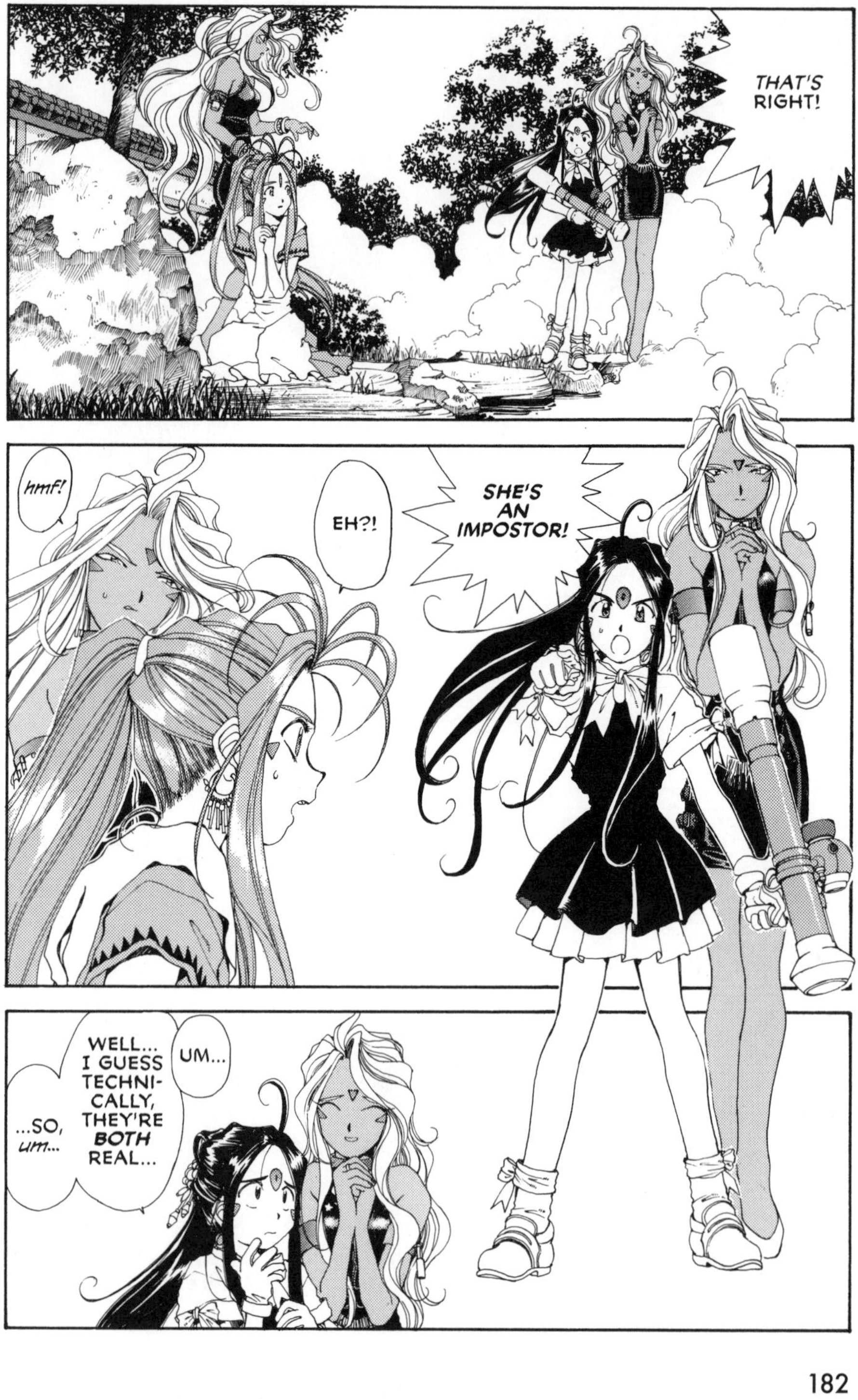
THAT'S RIGHT!
SHE'S AN IMPOSTOR!
EH?!
hmf!
UM...
WELL... I GUESS TECHNICALLY, THEY'RE BOTH REAL...
...SO, um...

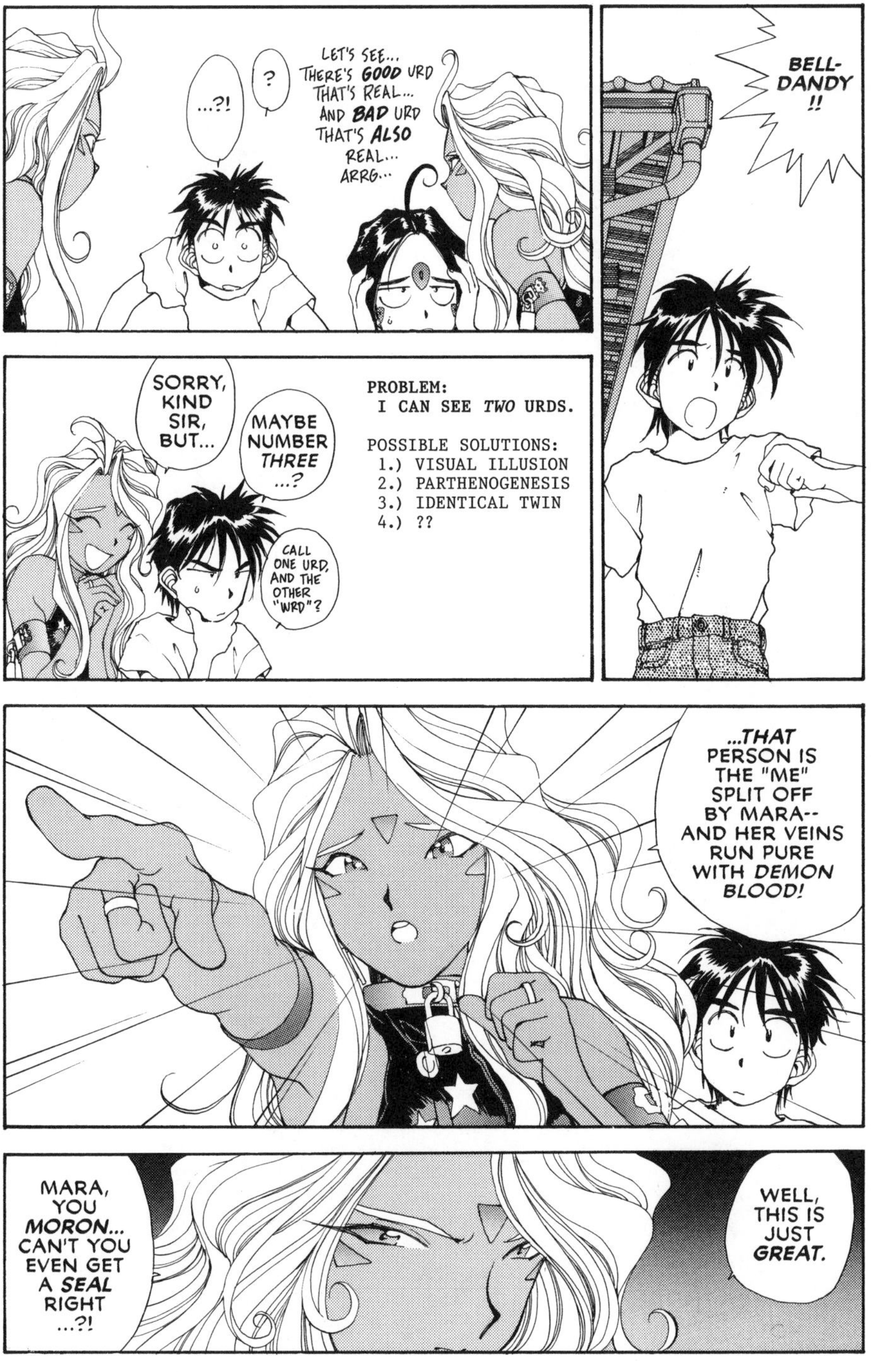
BELL-DANDY !!
LET'S SEE... THERE'S GOOD URD THAT'S REAL... AND BAD URD THAT'S ALSO REAL... ARRG...
?
...?!
PROBLEM:
I CAN SEE TWO URDS.
POSSIBLE SOLUTIONS:
1.) VISUAL ILLUSION
2.) PARTHENOGENESIS
3.) IDENTICAL TWIN
4.) ??
MAYBE NUMBER THREE ...?
SORRY, KIND SIR, BUT...
CALL ONE URD, AND THE OTHER "WRD"?
...THAT PERSON IS THE "ME" SPLIT OFF BY MARA-- AND HER VEINS RUN PURE WITH DEMON BLOOD!
WELL, THIS IS JUST GREAT.
MARA, YOU MORON... CAN'T YOU EVEN GET A SEAL RIGHT ...?!

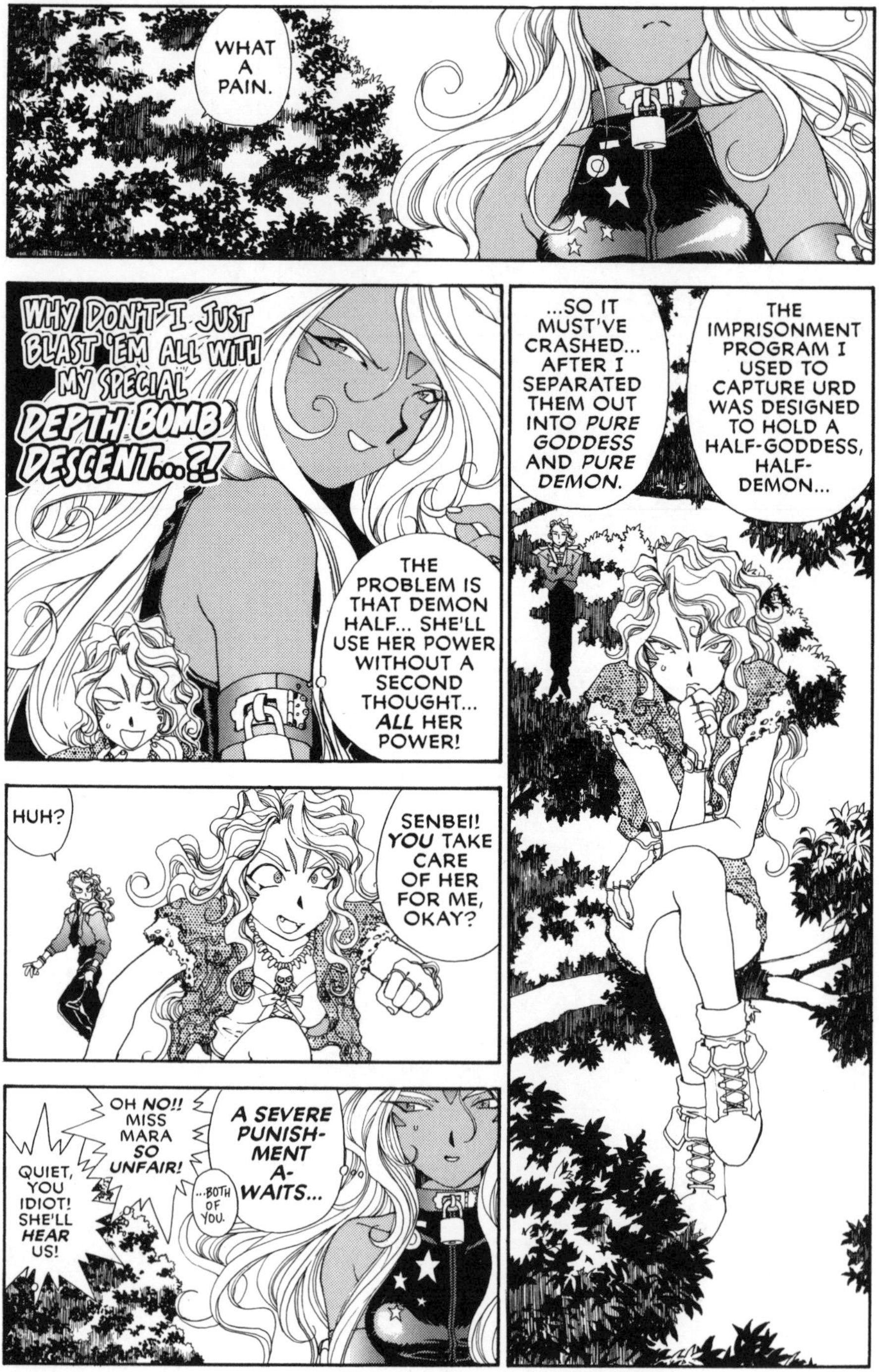
WHAT A PAIN.
THE IMPRISONMENT PROGRAM I USED TO CAPTURE URD WAS DESIGNED TO HOLD A HALF-GODDESS, HALF-DEMON...
...SO IT MUST'VE CRASHED... AFTER I SEPARATED THEM OUT INTO *PURE GODDESS* AND *PURE DEMON.*
WHY DON'T I JUST BLAST 'EM ALL WITH MY SPECIAL DEPTH BOMB DESCENT...?!
THE PROBLEM IS THAT DEMON HALF... SHE'LL USE HER POWER WITHOUT A SECOND THOUGHT... *ALL* HER POWER!
SENBEI! *YOU* TAKE CARE OF HER FOR ME, OKAY?
HUH?
A SEVERE PUNISH-MENT A-WAITS...
...BOTH OF YOU.
OH *NO!!* MISS MARA *SO UNFAIR!*
QUIET, YOU IDIOT! SHE'LL *HEAR* US!

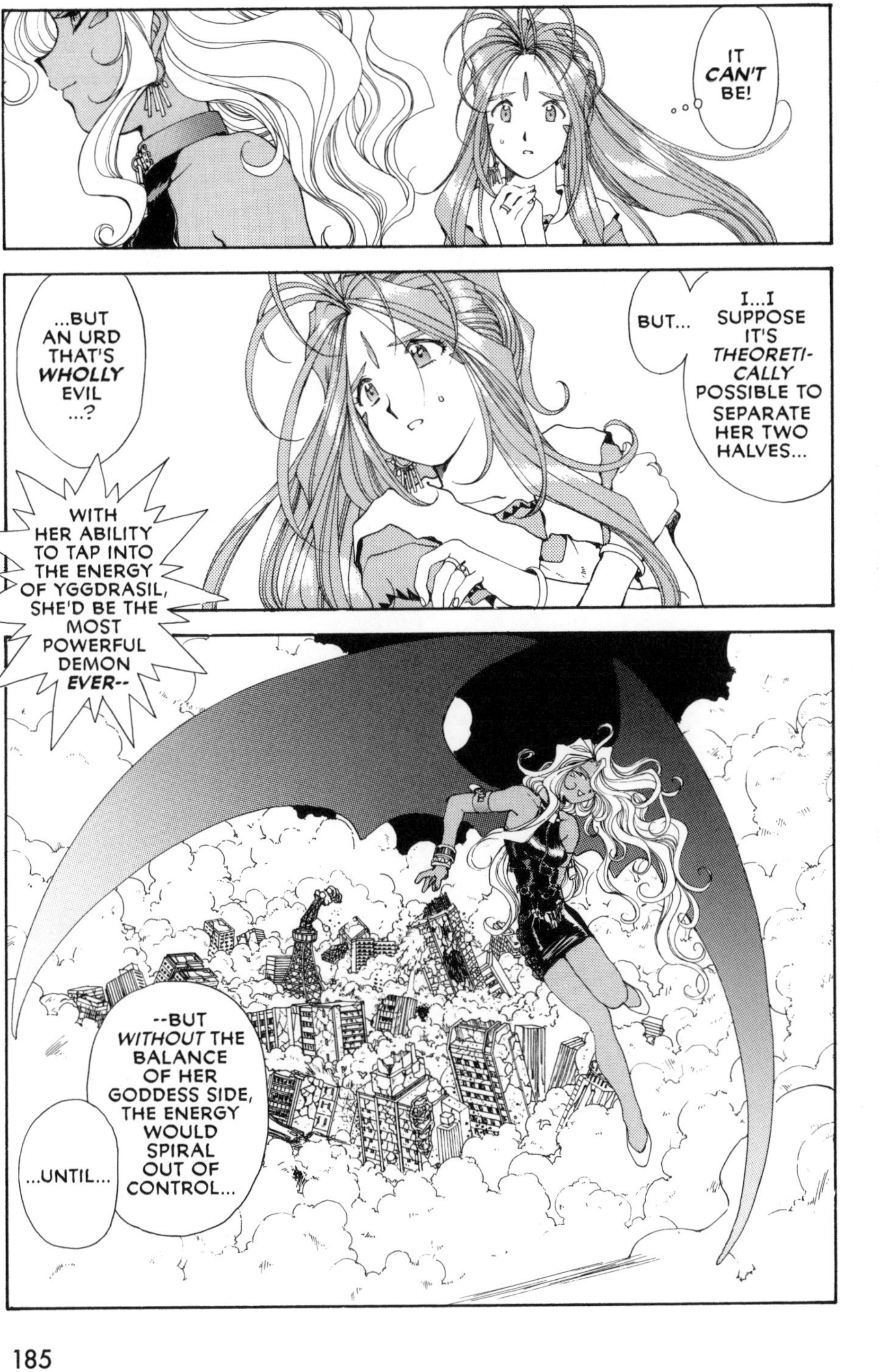

IT CAN'T BE!
I...I SUPPOSE IT'S THEORETICALLY POSSIBLE TO SEPARATE HER TWO HALVES...
BUT...
...BUT AN URD THAT'S WHOLLY EVIL ...?
WITH HER ABILITY TO TAP INTO THE ENERGY OF YGGDRASIL, SHE'D BE THE MOST POWERFUL DEMON EVER--
--BUT WITHOUT THE BALANCE OF HER GODDESS SIDE, THE ENERGY WOULD SPIRAL OUT OF CONTROL...
...UNTIL...

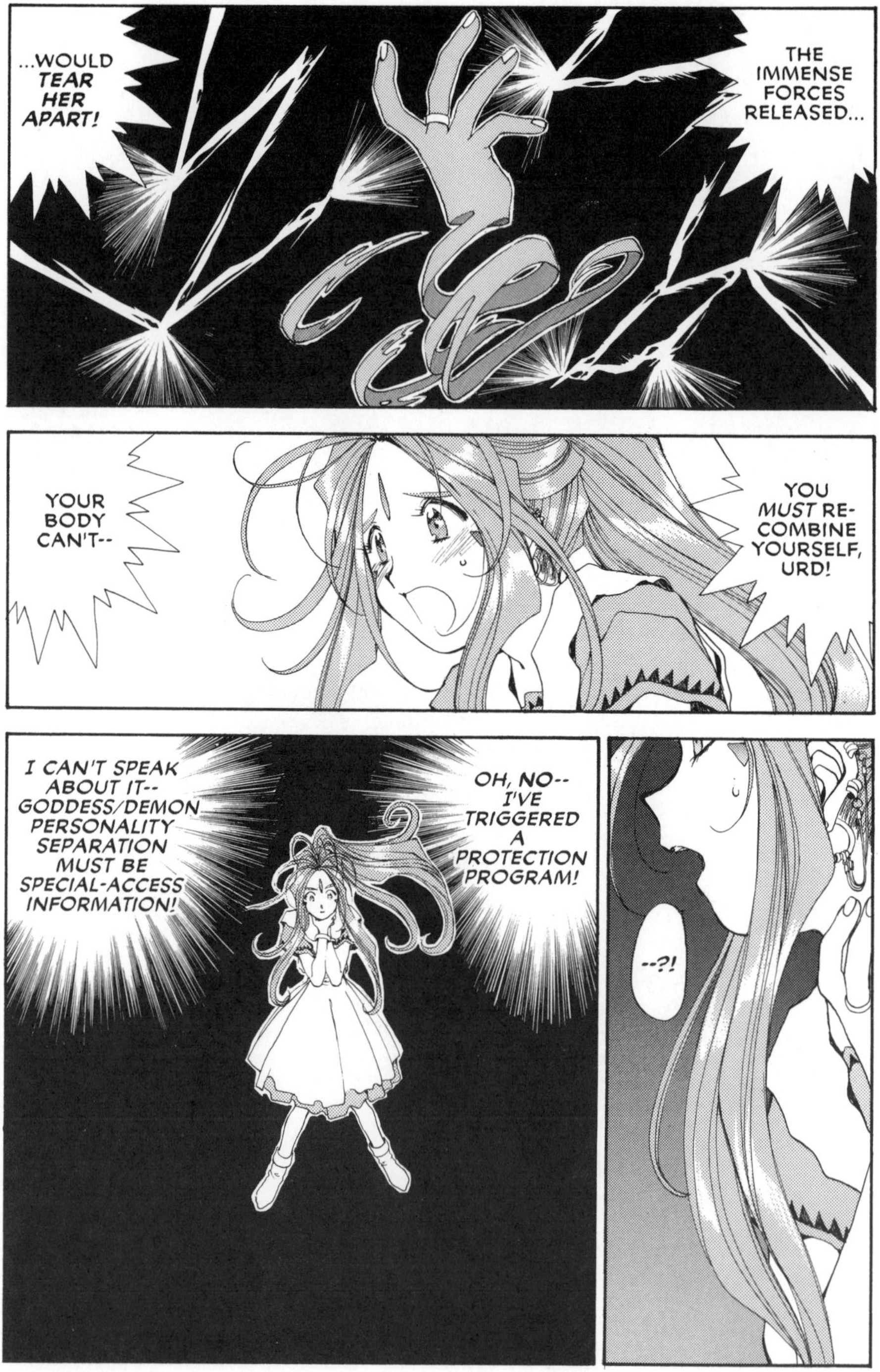
THE IMMENSE FORCES RELEASED...
...WOULD TEAR HER APART!
YOU MUST RE-COMBINE YOURSELF, URD!
YOUR BODY CAN'T--
--?!
OH, NO-- I'VE TRIGGERED A PROTECTION PROGRAM!
I CAN'T SPEAK ABOUT IT-- GODDESS/DEMON PERSONALITY SEPARATION MUST BE SPECIAL-ACCESS INFORMATION!

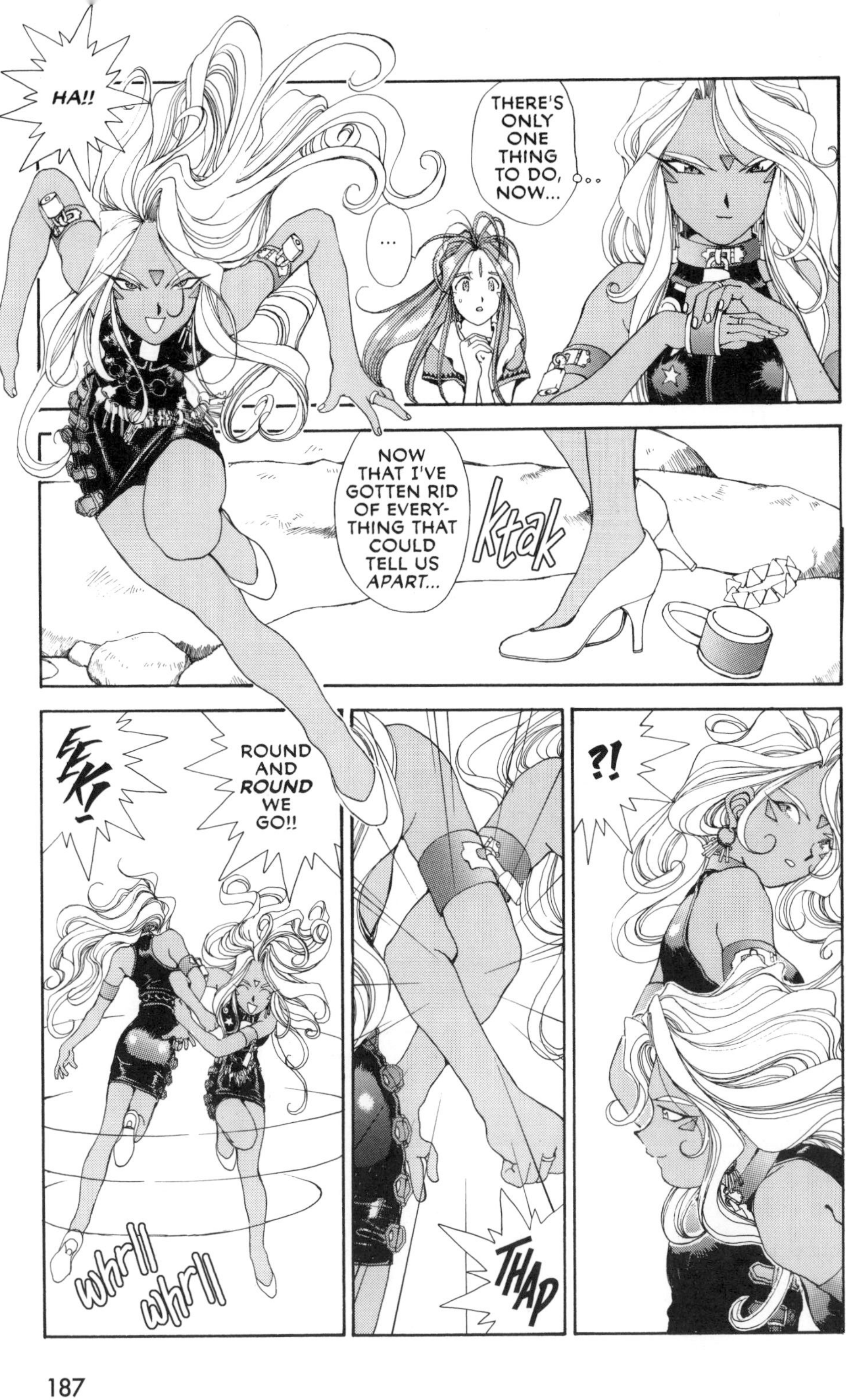
...
THERE'S ONLY ONE THING TO DO, NOW...
NOW THAT I'VE GOTTEN RID OF EVERY-THING THAT COULD TELL US APART...
ktak
HA!!
EEK!
ROUND AND ROUND WE GO!!
whrll whrll
THAP
?!

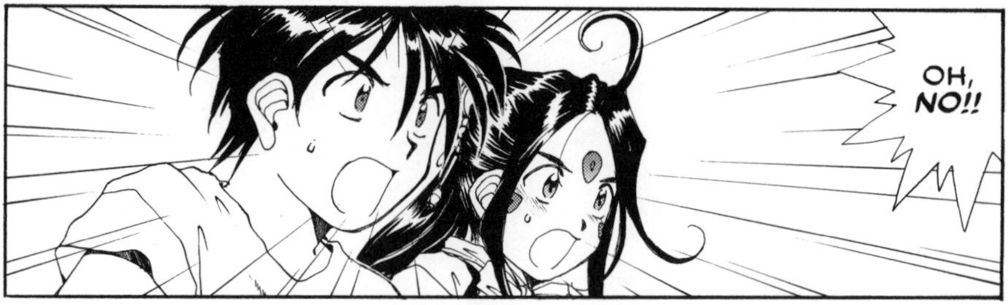
OH, ***NO!!***

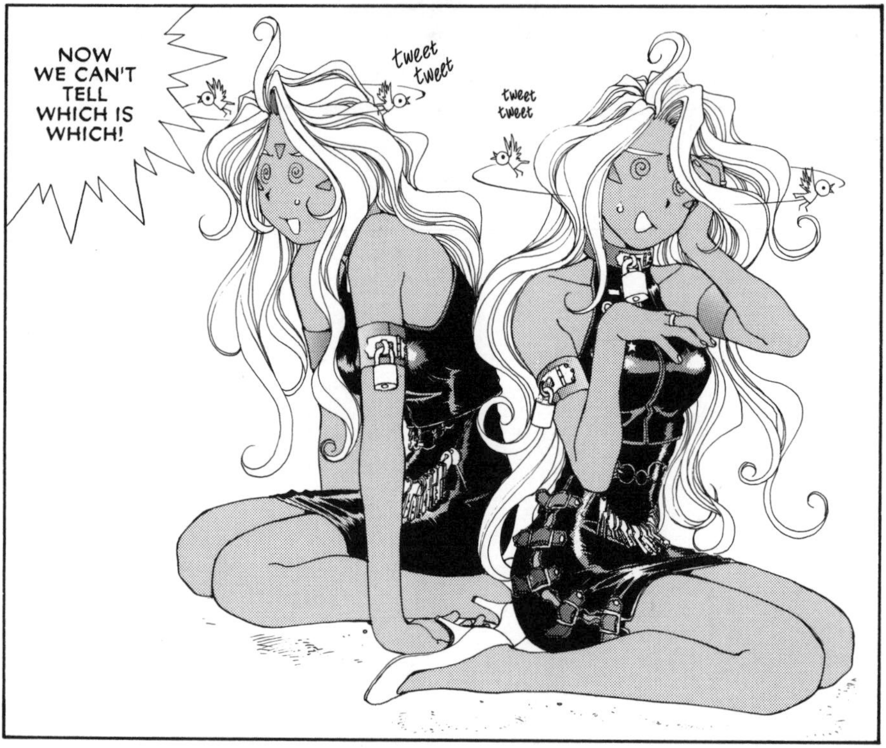
tweet tweet
tweet tweet
NOW WE CAN'T TELL WHICH IS WHICH!

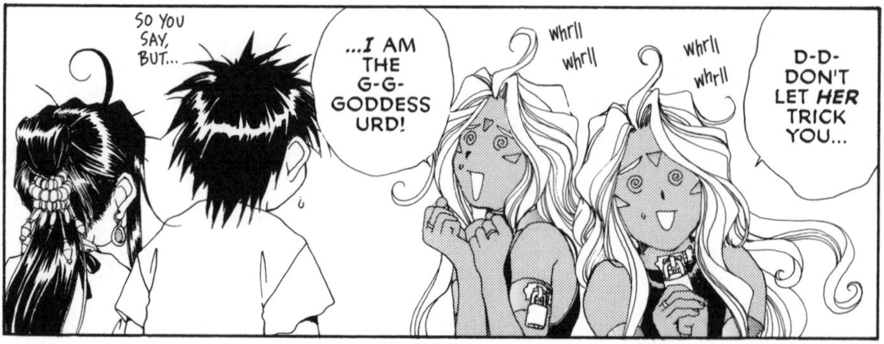
D-D-DON'T LET ***HER*** TRICK YOU...
whrll whrll
whrll whrll
...***I*** AM THE G-G-GODDESS URD!
SO YOU SAY, BUT...

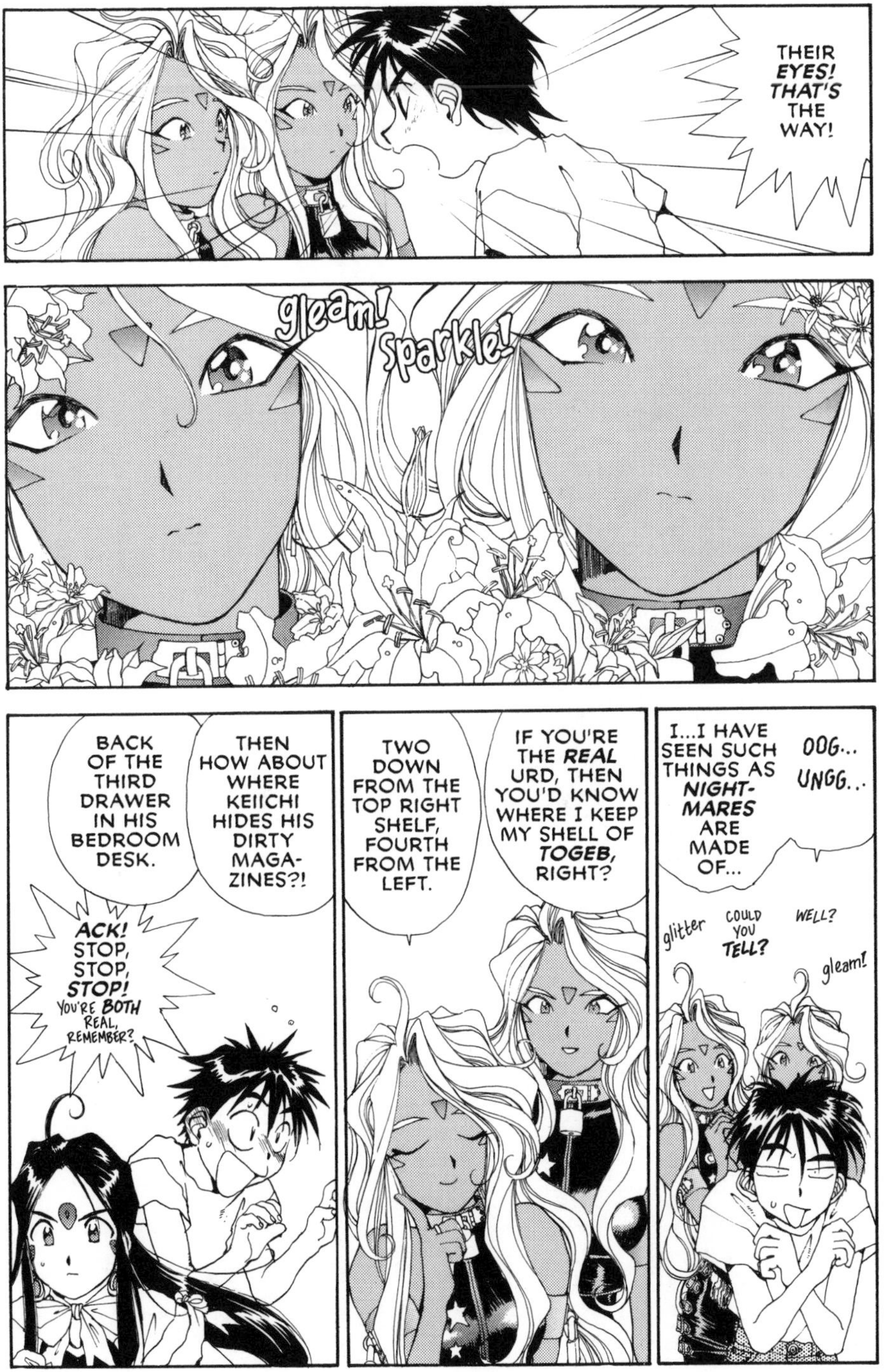
THEIR *EYES! THAT'S* THE WAY!
gleam!
sparkle!
OOG... UNGG...
I...I HAVE SEEN SUCH THINGS AS *NIGHTMARES* ARE MADE OF...
WELL?
COULD YOU *TELL?*
glitter
gleam!
IF YOU'RE THE *REAL* URD, THEN YOU'D KNOW WHERE I KEEP MY SHELL OF *TOGEB,* RIGHT?
TWO DOWN FROM THE TOP RIGHT SHELF, FOURTH FROM THE LEFT.
THEN HOW ABOUT WHERE KEIICHI HIDES HIS DIRTY MAGA-ZINES?!
BACK OF THE THIRD DRAWER IN HIS BEDROOM DESK.
ACK! STOP, STOP, *STOP!* YOU'RE *BOTH* REAL, REMEMBER?

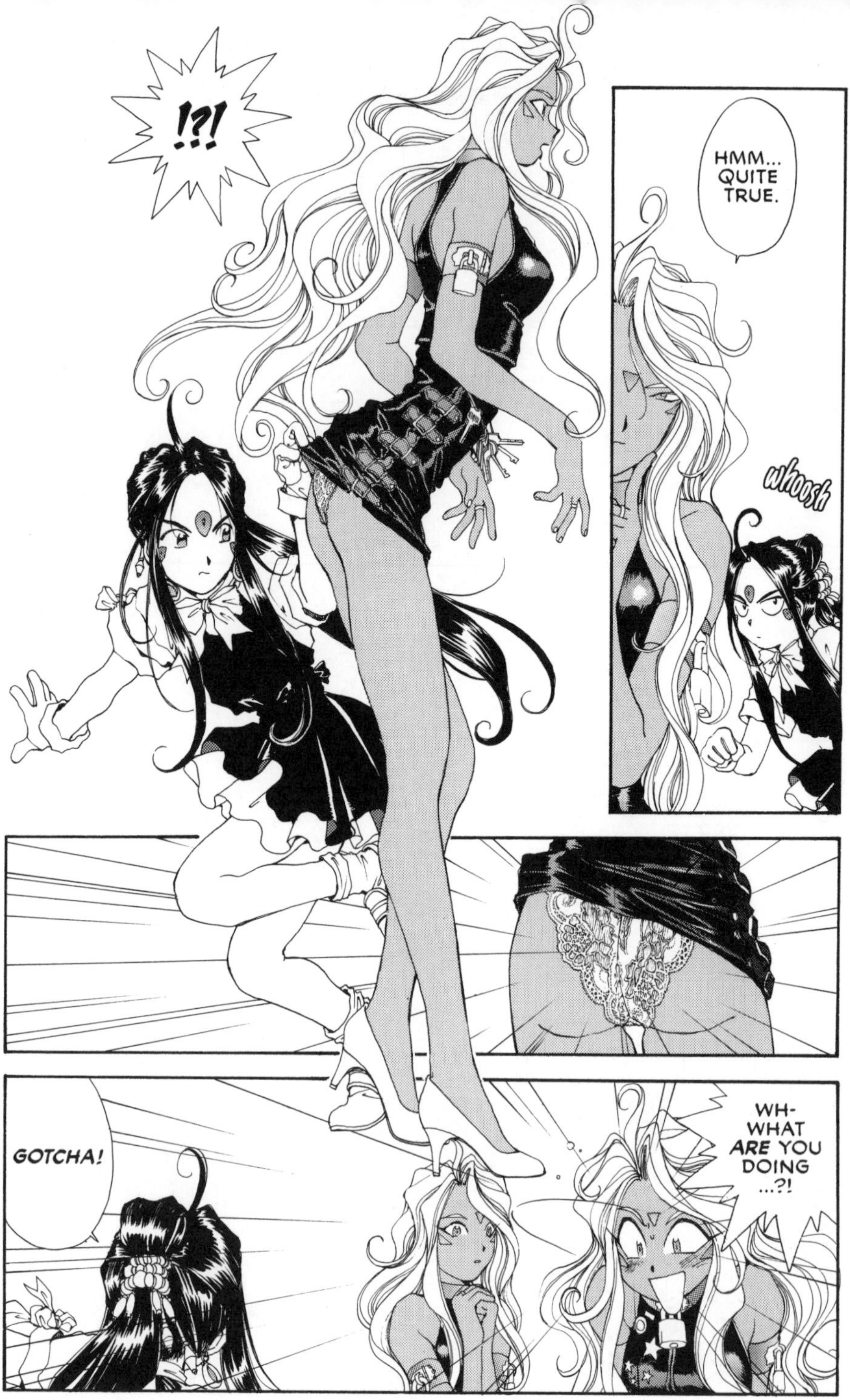
HMM... QUITE TRUE.
whoosh
!?!
WH- WHAT ARE YOU DOING ...?!
GOTCHA!

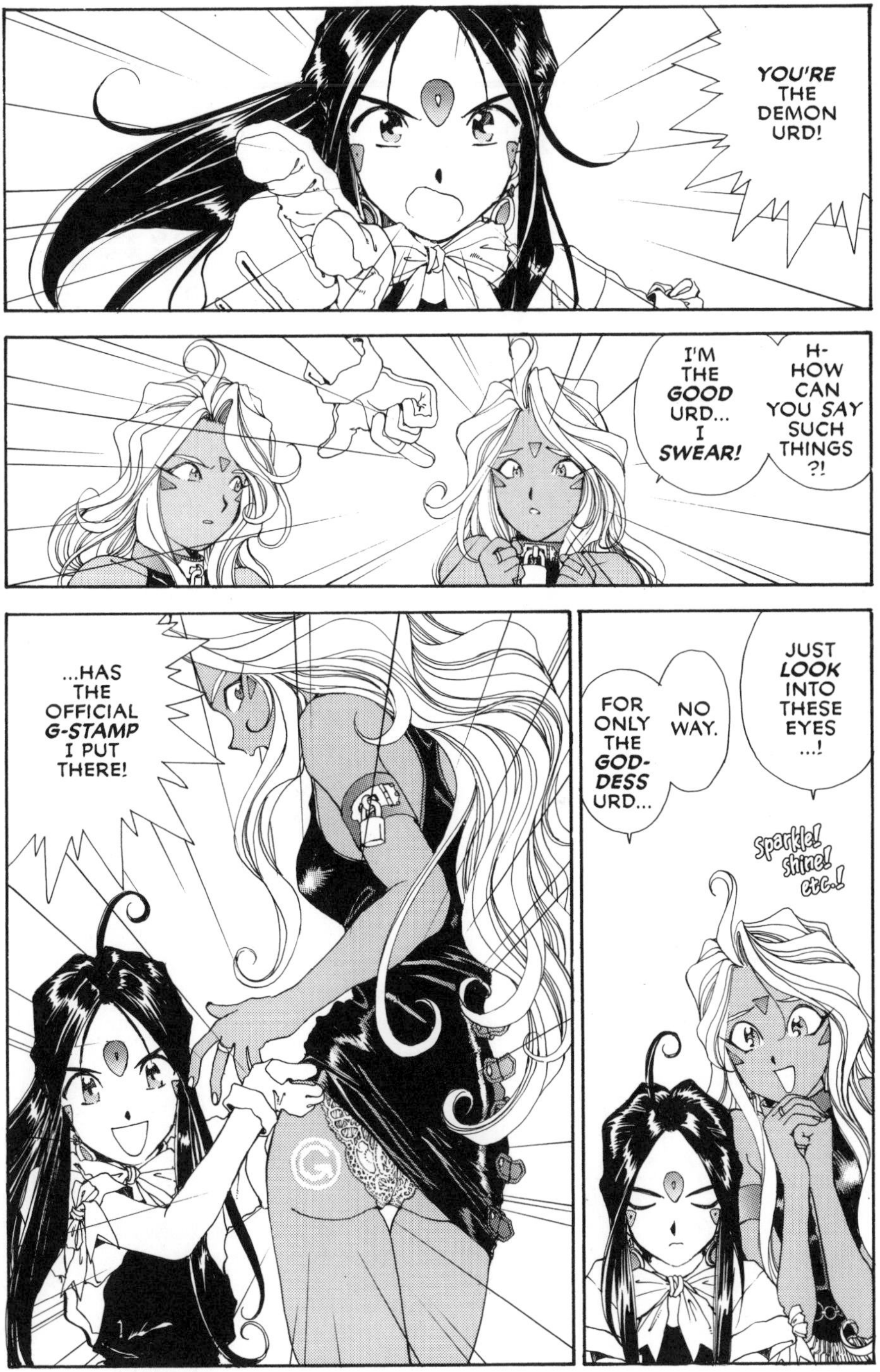
YOU'RE THE DEMON URD!
H-HOW CAN YOU SAY SUCH THINGS?!
I'M THE GOOD URD... I SWEAR!
JUST LOOK INTO THESE EYES...!
Sparkle! shine! etc.!
NO WAY.
FOR ONLY THE GOD-DESS URD...
...HAS THE OFFICIAL G-STAMP I PUT THERE!

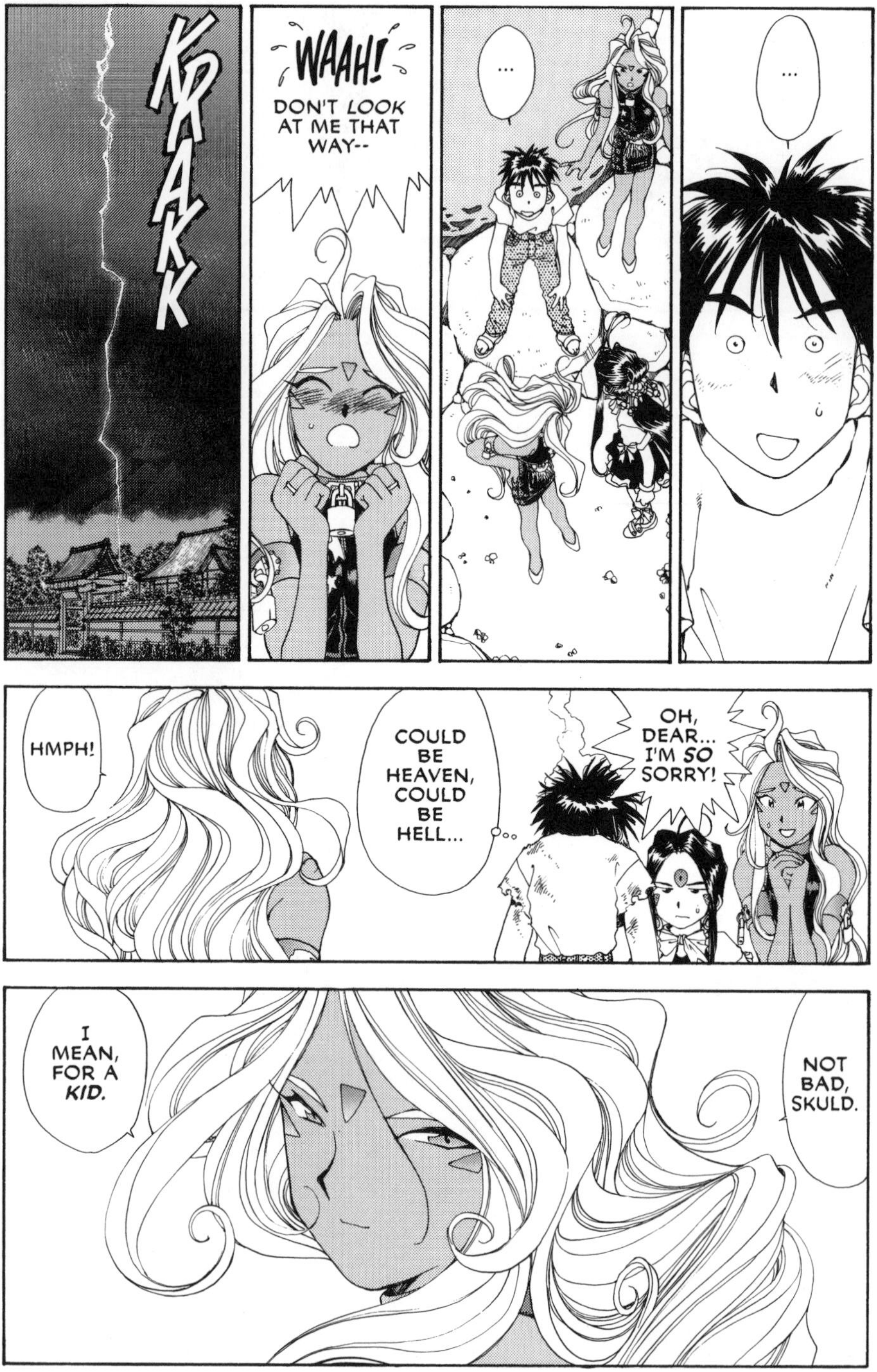
...
...
WAAH!
DON'T LOOK AT ME THAT WAY--
KRAAKK
OH, DEAR... I'M SO SORRY!
COULD BE HEAVEN, COULD BE HELL...
HMPH!
NOT BAD, SKULD.
I MEAN, FOR A KID.

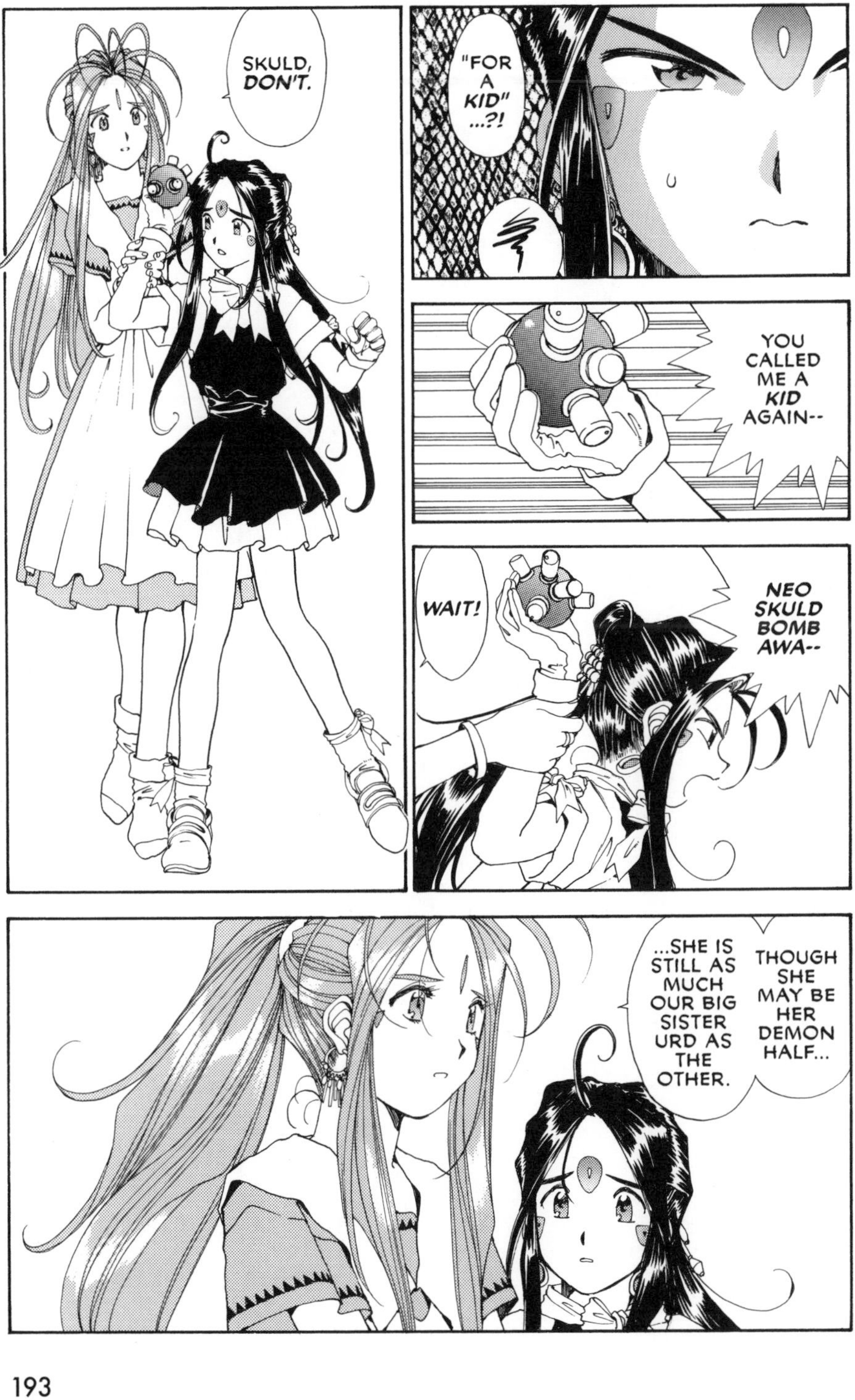
"FOR A KID" ...?!
YOU CALLED ME A KID AGAIN--
NEO SKULD BOMB AWA--
WAIT!
SKULD, DON'T.
THOUGH SHE MAY BE HER DEMON HALF...
...SHE IS STILL AS MUCH OUR BIG SISTER URD AS THE OTHER.

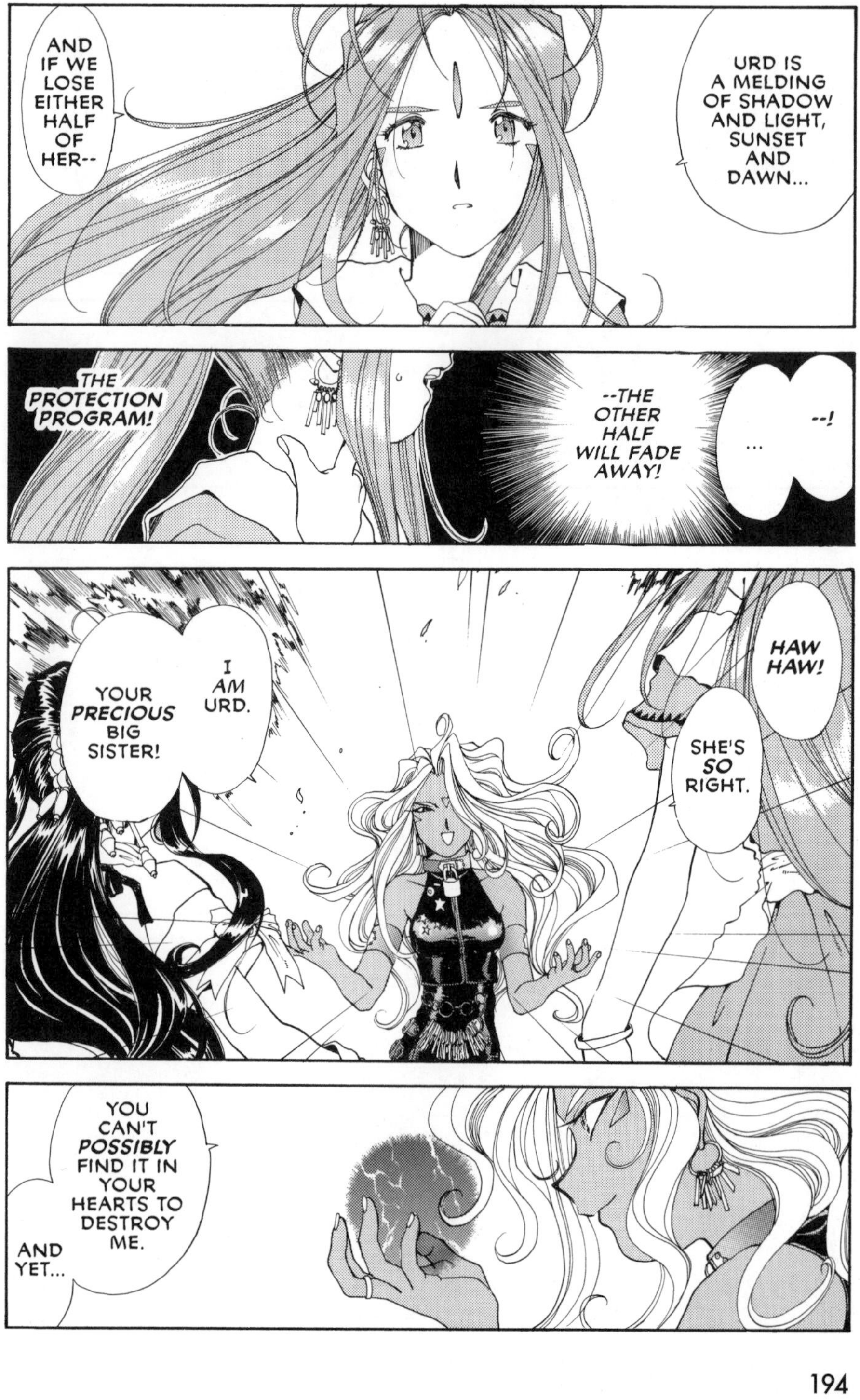
URD IS A MELDING OF SHADOW AND LIGHT, SUNSET AND DAWN...
AND IF WE LOSE EITHER HALF OF HER--
--! ...
--THE OTHER HALF WILL FADE AWAY!
THE PROTECTION PROGRAM!
HAW HAW!
SHE'S SO RIGHT.
I AM URD.
YOUR PRECIOUS BIG SISTER!
YOU CAN'T POSSIBLY FIND IT IN YOUR HEARTS TO DESTROY ME.
AND YET...

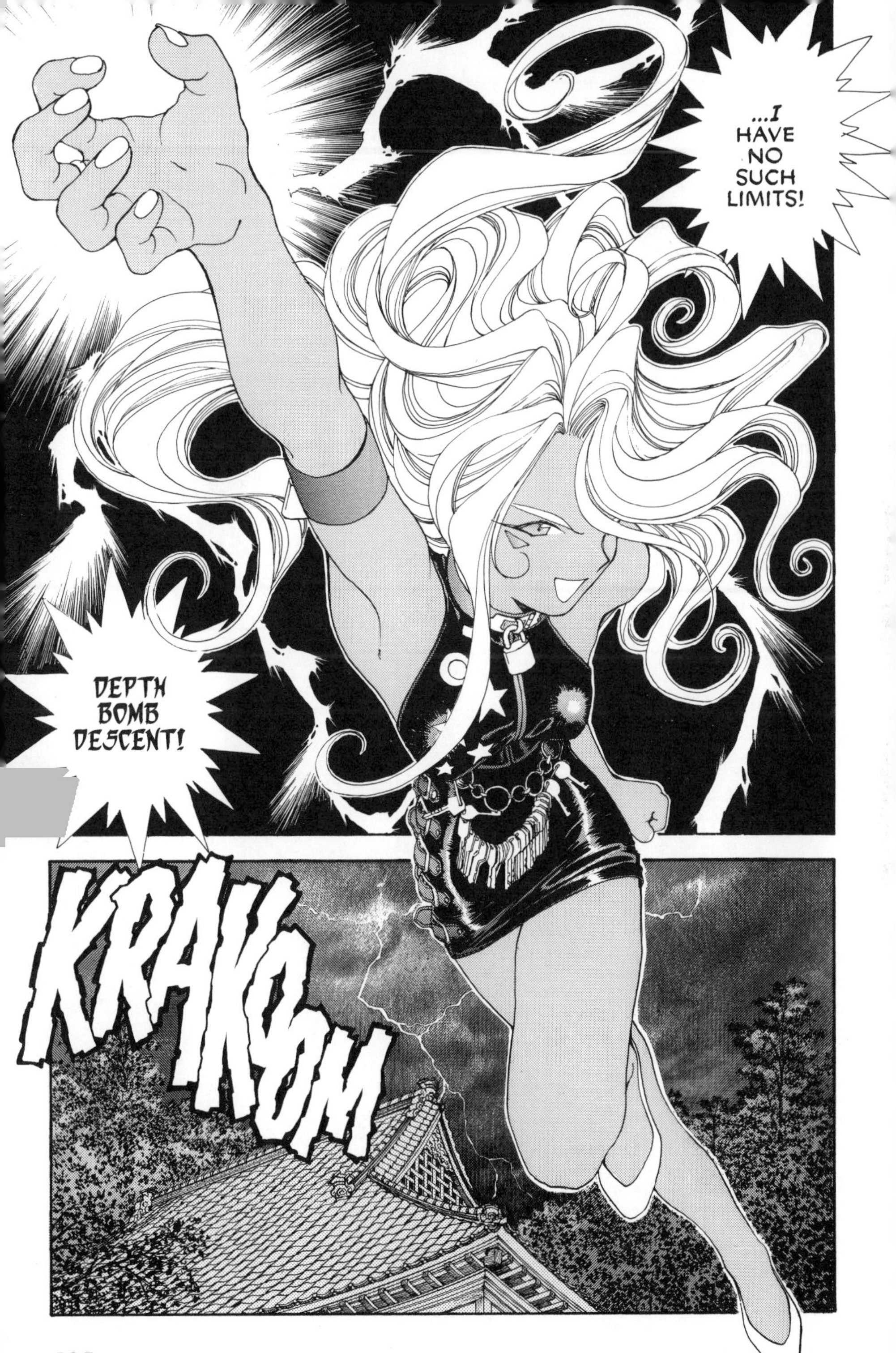
...I HAVE NO SUCH LIMITS!
DEPTH BOMB DESCENT!
KRAKOOM

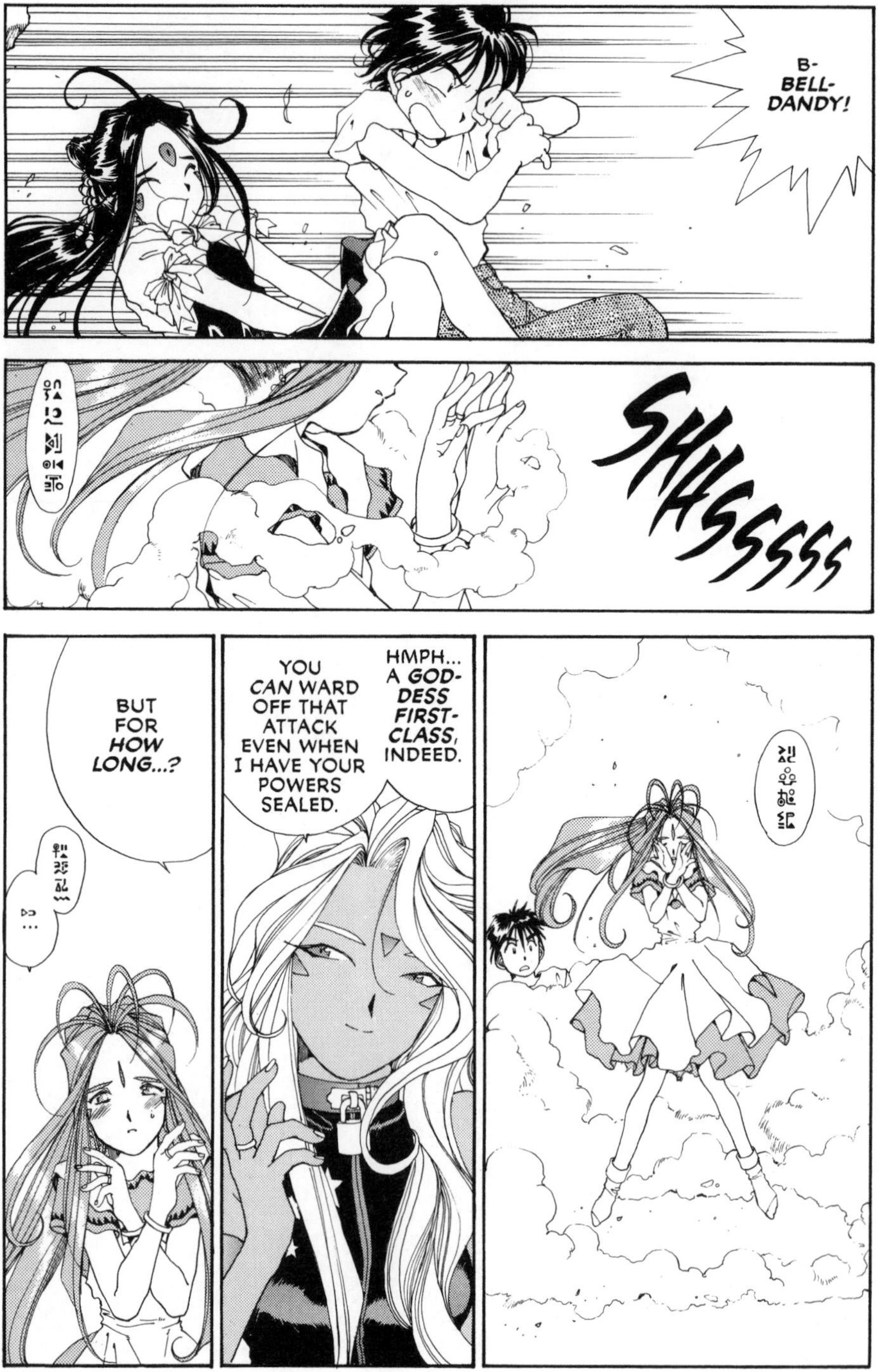
B-BELL-DANDY!
SHHSSSSS
HMPH... A *GOD-DESS FIRST-CLASS,* INDEED.
YOU *CAN* WARD OFF THAT ATTACK EVEN WHEN I HAVE YOUR POWERS SEALED.
BUT FOR *HOW LONG...?*

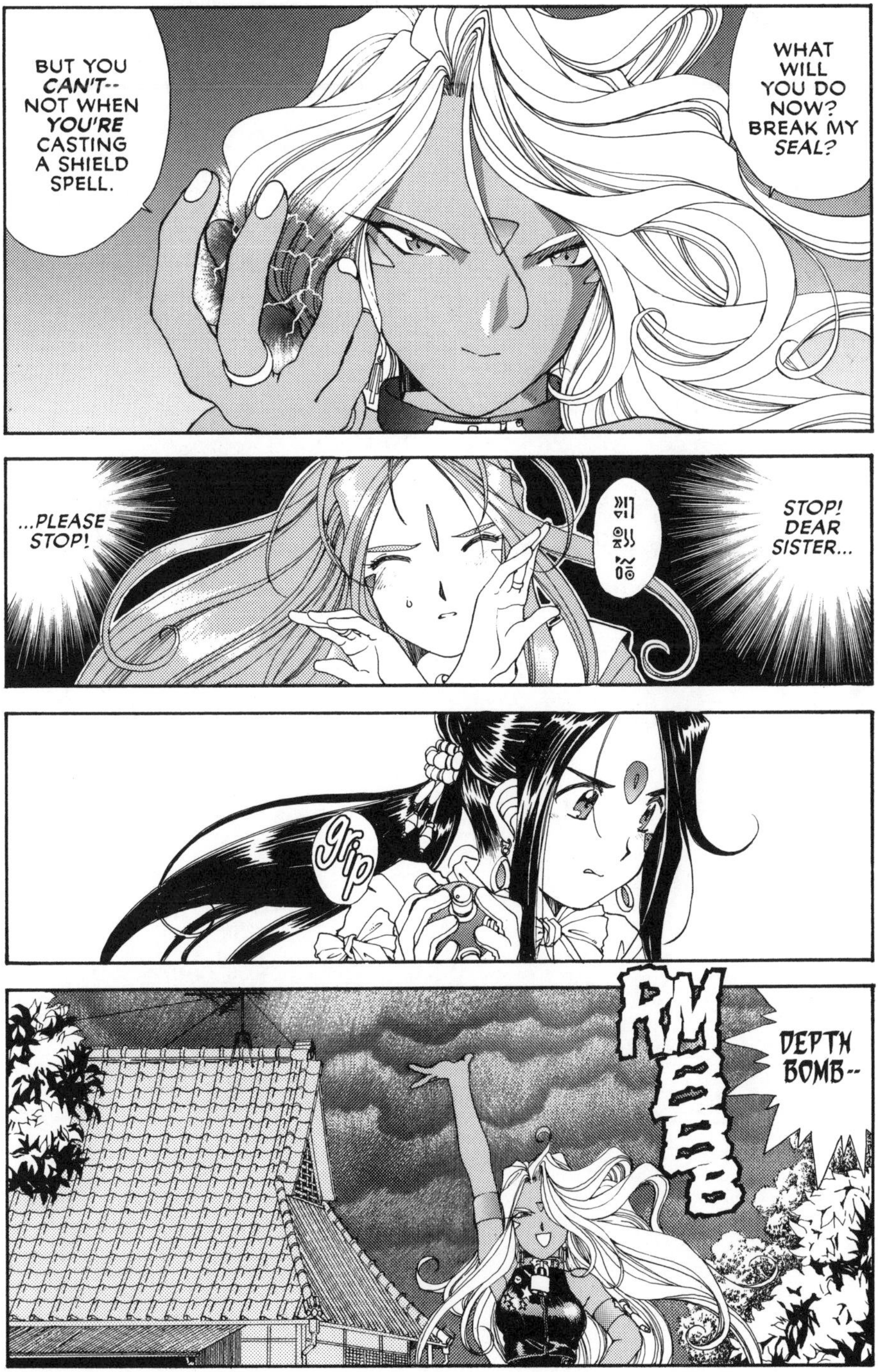
WHAT WILL YOU DO NOW? BREAK MY *SEAL?*
BUT YOU *CAN'T*-- NOT WHEN *YOU'RE* CASTING A SHIELD SPELL.
STOP! DEAR SISTER...
...PLEASE STOP!
grip
DEPTH BOMB--
RMBBB

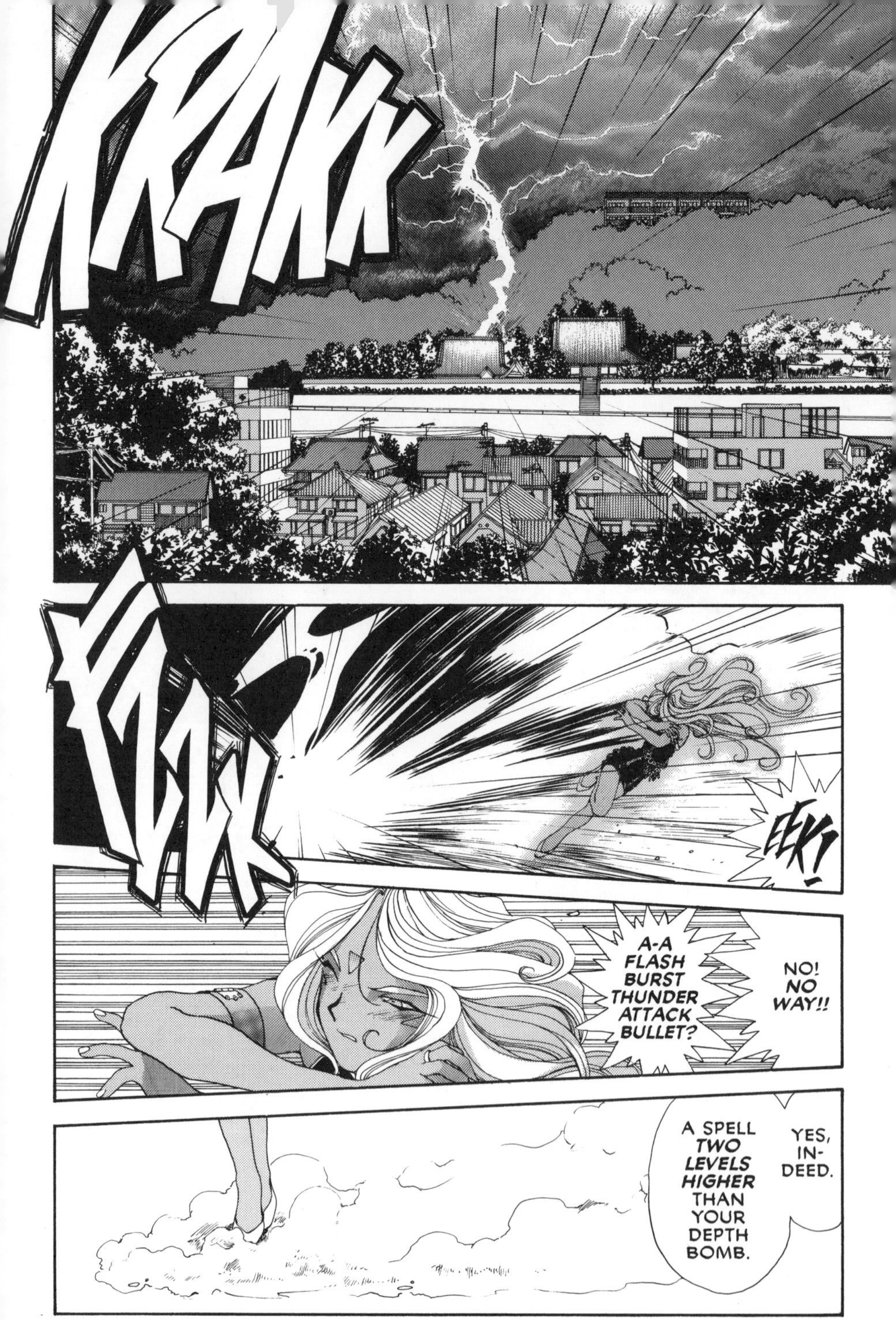
KRAKK
KRAKK
EEK!
NO! NO WAY!!
A-A FLASH BURST THUNDER ATTACK BULLET?
YES, IN-DEED.
A SPELL TWO LEVELS HIGHER THAN YOUR DEPTH BOMB.

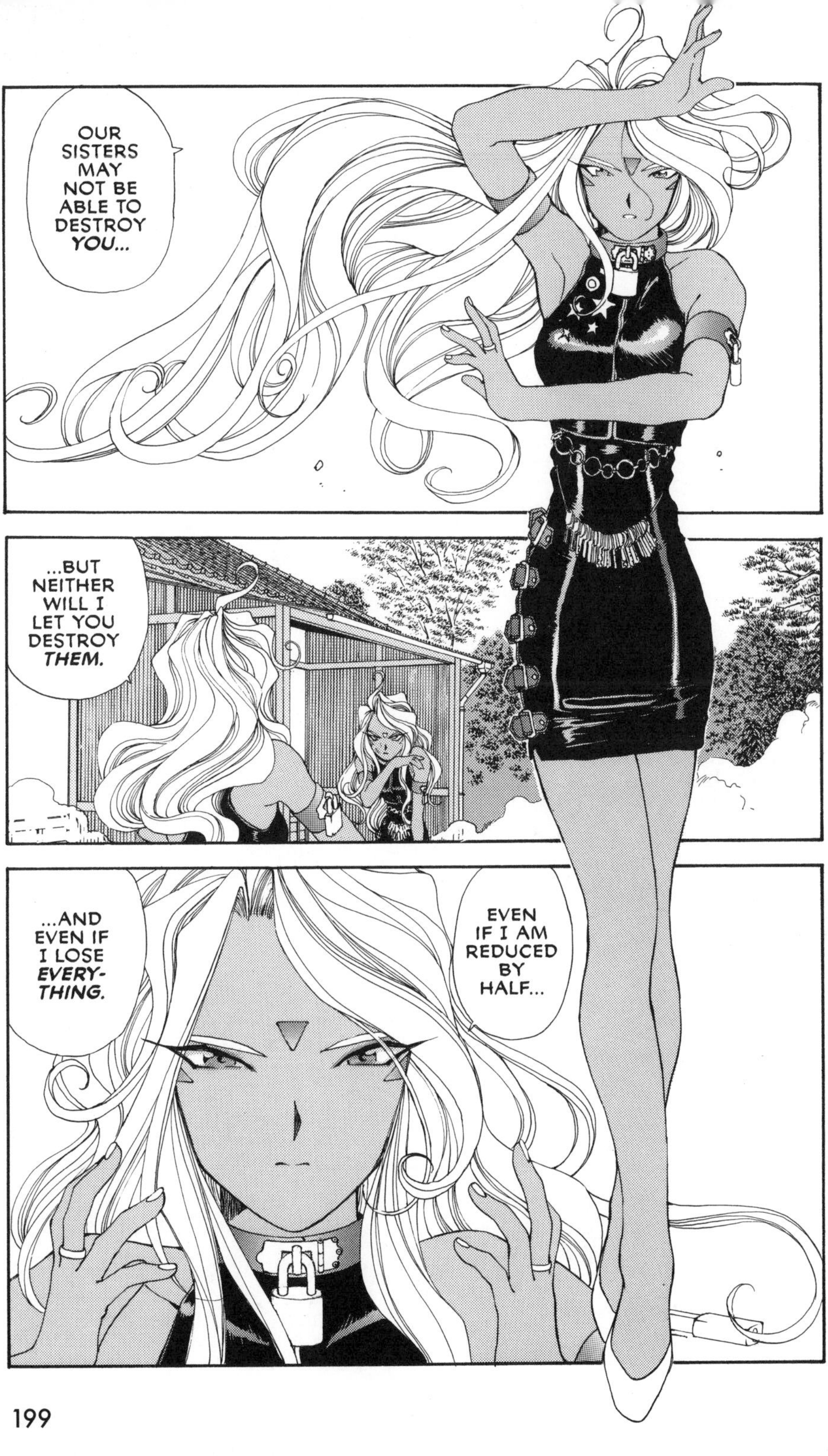
OUR SISTERS MAY NOT BE ABLE TO DESTROY *YOU*...
...BUT NEITHER WILL I LET YOU DESTROY *THEM.*
EVEN IF I AM REDUCED BY HALF...
...AND EVEN IF I LOSE *EVERY-THING.*

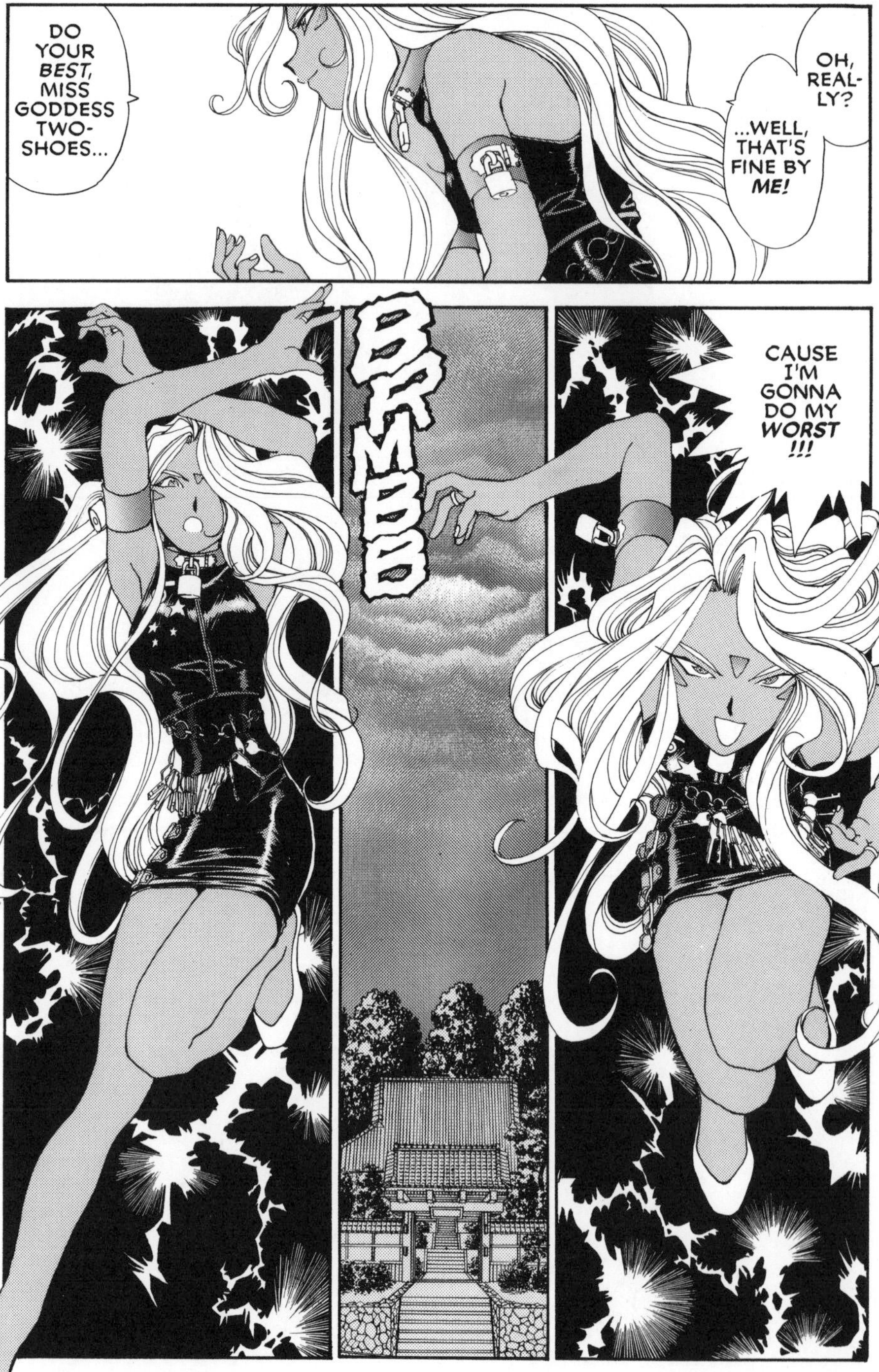
DO YOUR *BEST,* MISS GODDESS TWO-SHOES...
OH, REAL-LY? ...WELL, THAT'S FINE BY *ME!*
BRMBB
CAUSE I'M GONNA DO MY *WORST* !!!

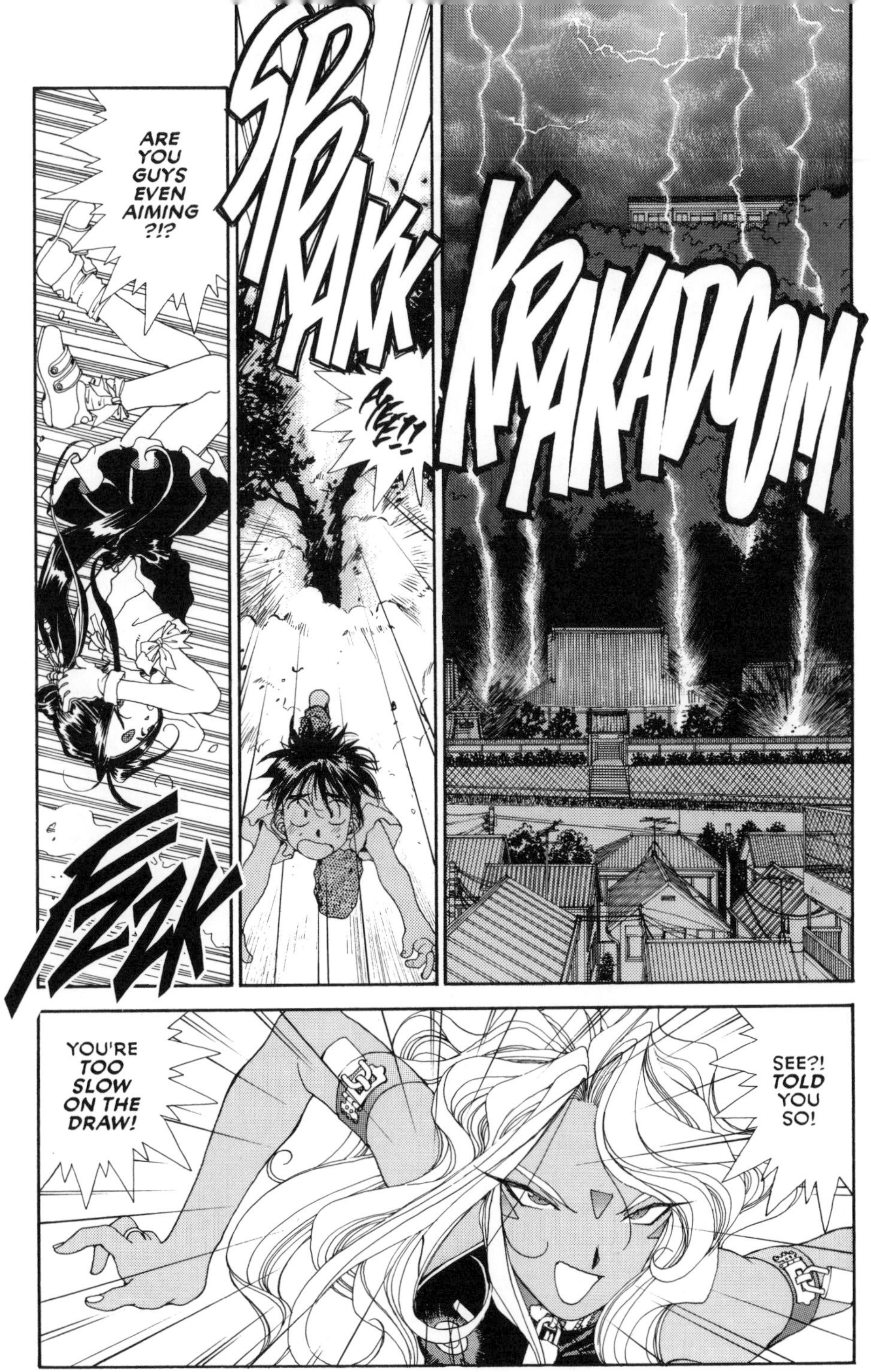
KRAKADOOM
SPRAKK
AIEE?!
ARE YOU GUYS EVEN AIMING ?!?
FZZK
SEE?! TOLD YOU SO!
YOU'RE TOO SLOW ON THE DRAW!

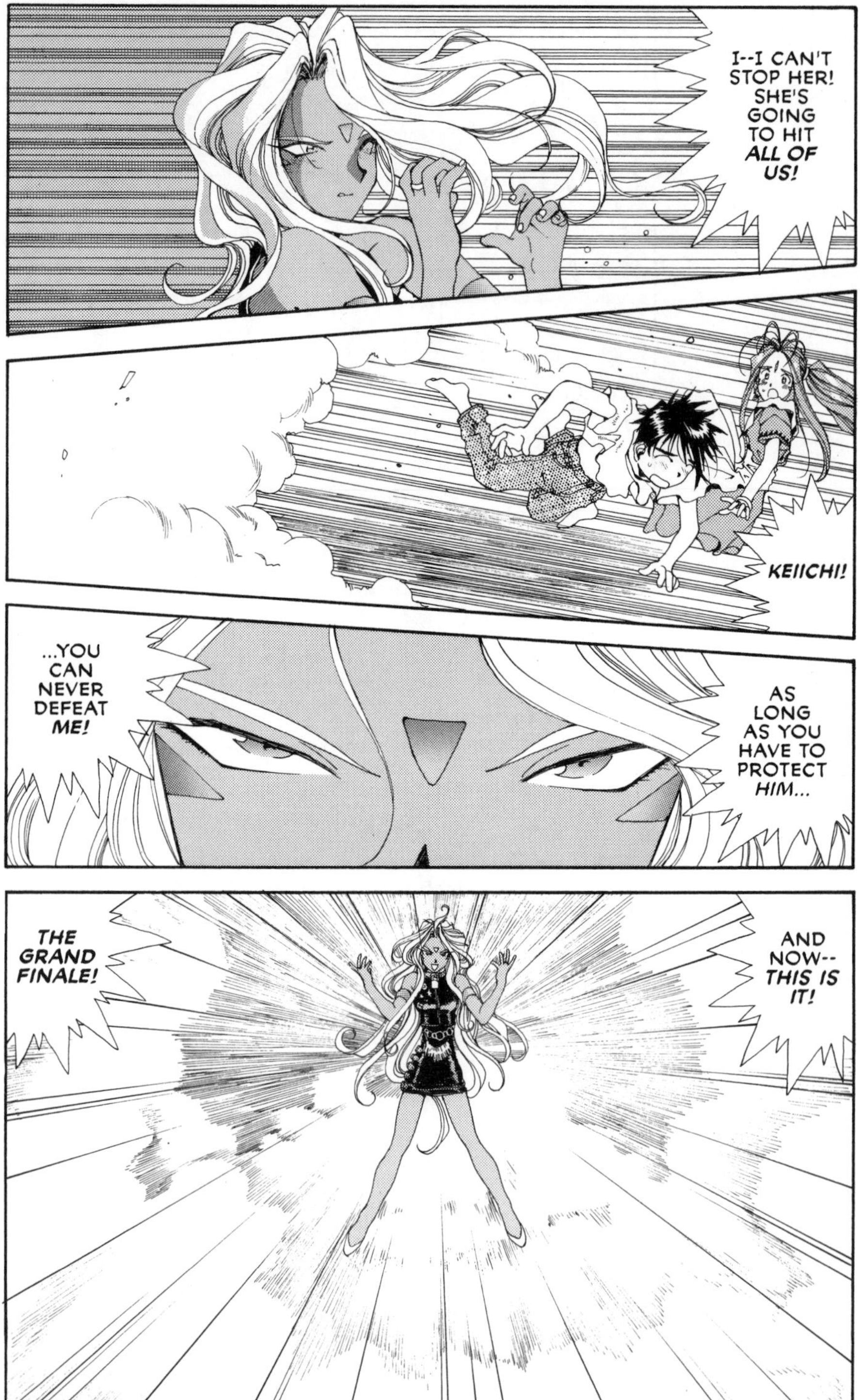
I--I CAN'T STOP HER! SHE'S GOING TO HIT ALL OF US!
KEIICHI!
AS LONG AS YOU HAVE TO PROTECT HIM...
...YOU CAN NEVER DEFEAT ME!
AND NOW-- THIS IS IT!
THE GRAND FINALE!

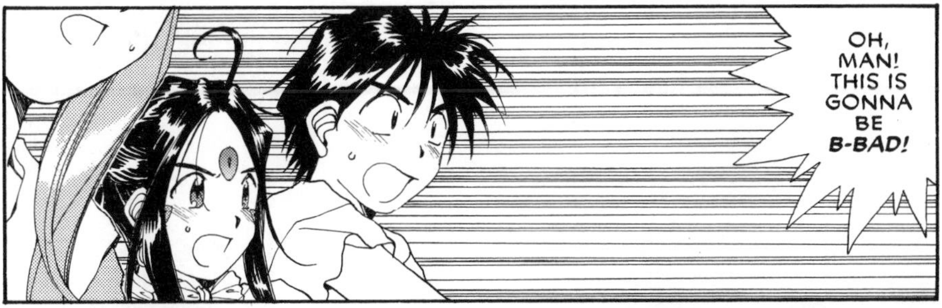
OH, MAN! THIS IS GONNA BE B-BAD!

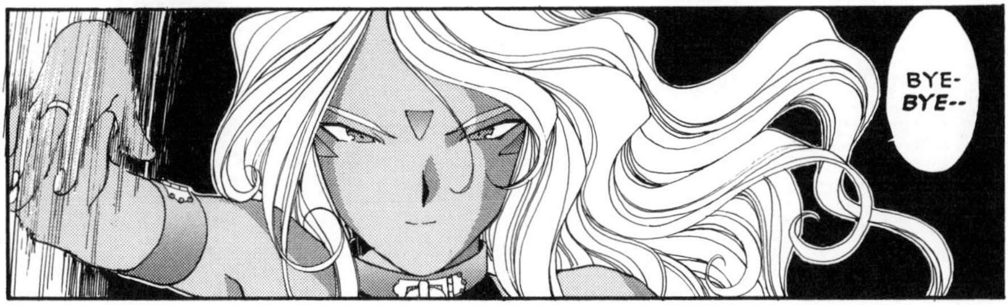
BYE-BYE--

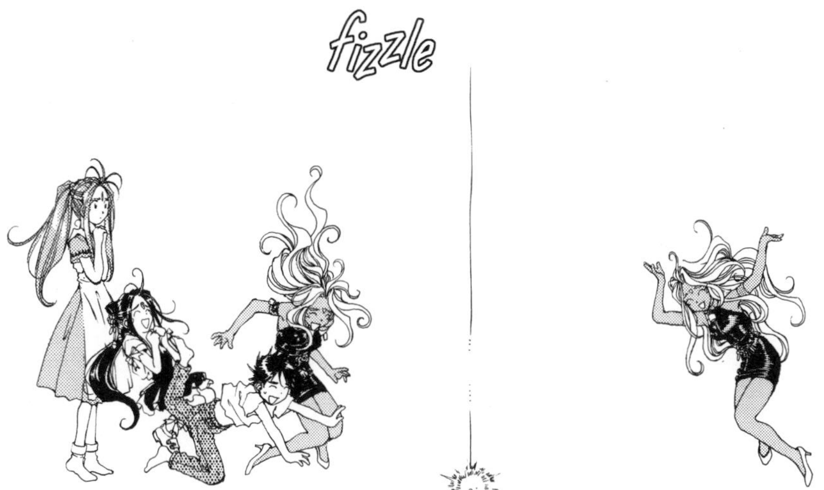
fizzle

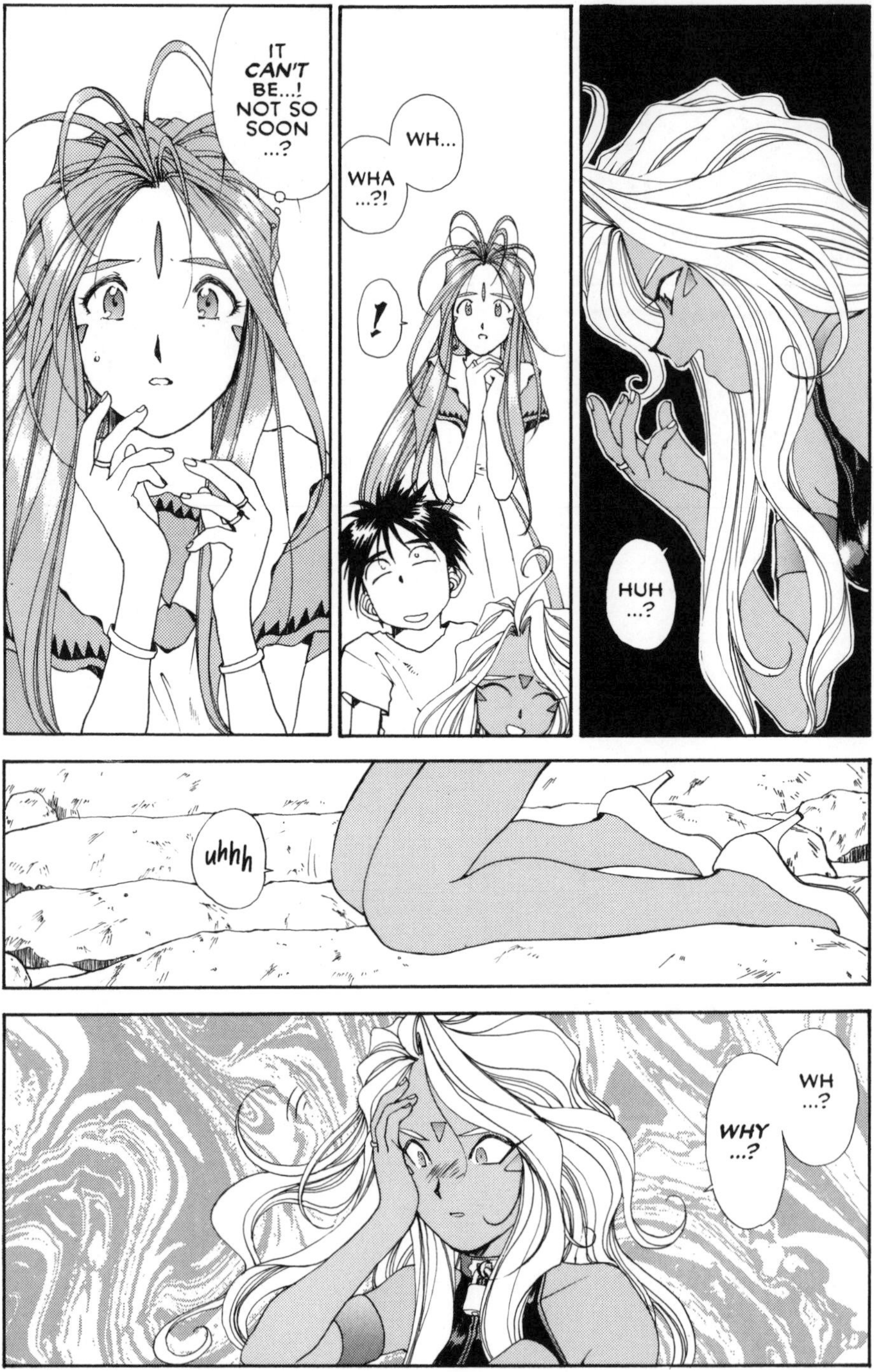
HUH ...?
WH...
WHA ...?!
!
IT CAN'T BE...! NOT SO SOON ...?
uhhh
WH ...?
WHY ...?

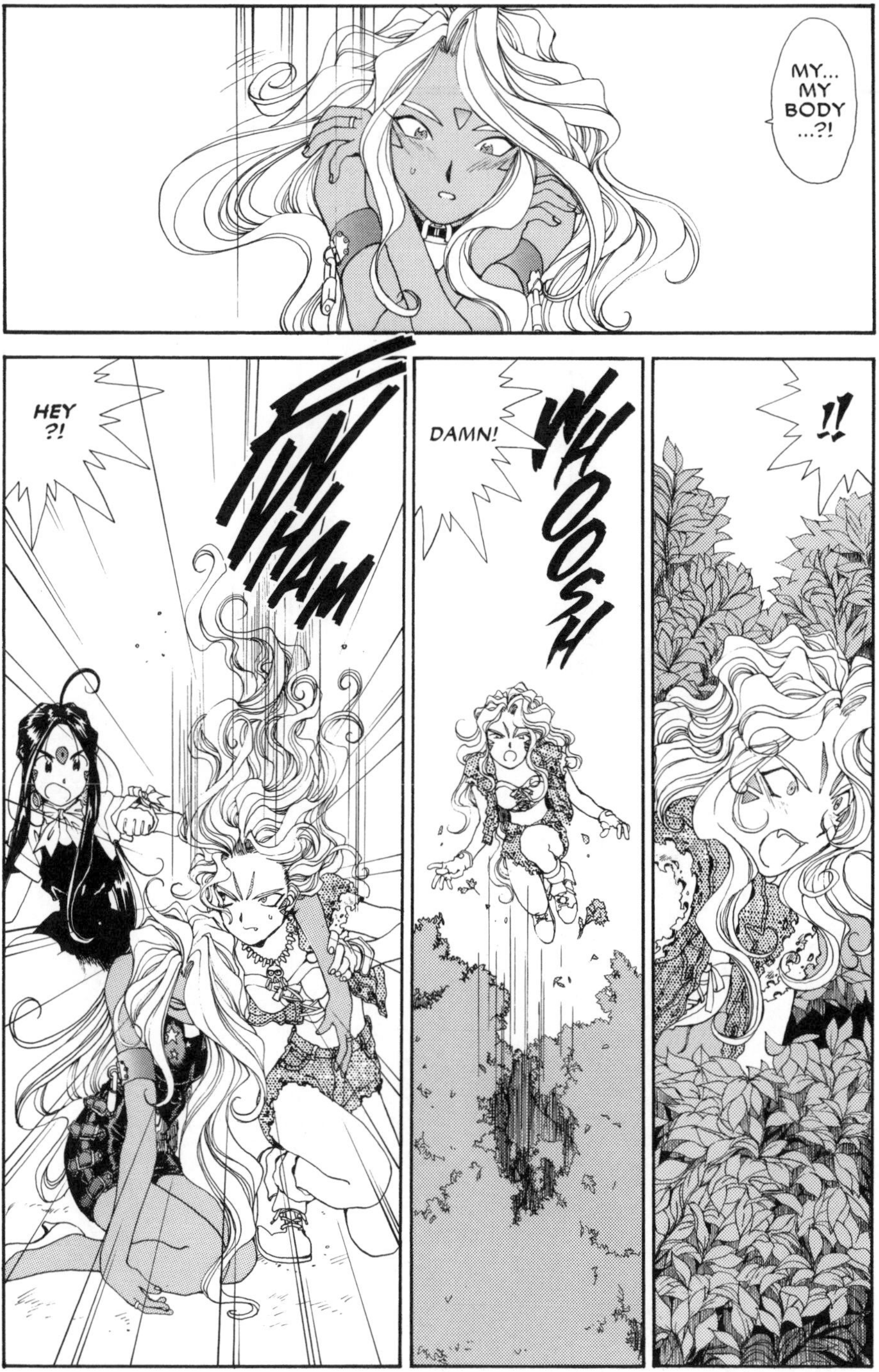
MY... MY BODY ...?!
!!
DAMN!
WHOOOSH
HEY ?!
FWHAM

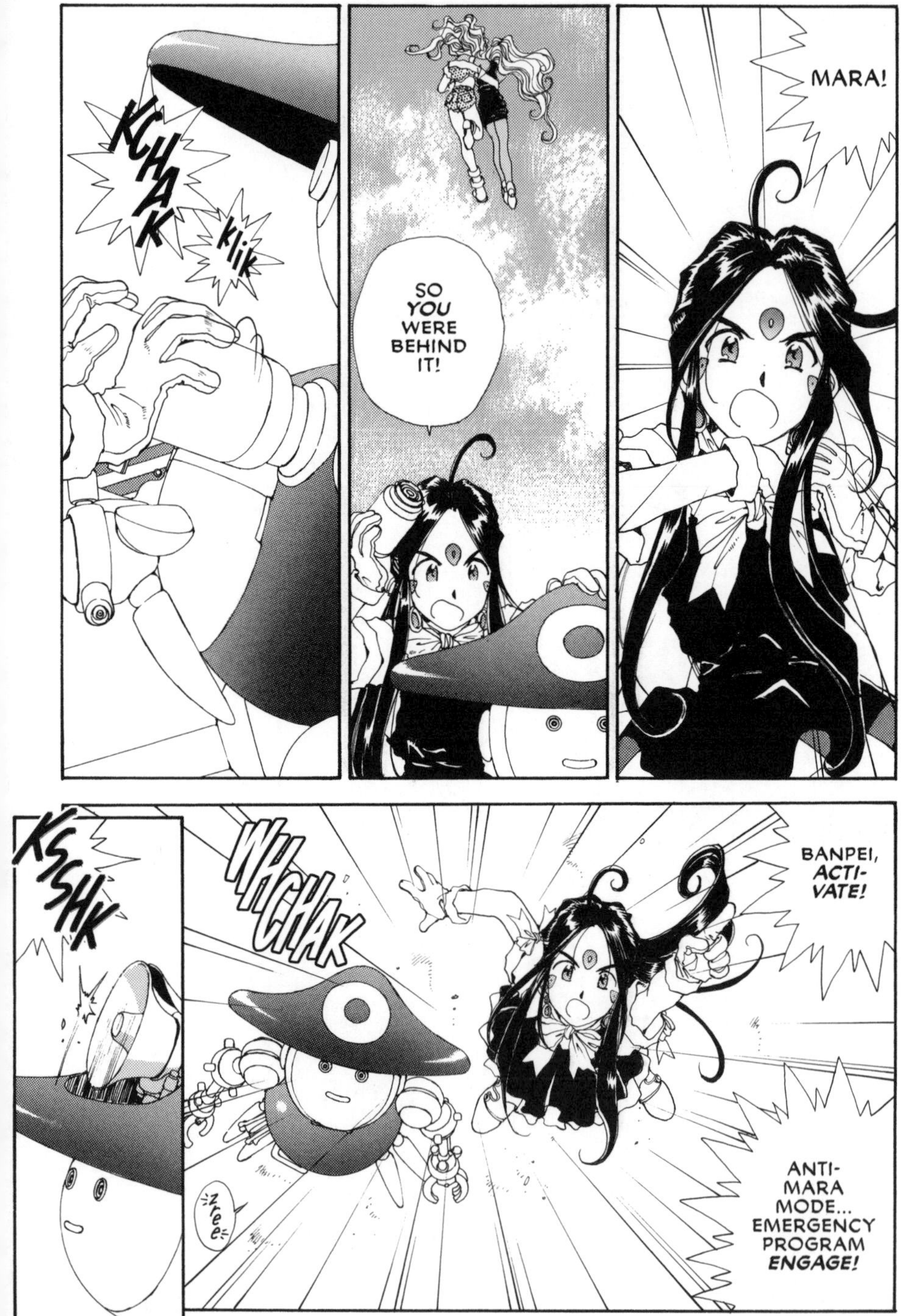
MARA!
SO *YOU* WERE BEHIND IT!
KCHAK
klik
BANPEI, *ACTIVATE!*
WHCHAK
ANTI-MARA MODE... EMERGENCY PROGRAM *ENGAGE!*
zree
KSSHK

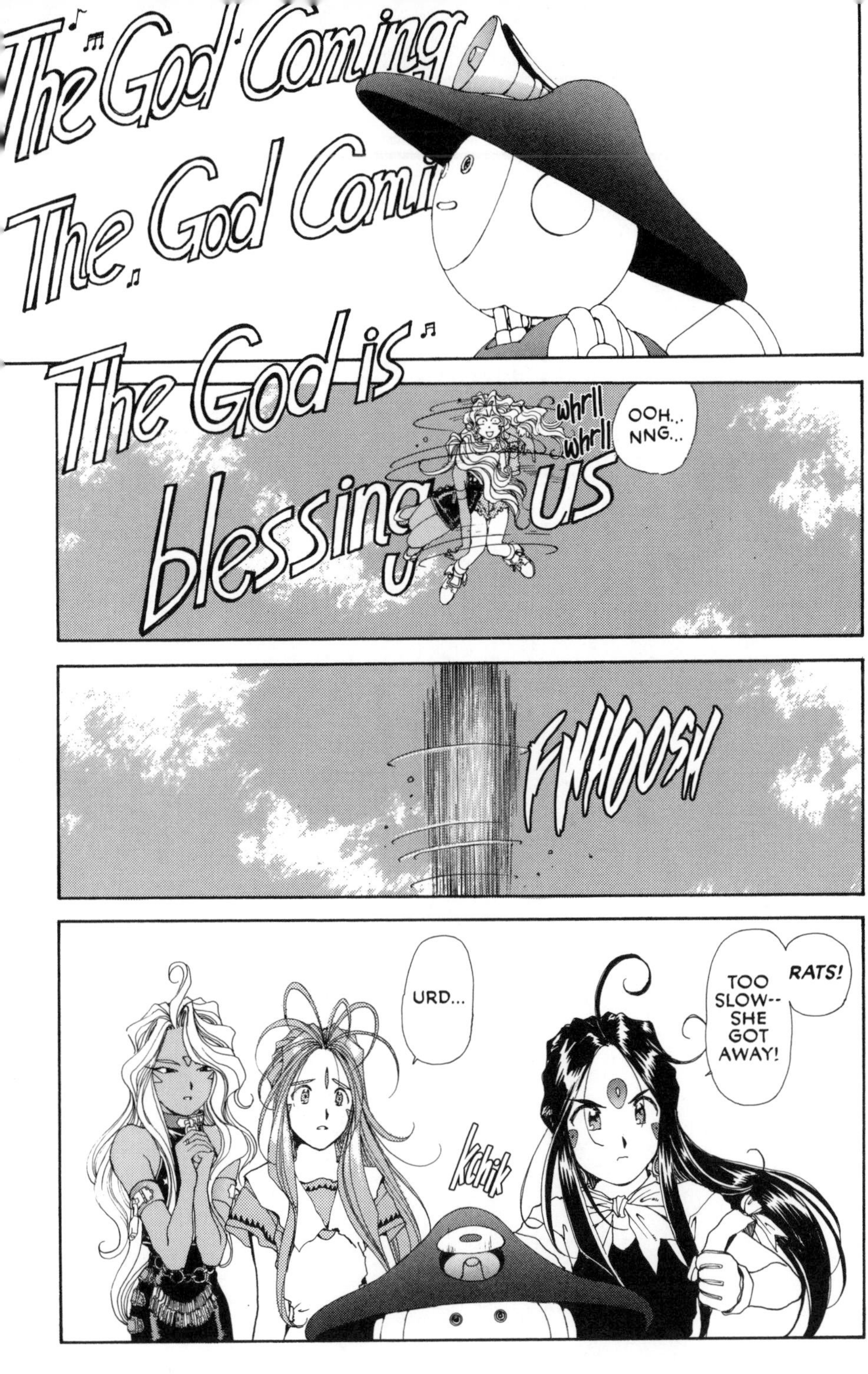

The God Coming
The God Comi
The God is blessing us
whrll
whrll
OOH... NNG...
FWHOOSH
RATS!
TOO SLOW-- SHE GOT AWAY!
URD...
kchik

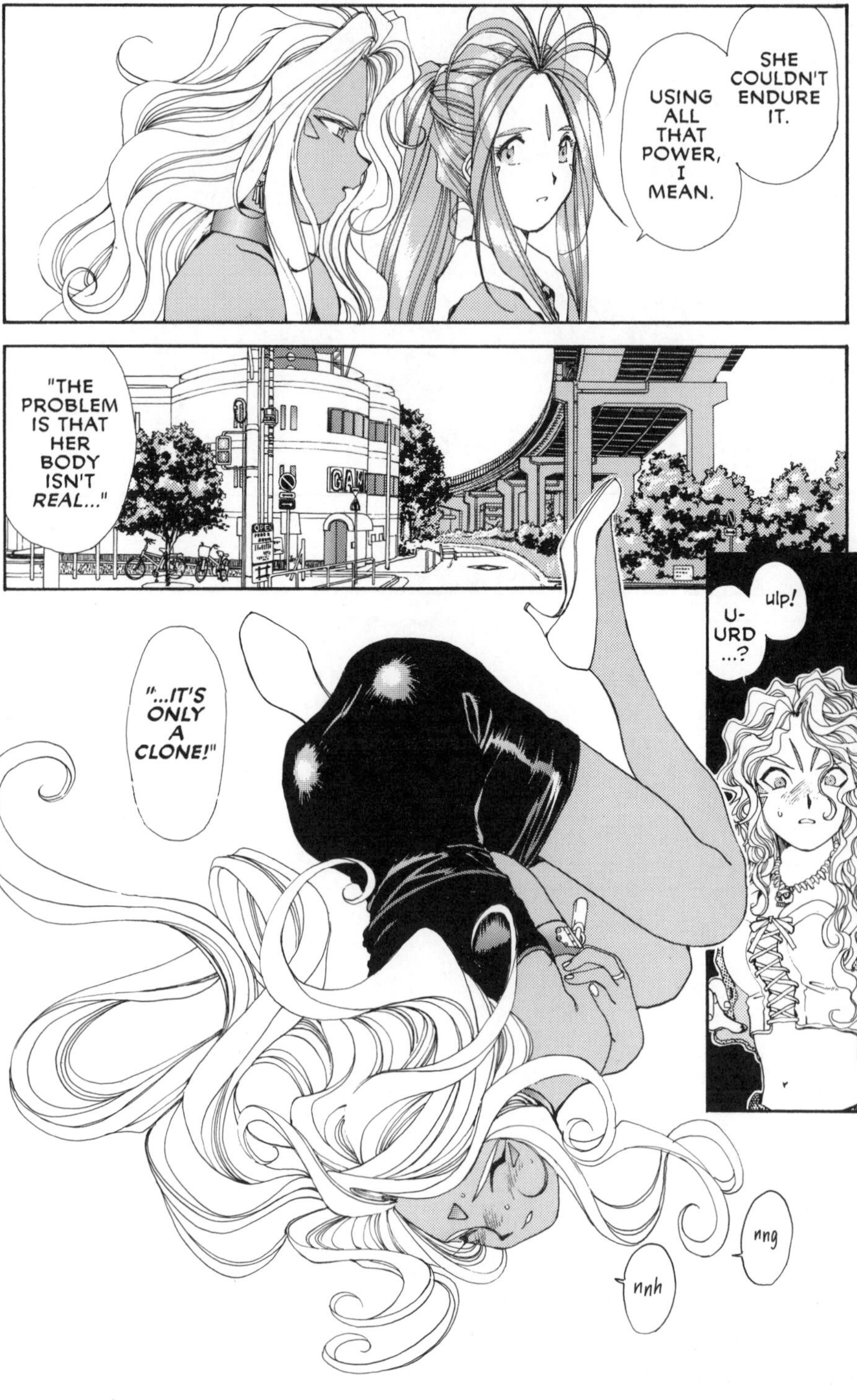
SHE COULDN'T ENDURE IT.
USING ALL THAT POWER, I MEAN.
"THE PROBLEM IS THAT HER BODY ISN'T *REAL*..."
ulp!
U-URD ...?
"...IT'S ONLY A CLONE!"
nng
nnh

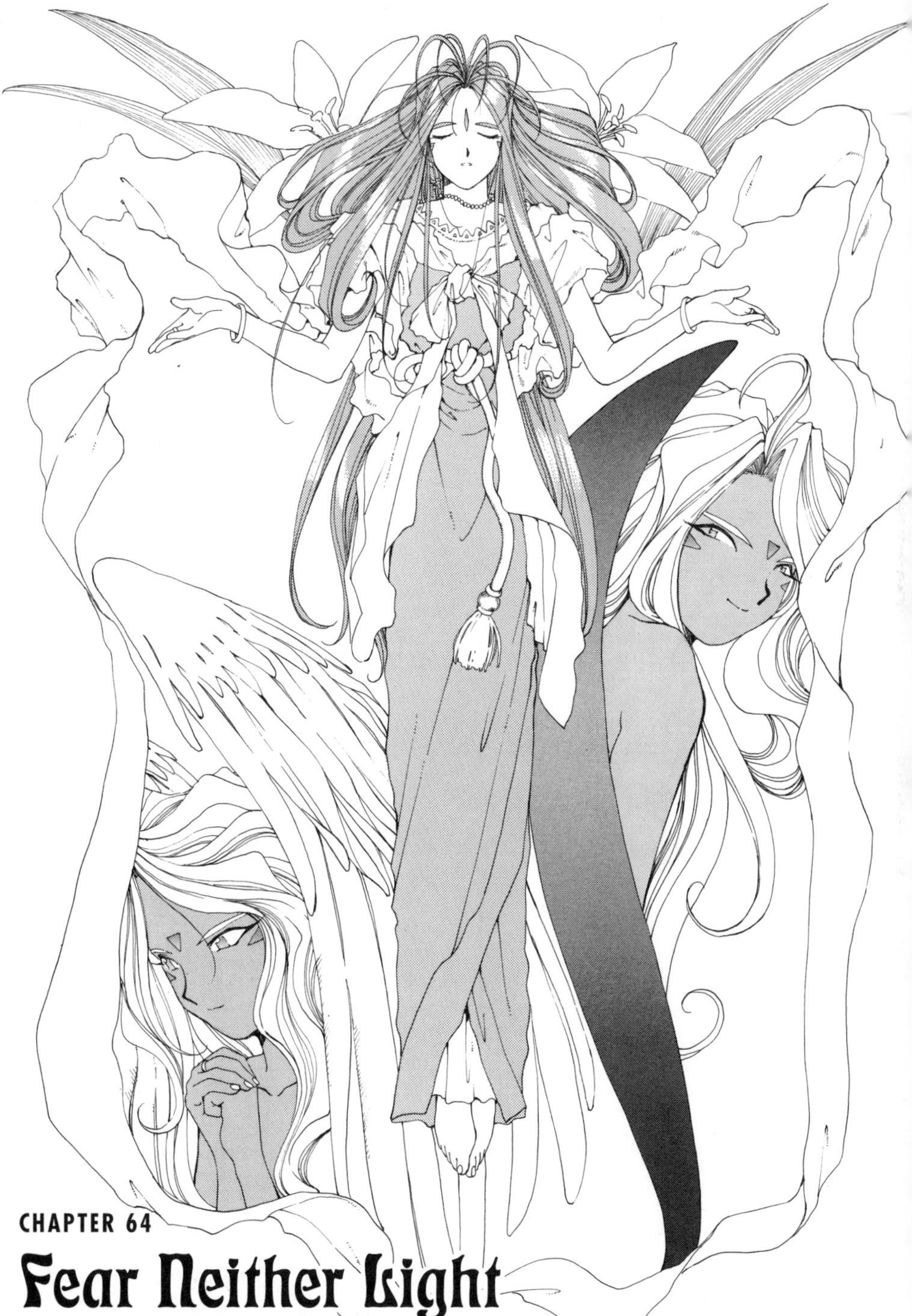

CHAPTER 64

Fear Neither Light nor Darkness

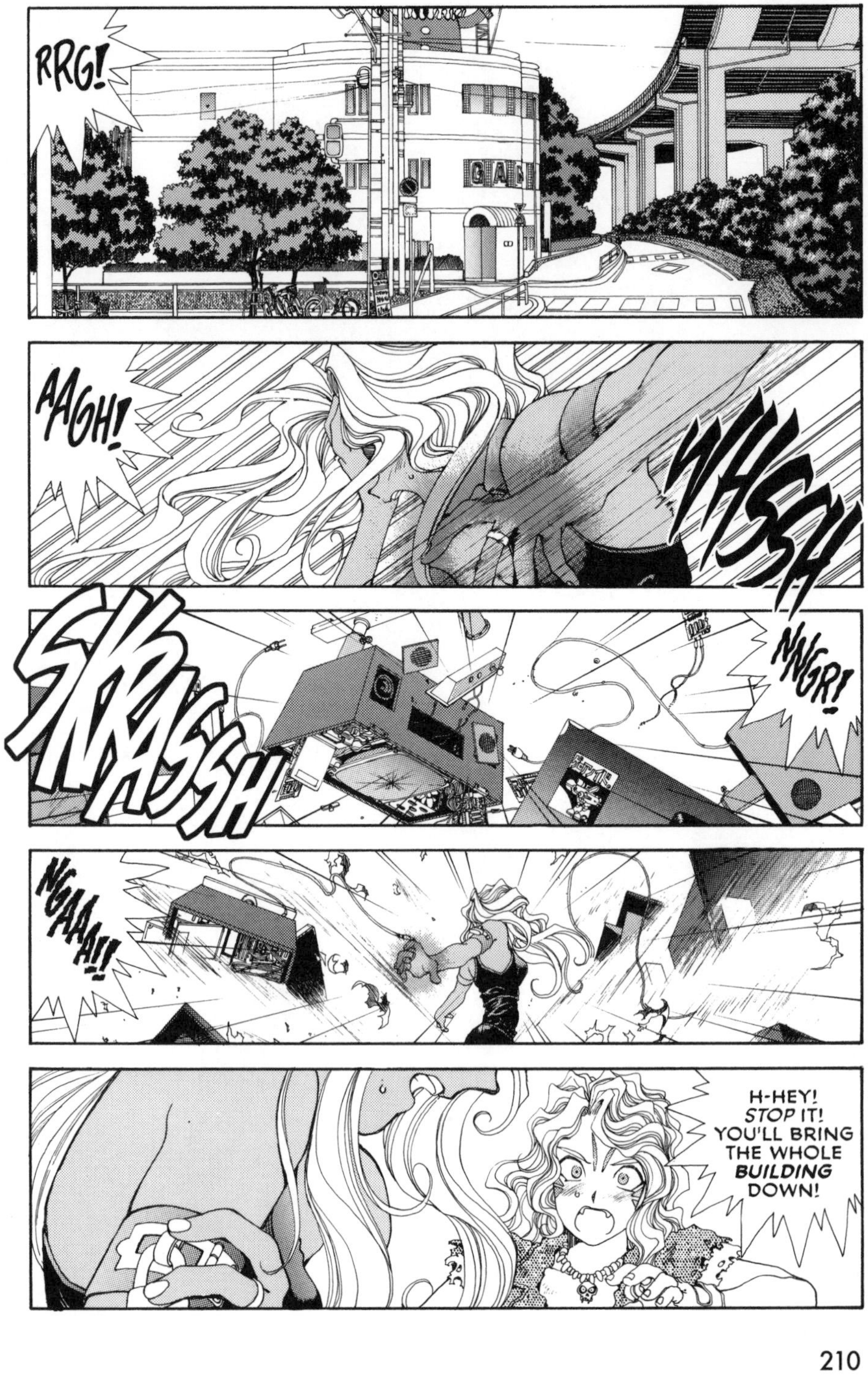
RRG!
WHSH
AAGH!
NNGR!
SKRASSH
NGAAAA!!
H-HEY! *STOP* IT! YOU'LL BRING THE WHOLE *BUILDING* DOWN!

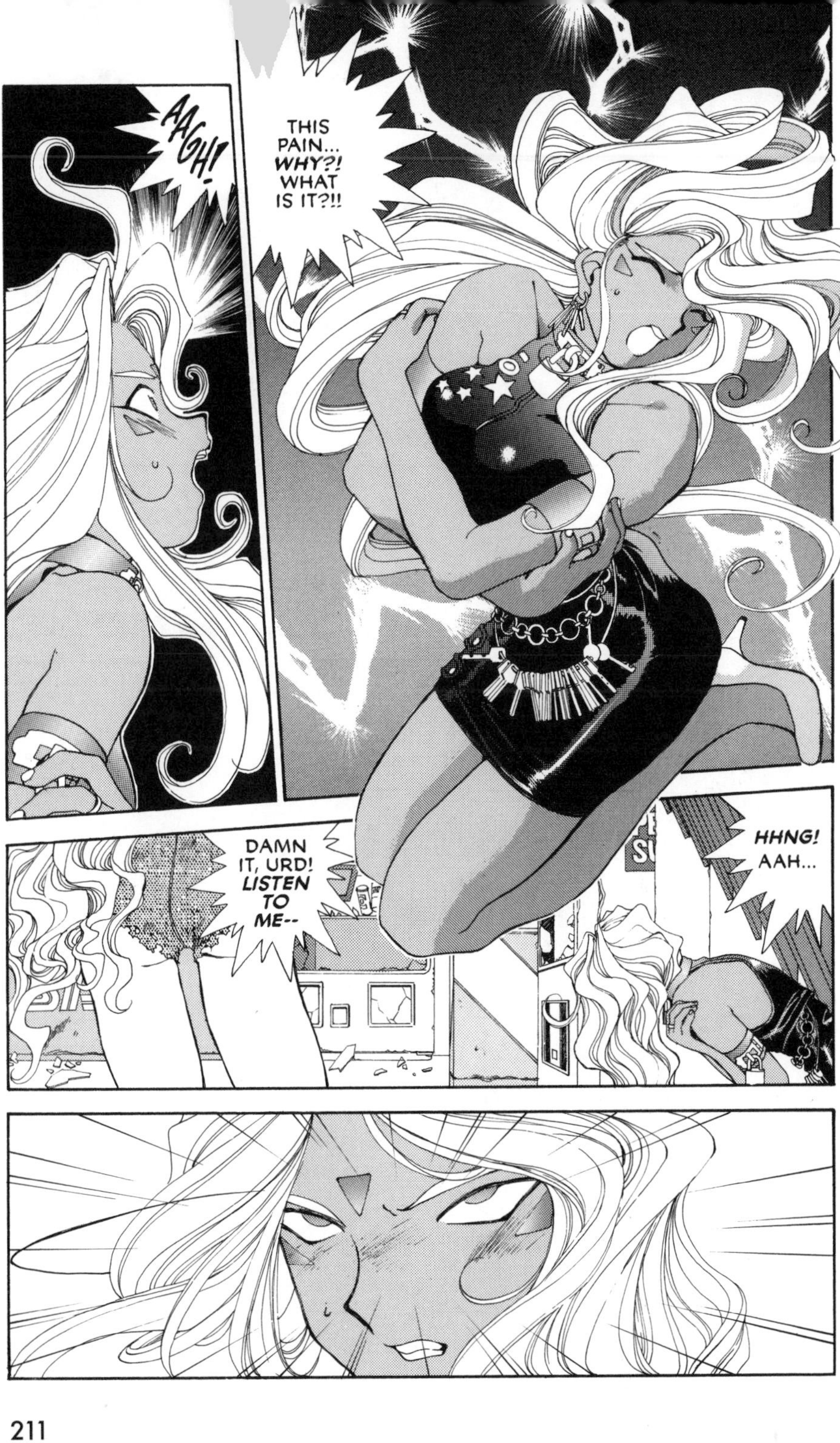
THIS PAIN... WHY?! WHAT IS IT?!!
AAGH!
HHNG! AAH...
DAMN IT, URD! LISTEN TO ME--

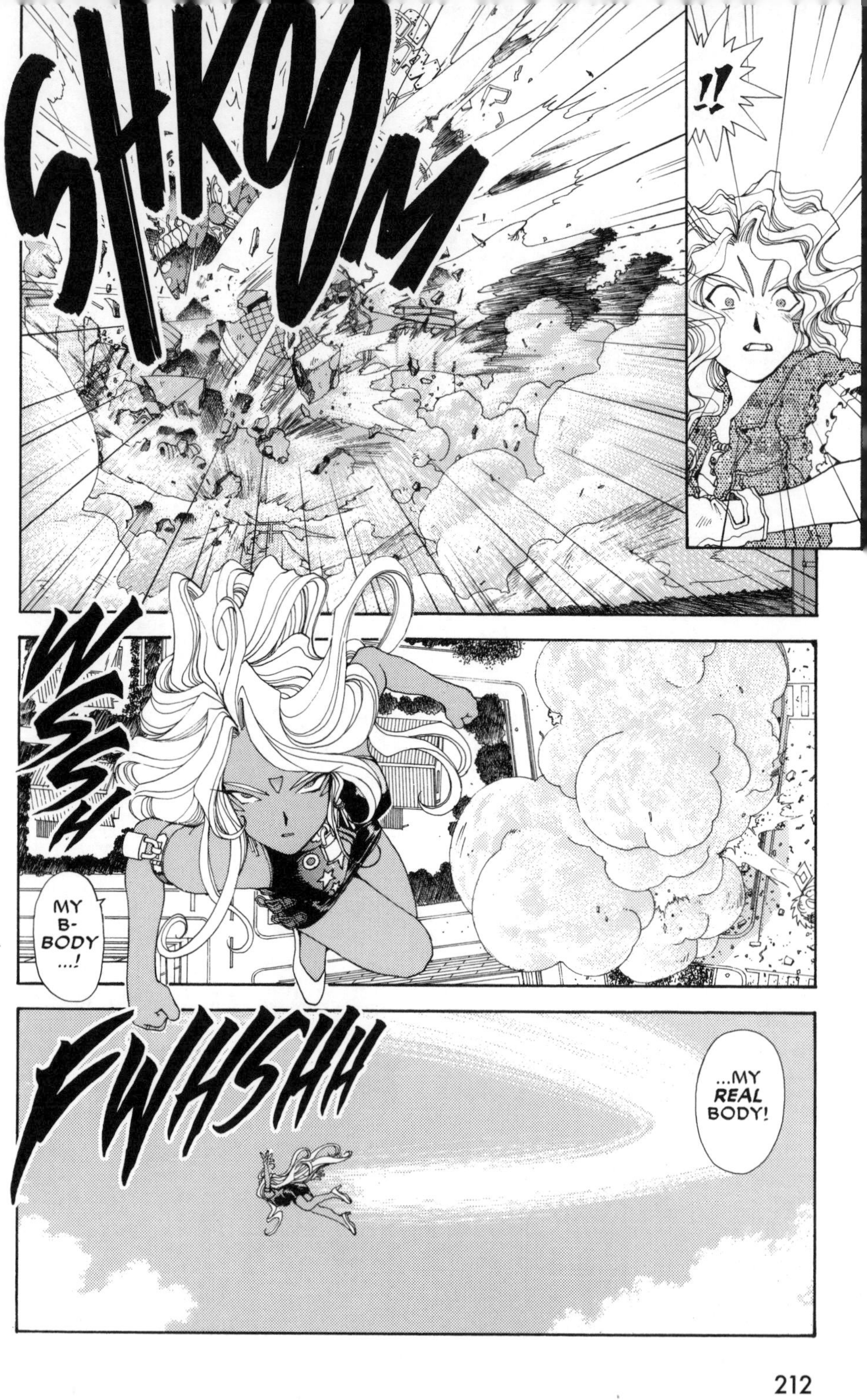
!!
SHKOOM
WSSH
MY B-BODY ...!
FWHSHH
...MY *REAL* BODY!

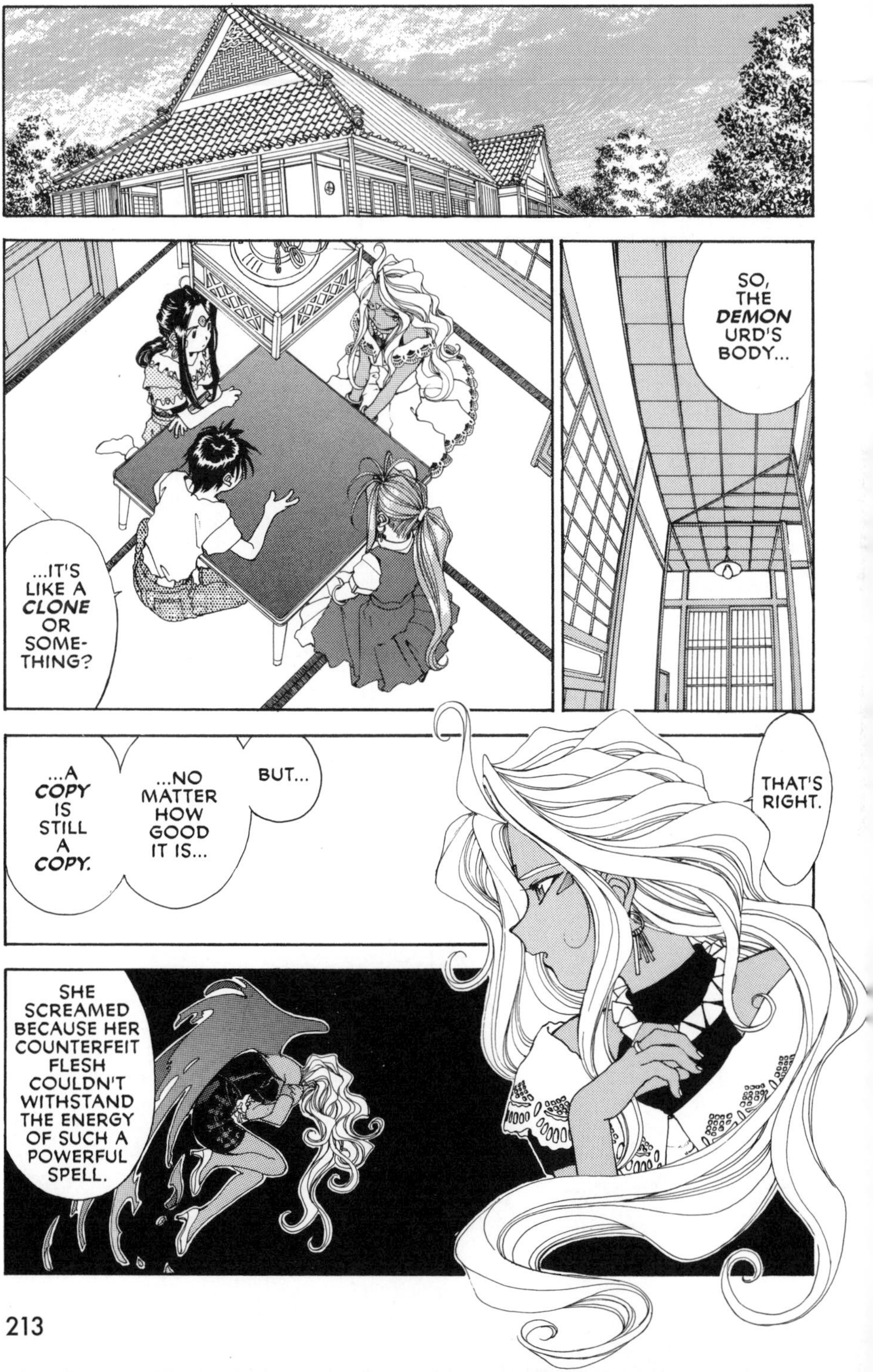
SO, THE DEMON URD'S BODY...
...IT'S LIKE A CLONE OR SOMETHING?
THAT'S RIGHT.
BUT...
...NO MATTER HOW GOOD IT IS...
...A COPY IS STILL A COPY.
SHE SCREAMED BECAUSE HER COUNTERFEIT FLESH COULDN'T WITHSTAND THE ENERGY OF SUCH A POWERFUL SPELL.

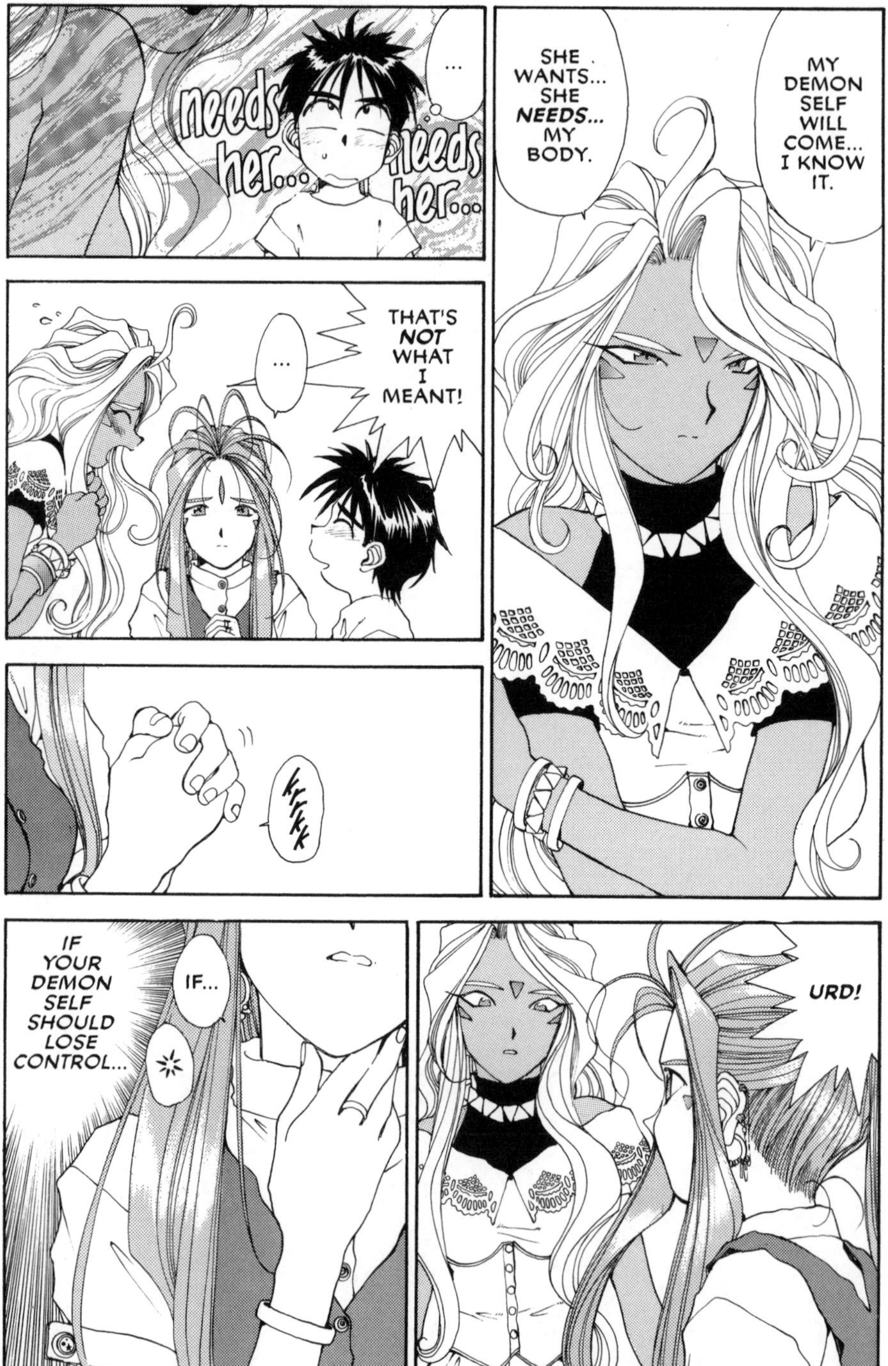
MY DEMON SELF WILL COME... I KNOW IT.
SHE WANTS... SHE *NEEDS*... MY BODY.
...
needs her...
needs her...
THAT'S *NOT* WHAT I MEANT!
...
krrkk
URD!
IF...
IF YOUR DEMON SELF SHOULD LOSE CONTROL...

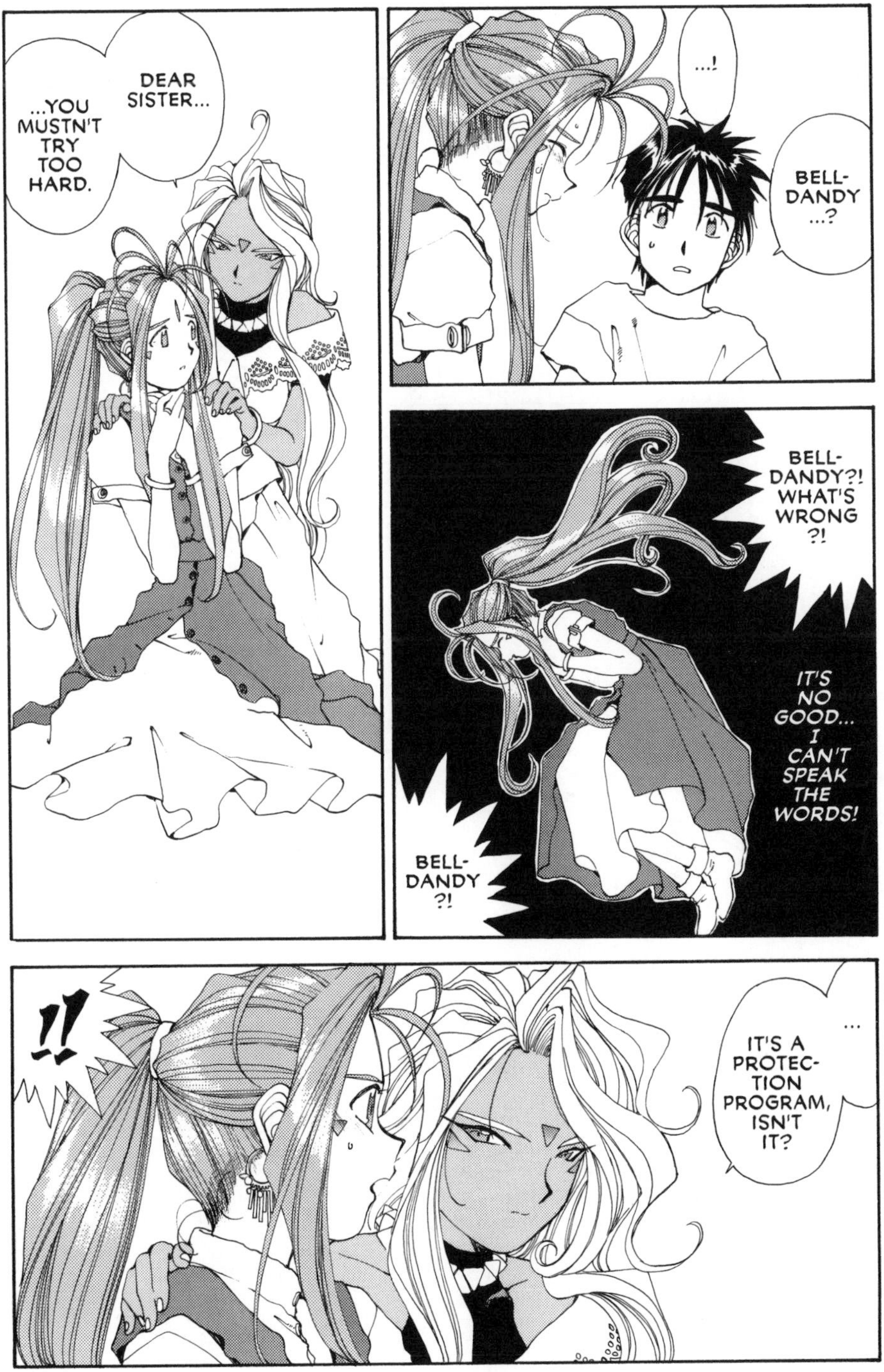
...!
BELL-DANDY ...?
BELL-DANDY?! WHAT'S WRONG ?!
IT'S NO GOOD... I CAN'T SPEAK THE WORDS!
BELL-DANDY ?!
DEAR SISTER...
...YOU MUSTN'T TRY TOO HARD.
... IT'S A PROTECTION PROGRAM, ISN'T IT?
!!

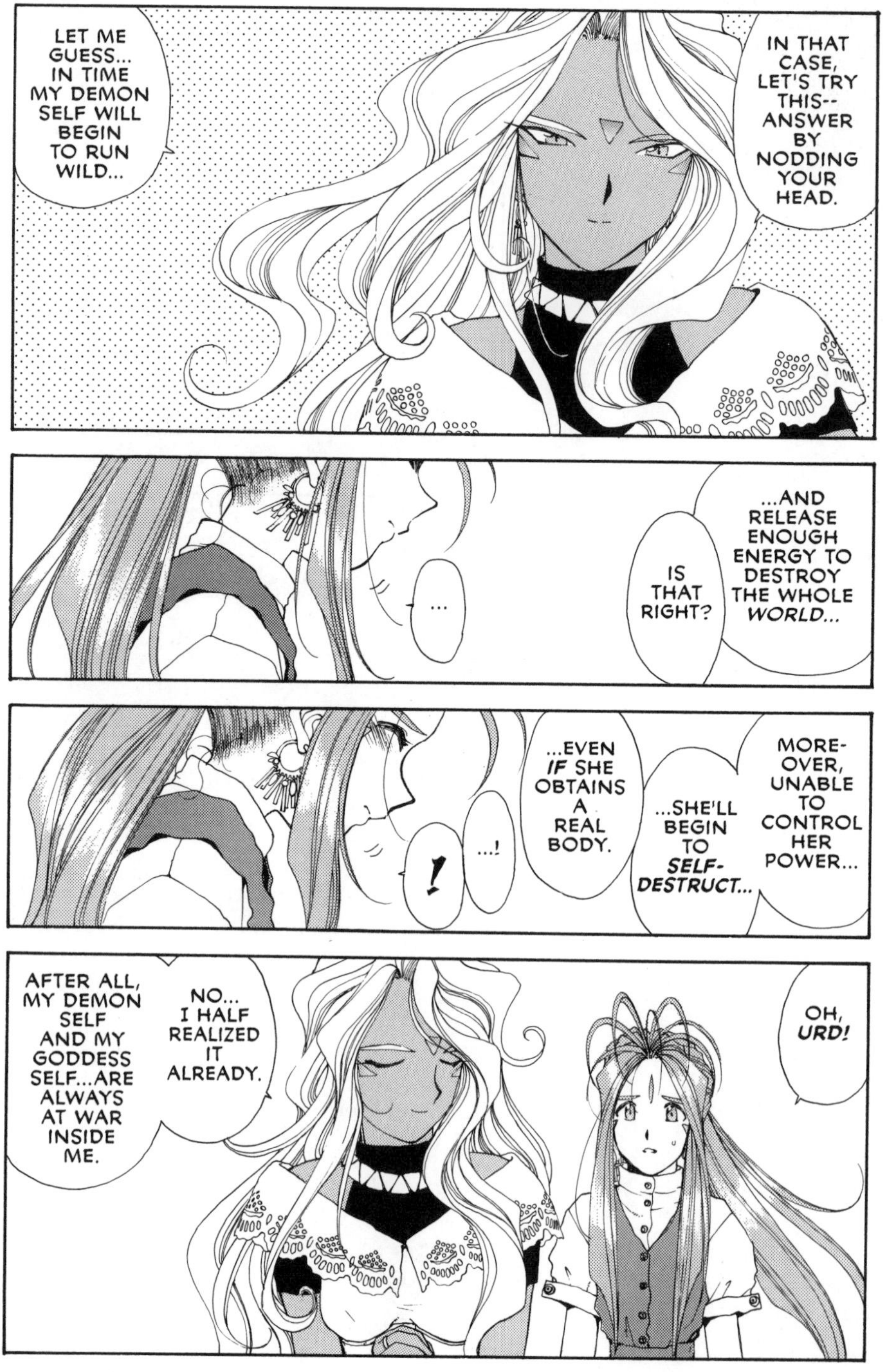
IN THAT CASE, LET'S TRY THIS-- ANSWER BY NODDING YOUR HEAD.
LET ME GUESS... IN TIME MY DEMON SELF WILL BEGIN TO RUN WILD...
...AND RELEASE ENOUGH ENERGY TO DESTROY THE WHOLE *WORLD...*
IS THAT RIGHT?
...
MORE-OVER, UNABLE TO CONTROL HER POWER...
...SHE'LL BEGIN TO *SELF-DESTRUCT...*
...EVEN *IF* SHE OBTAINS A REAL BODY.
...!
!
OH, *URD!*
NO... I HALF REALIZED IT ALREADY.
AFTER ALL, MY DEMON SELF AND MY GODDESS SELF...ARE ALWAYS AT WAR INSIDE ME.

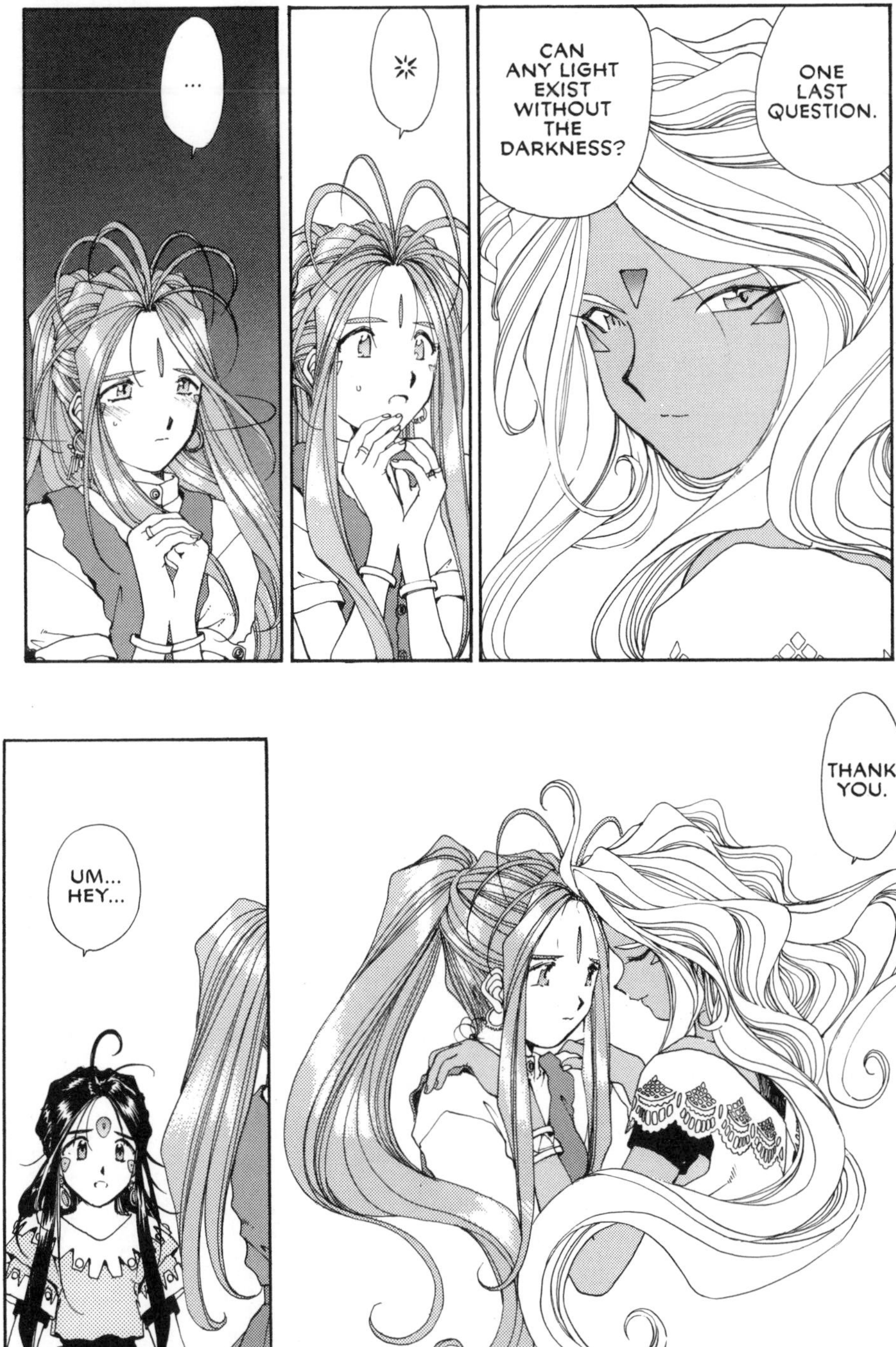
ONE LAST QUESTION.
CAN ANY LIGHT EXIST WITHOUT THE DARKNESS?
...
THANK YOU.
UM... HEY...

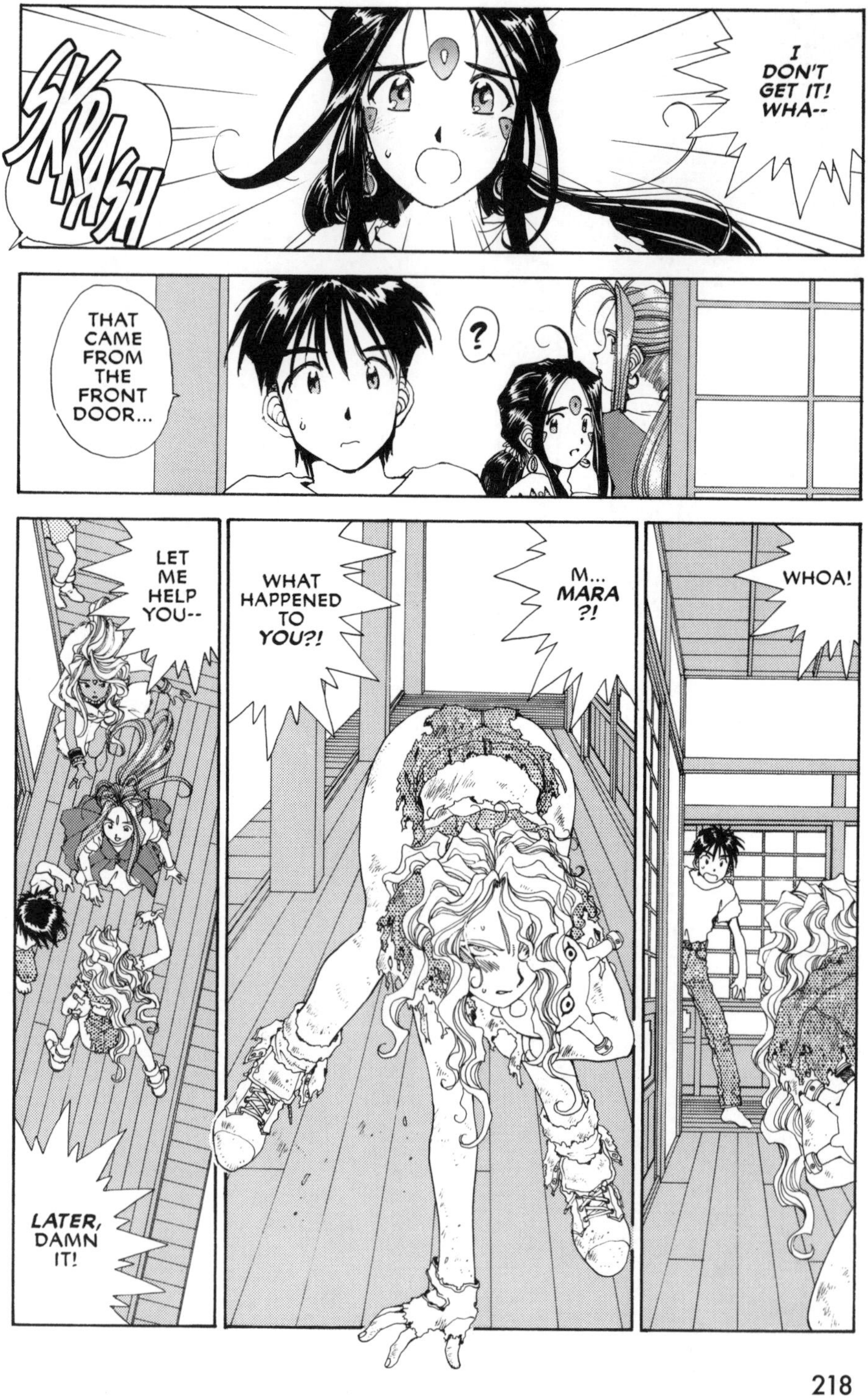
I DON'T GET IT! WHA--
SKRASH
?
THAT CAME FROM THE FRONT DOOR...
WHOA!
M... *MARA* ?!
WHAT HAPPENED TO *YOU*?!
LET ME HELP YOU--
LATER, DAMN IT!

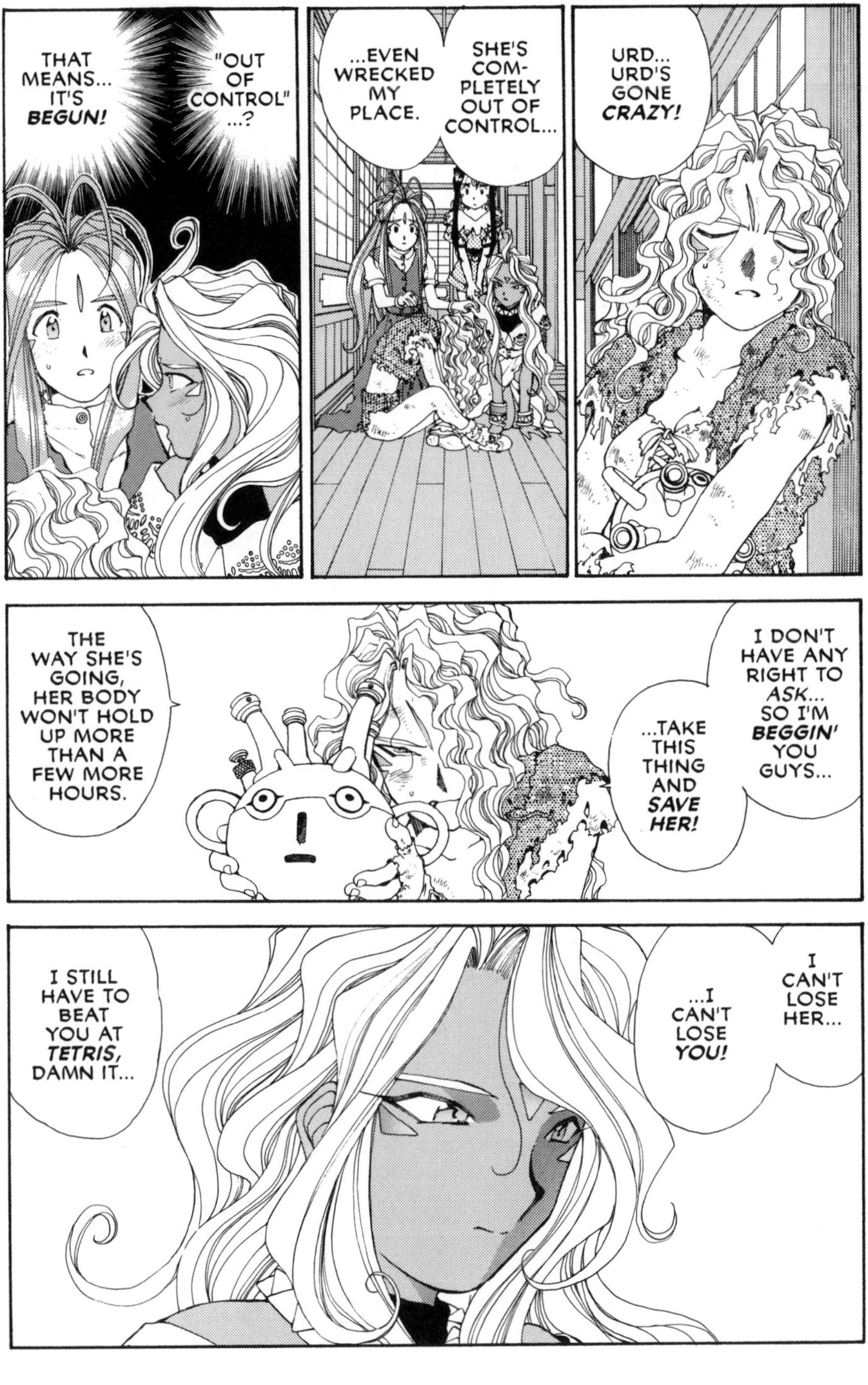
URD... URD'S GONE *CRAZY!*
SHE'S COMPLETELY OUT OF CONTROL...
...EVEN WRECKED MY PLACE.
"OUT OF CONTROL" ...?
THAT MEANS... IT'S *BEGUN!*
I DON'T HAVE ANY RIGHT TO *ASK*... SO I'M *BEGGIN'* YOU GUYS...
...TAKE THIS THING AND *SAVE HER!*
THE WAY SHE'S GOING, HER BODY WON'T HOLD UP MORE THAN A FEW MORE HOURS.
I CAN'T LOSE HER...
...I CAN'T LOSE *YOU!*
I STILL HAVE TO BEAT YOU AT *TETRIS,* DAMN IT...

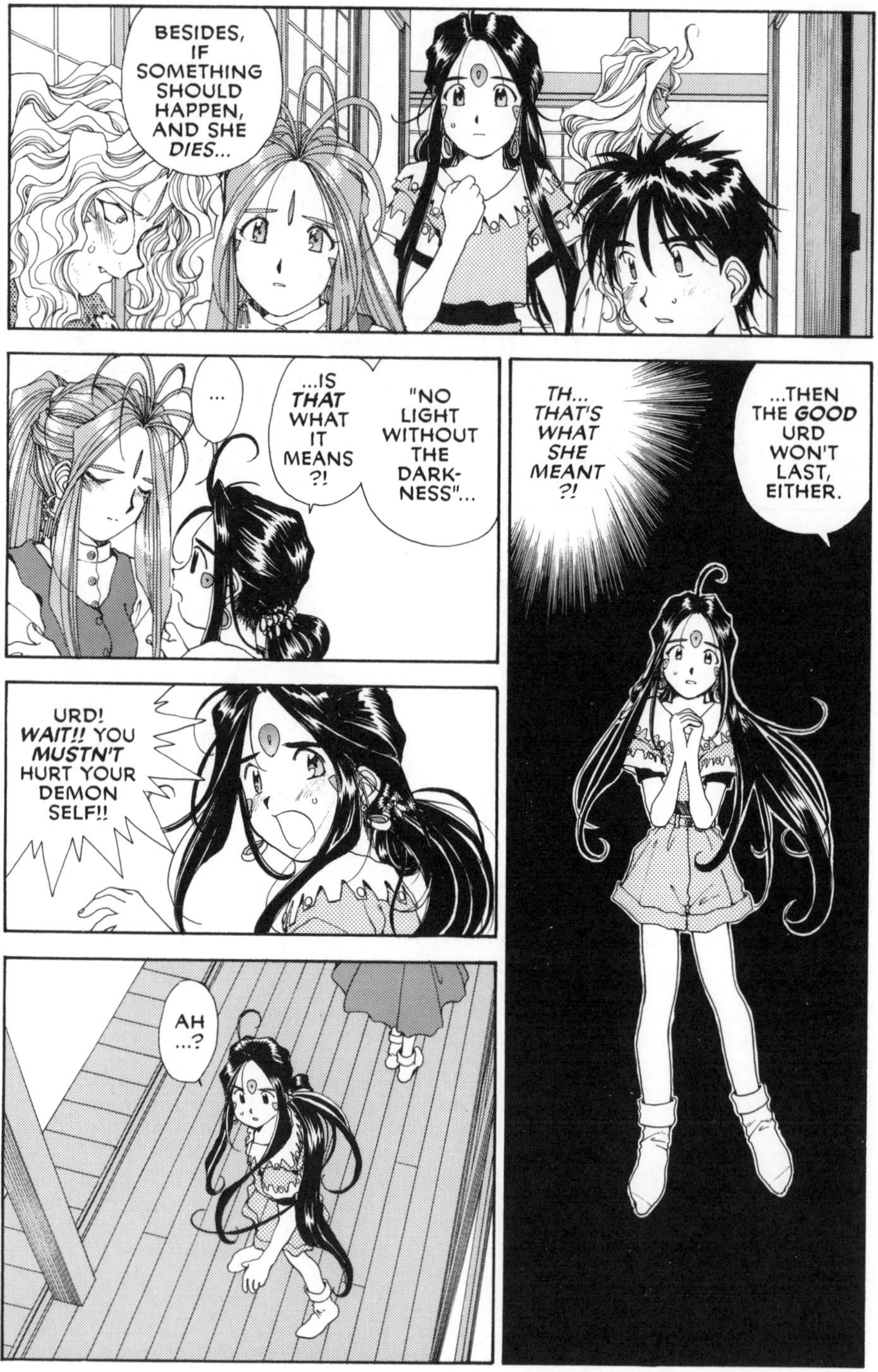

BESIDES, IF SOMETHING SHOULD HAPPEN, AND SHE *DIES*...
...THEN THE ***GOOD*** URD WON'T LAST, EITHER.
TH... THAT'S WHAT SHE MEANT ?!
"NO LIGHT WITHOUT THE DARKNESS"...
...IS ***THAT*** WHAT IT MEANS ?!
...
URD! ***WAIT!!*** YOU ***MUSTN'T*** HURT YOUR DEMON SELF!!
AH ...?

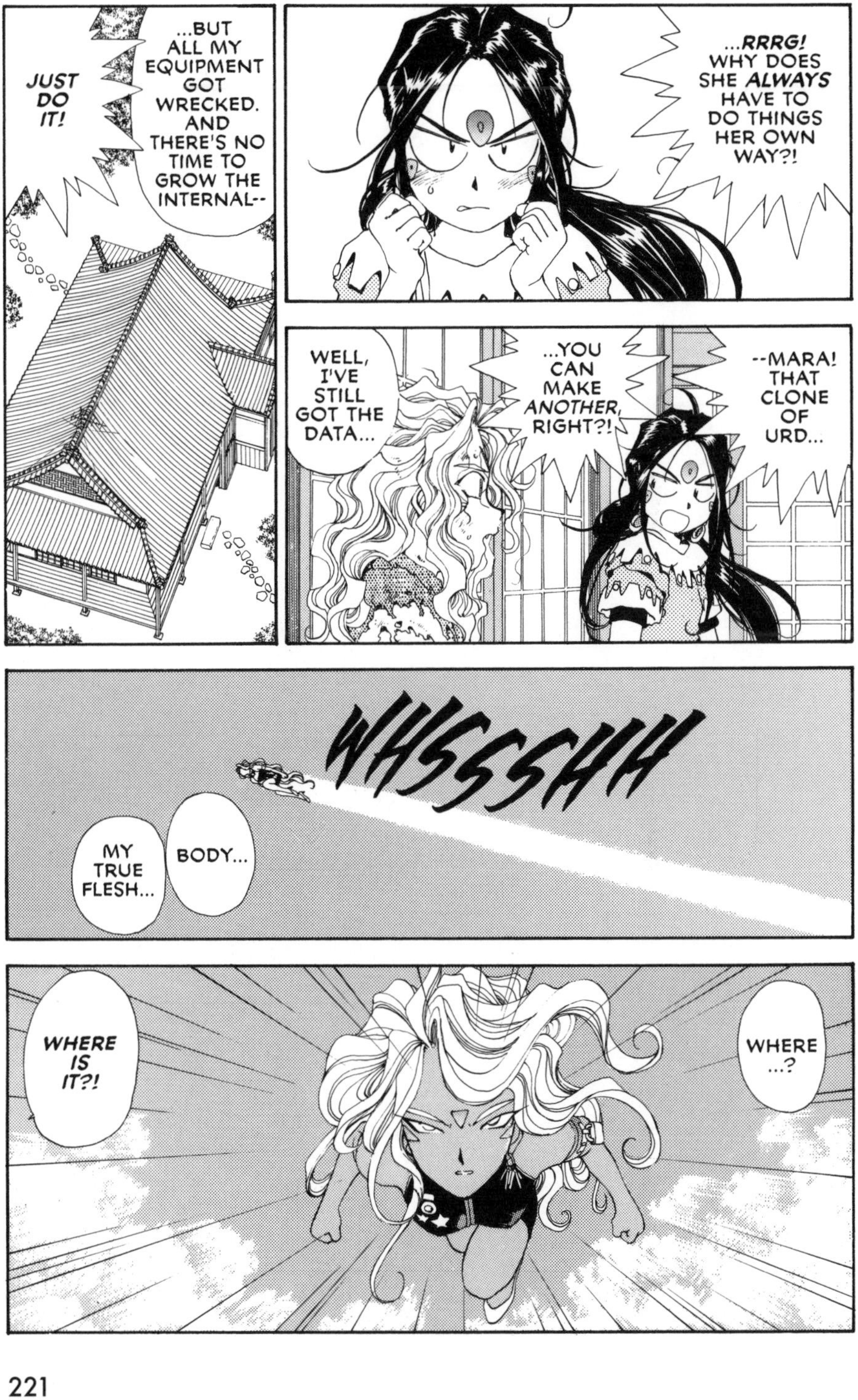
...RRRG! WHY DOES SHE ALWAYS HAVE TO DO THINGS HER OWN WAY?!
--MARA! THAT CLONE OF URD...
...YOU CAN MAKE ANOTHER, RIGHT?!
WELL, I'VE STILL GOT THE DATA...
...BUT ALL MY EQUIPMENT GOT WRECKED. AND THERE'S NO TIME TO GROW THE INTERNAL--
JUST DO IT!
WHSSSHH
BODY...
MY TRUE FLESH...
WHERE ...?
WHERE IS IT?!

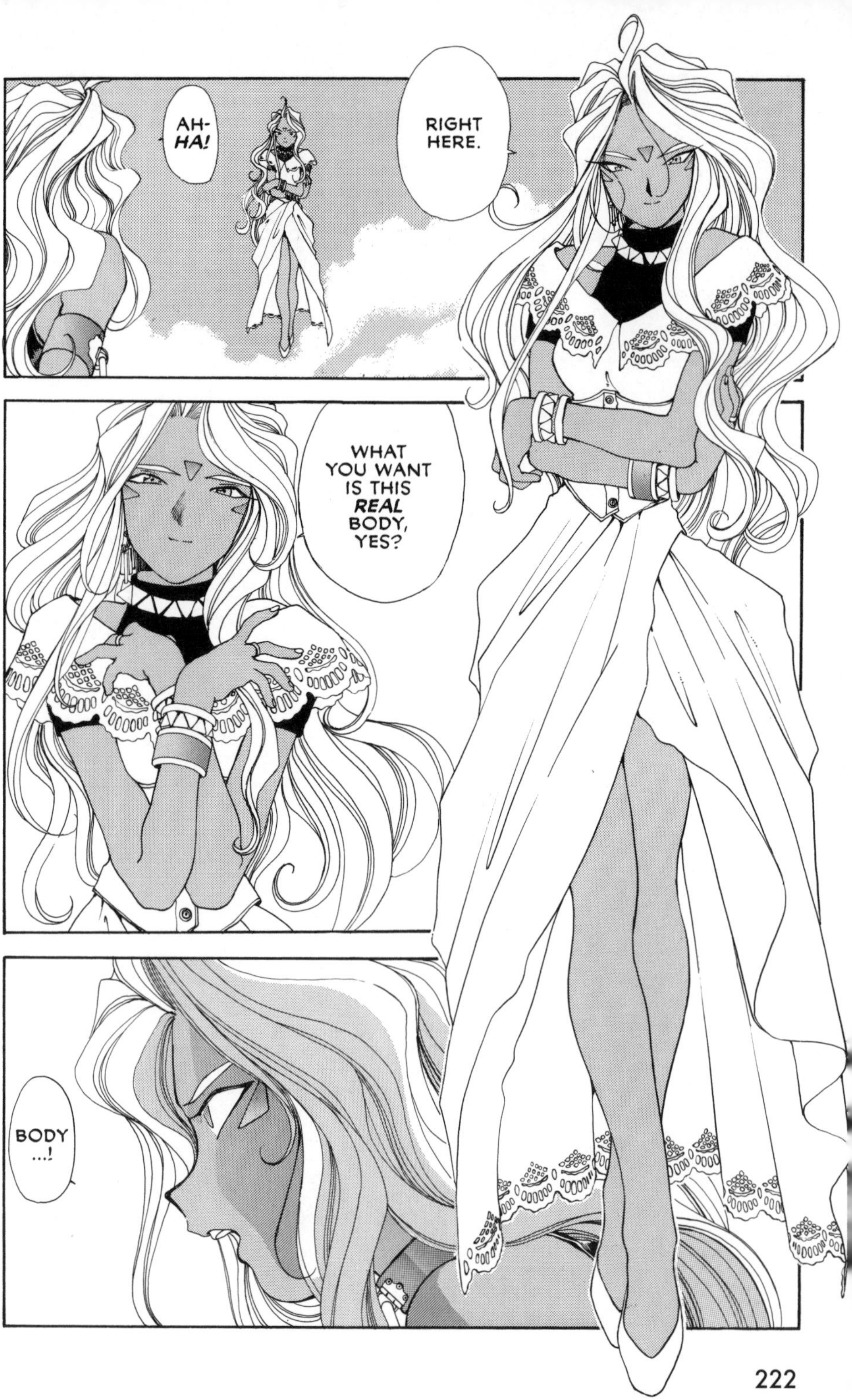
AH-
HA!
RIGHT HERE.
WHAT YOU WANT IS THIS *REAL* BODY, YES?
BODY ...!

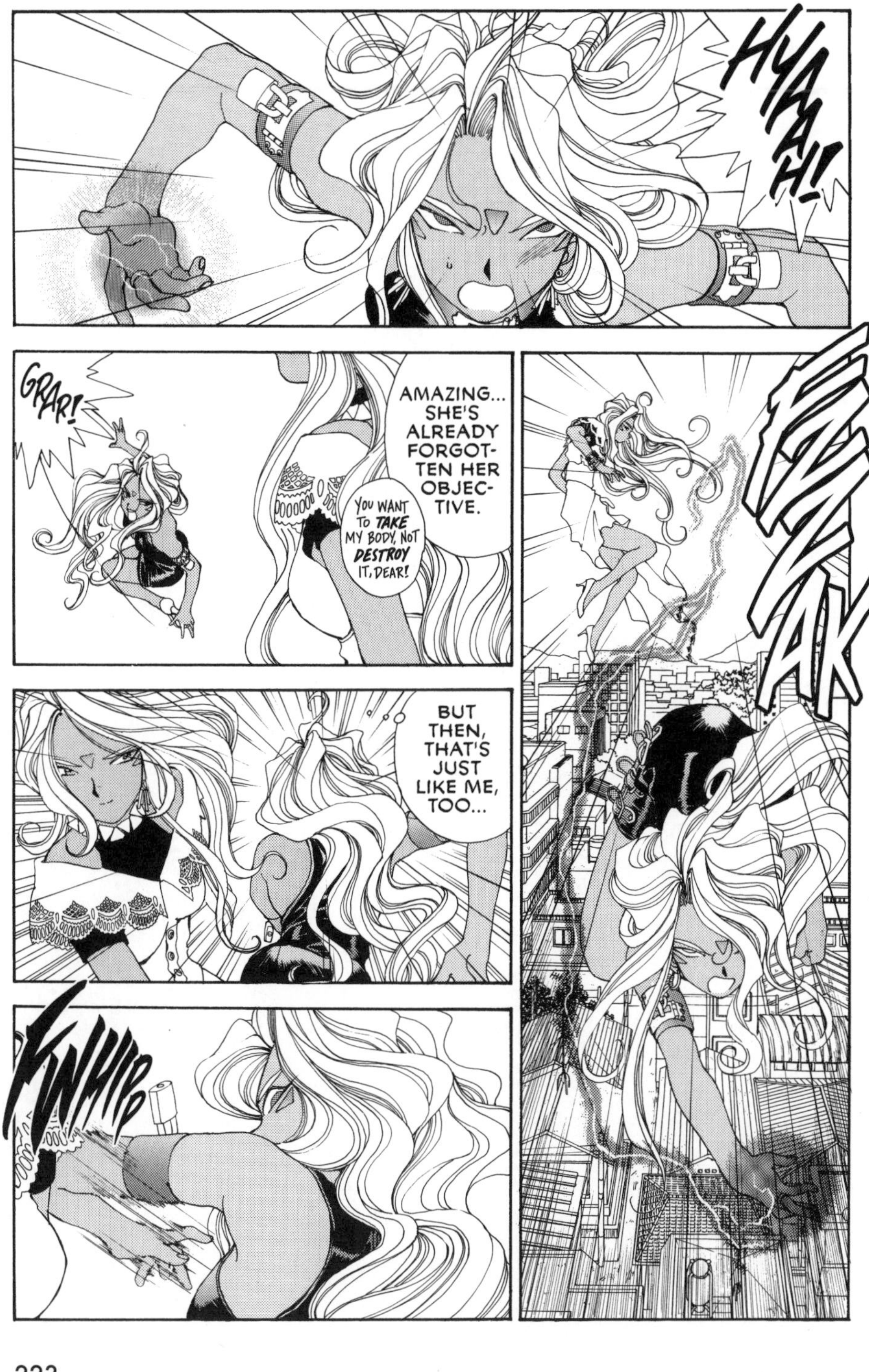
HYAAAH!
AMAZING... SHE'S ALREADY FORGOTTEN HER OBJECTIVE.
YOU WANT TO TAKE MY BODY, NOT DESTROY IT, DEAR!
GRAR!
BUT THEN, THAT'S JUST LIKE ME, TOO...
KWHIP

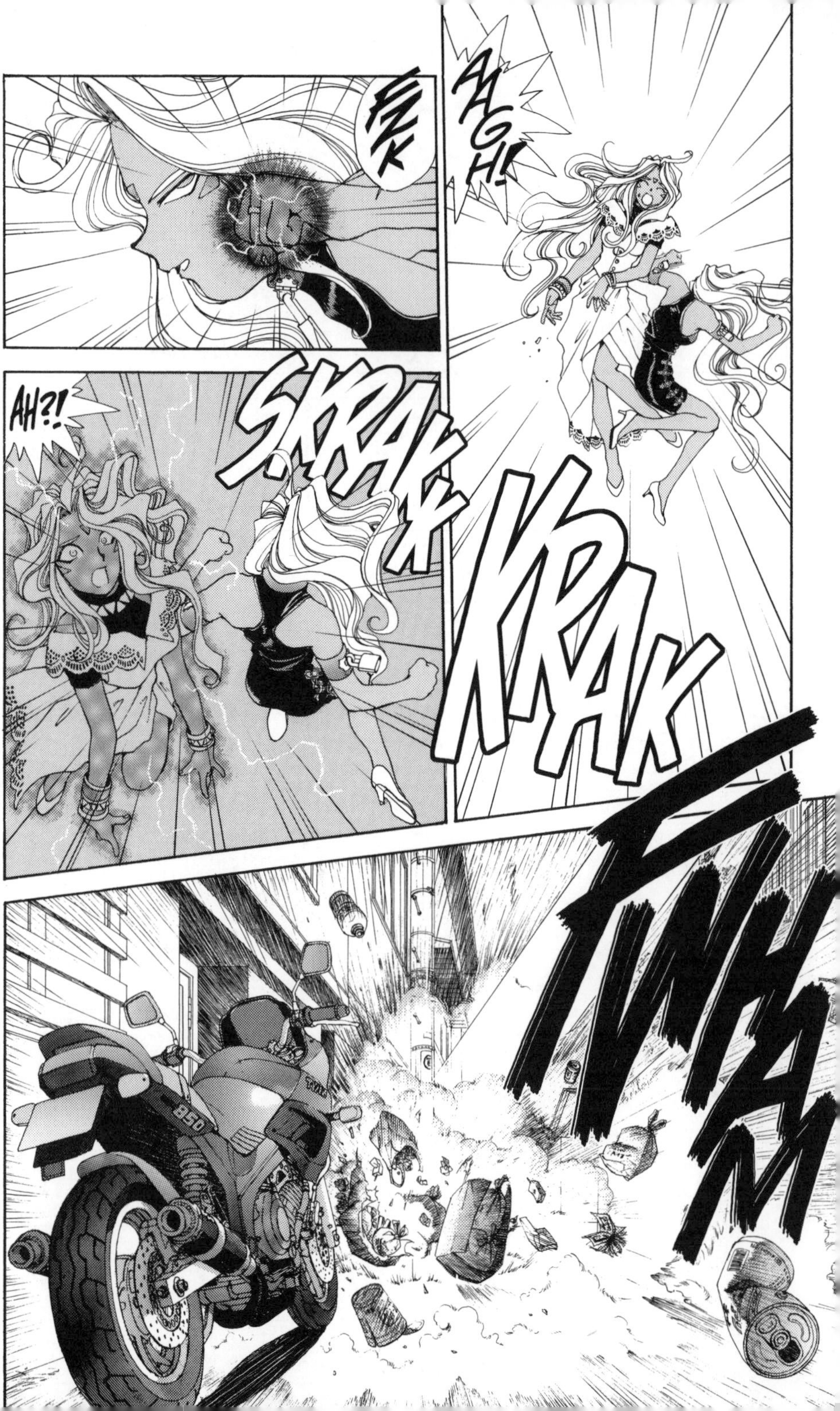
AAAGH!
EEK
AH?!
SKRAK
KRAK
THWAM
850

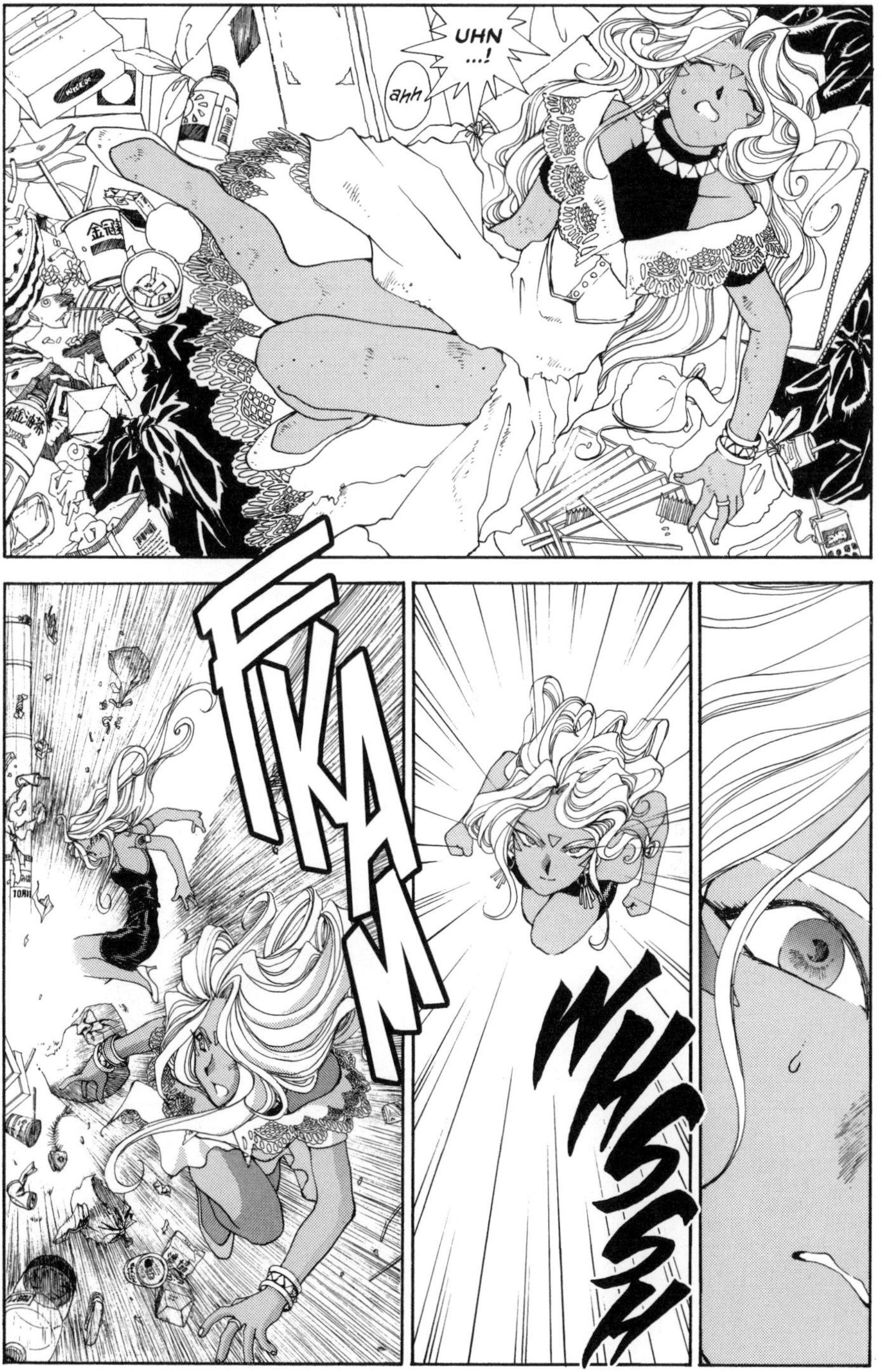
UHN ...!
ahh
WHSSH
FKAM

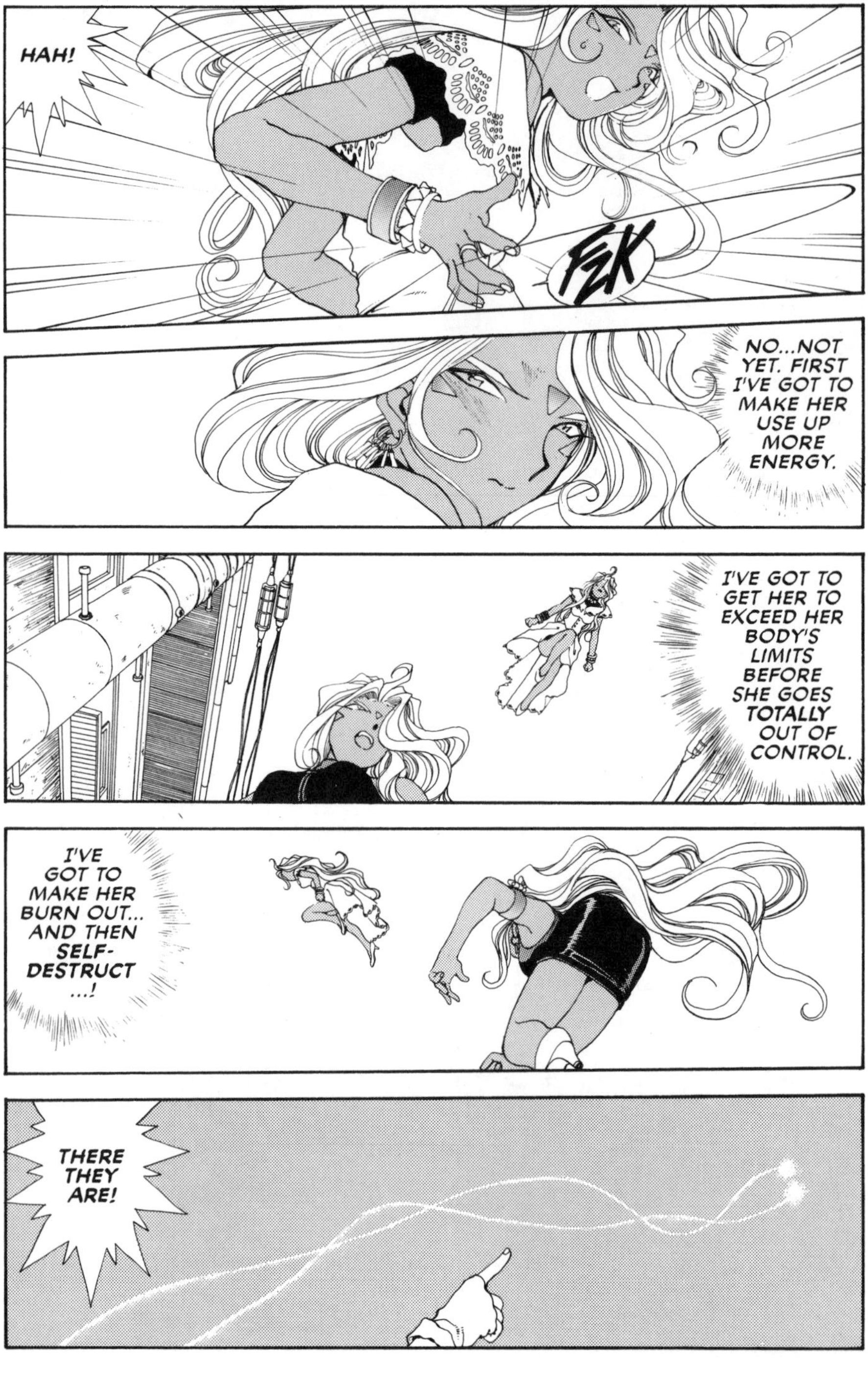
FZK
HAH!
NO...NOT YET. FIRST I'VE GOT TO MAKE HER USE UP MORE ENERGY.
I'VE GOT TO GET HER TO EXCEED HER BODY'S LIMITS BEFORE SHE GOES TOTALLY OUT OF CONTROL.
I'VE GOT TO MAKE HER BURN OUT... AND THEN SELF-DESTRUCT ...!
THERE THEY ARE!

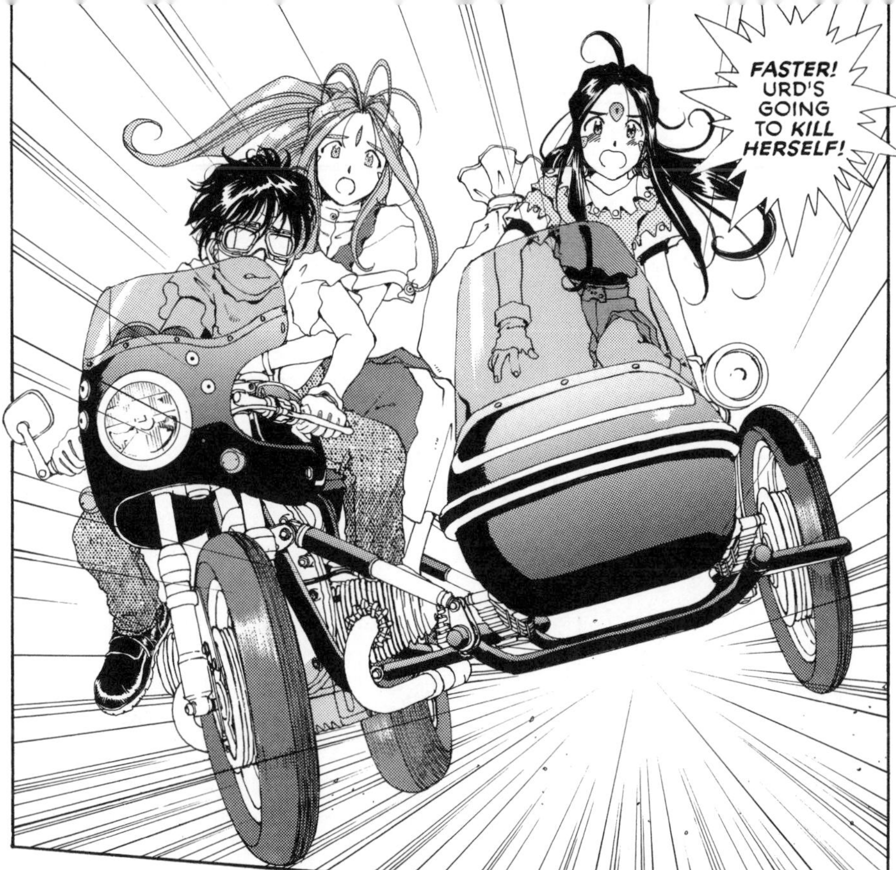
FASTER! URD'S GOING TO KILL HERSELF!
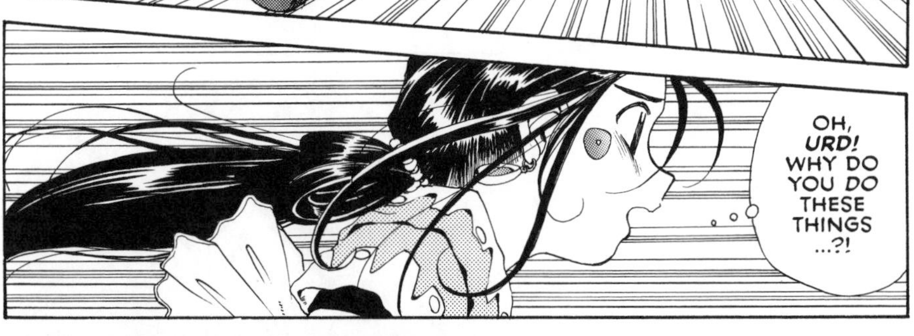
OH, URD! WHY DO YOU DO THESE THINGS ...?!
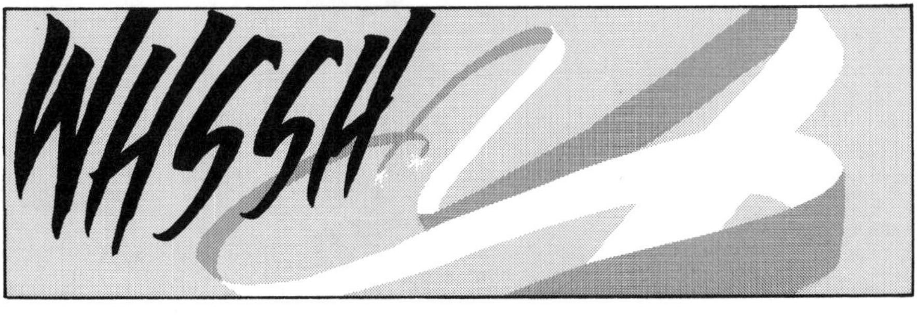
WHSSH

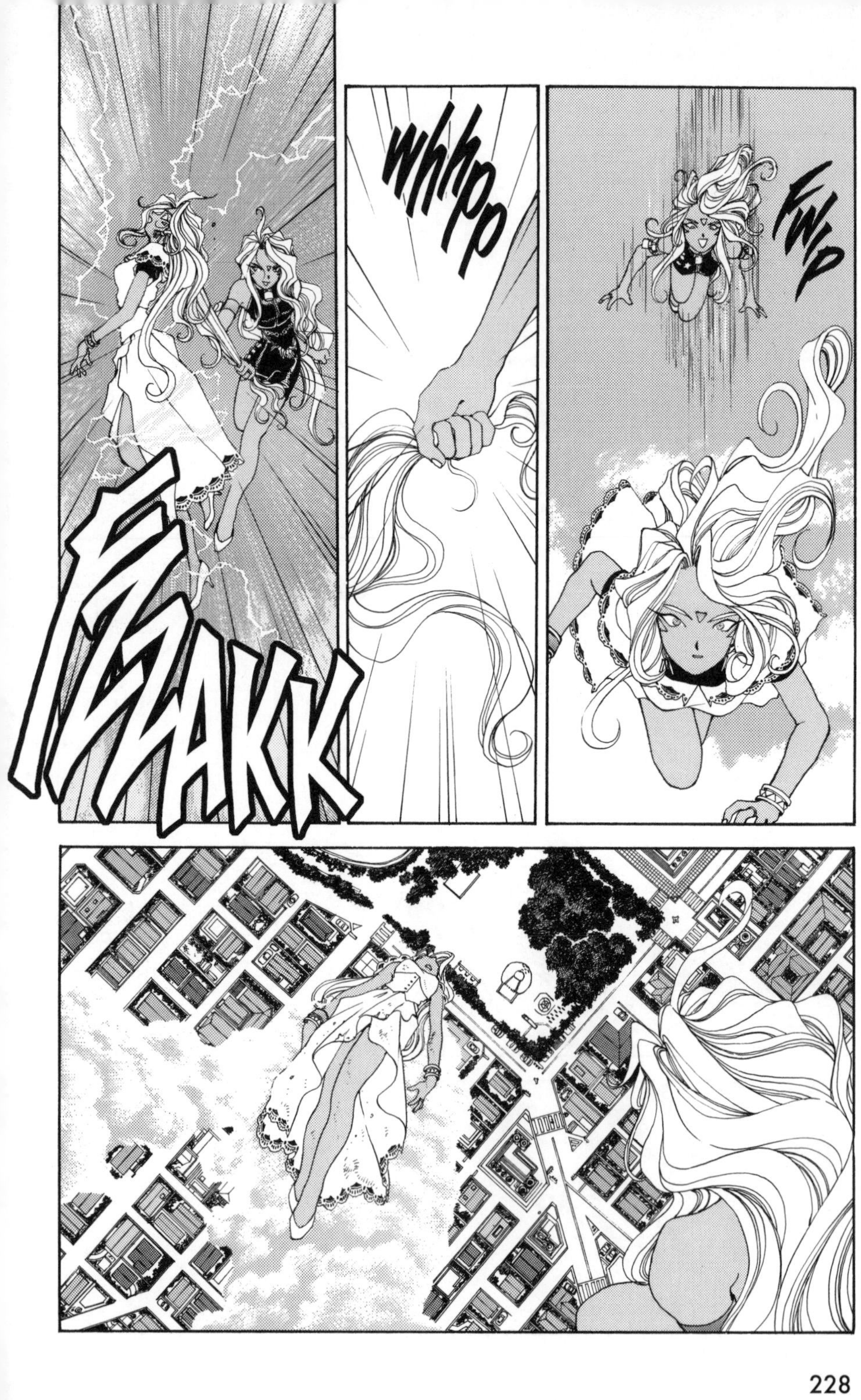
fwip
whhpp
ZZAKK

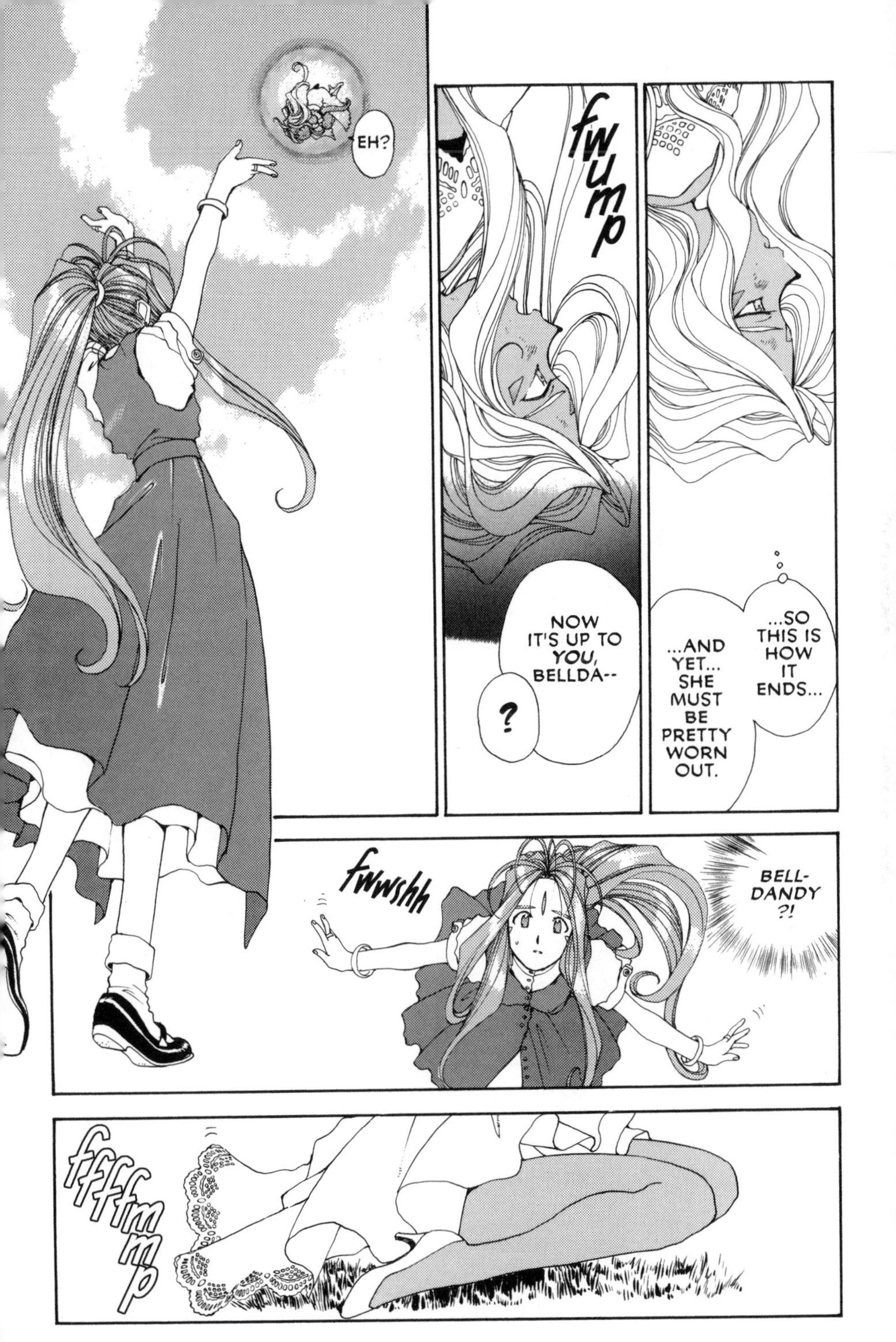
...SO THIS IS HOW IT ENDS...
...AND YET... SHE MUST BE PRETTY WORN OUT.
fwump
NOW IT'S UP TO *YOU*, BELLDA--
?
BELL-DANDY?!
fwwshh
EH?
ffffmmp

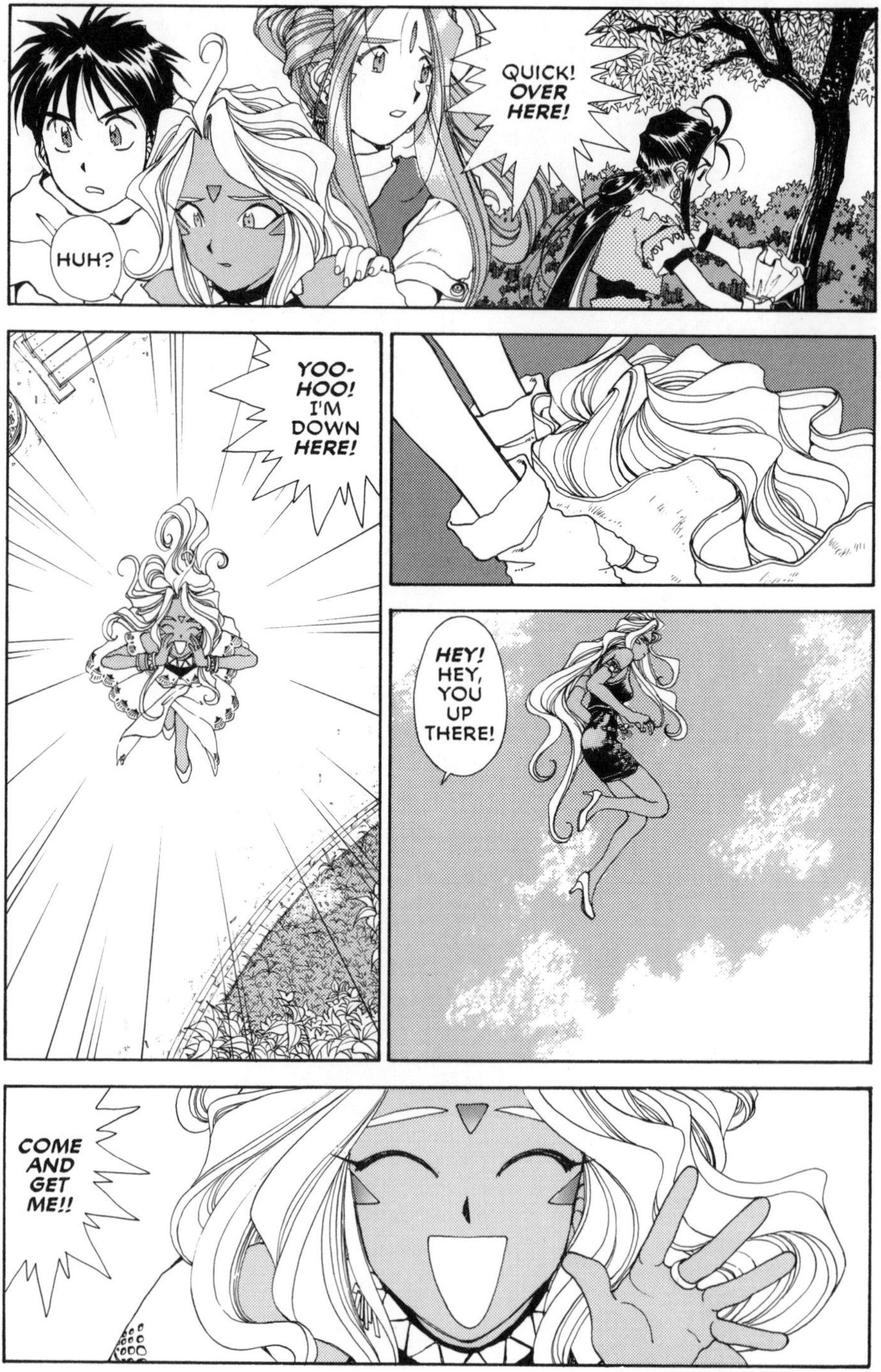
QUICK! OVER HERE!
HUH?
HEY! HEY, YOU UP THERE!
YOO-HOO! I'M DOWN HERE!
COME AND GET ME!!

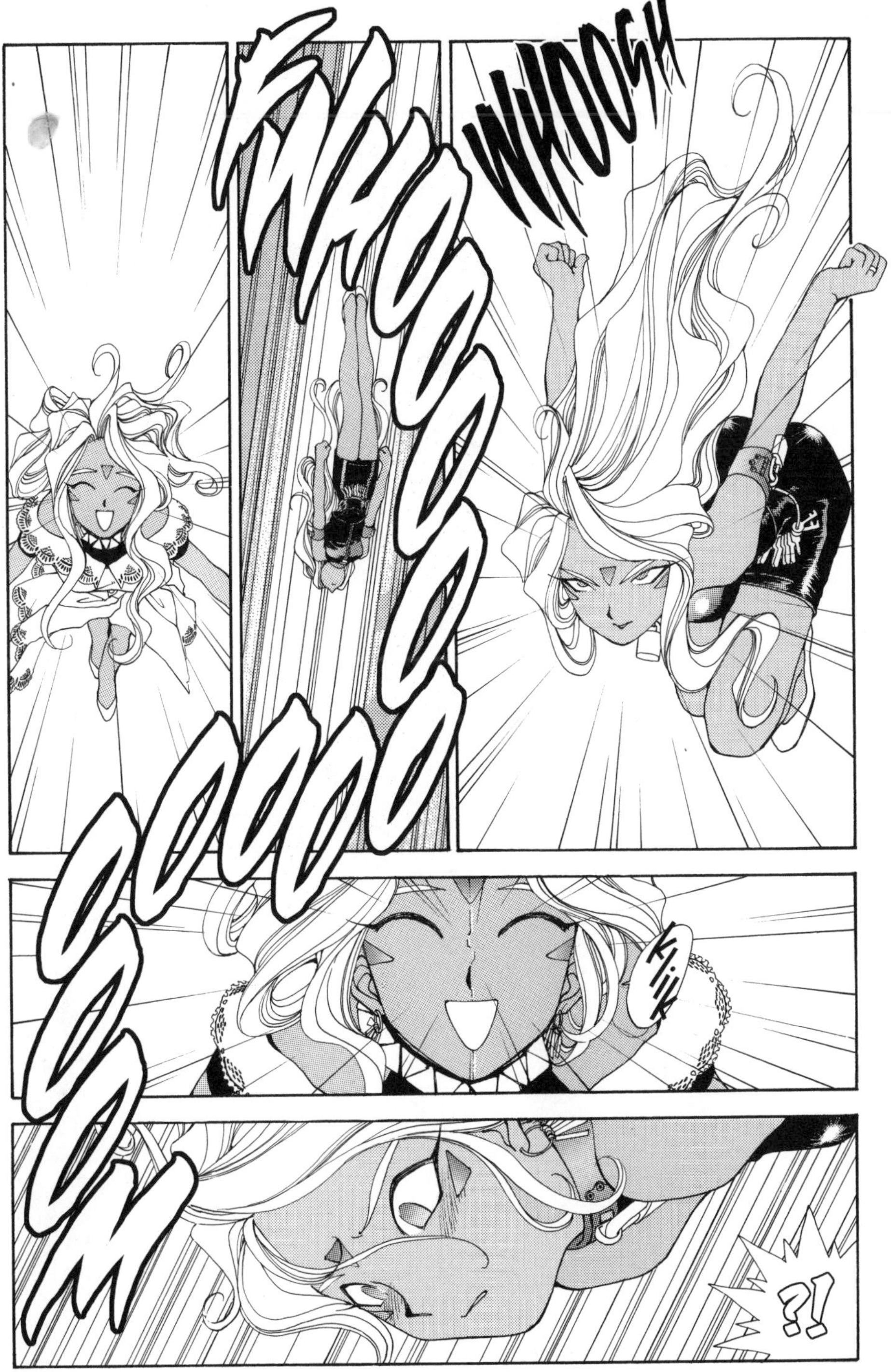
WHOOSH
KLIK
?!

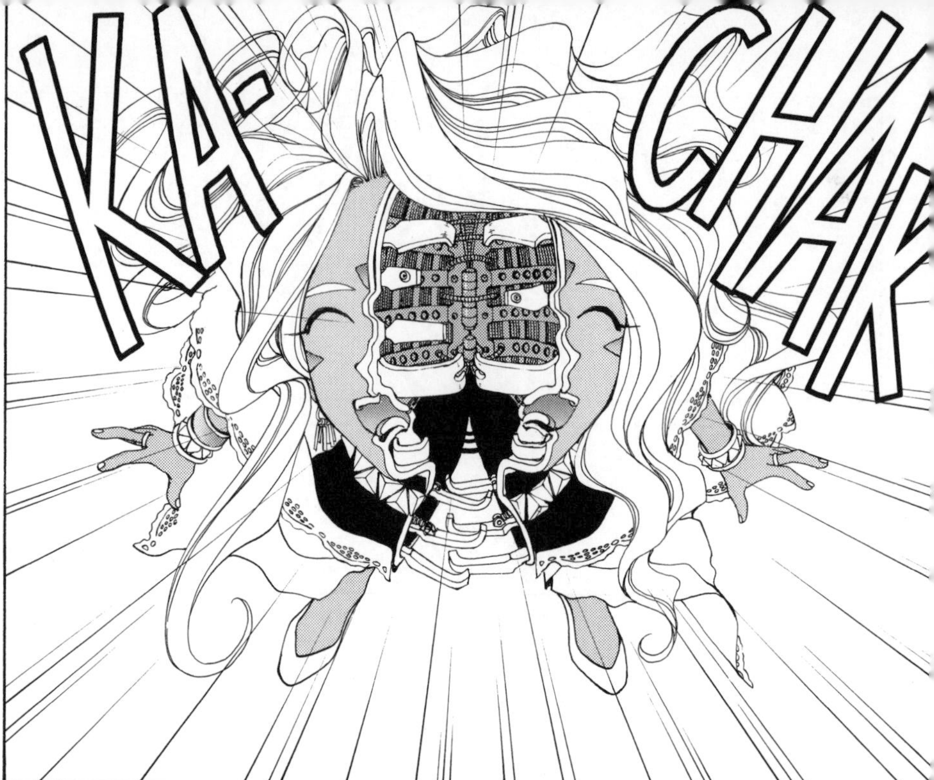
KA-CHAK
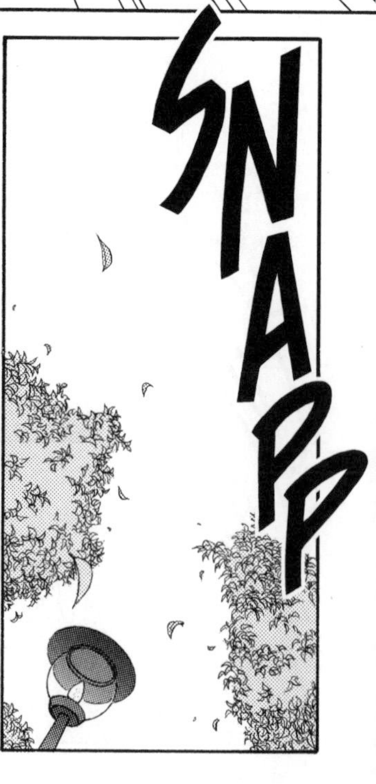
SNAPP
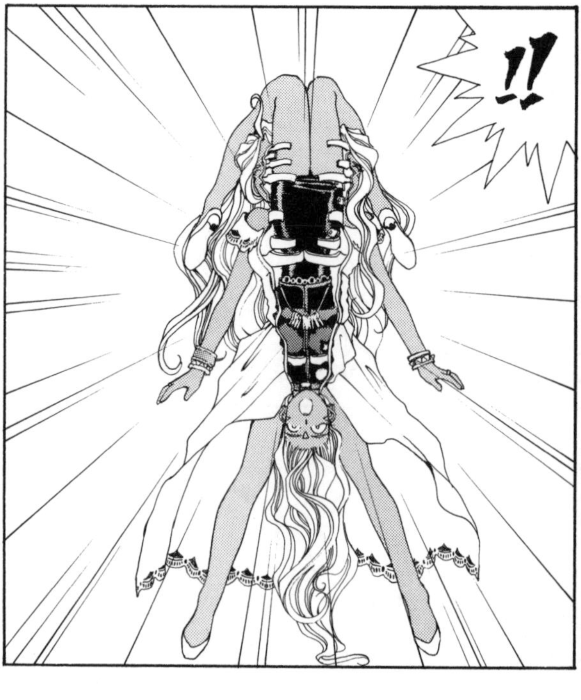
!!

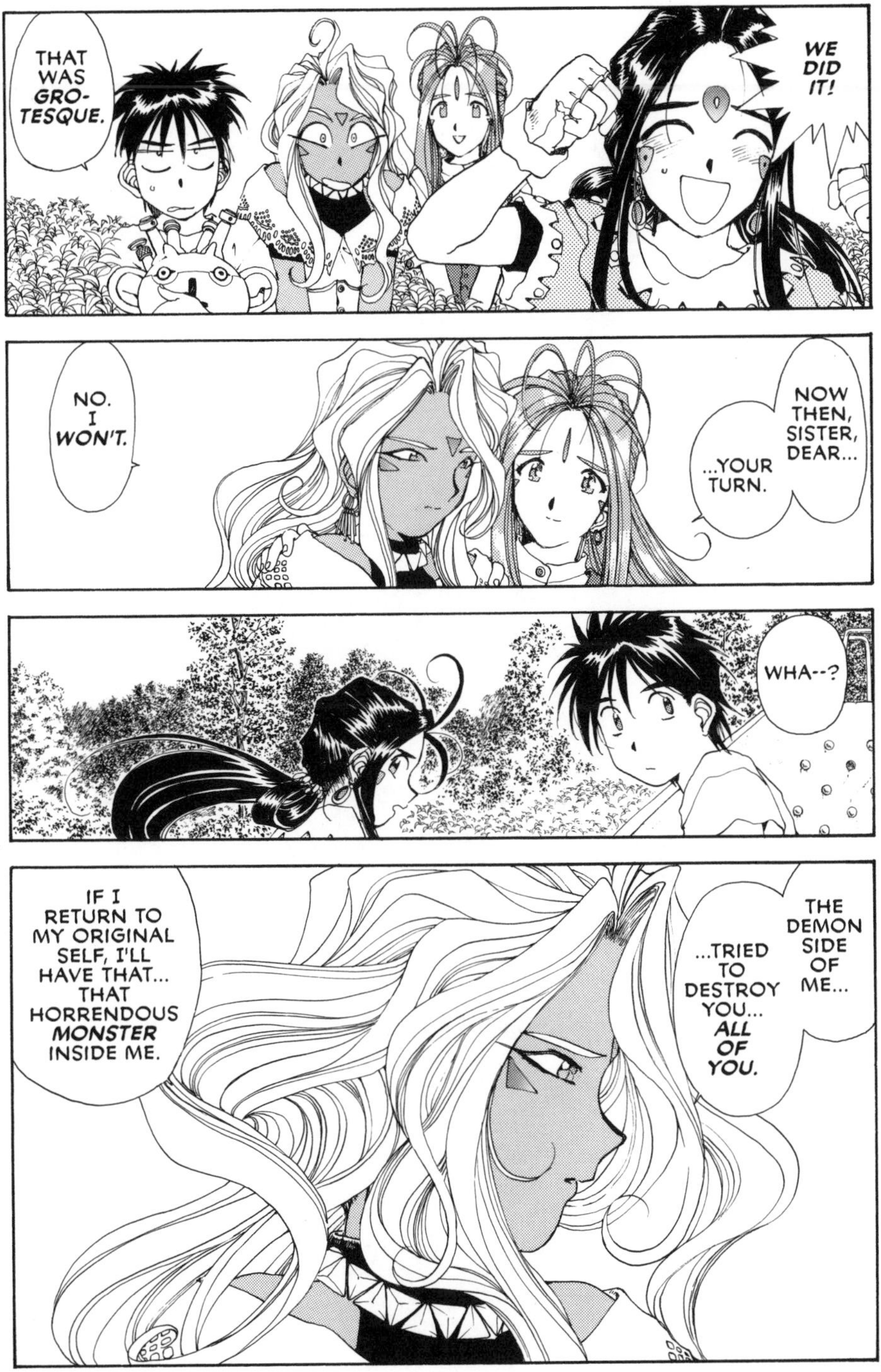
WE DID IT!
THAT WAS GROTESQUE.
NOW THEN, SISTER, DEAR...
...YOUR TURN.
NO. I WON'T.
WHA--?
THE DEMON SIDE OF ME...
...TRIED TO DESTROY YOU... ALL OF YOU.
IF I RETURN TO MY ORIGINAL SELF, I'LL HAVE THAT... THAT HORRENDOUS MONSTER INSIDE ME.

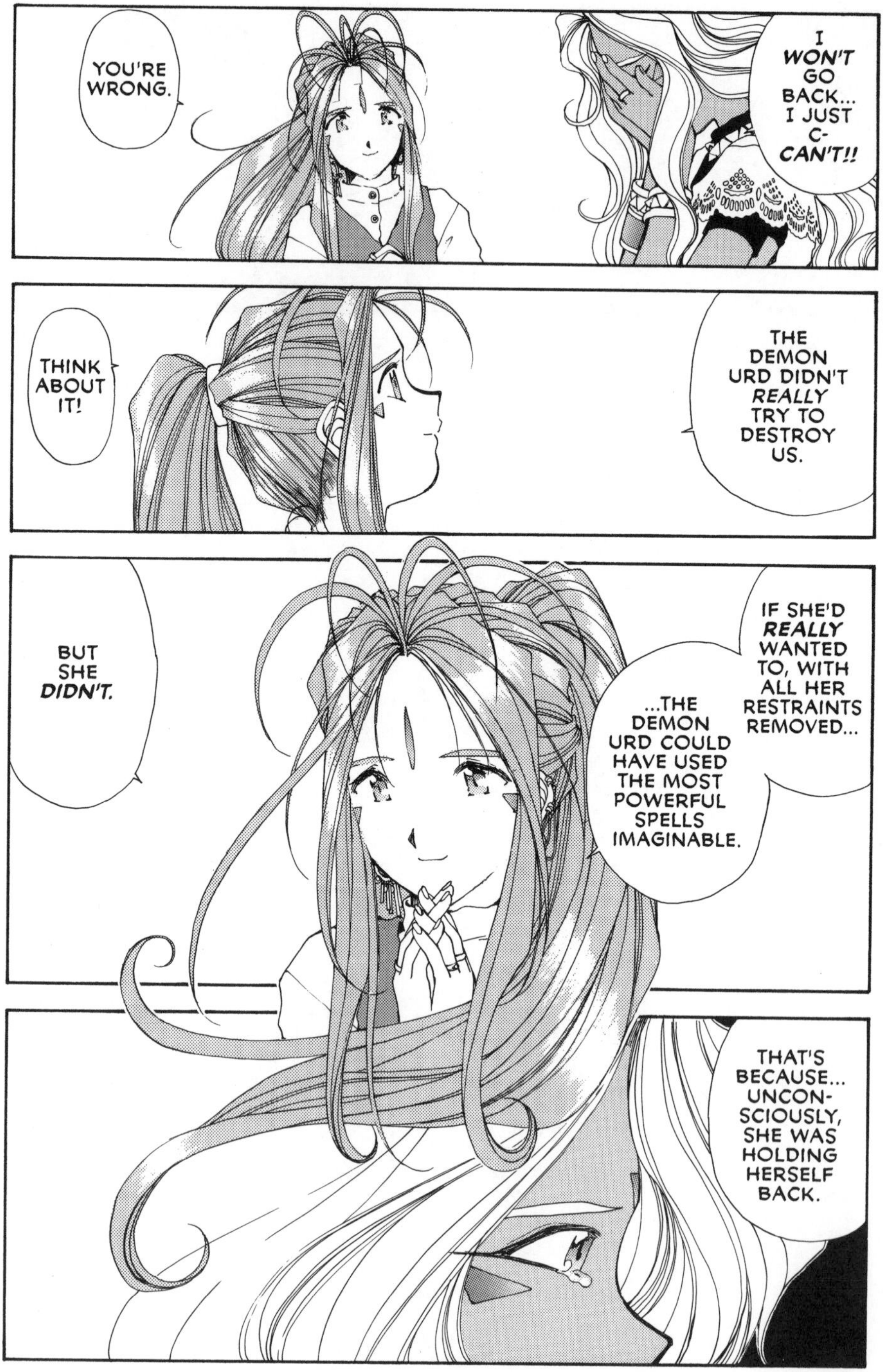
I *WON'T* GO BACK... I JUST C-*CAN'T!!*
YOU'RE WRONG.
THE DEMON URD DIDN'T *REALLY* TRY TO DESTROY US.
THINK ABOUT IT!
IF SHE'D *REALLY* WANTED TO, WITH ALL HER RESTRAINTS REMOVED...
...THE DEMON URD COULD HAVE USED THE MOST POWERFUL SPELLS IMAGINABLE.
BUT SHE *DIDN'T.*
THAT'S BECAUSE... UNCONSCIOUSLY, SHE WAS HOLDING HERSELF BACK.

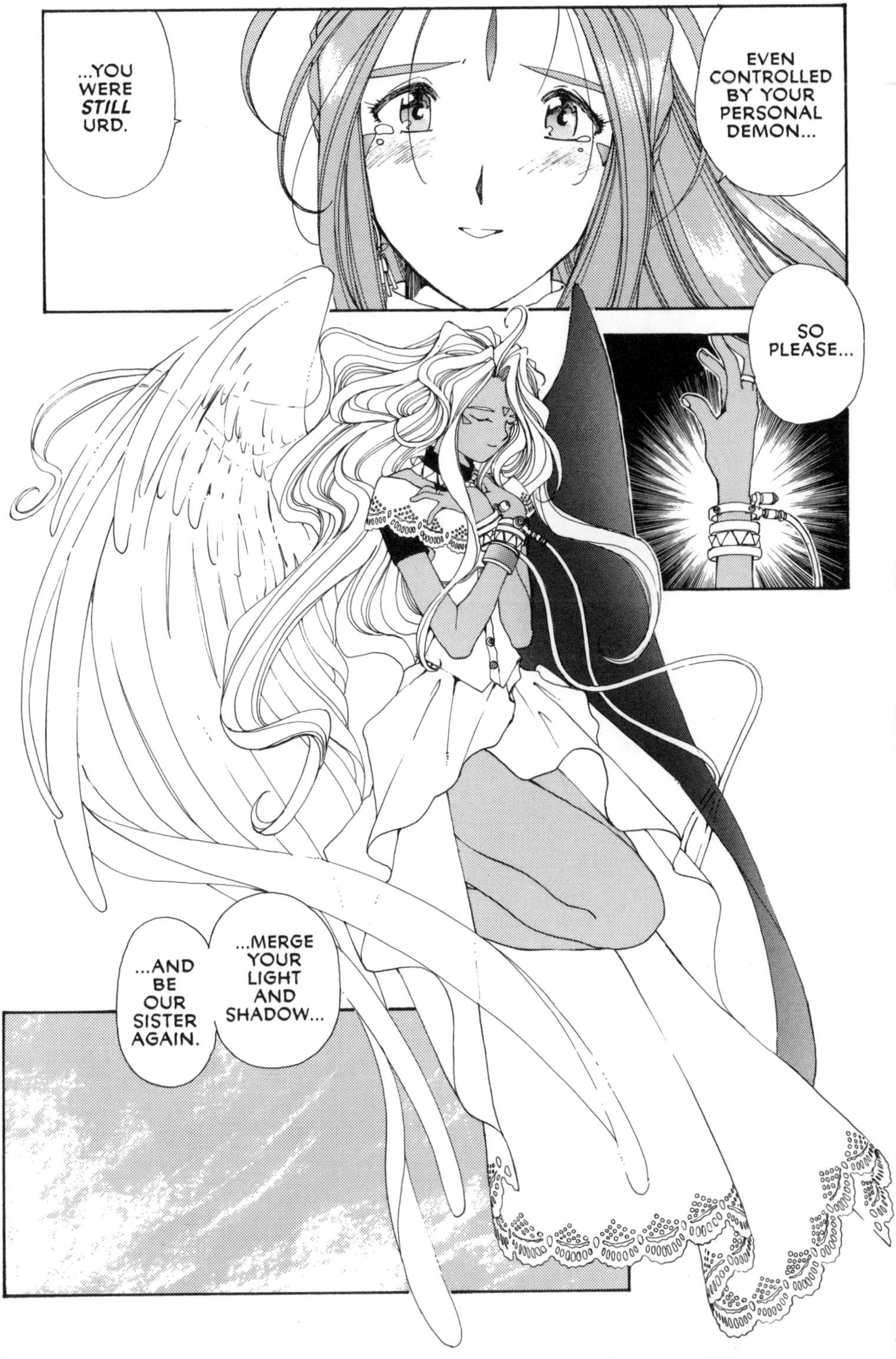
EVEN CONTROLLED BY YOUR PERSONAL DEMON...
...YOU WERE *STILL* URD.
SO PLEASE...
...MERGE YOUR LIGHT AND SHADOW...
...AND BE OUR SISTER AGAIN.

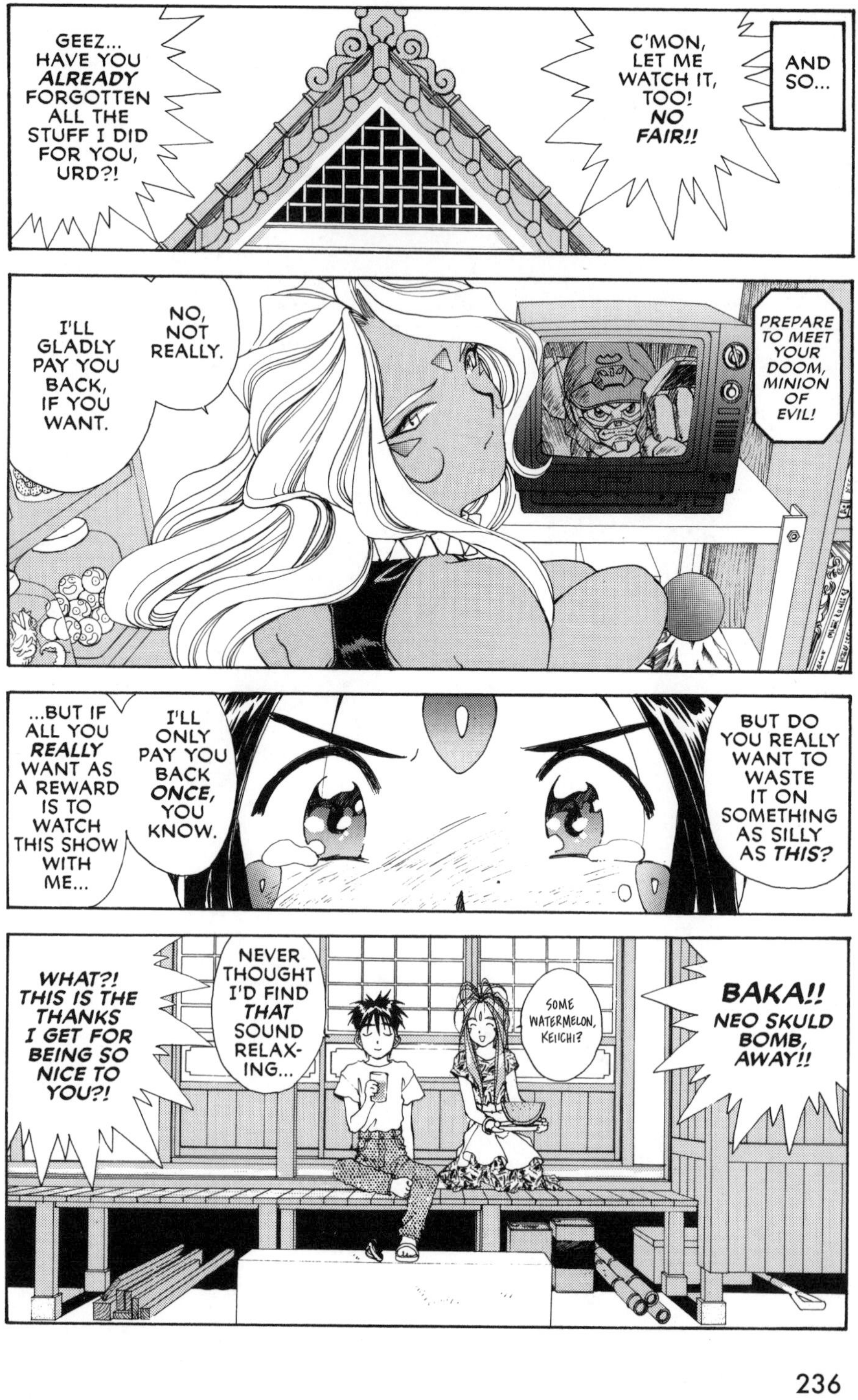
AND SO...
C'MON, LET ME WATCH IT, TOO! NO FAIR!!
GEEZ... HAVE YOU ALREADY FORGOTTEN ALL THE STUFF I DID FOR YOU, URD?!
PREPARE TO MEET YOUR DOOM, MINION OF EVIL!
NO, NOT REALLY.
I'LL GLADLY PAY YOU BACK, IF YOU WANT.
BUT DO YOU REALLY WANT TO WASTE IT ON SOMETHING AS SILLY AS THIS?
I'LL ONLY PAY YOU BACK ONCE, YOU KNOW.
...BUT IF ALL YOU REALLY WANT AS A REWARD IS TO WATCH THIS SHOW WITH ME...
BAKA!! NEO SKULD BOMB, AWAY!!
SOME WATERMELON, KEIICHI?
NEVER THOUGHT I'D FIND THAT SOUND RELAX-ING...
WHAT?! THIS IS THE THANKS I GET FOR BEING SO NICE TO YOU?!

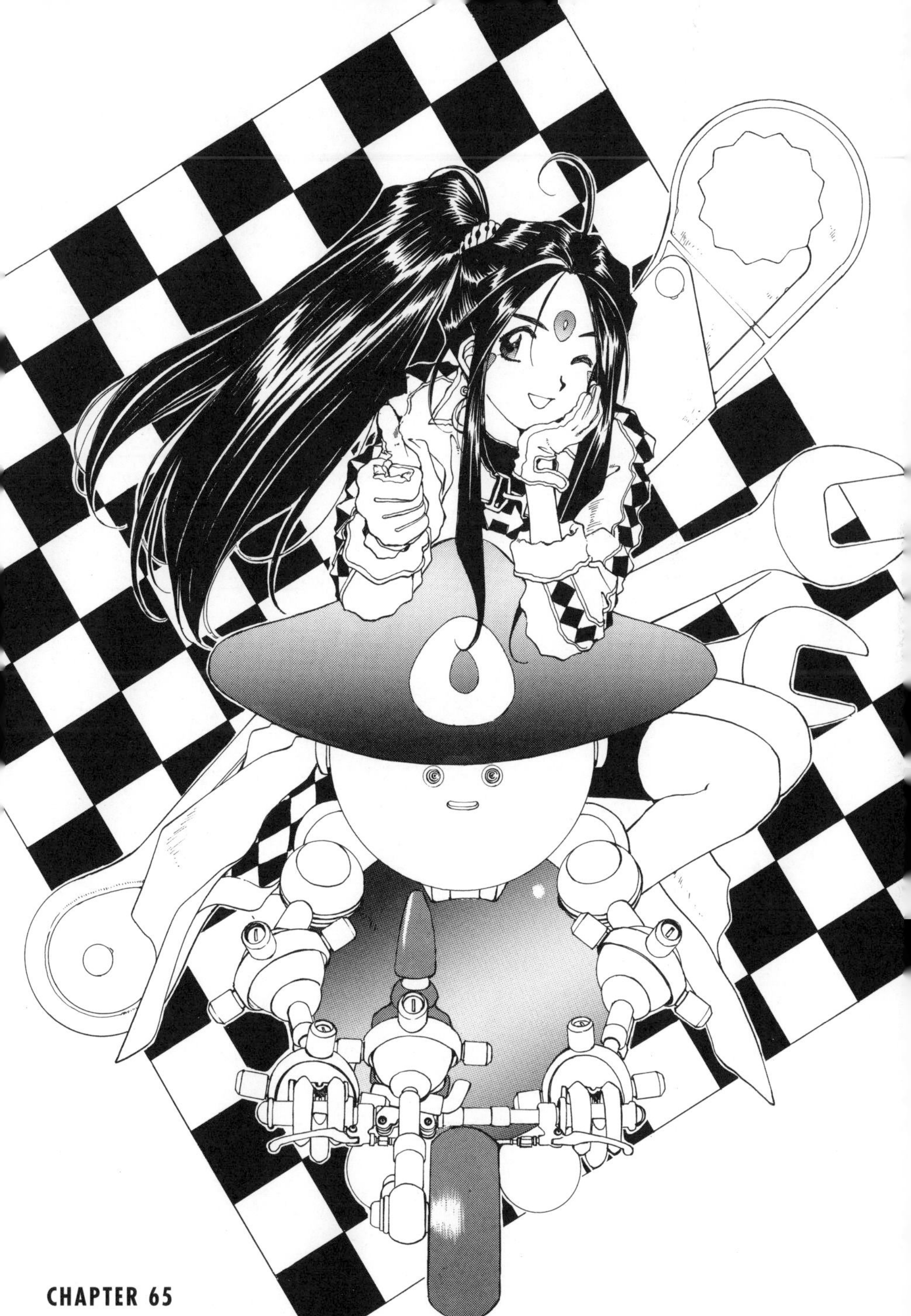

CHAPTER 65

Urd Mode Is Gentle Mode

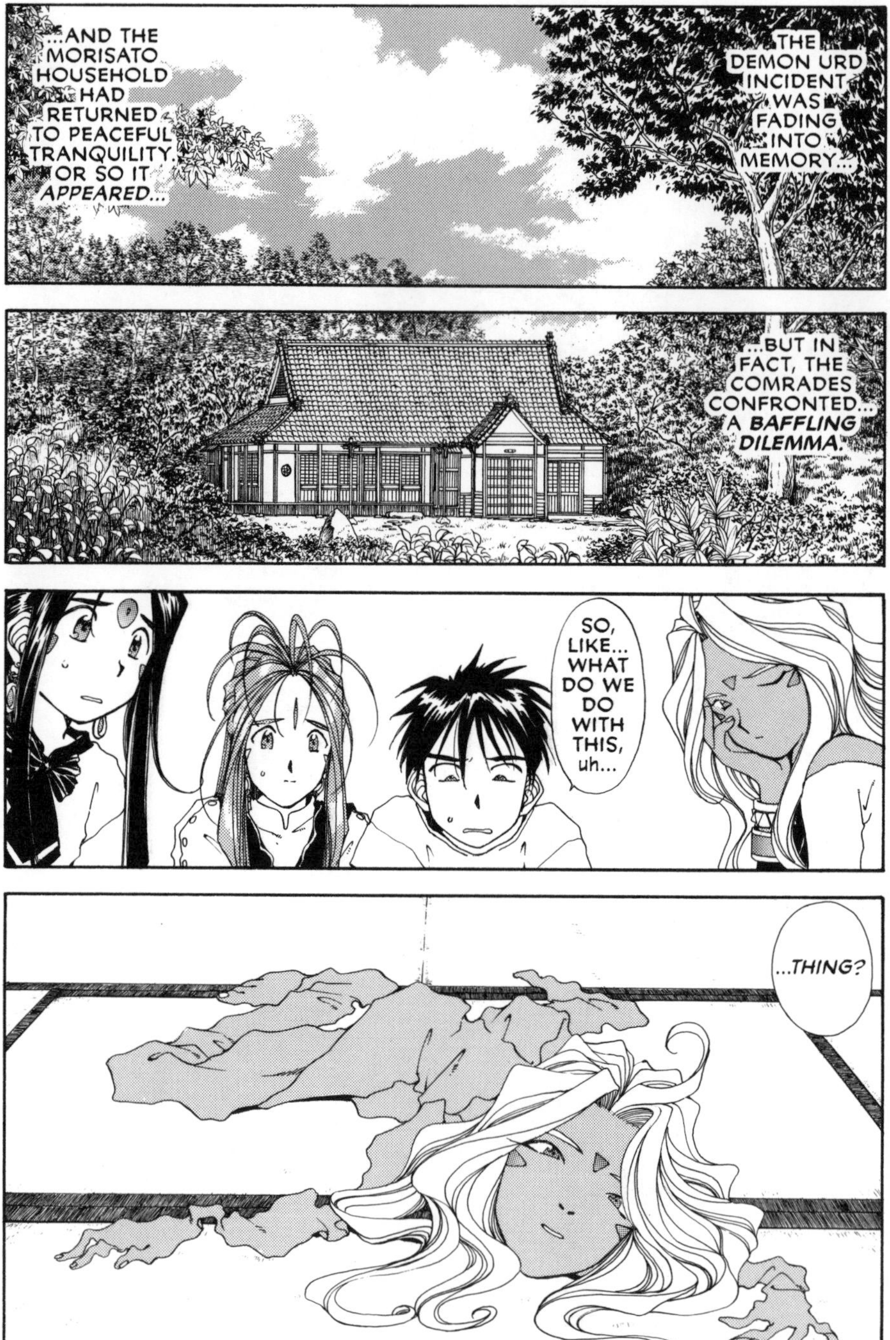
THE DEMON URD INCIDENT WAS FADING INTO MEMORY...
...AND THE MORISATO HOUSEHOLD HAD RETURNED TO PEACEFUL TRANQUILITY. OR SO IT *APPEARED*...
...BUT IN FACT, THE COMRADES CONFRONTED... A ***BAFFLING DILEMMA.***
SO, LIKE... WHAT DO WE DO WITH THIS, uh...
...*THING?*

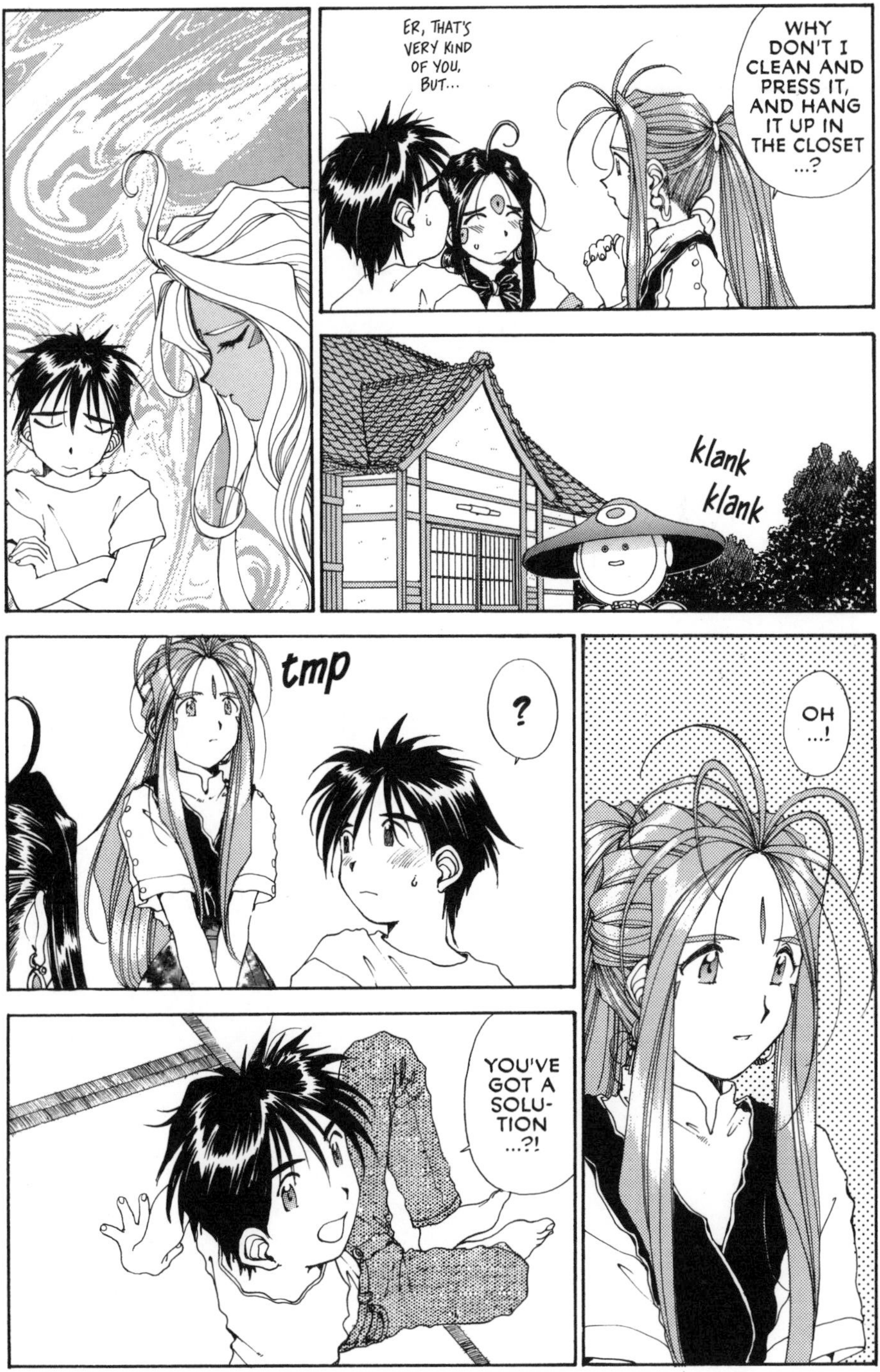
WHY DON'T I CLEAN AND PRESS IT, AND HANG IT UP IN THE CLOSET ...?
ER, THAT'S VERY KIND OF YOU, BUT...
klank klank
OH ...!
tmp
?
YOU'VE GOT A SOLU-TION ...?!

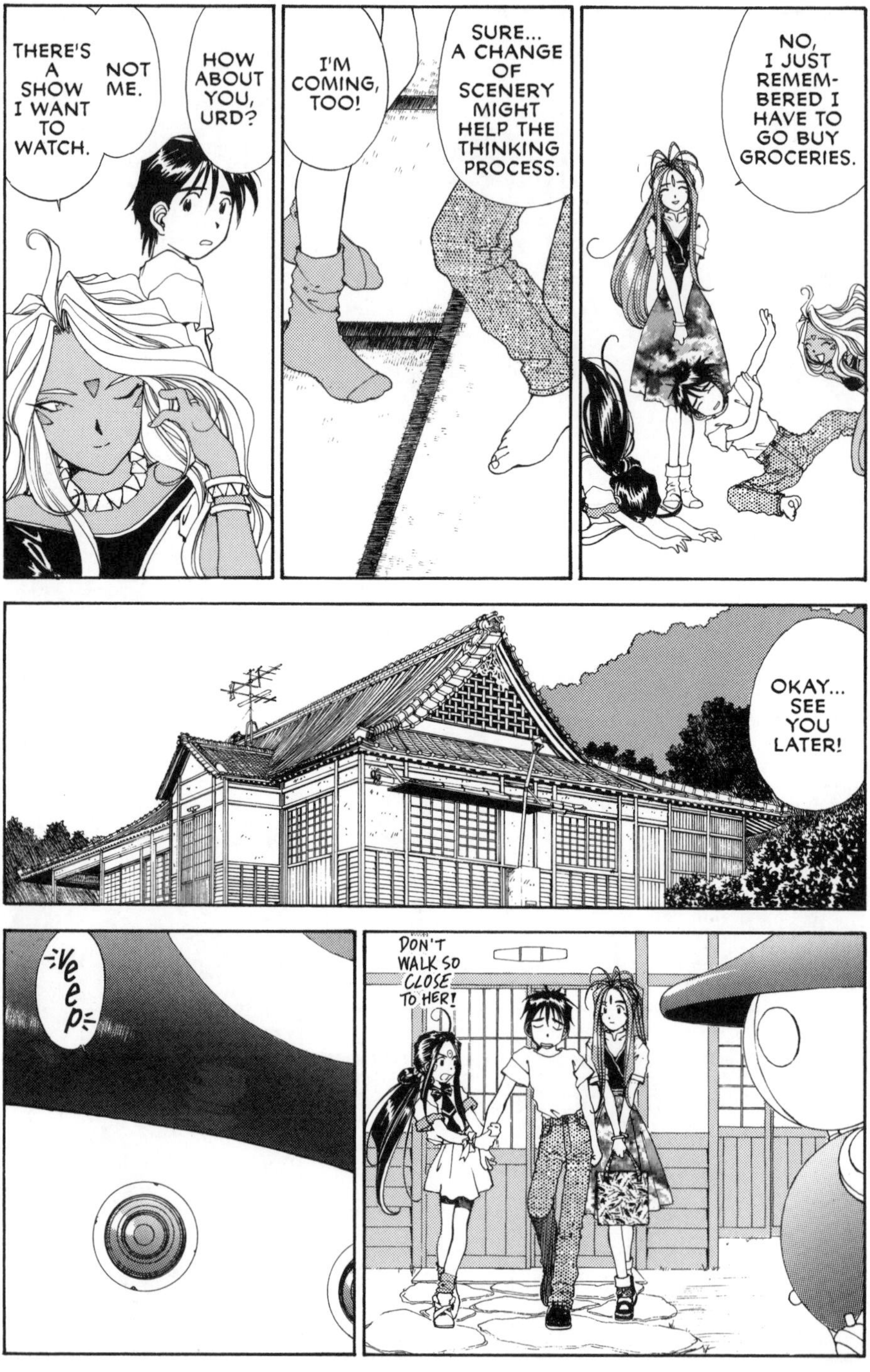
HOW ABOUT YOU, URD?
NOT ME.
THERE'S A SHOW I WANT TO WATCH.
I'M COMING, TOO!
SURE... A CHANGE OF SCENERY MIGHT HELP THE THINKING PROCESS.
NO, I JUST REMEMBERED I HAVE TO GO BUY GROCERIES.
OKAY... SEE YOU LATER!
Veep
DON'T WALK SO CLOSE TO HER!

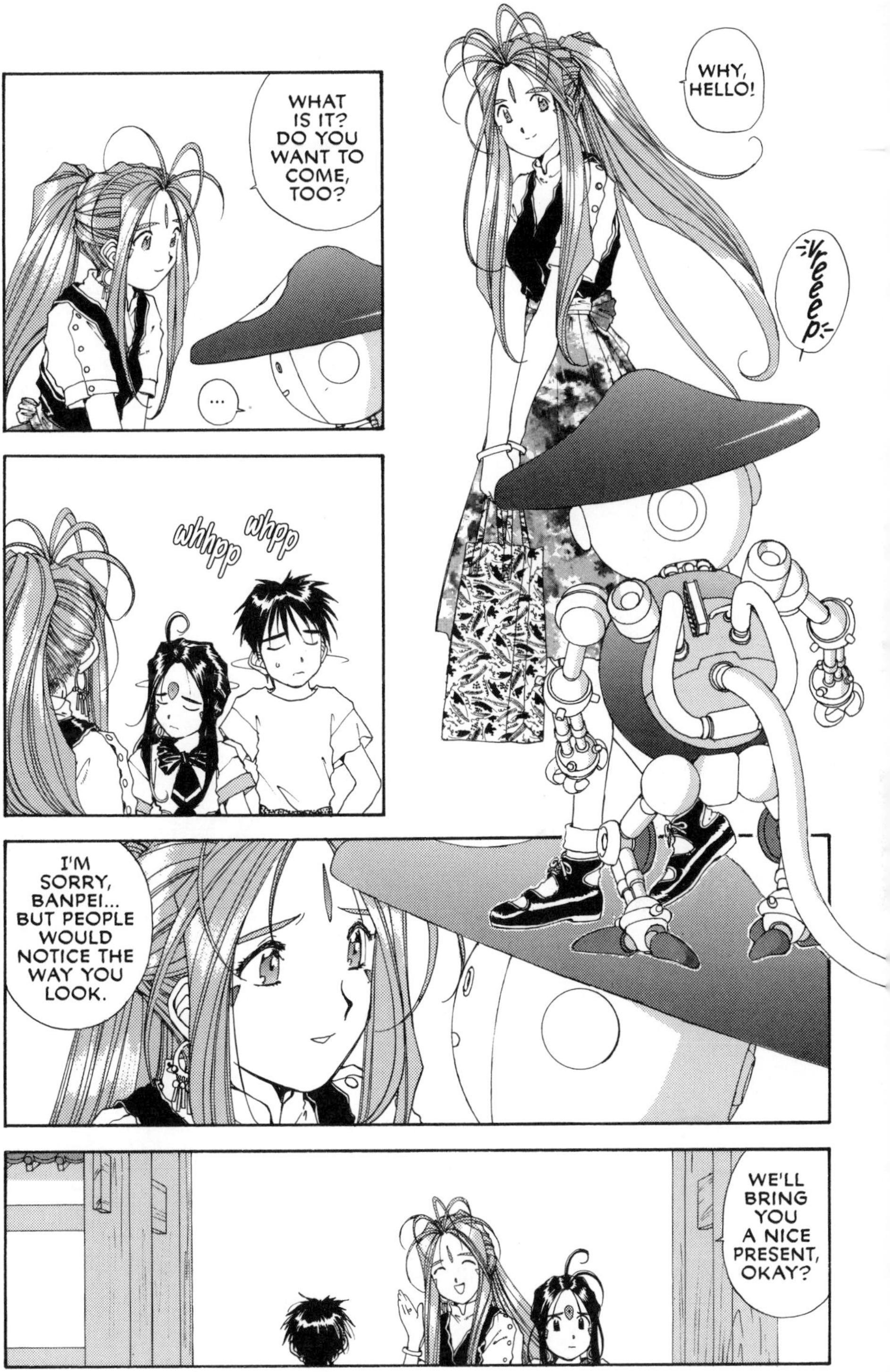
WHY, HELLO!
vreeep
WHAT IS IT? DO YOU WANT TO COME, TOO?
...
whpp
whhpp
I'M SORRY, BANPEI... BUT PEOPLE WOULD NOTICE THE WAY YOU LOOK.
WE'LL BRING YOU A NICE PRESENT, OKAY?

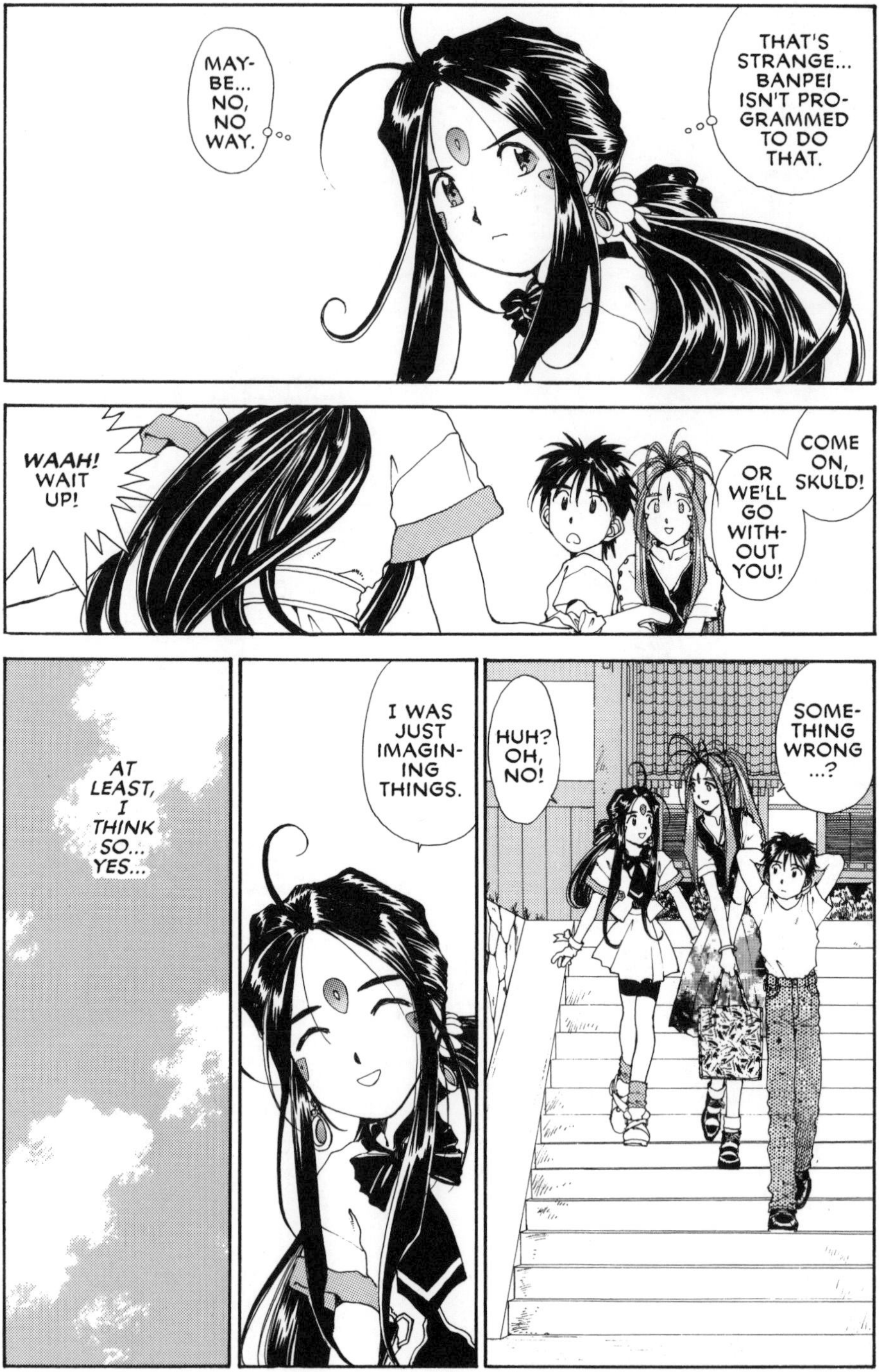
THAT'S STRANGE... BANPEI ISN'T PRO-GRAMMED TO DO THAT.
MAY-BE... NO, NO WAY.
COME ON, SKULD!
OR WE'LL GO WITH-OUT YOU!
WAAH! WAIT UP!
SOME-THING WRONG ...?
HUH? OH, NO!
I WAS JUST IMAGIN-ING THINGS.
AT LEAST, I THINK SO... YES...

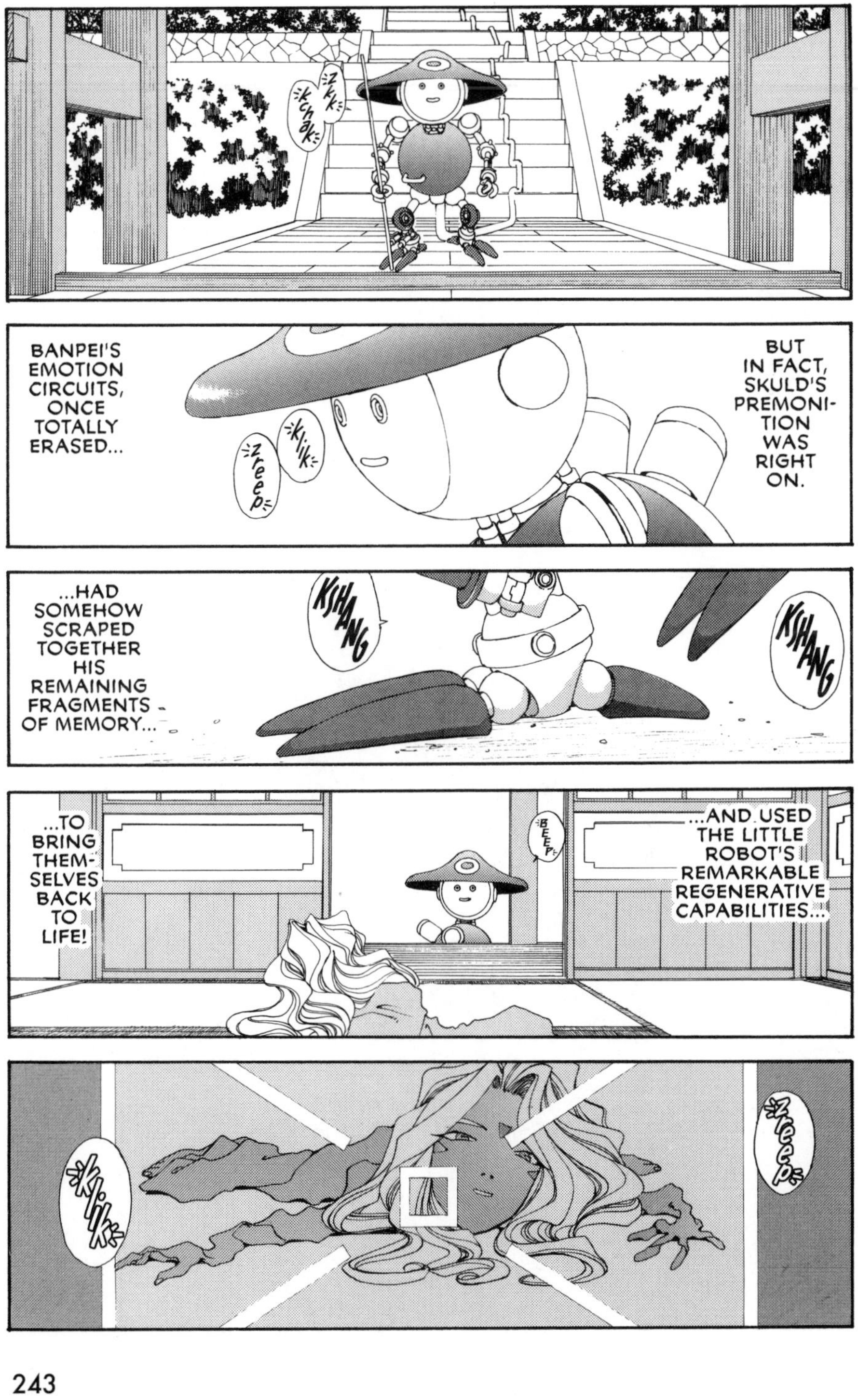
zkk kchak
BUT IN FACT, SKULD'S PREMONITION WAS RIGHT ON.
klik
zreep
BANPEI'S EMOTION CIRCUITS, ONCE TOTALLY ERASED...
KSHANG
KSHANG
...HAD SOMEHOW SCRAPED TOGETHER HIS REMAINING FRAGMENTS OF MEMORY...
...AND USED THE LITTLE ROBOT'S REMARKABLE REGENERATIVE CAPABILITIES...
BEEEP
...TO BRING THEMSELVES BACK TO LIFE!
zreep
klik

FWDD
KANG
KCHAK
chingg
KCHAK
skshhh

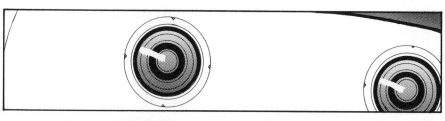

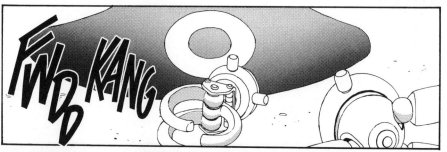

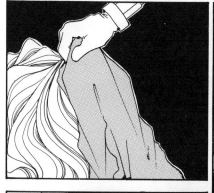

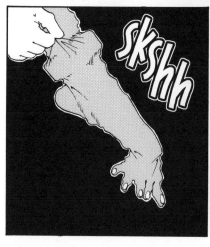

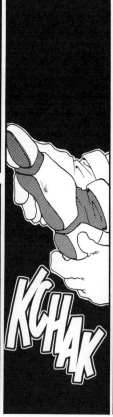

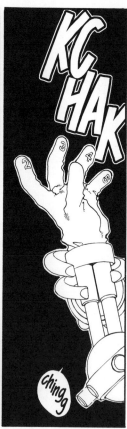

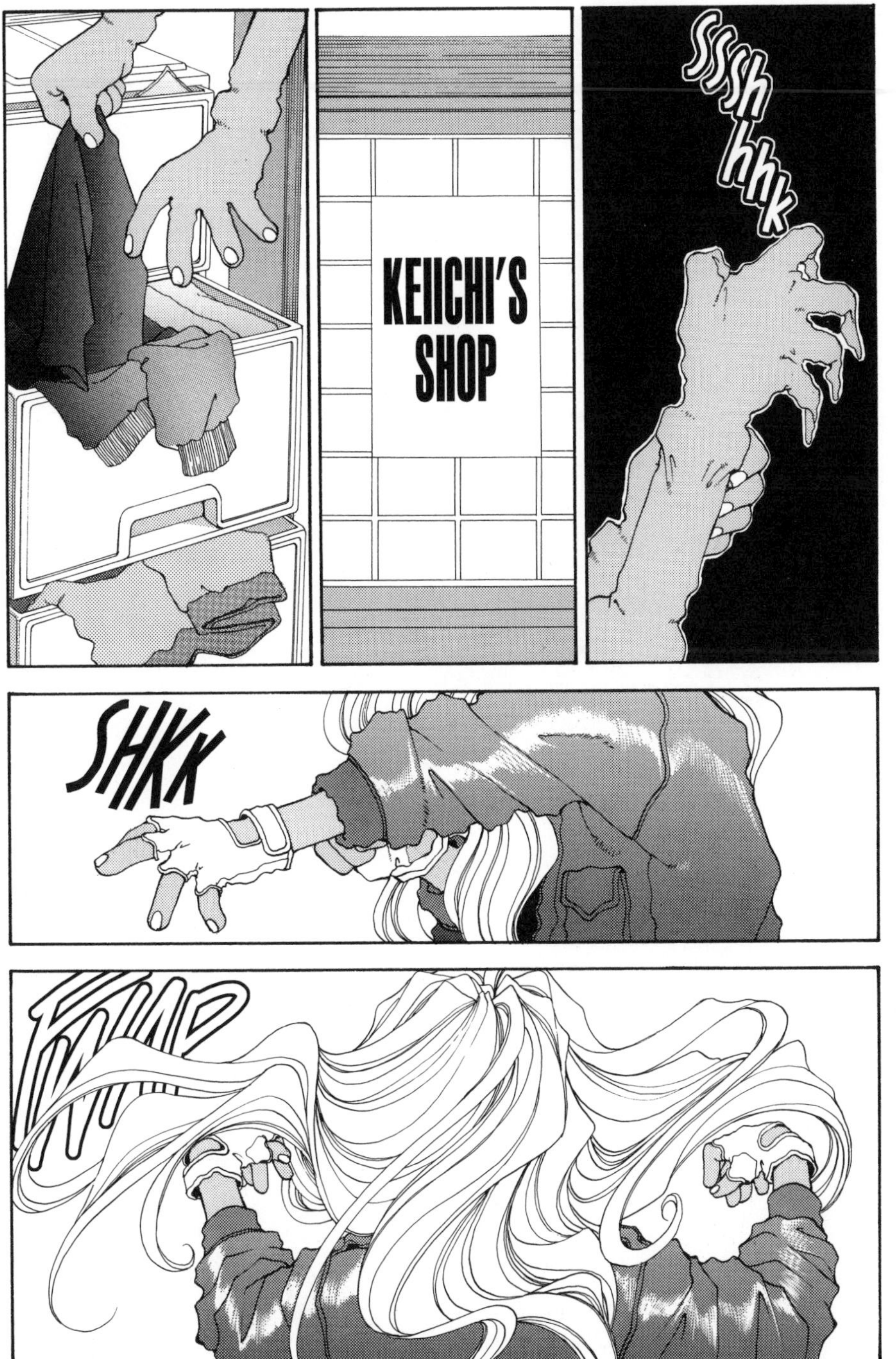
SSShhhk
KEIICHI'S SHOP
SHKK

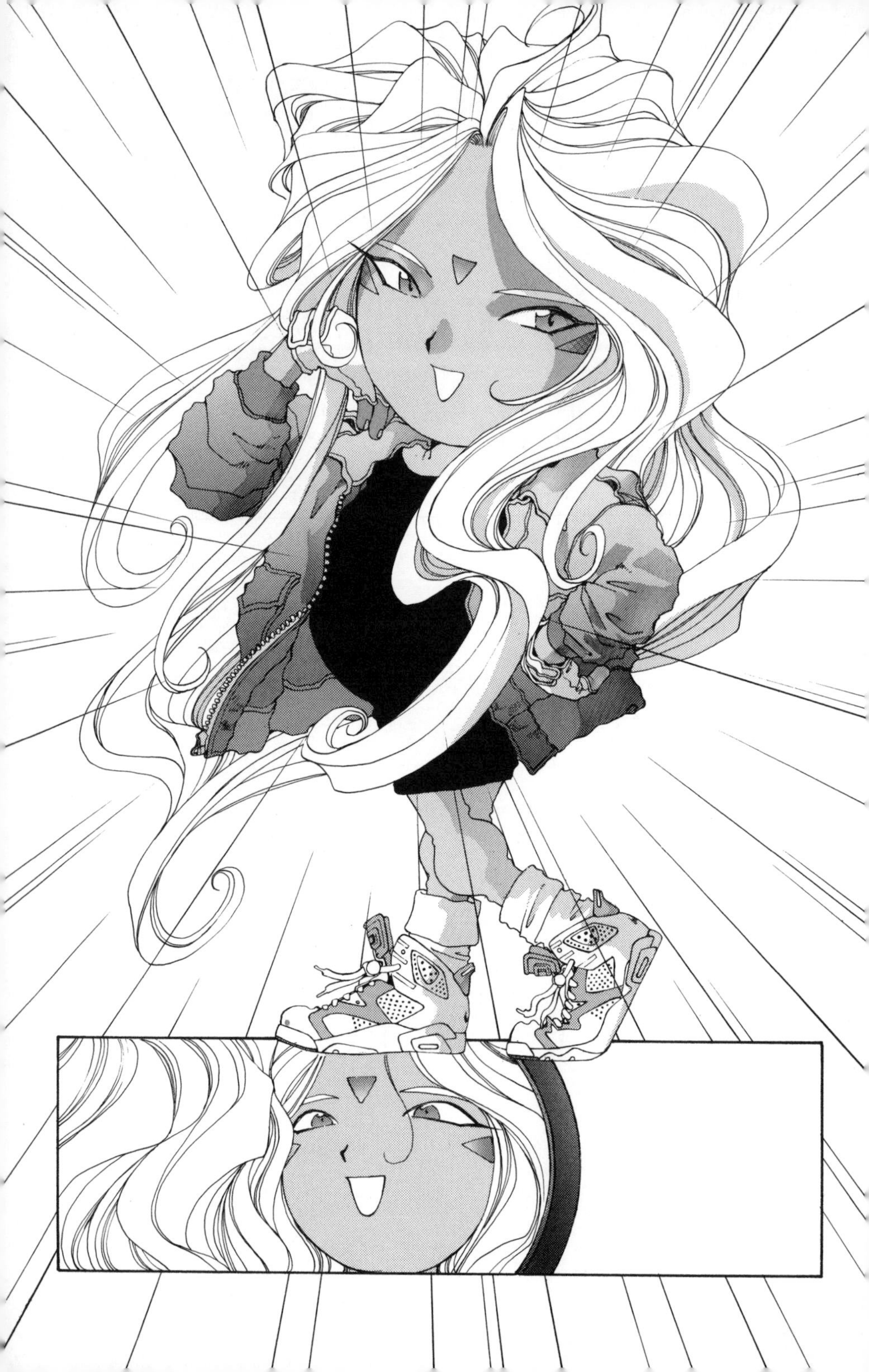

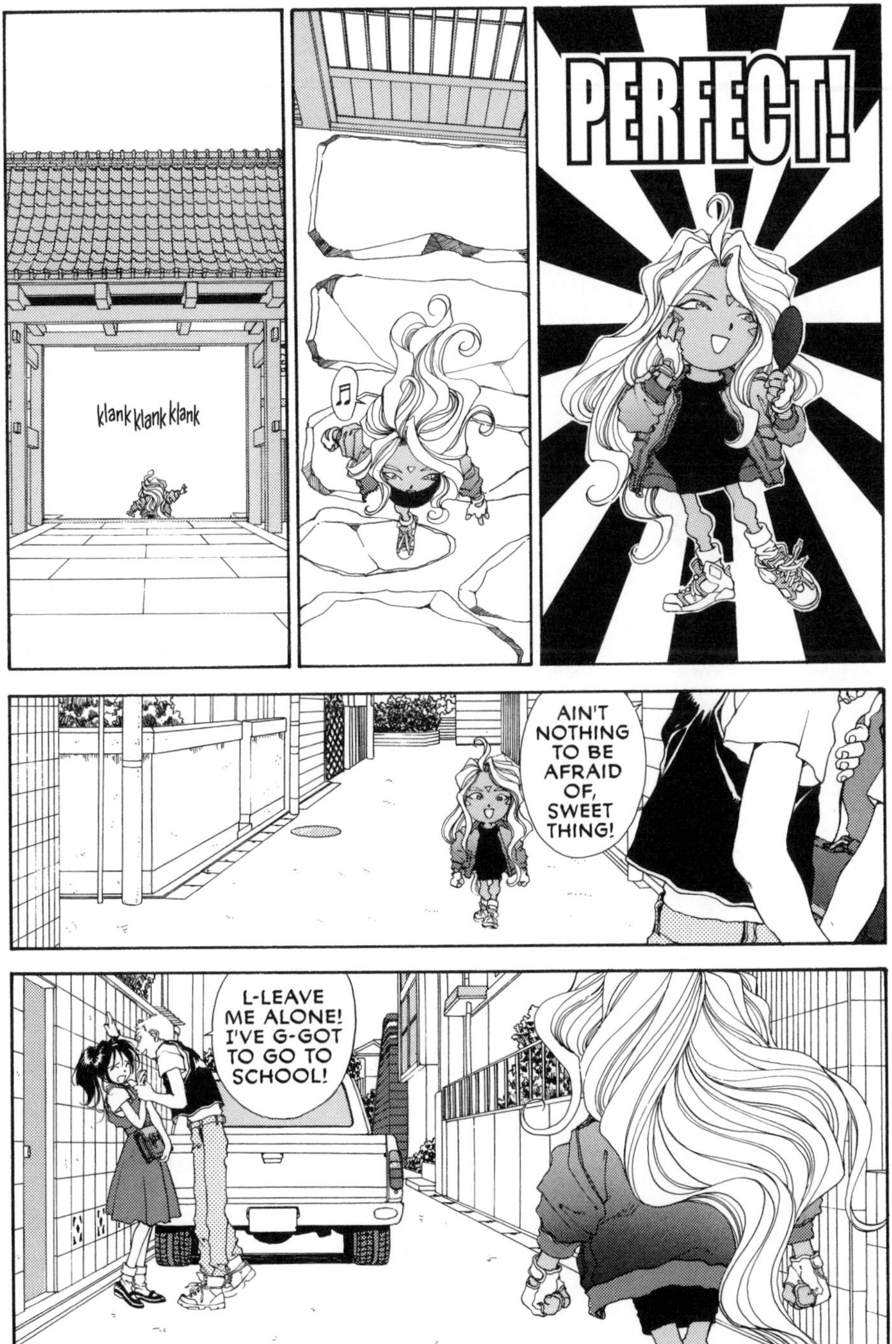
PERFECT!
♪
klank klank klank
AIN'T NOTHING TO BE AFRAID OF, SWEET THING!
L-LEAVE ME ALONE! I'VE G-GOT TO GO TO SCHOOL!

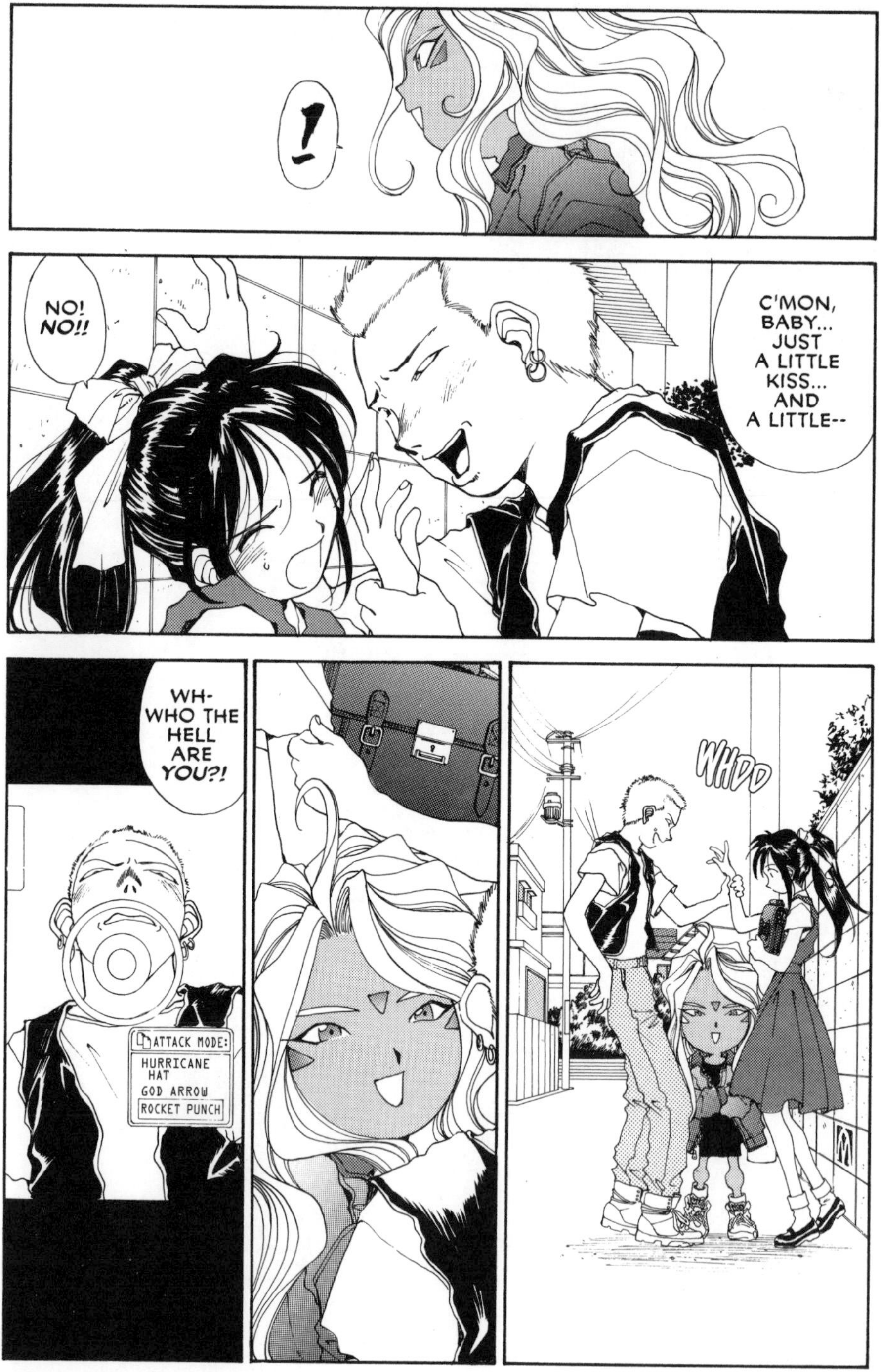
!
C'MON, BABY... JUST A LITTLE KISS... AND A LITTLE--
NO! *NO!!*
WHDD
WH- WHO THE HELL ARE *YOU?!*
ATTACK MODE:
HURRICANE HAT
GOD ARROW
ROCKET PUNCH

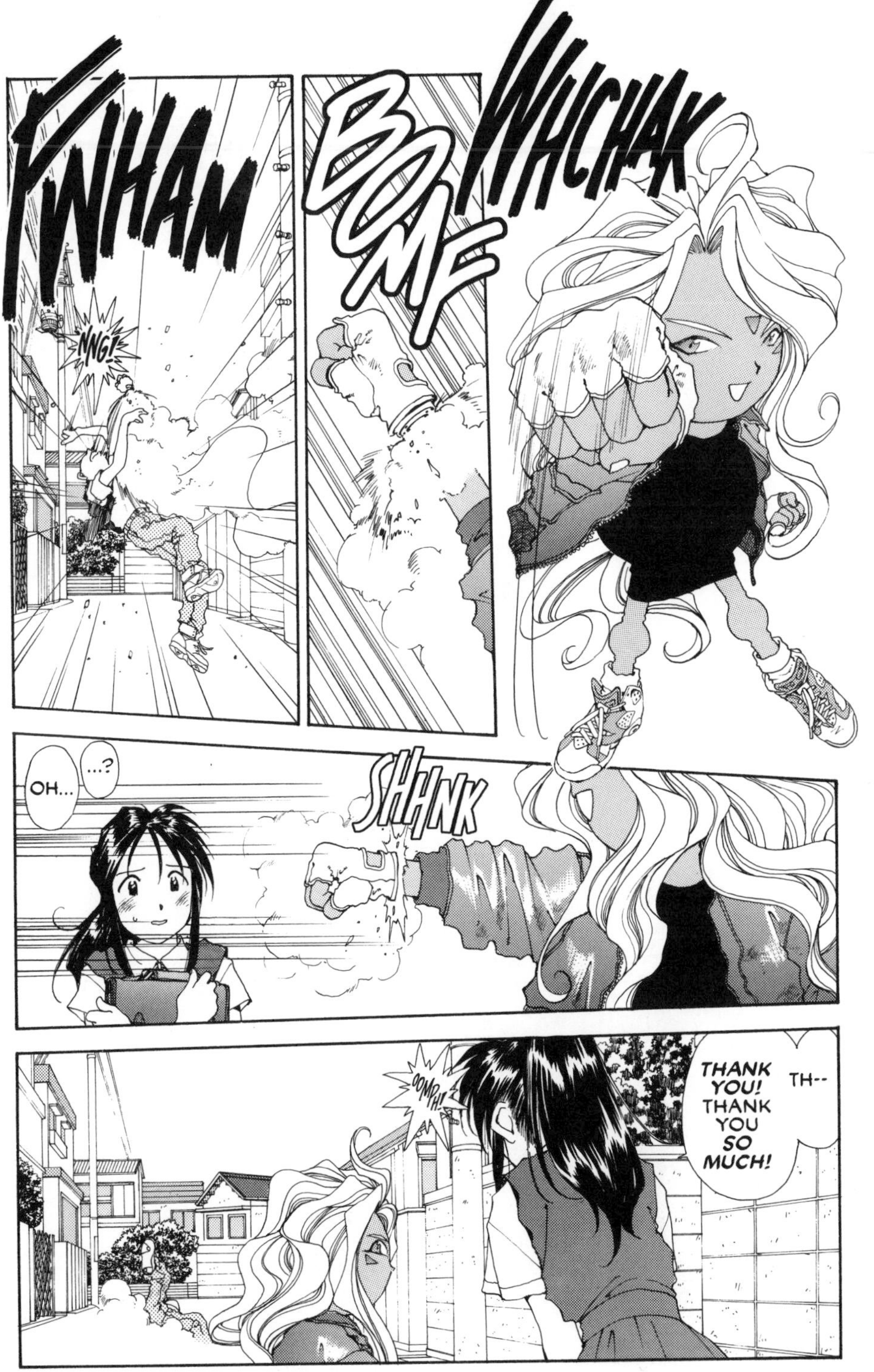
WHCHAK
BOMF
FWHAM
NNG!
SHHNK
...?
OH...
TH--
THANK YOU! THANK YOU SO MUCH!
OOMPH!

um...   ...?

EXCUSE ME, BUT... YOUR NAME?

K-CHAK

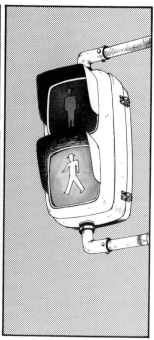

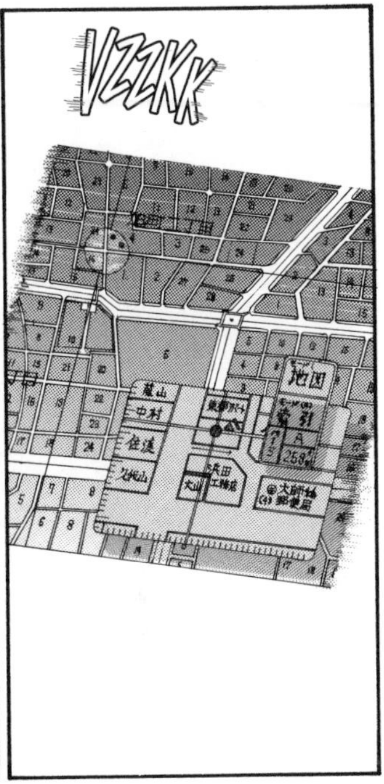
VZZKK
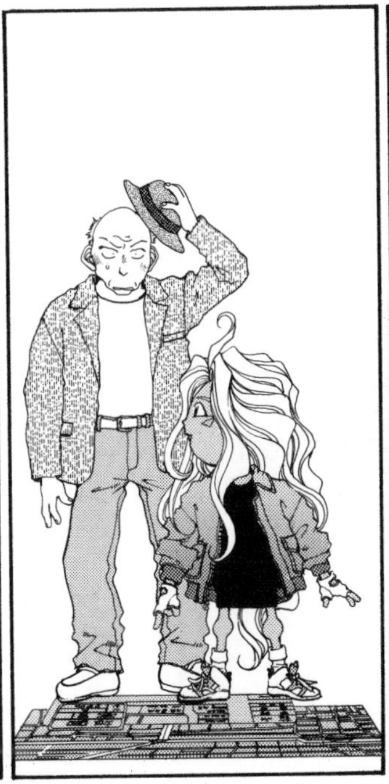
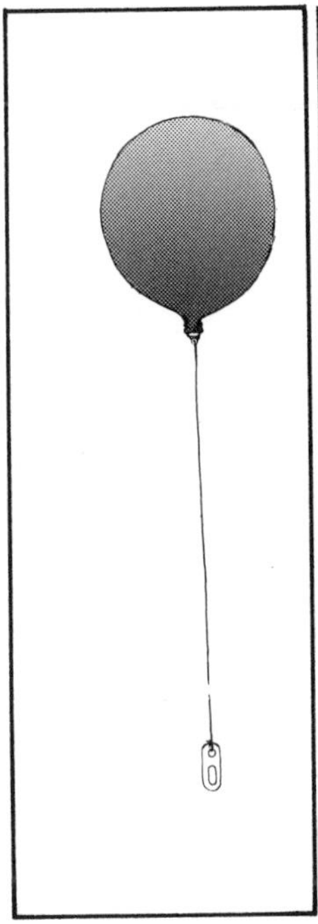
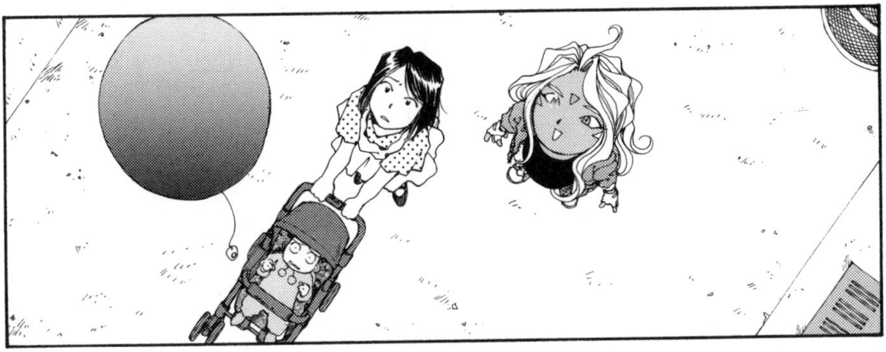
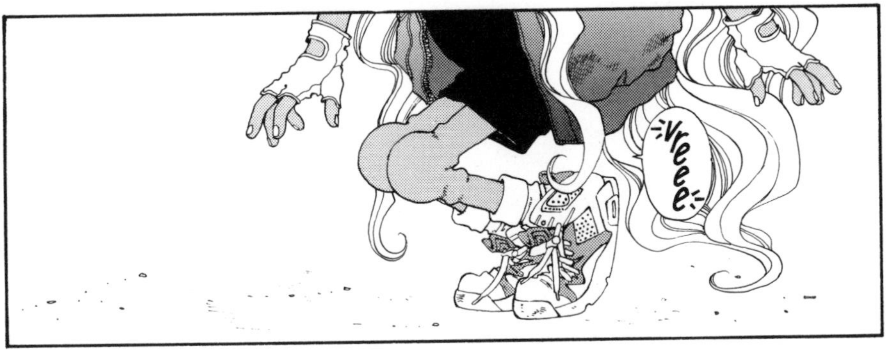
Vreeee

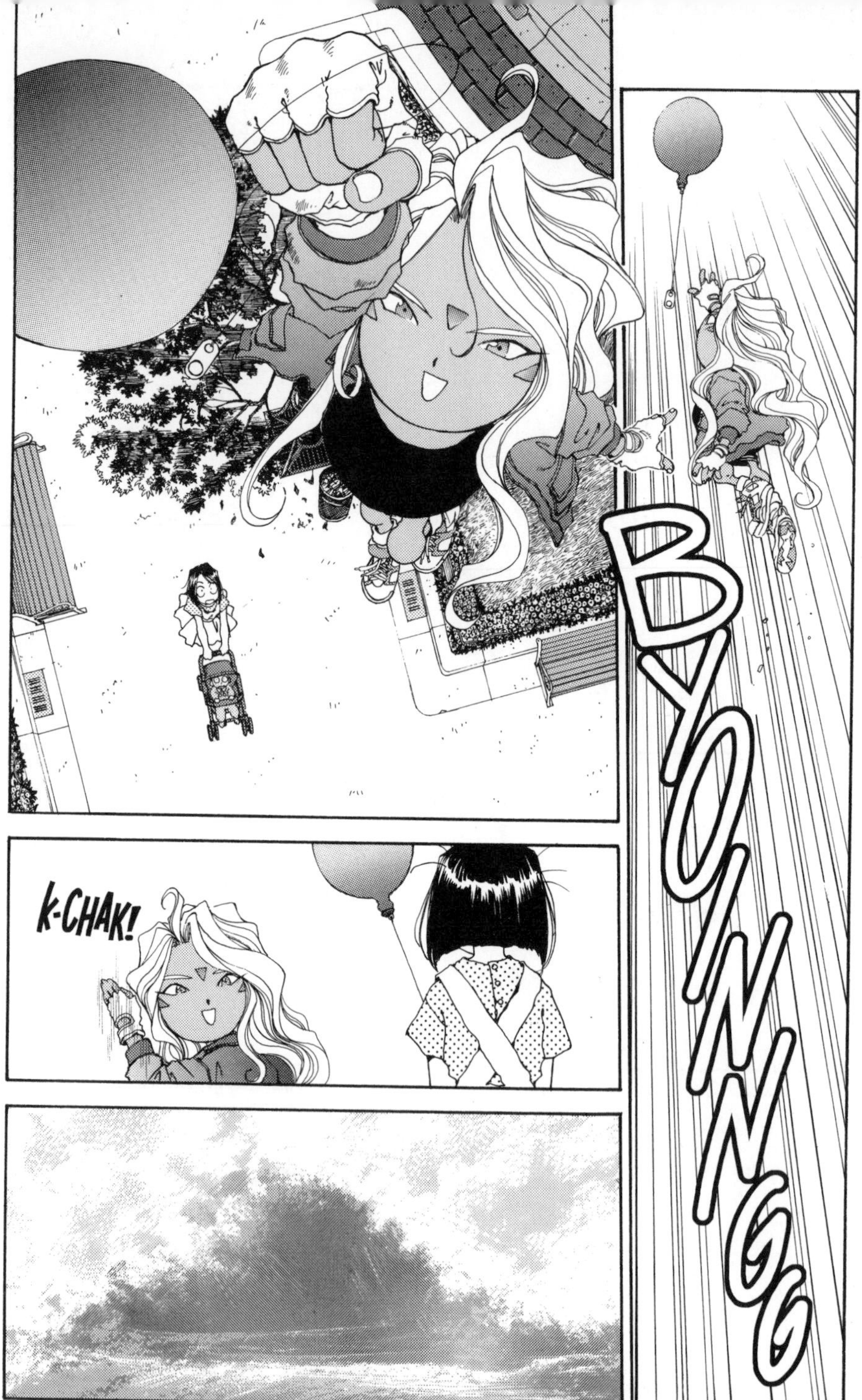
BYOINNGG
K-CHAK!

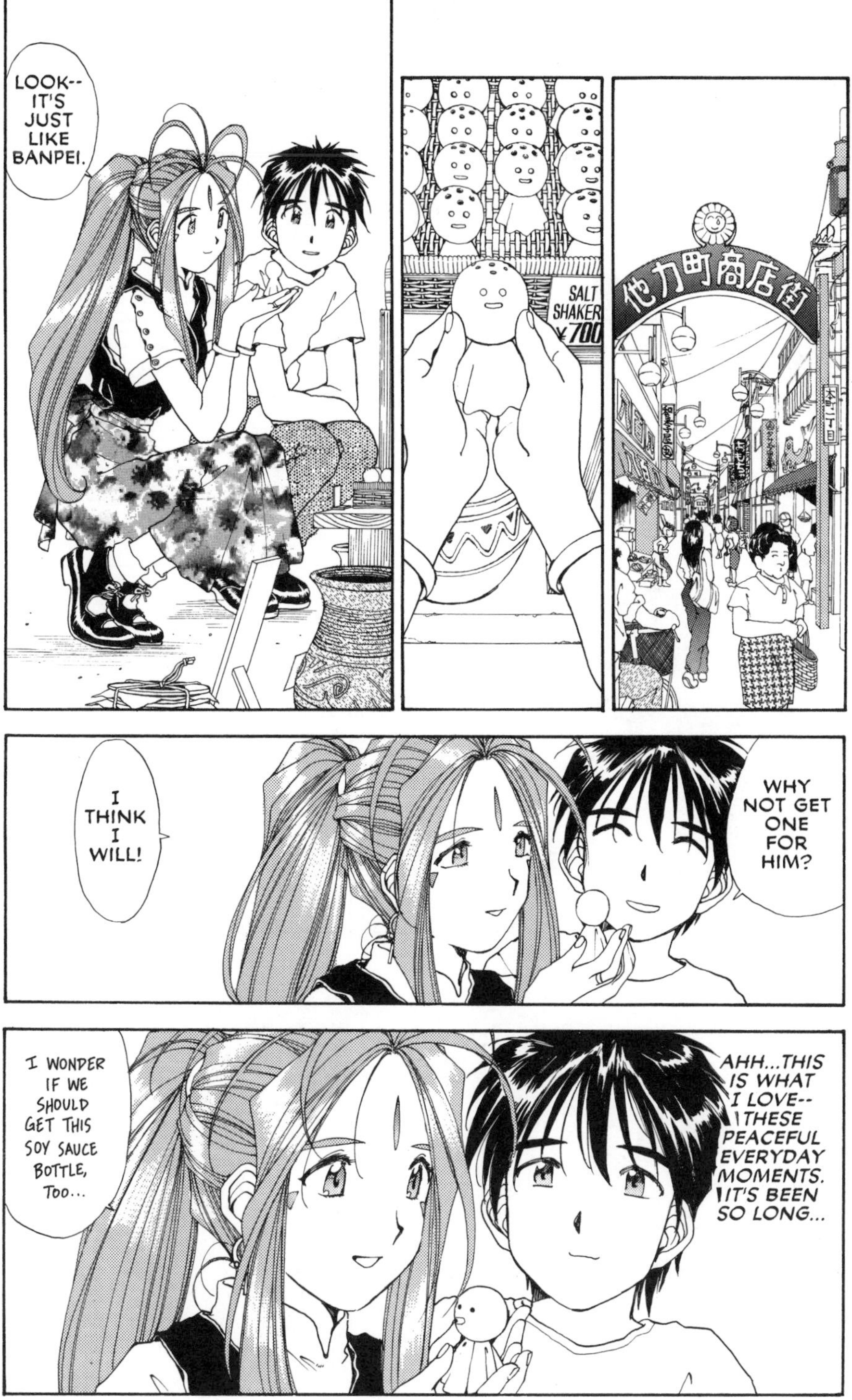
他力町商店街
本町二丁目
SALT SHAKER ¥700
LOOK-- IT'S JUST LIKE BANPEI.
WHY NOT GET ONE FOR HIM?
I THINK I WILL!
AHH...THIS IS WHAT I LOVE-- THESE PEACEFUL EVERYDAY MOMENTS. IT'S BEEN SO LONG...
I WONDER IF WE SHOULD GET THIS SOY SAUCE BOTTLE, TOO...

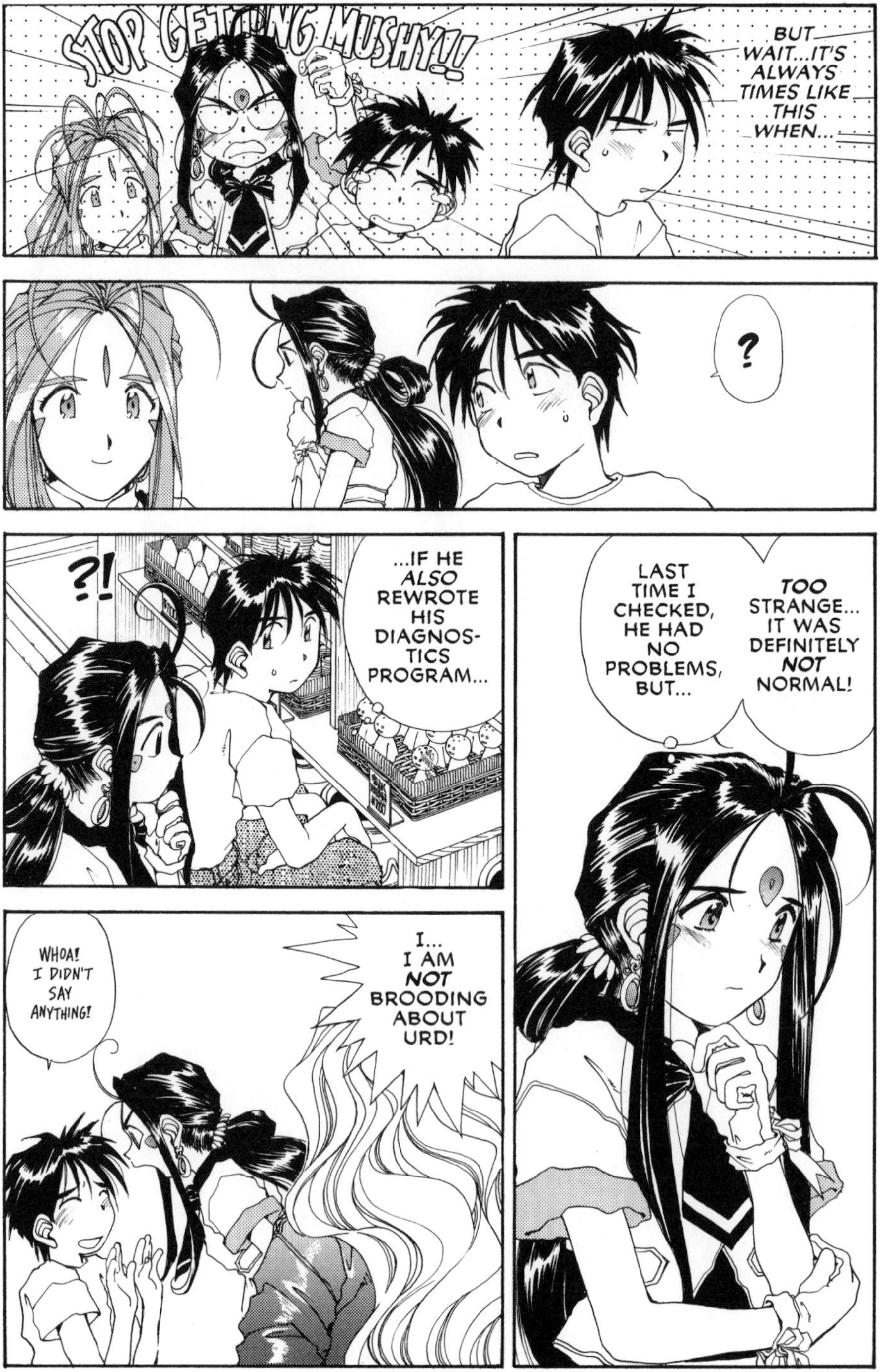
BUT WAIT...IT'S ALWAYS TIMES LIKE THIS WHEN...
STOP GET NG MUSHY!!
?
TOO STRANGE... IT WAS DEFINITELY NOT NORMAL!
LAST TIME I CHECKED, HE HAD NO PROBLEMS, BUT...
...IF HE ALSO REWROTE HIS DIAGNOSTICS PROGRAM...
?!
I... I AM NOT BROODING ABOUT URD!
WHOA! I DIDN'T SAY ANYTHING!

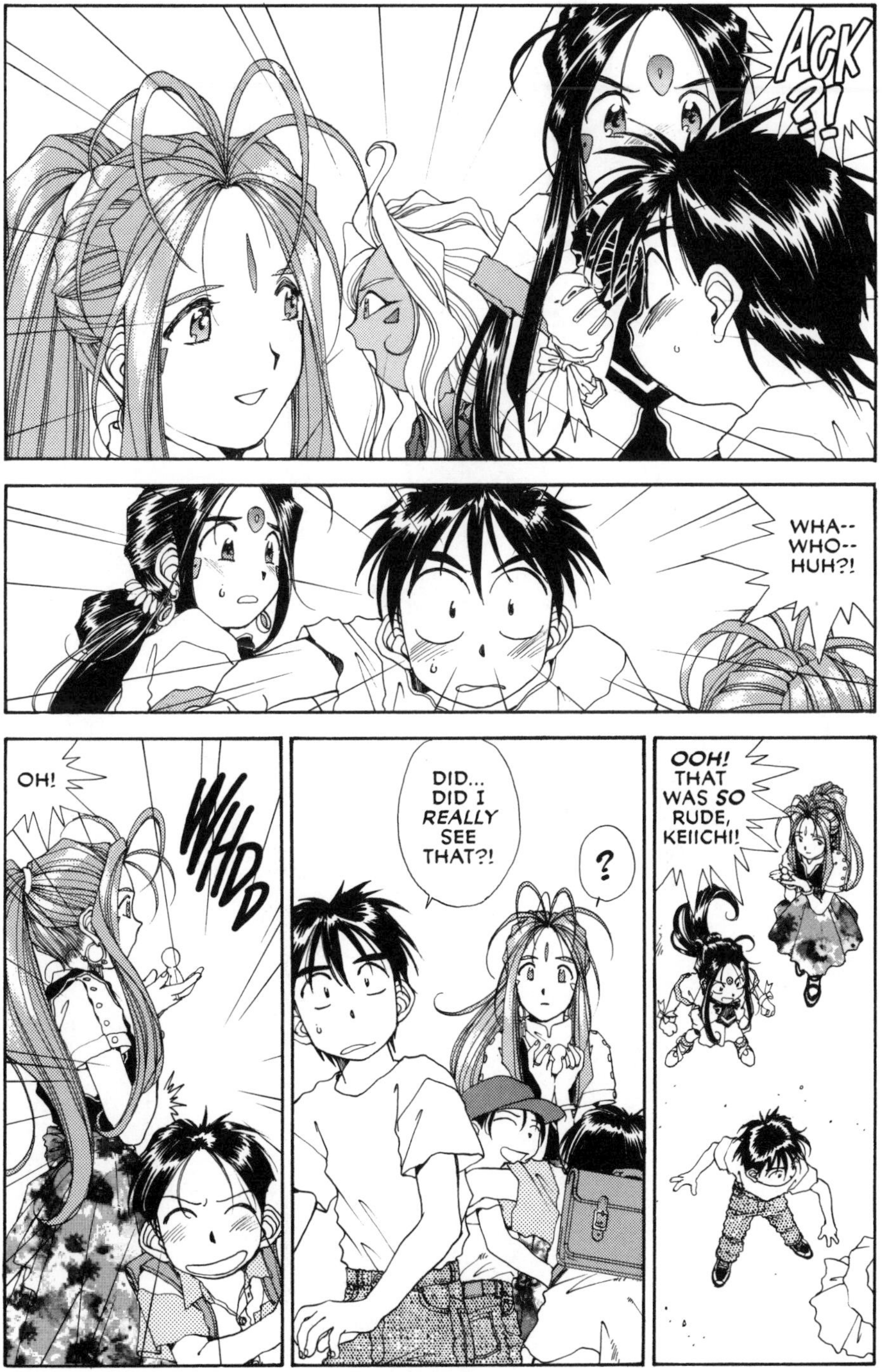
ACK ?!
WHA-- WHO-- HUH?!
OOH! THAT WAS *SO* RUDE, KEIICHI!
DID... DID I *REALLY* SEE THAT?!
?
OH!
WHDD

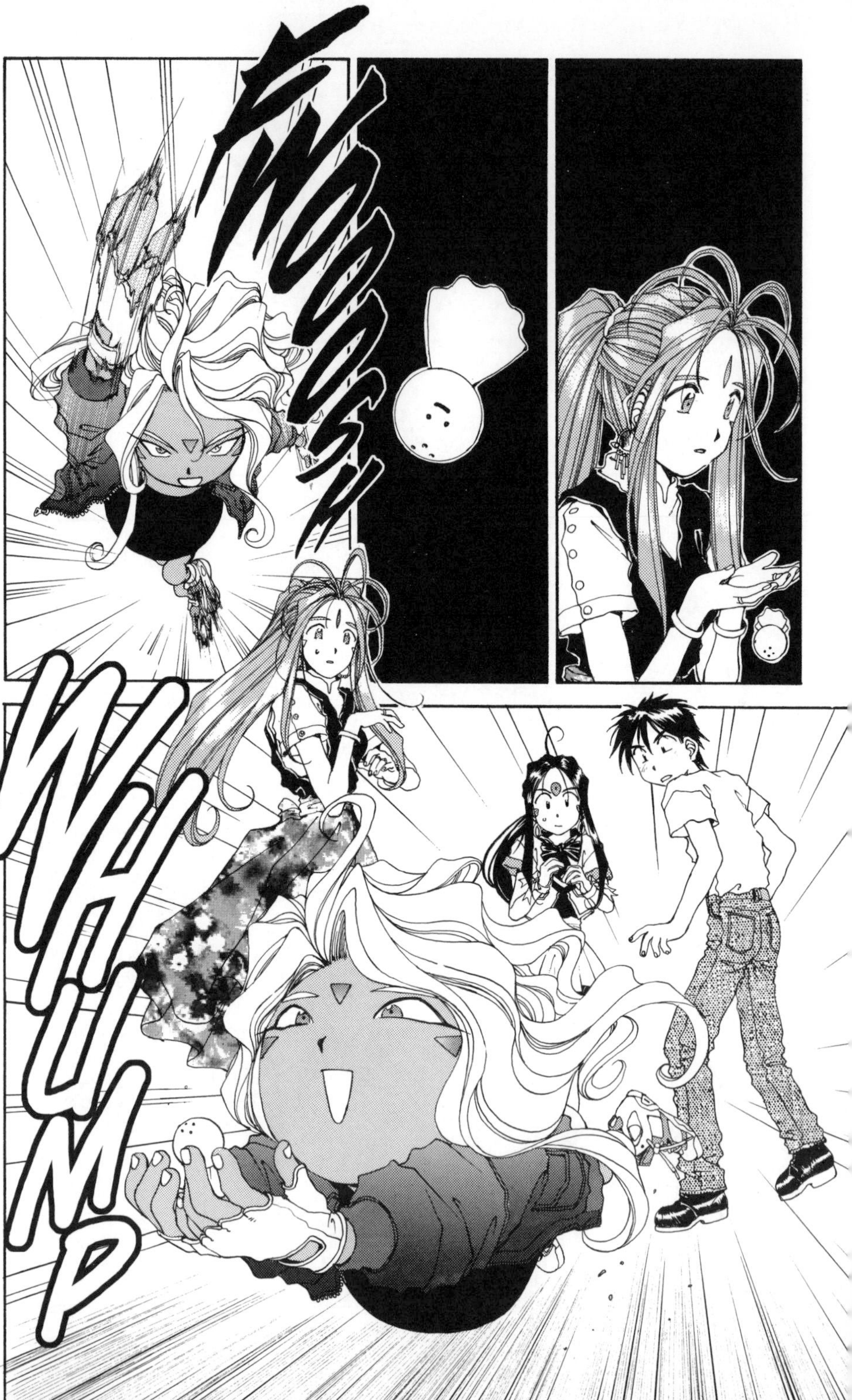
FWOOOSH
WHUMP

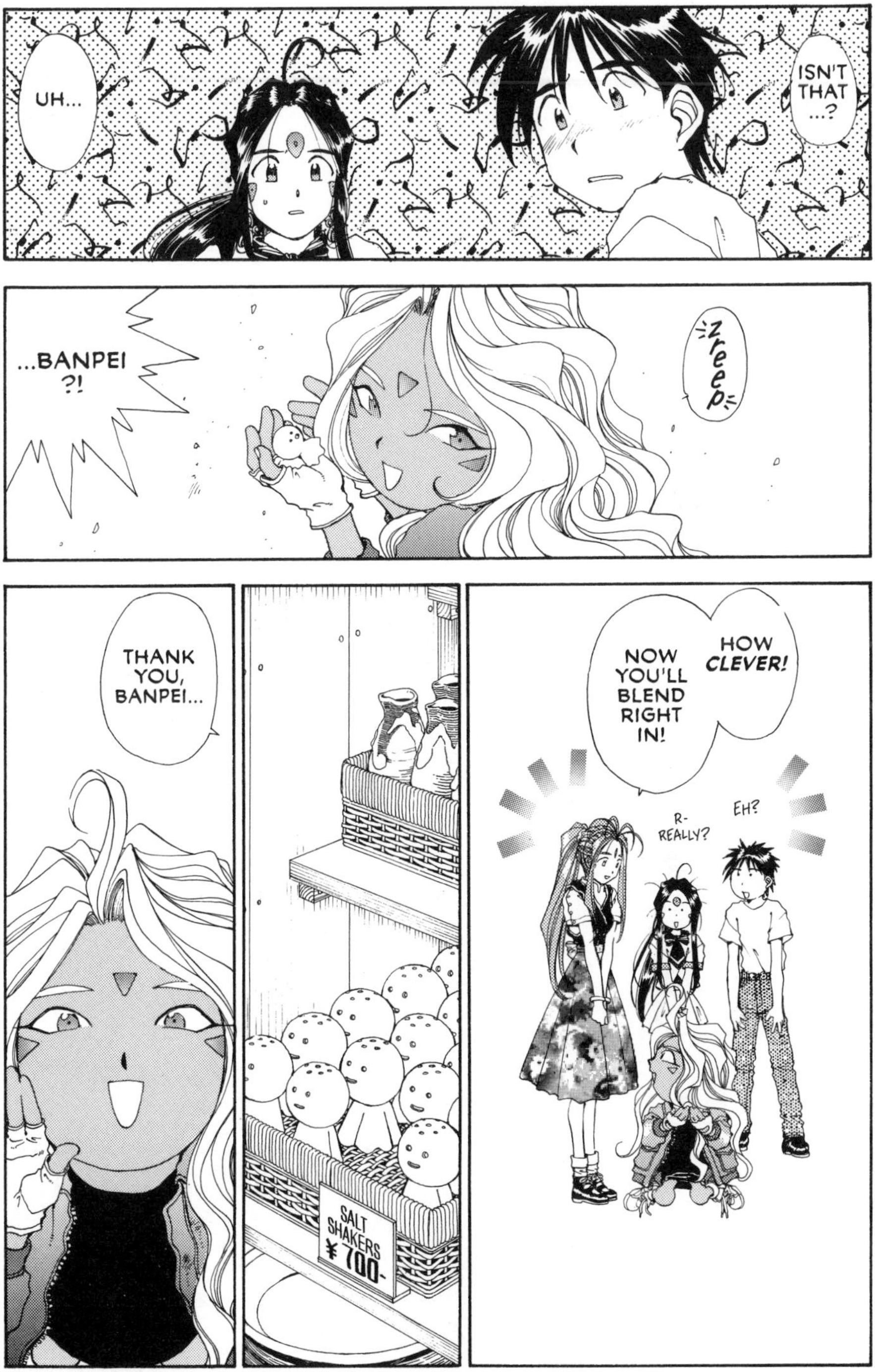
ISN'T THAT ...?
UH...
zreep
...BANPEI ?!
HOW CLEVER! NOW YOU'LL BLEND RIGHT IN!
EH?
R-REALLY?
SALT SHAKERS ¥700-
THANK YOU, BANPEI...

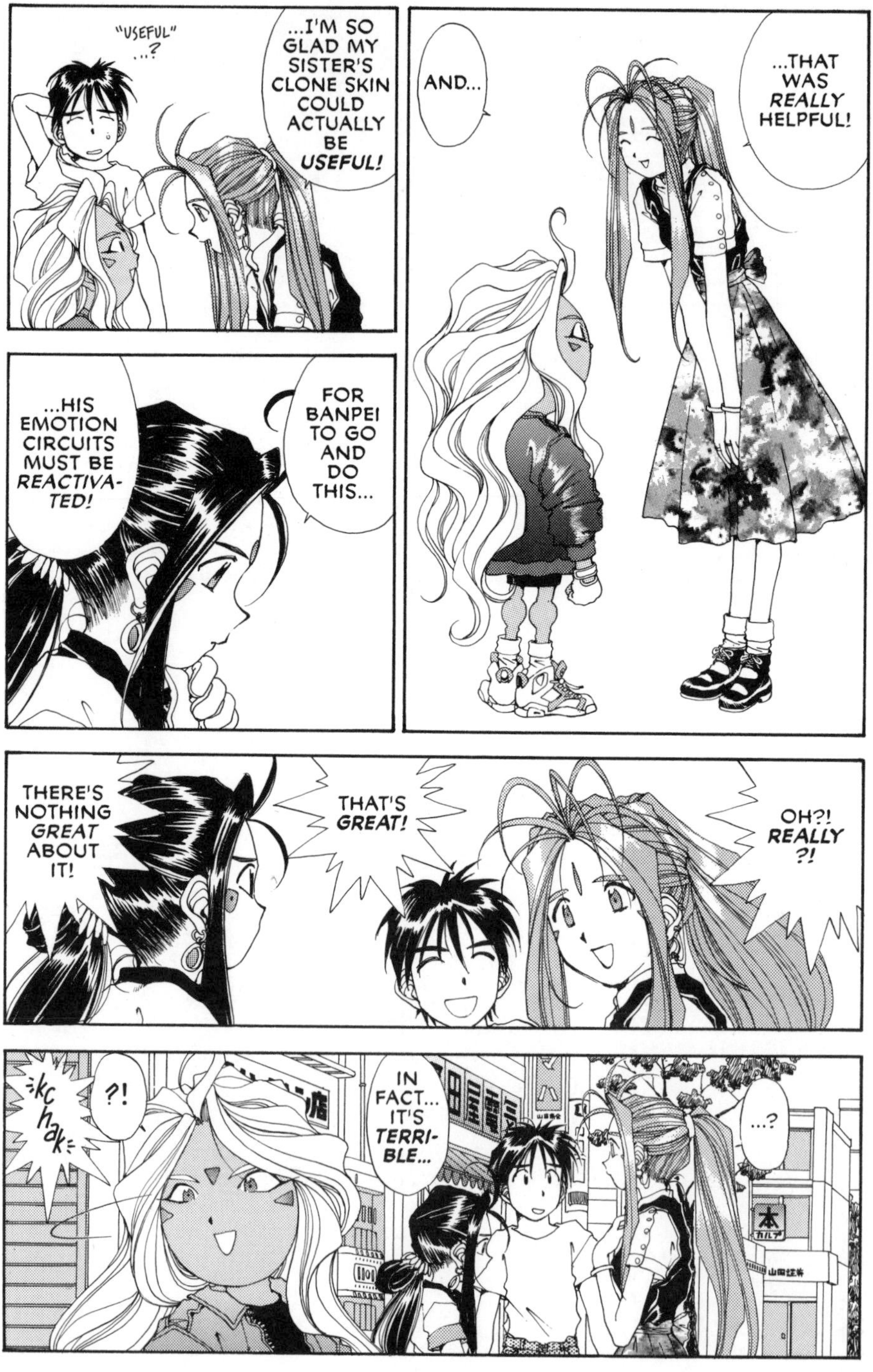
...THAT WAS *REALLY* HELPFUL!
AND...
...I'M SO GLAD MY SISTER'S CLONE SKIN COULD ACTUALLY BE *USEFUL!*
"USEFUL" ...?
FOR BANPEI TO GO AND DO THIS...
...HIS EMOTION CIRCUITS MUST BE *REACTIVATED!*
OH?! *REALLY ?!*
THAT'S *GREAT!*
THERE'S NOTHING *GREAT* ABOUT IT!
...?
IN FACT... IT'S *TERRIBLE...*
?!
KCHAK

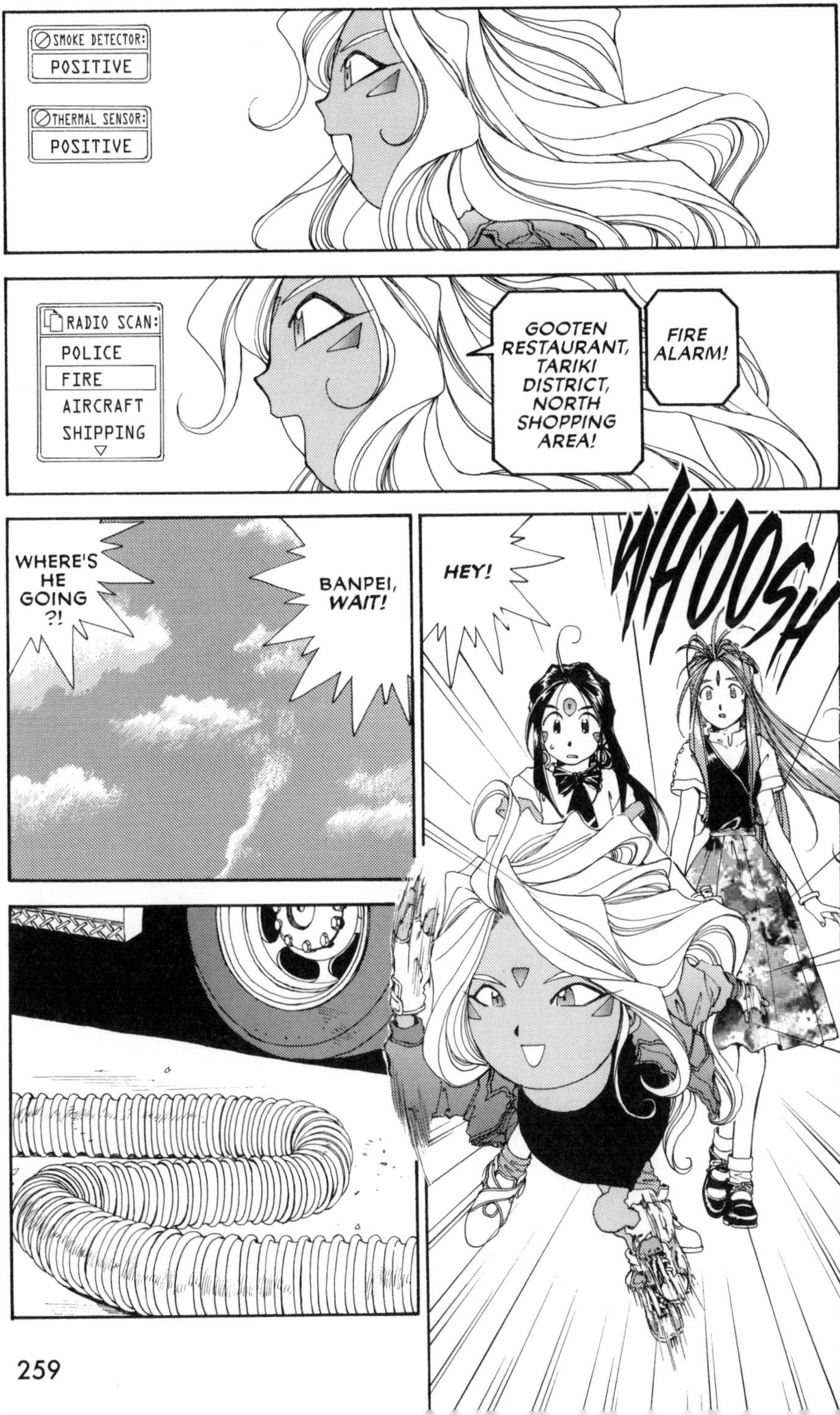
SMOKE DETECTOR:
POSITIVE
THERMAL SENSOR:
POSITIVE
RADIO SCAN:
POLICE
FIRE
AIRCRAFT
SHIPPING
FIRE ALARM!
GOOTEN RESTAURANT, TARIKI DISTRICT, NORTH SHOPPING AREA!
WHOOSH
HEY!
BANPEI, WAIT!
WHERE'S HE GOING ?!

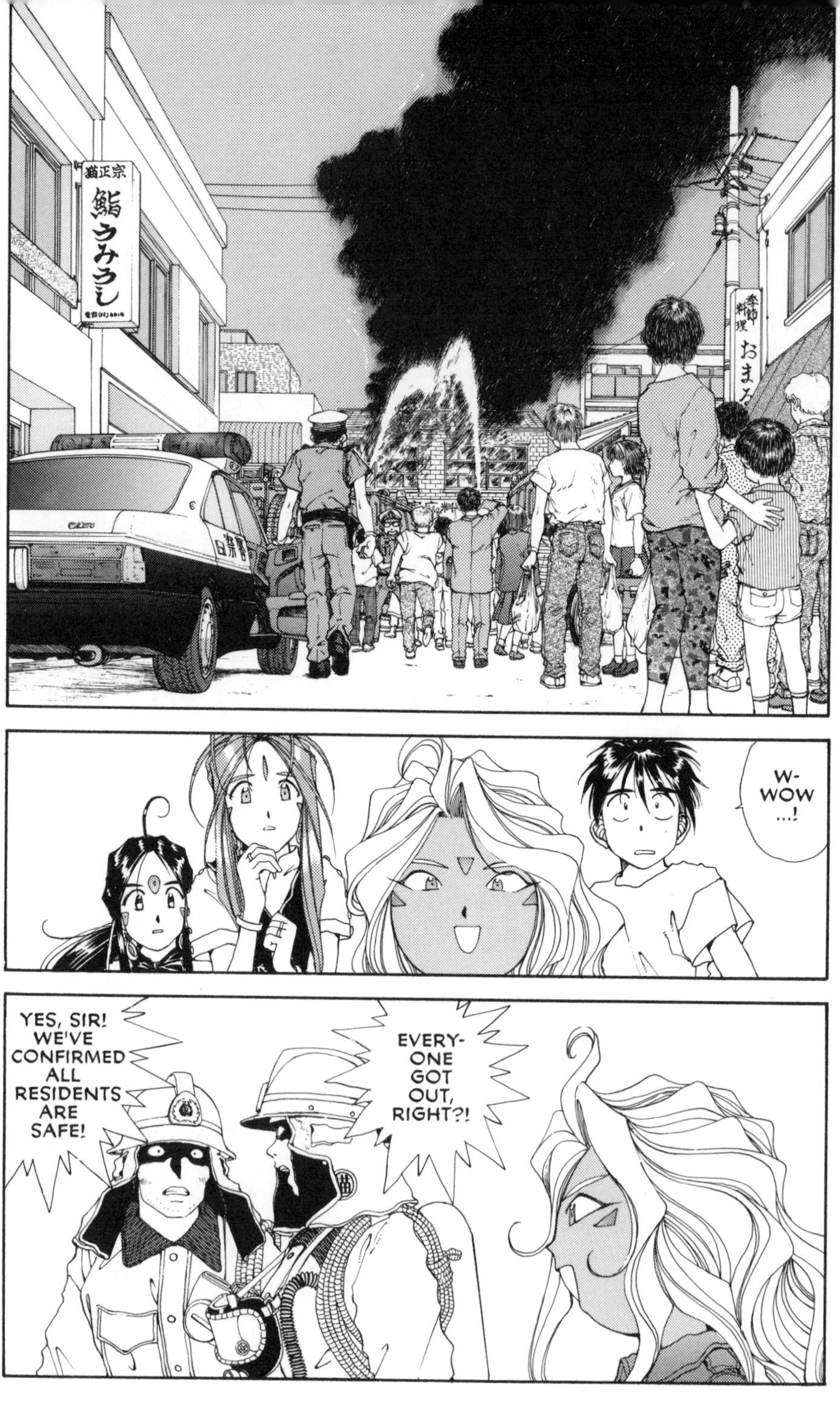
猫正宗
鮨 うみうし
W-WOW ...!
EVERY-ONE GOT OUT, RIGHT?!
YES, SIR! WE'VE CONFIRMED ALL RESIDENTS ARE SAFE!

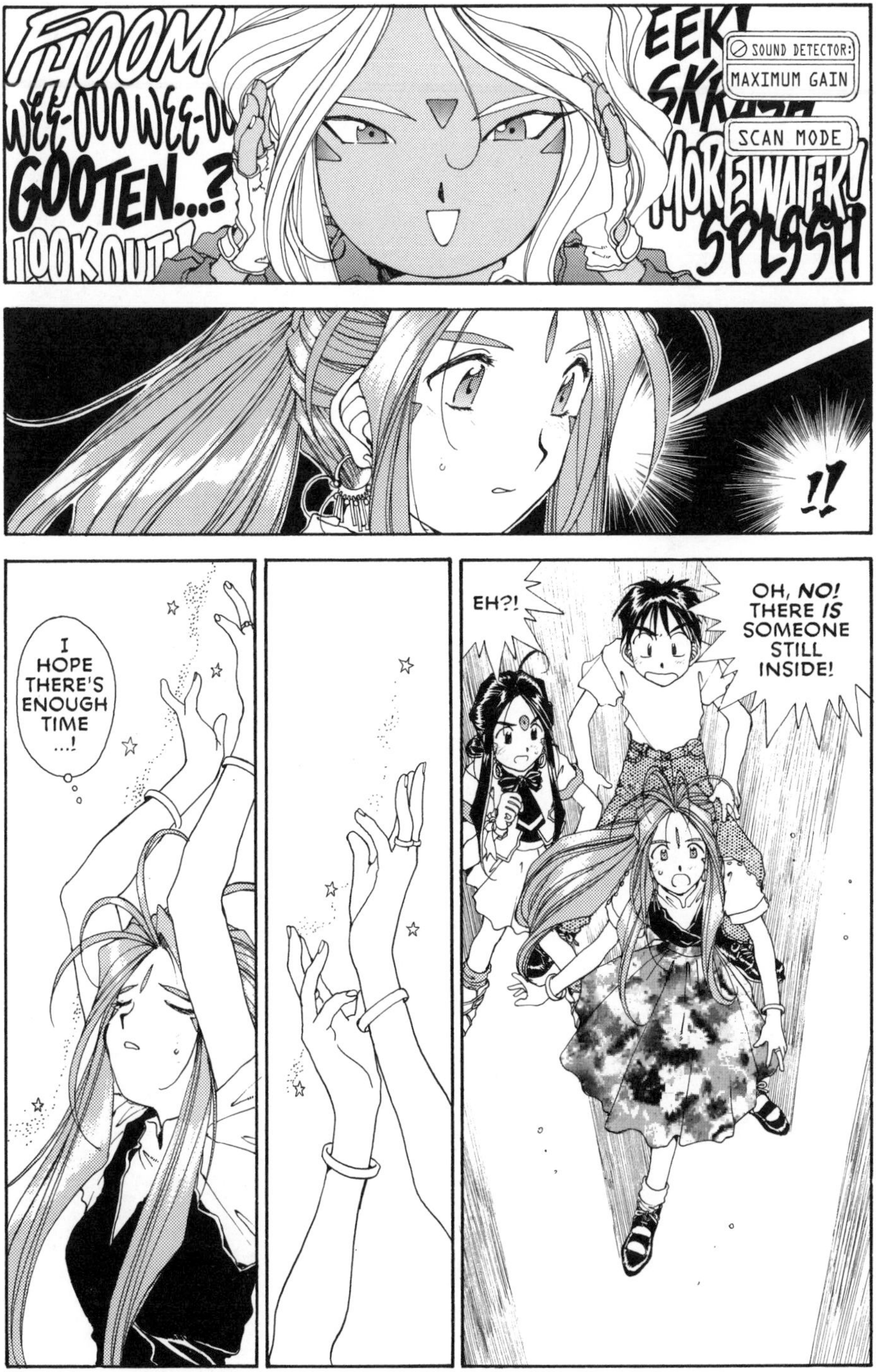
SOUND DETECTOR:
MAXIMUM GAIN
SCAN MODE
EEK!
MORE WATER!
SPLASH
FHOOM
WEE-OOO WEE-OO
GOOTEN...?
LOOKOUT!
!!
OH, *NO!* THERE *IS* SOMEONE STILL INSIDE!
EH?!
I HOPE THERE'S ENOUGH TIME ...!

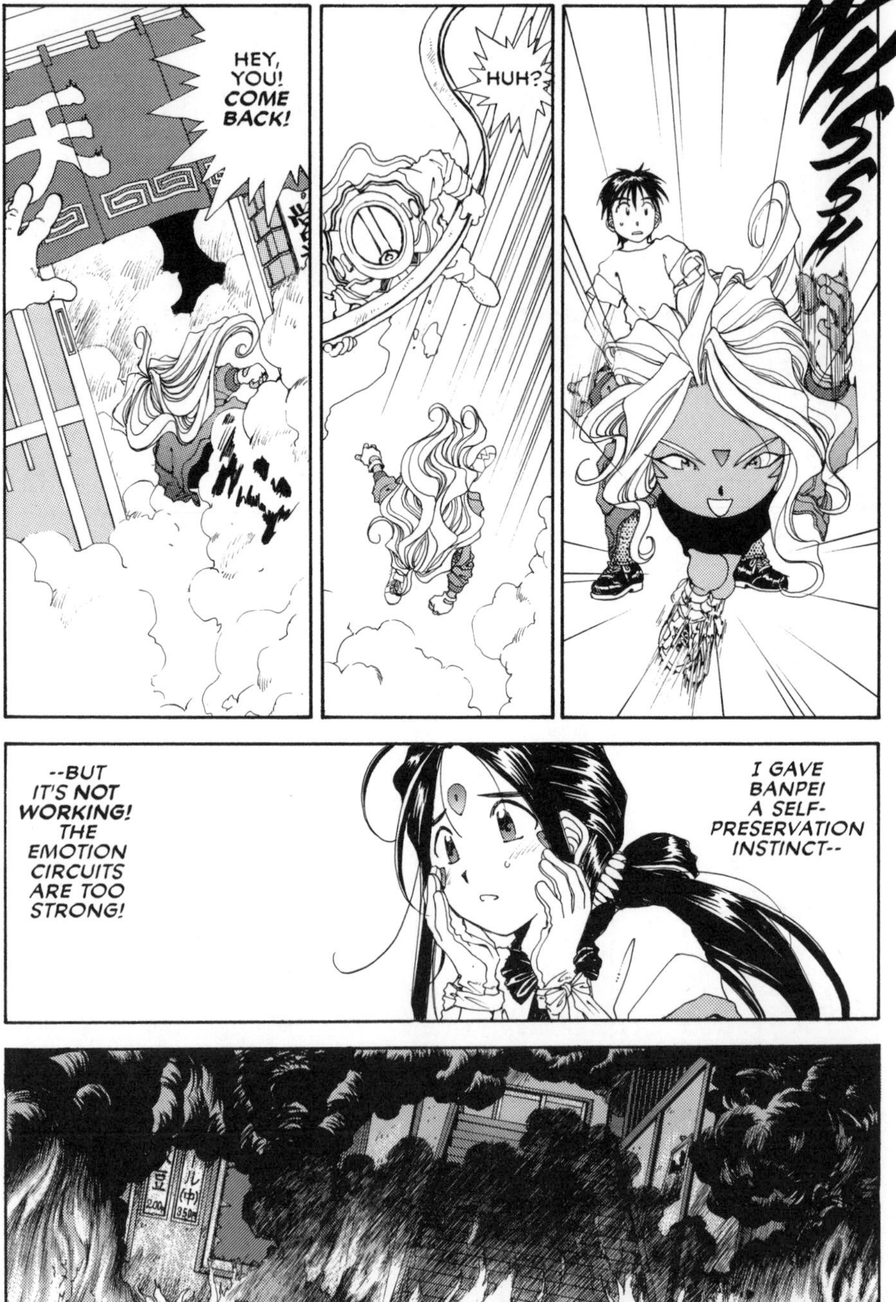
HUH?
HEY, YOU! COME BACK!
I GAVE BANPEI A SELF-PRESERVATION INSTINCT--
--BUT IT'S NOT WORKING! THE EMOTION CIRCUITS ARE TOO STRONG!

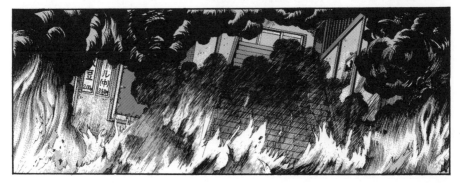

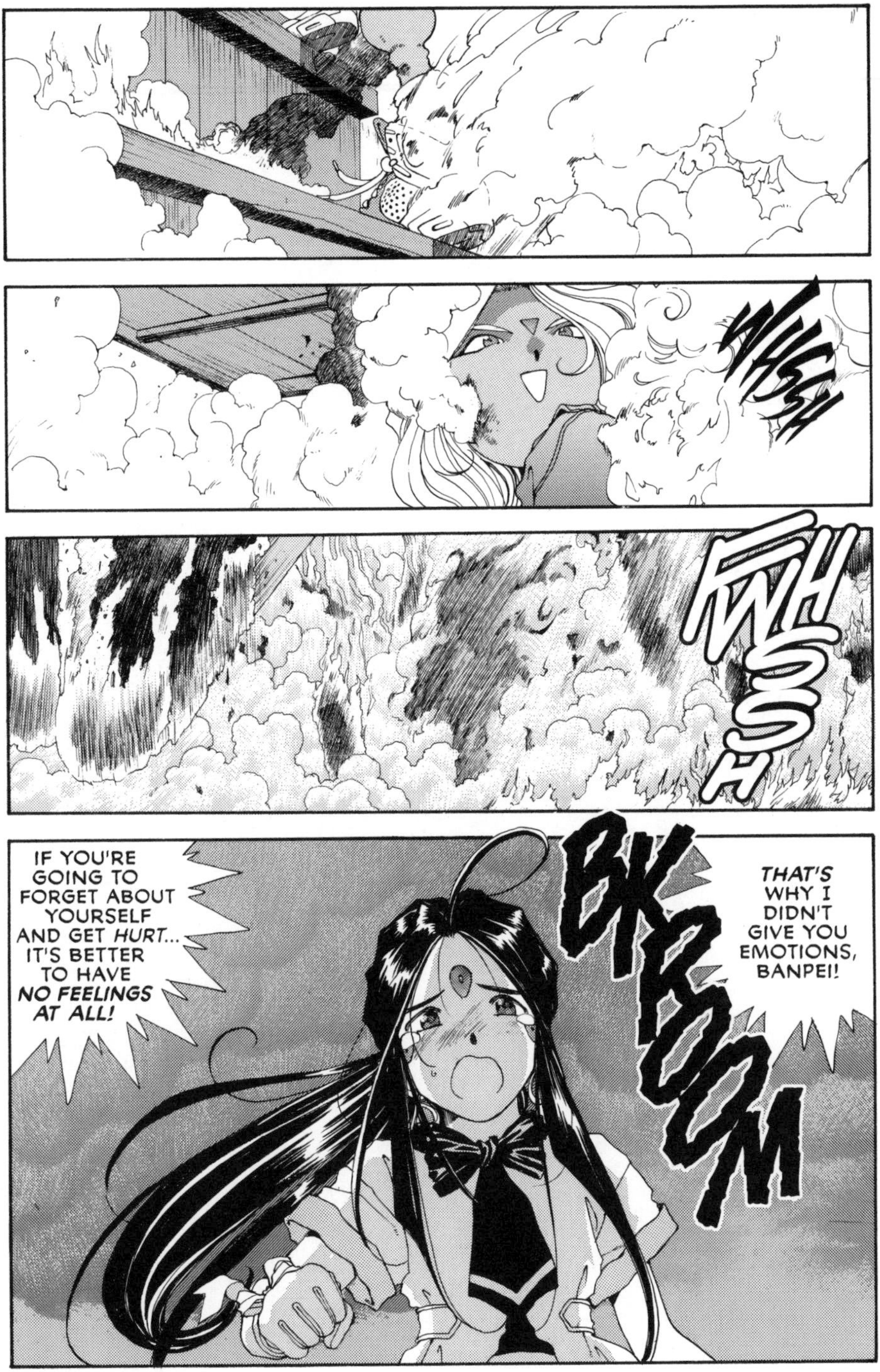
WHSSH
FWHSSH
IF YOU'RE GOING TO FORGET ABOUT YOURSELF AND GET *HURT*... IT'S BETTER TO HAVE ***NO FEELINGS AT ALL!***
BKBOOM
THAT'S WHY I DIDN'T GIVE YOU EMOTIONS, BANPEI!

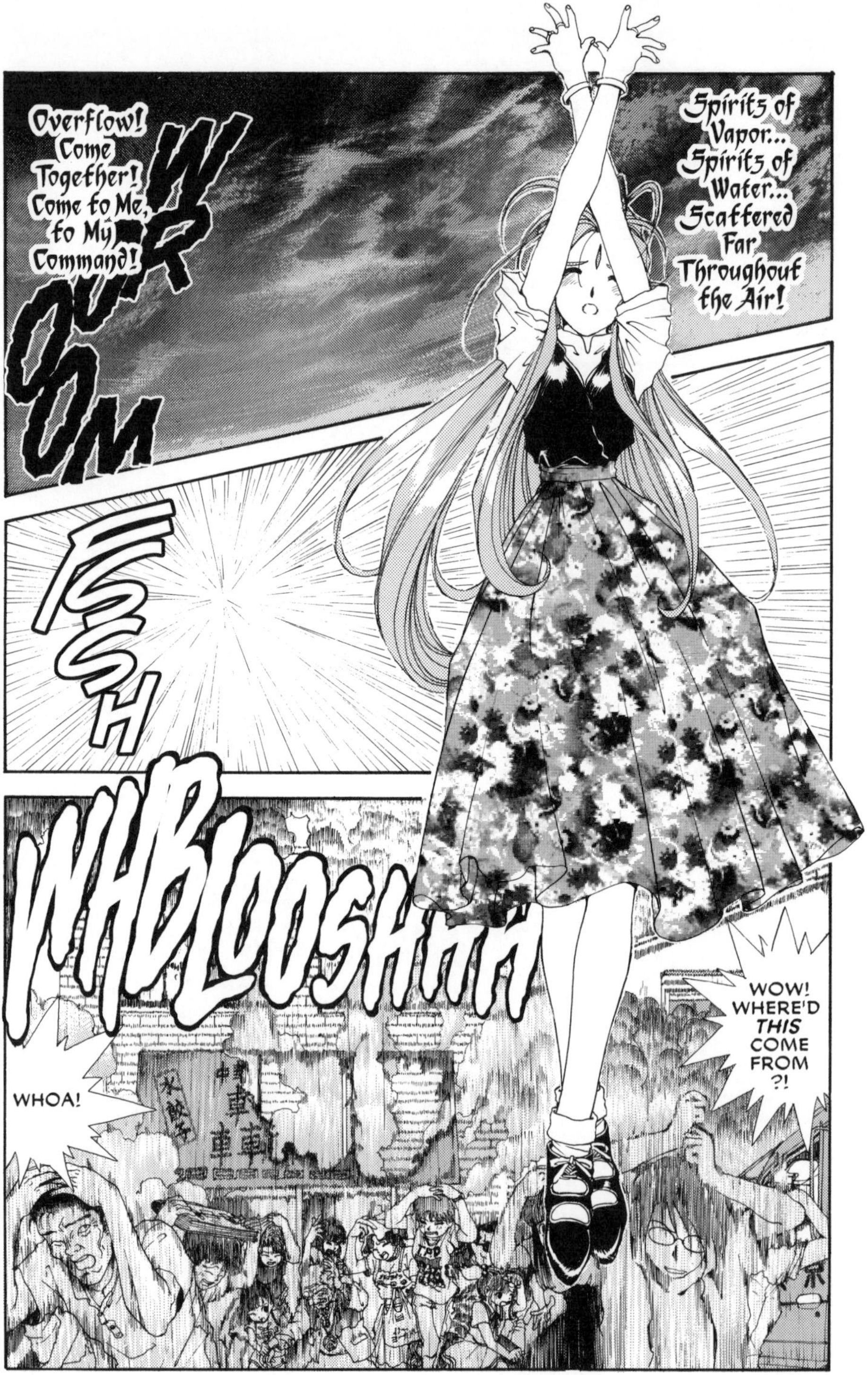
Spirits of Vapor... Spirits of Water... Scattered Far Throughout the Air!
Overflow! Come Together! Come to Me, to My Command!
WOOM
FSSH
WHBLOOSHHH
WOW! WHERE'D THIS COME FROM ?!
WHOA!

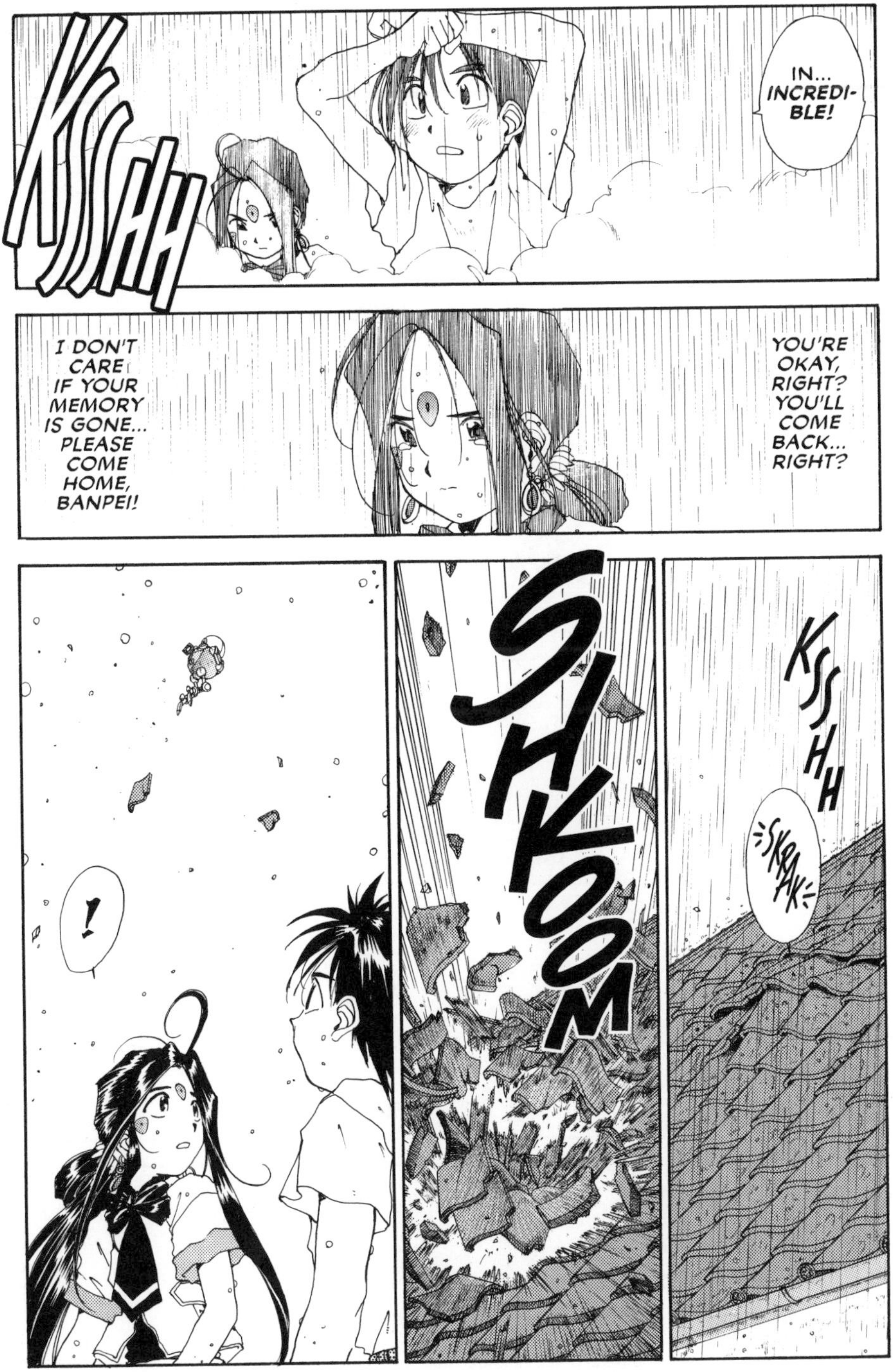
IN... INCREDI-BLE!
KSSHH
YOU'RE OKAY, RIGHT? YOU'LL COME BACK... RIGHT?
I DON'T CARE IF YOUR MEMORY IS GONE... PLEASE COME HOME, BANPEI!
KSSHH
SKRAK
SHKOOM
!

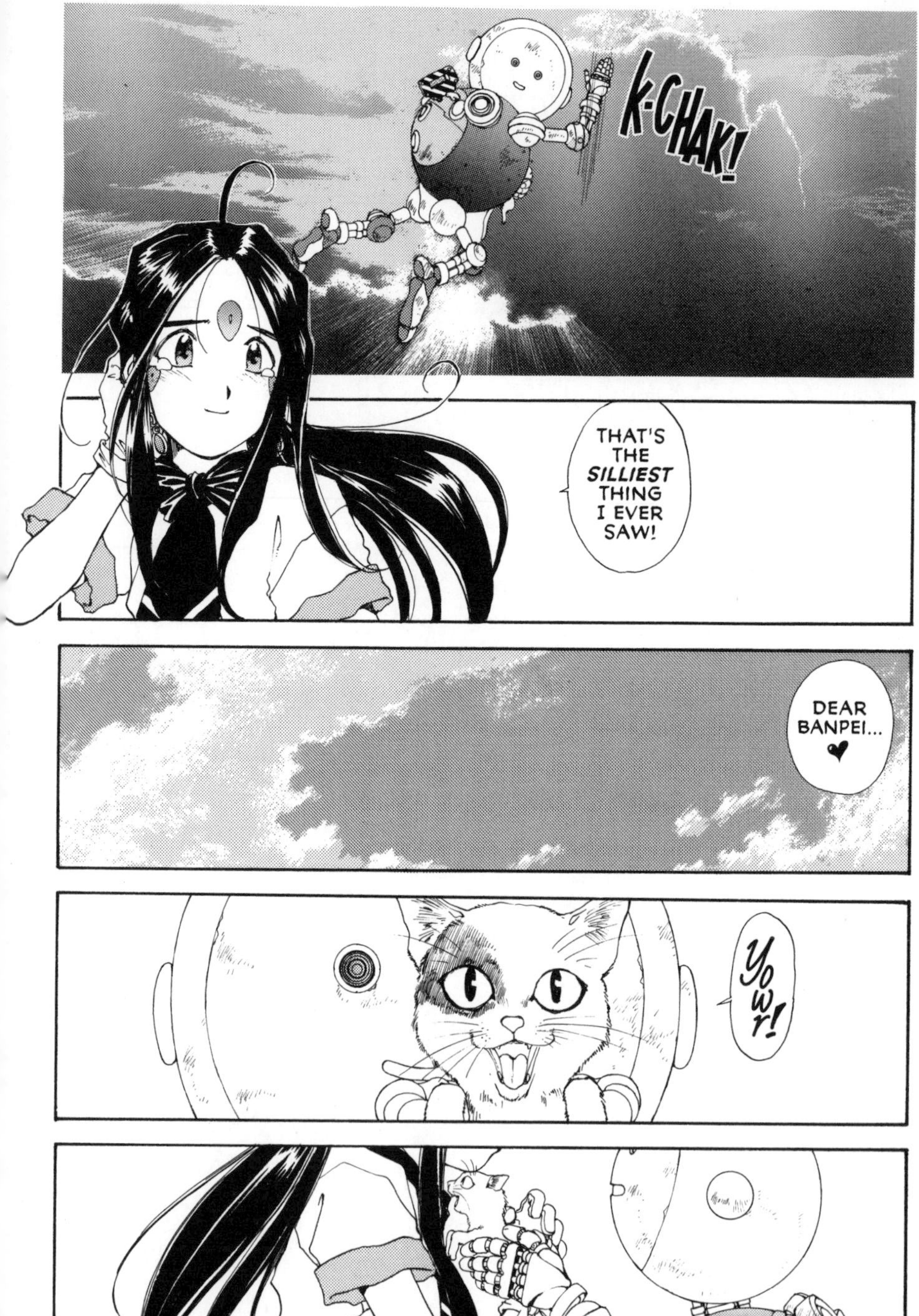
K-CHAK!
THAT'S THE *SILLIEST* THING I EVER SAW!
DEAR BANPEI... ♥
Yowr!

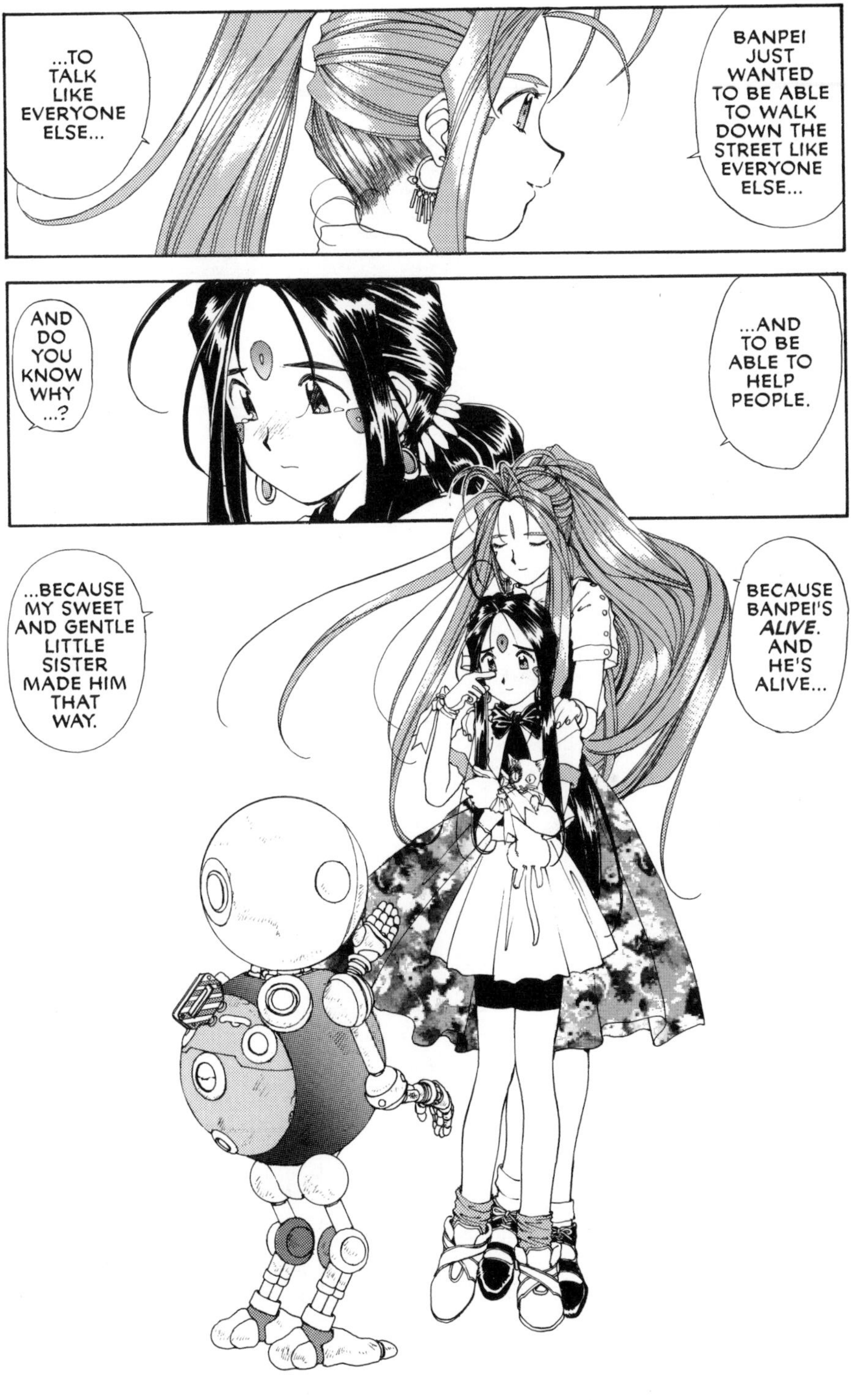
BANPEI JUST WANTED TO BE ABLE TO WALK DOWN THE STREET LIKE EVERYONE ELSE...
...TO TALK LIKE EVERYONE ELSE...
...AND TO BE ABLE TO HELP PEOPLE.
AND DO YOU KNOW WHY ...?
BECAUSE BANPEI'S *ALIVE*. AND HE'S ALIVE...
...BECAUSE MY SWEET AND GENTLE LITTLE SISTER MADE HIM THAT WAY.

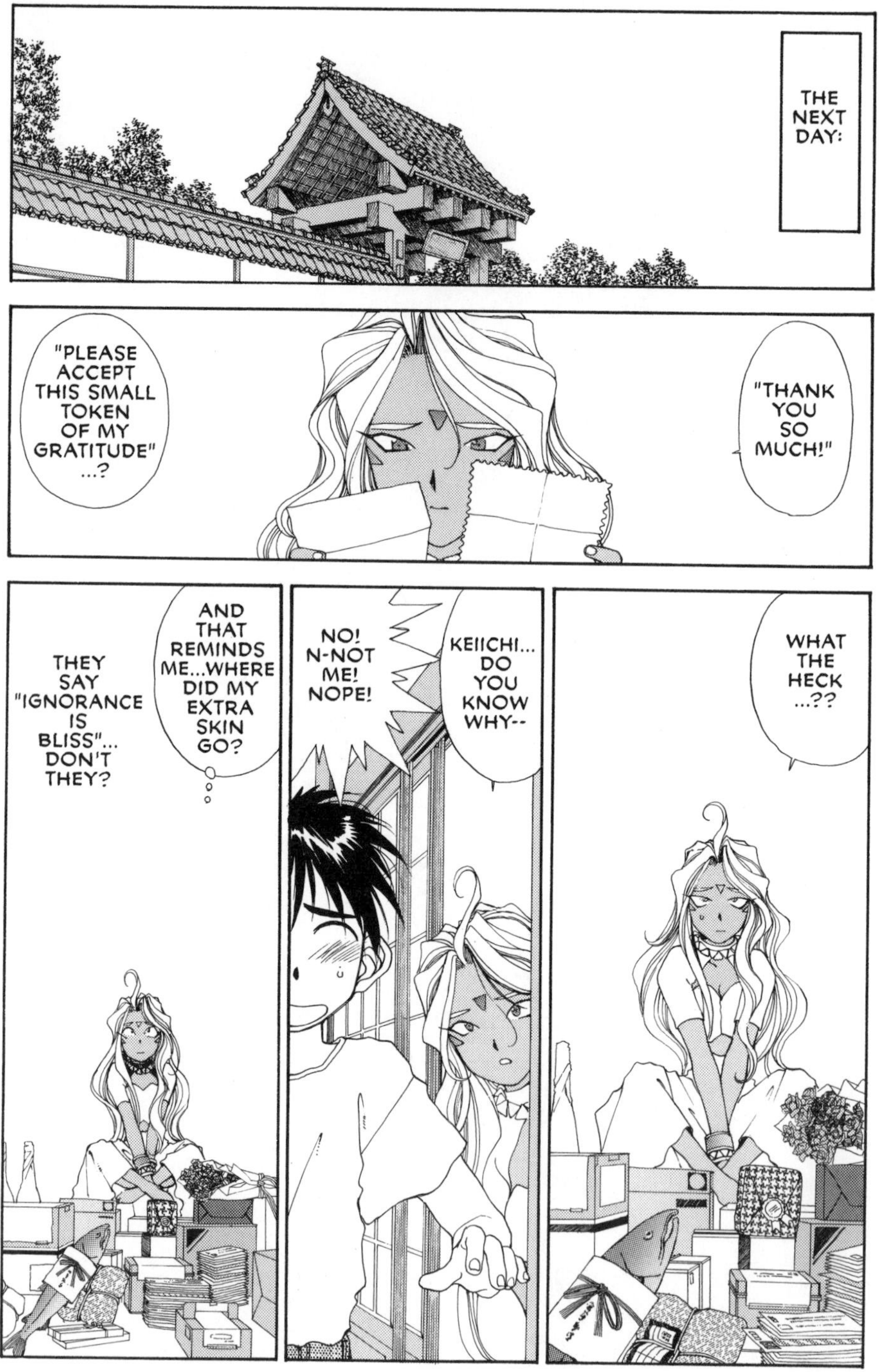
THE NEXT DAY:
"THANK YOU SO MUCH!"
"PLEASE ACCEPT THIS SMALL TOKEN OF MY GRATITUDE" ...?
WHAT THE HECK ...??
KEIICHI... DO YOU KNOW WHY--
NO! N-NOT ME! NOPE!
AND THAT REMINDS ME...WHERE DID MY EXTRA SKIN GO?
THEY SAY "IGNORANCE IS BLISS"... DON'T THEY?

MINI-GODDESSES THEATER OF LOVE!

UP-IN-YOUR-FACE PERIOD DRAMA!
◆ STARRING URD! THE UNFORGIVABLE! THE BORED! ◆

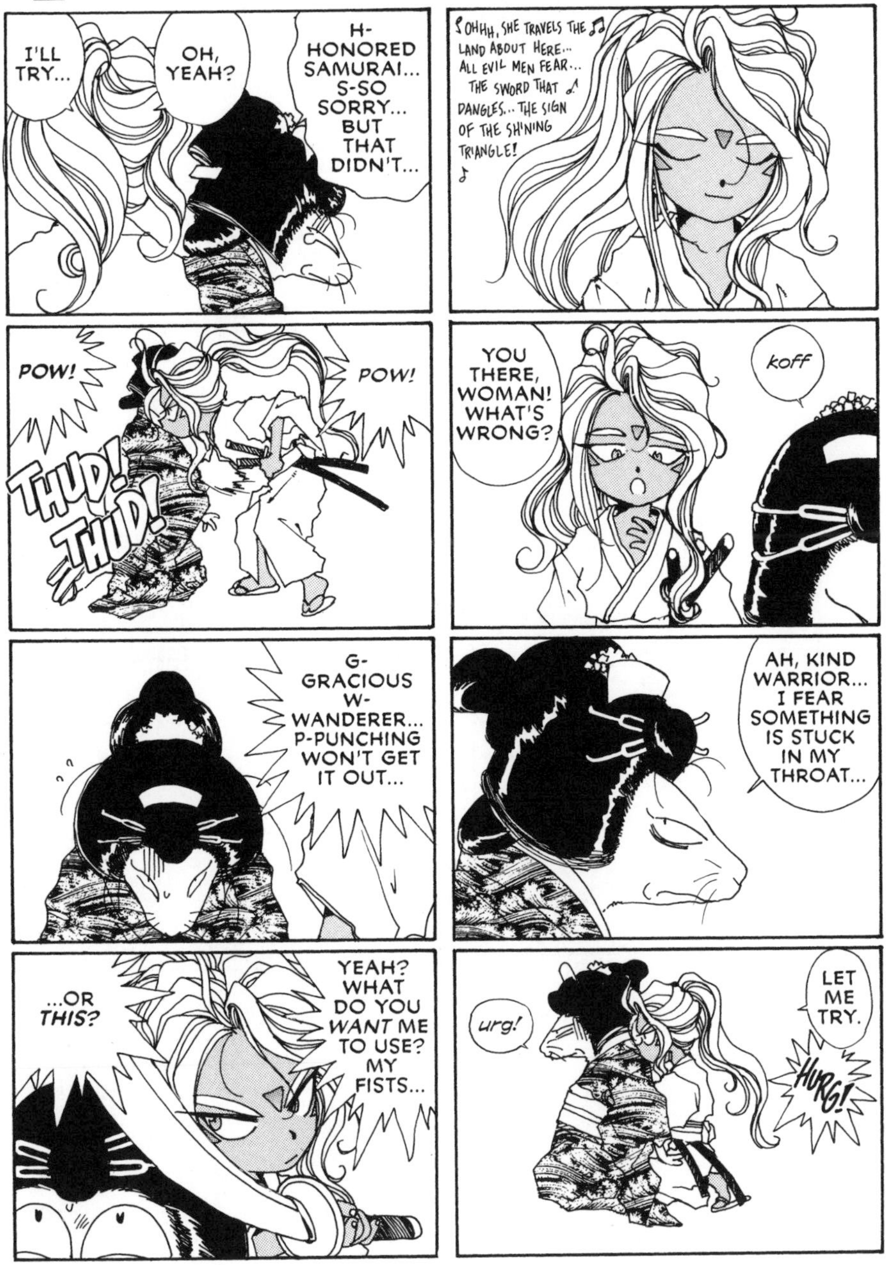

OHHH, SHE TRAVELS THE LAND ABOUT HERE... ALL EVIL MEN FEAR... THE SWORD THAT DANGLES... THE SIGN OF THE SHINING TRIANGLE!
YOU THERE, WOMAN! WHAT'S WRONG?
koff
AH, KIND WARRIOR... I FEAR SOMETHING IS STUCK IN MY THROAT...
LET ME TRY.
urg!
HURG!
H- HONORED SAMURAI... S-SO SORRY... BUT THAT DIDN'T...
OH, YEAH?
I'LL TRY...
POW!
POW!
THUD! THUD!
G- GRACIOUS W- WANDERER... P-PUNCHING WON'T GET IT OUT...
YEAH? WHAT DO YOU WANT ME TO USE? MY FISTS...
...OR THIS?

MINI-GODDESSES THEATER OF LOVE!

◆ WE'VE PUT THE BAND ON HOLD ◆

LITTLE GAN, ◆THE FAITHFUL RAT-AINER◆

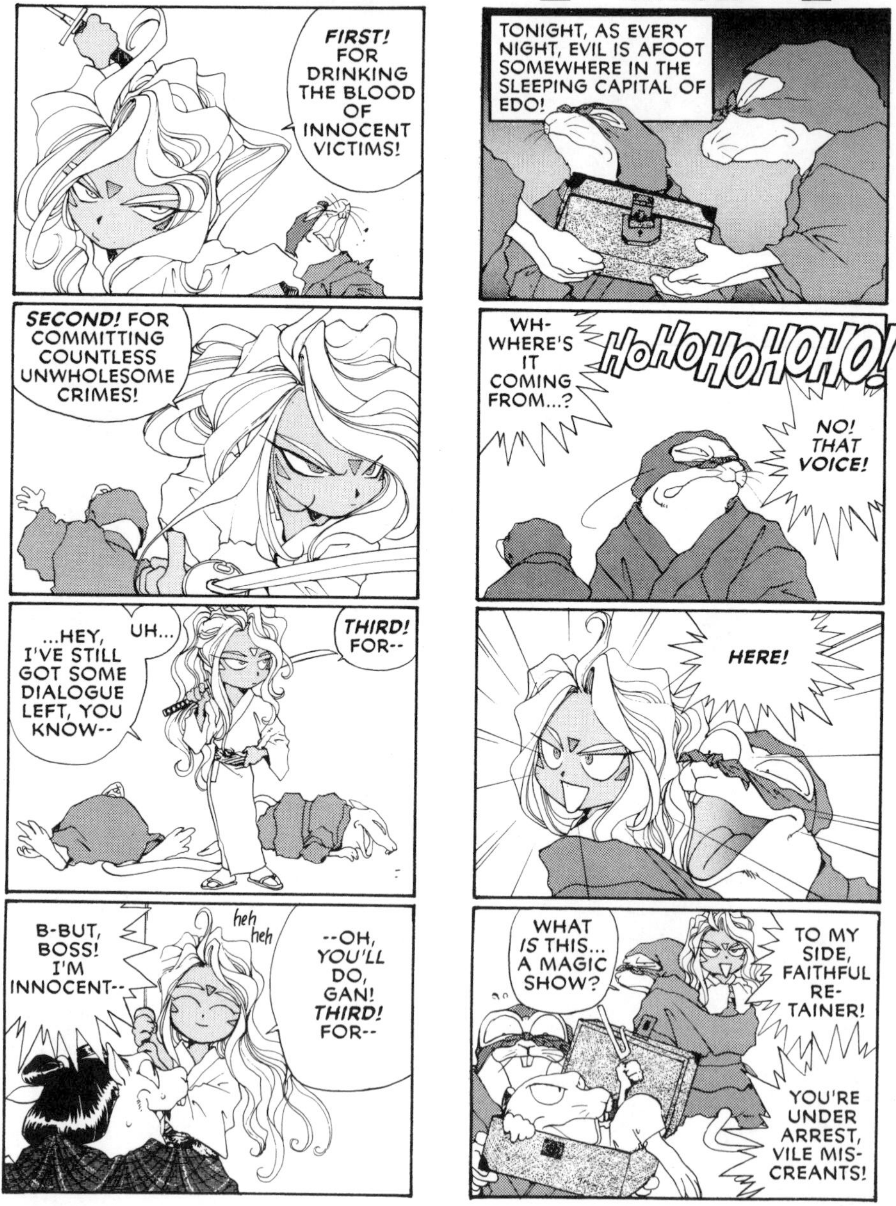
TONIGHT, AS EVERY NIGHT, EVIL IS AFOOT SOMEWHERE IN THE SLEEPING CAPITAL OF EDO!
HOHOHOHOHOHO!
WH- WHERE'S IT COMING FROM...?
NO! THAT VOICE!
HERE!
TO MY SIDE, FAITHFUL RE- TAINER!
WHAT IS THIS... A MAGIC SHOW?
YOU'RE UNDER ARREST, VILE MIS- CREANTS!
FIRST! FOR DRINKING THE BLOOD OF INNOCENT VICTIMS!
SECOND! FOR COMMITTING COUNTLESS UNWHOLESOME CRIMES!
THIRD! FOR--
UH...
...HEY, I'VE STILL GOT SOME DIALOGUE LEFT, YOU KNOW--
--OH, YOU'LL DO, GAN! THIRD! FOR--
heh heh
B-BUT, BOSS! I'M INNOCENT--

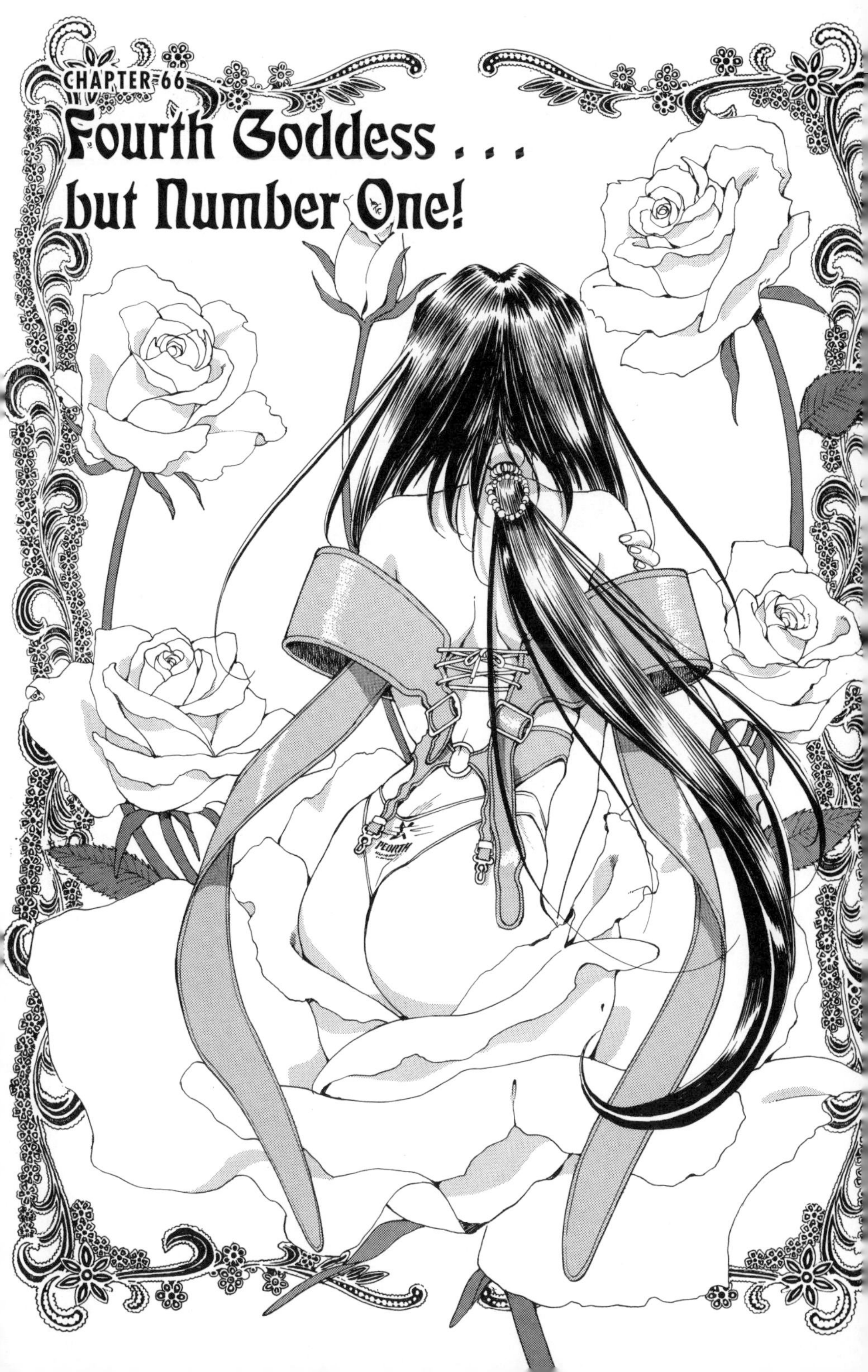
CHAPTER 66
Fourth Goddess . . .
but Number One!
PEORTH

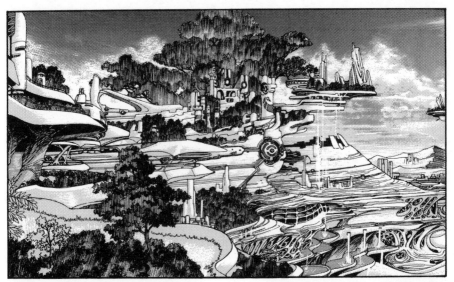

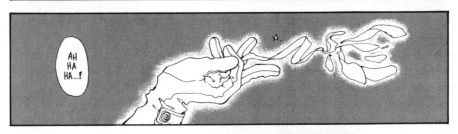

HEH...
AH HA HA...!
IT COMES... I CAN FEEL IT.
...A HEART CRYING OUT FOR *HELP*...

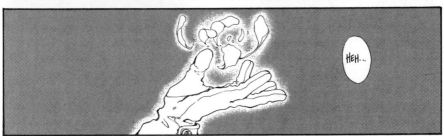

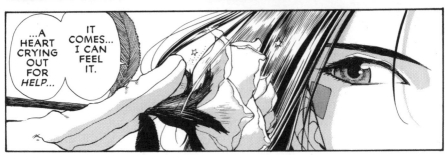

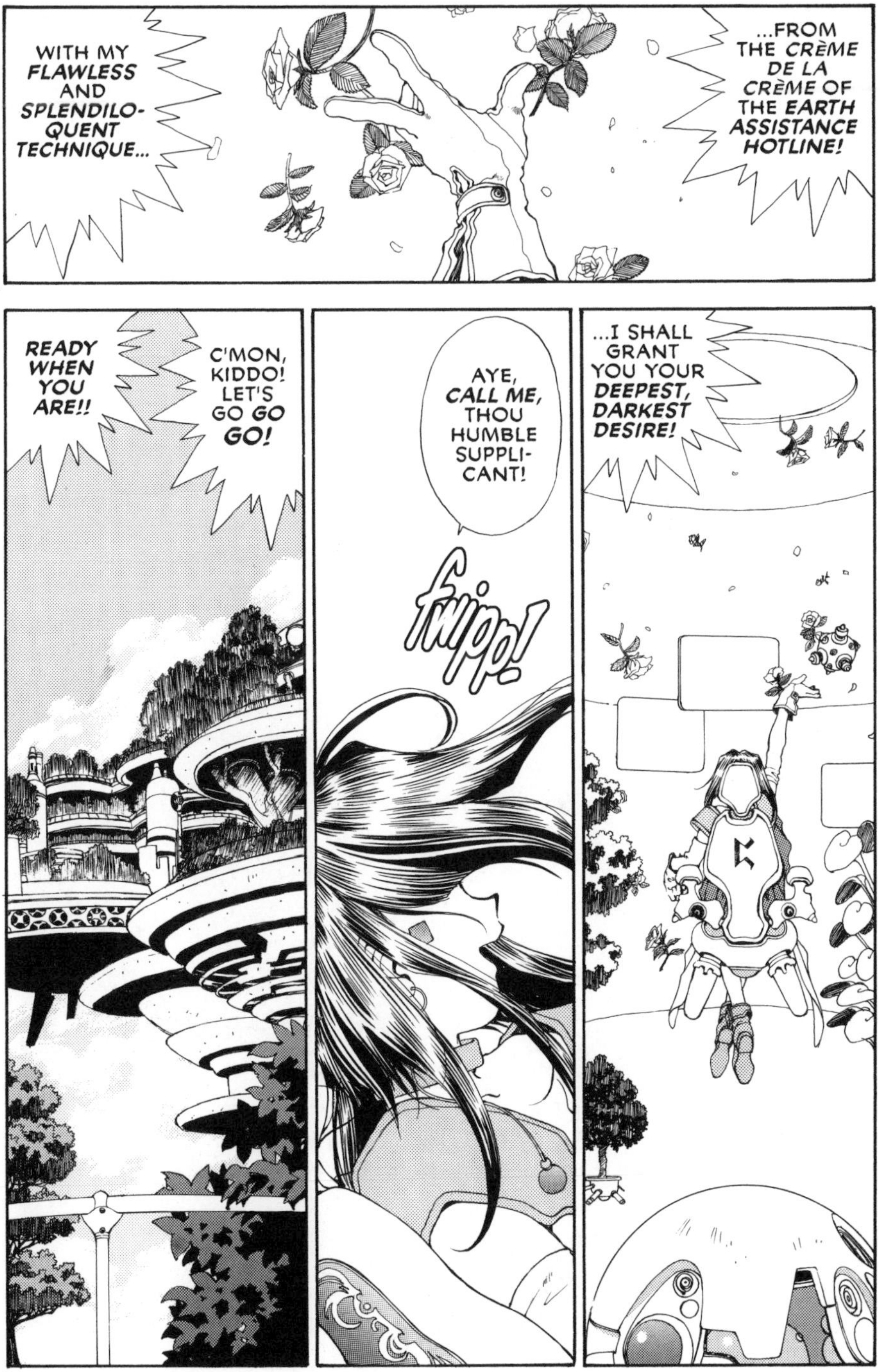
...FROM THE CRÈME DE LA CRÈME OF THE EARTH ASSISTANCE HOTLINE!
WITH MY FLAWLESS AND SPLENDILOQUENT TECHNIQUE...
...I SHALL GRANT YOU YOUR DEEPEST, DARKEST DESIRE!
AYE, CALL ME, THOU HUMBLE SUPPLICANT!
fwipp!
C'MON, KIDDO! LET'S GO GO GO!
READY WHEN YOU ARE!!

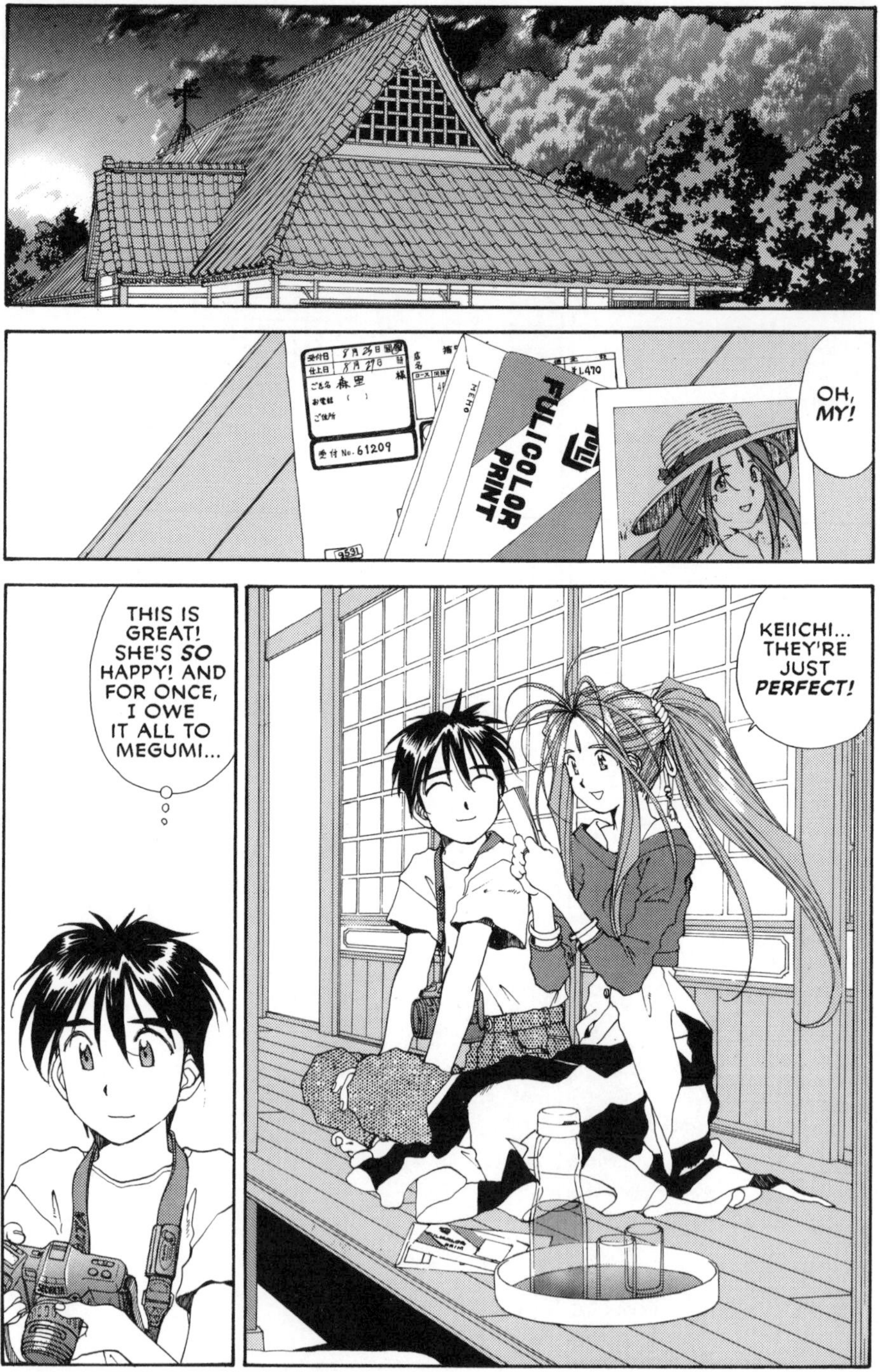
FUJICOLOR PRINT
OH, *MY!*
KEIICHI... THEY'RE JUST *PERFECT!*
THIS IS GREAT! SHE'S *SO* HAPPY! AND FOR ONCE, I OWE IT ALL TO MEGUMI...

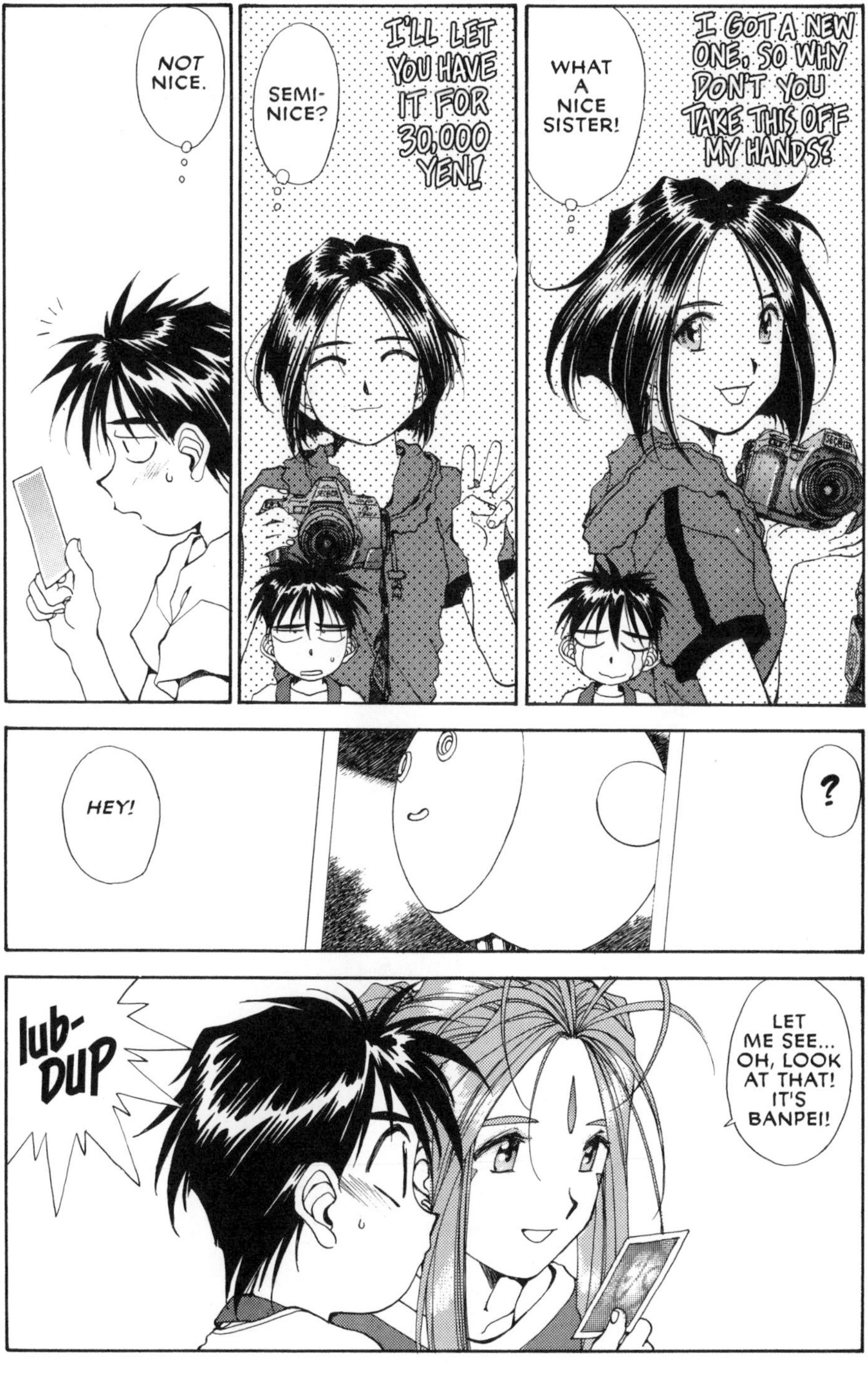
I GOT A NEW ONE, SO WHY DON'T YOU TAKE THIS OFF MY HANDS?
WHAT A NICE SISTER!
I'LL LET YOU HAVE IT FOR 30,000 YEN!
SEMI-NICE?
NOT NICE.
?
HEY!
LET ME SEE... OH, LOOK AT THAT! IT'S BANPEI!
lub-DUP

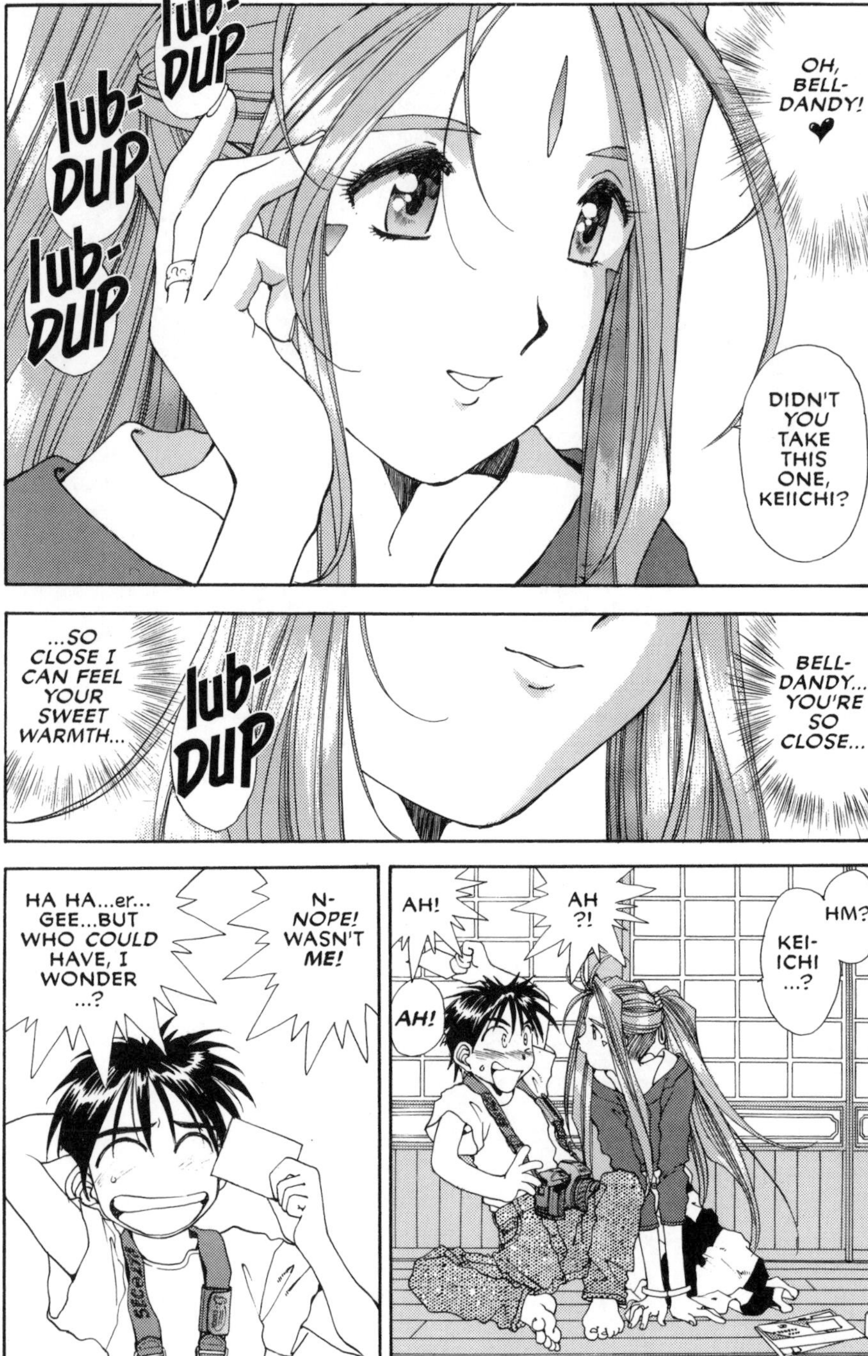
OH, BELL-DANDY! ❤
DIDN'T YOU TAKE THIS ONE, KEIICHI?
lub-DUP
lub-DUP
lub-DUP
BELL-DANDY... YOU'RE SO CLOSE...
lub-DUP
...SO CLOSE I CAN FEEL YOUR SWEET WARMTH...
HM? KEI-ICHI ...?
AH ?!
AH!
AH!
N-NOPE! WASN'T *ME!*
HA HA...er... GEE...BUT WHO *COULD* HAVE, I WONDER ...?

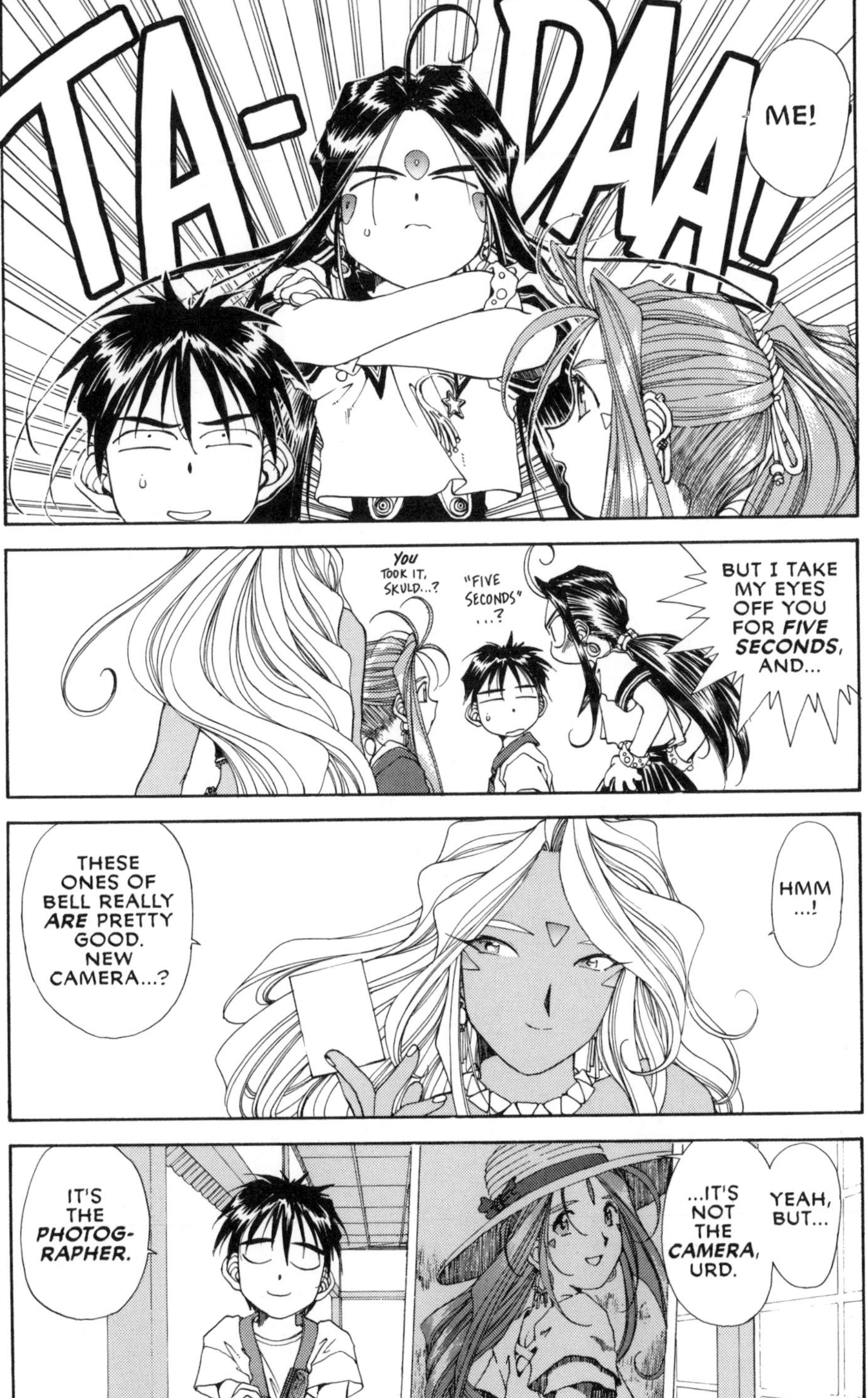
TA-DAA!
ME!
BUT I TAKE MY EYES OFF YOU FOR *FIVE SECONDS*, AND...
"FIVE SECONDS" ...?
YOU TOOK IT, SKULD...?
HMM ...!
THESE ONES OF BELL REALLY *ARE* PRETTY GOOD. NEW CAMERA...?
YEAH, BUT...
...IT'S NOT THE *CAMERA*, URD.
IT'S THE *PHOTOGRAPHER*.

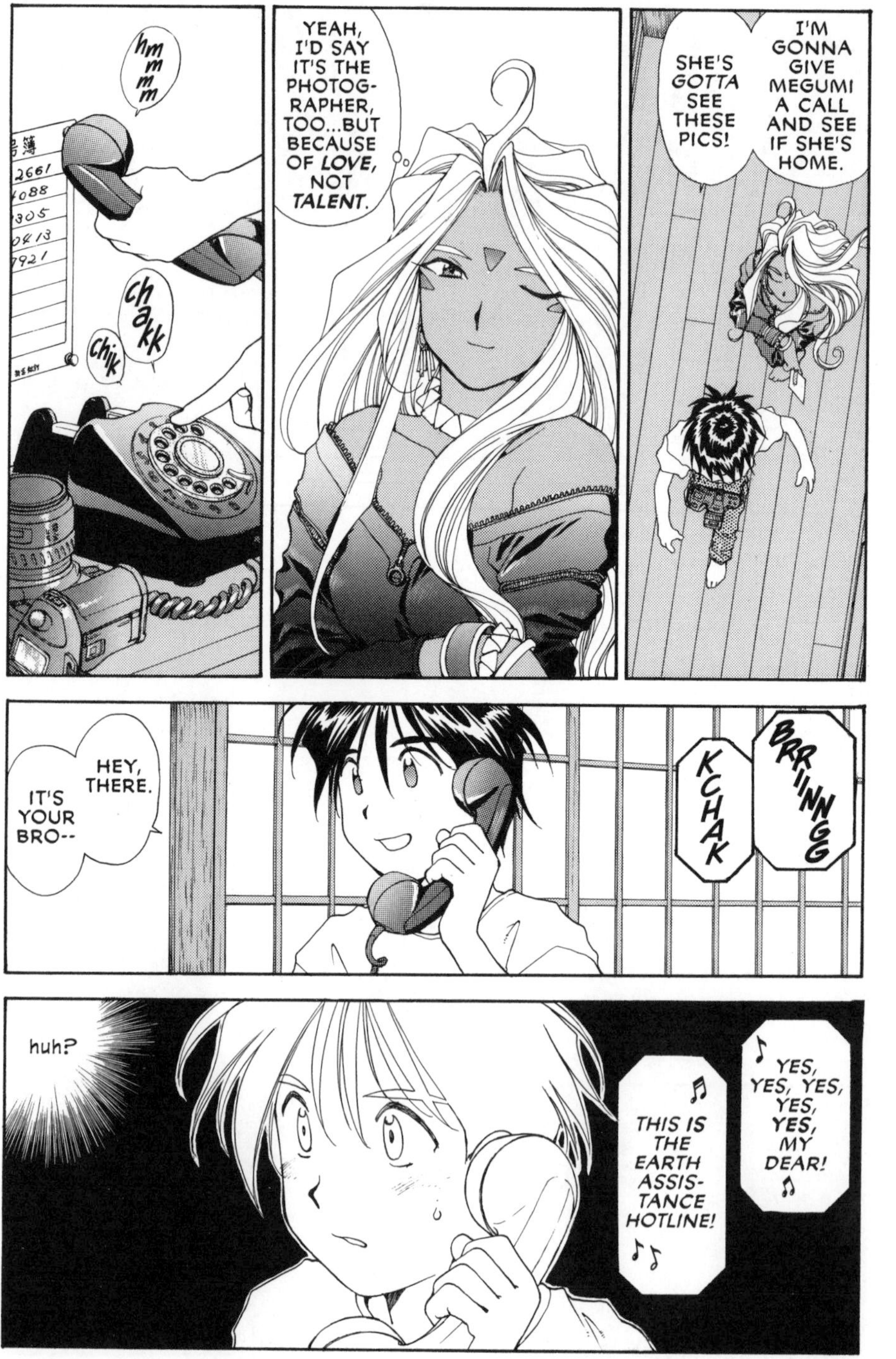
I'M GONNA GIVE MEGUMI A CALL AND SEE IF SHE'S HOME.
SHE'S *GOTTA* SEE THESE PICS!
YEAH, I'D SAY IT'S THE PHOTOG-RAPHER, TOO...BUT BECAUSE OF ***LOVE***, NOT ***TALENT***.
hmmmm
chakk
chik
BRRIINNGG
KCHAK
HEY, THERE.
IT'S YOUR BRO--
♪ YES, YES, YES, YES, **YES**, MY DEAR! ♪
♪ *THIS* ***IS*** *THE EARTH ASSIS-TANCE HOTLINE!* ♪♪
huh?

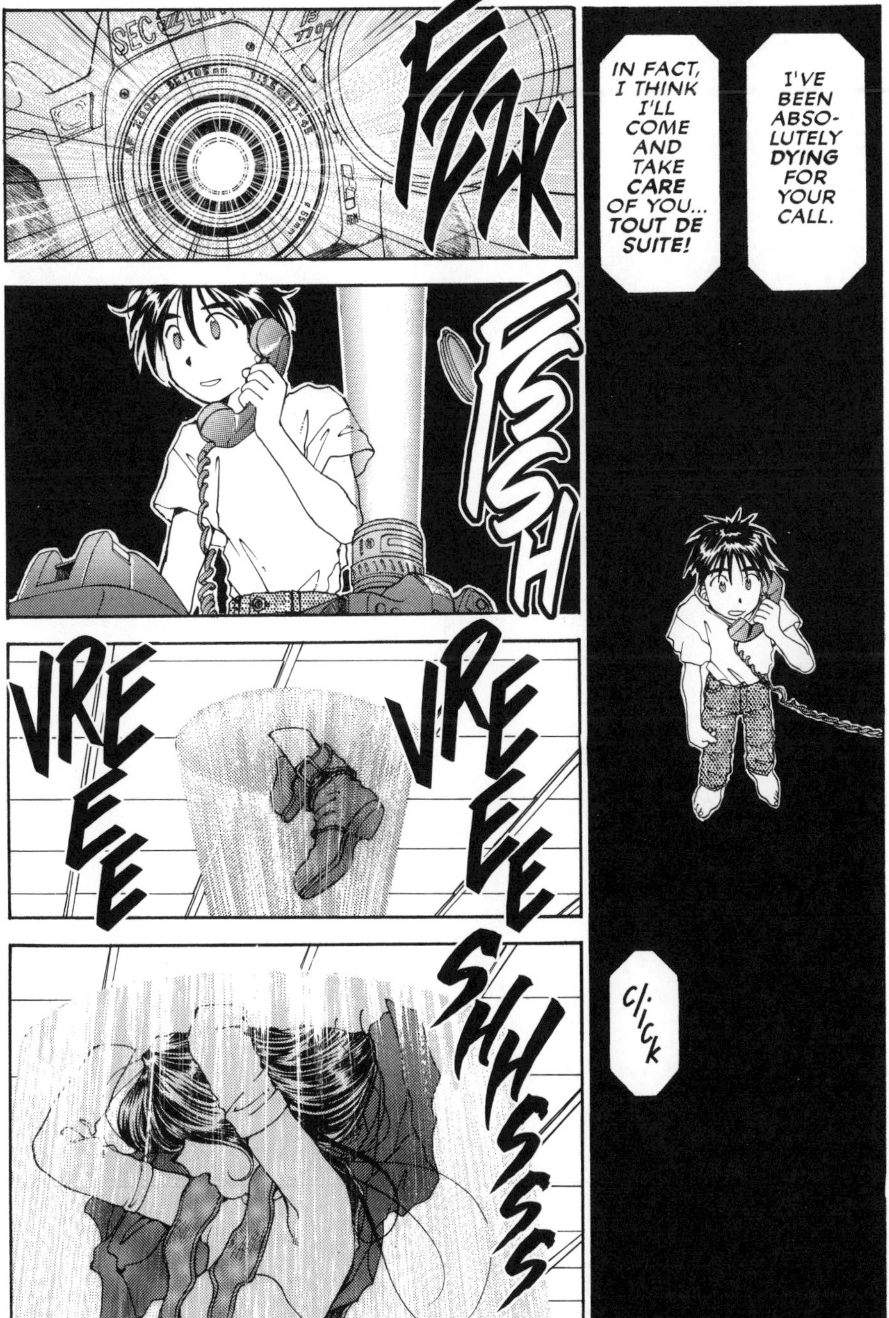
I'VE BEEN ABSOLUTELY DYING FOR YOUR CALL.
IN FACT, I THINK I'LL COME AND TAKE CARE OF YOU... TOUT DE SUITE!
CLICK
FZZK
FSSH
VREEE
VREEE
SHHSSSS

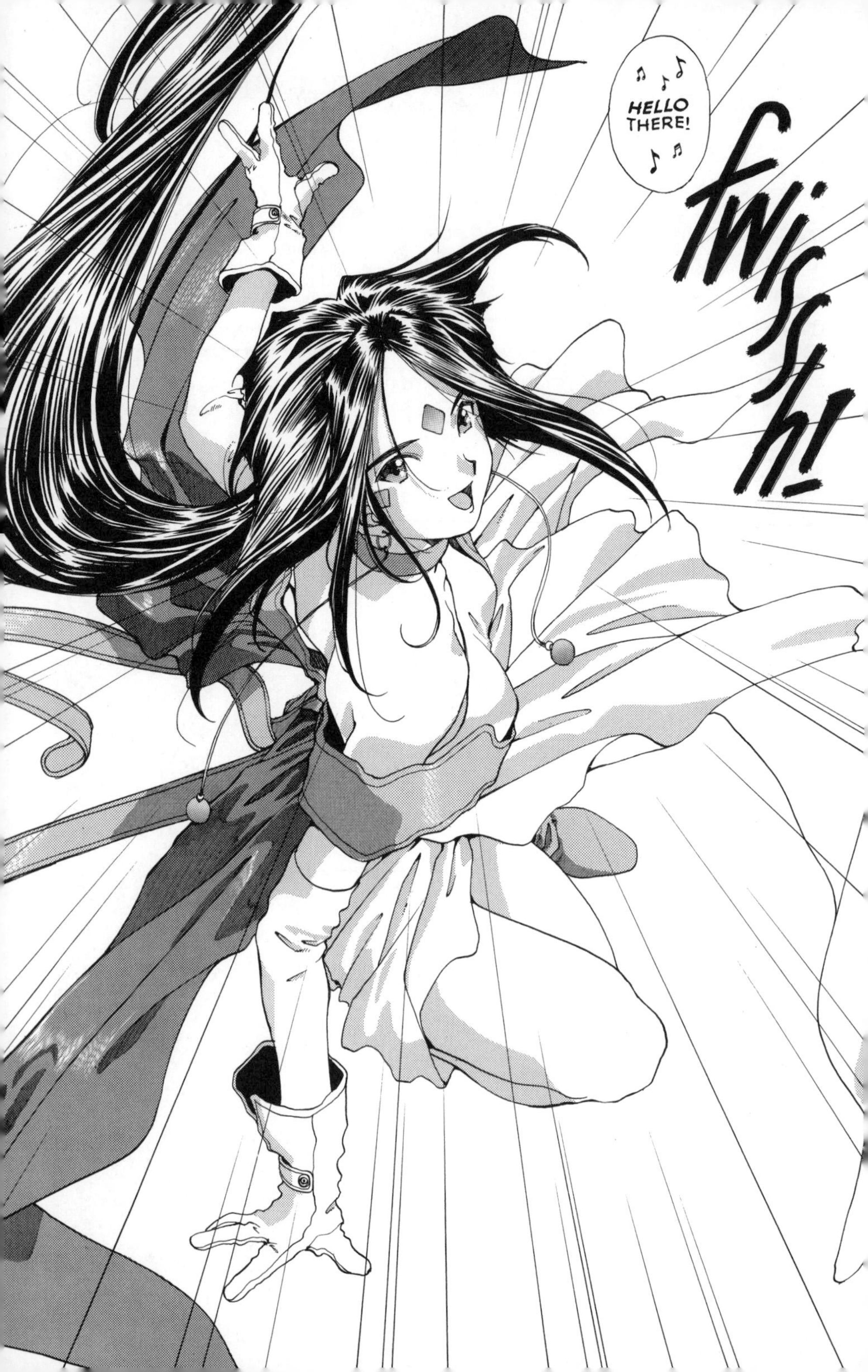
♫ ♪ ♪
HELLO THERE!
♪ ♫
fwissh!

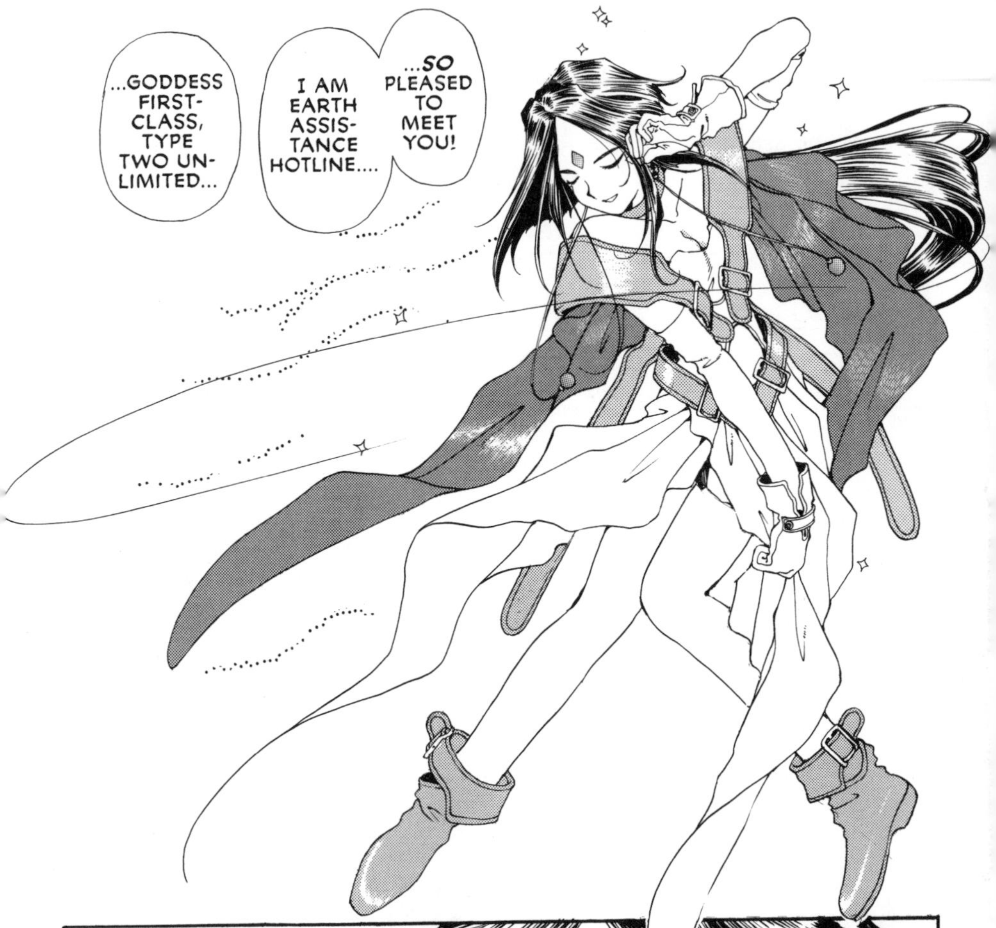
...SO PLEASED TO MEET YOU!
I AM EARTH ASSISTANCE HOTLINE....
...GODDESS FIRST-CLASS, TYPE TWO UNLIMITED...

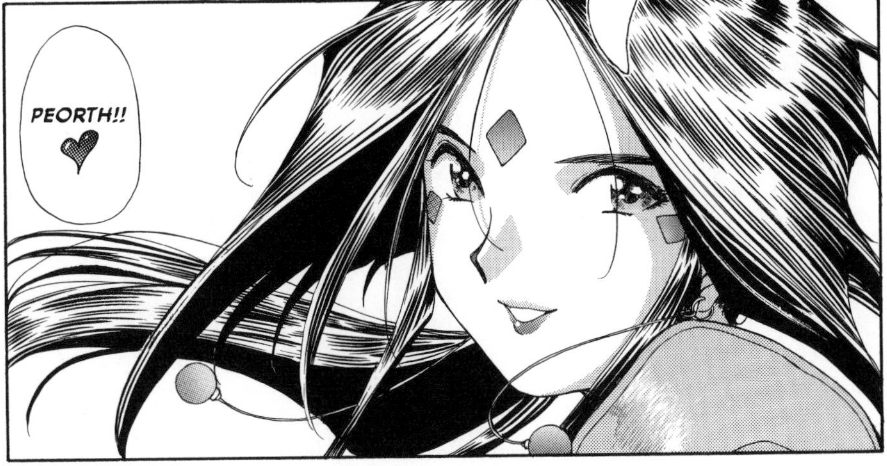
PEORTH!! ♥

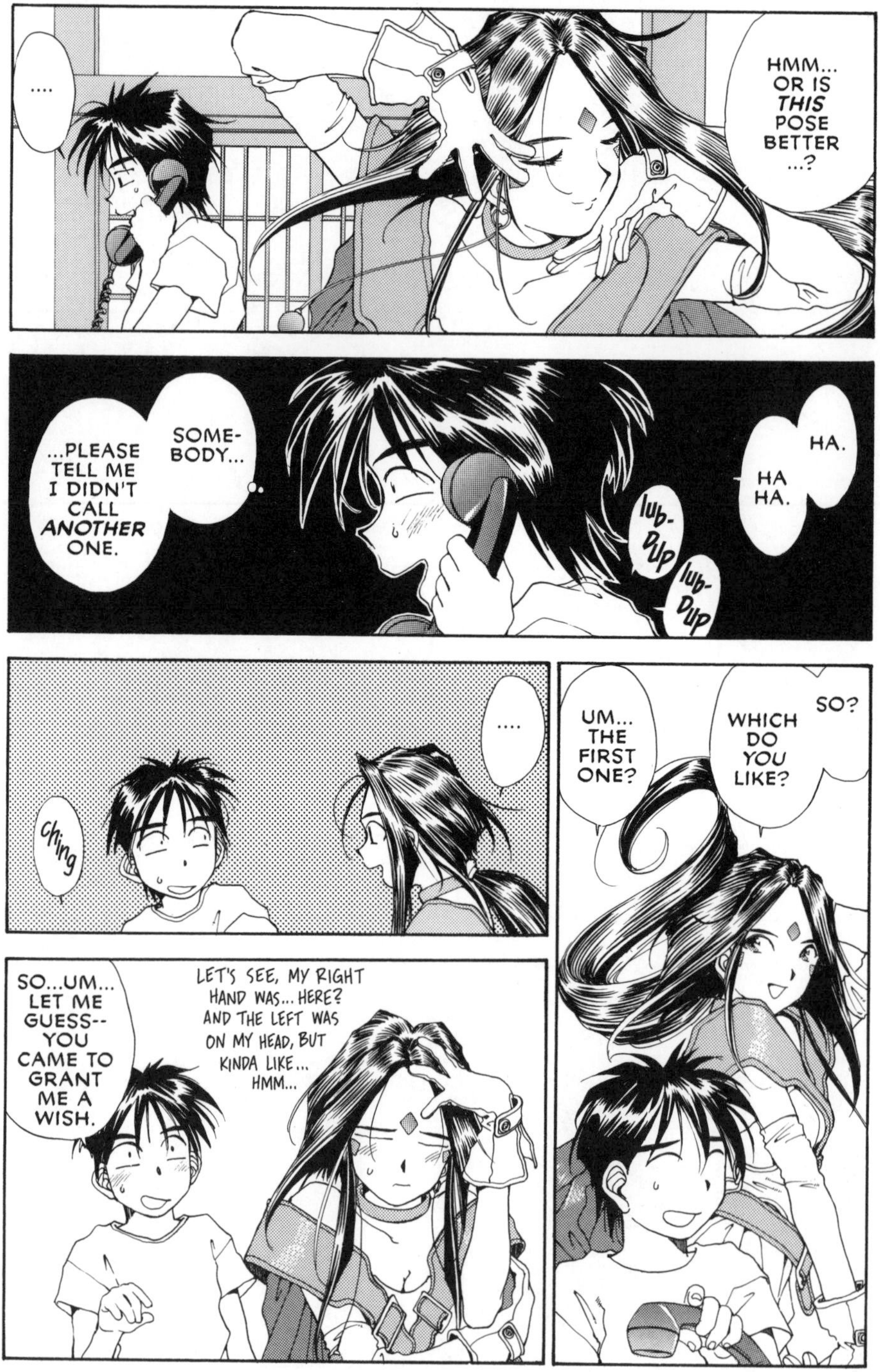
HMM... OR IS *THIS* POSE BETTER ...?
....
HA.
HA HA.
lub-DUP
lub-DUP
SOME-BODY...
...PLEASE TELL ME I DIDN'T CALL ***ANOTHER*** ONE.
SO?
WHICH DO *YOU* LIKE?
UM... THE FIRST ONE?
....
ching
LET'S SEE, MY RIGHT HAND WAS... HERE? AND THE LEFT WAS ON MY HEAD, BUT KINDA LIKE... HMM...
SO...UM... LET ME GUESS-- YOU CAME TO GRANT ME A WISH.

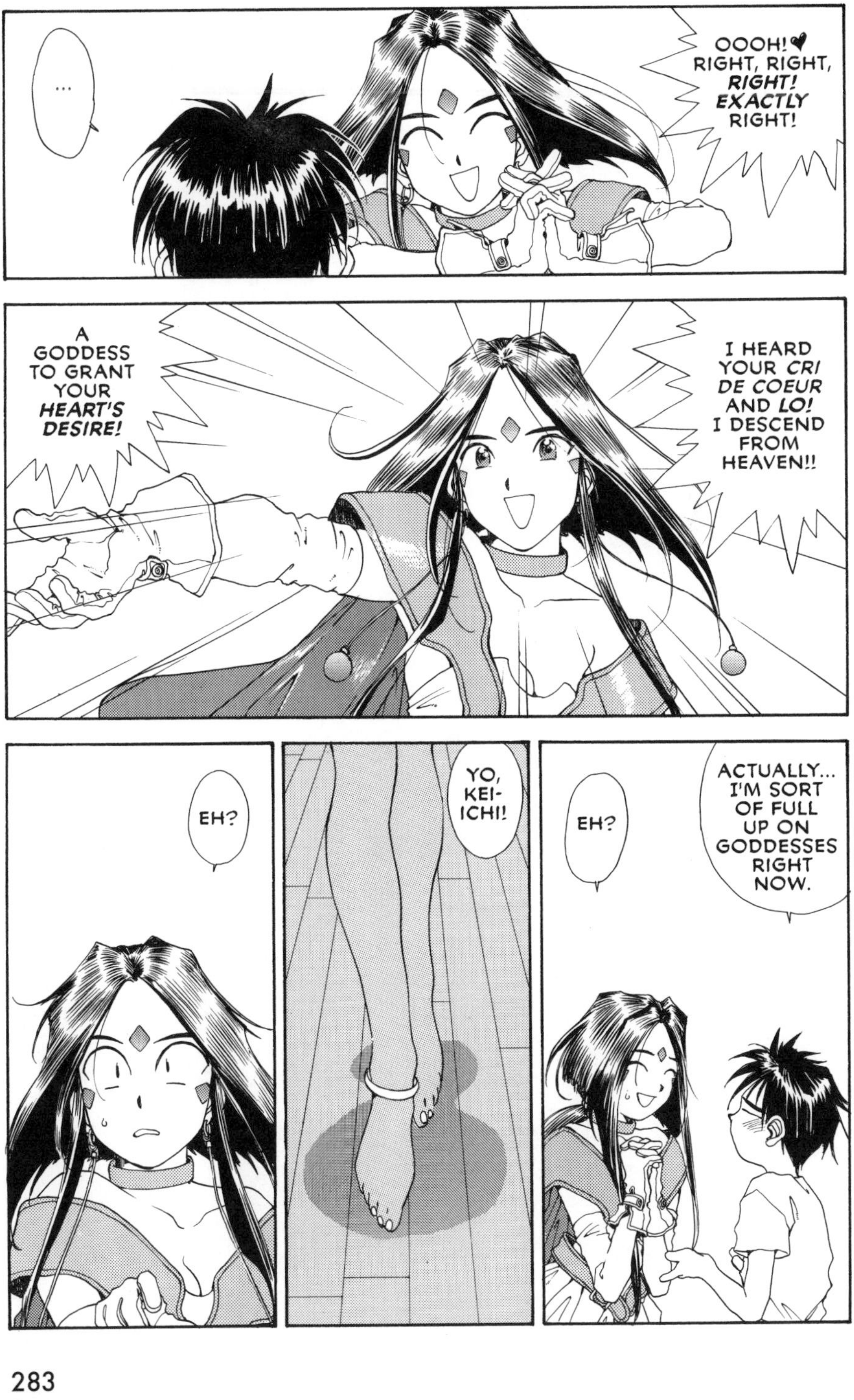
OOOH!♥ RIGHT, RIGHT, RIGHT! EXACTLY RIGHT!
...
I HEARD YOUR CRI DE COEUR AND LO! I DESCEND FROM HEAVEN!!
A GODDESS TO GRANT YOUR HEART'S DESIRE!
ACTUALLY... I'M SORT OF FULL UP ON GODDESSES RIGHT NOW.
EH?
YO, KEI-ICHI!
EH?

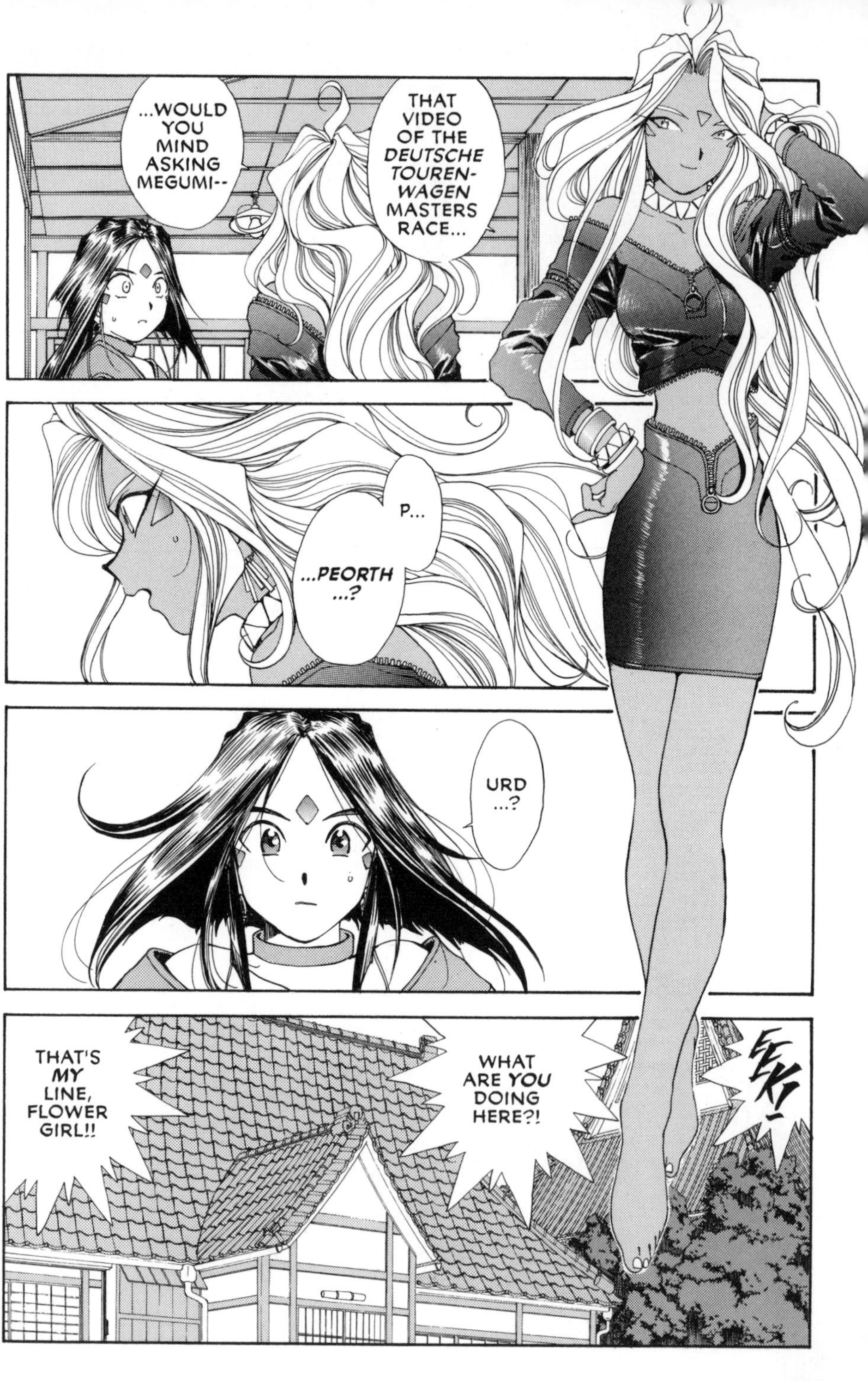
THAT VIDEO OF THE *DEUTSCHE TOURENWAGEN* MASTERS RACE...
...WOULD YOU MIND ASKING MEGUMI--
P...
...*PEORTH* ...?
URD ...?
EEK!
WHAT ARE *YOU* DOING HERE?!
THAT'S *MY* LINE, FLOWER GIRL!!

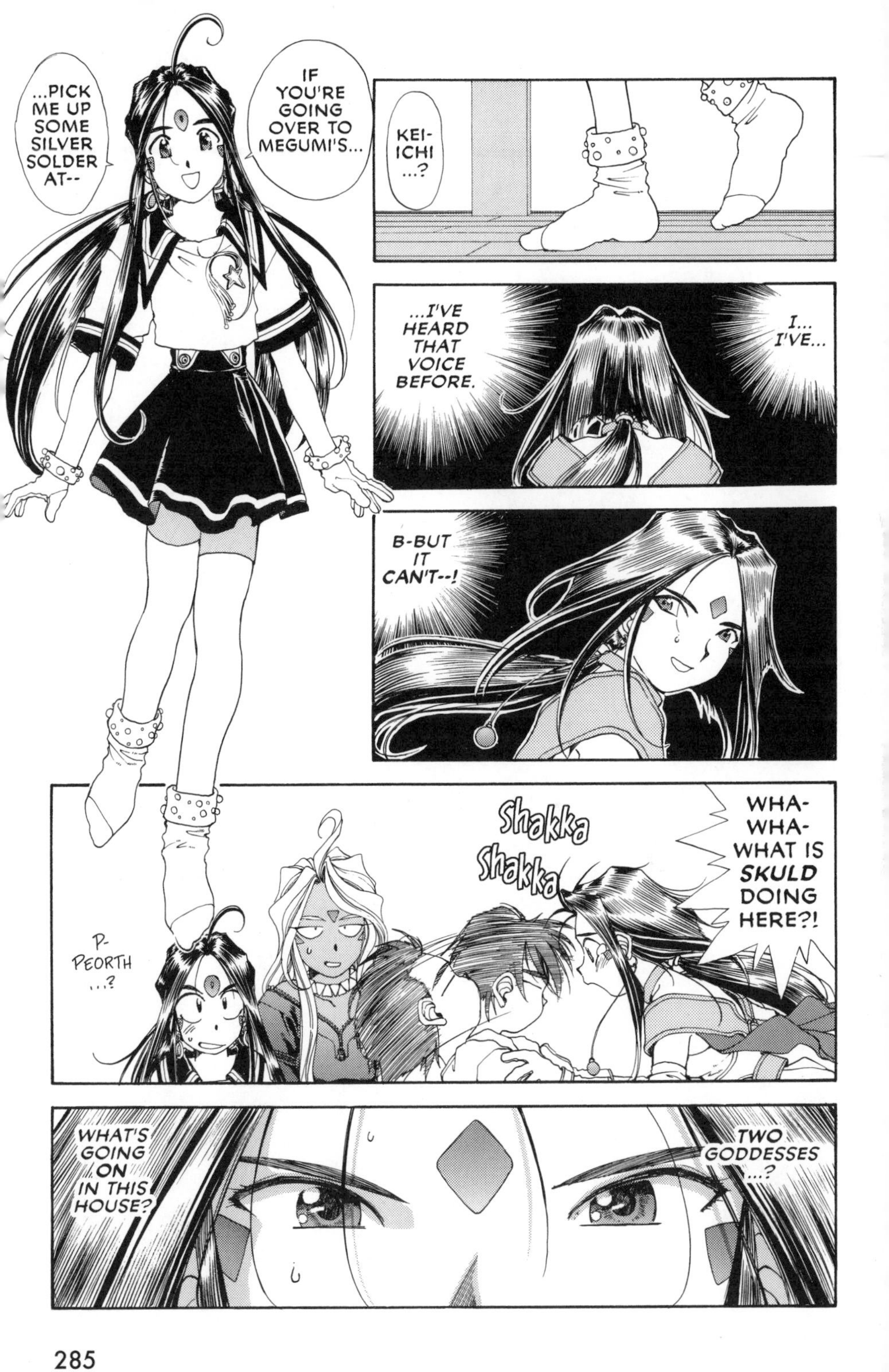
IF YOU'RE GOING OVER TO MEGUMI'S...
...PICK ME UP SOME SILVER SOLDER AT--
KEI-ICHI ...?
I... I'VE...
...I'VE HEARD THAT VOICE BEFORE.
B-BUT IT CAN'T--!
WHA-WHA-WHAT IS SKULD DOING HERE?!
Shakka Shakka
P-PEORTH ...?
TWO GODDESSES ...?
WHAT'S GOING ON IN THIS HOUSE?

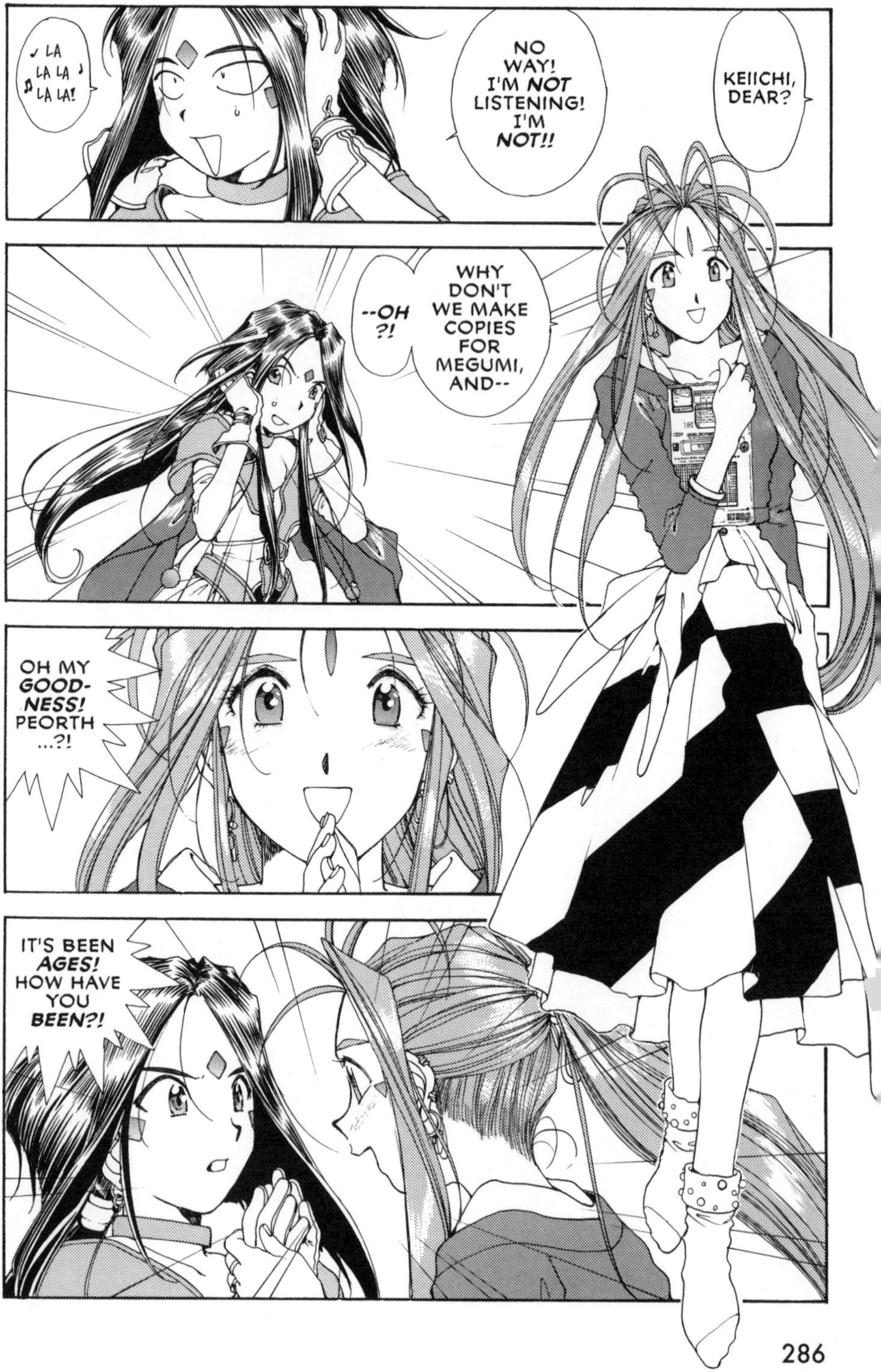
KEIICHI, DEAR?
NO WAY! I'M NOT LISTENING! I'M NOT!!
LA LA LA LA LA LA!
WHY DON'T WE MAKE COPIES FOR MEGUMI, AND--
--OH ?!
OH MY GOODNESS! PEORTH ...?!
IT'S BEEN AGES! HOW HAVE YOU BEEN?!

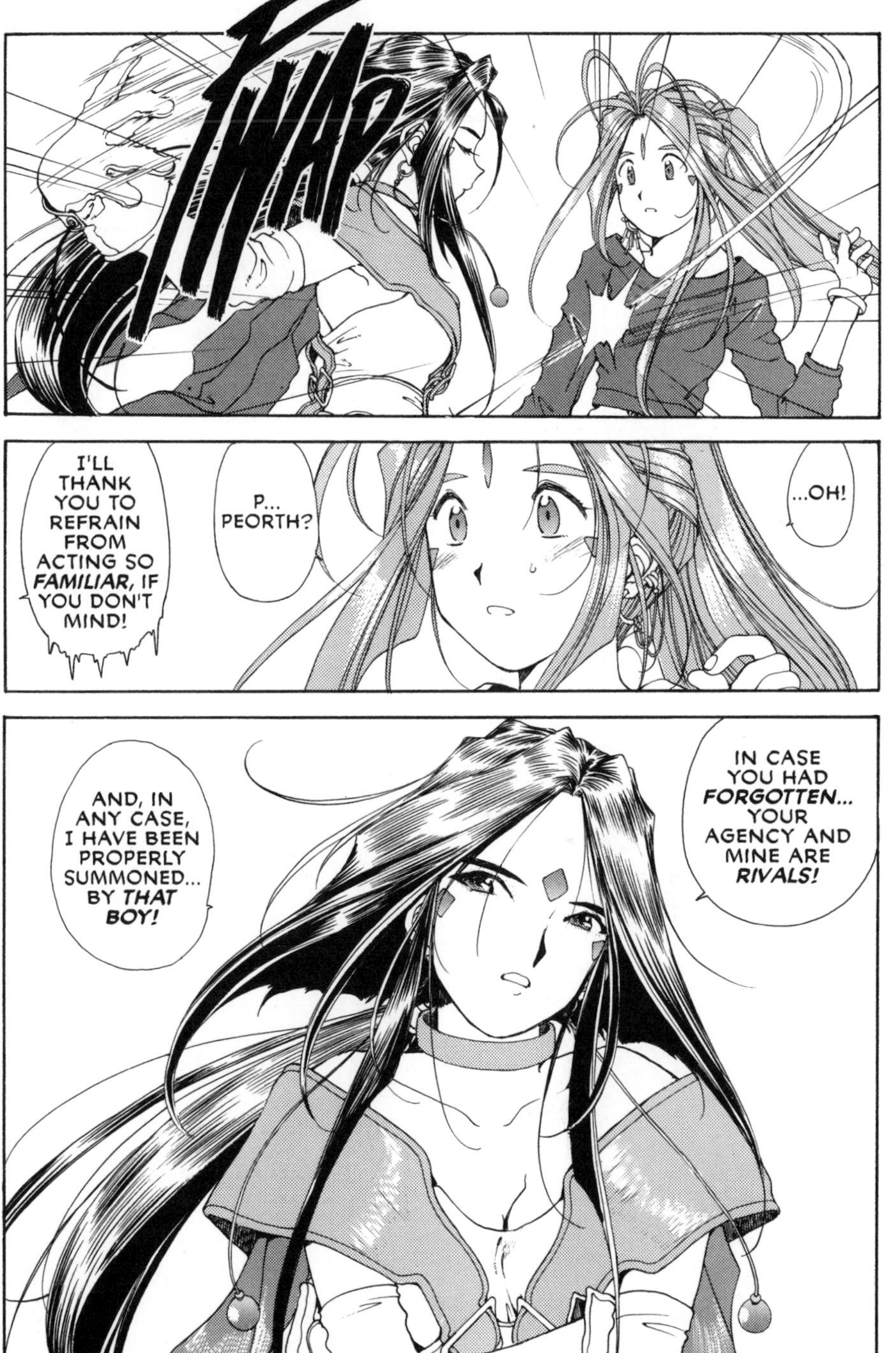
THWAP
...OH!
P... PEORTH?
I'LL THANK YOU TO REFRAIN FROM ACTING SO *FAMILIAR*, IF YOU DON'T MIND!
IN CASE YOU HAD *FORGOTTEN...* YOUR AGENCY AND MINE ARE *RIVALS!*
AND, IN ANY CASE, I HAVE BEEN PROPERLY SUMMONED... BY *THAT BOY!*

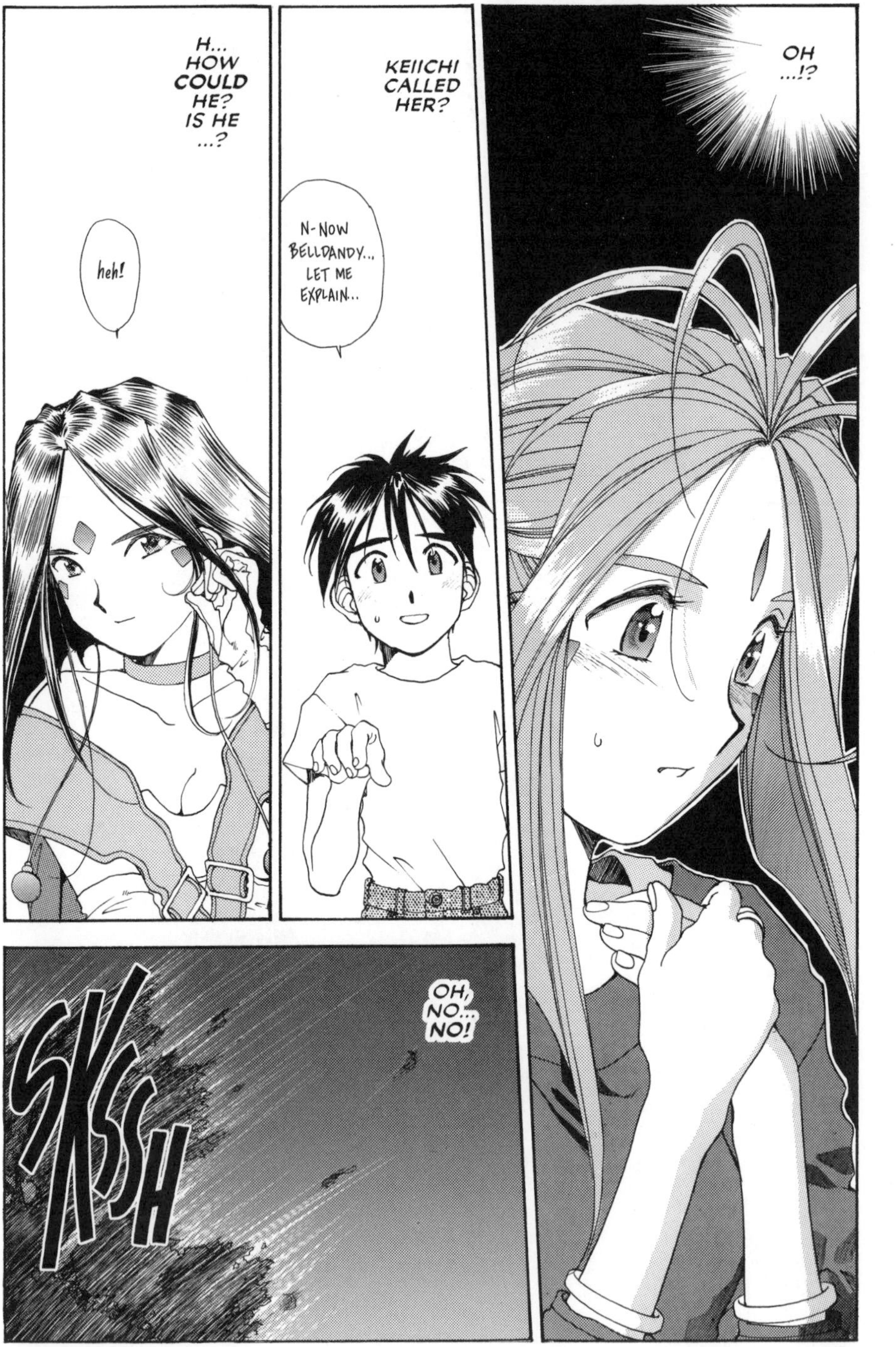
OH ...!?
KEIICHI CALLED HER?
N-NOW BELLDANDY... LET ME EXPLAIN...
H... HOW COULD HE? IS HE ...?
heh!
OH, NO... NO!
SKSSH

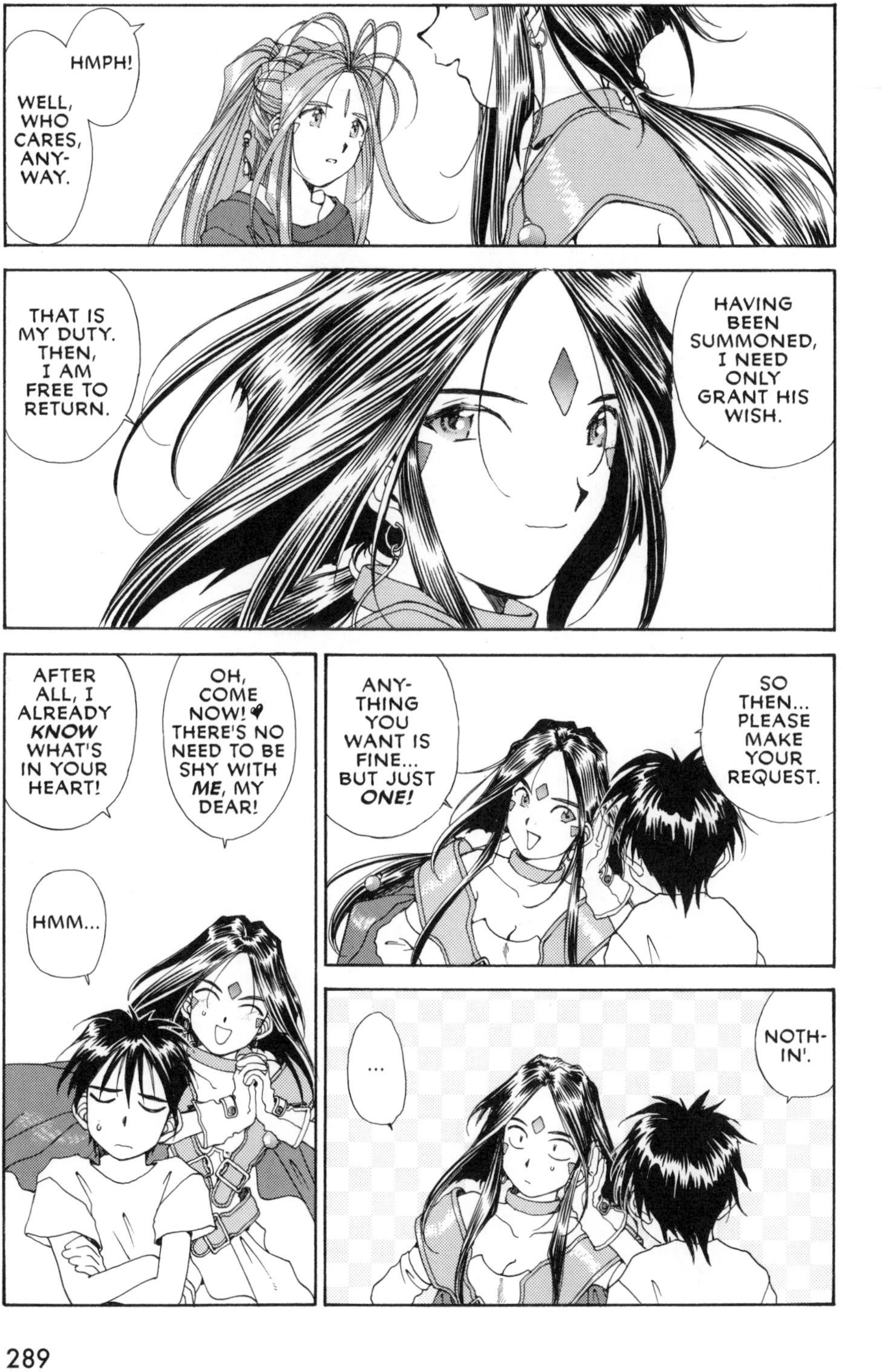
HMPH! WELL, WHO CARES, ANYWAY.
HAVING BEEN SUMMONED, I NEED ONLY GRANT HIS WISH.
THAT IS MY DUTY. THEN, I AM FREE TO RETURN.
SO THEN... PLEASE MAKE YOUR REQUEST.
ANYTHING YOU WANT IS FINE... BUT JUST ONE!
NOTHIN'.
...
OH, COME NOW! ♥ THERE'S NO NEED TO BE SHY WITH ME, MY DEAR!
AFTER ALL, I ALREADY KNOW WHAT'S IN YOUR HEART!
HMM...

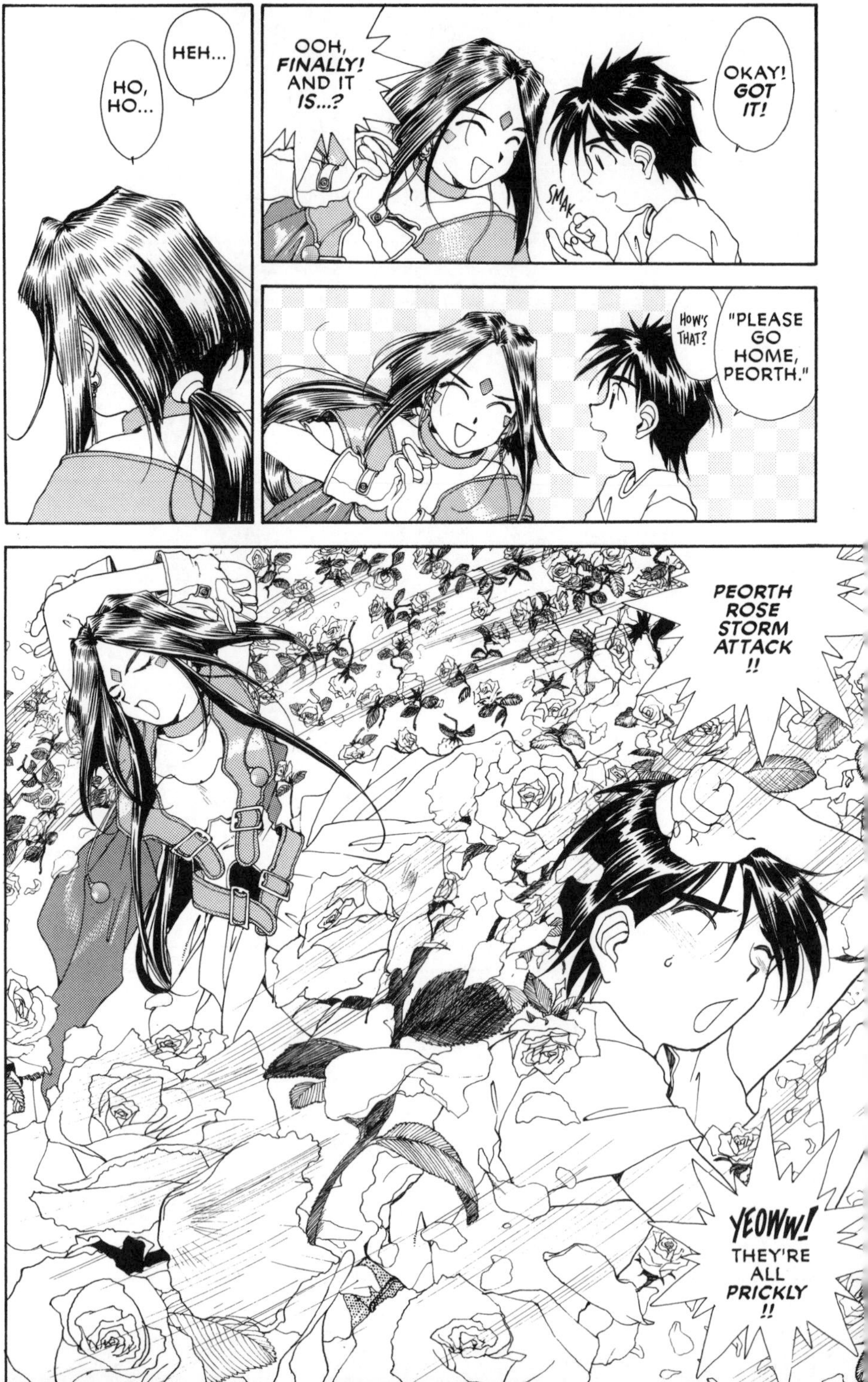
OKAY! GOT IT!
SMAK
OOH, FINALLY! AND IT IS...?
"PLEASE GO HOME, PEORTH."
HOW'S THAT?
HEH...
HO, HO...
PEORTH ROSE STORM ATTACK !!
YEOWW! THEY'RE ALL PRICKLY !!

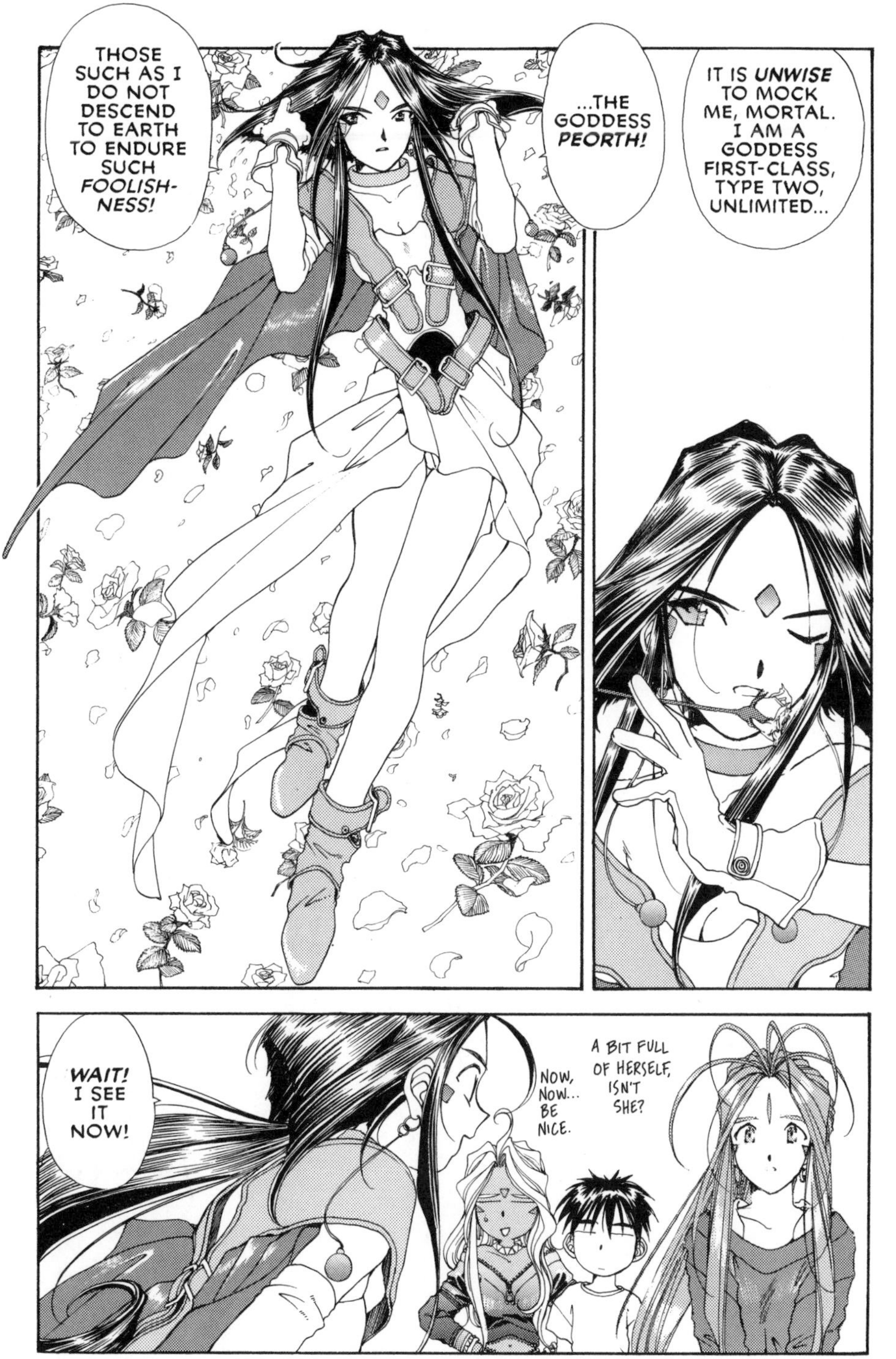
IT IS UNWISE TO MOCK ME, MORTAL. I AM A GODDESS FIRST-CLASS, TYPE TWO, UNLIMITED...
...THE GODDESS PEORTH!
THOSE SUCH AS I DO NOT DESCEND TO EARTH TO ENDURE SUCH FOOLISHNESS!
A BIT FULL OF HERSELF, ISN'T SHE?
NOW, NOW... BE NICE.
WAIT! I SEE IT NOW!

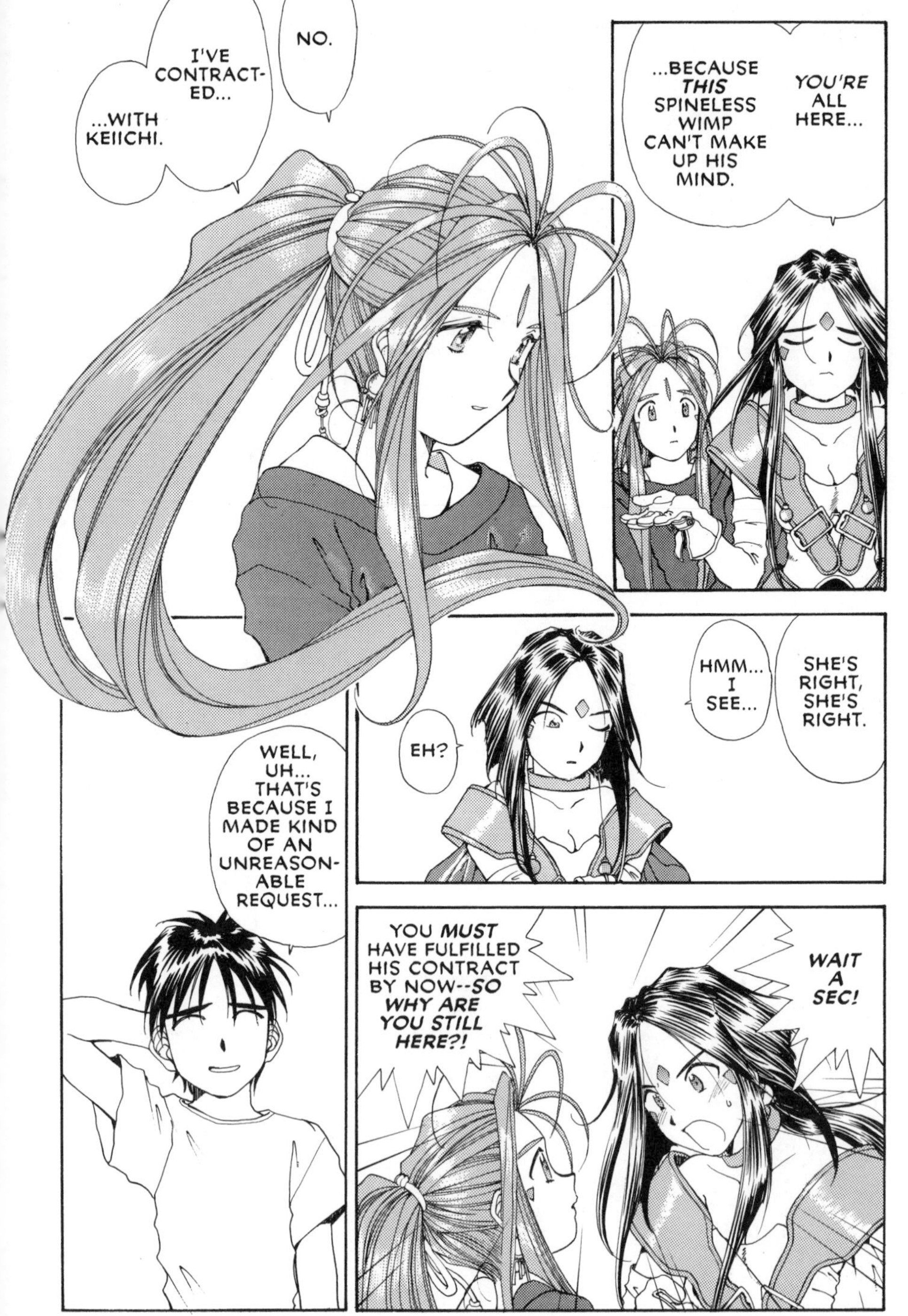
YOU'RE ALL HERE...
...BECAUSE THIS SPINELESS WIMP CAN'T MAKE UP HIS MIND.
NO.
I'VE CONTRACT-ED...
...WITH KEIICHI.
SHE'S RIGHT, SHE'S RIGHT.
HMM... I SEE...
EH?
WAIT A SEC!
YOU MUST HAVE FULFILLED HIS CONTRACT BY NOW--SO WHY ARE YOU STILL HERE?!
WELL, UH... THAT'S BECAUSE I MADE KIND OF AN UNREASON-ABLE REQUEST...

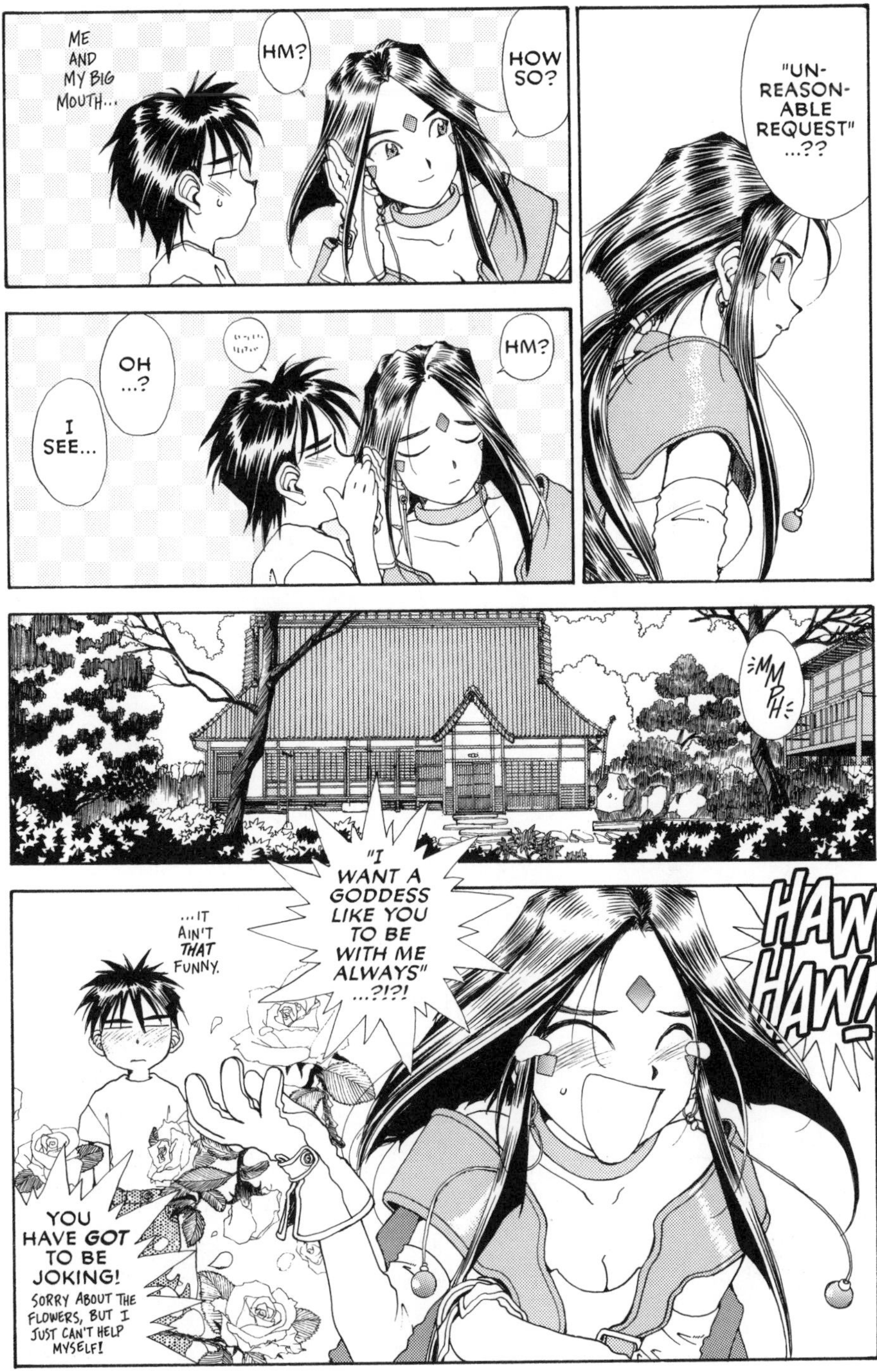
"UN-REASONABLE REQUEST" ...??
HOW SO?
HM?
ME AND MY BIG MOUTH...
HM?
OH ...?
I SEE...
MMPH
HAW HAW!
"I WANT A GODDESS LIKE YOU TO BE WITH ME ALWAYS" ...?!?!
...IT AIN'T THAT FUNNY.
YOU HAVE GOT TO BE JOKING!
SORRY ABOUT THE FLOWERS, BUT I JUST CAN'T HELP MYSELF!

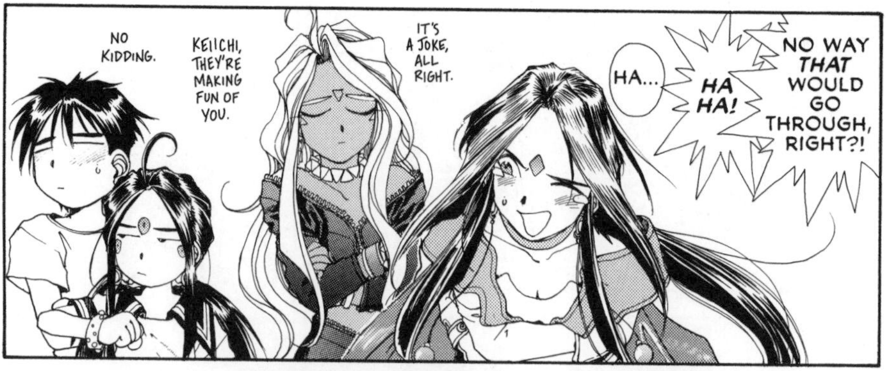
HA...
HA HA!
NO WAY *THAT* WOULD GO THROUGH, RIGHT?!
IT'S A JOKE, ALL RIGHT.
KEIICHI, THEY'RE MAKING FUN OF YOU.
NO KIDDING.

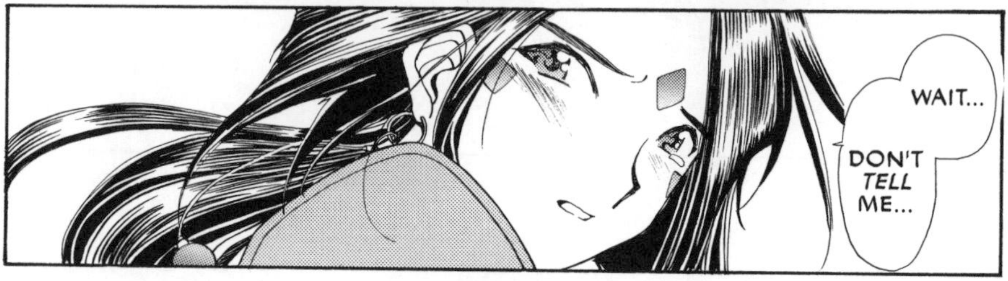
WAIT...
DON'T *TELL* ME...

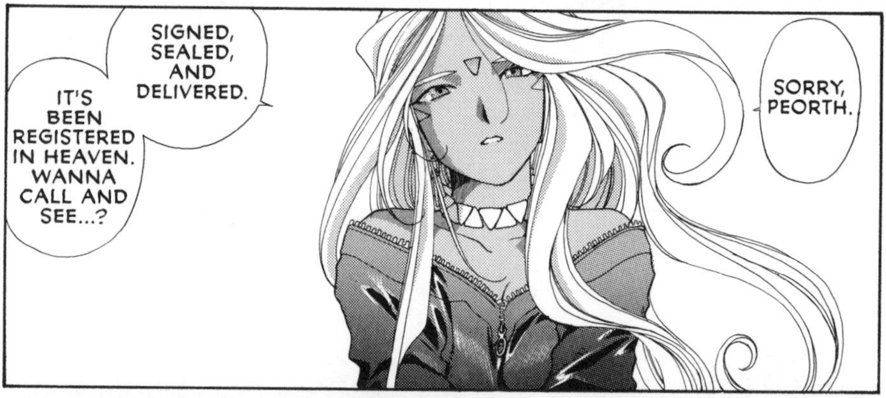
SORRY, PEORTH.
SIGNED, SEALED, AND DELIVERED.
IT'S BEEN REGISTERED IN HEAVEN. WANNA CALL AND SEE...?

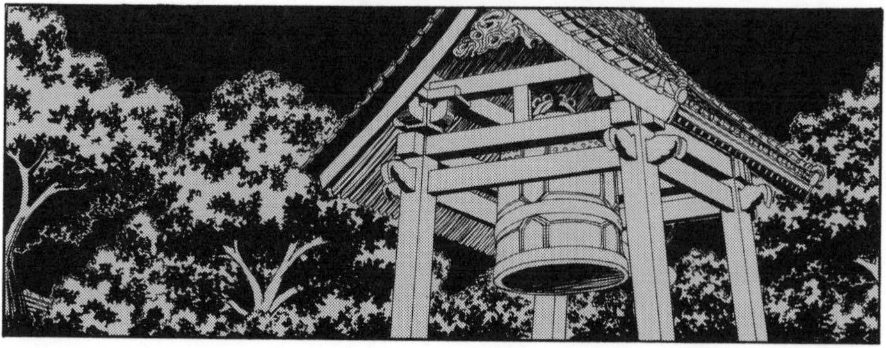

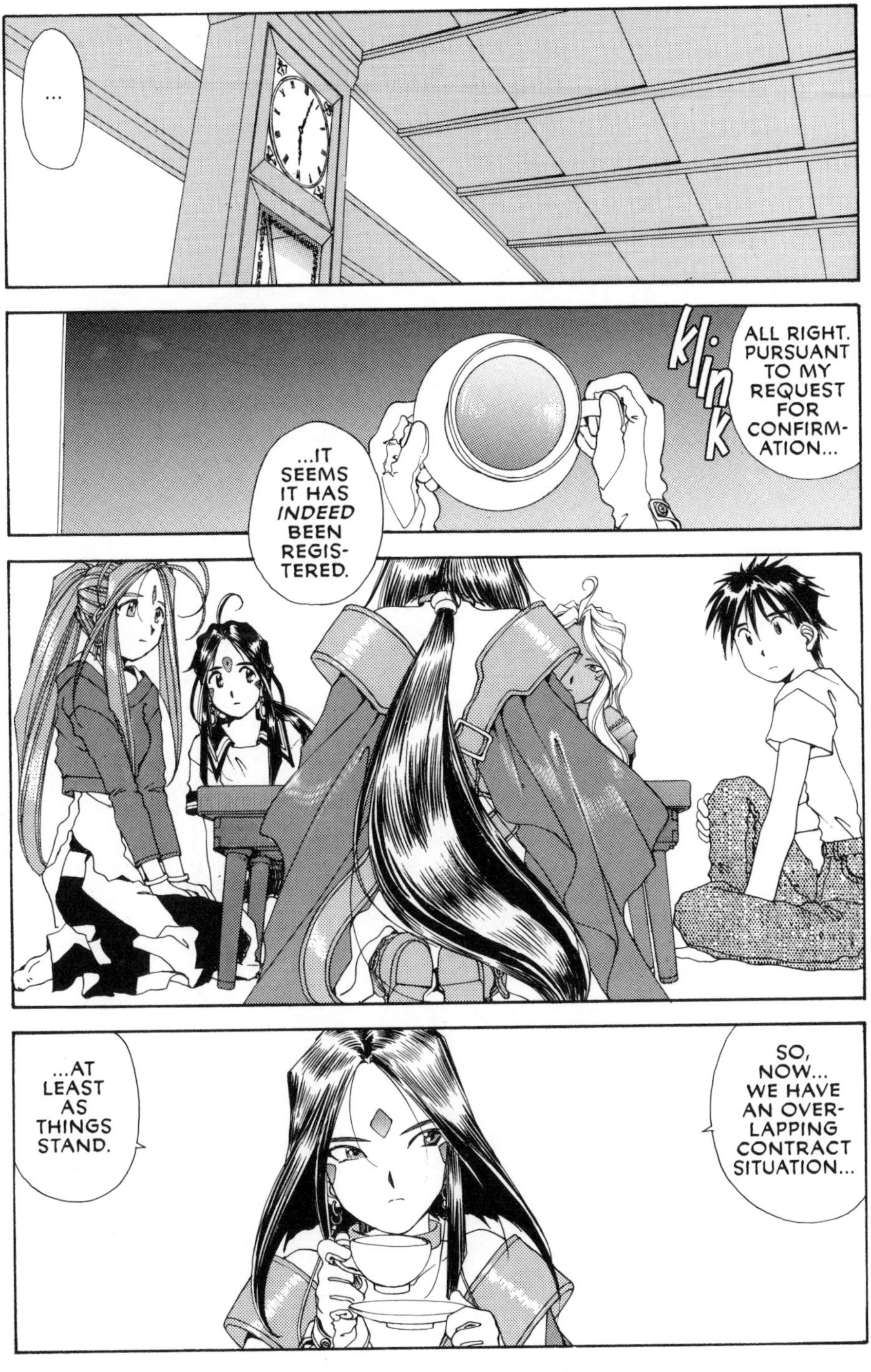
...
ALL RIGHT. PURSUANT TO MY REQUEST FOR CONFIRMATION...
klink
...IT SEEMS IT HAS *INDEED* BEEN REGISTERED.
SO, NOW... WE HAVE AN OVERLAPPING CONTRACT SITUATION...
...AT LEAST AS THINGS STAND.

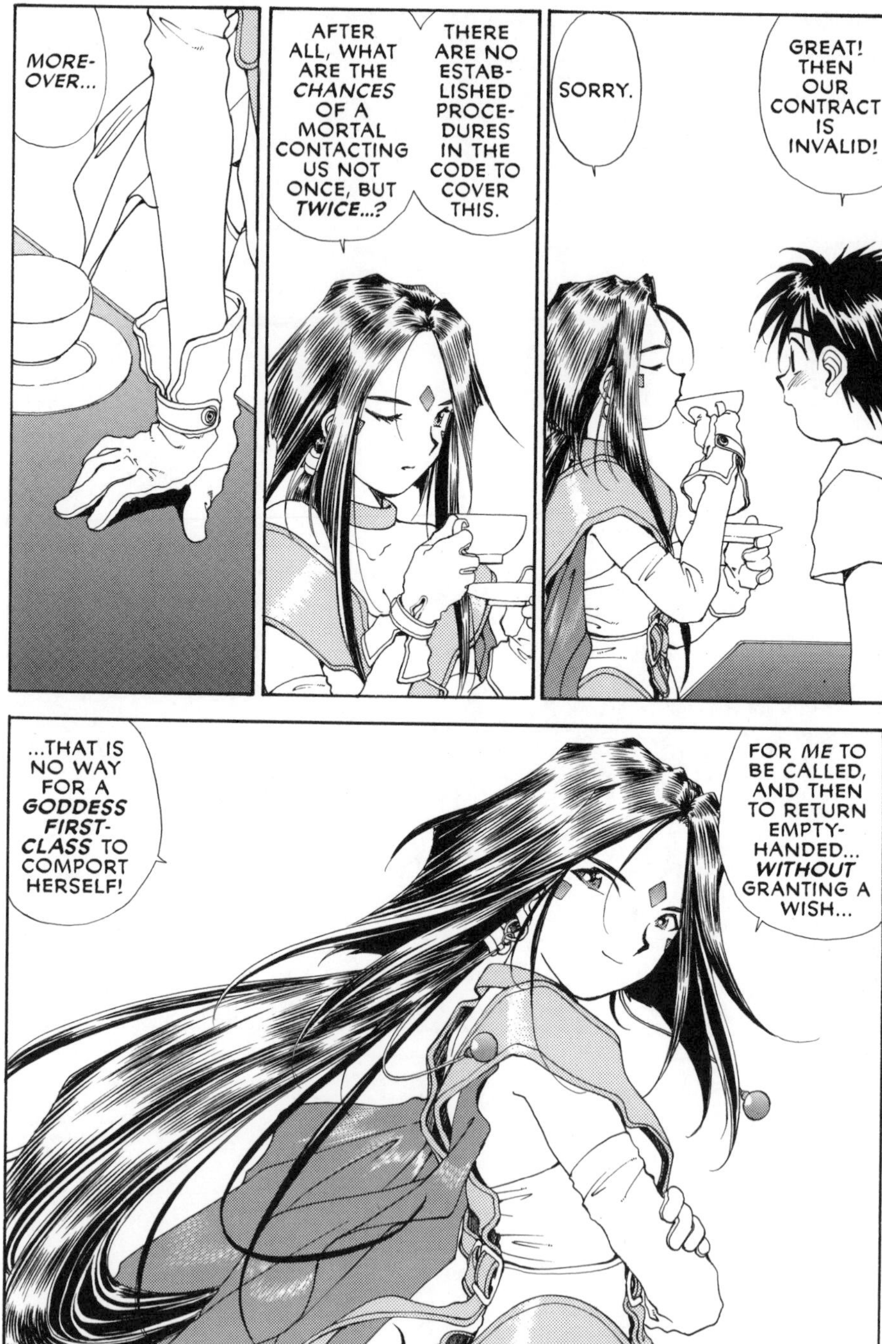

GREAT! THEN OUR CONTRACT IS INVALID!
SORRY.
THERE ARE NO ESTABLISHED PROCEDURES IN THE CODE TO COVER THIS.
AFTER ALL, WHAT ARE THE *CHANCES* OF A MORTAL CONTACTING US NOT ONCE, BUT *TWICE...?*
MOREOVER...
FOR *ME* TO BE CALLED, AND THEN TO RETURN EMPTY-HANDED... *WITHOUT* GRANTING A WISH...
...THAT IS NO WAY FOR A *GODDESS FIRST-CLASS* TO COMPORT HERSELF!

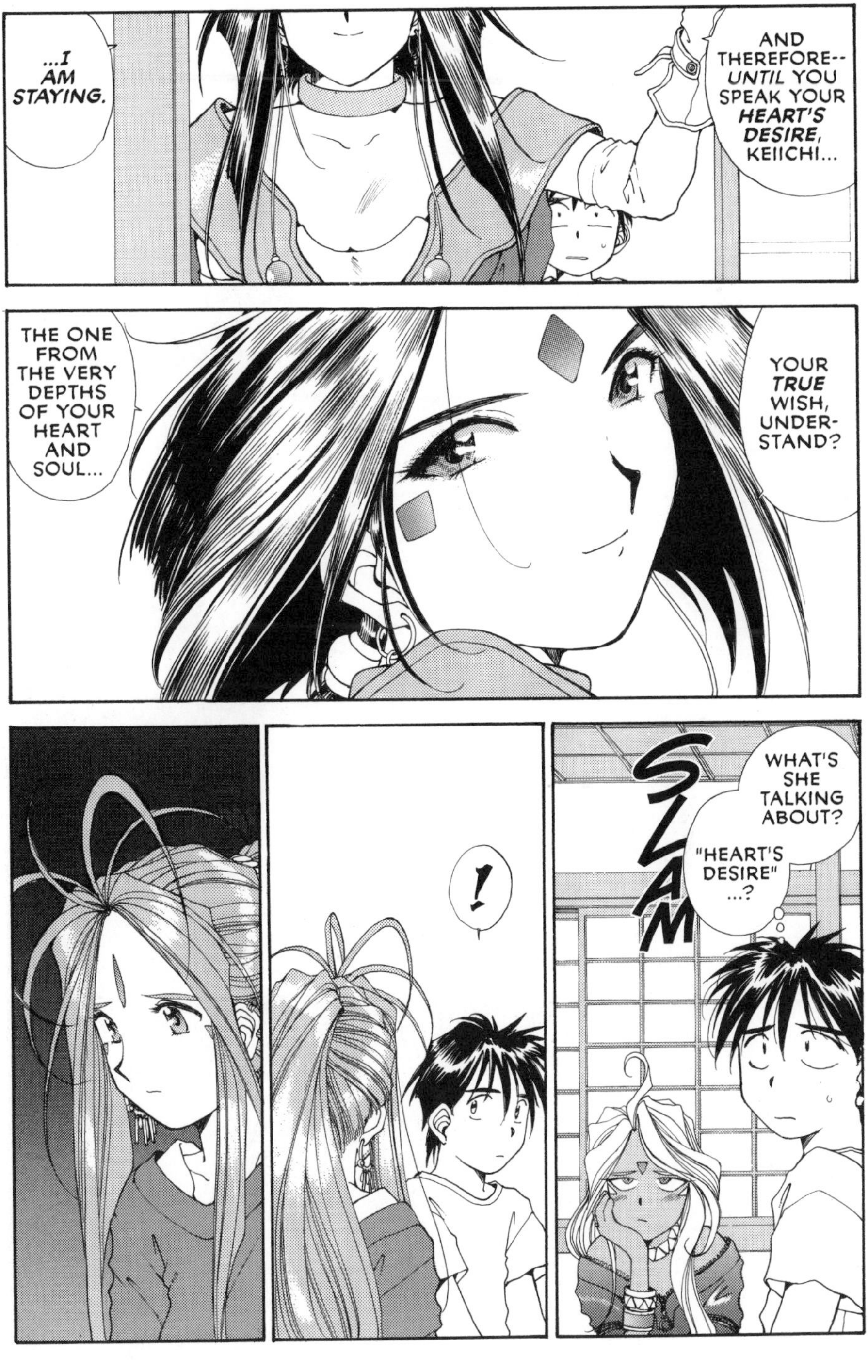
AND THEREFORE-- UNTIL YOU SPEAK YOUR HEART'S DESIRE, KEIICHI...
...I AM STAYING.
YOUR TRUE WISH, UNDERSTAND?
THE ONE FROM THE VERY DEPTHS OF YOUR HEART AND SOUL...
SLAM
WHAT'S SHE TALKING ABOUT?
"HEART'S DESIRE" ...?
!

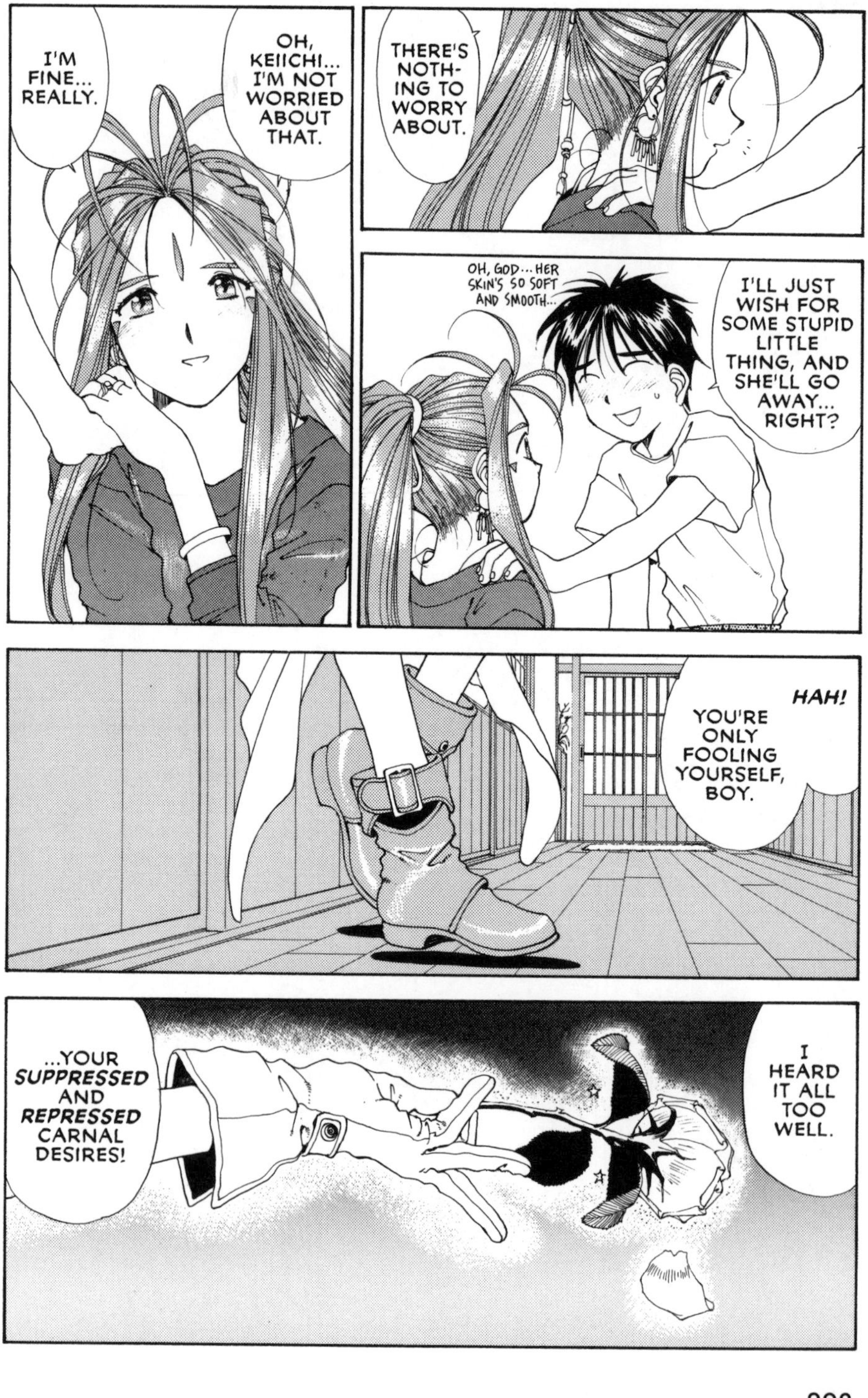
THERE'S NOTH-ING TO WORRY ABOUT.
OH, GOD... HER SKIN'S SO SOFT AND SMOOTH...
I'LL JUST WISH FOR SOME STUPID LITTLE THING, AND SHE'LL GO AWAY... RIGHT?
OH, KEIICHI... I'M NOT WORRIED ABOUT THAT.
I'M FINE... REALLY.
HAH!
YOU'RE ONLY FOOLING YOURSELF, BOY.
I HEARD IT ALL TOO WELL.
...YOUR *SUPPRESSED* AND *REPRESSED* CARNAL DESIRES!

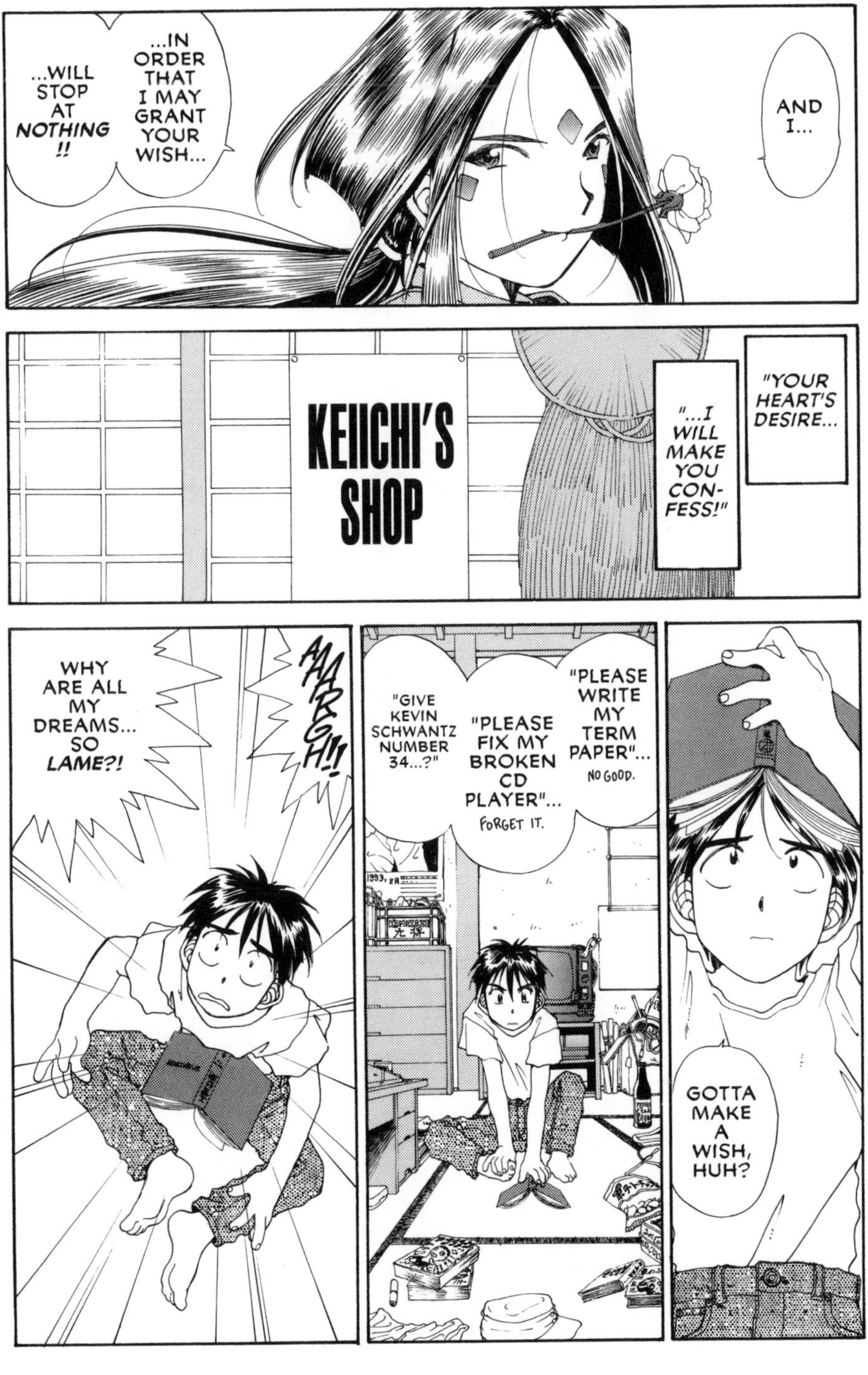
AND I...
...IN ORDER THAT I MAY GRANT YOUR WISH...
...WILL STOP AT *NOTHING* !!
"YOUR HEART'S DESIRE...
"...I WILL MAKE YOU CONFESS!"
KEIICHI'S SHOP
GOTTA MAKE A WISH, HUH?
"PLEASE WRITE MY TERM PAPER"... NO GOOD.
"PLEASE FIX MY BROKEN CD PLAYER"... FORGET IT.
"GIVE KEVIN SCHWANTZ NUMBER 34...?"
AAARGH!!
WHY ARE ALL MY DREAMS... SO *LAME?!*

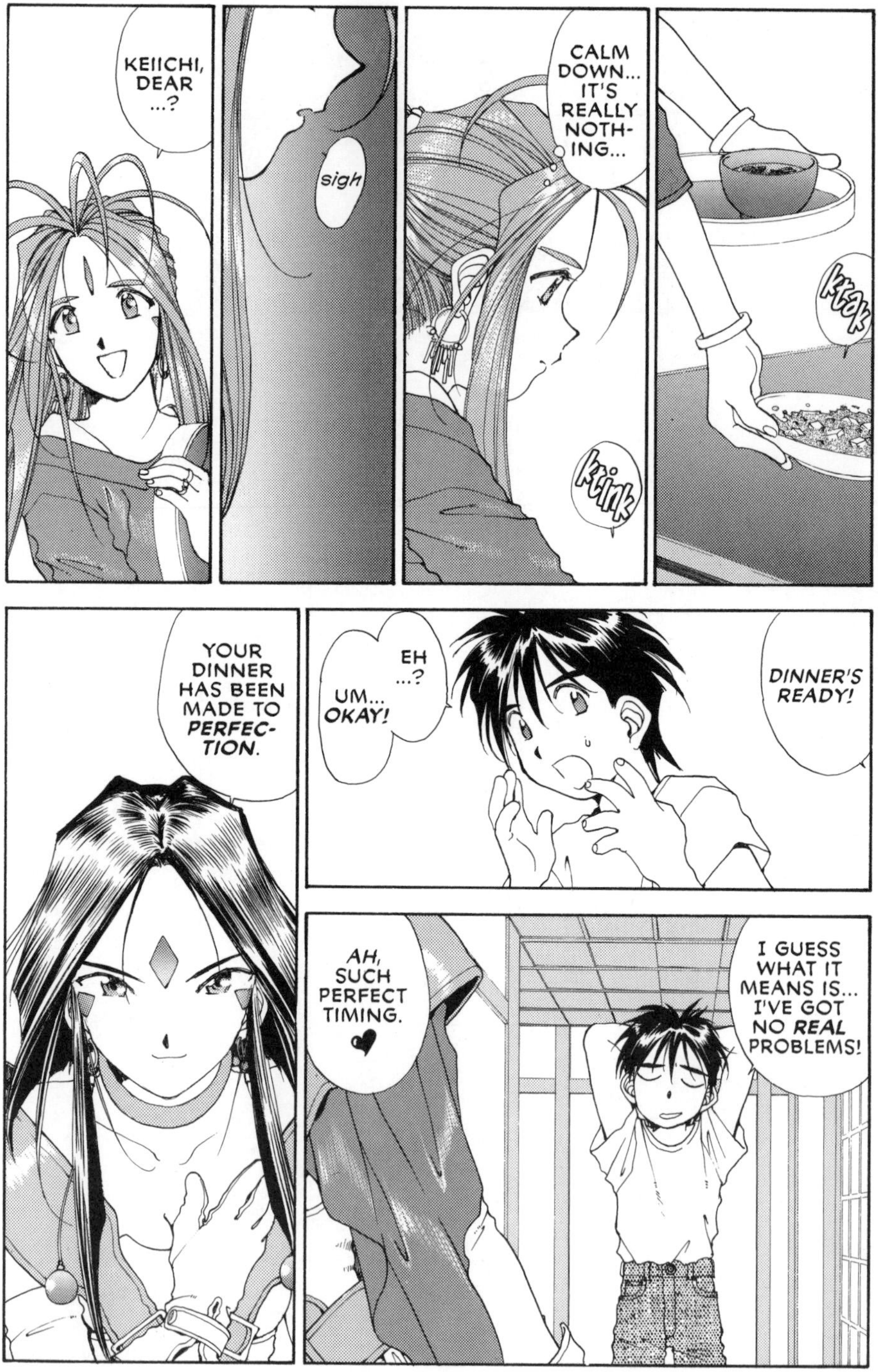
ktak
CALM DOWN... IT'S REALLY NOTHING...
ktink
sigh
KEIICHI, DEAR ...?
DINNER'S READY!
EH ...? UM... **OKAY!**
I GUESS WHAT IT MEANS IS... I'VE GOT NO **REAL** PROBLEMS!
AH, SUCH PERFECT TIMING. ♥
YOUR DINNER HAS BEEN MADE TO **PERFECTION**.

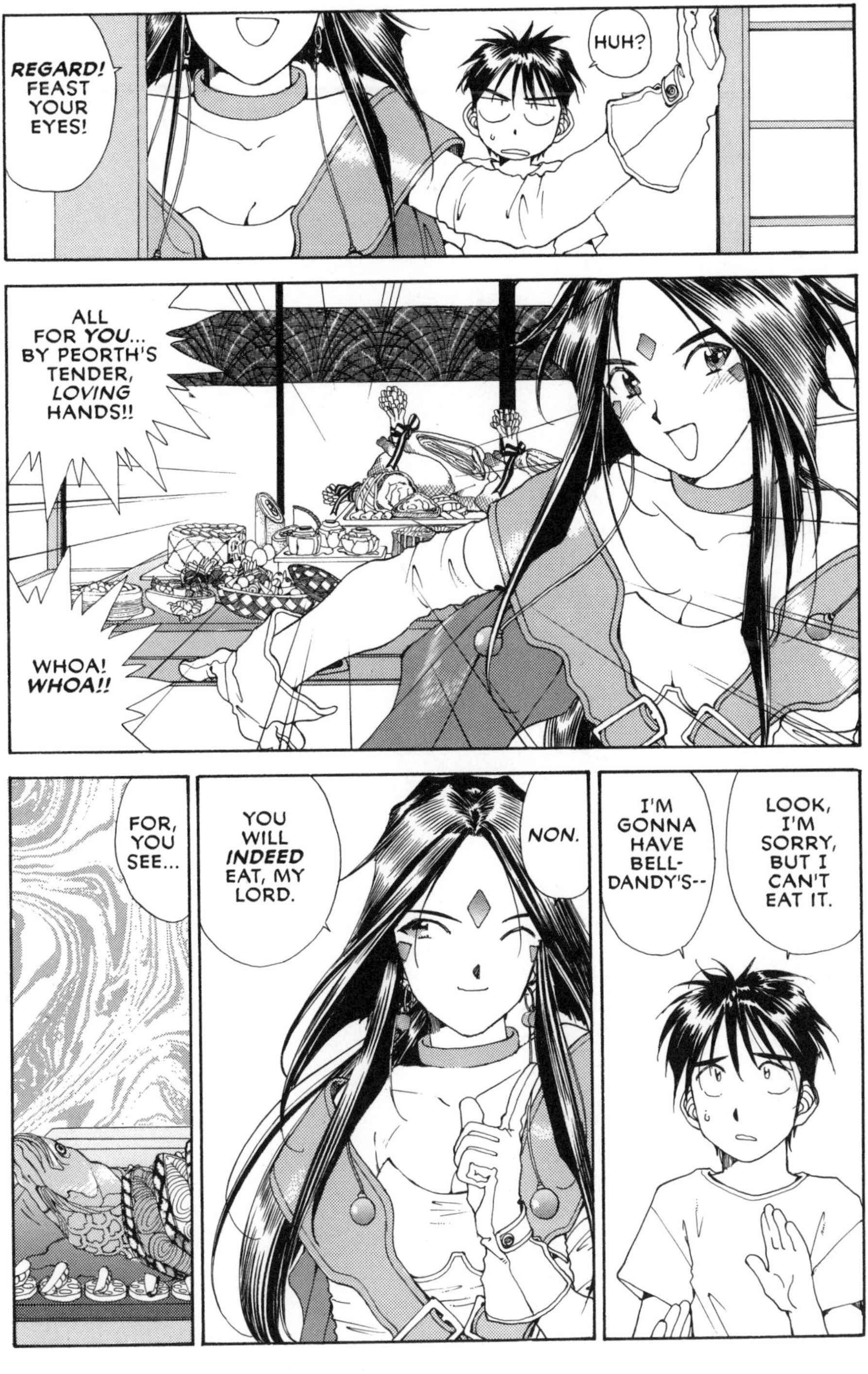
HUH?
REGARD! FEAST YOUR EYES!
ALL FOR YOU... BY PEORTH'S TENDER, LOVING HANDS!!
WHOA! WHOA!!
LOOK, I'M SORRY, BUT I CAN'T EAT IT.
I'M GONNA HAVE BELL-DANDY'S--
NON.
YOU WILL INDEED EAT, MY LORD.
FOR, YOU SEE...

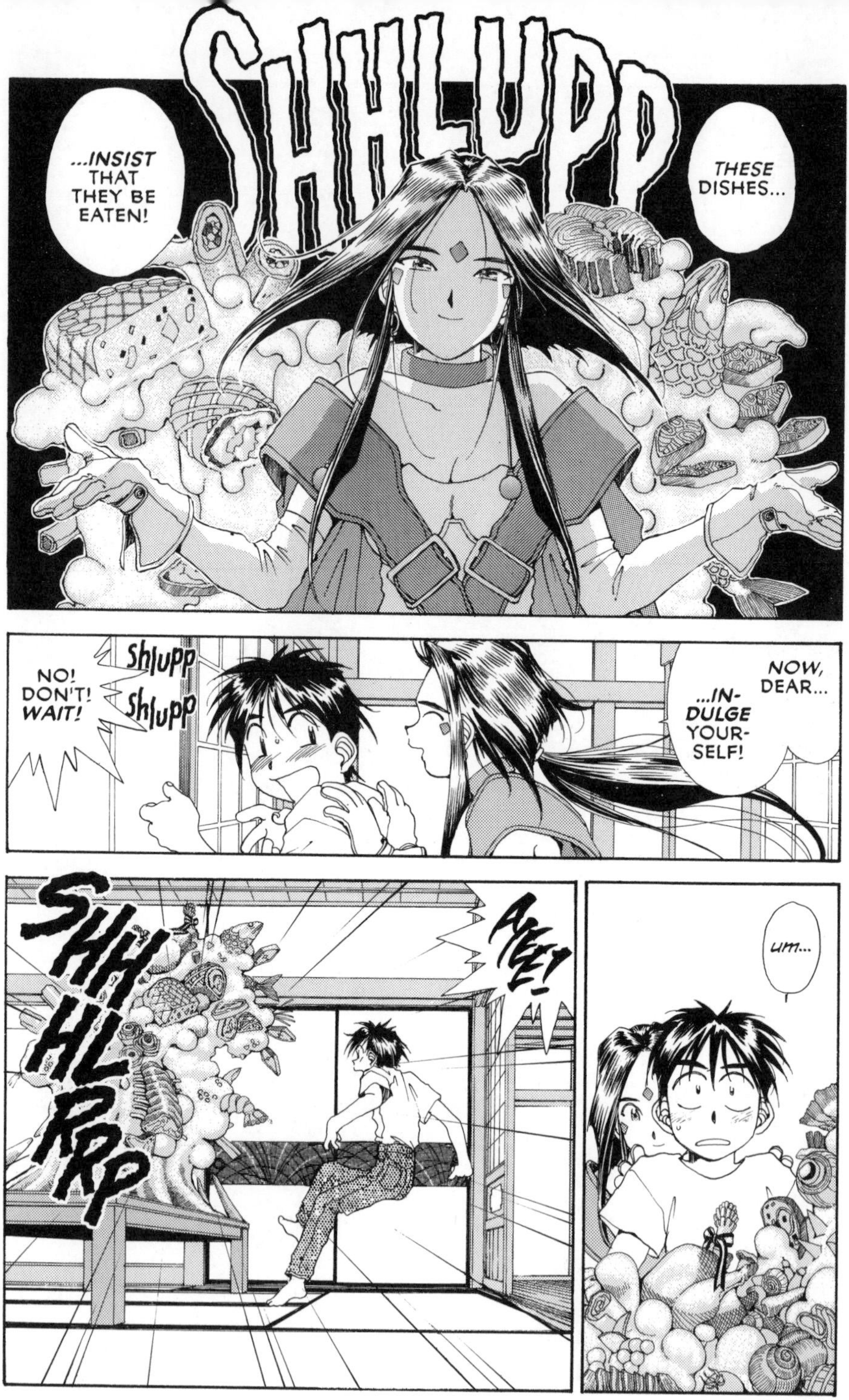
SHHLUPP
THESE DISHES...
...INSIST THAT THEY BE EATEN!
NOW, DEAR...
...IN-DULGE YOUR-SELF!
Shlupp
Shlupp
NO! DON'T! WAIT!
um...
AIEE!
SHHHLRRP

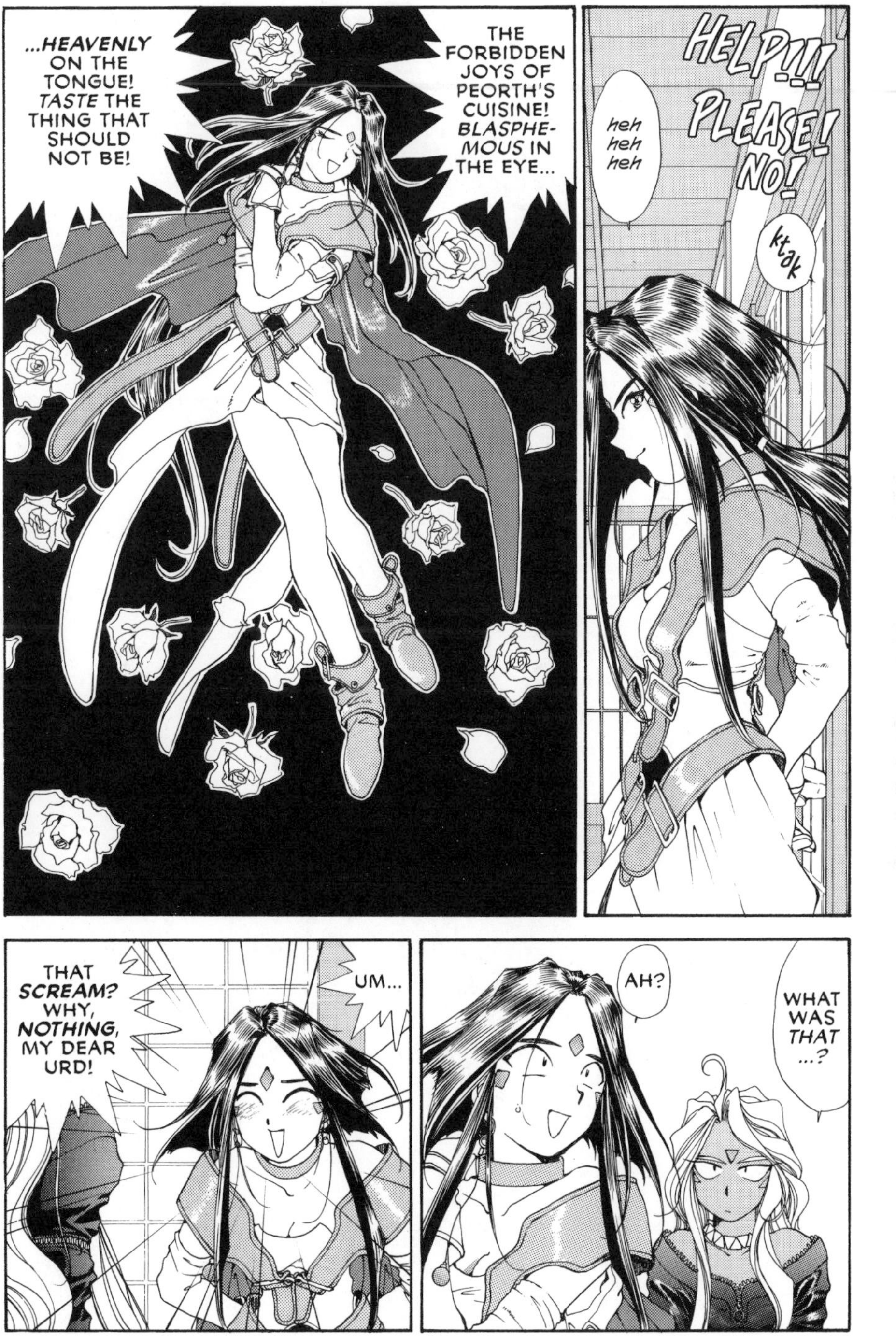
HELP!!! PLEASE! NO!
heh heh heh
ktak
THE FORBIDDEN JOYS OF PEORTH'S CUISINE! BLASPHEMOUS IN THE EYE...
...HEAVENLY ON THE TONGUE! TASTE THE THING THAT SHOULD NOT BE!
WHAT WAS THAT ...?
AH?
UM...
THAT SCREAM? WHY, NOTHING, MY DEAR URD!

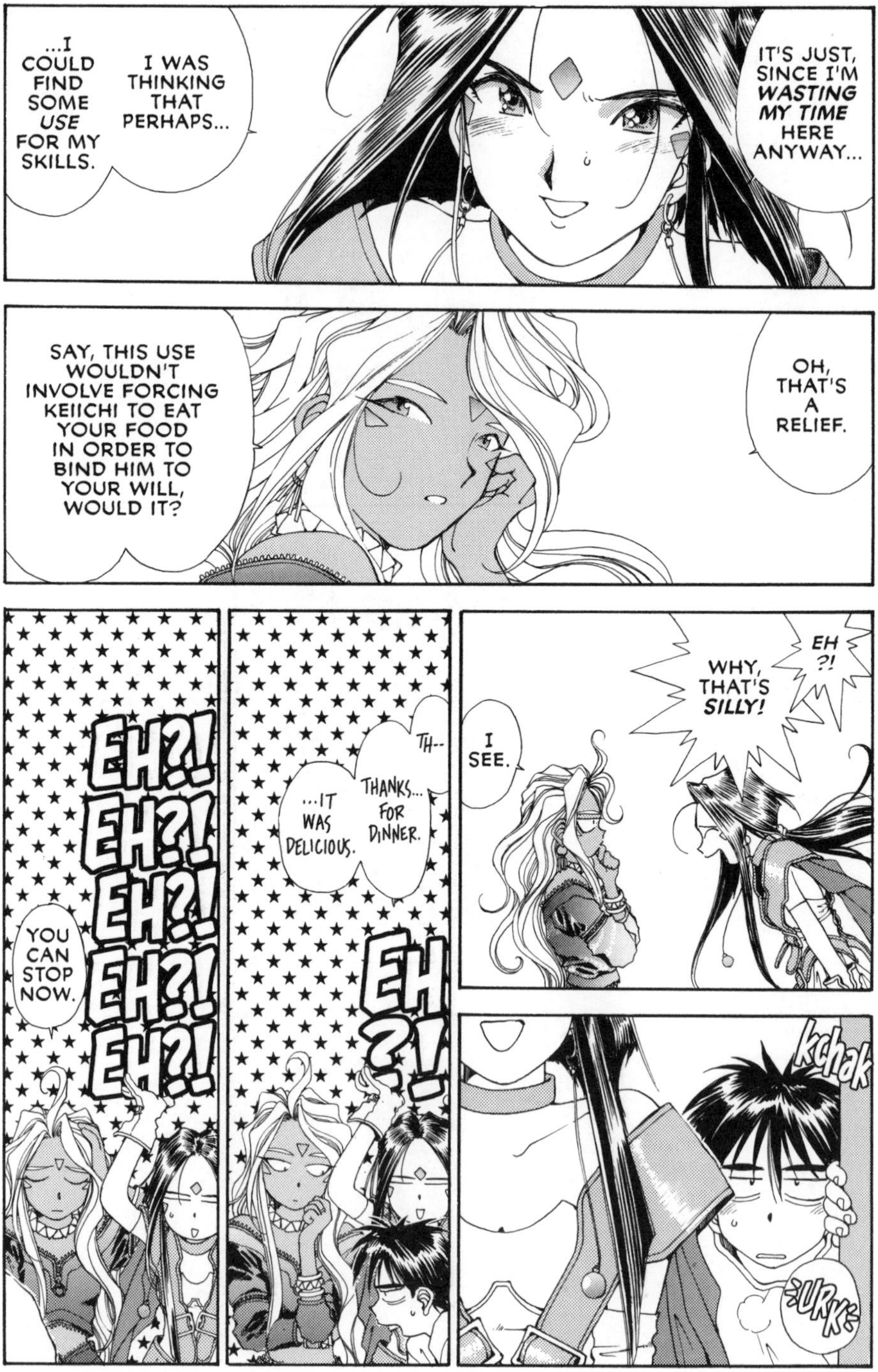
IT'S JUST, SINCE I'M *WASTING MY TIME* HERE ANYWAY...
I WAS THINKING THAT PERHAPS...
...I COULD FIND SOME *USE* FOR MY SKILLS.
OH, THAT'S A RELIEF.
SAY, THIS USE WOULDN'T INVOLVE FORCING KEIICHI TO EAT YOUR FOOD IN ORDER TO BIND HIM TO YOUR WILL, WOULD IT?
EH ?!
WHY, THAT'S *SILLY!*
I SEE.
kchak
URK
TH--
THANKS... FOR DINNER.
...IT WAS DELICIOUS.
EH ?!
EH?! EH?! EH?! EH?! EH?!
YOU CAN STOP NOW.

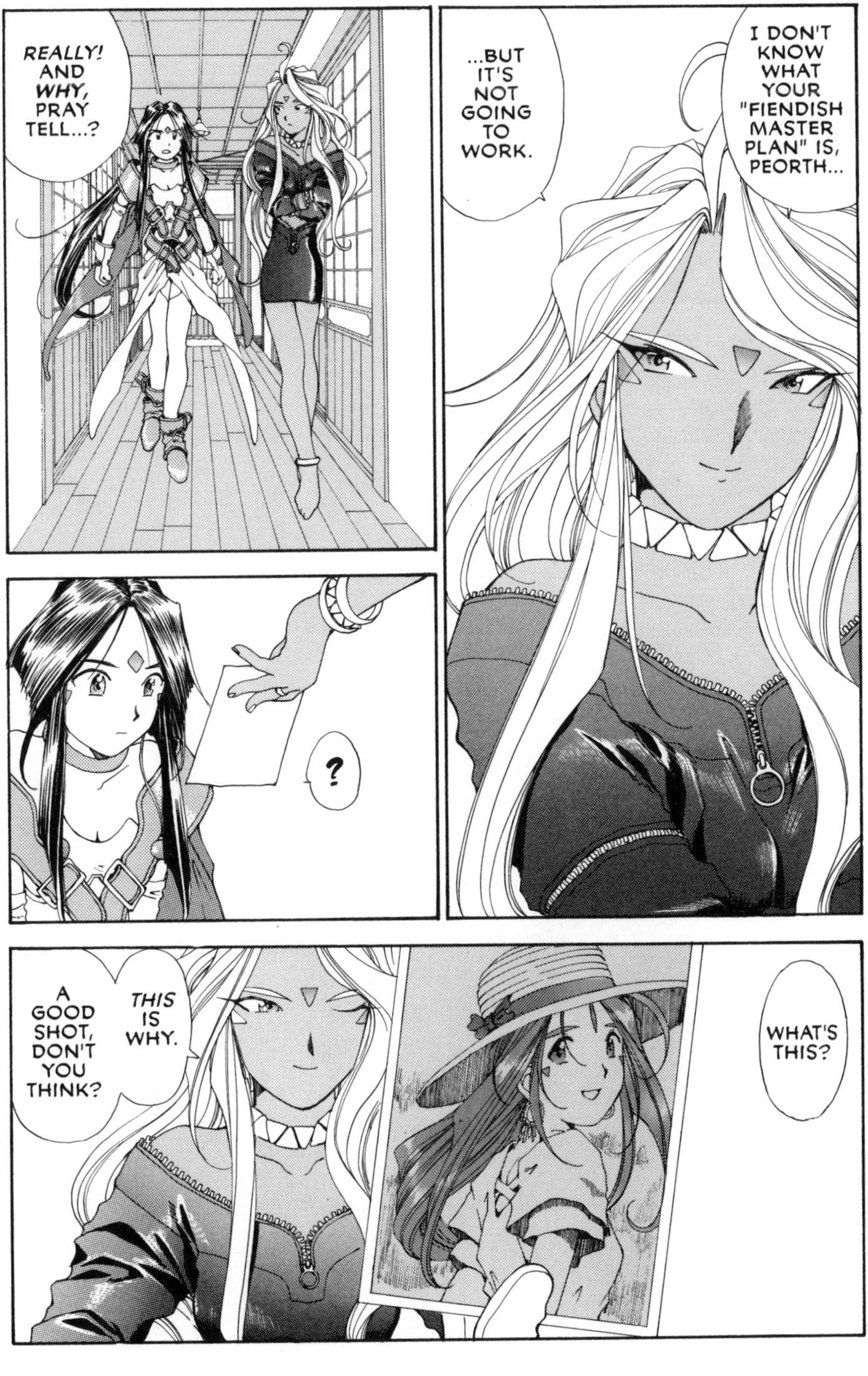
I DON'T KNOW WHAT YOUR "FIENDISH MASTER PLAN" IS, PEORTH...
...BUT IT'S NOT GOING TO WORK.
REALLY! AND *WHY*, PRAY TELL...?
?
WHAT'S THIS?
THIS IS WHY.
A GOOD SHOT, DON'T YOU THINK?

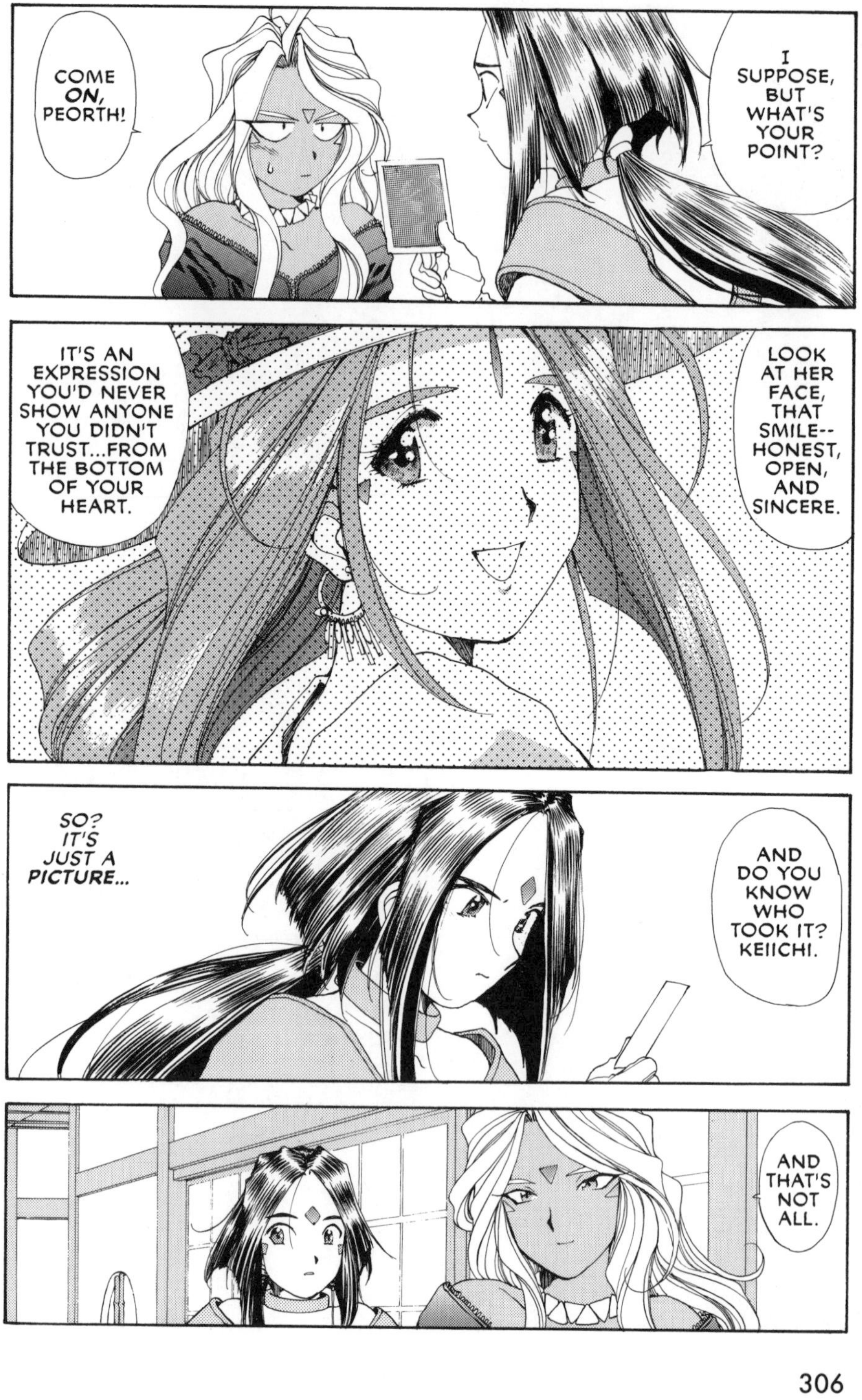
COME ON, PEORTH!
I SUPPOSE, BUT WHAT'S YOUR POINT?
IT'S AN EXPRESSION YOU'D NEVER SHOW ANYONE YOU DIDN'T TRUST...FROM THE BOTTOM OF YOUR HEART.
LOOK AT HER FACE, THAT SMILE--HONEST, OPEN, AND SINCERE.
SO? IT'S JUST A PICTURE...
AND DO YOU KNOW WHO TOOK IT? KEIICHI.
AND THAT'S NOT ALL.

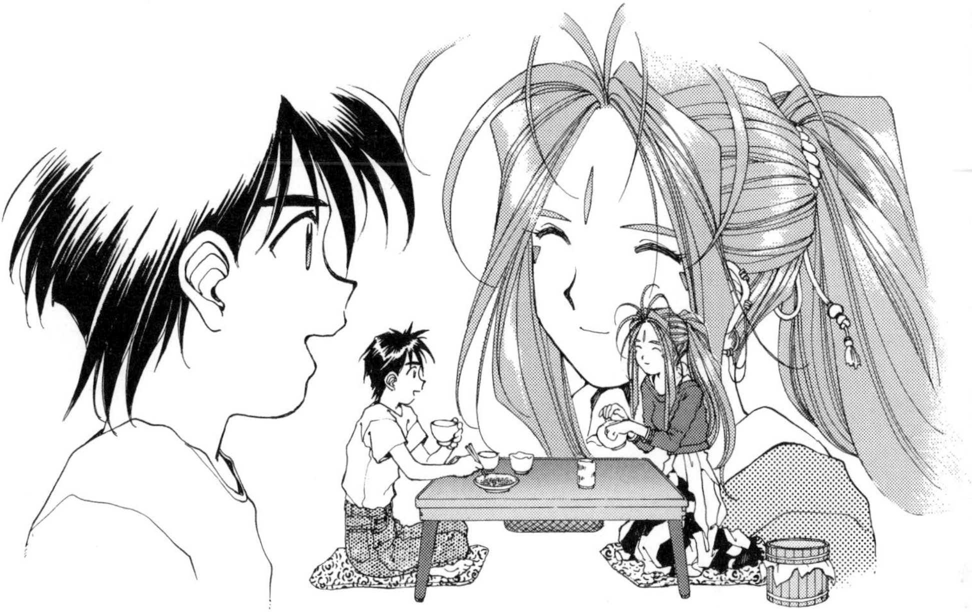

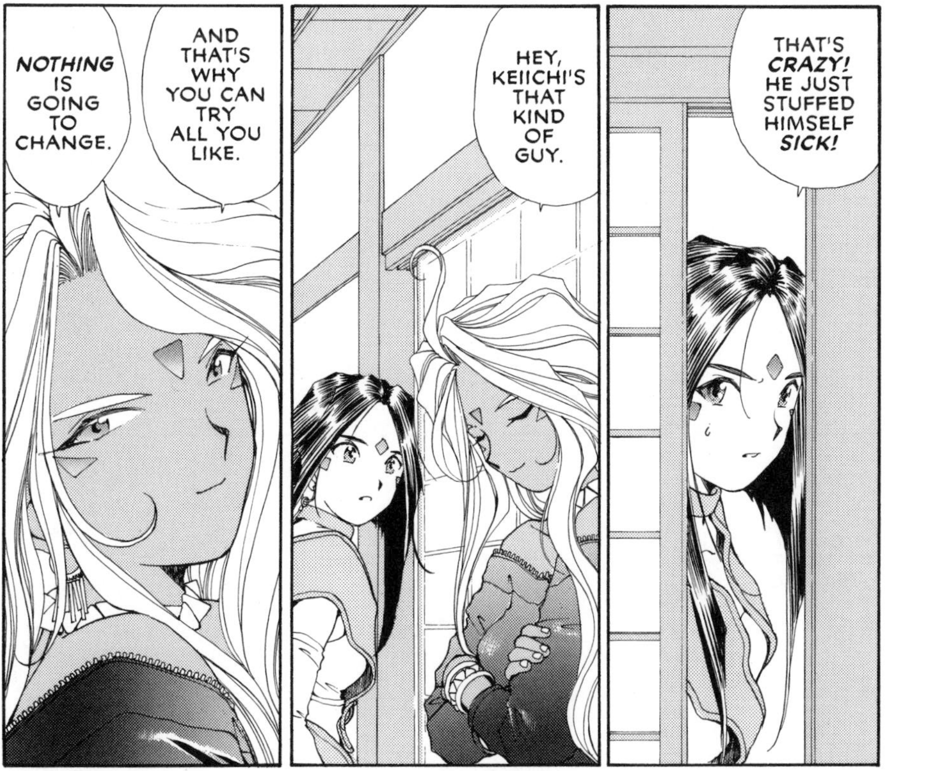
THAT'S *CRAZY!* HE JUST STUFFED HIMSELF *SICK!*
HEY, KEIICHI'S THAT KIND OF GUY.
AND THAT'S WHY YOU CAN TRY ALL YOU LIKE.
NOTHING IS GOING TO CHANGE.

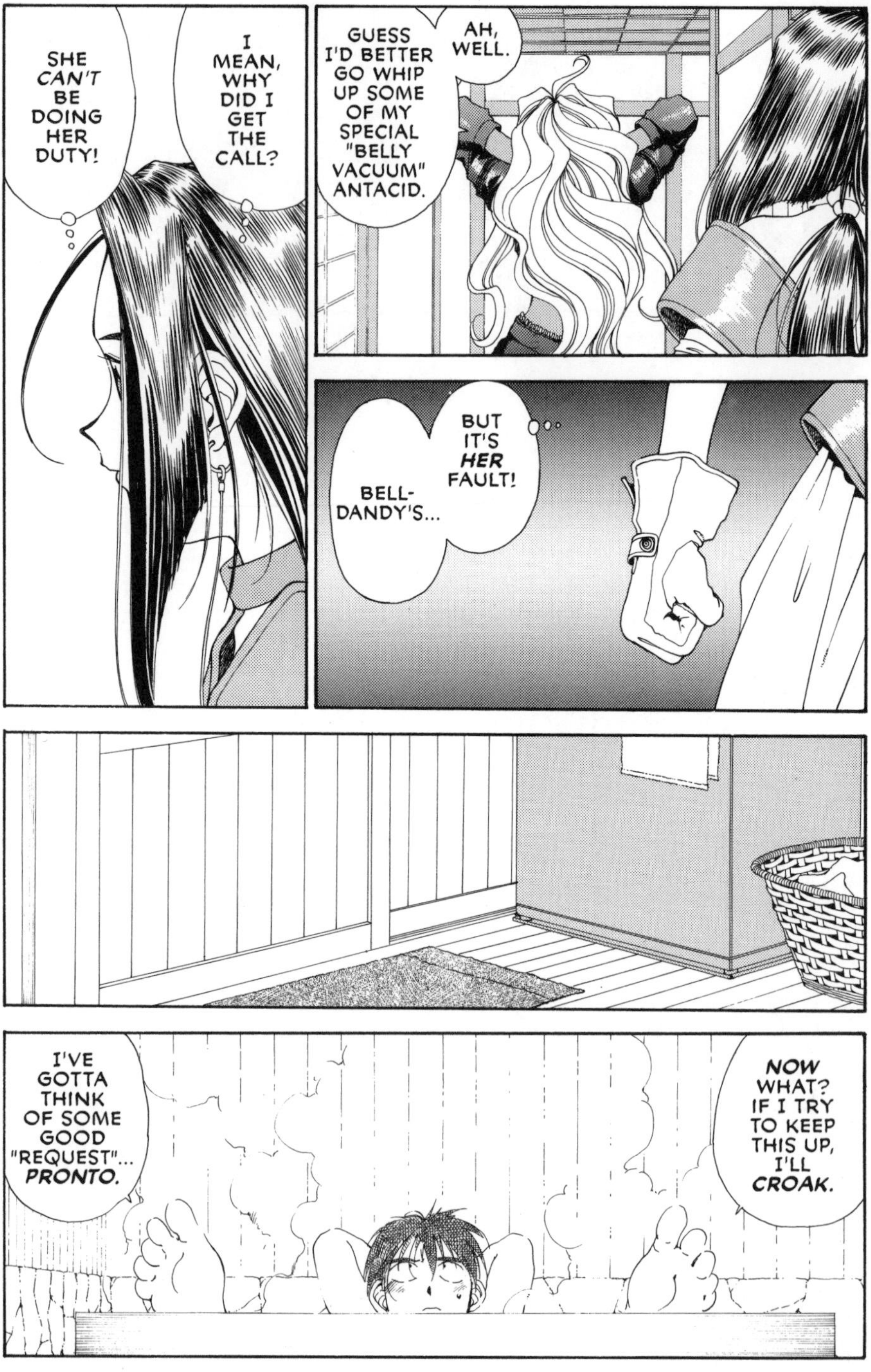
AH, WELL.
GUESS I'D BETTER GO WHIP UP SOME OF MY SPECIAL "BELLY VACUUM" ANTACID.
BUT IT'S *HER* FAULT!
BELL-DANDY'S...
I MEAN, WHY DID I GET THE CALL?
SHE *CAN'T* BE DOING HER DUTY!
NOW WHAT? IF I TRY TO KEEP THIS UP, I'LL *CROAK.*
I'VE GOTTA THINK OF SOME GOOD "REQUEST"... *PRONTO.*

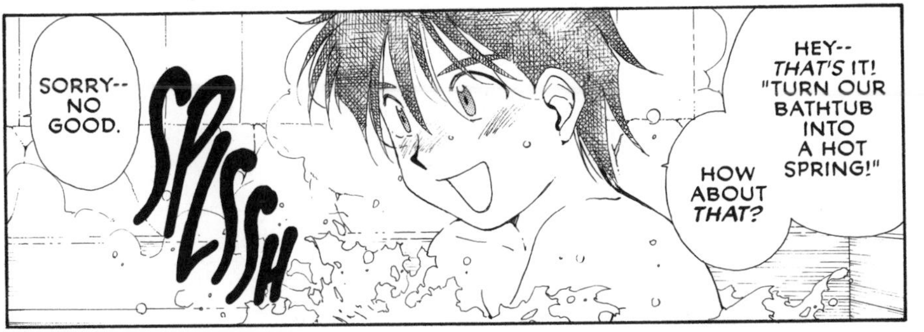
HEY-- THAT'S IT! "TURN OUR BATHTUB INTO A HOT SPRING!"
HOW ABOUT THAT?
SPLSSH
SORRY-- NO GOOD.

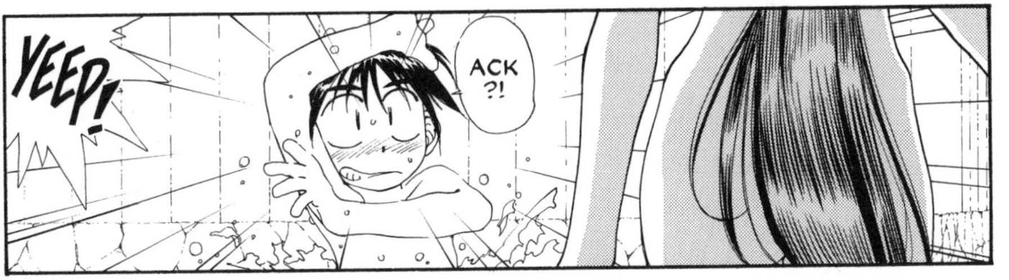
ACK ?!
YEEP!

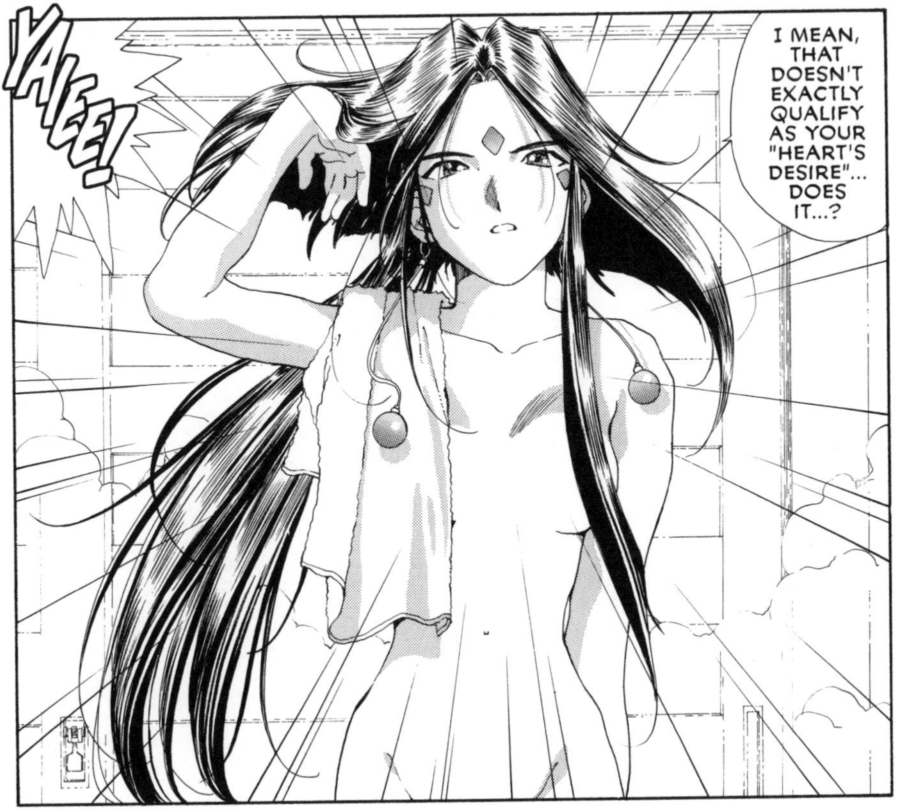
I MEAN, THAT DOESN'T EXACTLY QUALIFY AS YOUR "HEART'S DESIRE"... DOES IT...?
YAIEE!

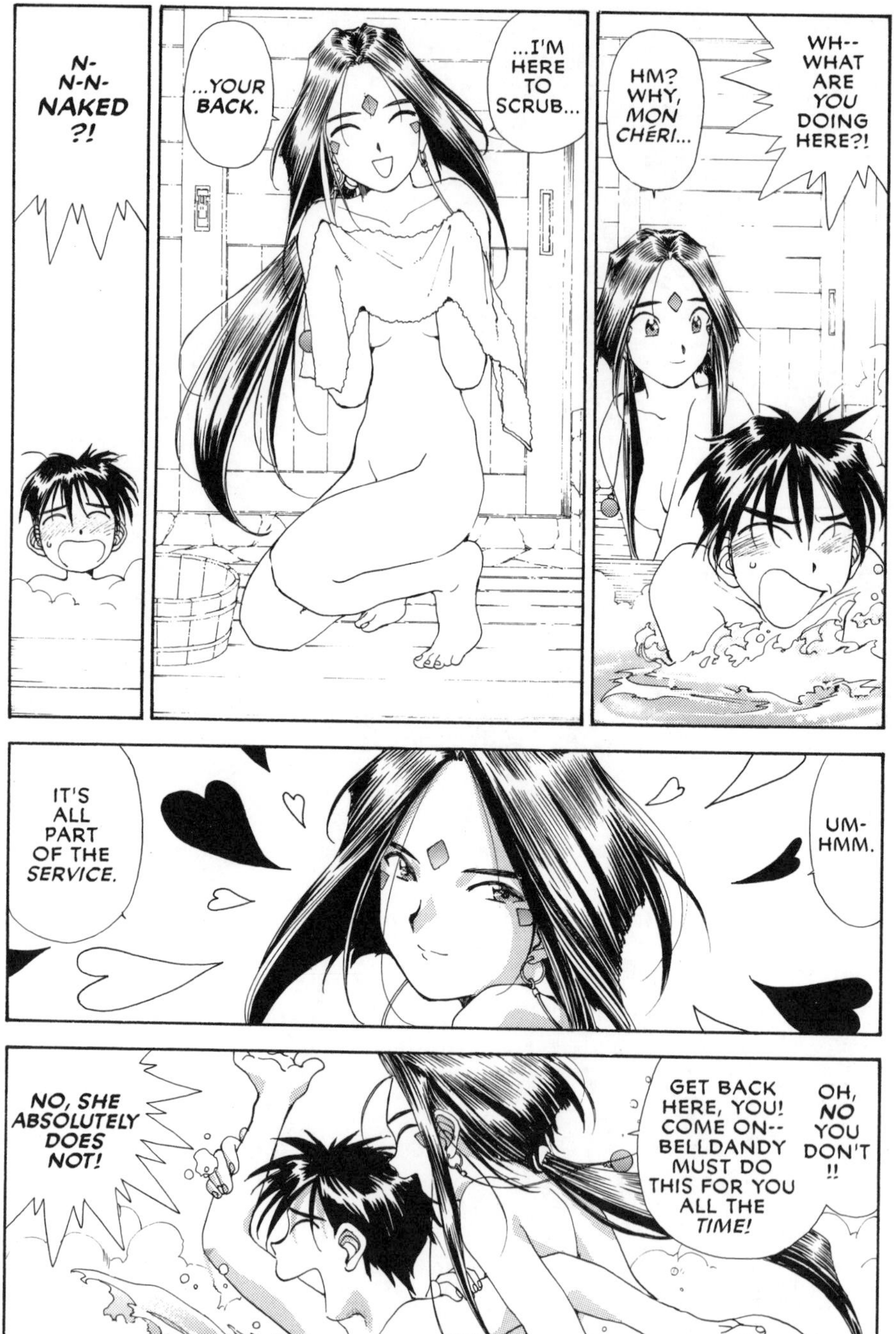
WH-- WHAT ARE YOU DOING HERE?!
HM? WHY, MON CHÉRI...
...I'M HERE TO SCRUB...
...YOUR BACK.
N-N-N-NAKED?!
UM-HMM.
IT'S ALL PART OF THE SERVICE.
OH, NO YOU DON'T!!
GET BACK HERE, YOU! COME ON-- BELLDANDY MUST DO THIS FOR YOU ALL THE TIME!
NO, SHE ABSOLUTELY DOES NOT!

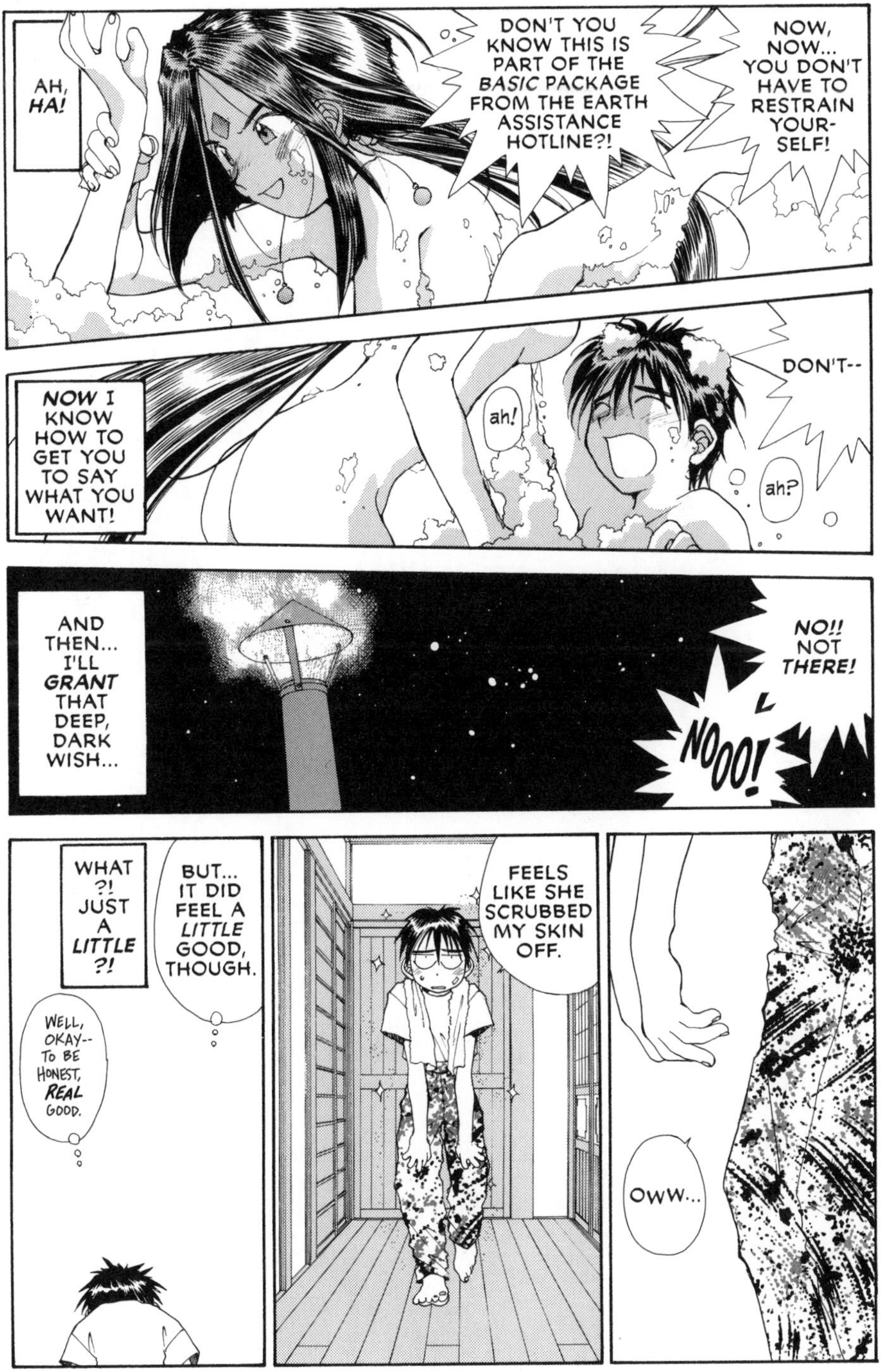
NOW, NOW... YOU DON'T HAVE TO RESTRAIN YOUR-SELF!
DON'T YOU KNOW THIS IS PART OF THE BASIC PACKAGE FROM THE EARTH ASSISTANCE HOTLINE?!
AH, HA!
DON'T--
ah?
ah!
NOW I KNOW HOW TO GET YOU TO SAY WHAT YOU WANT!
NO!! NOT THERE!
NOOO!
AND THEN... I'LL GRANT THAT DEEP, DARK WISH...
OWW...
FEELS LIKE SHE SCRUBBED MY SKIN OFF.
BUT... IT DID FEEL A LITTLE GOOD, THOUGH.
WHAT?! JUST A LITTLE?!
WELL, OKAY-- TO BE HONEST, REAL GOOD.

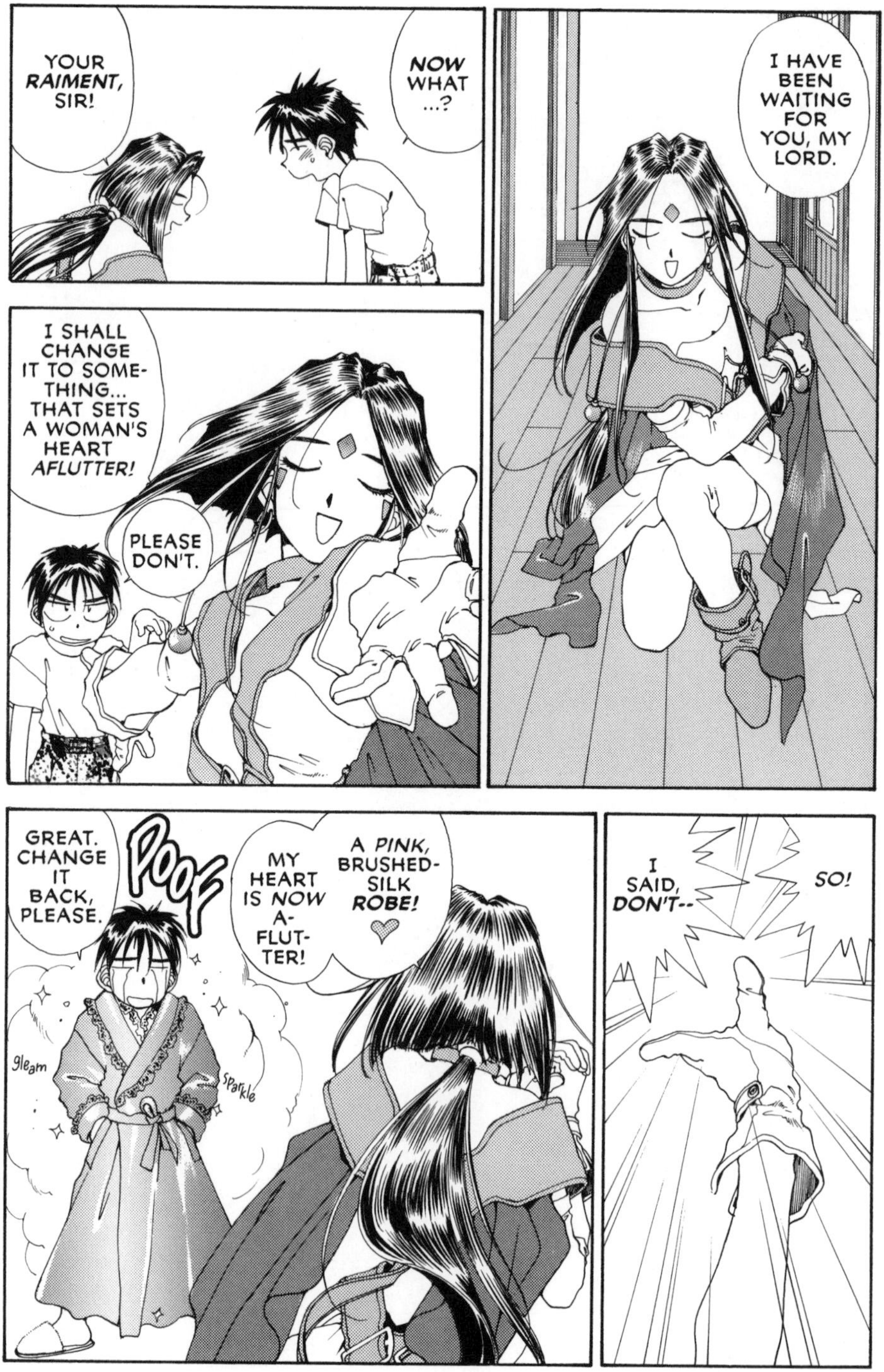
I HAVE BEEN WAITING FOR YOU, MY LORD.
NOW WHAT ...?
YOUR *RAIMENT*, SIR!
I SHALL CHANGE IT TO SOMETHING... THAT SETS A WOMAN'S HEART *AFLUTTER!*
PLEASE DON'T.
I SAID, *DON'T--*
SO!
A *PINK*, BRUSHED-SILK *ROBE!* ♡
MY HEART IS *NOW* A-FLUTTER!
POOF
GREAT. CHANGE IT BACK, PLEASE.
gleam
sparkle

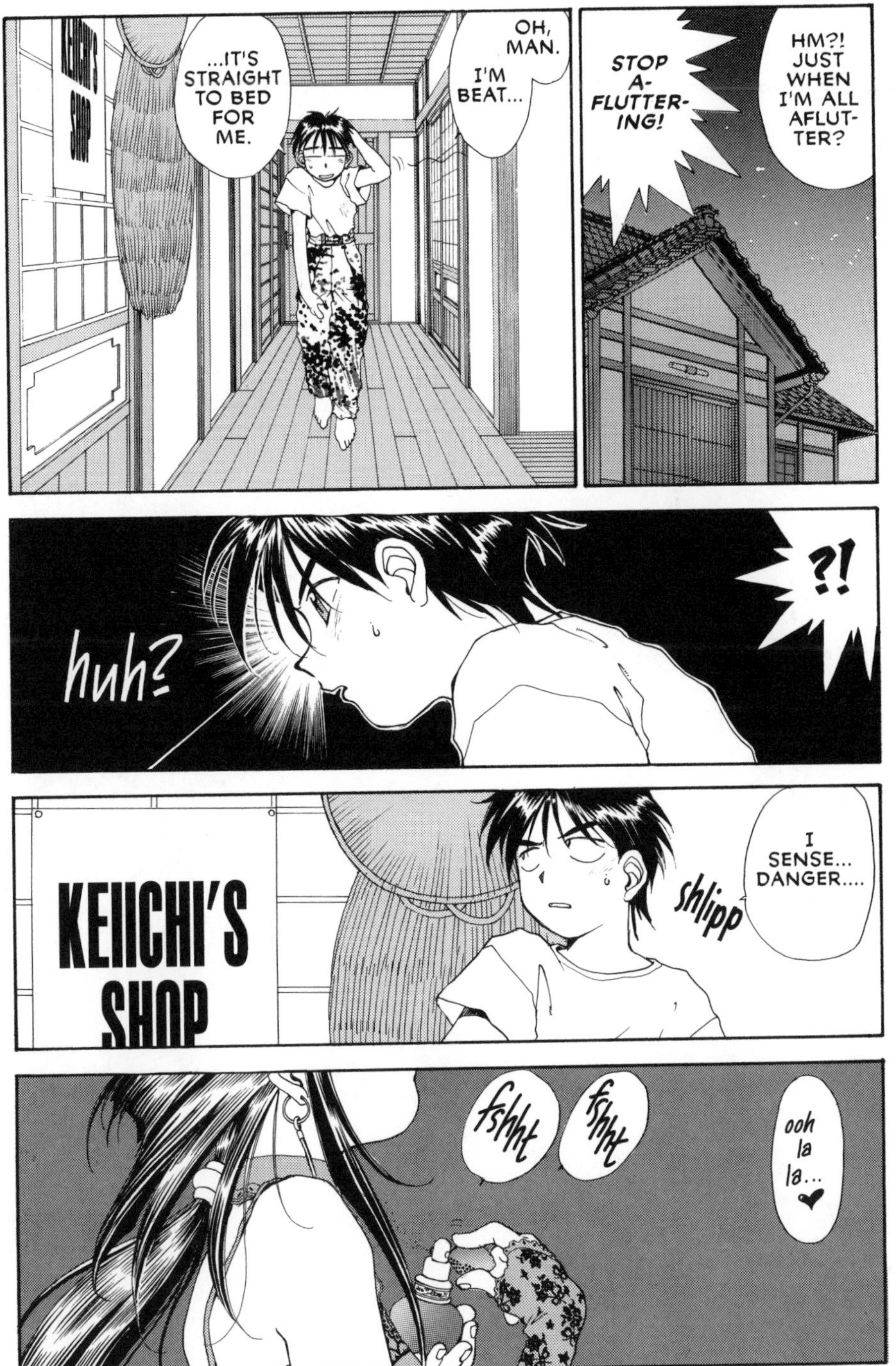
HM?! JUST WHEN I'M ALL AFLUTTER?
STOP A-FLUTTERING!
OH, MAN. I'M BEAT...
...IT'S STRAIGHT TO BED FOR ME.
KEIICHI'S SHOP
?!
huh?
I SENSE... DANGER....
shlipp
KEIICHI'S SHOP
ooh la la...
fshht
fshht

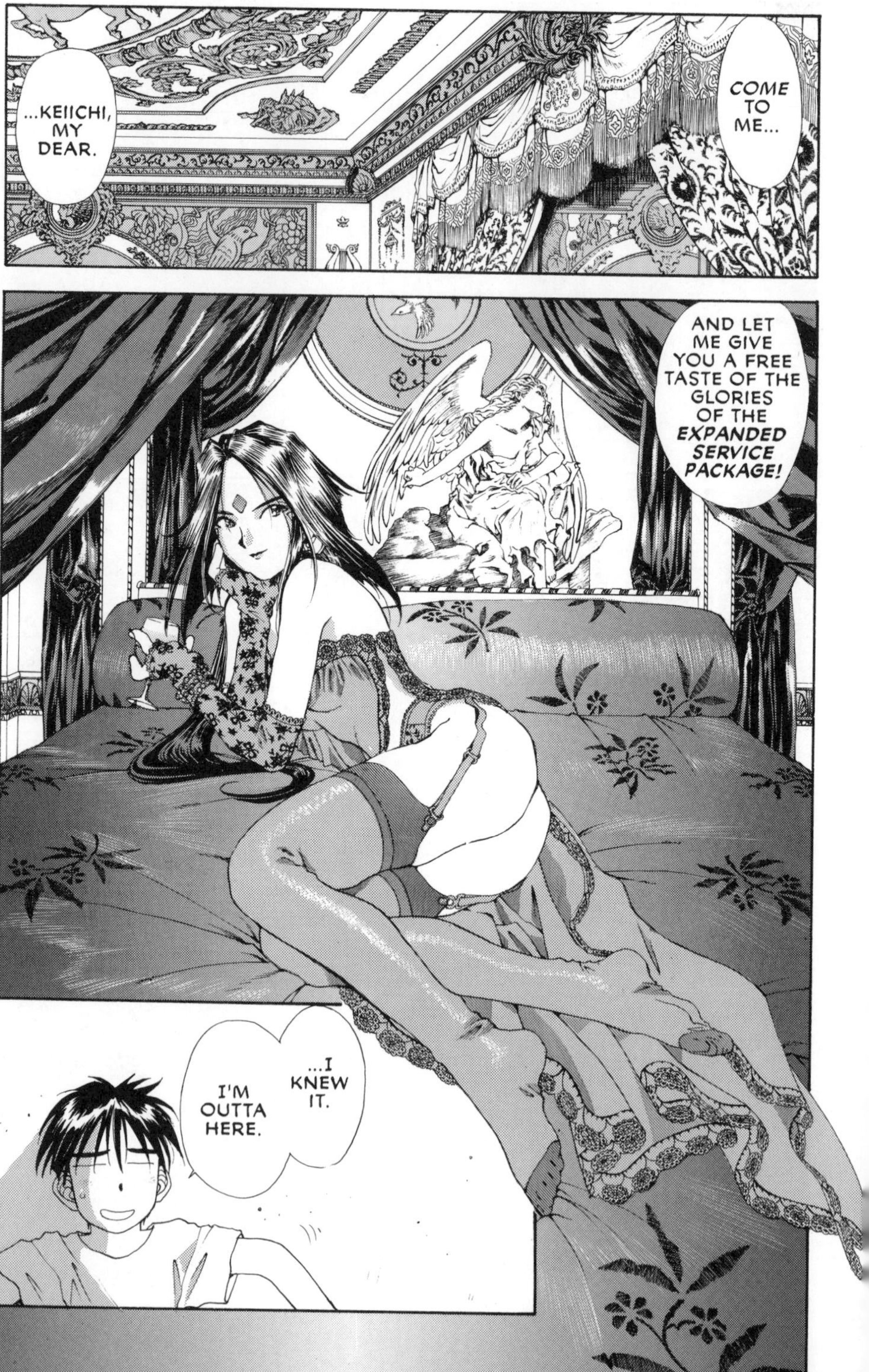
COME TO ME...
...KEIICHI, MY DEAR.
AND LET ME GIVE YOU A FREE TASTE OF THE GLORIES OF THE *EXPANDED SERVICE PACKAGE!*
...I KNEW IT.
I'M OUTTA HERE.

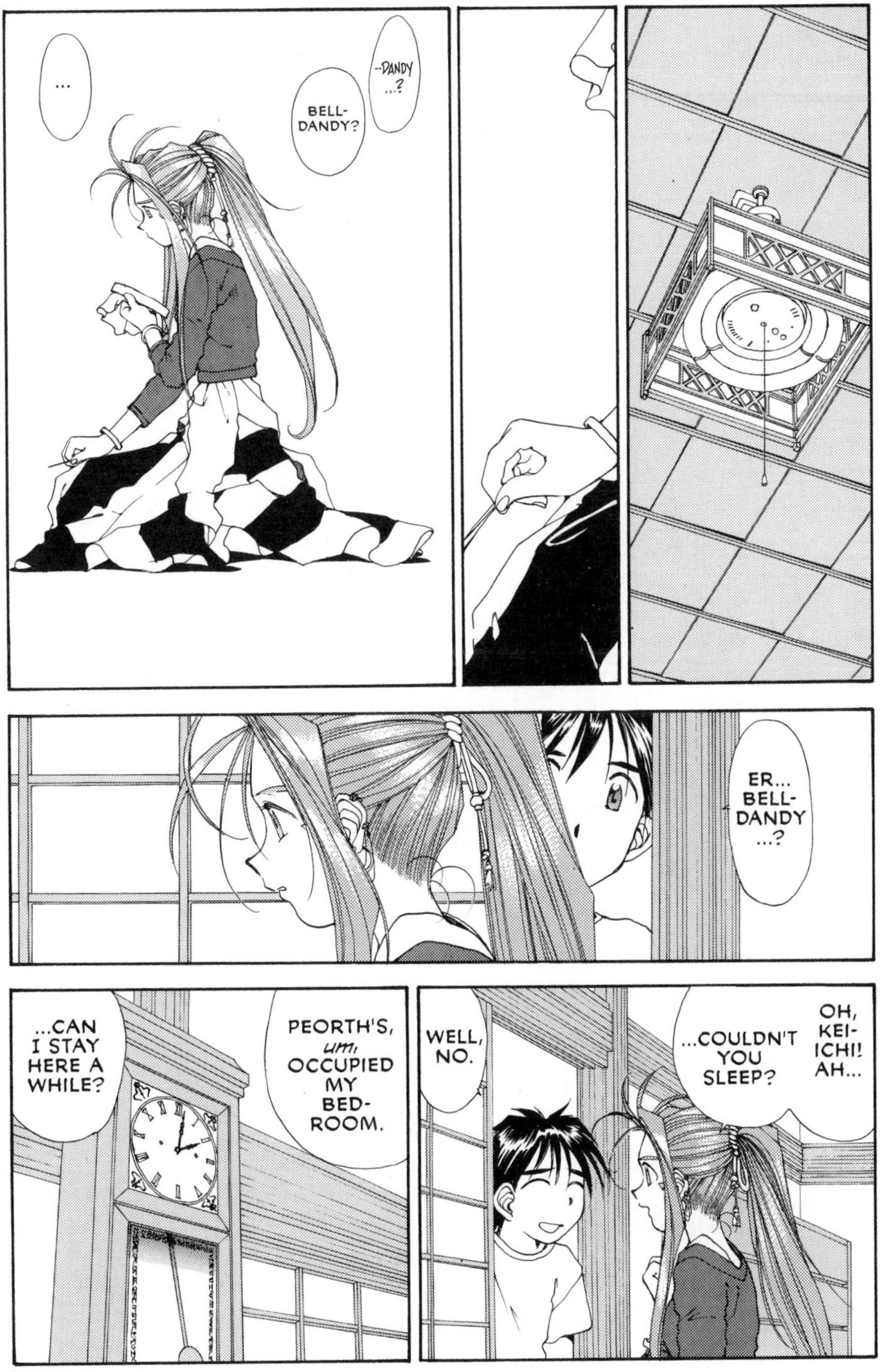
--DANDY ...?
BELL-DANDY?
...
ER... BELL-DANDY ...?
OH, KEI-ICHI! AH...
...COULDN'T YOU SLEEP?
WELL, NO.
PEORTH'S, *um,* OCCUPIED MY BED-ROOM.
...CAN I STAY HERE A WHILE?

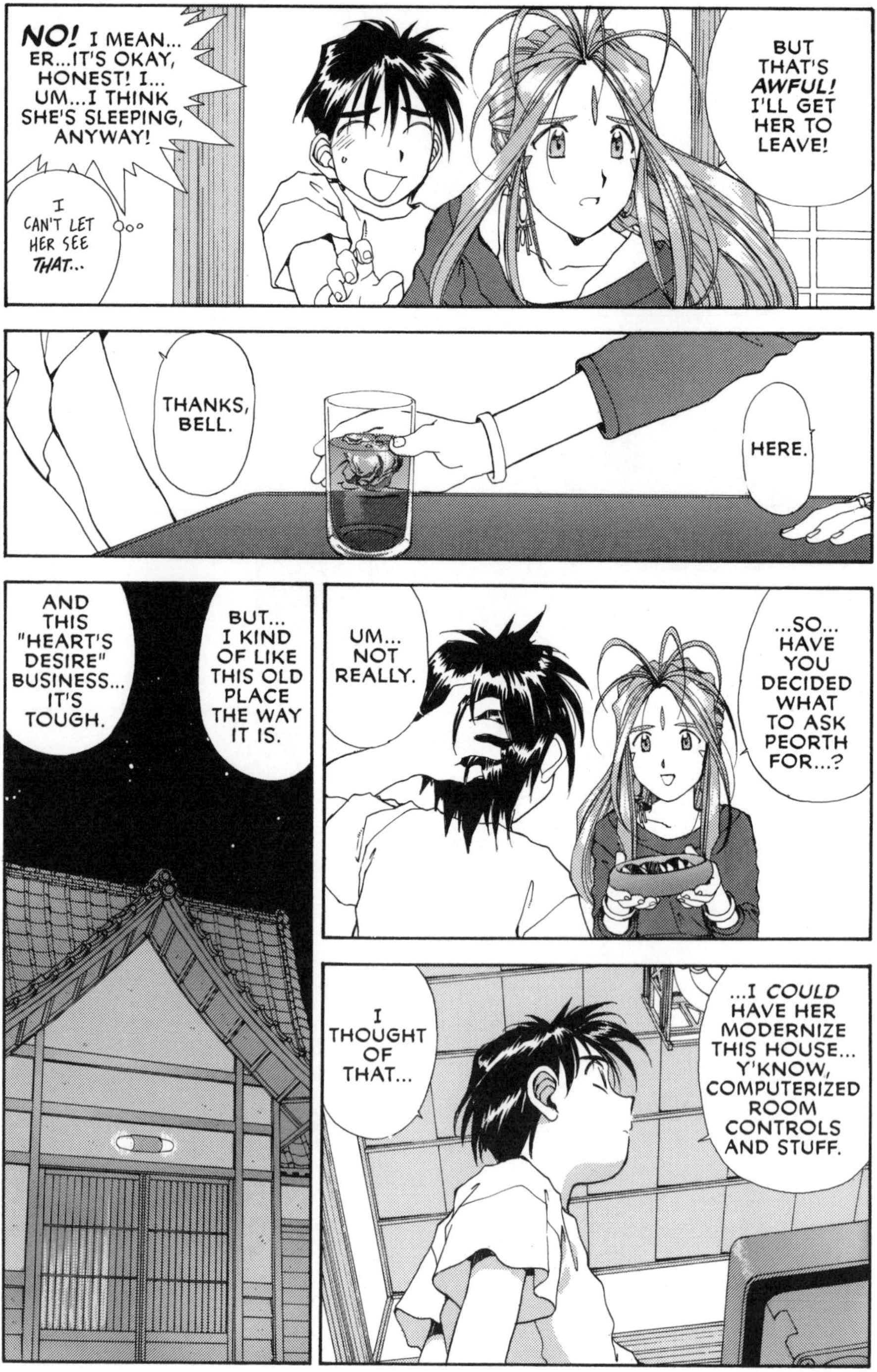
BUT THAT'S *AWFUL!* I'LL GET HER TO LEAVE!
NO! I MEAN... ER...IT'S OKAY, HONEST! I... UM...I THINK SHE'S SLEEPING, ANYWAY!
I CAN'T LET HER SEE *THAT*...
HERE.
THANKS, BELL.
...SO... HAVE YOU DECIDED WHAT TO ASK PEORTH FOR...?
UM... NOT REALLY.
...I *COULD* HAVE HER MODERNIZE THIS HOUSE... Y'KNOW, COMPUTERIZED ROOM CONTROLS AND STUFF.
I THOUGHT OF THAT...
BUT... I KIND OF LIKE THIS OLD PLACE THE WAY IT IS.
AND THIS "HEART'S DESIRE" BUSINESS... IT'S TOUGH.

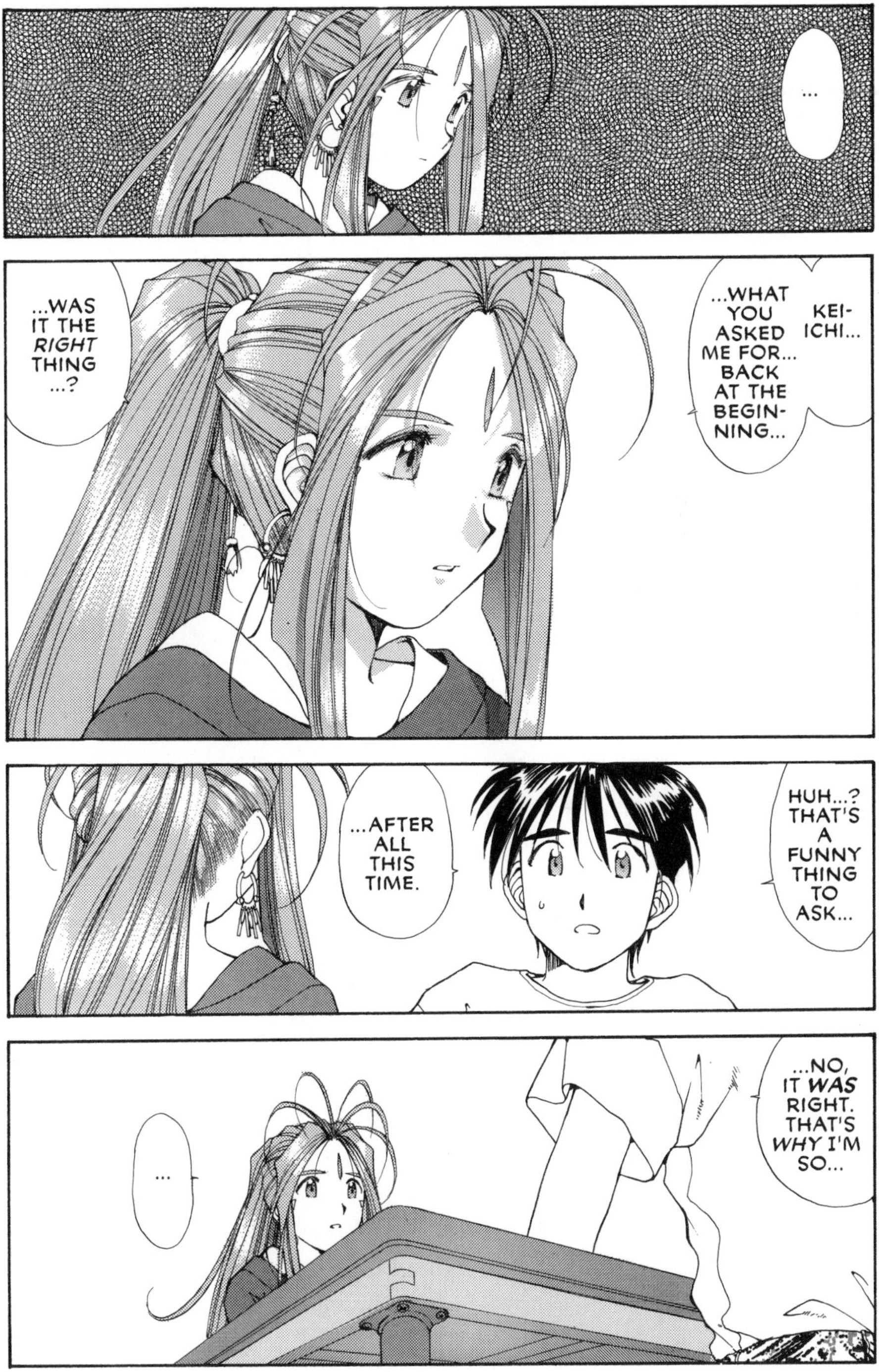
...
KEICHI... ...WHAT YOU ASKED ME FOR... BACK AT THE BEGINNING...
...WAS IT THE *RIGHT* THING...?
HUH...? THAT'S A FUNNY THING TO ASK...
...AFTER ALL THIS TIME.
...NO, IT ***WAS*** RIGHT. THAT'S *WHY* I'M SO...
...

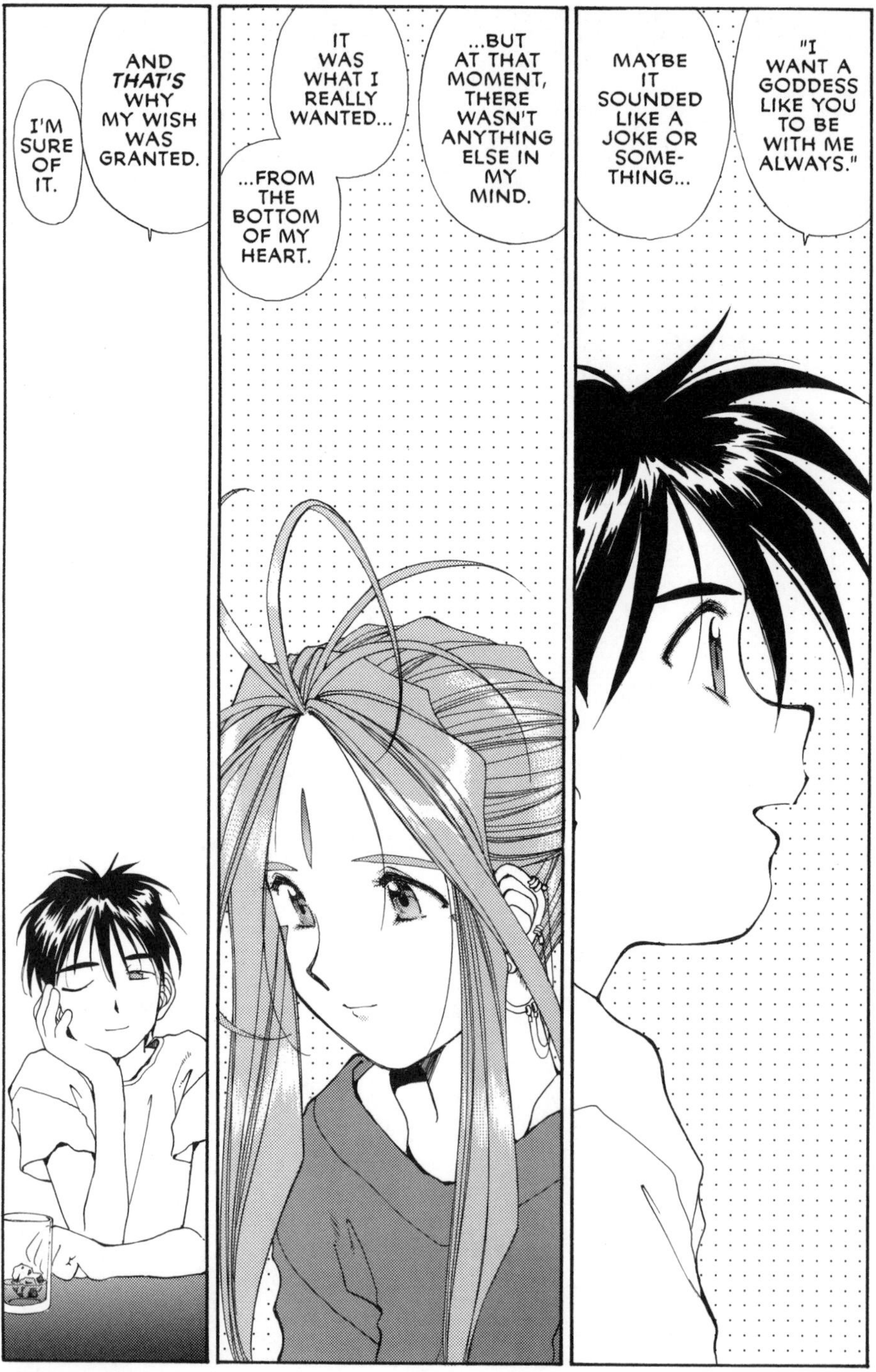
"I WANT A GODDESS LIKE YOU TO BE WITH ME ALWAYS."
MAYBE IT SOUNDED LIKE A JOKE OR SOME-THING...
...BUT AT THAT MOMENT, THERE WASN'T ANYTHING ELSE IN MY MIND.
IT WAS WHAT I REALLY WANTED...
...FROM THE BOTTOM OF MY HEART.
AND *THAT'S* WHY MY WISH WAS GRANTED.
I'M SURE OF IT.

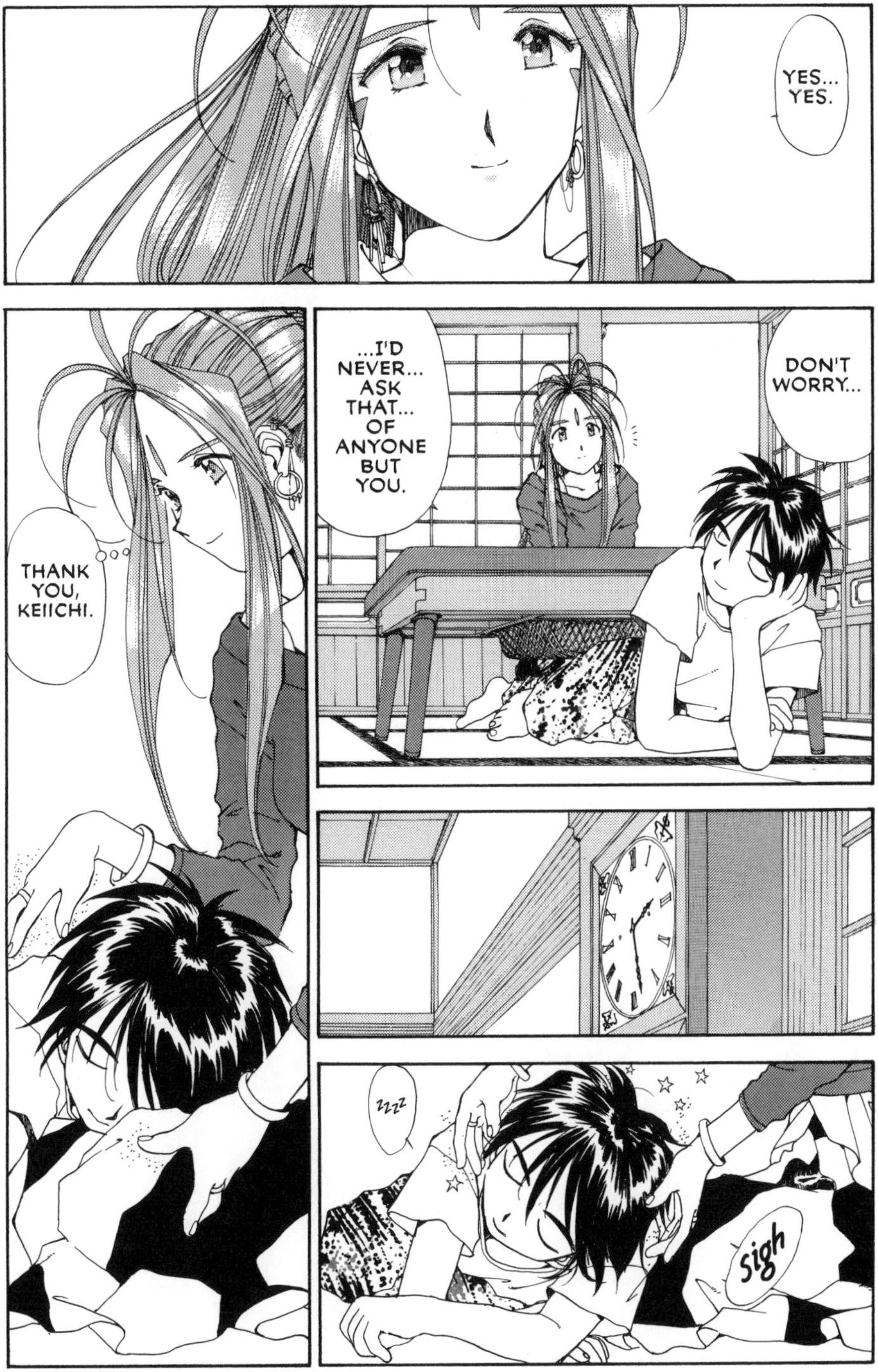
YES... YES.
DON'T WORRY...
...I'D NEVER... ASK THAT... OF ANYONE BUT YOU.
zzzz
sigh
THANK YOU, KEIICHI.

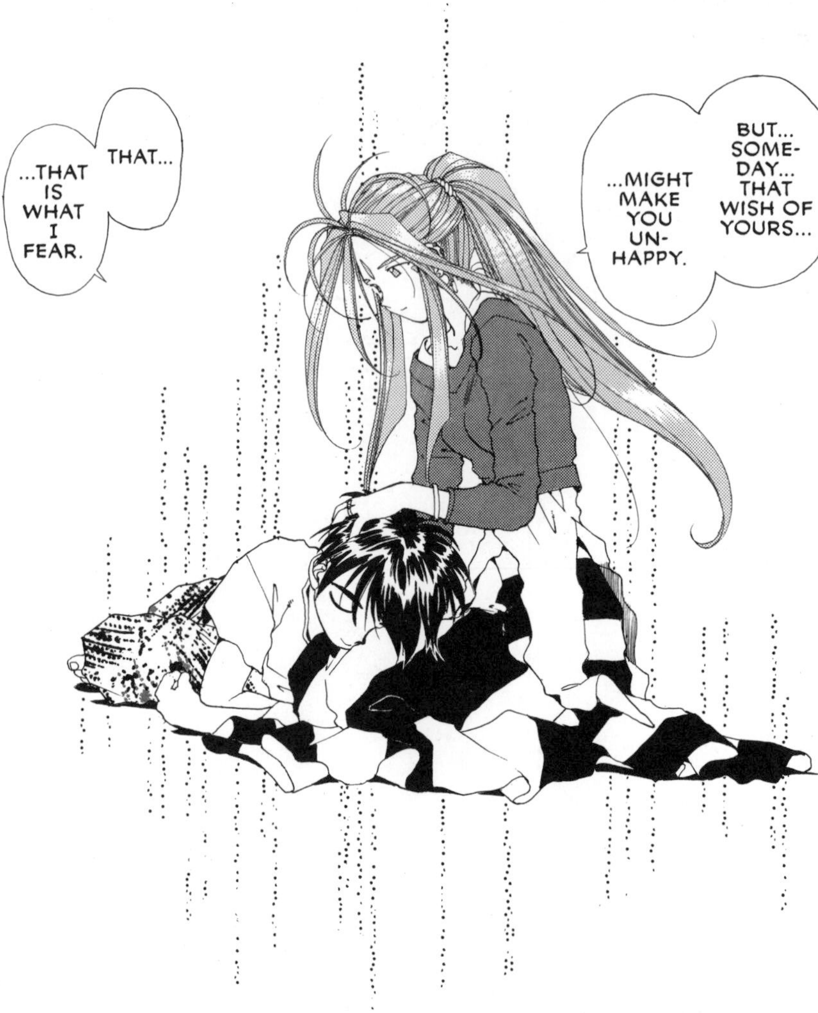
BUT... SOME-DAY... THAT WISH OF YOURS...
...MIGHT MAKE YOU UN-HAPPY.
THAT...
...THAT IS WHAT I FEAR.

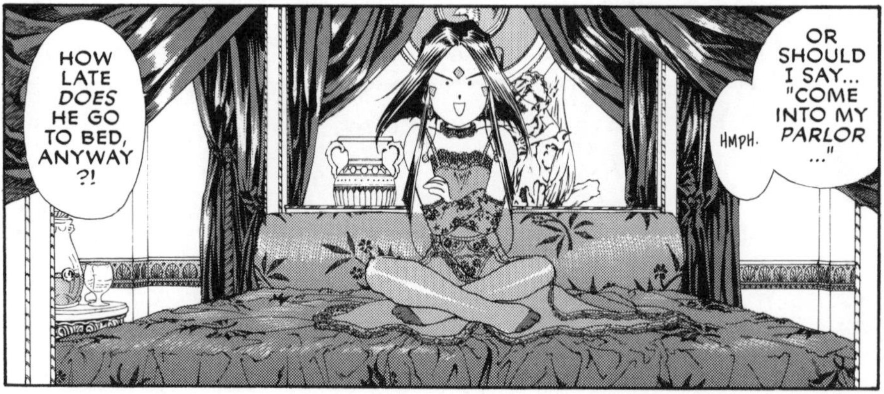
OR SHOULD I SAY... "COME INTO MY *PARLOR* ..."
HMPH.
HOW LATE *DOES* HE GO TO BED, ANYWAY?!

CHAPTER 67

Are You Being Served?

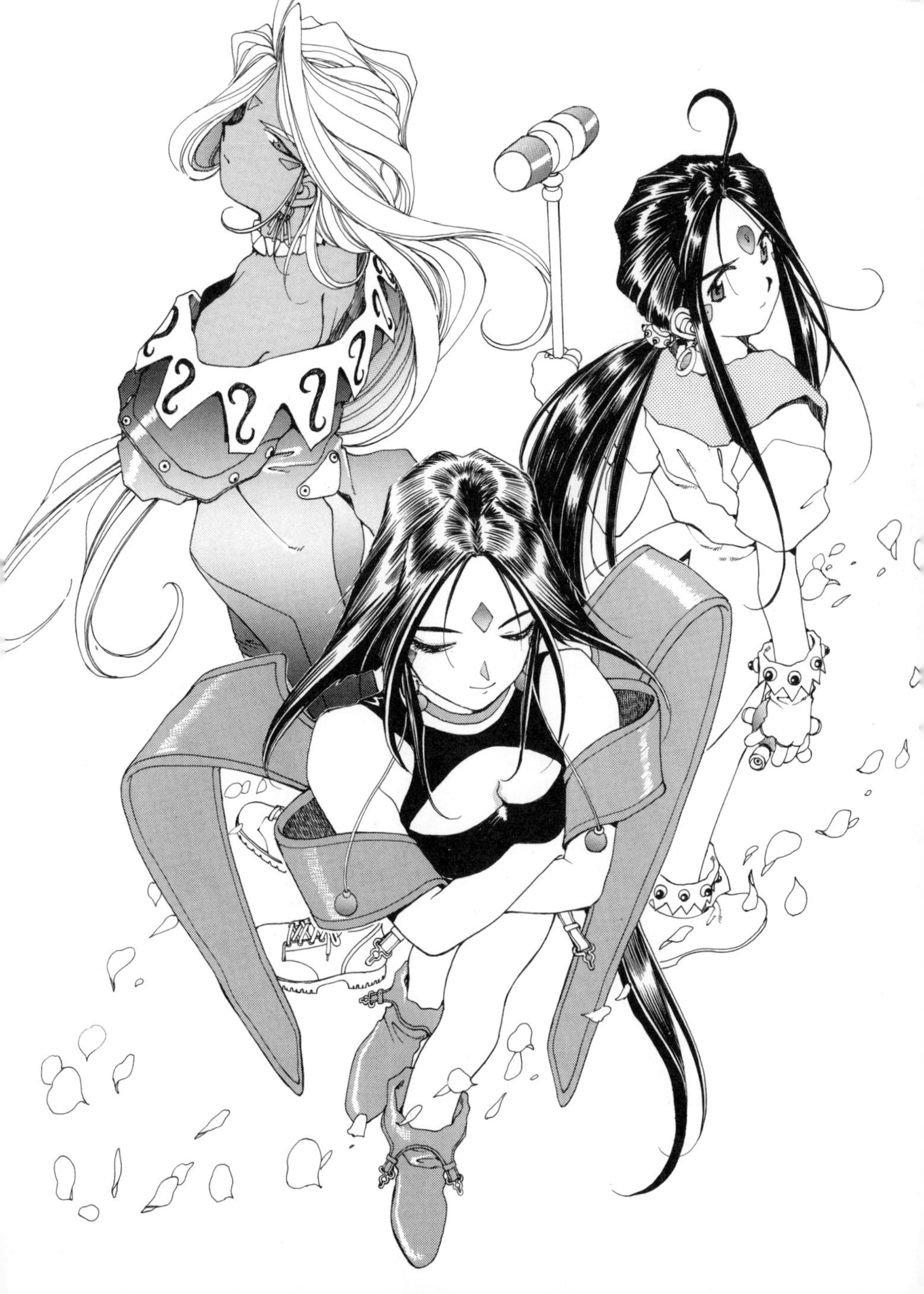

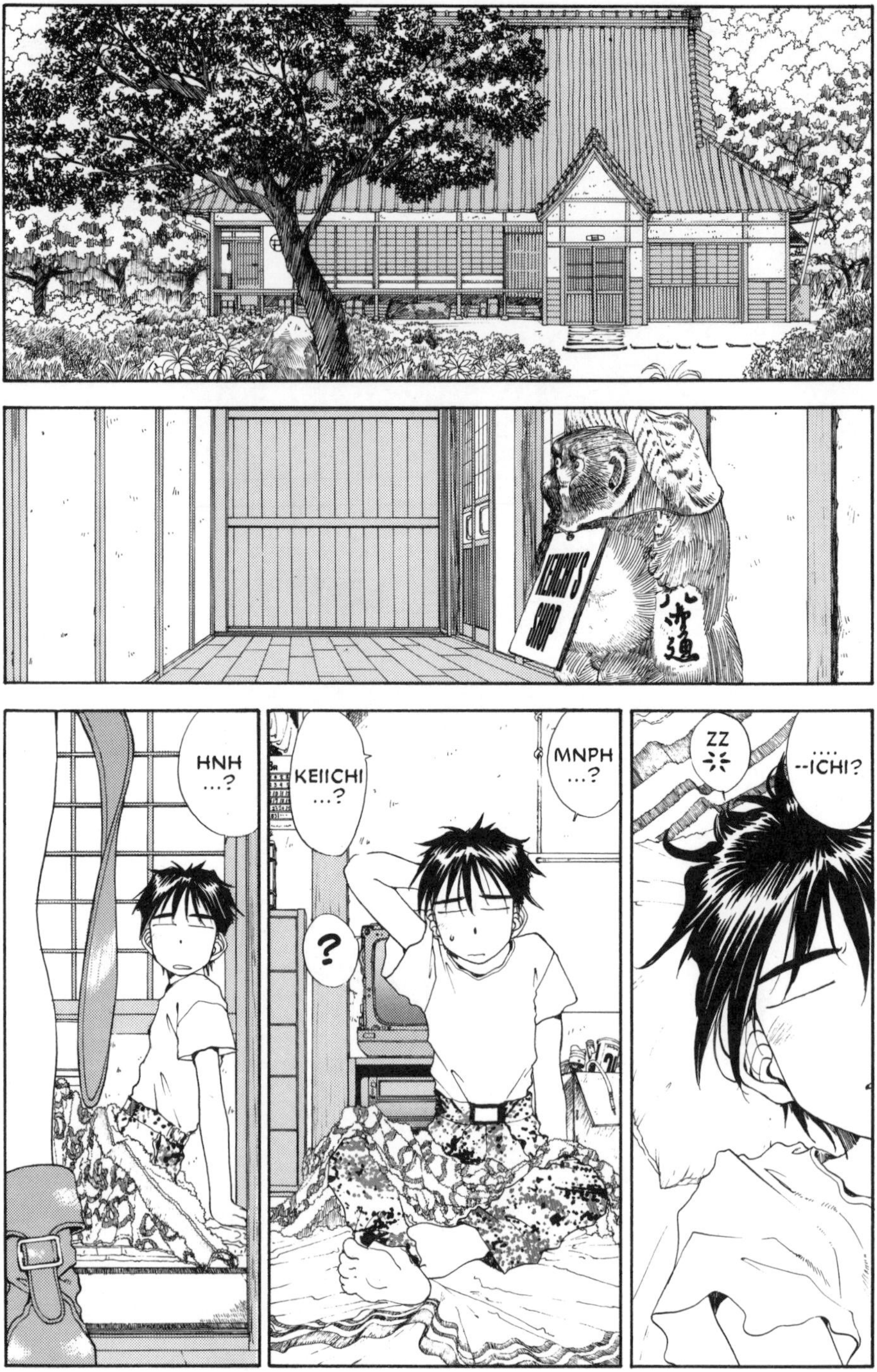
KEIICHI'S SHOP
....
--ICHI?
ZZ
MNPH
...?
KEIICHI
...?
?
HNH
...?

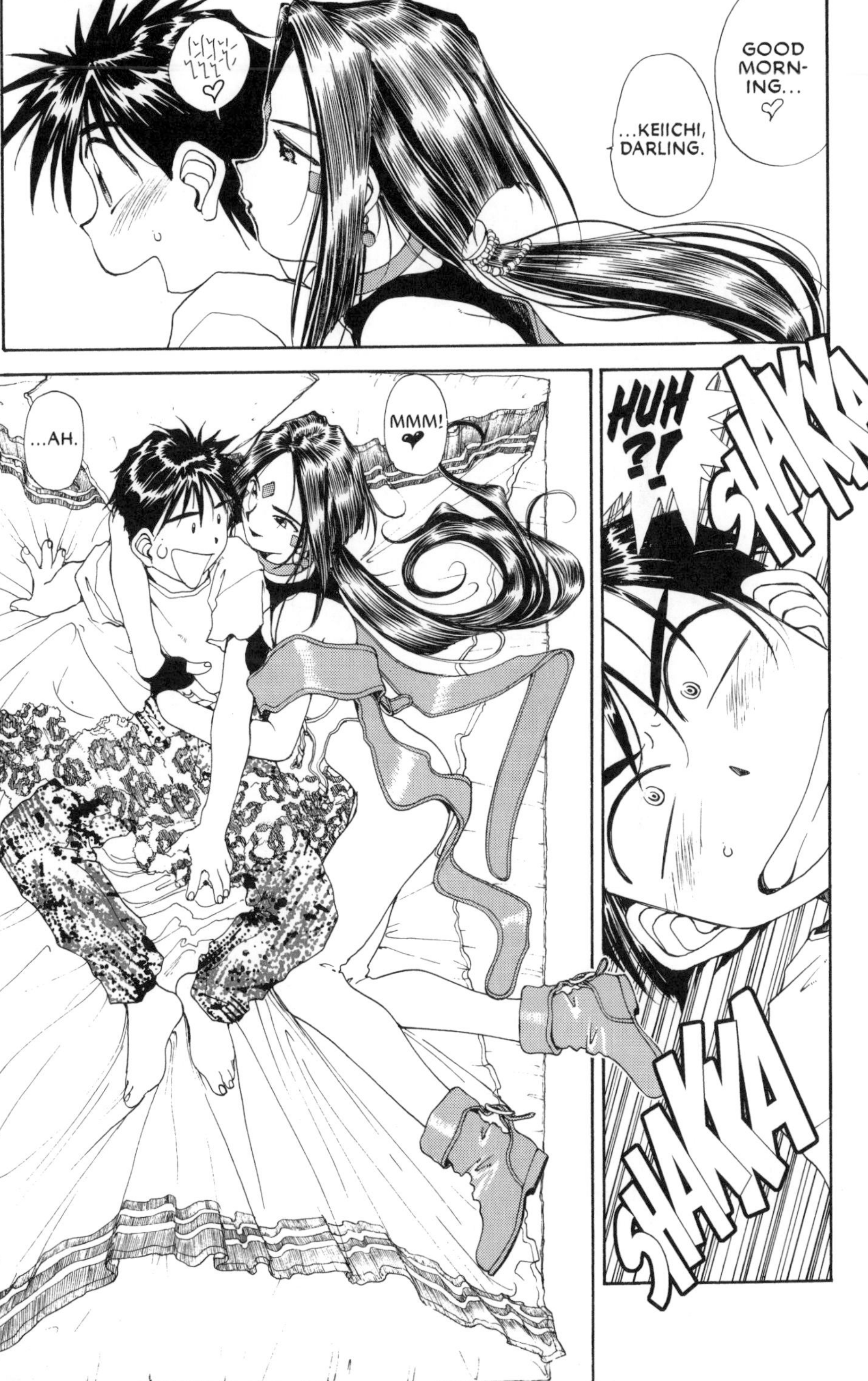
GOOD MORN-ING... ♡
...KEIICHI, DARLING.
HUH ?!
SHAKKA
SHAKKA
MMM! ♥
...AH.

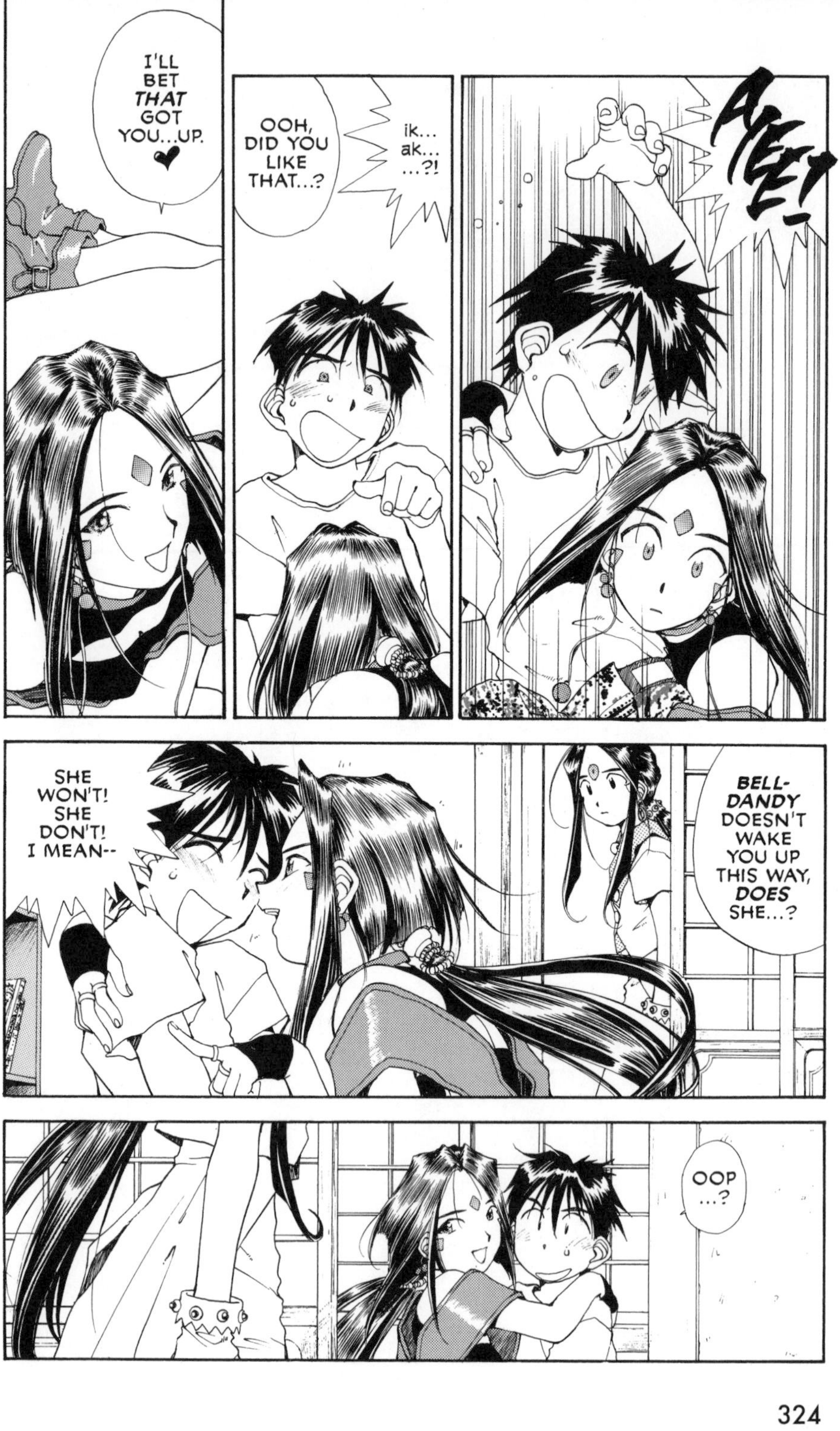
AIEEE!
OOH, DID YOU LIKE THAT...?
ik... ak... ...?!
I'LL BET THAT GOT YOU...UP. ♥
BELL-DANDY DOESN'T WAKE YOU UP THIS WAY, DOES SHE...?
SHE WON'T! SHE DON'T! I MEAN--
OOP ...?

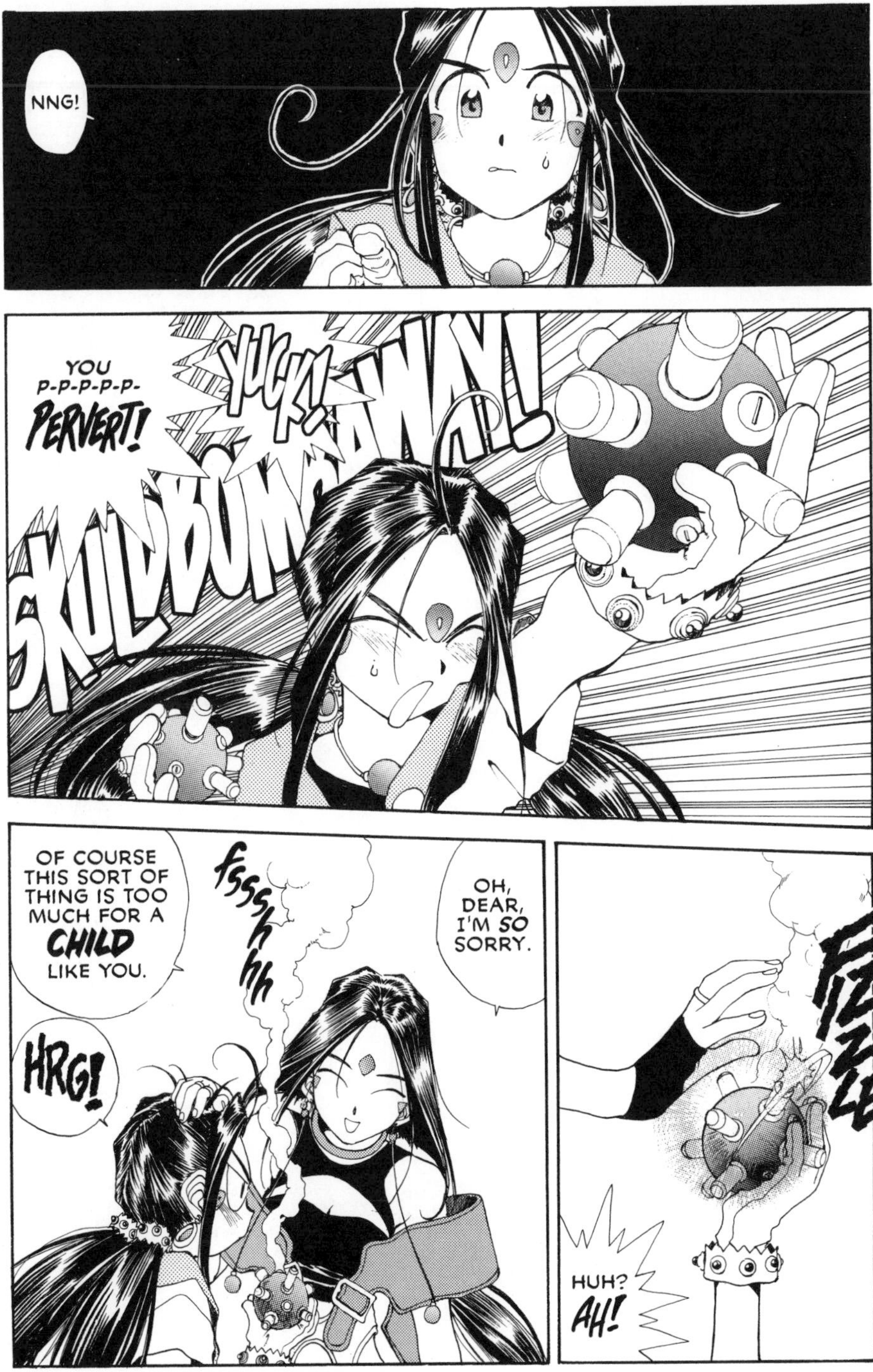
NNG!
YOU P-P-P-P-P-P-PERVERT!
YUCK!
SKULDBOMB
AWAY!
OF COURSE THIS SORT OF THING IS TOO MUCH FOR A CHILD LIKE YOU.
fssshhh
OH, DEAR, I'M SO SORRY.
HRG!
FIZZZLE
HUH? AH!

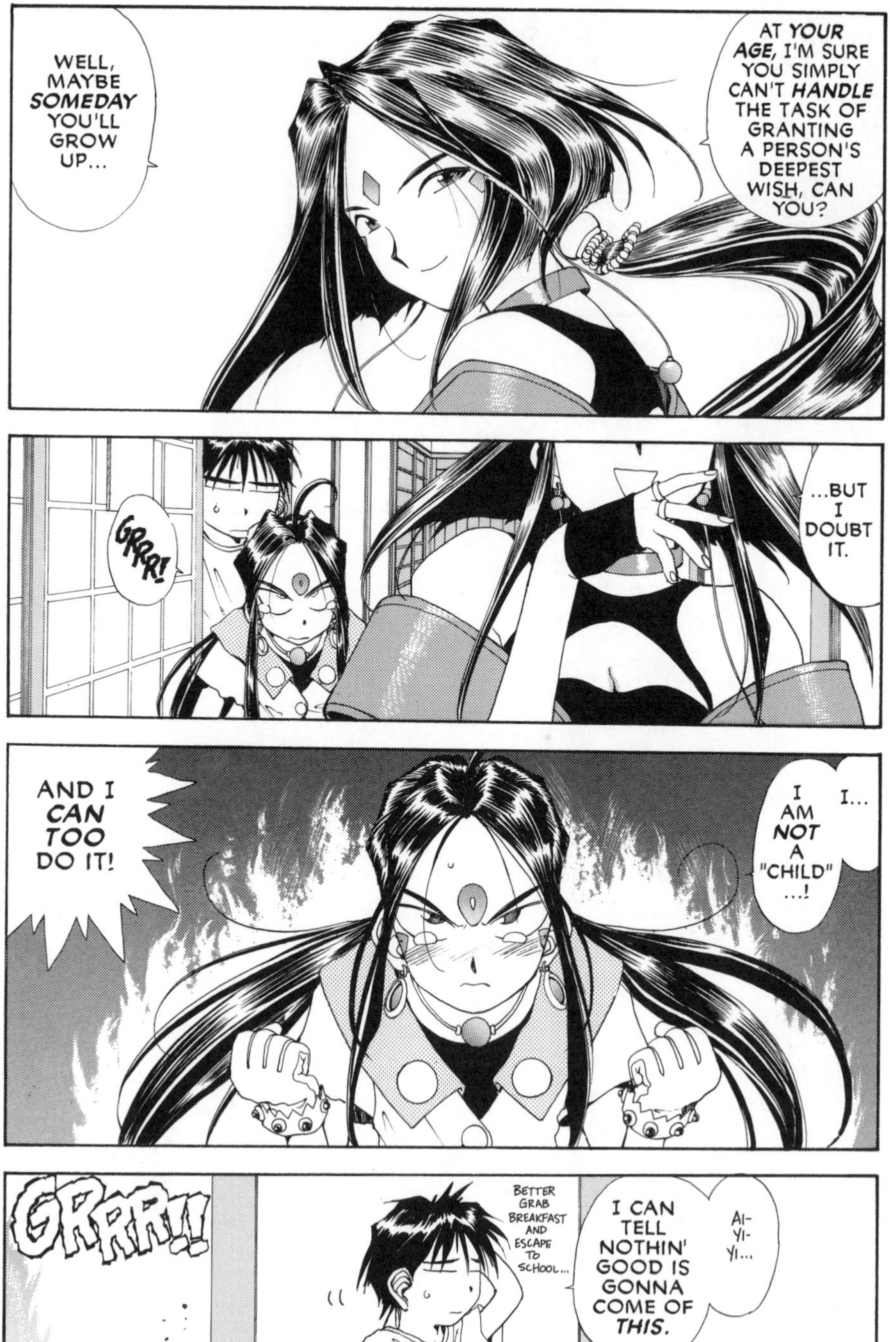
AT YOUR AGE, I'M SURE YOU SIMPLY CAN'T HANDLE THE TASK OF GRANTING A PERSON'S DEEPEST WISH, CAN YOU?
WELL, MAYBE SOMEDAY YOU'LL GROW UP...
...BUT I DOUBT IT.
GRRR!
I...
I AM NOT A "CHILD" ...!
AND I CAN TOO DO IT!
AI-YI-YI...
I CAN TELL NOTHIN' GOOD IS GONNA COME OF THIS.
BETTER GRAB BREAKFAST AND ESCAPE TO SCHOOL...
GRRR!!

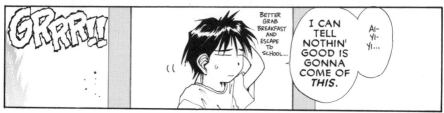

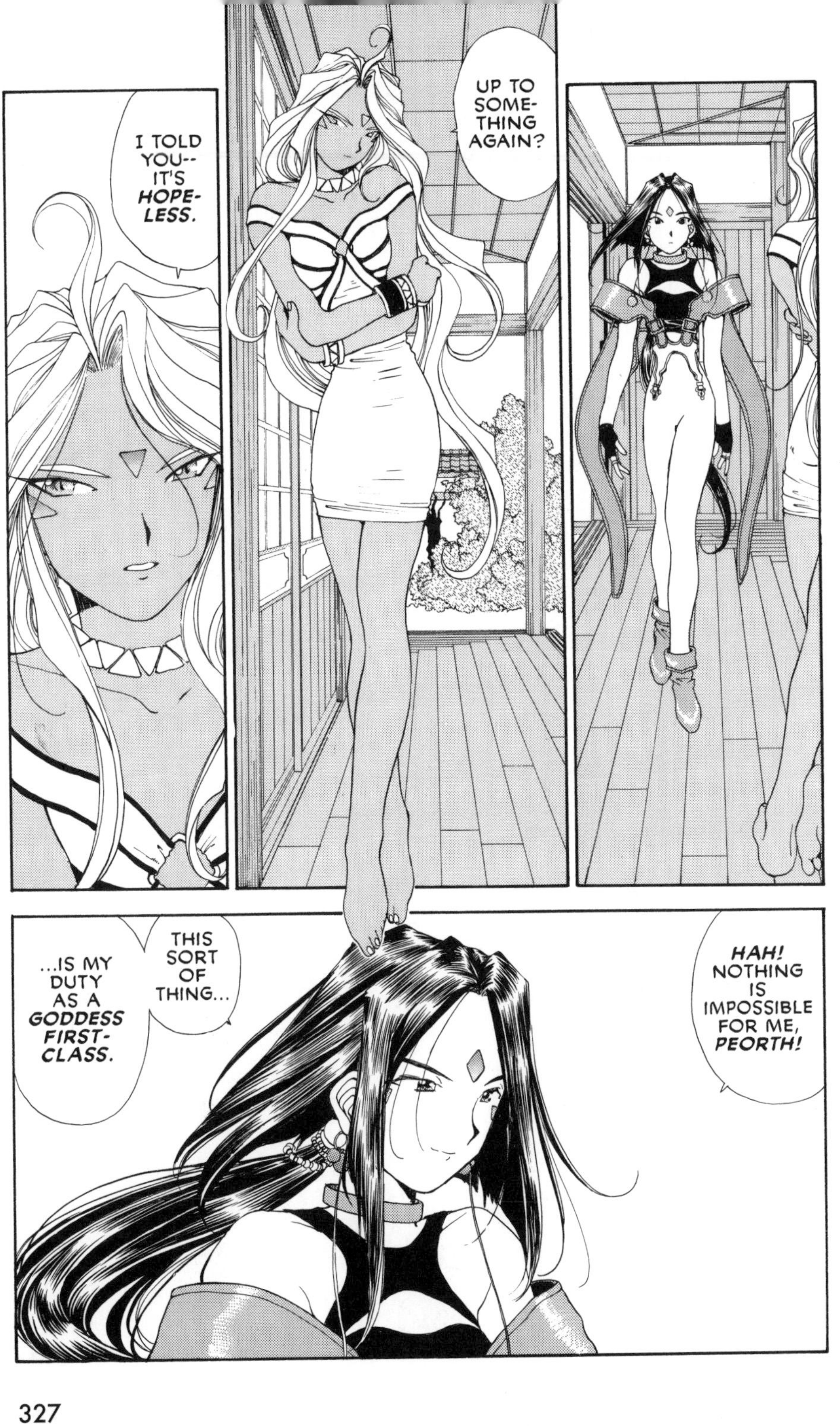
UP TO SOME-THING AGAIN?
I TOLD YOU-- IT'S *HOPE-LESS.*
HAH! NOTHING IS IMPOSSIBLE FOR ME, *PEORTH!*
THIS SORT OF THING...
...IS MY DUTY AS A *GODDESS FIRST-CLASS.*

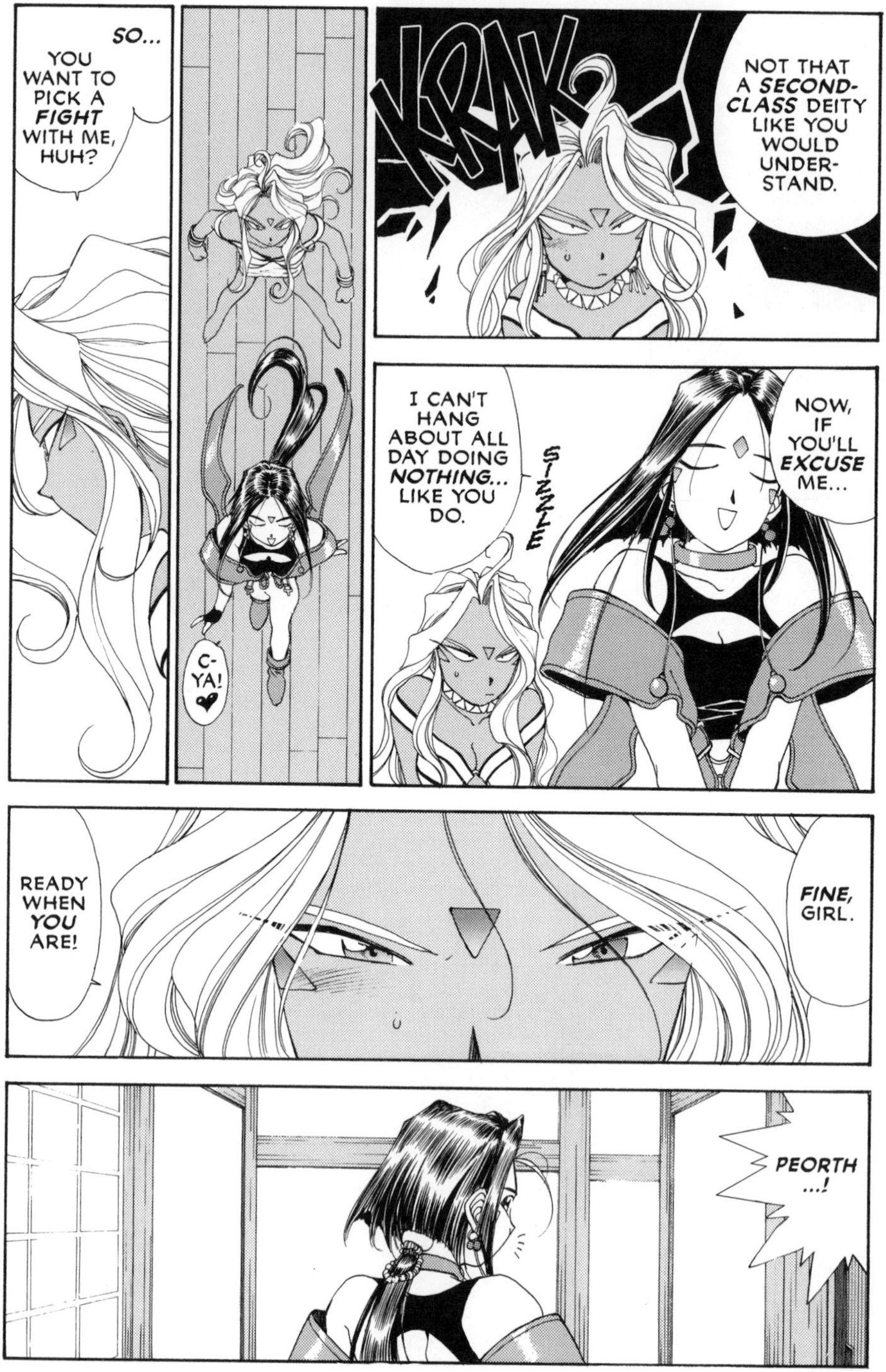
KRAK
NOT THAT A **SECOND-CLASS** DEITY LIKE YOU WOULD UNDER-STAND.
NOW, IF YOU'LL **EXCUSE** ME...
I CAN'T HANG ABOUT ALL DAY DOING **NOTHING**... LIKE YOU DO.
SIZZLE
C-YA! ❤
SO...
YOU WANT TO PICK A **FIGHT** WITH ME, HUH?
FINE, GIRL.
READY WHEN **YOU** ARE!
PEORTH ...!

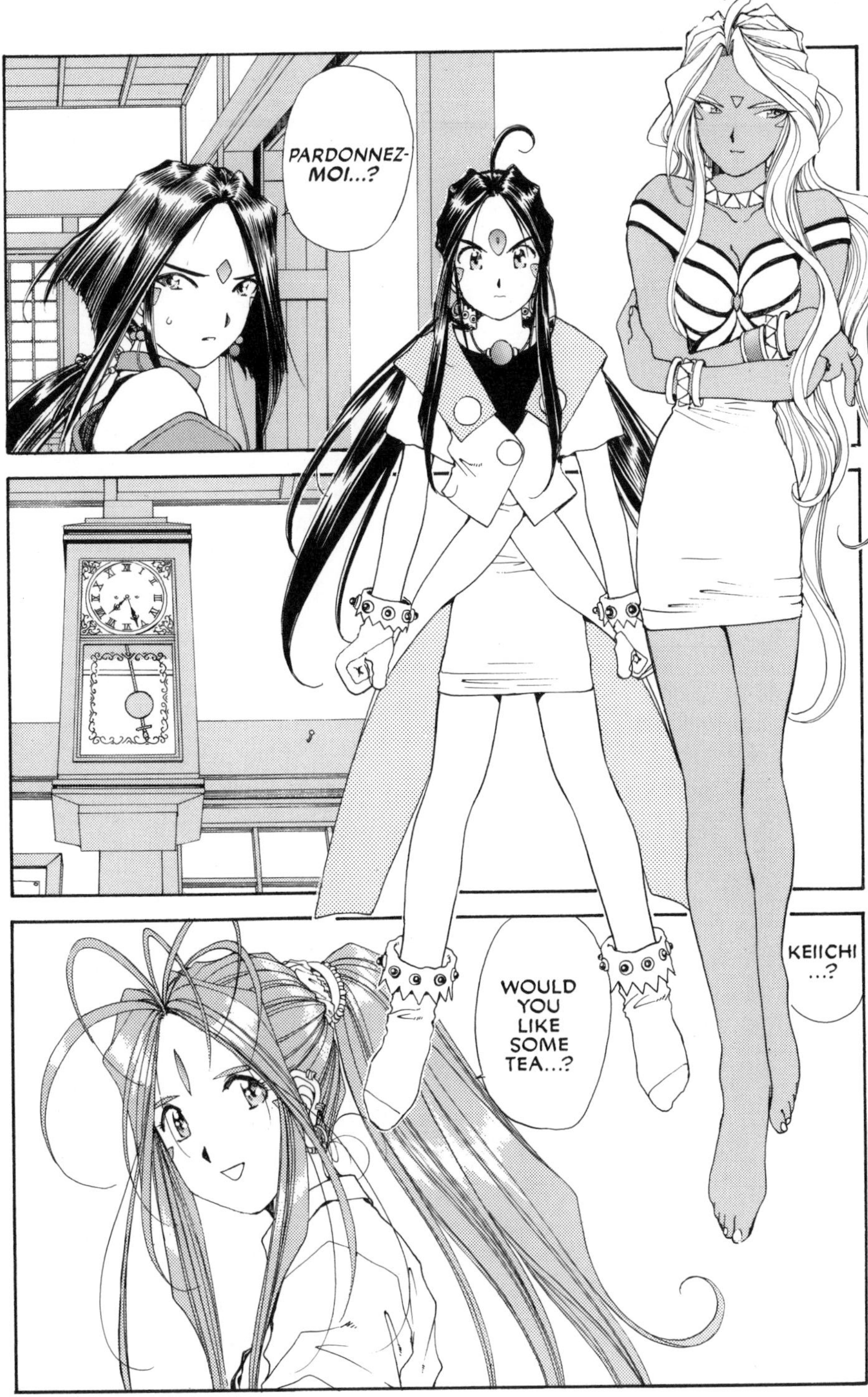
PARDONNEZ-MOI...?
KEIICHI ...?
WOULD YOU LIKE SOME TEA...?

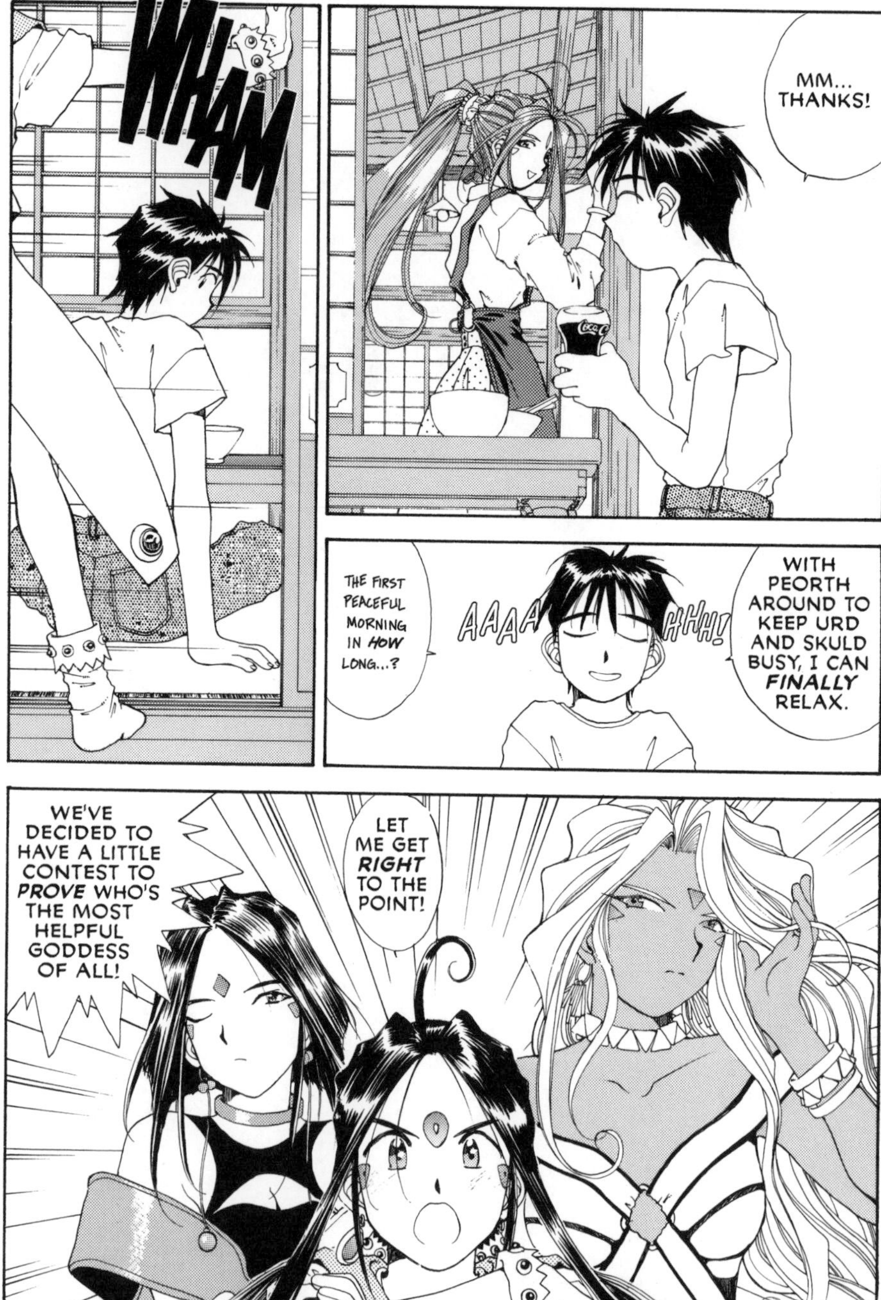
MM... THANKS!
WITH PEORTH AROUND TO KEEP URD AND SKULD BUSY, I CAN *FINALLY* RELAX.
AAAAHHHH!
THE FIRST PEACEFUL MORNING IN *HOW* LONG...?
WHAM
LET ME GET *RIGHT* TO THE POINT!
WE'VE DECIDED TO HAVE A LITTLE CONTEST TO *PROVE* WHO'S THE MOST HELPFUL GODDESS OF ALL!

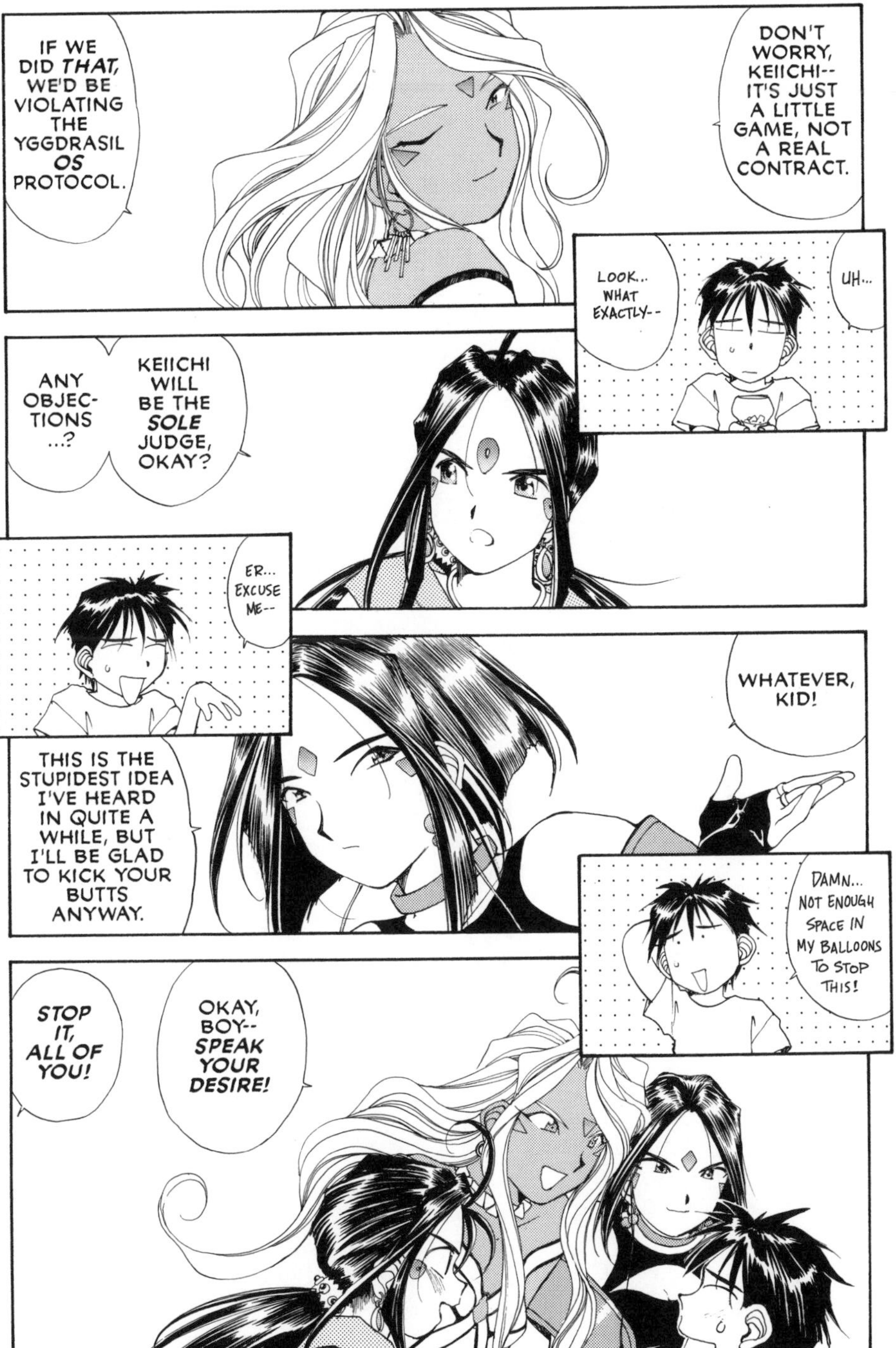
DON'T WORRY, KEIICHI-- IT'S JUST A LITTLE GAME, NOT A REAL CONTRACT.
IF WE DID *THAT,* WE'D BE VIOLATING THE YGGDRASIL *OS* PROTOCOL.
UH...
LOOK... WHAT EXACTLY--
KEIICHI WILL BE THE *SOLE* JUDGE, OKAY?
ANY OBJECTIONS ...?
ER... EXCUSE ME--
WHATEVER, KID!
THIS IS THE STUPIDEST IDEA I'VE HEARD IN QUITE A WHILE, BUT I'LL BE GLAD TO KICK YOUR BUTTS ANYWAY.
DAMN... NOT ENOUGH SPACE IN MY BALLOONS TO STOP THIS!
OKAY, BOY-- *SPEAK YOUR DESIRE!*
STOP IT, ALL OF YOU!

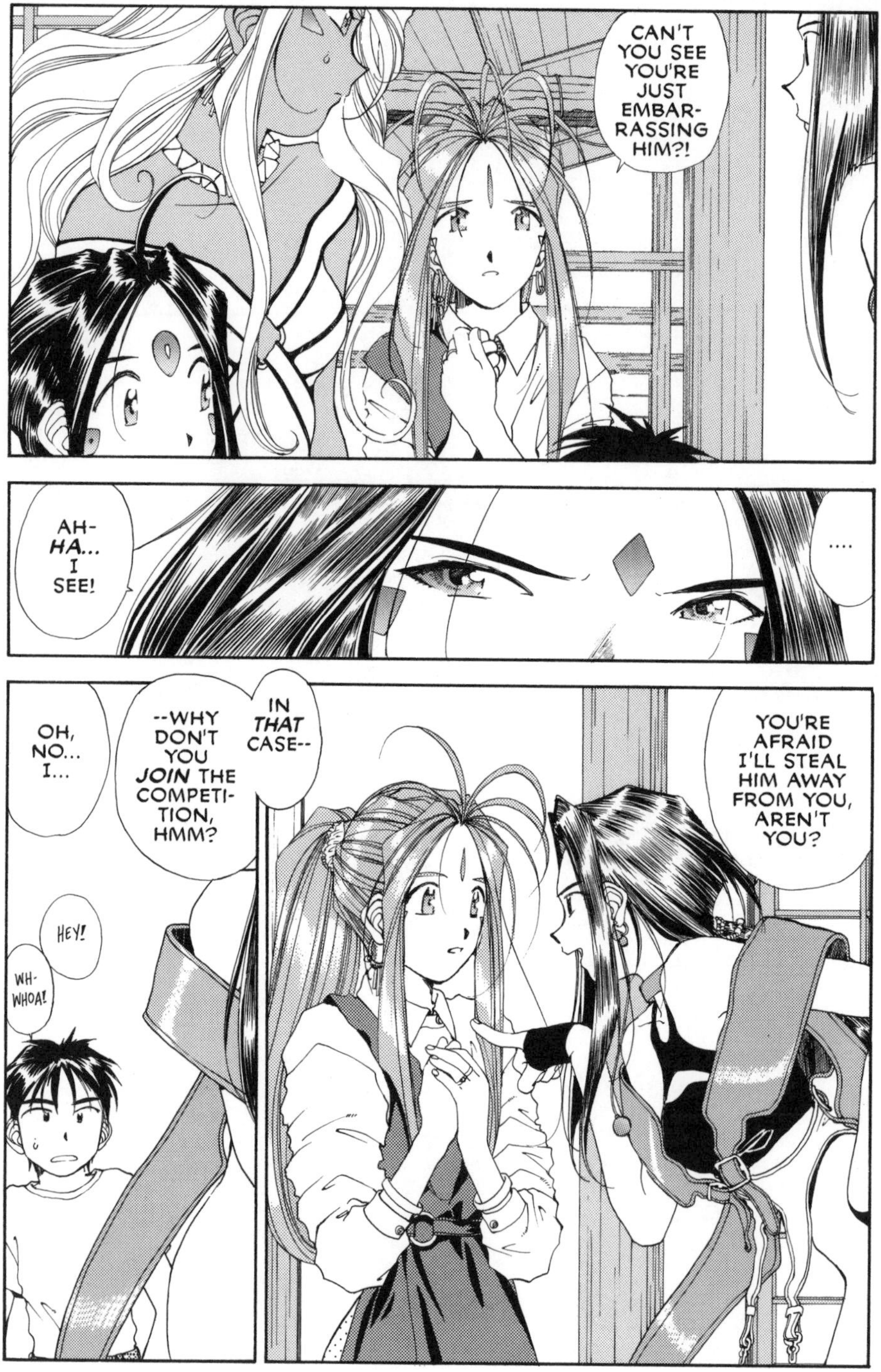

CAN'T YOU SEE YOU'RE JUST EMBARRASSING HIM?!
....
AH-*HA*... I SEE!
YOU'RE AFRAID I'LL STEAL HIM AWAY FROM YOU, AREN'T YOU?
IN *THAT* CASE--
--WHY DON'T YOU *JOIN* THE COMPETITION, HMM?
OH, NO... I...
HEY!
WH-WHOA!

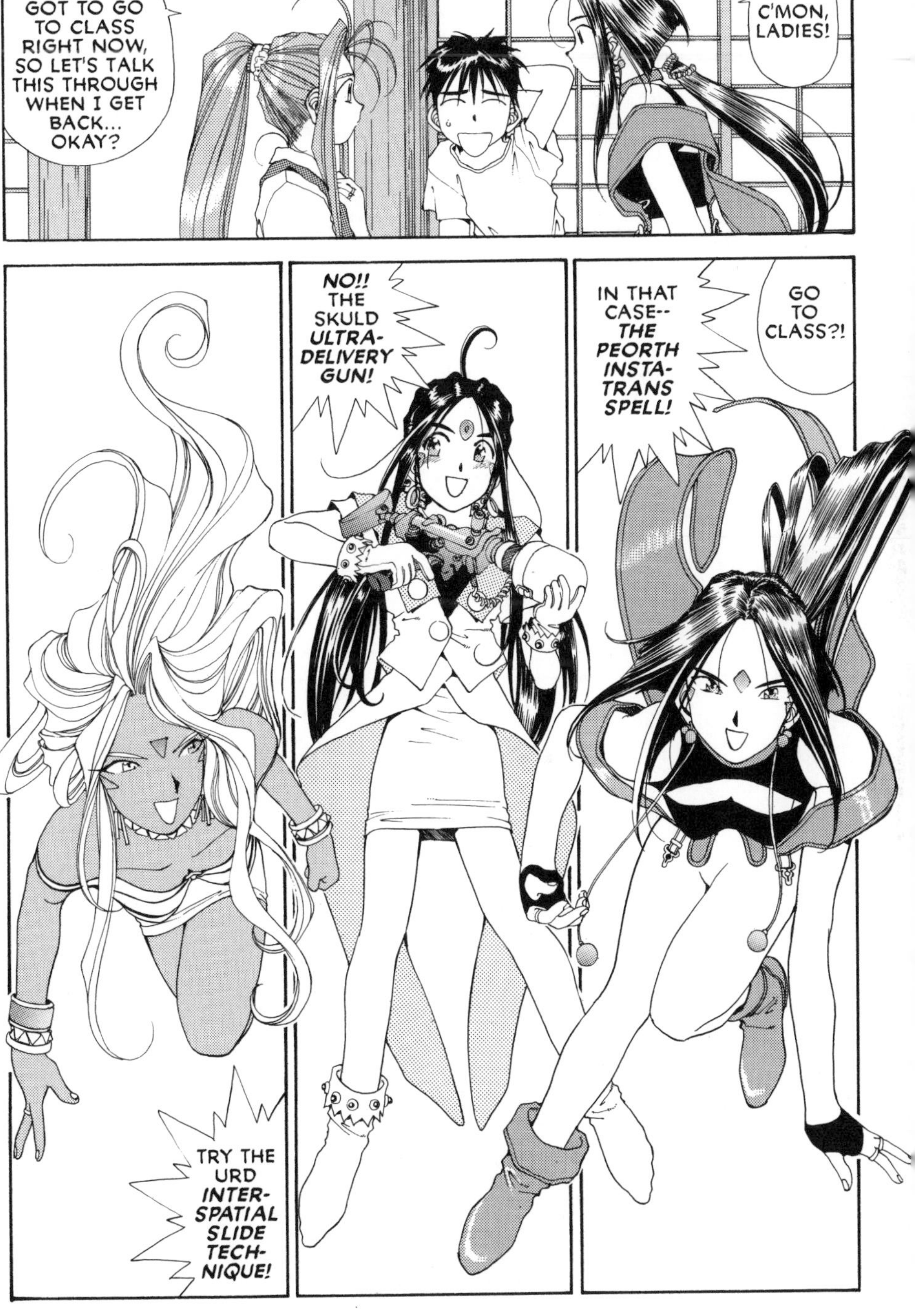
C'MON, LADIES!
LOOK--I'VE GOT TO GO TO CLASS RIGHT NOW, SO LET'S TALK THIS THROUGH WHEN I GET BACK... OKAY?
GO TO CLASS?!
IN THAT CASE-- *THE PEORTH INSTA-TRANS SPELL!*
NO!! THE SKULD *ULTRA-DELIVERY GUN!*
TRY THE URD *INTER-SPATIAL SLIDE TECHNIQUE!*

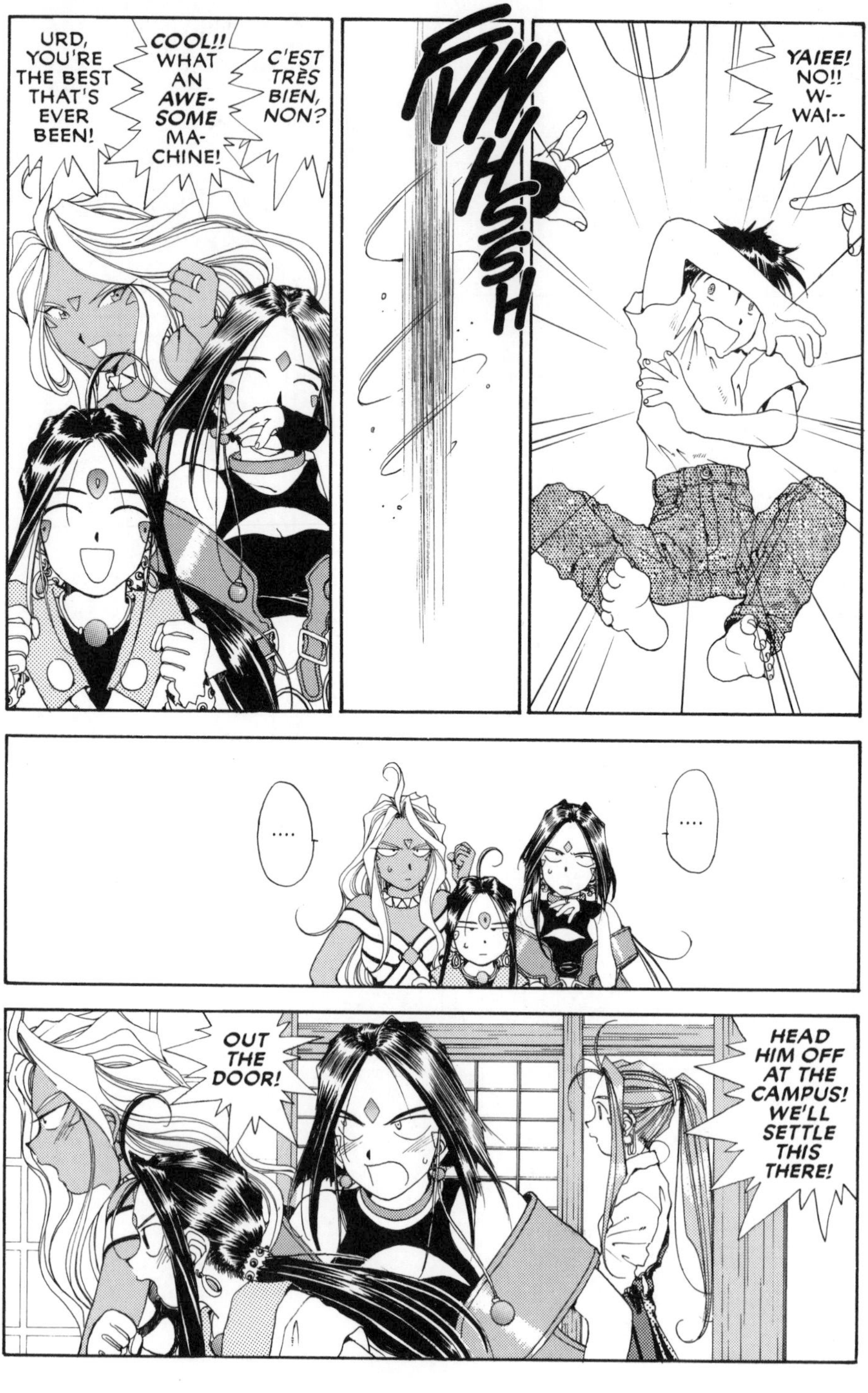
YAIEE! NO!! W-WAI--
FWHSSH
C'EST TRÈS BIEN, NON?
COOL!! WHAT AN AWESOME MACHINE!
URD, YOU'RE THE BEST THAT'S EVER BEEN!
....
....
HEAD HIM OFF AT THE CAMPUS! WE'LL SETTLE THIS THERE!
OUT THE DOOR!

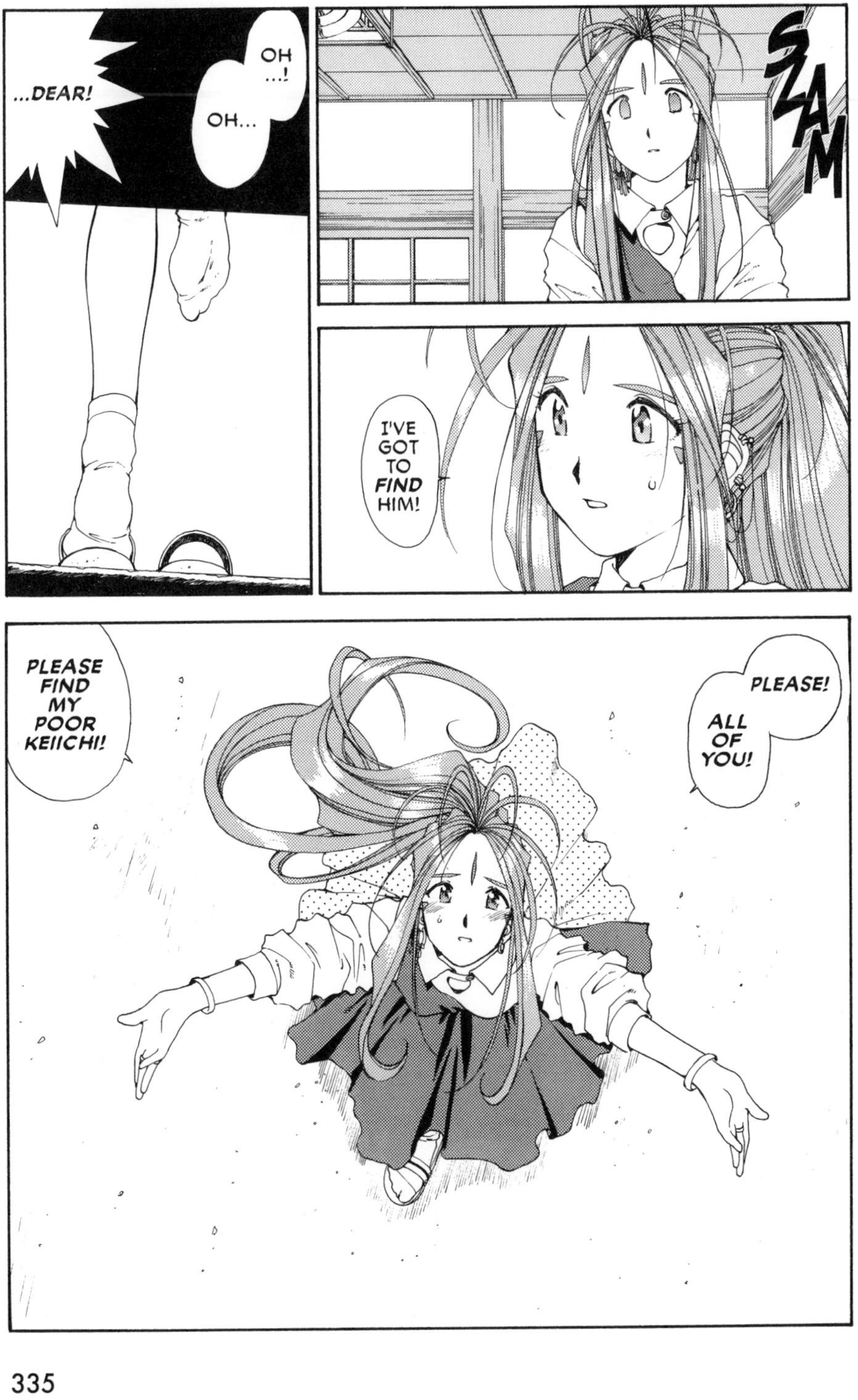
SLAM
I'VE GOT TO FIND HIM!
OH ...!
OH...
...DEAR!
PLEASE!
ALL OF YOU!
PLEASE FIND MY POOR KEIICHI!

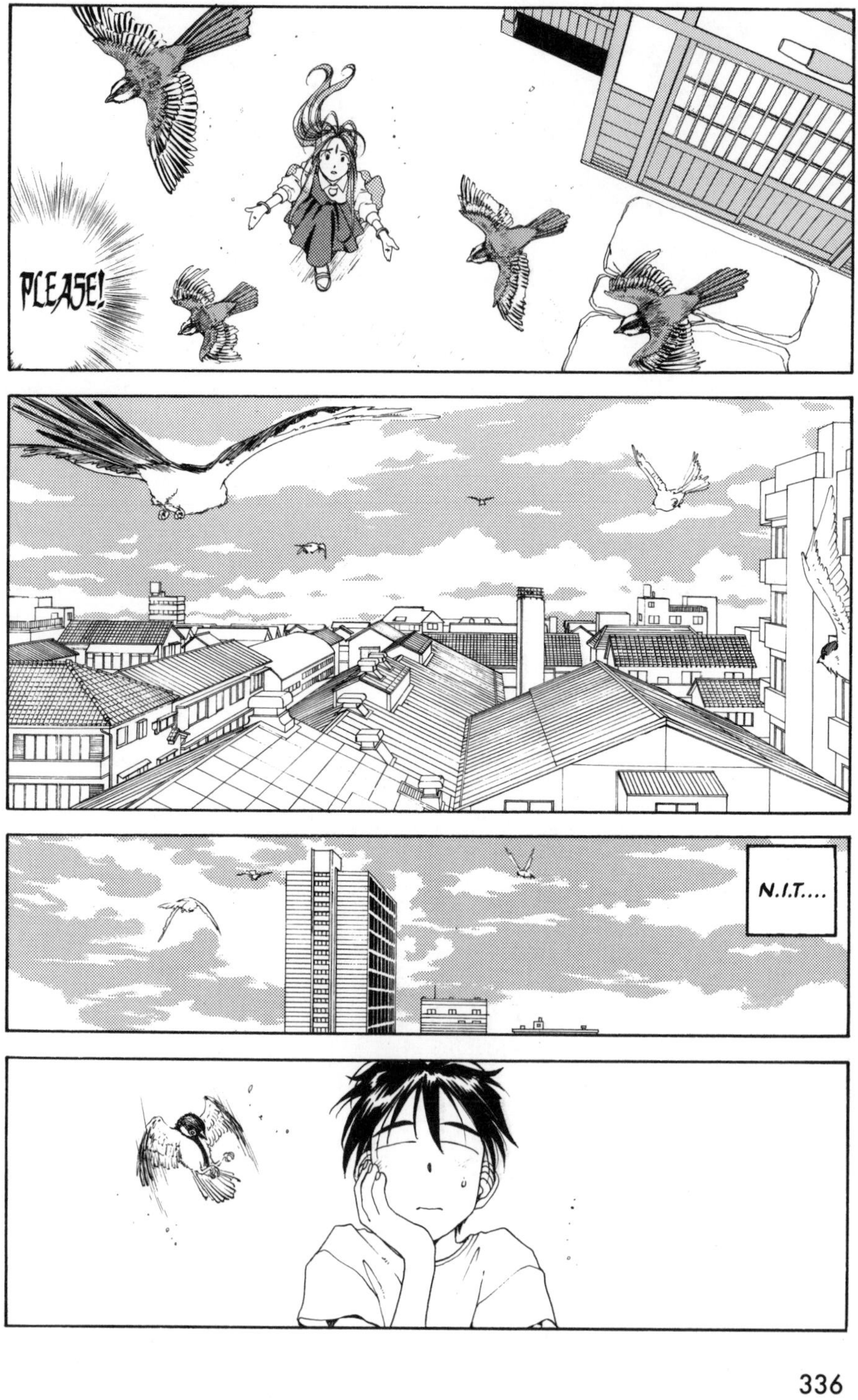
PLEASE!
N.I.T....

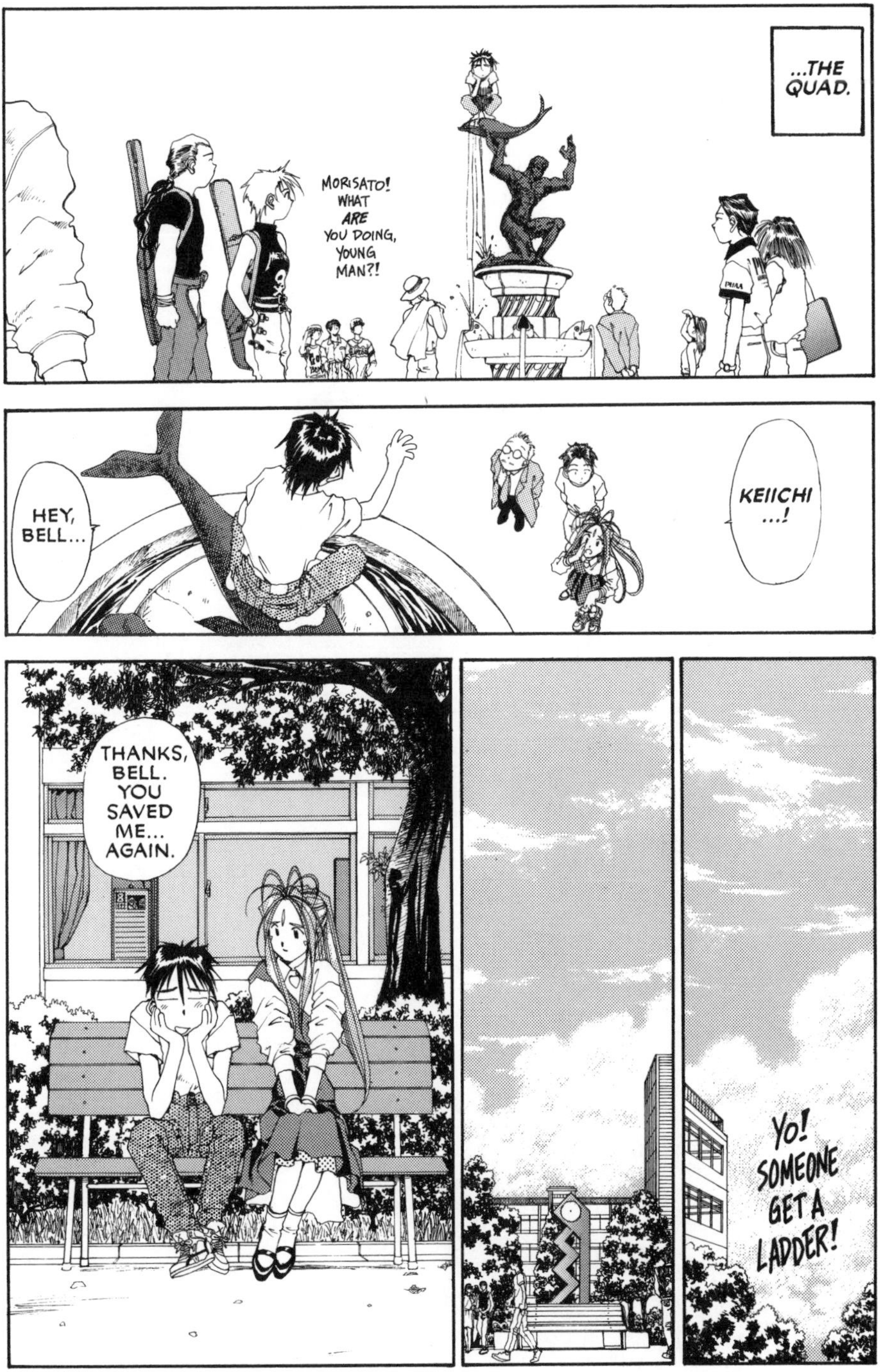
...THE QUAD.
MORISATO! WHAT ARE YOU DOING, YOUNG MAN?!
KEIICHI ...!
HEY, BELL...
YO! SOMEONE GET A LADDER!
THANKS, BELL. YOU SAVED ME... AGAIN.

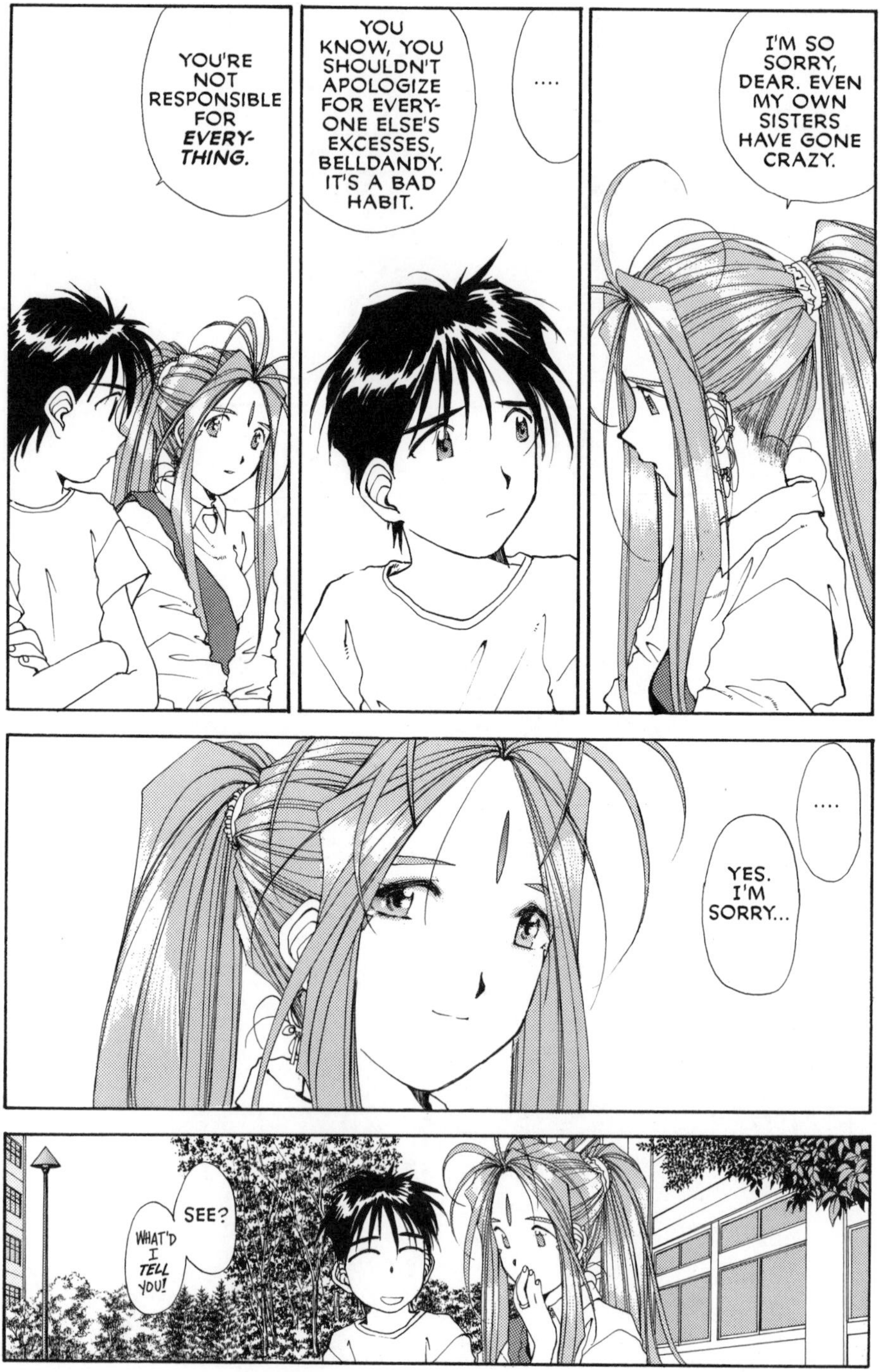
I'M SO SORRY, DEAR. EVEN MY OWN SISTERS HAVE GONE CRAZY.
....
YOU KNOW, YOU SHOULDN'T APOLOGIZE FOR EVERY-ONE ELSE'S EXCESSES, BELLDANDY. IT'S A BAD HABIT.
YOU'RE NOT RESPONSIBLE FOR *EVERY-THING.*
....
YES. I'M SORRY...
SEE?
WHAT'D I *TELL* YOU!

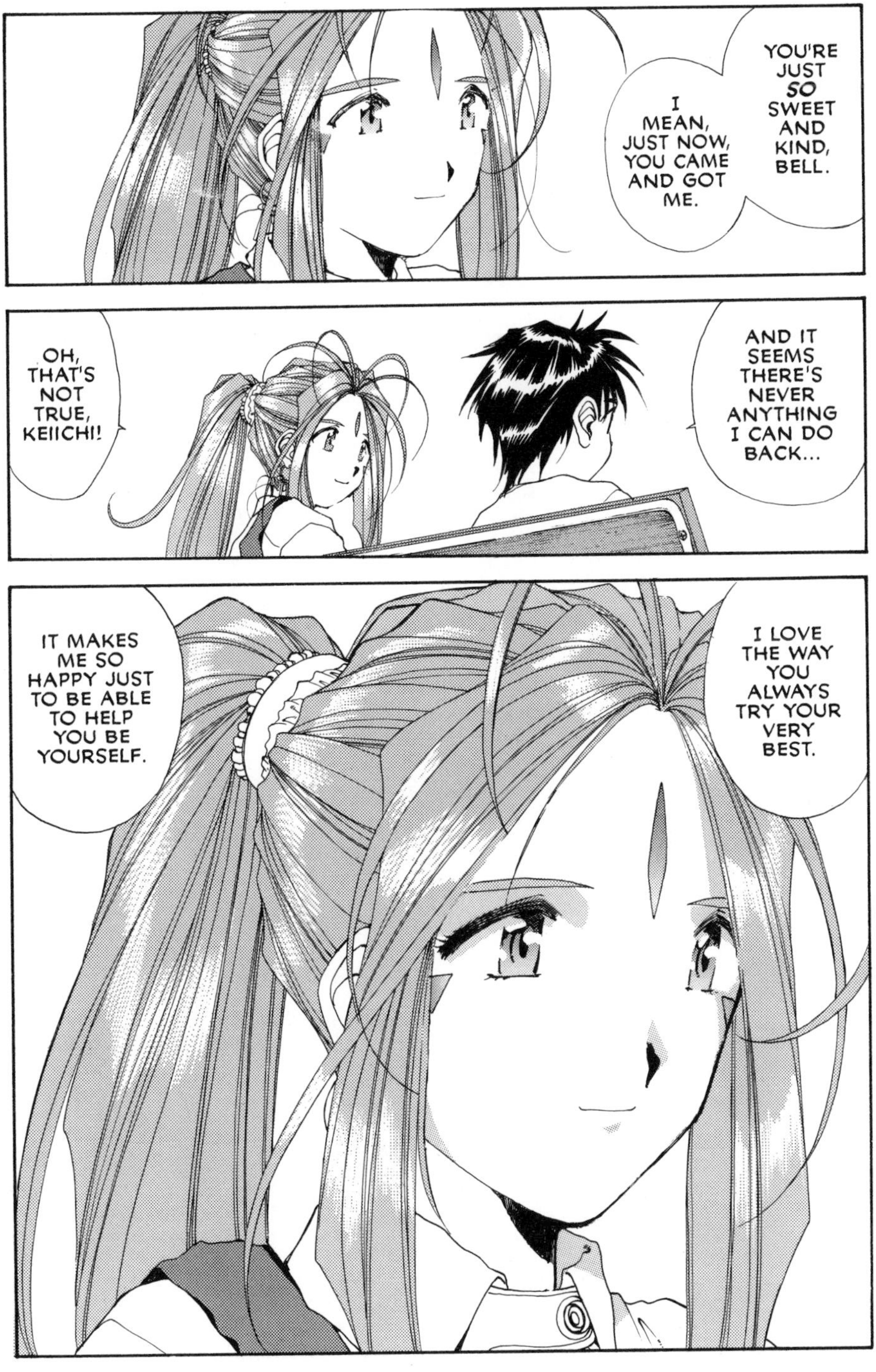
YOU'RE JUST *SO* SWEET AND KIND, BELL.
I MEAN, JUST NOW, YOU CAME AND GOT ME.
AND IT SEEMS THERE'S NEVER ANYTHING I CAN DO BACK...
OH, THAT'S NOT TRUE, KEIICHI!
I LOVE THE WAY YOU ALWAYS TRY YOUR VERY BEST.
IT MAKES ME SO HAPPY JUST TO BE ABLE TO HELP YOU BE YOURSELF.

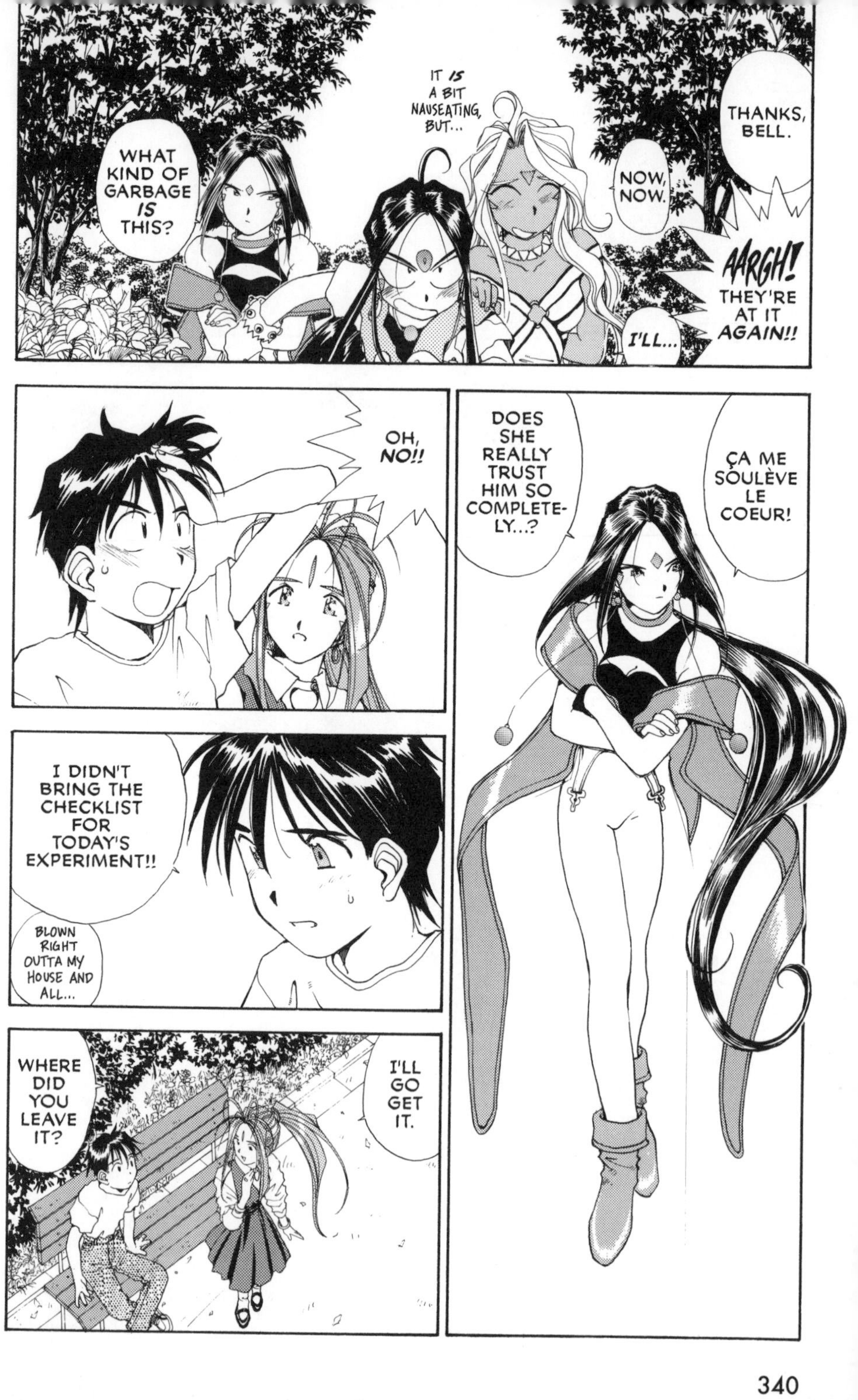
THANKS, BELL.
AARGH! THEY'RE AT IT AGAIN!!
I'LL...
NOW, NOW.
IT IS A BIT NAUSEATING, BUT...
WHAT KIND OF GARBAGE IS THIS?
ÇA ME SOULÈVE LE COEUR!
DOES SHE REALLY TRUST HIM SO COMPLETE-LY...?
OH, NO!!
I DIDN'T BRING THE CHECKLIST FOR TODAY'S EXPERIMENT!!
BLOWN RIGHT OUTTA MY HOUSE AND ALL...
I'LL GO GET IT.
WHERE DID YOU LEAVE IT?

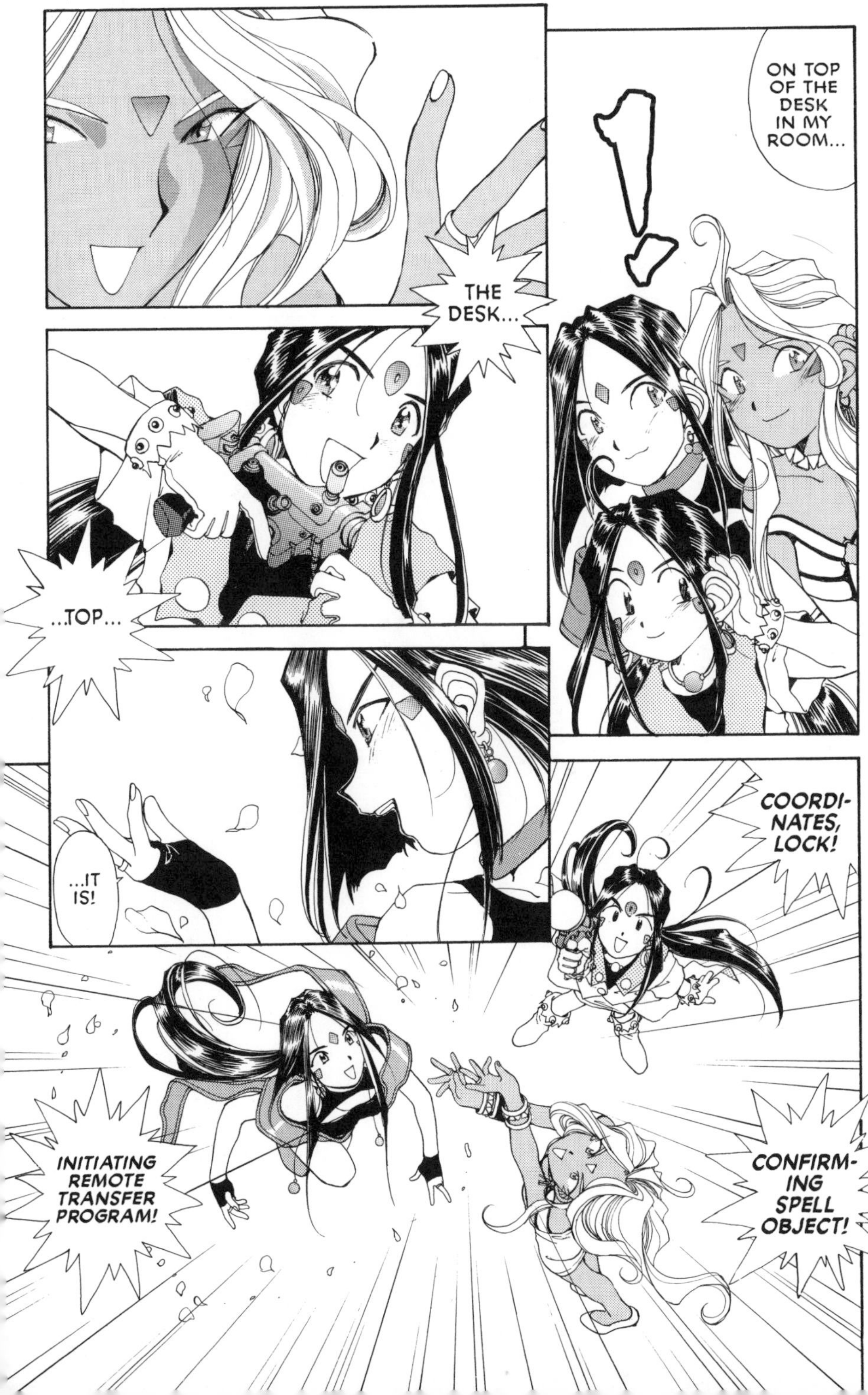
ON TOP OF THE DESK IN MY ROOM...
THE DESK...
...TOP...
...IT IS!
COORDI-NATES, LOCK!
CONFIRM-ING SPELL OBJECT!
INITIATING REMOTE TRANSFER PROGRAM!

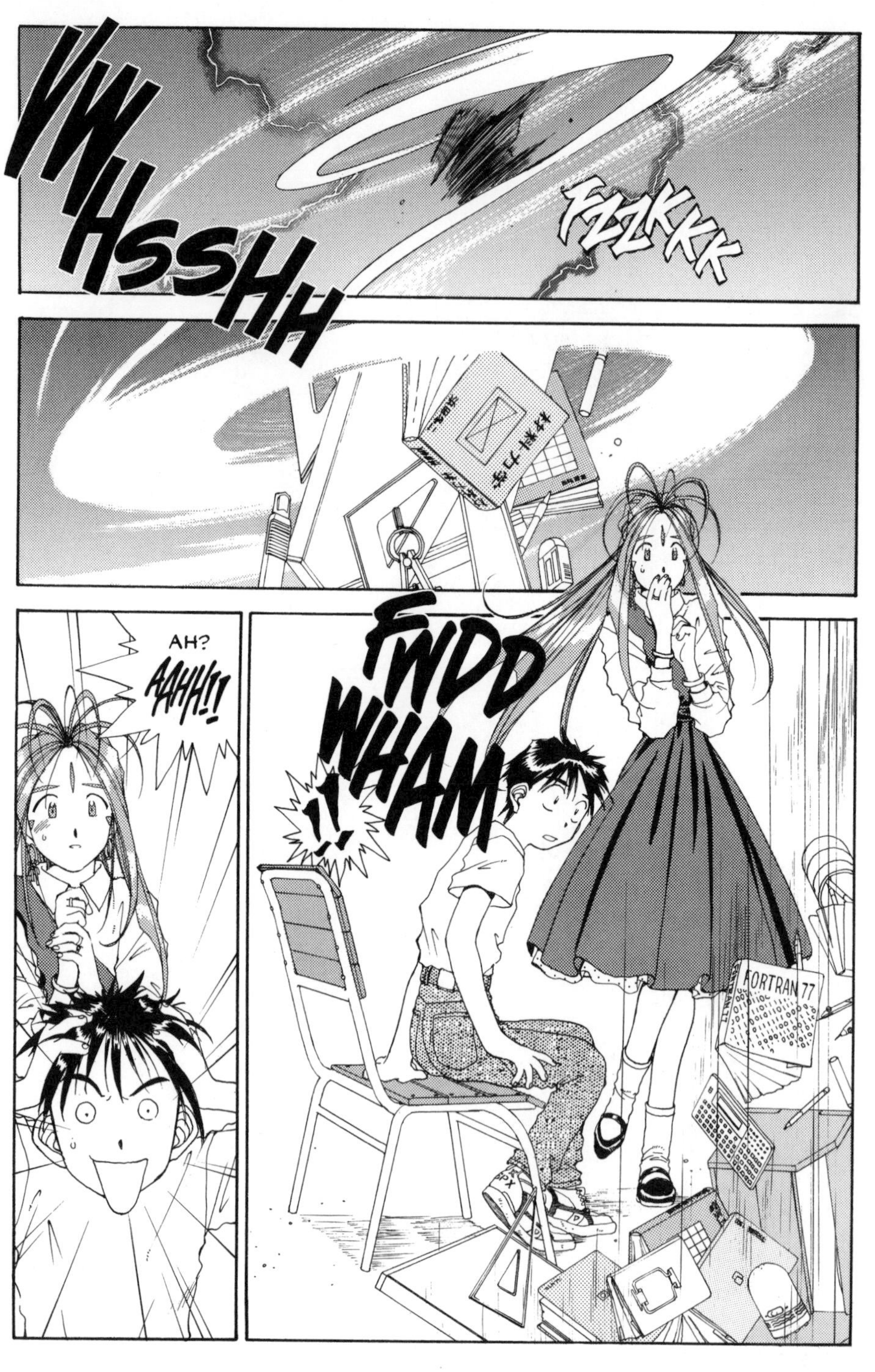
FZZKKK
VWHSSHH
FWDD
WHAM
!!
FORTRAN 77
AH?
AAHH!!

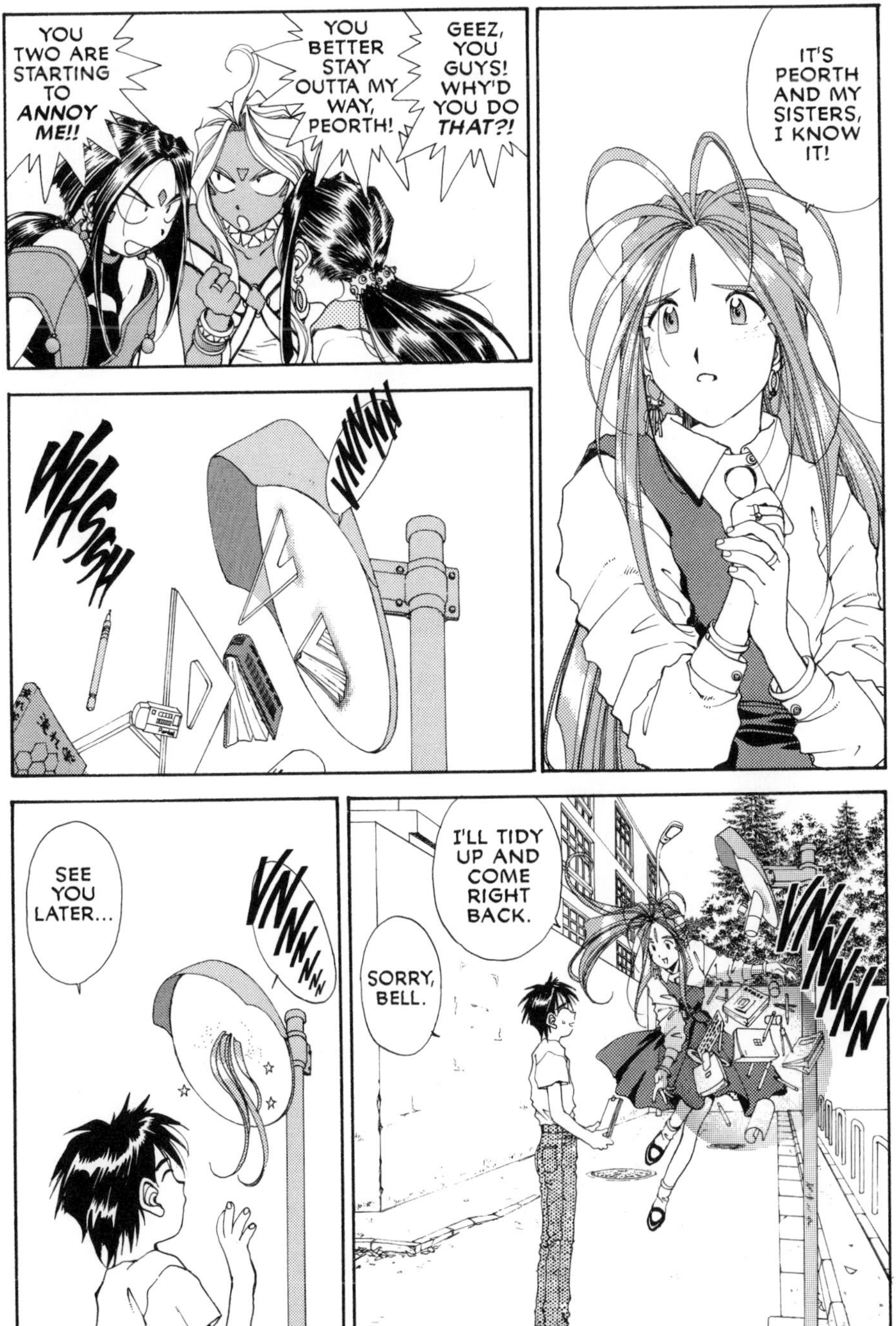
IT'S PEORTH AND MY SISTERS, I KNOW IT!
GEEZ, YOU GUYS! WHY'D YOU DO *THAT?!*
YOU BETTER STAY OUTTA MY WAY, PEORTH!
YOU TWO ARE STARTING TO *ANNOY ME!!*
VNNNNN
WHSSH
VNNNNNNN
I'LL TIDY UP AND COME RIGHT BACK.
SORRY, BELL.
VNNNNNNN
SEE YOU LATER...

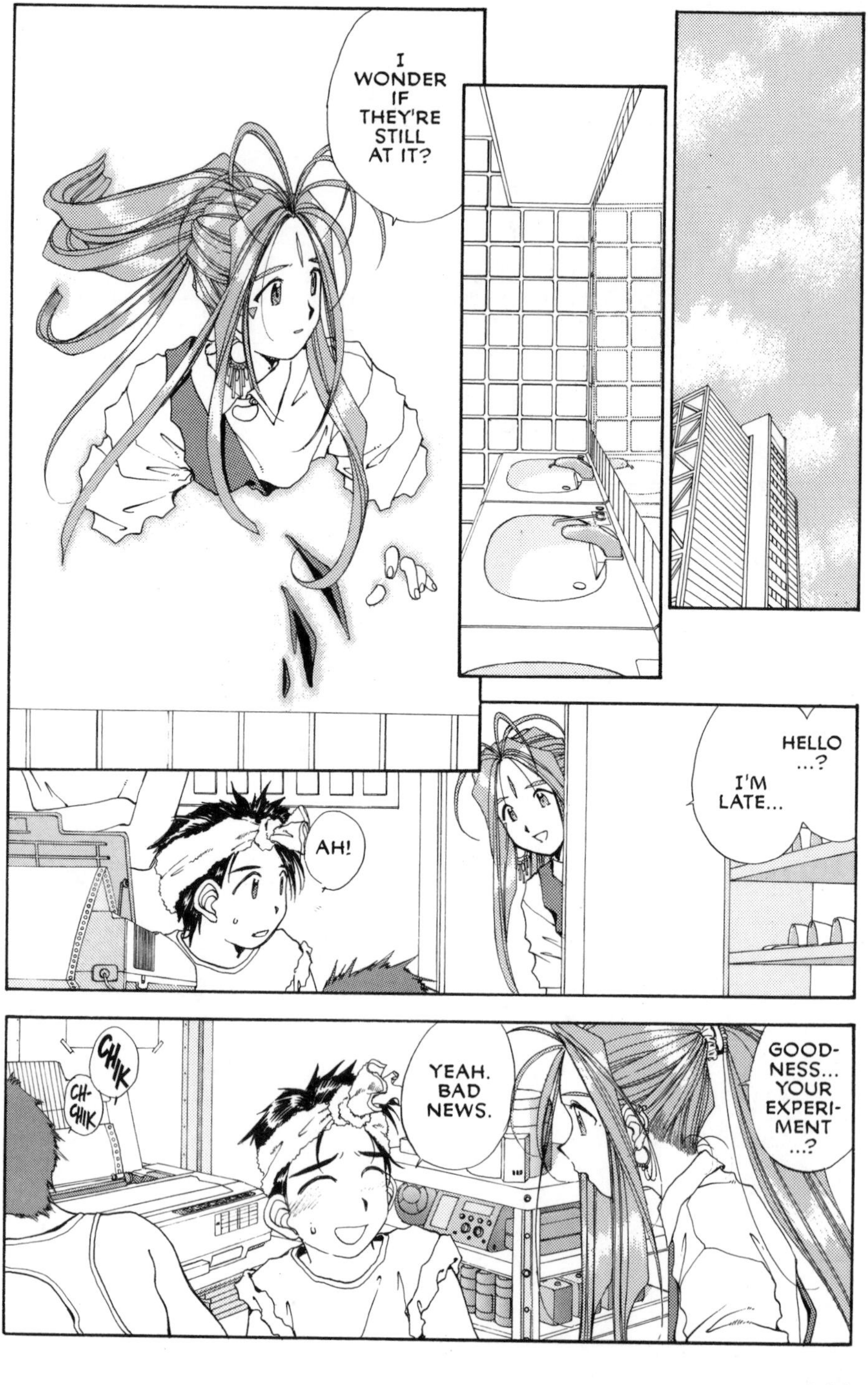
I WONDER IF THEY'RE STILL AT IT?
HELLO ...?
I'M LATE...
AH!
GOOD-NESS... YOUR EXPERI-MENT ...?
YEAH. BAD NEWS.
CHIK
CH-CHIK

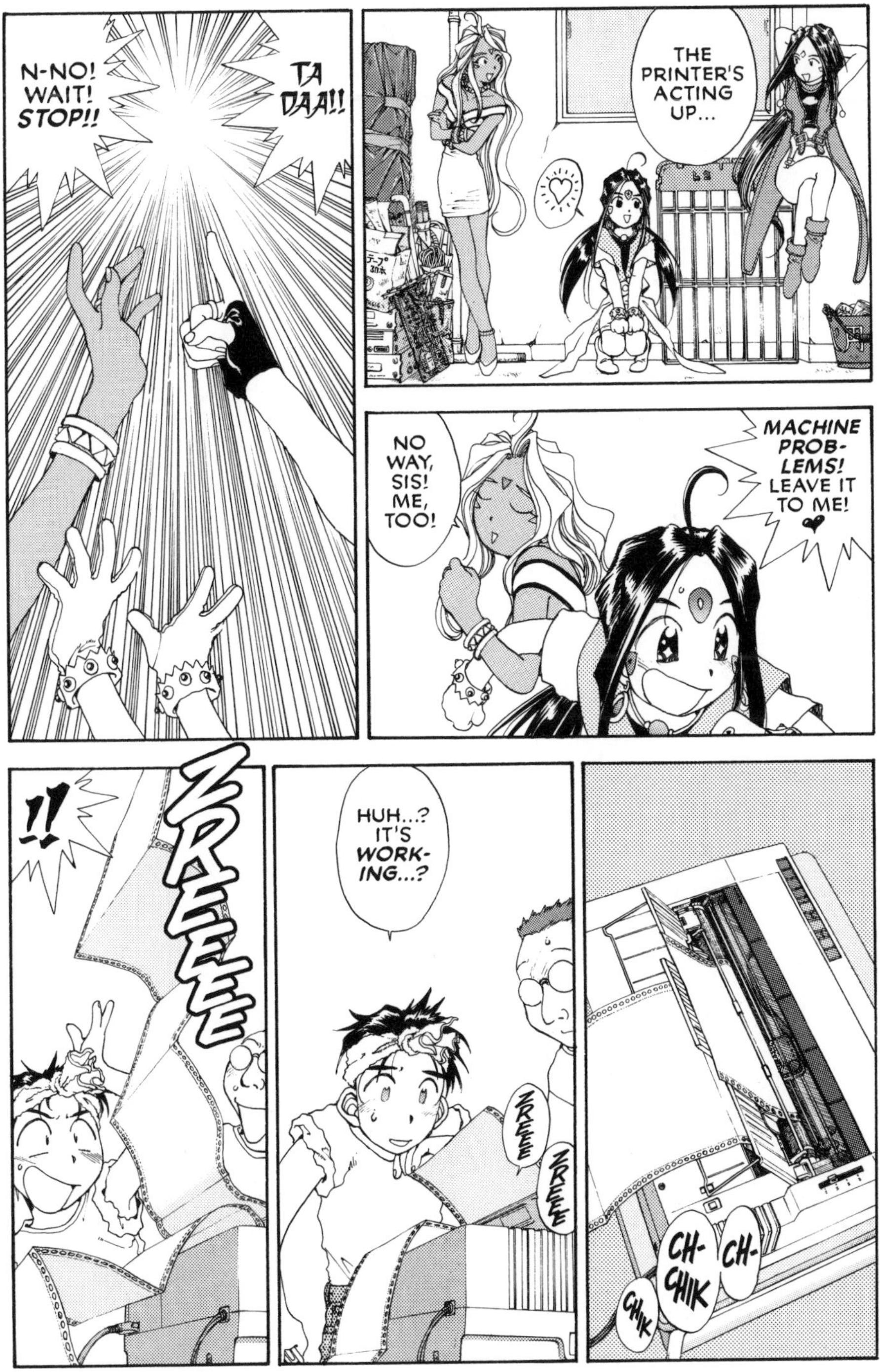
THE PRINTER'S ACTING UP...
♡
MACHINE PROBLEMS! LEAVE IT TO ME! ❤
NO WAY, SIS! ME, TOO!
TA DAA!!
N-NO! WAIT! STOP!!
CH-CHIK
CH-CHIK
HUH...? IT'S WORKING...?
ZREEE
ZREEE
ZREEEE
!!

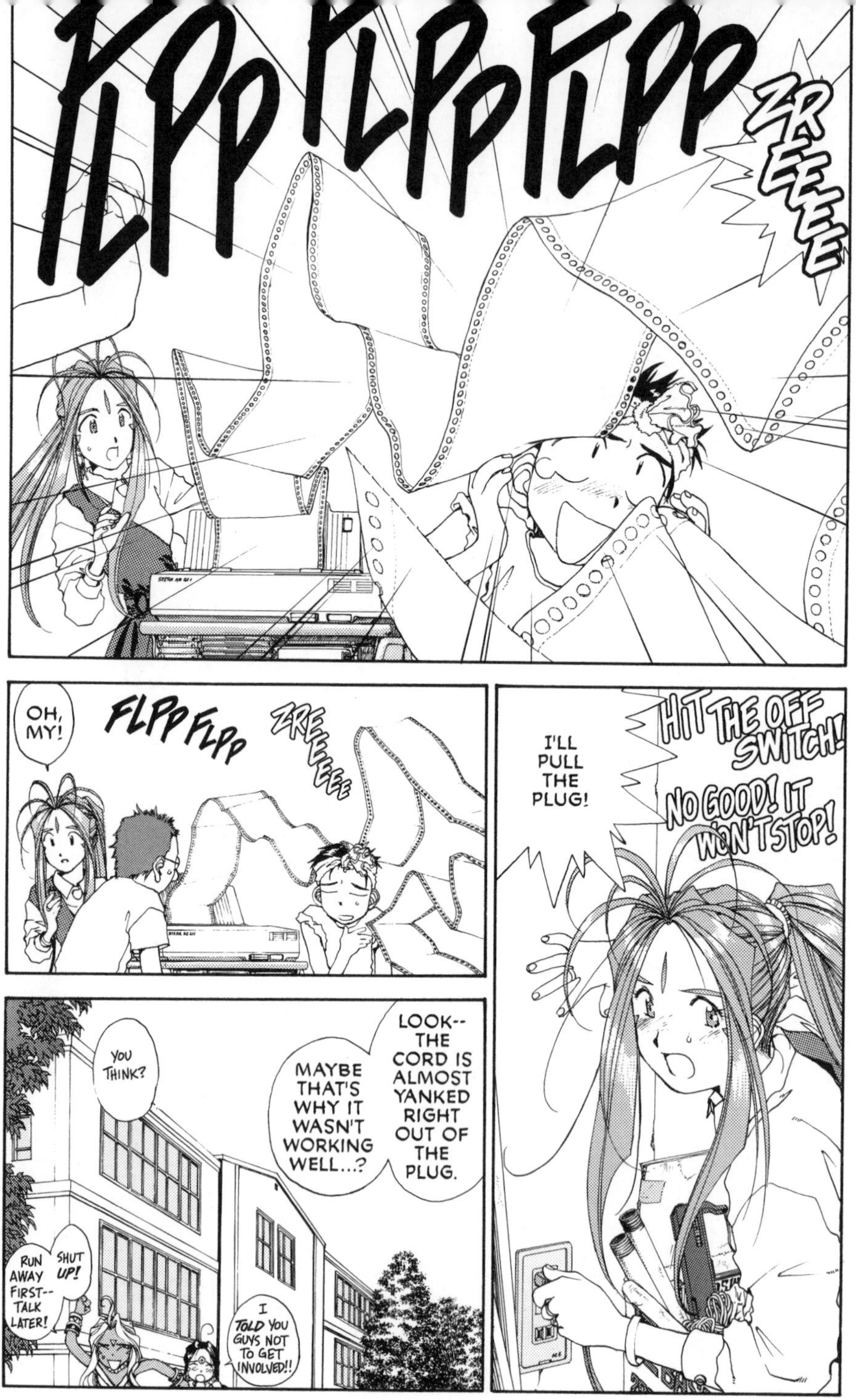
FLPP FLPP FLPP
ZREEEEE
HIT THE OFF SWITCH!
NO GOOD! IT WON'T STOP!
I'LL PULL THE PLUG!
OH, MY!
FLPP FLPP
ZREEEEE
LOOK-- THE CORD IS ALMOST YANKED RIGHT OUT OF THE PLUG.
MAYBE THAT'S WHY IT WASN'T WORKING WELL...?
YOU THINK?
I TOLD YOU GUYS NOT TO GET INVOLVED!!
SHUT UP!
RUN AWAY FIRST-- TALK LATER!

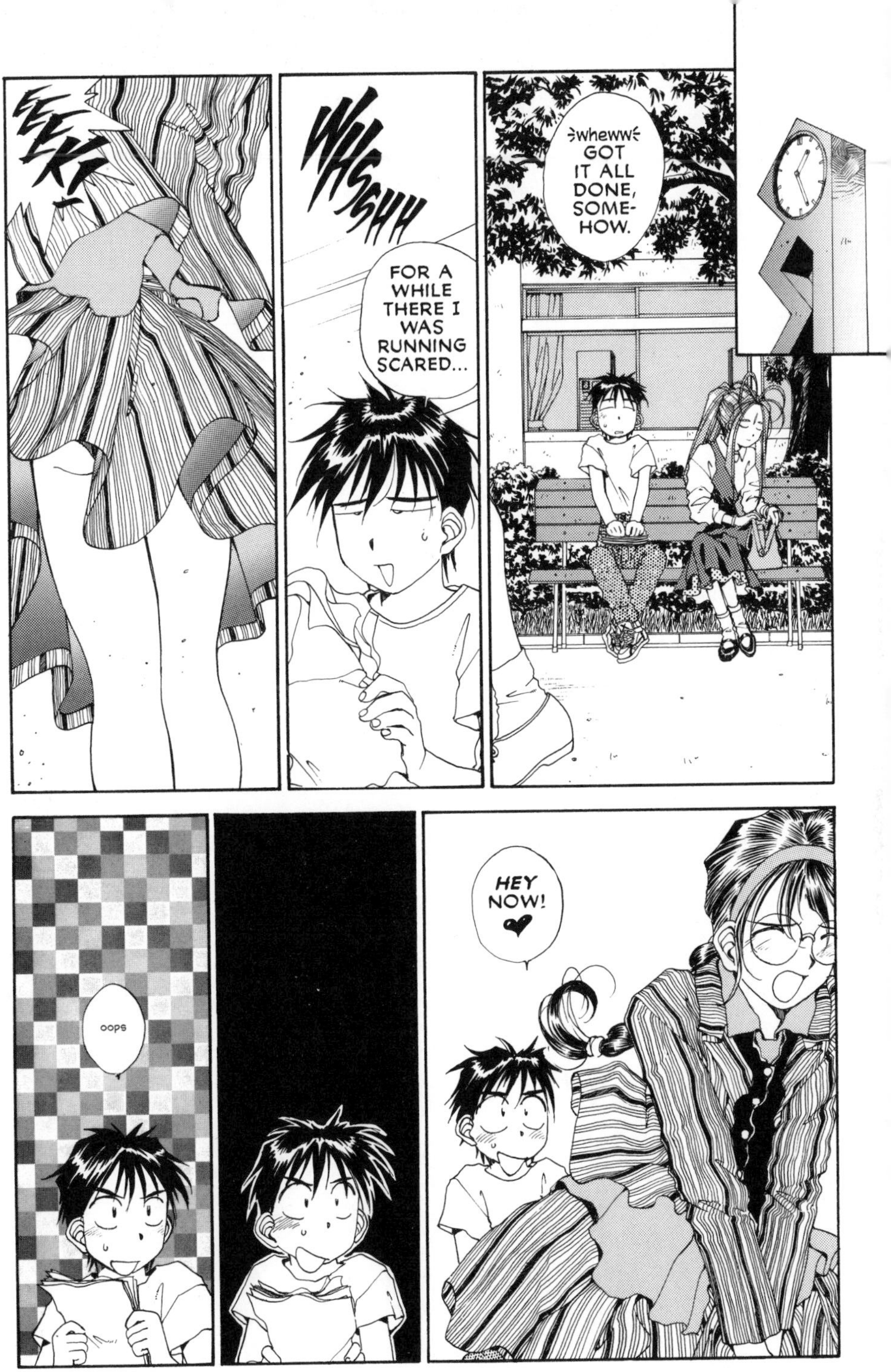

wheww
GOT IT ALL DONE, SOME-HOW.
WHSSHH
FOR A WHILE THERE I WAS RUNNING SCARED...
EEEK!
HEY NOW! ♥
oops

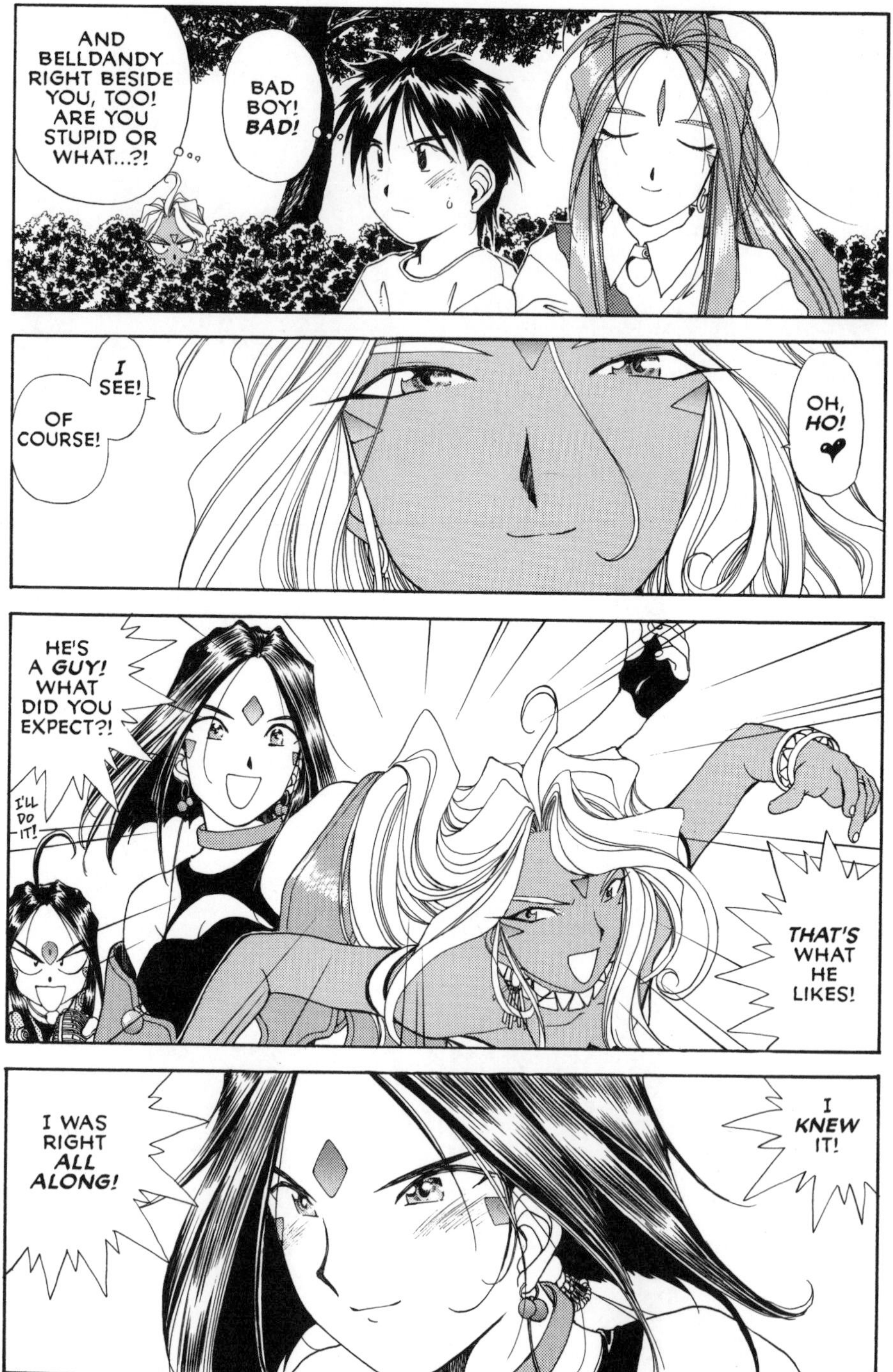
BAD BOY! BAD!
AND BELLDANDY RIGHT BESIDE YOU, TOO! ARE YOU STUPID OR WHAT...?!
OH, HO! ♥
I SEE!
OF COURSE!
THAT'S WHAT HE LIKES!
HE'S A GUY! WHAT DID YOU EXPECT?!
I'LL DO IT!
I KNEW IT!
I WAS RIGHT ALL ALONG!

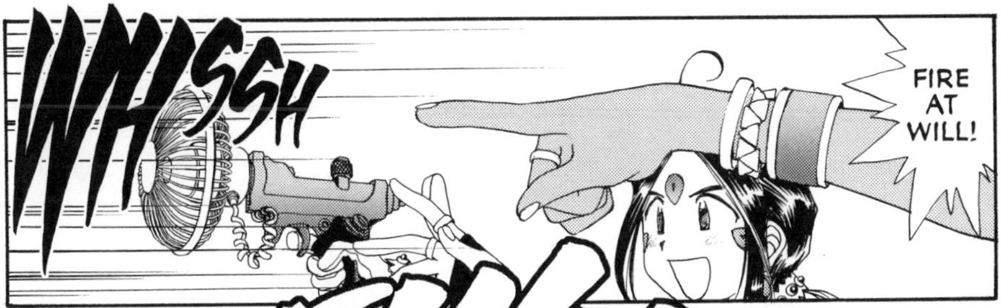
FIRE AT WILL!
WHISSH
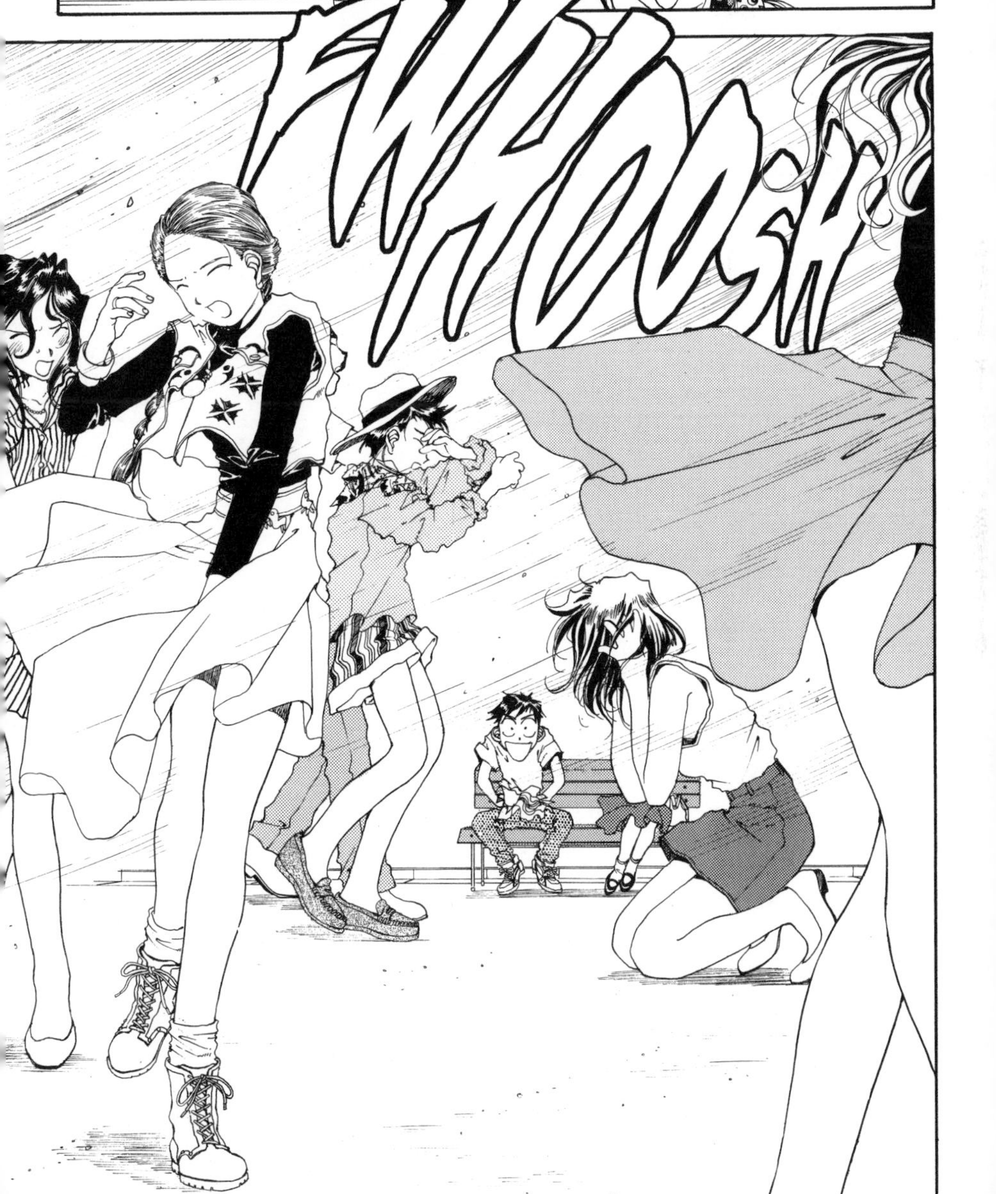
FWHOOSH

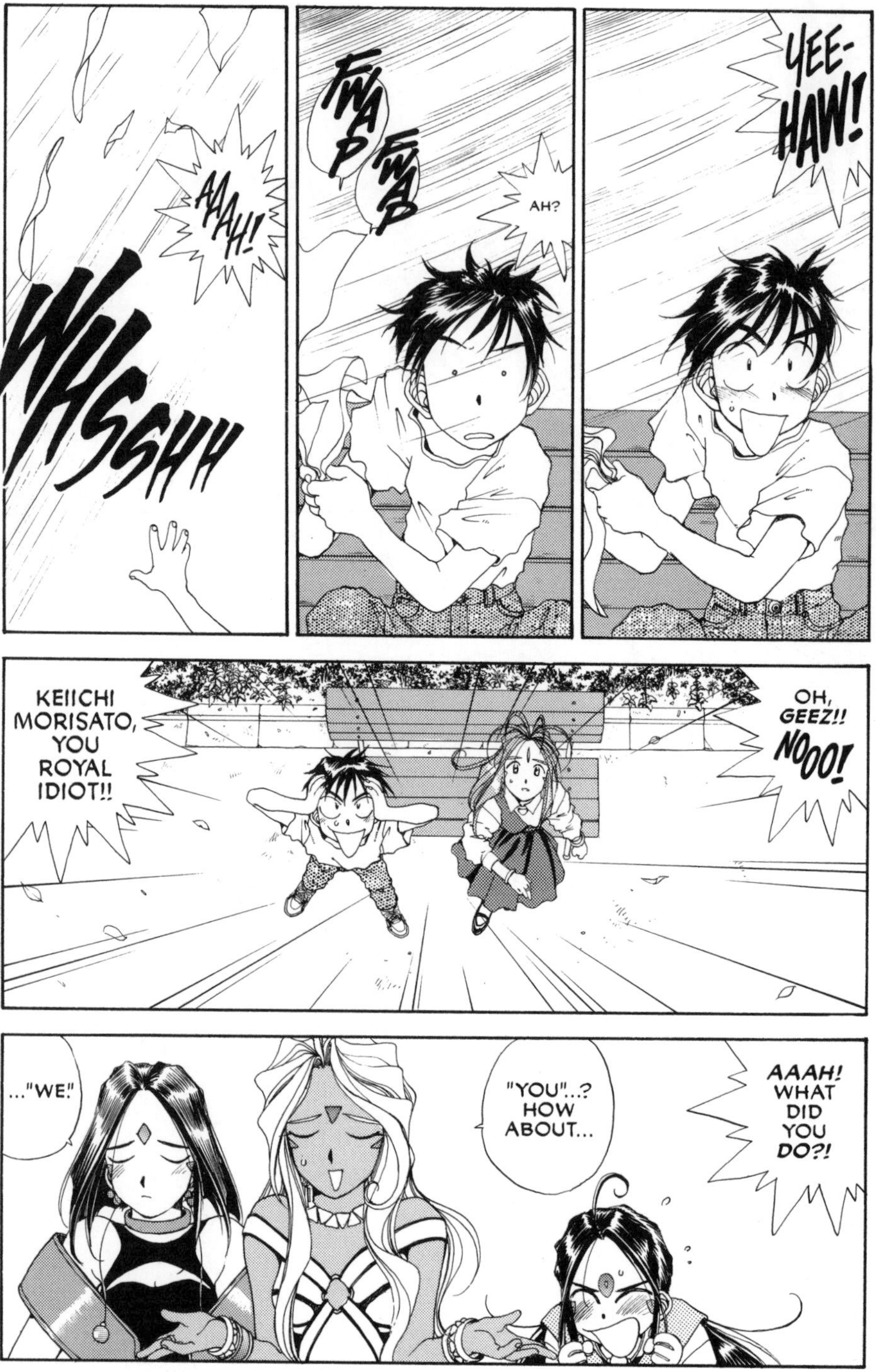
YEE-HAW!
FWAP FWAP
AH?
AAAH!
WHSSHH
OH, GEEZ!! NOOO!
KEIICHI MORISATO, YOU ROYAL IDIOT!!
AAAH! WHAT DID YOU DO?!
"YOU"..? HOW ABOUT...
..."WE."

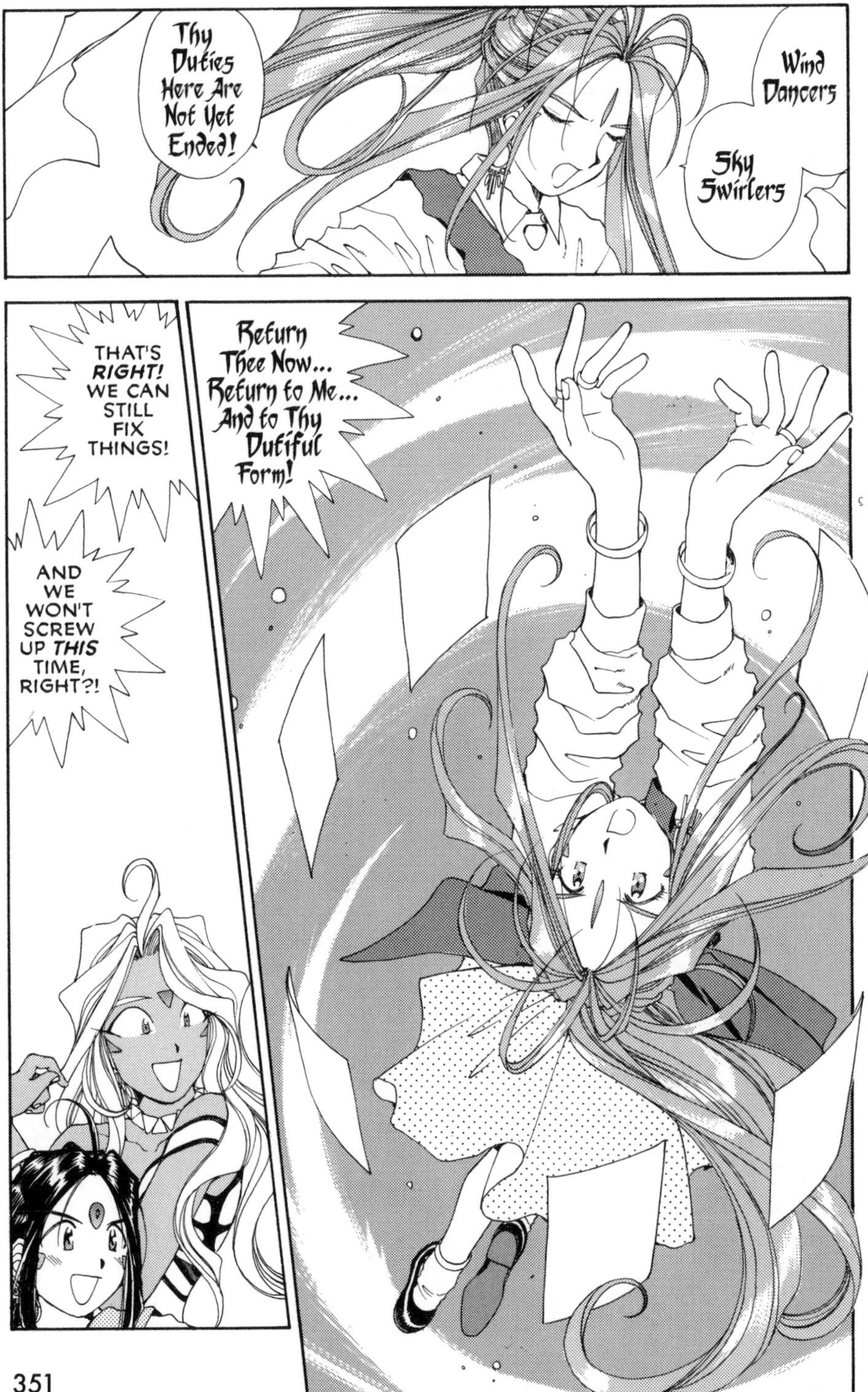
Wind Dancers
Sky Swirlers
Thy Duties Here Are Not Yet Ended!
Return Thee Now... Return to Me... And to Thy Dutiful Form!
THAT'S RIGHT! WE CAN STILL FIX THINGS!
AND WE WON'T SCREW UP THIS TIME, RIGHT?!

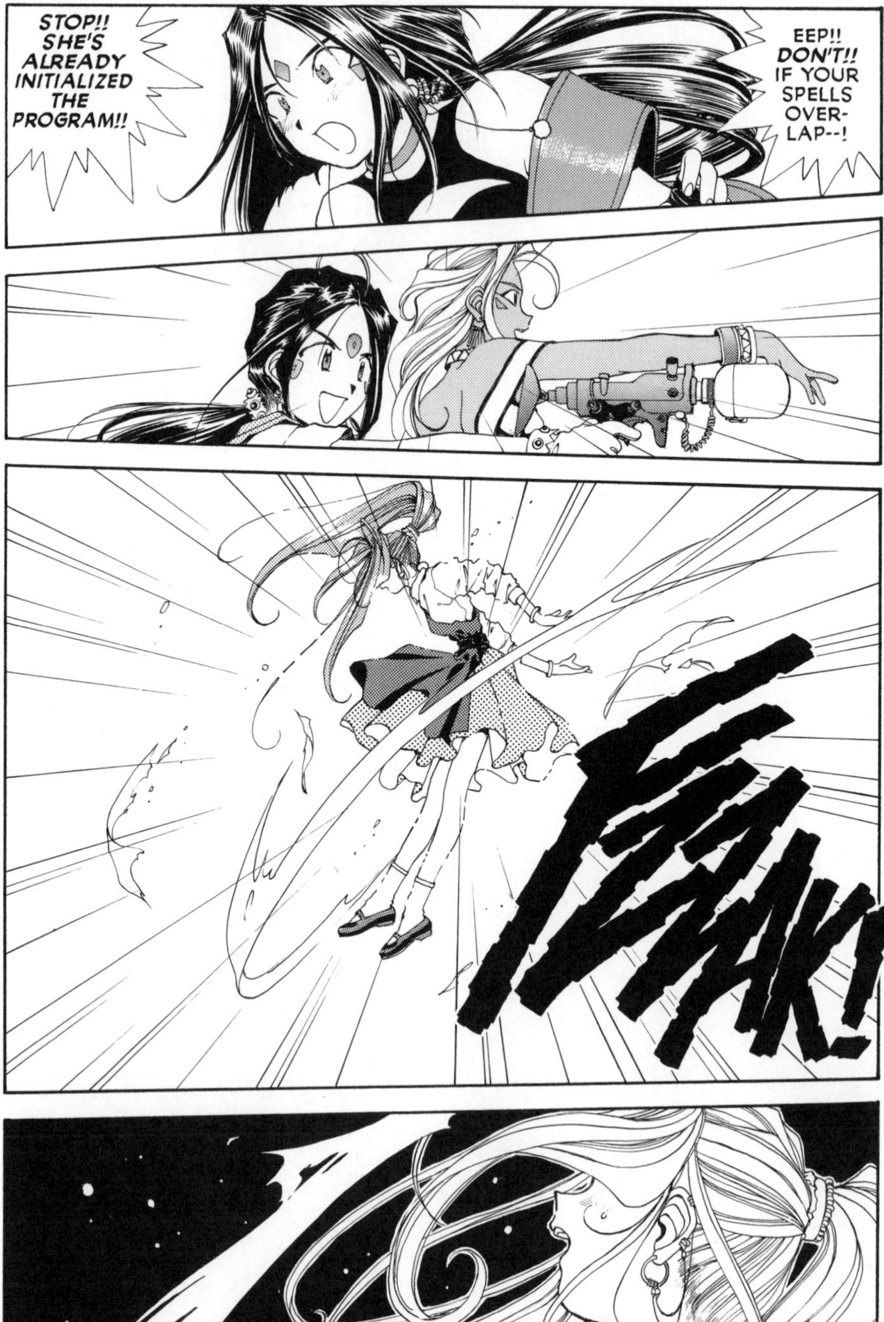
EEP!! DON'T!! IF YOUR SPELLS OVER-LAP--!
STOP!! SHE'S ALREADY INITIALIZED THE PROGRAM!!
FZAK!

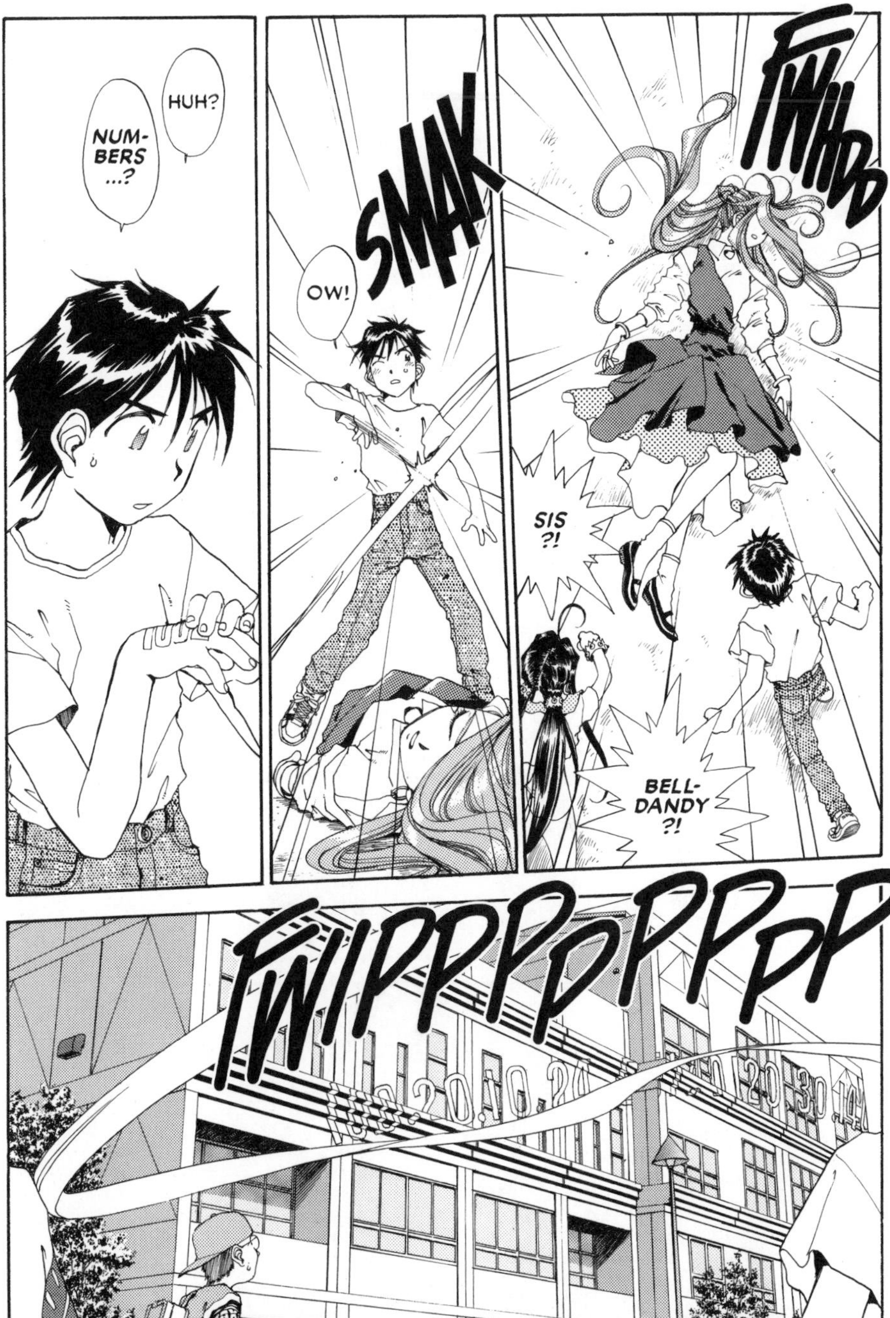
HUH?
NUM-
BERS
...?
SMAK
OW!
FWHOO
SIS
?!
BELL-
DANDY
?!
FWIPPPPPPPP

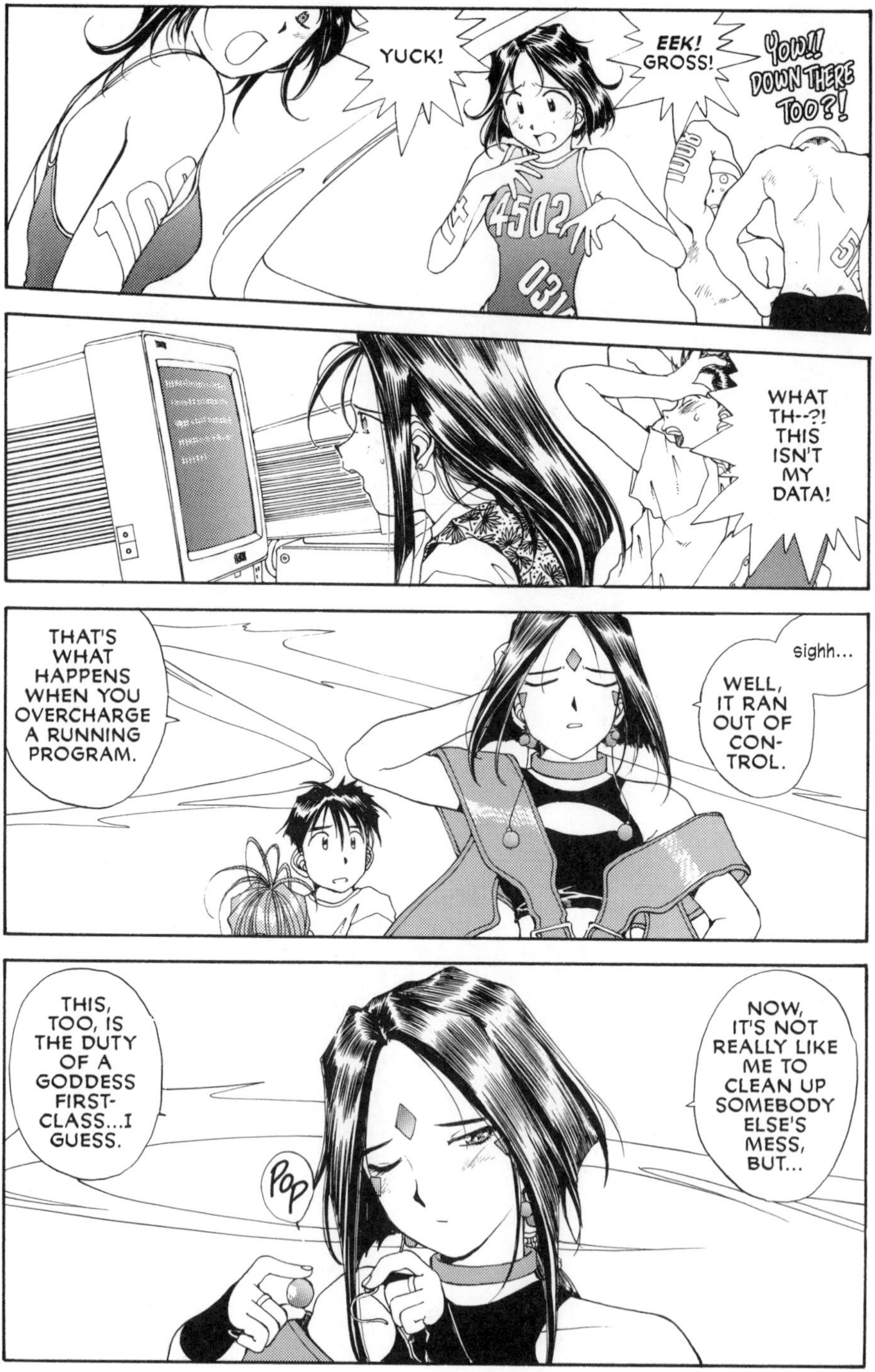
YOW!! DOWN THERE TOO?!
EEK! GROSS!
YUCK!
WHAT TH--?! THIS ISN'T MY DATA!
sighh...
WELL, IT RAN OUT OF CON-TROL.
THAT'S WHAT HAPPENS WHEN YOU OVERCHARGE A RUNNING PROGRAM.
NOW, IT'S NOT REALLY LIKE ME TO CLEAN UP SOMEBODY ELSE'S MESS, BUT...
POP
THIS, TOO, IS THE DUTY OF A GODDESS FIRST-CLASS...I GUESS.

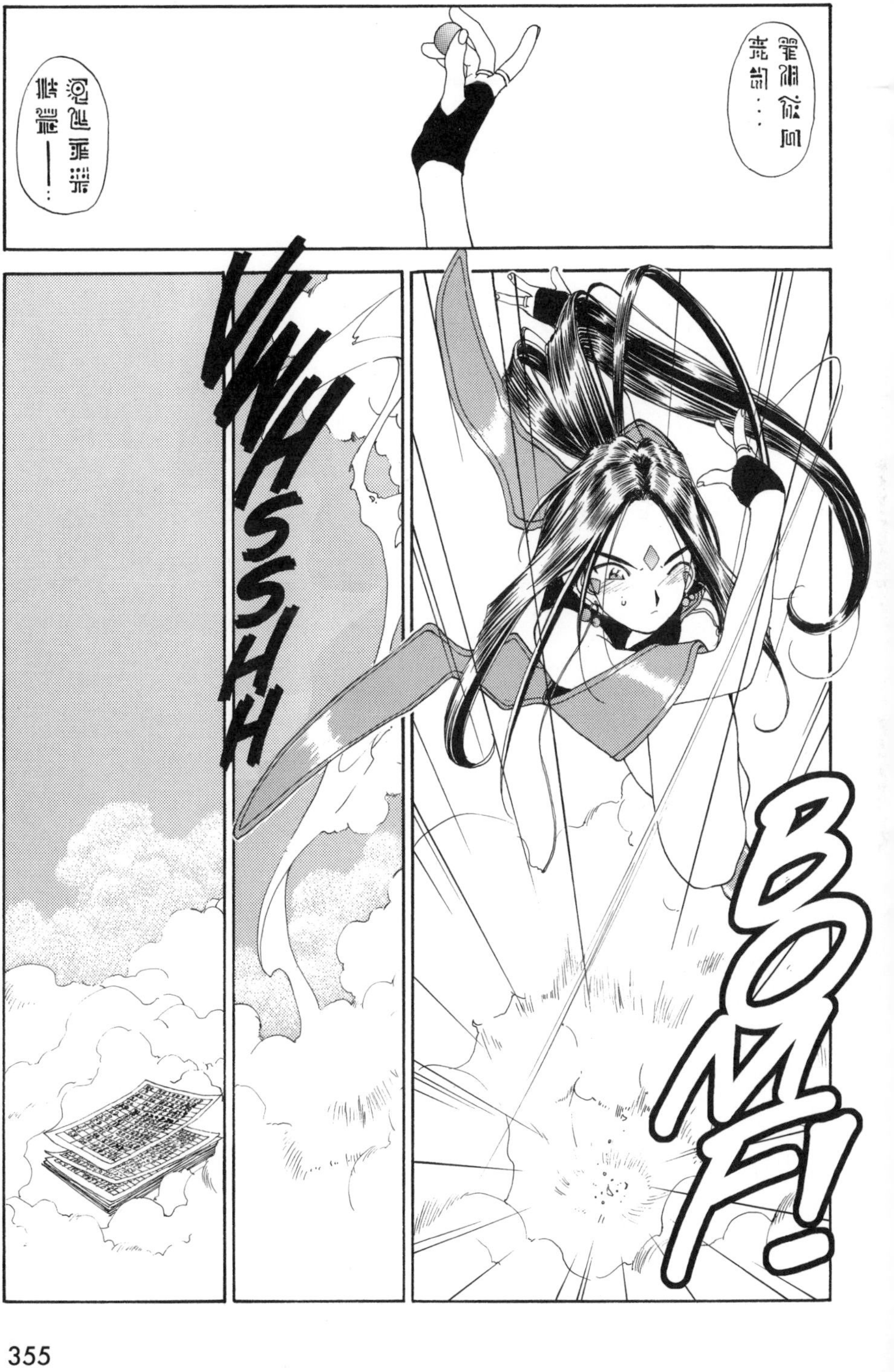
BOMF!
WHSSHH

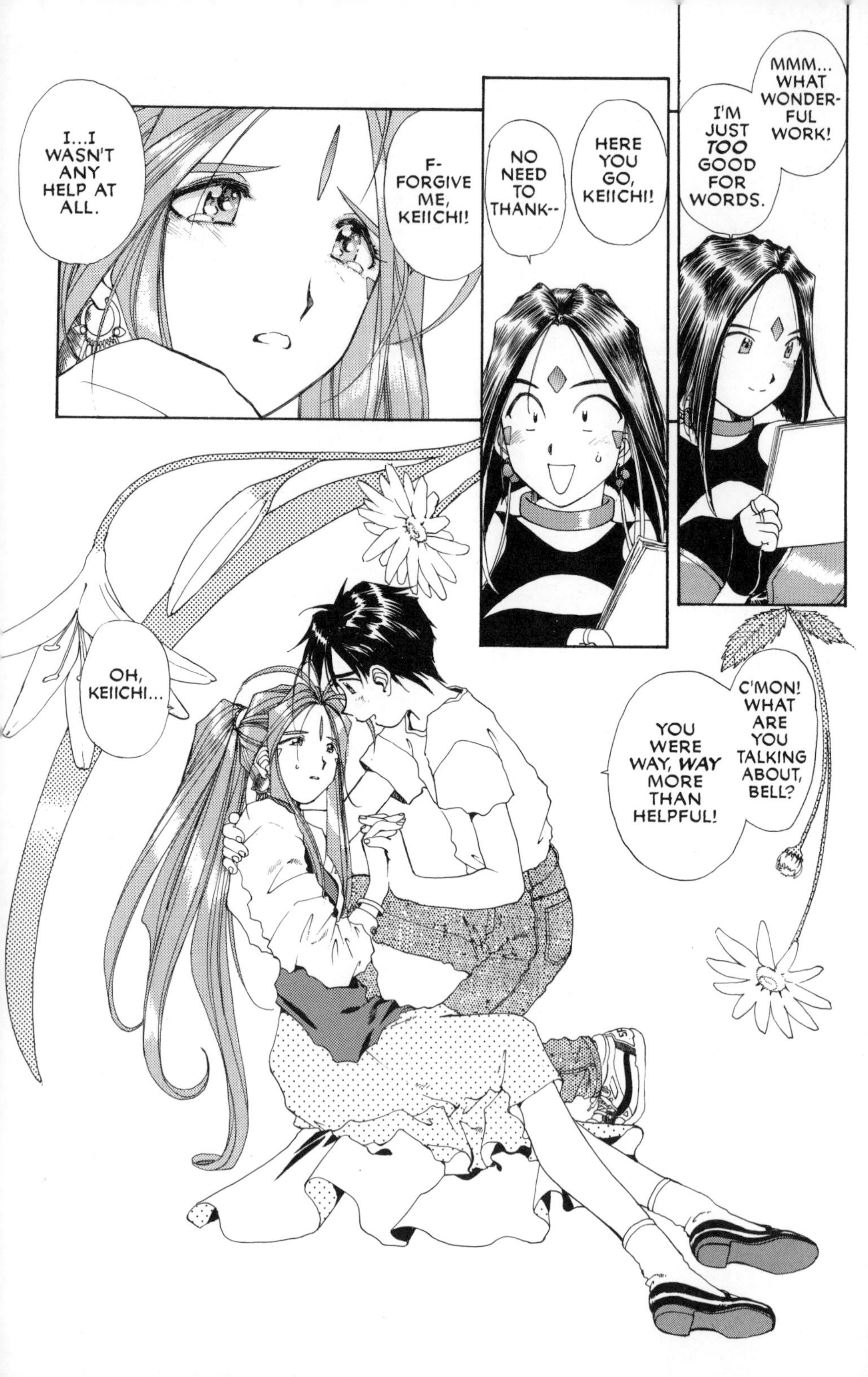

MMM... WHAT WONDERFUL WORK!
I'M JUST *TOO* GOOD FOR WORDS.
HERE YOU GO, KEIICHI!
NO NEED TO THANK--
F-FORGIVE ME, KEIICHI!
I...I WASN'T ANY HELP AT ALL.
C'MON! WHAT ARE YOU TALKING ABOUT, BELL?
YOU WERE WAY, *WAY* MORE THAN HELPFUL!
OH, KEIICHI...

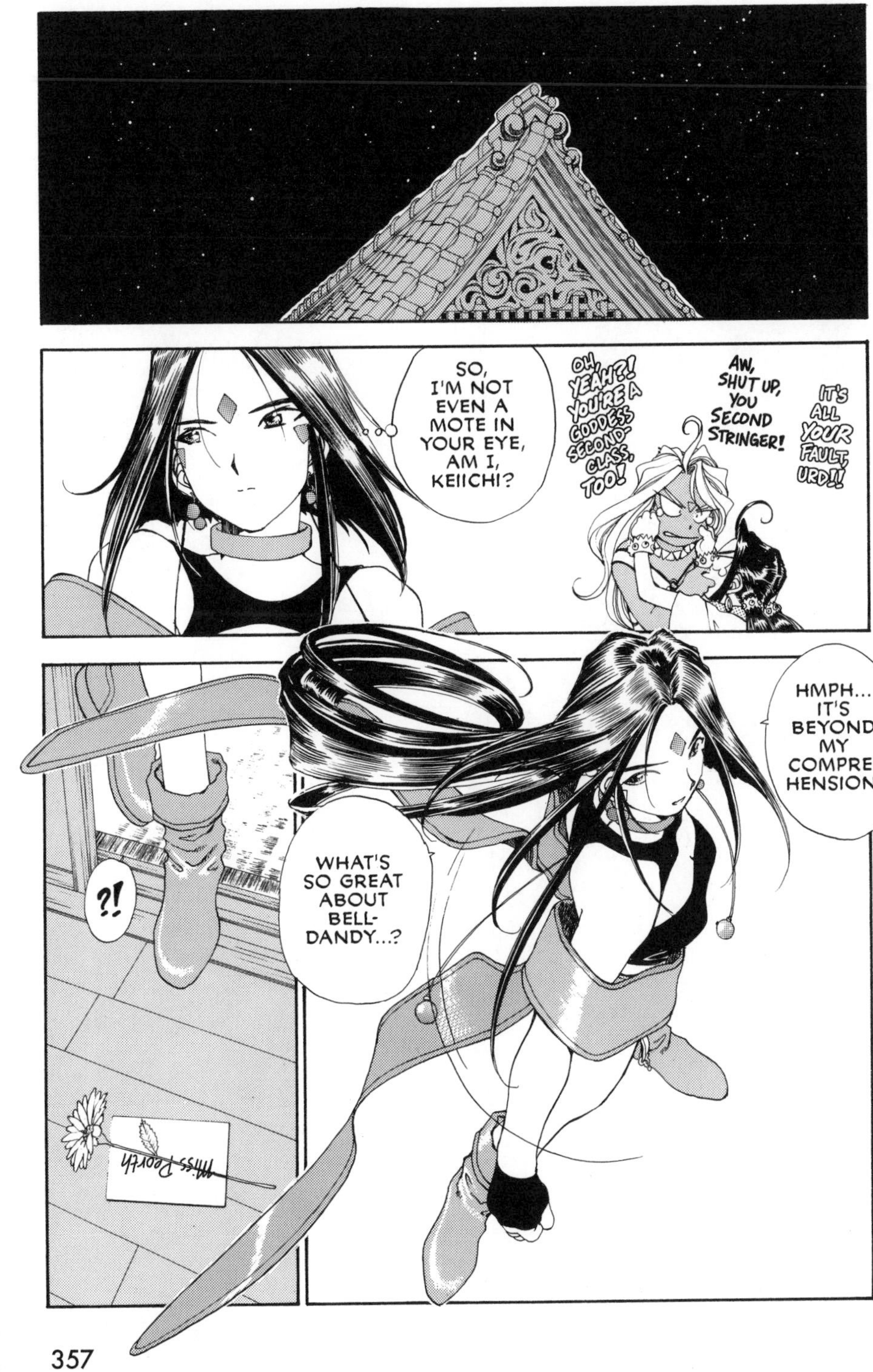
IT'S ALL YOUR FAULT, URD!!
AW, SHUT UP, YOU SECOND STRINGER!
OH, YEAH?! YOU'RE A GODDESS SECOND-CLASS, TOO!
SO, I'M NOT EVEN A MOTE IN YOUR EYE, AM I, KEIICHI?
HMPH... IT'S BEYOND MY COMPREHENSION!
WHAT'S SO GREAT ABOUT BELL-DANDY...?
?!
Miss Peorth

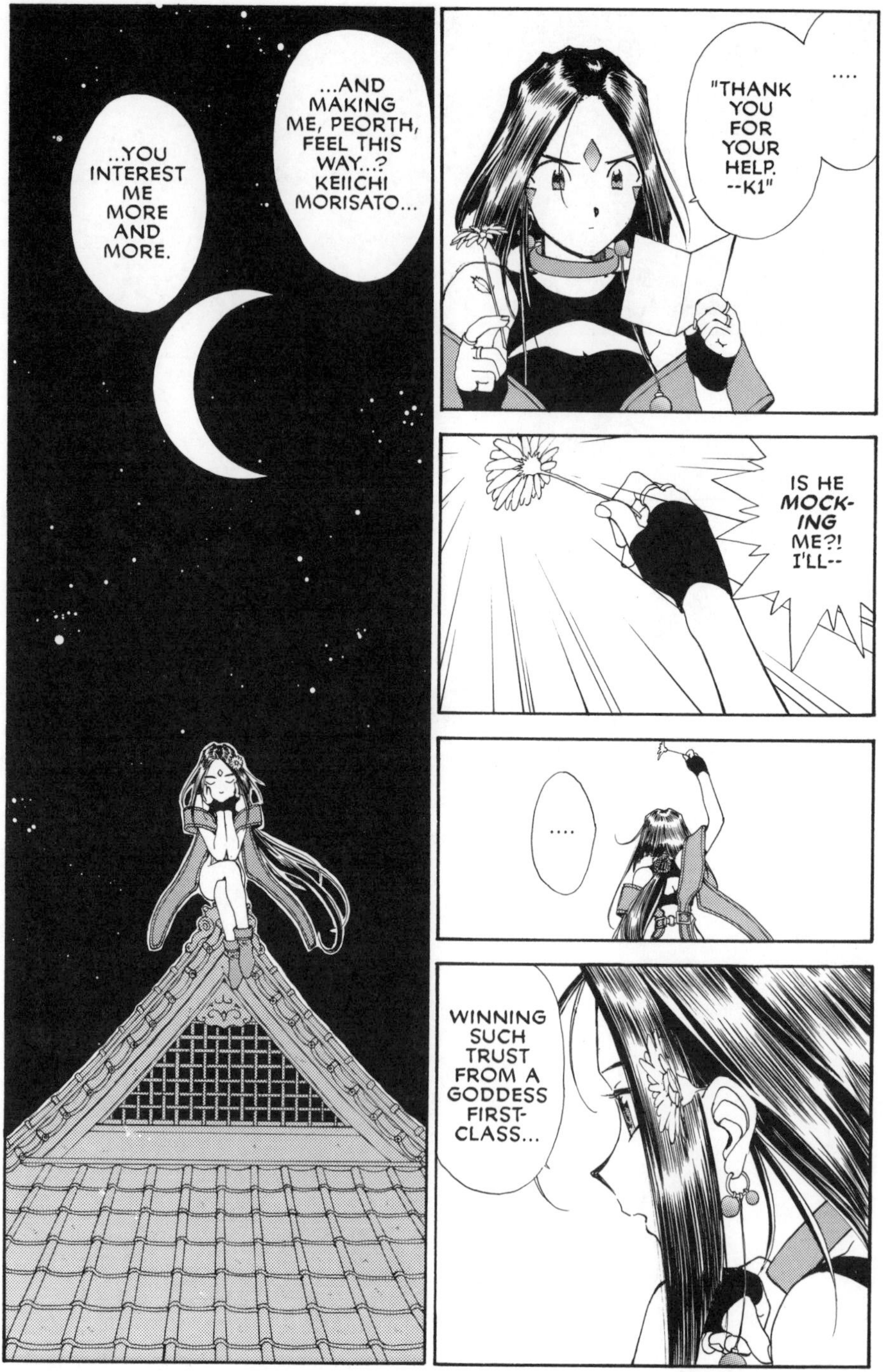
....
"THANK YOU FOR YOUR HELP. --K1"
IS HE MOCKING ME?! I'LL--
....
WINNING SUCH TRUST FROM A GODDESS FIRST-CLASS...
...AND MAKING ME, PEORTH, FEEL THIS WAY...? KEIICHI MORISATO...
...YOU INTEREST ME MORE AND MORE.

MINI-GODDESSES THEATER OF LOVE!

GAN (AND HIS LITTLE FRIENDS)

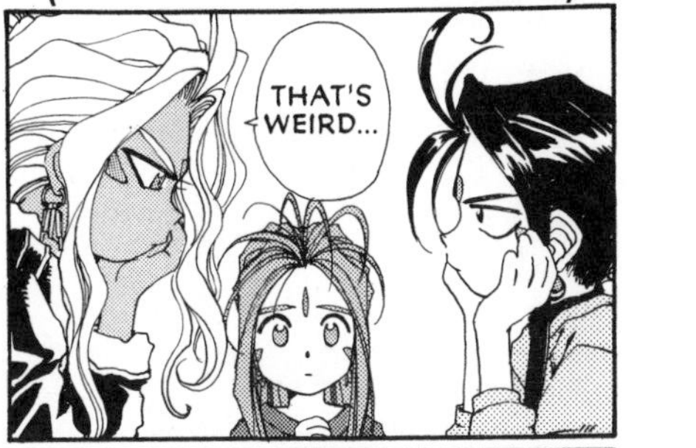
THAT'S WEIRD...

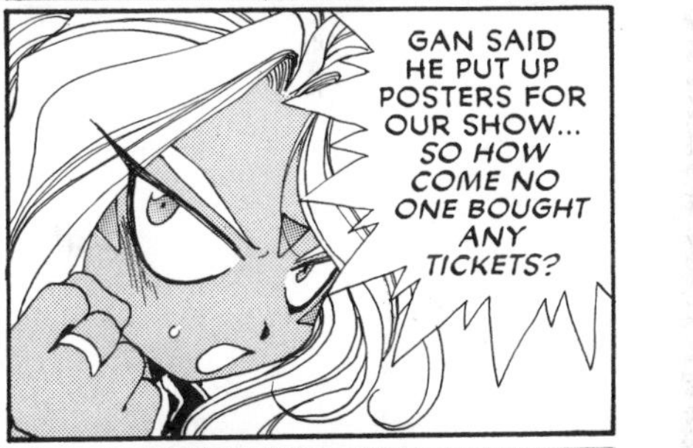
GAN SAID HE PUT UP POSTERS FOR OUR SHOW... *SO HOW COME NO ONE BOUGHT ANY TICKETS?*

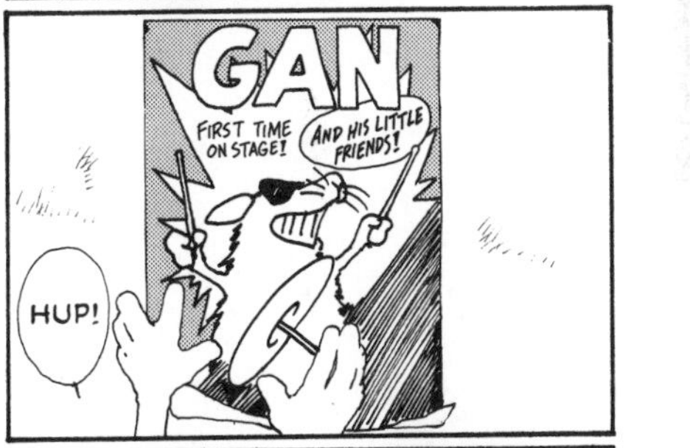
GAN
AND HIS LITTLE FRIENDS!
FIRST TIME ON STAGE!
HUP!

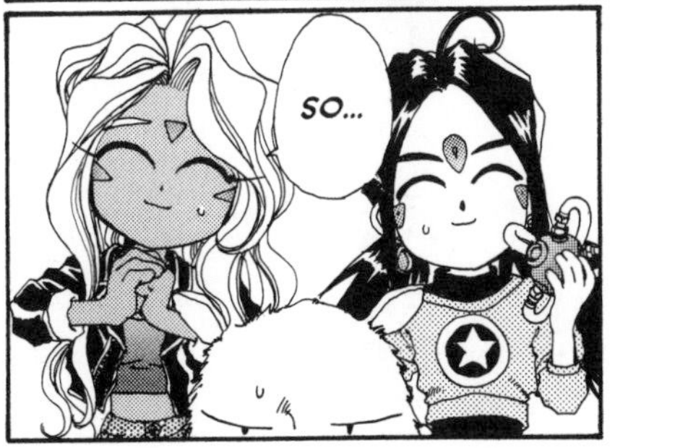
SO...

PRIMITIVE ECONOMIC DISTRIBUTION SYSTEMS 101

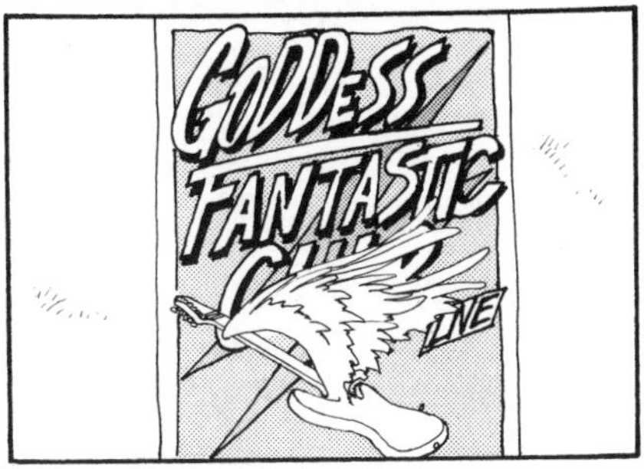
GODDESS
FANTASTIC
LIVE

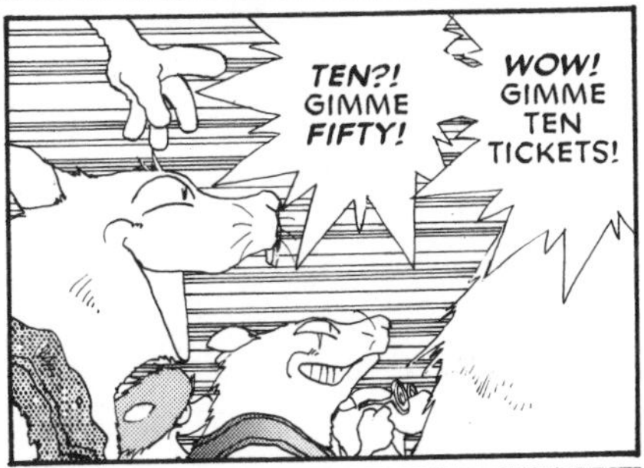
WOW! GIMME TEN TICKETS!
TEN?! GIMME *FIFTY!*

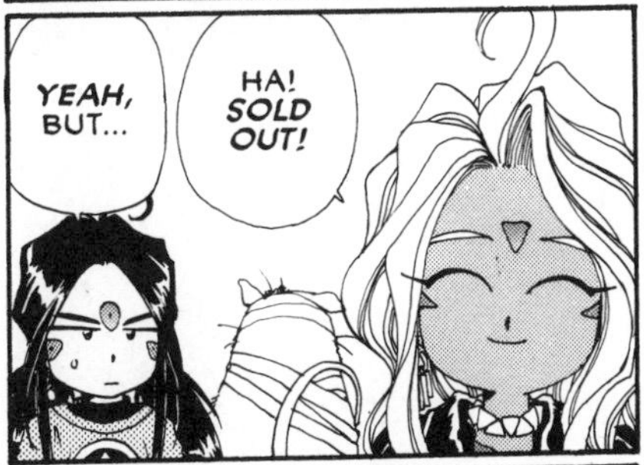
HA! *SOLD OUT!*
YEAH, BUT...

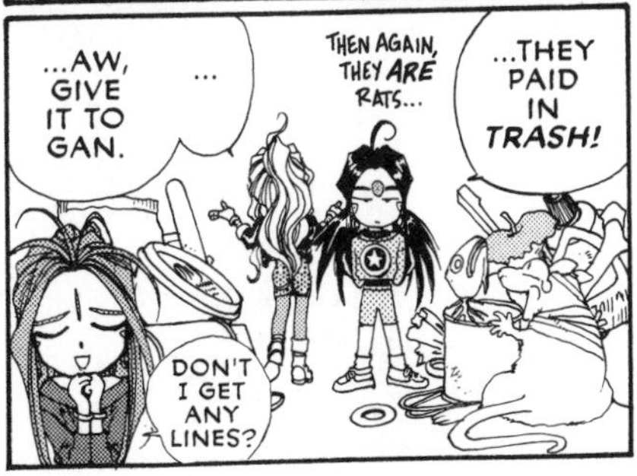
...THEY PAID IN *TRASH!*
THEN AGAIN, THEY *ARE* RATS...
...
...AW, GIVE IT TO GAN.
DON'T I GET ANY LINES?

MINI-GODDESSES THEATER OF LOVE!

◆ WRITE? WRONG! ◆

◆ "I'M RUNNING OUT OF PATIENCE..." ◆

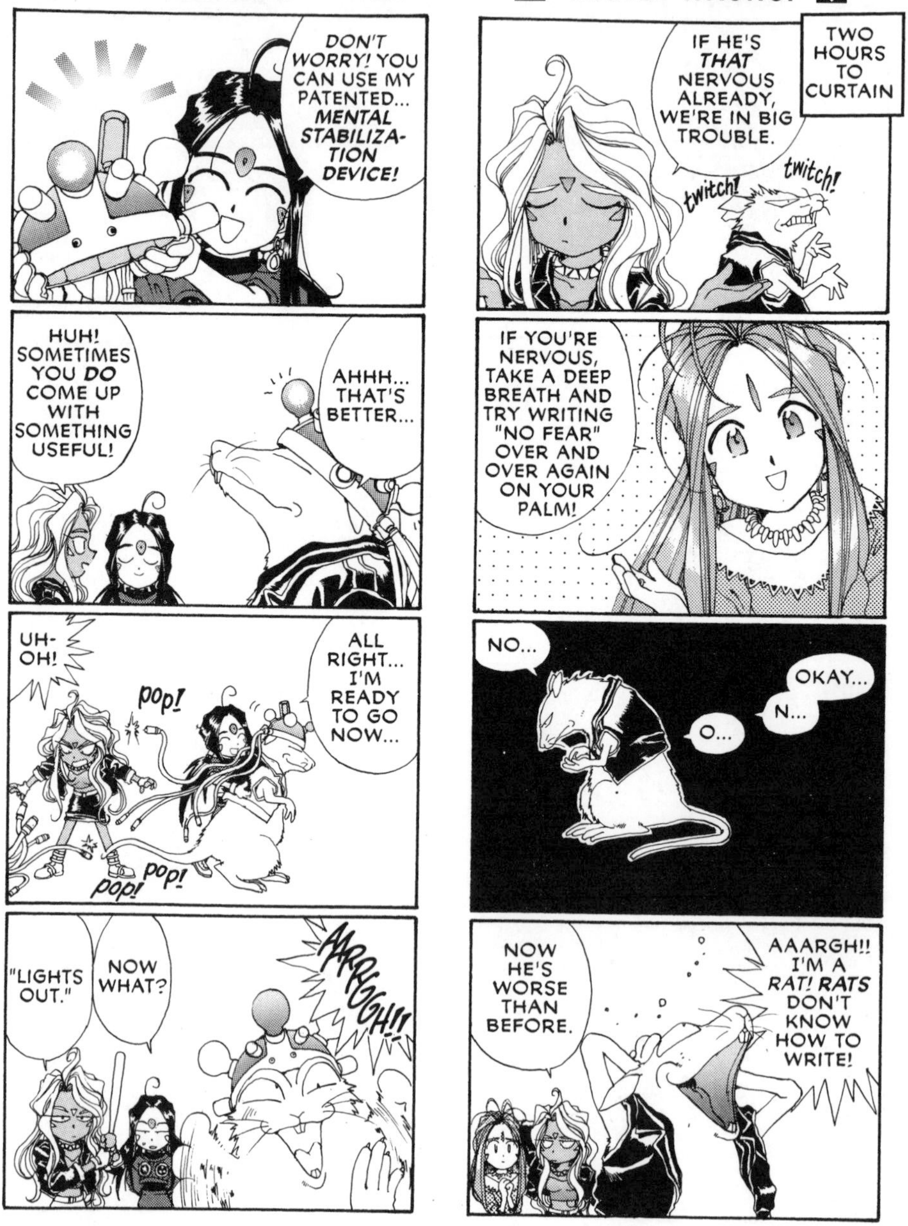

TWO HOURS TO CURTAIN
IF HE'S *THAT* NERVOUS ALREADY, WE'RE IN BIG TROUBLE.
twitch!
twitch!
IF YOU'RE NERVOUS, TAKE A DEEP BREATH AND TRY WRITING "NO FEAR" OVER AND OVER AGAIN ON YOUR PALM!
OKAY...
N...
O...
NO...
AAARGH!! I'M A *RAT! RATS* DON'T KNOW HOW TO WRITE!
NOW HE'S WORSE THAN BEFORE.
DON'T *WORRY!* YOU CAN USE MY PATENTED... *MENTAL STABILIZATION DEVICE!*
AHHH... THAT'S BETTER...
HUH! SOMETIMES YOU *DO* COME UP WITH SOMETHING USEFUL!
ALL RIGHT... I'M READY TO GO NOW...
UH-OH!
pop!
pop!
pop!
AARRGH!!
NOW WHAT?
"LIGHTS OUT."

MINI-GODDESSES THEATER OF LOVE!

SORRY ABOUT THE TINY PRINT IN THE PLOT SUMMARY...GOOD LUCK!

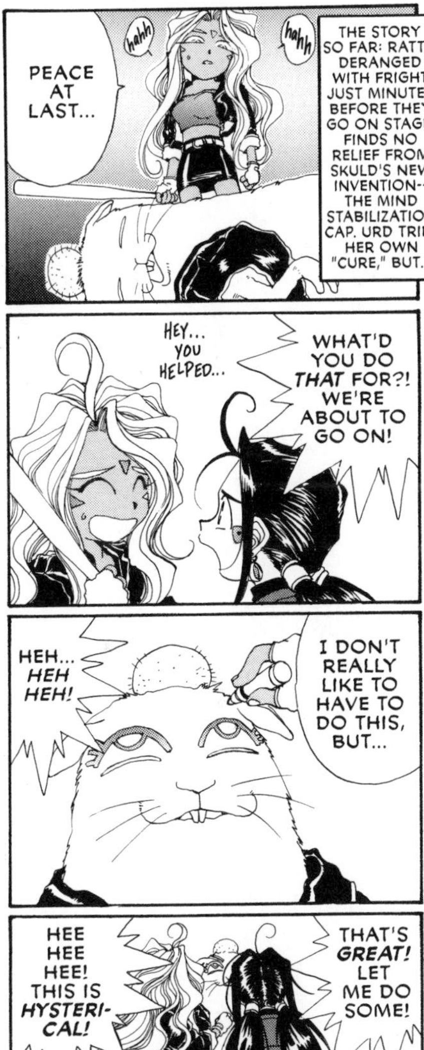
hahh
hahh
PEACE AT LAST...
THE STORY SO FAR: RATTY, DERANGED WITH FRIGHT JUST MINUTES BEFORE THEY GO ON STAGE, FINDS NO RELIEF FROM SKULD'S NEW INVENTION--THE MIND STABILIZATION CAP. URD TRIES HER OWN "CURE," BUT...
WHAT'D YOU DO THAT FOR?! WE'RE ABOUT TO GO ON!
HEY... YOU HELPED...
I DON'T REALLY LIKE TO HAVE TO DO THIS, BUT...
HEH... HEH HEH!
THAT'S GREAT! LET ME DO SOME!
HEE HEE HEE! THIS IS HYSTERICAL!

THEIR PURPOSE FORGOTTEN, THREE GODDESSES AND ONE RAT--ADRIFT IN THE SEA OF TIME!!

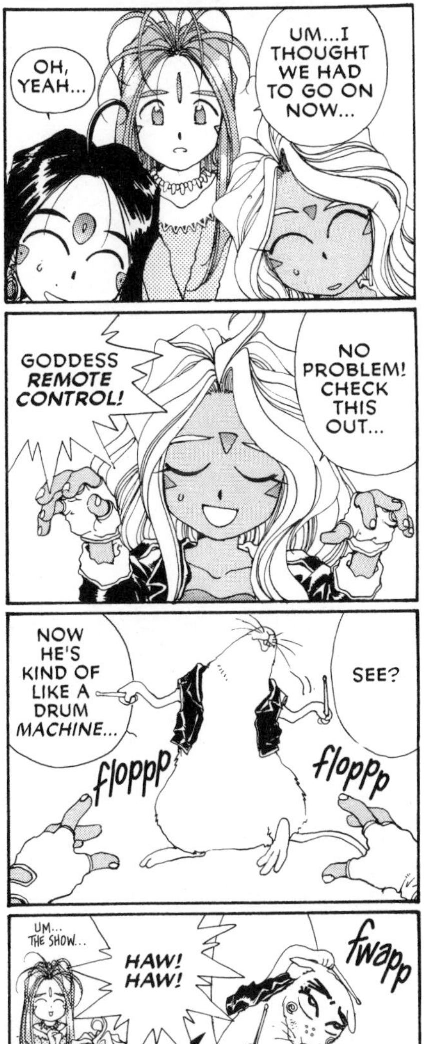
UM...I THOUGHT WE HAD TO GO ON NOW...
OH, YEAH...
NO PROBLEM! CHECK THIS OUT...
GODDESS REMOTE CONTROL!
SEE?
NOW HE'S KIND OF LIKE A DRUM MACHINE...
floppp
floppp
fwapp
fwapp
HAW! HAW!
UM... THE SHOW...

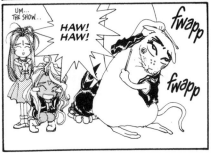

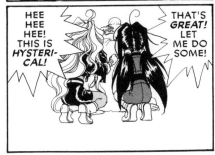

MINI-GODDESSES THEATER OF LOVE!

◆ HEAR THE ROAR OF MY SPIRIT! SHAKE TO THE BEAT OF MY HEART! THIS IS ROCK AND ROLL! ◆

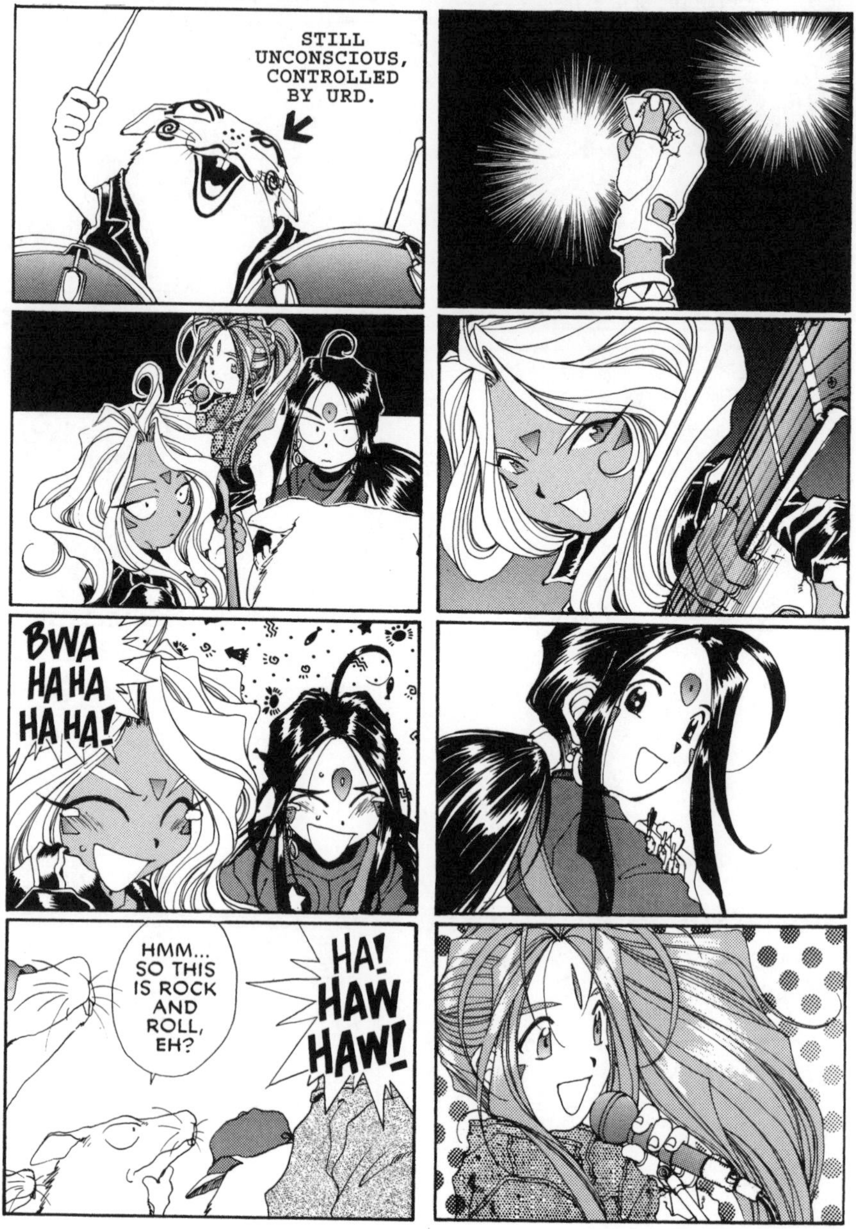
STILL UNCONSCIOUS, CONTROLLED BY URD.
BWA HA HA HA HA!
HA! HAW HAW!
HMM... SO THIS IS ROCK AND ROLL, EH?

OH MY GODDESS!

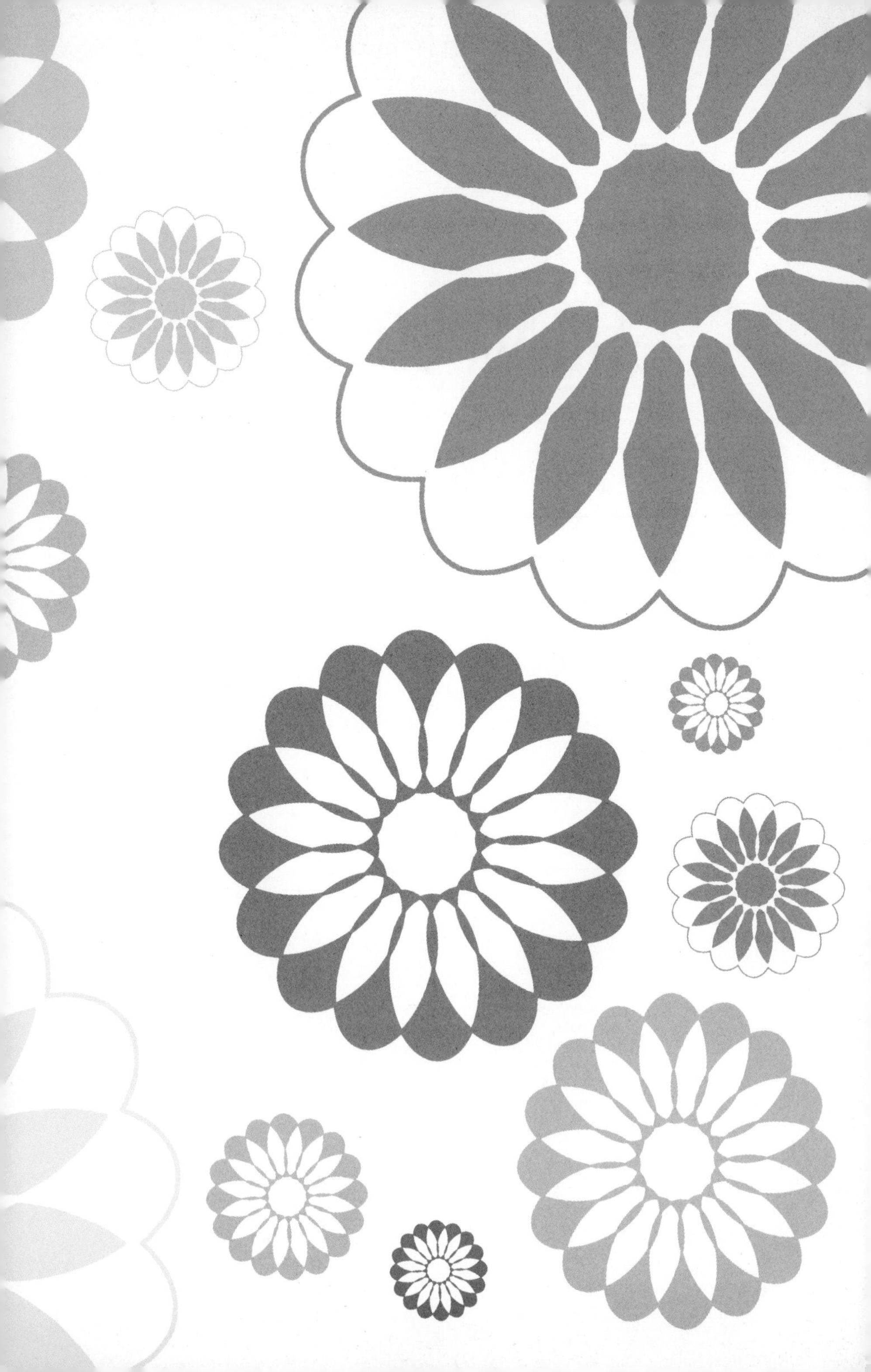

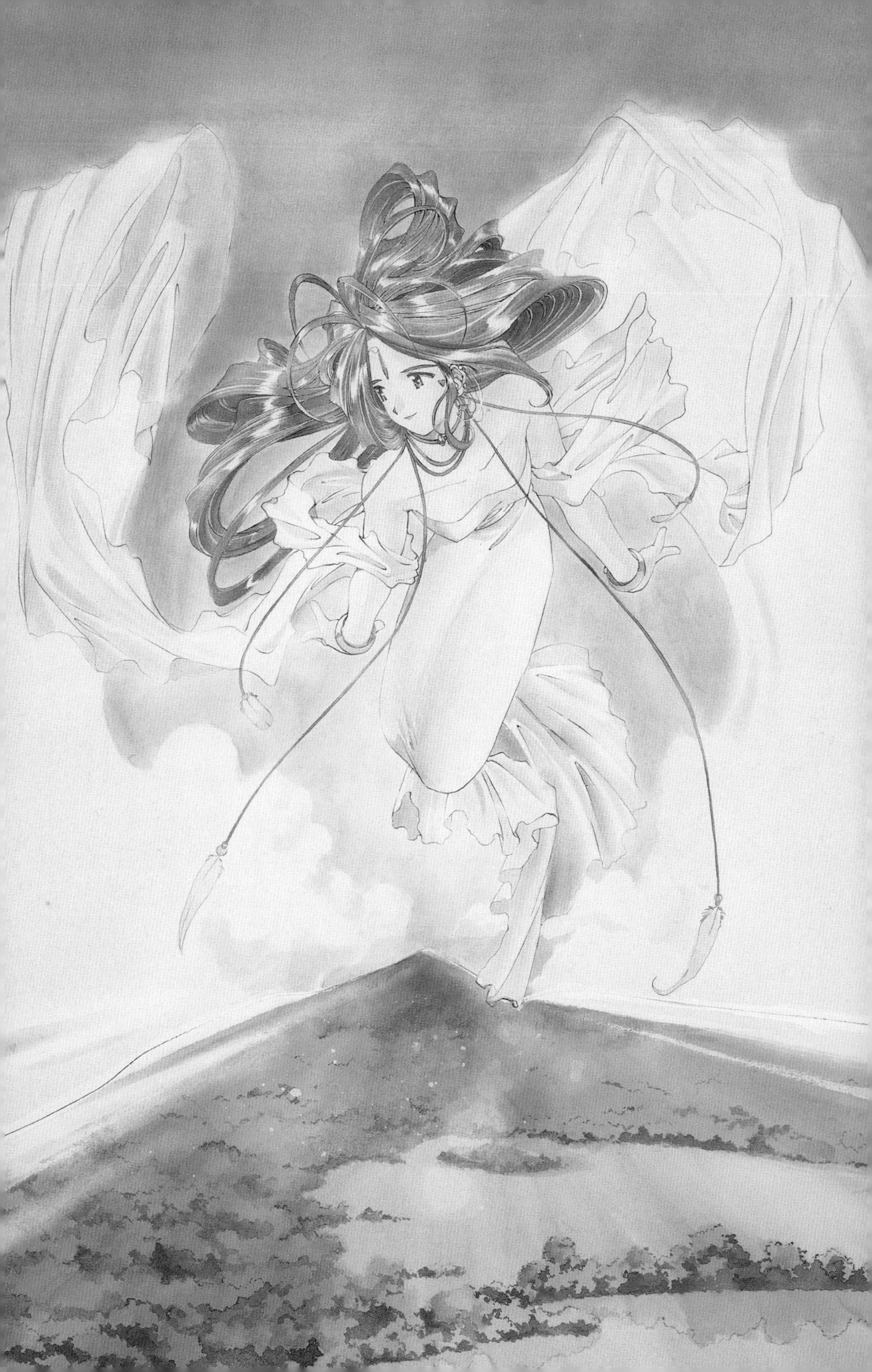

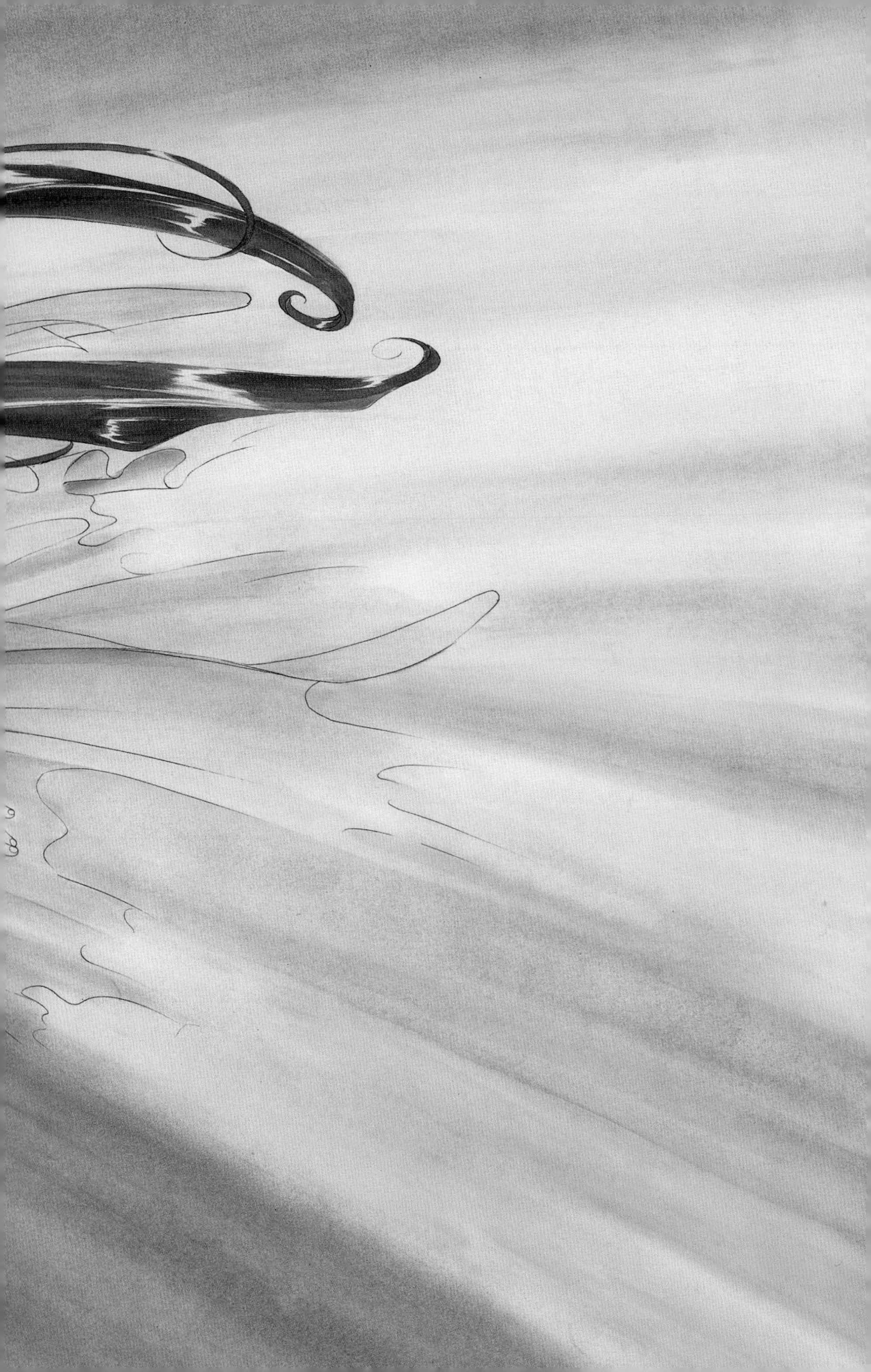

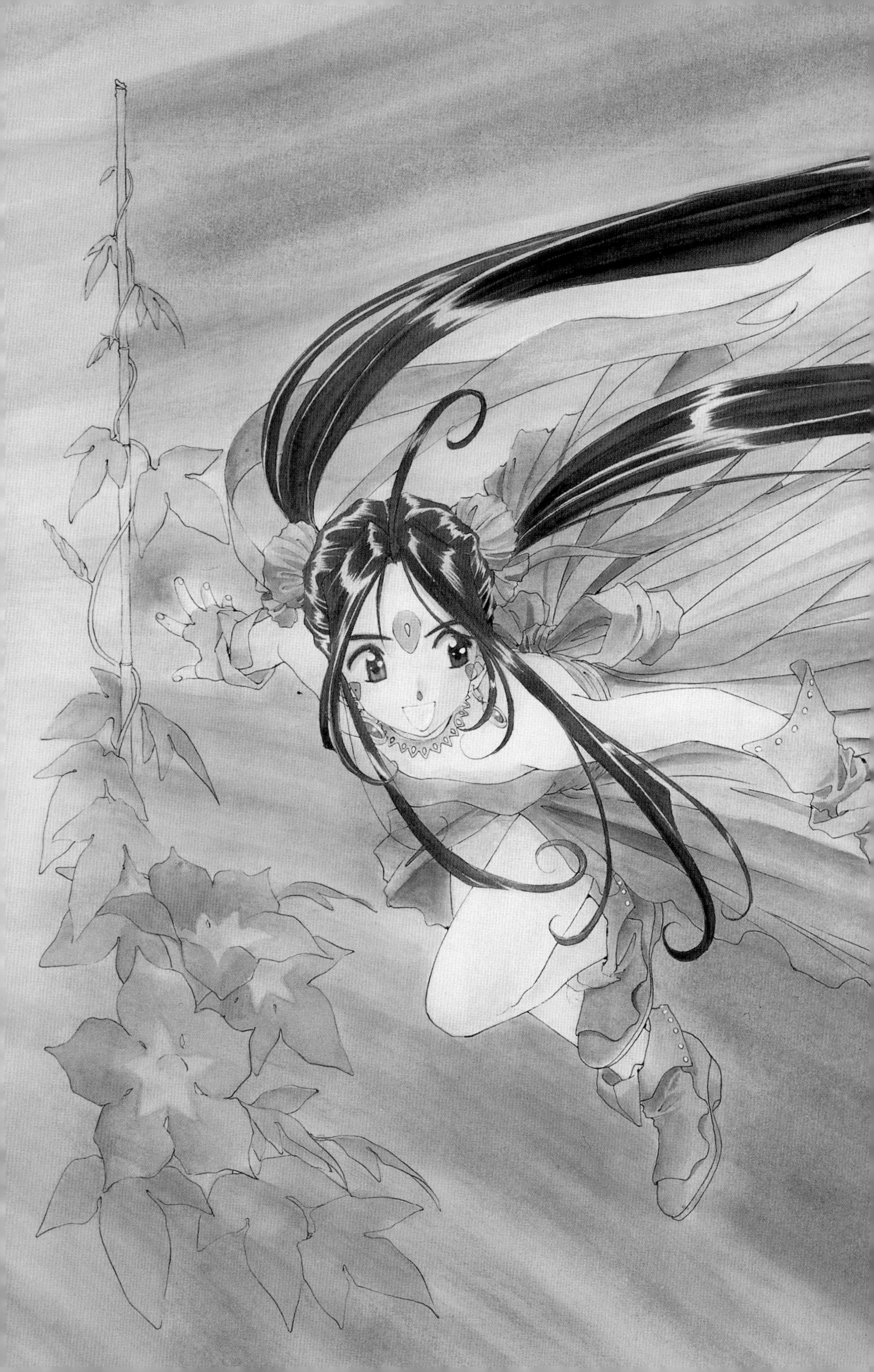

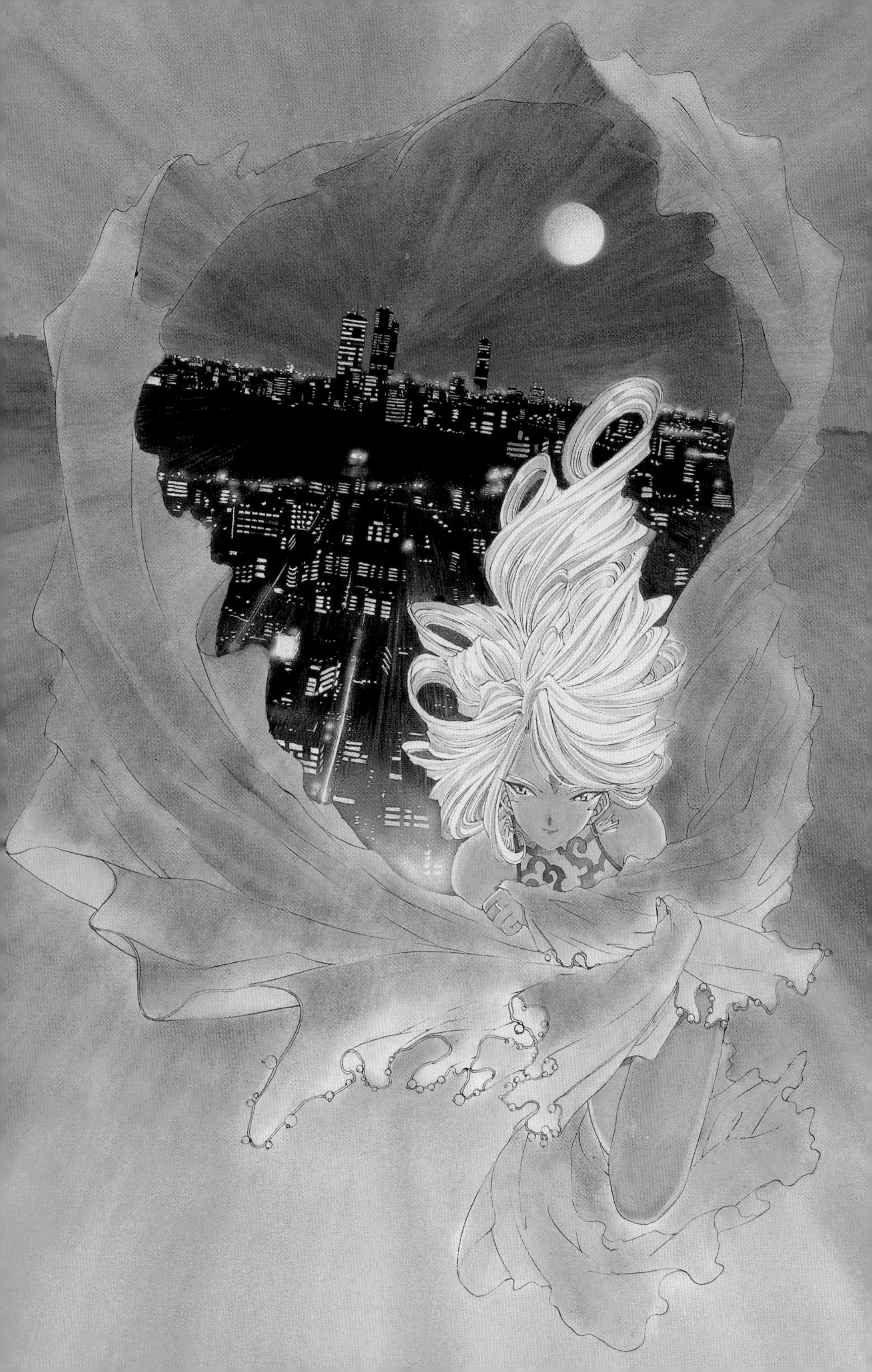

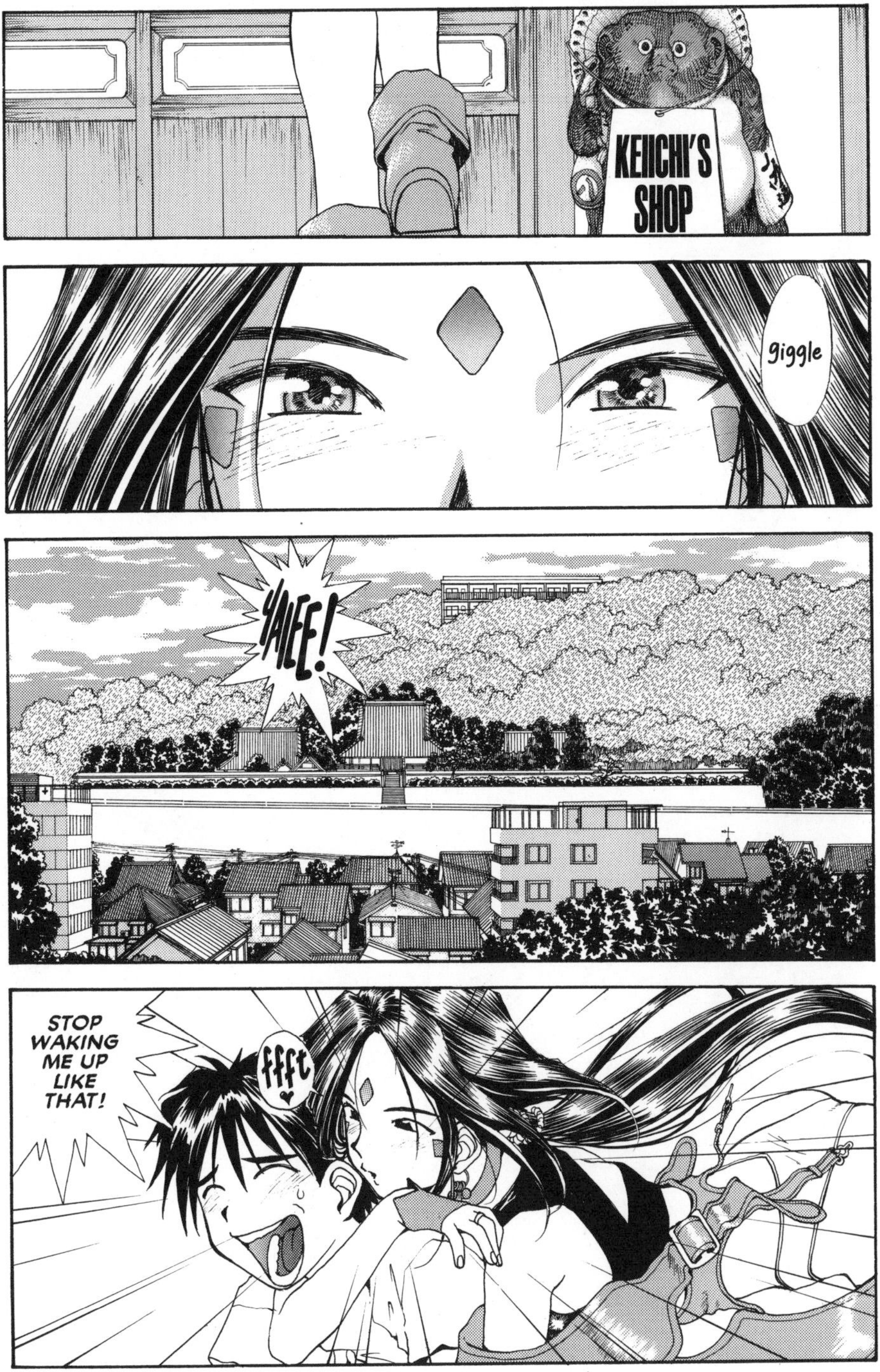
KEIICHI'S SHOP
giggle
YAIEE!
ffft
STOP WAKING ME UP LIKE THAT!

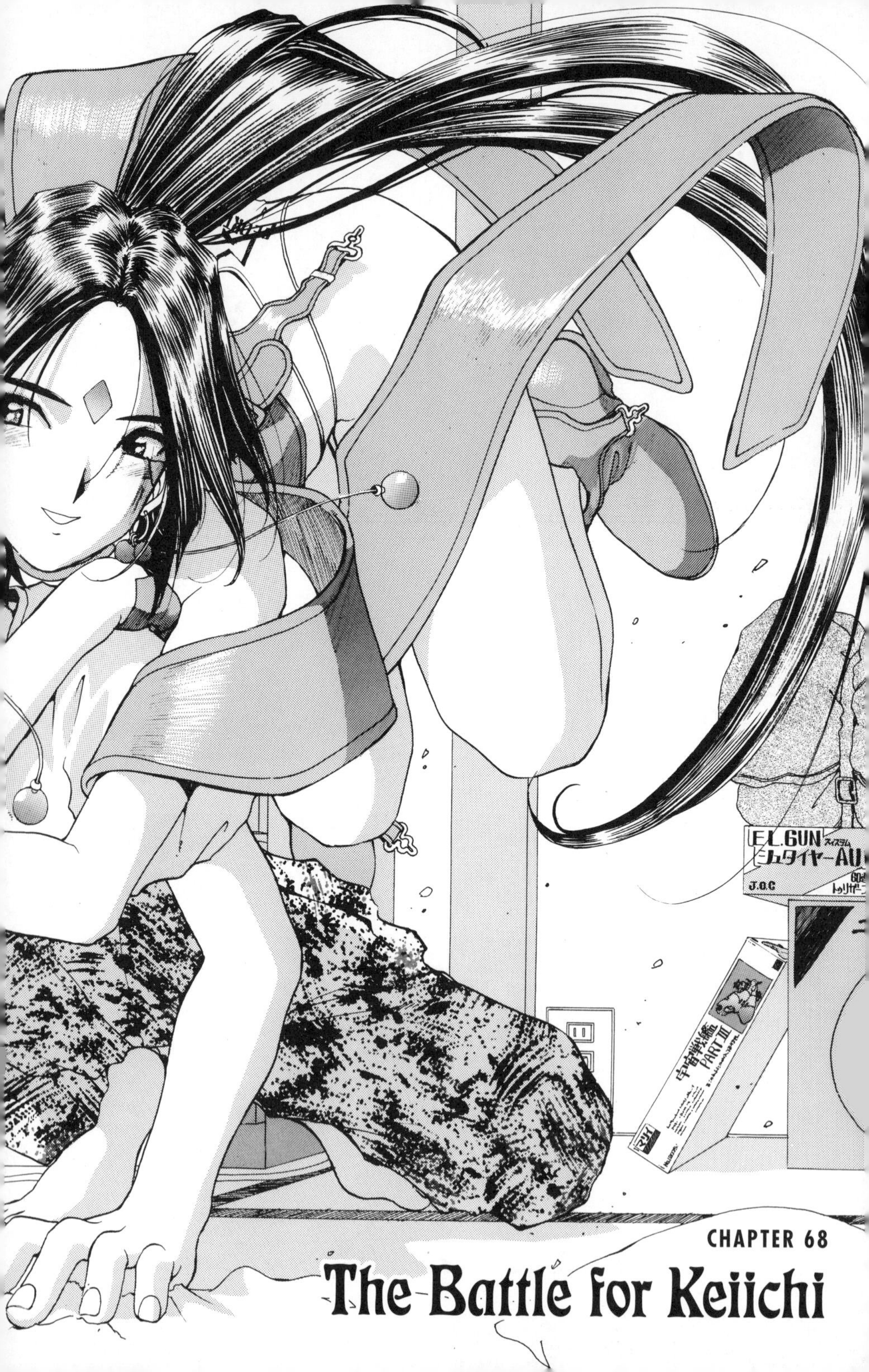
E.L.GUN
J.O.C
PART III

CHAPTER 68

The Battle for Keiichi

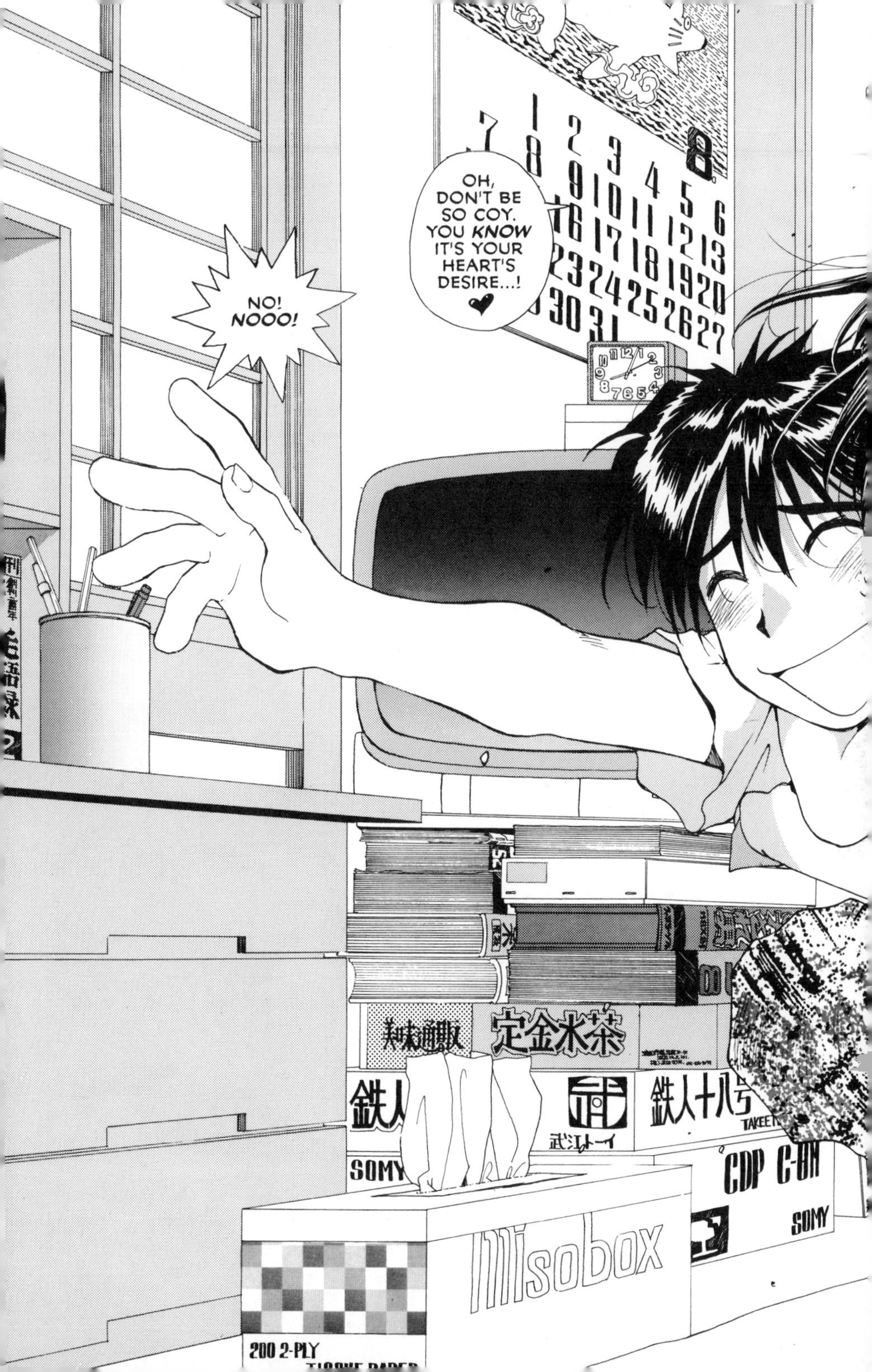
OH, DON'T BE SO COY. YOU *KNOW* IT'S YOUR HEART'S DESIRE...! ♥
NO! *NOOO!*

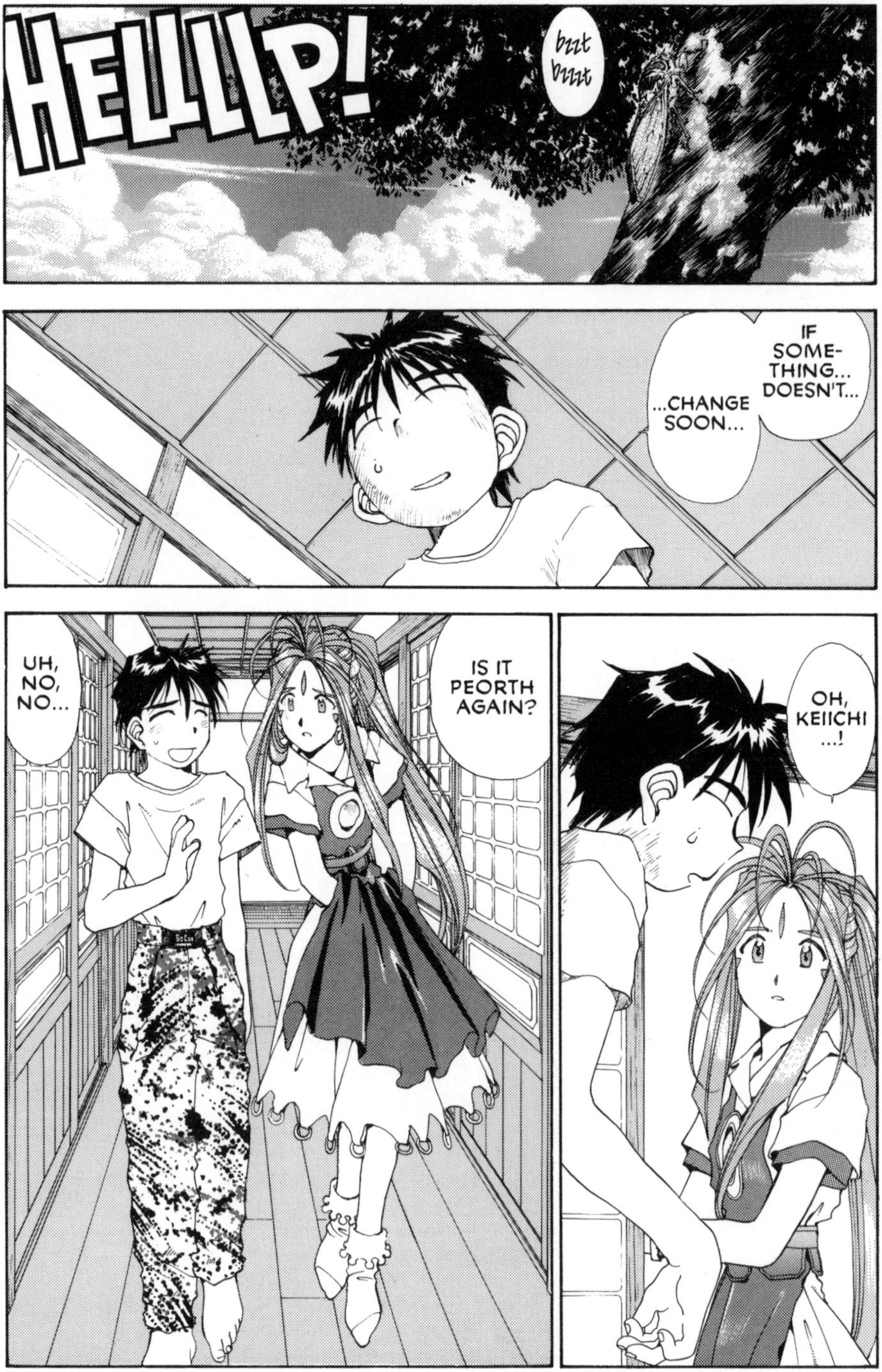
HELLLP!
bzzt bzzzt
IF SOME-THING... DOESN'T...
...CHANGE SOON...
OH, KEIICHI ...!
IS IT PEORTH AGAIN?
UH, NO, NO...

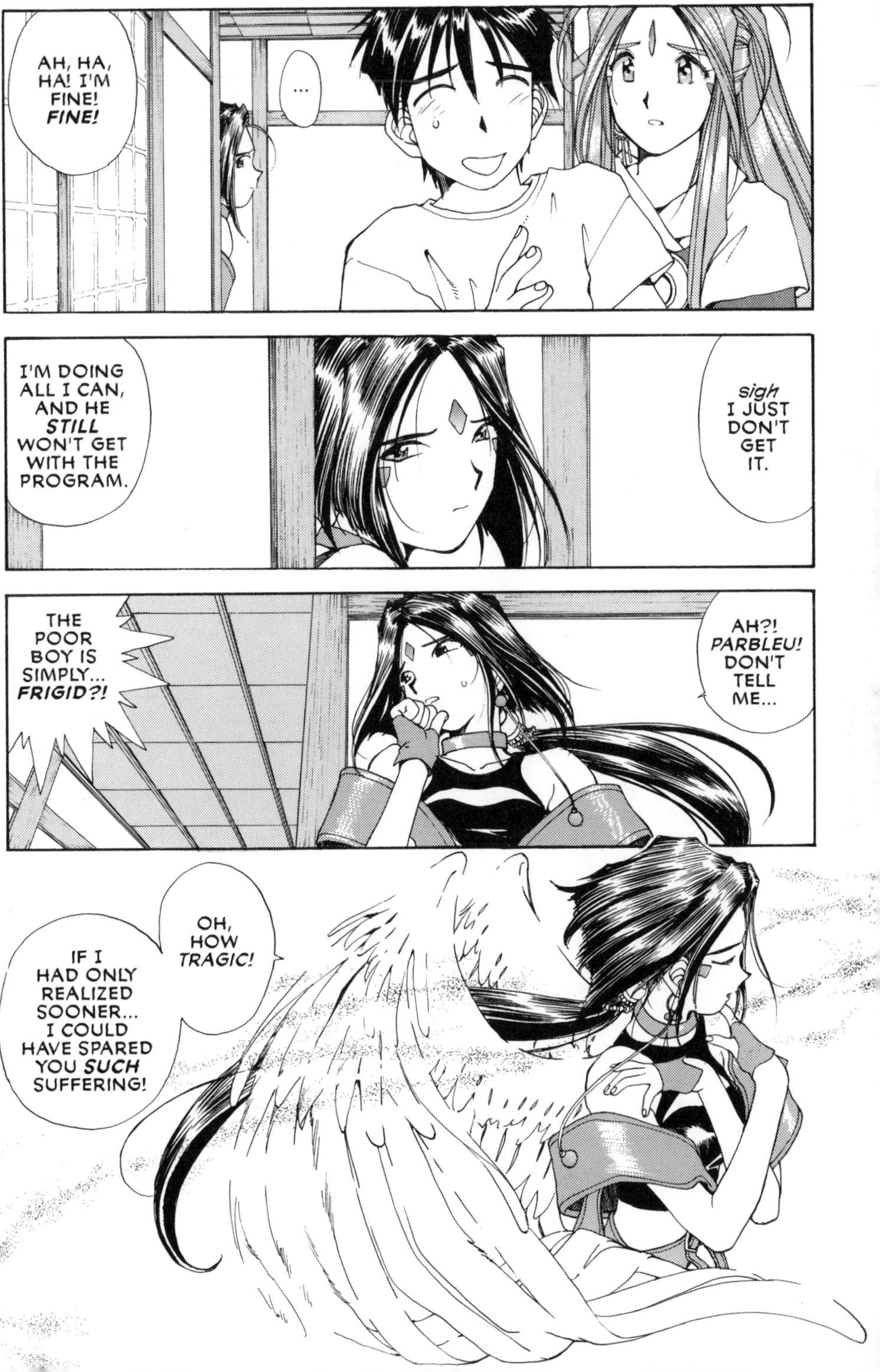
...
AH, HA, HA! I'M FINE! *FINE!*
sigh I JUST DON'T GET IT.
I'M DOING ALL I CAN, AND HE *STILL* WON'T GET WITH THE PROGRAM.
AH?! *PARBLEU!* DON'T TELL ME...
THE POOR BOY IS SIMPLY... *FRIGID?!*
OH, HOW *TRAGIC!*
IF I HAD ONLY REALIZED SOONER... I COULD HAVE SPARED YOU *SUCH* SUFFERING!

HAVE FAITH, DEAR KEIICHI!
PEORTH SHALL SAVE THEE!
URD'S ROOM
NOW, THEN...
...HMM... WHICH ONE IS IT?
SUPER GROWTH POTION *GIANT X*...
...*M-BOY*-TYPE OXYGUM...
WHERE IS THE ONLY ONE THAT *MATTERS* ...?
THIS IS ALL SO POINTLESS, URD.
AH! *HERE* WE ARE!
LOVE SEEDS!

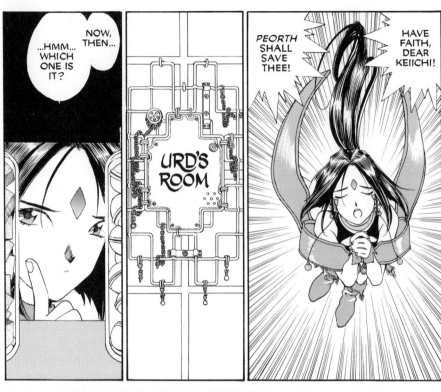

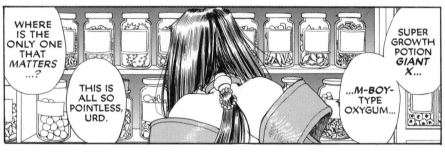

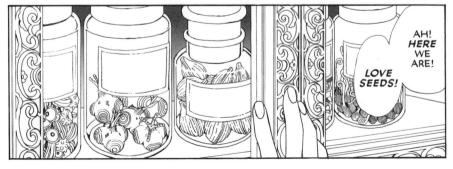

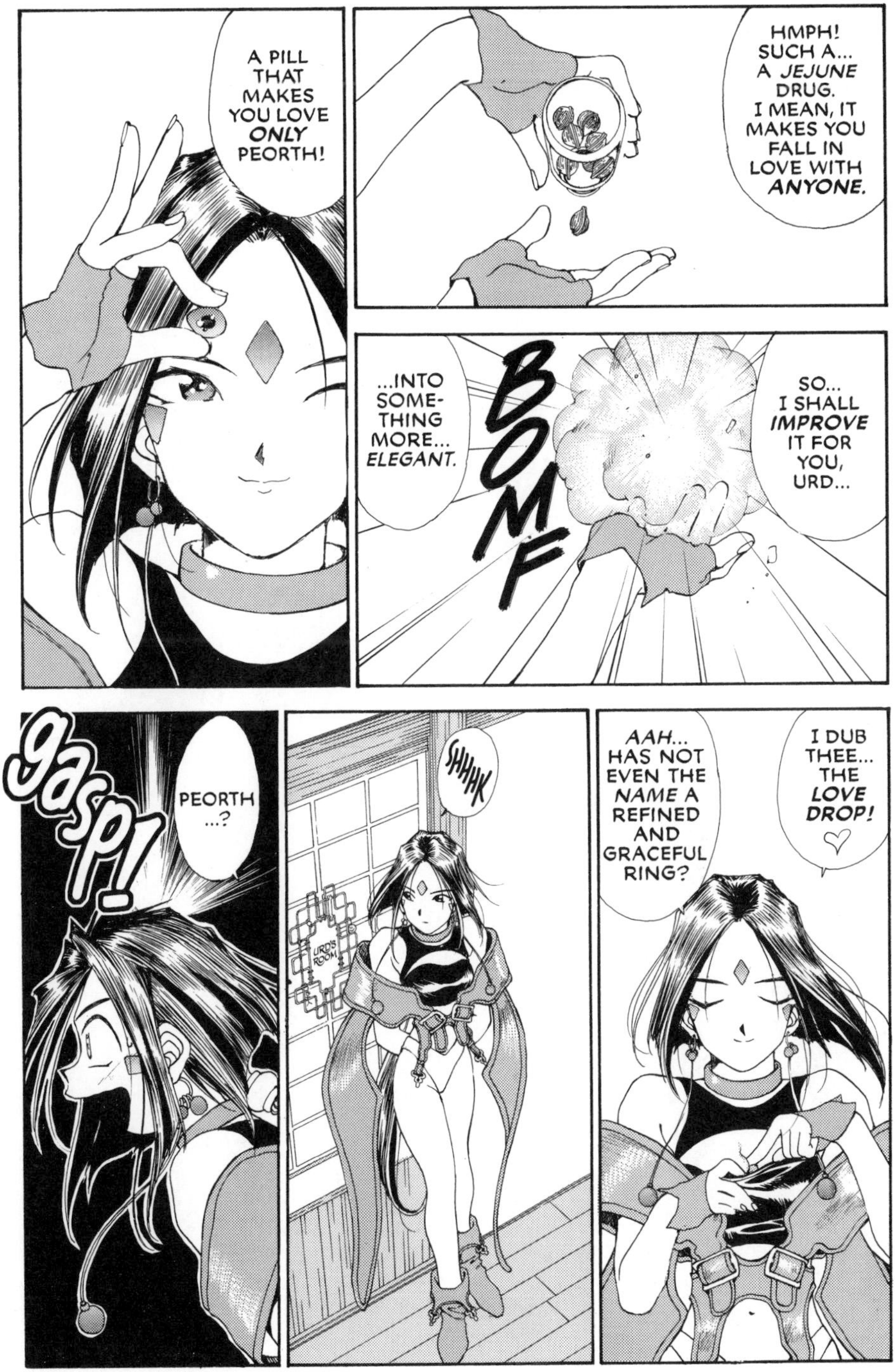
HMPH! SUCH A... A JEJUNE DRUG. I MEAN, IT MAKES YOU FALL IN LOVE WITH ANYONE.
SO... I SHALL IMPROVE IT FOR YOU, URD...
...INTO SOME-THING MORE... ELEGANT.
BOMF
A PILL THAT MAKES YOU LOVE ONLY PEORTH!
I DUB THEE... THE LOVE DROP! ♡
AAH... HAS NOT EVEN THE NAME A REFINED AND GRACEFUL RING?
SHHHK
URD'S ROOM
gasp!
PEORTH ...?

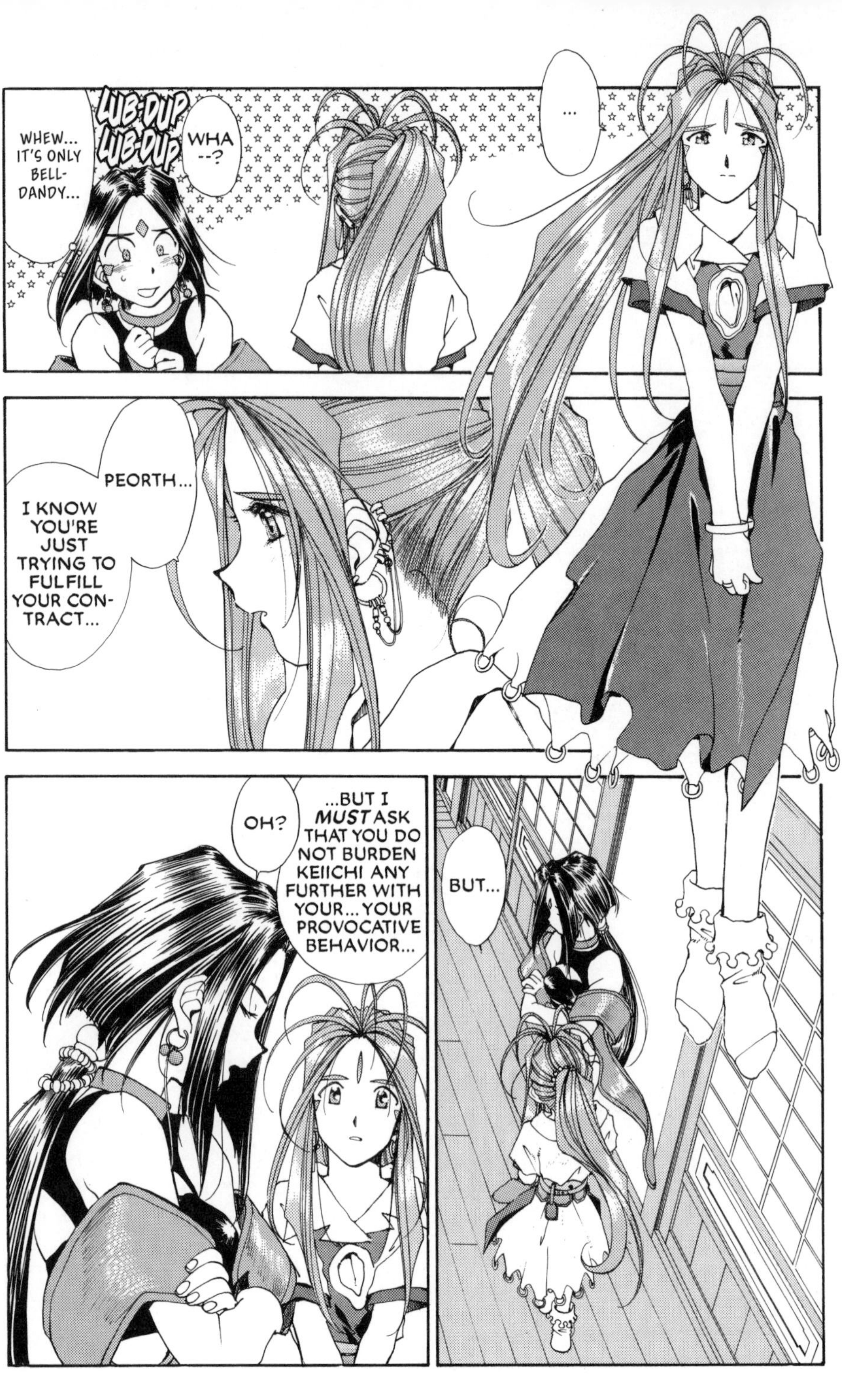

...
WHA --?
LUB-DUP LUB-DUP
WHEW... IT'S ONLY BELL-DANDY...
PEORTH...
I KNOW YOU'RE JUST TRYING TO FULFILL YOUR CON-TRACT...
BUT...
...BUT I *MUST* ASK THAT YOU DO NOT BURDEN KEIICHI ANY FURTHER WITH YOUR... YOUR PROVOCATIVE BEHAVIOR...
OH?

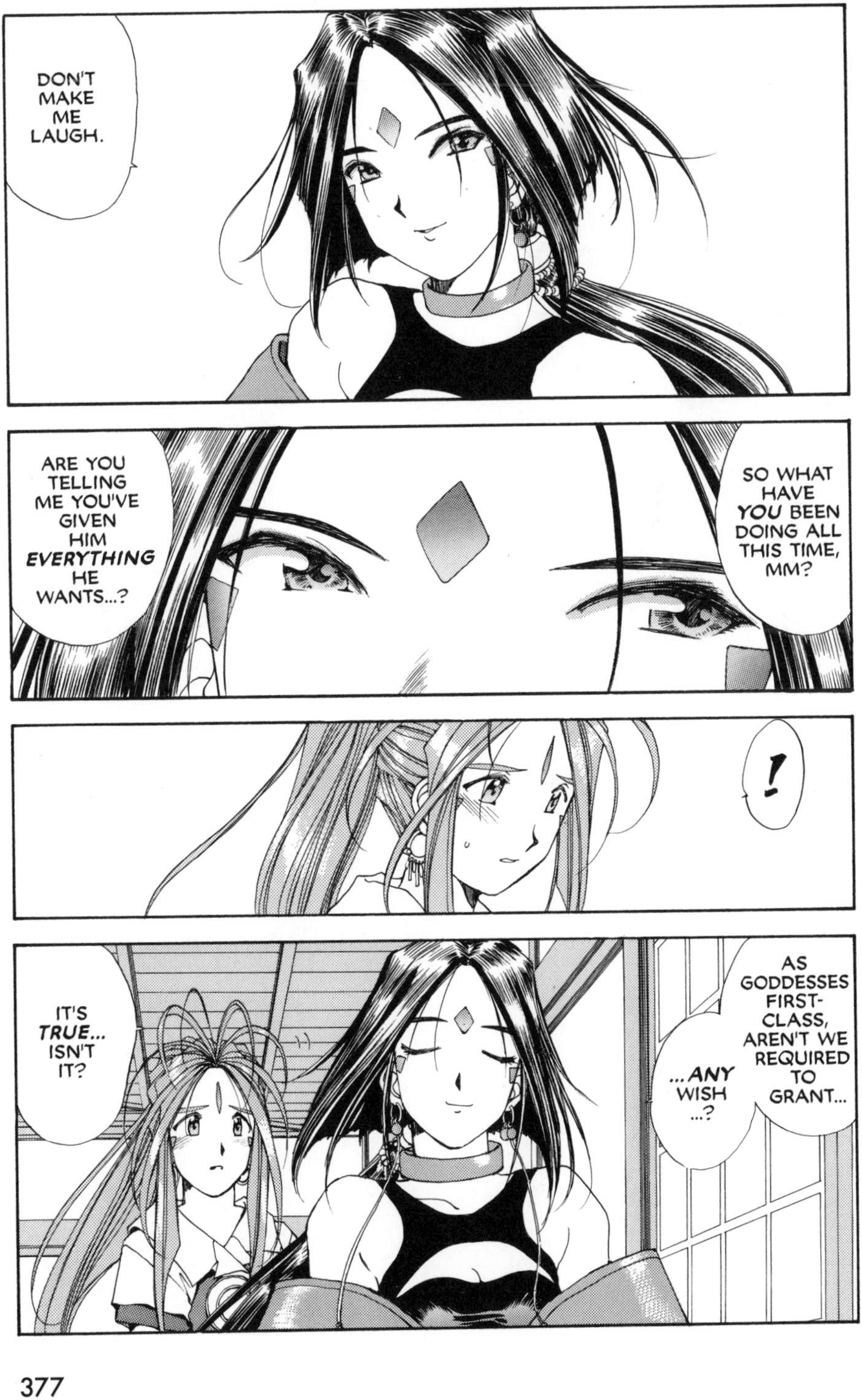
DON'T MAKE ME LAUGH.
SO WHAT HAVE *YOU* BEEN DOING ALL THIS TIME, MM?
ARE YOU TELLING ME YOU'VE GIVEN HIM *EVERYTHING* HE WANTS...?
!
AS GODDESSES FIRST-CLASS, AREN'T WE REQUIRED TO GRANT...
...*ANY* WISH ...?
IT'S *TRUE*... ISN'T IT?

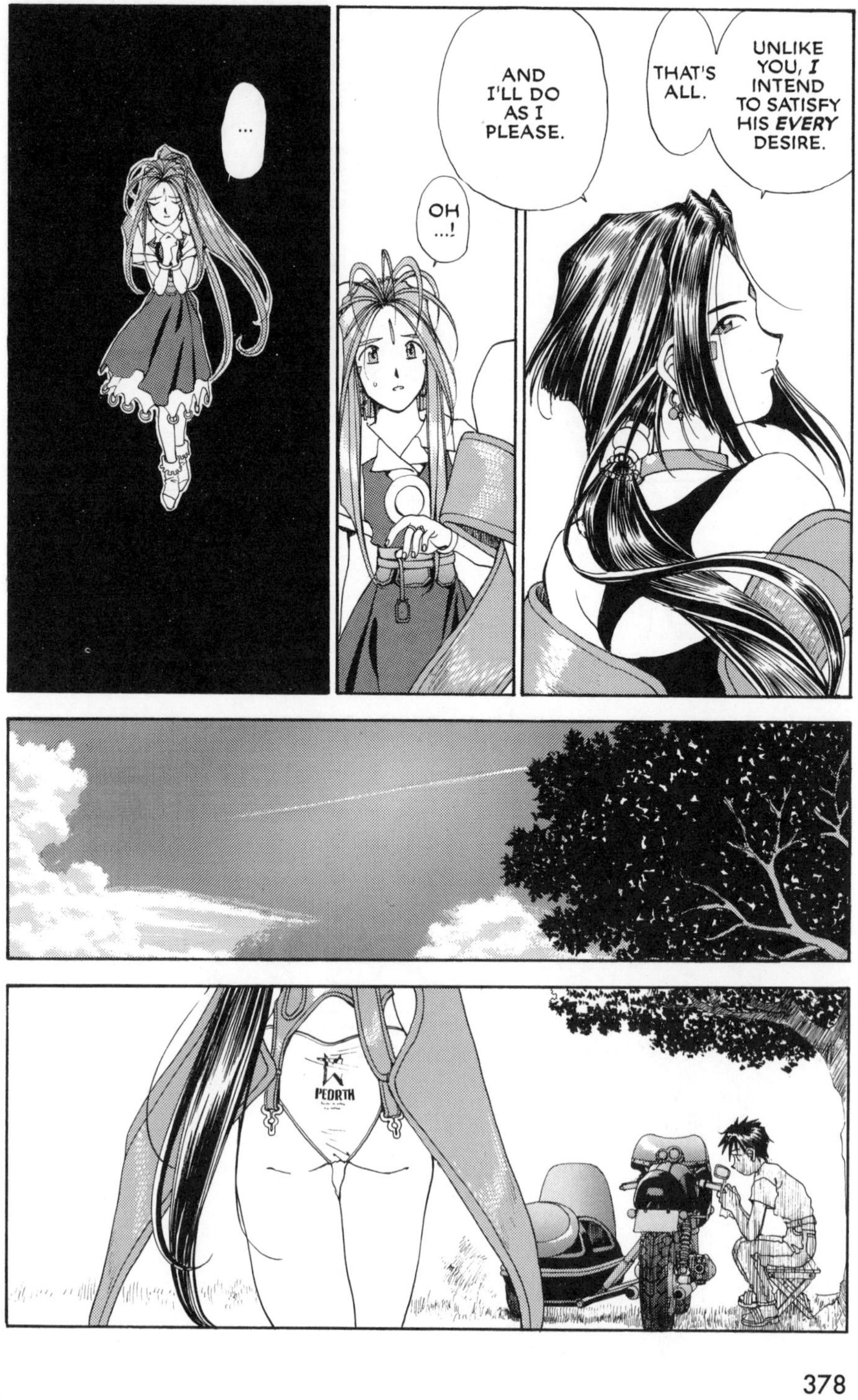
UNLIKE YOU, *I* INTEND TO SATISFY HIS *EVERY* DESIRE.
THAT'S ALL.
AND I'LL DO AS I PLEASE.
OH ...!
...
PEORTH

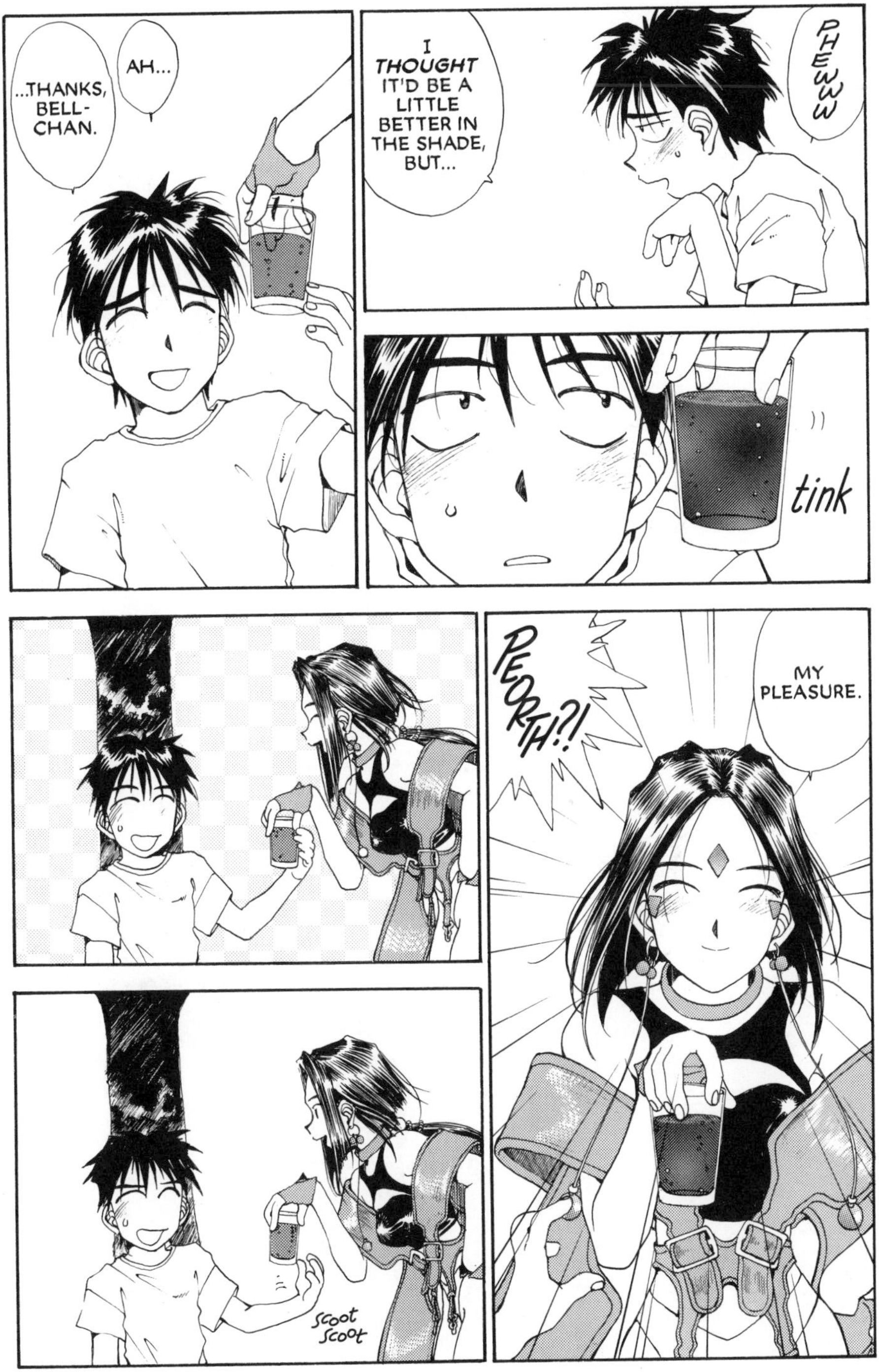
PHEWWW
I THOUGHT IT'D BE A LITTLE BETTER IN THE SHADE, BUT...
tink
AH...
...THANKS, BELL-CHAN.
MY PLEASURE.
PEORTH?!
scoot scoot

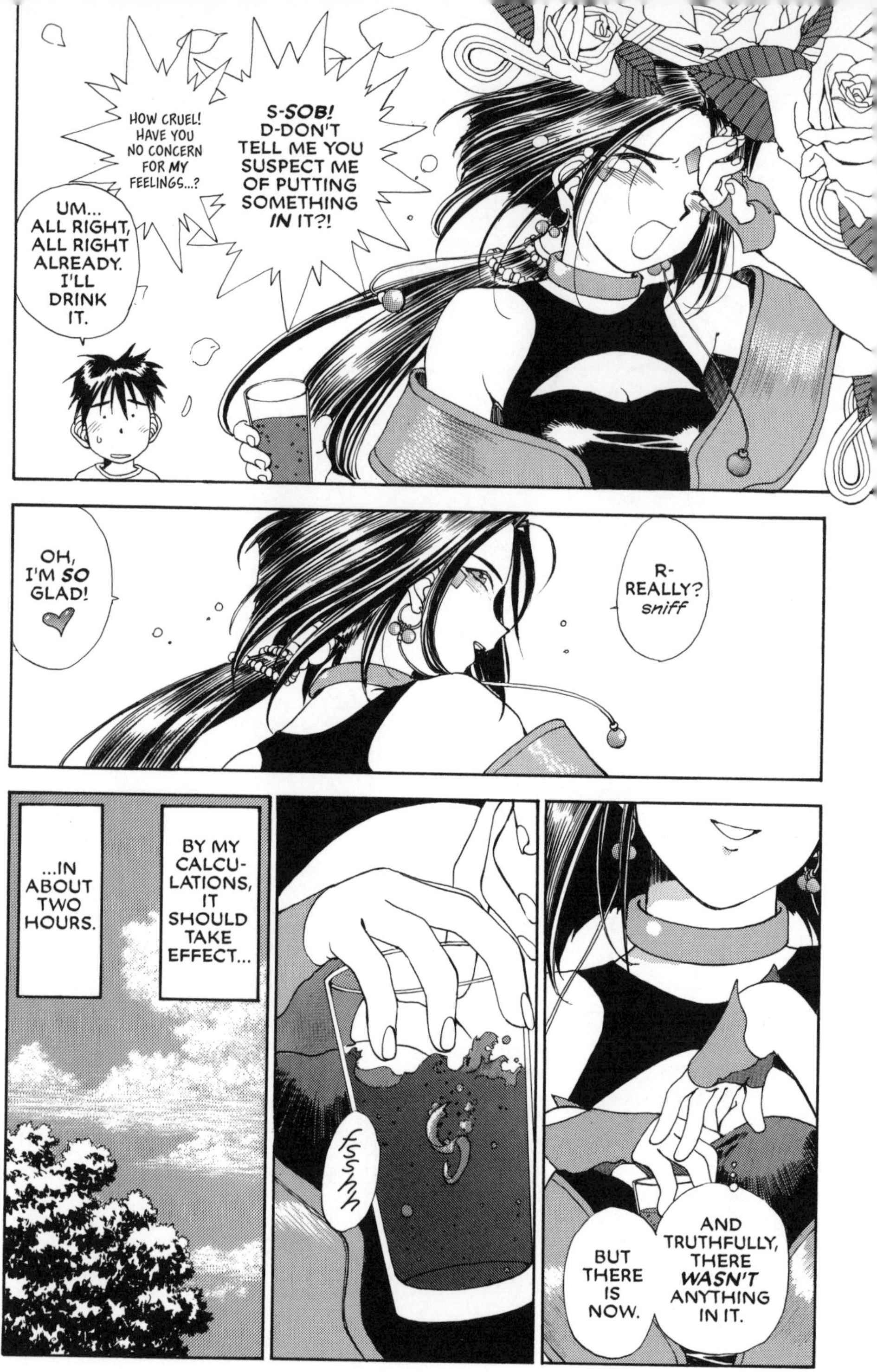
S-*SOB!* D-DON'T TELL ME YOU SUSPECT ME OF PUTTING SOMETHING *IN* IT?!
HOW CRUEL! HAVE YOU NO CONCERN FOR MY FEELINGS...?
UM... ALL RIGHT, ALL RIGHT ALREADY. I'LL DRINK IT.
R-REALLY? *sniff*
OH, I'M *SO* GLAD!
AND TRUTHFULLY, THERE *WASN'T* ANYTHING IN IT.
BUT THERE IS NOW.
BY MY CALCULATIONS, IT SHOULD TAKE EFFECT...
...IN ABOUT TWO HOURS.

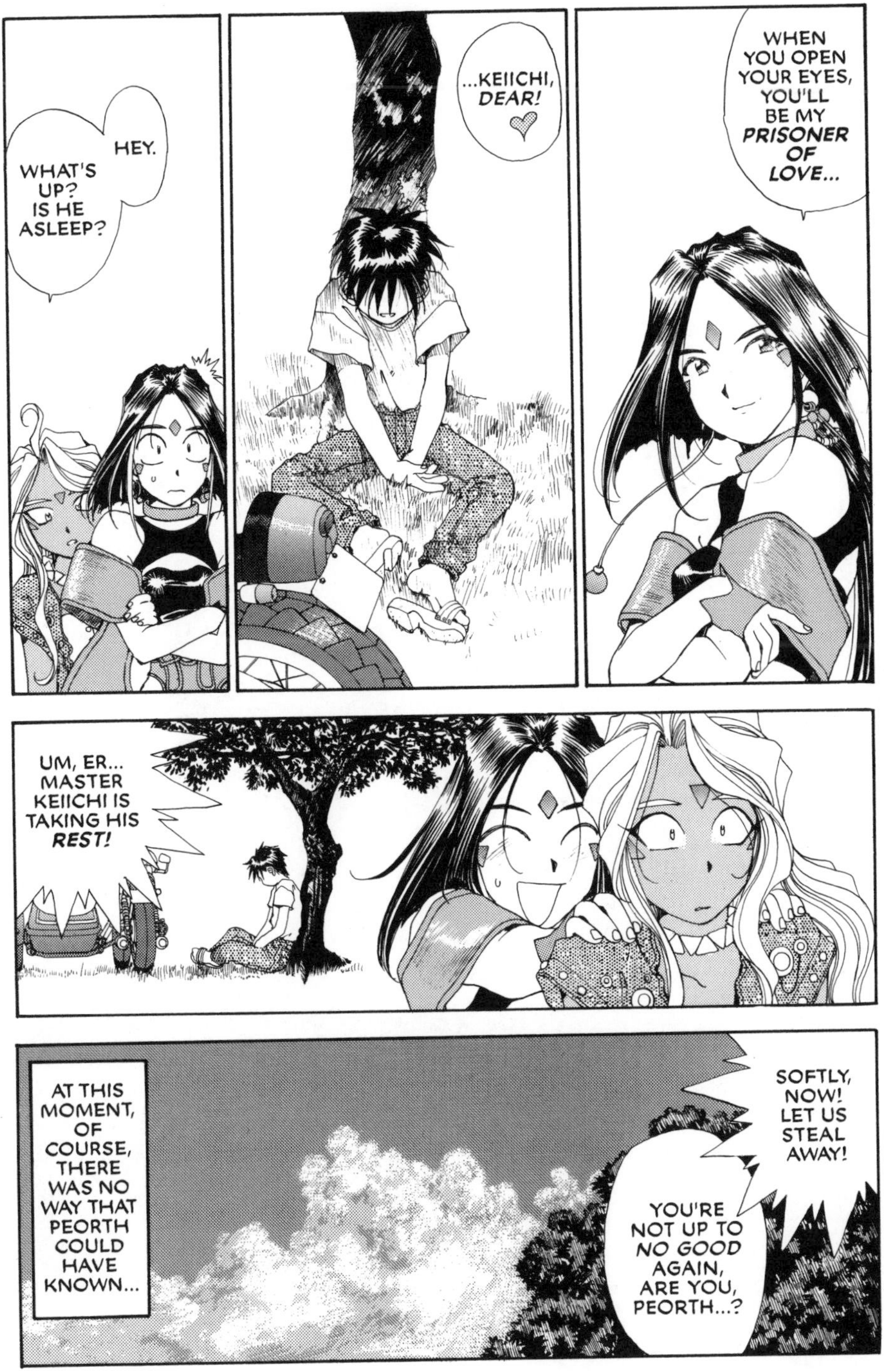
WHEN YOU OPEN YOUR EYES, YOU'LL BE MY *PRISONER OF LOVE...*
...KEIICHI, *DEAR!*
HEY.
WHAT'S UP? IS HE ASLEEP?
UM, ER... MASTER KEIICHI IS TAKING HIS *REST!*
SOFTLY, NOW! LET US STEAL AWAY!
YOU'RE NOT UP TO *NO GOOD* AGAIN, ARE YOU, PEORTH...?
AT THIS MOMENT, OF COURSE, THERE WAS NO WAY THAT PEORTH COULD HAVE KNOWN...

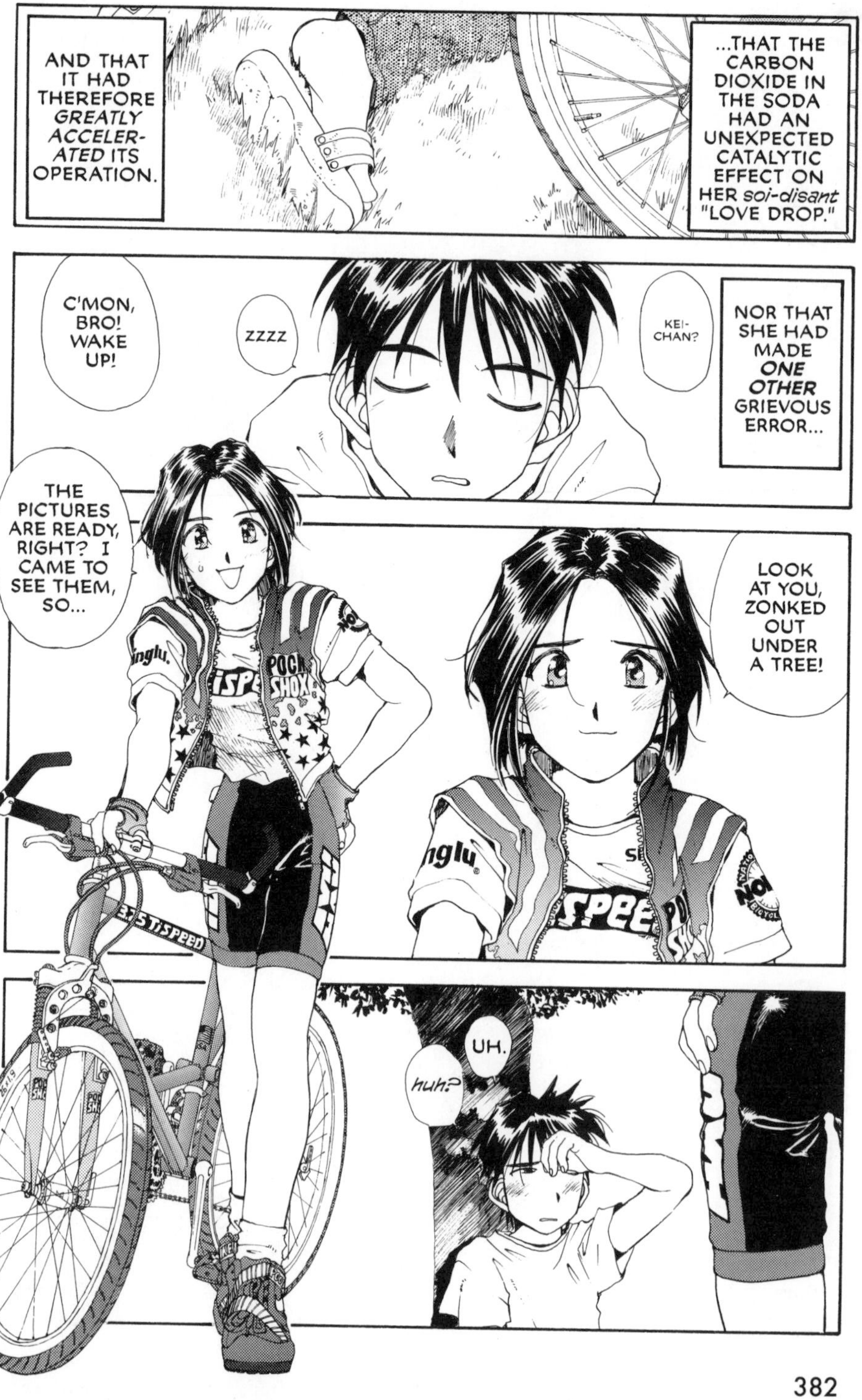
...THAT THE CARBON DIOXIDE IN THE SODA HAD AN UNEXPECTED CATALYTIC EFFECT ON HER *soi-disant* "LOVE DROP."
AND THAT IT HAD THEREFORE *GREATLY ACCELER-ATED* ITS OPERATION.
NOR THAT SHE HAD MADE ***ONE OTHER*** GRIEVOUS ERROR...
KEI-CHAN?
ZZZZ
C'MON, BRO! WAKE UP!
LOOK AT YOU, ZONKED OUT UNDER A TREE!
UH.
huh?
THE PICTURES ARE READY, RIGHT? I CAME TO SEE THEM, SO...

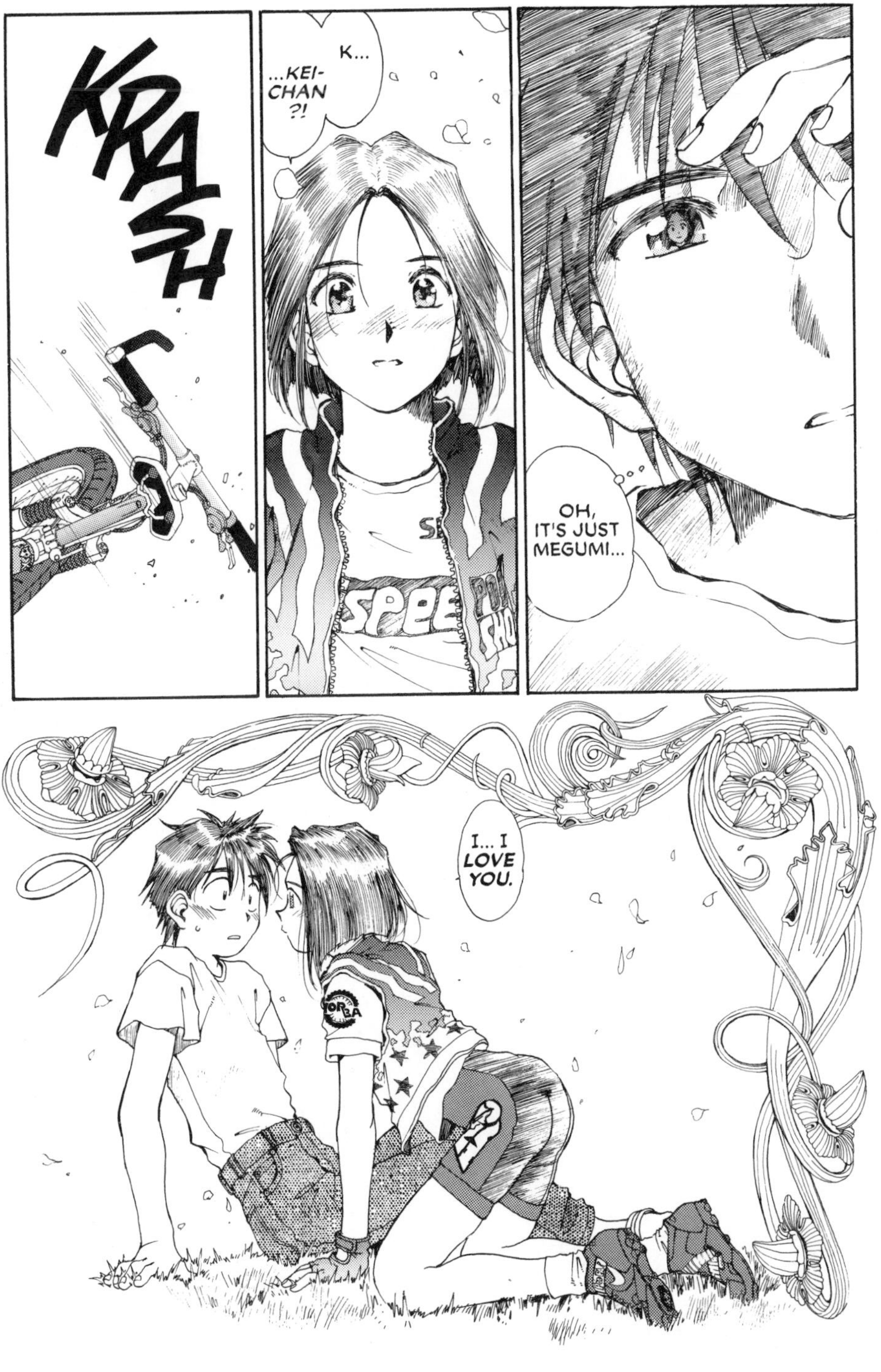
OH, IT'S JUST MEGUMI...
K...
...KEI-CHAN ?!
KRASH
I... I *LOVE* YOU.

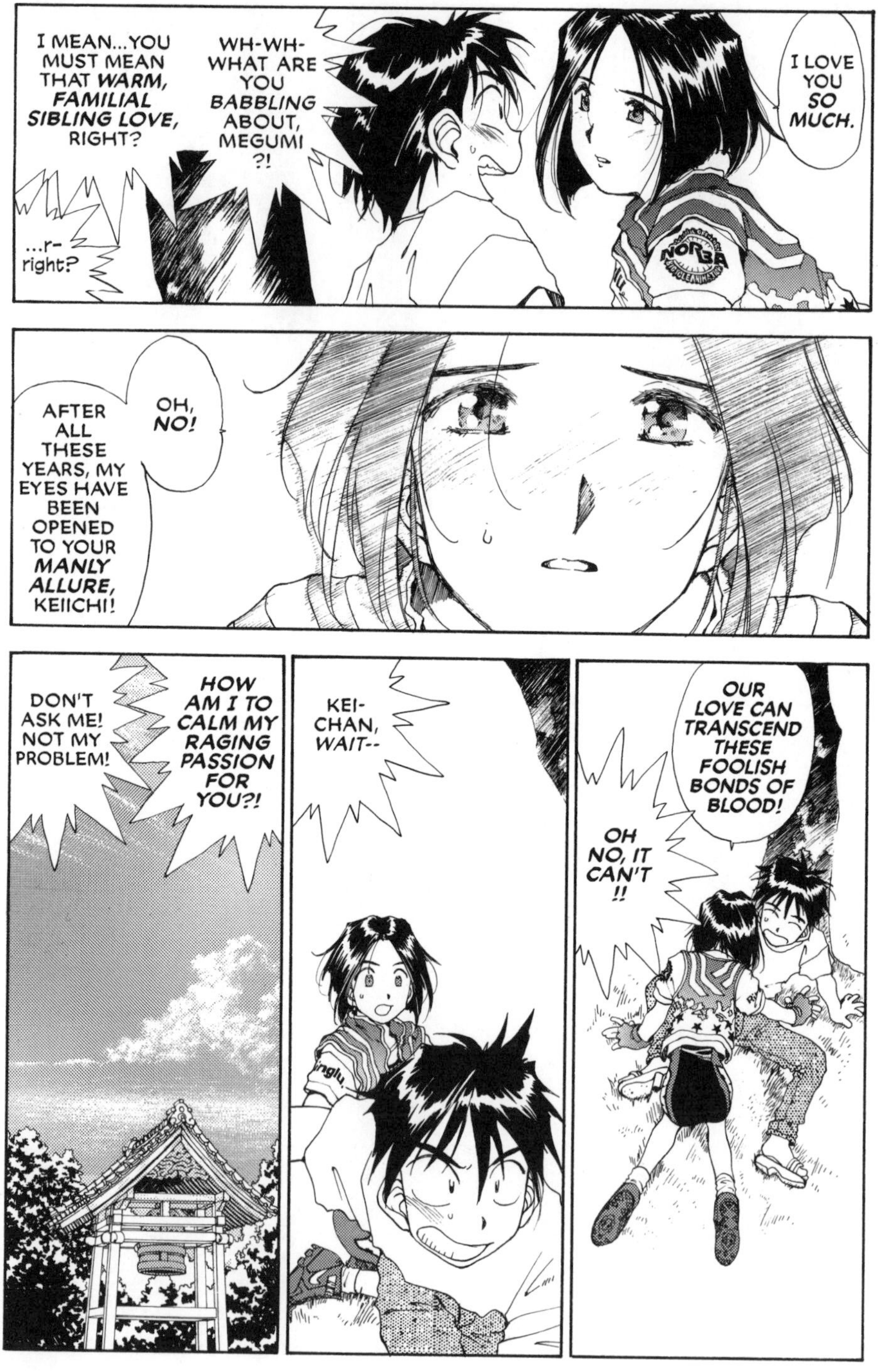
I LOVE YOU SO MUCH.
WH-WH-WHAT ARE YOU BABBLING ABOUT, MEGUMI?!
I MEAN...YOU MUST MEAN THAT WARM, FAMILIAL SIBLING LOVE, RIGHT?
...r-right?
OH, NO!
AFTER ALL THESE YEARS, MY EYES HAVE BEEN OPENED TO YOUR MANLY ALLURE, KEIICHI!
OUR LOVE CAN TRANSCEND THESE FOOLISH BONDS OF BLOOD!
OH NO, IT CAN'T!!
KEI-CHAN, WAIT--
HOW AM I TO CALM MY RAGING PASSION FOR YOU?!
DON'T ASK ME! NOT MY PROBLEM!

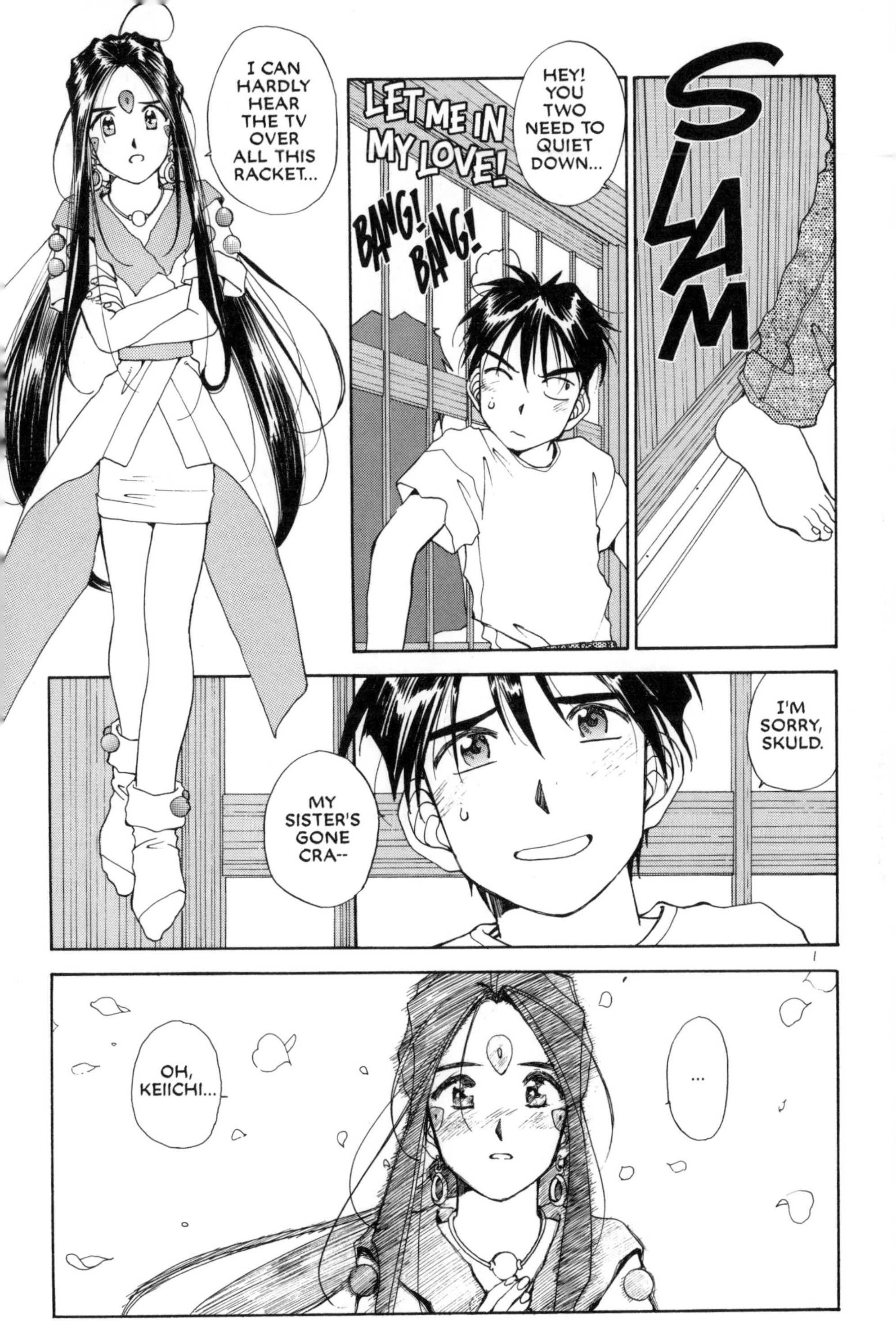
SLAM
LET ME IN MY LOVE!
BANG! BANG!
HEY! YOU TWO NEED TO QUIET DOWN...
I CAN HARDLY HEAR THE TV OVER ALL THIS RACKET...
I'M SORRY, SKULD.
MY SISTER'S GONE CRA--
...
OH, KEIICHI...

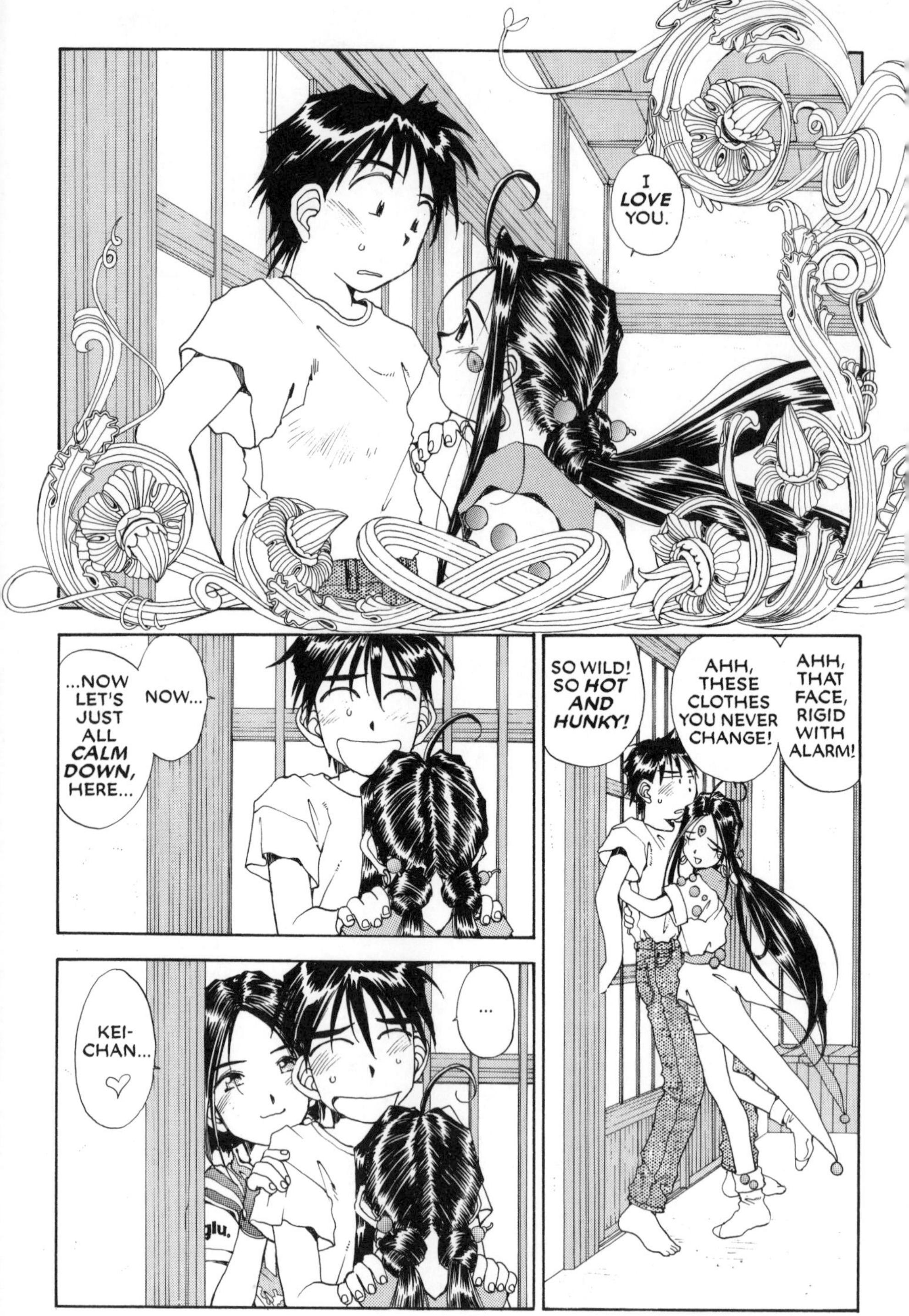
I *LOVE* YOU.
AHH, THAT FACE, RIGID WITH ALARM!
AHH, THESE CLOTHES YOU NEVER CHANGE!
SO WILD! SO *HOT AND HUNKY!*
NOW...
...NOW LET'S JUST ALL *CALM DOWN,* HERE...
...
KEI-CHAN... ♡

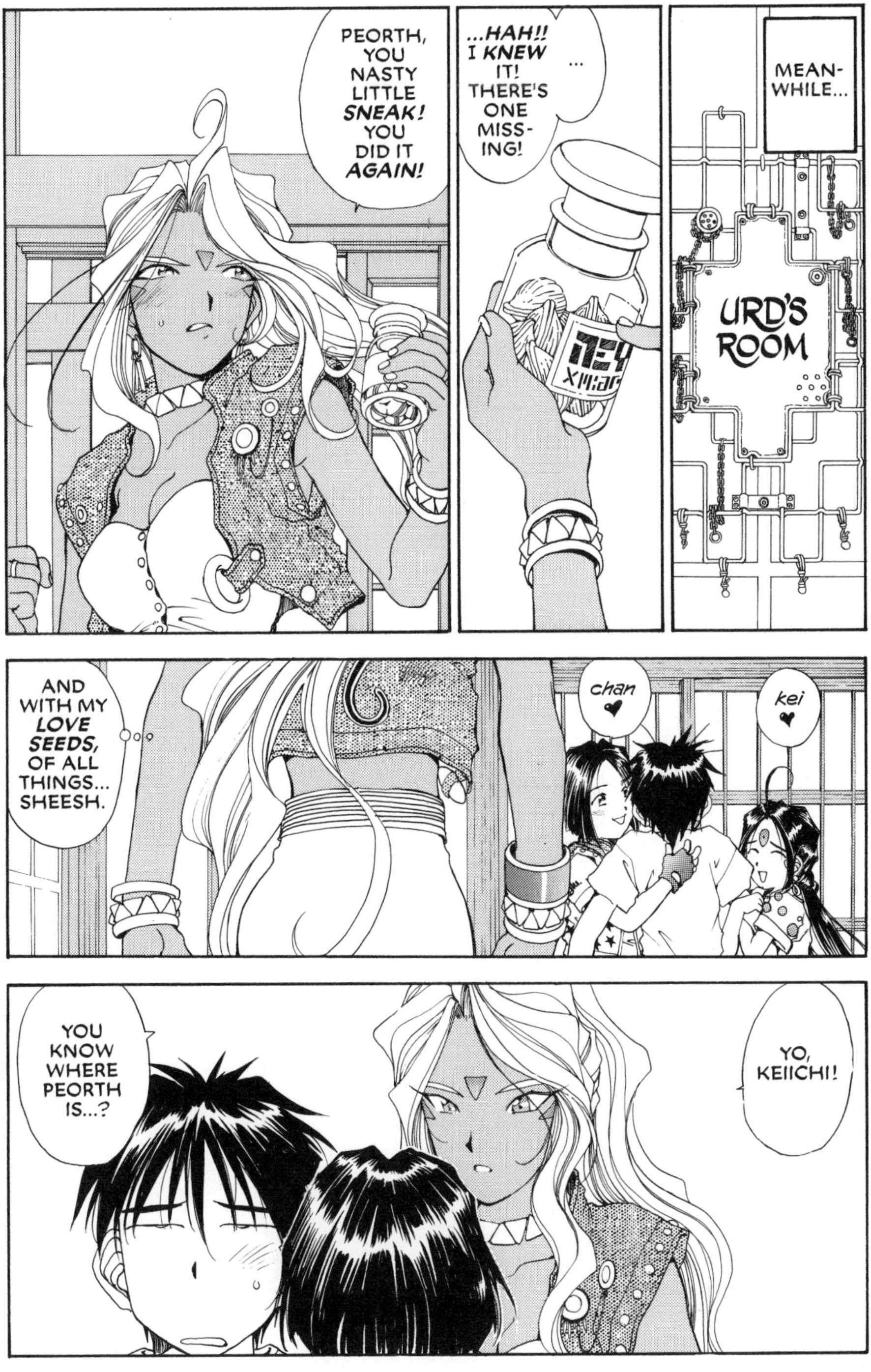
MEAN-WHILE...
URD'S ROOM
...
...HAH!! I KNEW IT! THERE'S ONE MISSING!
PEORTH, YOU NASTY LITTLE SNEAK! YOU DID IT AGAIN!
kei ♥
chan ♥
AND WITH MY LOVE SEEDS, OF ALL THINGS... SHEESH.
YO, KEIICHI!
YOU KNOW WHERE PEORTH IS...?

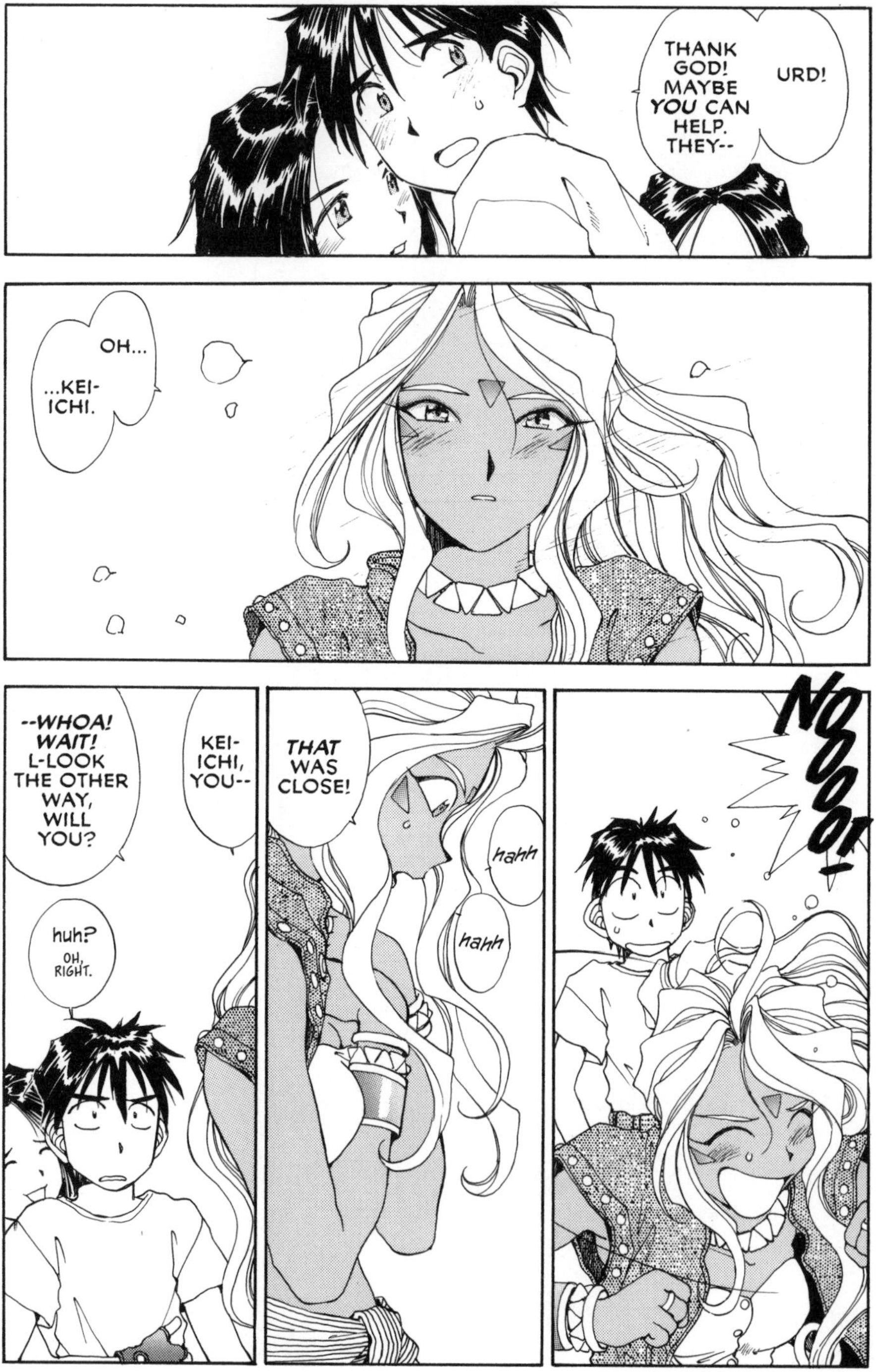
URD!
THANK GOD! MAYBE *YOU* CAN HELP. THEY--
OH...
...KEI-ICHI.
NOOOOO!
THAT WAS CLOSE!
hahh
hahh
KEI-ICHI, YOU--
--WHOA! WAIT! L-LOOK THE OTHER WAY, WILL YOU?
huh? OH, RIGHT.

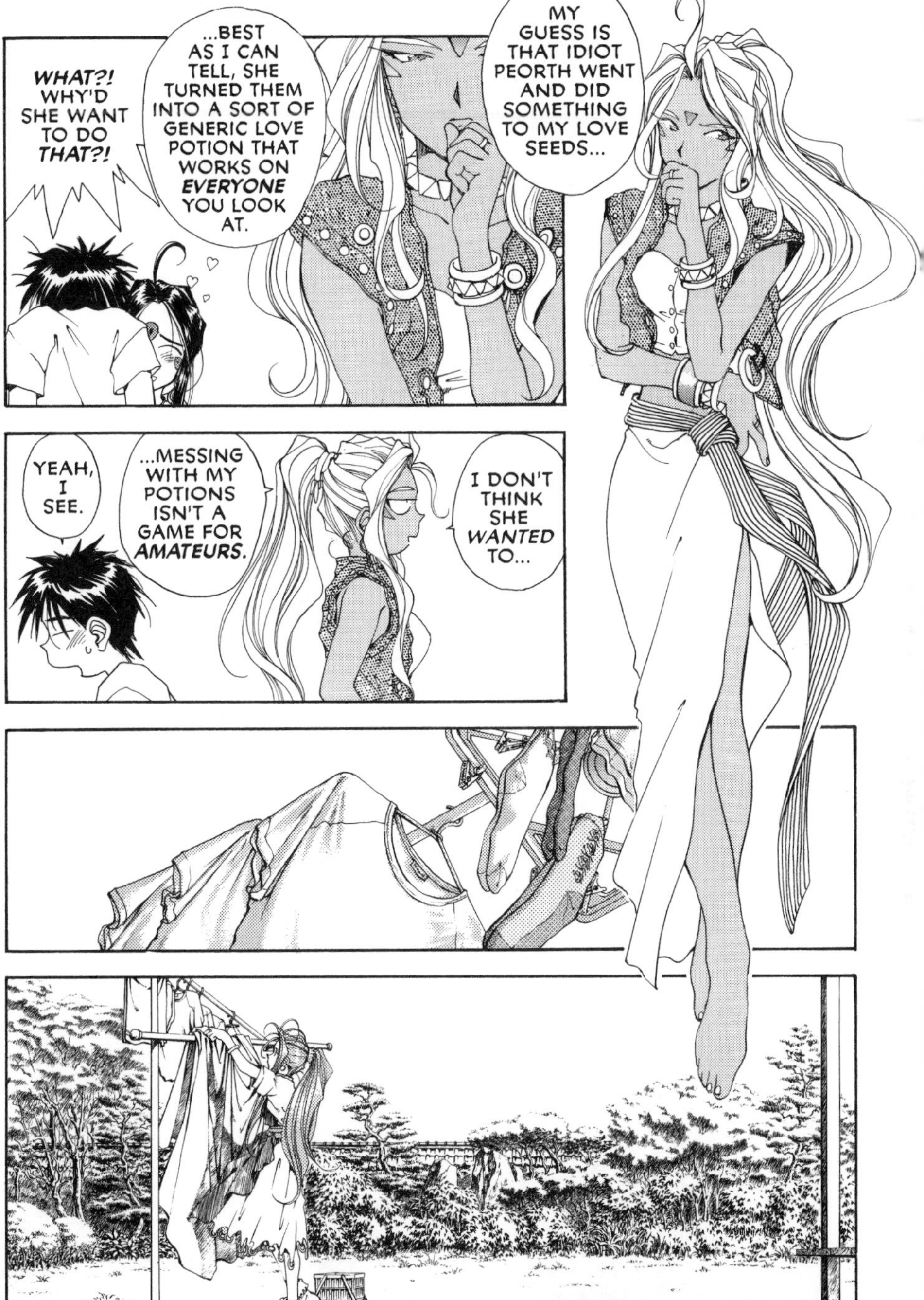
MY GUESS IS THAT IDIOT PEORTH WENT AND DID SOMETHING TO MY LOVE SEEDS...
...BEST AS I CAN TELL, SHE TURNED THEM INTO A SORT OF GENERIC LOVE POTION THAT WORKS ON *EVERYONE* YOU LOOK AT.
WHAT?! WHY'D SHE WANT TO DO *THAT?!*
I DON'T THINK SHE *WANTED* TO...
...MESSING WITH MY POTIONS ISN'T A GAME FOR *AMATEURS.*
YEAH, I SEE.

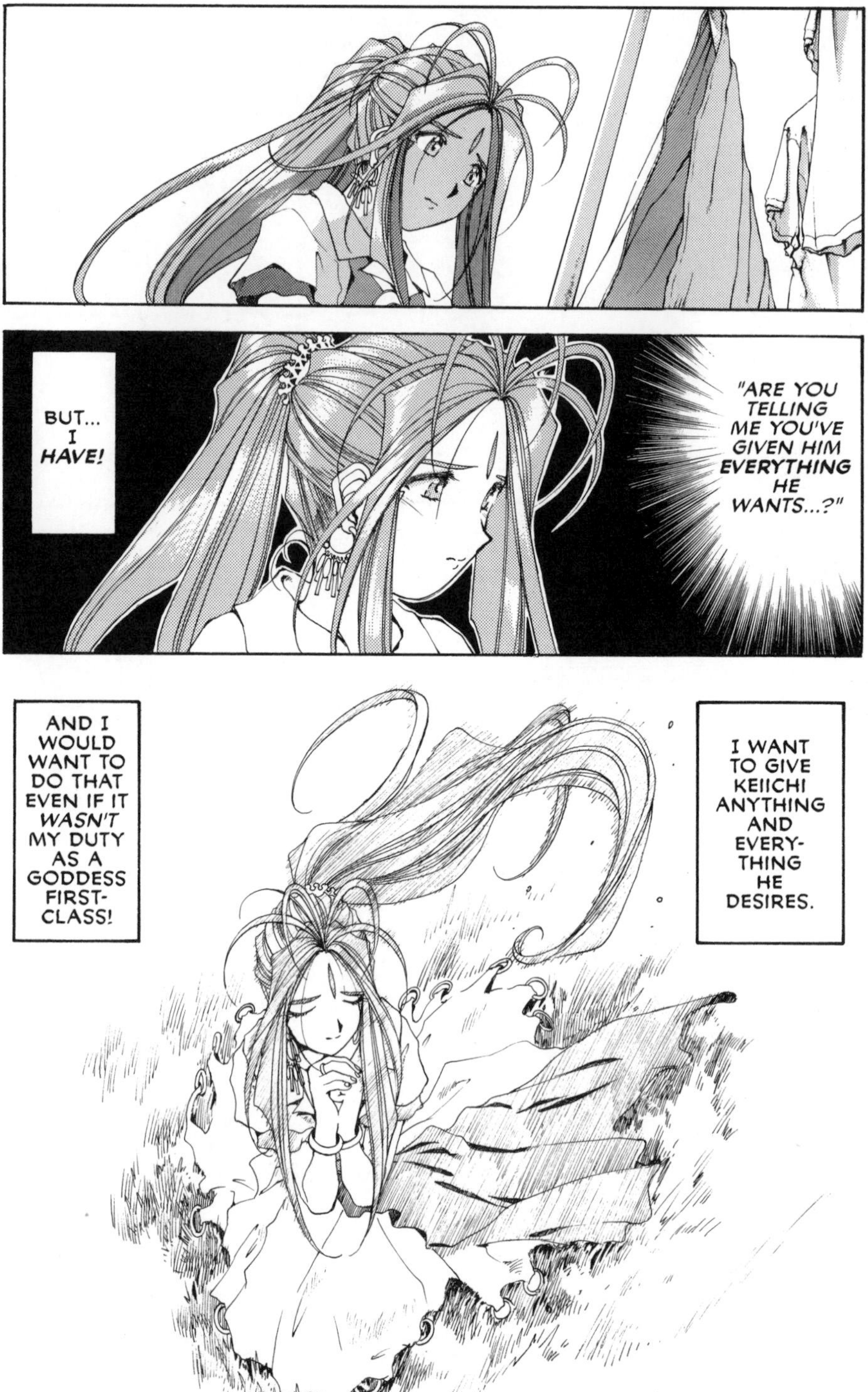
"ARE YOU TELLING ME YOU'VE GIVEN HIM **EVERYTHING** HE WANTS...?"
BUT... I *HAVE!*
I WANT TO GIVE KEIICHI ANYTHING AND EVERY-THING HE DESIRES.
AND I WOULD WANT TO DO THAT EVEN IF IT *WASN'T* MY DUTY AS A GODDESS FIRST-CLASS!

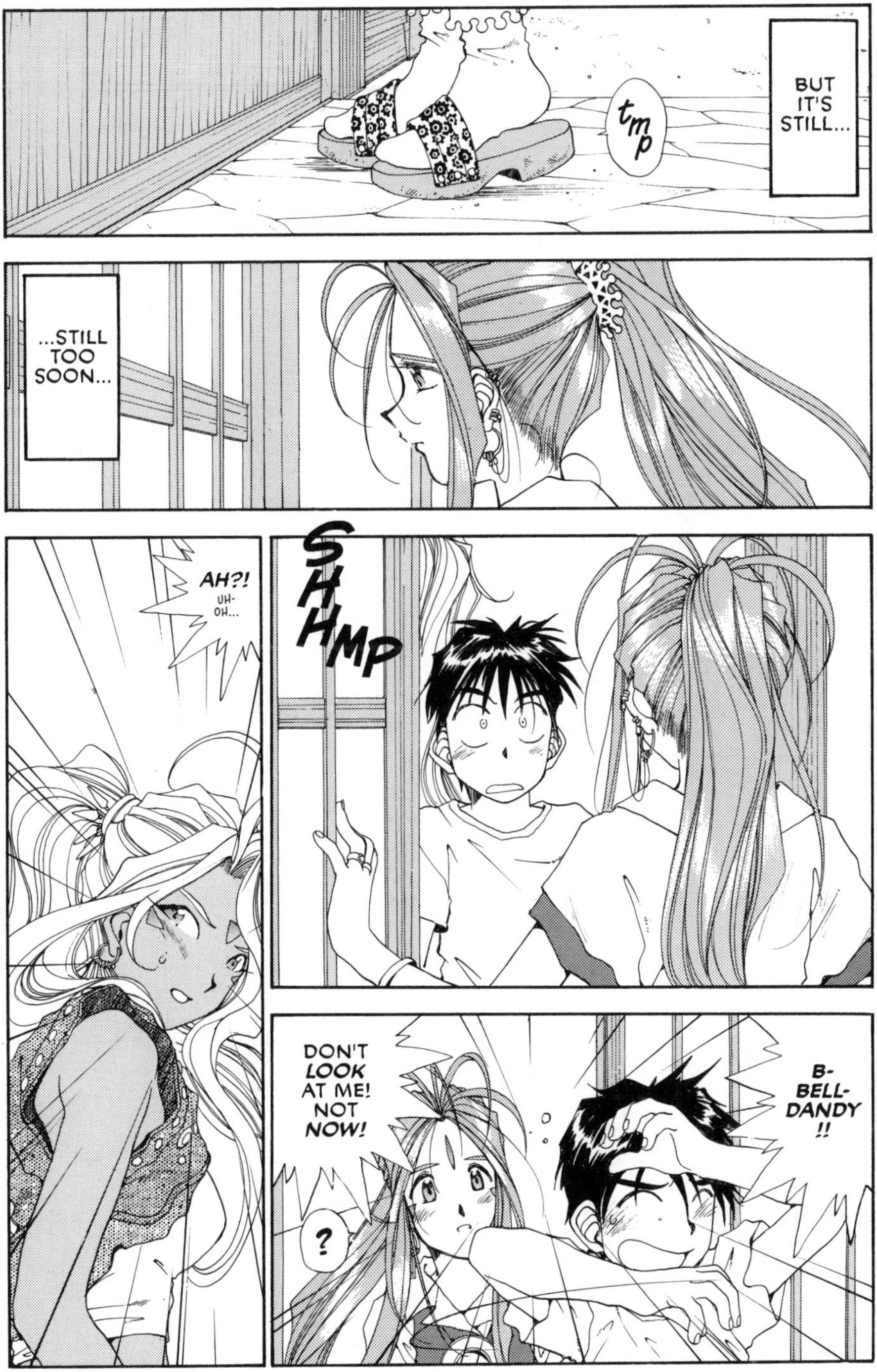
BUT IT'S STILL...
tmp
...STILL TOO SOON...
SHHMP
B-BELL-DANDY!!
DON'T LOOK AT ME! NOT NOW!
?
AH?!
UH-OH...

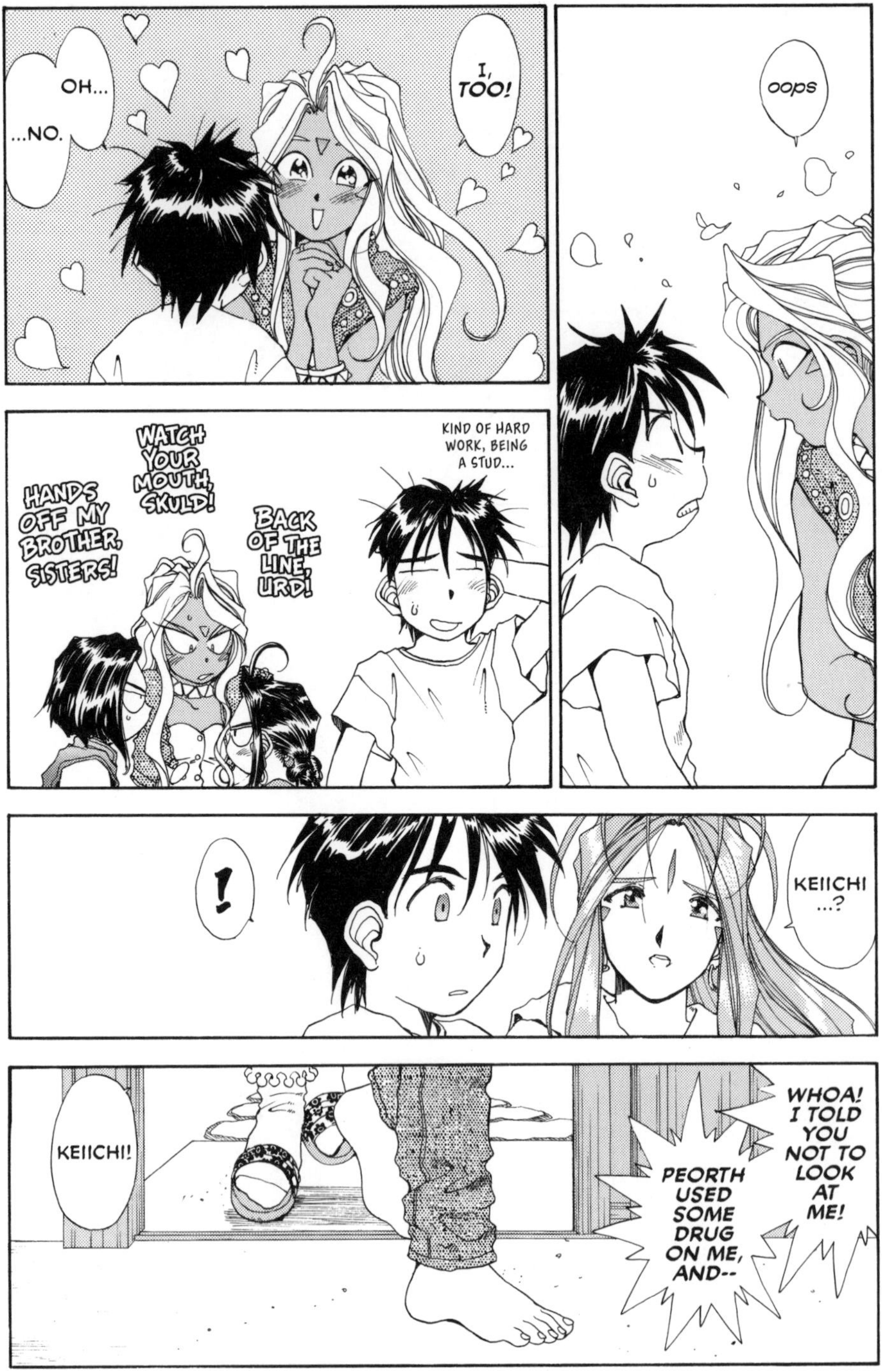
oops
I, TOO!
OH...
...NO.
KIND OF HARD WORK, BEING A STUD...
BACK OF THE LINE, URD!
WATCH YOUR MOUTH, SKULD!
HANDS OFF MY BROTHER, SISTERS!
KEIICHI ...?
!
WHOA! I TOLD YOU NOT TO LOOK AT ME!
PEORTH USED SOME DRUG ON ME, AND--
KEIICHI!

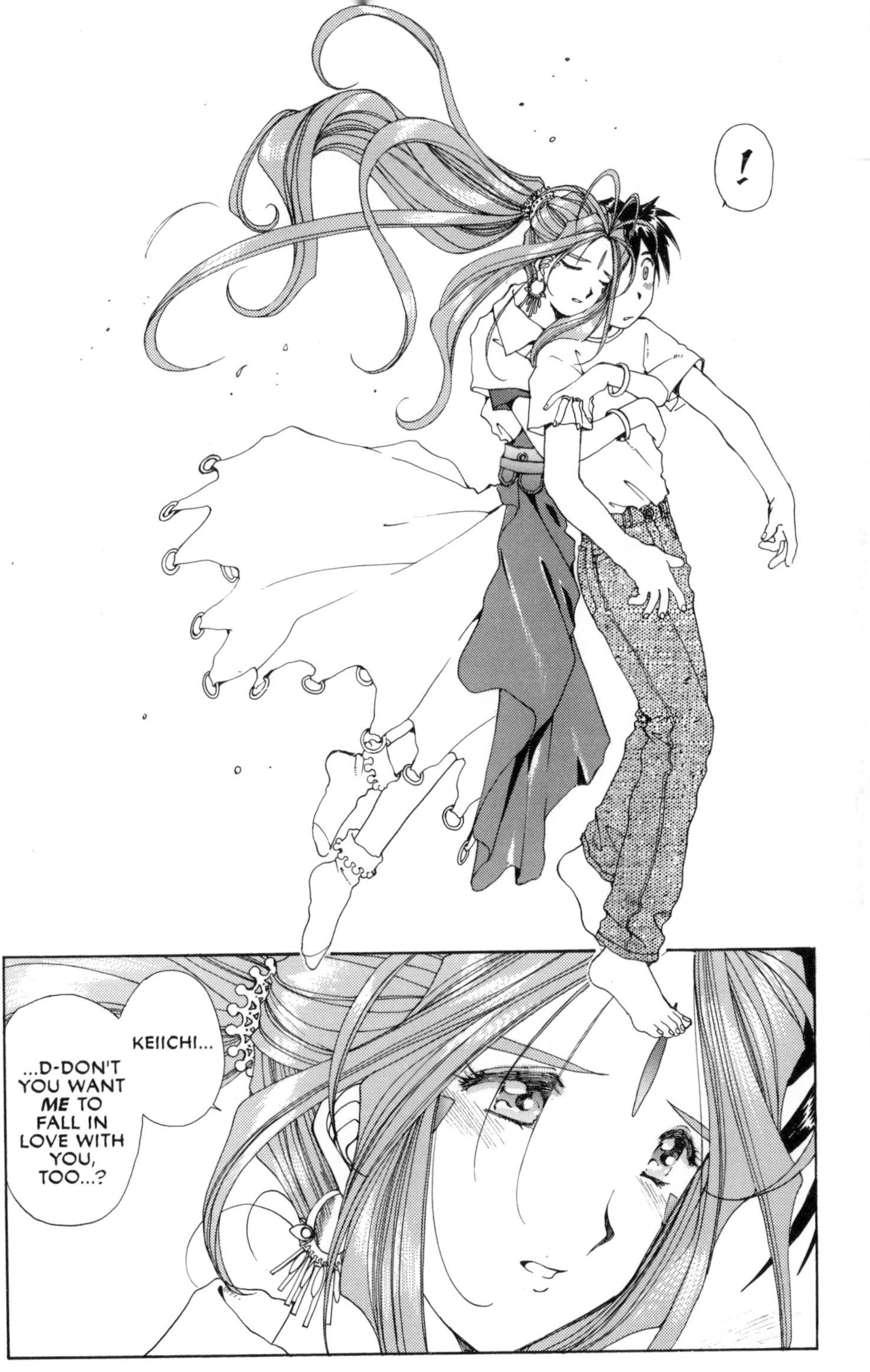
!
KEIICHI...
...D-DON'T YOU WANT *ME* TO FALL IN LOVE WITH YOU, TOO...?

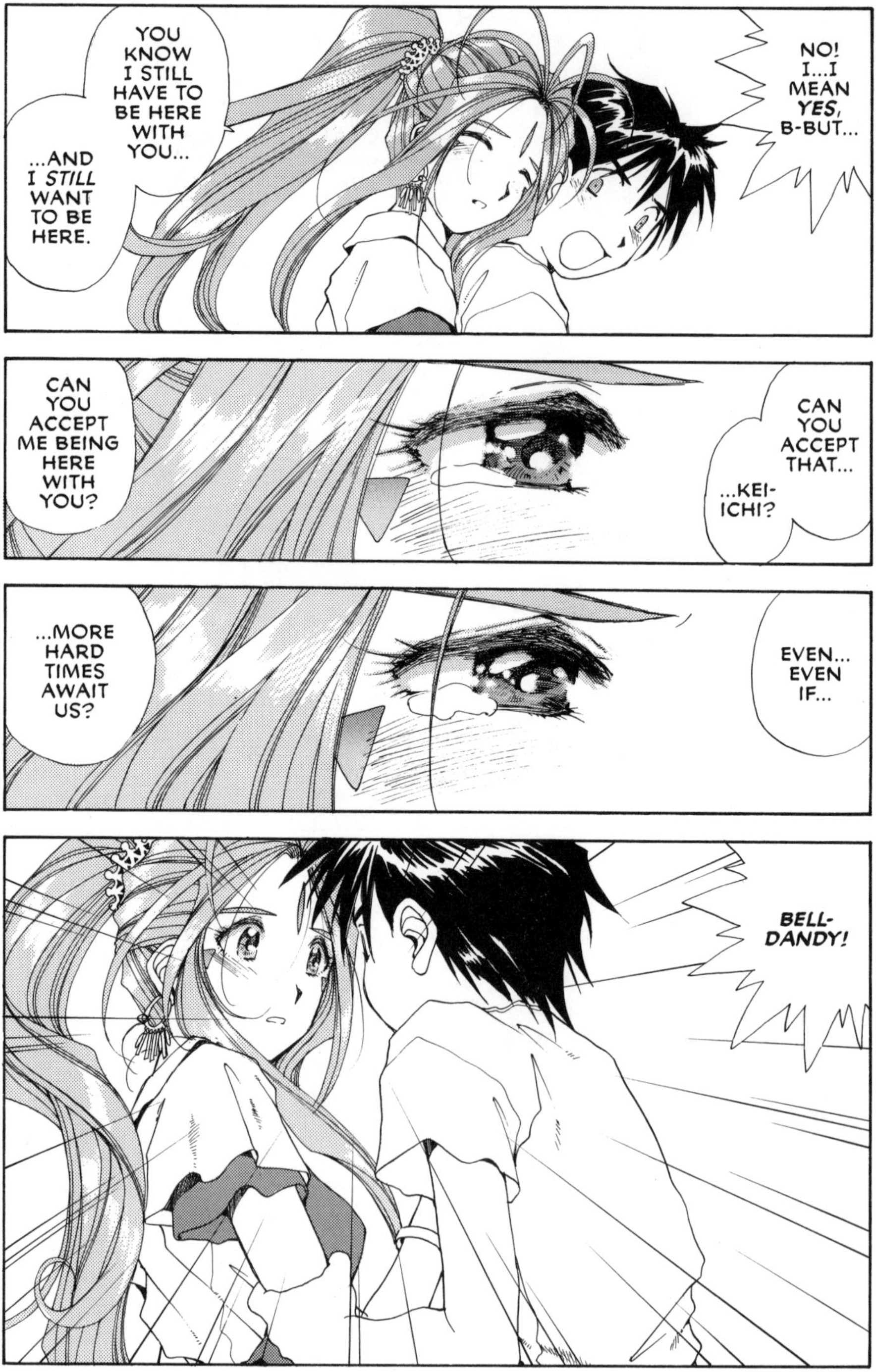
NO! I...I MEAN *YES*, B-BUT...
YOU KNOW I STILL HAVE TO BE HERE WITH YOU...
...AND I *STILL* WANT TO BE HERE.
CAN YOU ACCEPT THAT...
...KEI-ICHI?
CAN YOU ACCEPT ME BEING HERE WITH YOU?
EVEN... EVEN IF...
...MORE HARD TIMES AWAIT US?
BELL-DANDY!

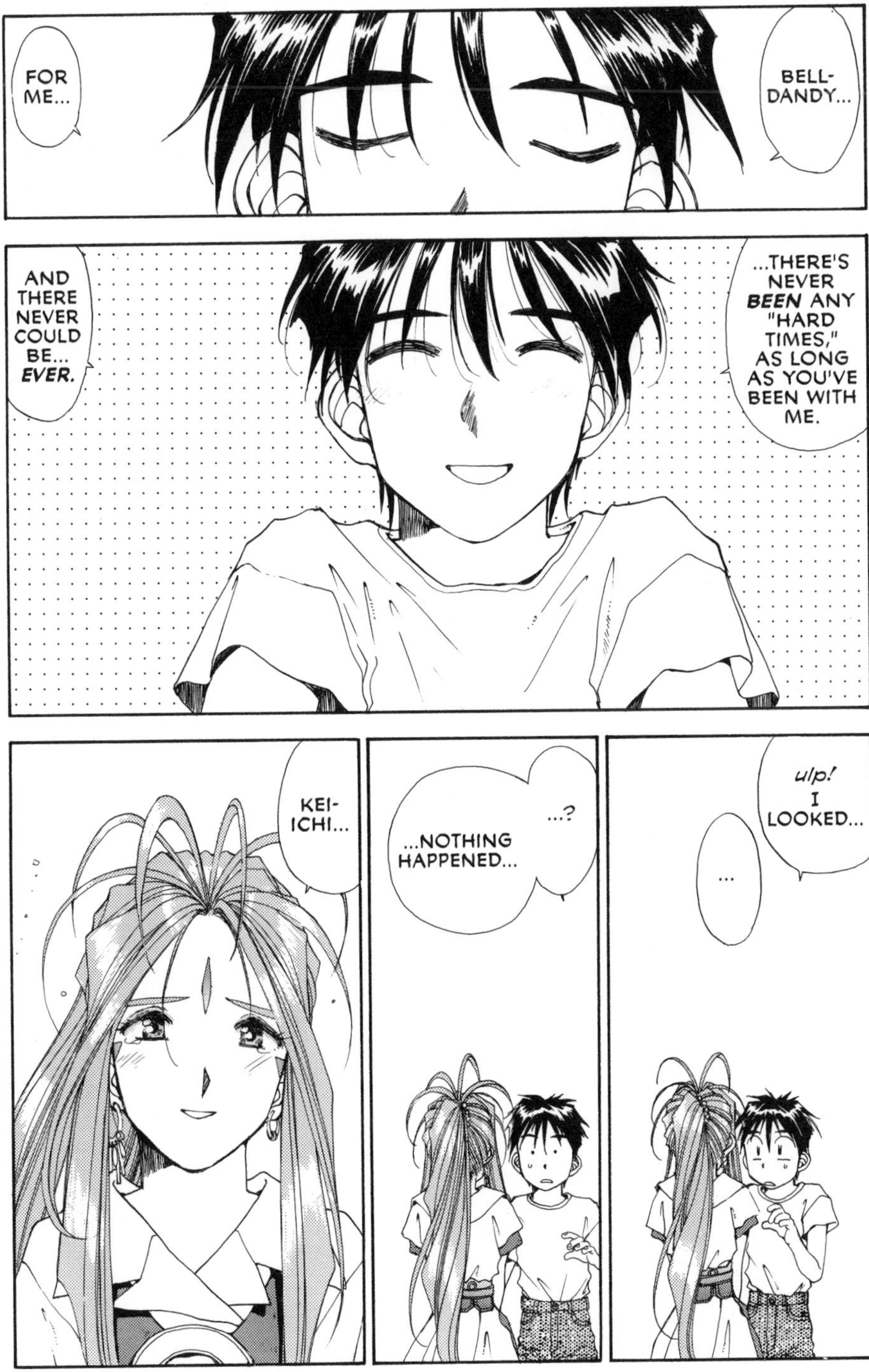
BELL-DANDY...
FOR ME...
...THERE'S NEVER *BEEN* ANY "HARD TIMES," AS LONG AS YOU'VE BEEN WITH ME.
AND THERE NEVER COULD BE... *EVER.*
ulp! I LOOKED...
...
...?
...NOTHING HAPPENED...
KEI-ICHI...

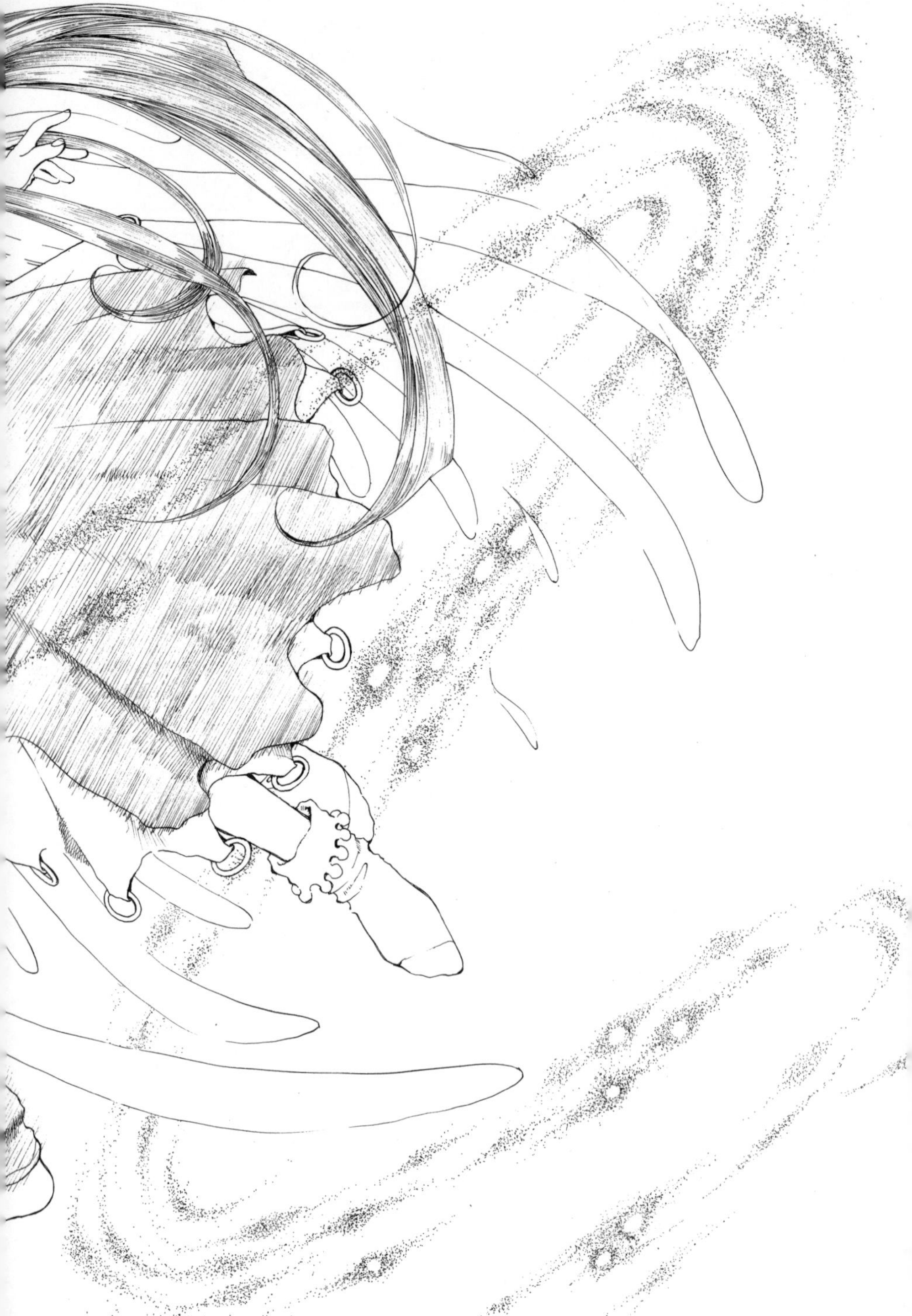

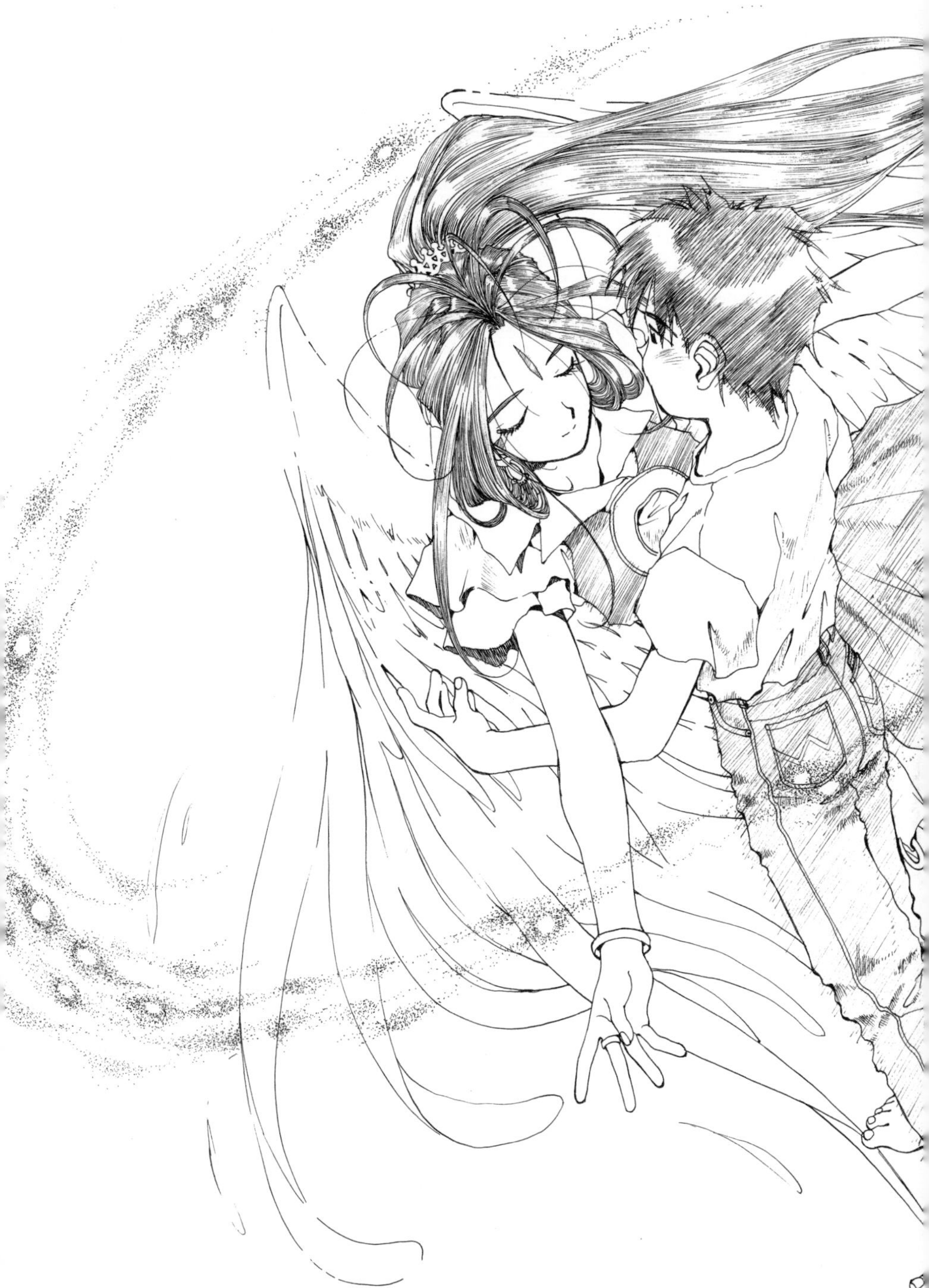

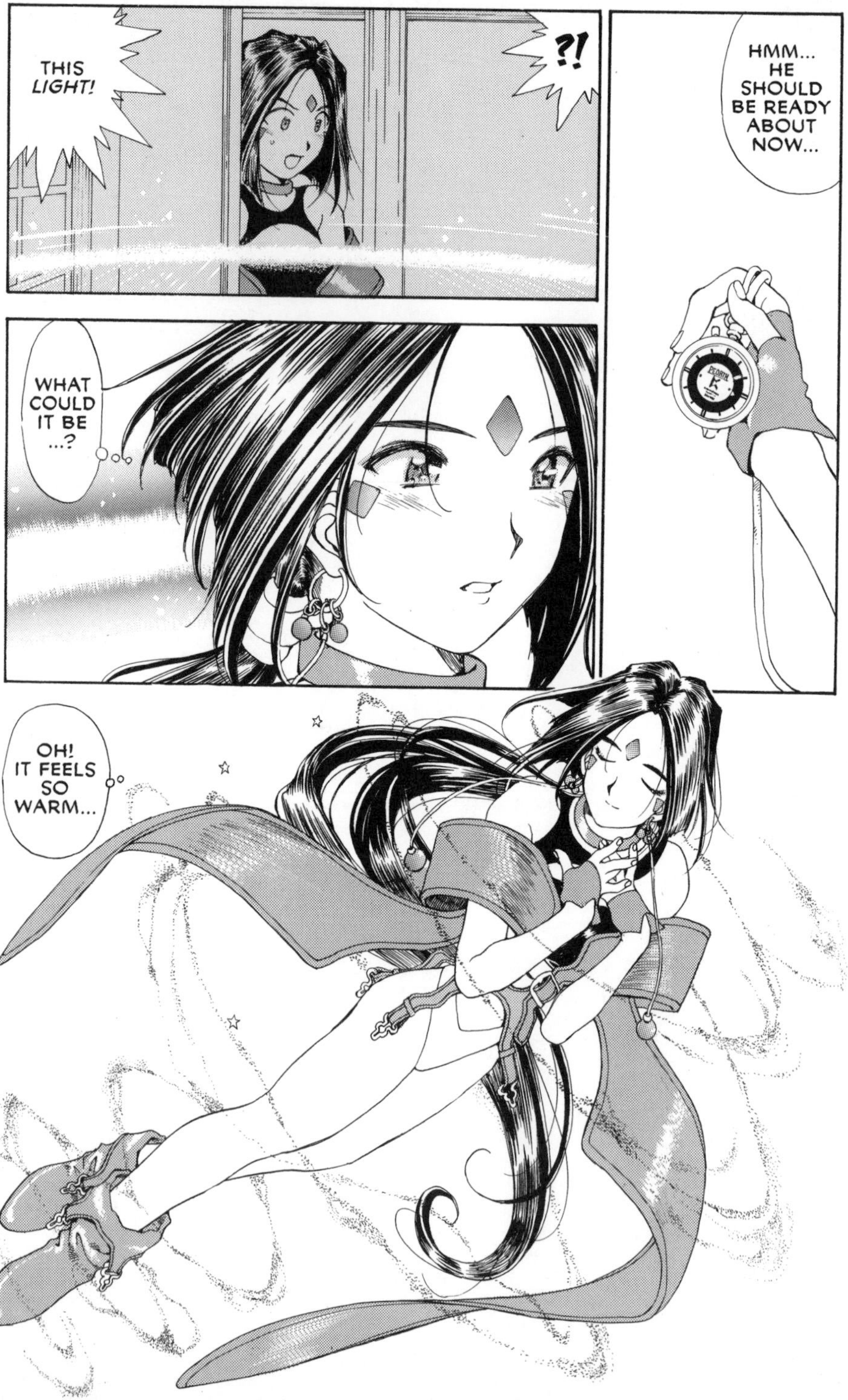
HMM... HE SHOULD BE READY ABOUT NOW...
?!
THIS *LIGHT!*
WHAT COULD IT BE ...?
OH! IT FEELS SO WARM...

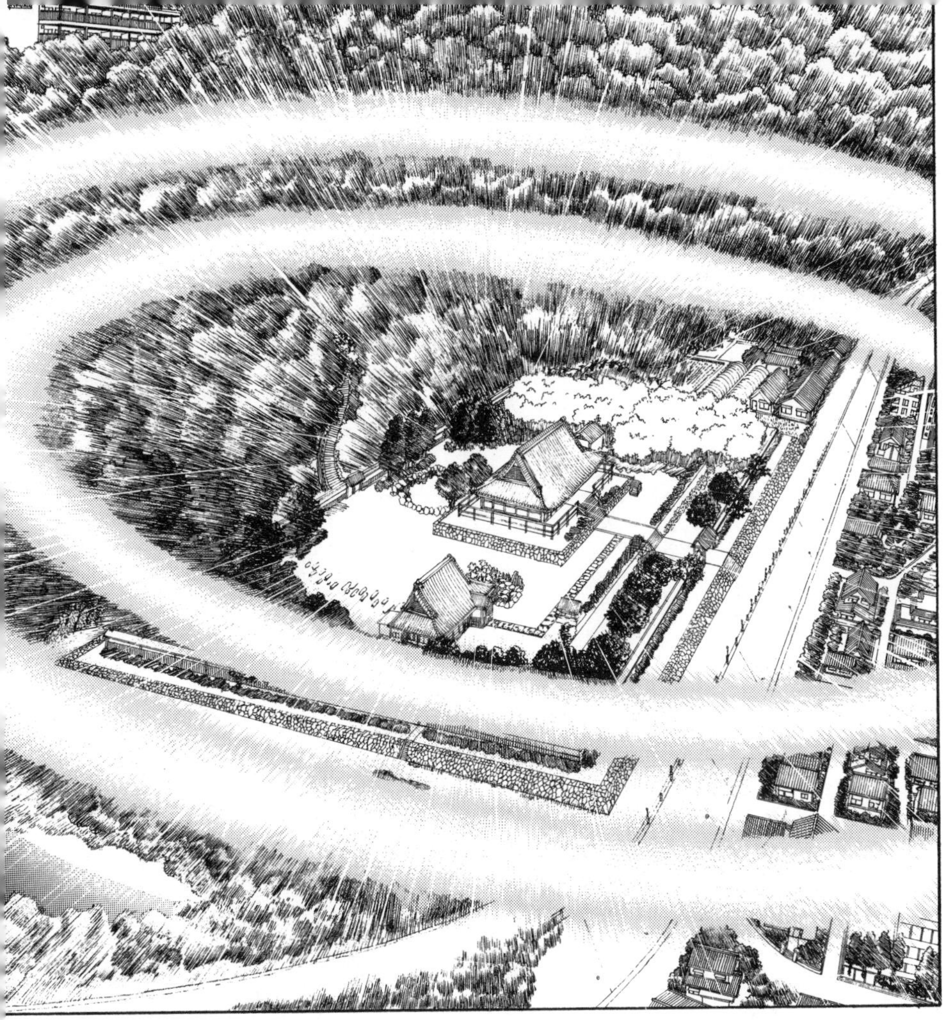

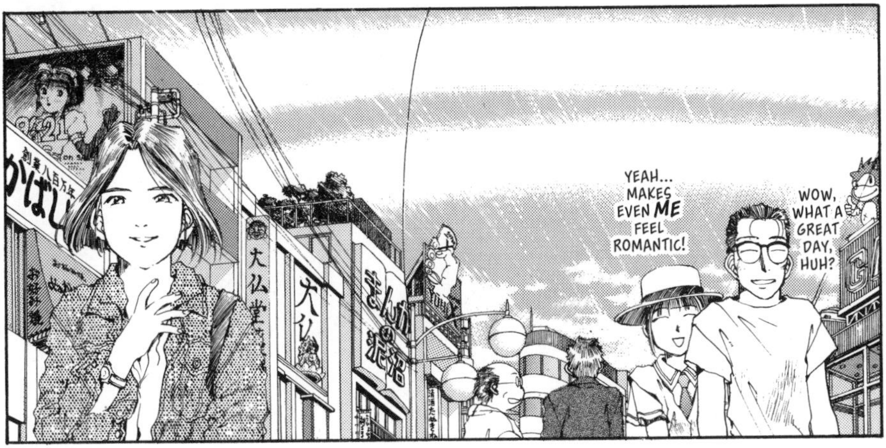

WOW, WHAT A GREAT DAY, HUH?
YEAH... MAKES EVEN ME FEEL ROMANTIC!

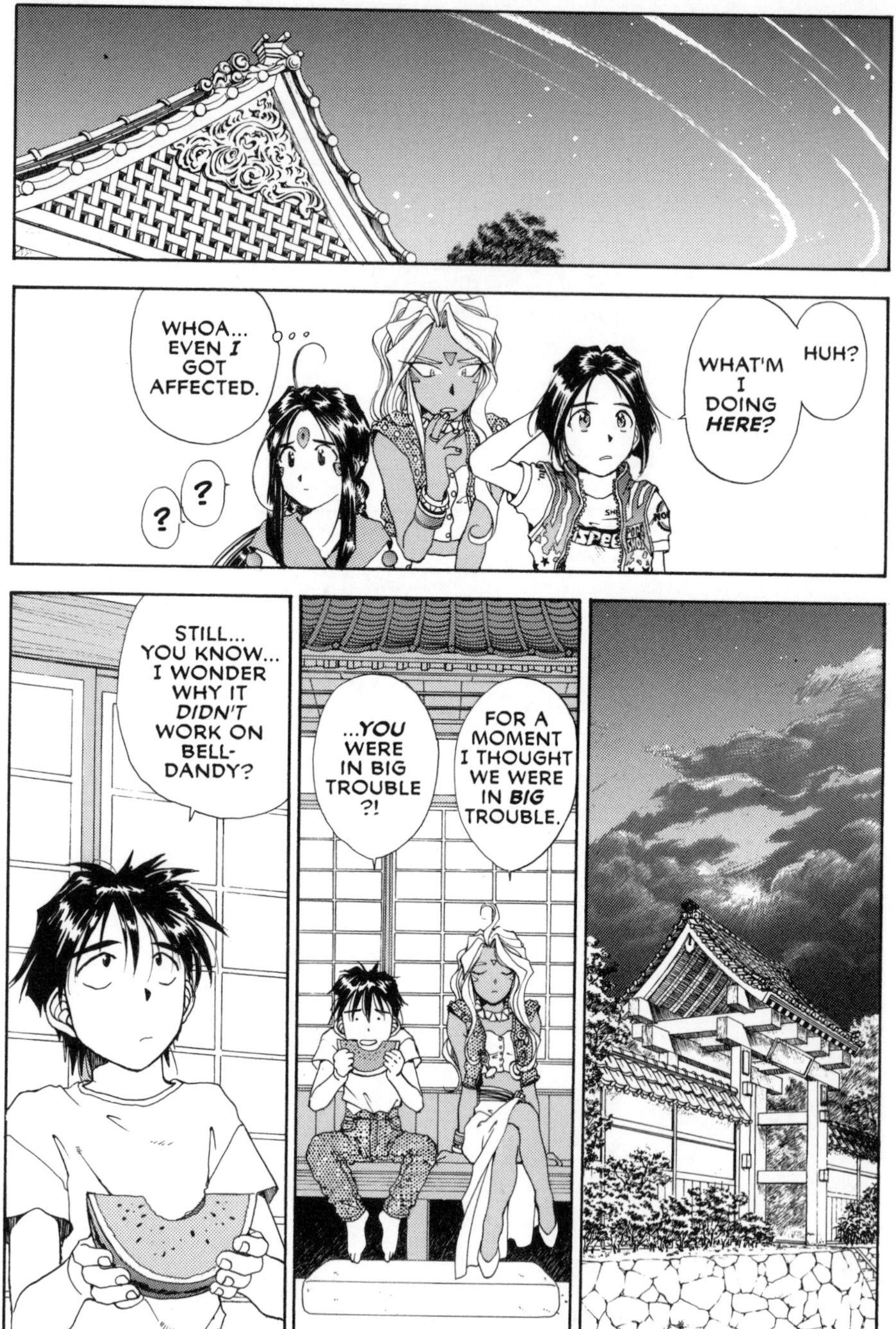
HUH?
WHAT'M I DOING *HERE?*
WHOA... EVEN *I* GOT AFFECTED.
?
?
FOR A MOMENT I THOUGHT WE WERE IN *BIG* TROUBLE.
...*YOU* WERE IN BIG TROUBLE ?!
STILL... YOU KNOW... I WONDER WHY IT *DIDN'T* WORK ON BELL-DANDY?

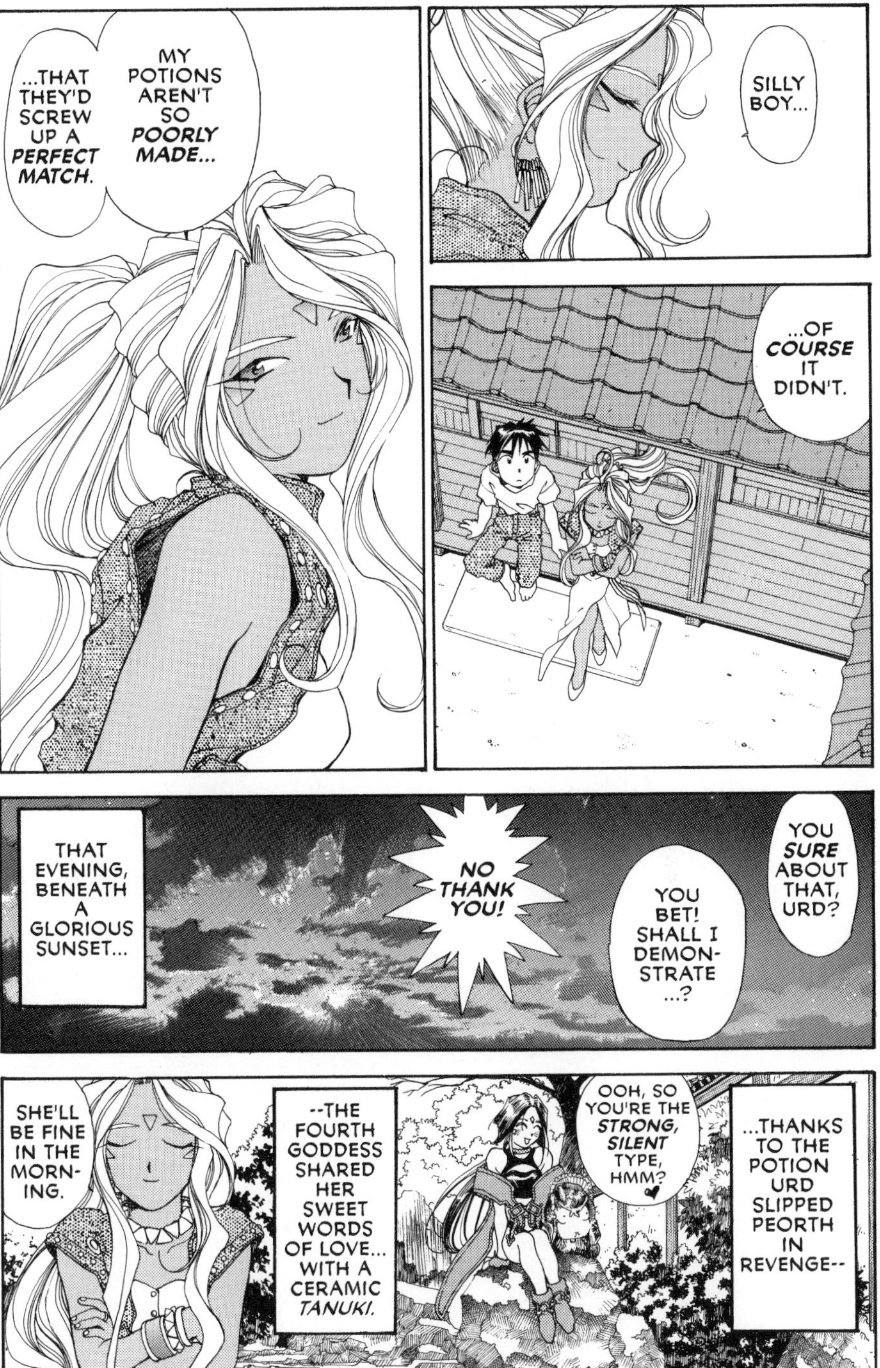
SILLY BOY...
...OF *COURSE* IT DIDN'T.
MY POTIONS AREN'T SO *POORLY MADE*...
...THAT THEY'D SCREW UP A *PERFECT MATCH*.
YOU *SURE* ABOUT THAT, URD?
YOU BET! SHALL I DEMON-STRATE ...?
NO THANK YOU!
THAT EVENING, BENEATH A GLORIOUS SUNSET...
...THANKS TO THE POTION URD SLIPPED PEORTH IN REVENGE--
OOH, SO YOU'RE THE *STRONG, SILENT* TYPE, HMM? ♥
--THE FOURTH GODDESS SHARED HER SWEET WORDS OF LOVE... WITH A CERAMIC *TANUKI*.
SHE'LL BE FINE IN THE MORN-ING.

THE ADVENTURES OF THE MINI-GODDESSES

◆SO YOU STARTED A BAND-- *NOW* WHAT?◆

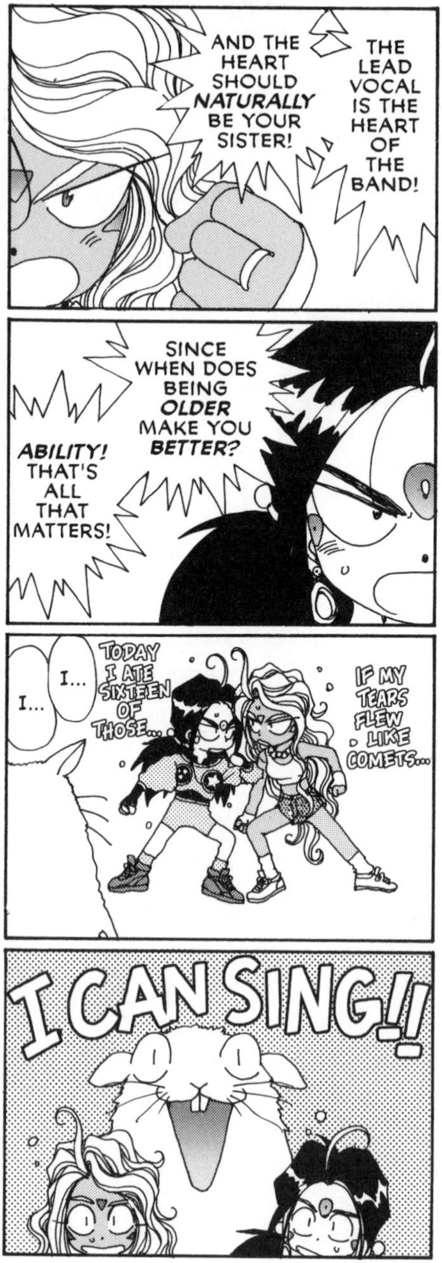

THE LEAD VOCAL IS THE HEART OF THE BAND!
AND THE HEART SHOULD *NATURALLY* BE YOUR SISTER!
SINCE WHEN DOES BEING *OLDER* MAKE YOU *BETTER?*
ABILITY! THAT'S ALL THAT MATTERS!
IF MY TEARS FLEW LIKE COMETS...
TODAY I ATE SIXTEEN OF THOSE...
I...
I...
I CAN SING!!

◆THE SECRET OF SONG◆

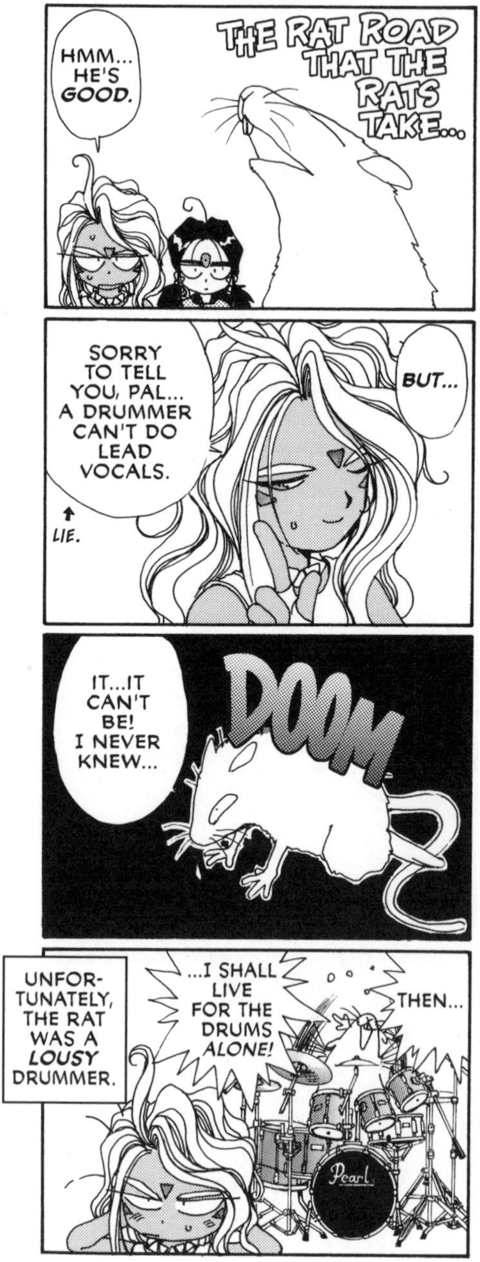

THE RAT ROAD THAT THE RATS TAKE...
HMM... HE'S *GOOD.*
BUT...
SORRY TO TELL YOU, PAL... A DRUMMER CAN'T DO LEAD VOCALS.
↑ LIE.
DOOM
IT...IT CAN'T BE! I NEVER KNEW...
THEN...
...I SHALL LIVE FOR THE DRUMS *ALONE!*
UNFORTUNATELY, THE RAT WAS A *LOUSY* DRUMMER.
Pearl

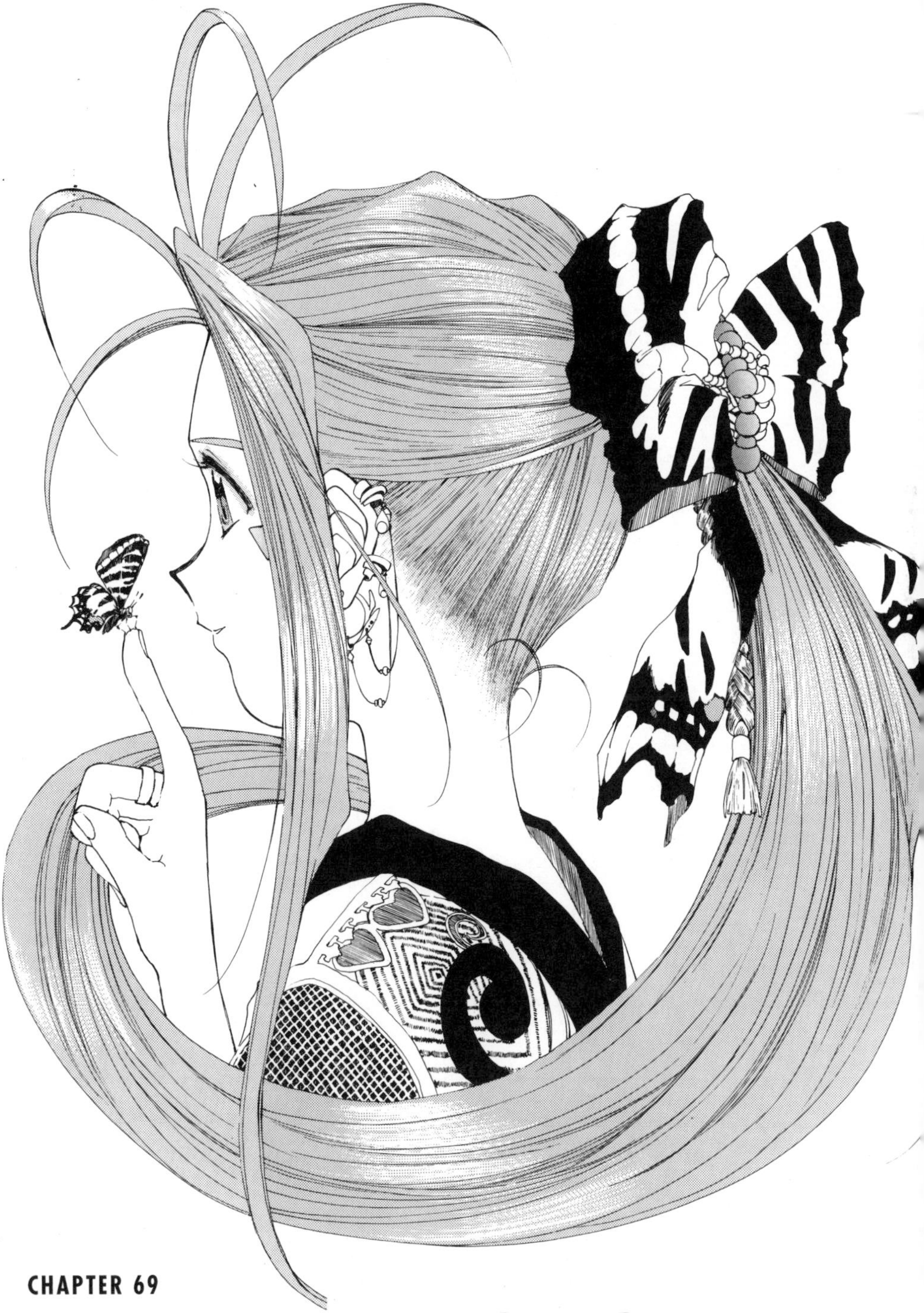

CHAPTER 69

Okay, This Is the Real Date

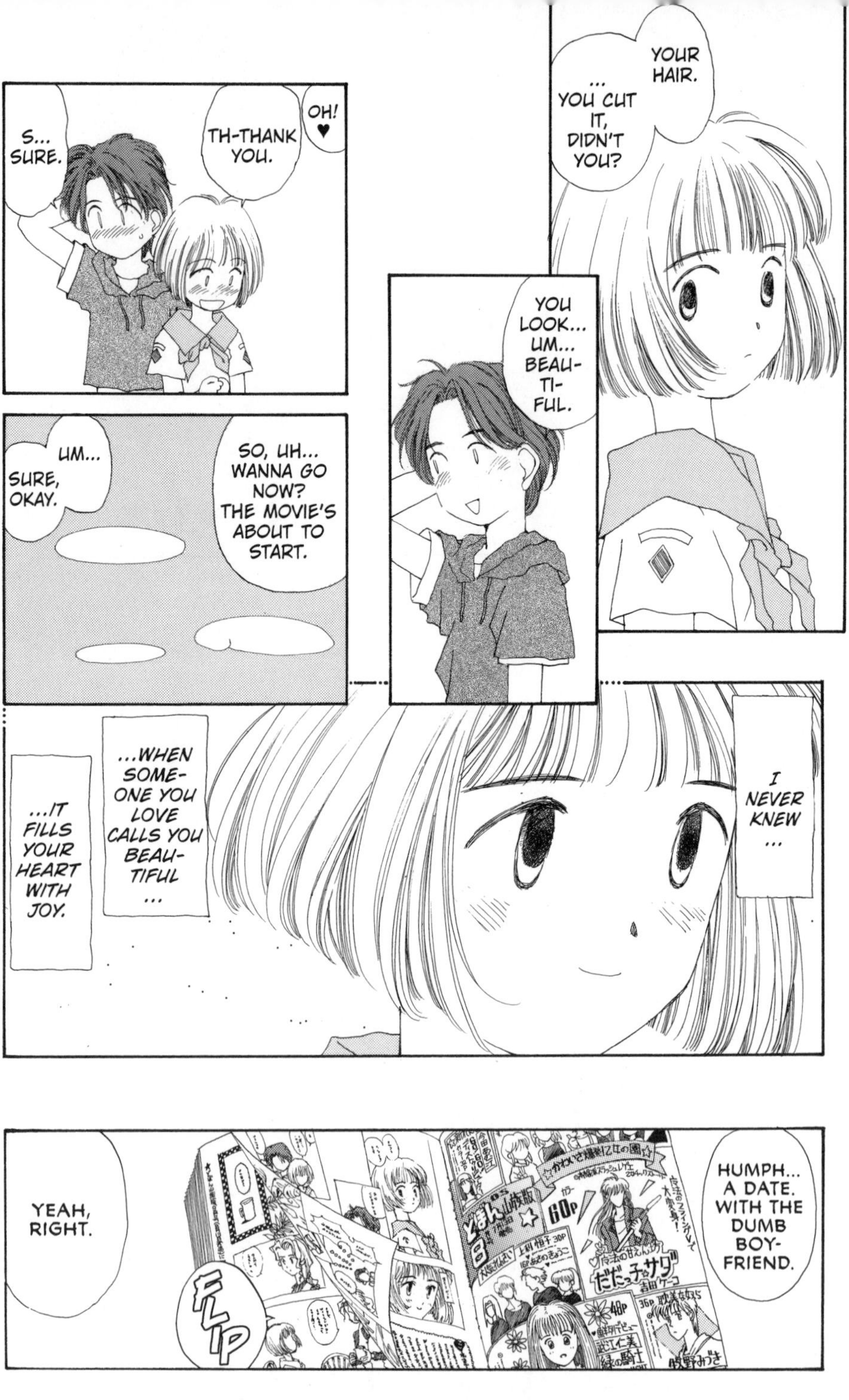

YOUR HAIR.
...YOU CUT IT, DIDN'T YOU?
YOU LOOK... UM... BEAU-TI-FUL.
OH! ♥
TH-THANK YOU.
S... SURE.
SO, UH... WANNA GO NOW? THE MOVIE'S ABOUT TO START.
UM... SURE, OKAY.
I NEVER KNEW...
...WHEN SOME-ONE YOU LOVE CALLS YOU BEAU-TIFUL...
...IT FILLS YOUR HEART WITH JOY.
HUMPH... A DATE. WITH THE DUMB BOY-FRIEND.
FLIP
YEAH, RIGHT.

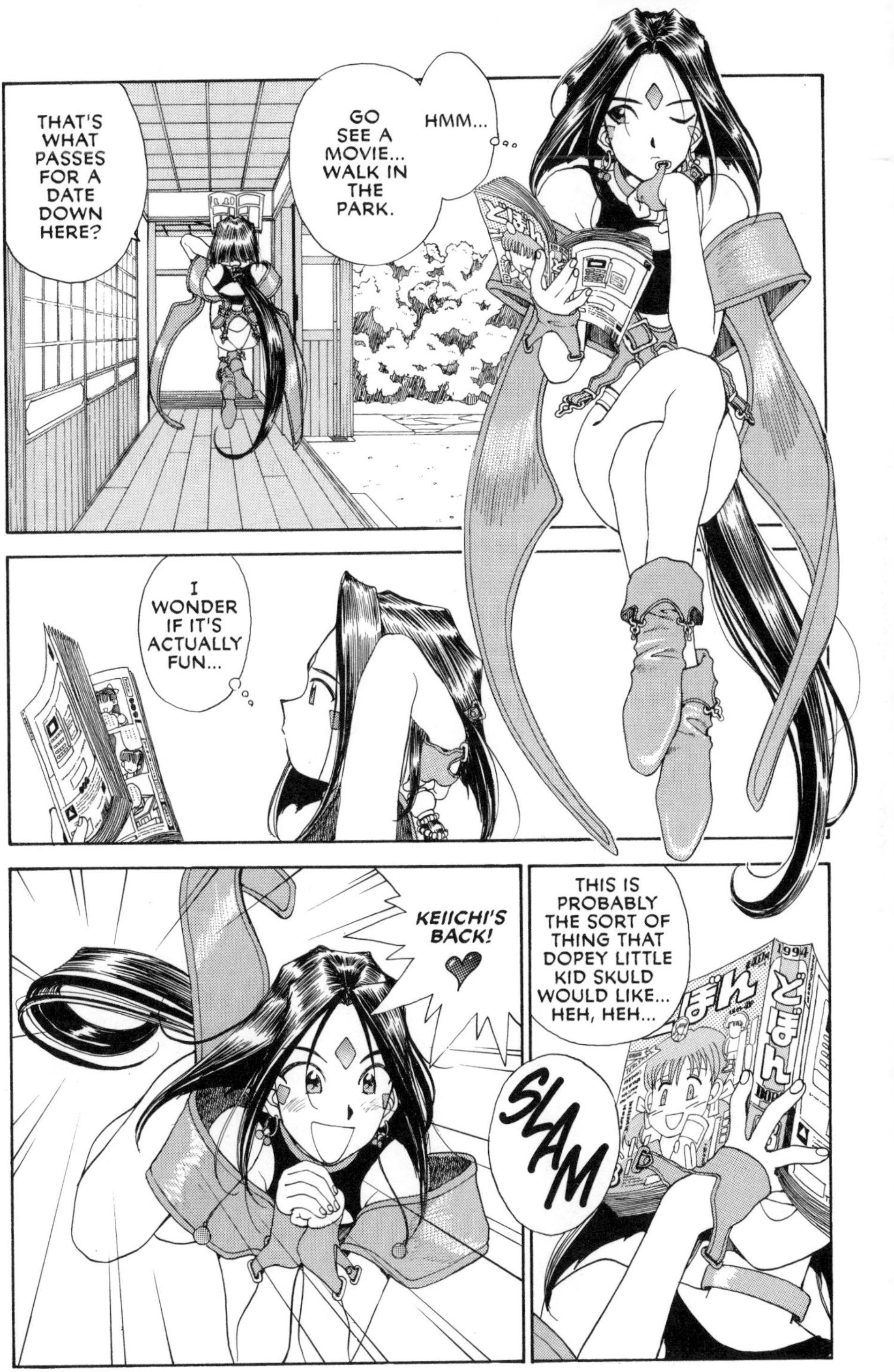
HMM...
GO SEE A MOVIE... WALK IN THE PARK.
THAT'S WHAT PASSES FOR A DATE DOWN HERE?
I WONDER IF IT'S ACTUALLY FUN...
THIS IS PROBABLY THE SORT OF THING THAT DOPEY LITTLE KID SKULD WOULD LIKE... HEH, HEH...
SLAM
KEIICHI'S BACK!

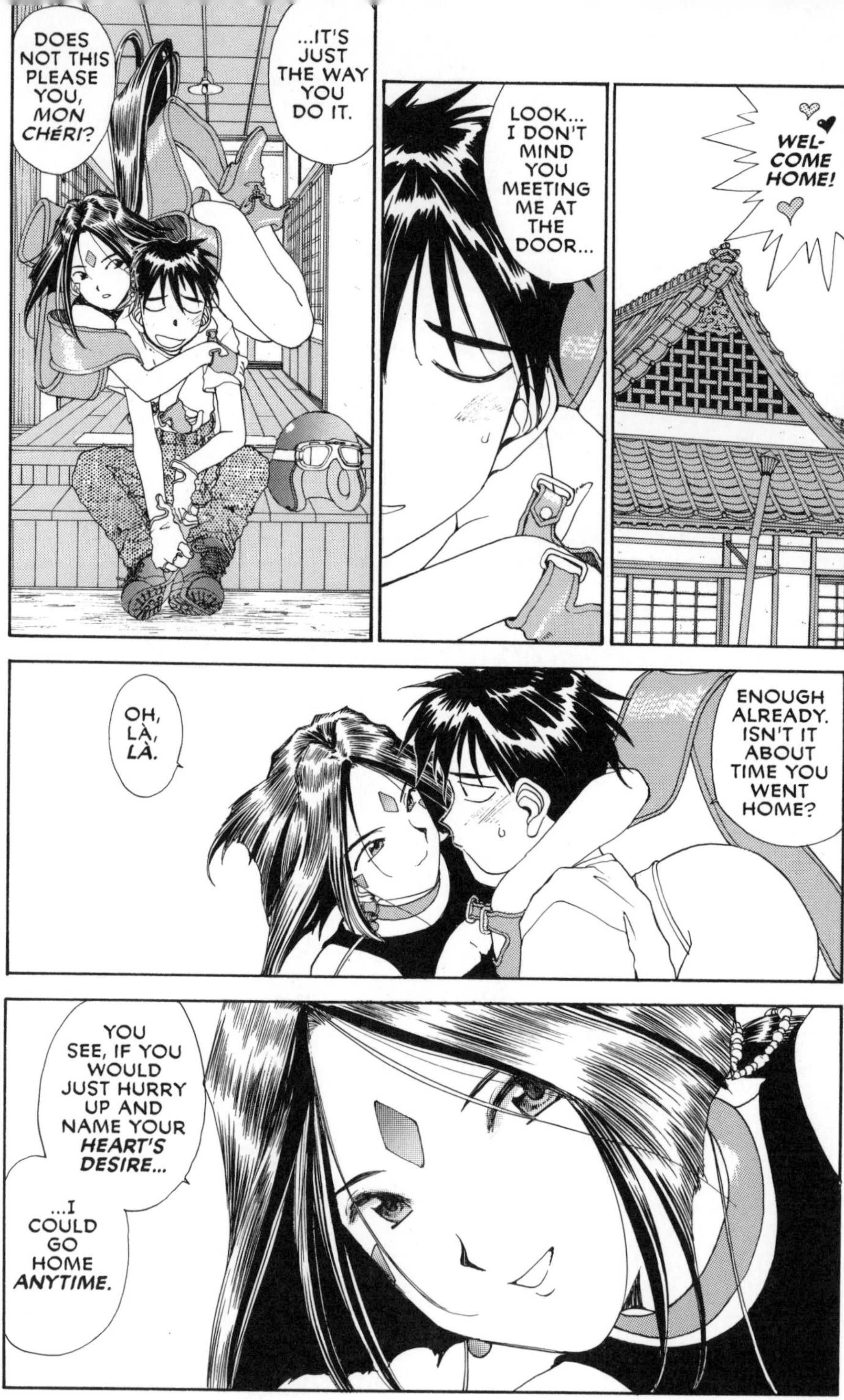
WEL-
COME
HOME!
LOOK...
I DON'T
MIND
YOU
MEETING
ME AT
THE
DOOR...
...IT'S
JUST
THE WAY
YOU
DO IT.
DOES
NOT THIS
PLEASE
YOU,
*MON
CHÉRI*?
ENOUGH
ALREADY.
ISN'T IT
ABOUT
TIME YOU
WENT
HOME?
OH,
LÀ,
LÀ.
YOU
SEE, IF YOU
WOULD
JUST HURRY
UP AND
NAME YOUR
***HEART'S
DESIRE***...
...I
COULD
GO
HOME
ANYTIME.

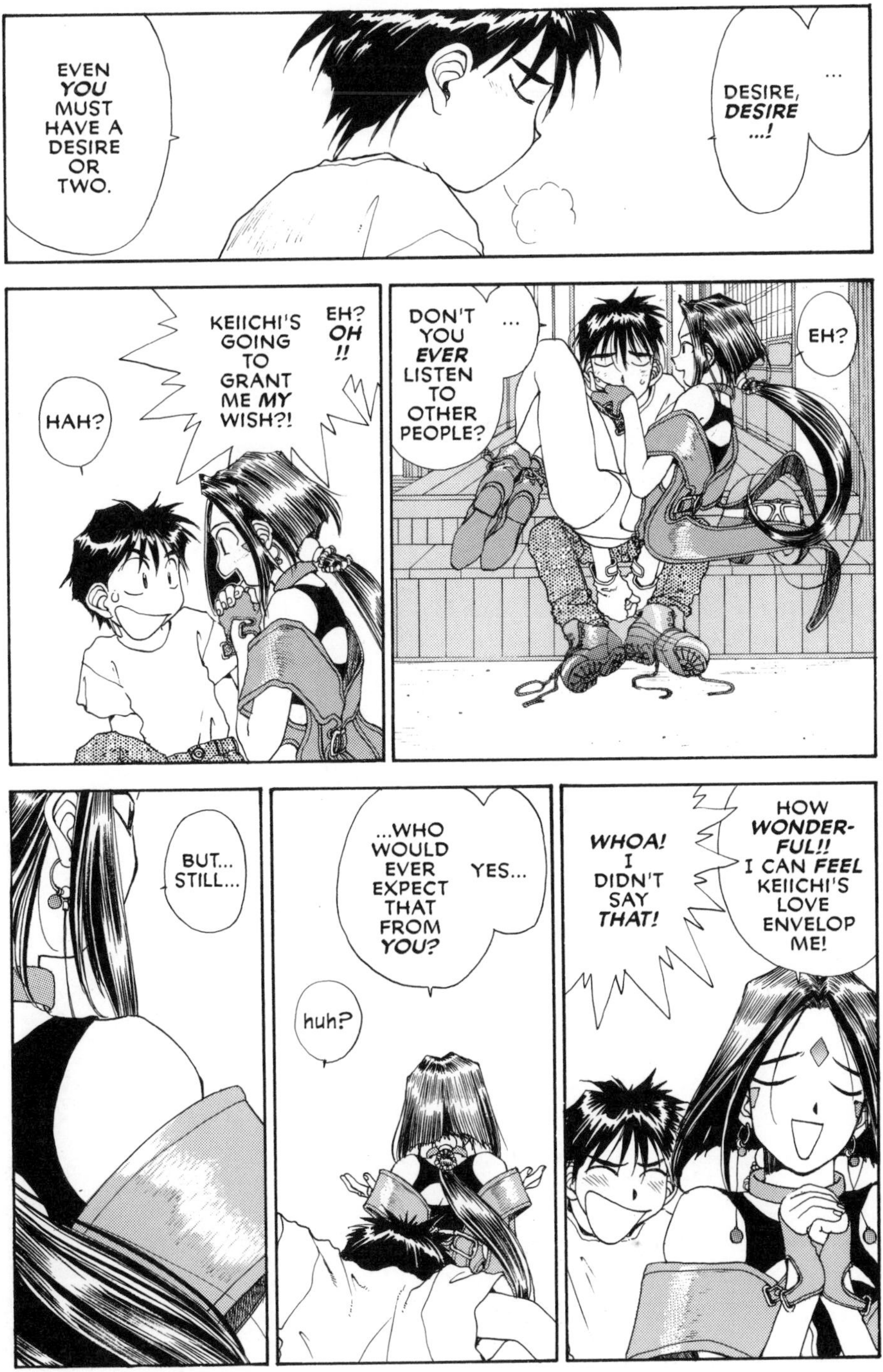
... DESIRE, DESIRE ...!
EVEN YOU MUST HAVE A DESIRE OR TWO.
EH?
...
DON'T YOU EVER LISTEN TO OTHER PEOPLE?
EH? OH !!
KEIICHI'S GOING TO GRANT ME MY WISH?!
HAH?
HOW WONDER-FUL!! I CAN FEEL KEIICHI'S LOVE ENVELOP ME!
WHOA! I DIDN'T SAY THAT!
YES...
...WHO WOULD EVER EXPECT THAT FROM YOU?
huh?
BUT... STILL...

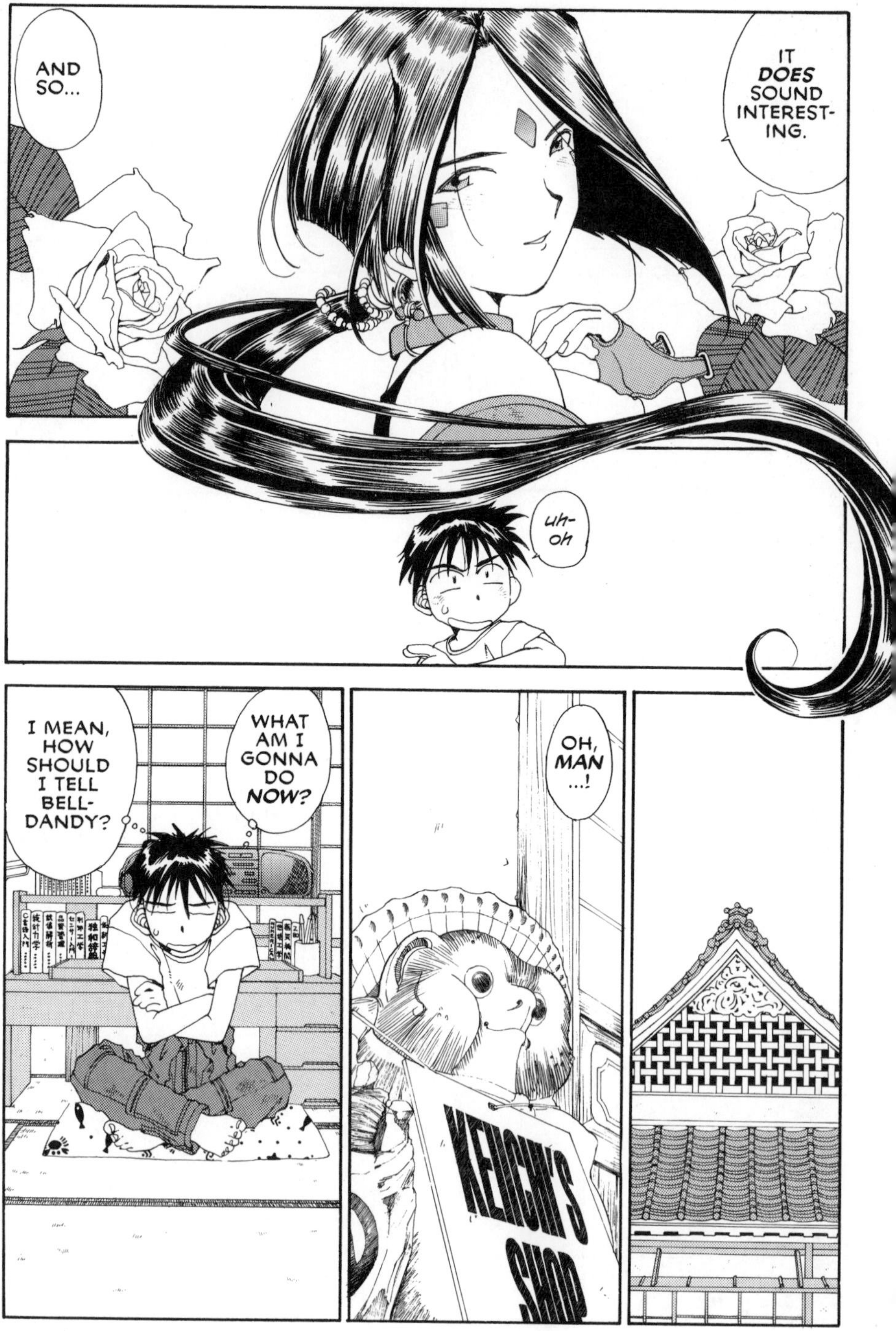
IT *DOES* SOUND INTEREST-ING.
AND SO...
uh-oh
OH, *MAN* ...!
KEIICHI'S SHOP
WHAT AM I GONNA DO *NOW?*
I MEAN, HOW SHOULD I TELL BELL-DANDY?

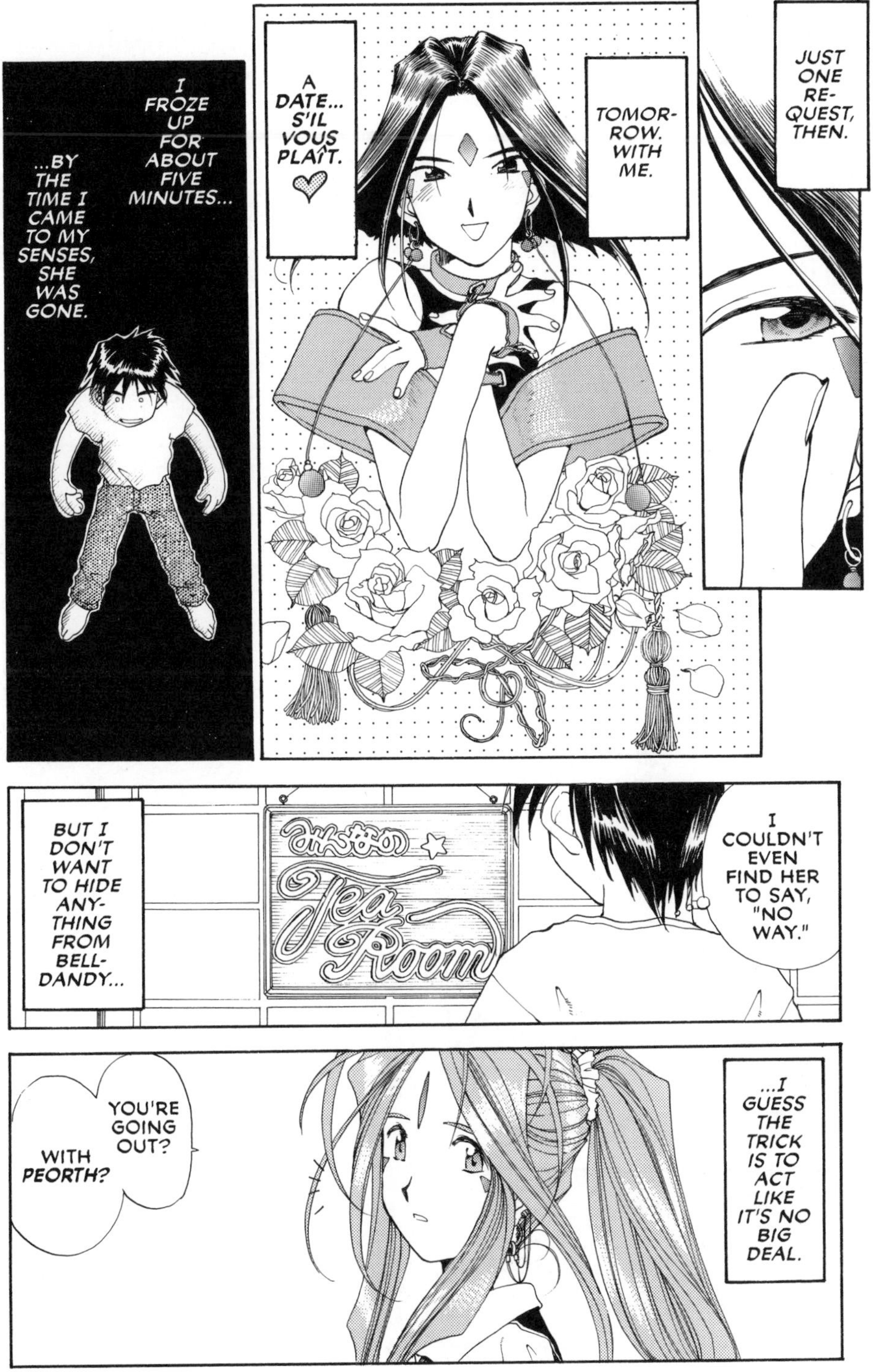
JUST ONE RE-QUEST, THEN.
TOMOR-ROW. WITH ME.
A DATE... S'IL VOUS PLAÎT.
I FROZE UP FOR ABOUT FIVE MINUTES...
...BY THE TIME I CAME TO MY SENSES, SHE WAS GONE.
I COULDN'T EVEN FIND HER TO SAY, "NO WAY."
みんなの Tea Room
BUT I DON'T WANT TO HIDE ANY-THING FROM BELL-DANDY...
...I GUESS THE TRICK IS TO ACT LIKE IT'S NO BIG DEAL.
YOU'RE GOING OUT?
WITH PEORTH?

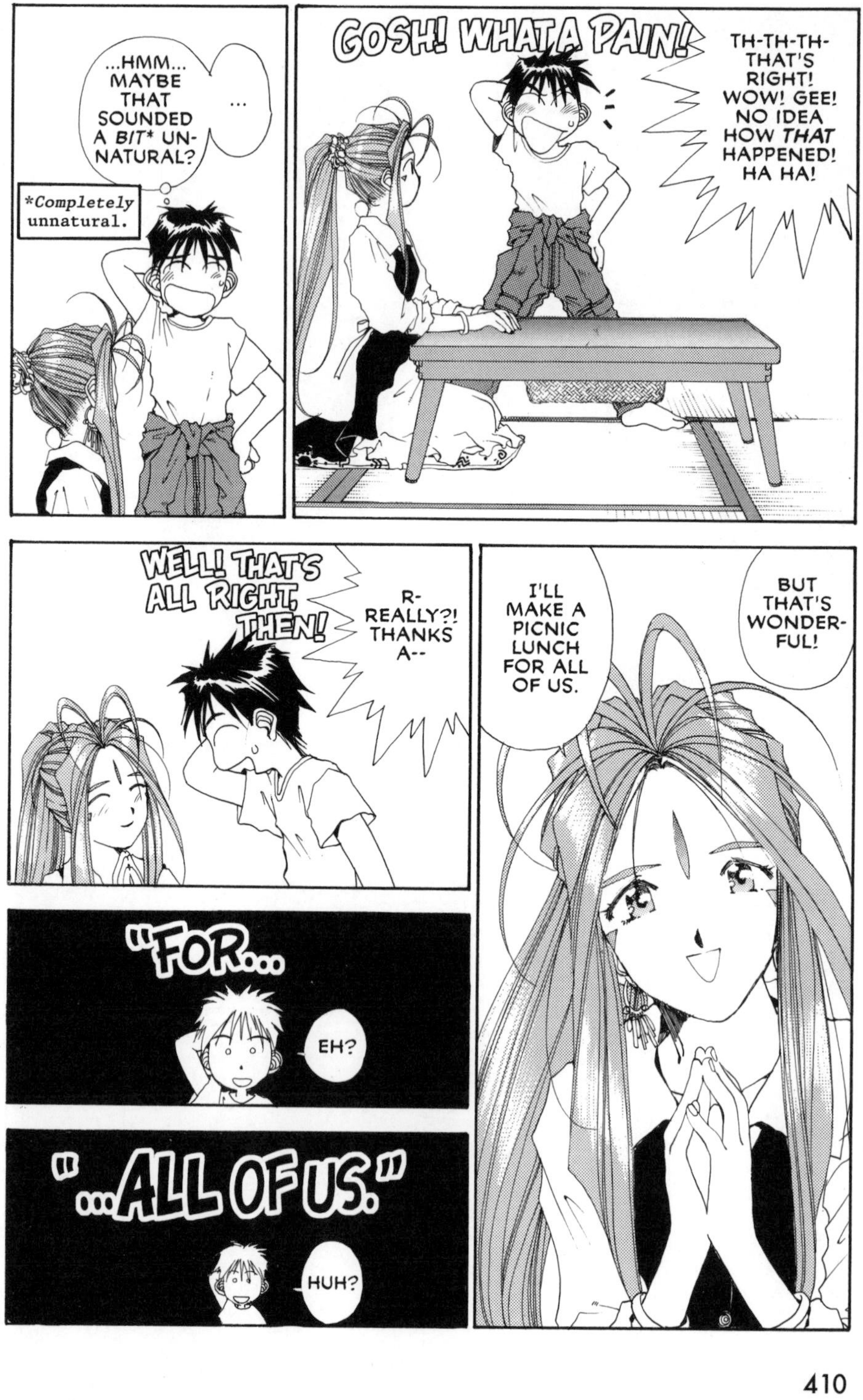
TH-TH-TH-THAT'S RIGHT! WOW! GEE! NO IDEA HOW *THAT* HAPPENED! HA HA!
GOSH! WHAT A PAIN!
...HMM... MAYBE THAT SOUNDED A *BIT** UN-NATURAL?
...
*Completely unnatural.
BUT THAT'S WONDER-FUL!
I'LL MAKE A PICNIC LUNCH FOR ALL OF US.
WELL! THAT'S ALL RIGHT, THEN!
R-REALLY?! THANKS A--
"FOR...
EH?
"...ALL OF US."
HUH?

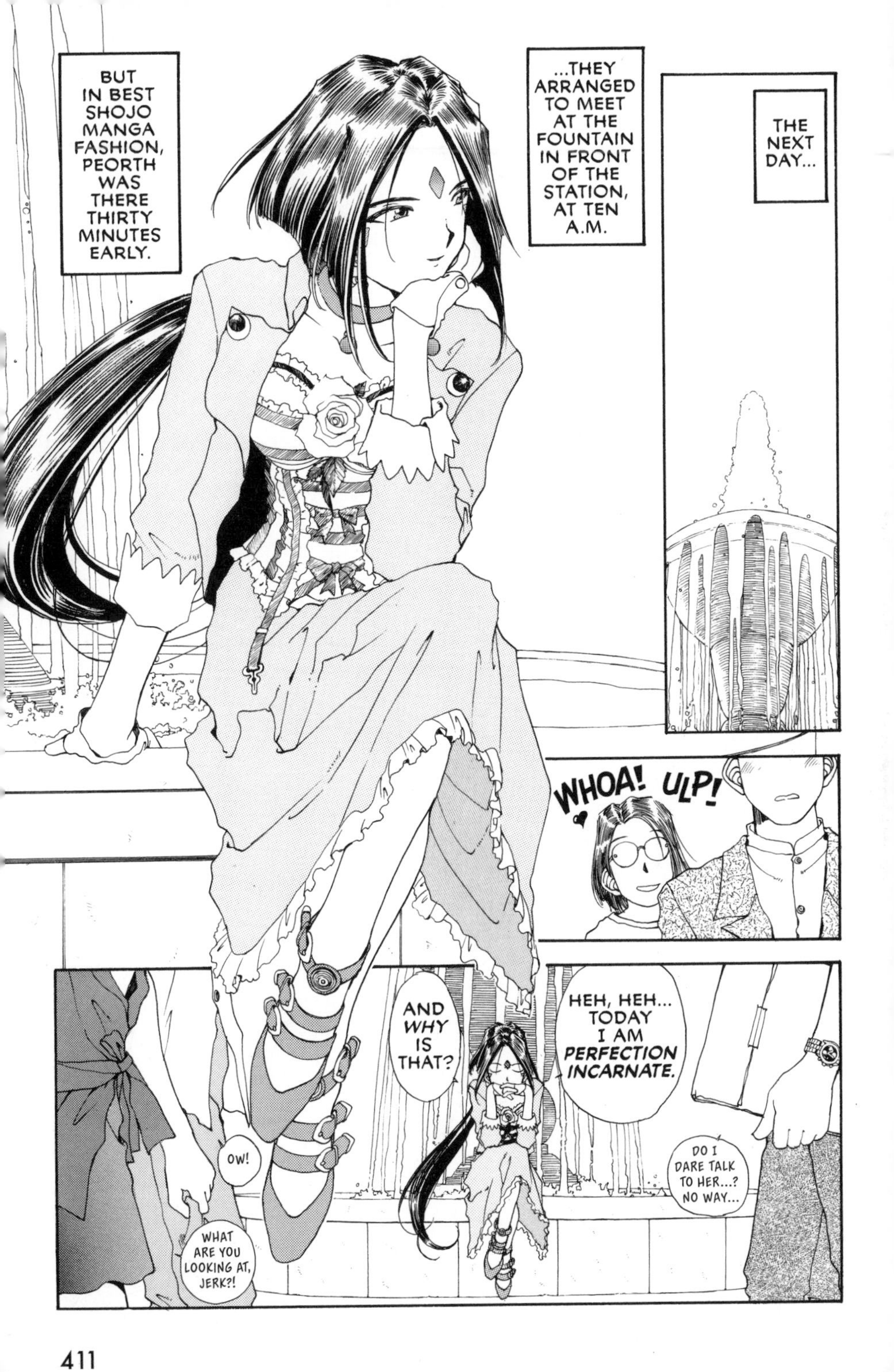
THE NEXT DAY...
...THEY ARRANGED TO MEET AT THE FOUNTAIN IN FRONT OF THE STATION, AT TEN A.M.
BUT IN BEST SHOJO MANGA FASHION, PEORTH WAS THERE THIRTY MINUTES EARLY.
WHOA! ULP!
DO I DARE TALK TO HER...? NO WAY...
HEH, HEH... TODAY I AM *PERFECTION INCARNATE.*
AND *WHY* IS THAT?
OW!
WHAT ARE YOU LOOKING AT, JERK?!

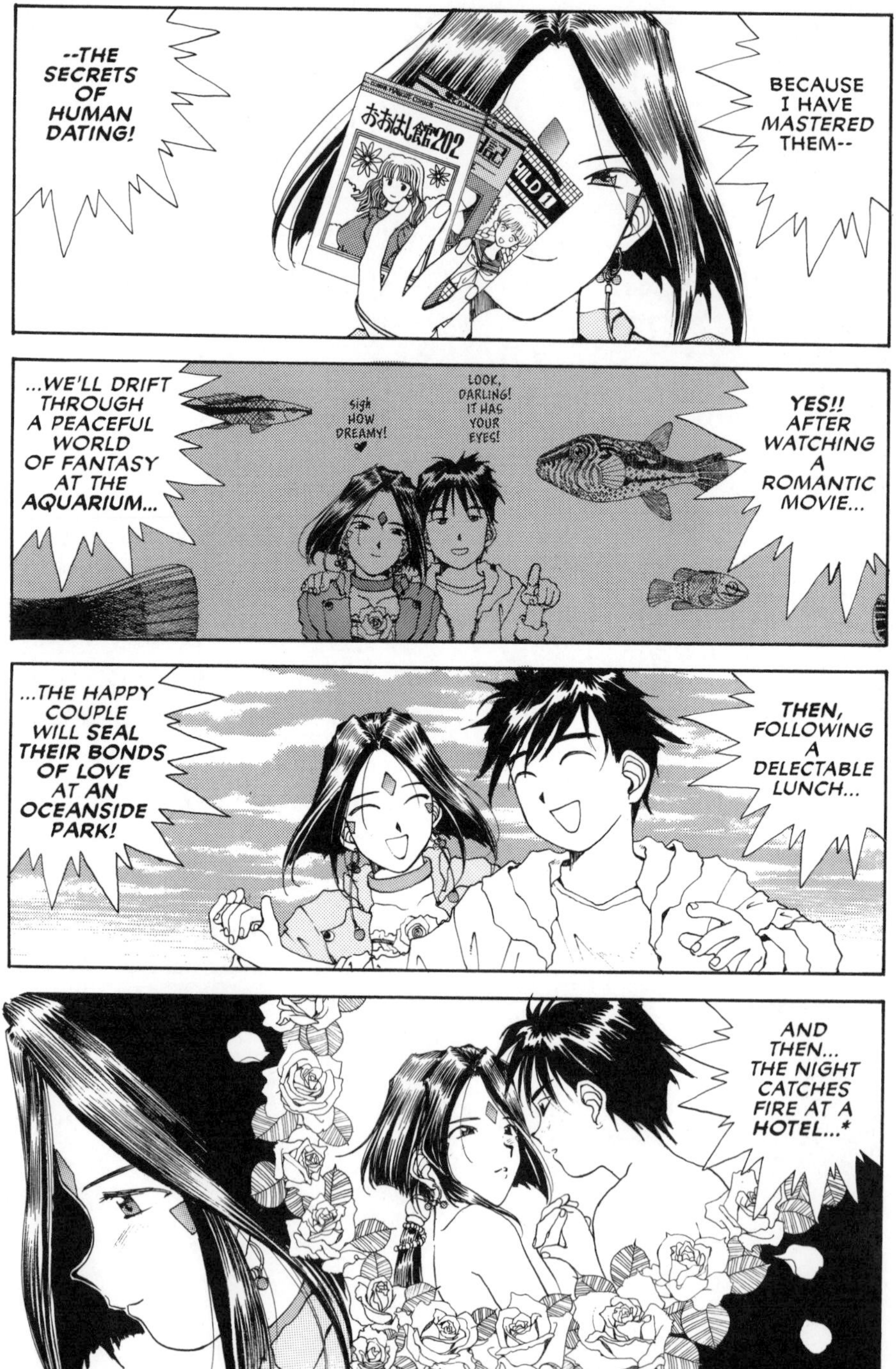
BECAUSE I HAVE MASTERED THEM--
--THE SECRETS OF HUMAN DATING!
おおはし館202
YES!! AFTER WATCHING A ROMANTIC MOVIE...
...WE'LL DRIFT THROUGH A PEACEFUL WORLD OF FANTASY AT THE AQUARIUM...
LOOK, DARLING! IT HAS YOUR EYES!
Sigh HOW DREAMY!
THEN, FOLLOWING A DELECTABLE LUNCH...
...THE HAPPY COUPLE WILL SEAL THEIR BONDS OF LOVE AT AN OCEANSIDE PARK!
AND THEN... THE NIGHT CATCHES FIRE AT A HOTEL...*

*She's been reading those *josei* manga too...

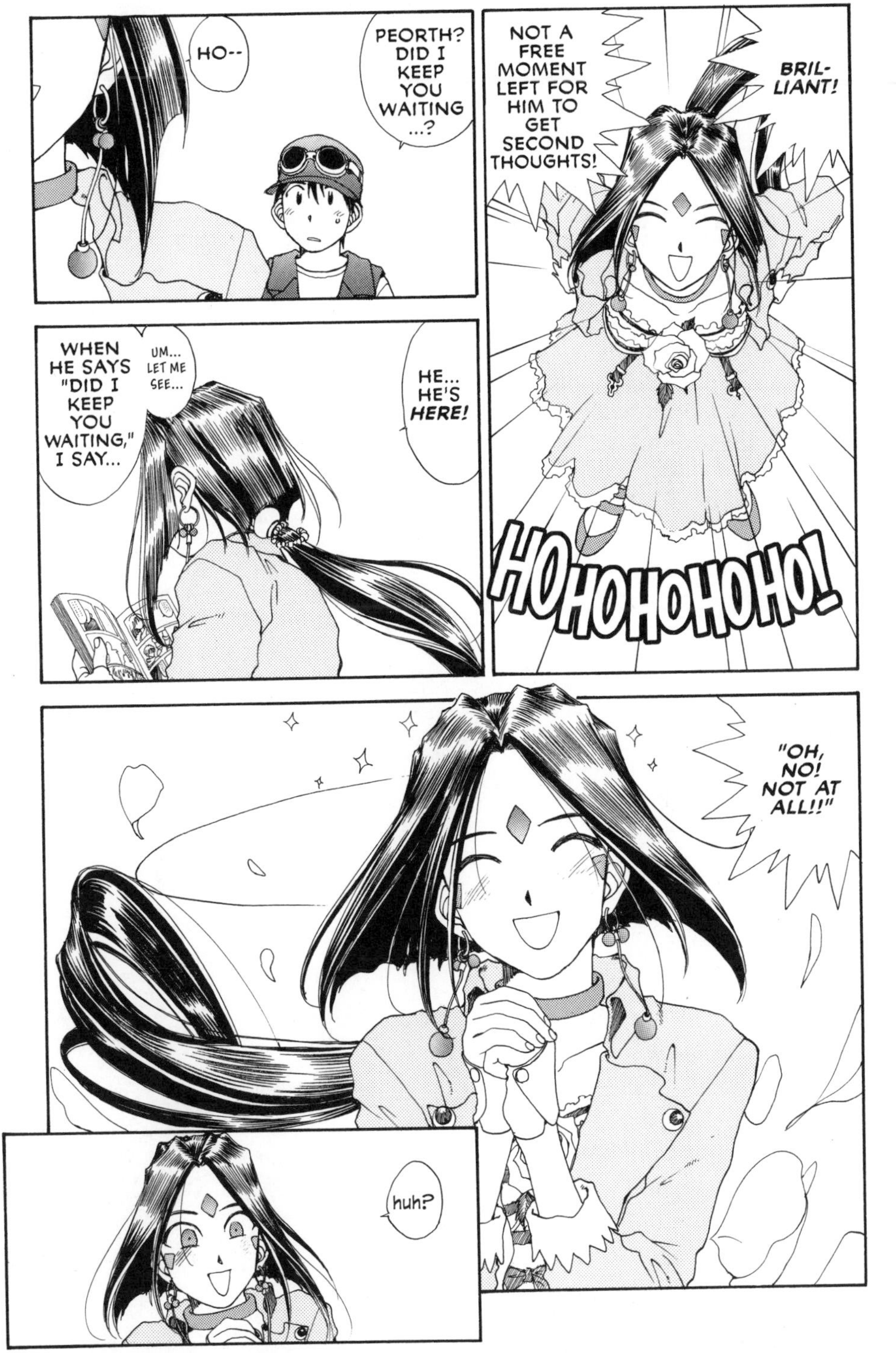

PEORTH? DID I KEEP YOU WAITING ...?
HO--
HE... HE'S *HERE!*
WHEN HE SAYS "DID I KEEP YOU WAITING," I SAY...
UM... LET ME SEE...
NOT A FREE MOMENT LEFT FOR HIM TO GET SECOND THOUGHTS!
BRIL-LIANT!
HOHOHOHOHOHO!
"OH, NO! NOT AT ALL!!"
huh?

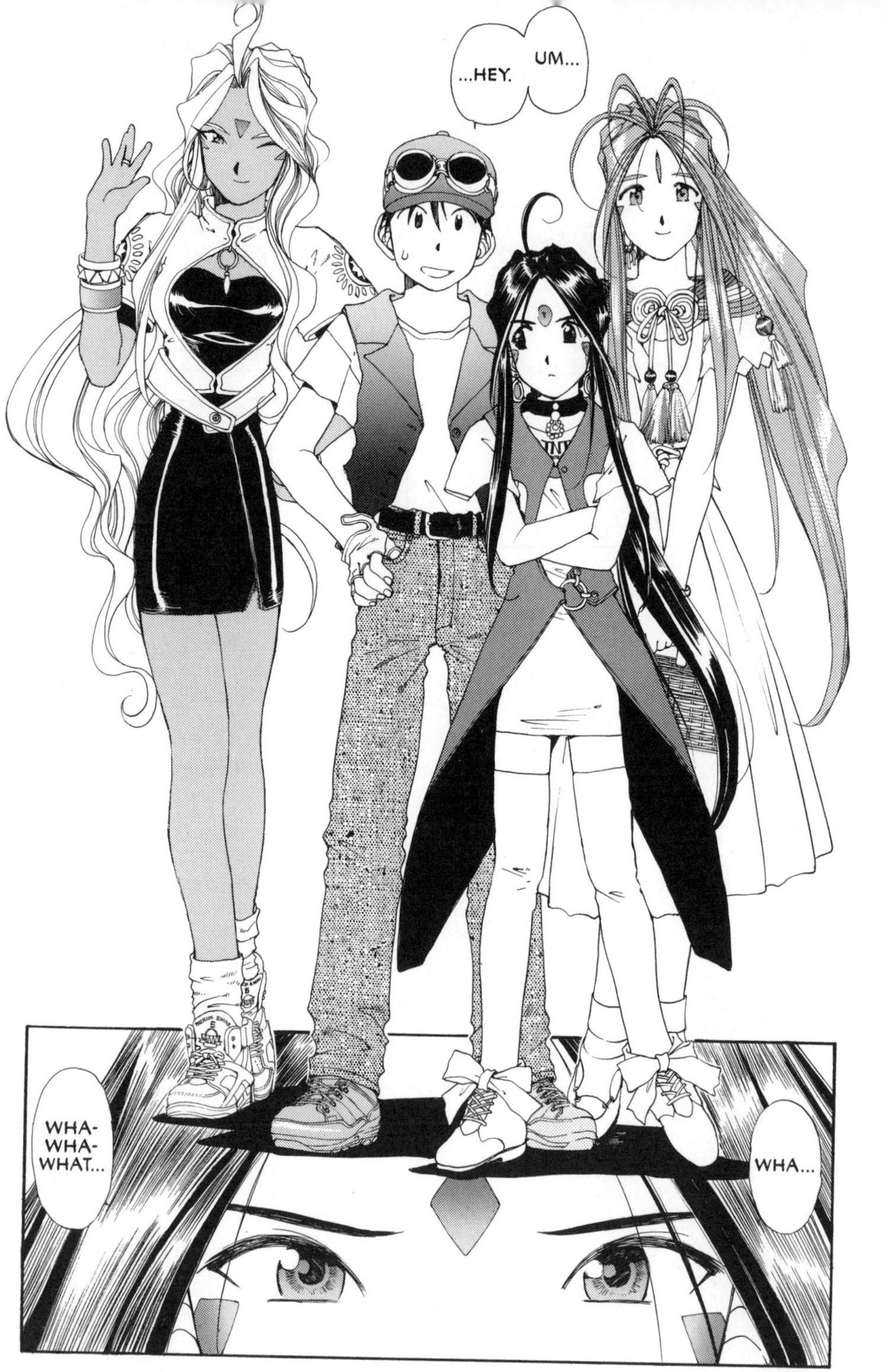
UM... ...HEY.
WHA...
WHA- WHA- WHAT...

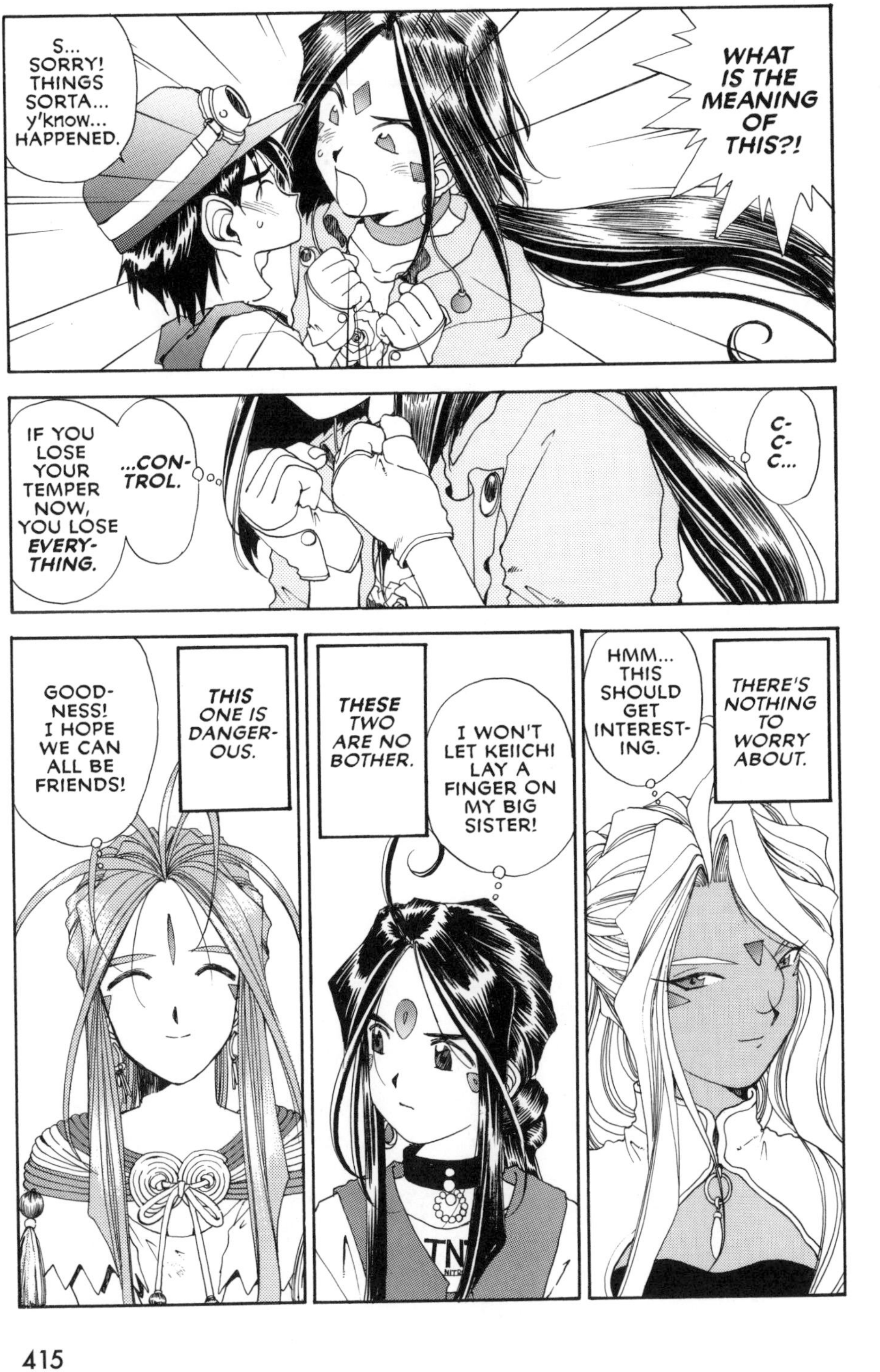
WHAT IS THE MEANING OF THIS?!
S... SORRY! THINGS SORTA... y'know... HAPPENED.
C-C-C...
...CON-TROL.
IF YOU LOSE YOUR TEMPER NOW, YOU LOSE *EVERYTHING.*
THERE'S NOTHING TO WORRY ABOUT.
HMM... THIS SHOULD GET INTEREST-ING.
THESE TWO ARE NO BOTHER.
I WON'T LET KEIICHI LAY A FINGER ON MY BIG SISTER!
THIS ONE IS DANGER-OUS.
GOOD-NESS! I HOPE WE CAN ALL BE FRIENDS!

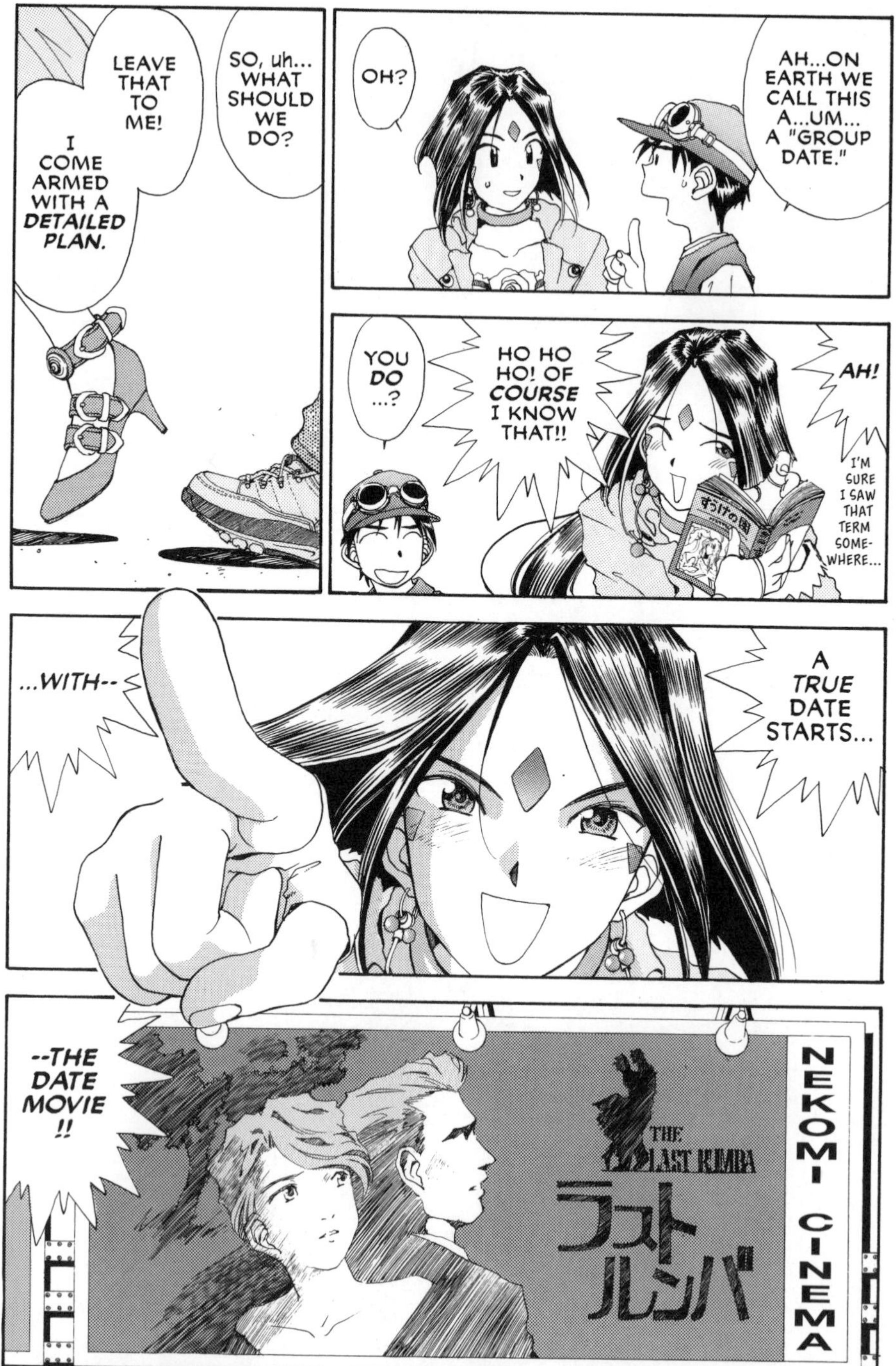
AH...ON EARTH WE CALL THIS A...UM... A "GROUP DATE."
OH?
AH!
I'M SURE I SAW THAT TERM SOME-WHERE...
HO HO HO! OF COURSE I KNOW THAT!!
YOU DO ...?
SO, uh... WHAT SHOULD WE DO?
LEAVE THAT TO ME!
I COME ARMED WITH A DETAILED PLAN.
A TRUE DATE STARTS...
...WITH--
NEKOMI CINEMA
THE LAST RUMBA
ラストルンバ
--THE DATE MOVIE!!

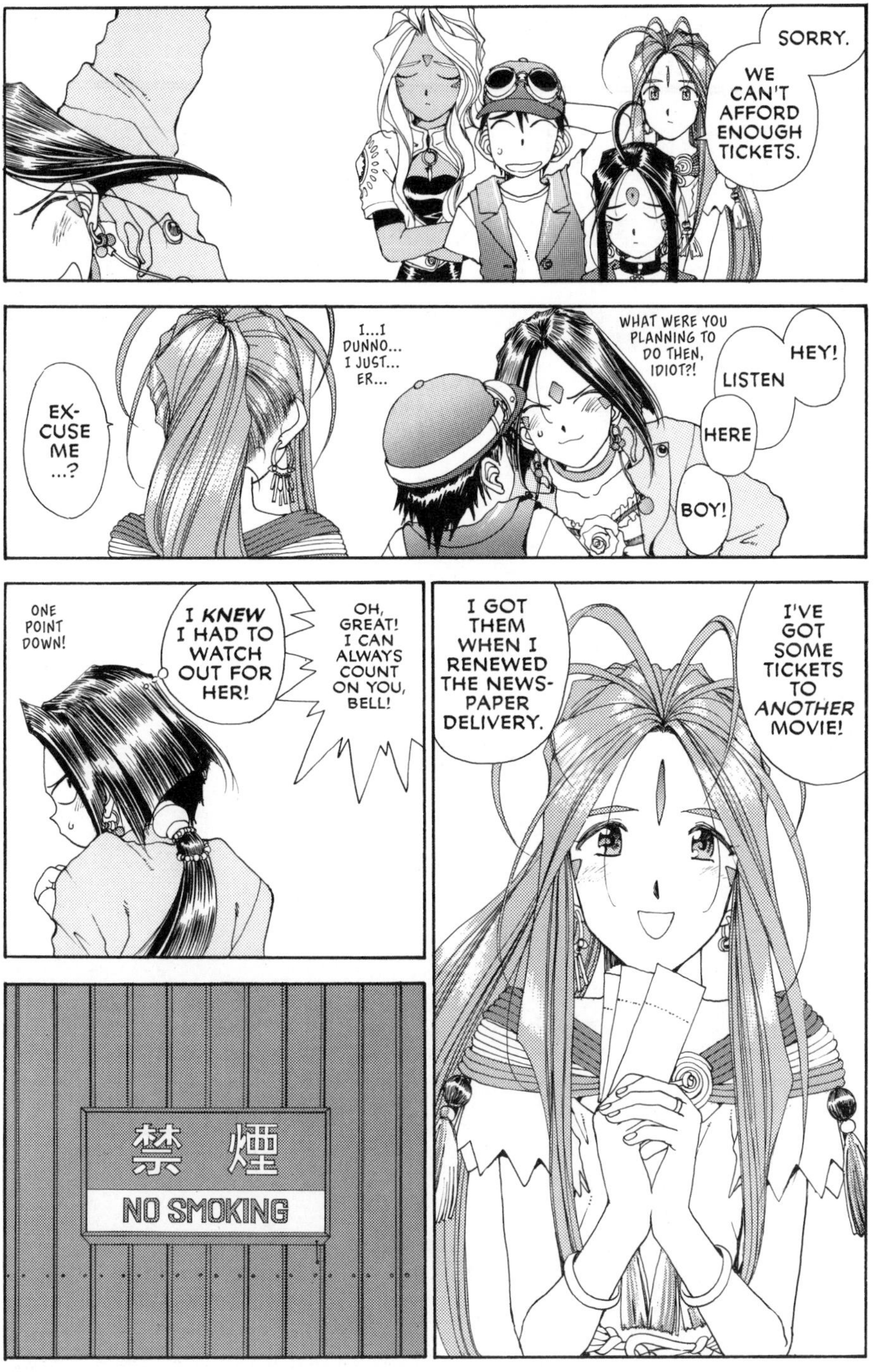
SORRY.
WE CAN'T AFFORD ENOUGH TICKETS.
HEY!
LISTEN
HERE
BOY!
WHAT WERE YOU PLANNING TO DO THEN, IDIOT?!
I...I DUNNO... I JUST... ER...
EX-CUSE ME ...?
I'VE GOT SOME TICKETS TO *ANOTHER* MOVIE!
I GOT THEM WHEN I RENEWED THE NEWS-PAPER DELIVERY.
OH, GREAT! I CAN ALWAYS COUNT ON YOU, BELL!
I *KNEW* I HAD TO WATCH OUT FOR HER!
ONE POINT DOWN!
禁煙
NO SMOKING

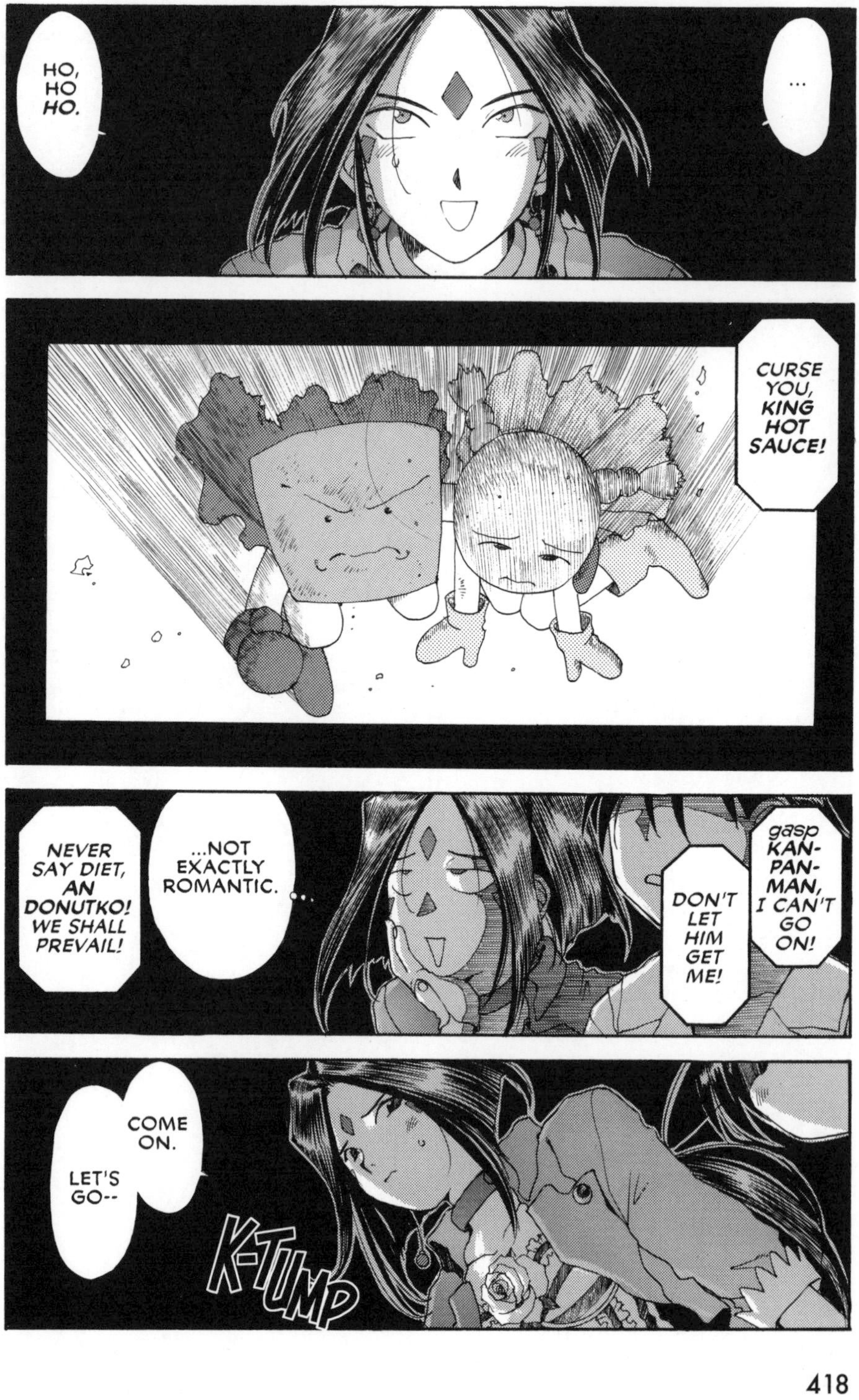
...
HO, HO HO.
CURSE YOU, KING HOT SAUCE!
gasp KAN-PAN-MAN, I CAN'T GO ON!
DON'T LET HIM GET ME!
...NOT EXACTLY ROMANTIC.
NEVER SAY DIET, AN DONUTKO! WE SHALL PREVAIL!
COME ON.
LET'S GO--
K-TUMP

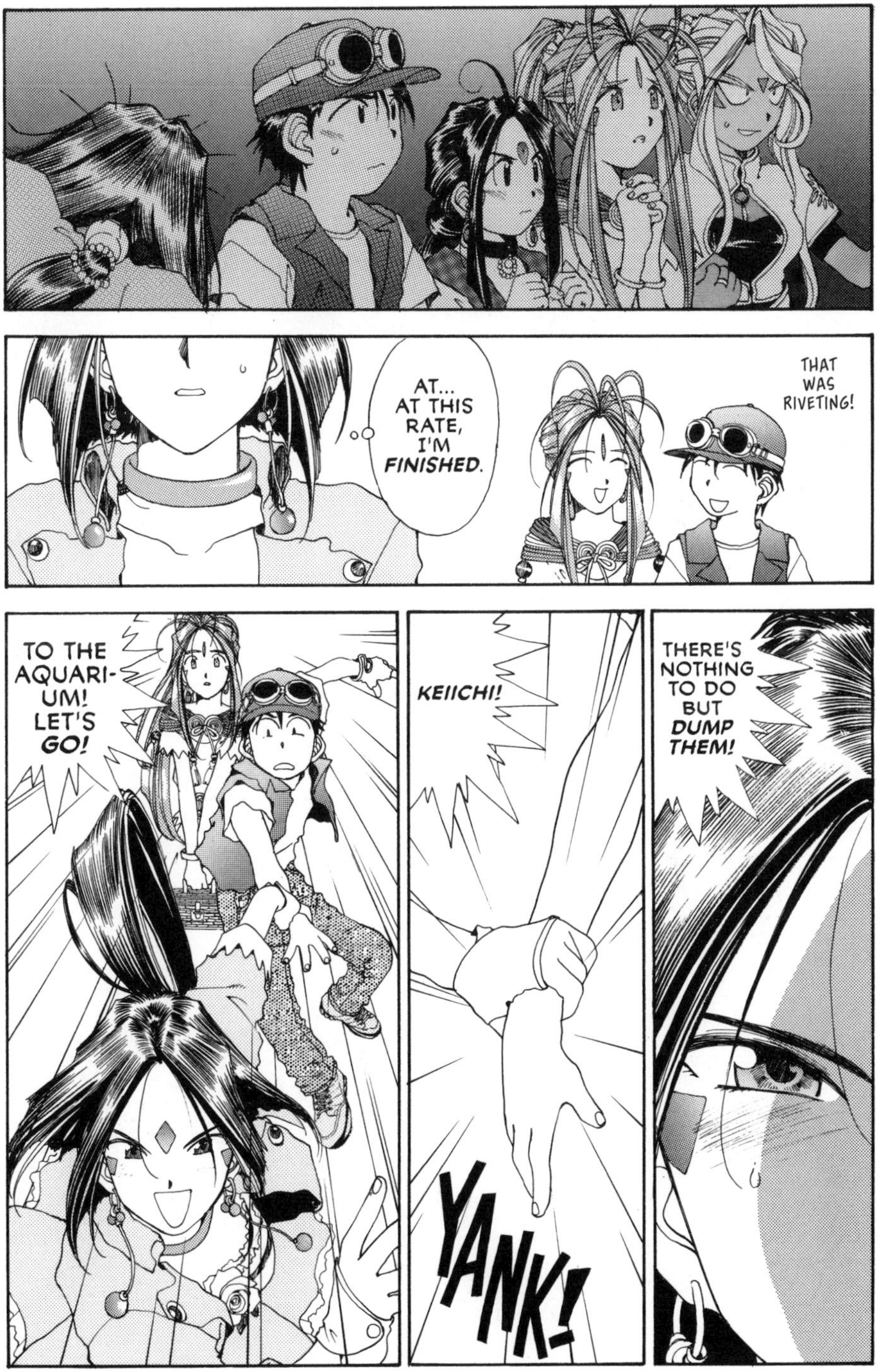
THAT WAS RIVETING!
AT... AT THIS RATE, I'M *FINISHED*.
THERE'S NOTHING TO DO BUT *DUMP THEM!*
KEIICHI!
YANK!
TO THE AQUARIUM! LET'S *GO!*

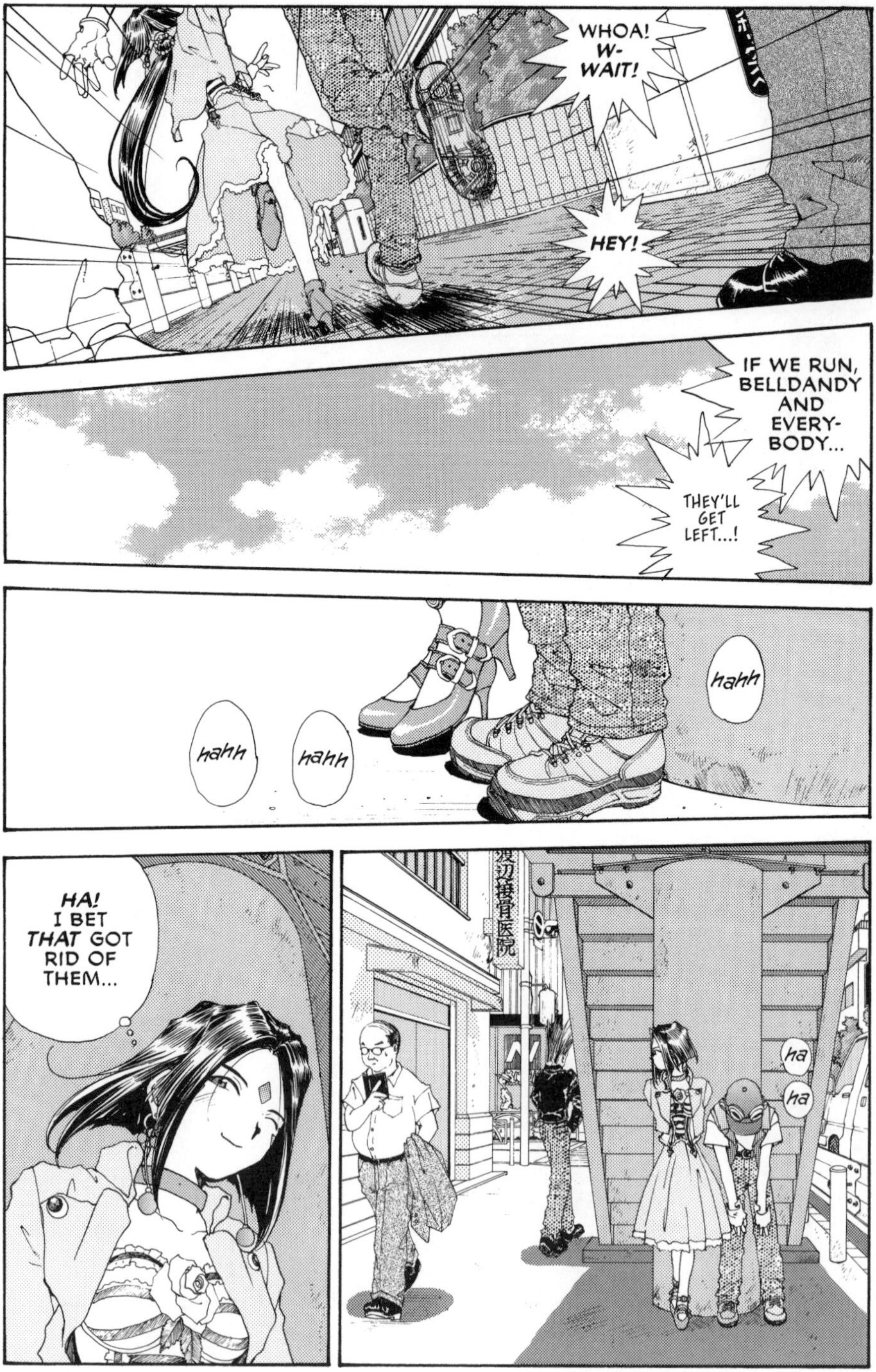
WHOA! W-WAIT!
HEY!
IF WE RUN, BELLDANDY AND EVERY-BODY...
THEY'LL GET LEFT...!
hahh
hahh
hahh
渡辺接骨医院
ha
ha
HA! I BET THAT GOT RID OF THEM...

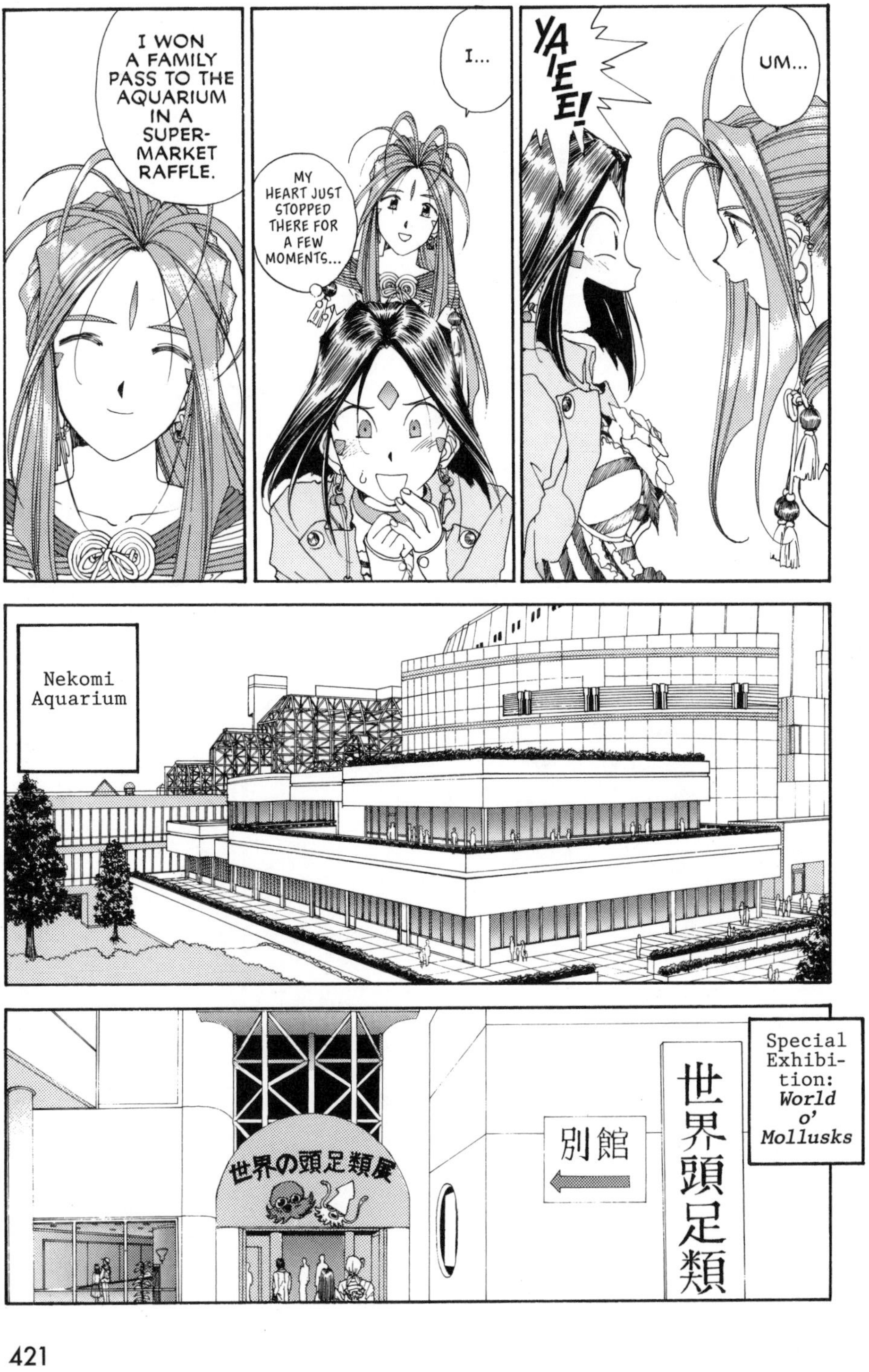
I WON A FAMILY PASS TO THE AQUARIUM IN A SUPER-MARKET RAFFLE.
I...
MY HEART JUST STOPPED THERE FOR A FEW MOMENTS...
YAIEE!
UM...
Nekomi Aquarium
Special Exhibition: World o' Mollusks
世界頭足類
別館
世界の頭足類展

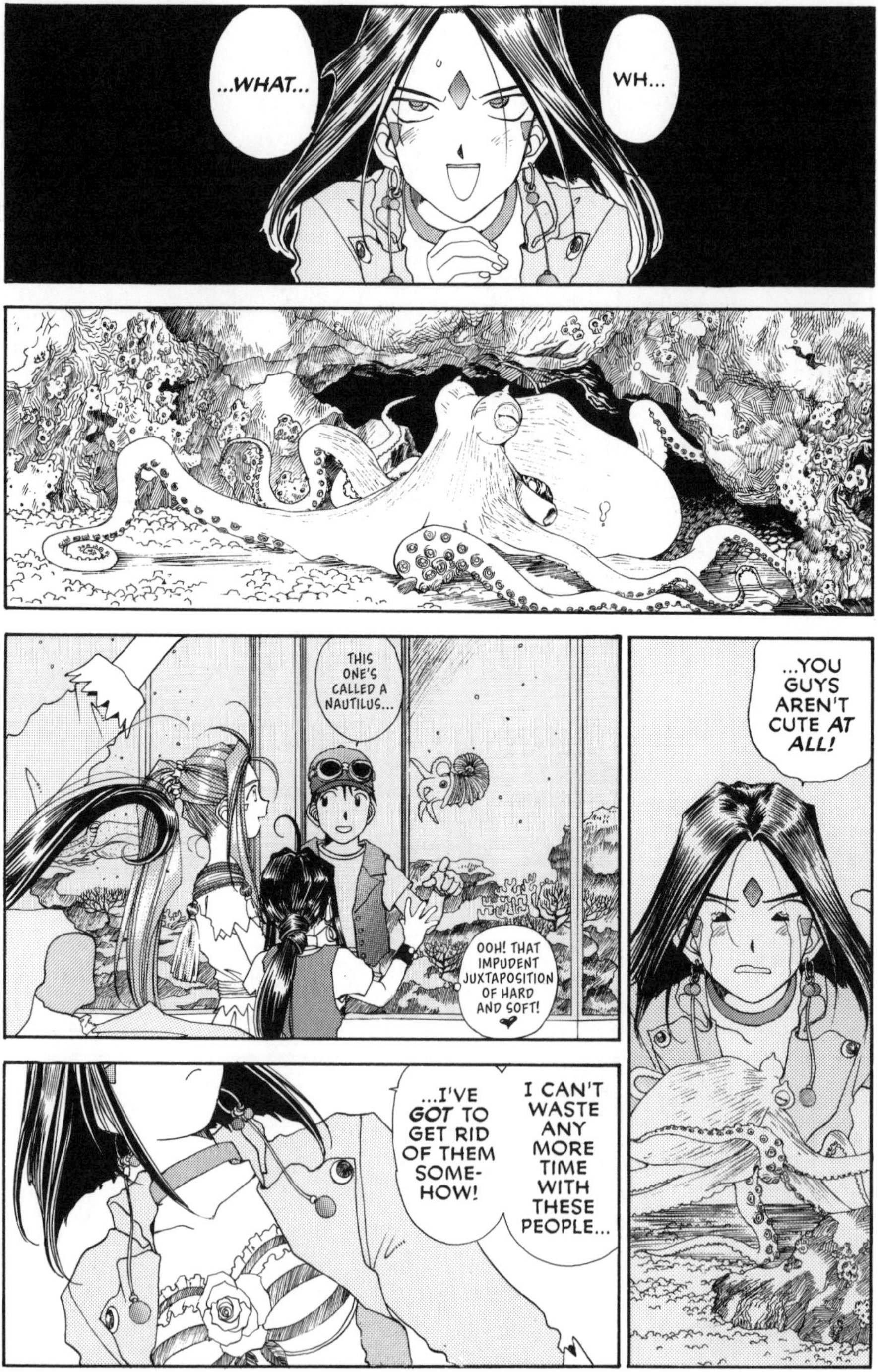
WH...
...WHAT...
...YOU GUYS AREN'T CUTE AT ALL!
THIS ONE'S CALLED A NAUTILUS...
OOH! THAT IMPUDENT JUXTAPOSITION OF HARD AND SOFT! ♥
I CAN'T WASTE ANY MORE TIME WITH THESE PEOPLE...
...I'VE GOT TO GET RID OF THEM SOME-HOW!

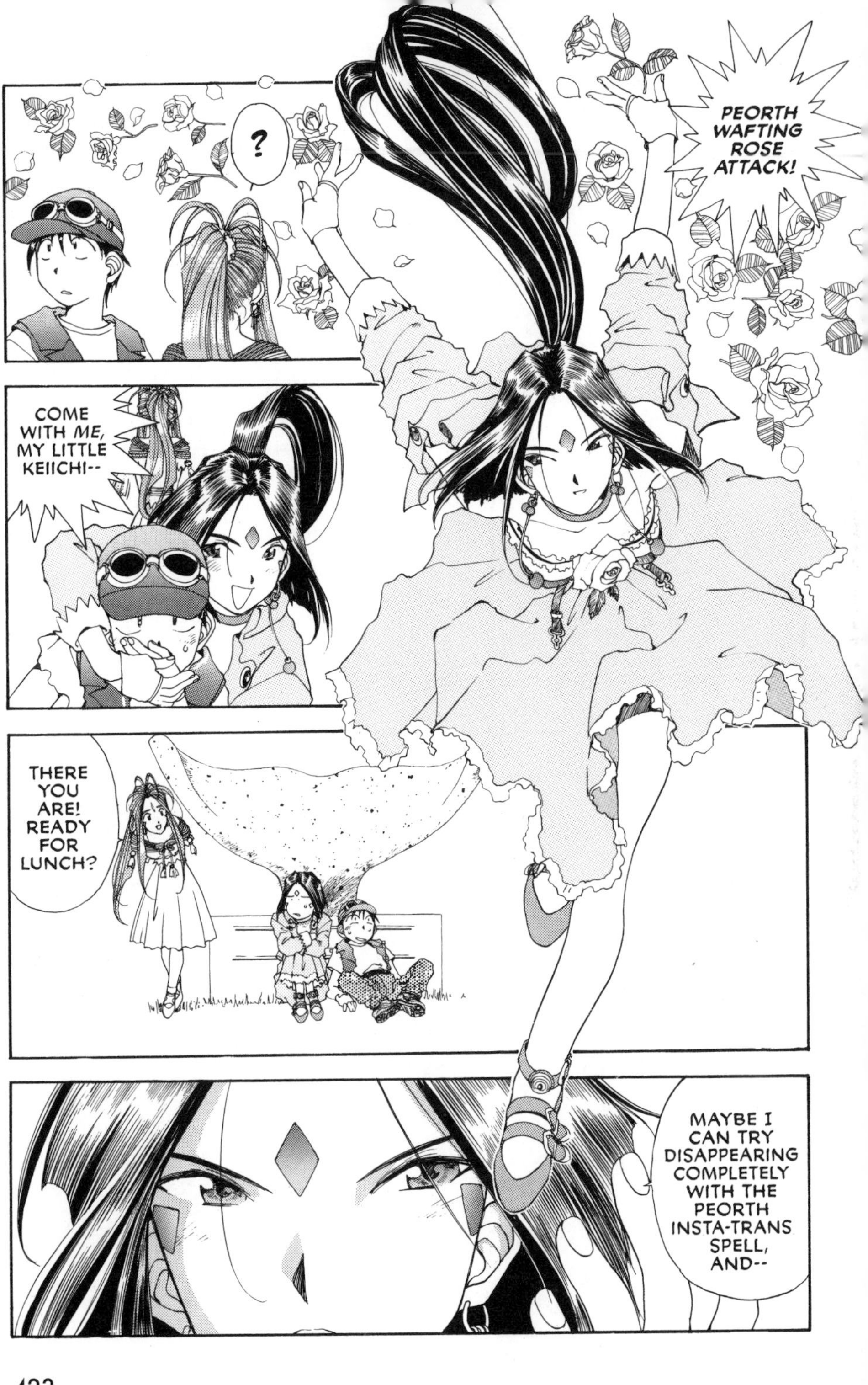
PEORTH WAFTING ROSE ATTACK!
?
COME WITH *ME*, MY LITTLE KEIICHI--
THERE YOU ARE! READY FOR LUNCH?
MAYBE I CAN TRY DISAPPEARING COMPLETELY WITH THE PEORTH INSTA-TRANS SPELL, AND--

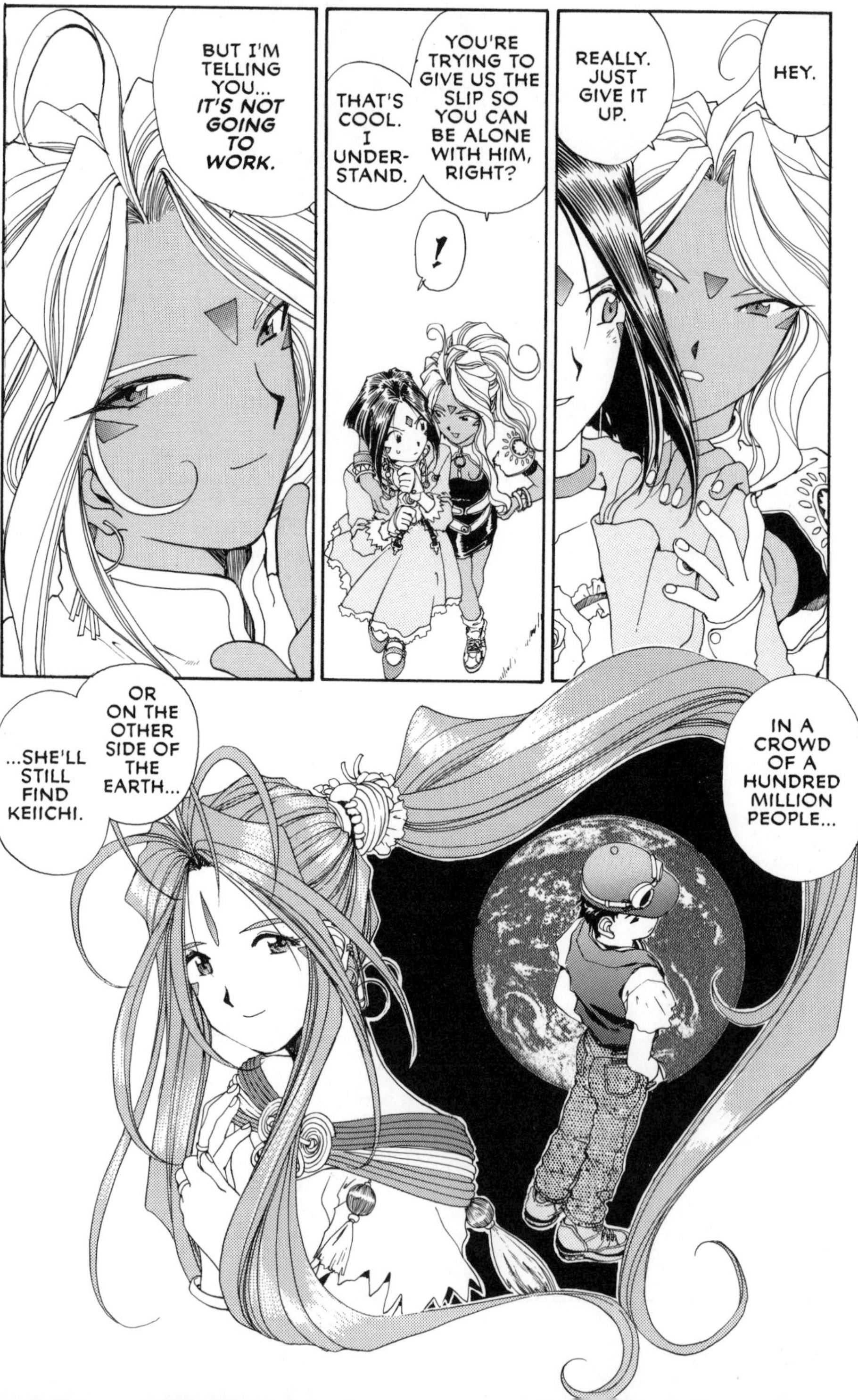
HEY.
REALLY. JUST GIVE IT UP.
YOU'RE TRYING TO GIVE US THE SLIP SO YOU CAN BE ALONE WITH HIM, RIGHT?
THAT'S COOL. I UNDER-STAND.
!
BUT I'M TELLING YOU... *IT'S NOT GOING TO WORK.*
IN A CROWD OF A HUNDRED MILLION PEOPLE...
OR ON THE OTHER SIDE OF THE EARTH...
...SHE'LL STILL FIND KEIICHI.

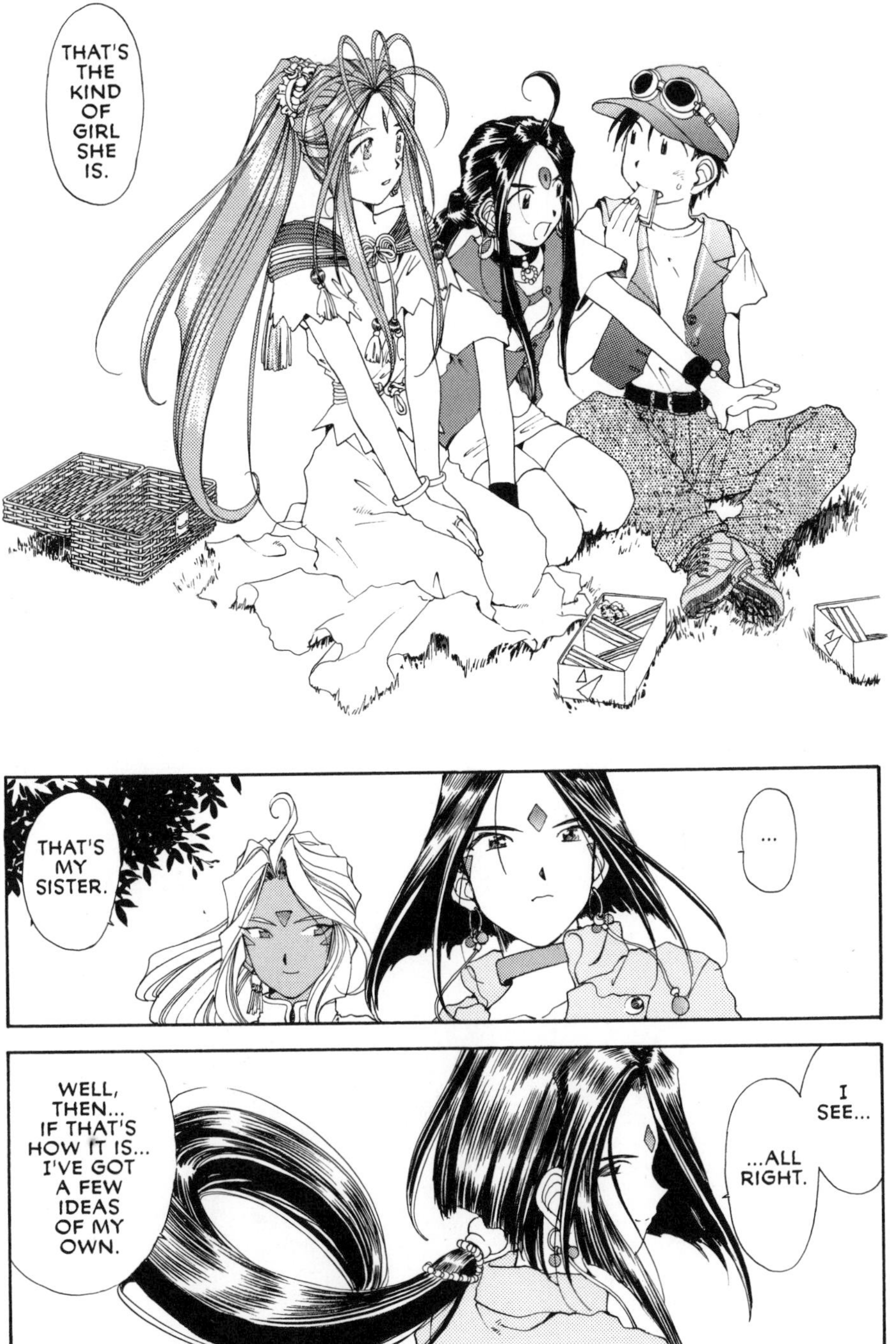
THAT'S THE KIND OF GIRL SHE IS.
...
THAT'S MY SISTER.
I SEE...
...ALL RIGHT.
WELL, THEN... IF THAT'S HOW IT IS... I'VE GOT A FEW IDEAS OF MY OWN.

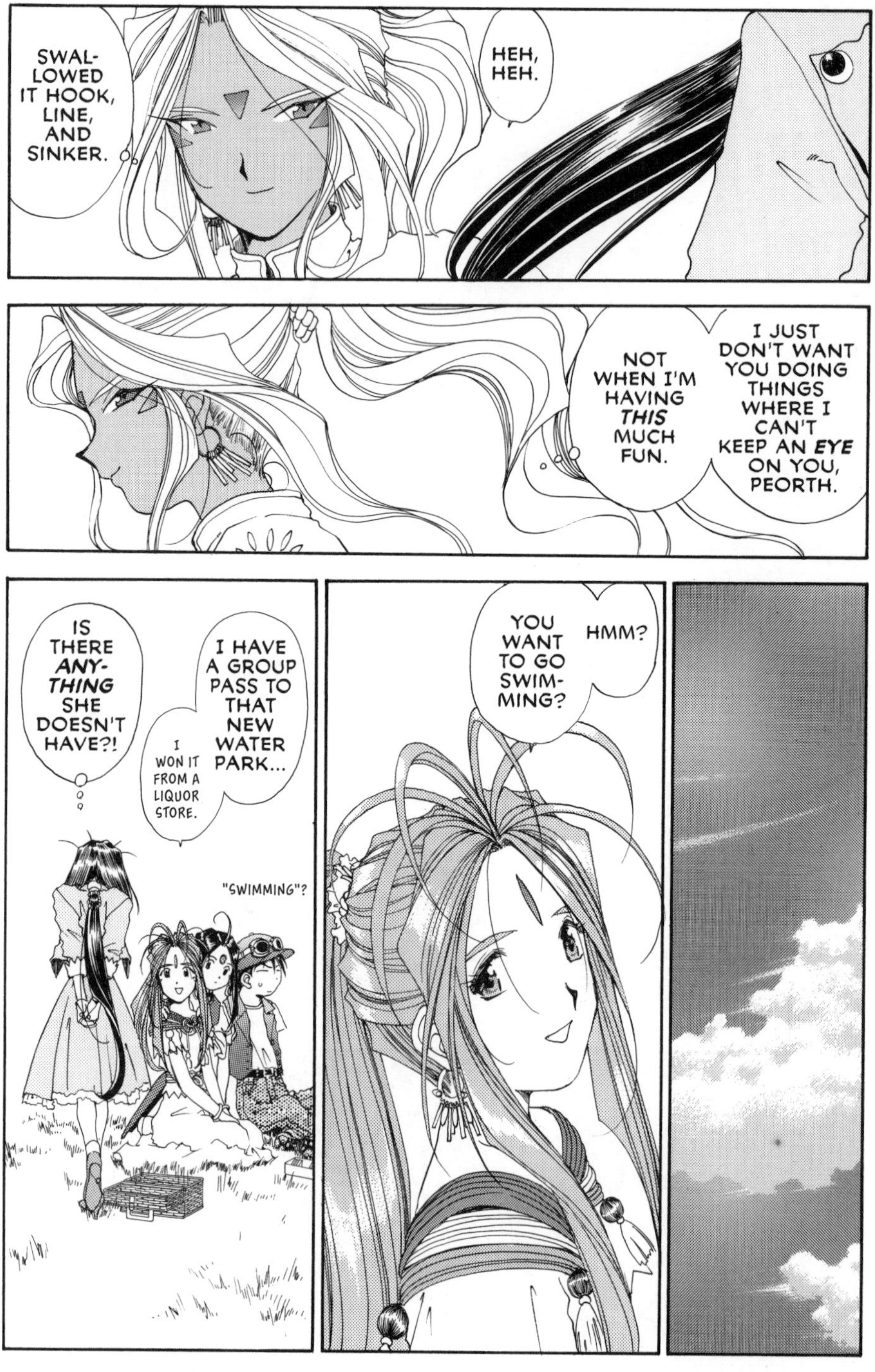
HEH, HEH.
SWAL-LOWED IT HOOK, LINE, AND SINKER.
I JUST DON'T WANT YOU DOING THINGS WHERE I CAN'T KEEP AN *EYE* ON YOU, PEORTH.
NOT WHEN I'M HAVING *THIS* MUCH FUN.
HMM?
YOU WANT TO GO SWIMMING?
I HAVE A GROUP PASS TO THAT NEW WATER PARK...
I WON IT FROM A LIQUOR STORE.
IS THERE *ANYTHING* SHE DOESN'T HAVE?!
"SWIMMING"?

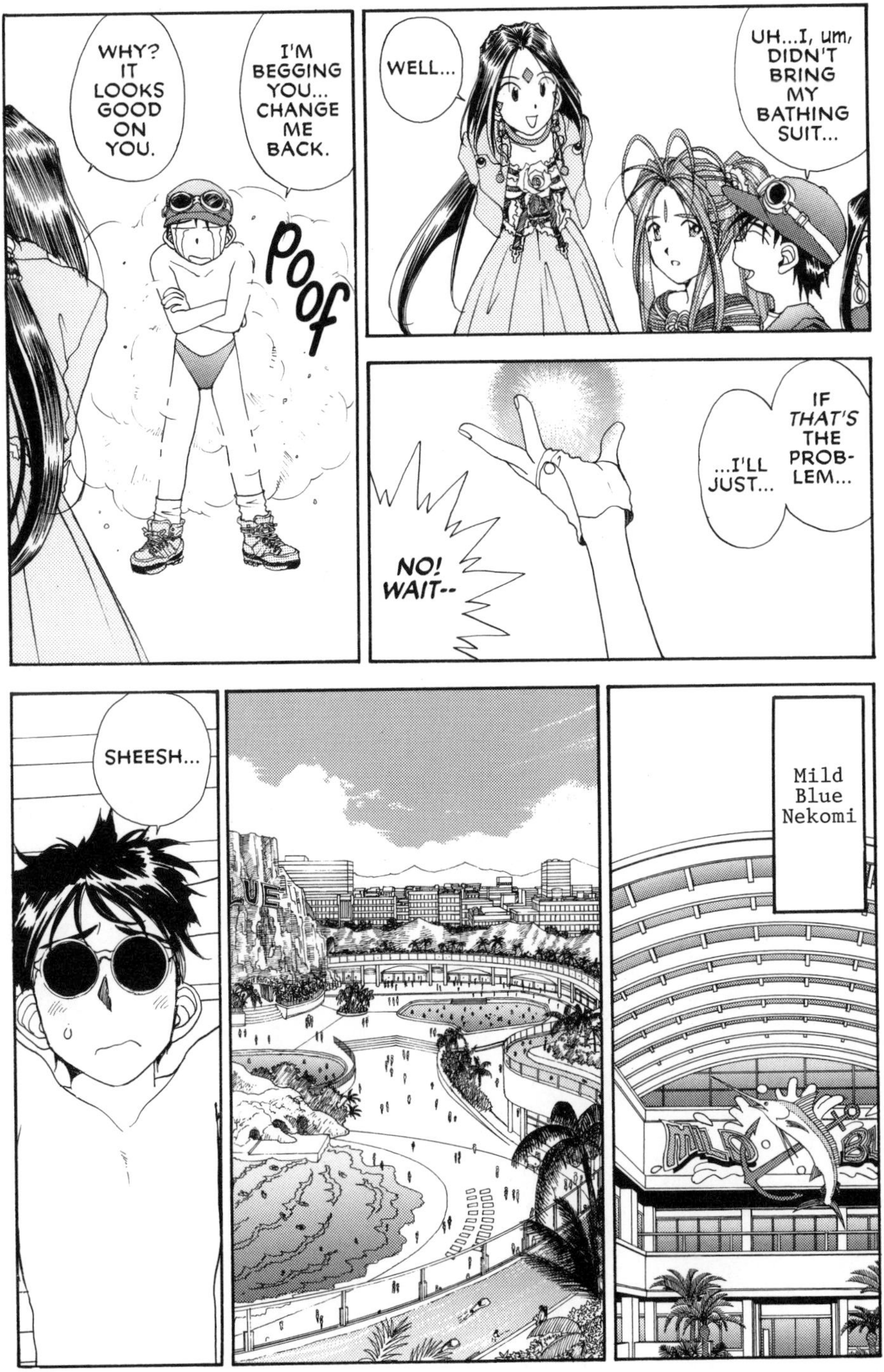
UH...I, um, DIDN'T BRING MY BATHING SUIT...
WELL...
IF THAT'S THE PROB-LEM...
...I'LL JUST...
NO! WAIT--
POOF
I'M BEGGING YOU... CHANGE ME BACK.
WHY? IT LOOKS GOOD ON YOU.
Mild Blue Nekomi
SHEESH...

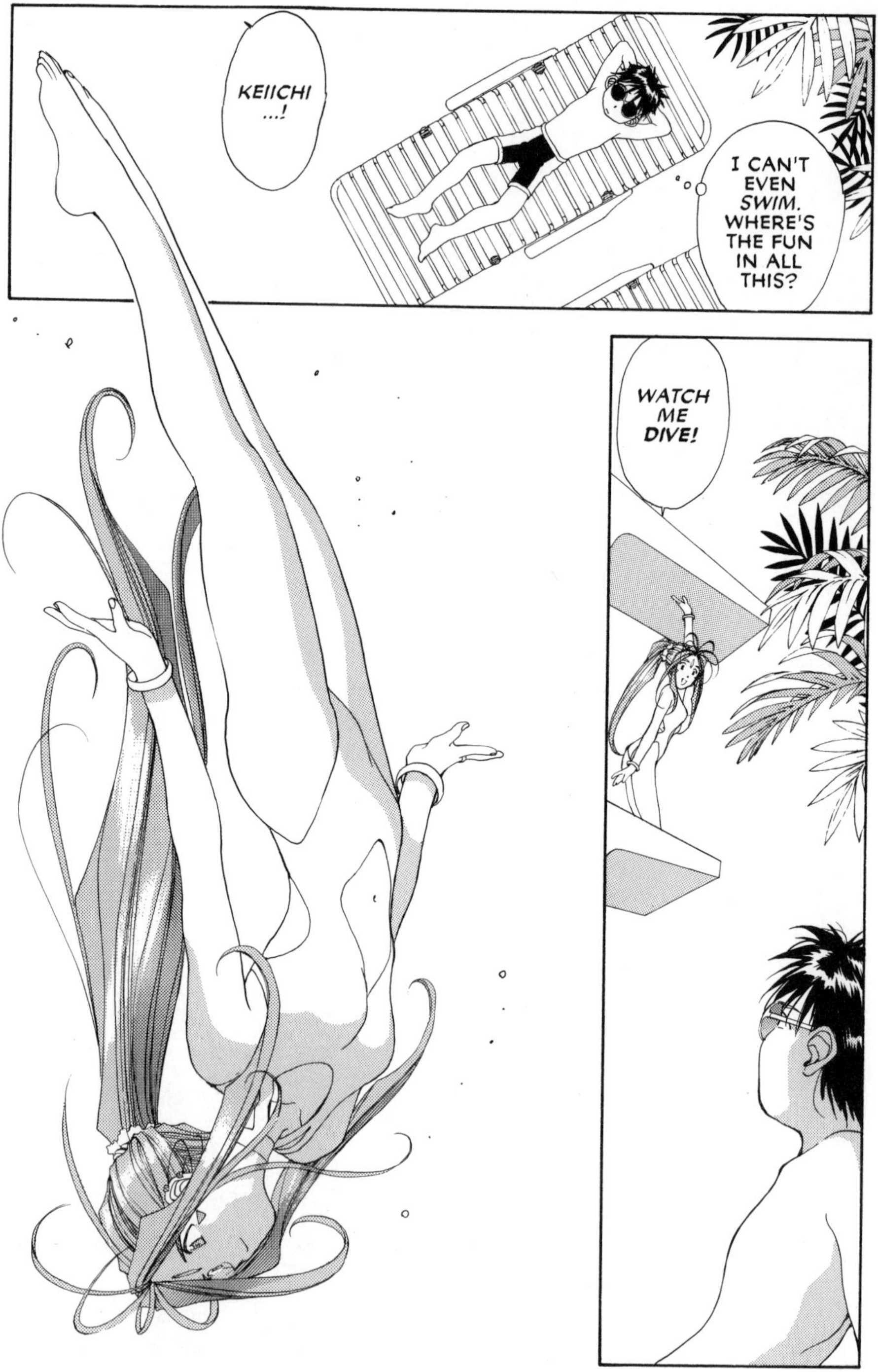
I CAN'T EVEN *SWIM*. WHERE'S THE FUN IN ALL THIS?
KEIICHI ...!
WATCH ME **DIVE!**

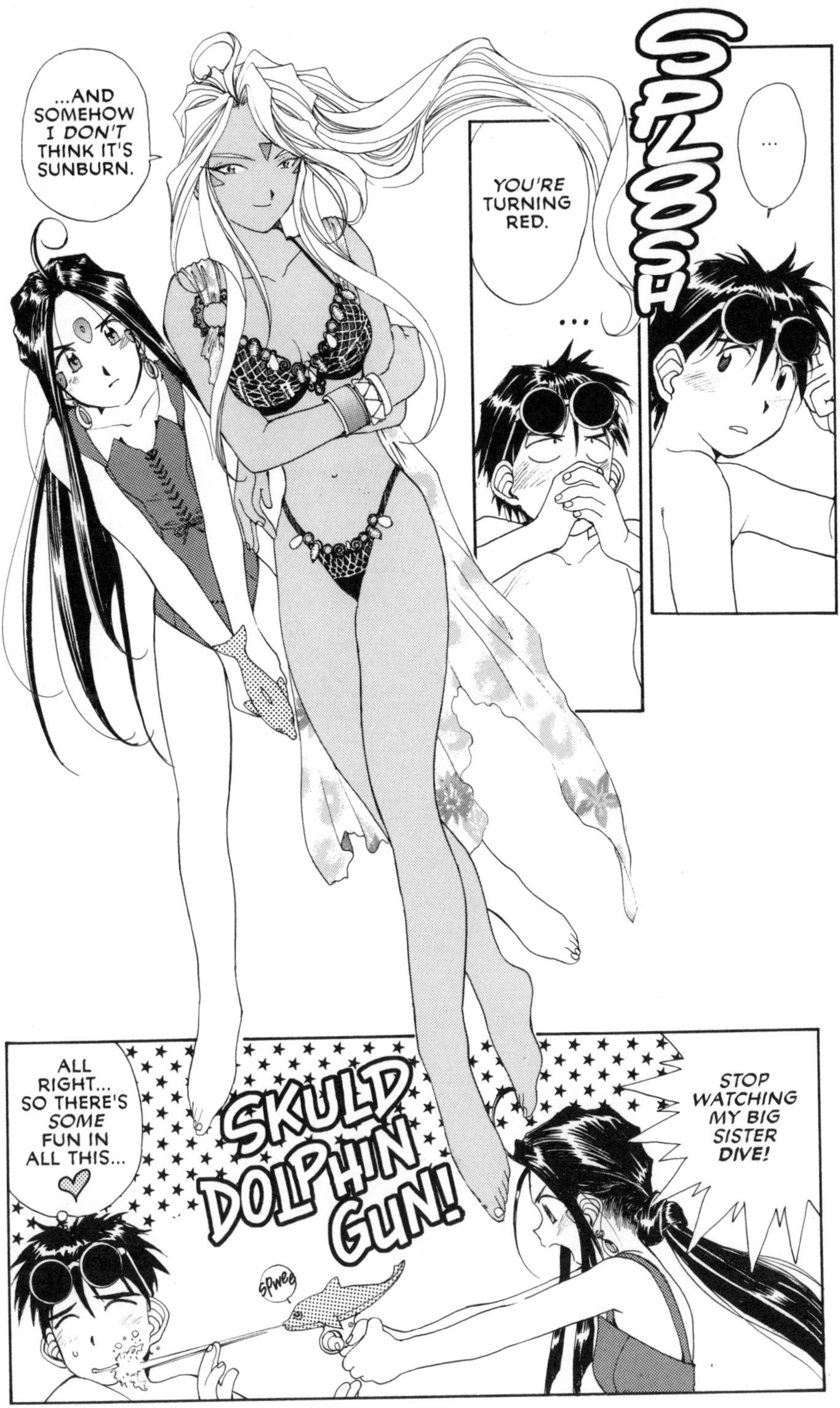
SPLOOSH
...
YOU'RE TURNING RED.
...
...AND SOMEHOW I *DON'T* THINK IT'S SUNBURN.
STOP WATCHING MY BIG SISTER DIVE!
SKULD DOLPHIN GUN!
SPWEE
ALL RIGHT... SO THERE'S *SOME* FUN IN ALL THIS...

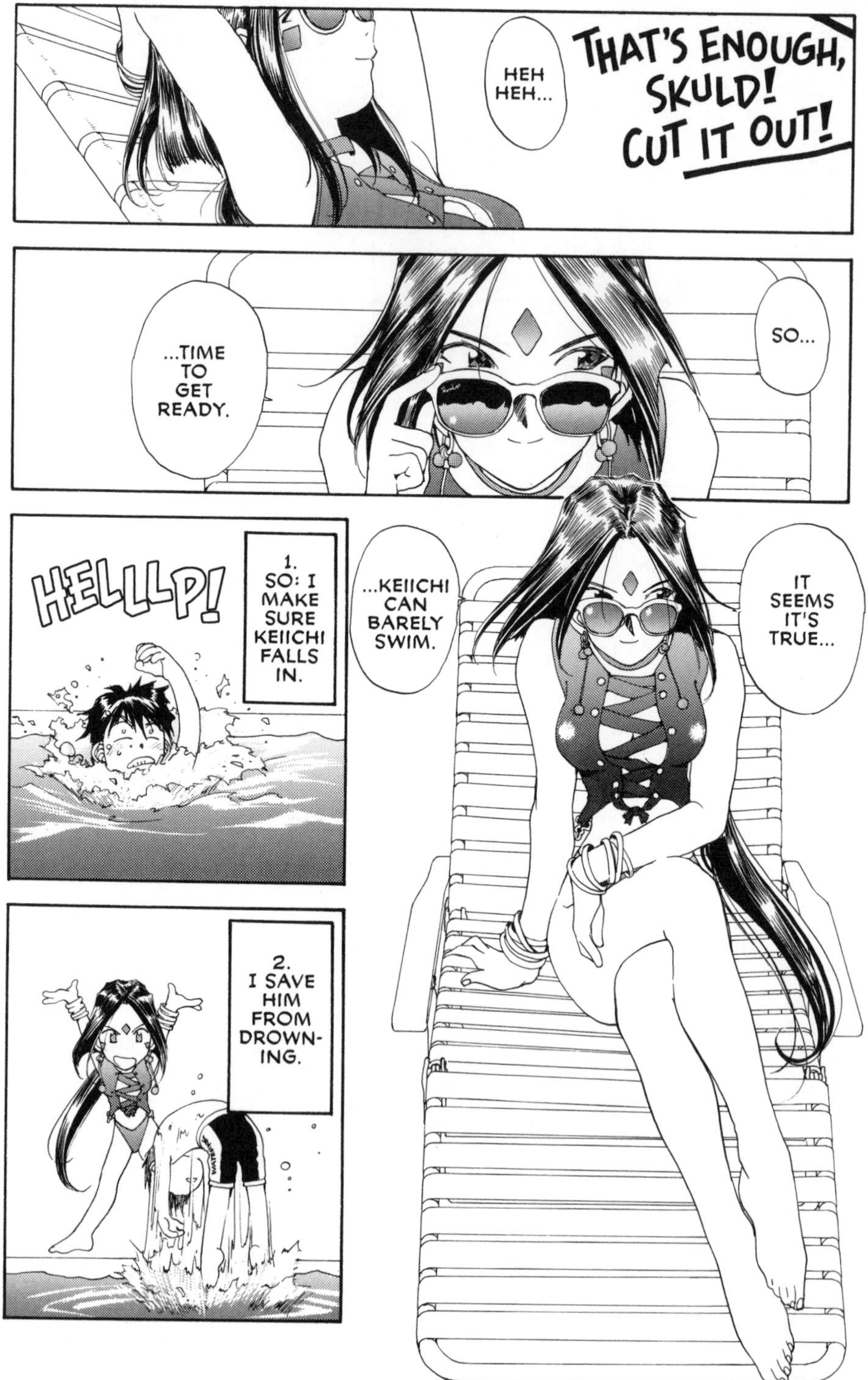
THAT'S ENOUGH, SKULD! CUT IT OUT!
HEH HEH...
SO...
...TIME TO GET READY.
IT SEEMS IT'S TRUE...
...KEIICHI CAN BARELY SWIM.
1. SO: I MAKE SURE KEIICHI FALLS IN.
HELLLP!
2. I SAVE HIM FROM DROWNING.

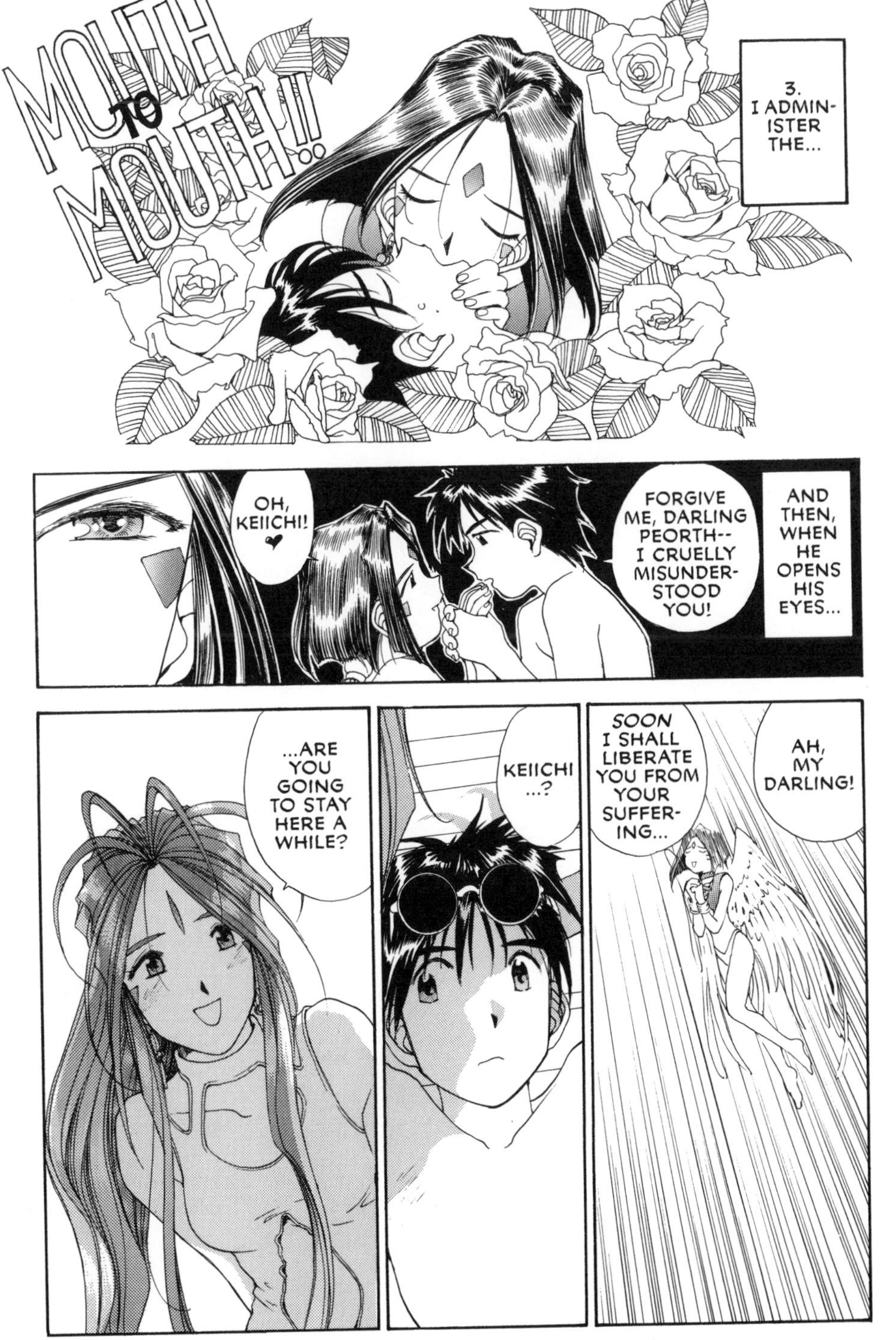
3. I ADMINISTER THE...
MOUTH TO MOUTH!!
AND THEN, WHEN HE OPENS HIS EYES...
FORGIVE ME, DARLING PEORTH-- I CRUELLY MISUNDERSTOOD YOU!
OH, KEIICHI! ♥
AH, MY DARLING!
SOON I SHALL LIBERATE YOU FROM YOUR SUFFERING...
KEIICHI ...?
...ARE YOU GOING TO STAY HERE A WHILE?

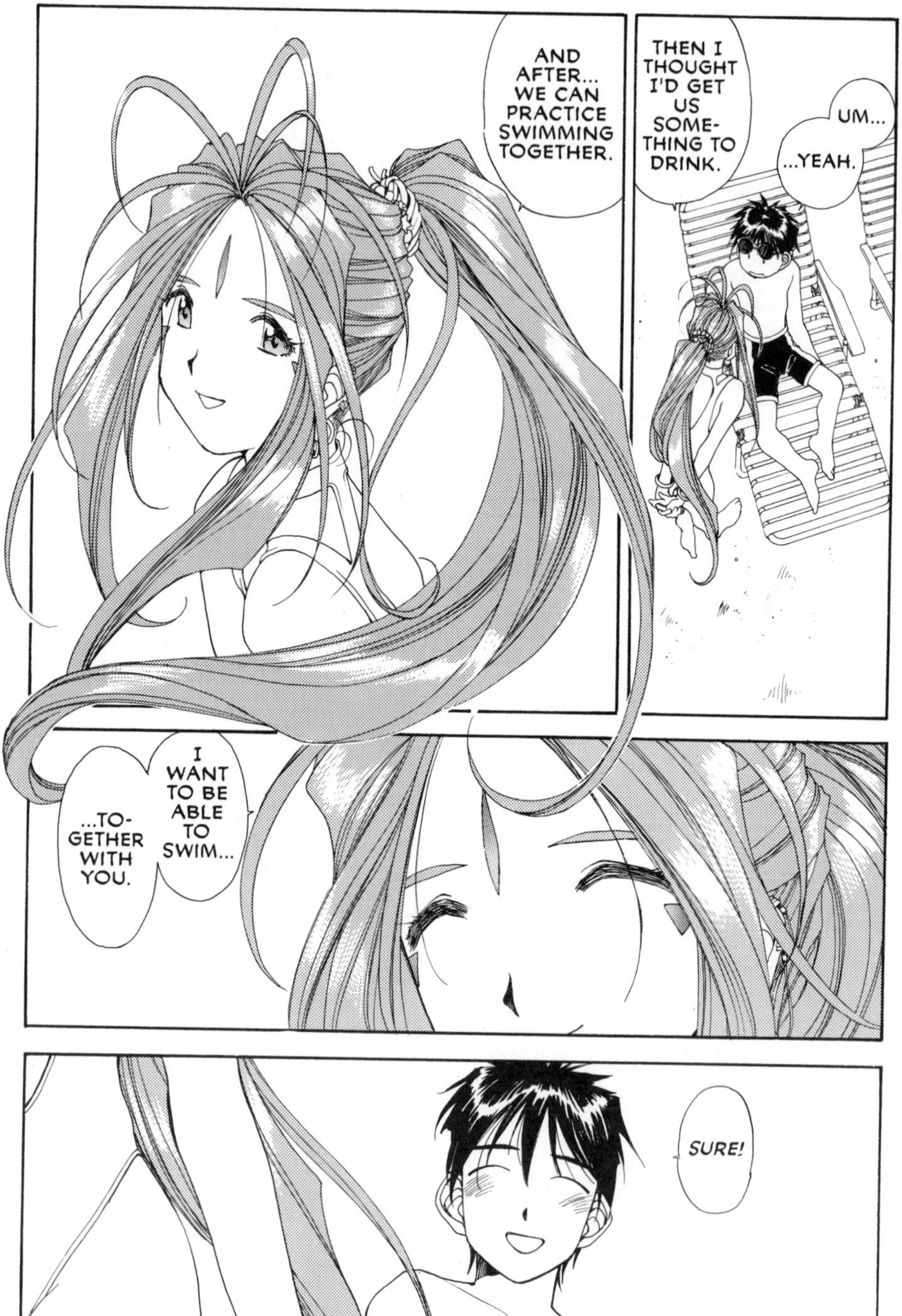
THEN I THOUGHT I'D GET US SOME-THING TO DRINK.
UM...
...YEAH.
AND AFTER... WE CAN PRACTICE SWIMMING TOGETHER.
I WANT TO BE ABLE TO SWIM...
...TO-GETHER WITH YOU.
SURE!

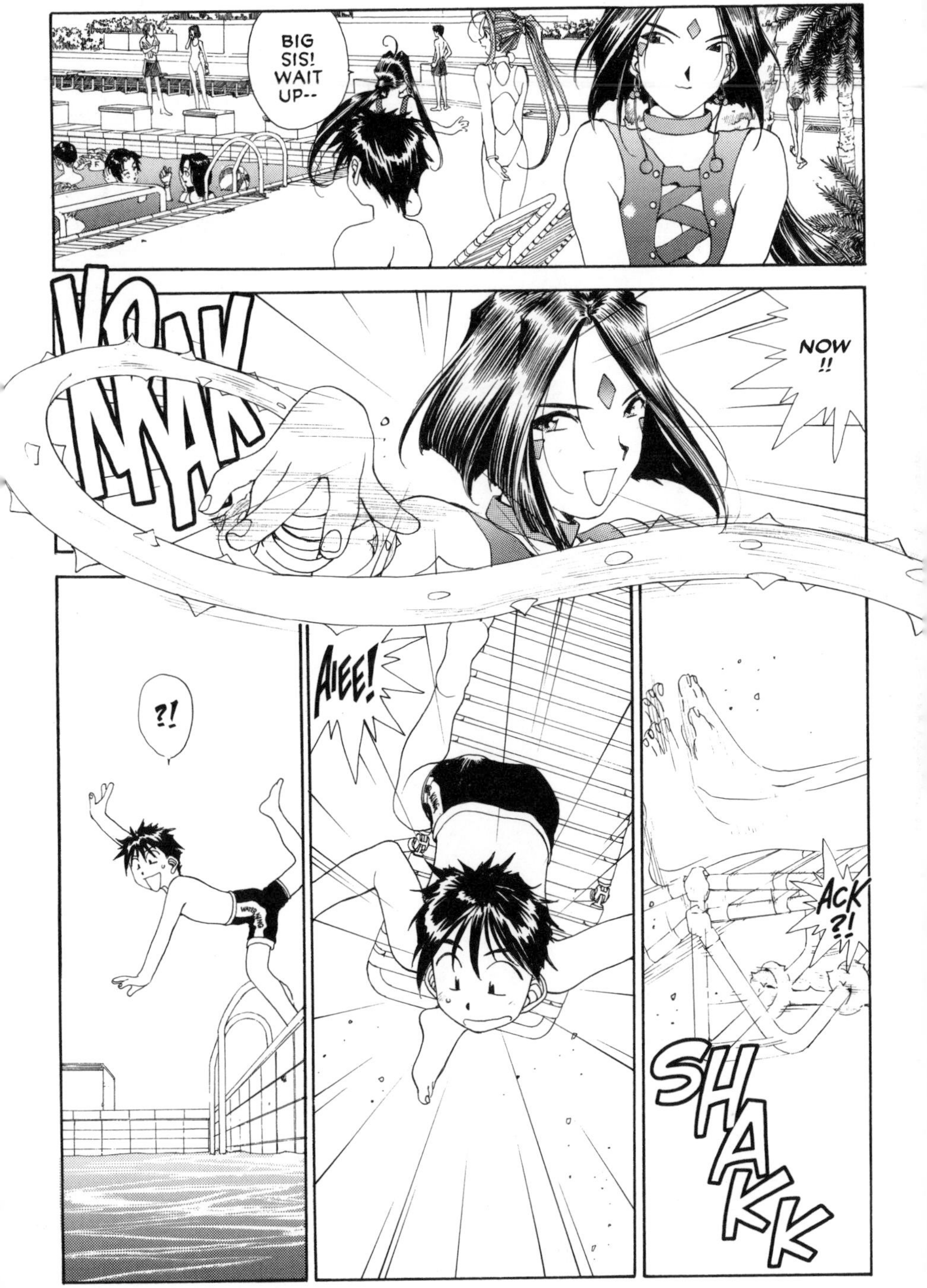
BIG SIS! WAIT UP--
NOW!!
ACK?!
SHAKK
AIEE!
?!

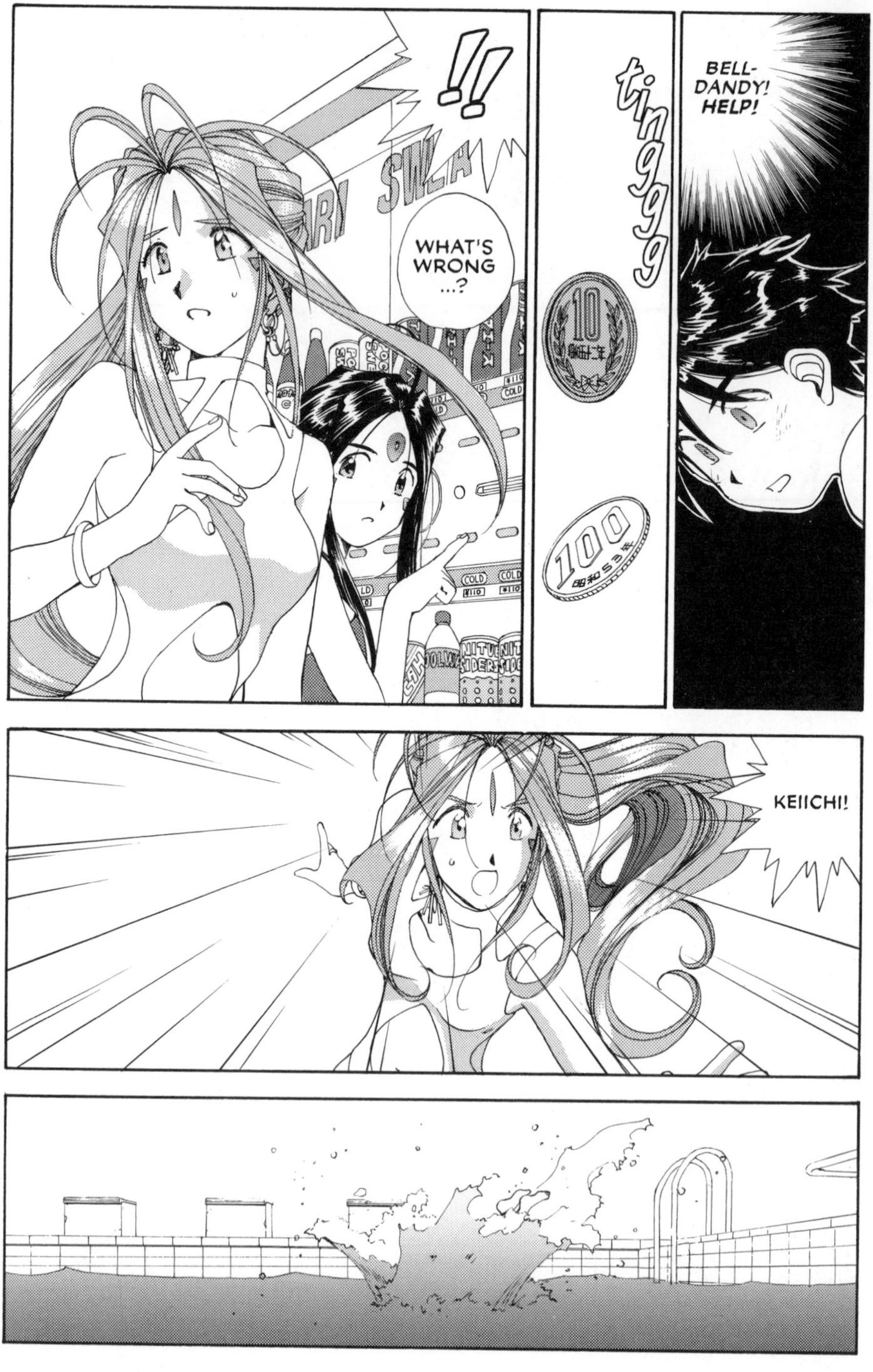
BELL-DANDY! HELP!
tinggg
!!
WHAT'S WRONG ...?
KEIICHI!

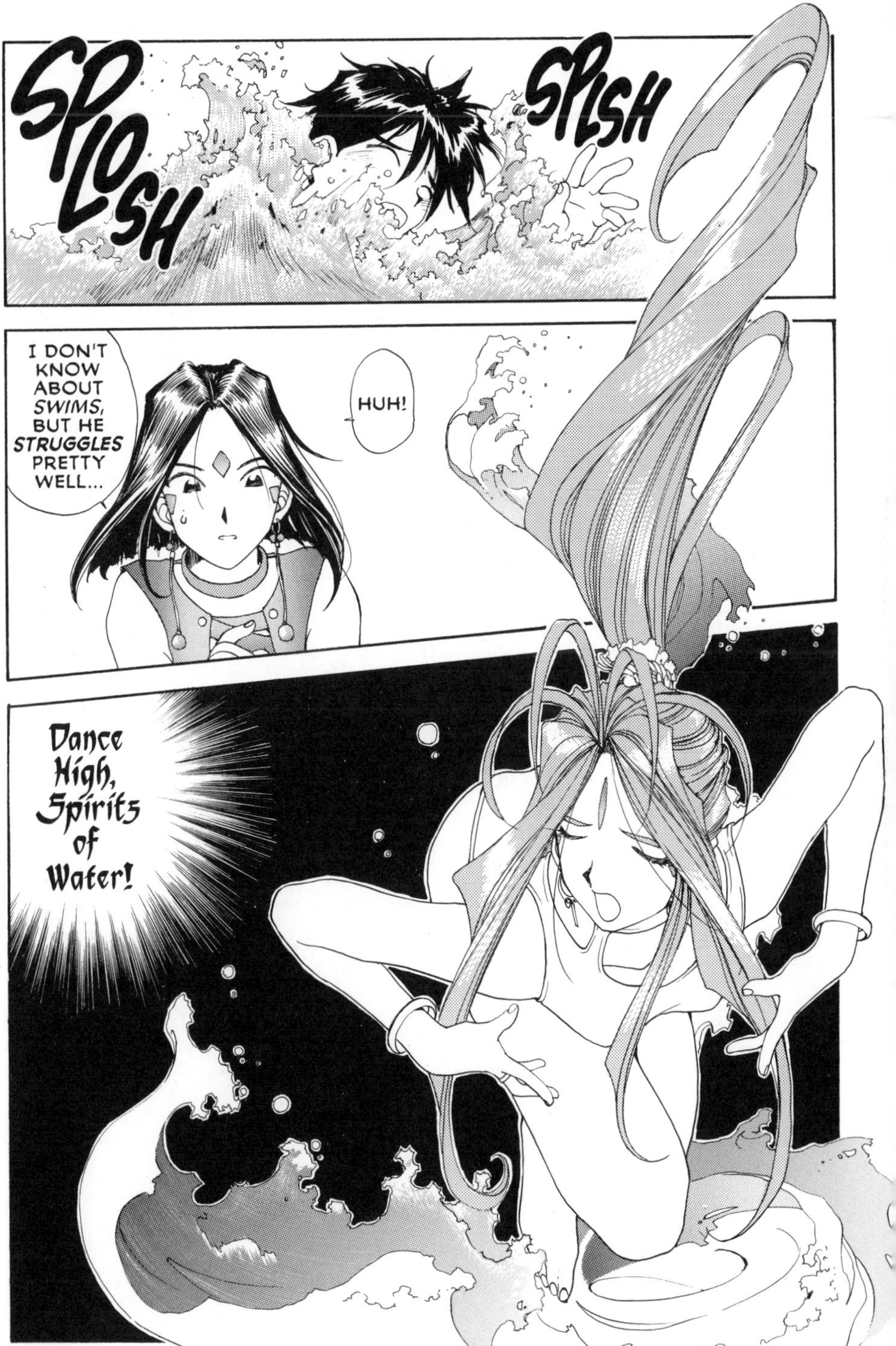
SPLISH
SPLOSH
HUH!
I DON'T KNOW ABOUT SWIMS, BUT HE STRUGGLES PRETTY WELL...
Dance High, Spirits of Water!

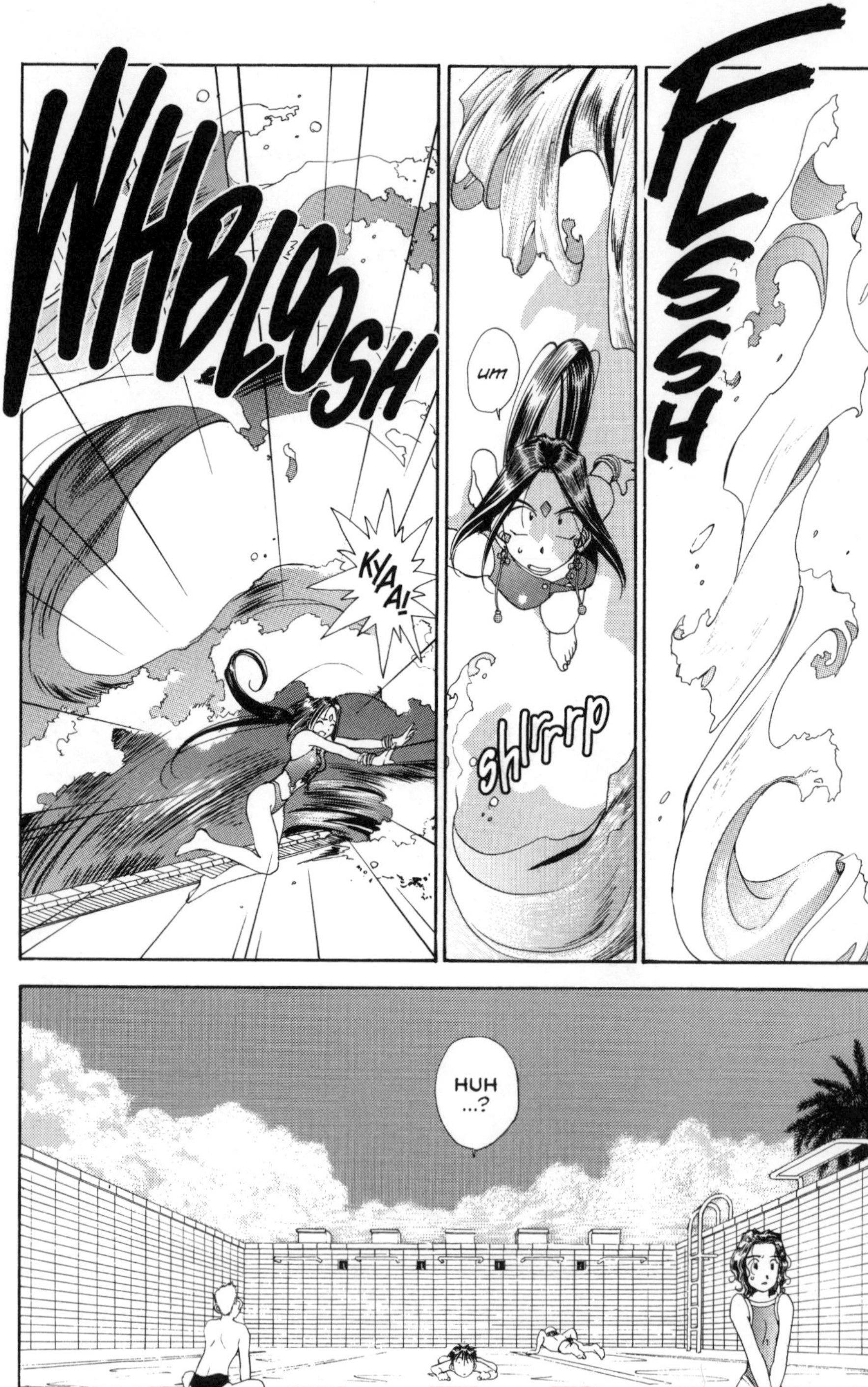
FLLSSH
um
shlrrrp
WHABLOOSH
KYAA!
HUH ...?

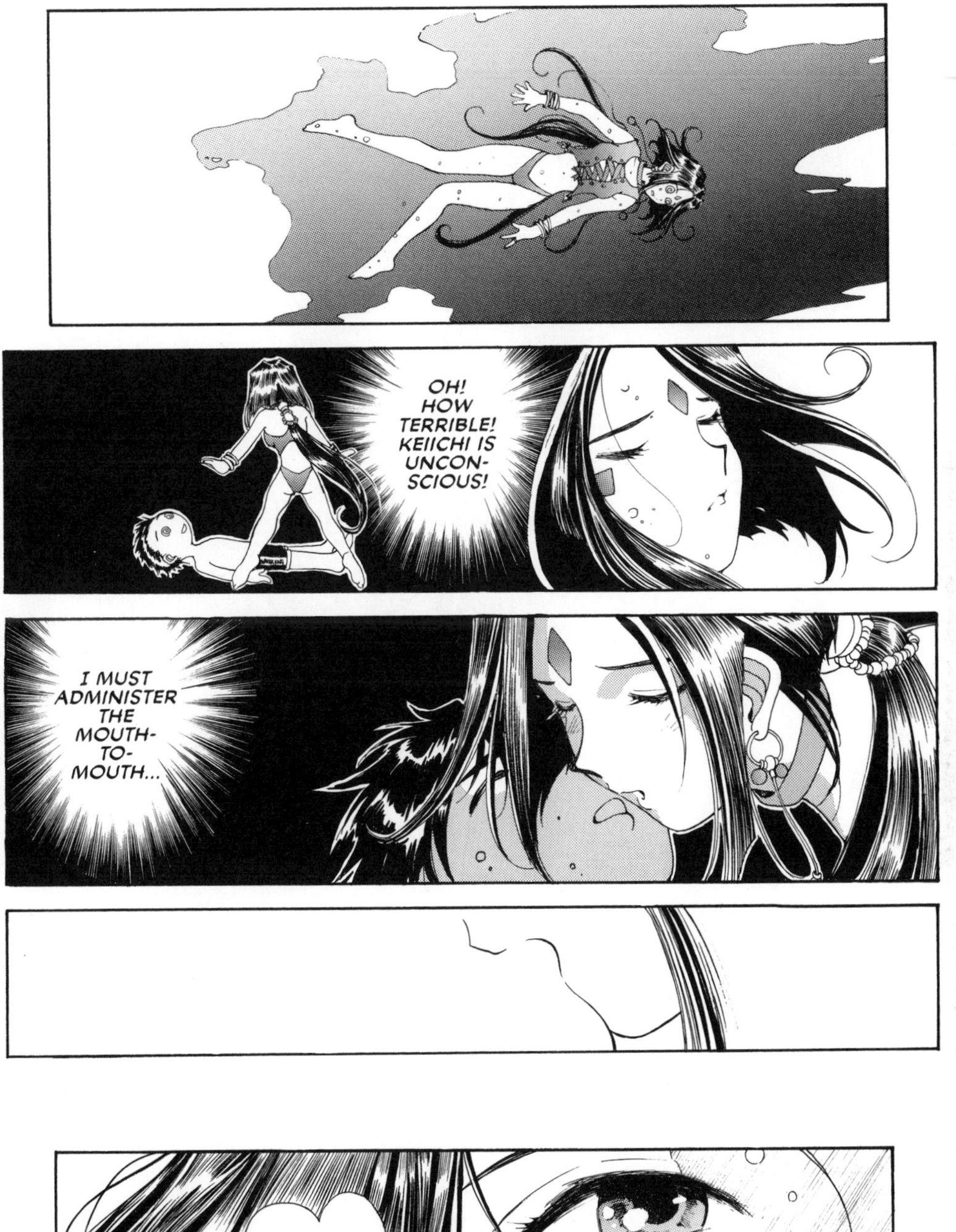
OH! HOW TERRIBLE! KEIICHI IS UNCON- SCIOUS!
I MUST ADMINISTER THE MOUTH- TO- MOUTH...
mm mmmm

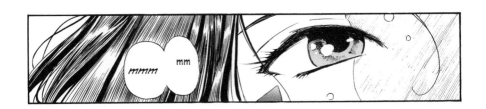

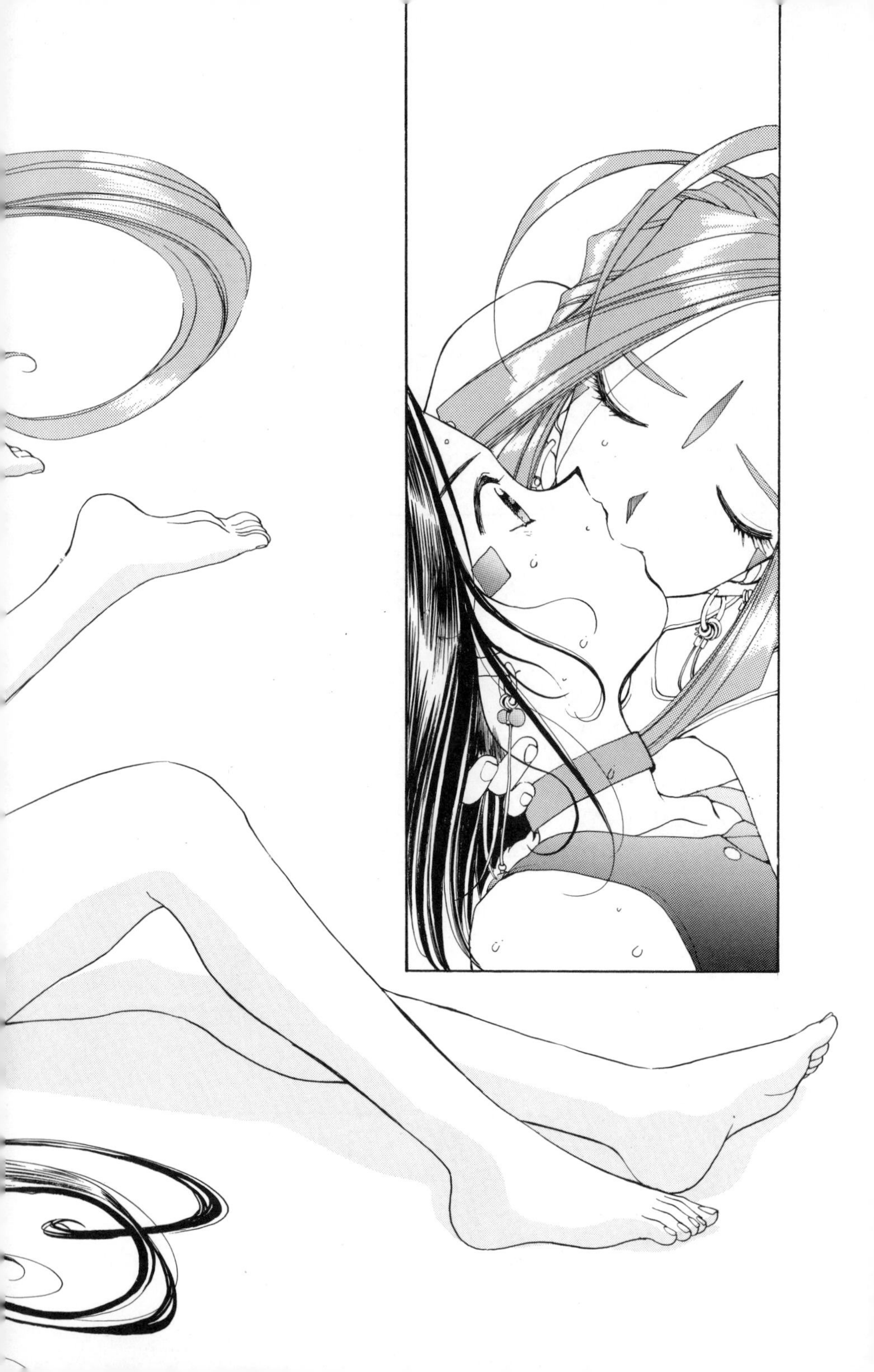

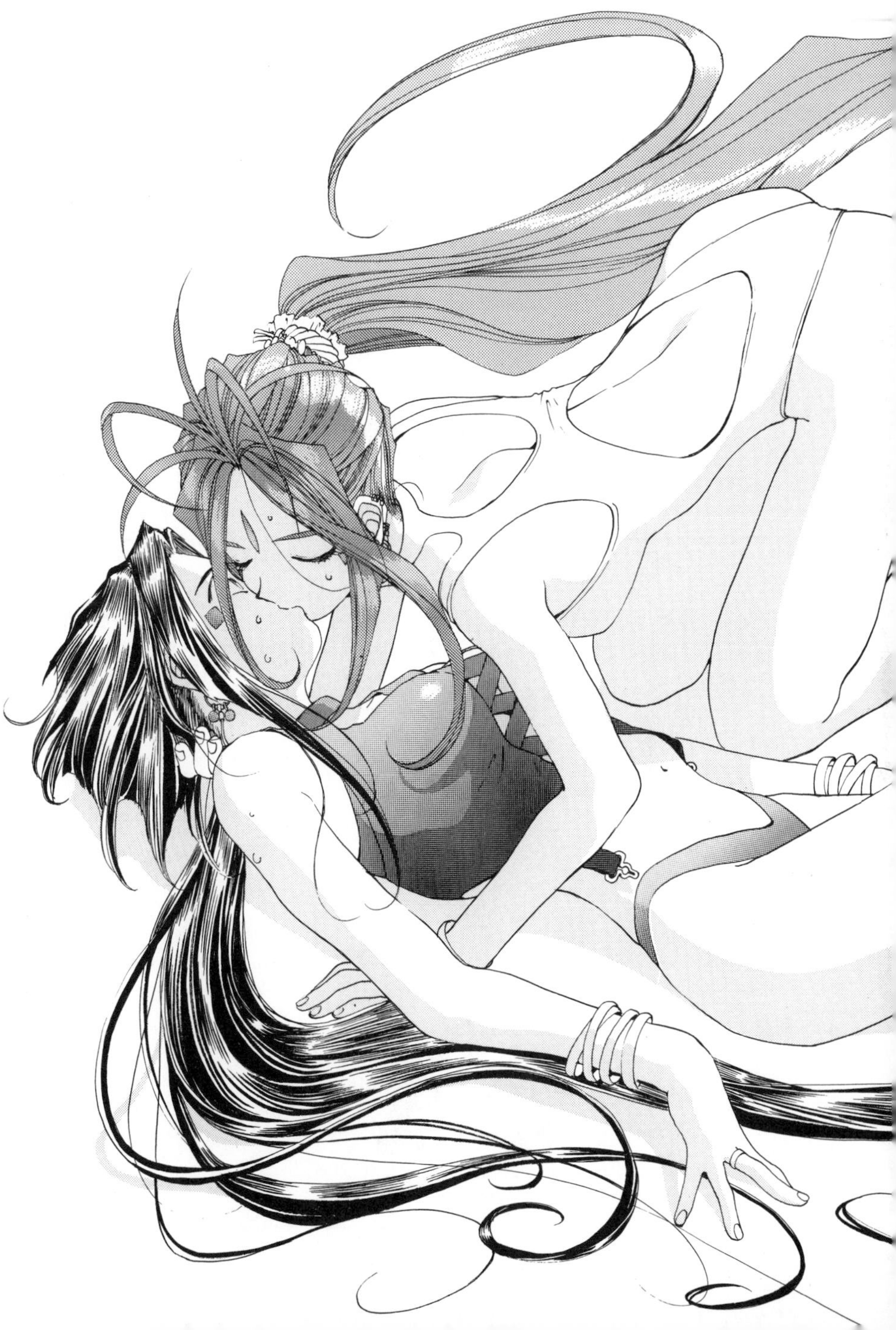

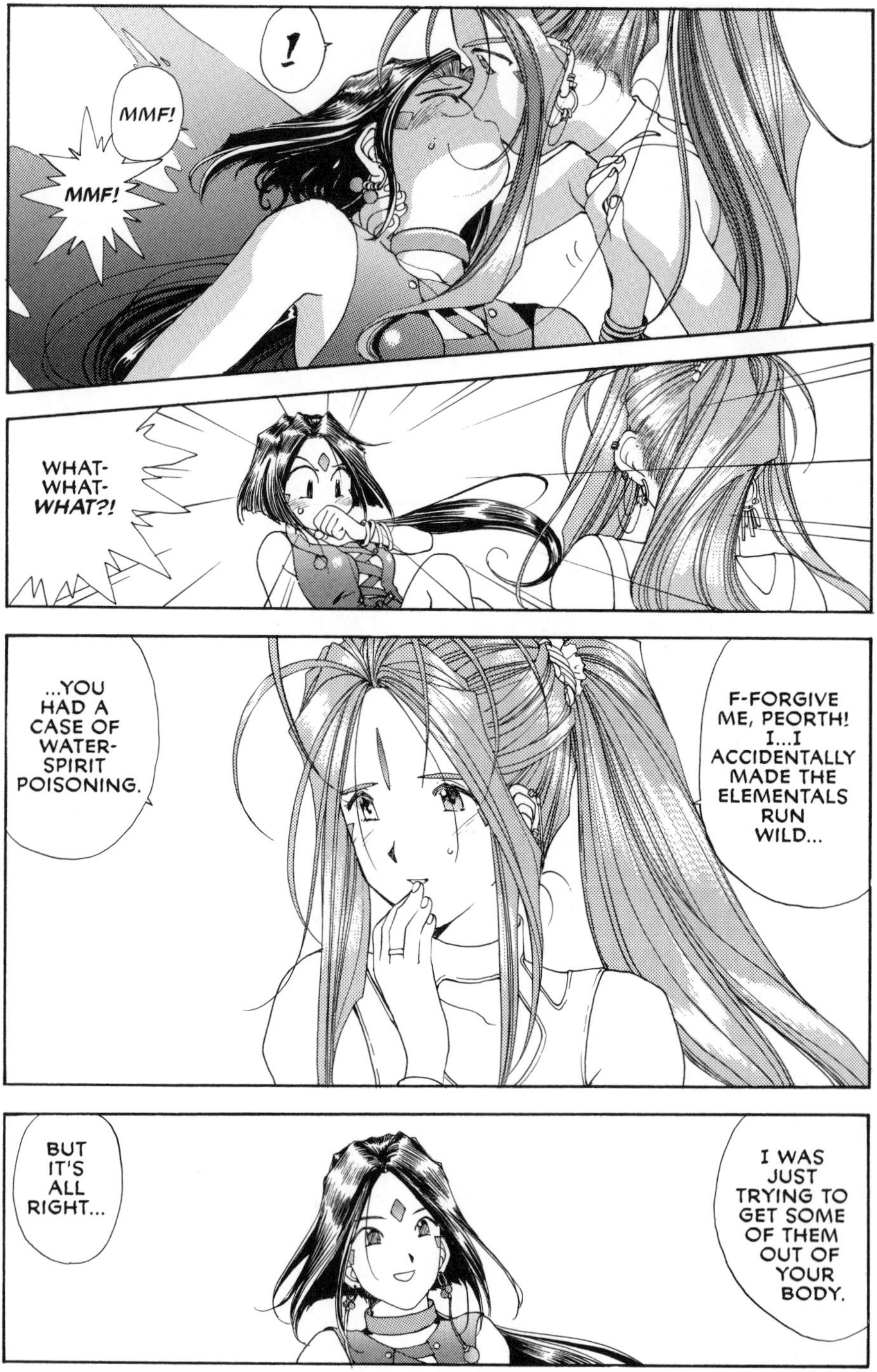
!
MMF!
MMF!
WHAT-WHAT-WHAT?!
F-FORGIVE ME, PEORTH! I...I ACCIDENTALLY MADE THE ELEMENTALS RUN WILD...
...YOU HAD A CASE OF WATER-SPIRIT POISONING.
I WAS JUST TRYING TO GET SOME OF THEM OUT OF YOUR BODY.
BUT IT'S ALL RIGHT...

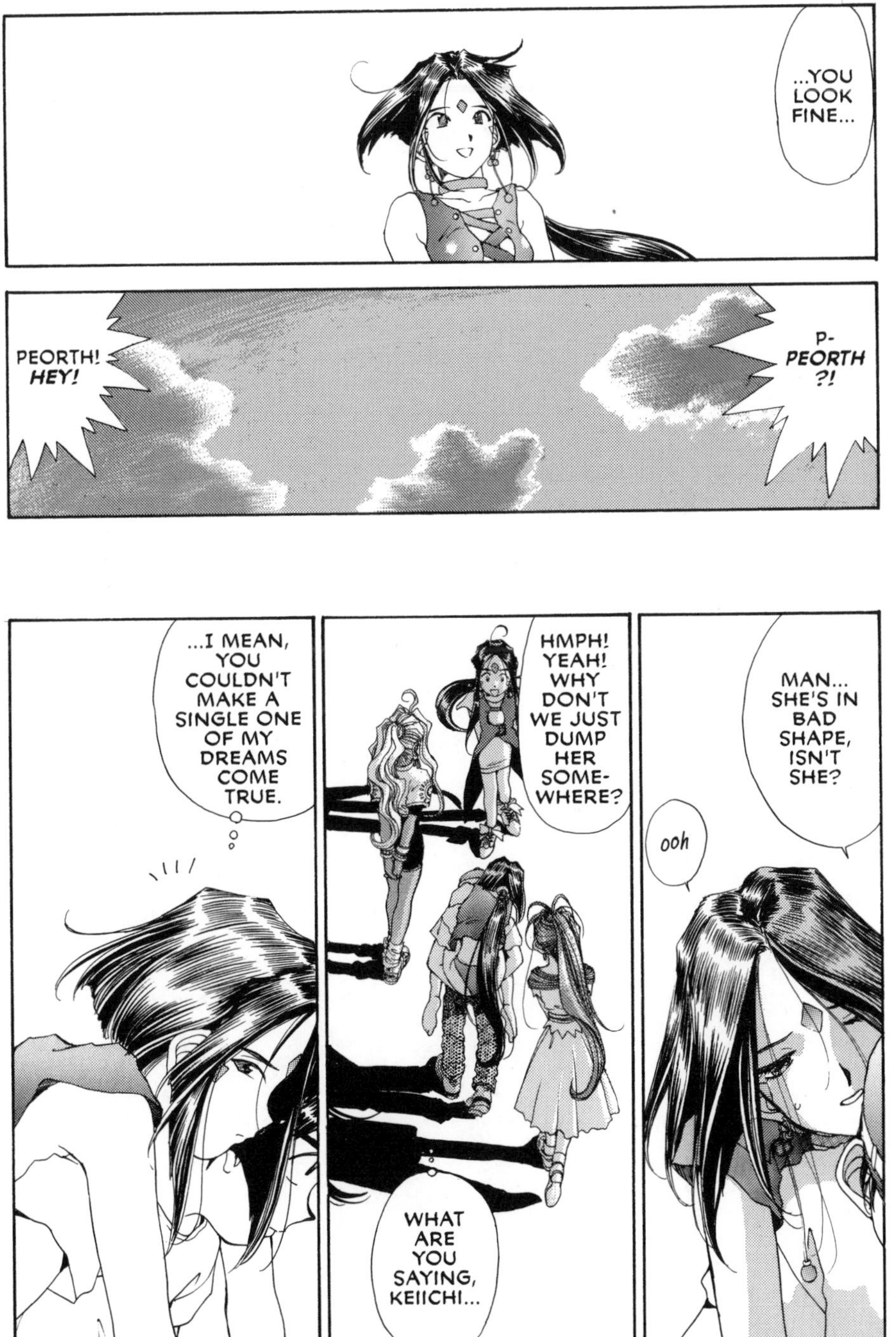
...YOU LOOK FINE...
P- PEORTH?!
PEORTH! HEY!
MAN... SHE'S IN BAD SHAPE, ISN'T SHE?
ooh
HMPH! YEAH! WHY DON'T WE JUST DUMP HER SOME-WHERE?
WHAT ARE YOU SAYING, KEIICHI...
...I MEAN, YOU COULDN'T MAKE A SINGLE ONE OF MY DREAMS COME TRUE.

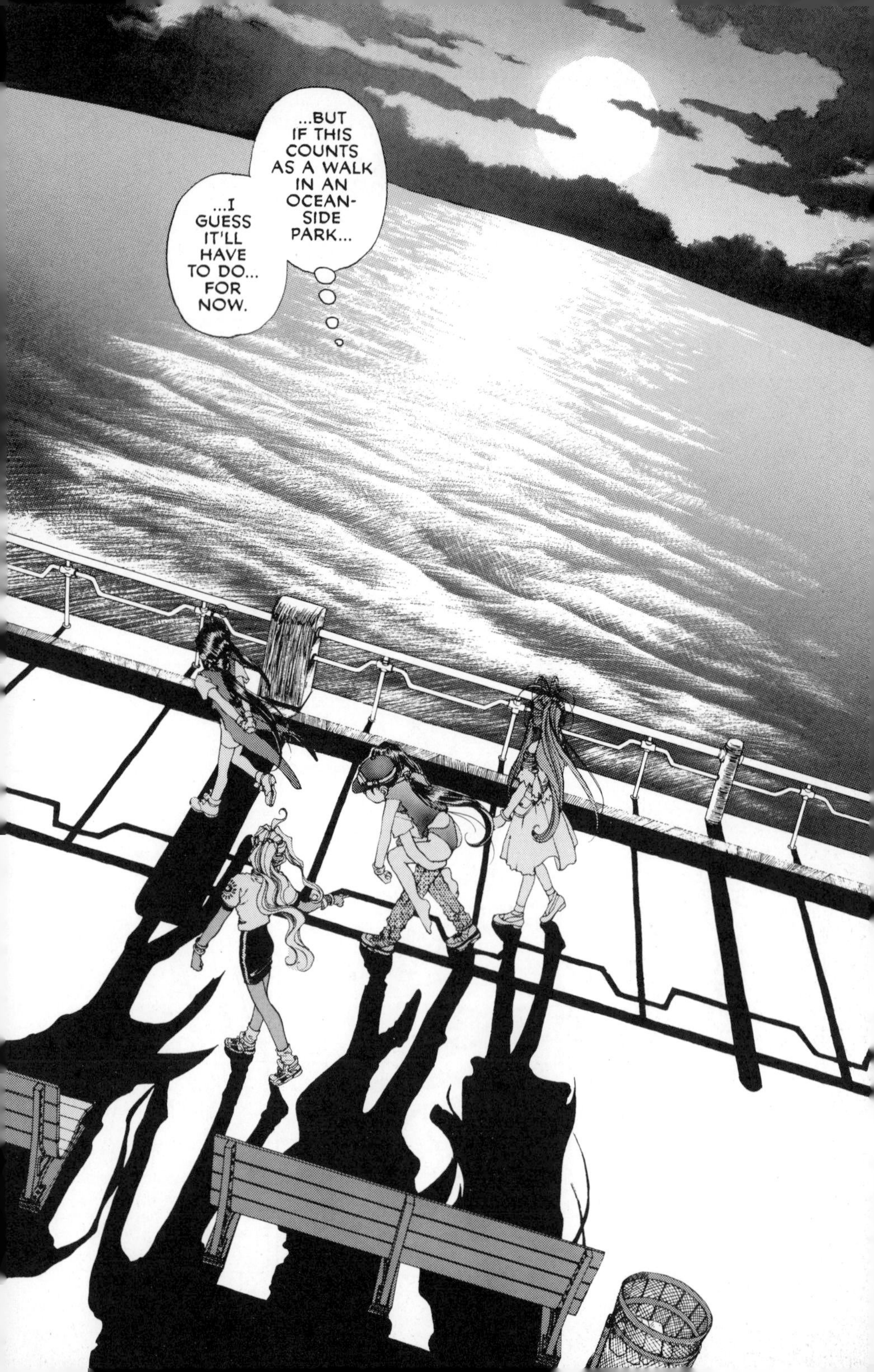
...BUT IF THIS COUNTS AS A WALK IN AN OCEAN-SIDE PARK...
...I GUESS IT'LL HAVE TO DO... FOR NOW.

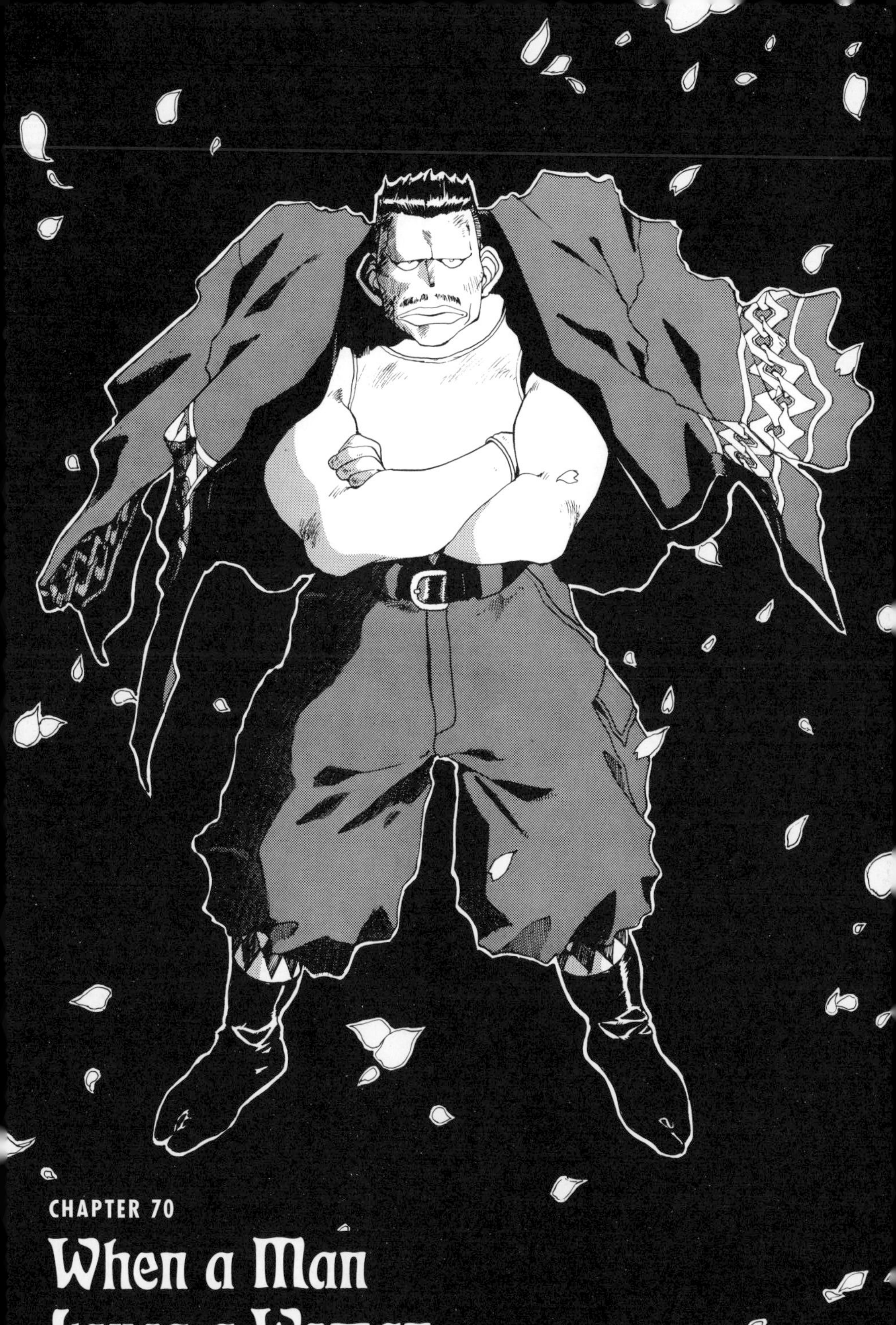

CHAPTER 70

When a Man Loves a Woman

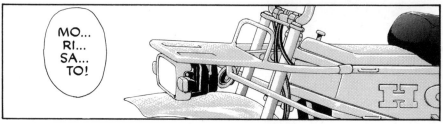

MO...
RI...
SA...
TO!

I'M
BRINGIN'
YUH AN
OFFICIAL
NOTICE FROM
DA *SUPREME
EXECUTIVE
COMMITTEE*--

...

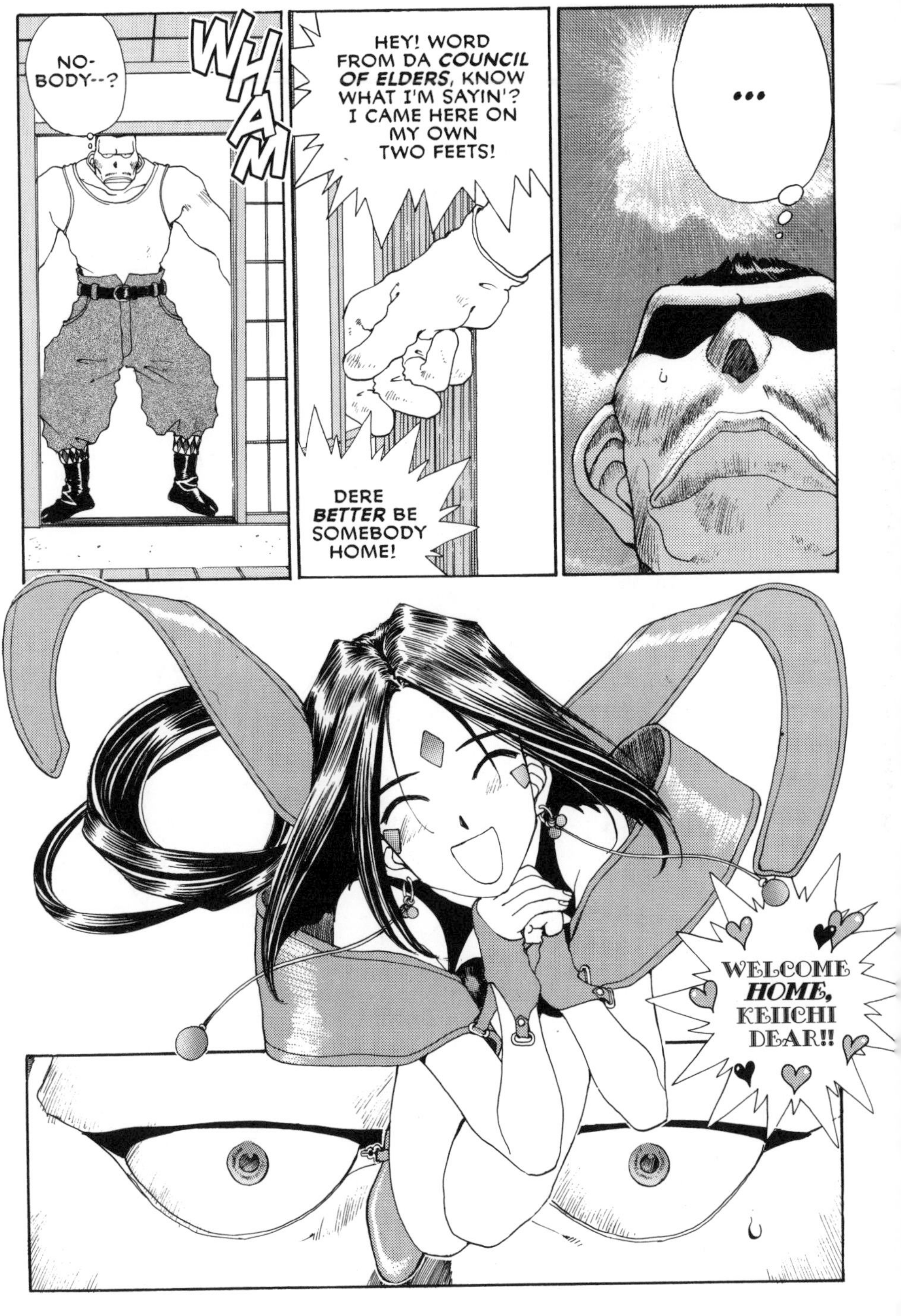
WHAM
NO-BODY--?
HEY! WORD FROM DA *COUNCIL OF ELDERS*, KNOW WHAT I'M SAYIN'? I CAME HERE ON MY OWN TWO FEETS!
DERE *BETTER* BE SOMEBODY HOME!
...
WELCOME *HOME*, KEIICHI DEAR!!

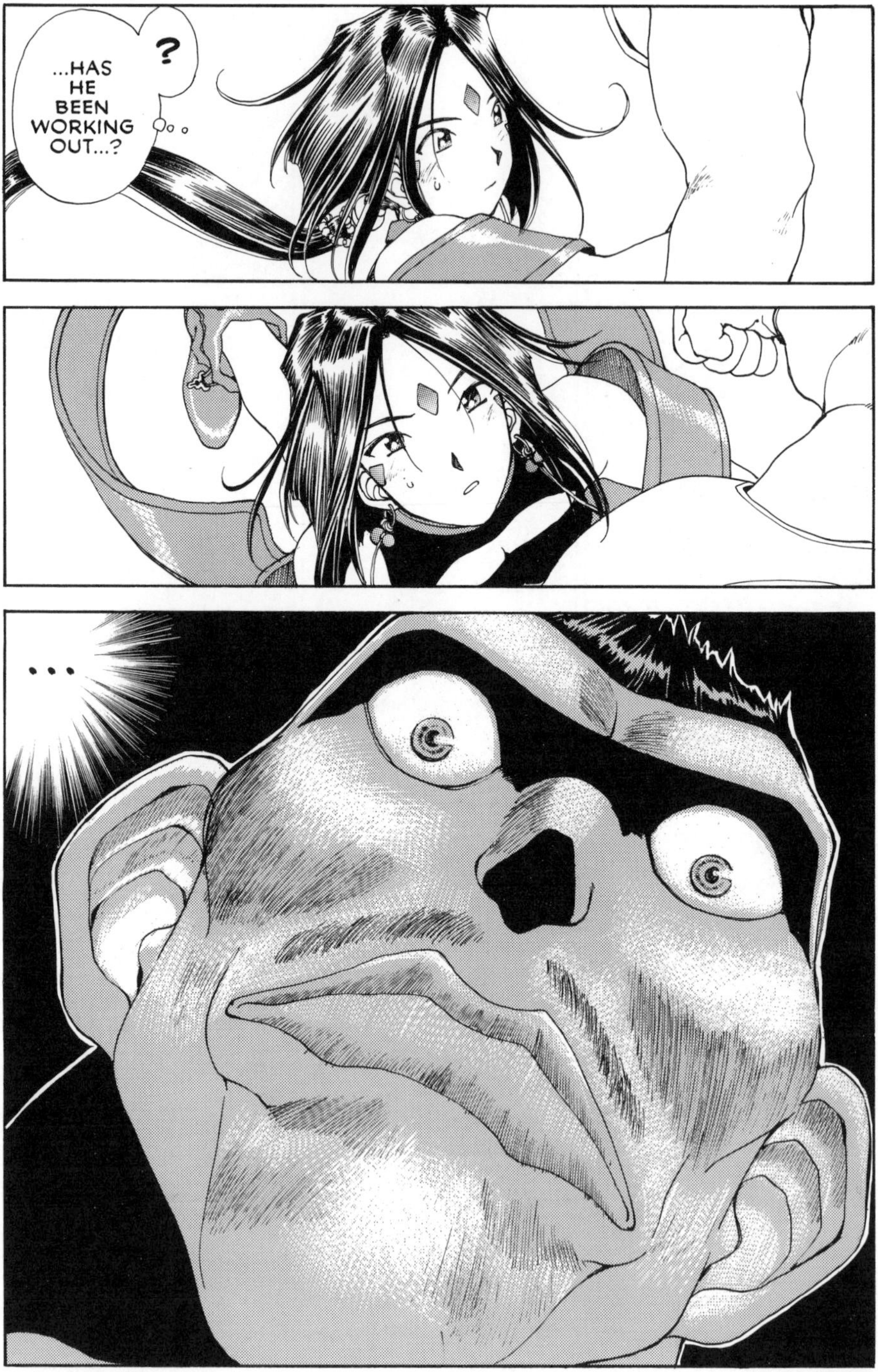
?
...HAS HE BEEN WORKING OUT...?
...

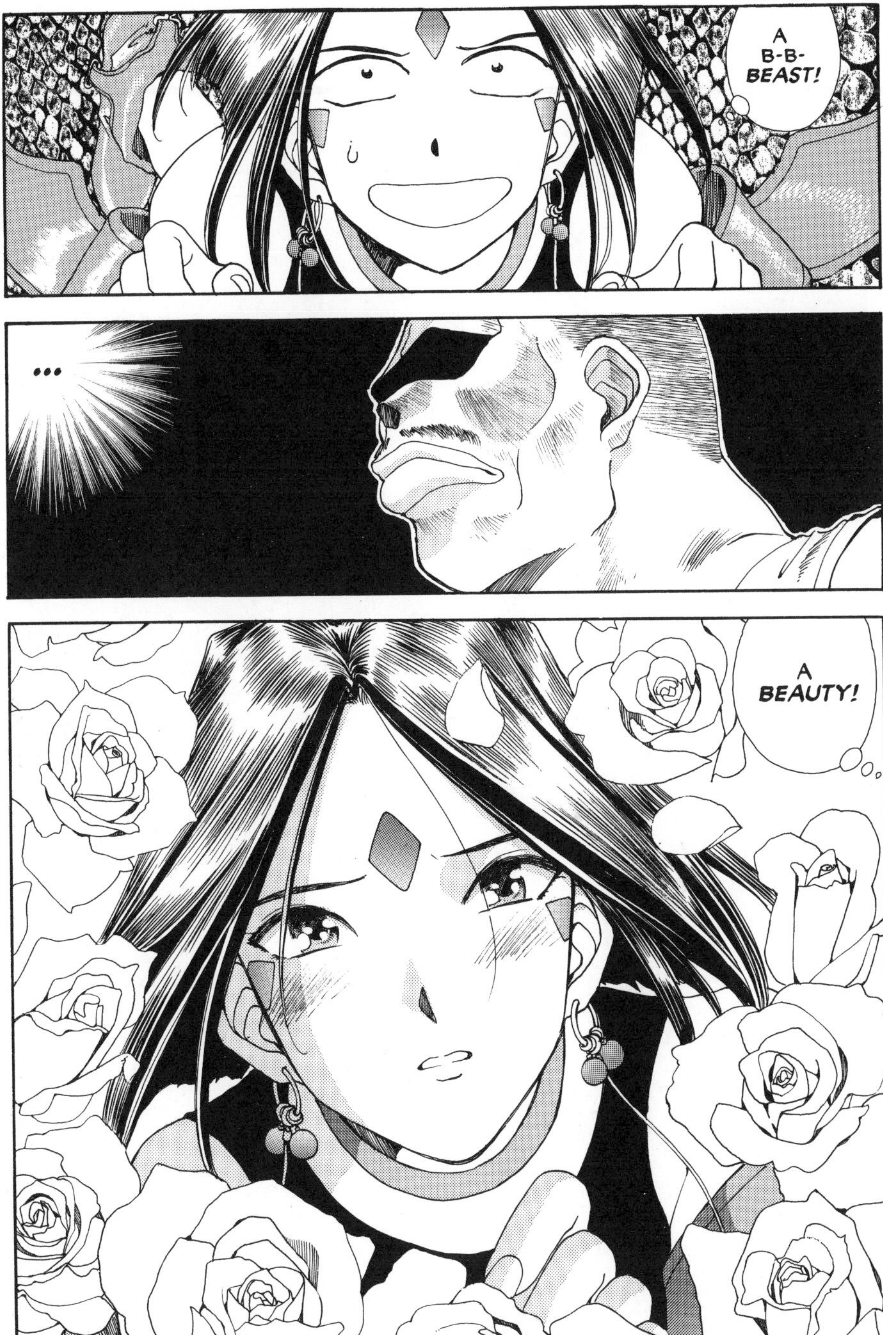
A B-B-BEAST!
...
A BEAUTY!

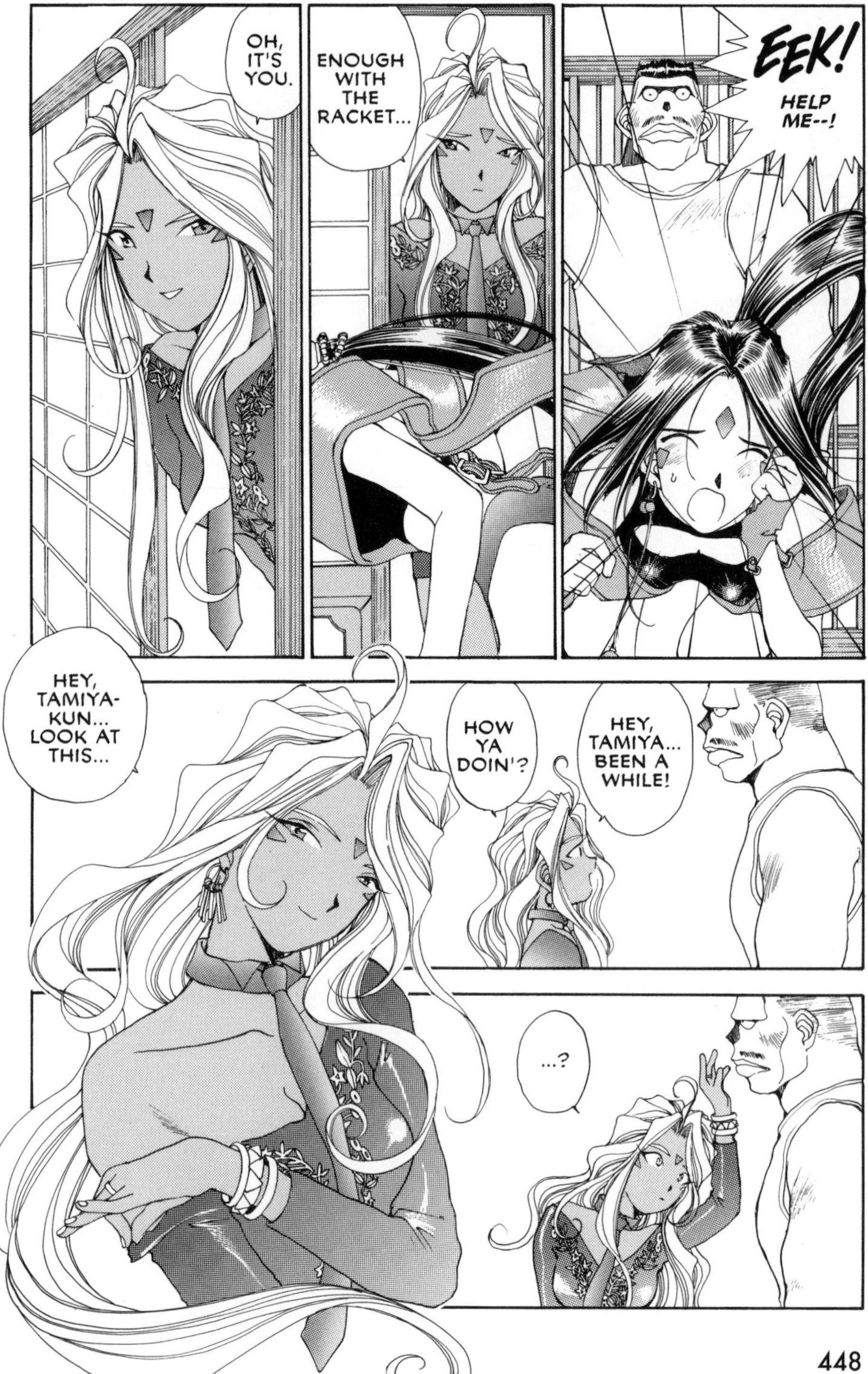

OH, IT'S YOU.
ENOUGH WITH THE RACKET...
EEK!
HELP ME--!
HEY, TAMIYA-KUN... LOOK AT THIS...
HOW YA DOIN'?
HEY, TAMIYA... BEEN A WHILE!
...?

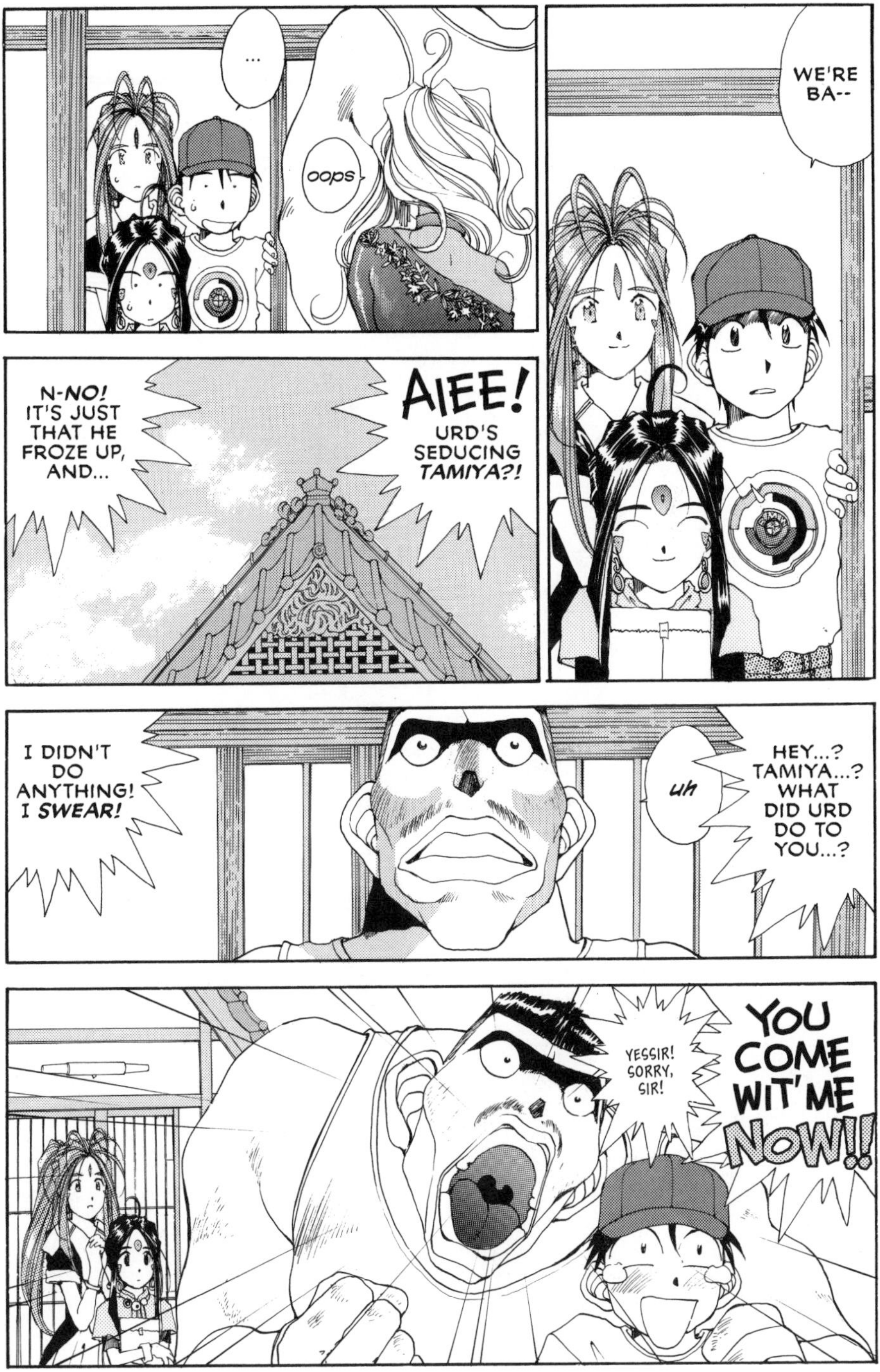

WE'RE BA--
...
oops
AIEE! URD'S SEDUCING TAMIYA?!
N-NO! IT'S JUST THAT HE FROZE UP, AND...
HEY...? TAMIYA...? WHAT DID URD DO TO YOU...?
uh
I DIDN'T DO ANYTHING! I SWEAR!
YOU COME WIT'ME NOW!!
YESSIR! SORRY, SIR!

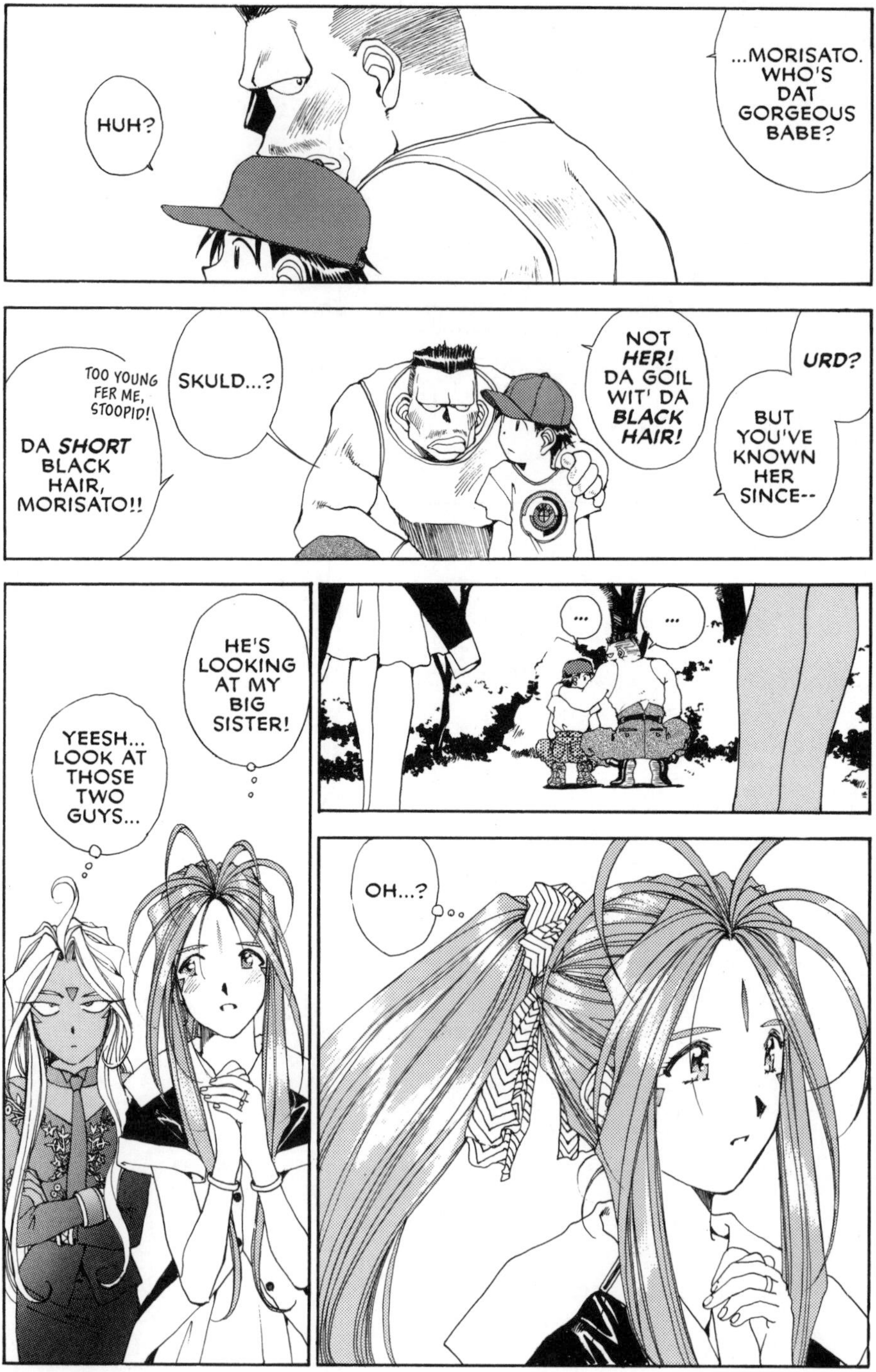
...MORISATO. WHO'S DAT GORGEOUS BABE?
HUH?
URD?
BUT YOU'VE KNOWN HER SINCE--
NOT HER! DA GOIL WIT' DA BLACK HAIR!
SKULD...?
TOO YOUNG FER ME, STOOPID!
DA SHORT BLACK HAIR, MORISATO!!
...
...
OH...?
HE'S LOOKING AT MY BIG SISTER!
YEESH... LOOK AT THOSE TWO GUYS...

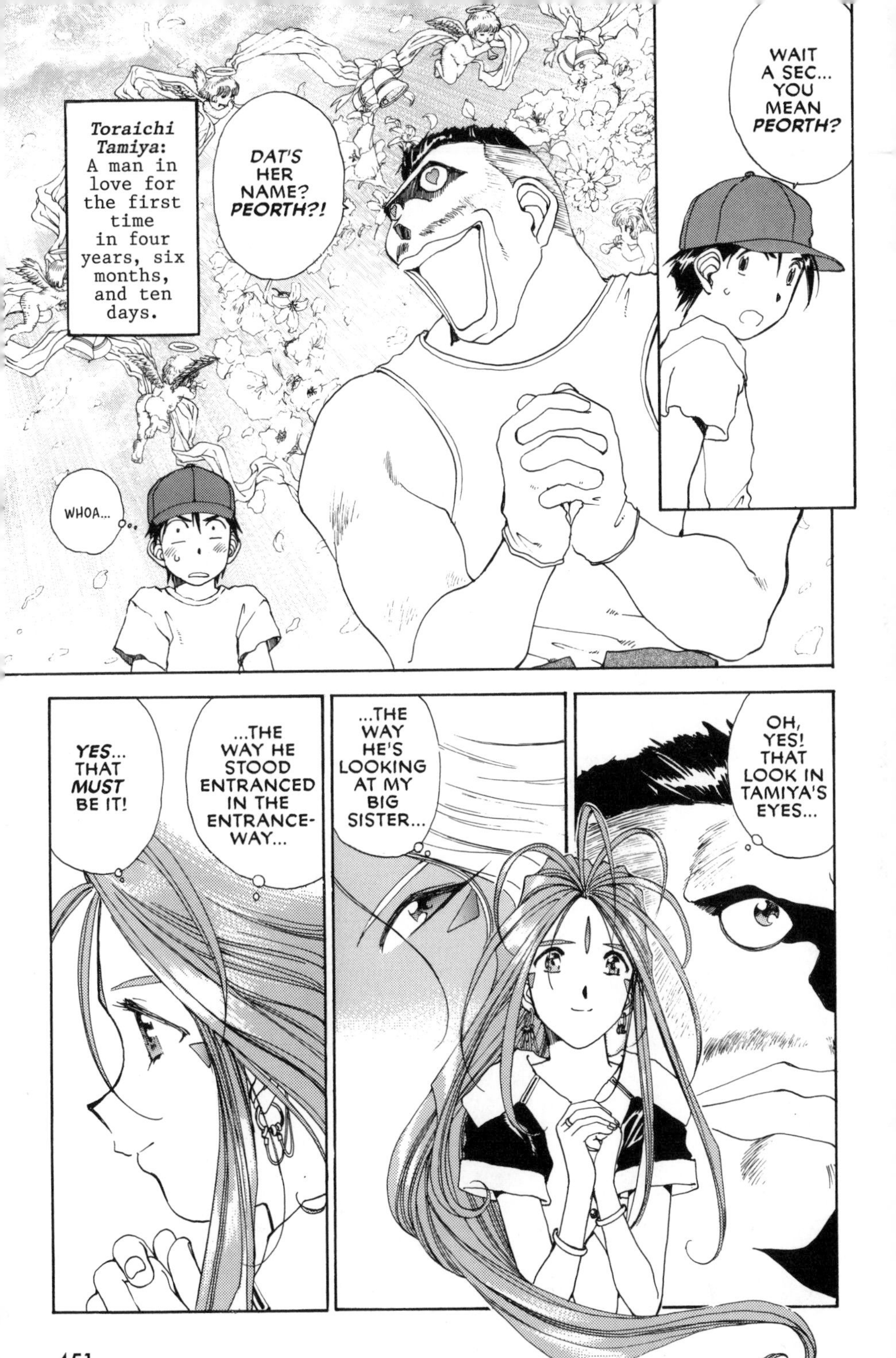
WAIT A SEC... YOU MEAN *PEORTH?*
DAT'S HER NAME? *PEORTH?!*
Toraichi Tamiya: A man in love for the first time in four years, six months, and ten days.
WHOA...
OH, YES! THAT LOOK IN TAMIYA'S EYES...
...THE WAY HE'S LOOKING AT MY BIG SISTER...
...THE WAY HE STOOD ENTRANCED IN THE ENTRANCE-WAY...
YES... THAT *MUST* BE IT!

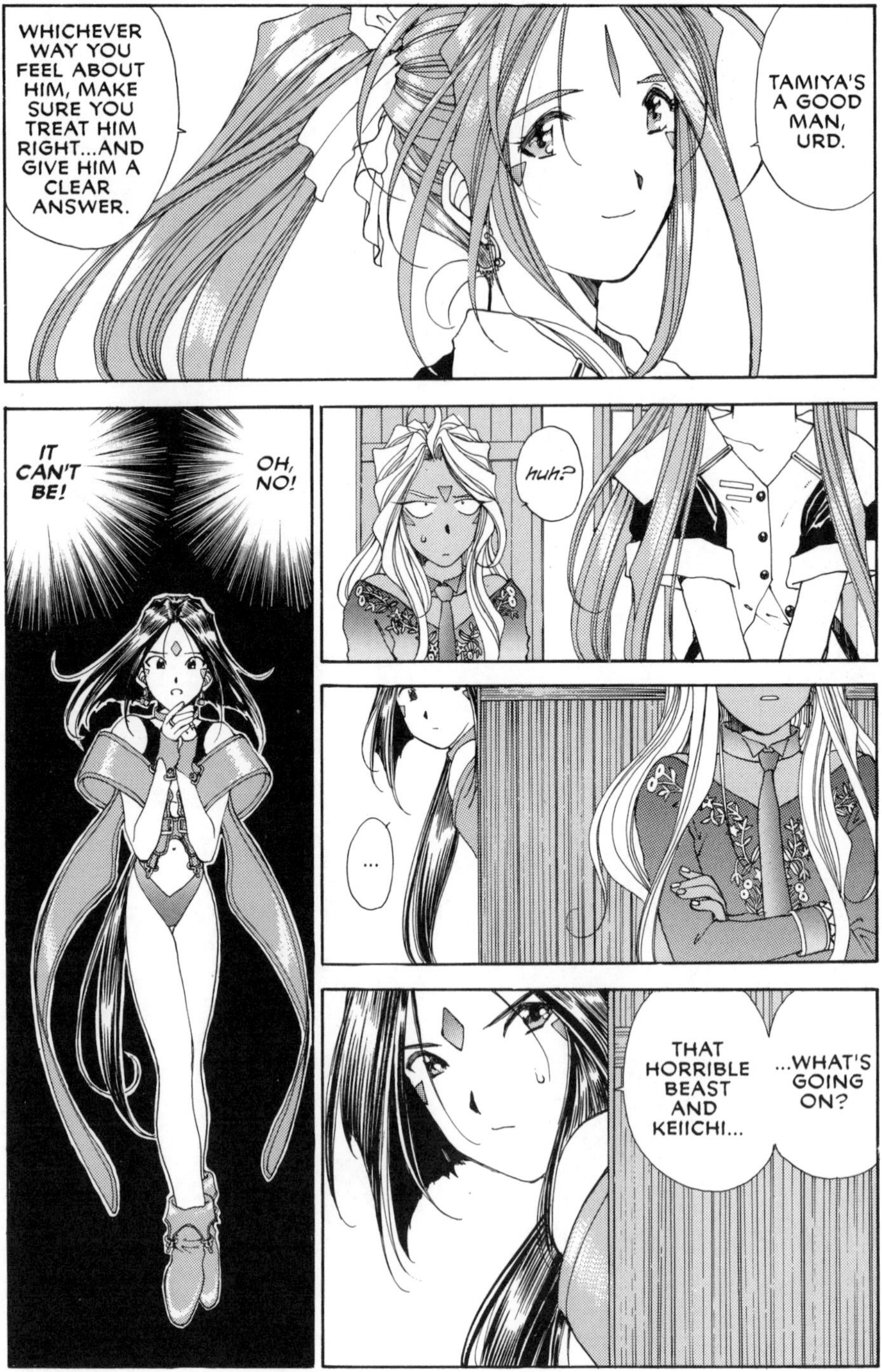
TAMIYA'S A GOOD MAN, URD.
WHICHEVER WAY YOU FEEL ABOUT HIM, MAKE SURE YOU TREAT HIM RIGHT...AND GIVE HIM A CLEAR ANSWER.
huh?
...
...WHAT'S GOING ON?
THAT HORRIBLE BEAST AND KEIICHI...
OH, NO!
IT CAN'T BE!

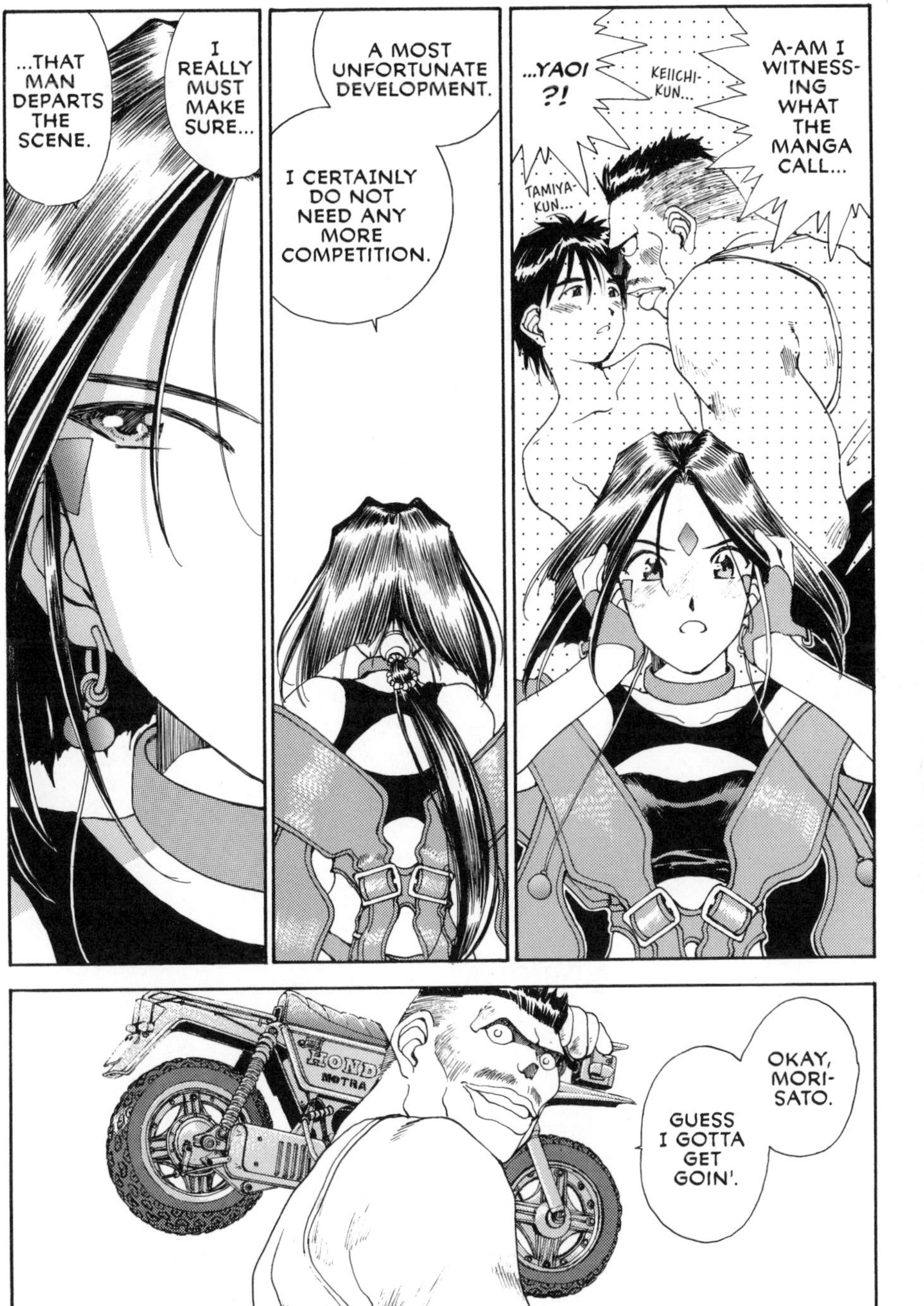
A-AM I WITNESSING WHAT THE MANGA CALL...
KEIICHI-KUN...
...YAOI ?!
TAMIYA-KUN...
A MOST UNFORTUNATE DEVELOPMENT.
I CERTAINLY DO NOT NEED ANY MORE COMPETITION.
I REALLY MUST MAKE SURE...
...THAT MAN DEPARTS THE SCENE.
HONDA
MOTRA
OKAY, MORI-SATO.
GUESS I GOTTA GET GOIN'.

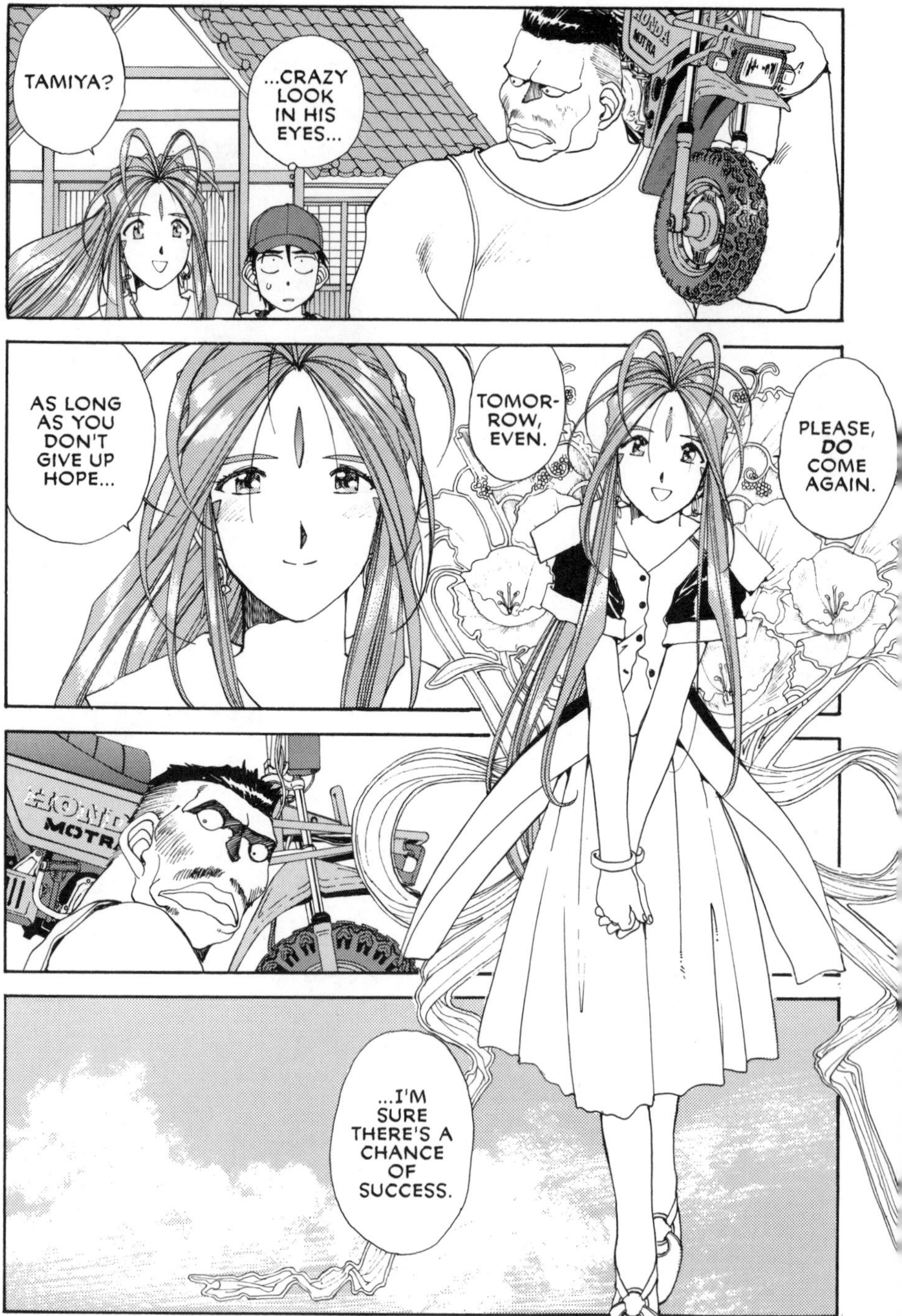
...CRAZY LOOK IN HIS EYES...
TAMIYA?
HONDA MOTRA
PLEASE, *DO* COME AGAIN.
TOMOR-ROW, EVEN.
AS LONG AS YOU DON'T GIVE UP HOPE...
HONDA MOTRA
...I'M SURE THERE'S A CHANCE OF SUCCESS.

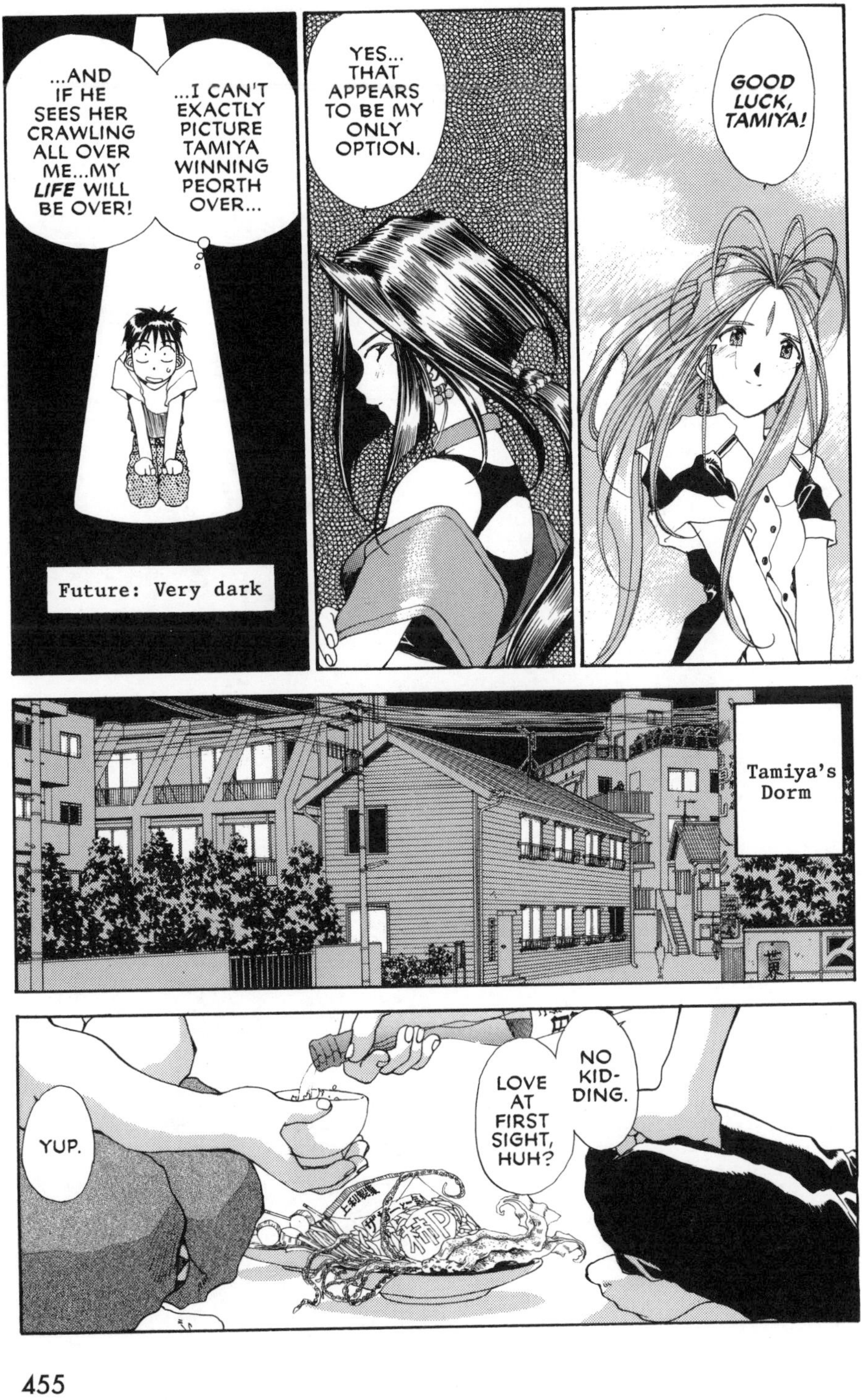
GOOD LUCK, TAMIYA!
YES... THAT APPEARS TO BE MY ONLY OPTION.
...I CAN'T EXACTLY PICTURE TAMIYA WINNING PEORTH OVER...
...AND IF HE SEES HER CRAWLING ALL OVER ME...MY *LIFE* WILL BE OVER!
Future: Very dark
Tamiya's Dorm
NO KID-DING.
LOVE AT FIRST SIGHT, HUH?
YUP.

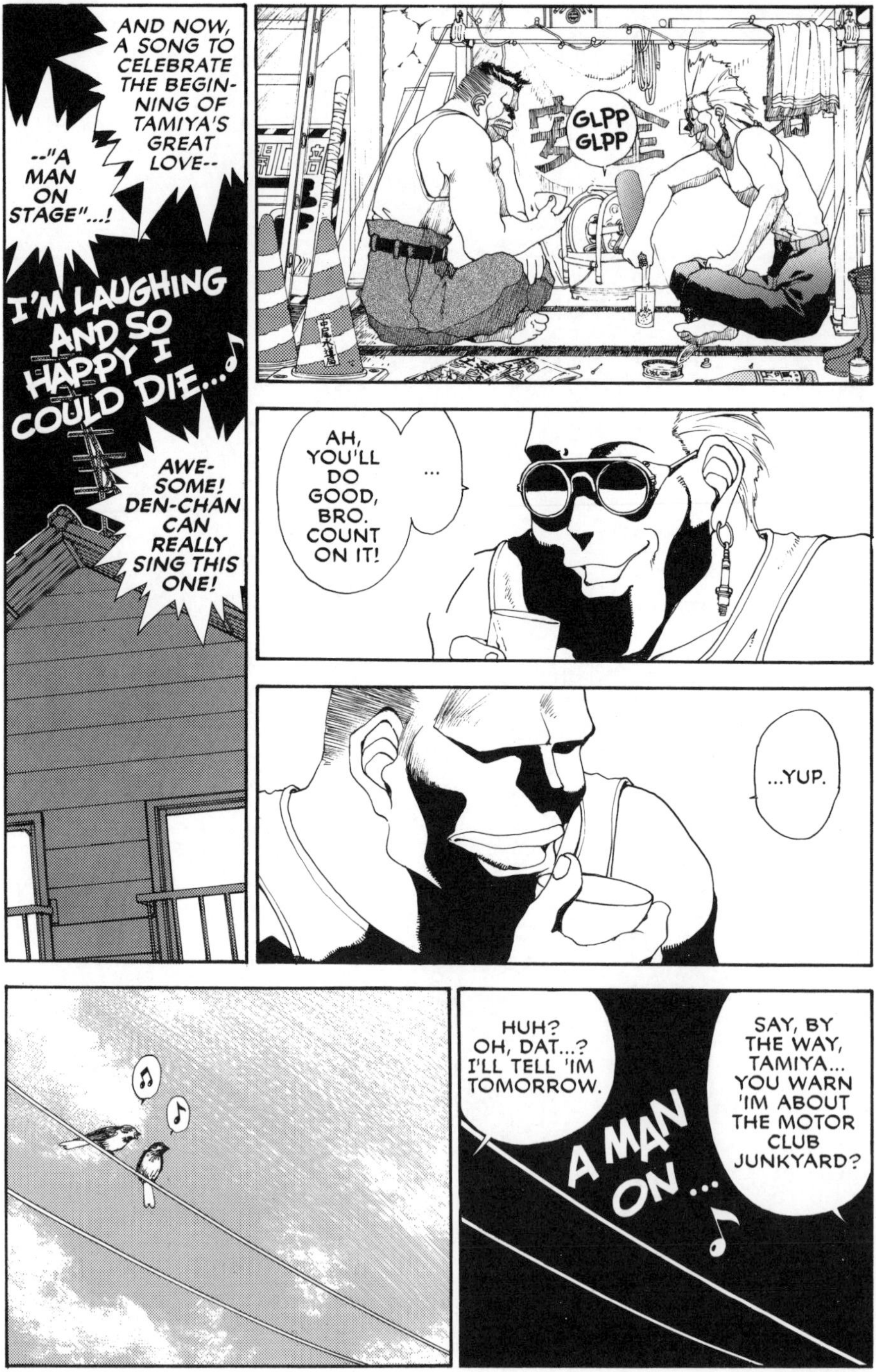
GLPP GLPP
...
AH, YOU'LL DO GOOD, BRO. COUNT ON IT!
...YUP.
AND NOW, A SONG TO CELEBRATE THE BEGIN-NING OF TAMIYA'S GREAT LOVE--
--"A MAN ON STAGE"...!
I'M LAUGHING AND SO HAPPY I COULD DIE...♪
AWE-SOME! DEN-CHAN CAN REALLY SING THIS ONE!
SAY, BY THE WAY, TAMIYA... YOU WARN 'IM ABOUT THE MOTOR CLUB JUNKYARD?
HUH? OH, DAT...? I'LL TELL 'IM TOMORROW.
A MAN ON...♪

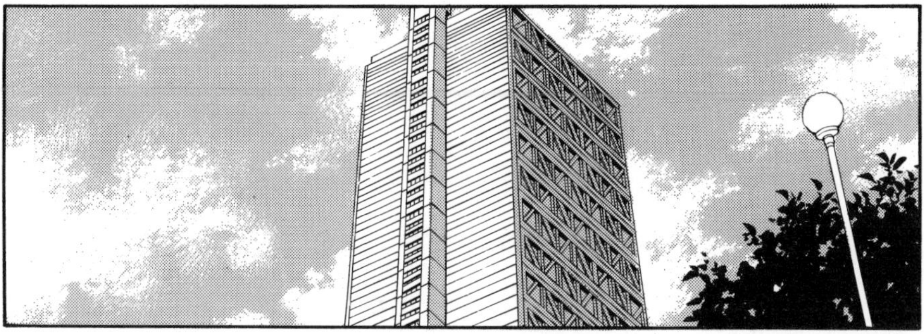

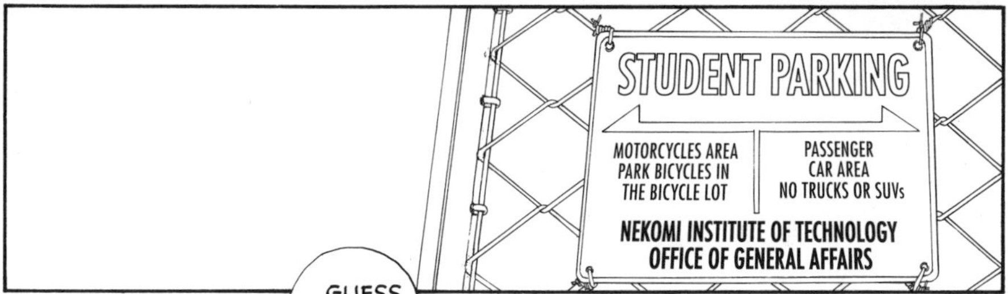
STUDENT PARKING
MOTORCYCLES AREA
PARK BICYCLES IN
THE BICYCLE LOT
PASSENGER
CAR AREA
NO TRUCKS OR SUVs
NEKOMI INSTITUTE OF TECHNOLOGY
OFFICE OF GENERAL AFFAIRS

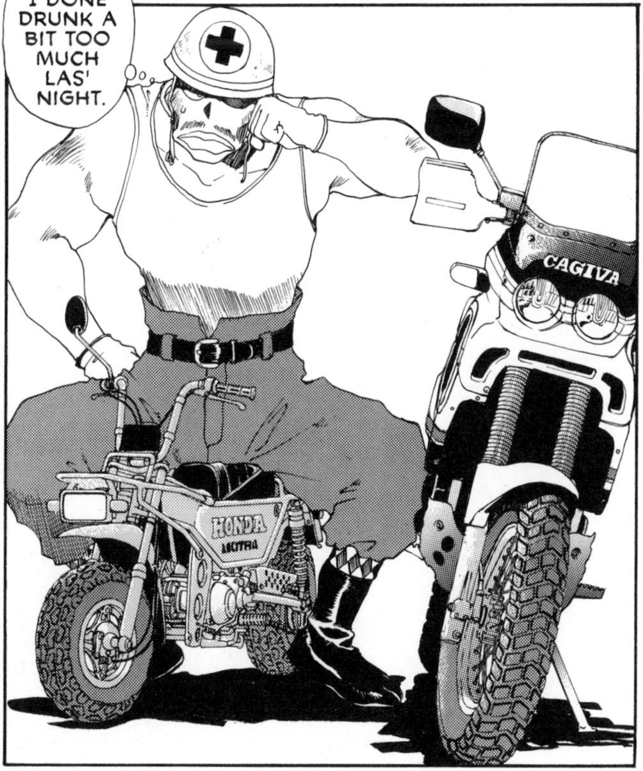
...GUESS I DONE DRUNK A BIT TOO MUCH LAS' NIGHT.
CAGIVA
HONDA

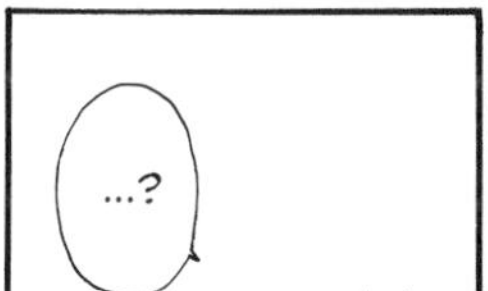
...?

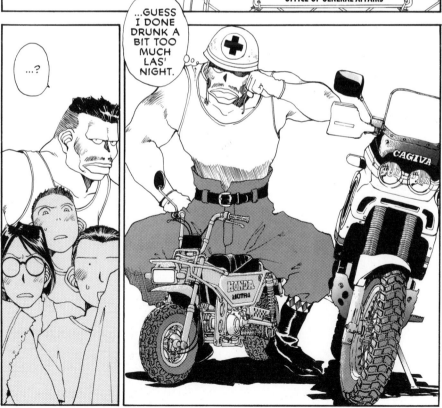

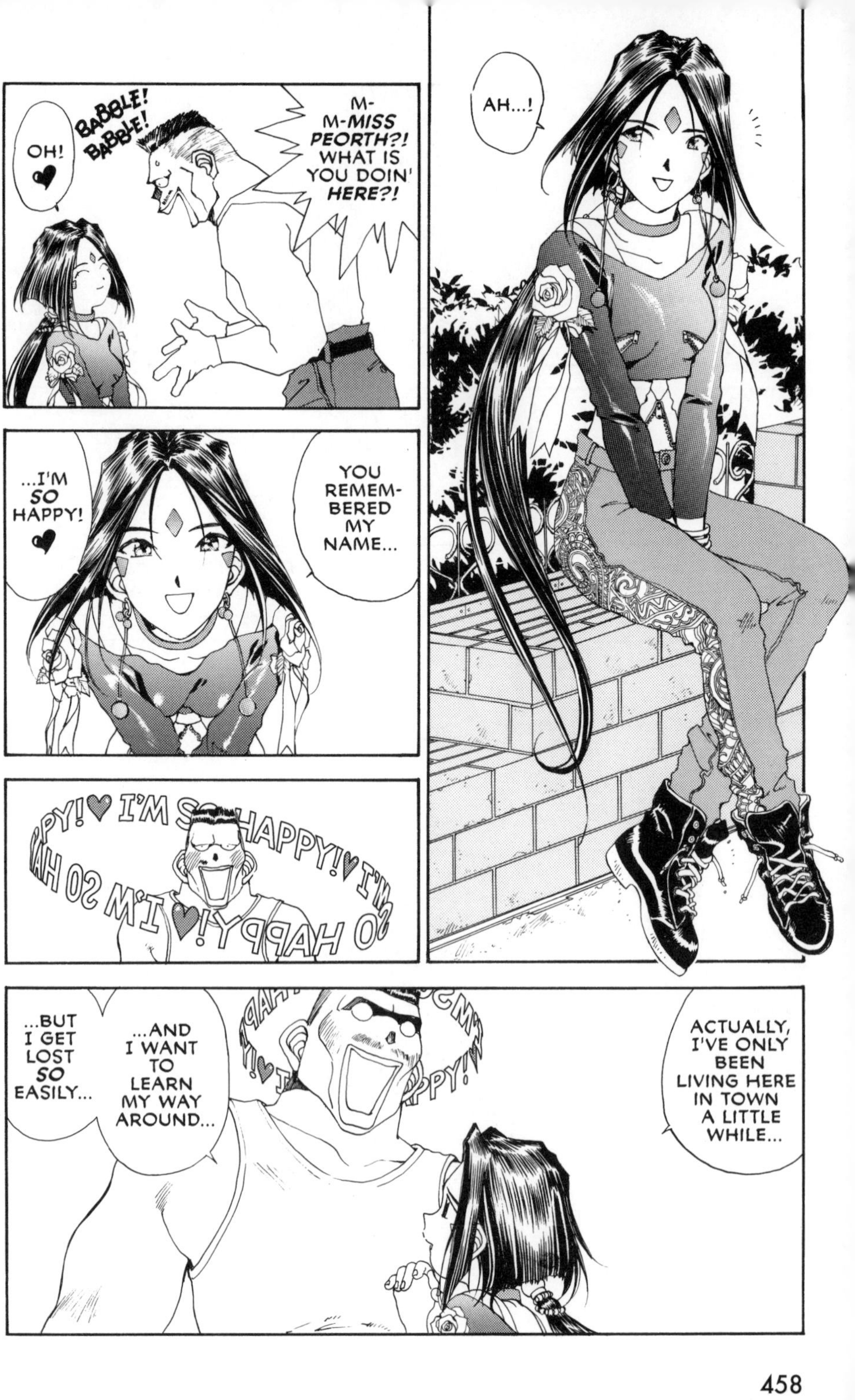
AH...!
M-M-*MISS PEORTH?!* WHAT IS YOU DOIN' *HERE?!*
BABBLE! BABBLE!
OH! ♥
YOU REMEMBERED MY NAME...
...I'M *SO* HAPPY! ♥
I'M SO HAPPY!♥ I'M SO HAPPY!♥ I'M SO HAPPY!♥
ACTUALLY, I'VE ONLY BEEN LIVING HERE IN TOWN A LITTLE WHILE...
...AND I WANT TO LEARN MY WAY AROUND...
...BUT I GET LOST *SO* EASILY...

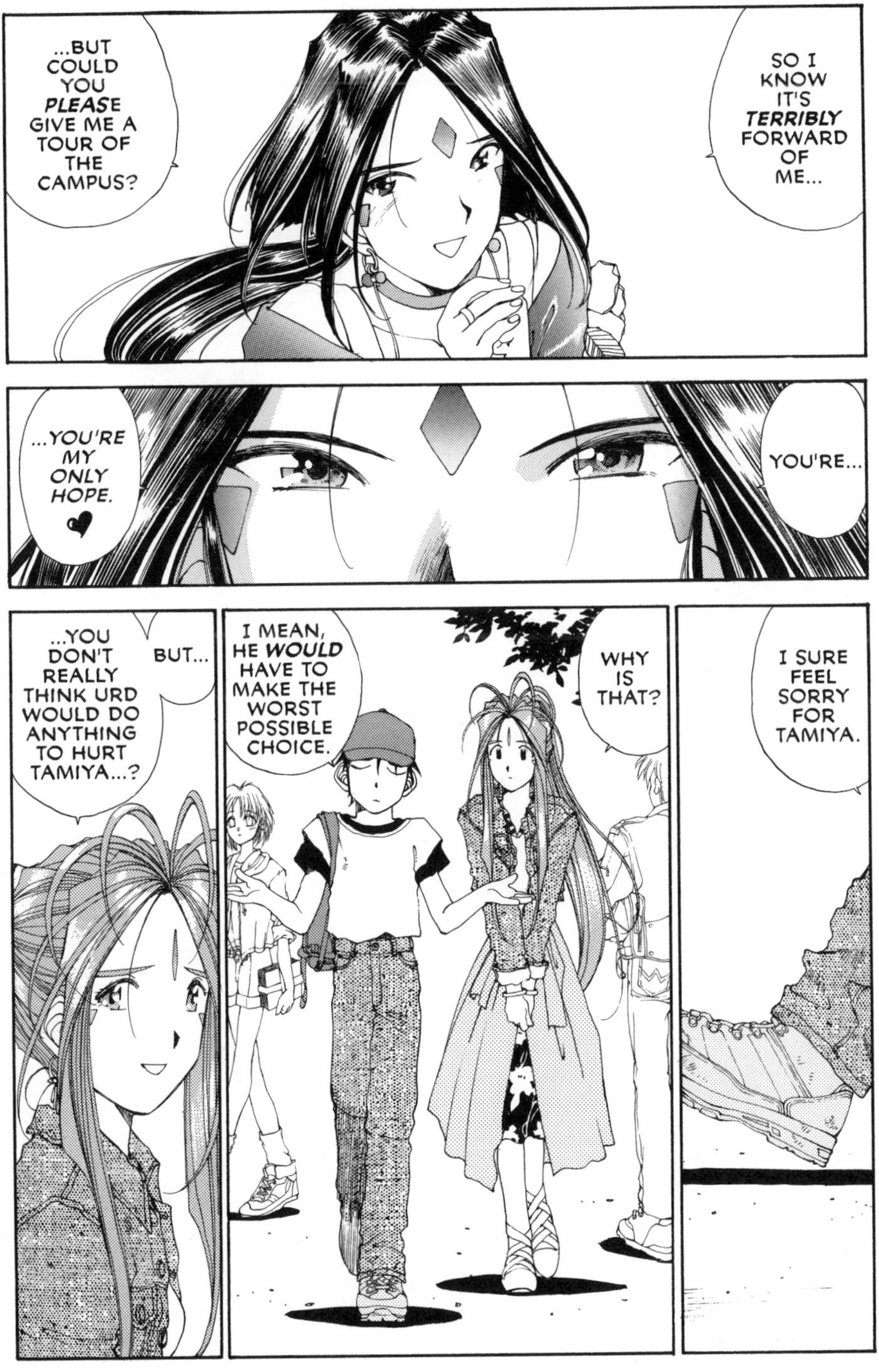
SO I KNOW IT'S *TERRIBLY* FORWARD OF ME...
...BUT COULD YOU *PLEASE* GIVE ME A TOUR OF THE CAMPUS?
YOU'RE...
...YOU'RE MY ONLY HOPE. ♥
I SURE FEEL SORRY FOR TAMIYA.
WHY IS THAT?
I MEAN, HE *WOULD* HAVE TO MAKE THE WORST POSSIBLE CHOICE.
BUT...
...YOU DON'T REALLY THINK URD WOULD DO ANYTHING TO HURT TAMIYA...?

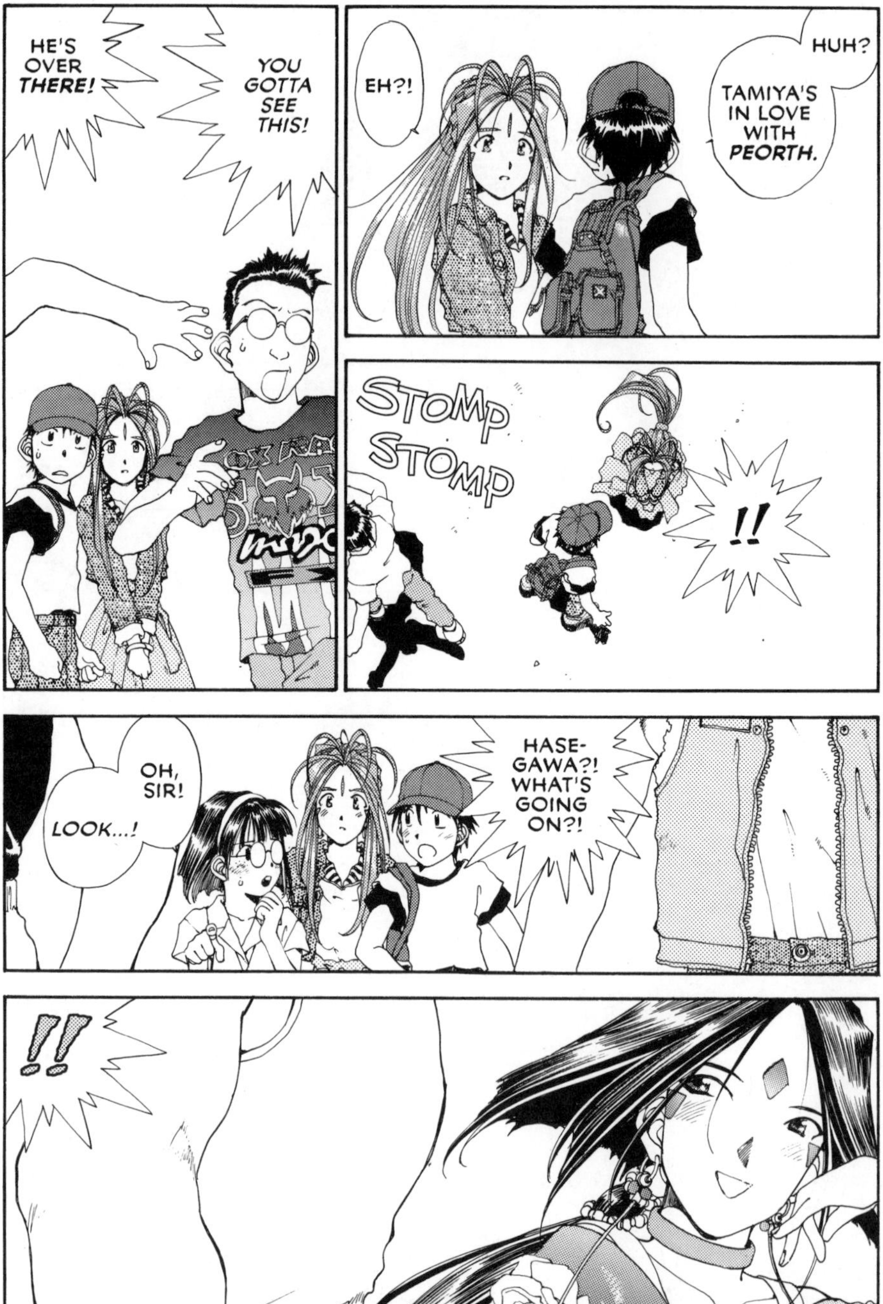
HUH?
TAMIYA'S IN LOVE WITH PEORTH.
EH?!
STOMP STOMP
!!
YOU GOTTA SEE THIS!
HE'S OVER THERE!
HASE-GAWA?! WHAT'S GOING ON?!
OH, SIR!
LOOK...!
!!

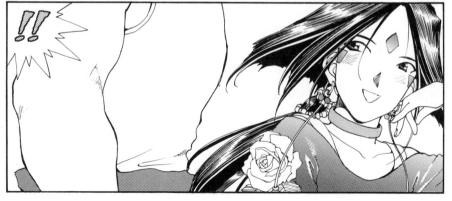

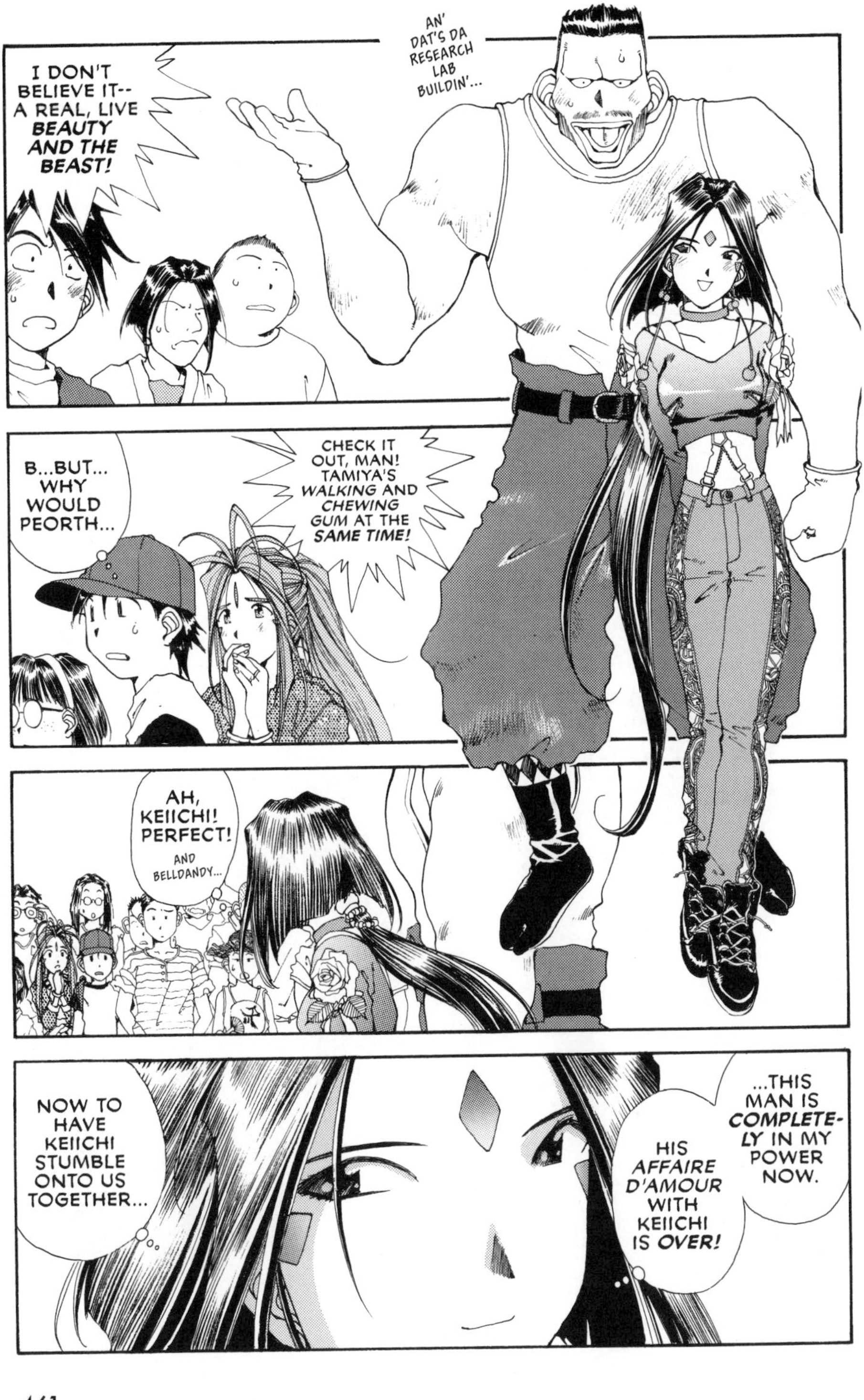
AN' DAT'S DA RESEARCH LAB BUILDIN'...
I DON'T BELIEVE IT-- A REAL, LIVE *BEAUTY AND THE BEAST!*
B...BUT... WHY WOULD PEORTH...
CHECK IT OUT, MAN! TAMIYA'S *WALKING* AND *CHEWING* GUM AT THE *SAME TIME!*
AH, KEIICHI! PERFECT!
AND BELLDANDY...
NOW TO HAVE KEIICHI STUMBLE ONTO US TOGETHER...
...THIS MAN IS *COMPLETELY* IN MY POWER NOW.
HIS *AFFAIRE D'AMOUR* WITH KEIICHI IS *OVER!*

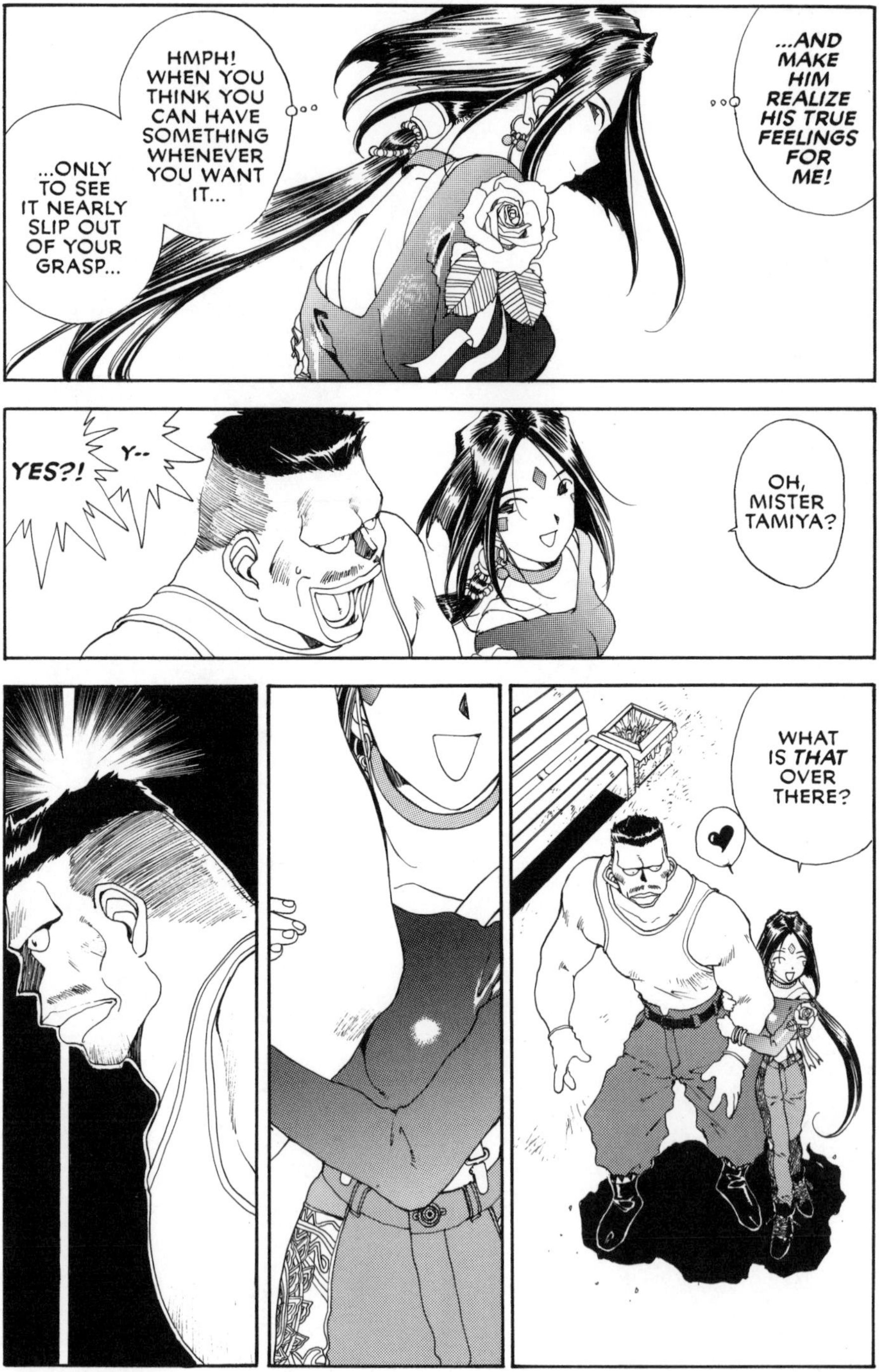
HMPH! WHEN YOU THINK YOU CAN HAVE SOMETHING WHENEVER YOU WANT IT...
...ONLY TO SEE IT NEARLY SLIP OUT OF YOUR GRASP...
...AND MAKE HIM REALIZE HIS TRUE FEELINGS FOR ME!
OH, MISTER TAMIYA?
Y--
YES?!
WHAT IS THAT OVER THERE?

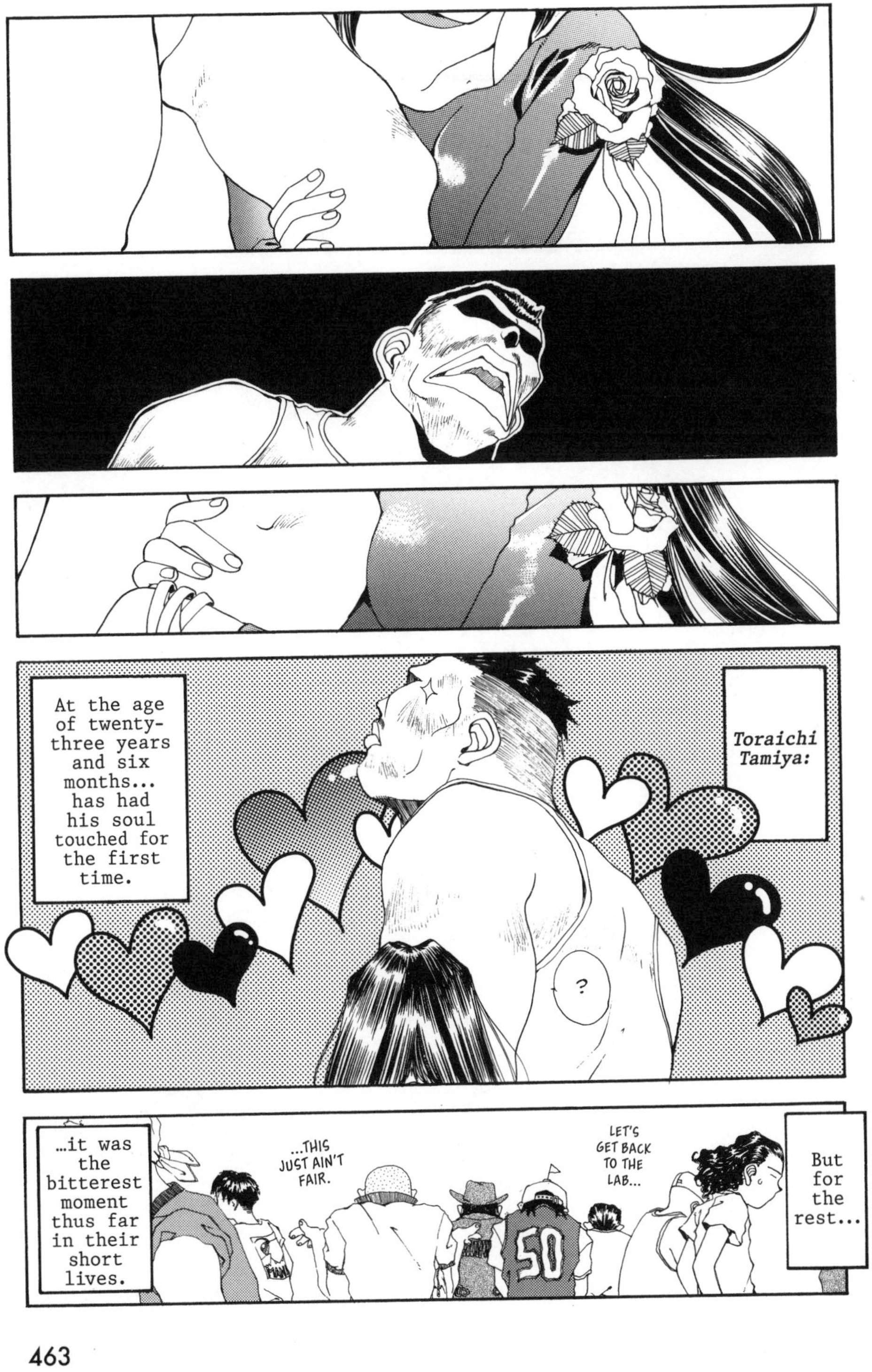
Toraichi Tamiya:
At the age of twenty-three years and six months... has had his soul touched for the first time.
?
But for the rest...
LET'S GET BACK TO THE LAB...
...THIS JUST AIN'T FAIR.
...it was the bitterest moment thus far in their short lives.

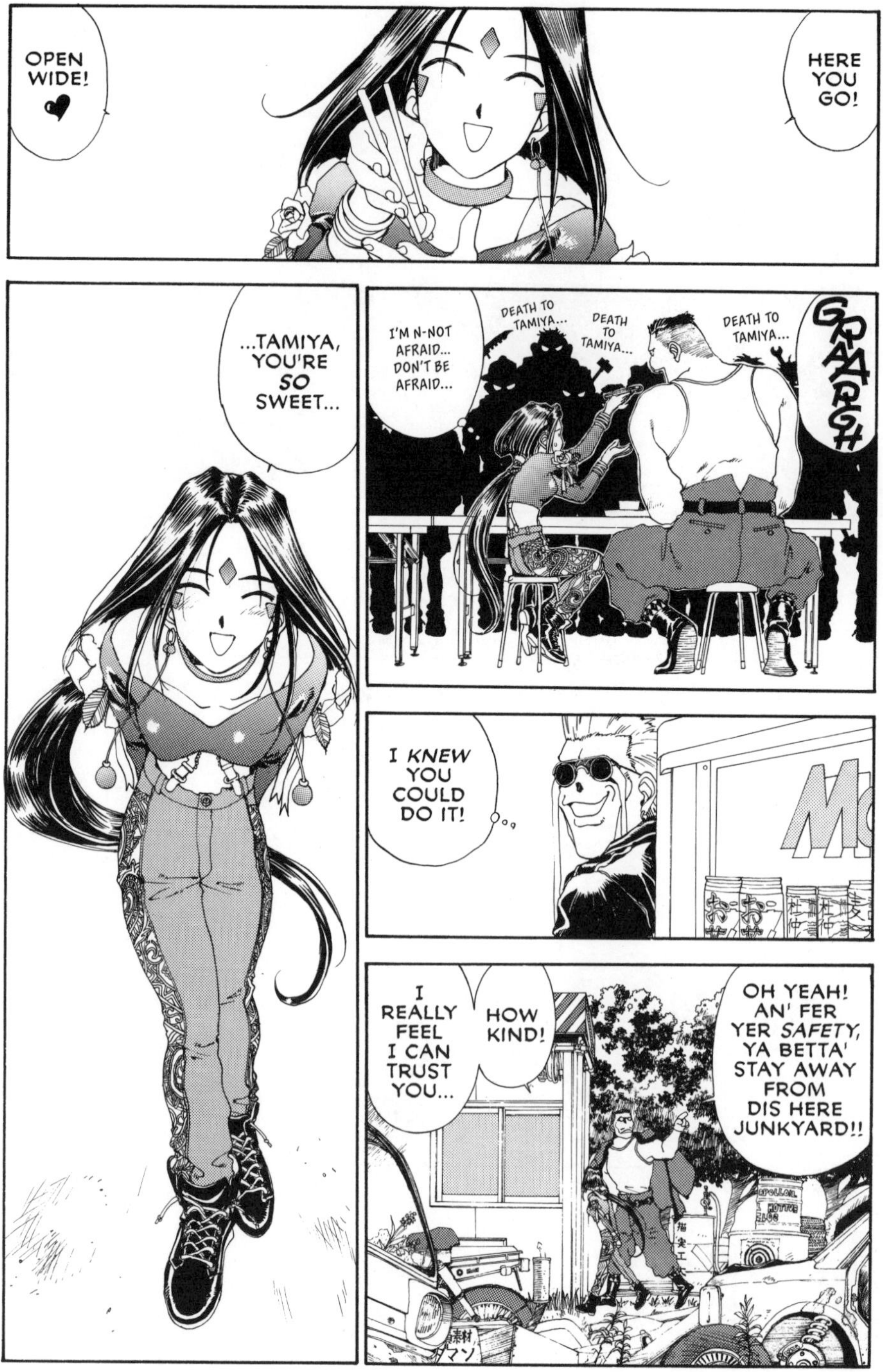
HERE YOU GO!
OPEN WIDE! ♥
GRAAARGH
DEATH TO TAMIYA...
DEATH TO TAMIYA...
DEATH TO TAMIYA...
I'M N-NOT AFRAID... DON'T BE AFRAID...
I KNEW YOU COULD DO IT!
OH YEAH! AN' FER YER SAFETY, YA BETTA' STAY AWAY FROM DIS HERE JUNKYARD!!
HOW KIND!
I REALLY FEEL I CAN TRUST YOU...
...TAMIYA, YOU'RE SO SWEET...

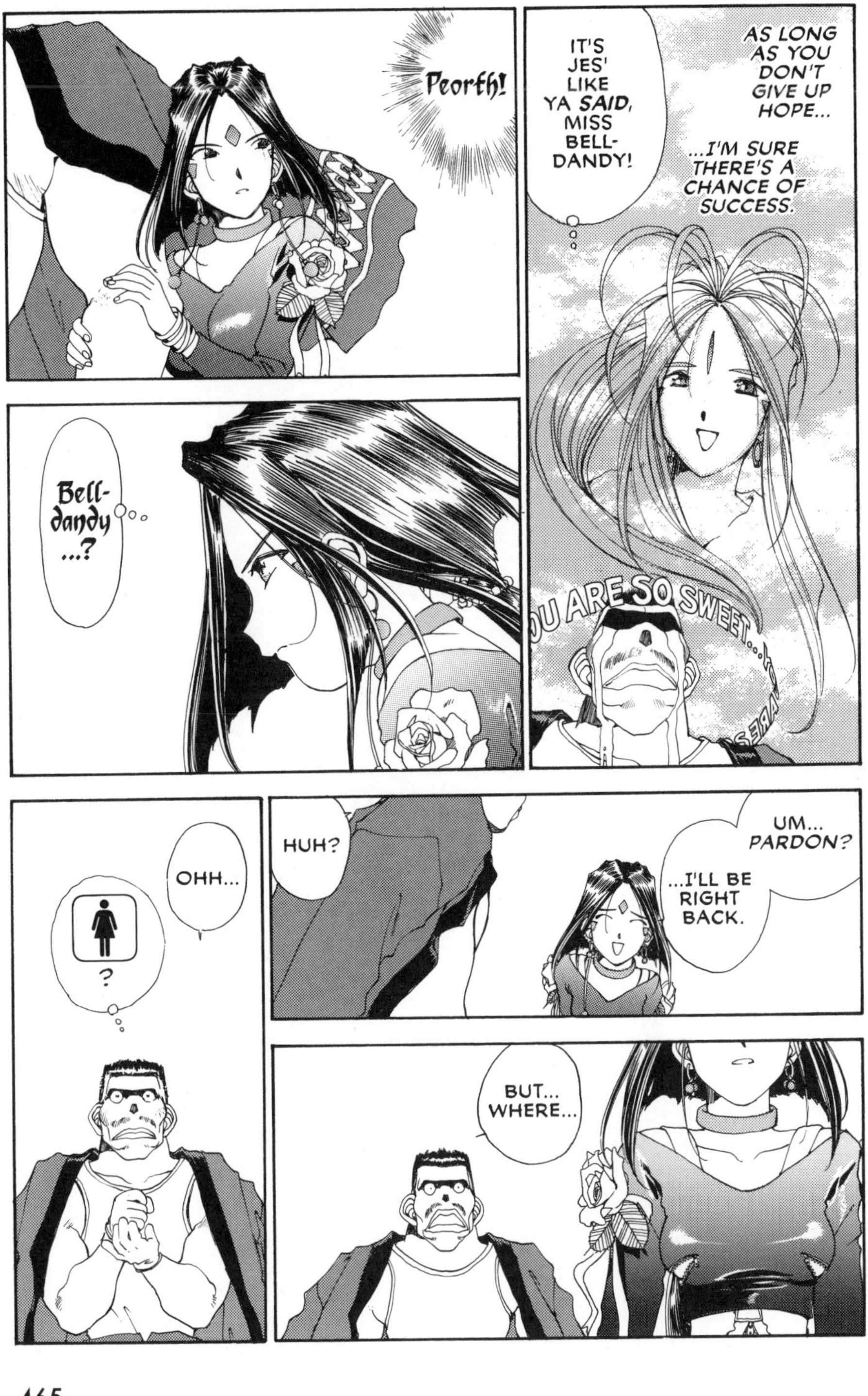

AS LONG AS YOU DON'T GIVE UP HOPE...
...I'M SURE THERE'S A CHANCE OF SUCCESS.
IT'S JES' LIKE YA *SAID*, MISS BELL-DANDY!
OU ARE SO SWEET...
Peorth!
Bell-dandy ...?
UM... *PARDON?*
...I'LL BE RIGHT BACK.
HUH?
BUT... WHERE...
OHH...
?

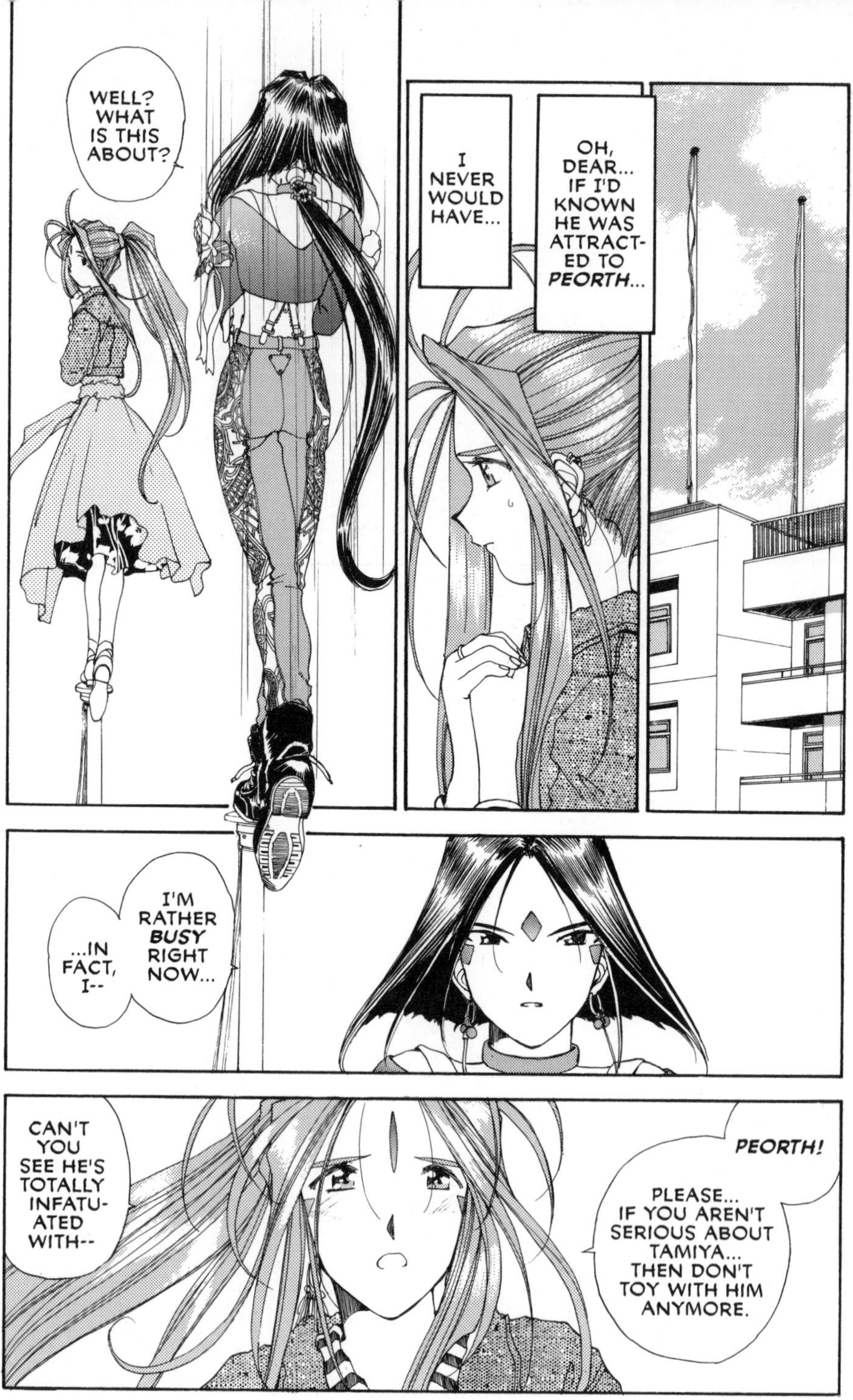

OH, DEAR... IF I'D KNOWN HE WAS ATTRACT-ED TO *PEORTH*...
I NEVER WOULD HAVE...
WELL? WHAT IS THIS ABOUT?
I'M RATHER *BUSY* RIGHT NOW...
...IN FACT, I--
PEORTH!
PLEASE... IF YOU AREN'T SERIOUS ABOUT TAMIYA... THEN DON'T TOY WITH HIM ANYMORE.
CAN'T YOU SEE HE'S TOTALLY INFATU-ATED WITH--

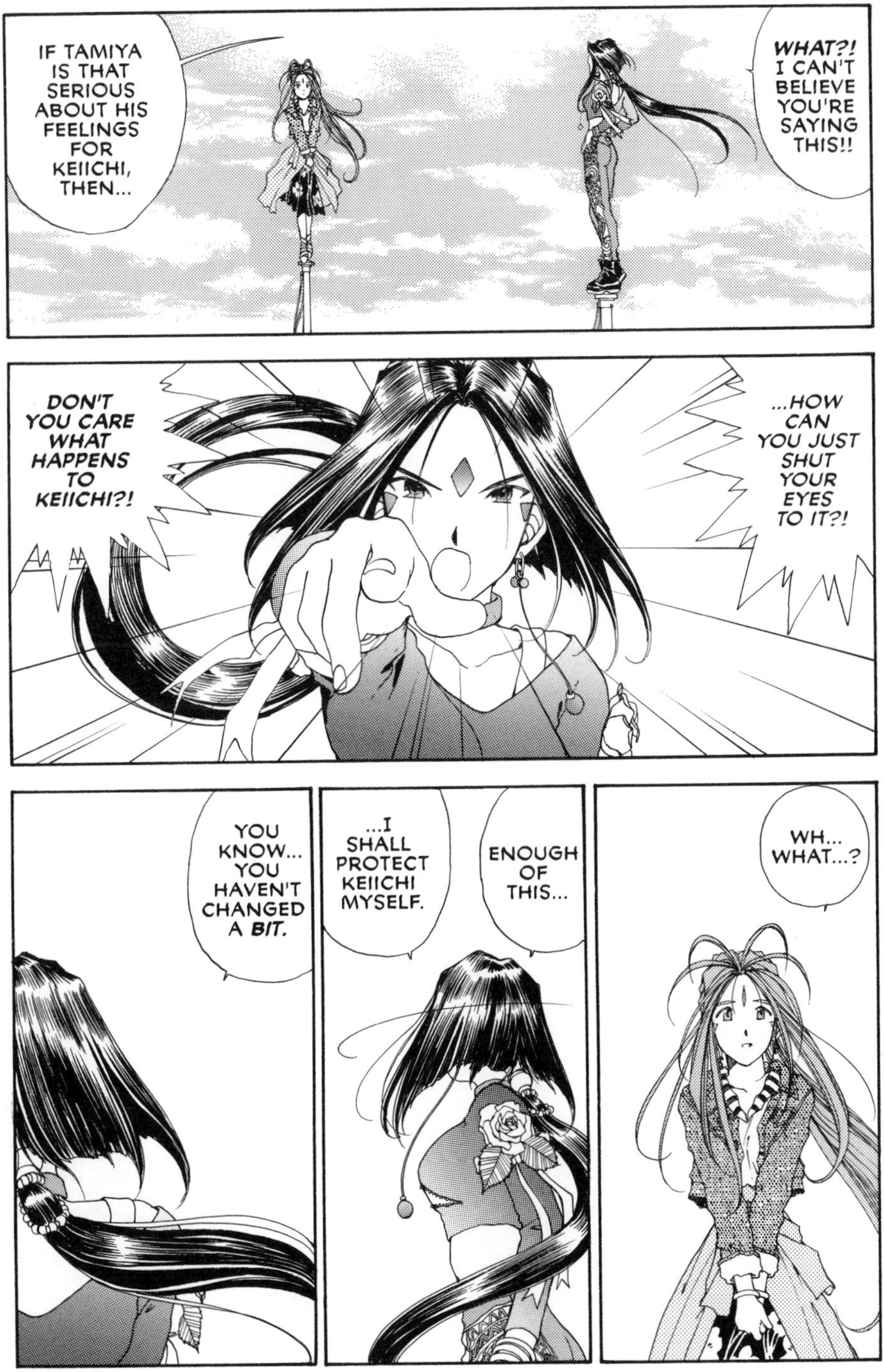
IF TAMIYA IS THAT SERIOUS ABOUT HIS FEELINGS FOR KEIICHI, THEN...
WHAT?! I CAN'T BELIEVE YOU'RE SAYING THIS!!
DON'T YOU CARE WHAT HAPPENS TO KEIICHI?!
...HOW CAN YOU JUST SHUT YOUR EYES TO IT?!
YOU KNOW... YOU HAVEN'T CHANGED A *BIT.*
...I SHALL PROTECT KEIICHI MYSELF.
ENOUGH OF THIS...
WH... WHAT...?

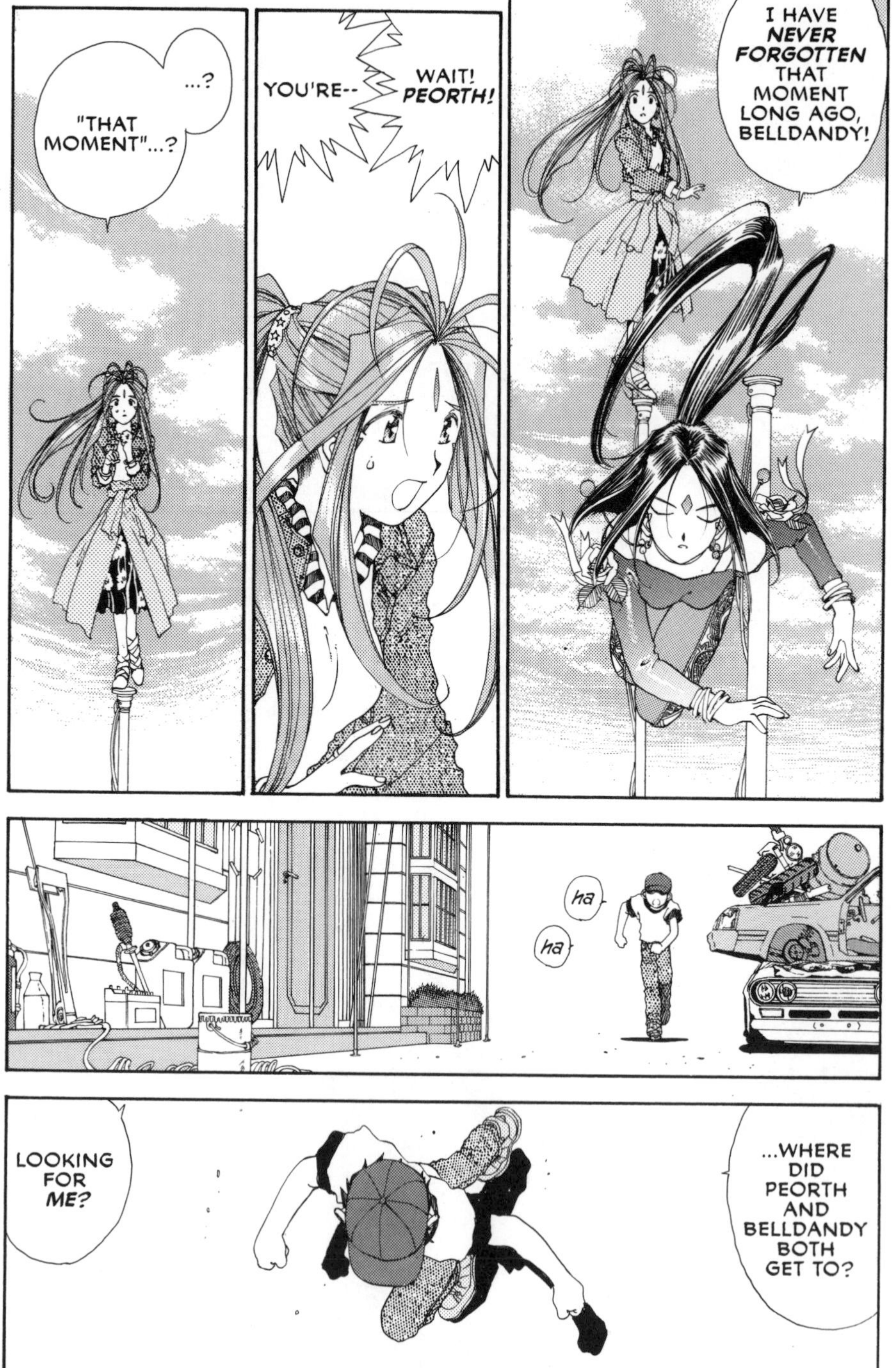
I HAVE NEVER FORGOTTEN THAT MOMENT LONG AGO, BELLDANDY!
WAIT! PEORTH!
YOU'RE--
...?
"THAT MOMENT"...?
ha
ha
...WHERE DID PEORTH AND BELLDANDY BOTH GET TO?
LOOKING FOR ME?

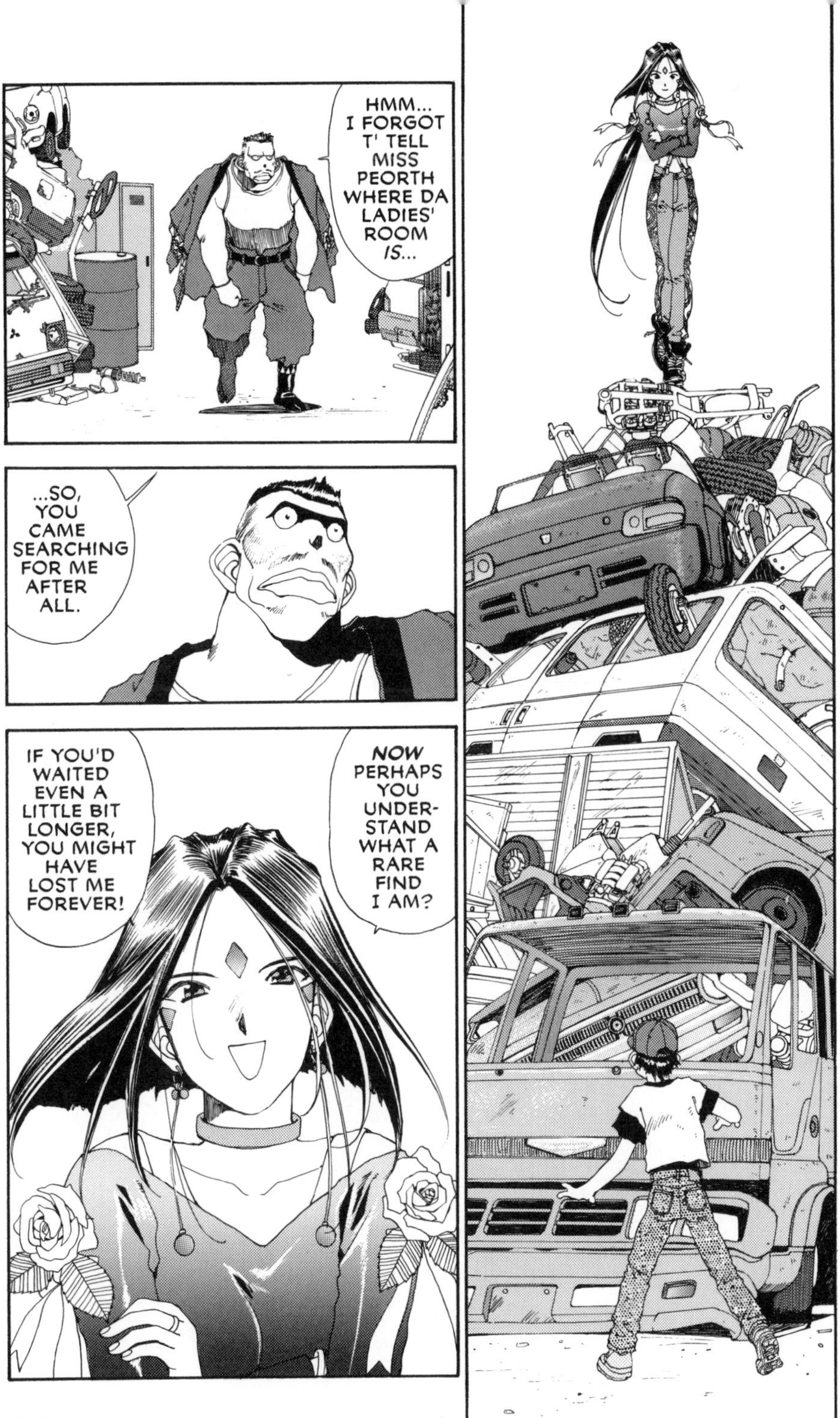
HMM... I FORGOT T' TELL MISS PEORTH WHERE DA LADIES' ROOM *IS*...
...SO, YOU CAME SEARCHING FOR ME AFTER ALL.
NOW PERHAPS YOU UNDER-STAND WHAT A RARE FIND I AM?
IF YOU'D WAITED EVEN A LITTLE BIT LONGER, YOU MIGHT HAVE LOST ME FOREVER!

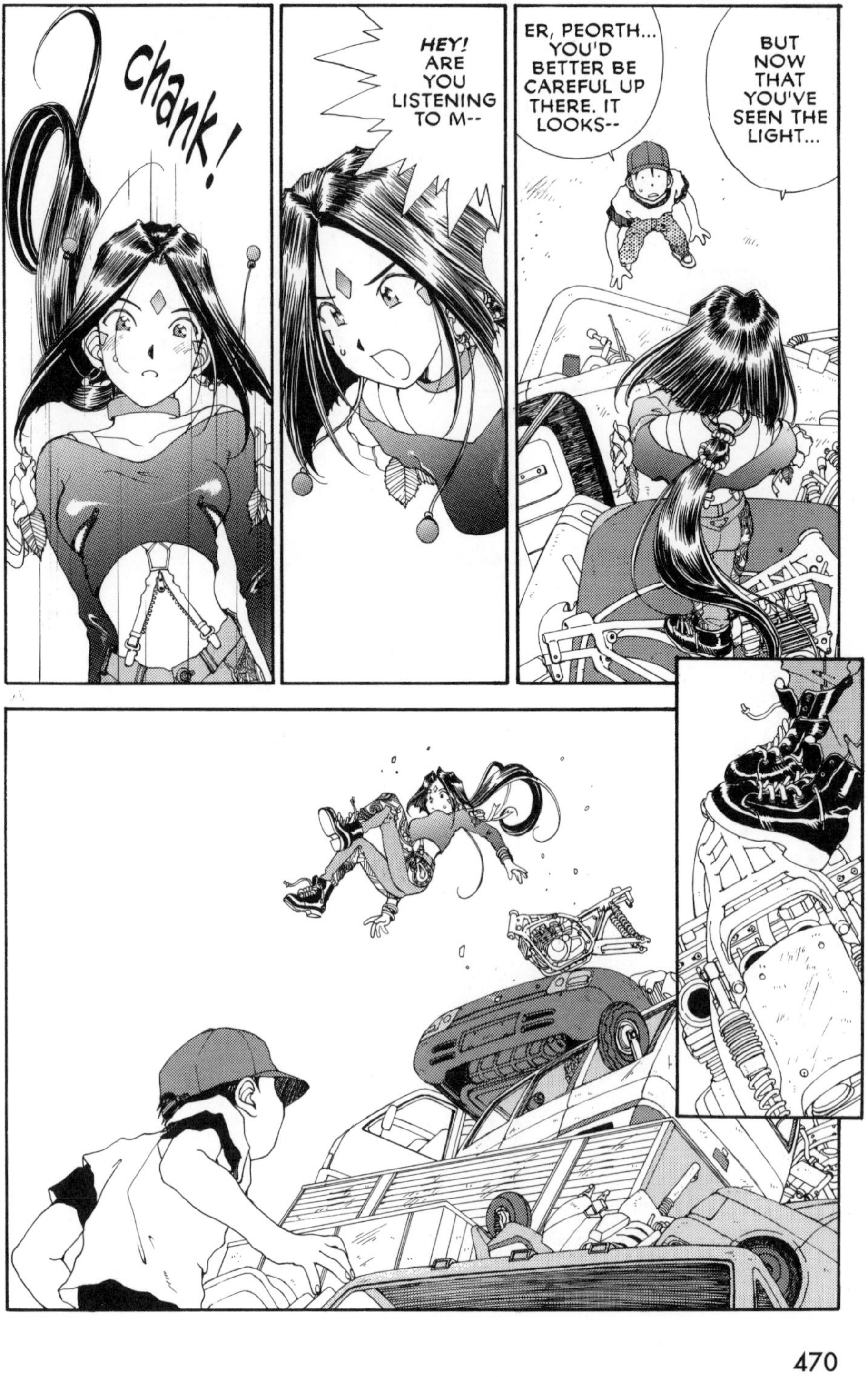
BUT NOW THAT YOU'VE SEEN THE LIGHT...
ER, PEORTH... YOU'D BETTER BE CAREFUL UP THERE. IT LOOKS--
HEY! ARE YOU LISTENING TO M--
chank!

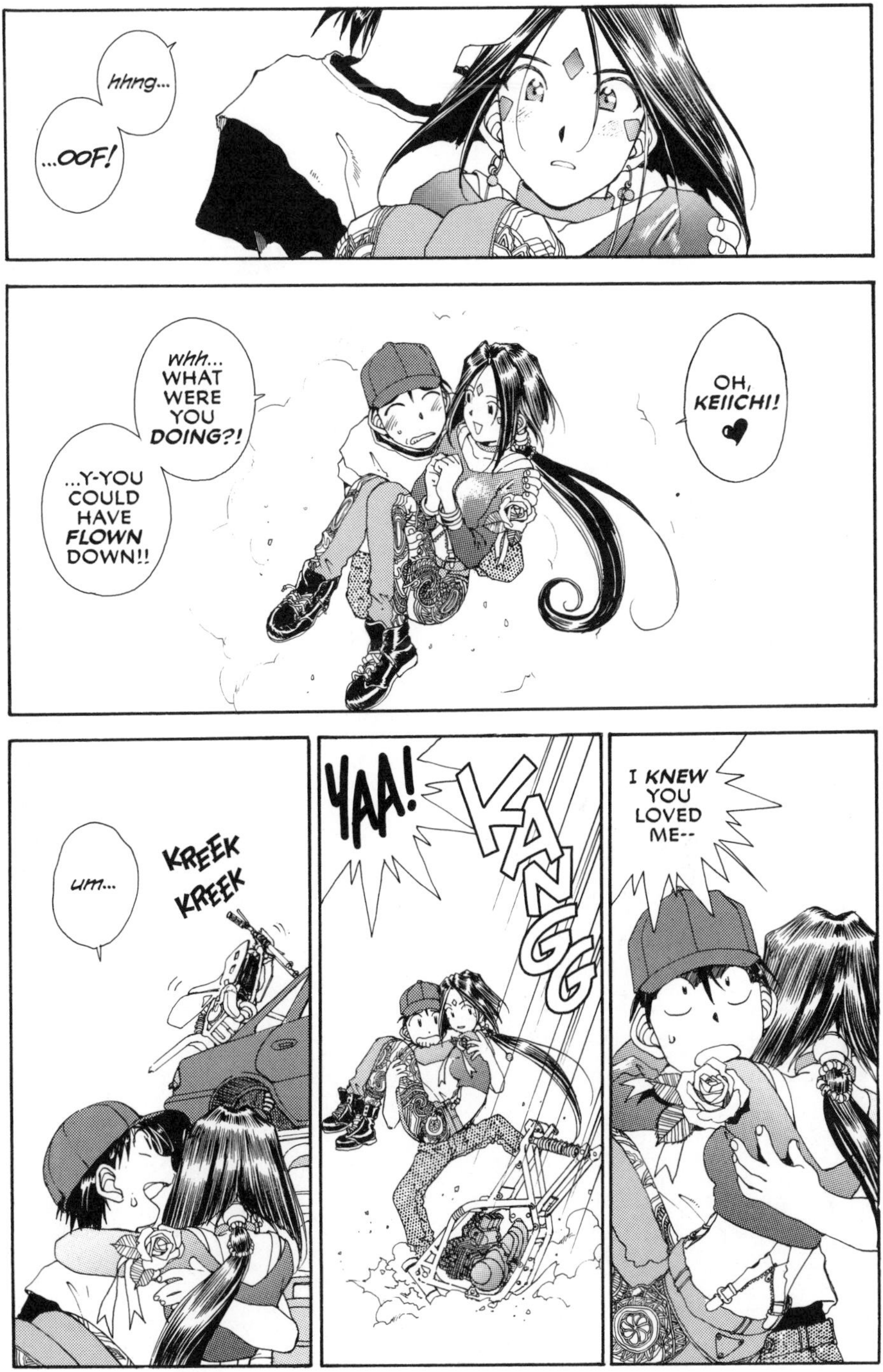
hhng...
...OOF!
whh... WHAT WERE YOU DOING?!
...Y-YOU COULD HAVE FLOWN DOWN!!
OH, KEIICHI! ♥
um...
KREEK KREEK
YAA!
KANGG
I KNEW YOU LOVED ME--

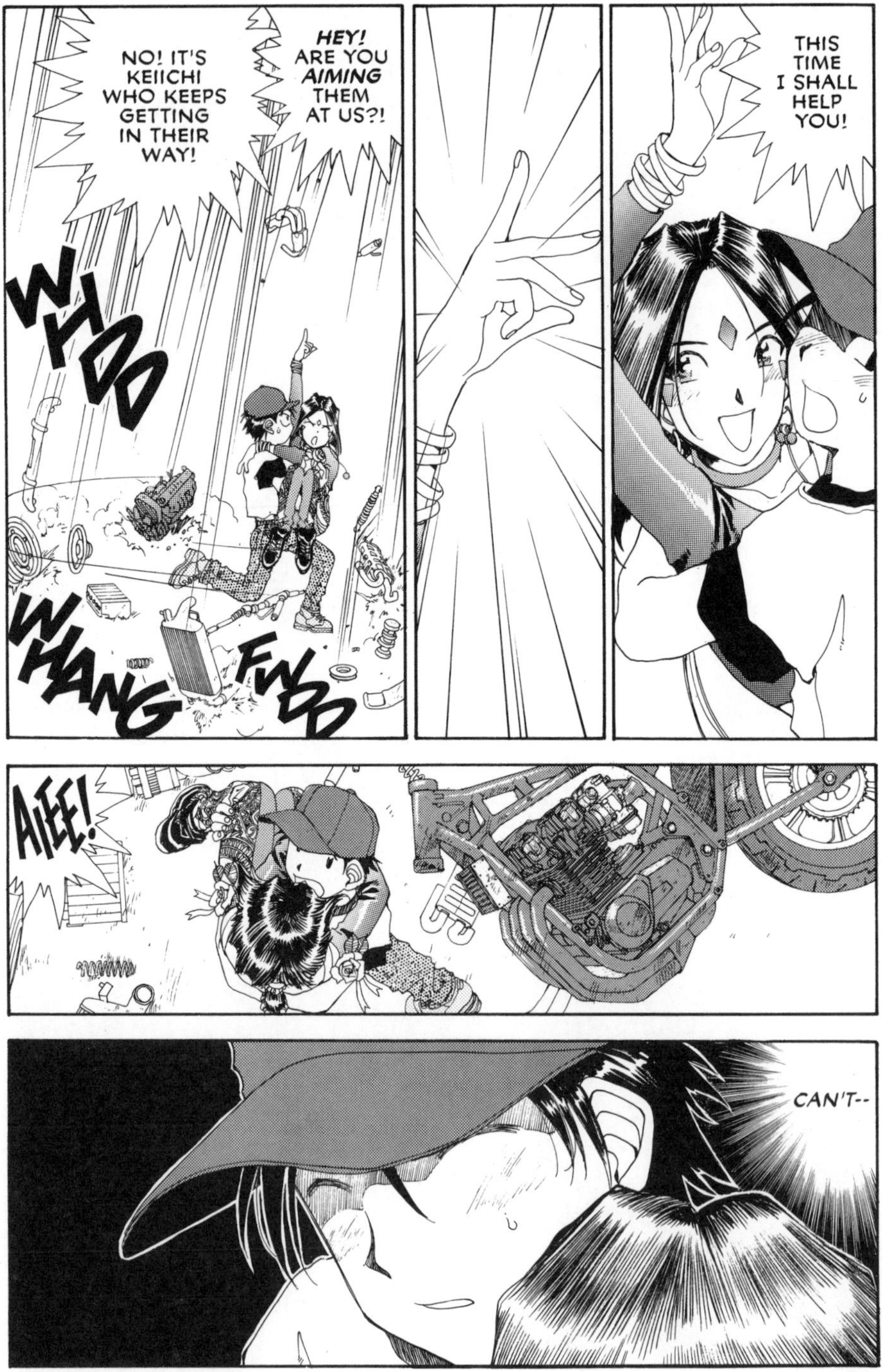
THIS TIME I SHALL HELP YOU!
HEY! ARE YOU AIMING THEM AT US?!
NO! IT'S KEIICHI WHO KEEPS GETTING IN THEIR WAY!
WHOO
FWOO
WHANG
AIEEE!
CAN'T--

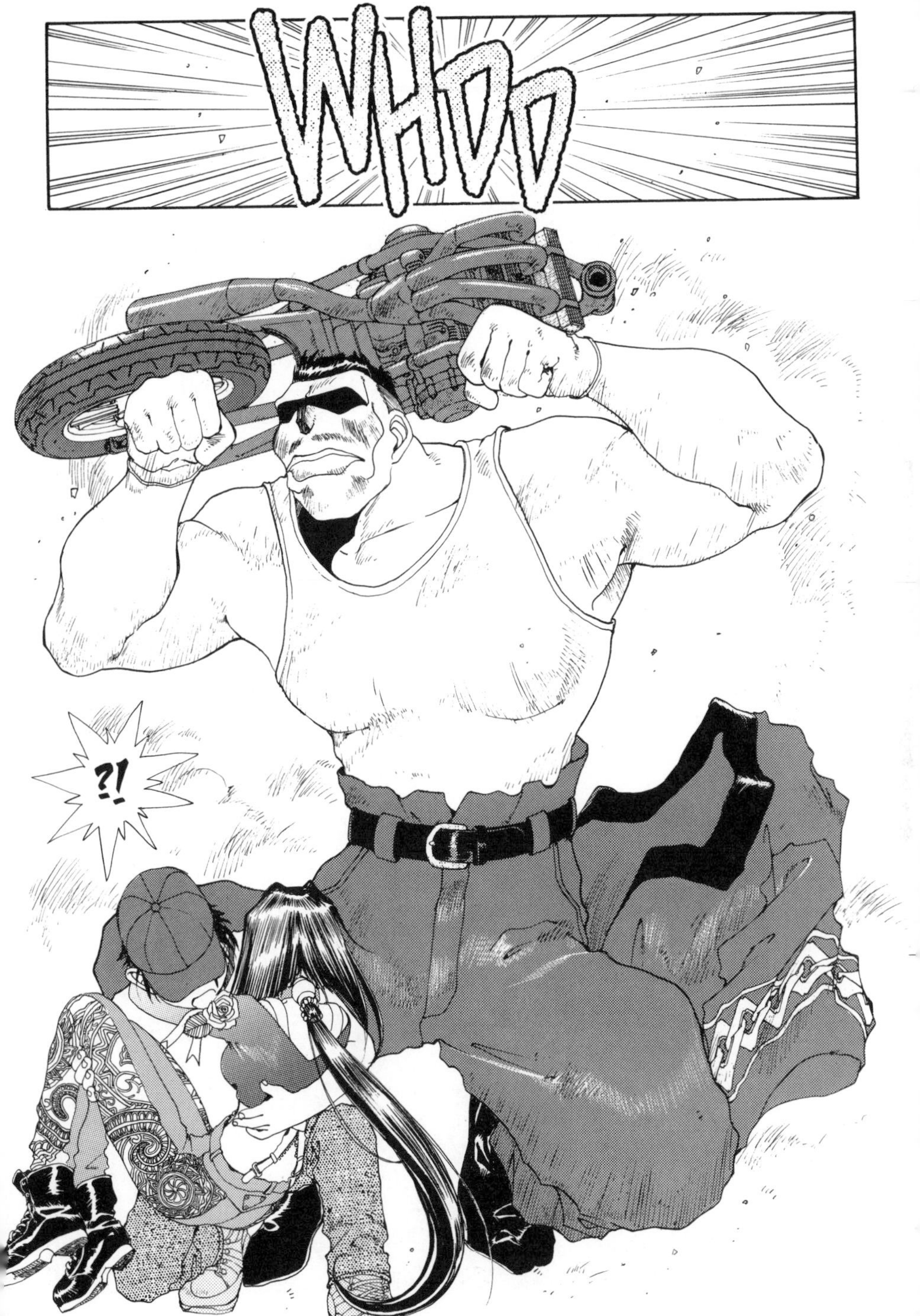
WHOO
?!

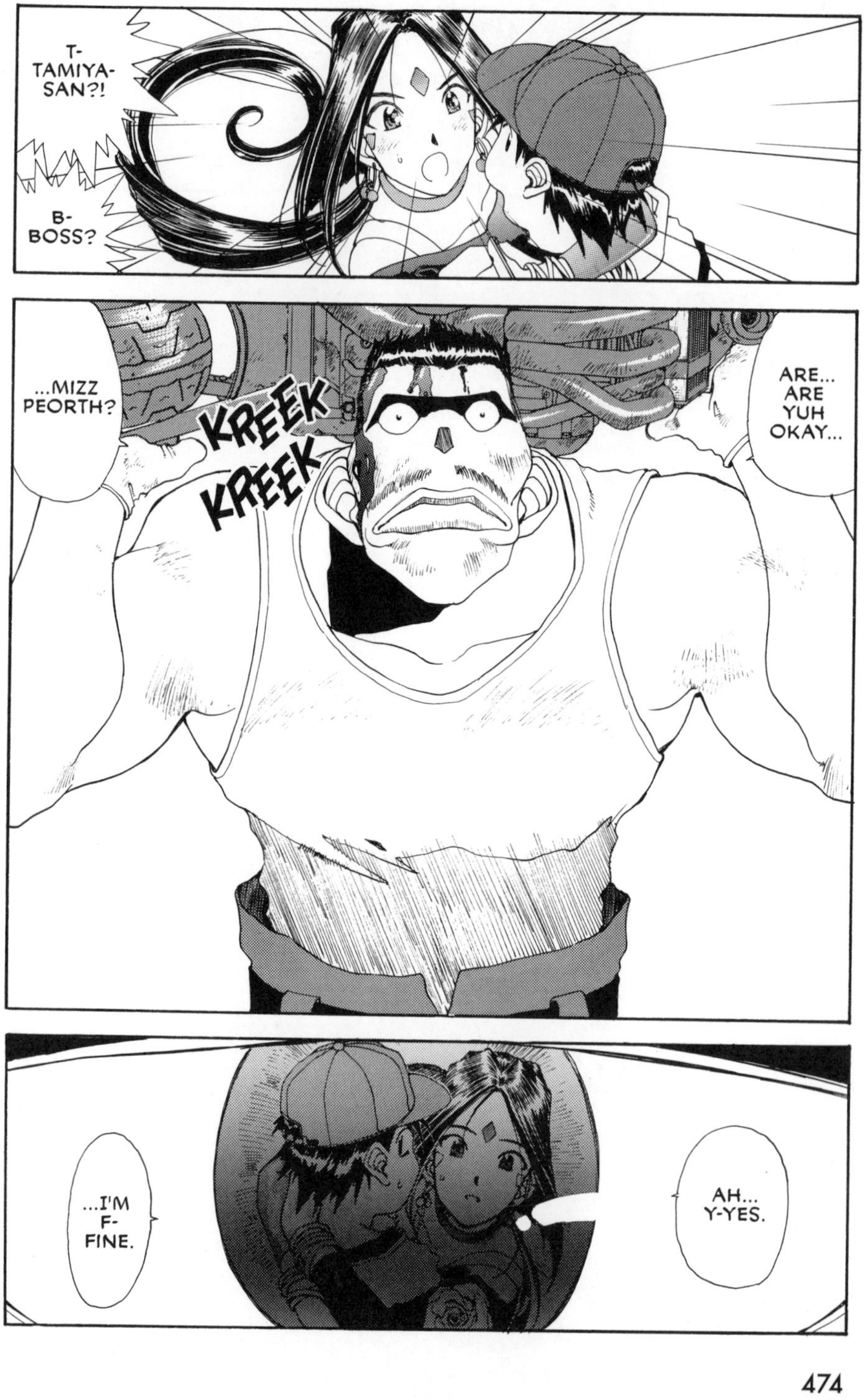
T-TAMIYA-SAN?!
B-BOSS?
ARE... ARE YUH OKAY...
...MIZZ PEORTH?
KREEK KREEK
AH... Y-YES.
...I'M F-FINE.

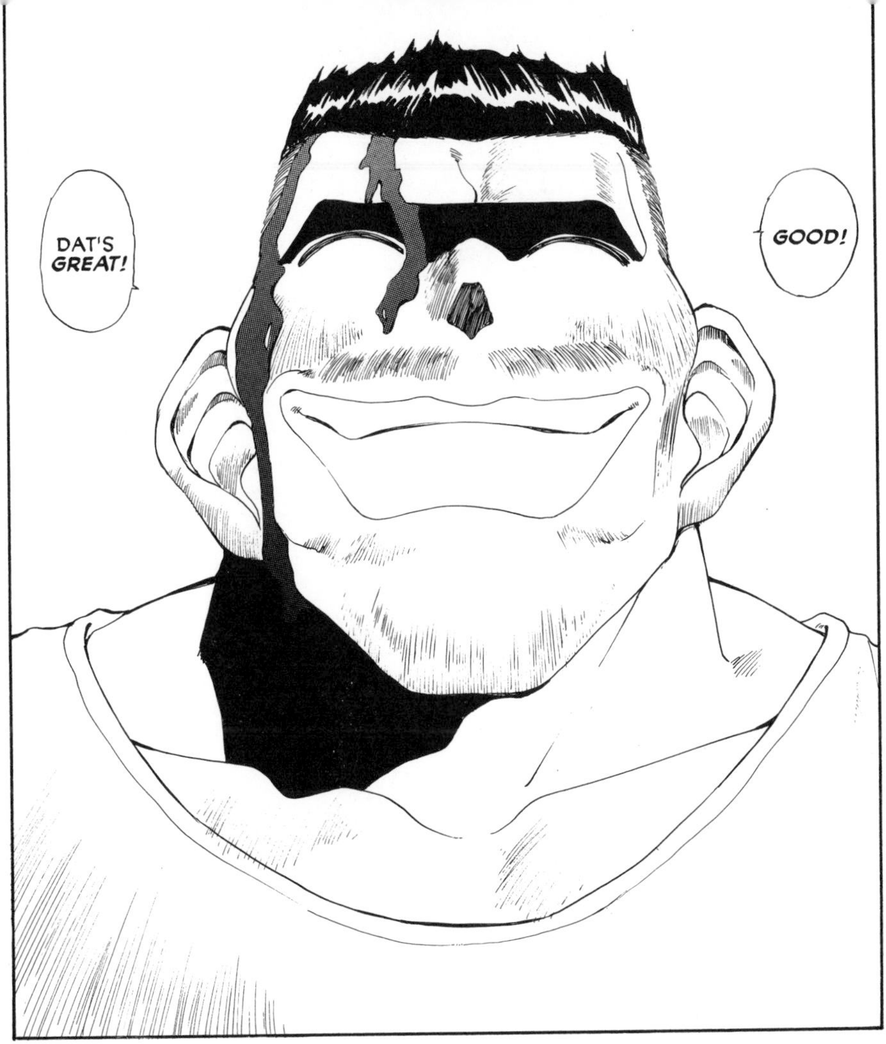
GOOD!
DAT'S GREAT!
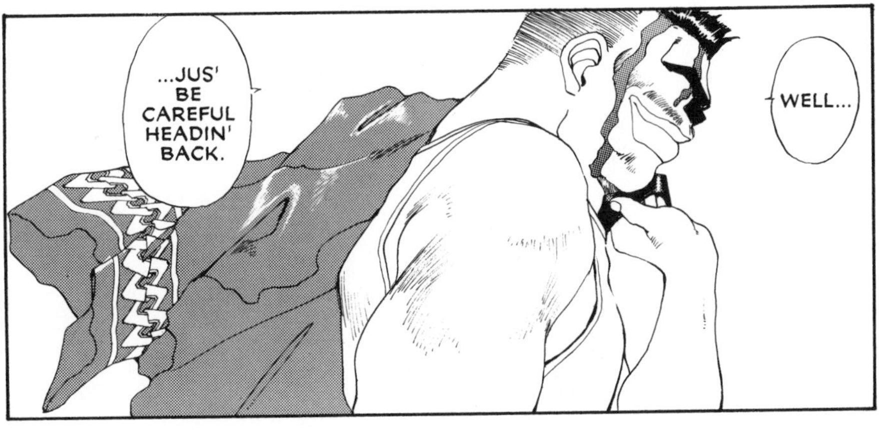
WELL...
...JUS' BE CAREFUL HEADIN' BACK.

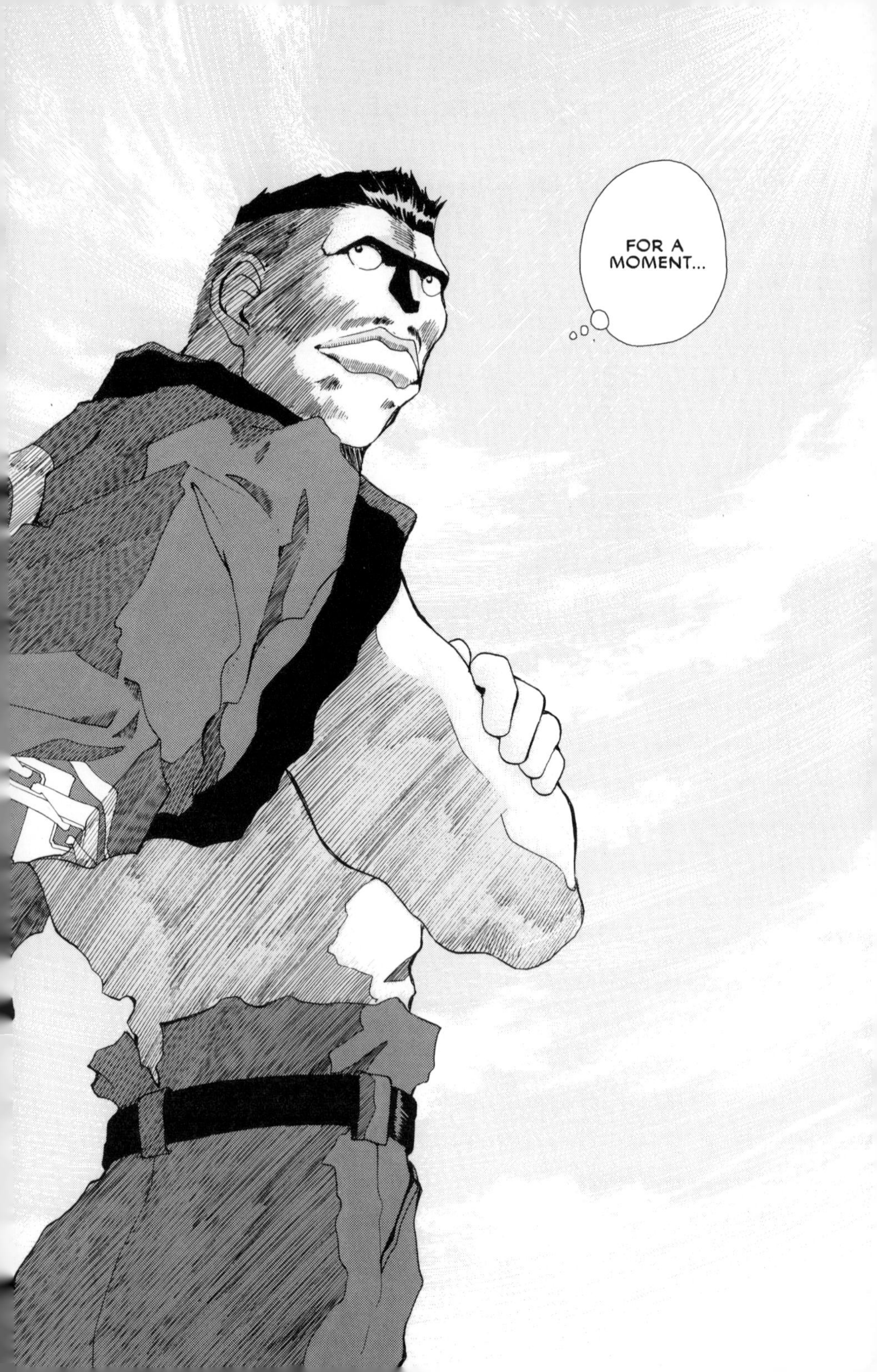
FOR A MOMENT...

...I FEEL
I CAUGHT
A GLIMPSE
O' HEAVEN.

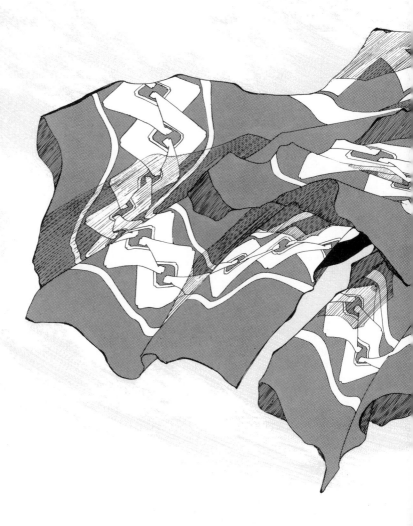

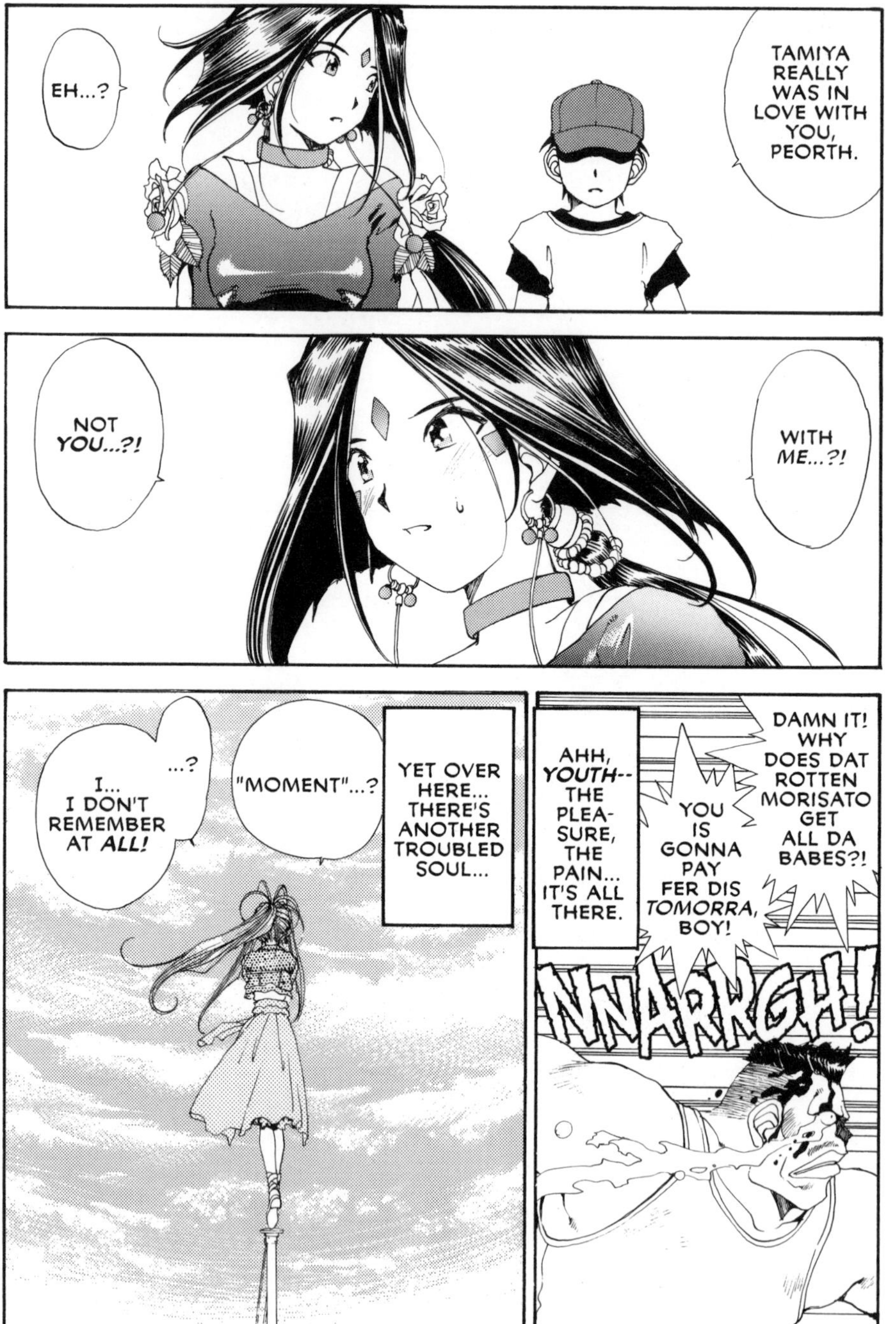
TAMIYA REALLY WAS IN LOVE WITH YOU, PEORTH.
EH...?
WITH *ME...?!*
NOT *YOU...?!*
DAMN IT! WHY DOES DAT ROTTEN MORISATO GET ALL DA BABES?!
YOU IS GONNA PAY FER DIS *TOMORRA,* BOY!
NNARRGH!
AHH, *YOUTH*-- THE PLEA-SURE, THE PAIN... IT'S ALL THERE.
YET OVER HERE... THERE'S ANOTHER TROUBLED SOUL...
"MOMENT"...?
...? I... I DON'T REMEMBER AT *ALL!*

CHAPTER 71

Meeting a Goddess's Troubles Halfway

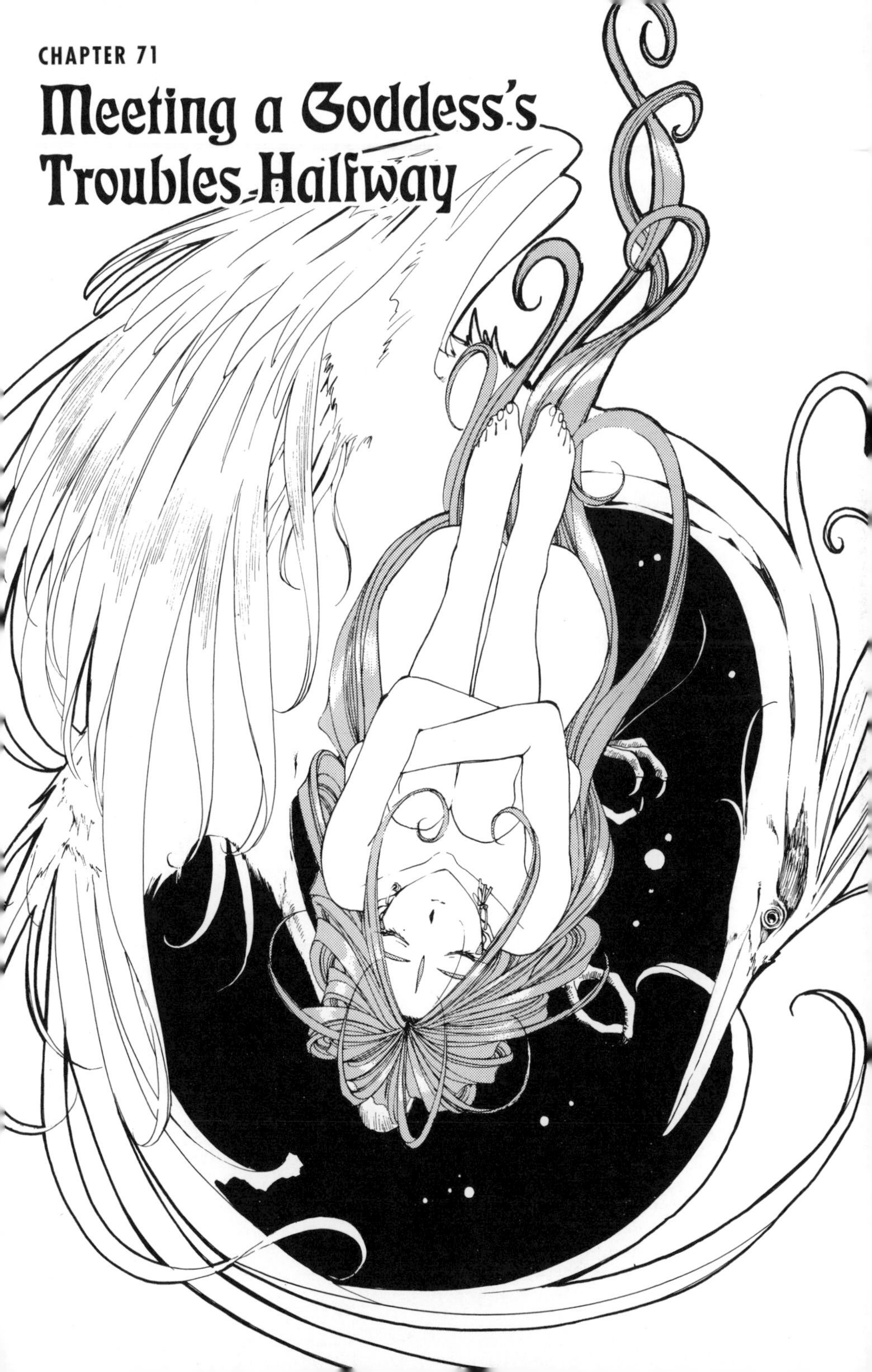

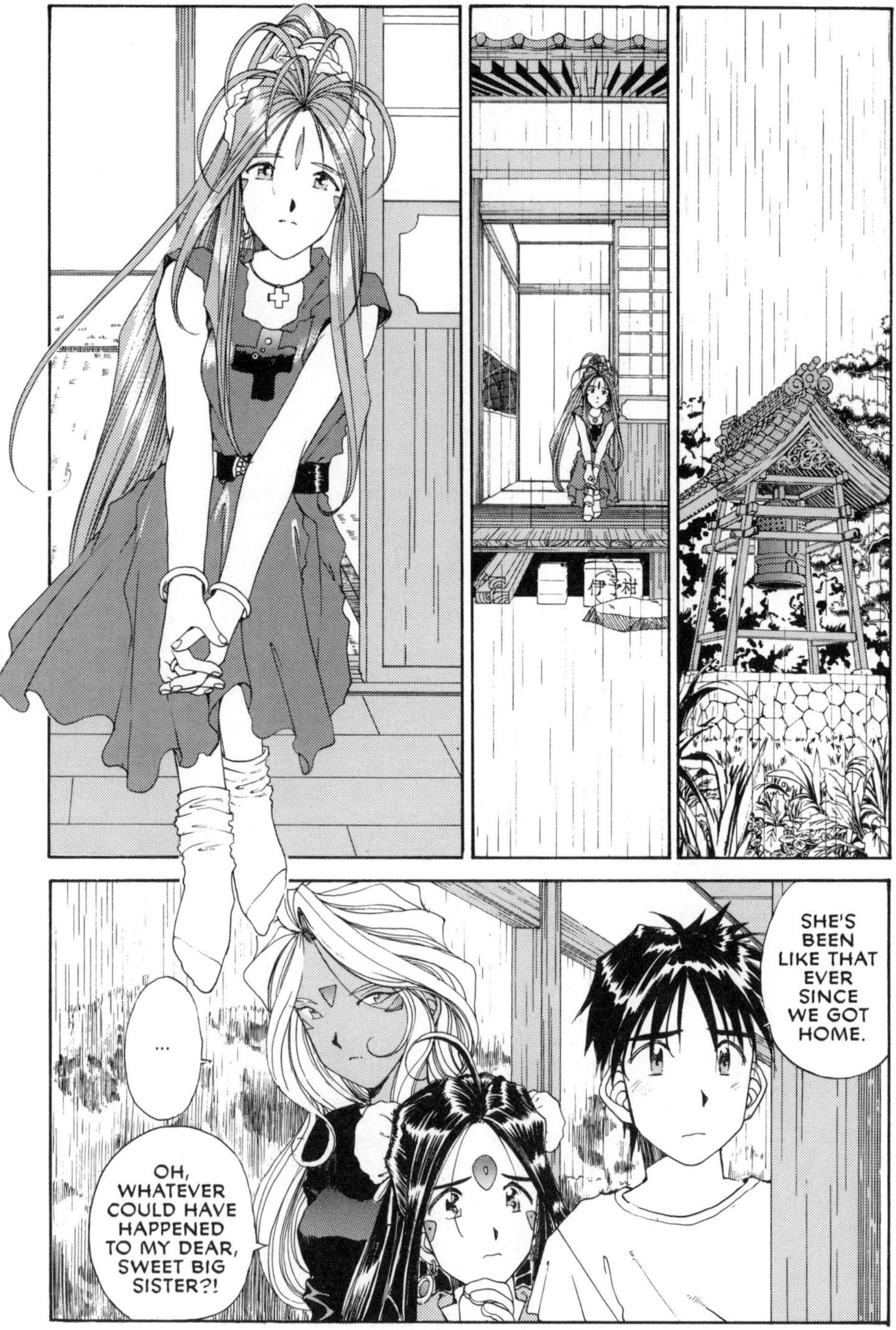
伊予柑
SHE'S BEEN LIKE THAT EVER SINCE WE GOT HOME.
...
OH, WHATEVER COULD HAVE HAPPENED TO MY DEAR, SWEET BIG SISTER?!

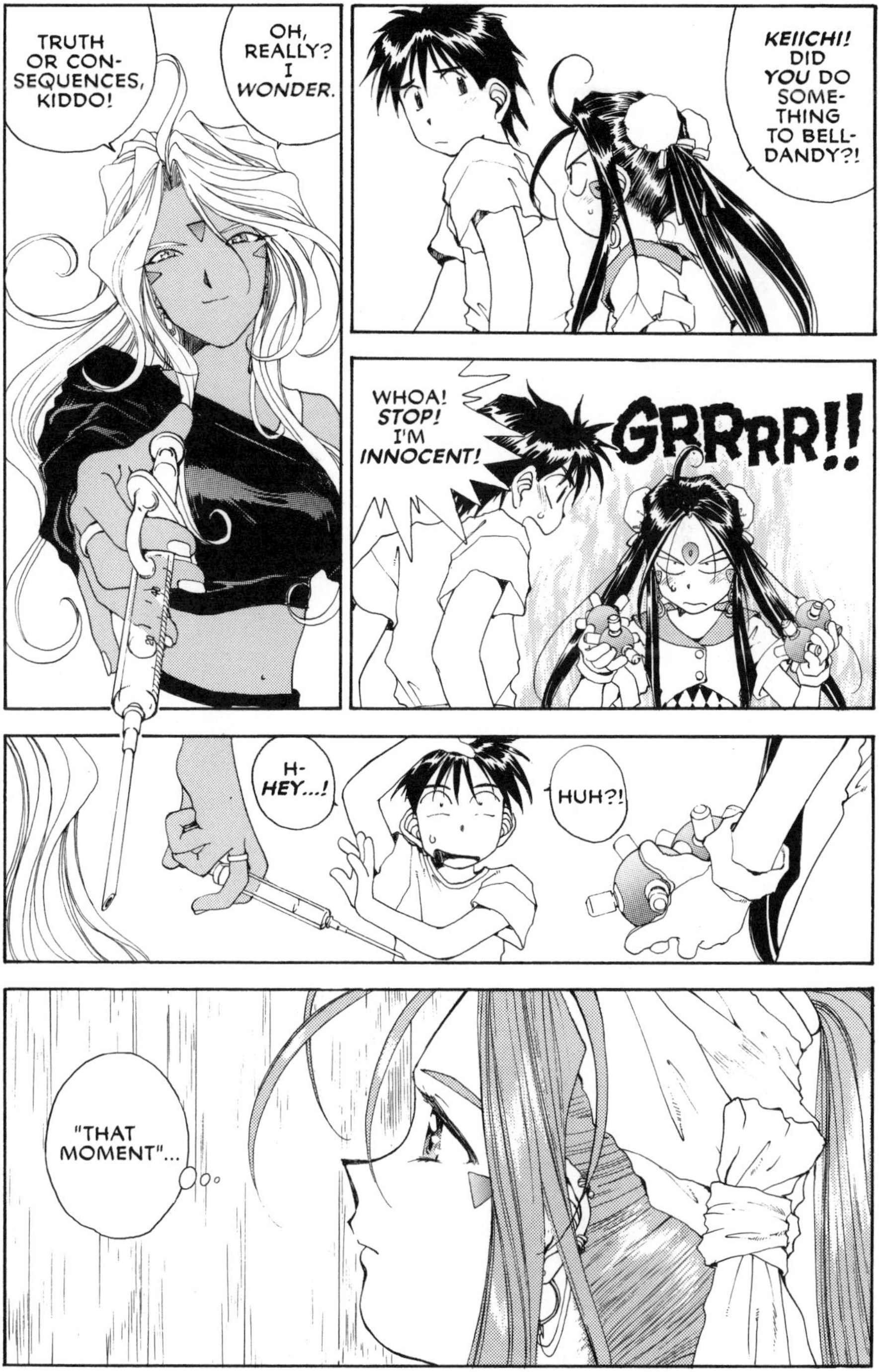
KEIICHI! DID YOU DO SOME-THING TO BELL-DANDY?!
GRRRR!!
WHOA! STOP! I'M INNOCENT!
OH, REALLY? I WONDER.
TRUTH OR CON-SEQUENCES, KIDDO!
HUH?!
H-HEY...!
"THAT MOMENT"...

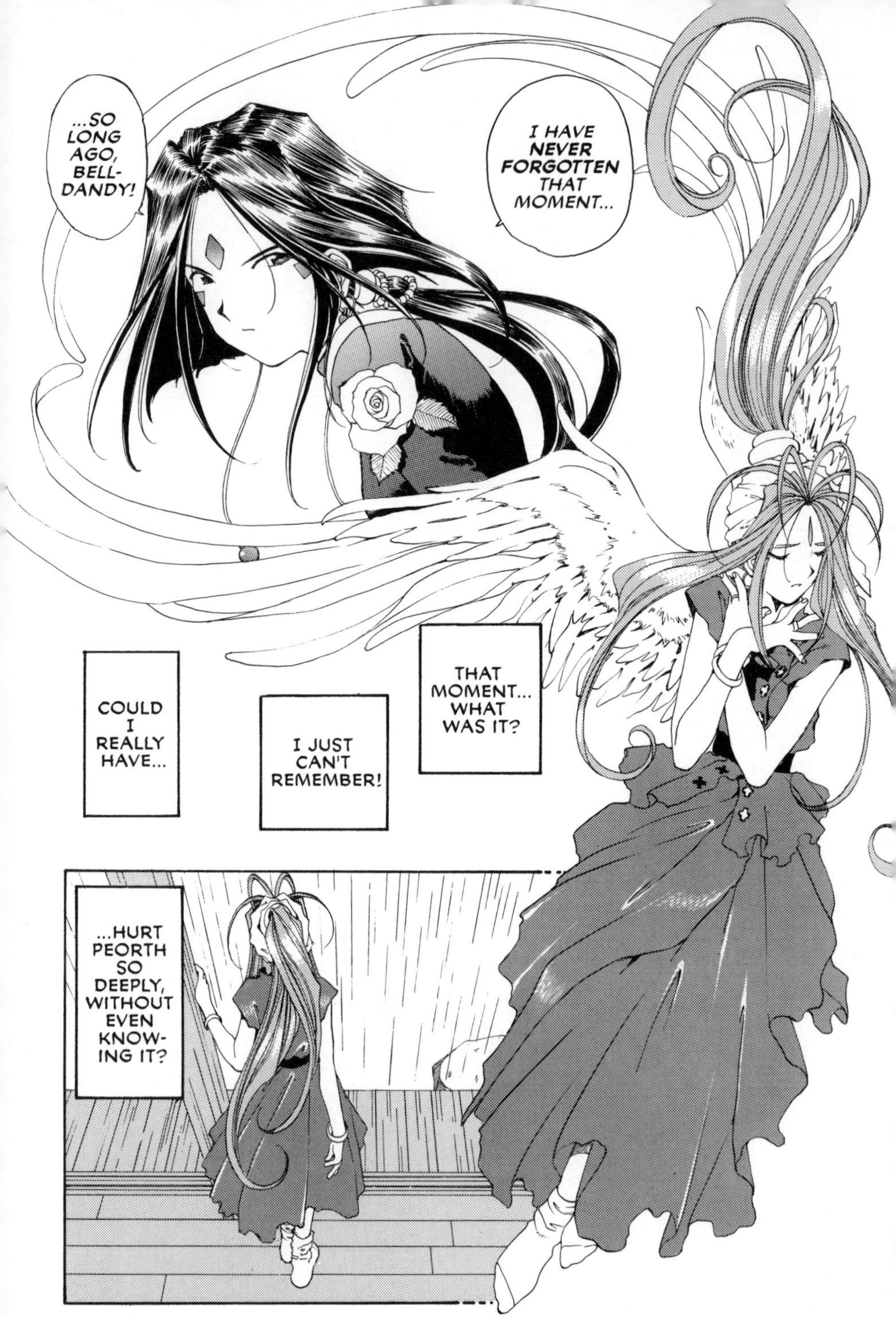
I HAVE NEVER FORGOTTEN THAT MOMENT...
...SO LONG AGO, BELL-DANDY!
THAT MOMENT... WHAT WAS IT?
I JUST CAN'T REMEMBER!
COULD I REALLY HAVE...
...HURT PEORTH SO DEEPLY, WITHOUT EVEN KNOWING IT?

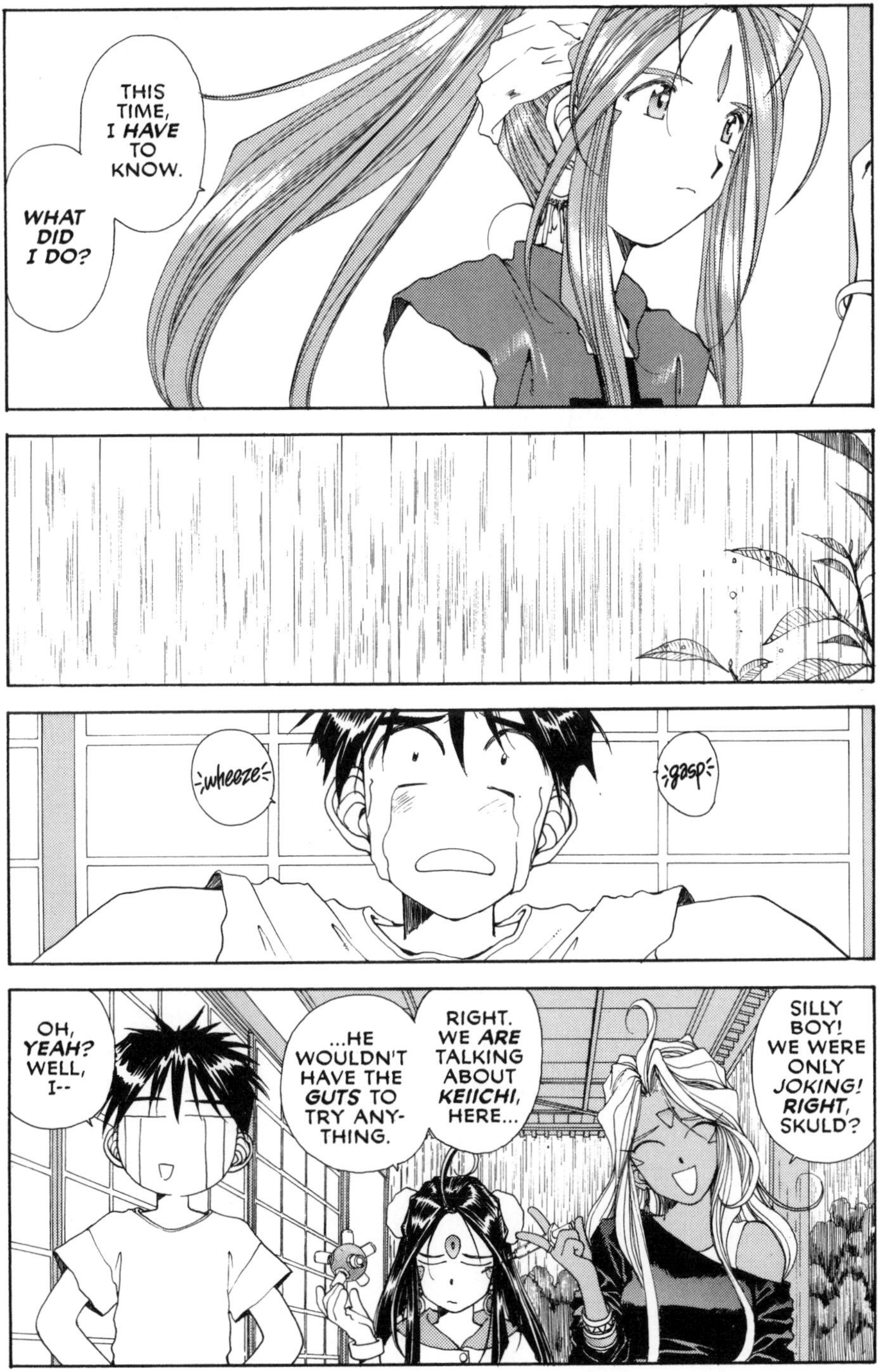
THIS TIME, I HAVE TO KNOW.
WHAT DID I DO?
gasp
wheeze
SILLY BOY! WE WERE ONLY JOKING! RIGHT, SKULD?
RIGHT. WE ARE TALKING ABOUT KEIICHI, HERE...
...HE WOULDN'T HAVE THE GUTS TO TRY ANY-THING.
OH, YEAH? WELL, I--

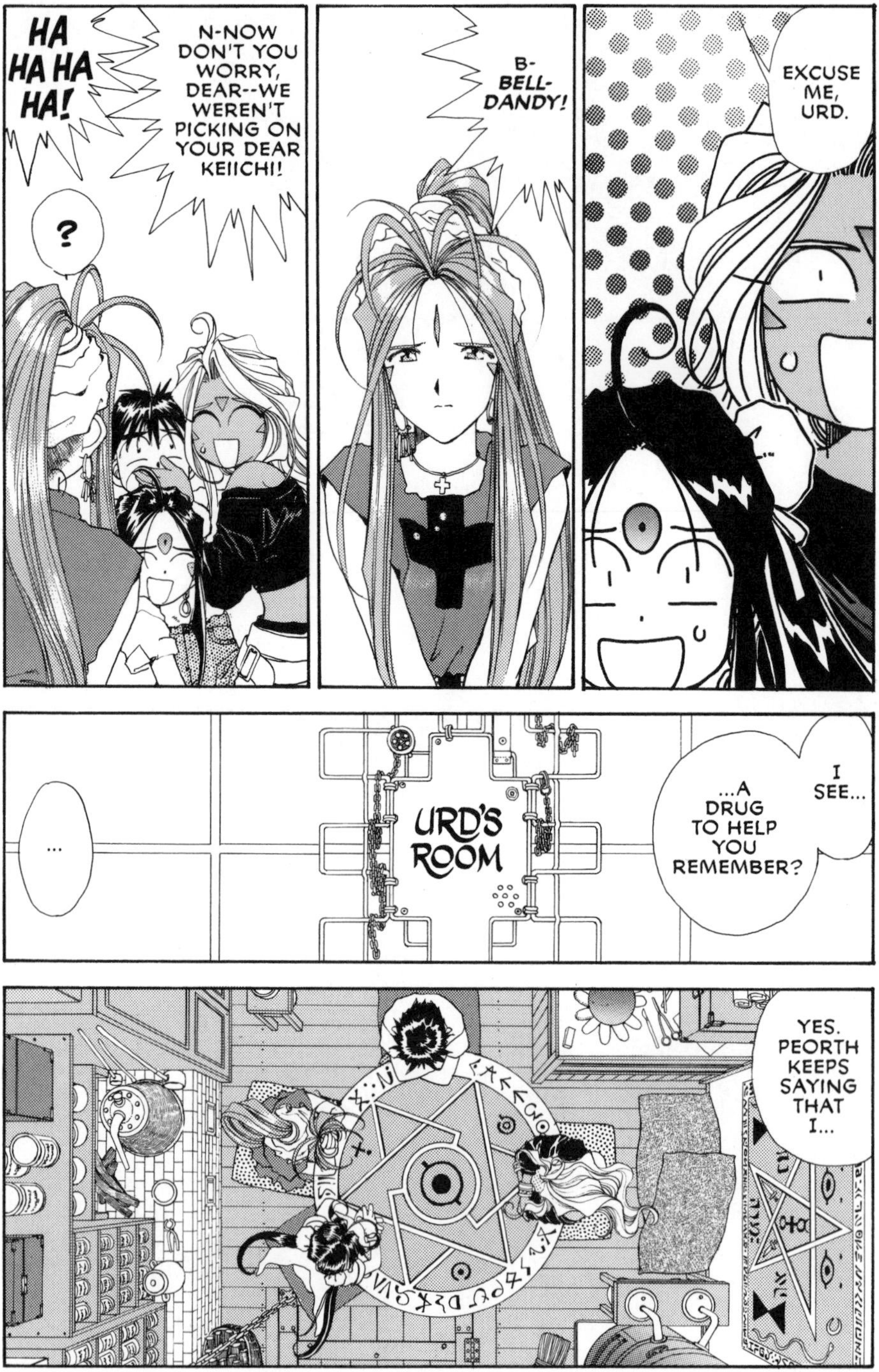
EXCUSE ME, URD.
B- BELL-DANDY!
N-NOW DON'T YOU WORRY, DEAR--WE WEREN'T PICKING ON YOUR DEAR KEIICHI!
HA HA HA HA!
?
I SEE...
...A DRUG TO HELP YOU REMEMBER?
URD'S ROOM
...
YES. PEORTH KEEPS SAYING THAT I...

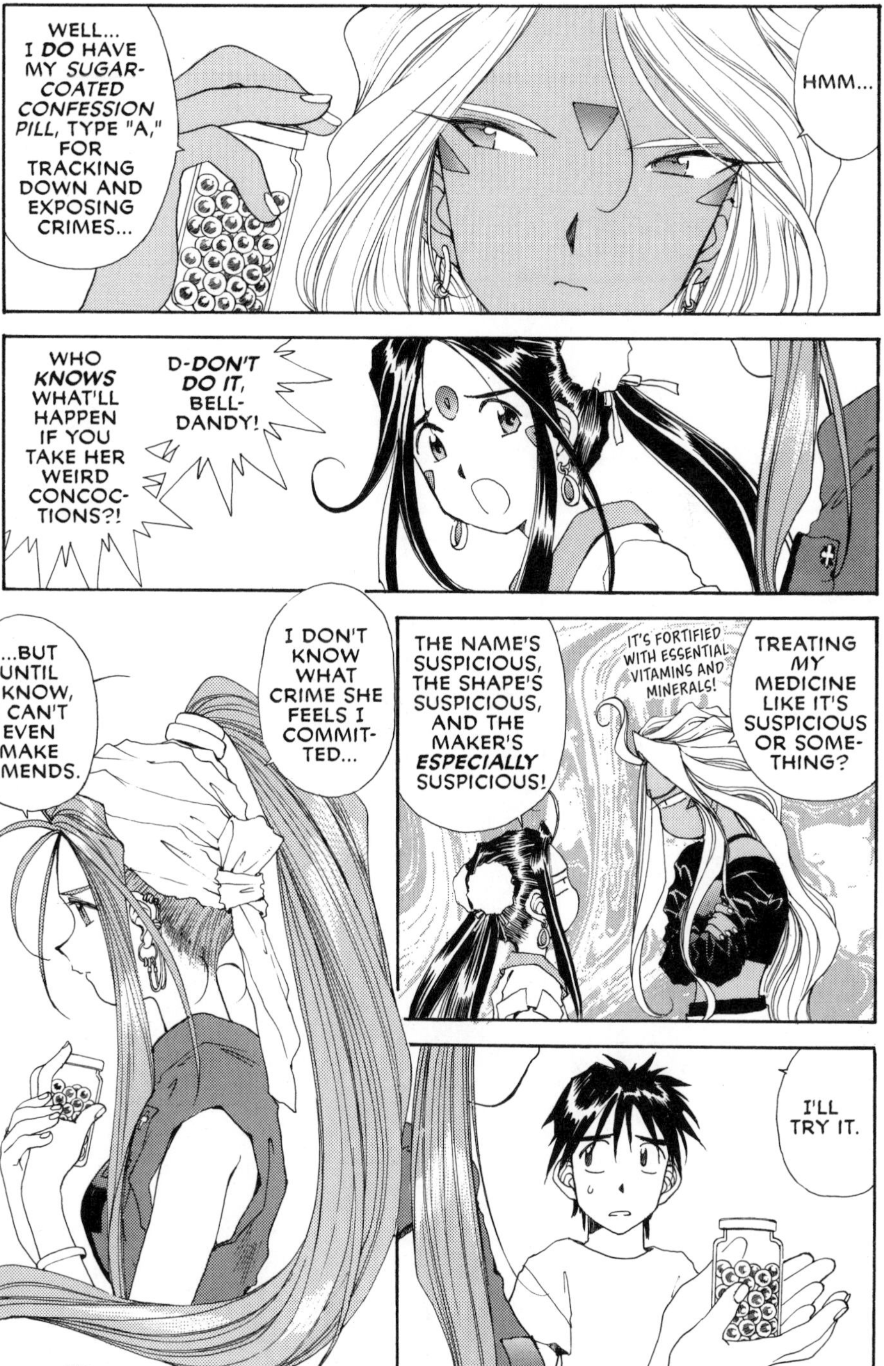
HMM...
WELL... I DO HAVE MY SUGAR-COATED CONFESSION PILL, TYPE "A," FOR TRACKING DOWN AND EXPOSING CRIMES...
D-DON'T DO IT, BELL-DANDY!
WHO KNOWS WHAT'LL HAPPEN IF YOU TAKE HER WEIRD CONCOC-TIONS?!
TREATING MY MEDICINE LIKE IT'S SUSPICIOUS OR SOME-THING?
IT'S FORTIFIED WITH ESSENTIAL VITAMINS AND MINERALS!
THE NAME'S SUSPICIOUS, THE SHAPE'S SUSPICIOUS, AND THE MAKER'S ESPECIALLY SUSPICIOUS!
I DON'T KNOW WHAT CRIME SHE FEELS I COMMIT-TED...
...BUT UNTIL I KNOW, I CAN'T EVEN MAKE AMENDS.
I'LL TRY IT.

...ANY-THING.

I DON'T FEEL...

Ten Minutes Later

GRRR

WHAT A RELIEF! IT DOESN'T WORK!

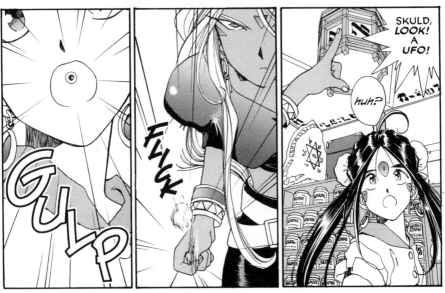

GULP

FLICK

SKULD, *LOOK!* A UFO!

huh?

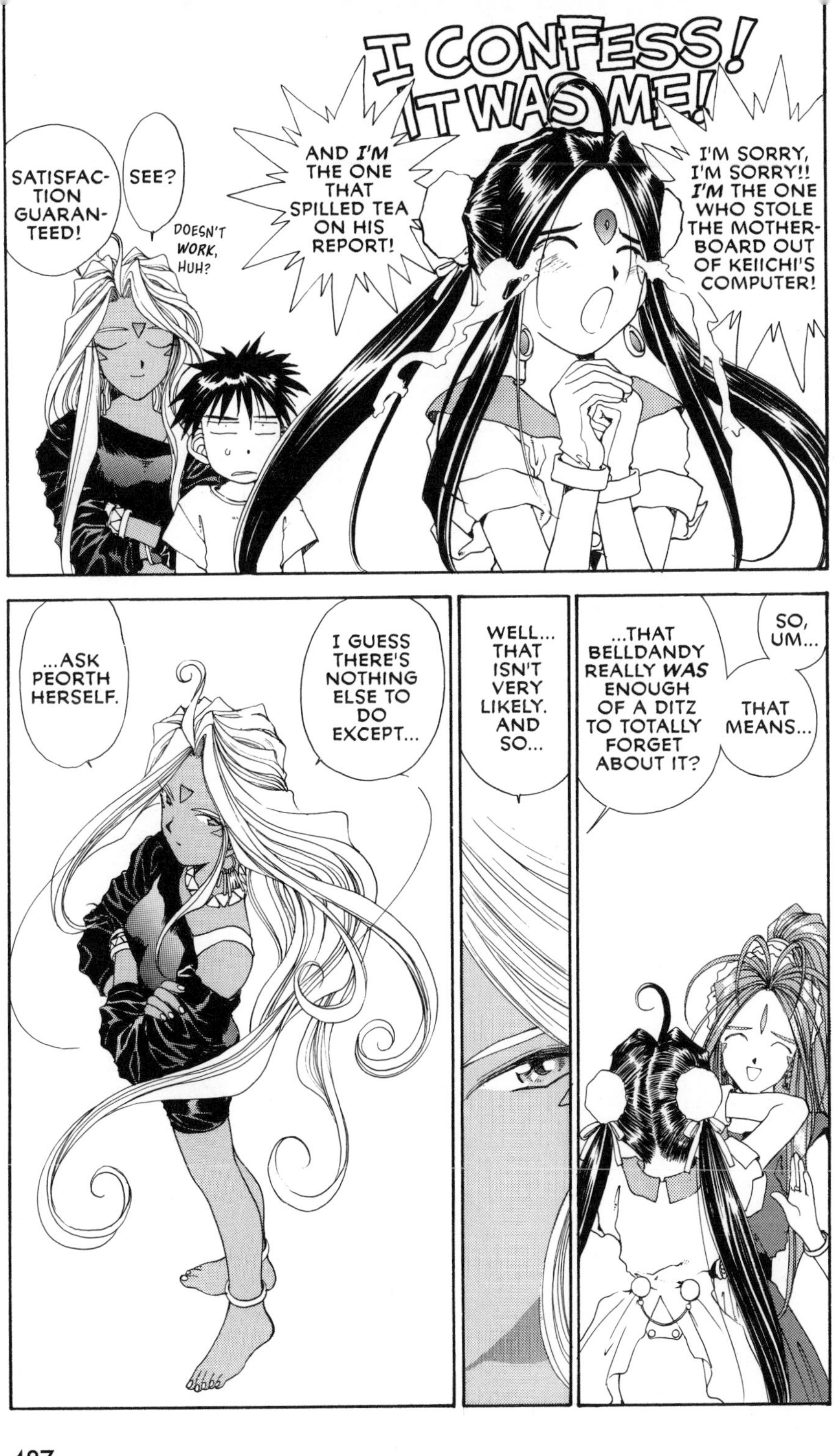
I CONFESS! IT WAS ME!
I'M SORRY, I'M SORRY!! *I'M* THE ONE WHO STOLE THE MOTHER-BOARD OUT OF KEIICHI'S COMPUTER!
AND *I'M* THE ONE THAT SPILLED TEA ON HIS REPORT!
SEE?
SATISFAC-TION GUARAN-TEED!
DOESN'T *WORK*, HUH?
SO, UM...
THAT MEANS...
...THAT BELLDANDY REALLY *WAS* ENOUGH OF A DITZ TO TOTALLY FORGET ABOUT IT?
WELL... THAT ISN'T VERY LIKELY. AND SO...
I GUESS THERE'S NOTHING ELSE TO DO EXCEPT...
...ASK PEORTH HERSELF.

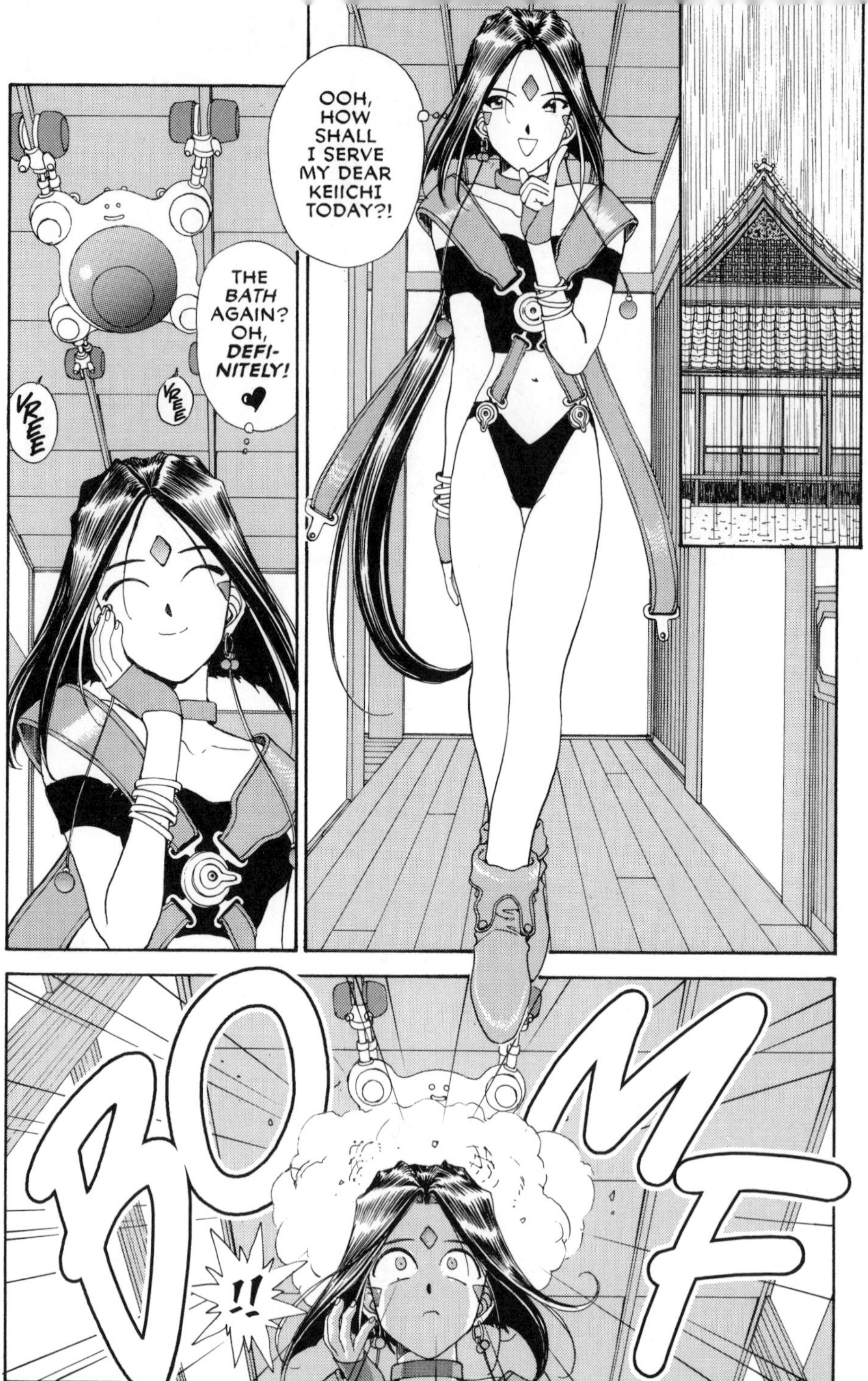
OOH, HOW SHALL I SERVE MY DEAR KEIICHI TODAY?!
VREE
VREE
THE BATH AGAIN? OH, DEFINITELY! ♥
BOMF
!!

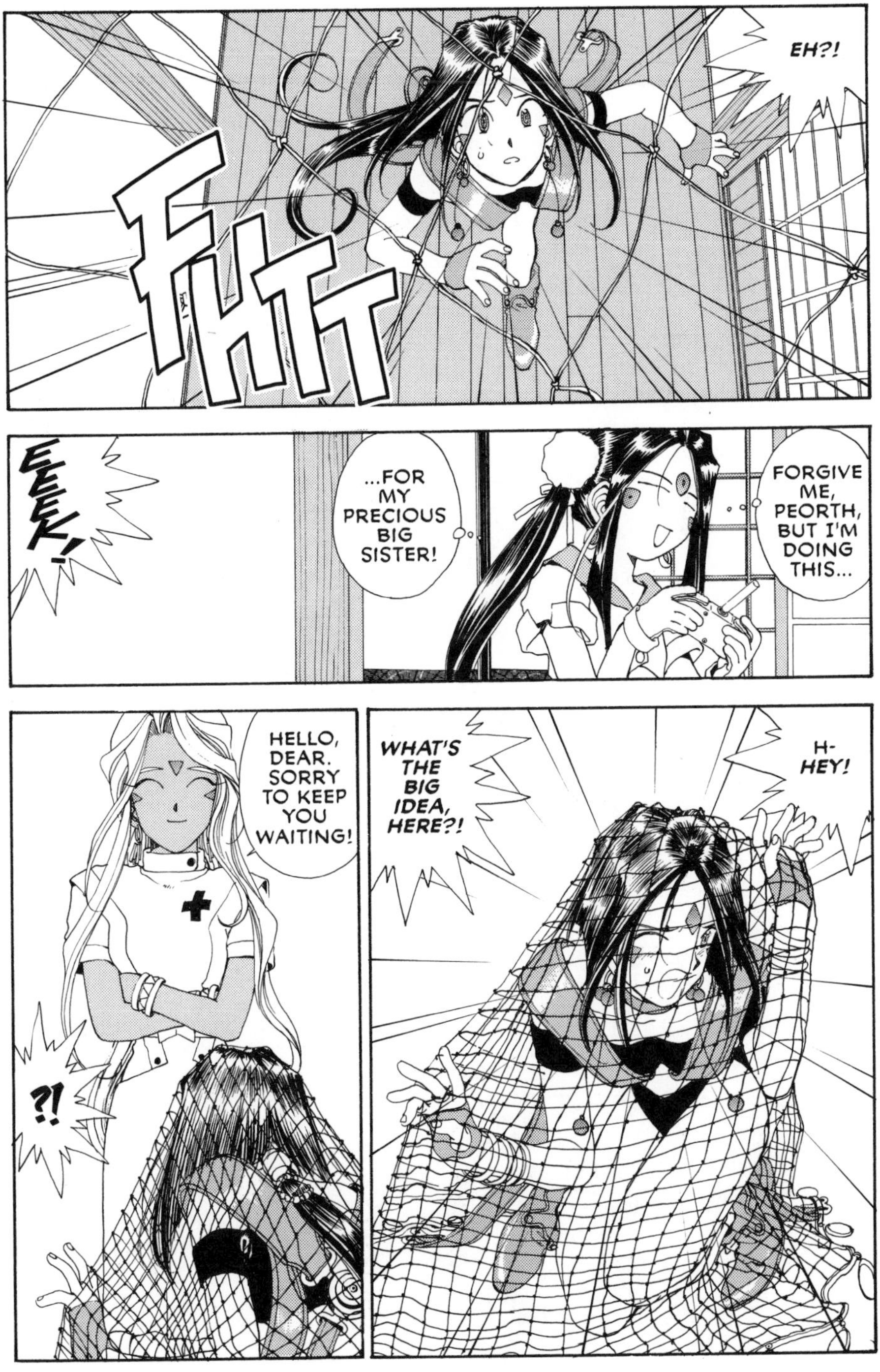
EH?!
FHTT
FORGIVE ME, PEORTH, BUT I'M DOING THIS...
...FOR MY PRECIOUS BIG SISTER!
EEEEK!
H-HEY!
WHAT'S THE BIG IDEA, HERE?!
HELLO, DEAR. SORRY TO KEEP YOU WAITING!
?!

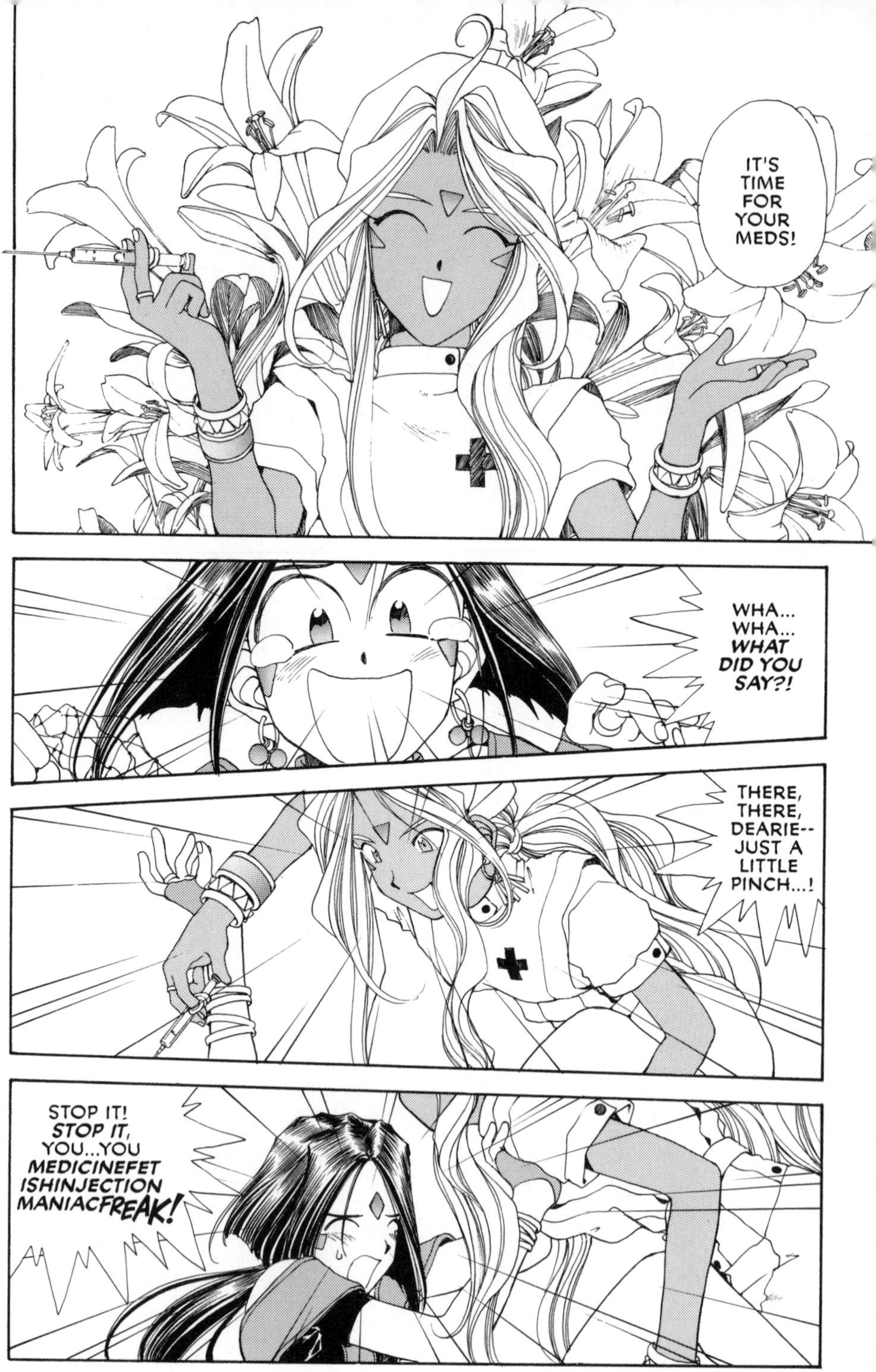
IT'S TIME FOR YOUR MEDS!
WHA... WHA... WHAT DID YOU SAY?!
THERE, THERE, DEARIE-- JUST A LITTLE PINCH...!
STOP IT! STOP IT, YOU...YOU MEDICINEFET ISHINJECTION MANIACFREAK!

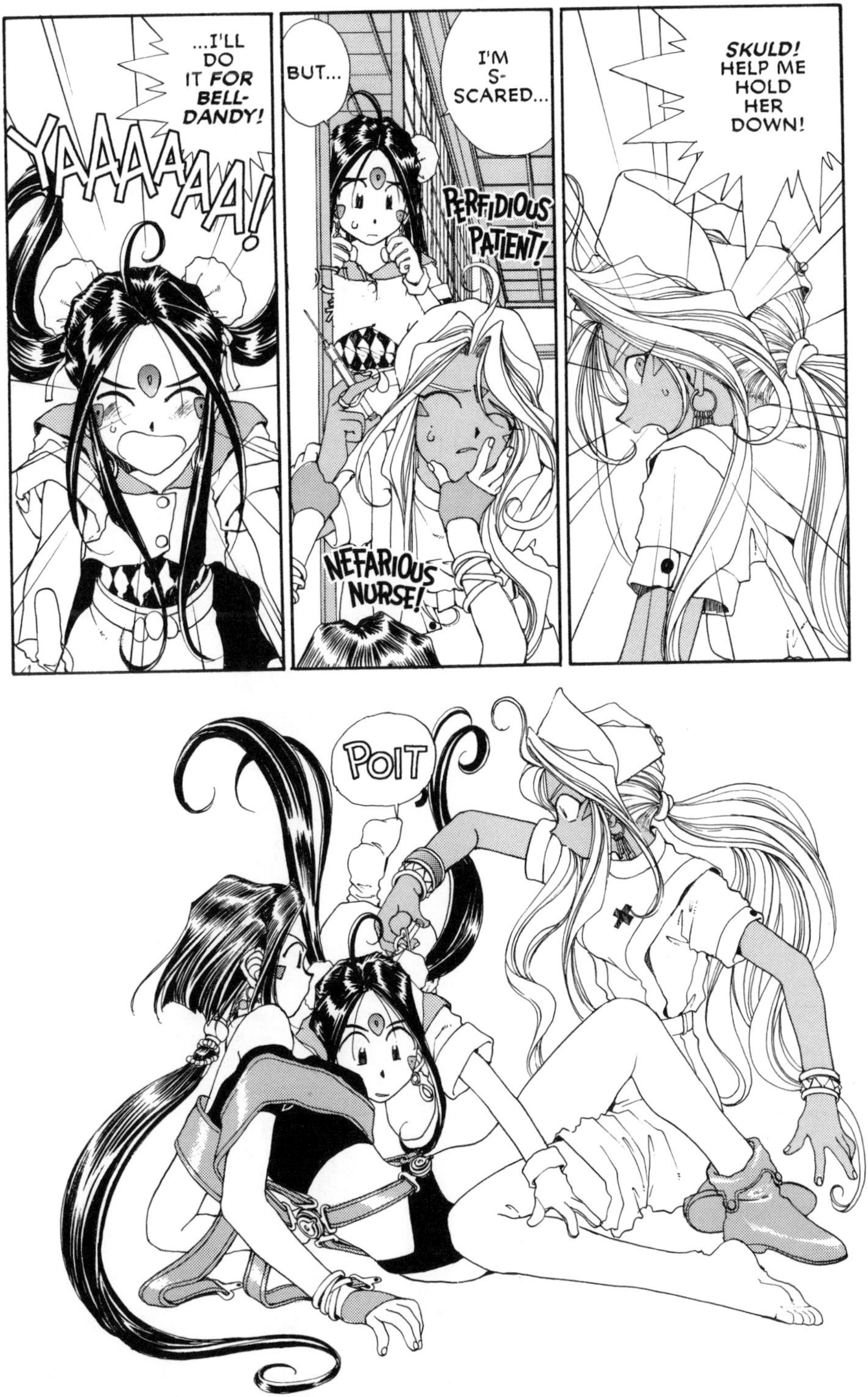
SKULD! HELP ME HOLD HER DOWN!
I'M S-SCARED...
BUT...
PERFIDIOUS PATIENT!
NEFARIOUS NURSE!
...I'LL DO IT FOR BELL-DANDY!
YAAAAAAA!
POIT

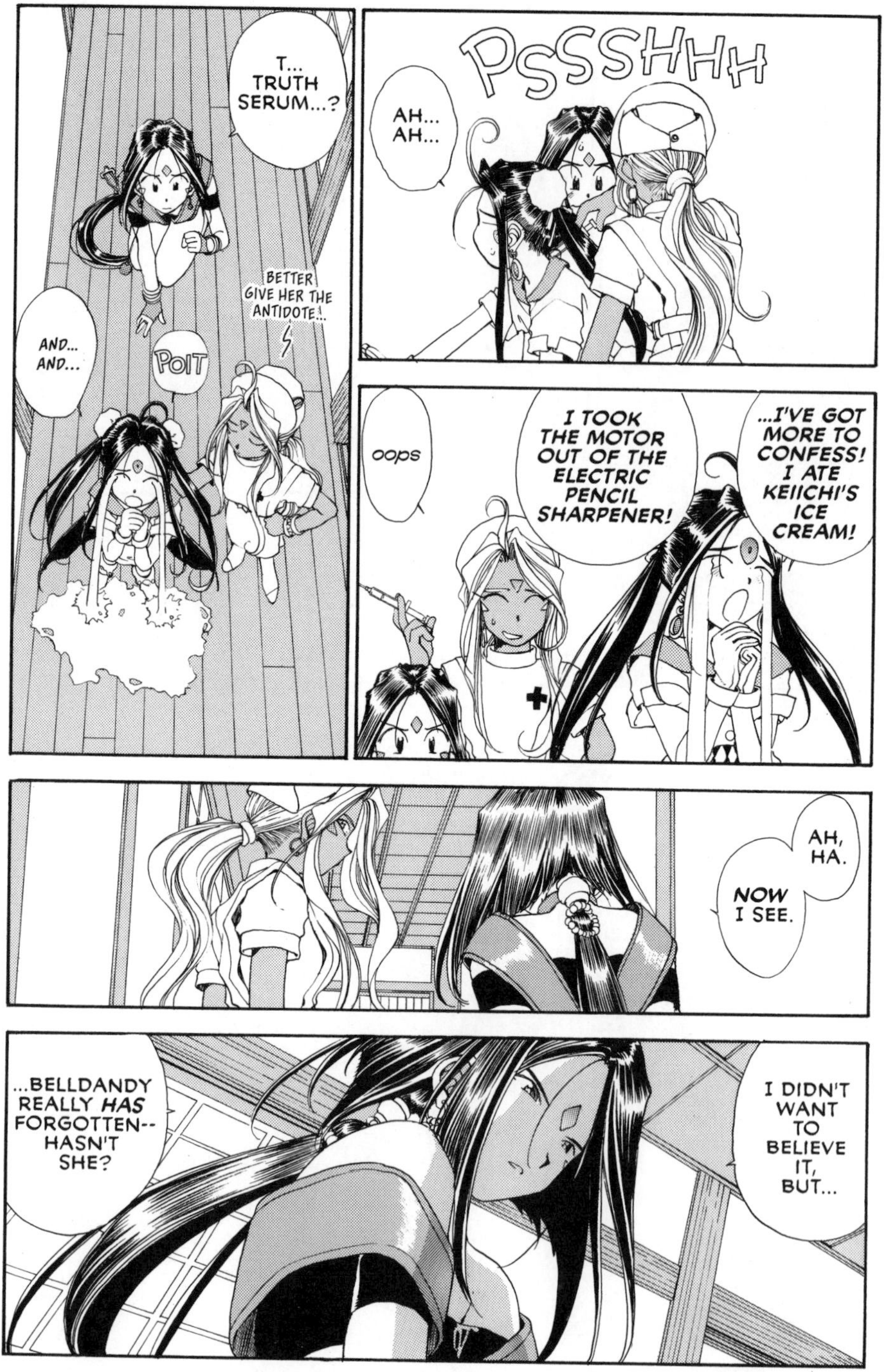
T... TRUTH SERUM...?
AND... AND...
POIT
BETTER GIVE HER THE ANTIDOTE...
PSSSHHH
AH... AH...
...I'VE GOT MORE TO CONFESS! I ATE KEIICHI'S ICE CREAM!
I TOOK THE MOTOR OUT OF THE ELECTRIC PENCIL SHARPENER!
oops
AH, HA. NOW I SEE.
I DIDN'T WANT TO BELIEVE IT, BUT...
...BELLDANDY REALLY HAS FORGOTTEN--HASN'T SHE?

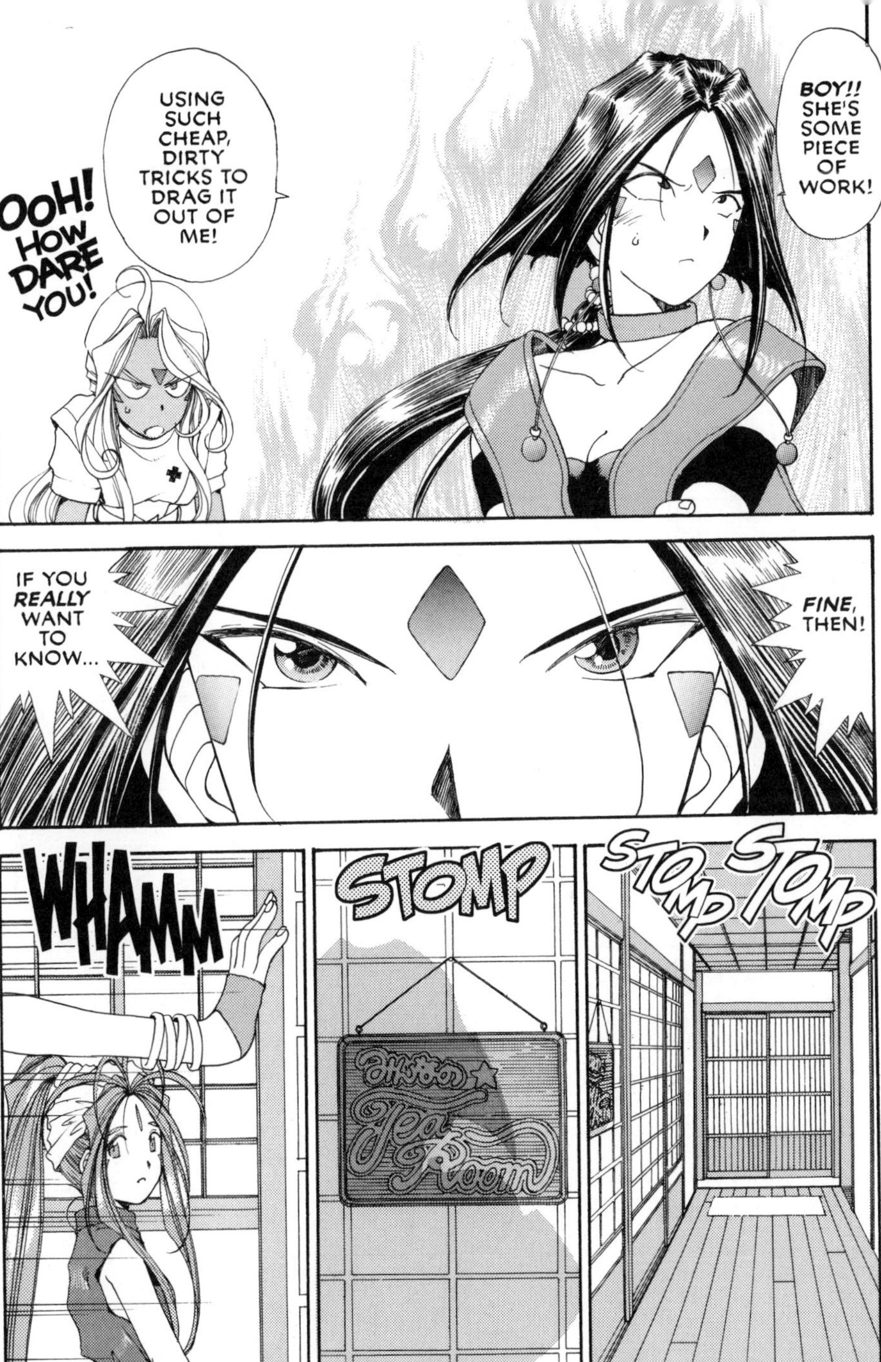
OOH! HOW DARE YOU!
USING SUCH CHEAP, DIRTY TRICKS TO DRAG IT OUT OF ME!
BOY!! SHE'S SOME PIECE OF WORK!
IF YOU REALLY WANT TO KNOW...
FINE, THEN!
WHAMM
STOMP
Tea Room
STOMP STOMP

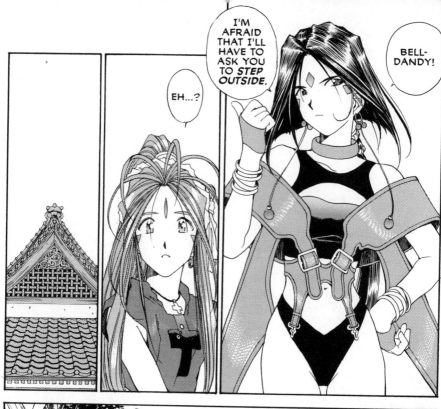

I'M AFRAID THAT I'LL HAVE TO ASK YOU TO *STEP OUTSIDE.*

EH...?

BELL-DANDY!

SSH!

...I WONDER WHAT SHE'S GOING TO DO?

I...

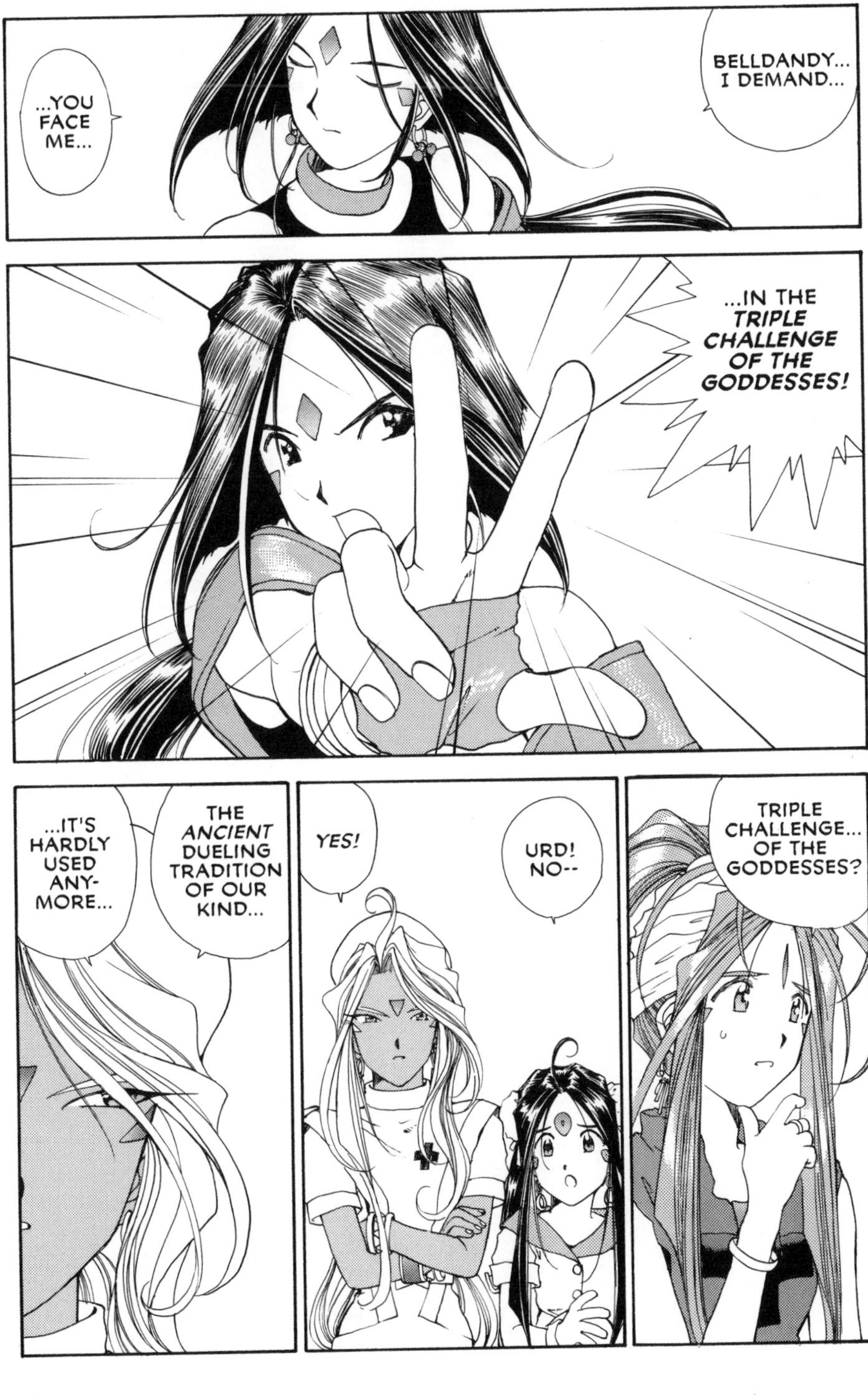
BELLDANDY... I DEMAND...
...YOU FACE ME...
...IN THE *TRIPLE CHALLENGE* OF THE *GODDESSES!*
TRIPLE CHALLENGE... OF THE GODDESSES?
URD! NO--
YES!
THE *ANCIENT* DUELING TRADITION OF OUR KIND...
...IT'S HARDLY USED ANY-MORE...

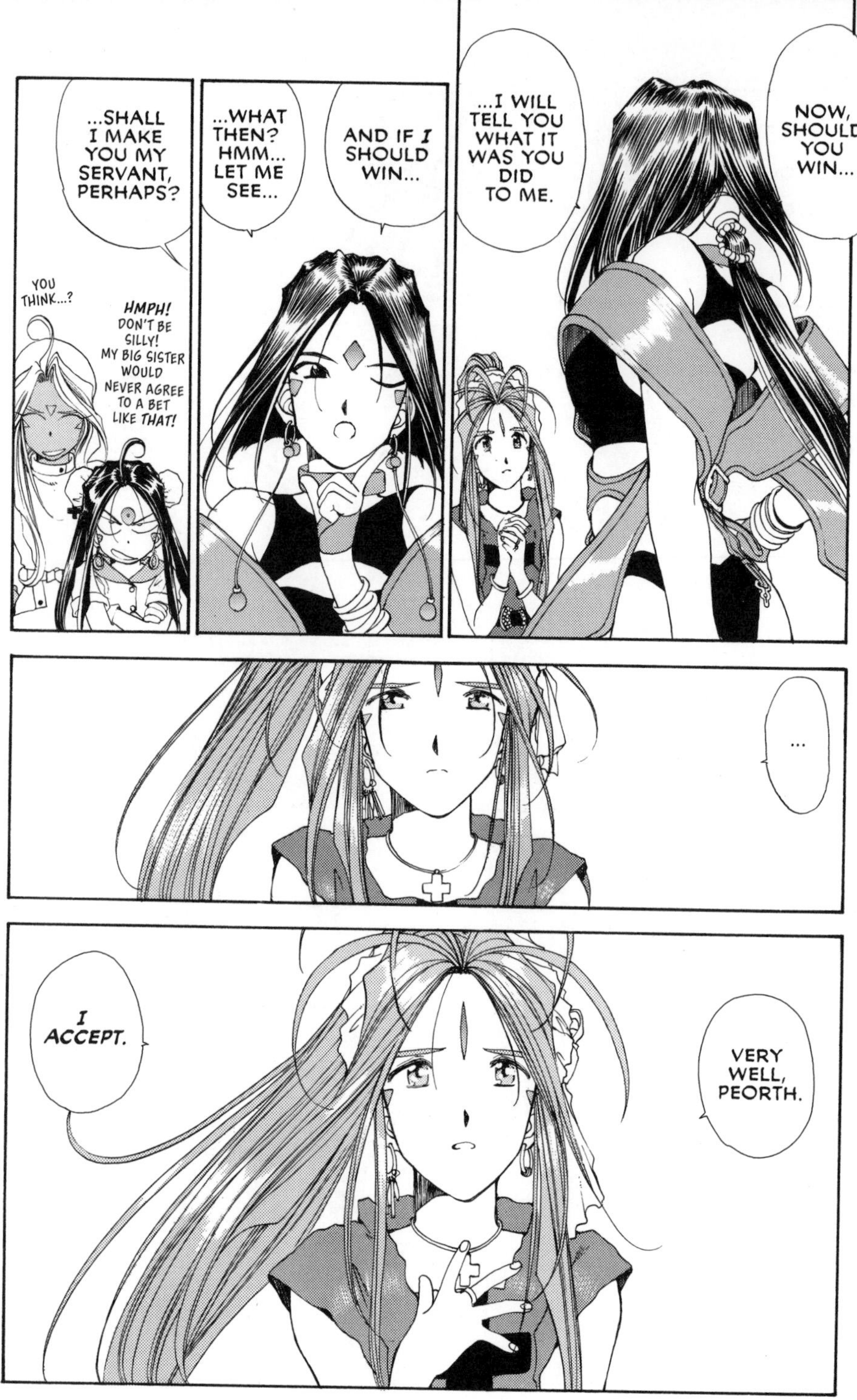
NOW, SHOULD YOU WIN...
...I WILL TELL YOU WHAT IT WAS YOU DID TO ME.
AND IF *I* SHOULD WIN...
...WHAT THEN? HMM... LET ME SEE...
...SHALL I MAKE YOU MY SERVANT, PERHAPS?
HMPH! DON'T BE SILLY! MY BIG SISTER WOULD NEVER AGREE TO A BET LIKE *THAT!*
YOU THINK...?
...
VERY WELL, PEORTH.
I ACCEPT.

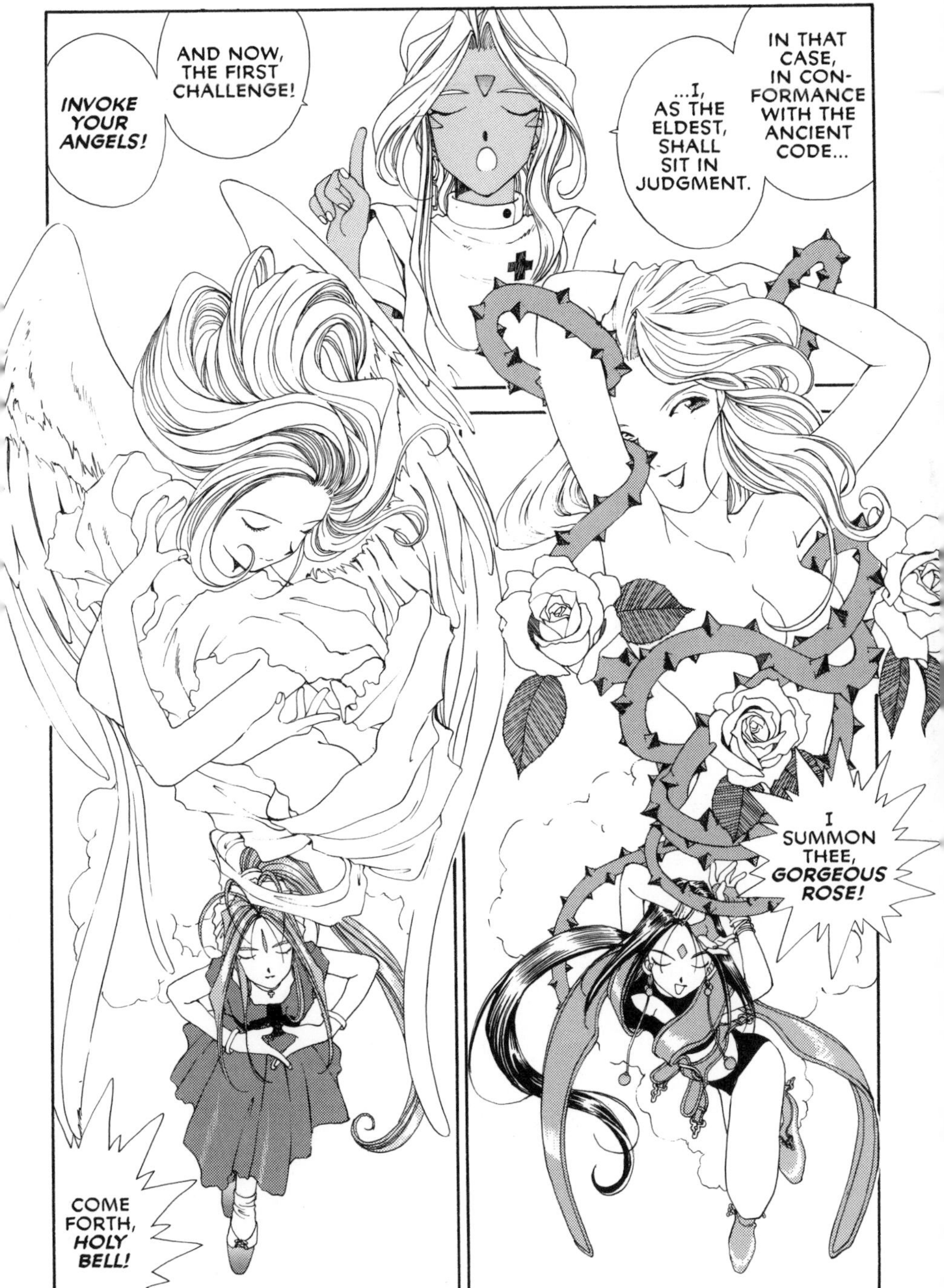
IN THAT CASE, IN CONFORMANCE WITH THE ANCIENT CODE...
...I, AS THE ELDEST, SHALL SIT IN JUDGMENT.
AND NOW, THE FIRST CHALLENGE!
INVOKE YOUR ANGELS!
I SUMMON THEE, ***GORGEOUS ROSE!***
COME FORTH, ***HOLY BELL!***

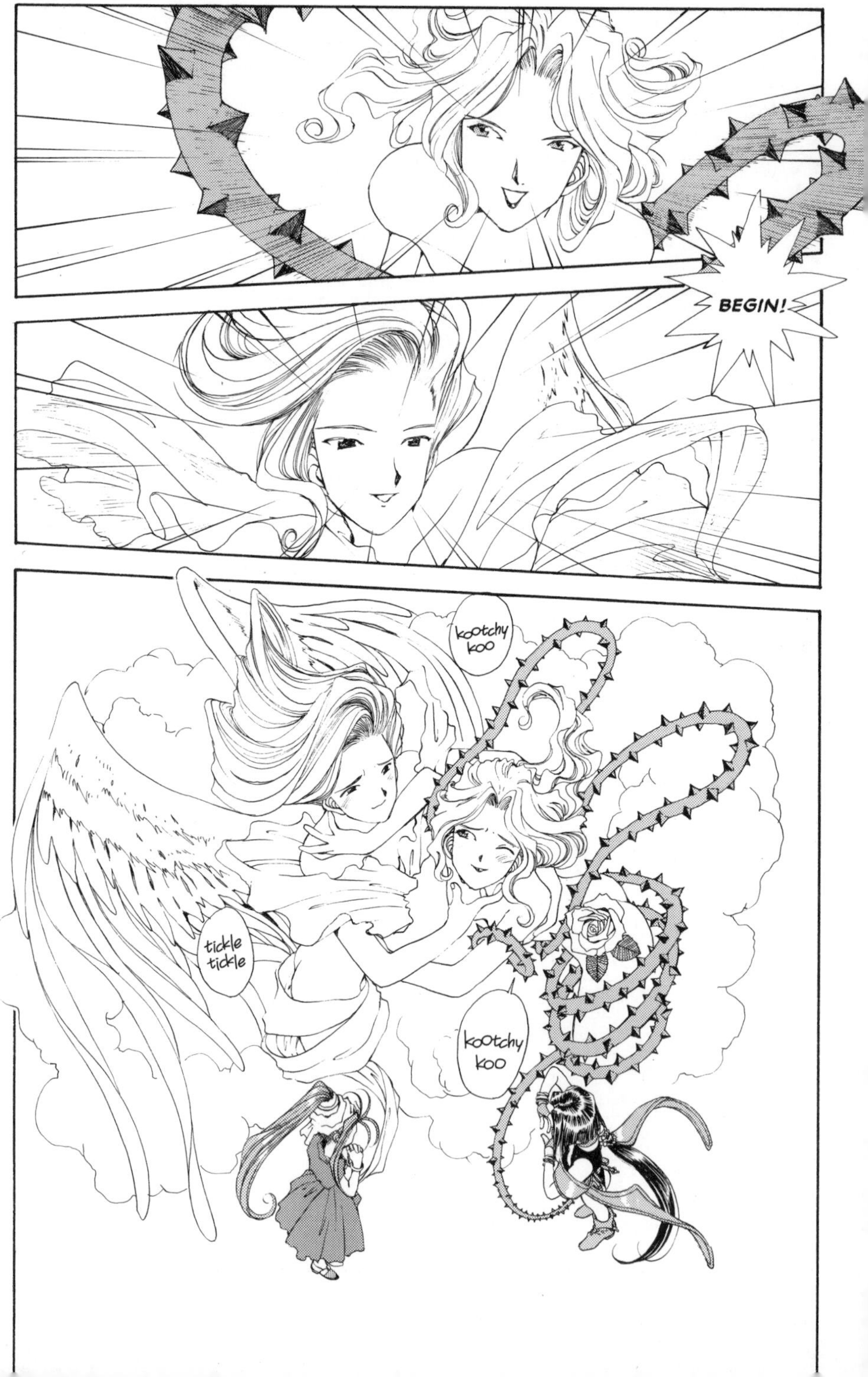
BEGIN!
kootchy koo
kootchy koo
tickle tickle

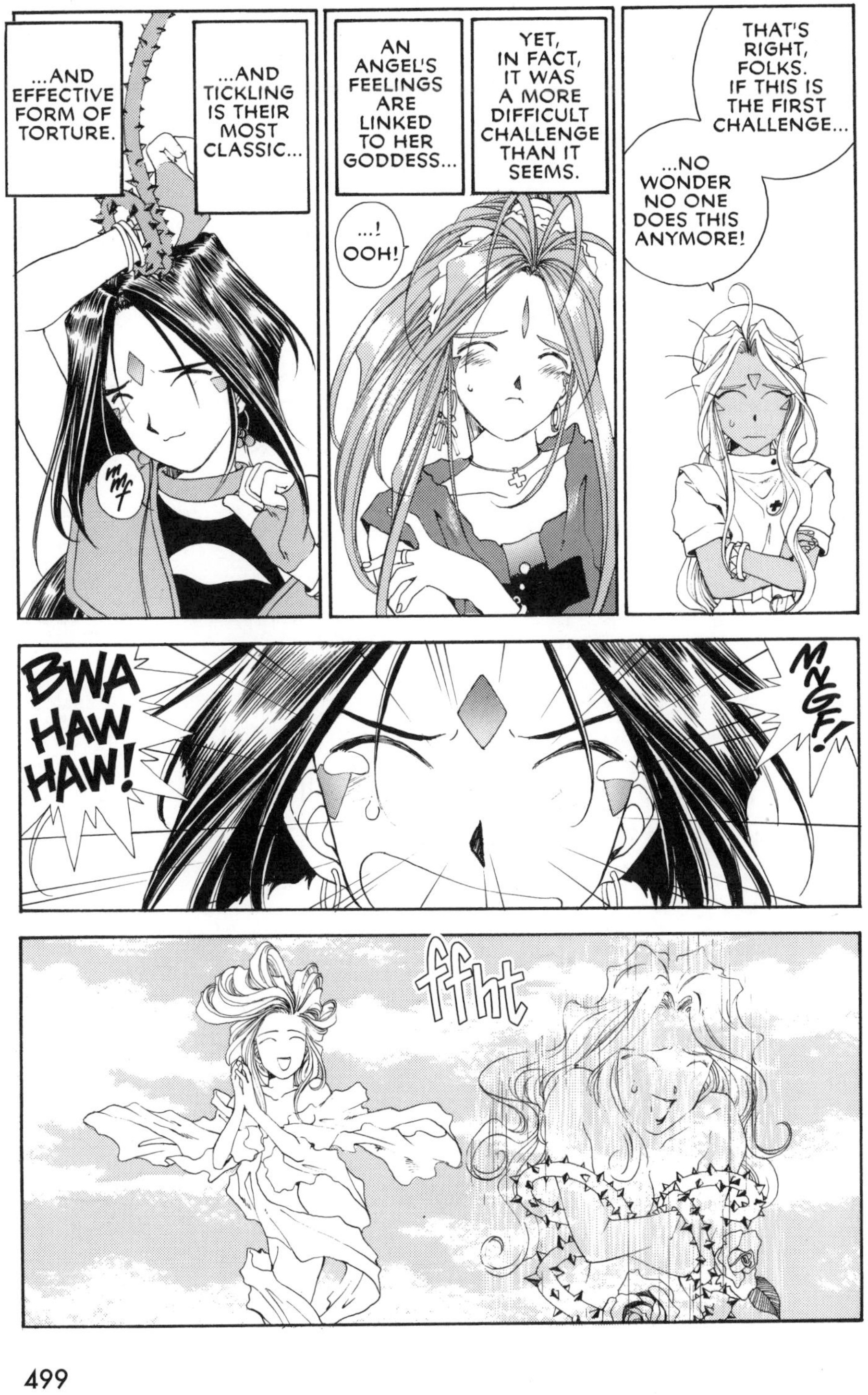

...AND TICKLING IS THEIR MOST CLASSIC...
...AND EFFECTIVE FORM OF TORTURE.
MMF
AN ANGEL'S FEELINGS ARE LINKED TO HER GODDESS...
YET, IN FACT, IT WAS A MORE DIFFICULT CHALLENGE THAN IT SEEMS.
...! OOH!
THAT'S RIGHT, FOLKS. IF THIS IS THE FIRST CHALLENGE...
...NO WONDER NO ONE DOES THIS ANYMORE!
BWA HAW HAW!
MNGF!
ffht

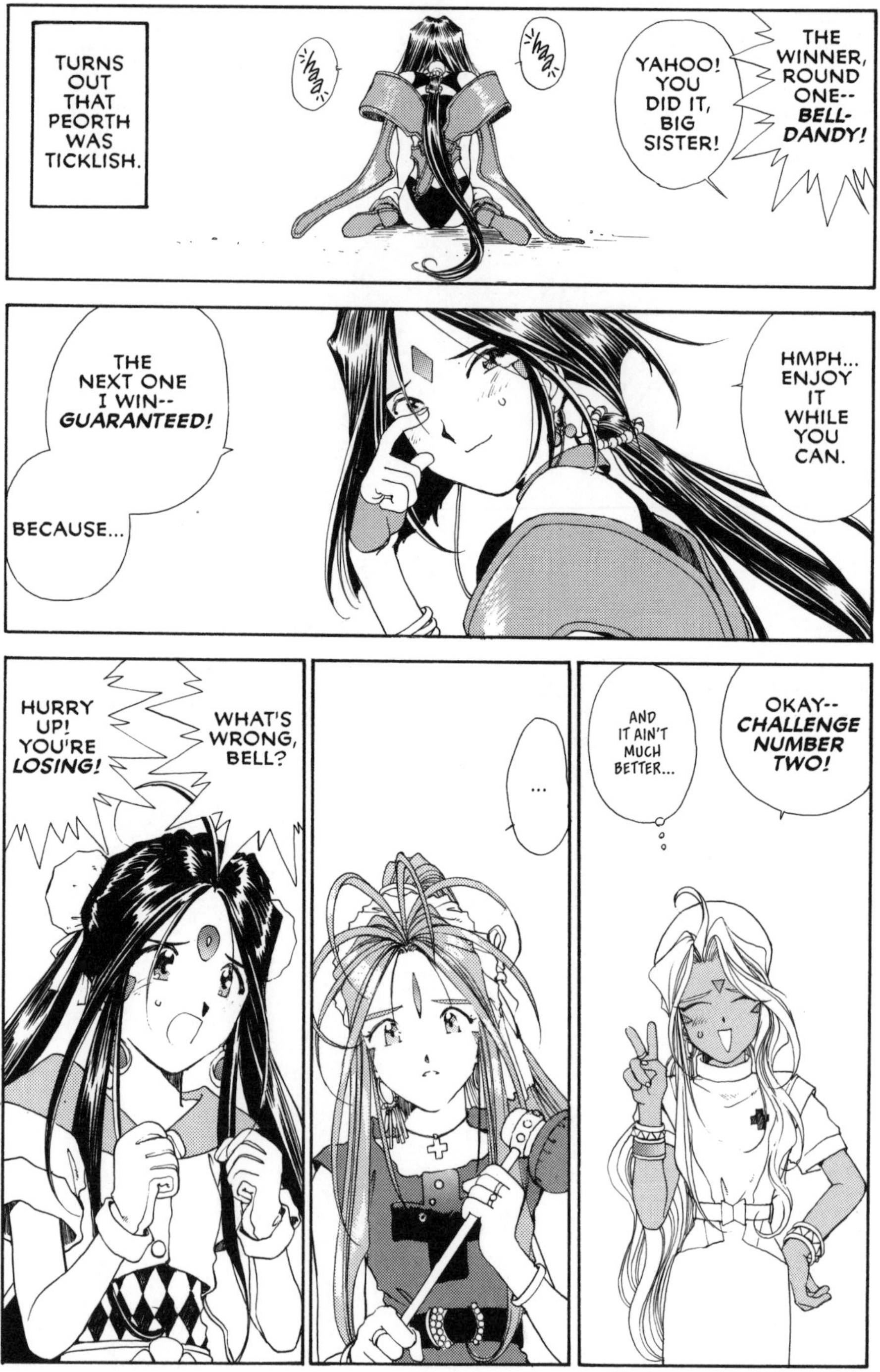
THE WINNER, ROUND ONE-- *BELL-DANDY!*
YAHOO! YOU DID IT, BIG SISTER!
TURNS OUT THAT PEORTH WAS TICKLISH.
HMPH... ENJOY IT WHILE YOU CAN.
THE NEXT ONE I WIN-- *GUARANTEED!*
BECAUSE...
OKAY-- *CHALLENGE NUMBER TWO!*
AND IT AIN'T MUCH BETTER...
...
WHAT'S WRONG, BELL?
HURRY UP! YOU'RE *LOSING!*

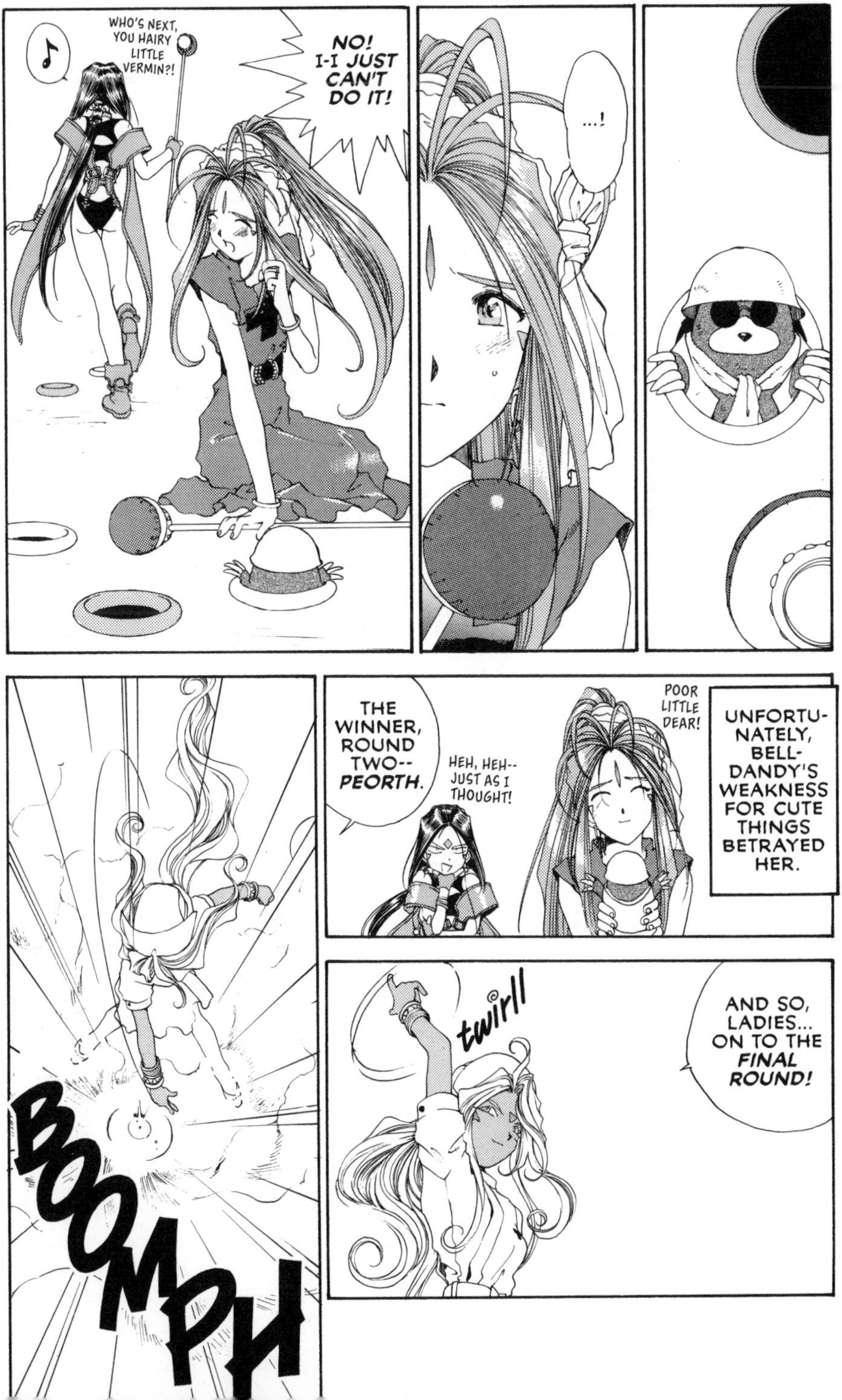

♪
WHO'S NEXT, YOU HAIRY LITTLE VERMIN?!
NO! I-I JUST CAN'T DO IT!
...!
BOOMPH
THE WINNER, ROUND TWO-- PEORTH.
HEH, HEH-- JUST AS I THOUGHT!
POOR LITTLE DEAR!
UNFORTU-NATELY, BELL-DANDY'S WEAKNESS FOR CUTE THINGS BETRAYED HER.
twirl!
AND SO, LADIES... ON TO THE FINAL ROUND!

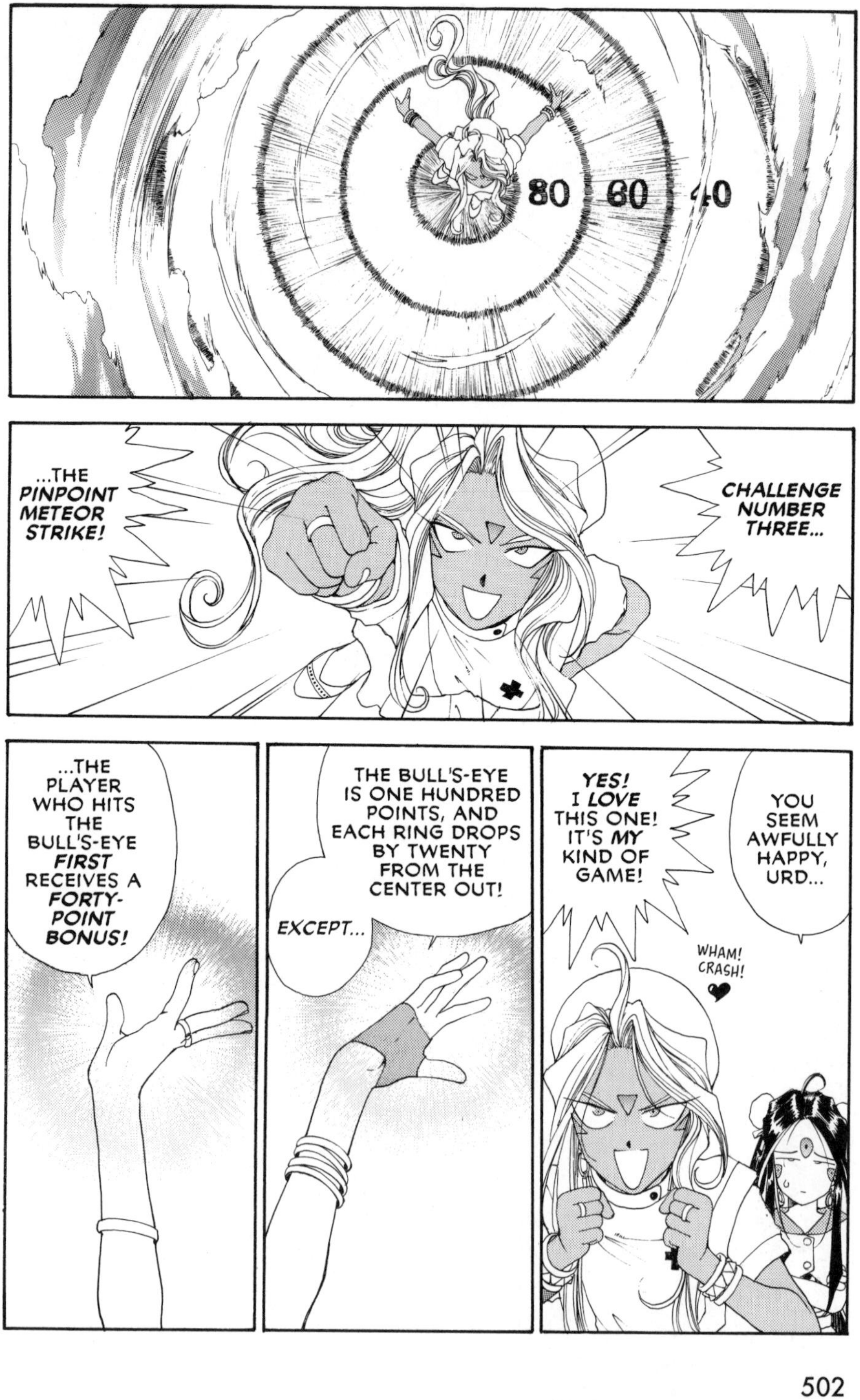
80
60
40
CHALLENGE NUMBER THREE...
...THE PINPOINT METEOR STRIKE!
YOU SEEM AWFULLY HAPPY, URD...
YES! I LOVE THIS ONE! IT'S MY KIND OF GAME!
WHAM! CRASH!
THE BULL'S-EYE IS ONE HUNDRED POINTS, AND EACH RING DROPS BY TWENTY FROM THE CENTER OUT!
EXCEPT...
...THE PLAYER WHO HITS THE BULL'S-EYE FIRST RECEIVES A FORTY-POINT BONUS!

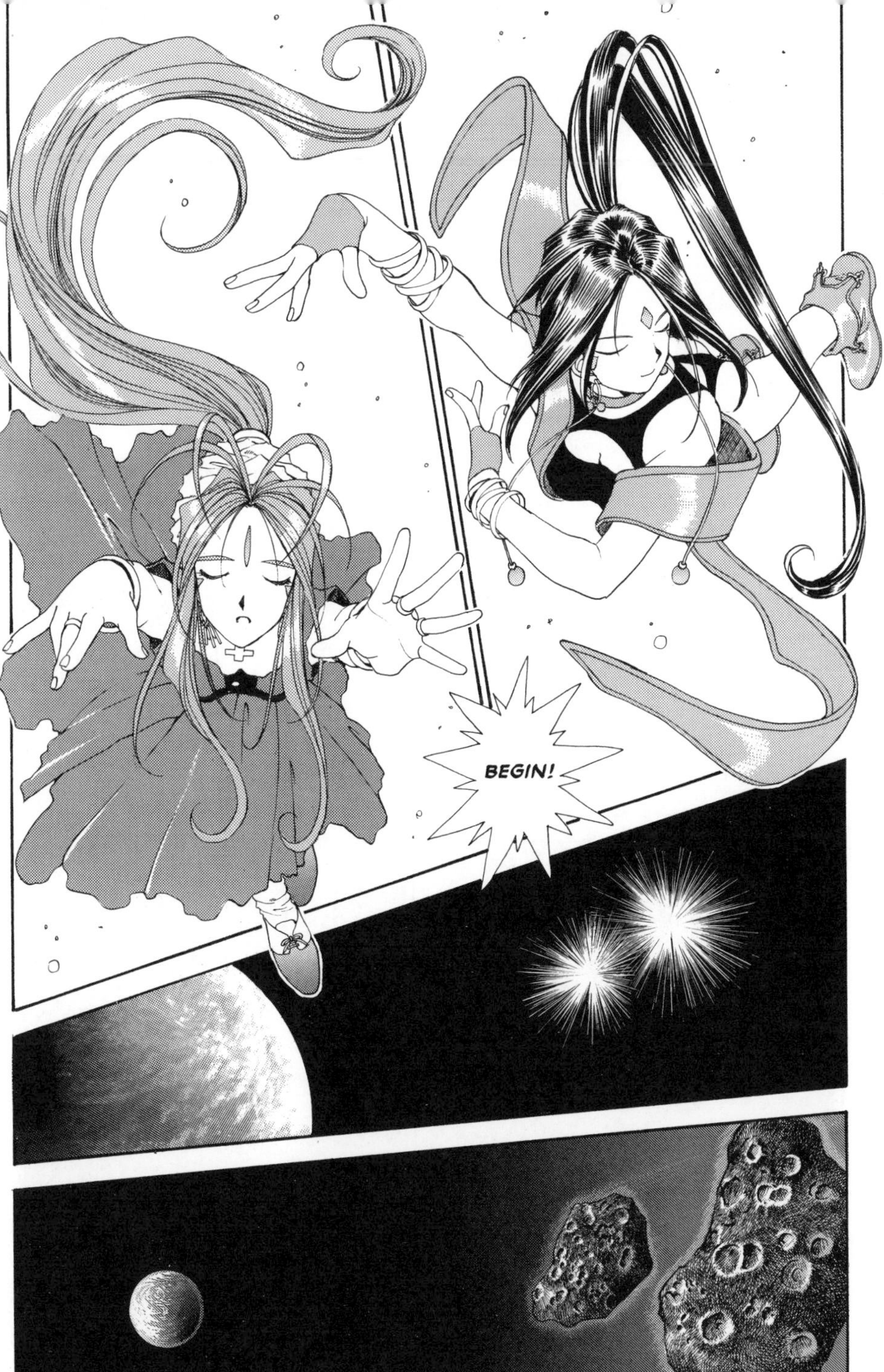
BEGIN!

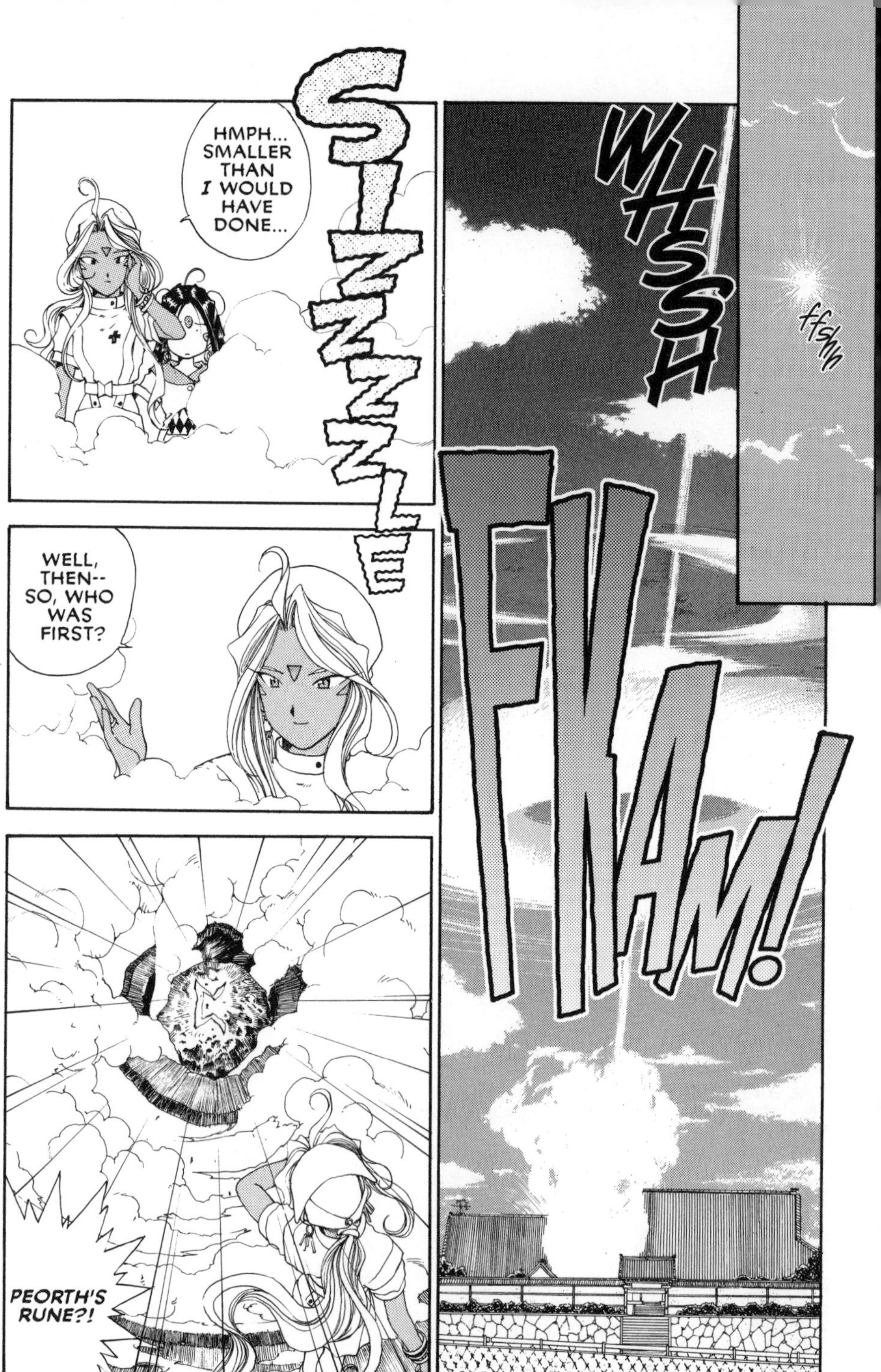

ffshh
WHSSH
FWAM!
SIZZZZLE
HMPH... SMALLER THAN *I* WOULD HAVE DONE...
WELL, THEN-- SO, WHO WAS FIRST?
PEORTH'S RUNE?!

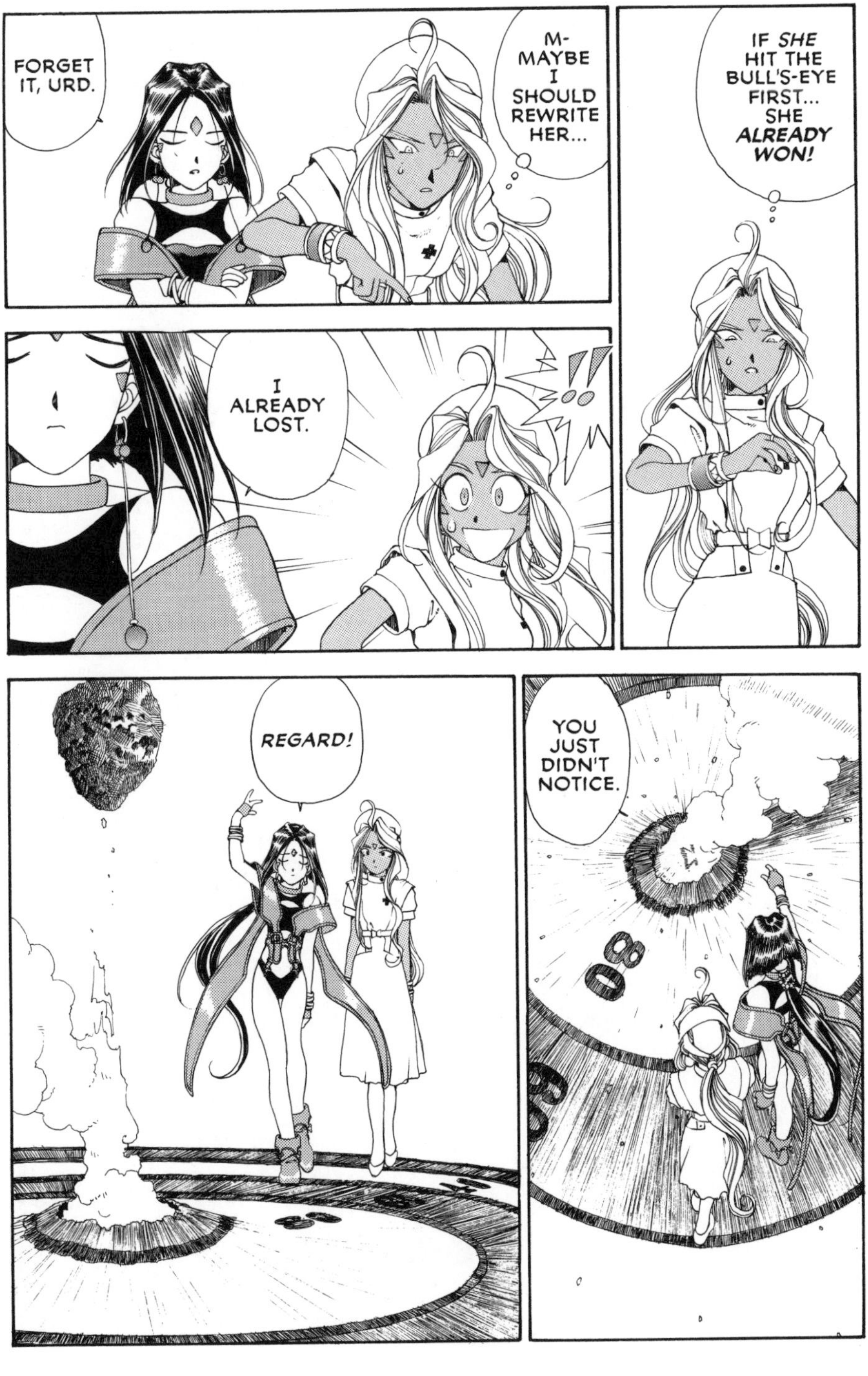
M-MAYBE I SHOULD REWRITE HER...
FORGET IT, URD.
IF *SHE* HIT THE BULL'S-EYE FIRST... SHE *ALREADY WON!*
I ALREADY LOST.
!!
REGARD!
YOU JUST DIDN'T NOTICE.

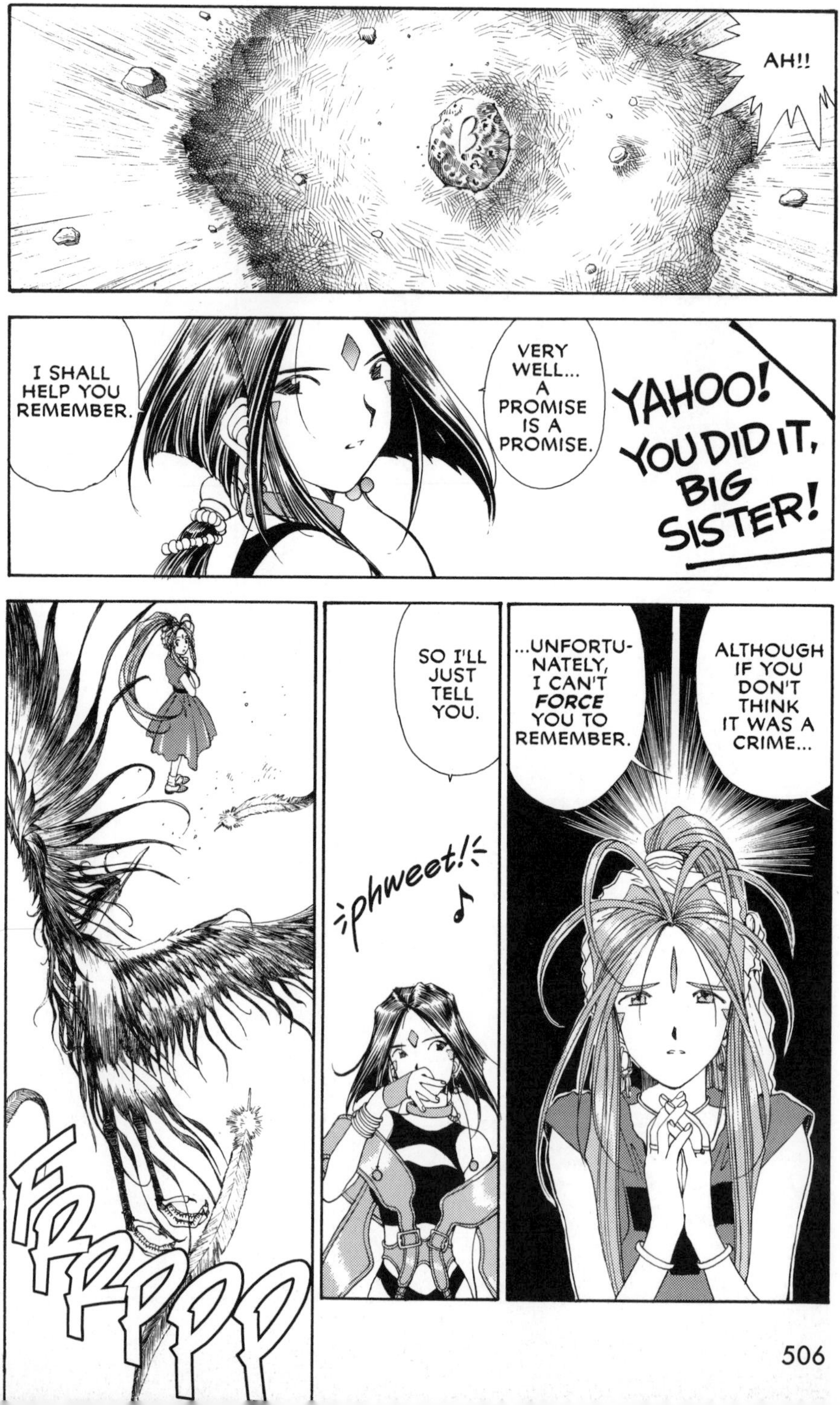
AH!!
YAHOO! YOU DID IT, BIG SISTER!
VERY WELL... A PROMISE IS A PROMISE.
I SHALL HELP YOU REMEMBER.
ALTHOUGH IF YOU DON'T THINK IT WAS A CRIME...
...UNFORTUNATELY, I CAN'T *FORCE* YOU TO REMEMBER.
SO I'LL JUST TELL YOU.
phweet! ♪
FRRPPP

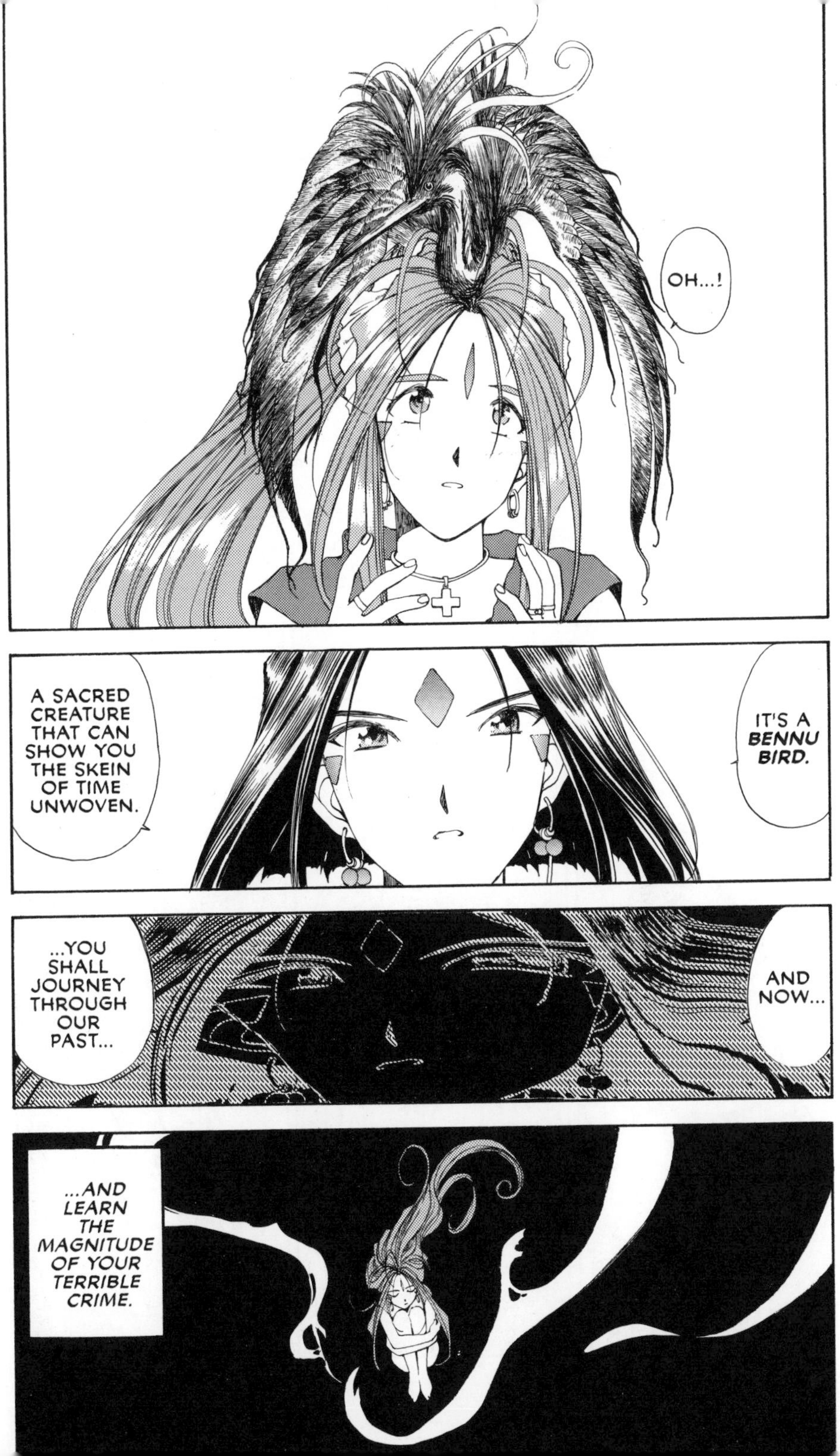
OH...!
IT'S A BENNU BIRD.
A SACRED CREATURE THAT CAN SHOW YOU THE SKEIN OF TIME UNWOVEN.
AND NOW...
...YOU SHALL JOURNEY THROUGH OUR PAST...
...AND LEARN THE MAGNITUDE OF YOUR TERRIBLE CRIME.

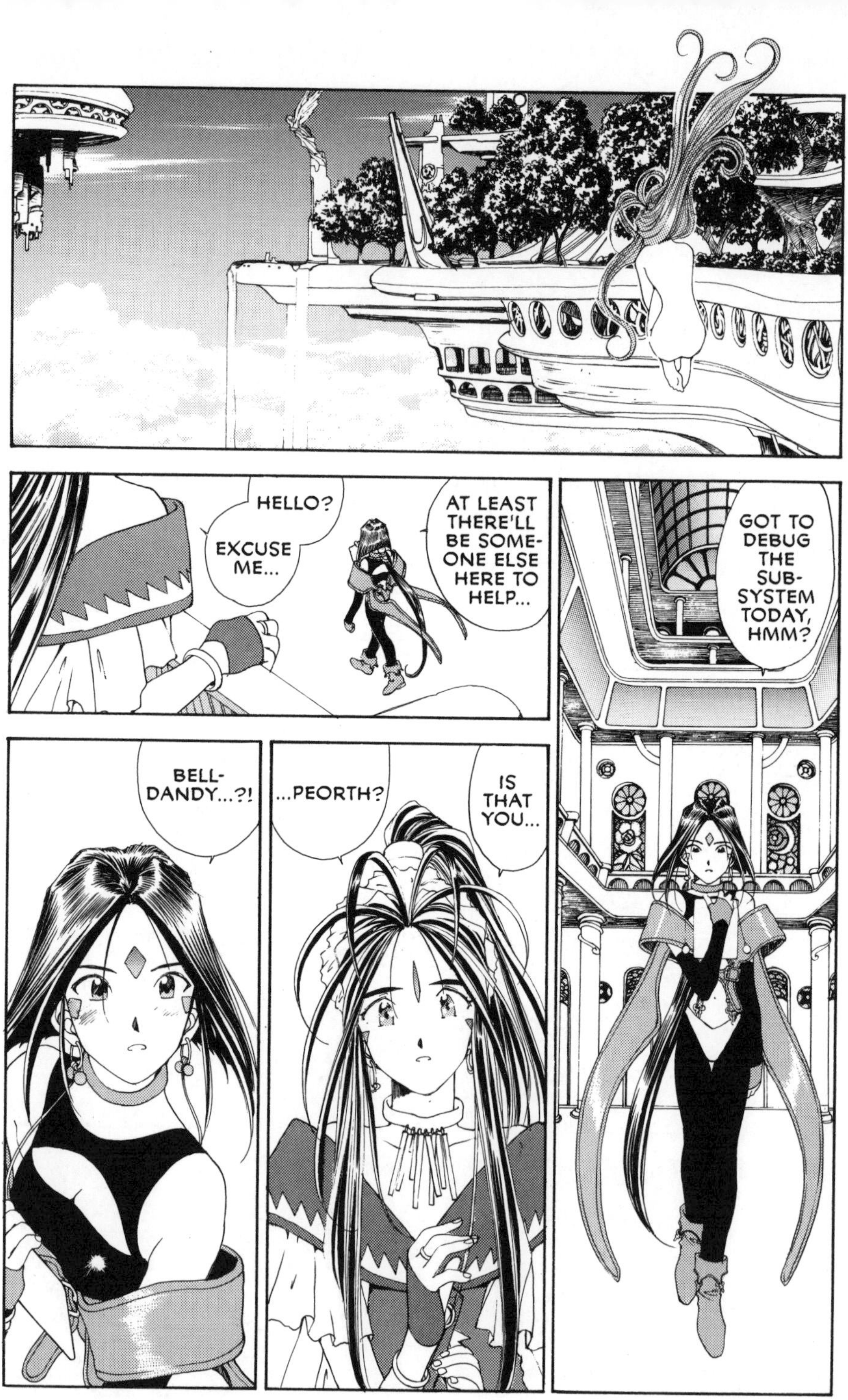
GOT TO DEBUG THE SUB-SYSTEM TODAY, HMM?
AT LEAST THERE'LL BE SOME-ONE ELSE HERE TO HELP...
HELLO?
EXCUSE ME...
IS THAT YOU...
...PEORTH?
BELL-DANDY...?!

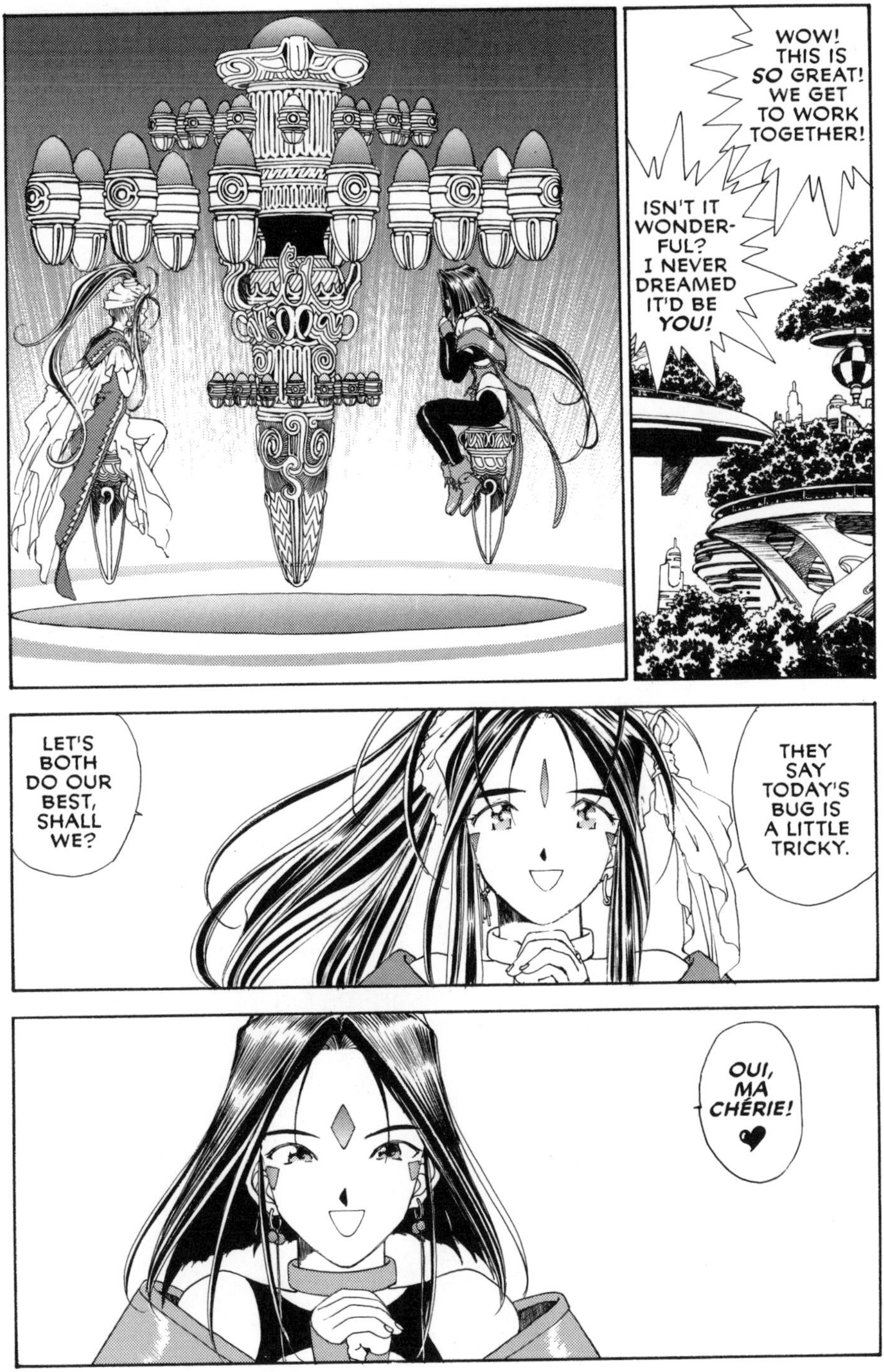
WOW! THIS IS *SO* GREAT! WE GET TO WORK TOGETHER!
ISN'T IT WONDER-FUL? I NEVER DREAMED IT'D BE *YOU!*
THEY SAY TODAY'S BUG IS A LITTLE TRICKY.
LET'S BOTH DO OUR BEST, SHALL WE?
OUI, MA CHÉRIE! ♥

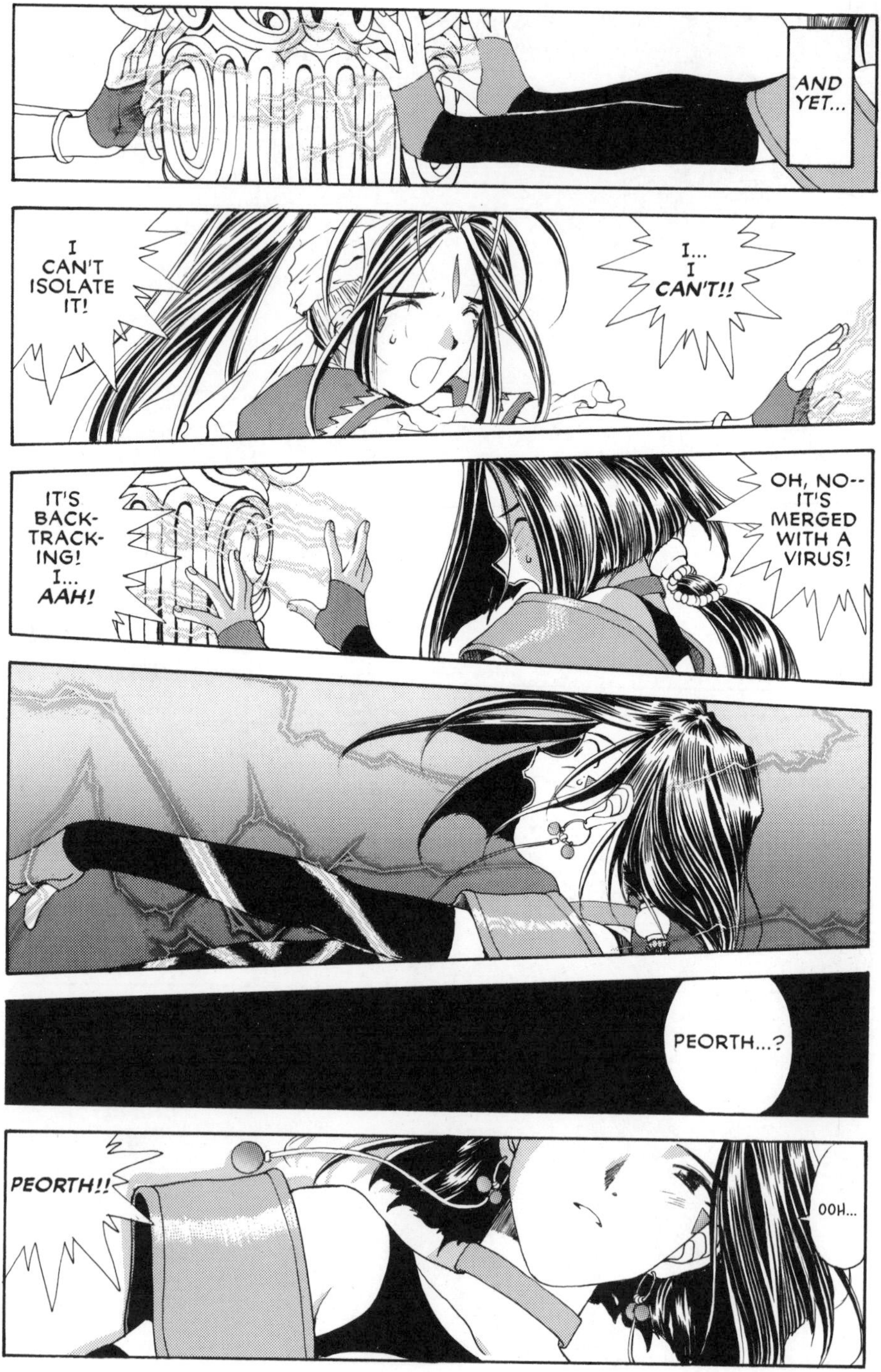
AND YET...
I... I CAN'T!!
I CAN'T ISOLATE IT!
OH, NO-- IT'S MERGED WITH A VIRUS!
IT'S BACK-TRACKING! I... AAH!
PEORTH...?
OOH...
PEORTH!!

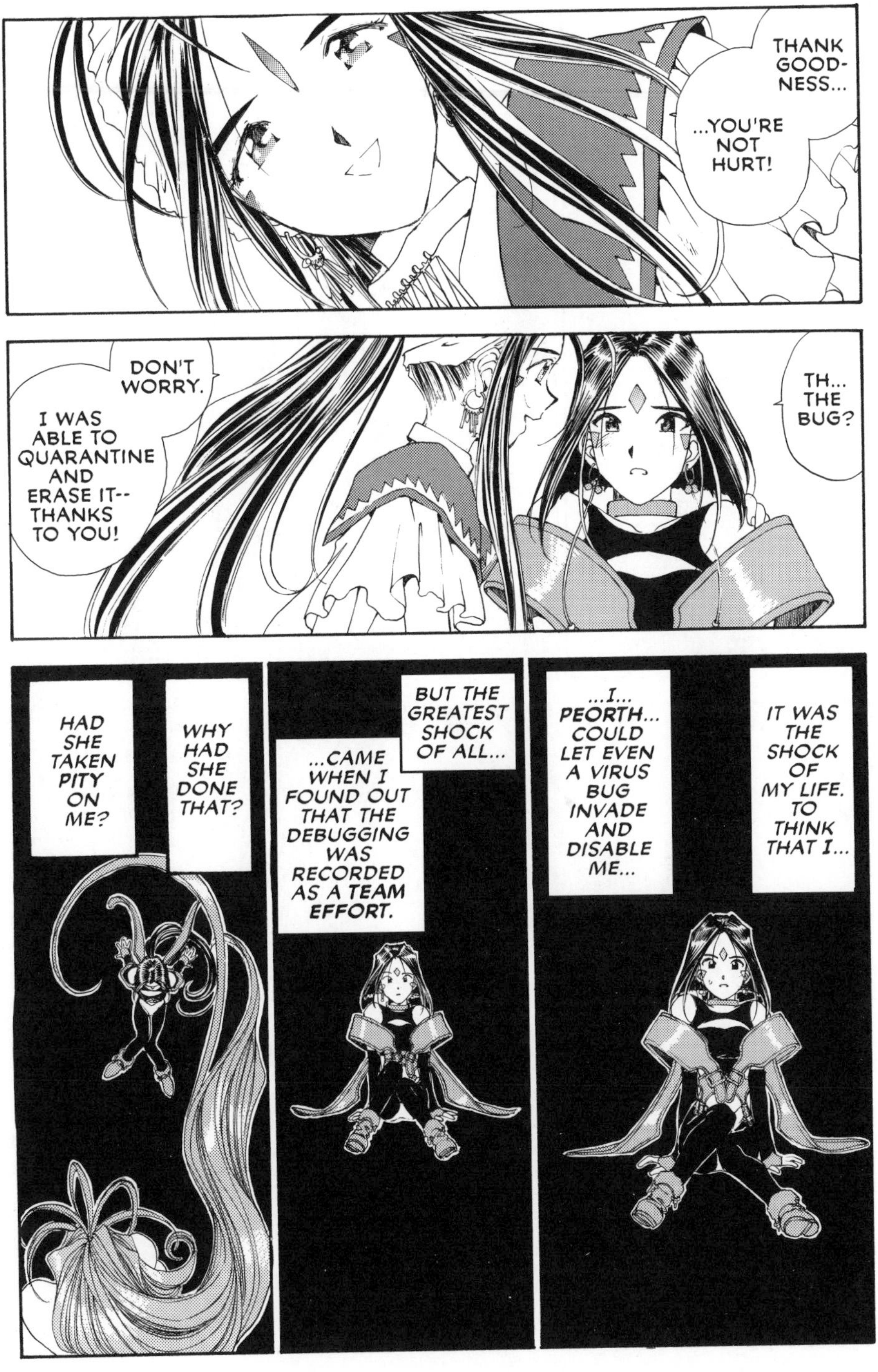
THANK GOODNESS...
...YOU'RE NOT HURT!
TH... THE BUG?
DON'T WORRY.
I WAS ABLE TO QUARANTINE AND ERASE IT-- THANKS TO YOU!
IT WAS THE SHOCK OF MY LIFE. TO THINK THAT I...
...I... PEORTH... COULD LET EVEN A VIRUS BUG INVADE AND DISABLE ME...
BUT THE GREATEST SHOCK OF ALL...
...CAME WHEN I FOUND OUT THAT THE DEBUGGING WAS RECORDED AS A TEAM EFFORT.
WHY HAD SHE DONE THAT?
HAD SHE TAKEN PITY ON ME?

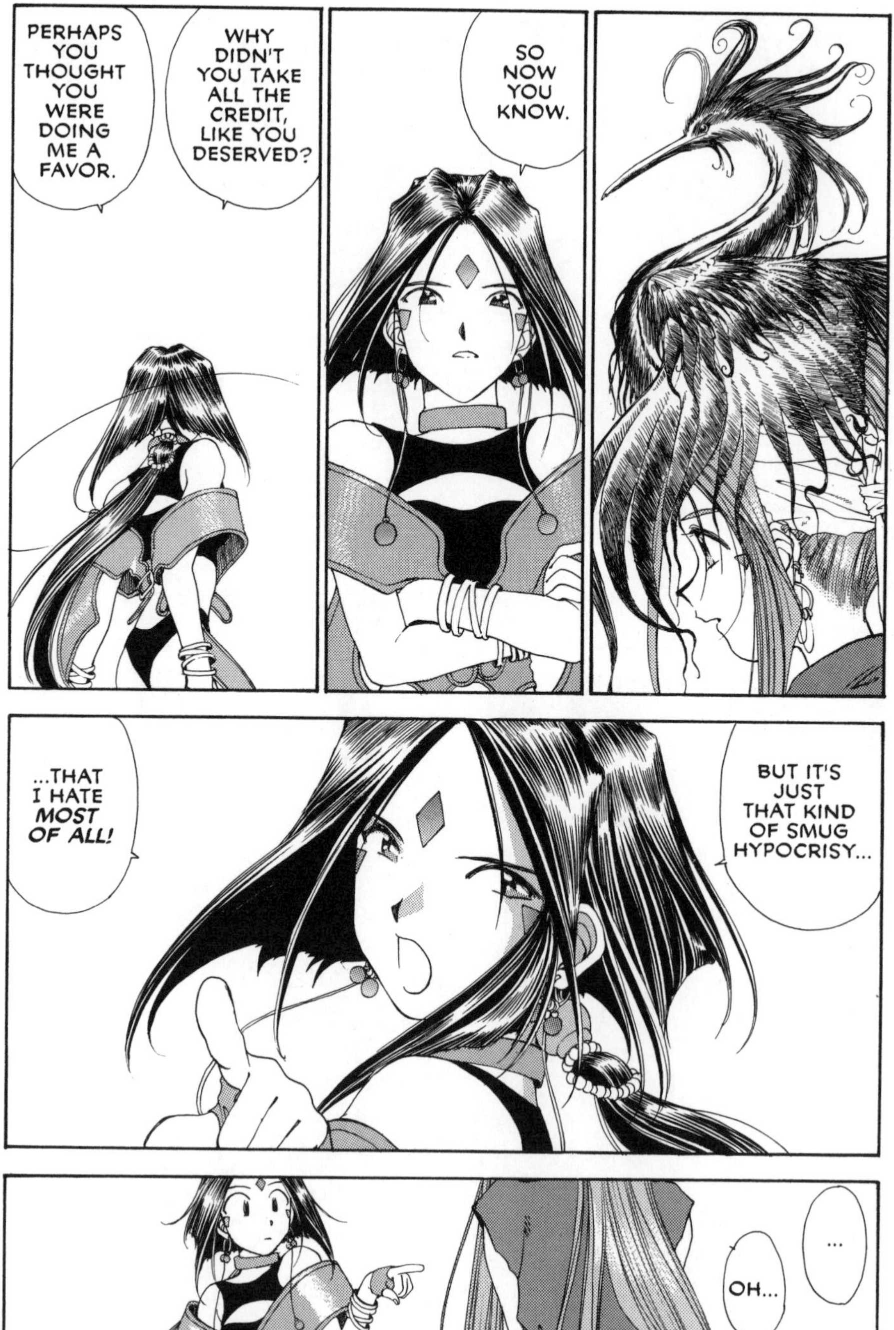
SO NOW YOU KNOW.
WHY DIDN'T YOU TAKE ALL THE CREDIT, LIKE YOU DESERVED?
PERHAPS YOU THOUGHT YOU WERE DOING ME A FAVOR.
BUT IT'S JUST THAT KIND OF SMUG HYPOCRISY...
...THAT I HATE *MOST OF ALL!*
...
OH...

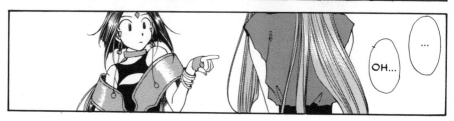

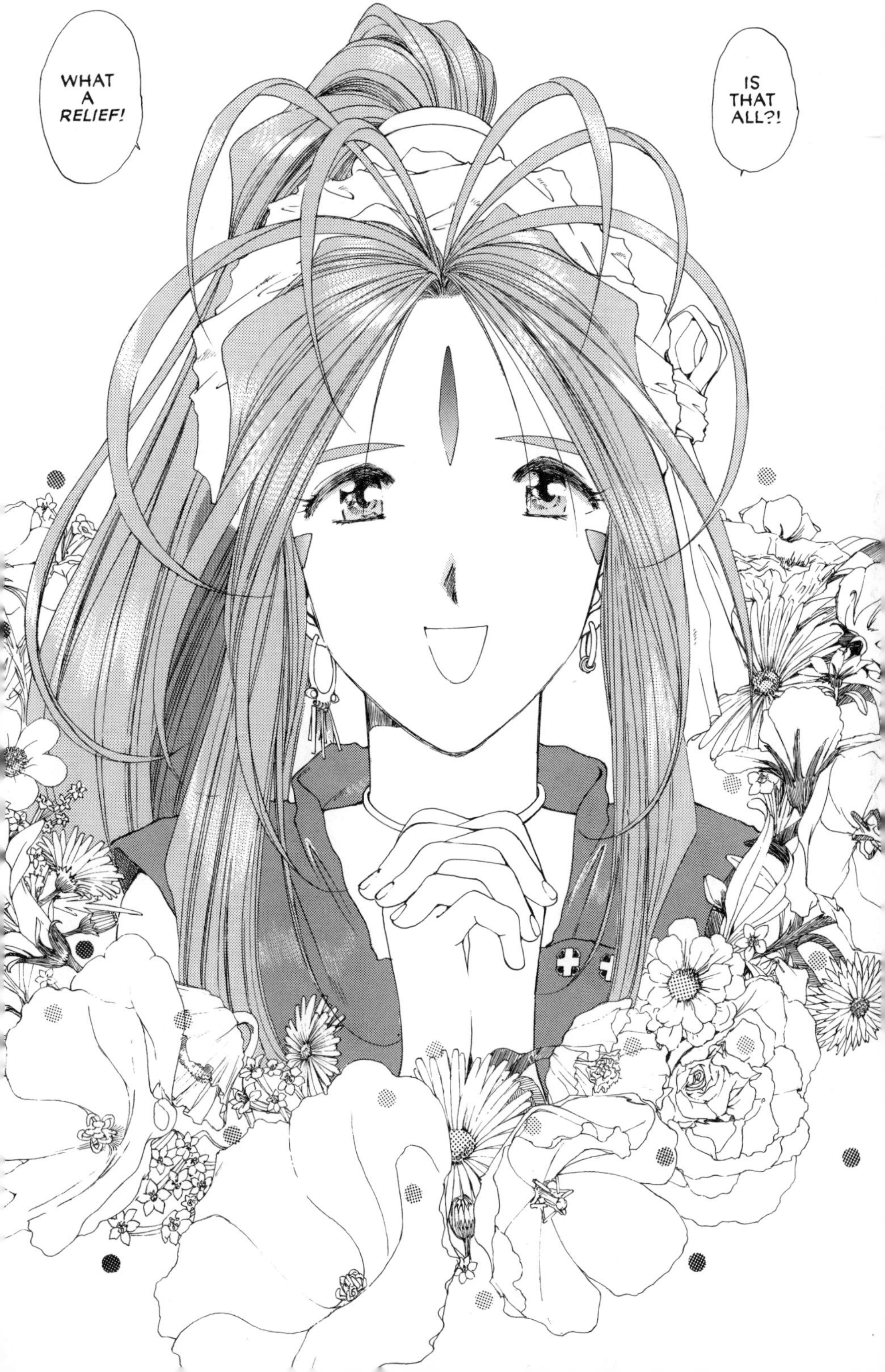
IS THAT ALL?!
WHAT A *RELIEF!*

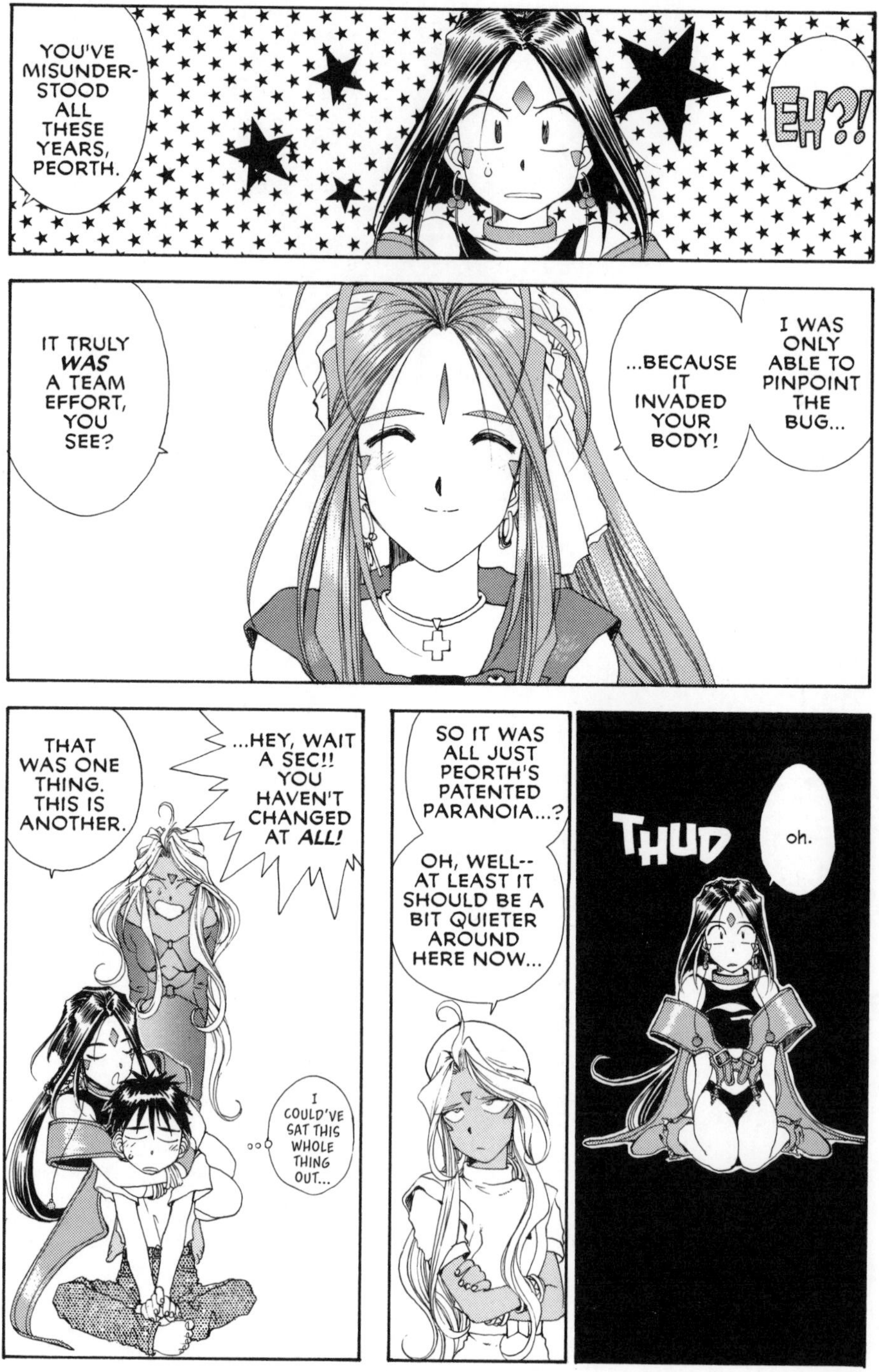
EH?!
YOU'VE MISUNDER-STOOD ALL THESE YEARS, PEORTH.
I WAS ONLY ABLE TO PINPOINT THE BUG...
...BECAUSE IT INVADED YOUR BODY!
IT TRULY *WAS* A TEAM EFFORT, YOU SEE?
THUD
oh.
SO IT WAS ALL JUST PEORTH'S PATENTED PARANOIA...?
OH, WELL-- AT LEAST IT SHOULD BE A BIT QUIETER AROUND HERE NOW...
...HEY, WAIT A SEC!! YOU HAVEN'T CHANGED AT *ALL!*
THAT WAS ONE THING. THIS IS ANOTHER.
I COULD'VE SAT THIS WHOLE THING OUT...

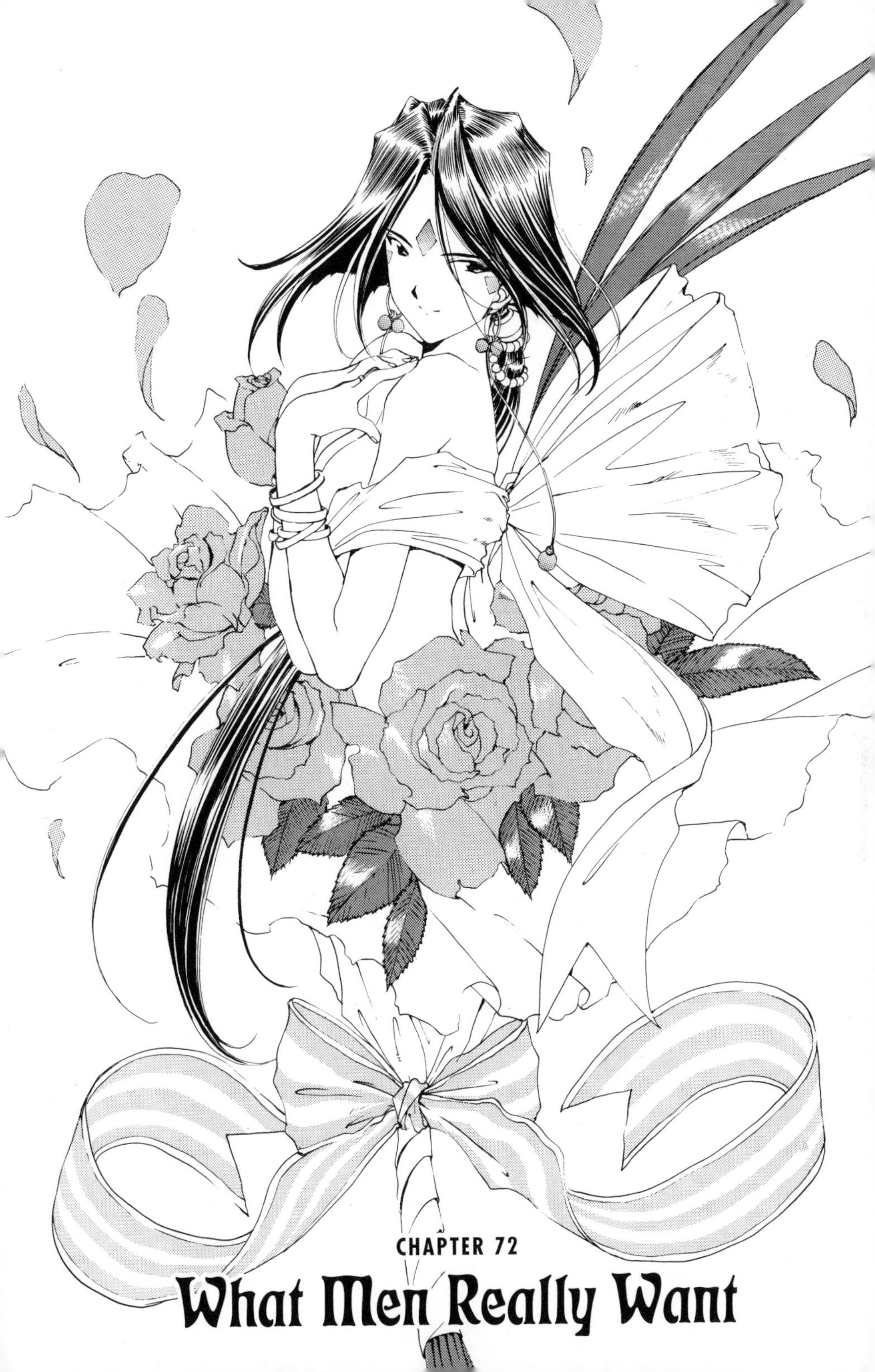

CHAPTER 72

What Men Really Want

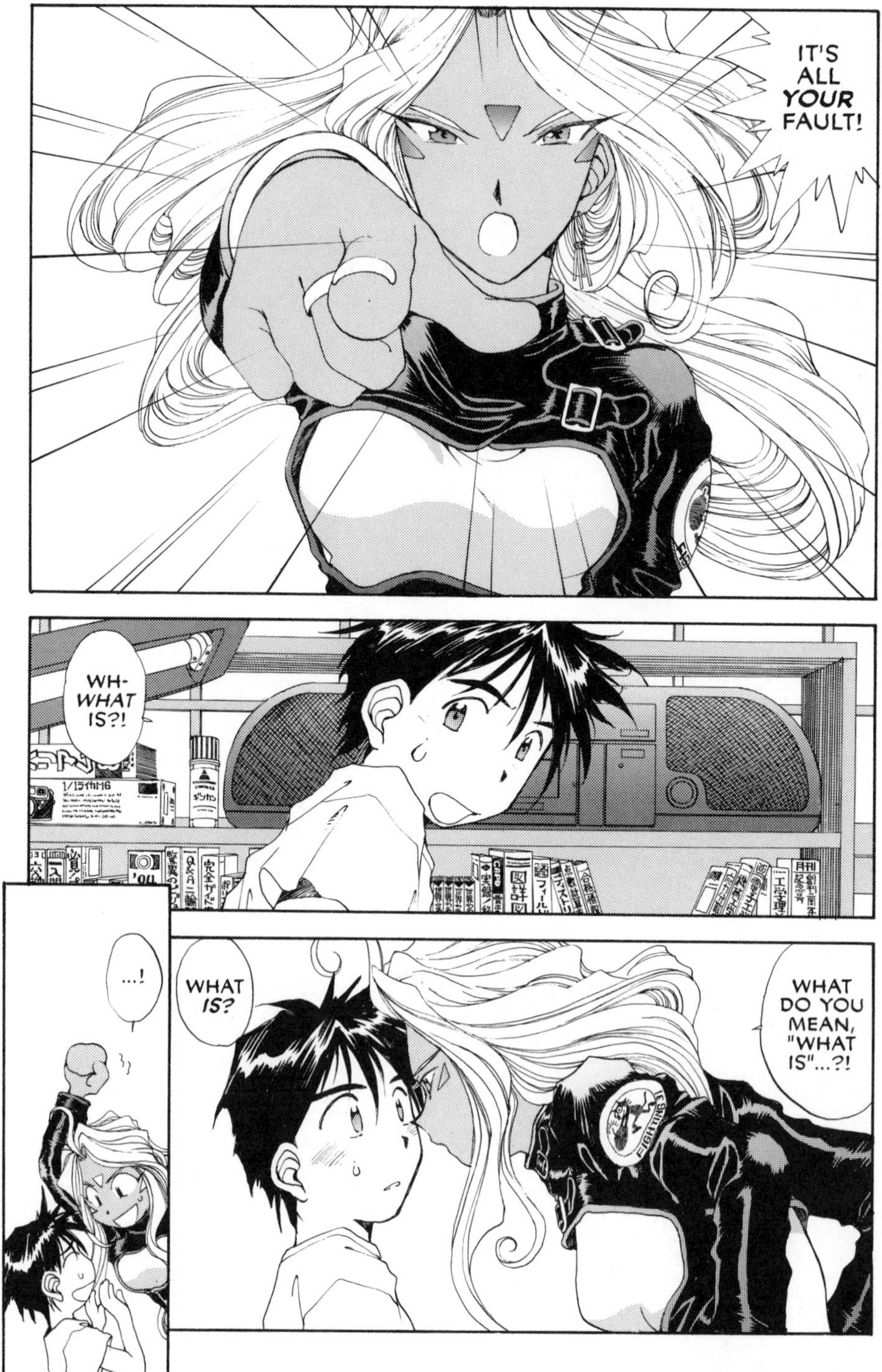

IT'S ALL *YOUR* FAULT!
WH- *WHAT* IS?!
WHAT DO YOU MEAN, "WHAT IS"...?!
WHAT *IS*?
...!

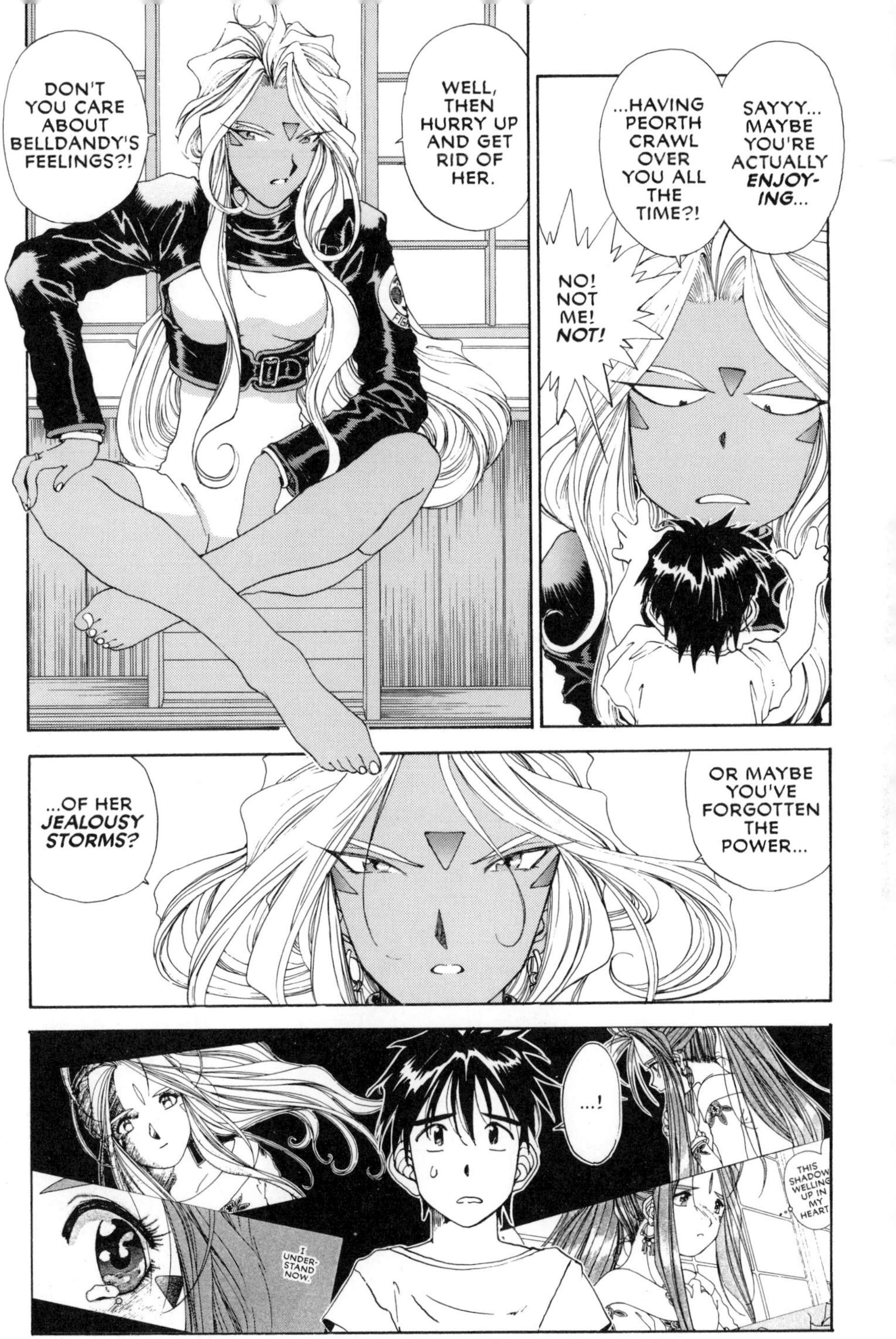

SAYYY... MAYBE YOU'RE ACTUALLY *ENJOYING*...
...HAVING PEORTH CRAWL OVER YOU ALL THE TIME?!
NO! NOT ME! *NOT!*
WELL, THEN HURRY UP AND GET RID OF HER.
DON'T YOU CARE ABOUT BELLDANDY'S FEELINGS?!
OR MAYBE YOU'VE FORGOTTEN THE POWER...
...OF HER *JEALOUSY STORMS?*
...!
THIS SHADOW WELLING UP IN MY HEART
I UNDERSTAND NOW.

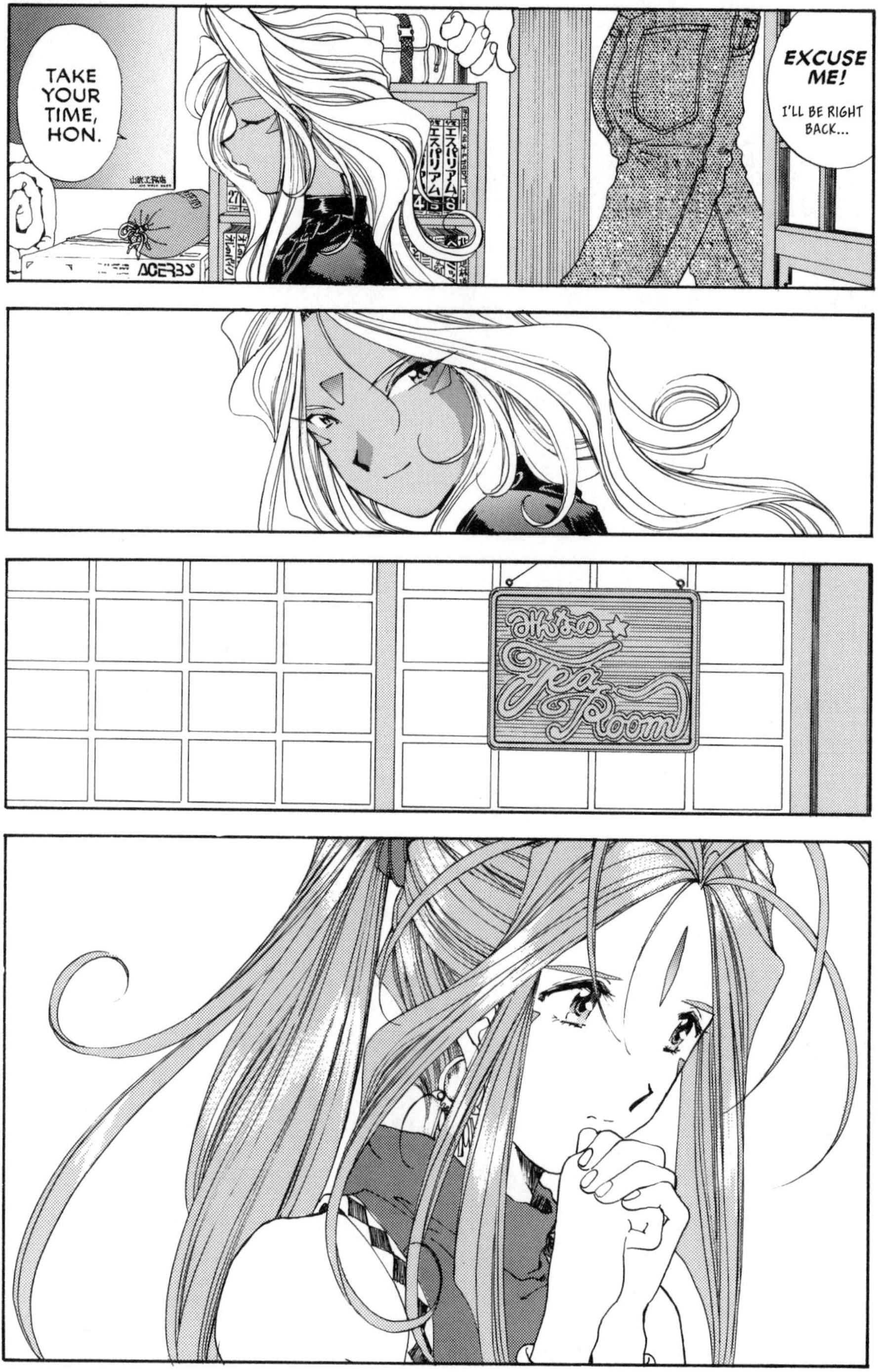
EXCUSE ME!
I'LL BE RIGHT BACK...
TAKE YOUR TIME, HON.
みんなの☆
Tea Room

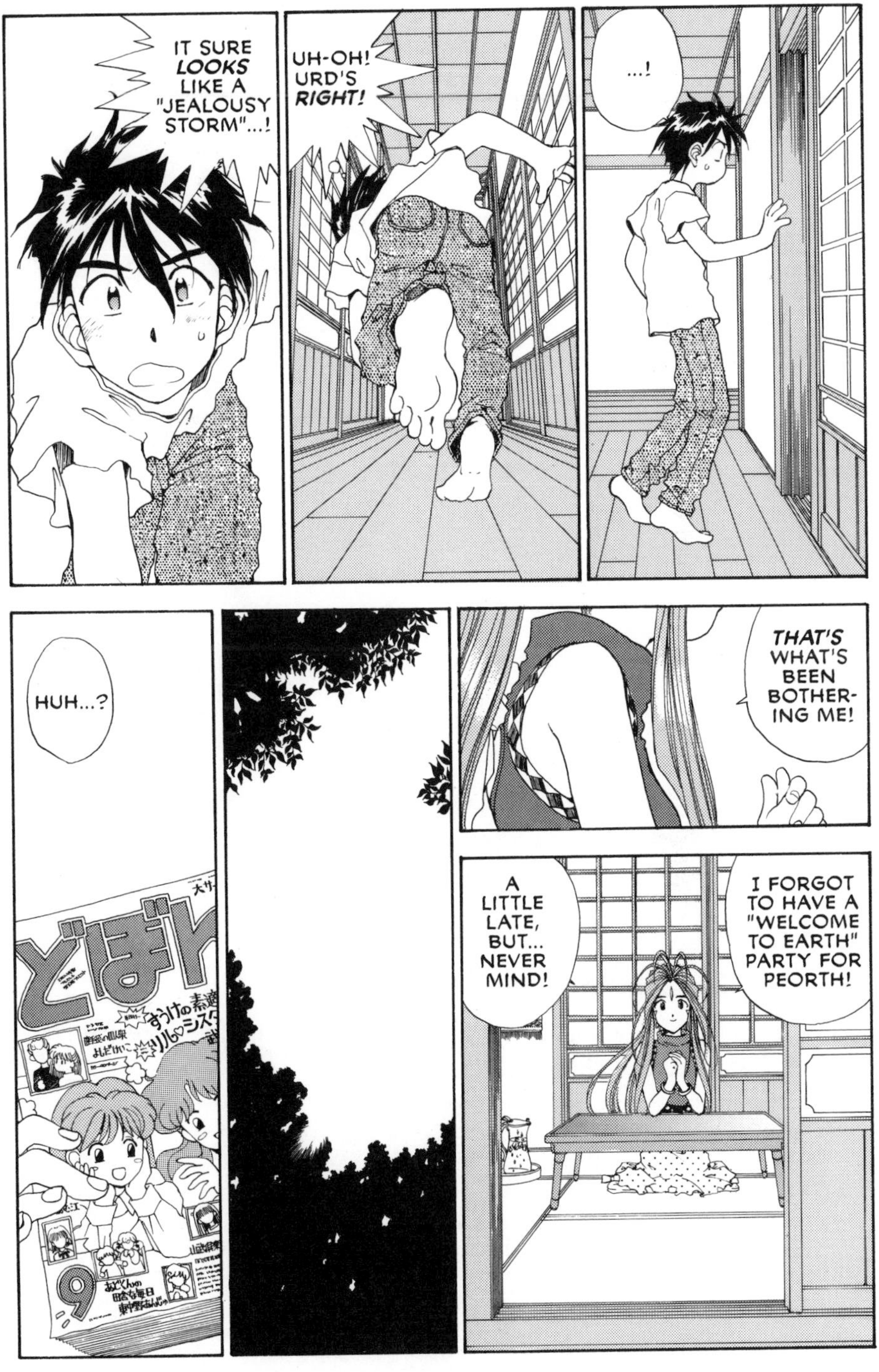

...!
UH-OH! URD'S RIGHT!
IT SURE LOOKS LIKE A "JEALOUSY STORM"...!
THAT'S WHAT'S BEEN BOTHERING ME!
I FORGOT TO HAVE A "WELCOME TO EARTH" PARTY FOR PEORTH!
A LITTLE LATE, BUT... NEVER MIND!
HUH...?

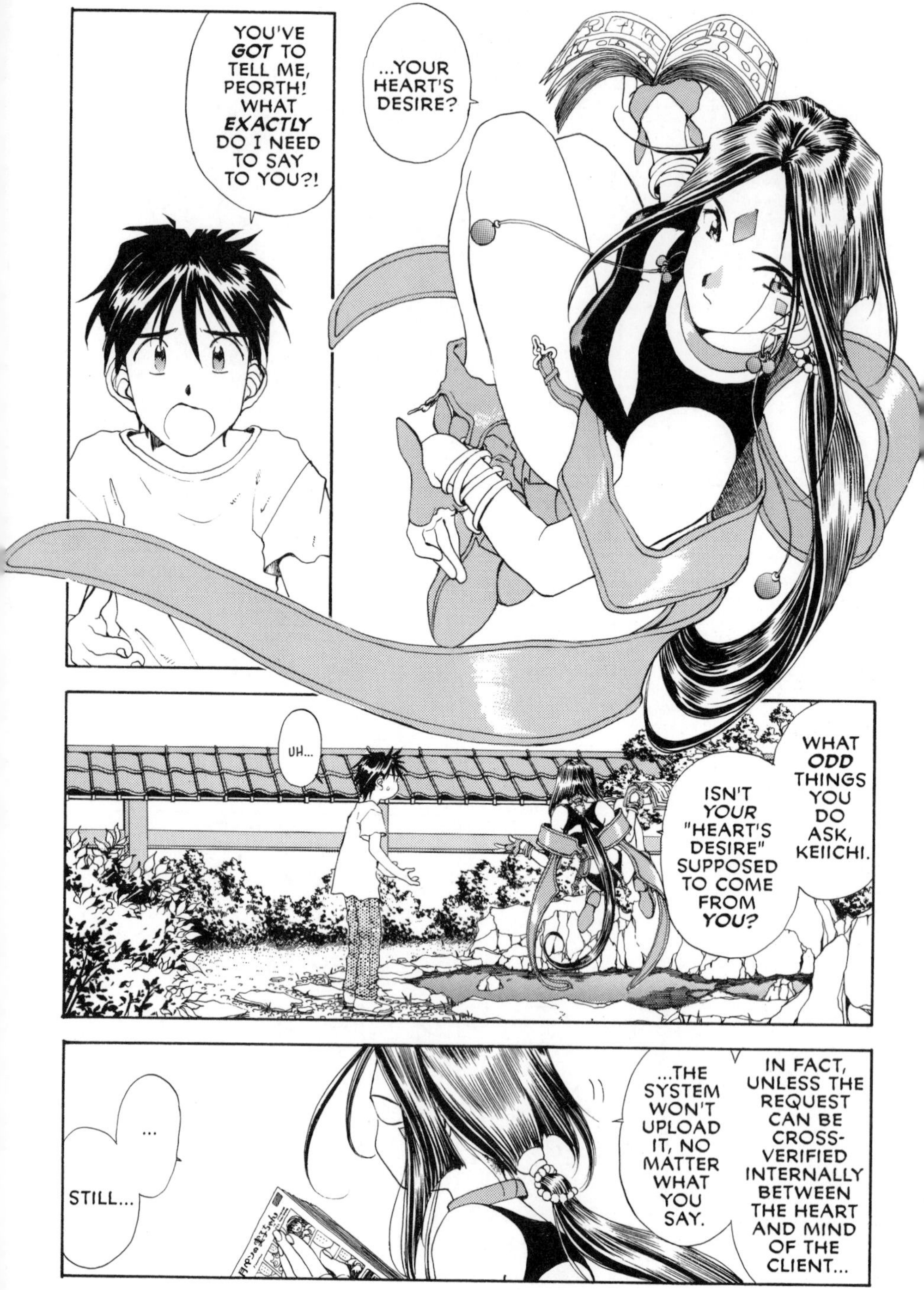
...YOUR HEART'S DESIRE?
YOU'VE *GOT* TO TELL ME, PEORTH! WHAT *EXACTLY* DO I NEED TO SAY TO YOU?!
WHAT *ODD* THINGS YOU DO ASK, KEIICHI.
ISN'T *YOUR* "HEART'S DESIRE" SUPPOSED TO COME FROM *YOU?*
UH...
IN FACT, UNLESS THE REQUEST CAN BE CROSS-VERIFIED INTERNALLY BETWEEN THE HEART AND MIND OF THE CLIENT...
...THE SYSTEM WON'T UPLOAD IT, NO MATTER WHAT YOU SAY.
...
STILL...

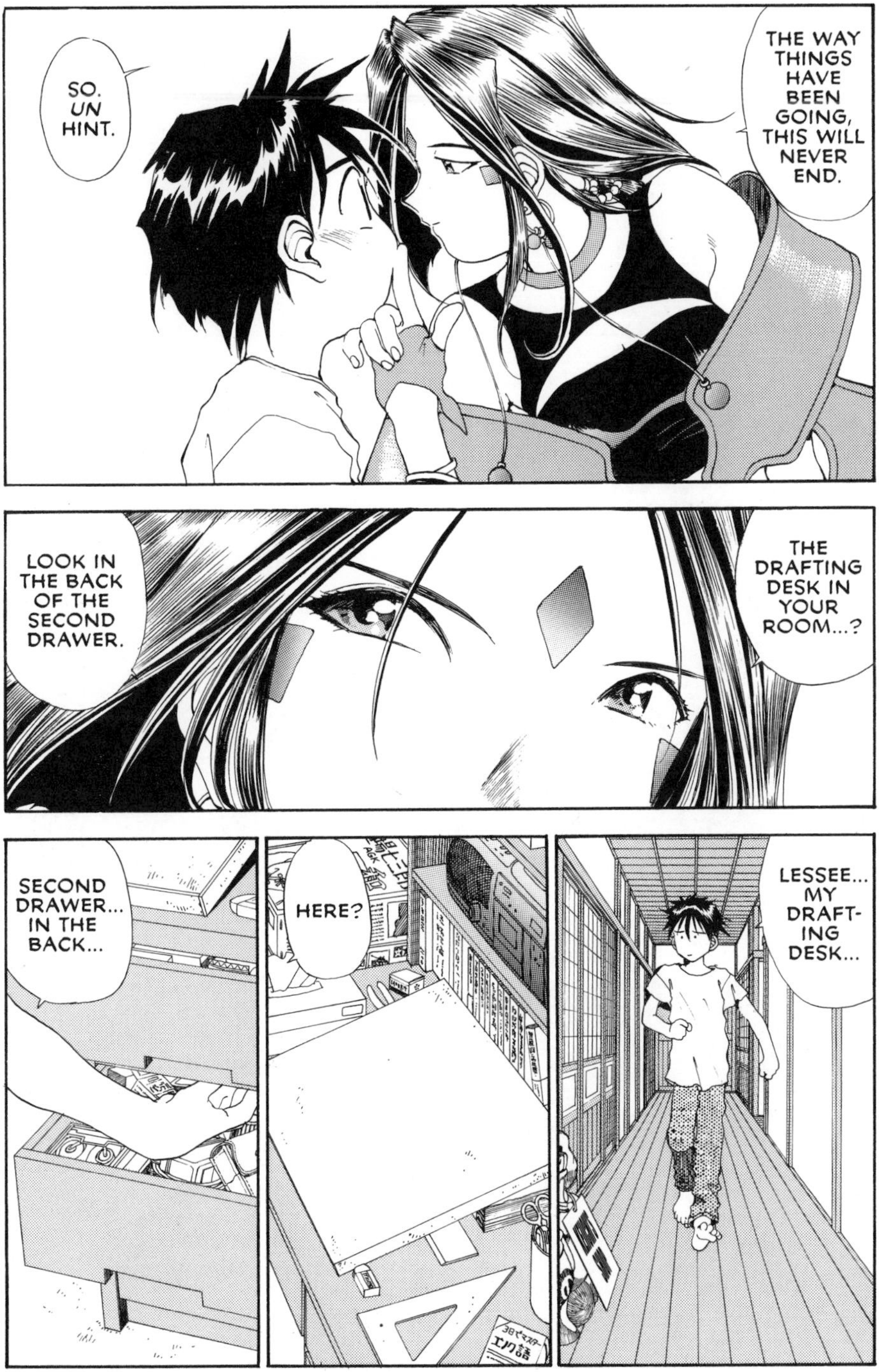
THE WAY THINGS HAVE BEEN GOING, THIS WILL NEVER END.
SO. *UN* HINT.
THE DRAFTING DESK IN YOUR ROOM...?
LOOK IN THE BACK OF THE SECOND DRAWER.
LESSEE... MY DRAFT-ING DESK...
HERE?
SECOND DRAWER... IN THE BACK...

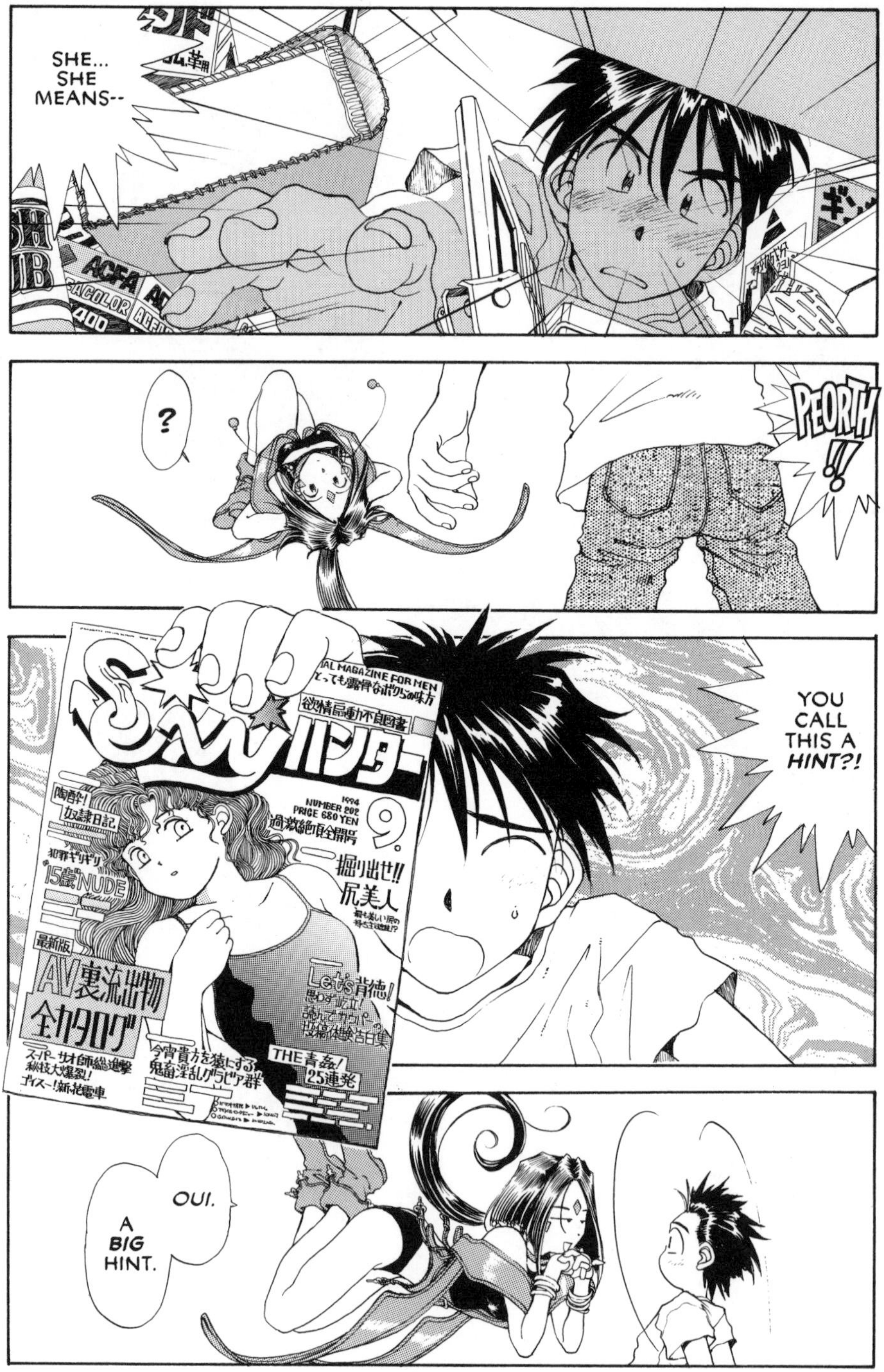
SHE... SHE MEANS--
PEORTH!!
?
YOU CALL THIS A HINT?!
ハンター
1994 NUMBER 202 PRICE 680 YEN
9.
掘り出せ!! 尻美人
AV裏流出物 全カタログ
THE青姦! 25連発
OUI.
A BIG HINT.

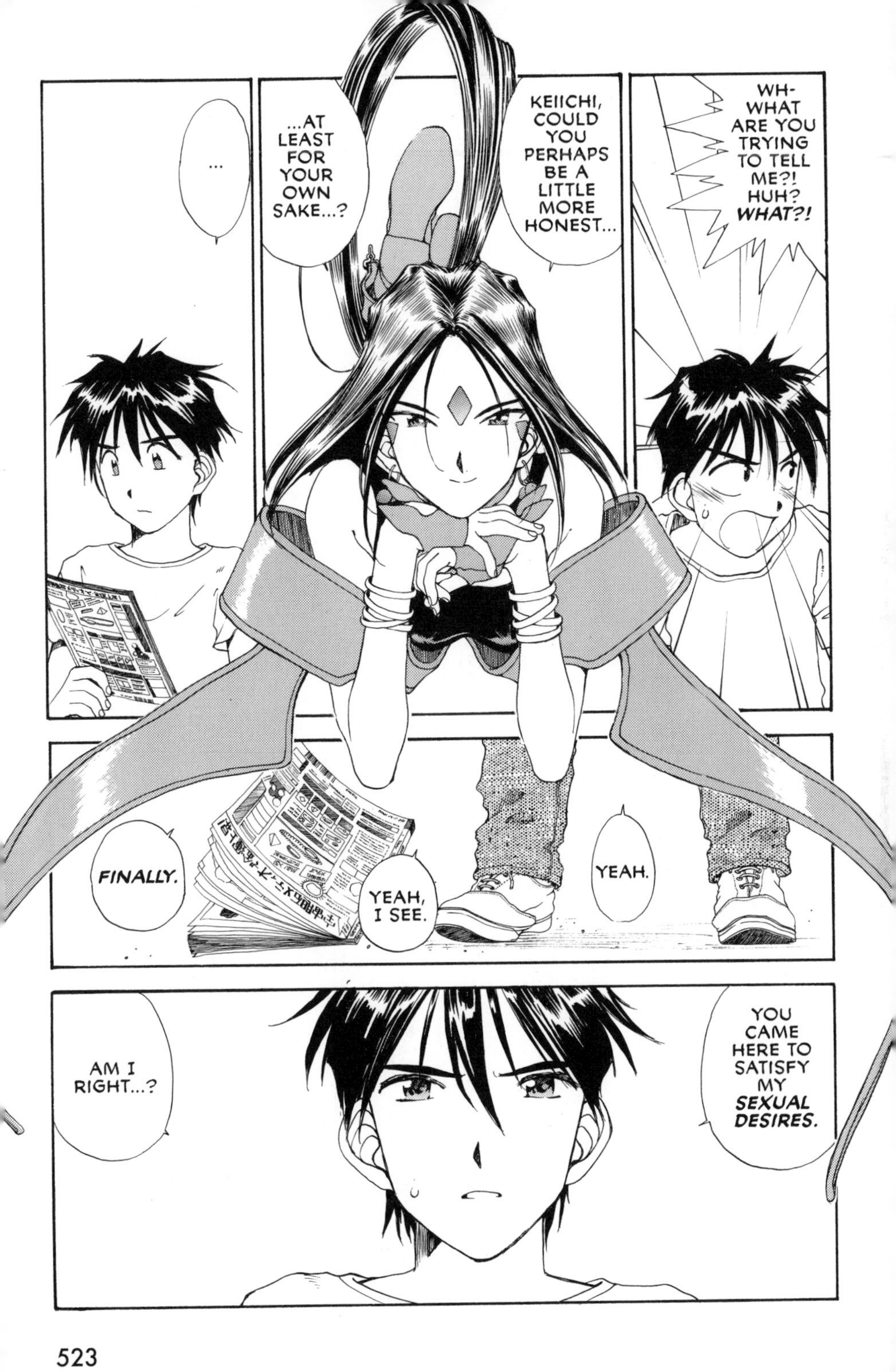
WH- WHAT ARE YOU TRYING TO TELL ME?! HUH? WHAT?!
KEIICHI, COULD YOU PERHAPS BE A LITTLE MORE HONEST...
...AT LEAST FOR YOUR OWN SAKE...?
...
YEAH.
YEAH, I SEE.
FINALLY.
YOU CAME HERE TO SATISFY MY SEXUAL DESIRES.
AM I RIGHT...?

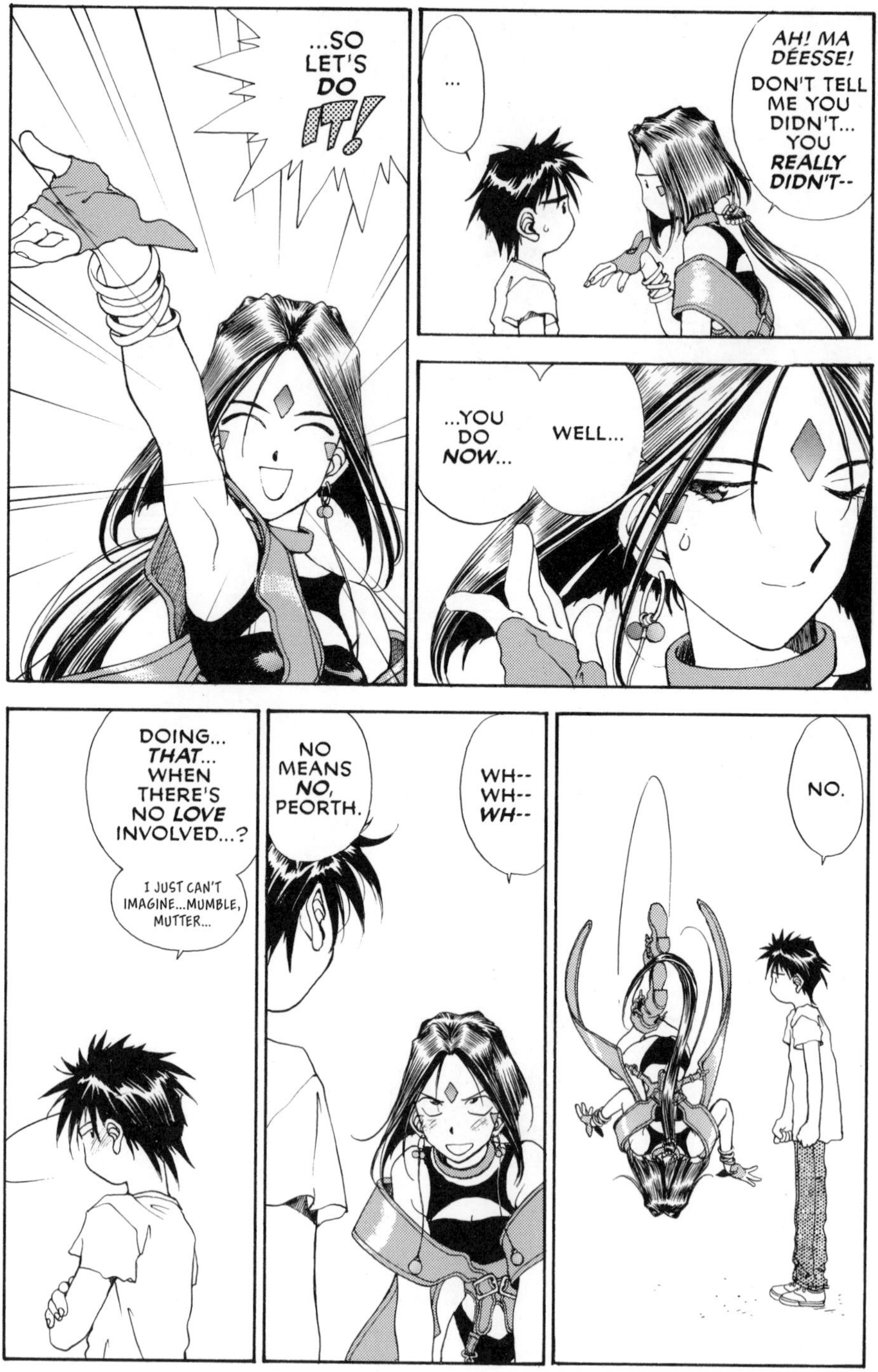
AH! MA DÉESSE! DON'T TELL ME YOU DIDN'T... YOU REALLY DIDN'T--
...
WELL...
...YOU DO NOW...
...SO LET'S DO IT!
NO.
WH-- WH-- WH--
NO MEANS NO, PEORTH.
DOING... THAT... WHEN THERE'S NO LOVE INVOLVED...?
I JUST CAN'T IMAGINE...MUMBLE, MUTTER...

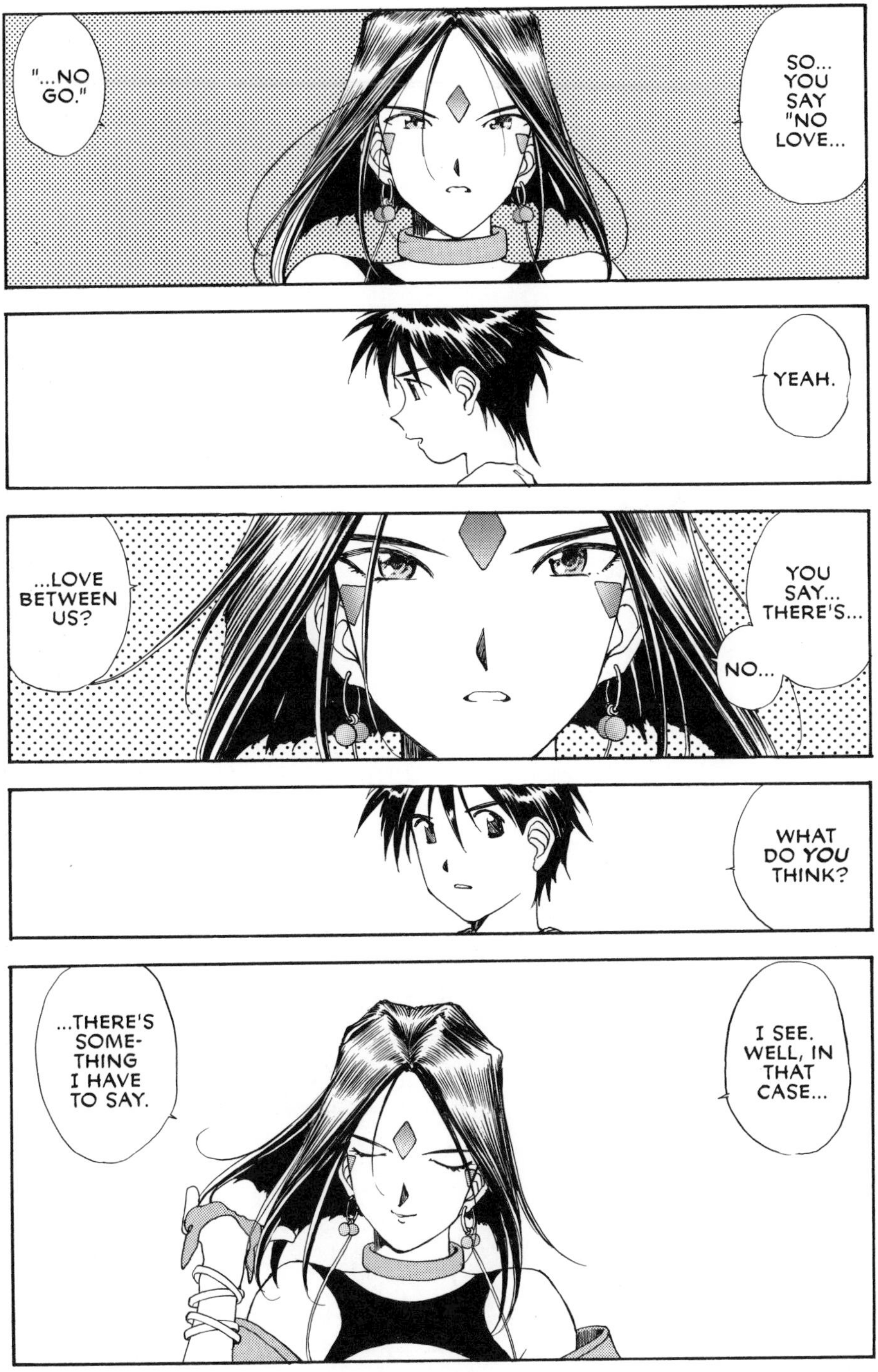
SO... YOU SAY "NO LOVE...
"...NO GO."
YEAH.
YOU SAY... THERE'S...
NO...
...LOVE BETWEEN US?
WHAT DO *YOU* THINK?
I SEE. WELL, IN THAT CASE...
...THERE'S SOME-THING I HAVE TO SAY.

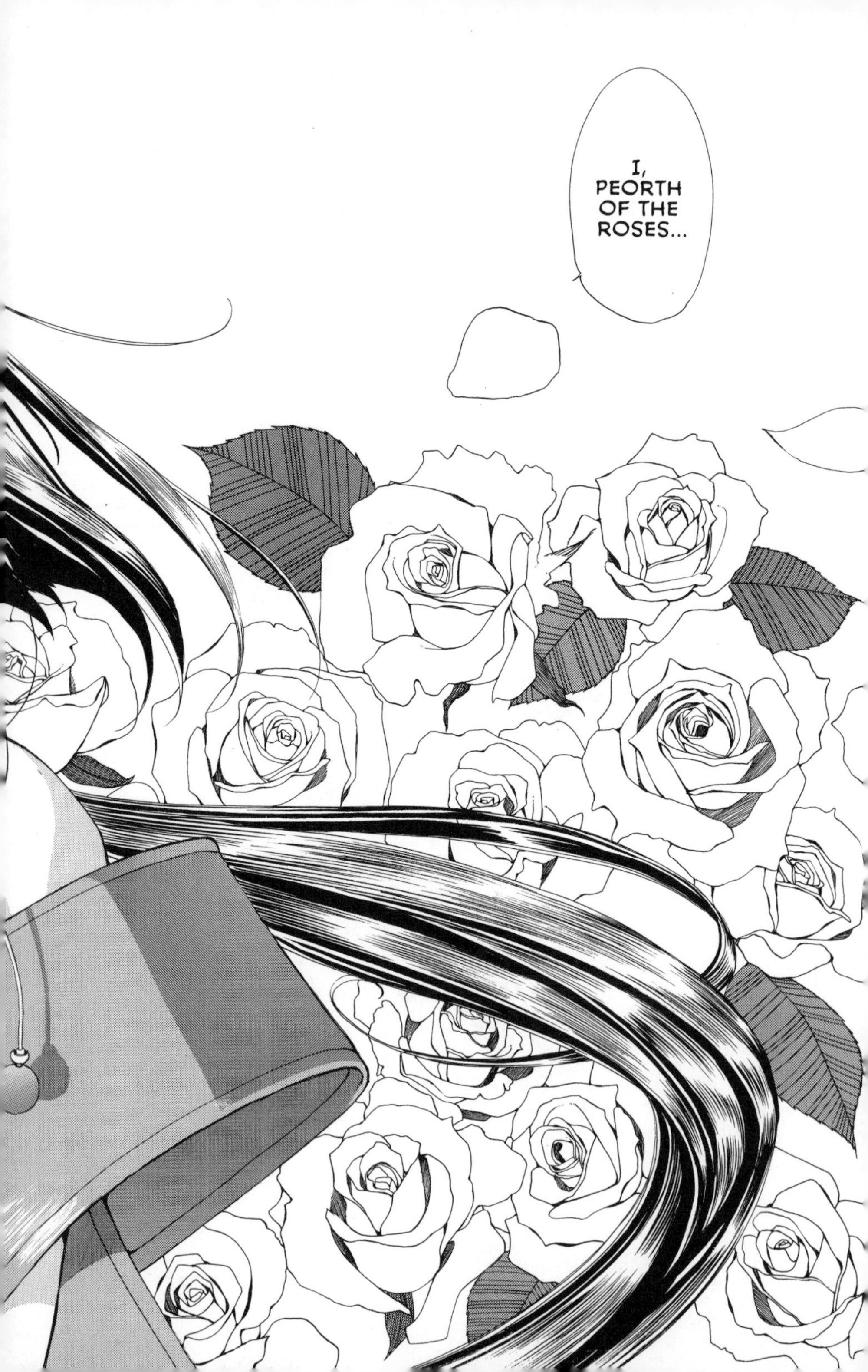
I, PEORTH OF THE ROSES...

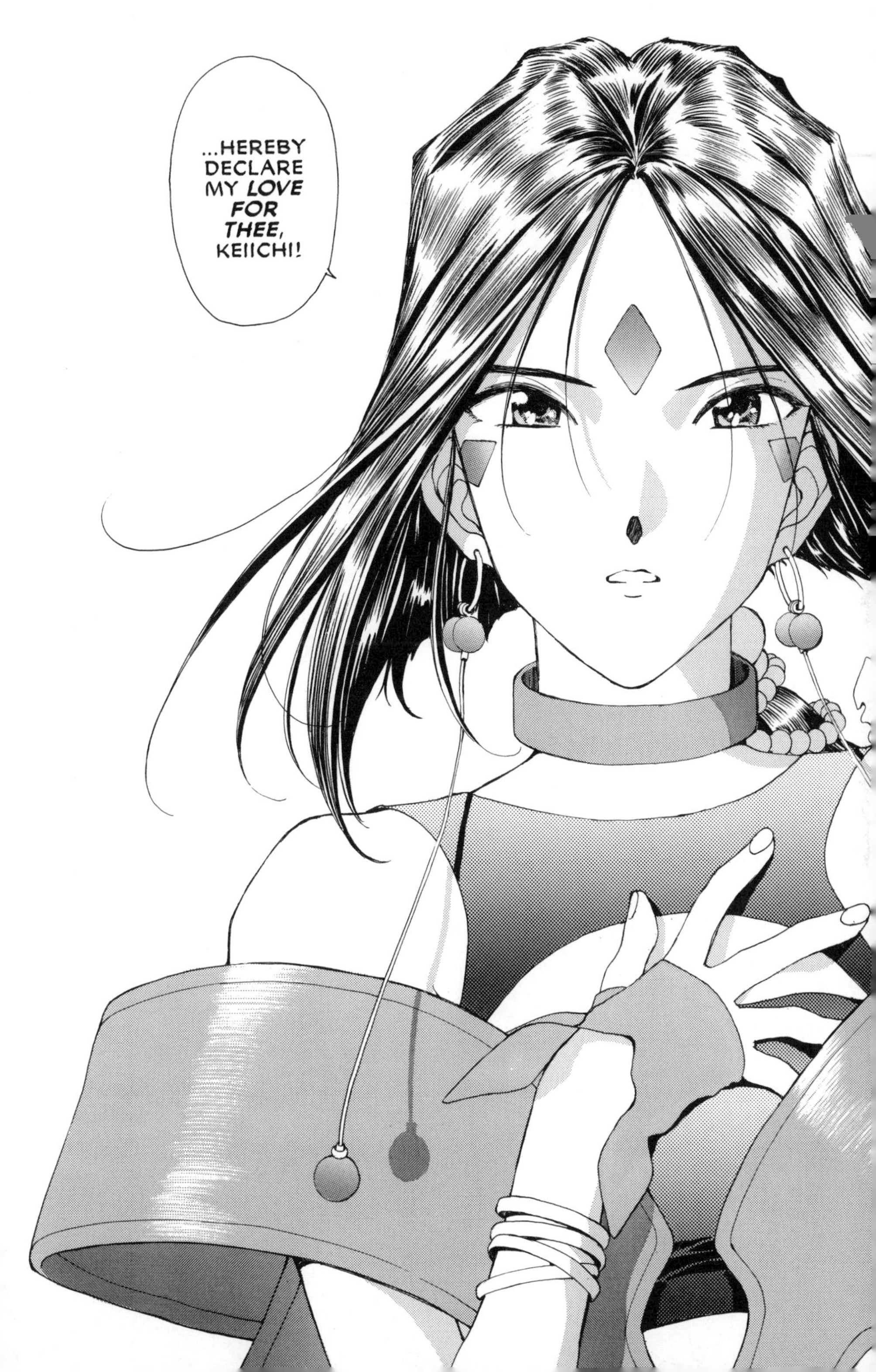
...HEREBY DECLARE MY *LOVE FOR THEE*, KEIICHI!

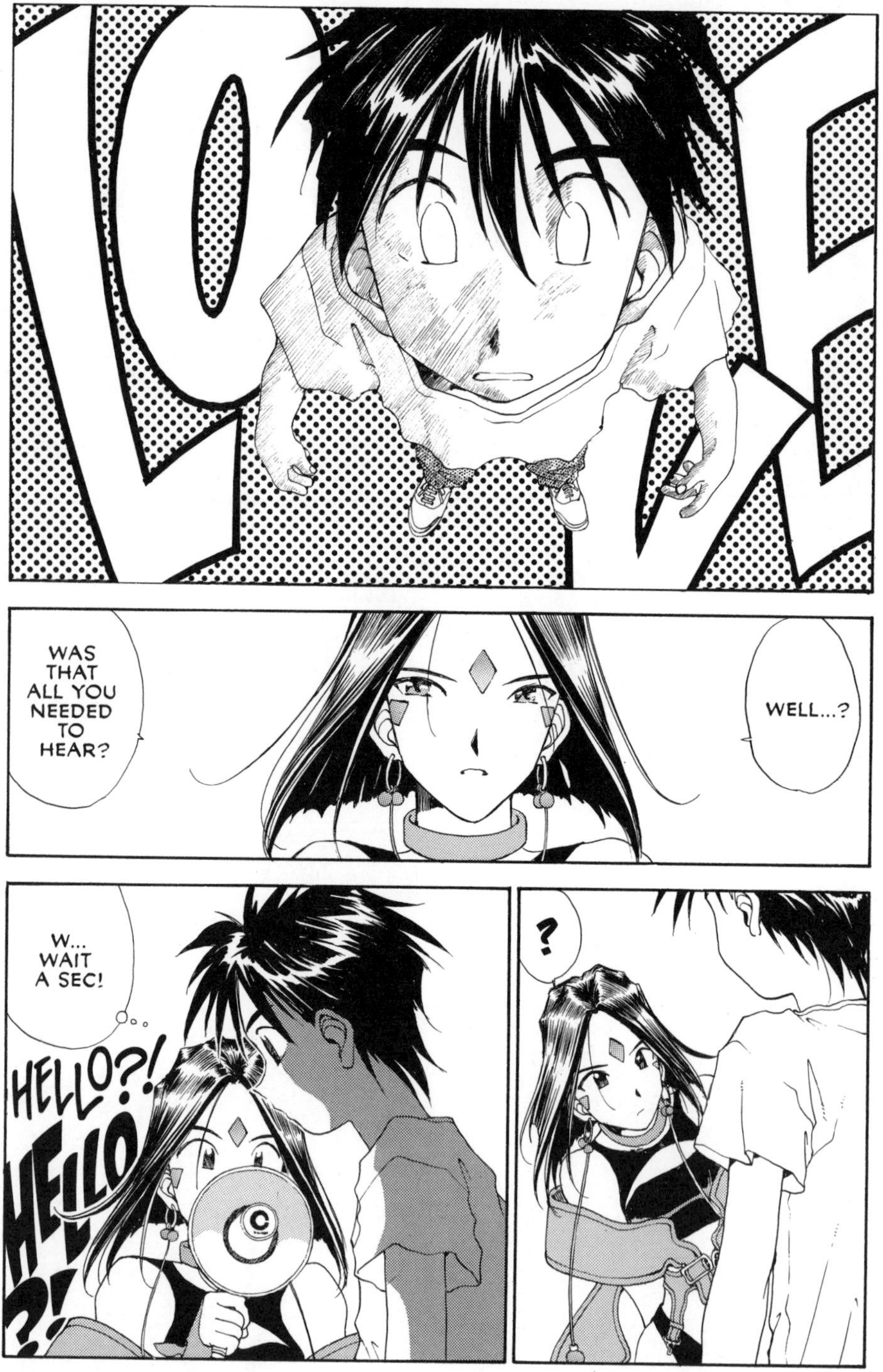
WELL...?
WAS THAT ALL YOU NEEDED TO HEAR?
?
W... WAIT A SEC!
HELLO?!
HELLO?!

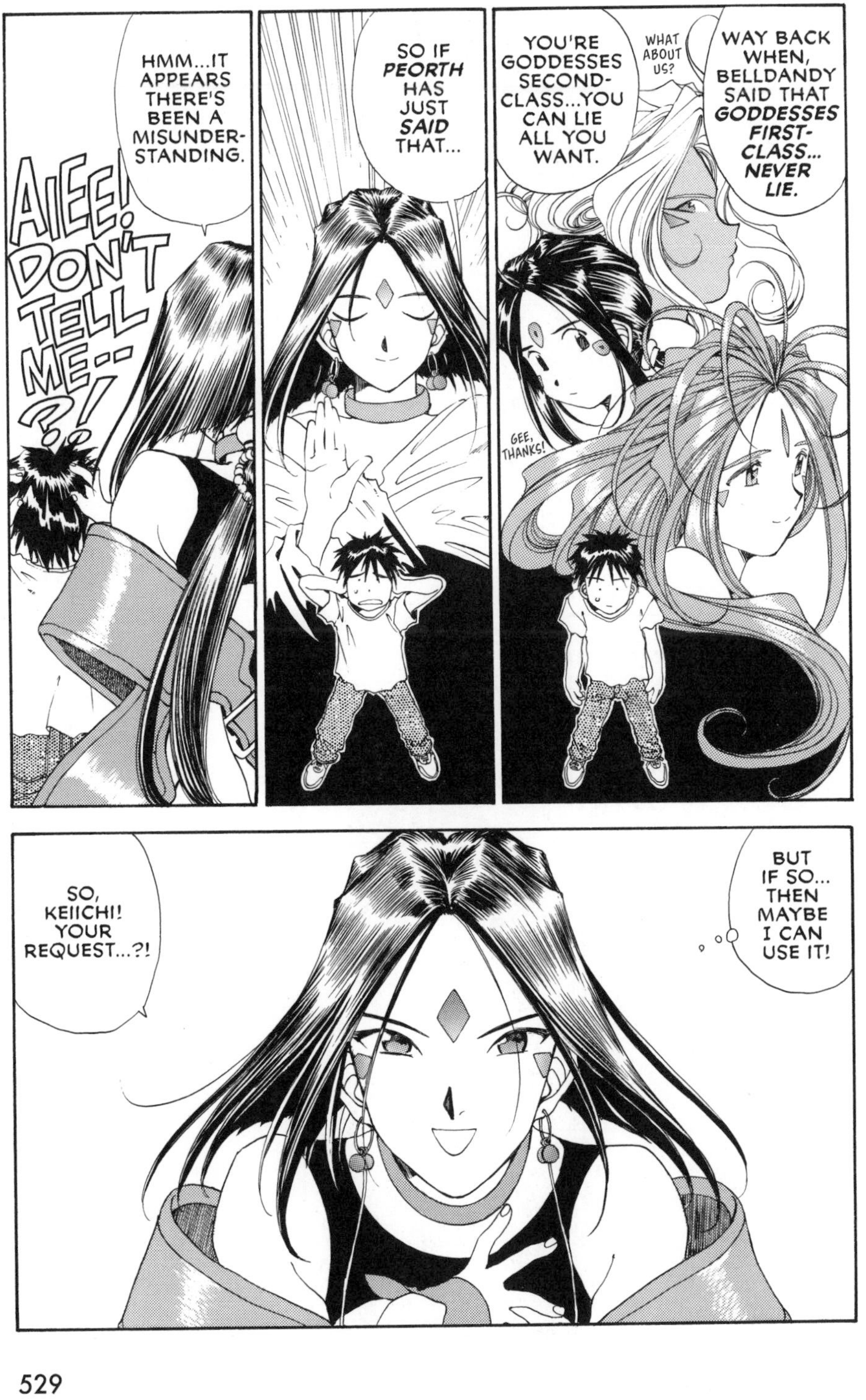
WAY BACK WHEN, BELLDANDY SAID THAT GODDESSES FIRST-CLASS... NEVER LIE.
WHAT ABOUT US?
YOU'RE GODDESSES SECOND-CLASS...YOU CAN LIE ALL YOU WANT.
GEE, THANKS!
SO IF PEORTH HAS JUST SAID THAT...
HMM...IT APPEARS THERE'S BEEN A MISUNDERSTANDING.
AIEEE! DON'T TELL ME...?!
BUT IF SO... THEN MAYBE I CAN USE IT!
SO, KEIICHI! YOUR REQUEST...?!

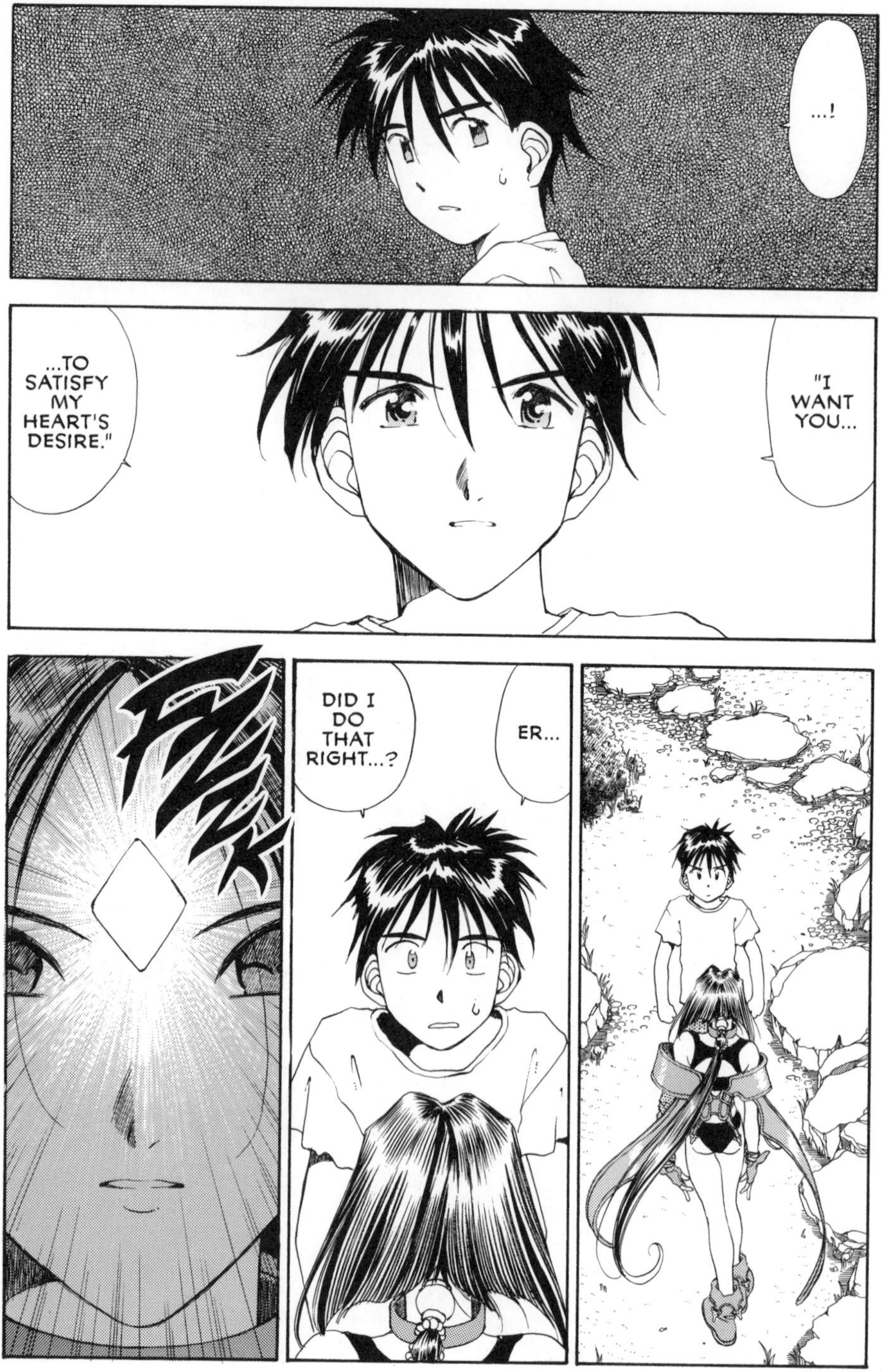
...!
"I WANT YOU...
...TO SATISFY MY HEART'S DESIRE."
ER...
DID I DO THAT RIGHT...?

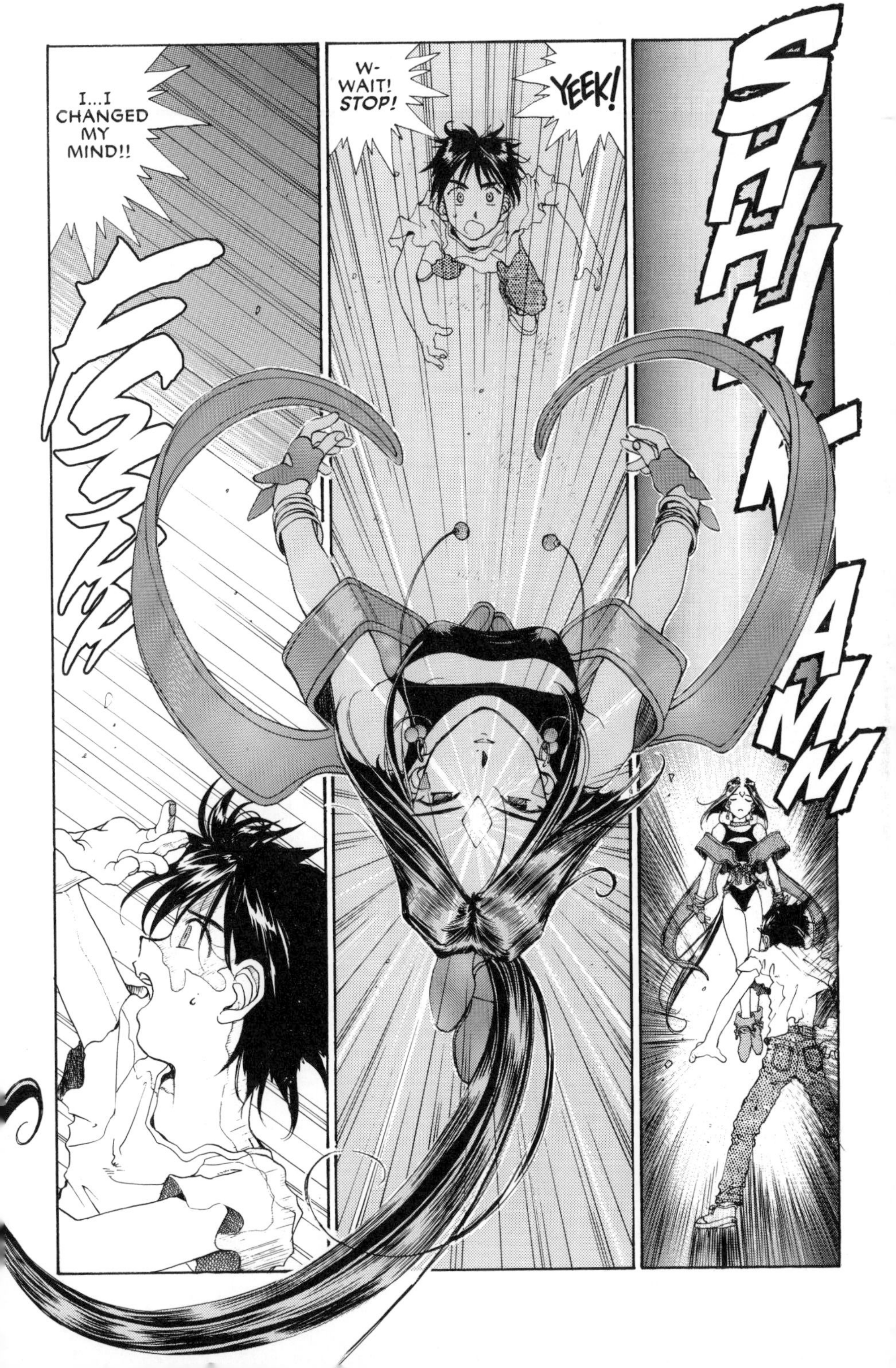
YEEK!
W-WAIT! STOP!
I...I CHANGED MY MIND!!

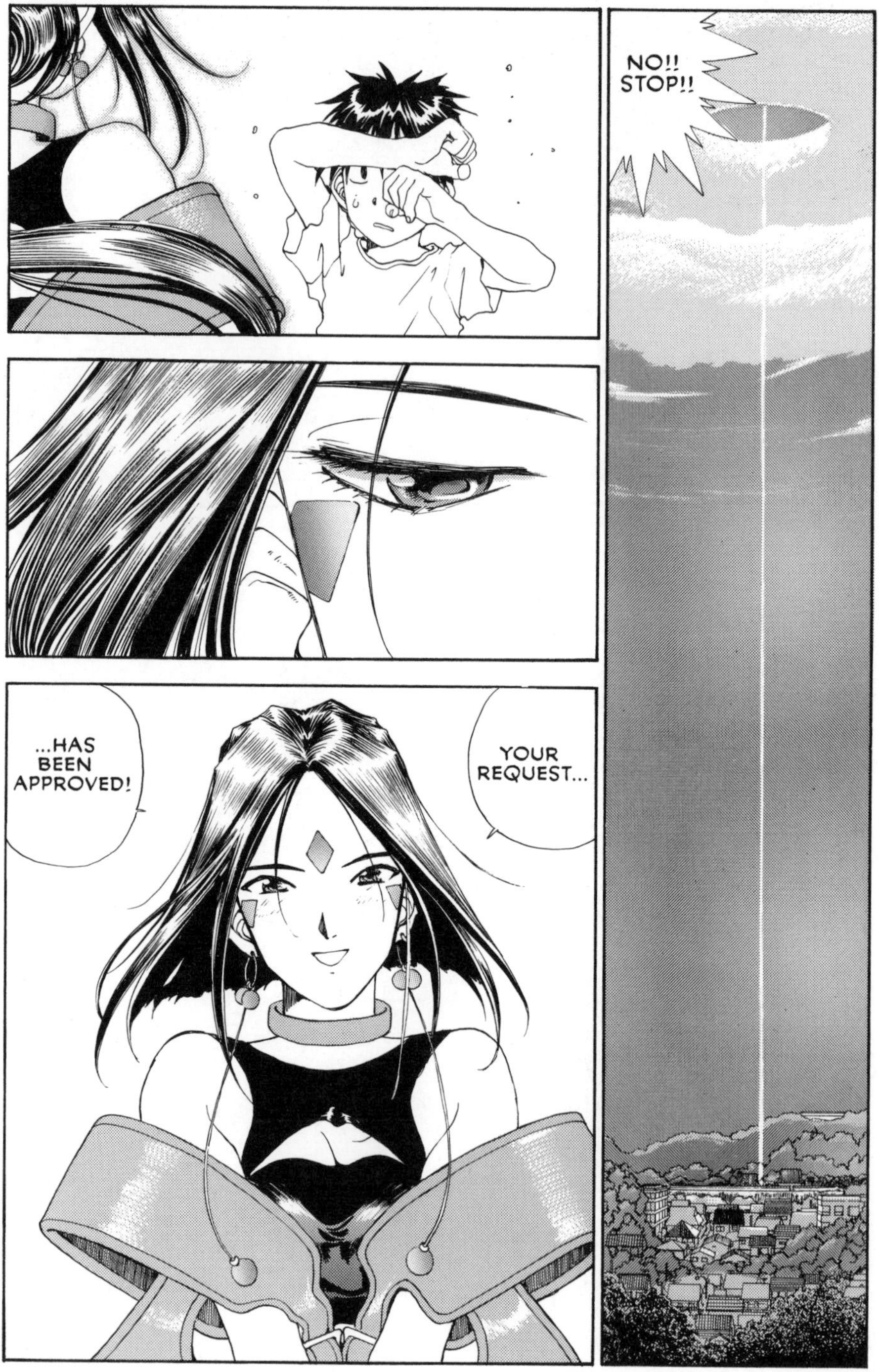
NO!! STOP!!
YOUR REQUEST...
...HAS BEEN APPROVED!

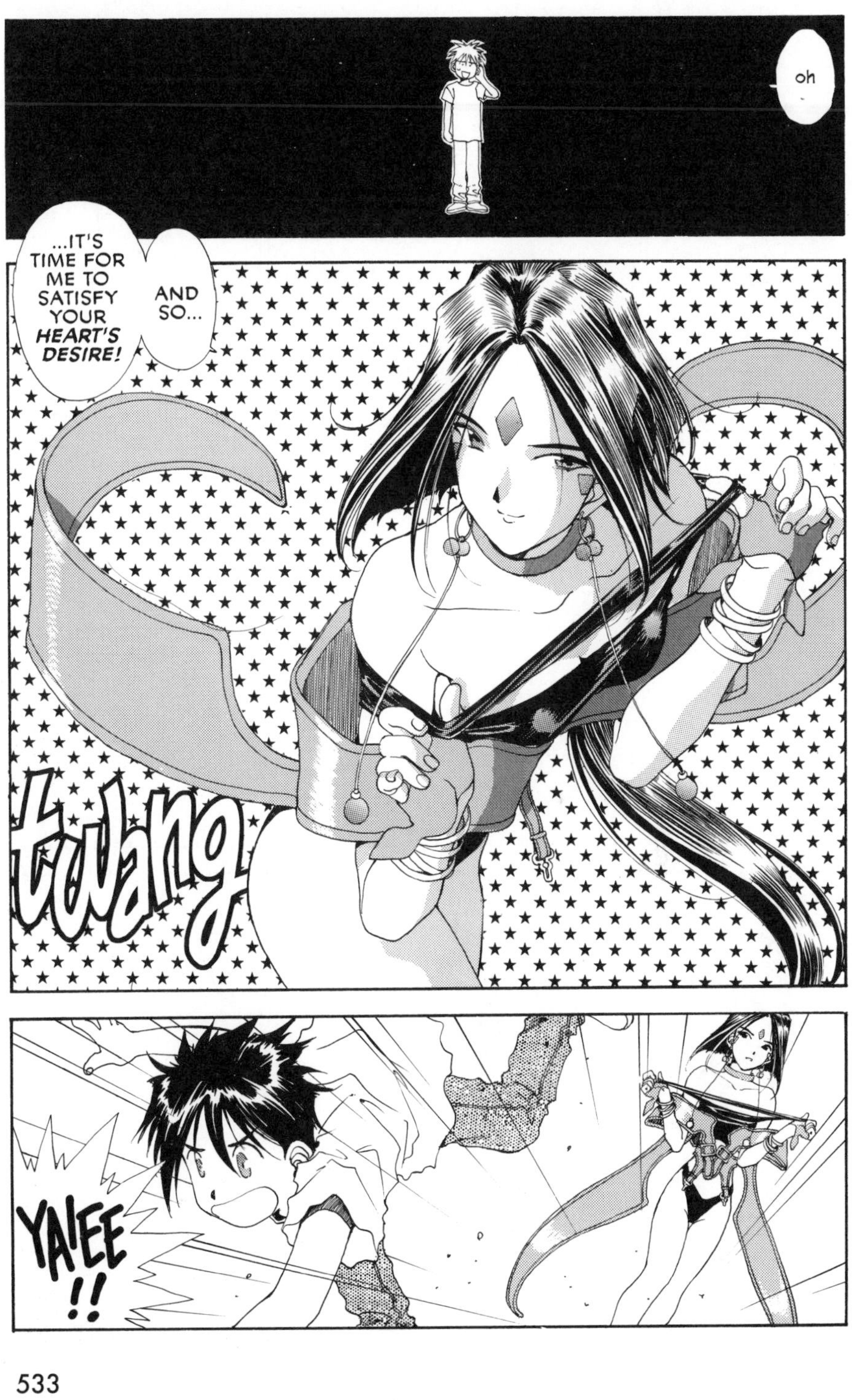
oh
AND SO...
...IT'S TIME FOR ME TO SATISFY YOUR *HEART'S DESIRE!*
twang
YAIEE!!

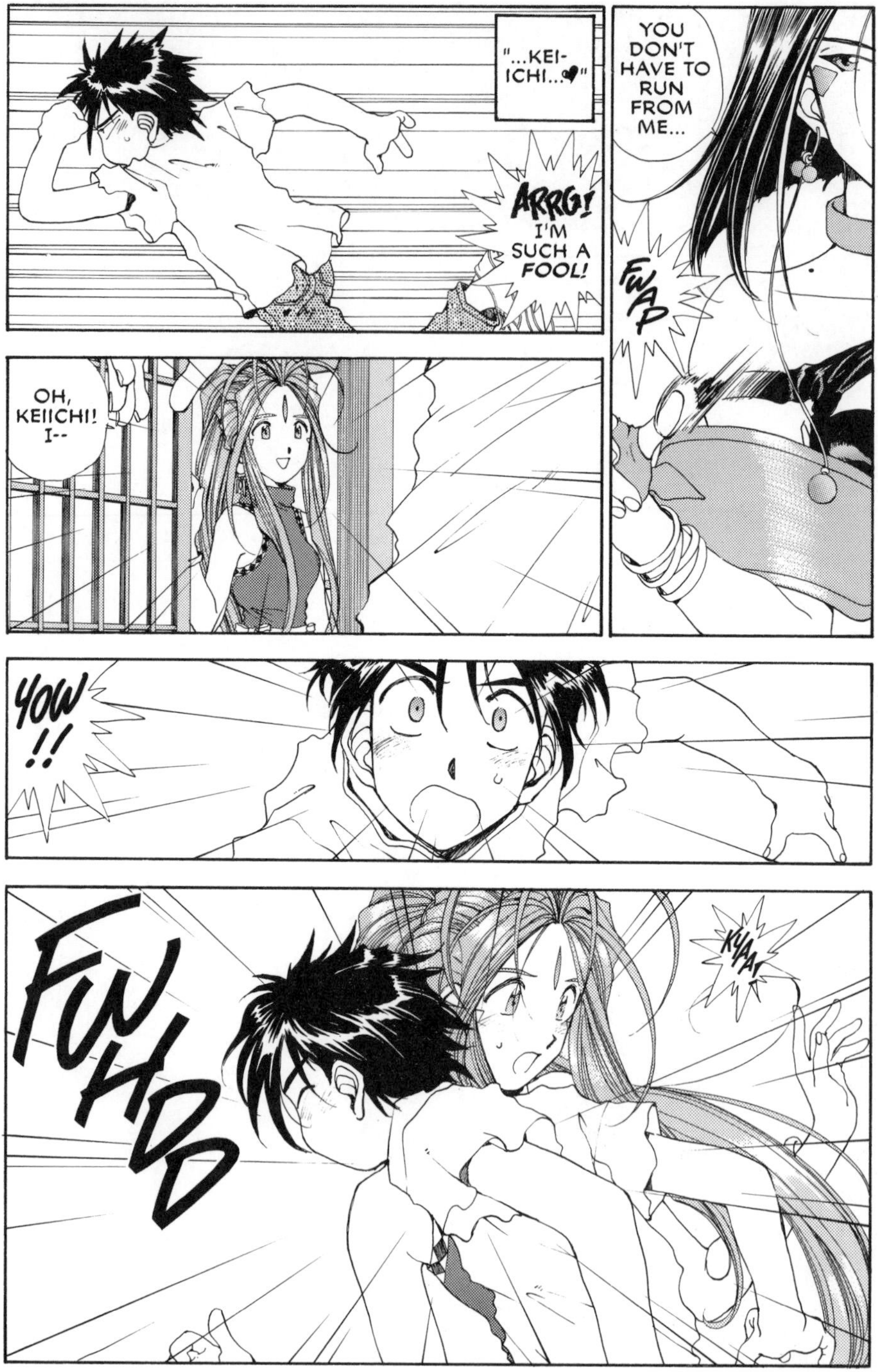
YOU DON'T HAVE TO RUN FROM ME...
FWAP
"...KEI-ICHI...♥"
ARRG! I'M SUCH A FOOL!
OH, KEIICHI! I--
YOW!!
KYAA!
FUHDD

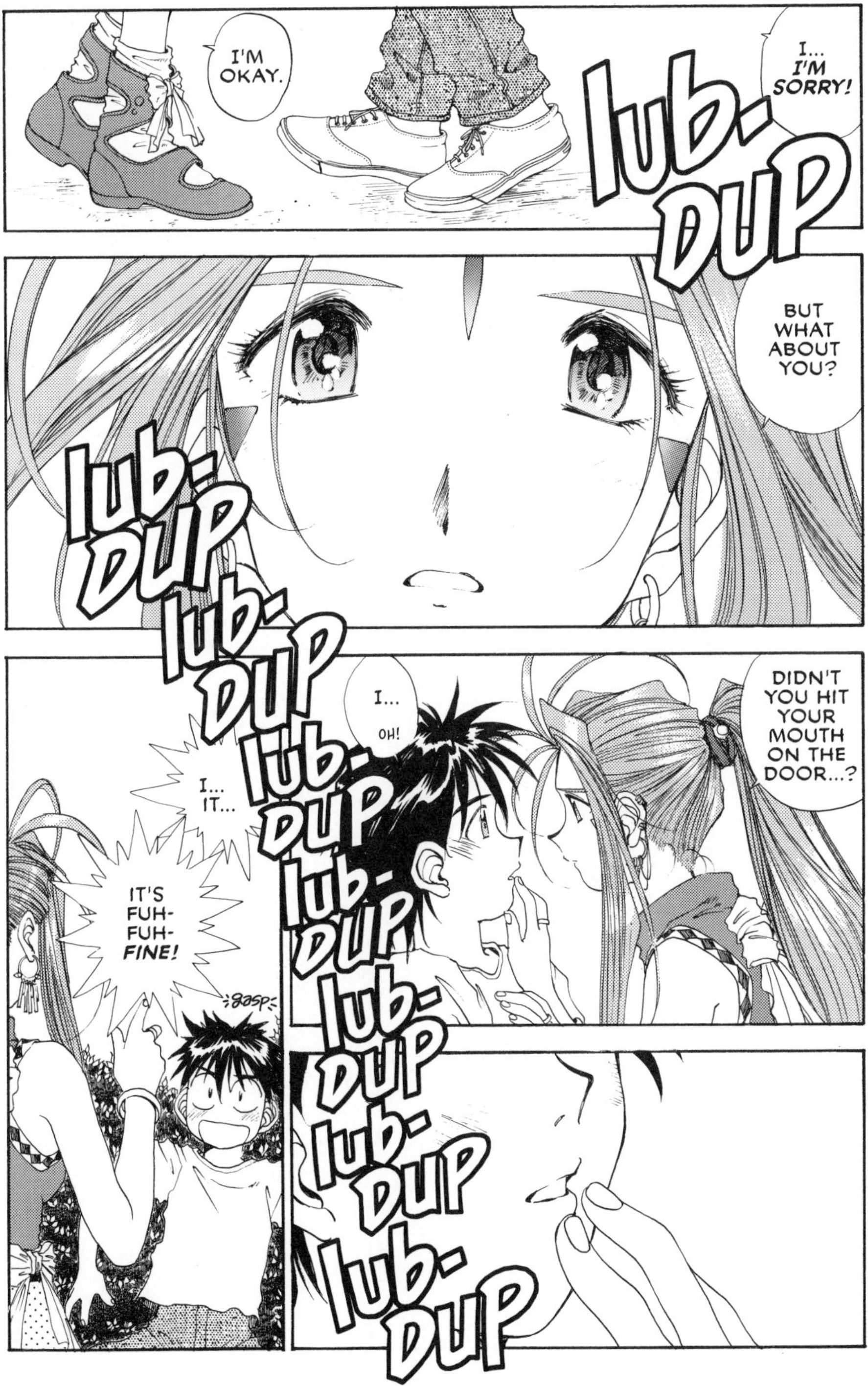
I... I'M SORRY!
I'M OKAY.
lub-DUP
BUT WHAT ABOUT YOU?
lub-DUP lub-DUP lub-DUP lub-DUP lub-DUP lub-DUP lub-DUP
DIDN'T YOU HIT YOUR MOUTH ON THE DOOR...?
I...
OH!
I... IT...
IT'S FUH-FUH-FINE!
gasp

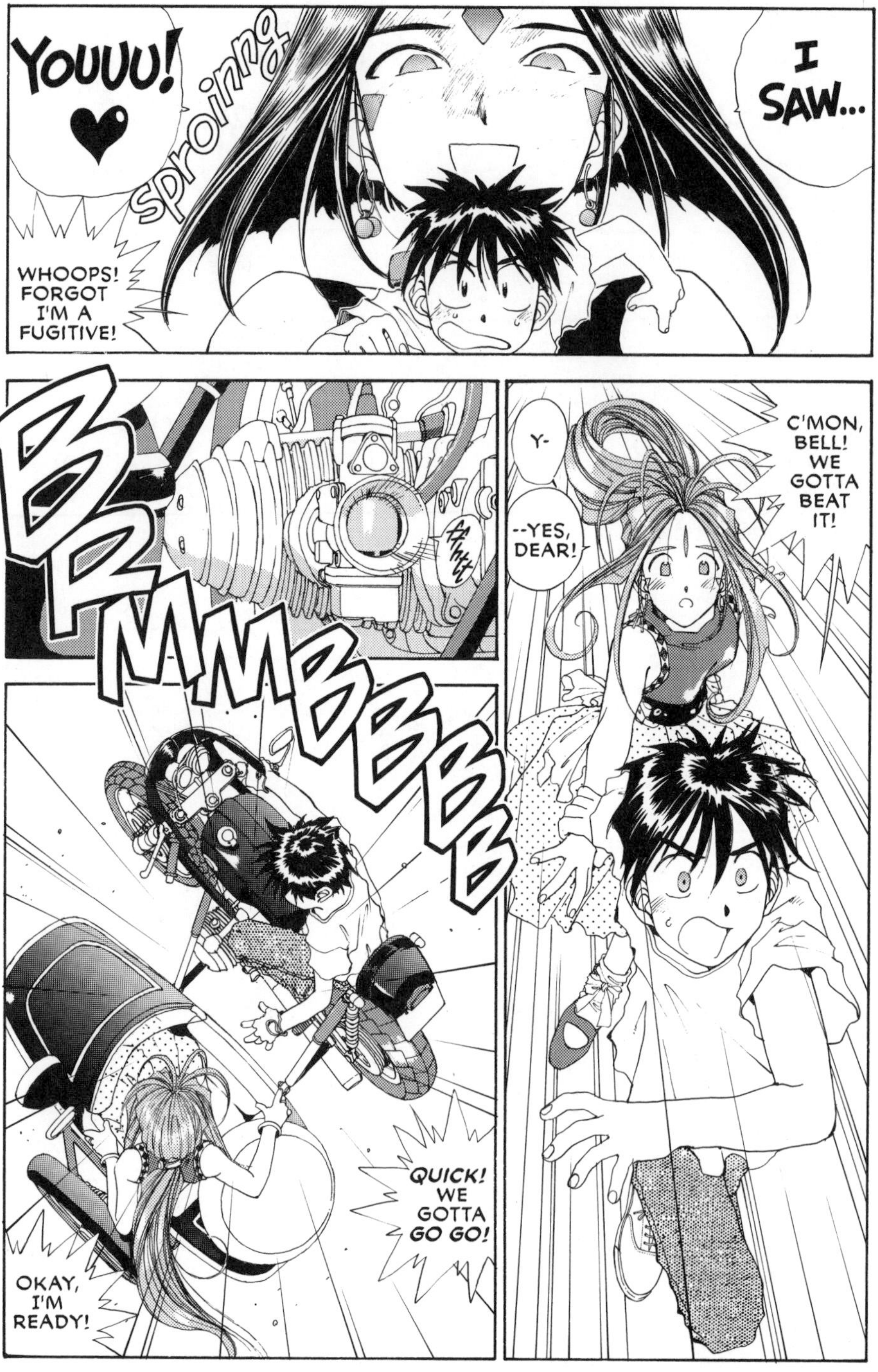
I SAW...
YOUUU! ♥
sproinng
WHOOPS! FORGOT I'M A FUGITIVE!
C'MON, BELL! WE GOTTA BEAT IT!
Y-
--YES, DEAR!
BRMMBBBB
QUICK! WE GOTTA GO GO!
OKAY, I'M READY!

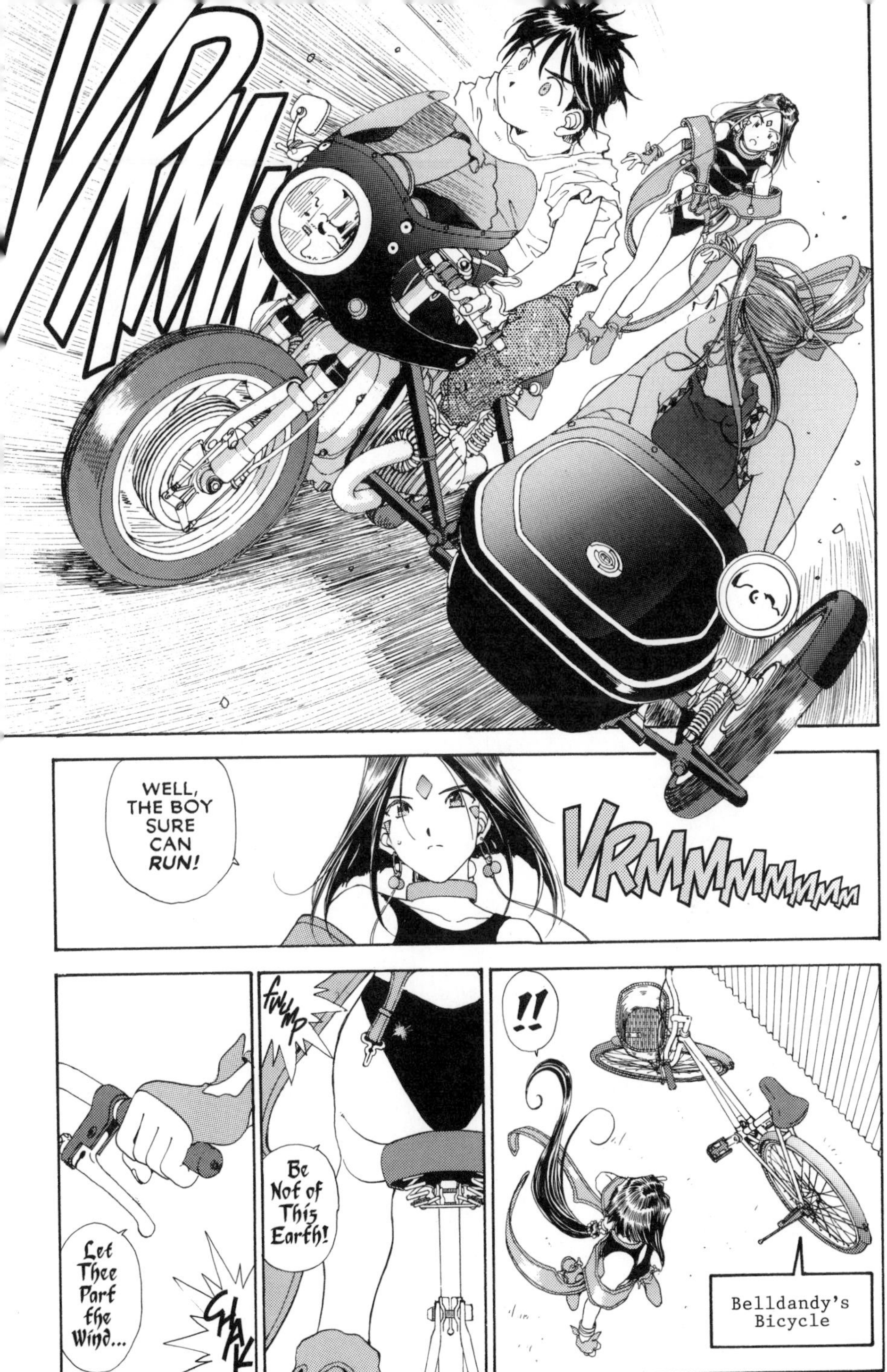
VRMM
VRMMMMMMMM
WELL, THE BOY SURE CAN RUN!
!!
Belldandy's Bicycle
FWUMP
Be Not of This Earth!
Let Thee Part the Wind...
CHAK

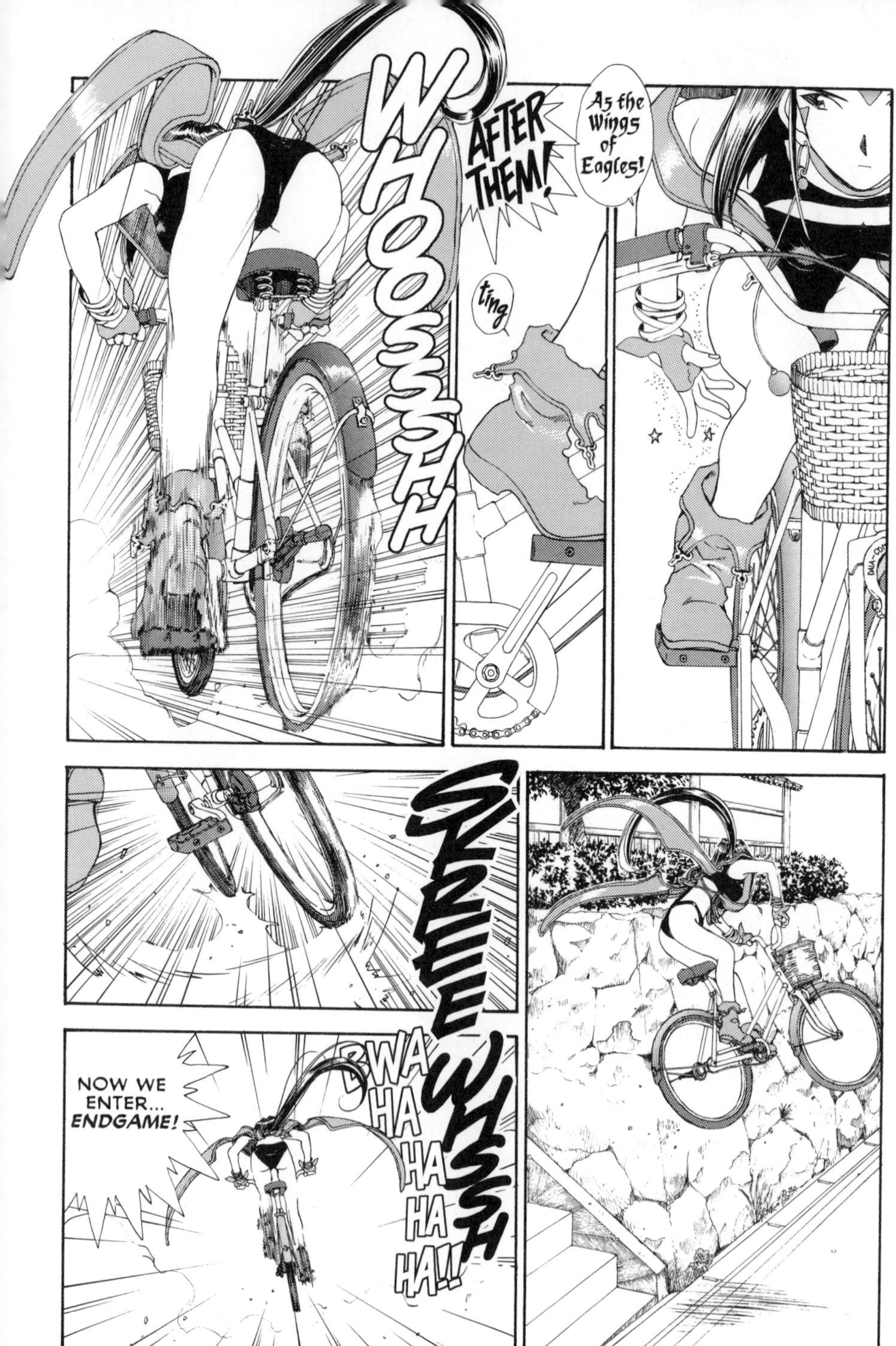
As the Wings of Eagles!
ting
AFTER THEM!
WHOOSSHH
SKREEEWHISSH
NOW WE ENTER... ENDGAME!
BWAHAHAHAHA!!

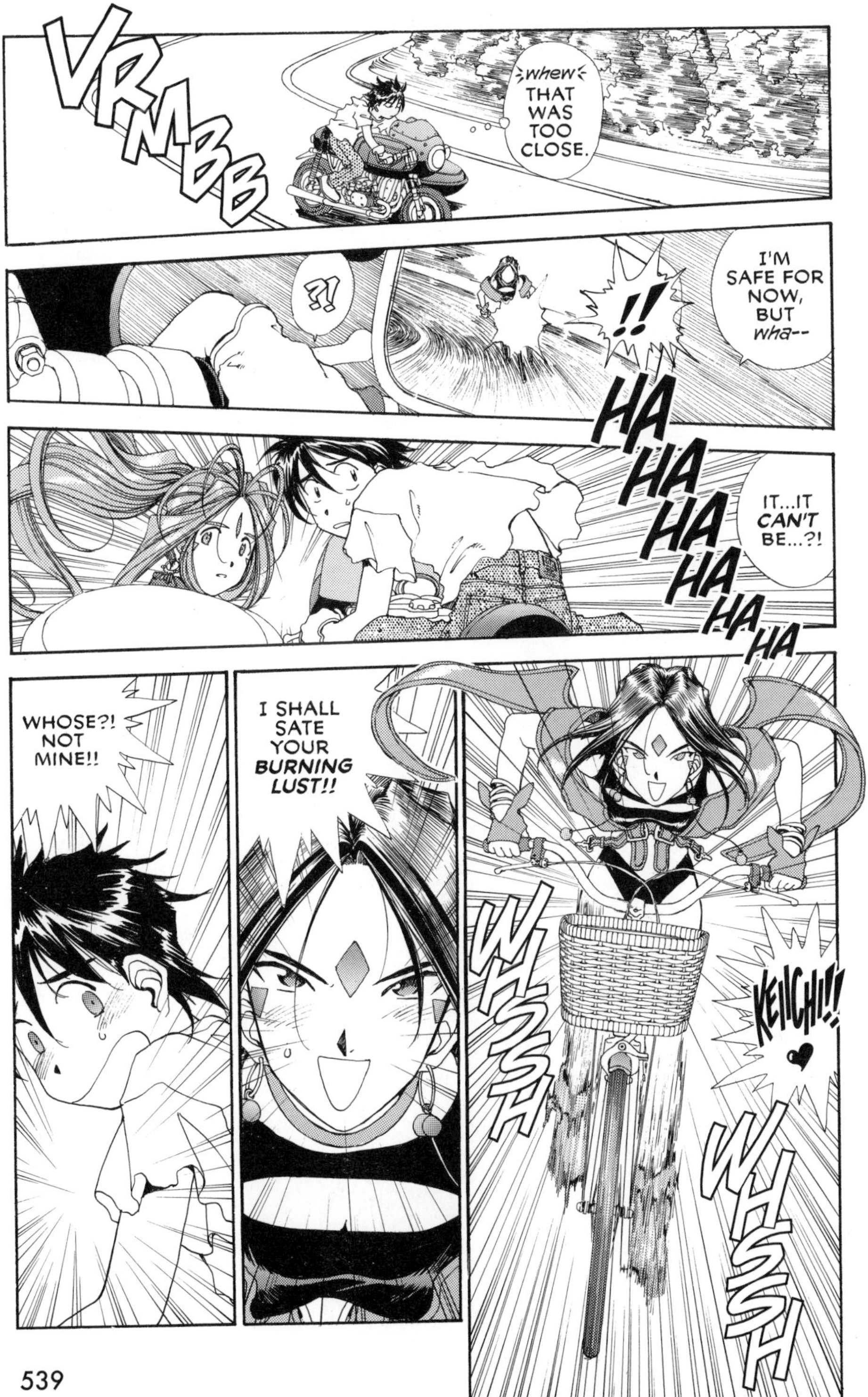
VRMBB
whew THAT WAS TOO CLOSE.
I'M SAFE FOR NOW, BUT wha--
!!
?!
HA HA HA HA HA HA HA
IT...IT CAN'T BE...?!
KEIICHI!! ♥
WHSSH
WHSSH
I SHALL SATE YOUR BURNING LUST!!
WHOSE?! NOT MINE!!

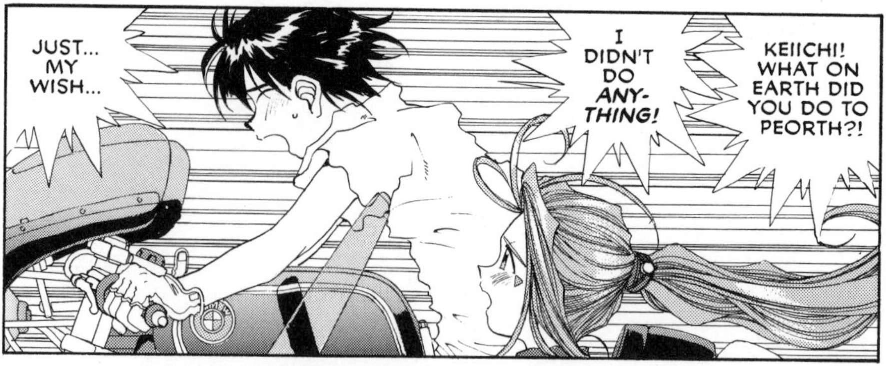
KEIICHI! WHAT ON EARTH DID YOU DO TO PEORTH?!
I DIDN'T DO *ANYTHING!*
JUST... MY WISH...
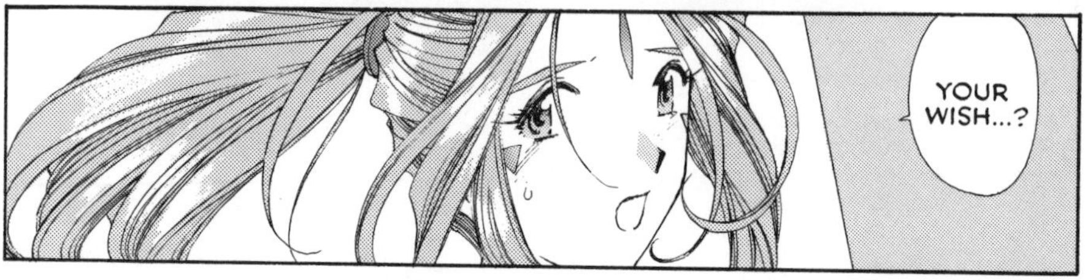
YOUR WISH...?
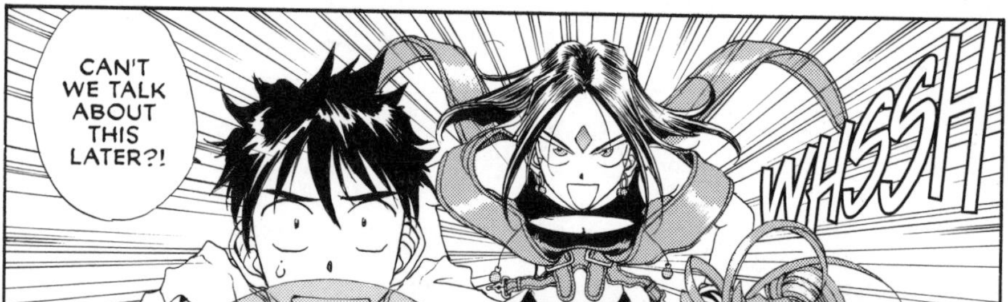
WHSSH
CAN'T WE TALK ABOUT THIS LATER?!
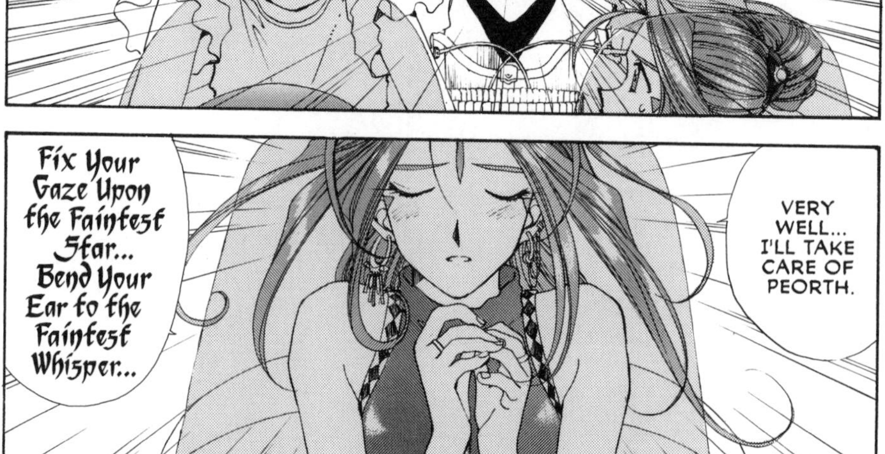
VERY WELL... I'LL TAKE CARE OF PEORTH.
Fix Your Gaze Upon the Faintest Star... Bend Your Ear to the Faintest Whisper...

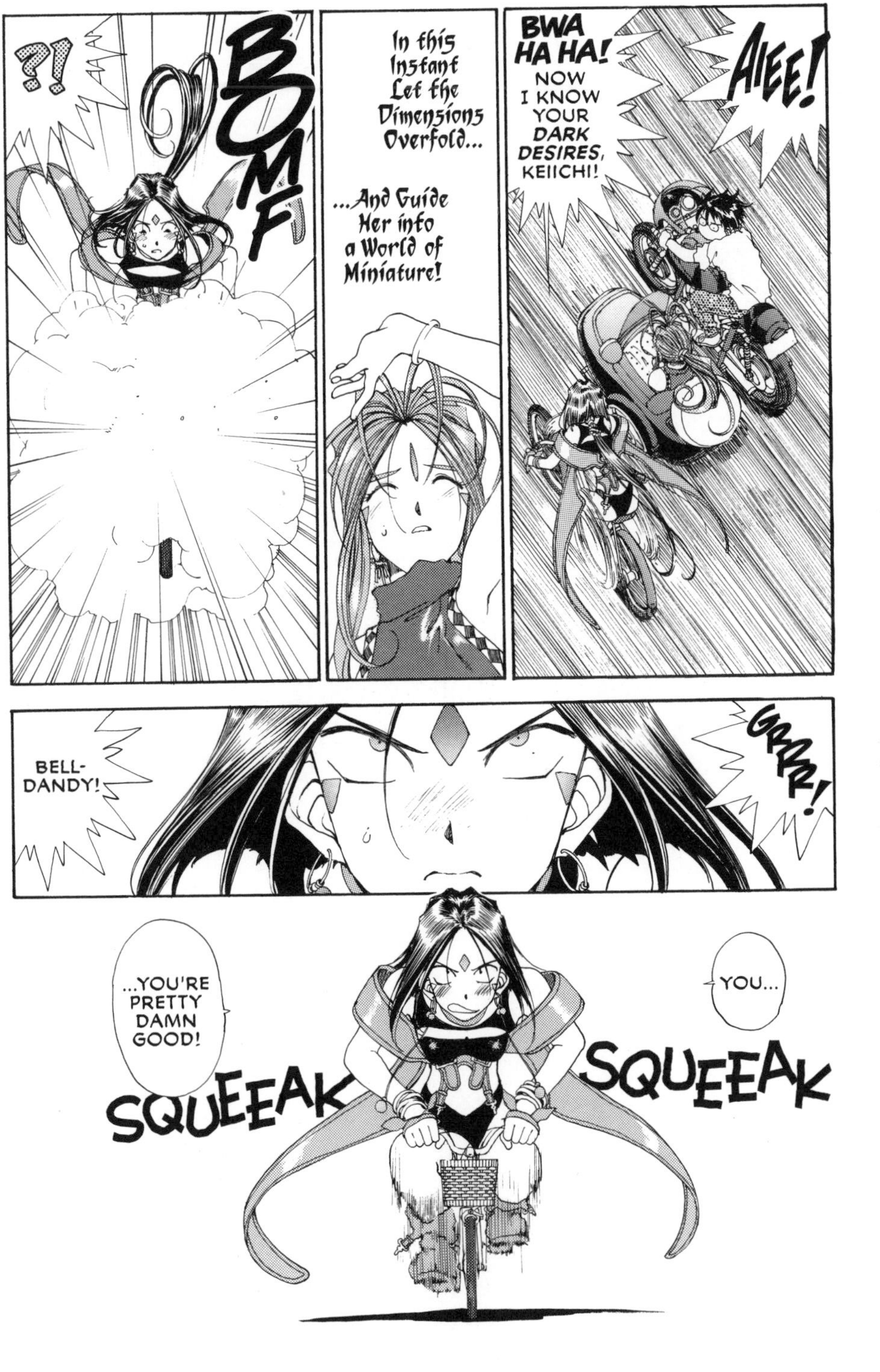
AIEEE!
BWA HA HA! NOW I KNOW YOUR DARK DESIRES, KEIICHI!
In this Instant Let the Dimensions Overfold...
...And Guide Her into a World of Miniature!
BOMF
?!
GRRR!
BELL-DANDY!
YOU...
...YOU'RE PRETTY DAMN GOOD!
SQUEEAK
SQUEEAK

...WHAT TH--?

BRP-BRP

NICE ONE, BELL! ♥

GREAT! YOU DID IT!

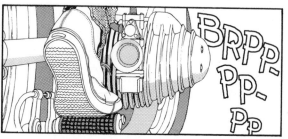

BRPP-PP-PP

DANG... AND I FORGOT MY WALLET, TOO.

RIGHT! THE *MOTOR CLUB!*

klik

BRP

ARGH! OUT OF GAS!?

60 80
80920

20

10
0

2824

▲ SWITCHING TO THE RESERVE TANK.

542

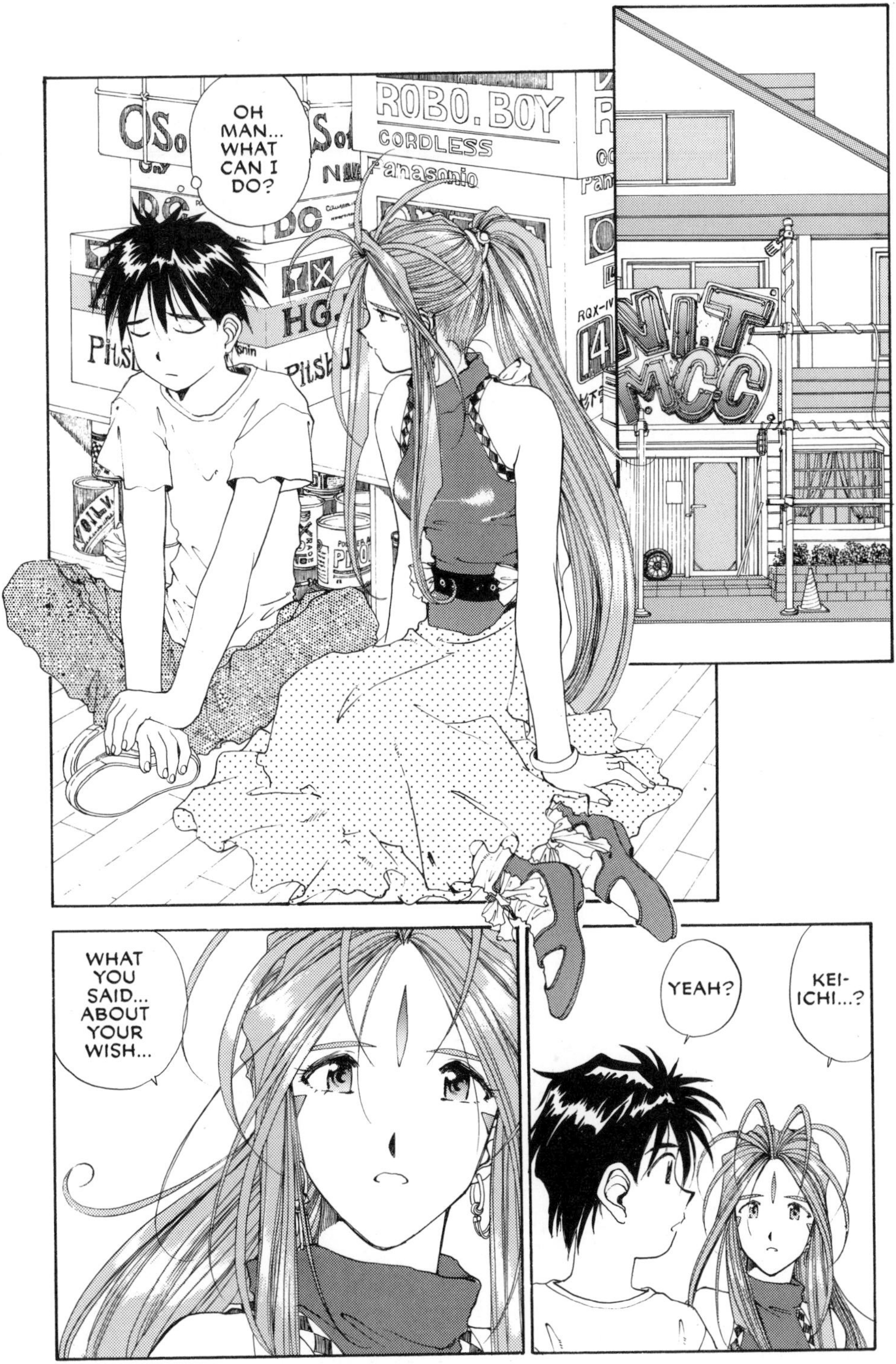
N.I.T
MCC
ROBO. BOY
CORDLESS
OH MAN... WHAT CAN I DO?
KEI-ICHI...?
YEAH?
WHAT YOU SAID... ABOUT YOUR WISH...

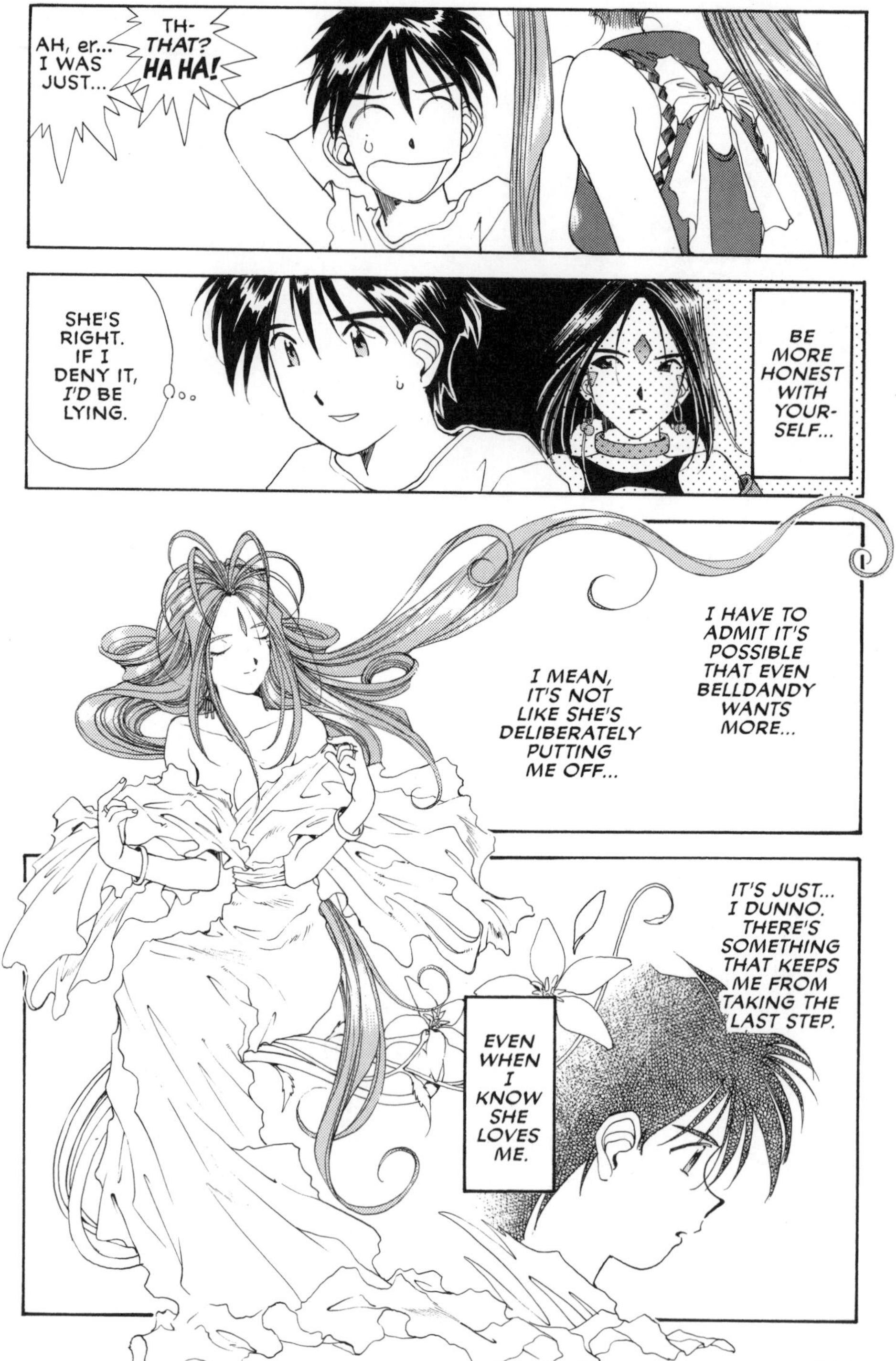
TH- THAT? HA HA!
AH, er... I WAS JUST...
BE MORE HONEST WITH YOUR-SELF...
SHE'S RIGHT. IF I DENY IT, I'D BE LYING.
I HAVE TO ADMIT IT'S POSSIBLE THAT EVEN BELLDANDY WANTS MORE...
I MEAN, IT'S NOT LIKE SHE'S DELIBERATELY PUTTING ME OFF...
IT'S JUST... I DUNNO. THERE'S SOMETHING THAT KEEPS ME FROM TAKING THE LAST STEP.
EVEN WHEN I KNOW SHE LOVES ME.

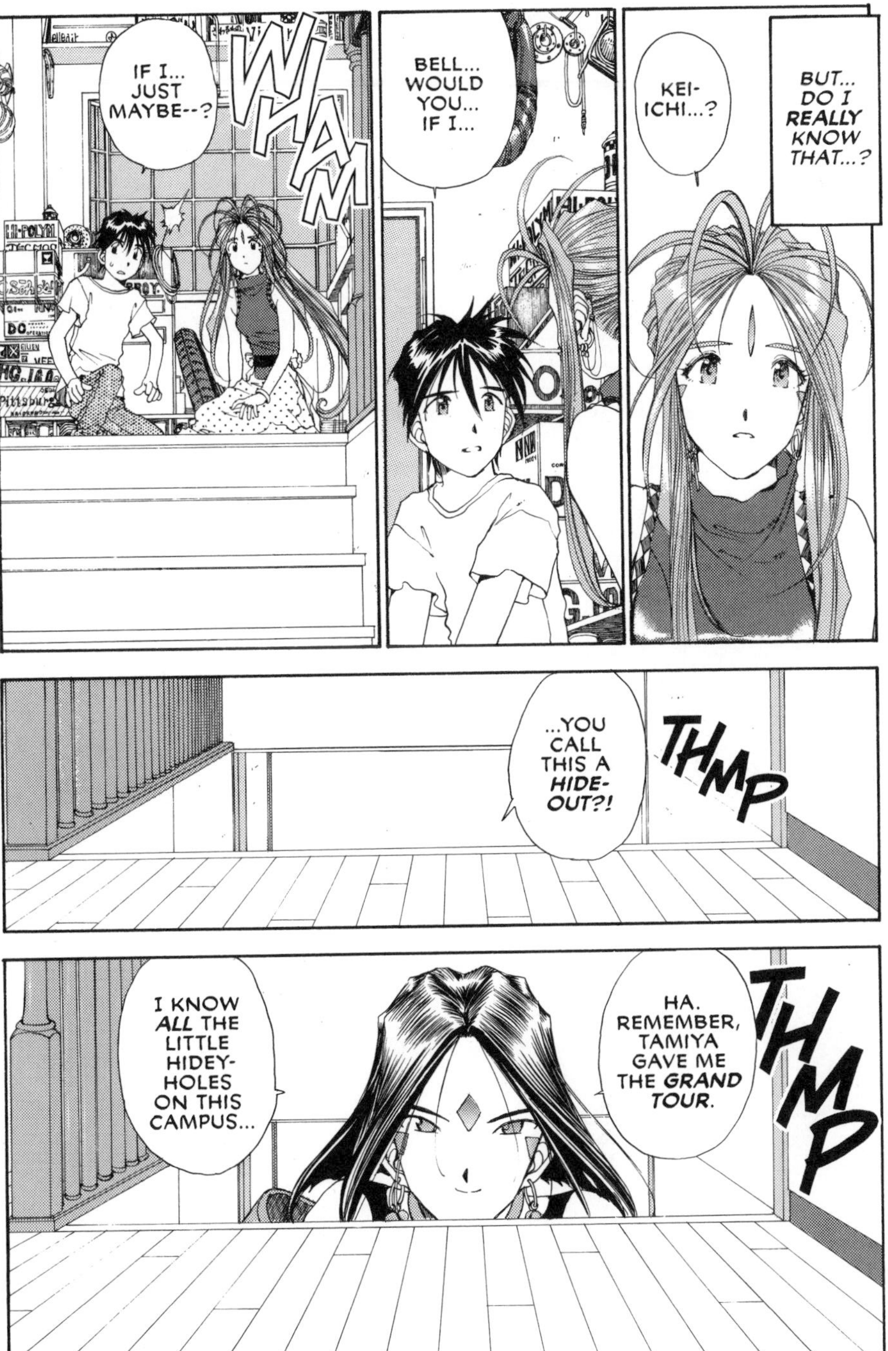
BUT... DO I REALLY KNOW THAT...?
KEI-ICHI...?
BELL... WOULD YOU... IF I...
IF I... JUST MAYBE--?
WHAM
THMP
...YOU CALL THIS A HIDE-OUT?!
THMP
HA. REMEMBER, TAMIYA GAVE ME THE GRAND TOUR.
I KNOW ALL THE LITTLE HIDEY-HOLES ON THIS CAMPUS...

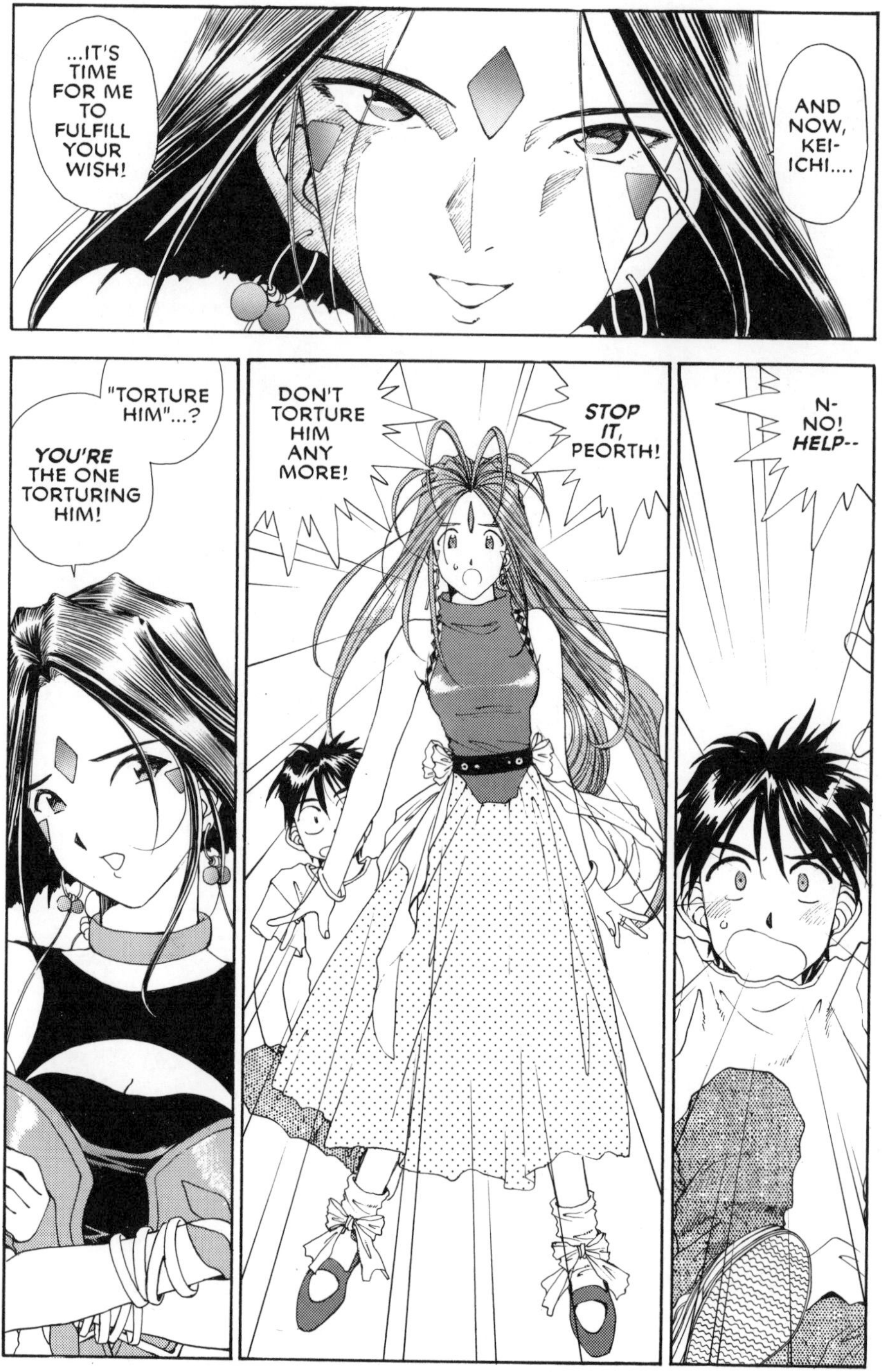
AND NOW, KEI-ICHI....
...IT'S TIME FOR ME TO FULFILL YOUR WISH!
N-NO! HELP--
STOP IT, PEORTH!
DON'T TORTURE HIM ANY MORE!
"TORTURE HIM"...?
YOU'RE THE ONE TORTURING HIM!

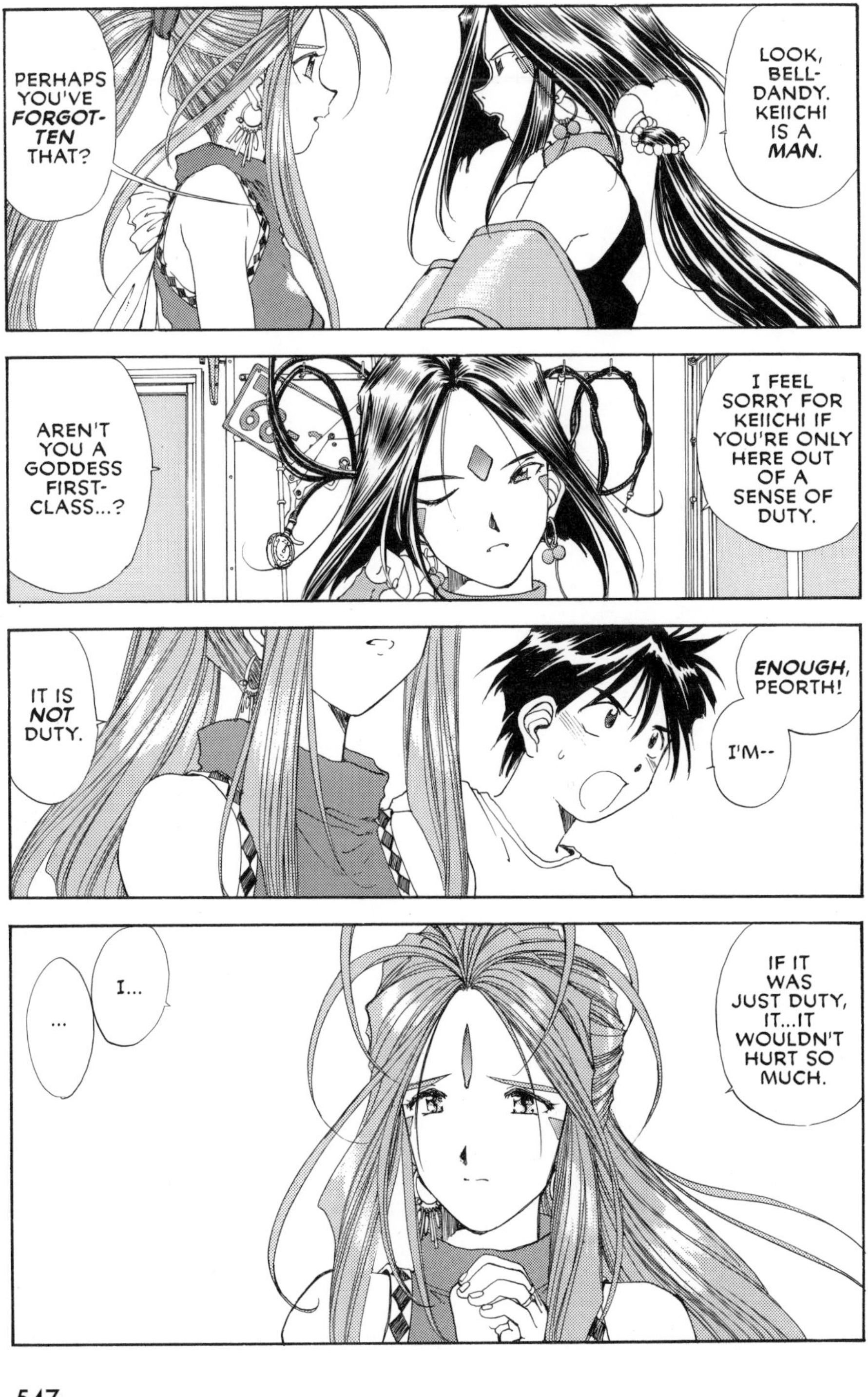
LOOK, BELL-DANDY. KEIICHI IS A *MAN*.
PERHAPS YOU'VE *FORGOTTEN* THAT?
I FEEL SORRY FOR KEIICHI IF YOU'RE ONLY HERE OUT OF A SENSE OF DUTY.
AREN'T YOU A GODDESS FIRST-CLASS...?
ENOUGH, PEORTH!
I'M--
IT IS *NOT* DUTY.
IF IT WAS JUST DUTY, IT...IT WOULDN'T HURT SO MUCH.
I...
...

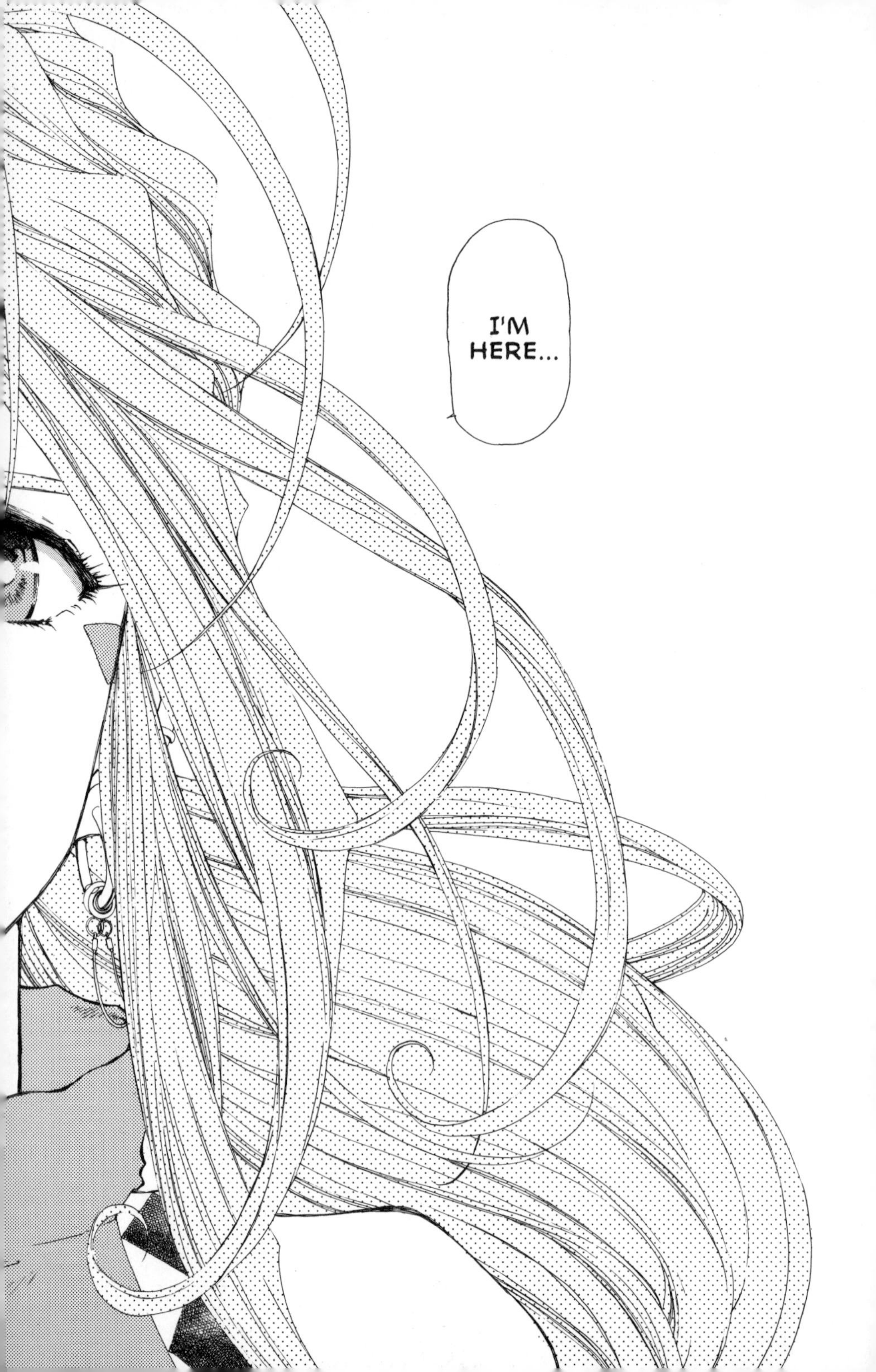
I'M HERE...

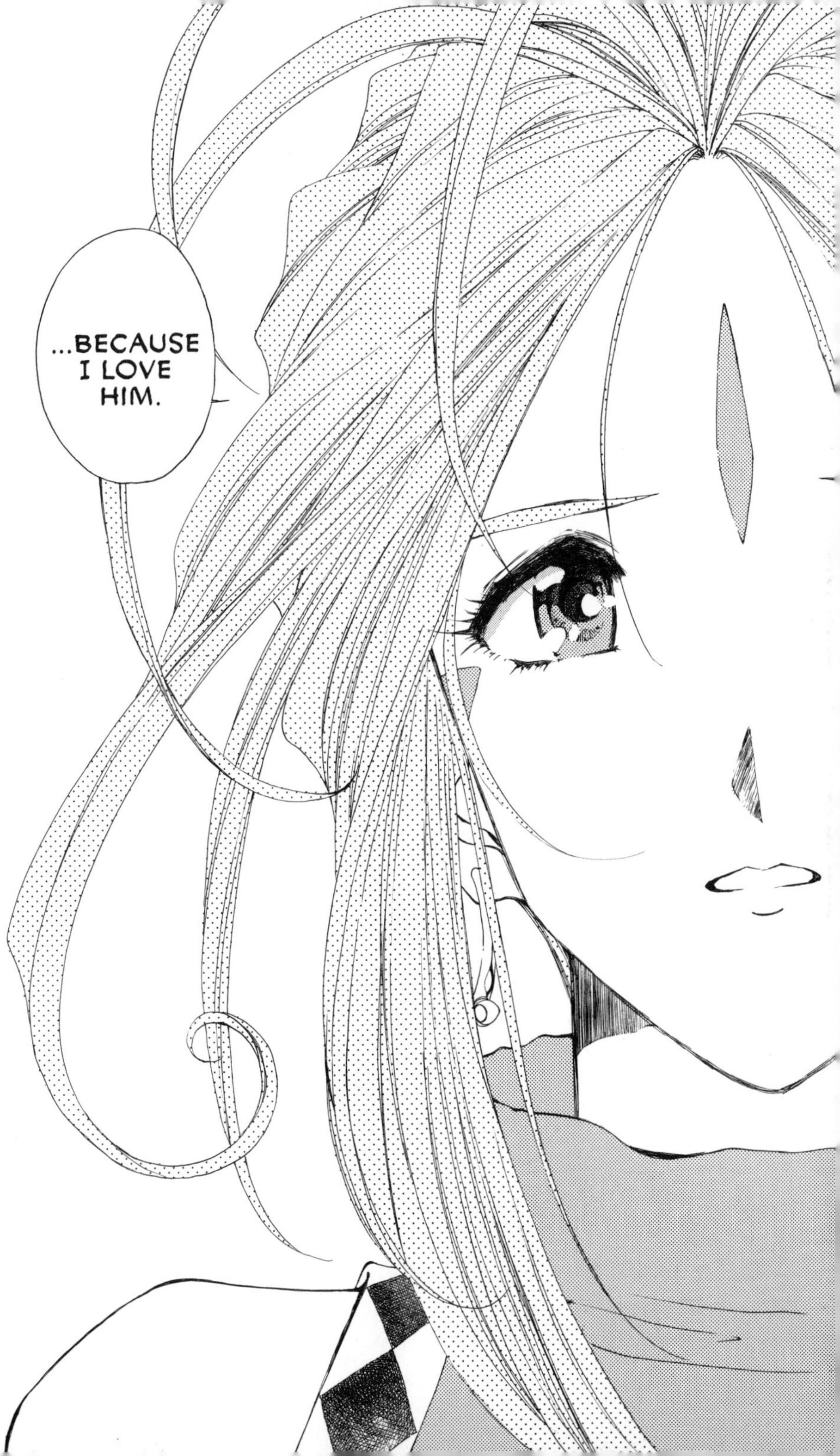
...BECAUSE I LOVE HIM.

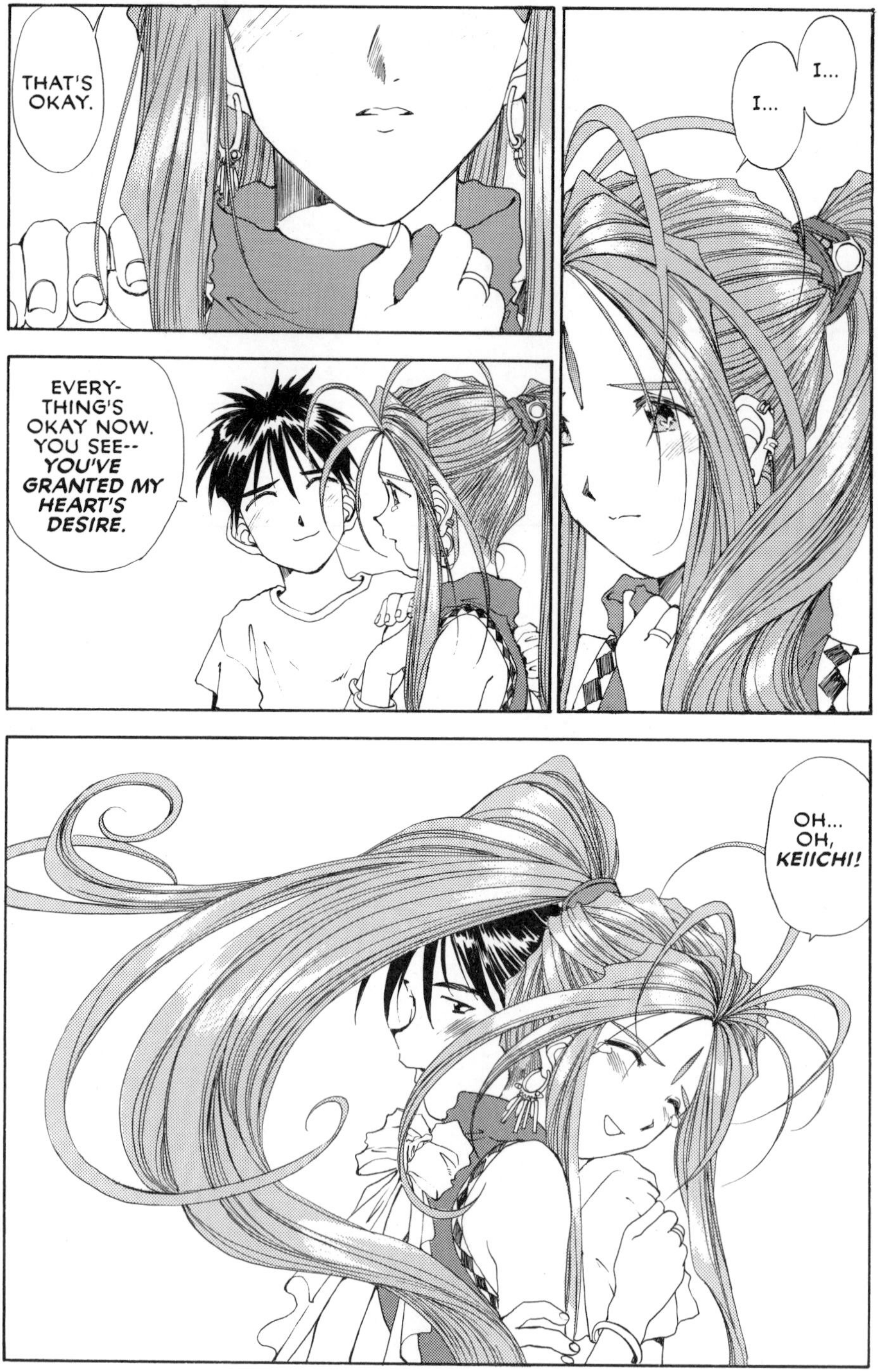

I... I...
THAT'S OKAY.
EVERYTHING'S OKAY NOW. YOU SEE-- *YOU'VE GRANTED MY HEART'S DESIRE.*
OH... OH, *KEIICHI!*

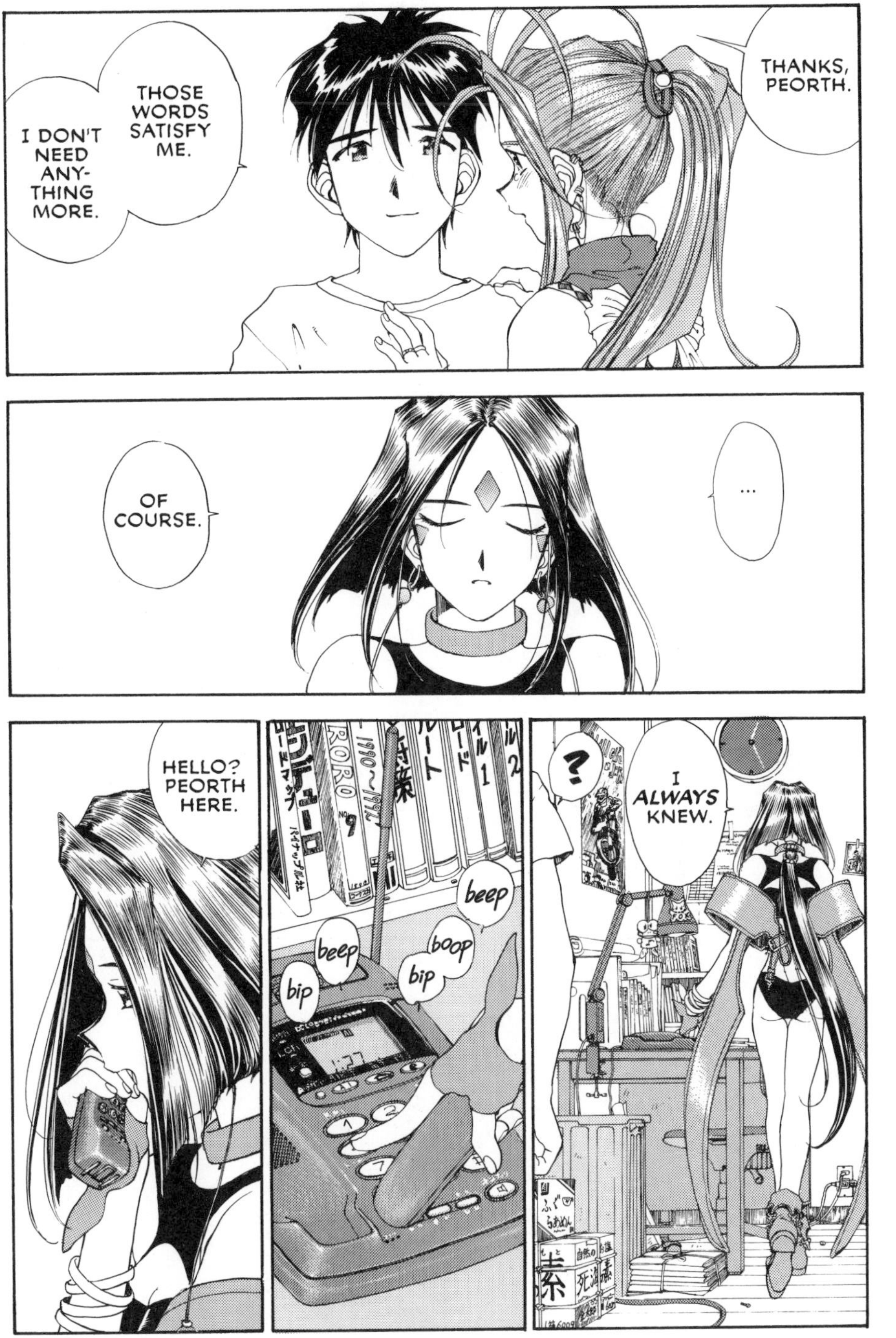
THANKS, PEORTH.
THOSE WORDS SATISFY ME.
I DON'T NEED ANY-THING MORE.
...
OF COURSE.
?
I ALWAYS KNEW.
beep
boop
bip
beep
bip
HELLO? PEORTH HERE.

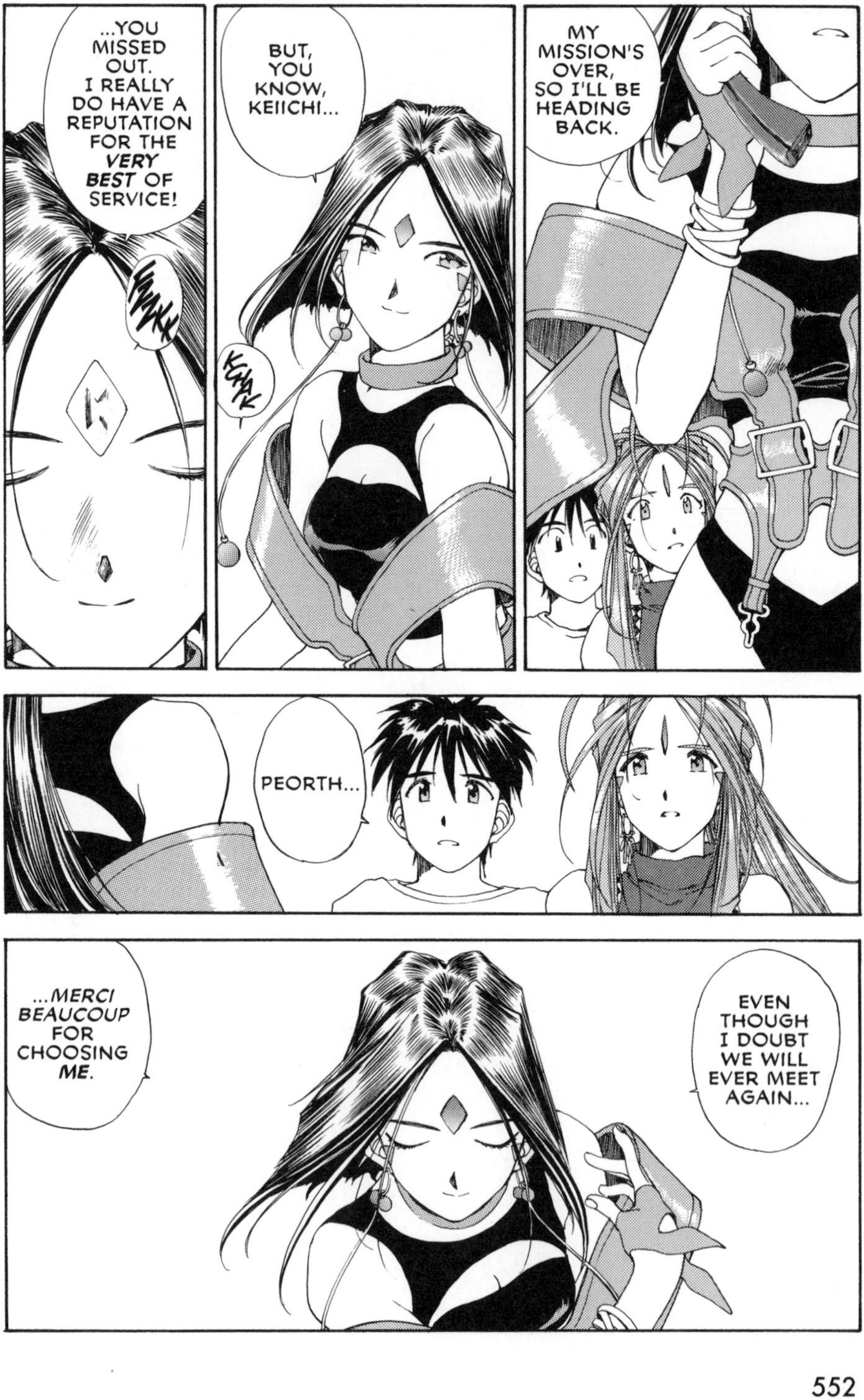
MY MISSION'S OVER, SO I'LL BE HEADING BACK.
BUT, YOU KNOW, KEIICHI...
...YOU MISSED OUT. I REALLY DO HAVE A REPUTATION FOR THE VERY BEST OF SERVICE!
PEORTH...
EVEN THOUGH I DOUBT WE WILL EVER MEET AGAIN...
...MERCI BEAUCOUP FOR CHOOSING ME.

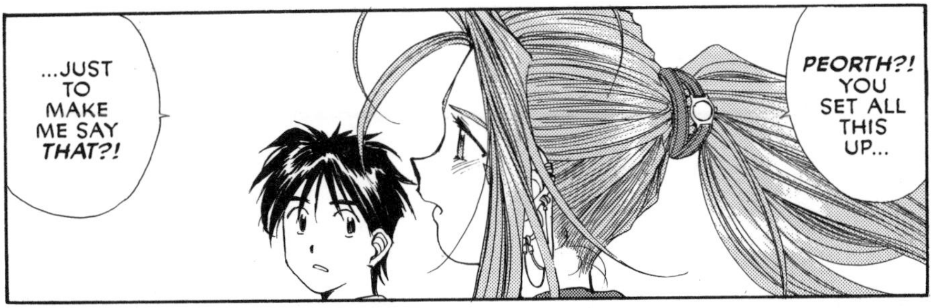
PEORTH?! YOU SET ALL THIS UP...
...JUST TO MAKE ME SAY THAT?!

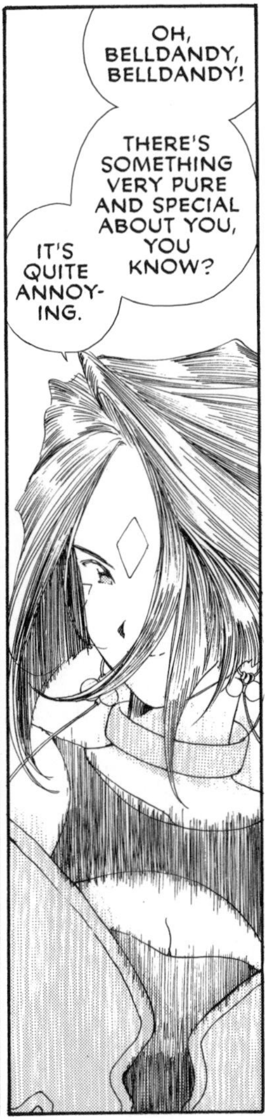
OH, BELLDANDY, BELLDANDY!
THERE'S SOMETHING VERY PURE AND SPECIAL ABOUT YOU, YOU KNOW?
IT'S QUITE ANNOY-ING.

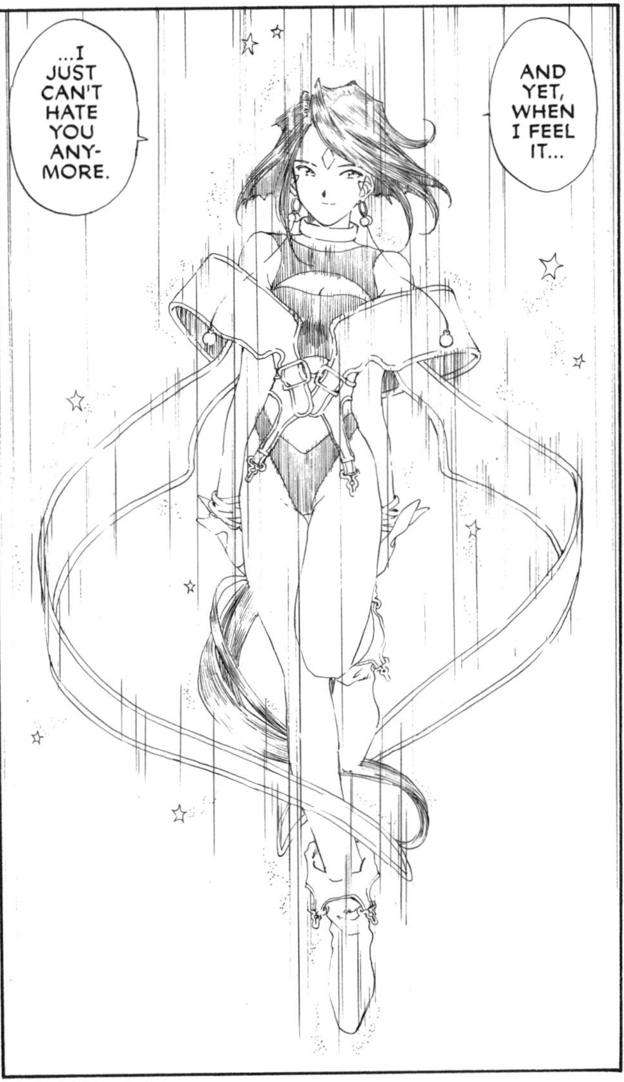
AND YET, WHEN I FEEL IT...
...I JUST CAN'T HATE YOU ANY-MORE.

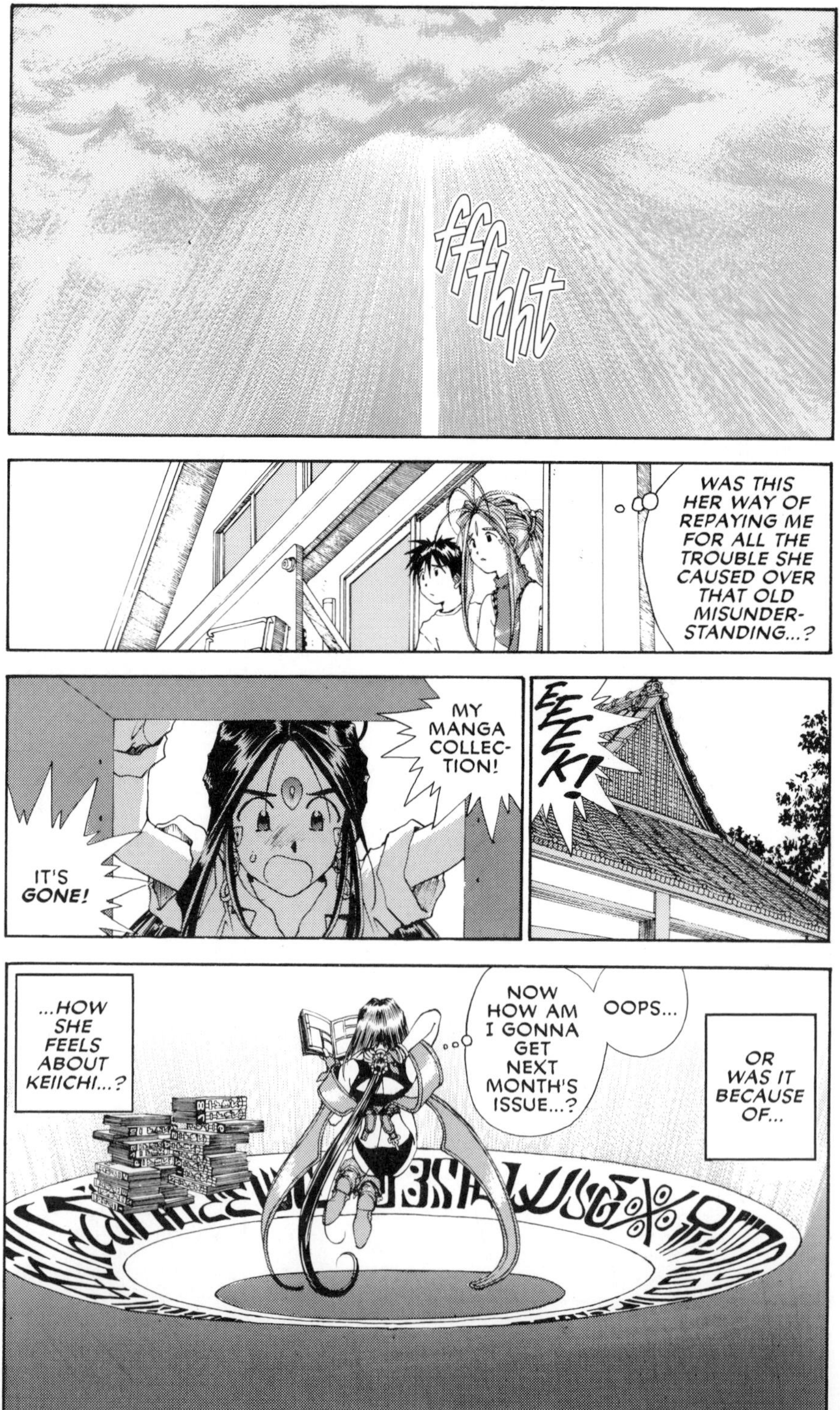
fffhht
WAS THIS HER WAY OF REPAYING ME FOR ALL THE TROUBLE SHE CAUSED OVER THAT OLD MISUNDER-STANDING...?
EEEEK!
MY MANGA COLLEC-TION!
IT'S GONE!
OR WAS IT BECAUSE OF...
OOPS...
NOW HOW AM I GONNA GET NEXT MONTH'S ISSUE...?
...HOW SHE FEELS ABOUT KEIICHI...?

THE ADVENTURES OF THE MINI-GODDESSES

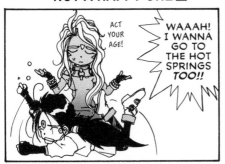

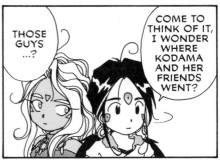

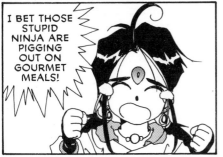

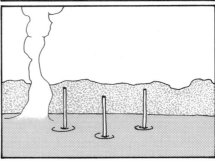

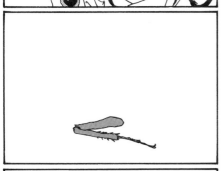

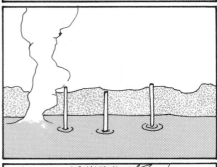

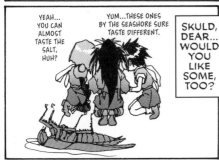

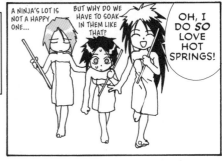

◇ A NINJA'S LOT IS NOT A HAPPY ONE ◇

COME TO THINK OF IT, I WONDER WHERE KODAMA AND HER FRIENDS WENT?
THOSE GUYS ...?
OH, I DO *SO* LOVE HOT SPRINGS!
BUT WHY DO WE HAVE TO SOAK IN THEM LIKE THAT?
A NINJA'S LOT IS NOT A HAPPY ONE...

◇ A NINJA'S LOT IS DEFINITELY NOT A HAPPY ONE ◇

WAAAH! I WANNA GO TO THE HOT SPRINGS *TOO!!*
ACT YOUR AGE!
I BET THOSE STUPID NINJA ARE PIGGING OUT ON GOURMET MEALS!
SKULD, DEAR... WOULD YOU LIKE SOME, TOO?
YUM...THESE ONES BY THE SEASHORE SURE TASTE DIFFERENT.
YEAH... YOU CAN ALMOST TASTE THE SALT, HUH?

THE ADVENTURES OF THE MINI-GODDESSES

MORISATO, YOU MAY HAVE BREASTS, BUT YOU'RE **STILL** A GUY!

(Might as well dig your grave right now!!)

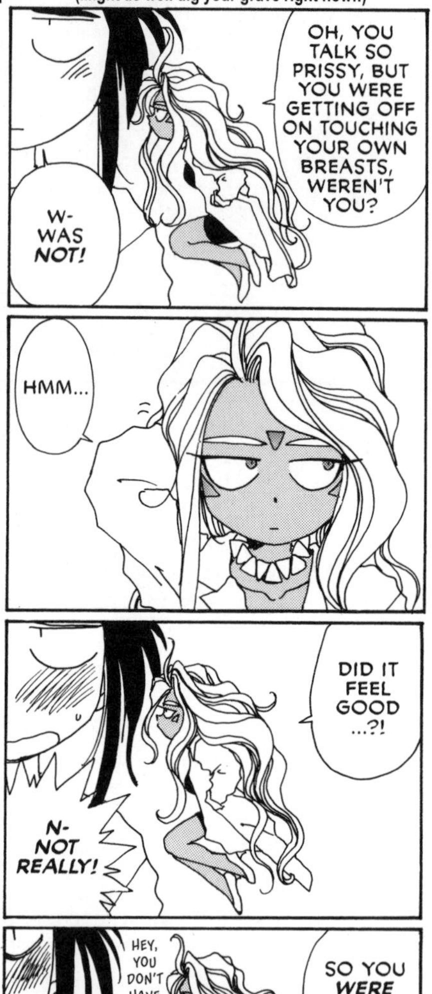
OH, YOU TALK SO PRISSY, BUT YOU WERE GETTING OFF ON TOUCHING YOUR OWN BREASTS, WEREN'T YOU?
W-WAS ***NOT!***
HMM...
DID IT FEEL GOOD ...?!
N-NOT REALLY!
SO YOU ***WERE*** DOING IT, THEN?
HEY, YOU DON'T HAVE TO CRY...
...!

OH MY MANGA-KA! (SPECIAL ROAD-TRIP EDITION) BATTLE! THE CHALLENGE OF THE FAKE FOOD SAMPLES!

AN ALMOST-TRUE STORY STARRING "KIKUKO INOGASHIRA" (PSEUDONYM— BELLDANDY'S VOICE ACTRESS)

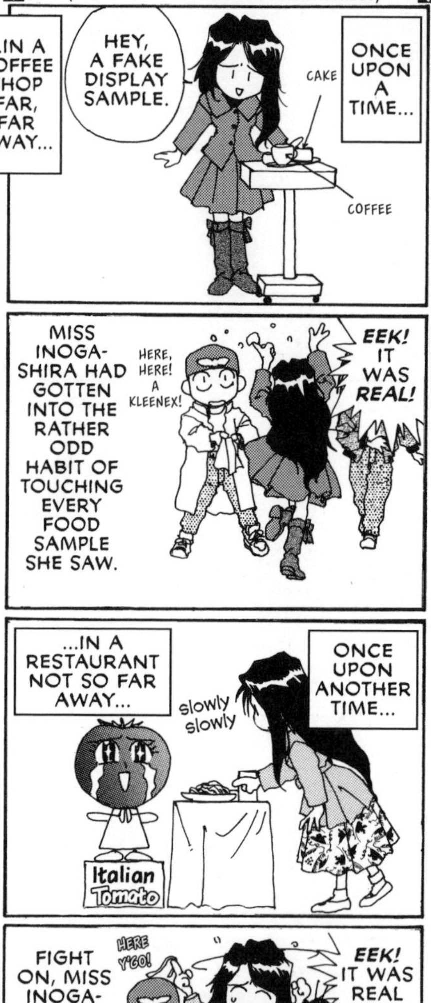
ONCE UPON A TIME...
CAKE
HEY, A FAKE DISPLAY SAMPLE.
COFFEE
...IN A COFFEE SHOP FAR, FAR AWAY...
EEK! IT WAS ***REAL!***
HERE, HERE! A KLEENEX!
MISS INOGA-SHIRA HAD GOTTEN INTO THE RATHER ODD HABIT OF TOUCHING EVERY FOOD SAMPLE SHE SAW.
ONCE UPON ANOTHER TIME...
slowly slowly
...IN A RESTAURANT NOT SO FAR AWAY...
Italian Tomato
EEK! IT WAS REAL ***AGAIN !!***
HERE Y'GO!
FIGHT ON, MISS INOGA-SHIRA! A WORLD OF REAL FOOD SAMPLES AWAITS YOU!

Any similarity with any person living or dead is purely coincidental! Honest! I swear!

Oh My Goddess!

ああっ女神さまっ

⑤

OMNIBUS

藤島康介
KOSUKE FUJISHIMA

Skuld, who loves to overengineer, has trouble understanding the simple appeal of a bicycle—until Sentaro, a boy in town, teaches her how to ride one. But Skuld is new to understanding love as well . . . Meanwhile, the girl on campus who can never get enough love (and worship), Sayoko Mishima, is willing to sell her soul to help demoness Mara defeat Belldandy . . . and turn Nekomi Tech into a literal castle where Queen Sayoko reigns supreme!

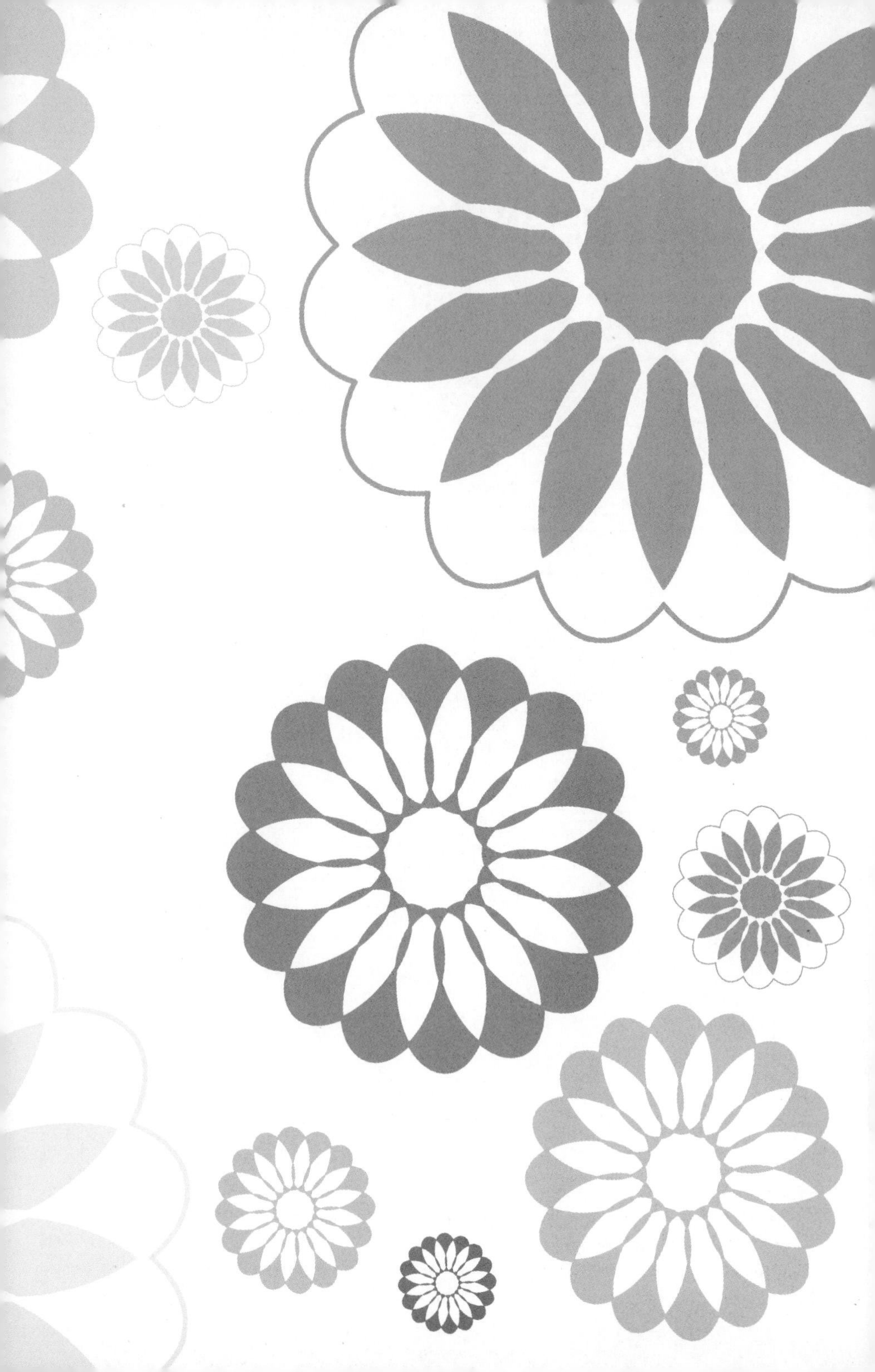

PRESIDENT AND PUBLISHER
Mike Richardson

EDITOR
Carl Gustav Horn

DESIGNER
Sarah Terry

DIGITAL ART TECHNICIAN
Christina McKenzie

English-language version
produced by Dark Horse Comics

OH MY GODDESS! Omnibus Book 4

Published by Dark Horse Manga
A division of Dark Horse Comics, Inc.
10956 SE Main Street
Milwaukie, OR 97222
DarkHorse.com

To find a comics shop in your area,
call the Comic Shop Locator Service
toll-free at 1-888-266-4226.

First edition: July 2016
ISBN 978-1-50670-052-6

1 3 5 7 9 10 8 6 4 2

Printed in China

OH MY GODDESS!

東京 TOKYO BABYLON

CLAMP

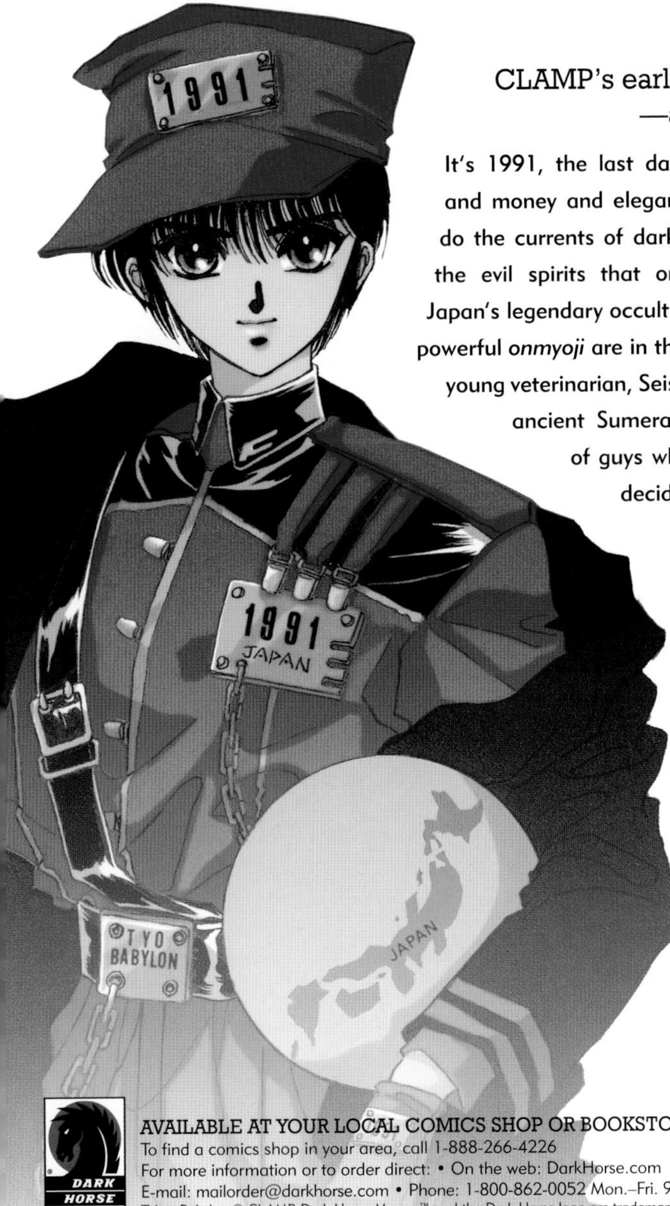
1991
1991
JAPAN
TYO
BABYLON
JAPAN

CLAMP's early epic of dangerous work —and dangerous attraction!

It's 1991, the last days of Japan's bubble economy, and money and elegance run through the streets. So do the currents of darkness beneath them, nourishing the evil spirits that only the arts of the *onmyoji*—Japan's legendary occultists—can combat. The two most powerful *onmyoji* are in the unlikely guises of a handsome young veterinarian, Seishiro, and the teenage heir to the ancient Sumeragi clan, Subaru—just a couple of guys whom Subaru's sister Hokuto has decided are destined to be together!

***"Tokyo Babylon** is CLAMP's first really great work."*
—Manga: The Complete Guide

Each omnibus-sized volume features over a dozen full-color bonus pages!

VOLUME ONE
ISBN 978-1-61655-116-2
$19.99

VOLUME TWO
ISBN 978-1-61655-189-6
$19.99

DARK HORSE MANGA
DarkHorse.com

AVAILABLE AT YOUR LOCAL COMICS SHOP OR BOOKSTORE!
To find a comics shop in your area, call 1-888-266-4226
For more information or to order direct: • On the web: DarkHorse.com
E-mail: mailorder@darkhorse.com • Phone: 1-800-862-0052 Mon.–Fri. 9 AM to 5 PM Pacific Time

CLAMP オキモノ キモノ
Mokona's
OKIMONO
KIMONO

CLAMP artist Mokona loves the art of traditional Japanese kimono. In fact, she designs kimono and kimono accessories herself and shares her love in *Okimono Kimono*, a fun and lavishly illustrated book full of drawings and photographs, interviews (including an interview with Onuki Ami of the J-pop duo Puffy AmiYumi), and exclusive short manga stories from the CLAMP artists!

From the creators of such titles as *Clover*, *Chobits*, *Cardcaptor Sakura*, *Magic Knight Rayearth*, and *Tsubasa*, *Okimono Kimono* is now available in English for the first time ever!

ISBN 978-1-59582-456-1
$12.99

ANGELIC LAYER

Story and Art by
CLAMP

YOUNG TEEN MISAKI SUZUHARA
has just arrived in Tokyo to attend the
prestigious Eriol Academy. But what really
excites her is Angelic Layer, the game where
you control an Angel—a miniature robot
fighter whose moves depend on your mind!
Before she knows it, Misaki is an up-and-
coming contender in Angelic Layer . . . and in
way over her not-very-tall head! How far can
enthusiasm take her in an arena full of much
more experienced fighters . . . and a game
full of secrets?

Don't miss the thrilling prequel to the
acclaimed CLAMP manga *Chobits*! These
omnibus-sized volumes feature not only the
full story of *Angelic Layer* but also gorgeous,
exclusive bonus color illustrations!

VOLUME ONE
978-1-61655-021-9

VOLUME TWO
978-1-61655-128-5

$19.99 each

CLOVER

The long-out-of-print classic from Japan's
shojo artist supergroup CLAMP!

Clover has never before
been available in English
in its original unflopped,
right-to-left reading
format—until now! Dark
Horse collects all four
volumes of *Clover* in one
bargain omnibus format,
including 17 pages of
bonus art in color!

"Edgy and genre-bending . . . *Clover* certainly challenges
people's perception of what shojo manga should be."
—Manga: *The Complete Guide*

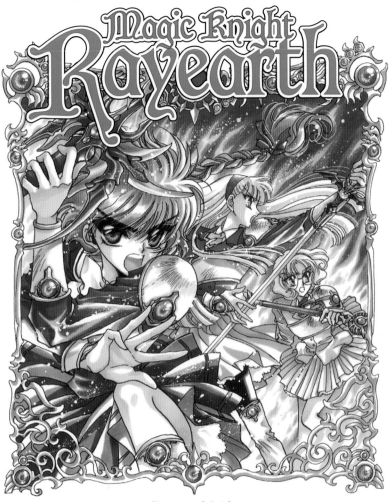

CLAMP

Chobits
ちょびっツ

IN NEAR-FUTURE JAPAN,
the hottest style for your personal computer, or "persocom," is in the shape of an attractive android! Hideki, a poor student, finds a persocom seemingly discarded in an alley. He takes the cute, amnesiac robot home and names her "Chi."

But who is this strange new persocom in his life? Hideki finds himself having to teach Chi how to get along in the everyday world, even while he and his friends try to solve the mystery of her origins. Is she one of the urban-legendary *Chobits*—persocoms built to have the riskiest functions of all: real emotions and free will?

CLAMP's best-selling manga in America is finally available in omnibus form! Containing dozens of bonus color pages, *Chobits* is an engaging, touching, exciting story.

BOOK 1
ISBN 978-1-59582-451-6
$24.99

BOOK 2
ISBN 978-1-59582-514-8
$24.99

STOP! This is the back of the book!

This manga collection is translated into English, but arranged in right-to-left reading format to maintain the artwork's visual orientation as originally drawn and published in Japan. If you've never read comics this way before, take a look at the diagram below to give yourself an idea of how to go about it. Basically, you'll be starting in the upper right-hand corner, and will read each word balloon and panel moving right to left. It may take a little getting used to, but you should get the hang of it very quickly. Have fun! If this is the millionth manga you've read this way, never mind. ^_^

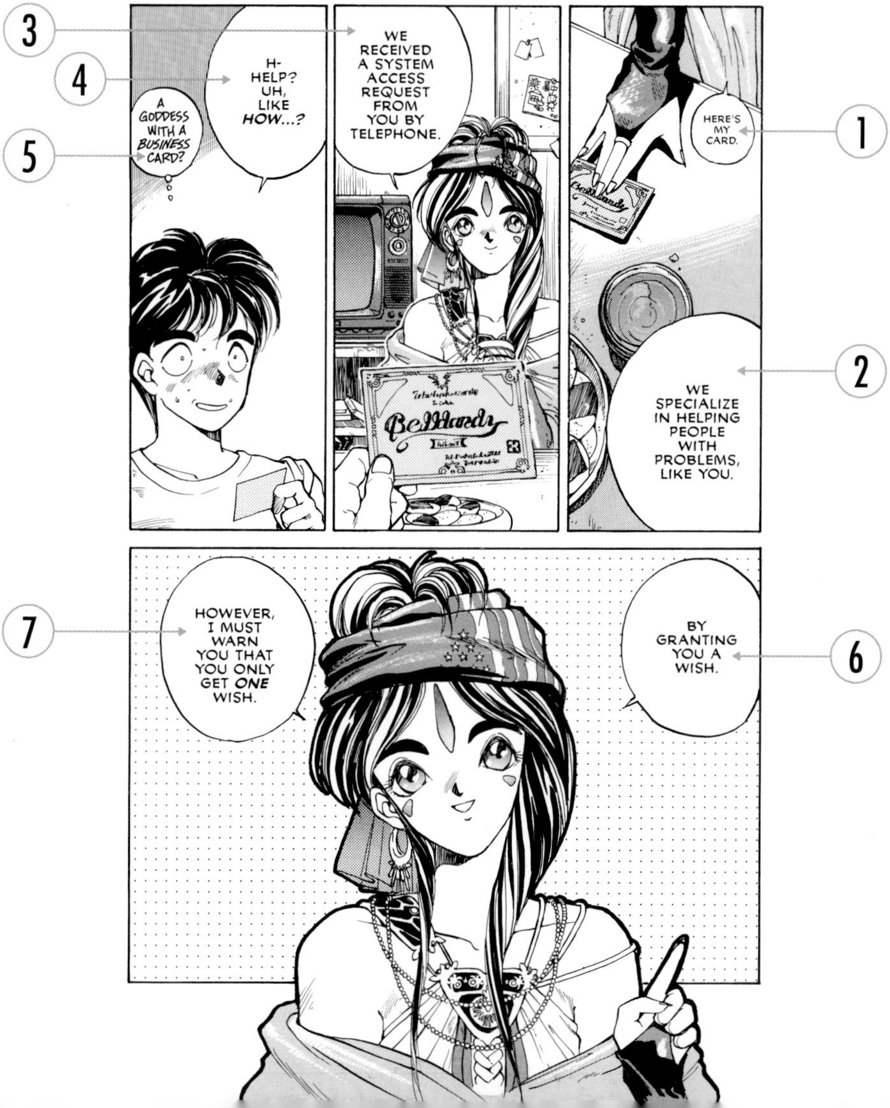
1
HERE'S MY CARD.
2
WE SPECIALIZE IN HELPING PEOPLE WITH PROBLEMS, LIKE YOU.
3
WE RECEIVED A SYSTEM ACCESS REQUEST FROM YOU BY TELEPHONE.
4
H-HELP? UH, LIKE *HOW...?*
5
A GODDESS WITH A *BUSINESS* CARD?
6
BY GRANTING YOU A WISH.
7
HOWEVER, I MUST WARN YOU THAT YOU ONLY GET *ONE* WISH.

Cardcaptor Sakura
カードキャプターさくら

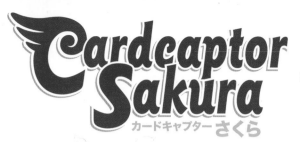

MANGA BY
CLAMP

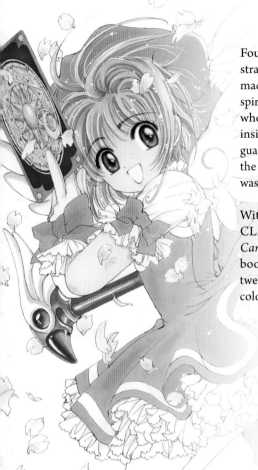

Fourth grader Sakura Kinomoto has found a strange book in her father's library—a book made by the wizard Clow to store dangerous spirits sealed within a set of magical cards. But when Sakura opens it up, there is nothing left inside but Kero-chan, the book's cute little guardian beast...who informs Sakura that since the Clow cards seem to have escaped while he was asleep, it's now her job to capture them!

With remastered image files straight from CLAMP, Dark Horse is proud to present *Cardcaptor Sakura* in omnibus form! Each book collects three volumes of the original twelve-volume series, and features thirty bonus color pages!

OMNIBUS BOOK 1
ISBN 978-1-59582-522-3

OMNIBUS BOOK 2
ISBN 978-1-59582-591-9

OMNIBUS BOOK 3
ISBN 978-1-59582-808-8

OMNIBUS BOOK 4
ISBN 978-1-59582-889-7

$19.99 each!

AVAILABLE AT YOUR LOCAL COMICS SHOP OR BOOKSTORE!
To find a comics shop in your area, call 1-888-266-4226
For more information or to order direct: • On the web: DarkHorse.com
E-mail: mailorder@darkhorse.com • Phone: 1-800-862-0052 Mon.–Fri. 9 AM to 5 PM Pacific Time

DarkHorse.com